From Tribute to Communal Sovereignty

NATIVE PEOPLES OF THE AMERICAS

Laurie Weinstein, Series Editor

From Tribute to Communal Sovereignty

The Tarascan and Caxcan Territories in Transition

Edited by
Andrew Roth-Seneff,
Robert V. Kemper,
and Julie Adkins

THE UNIVERSITY OF
ARIZONA PRESS

TUCSON

The University of Arizona Press
www.uapress.arizona.edu

Printed in the United States of America
20   19   18   17   16   15   6   5   4   3   2   1

ISBN-13: 978-0-8165-3158-5 (cloth)

Jacket designed by Miriam Warren
Jacket photo by Richard Barthelemy, courtesy of Colegio de Michoacán

Publication of this book is made possible in part by the proceeds of a permanent
endowment created with the assistance of a Challenge Grant from the National
Endowment for the Humanities, a federal agency.

Library of Congress Cataloging-in-Publication Data
From tribute to communal sovereignty : the Tarascan and Caxcan territories in
transition / edited by Andrew Roth-Seneff, Robert V. Kemper, and Julie Adkins.
    pages cm — (Native peoples of the Americas)
  Includes bibliographical references and index.
   ISBN 978-0-8165-3158-5 (cloth : alk. paper)
  1. Indians of Mexico—Mexico—Michoacán de Ocampo. 2. Indians of Mexico—
Mexico—Nueva Galicia. 3. Mexico—History—Spanish colony, 1540–1810.
4. Mexico—History—1810– I. Roth Seneff, A. (Andrés), editor. II. Kemper,
Robert V., 1945– editor. III. Adkins, Julie, 1960– editor.
  F1219.1.M55F76 2015
  972'.03—dc23
                              2014040043

Contents

Part IV   The Past in the Present

Foreword

Native Peoples of the Americas is a multivolume series that covers North, Middle, and South America. Each volume takes unique methodological approaches—archaeological, ethnographic, ecological, and/or ethnohistorical—to culture areas and regions and to themes that link areas across time and space. The series has been published by the University of Arizona Press since 2003 and includes *Native Peoples of the Gulf Coast of Mexico* by Alan Sandstrom and Hugo Garcia Valencia (2005), *Lifeways in the Northern Mayan Lowlands: New Approaches to Archaeology in the Yucatan Peninsula* by Jenifer Mathews and Bethany Morrison (2006), *Anthropologies of Guyana: Cultural Spaces in Northeastern Amazonia* by Neil Whitehead and Stephanie Aleman (2009) and *The Archaeology at El Perú-Waka': Performances of Ritual, Memory and Power*, edited by Olivia Navarro-Farr and Michelle Rich (in press).

From Tribute to Communal Sovereignty: The Tarascan and Caxcan Territories in Transition, edited by Andrew Roth-Seneff, Robert V. Kemper, and Julie Adkins, is an ambitious volume that covers the anthropology of western central Mexico. Much of the volume deals with the conflicts and casualties of the Spanish conquest. Disease, population decline, and famine, along with Catholicism and a Spanish political system, were all imposed on Native peoples. In some cases, these new socioreligious and political structures coexisted with Native ones; in other cases, they simply replaced them. Natives were not at all passive in accepting these new impositions. They fought back both overtly and covertly, as the Rebelión de Nueva Galicia suggests, when competing sides joined forces against a common Spanish enemy (Phillip C. Weigand, chapter 3).

Prehispanic peoples were not all one people, and their societies were diverse, from state-level societies, like that of the Tarascans, to mixed hunting-and-gathering and farming societies. The larger regional ethnic groups included the Tarascans (Purépecha) and Caxcanes. This volume uses archaeological, ethnohistorical, and ethnographic analyses to bring together the rich history of these peoples. From Robert V. Kemper and Julie Adkins's introduction to the region, with detailed census data and maps, to the final chapter by Andrew Roth-Seneff about the contemporary Purépecha and the evolution of their ritualized ceremonies of exchange, this book has a lot to offer both the scholar and the student of Middle America. The volume is constructed on the premise that the past is also in the present (the section head to part 4), with contributors looking at the stream of history from precontact to contemporary times. Well-known scholars of Middle America are all a part of this text, including the editors (Andrew Roth-Seneff, Robert V. Kemper, and Julie Adkins) and the contributors (Phil Weigand, Helen Perlstein Pollard, Hans Roskamp, Felipe Castro Gutiérrez, José Francisco Román Gutiérrez, Paul Liffman, and John Gledhill).

This volume is remarkable for another, more personal reason as well. Dr. Kemper died in the midst of finishing this volume. In fact, Dr. Roth-Seneff told me that Van was working on this book from his deathbed. Always the incessant worker, he barreled through everything with great enthusiasm and energy. Van was my mentor in graduate school. I knew him as a true bibliophile and collector of ethnographic facts. I would see him at meetings after graduate school, and he would pull me aside to show me the reams of data that he was working on. When he agreed to take on a book in this series, he was thrilled to show me the maps and tables of data he had collected for it. He was a one-of-a-kind person and a scholar, and his loss is deeply felt by all of us.

Laurie Weinstein, Ph.D.
Series Editor, Native Peoples of the Americas
Danbury, Connecticut, August 2014

Acknowledgments

For numerous reasons, some anticipated and many others that took us completely by surprise, this book's gestation has been long and difficult. As in any creative endeavor of these dimensions, many people have contributed, both facilitating field and archival research and providing important technical assistance. Both editors and authors deeply appreciate all these silent contributors, with many of whom we continue to collaborate. We would particularly like to mention the technical assistance so ably offered by the Geographical Information Systems Section of the Academic Services Area at the Colegio de Michoacán, in particular Marco Antonio Hernández. Likewise, in addition to the collaborating authors in the present volume, several specialists have contributed importantly to improving chapters and clarifying points concerning the languages, history, anthropology, and archaeology of central western Mexico, in particular Cristina Monzón at the Colegio de Michoacán, Carlos Paredes and Luis Vázquez at the Centro de Estudios Superiores de Antropología Social, Claudio Garibay at the Universidad Nacional Autónoma de México, and three anonymous reviewers.

During the creation of this book, as well as the process of getting it to press, we lost two key collaborators. Phillip C. Weigand (1934–2011) was a major creative force in the design and development of the ethnographic and historical baseline so vital to our understanding of the precolumbian organization of what is today central western Mexico, as well as the colonial organization and resistance during the first centuries of the Spanish Empire. Robert V. Kemper (1945–2013), with his pioneering studies of migration in central western Mexico during the twentieth century, his extensive ethnographic, geographical, and social-demographic data on the region, and his incredible bibliographic resources, was a vital force in the development and promotion of this volume. We acknowledge their distinguished careers and their contributions to our knowledge of the archaeology, anthropology, ethnohistory, and sociology of central western Mexico. We deeply regret their passing before the book reached its conclusion.

Under the able leadership of editor in chief Allyson Carter, the editorial team at the University of Arizona Press has made a major contribution to the realization and improvement of the book. Christopher Kaplan assisted in the formal aspects of getting the volume out, while Mary M. Hill carried out the major task of copyediting such a diverse and demanding text and Amanda Krause conducted a thorough review of the final draft. Finally, the series editor, Laurie Weinstein, was a patient and supportive presence throughout the very long process of defining and developing this volume, as well as steadfast in her encouragement throughout several difficult periods as the book was being completed.

From Tribute to Communal Sovereignty

I
Introduction

1

Ethnic Landscapes

Territoriality, Time Immemorial,
and the Twenty-First Century

Andrew Roth-Seneff

Continuities and Changes

An analysis of the populations and geographical concentrations of speakers of indigenous languages in central western Mexico points to both continuities and changes during the last five centuries. In part, the continuities concern ancestral territorial claims that date back to time immemorial and reflect the fact that core populations of indigenous language speakers have occupied places in or near their precolumbian territories since the Postclassic period (thirteenth to late fifteenth centuries). Present-day claims concerning territorial continuity are often oriented by ritual and sacred sites (Liffman 2010) or by archeological ruins shrouded in oral traditions (Roth-Seneff and Roskamp 2004), as well as by interpretations of place-names and colonial documents, especially land titles and codices (Roskamp 2010; Ruiz Medrano 2010). Though selective traditions (Williams 1977) are common, in many cases there is real historical depth to these arguments. The histories of central western indigenous populations have suffered from Western assumptions related to cultural change in rural subaltern populations. In the twentieth century it was all too common to employ the circular logic of a certain type of ethnographic analogy to defend claims of cultural continuity made by both anthropologists and members of indigenous communities themselves.

First, parallels were adduced between contemporary ethnographic descriptions and the foundational traditions of indigenous villages. Next, these parallels were used to support claims for a cultural base instituted in the sixteenth century that continued until at least the mid-twentieth century. That cultural base could be characterized as a precolumbian survival sustained through syncretism and resistance or as the outcome of Spanish colonial consolidation both before and after a catastrophic loss of indigenous population due to epidemics in the sixteenth century. Nonetheless, and regardless of the occidental or subaltern character of this postulated cultural base, it soon became evidence used to support the thesis, built on ethnographic analogy, of important continuities in indigenous communal organization from the sixteenth century to the present.

The circularity of these arguments now seems obvious: a cultural baseline is constructed by selectively stressing similarities between sixteenth- and twentieth-century descriptions of communal lifeways and ceremonial cycles while ignoring how communal institutions have adapted and changed over five centuries of state formation. This involves converting major periods of reform into a background: the changing modern world supposedly surrounded and encapsulated traditional society, only gradually penetrating it through the consolidation of New Spain in the Spanish Empire, the Bourbon reforms of the colonial state, Mexican independence and liberal reforms, revolution, agrarian reform, industrialization, and the North American Free Trade Agreement. This cultural baseline then becomes proof of an unchanging traditional community located, somehow, outside of the transforming forces of modernity. This selective construction of continuity is legitimized by assumptions related to the social fact of a dichotomy between traditional society and modern society (Durkheim 1997 [1893]; Maine 1986 [1861]; Tönnies 1957 [1887]); between rural and urban lifeways (Redfield 1953); between "hot" and "cold" societies (Lévi-Strauss 1966); or between unchanging societies that reduce conflict through ritual and those more open to revolution and technological change (Gluckman 1960).

Over the last four decades, historical and ethnographic research has made evident the very selective and circular nature of ethnographic analogies based on such dichotomies. The traditions of central western indigenous villages have developed and changed in modern times, and indigenous Mexico has played important and varied parts in this process. Indigenous traditions and customs are not an isolated reality opposed to modernity but, rather, involve practices and institutions that have been transformed in structure, function, and meaning during the construction of the modern world.

On the other hand, behind the claims to cultural continuity, especially those ethnic claims currently being made by representatives of the cultures of Original Peoples, lie histories of communal sovereignty and complex and contentious territorial transitions. As Helen Perlstein Pollard (chapter 5) notes, these histories involve the transition from the tributary empires, both precolumbian and Spanish, toward recently evolving claims of communal sovereignty. Robert Kemper and Julie Adkins (chapter 2) examined the areas of central western Mexico most densely populated by contemporary speakers of indigenous languages (specifically Purépecha [Tarascan], Nahuatl, Wixarika [Huichol], Hñähñu [Otomí], Tepehuan, and Cora) and encountered an important continuity. The most heavily populated core of speakers of all these languages continues to partially occupy the now-altered ancestral territories in which these languages have been spoken since at least the Neoclassic period (thirteenth to early sixteenth centuries).

As Kemper and Adkins demonstrate in chapter 2, the demographic and geographical information on indigenous languages spoken in central western

Mexico both attest to the historical continuity of those cultural groups and define the ethnic landscapes of this region. It is important to stress that these core groupings of indigenous language speakers and their settlements are entering the twenty-first century governed by a new model of the state, one that operates within a global economy. This horizon of change and its implications for these subaltern citizens of Mexico raise a myriad of issues concerning the past and its roles, both real and potential, in the present.

Legislating Free Determination

In the last half of the 1950s, the anthropologist Eric Wolf wrote two seminal articles (1955, 1957) concerned with the typology of communities formed under the pressures of colonial state consolidation during the construction of the Spanish Empire. As he would recognize later (1986), he was writing at a time when our ethnographic and historical knowledge of what could be generally described in the terms of the colonial process as "Christian Indian village communities" formed in the Spanish Empire was still quite limited. Little was known of the uneven development of such communities during a process of colonial state formation, while the varied, often contentious forms of subaltern participation in this process had yet to be explored by historians. Furthermore, the regional realities of these communities and their changes during five centuries of state reform had not been documented. Nevertheless, Wolf's seminal essays underlined one central aspect in the study of these communities, namely, the colonial corporate communal structure consolidated in the creation of Christian village communities and the subsequent prolonged history of political, economic, social, cultural, and legal efforts aimed at their disincorporation. Indeed, after the consolidation of Christian Indian village communities, the ensuing development of large agrarian estates (haciendas) was followed quickly by state reforms aimed at constructing a modern political economy, a process of *longue durée* that has led to complex, uneven, and incomplete processes of disincorporation that continue even today.

Hence, the major force behind the disincorporation of Indian village corporate communities has come from projects aimed at building a modern nation-state. It is commonplace to mention the Bourbon reforms, the liberal reforms of independent Mexico, the agrarian reforms that sought to transform peasants into farmers and workers by molding the corporate agrarian structure into larger, more technologically empowered and market-oriented productive units, and, finally, the current reforms aimed at opening up the country and its diversity to a global economy. These projects have been reflected in numerous legal reforms, the best known of which are Lerdo's Law (Ley de la desamortización, 1856), which abolished the corporately held properties of the Catholic Church and indigenous communities; Article 27 of the 1917 Constitution, which guaranteed agrarian reform and established supposedly modern corporate control over collective resources (water, forest, land) and coincided with a long period of policy making aimed at creating national autonomy through import substitution; and the more recent reform of Article 27, which ended state land redistribution through restitution or donation and made the privatization of the commons legally possible.

The sheer number of legal changes and their relation to changing state reforms over the last 250 years is symptomatic of the historical resilience of the Mexican rural corporate organizations clustered around local control over commons and collective identifications (Tortolero 2008). One initial and seldom-cited example of recent constitutional reform will serve to indicate both a basic issue in the legislation of ethnic landscapes in Mexico and the interrelations among constitutional changes, legislation, and international law, on the one hand, and recent important changes in the politics of identity and the practices of community in Indo-Mexican populations, on the other.

Since the Constitution of 1917, Article 115, which deals with municipal rights, the most basic of the three levels of government recognized by the Constitution (municipal, state, and federal), has been reformed a total of thirteen times. The eleventh reform occurred in 2001: a change accompanied by several other legislative acts, all of which were enacted into law through their publication in the *Diario Oficial de la Federacion* on the same day (August 14, 2001). On that day, Article 4 of the Constitution was extensively reformulated as Article 2. As we will see below, Article 4 was reformed in 1992 in order to recognize the multilingual and pluricultural nature of the Mexican nation in compliance with the terms of the Indigenous and Tribal Peoples in Independent Countries Convention 169 of the United Nations International Labor Organization, which was signed by Mexico in 1990. It was, however, a very limited constitutional compliance with Convention 169 and one that led to major debates and mobilizations concerned with autonomy, territoriality, and collective rights. In addition, on August 14, 2001, the terms for the legal implementation of the constitutional rights established by Article 2 came into effect through the publication of the Law of Indigenous Rights and Culture (known by the opposition as the Bartlett-Ortega-Cevallos Law after the legislators from the three dominant political parties who presented the proposal).

Various nongovernmental and indigenous organizations and groups vigorously questioned the new law. One of the central issues concerned the right of indigenous peoples to organize, cooperate, and associate as autonomous municipalities, or at intermunicipal and interstate levels not recognized in the federal Indigenous Law. Curiously, however, although published in the Official Federal Diary on the same day as this law and Article 2 of the Constitution, the reform of Article 115 did not become an issue of contention. This is surprising, since the change in this article, which is phrased in positive terms, states that "indigenous communities within the municipal precinct will be able to coordinate and associate in the terms and for the effects that the law foresees" (fol. 8389). In short, this reform of Article 115 only recognizes intercommunal organization and association within municipalities.

This constitutional proviso is quite powerful, since several efforts to establish state-level indigenous laws that are more flexible and empowering than the federal Law of Indigenous Rights and Culture have argued that Mexico's international conventions constitute commitments that render invalid any federal or state law that violates them (Godoy 2010). Hence, for example, while it could be argued that Convention 169 supersedes federal law, it can never supersede the Constitution. For this reason, the rights of cooperation and association relevant to all other indigenous rights established by international law and federal and state legislation are restricted constitutionally by Article 115 to within individual municipalities only.

This issue is not a new one, as it reflects the process of neoliberal reform of the Mexican state and the participation of Indo-Mexican populations in those reforms. Mexico was the first Latin American country and the second nation-state (after Norway) to sign Convention 169. This signing did away with the earlier Convention 107 on Indigenous Populations (established in 1957) in support of the then-dominant position of nationalist projects for the assimilation of indigenous populations into a homogeneous national culture with citizens holding constitutionally established individual rights (Hindley 1996:231).

It was in compliance with Convention 169 that in 1992 a new first paragraph was added to Article 4 of the Constitution: "The Mexican Nation has a pluricultural composition, originally based on its indigenous peoples. The law will protect and promote the development of their languages, cultures, uses, customs, resources and specific forms of social organization, and will guarantee their members effective access to the jurisdiction of the State. In the agrarian judgments and procedures in which they are part, their juridical practices and customs will be taken into account in the terms established by the law" (translated in Hindley 1996:234). This change, however, was accompanied by the reform of Article 27 of the Constitution. In effect, that article was changed on January 6, 1992, and its implementation was legislated 49 days later (February 24) through two key federal laws, whereas the paragraph on indigenous rights was added to Article 4 on January 28, 1992, and, as we have seen, the related federal legislation became law almost 10 years later, on August 14, 2001, accompanied by the reforms of Articles 2 and 115 of the Constitution.

Article 2 begins with the statement that "the Mexican Nation is unique and indivisible" (fol. 8176). It defines the indigenous communities that make up an indigenous people and recognizes the right of indigenous communities to "free determination," but only within the constitutional framework of "autonomy that assures national unity." It stipulates that this "free determination" will be established in the constitutions and laws of each state on the basis of ethnolinguistic and settlement criteria. Moreover, it enumerates the autonomy of "free determination" in relation to (1) internal forms of social, economic, political, and cultural organization and coexistence; (2) norms for the regulation and resolution of internal conflicts subject to the federal Constitution with respect to individual and human rights, as well as "the dignity and integrity of women"; (3) the norms, procedures, and practices for the election of representatives and authorities in a framework that respects the sovereignty of the federation and the states and assures gender equality; (4) norms for "preserving and enriching the language, knowledge and all other elements of culture and identity"; (5) guidelines for "conserving and improving the habitat and preserving lands in accordance with the terms of the Federal Constitution"; (6) access to natural resources within the habitat, except those in strategic areas and insofar as the acquired rights of third parties and community members are respected; (7) representation in municipal governments in municipalities with indigenous populations; and (8) access to due legal process that is respectful of custom and cultural specificities congruent with the federal Constitution and supported by interpreters and legal defense with knowledge of the language and culture of defendants. This section of Article 2 ends with the proviso that each state in the Mexican Federation will give greater precision to the terms of autonomy in their respective constitutions and laws in order to better express "the situations and aspirations" of their indigenous peoples, as well as the norms for recognizing indigenous communities as "public interest entities" (*entidades de interés público*).[1]

Collective Rights

The distinction between "interests" and "rights" (*intereses* vs. *derechos*) is highly politically charged, since a focus on public interest implies a politics of recognition of the indigenous population as a specific minority organization with certain prerogatives similar to those of political parties. It does not explicitly grant indigenous populations a legal identity as a group and ipso facto collective rights, what the Mexican anthropologist Guillermo de la Peña (1999) has termed "ethnic citizenship." Not surprisingly, three indigenous groups have challenged the validity of this aspect of Article 2.

The municipality of San Pedro Quiatoni in Oaxaca argued before the Mexican Supreme Court that indigenous peoples and communities should be recognized as "entities of public law" (*entidades de derecho público*), which would mean granting San Pedro Quiatoni legal identity as a people and as a community. However, in the same suit presented in 2001, residents of San Pedro Quiatoni also questioned the validity of the ratification process of the 2001 constitutional reform. As a constitutional tribunal, the validity of constitutional ratification lies outside the attributions of the Court. Hence, their suit was ruled beyond

Table 1.1. Legal Reforms and the Changing Ethnic Landscape.

Date	Legislation
1983	Eighth reform of Article 115 of the Constitution, granting greater financial autonomy to municipalities
1989	Creation of the National Commission for Indian Peoples under the auspices of the National Indigenous Institute
1990	Ratification (after Norway) of Convention 169 of the International Labor Organization concerned with "Indigenous and Tribal Peoples of Independent Countries"
1991	November: Reform of Article 27 of the Mexican Constitution
1992	May: The National Indigenous Institute changes its cabinet affiliation from the Ministry of Education to come under the Ministry of Social Development; October: Rigoberta Menchú is awarded the Nobel Peace Prize, Quincentenary Celebrations
1992	January 28: Reform of Article 4 of the Mexican Constitution
1993	"Year of Indigenous Peoples" in the United Nations
1994	January 1: North American Free Trade Agreement enters into effect; uprising of the Zapatista Army of National Liberation begins in Chiapas; January 19: The National Commission for the Integral Development and Social Justice of Indigenous peoples is created under the direction of the PRI politician Beatriz Paredes
1996	The Commission of Concord and Pacification (COCOPA in Spanish) presents the "Initiative for a Law of Indigenous Rights and Culture"; May 23: President Zedillo attends the concluding meeting of the National Forum on Indigenous Rights and Participation coordinated by Beatriz Paredes
2001	February–April: The COCOPA Law goes before Congress; the "Caravan for Indigenous Dignity" is under way, led by the Zapatista Army for National Liberation; the Third National Indigenous Congress is held in the Purépecha town of Nurío; the Zapatista Leadership appears in Congress in support of the COCOPA Law
2001	August 14: The Federal Law of Indigenous Rights and Culture is passed; the reforms of Article 4 are enacted and included in the new Article 2 of the Mexican Constitution; the eleventh reform of Article 115 is made official, establishing the Indigenous community's right to association and organization in municipalities
2002	April 23: Proposal for a law on the rights of indigenous peoples in the state of Michoacán de Ocampo; the Organización Nación P'urhépecha is founded
2011	June: reform of Article 1 of the Mexican Constitution establishing the human rights recognized both in the Constitution and in Mexico's international treaties

the Court's jurisdiction (Ansolabehere ms, paper presented in the V Congreso de la Red Latinoamericana de Antropología Jurídica, September 2006).

A second constitutional controversy involved the indigenous community of Zirahuén in the municipality of Salvador Escalante in the state of Michoacán. This case was brought in 2002. On that occasion the argument presented against the federal Congress and state legislators as the framers or ratifiers of Article 2 held that the constitutional reform reduced the rights and social and individual guarantees of the indigenous community, particularly with regard to their land rights and rights to natural resources. But the Court ruled in favor of Congress and the state legislators, noting that the Constitution recognizes a preferential right with reference to the natural resources of lands occupied by indigenous people or communities in relation to rights acquired by others. However, the Court also presented an interesting thesis with respect to the idea that Article 2 in some way reduced indigenous rights: given that the Constitution gives each state in the Union the task of regulating the implementation of Article 2, the terms of that article should be considered a *minimum* guarantee upon which each state could enlarge (Ansolabehere ms).

This principle of a minimum guarantee is also reflected in the 2011 reform of Article 1 of the Constitution, the second paragraph of which states that "the norms relevant to human rights will be interpreted in accordance with this constitution and with international treaties on this matter, favoring at all times the most ample protection for persons" (fol. 8284). The citizens of Cherán, Michoacán, cited this principle as established by the Mexican Constitution to argue successfully against local elections based on political parties and thereby gain the right to establish an electoral process and local government on the common-law basis of custom. In September 2011, the federal Judicial Electoral Tribunal resolved this issue in favor of Cherán and ordered that once the necessary conditions for the elections were satisfied, the state Congress should establish the dates for elections and the commencement of the new local custom-based government. By January 2012, Cherán had a local government composed of a council of *barrio* (roughly, ward) leaders and committees. Cherán's custom-based government also won a Supreme Court decision in May 2014 over the right to consultation and review of the state's constitutional reforms concerned with indigenous rights prior to their approval in March 2012.

Even before the Cherán ruling by that federal tribunal in 2011, the state of San Luis Potosí had reformed its Constitution (Article 9) and an indigenous law to grant legal identity to indigenous communities. The legislators were clear in their use of the Supreme Court's thesis that Article 2 of the Mexican Constitution establishes a minimum guarantee of the rights of indigenous peoples and communities as "entities of public interest," but San Luis Potosí's more ample guarantee consisted in recognizing the indigenous community as an "entity of public law." These reforms led to the creation of the Indigenous

Community Registry, in which each community so registered is endowed with a legal identity. Several surrounding states—Jalisco, Nayarit, and Guanajuato—have adopted the San Luis Potosí position as a model in their own process of constitutional reform and legislation.

Such legislation recognizes collective rights at the level of communal organization and, furthermore, respects the framework of Article 2 by basing the registry of the free determination of each community on ethnolinguistic and settlement criteria. It also respects the framework of Article 115, since association and cooperation only operate at the communal level within municipalities. Indeed, Article 115 recognizes that intermunicipal association and cooperation can be authorized with the support of two-thirds of the state legislators or, in the case of the organization of an Indo-Mexican people inhabiting more than one state, the support of two-thirds of each state legislature involved.

The process of consultation and legislation through which Mexico has adjusted its constitution and federal and state laws to accommodate international treaties and conventions makes it clear that the dominant focus for the collective rights of the indigenous population rests at the level of the community. As then-president Ernesto Zedillo argued in May 1996 at a meeting in the National Museum of Anthropology and History—held to present the conclusions of the National Enquiry on Indigenous Rights and Participation (*Consulta nacional sobre derechos y participación indígena*)—a new relationship between the state and the indigenous community was arising, one in which "indigenous communities should be the active subjects, and not the passive objects, of a development based on their cultural diversity, their traditions, and their customs" (author's translation from Roth-Seneff and Sosa 2003:137). This view was maintained in the reforms and legislation of 2001, in the efforts in San Luis Potosí, and, subsequently, in other state legislatures to recognize indigenous communities by granting them legal status as "entities of public law" and in Cherán's elimination of political parties in its 2012 custom-based municipal government.

Thus, there exists a clearly discernible position now amply legislated at the federal and state levels and supported by constitutional reform, namely, the recognition and guarantee of the right to associate and cooperate at the communal level as a form of free determination for indigenous peoples. With regard to Mexico's neoliberal reforms, this is clearly a central aspect of its indigenous policy and may crystallize into a mosaic of indigenous communities as the defining characteristic of Mexico's ethnic landscape in the twenty-first century. Nevertheless, we need to ask the larger historical and ethnographic question related to the congruence of this current legal model for defining the terms of indigenous peoples' association and participation both within Mexico and in relation to the larger global economy. In terms of the settlement patterns of the last five centuries in central western Mexico, language distribution, ritual representation of territoriality, processes of collective identity, and/or the forms of participation and resistance during different phases of Mexican state formation, the question arises as to whether the village community constitutes a unique level of organization for indigenous peoples. Are the settlements that were organized originally as indigenous Christian communities the only historically and ethnographically suitable collectivity for the public right to free association and participation? The chapters of this book address this question in rich and complex ways by focusing first on the past configurations and reconfigurations of the indigenous peoples and then relating them to the present conditions for indigenous groups in central western Mexico.

The Past in the Present

In his discussion of the colonial organization of the Tarascan or Purépecha population, Felipe Castro Gutiérrez (chapter 7) clearly documents how a form of social organization that was in fact a distinctive aspect of colonial government came to be seen not only as typical but as having existed since time immemorial.[2] Helen Perlstein Pollard (chapter 5) points out the structural similarity between the Tarascan and Spanish Empires in terms of their tributary organization. This offers another historical view that both helps explain the claims for such continuity and puts in question this time immemorial horizon. Indeed, both empires were organized around tribute from a subject population, but the organization of tribute was based on very different principles: on the one hand, the rights to dominion and the control of usufruct (Tarascan), and, on the other, the rights to territory and the control of property (Spanish). Thus it should come as no surprise that the primordial land titles studied by Hans Roskamp for the Tarascans (chapter 6) underline the theme of the timeless structure of the village community so relevant to litigation in the Spanish regime. Both Castro Gutiérrez and Roskamp document just how distinctive the Christian village community was as a colonial institution that linked town to state and church. Indeed, prior to the creation of the village structure conceived by the Spanish as a *república de indios* (Indian republic), the social organization in what would become the Viceroyalty of New Spain was considerably different.

As Phillip C. Weigand (chapters 3 and 4) has shown, Mesoamerica is a complex of civilizations, an ecumene linked by shared traditions and technologies but also diverse in its regional forms of organization and technological specialization. Weigand notes that the precolumbian populations of central western Mexico have all too frequently been seen through the lens of the recorded memory and traditions of the central Mexican civilizations, especially the Nahuatl-speaking populations of the Valley of Mexico and the central highlands of the east-west transvolcanic axis of mountains, high plains, and river valleys that so distinctly define Mexico's geography. However, a different picture emerges when we contrast this Culhua Mexica (or "Aztec") version of the precolumbian past with the recorded memory of different segments of the central western indigenous population during the first decades of Spanish control and, especially, with the historical register of conflicts and controversies over territorial dominion, rights to tribute, kinship legitimacy, marriage practices, inheritance, and settlement hierarchies. These sources help to resolve both the Aztec selective tradition, which describes the area surrounding the Tarascan state as a land of nomadic hunting and gathering warriors, and the contrasting descriptions of two rival conquering groups of Spaniards that operated in the central western regions in the first half of the sixteenth century: one (1530–42) associated with Nuño de Guzmán and subsequently Antonio de Mendoza, the first viceroy of New Spain; the other with Hernán Cortés (1522–29). Based on a thorough review of these sources and the archaeological register, Weigand (chapter 3) describes a complex cluster of civilizations in this central western region composed of the Tarascan state bordered to the west and northwest by a trans-Tarascan frontier characterized by small chiefdoms and states and with Uto-Aztec-speaking Caxcan states forming a northeastern frontier.

Upon the arrival of the Spanish, the Tarascans, a dominant and expanding empire, had successfully defended their realm from the neighboring Aztec or Culhua Mexica Empire centered in Tenochtitlan in the Valley of Mexico. Pollard (chapter 5) presents an archaeological record that reports strong continuities in material culture and ceremonial organization in the center of what became the Tarascan Empire, which in 1522 encompassed around 129,490 k^2 (50,000 square miles) of highly populated territory. The patterns of production and consumption of basic resources like pottery and obsidian, as well as the centralized distribution of precious commodities, suggest a transition from small competing states or chiefdoms to a major state alliance, which developed during the two centuries prior to the Spanish arrival. Similarly, the archaeological information on ceremonial sites and the settlement hierarchy reflected in their architecture suggest a ruling class that emerged from alliances involving the island population of Lake Pátzcuaro with people from the surrounding river basins. Indeed, by using this information as context for interpreting the early sixteenth-century indigenous testimonies concerning noble lineages and their relations or alliances with specific deities, Pollard argues for a continuous hierarchical alliance that constituted the Tarascan state, controlled and dominated by a Purépecha-speaking population.

In effect, the early sixteenth-century documents based on the Tarascan historical memory point to a complex society built around the logic of kindreds in which each individual's degree of kinship to a real or mythical ancestor defined her or his place in society. As Castro Gutiérrez notes, what appear to be lineages and eponymous groups are mentioned in these early colonial documents describing precolumbian customs and appear to define collective membership.

They also suggest that access to natural resources (land, water, forests, etc.) was organized on this logic of a clan with a hierarchy built on the principles of a kindred, that is, those members most closely related to real and/or mythical rulers controlled the usufruct of their more distant relations.

Both Roskamp and Castro Gutiérrez suggest that major transitions took place during the first two centuries of colonial administration. Kin-based control of usufruct and tribute was transformed into a village-based control of property, and tribute was displaced from the Purépecha nobility to the colonial state. By the end of the seventeenth century, the indigenous nobility had lost control over not only the city councils of Pátzcuaro, Tzintzuntzan, and Uruapan but also the collection of tribute from outlying settlements (*barrios*) traditionally controlled by those centers. This transition is documented in the land titles and indigenous documents of those indigenous villages and towns; and, as Roskamp shows, these colonial titles, or later versions of them, reappear in disputes over village territory or political jurisdiction in every major period of state reform up to the present.

As Castro Gutiérrez observes for the Tarascans, the ethnic landscape of the colonial period became village centered: an orientation sustained in disputes between village communities and municipal seats over questions of territory or political or religious jurisdiction, often supported by each community's historical documents and traditions. Despite a common language and culture, these village-based peasant corporations have only recently begun to transform into a collective Purépecha self-identification as a subaltern ethnic group in Mexico.

The colonial history of the trans-Tarascan frontier and Caxcan area north of the former Tarascan state was, however, strikingly different. In chapter 4, Weigand stresses the social, political, and economic impact of the Spanish arrival and conquest of the Culhua Mexica (Aztec) Empire, which put an end to a vitally important long-distance trade system intimately tied to the region. As José Francisco Román Gutiérrez (chapter 8) notes, when the Spanish reached the region—first to exploit its mineral resources and later to expand the colony—very few clearly identifiable settlements under colonial jurisdiction were established during several decades. Indeed, in order to initiate the settlement process, a major battle involving thousands of indigenous and Spanish troops was necessary. During three centuries of colonial government, this was the only occasion when a viceroy actually led an army into battle. As both Weigand and Román Gutiérrez document, the Mixtón War was the start of a prolonged rebellious movement that lasted into the first decades of the eighteenth century. This strong and prolonged resistance, which displaced the indigenous population to the more isolated areas of the western Sierra Madre and redistributed groups in other remote mountain areas above the Pacific coast, is an important historical background for Paul Liffman's (chapter 9) and John

Gledhill's (chapter 10) descriptions of the continued ritual and communal resistance and defense of territory in the present.

Liffman reviews the organization and historical depth of Huichol (Wixarika) ritual representations of territory. The dimensions and depth of these representations attest to centuries-old practices in the former trans-Tarascan and Caxcan regions of western Mexico. For instance, the Huichol ceremonial space extends over 145,028 k^2 (56,000 square miles). Liffman discloses both the cosmological and quotidian logics of this ceremonial space with its organization as a primordial exchange sphere between people and gods in which ceremonial offerings propitiate hunting and gathering and long-distance exchange. As Weigand and Román have documented, this area has formed part of a highly contentious and multicultural region since at least the Postclassic period (thirteenth to sixteenth centuries). Liffman presents contemporary aspects of these ongoing conflicts in the context of the Huichol's (Wixarika) continuing ritual conservation of territory and cosmological entitlement.

Another conflictive region in central western Mexico lies on the mountainous northwest Pacific coast of Michoacán, bordering on the modern state of Colima. Settlement in this area emerged from groups displaced during a colonial period of forced labor and struggle in the territories on the northern periphery of the former Tarascan Empire. As Gledhill documents, it was only by the end of the seventeenth century that Nahuatl became the lingua franca in this heterogeneous cultural region, and the strong community structure in this Nahuatl-speaking zone is a postcolonial construction. These communities arose during two centuries of struggle to preserve their territorial sovereignty against neighboring ranchers and outside interests attracted by the region's rich natural resources. As Gledhill shows, this has led to processes of disintegration such that only one community has managed to sustain territorial sovereignty into the twenty-first century. Unfortunately, this locality, Ostula, is now undergoing an extremely violent and difficult period of intervention by outside interests and regional groups, which Gledhill finds similar to the pressures exerted on the area at the end of the nineteenth century.

In these ethnographic and historical cases from central western Mexico, a common theme is the strong cohesive forces of ritual spheres of exchange both in the colonial construction of Christian village communities in Purépecha and Nahuatl groups in Michoacán and in territorially more extensive but demographically less inclusive Huichol (Wixarika) groups and their Cora and Tepehuan neighbors. Andrew Roth-Seneff (chapter 11) examines how in recent decades, especially in the twenty-first century, the Purépecha have begun a transition in which communally oriented spheres of ritual exchange have expanded, taking on an ethnic orientation. Through political struggles, demands for collective rights, and the celebration of cultural and ethnic revitalization,

Purépecha ceremonialism and ritual processes are becoming increasingly territorially extensive in their representations.

These changes are inseparable from the reforms that in the last three decades
have led to a new model of the state in Mexico. The past governmental focus
on building a nation-state through programs that promoted the acculturation
and assimilation of indigenous Mexico into a national mainstream has ceded its
place to a new emphasis on governing a multicultural nation integrated into the
global economy. Nevertheless, this new present contains a historically profound
and culturally very rich past, a powerful historical resource for contemporary
claims on communal sovereignty.

Notes

1. All translations are by the author.

2. Tarascan is the colonial term that was in use until around 1980, whereas
P'urhépecha is the current form of self-reference, and Purépecha is the current Spanish
orthography of P'urhépecha.

2

Indigenous Population Transformations in West-Central Mexico

Robert V. Kemper and Julie Adkins

During the time before the Conquest, all of the peoples of west-central Mexico were "indigenous," although there was no single designation for them, as came to be the case after the arrival of the Spaniards. The use of a term such as *indio* to refer to all the native peoples required that they be seen as the *same* rather than as *different* from each other (Bonfil Batalla 1996). Learning to recognize the presence of distinct population groups throughout the region has required archaeological research, ethnohistorical investigation, linguistic analysis, and cultural studies, nearly all of which have been carried out since the Mexican Revolution of 1910. This research has made use of the limited available historical resources (mainly located in local and national archives), government censuses and surveys, and firsthand fieldwork. Thus, the results from hundreds of independent projects provide the data for assessing the historical transformation of indigenous populations in west-central Mexico.

In this chapter, we offer an overview of these population transformations. One of the greatest challenges in examining "indigenous" populations is that the definition of the native communities has changed over time (Borah 1954). Carrying out systematic, longitudinal, comparative analysis depends on consistent data and their definitions; unfortunately, such data do not exist for our topic.

Given the detailed attention that the authors of other chapters give to particular populations in specific periods, ranging from the preconquest era to the present, we have taken a broader, regional perspective. We emphasize the changes in indigenous populations across the west-central region, with particular attention to the contemporary situation. Despite its limitations, the decennial census provides the only useful source of information to examine local and region-wide changes. The census uses a question about speaking an indigenous language (whether monolingually or bilingually) as the principal way to define the indigenous population. Elsewhere (Kemper and Adkins 2004), we have discussed at length the problems associated with this language-based approach to defining indigenous populations within specific regions. Suggestions have been made (e.g., Embriz Osorio and Ruíz Mondragón 2003) that new variables—including ones focused on localities and households—be added to those currently used in the national censuses. This would certainly improve our appreciation of the characteristics of the indigenous populations going forward but cannot help us to understand better the past.

The Period before the Arrival of the Spaniards

Archaeologists and ethnohistorians continue to seek out sites and archives that will reveal more information about the west-central region of Mexico prior to the early sixteenth century. They agree that much less is known about the populations occupying this vast region than is the case for the central highlands or the Maya Lowlands. For many scholars, the first priority was to understand the Aztecs and their empire; as a result, the west-central region was marginalized in terms of the number of scholars working there and projects being carried out. At present, numerous sites have been excavated within the region, ranging from Chemetla in southern Sinaloa to Chupícuaro in northeastern Michoacán to La Villita in the Río Balsas delta between Michoacán and Guerrero.

Unfortunately, scholars have not been able to reach a consensus on the size of the regional population at different periods before the arrival of the Spaniards. What is clear is that the Purépecha had consolidated their rule over the region of what is today the state of Michoacán and parts of Guanajuato and Jalisco. The other large population center was associated with Teuchitlán, located in what is today the state of Jalisco, and the people known as the Caxcanes. In addition, scattered settlements of what now are called the Cora and Huichol peoples were to be found in the rugged region where the borders of the modern states of Jalisco, Nayarit, and Durango come together.

The Conquest Period

According to Eric van Young, "Ethnologically speaking, at the eruption of the Europeans into the Center-West the macroregion included one great indigenous society of the complex, state-level Mesoamerican cultural type, the Tarascans; a number of more diminutive, city-state-level polities also sharing the core tradition, such as those of the upper Chapala Basin; and less advanced groups of hunter-gatherers and semi-sedentary farmers, mainly to the north and northeast, including those known into the colonial era by the pejorative Nahuatl name of Chichimecas" (2000:140).

The period of the early 1500s, when the Spaniards arrived in west-central Mexico, brought a great shock to the way of life that had emerged in important towns and their subsidiary *barrios* during the preceding two hundred years. For example, in the Lake Pátzcuaro region in the highlands of central Michoacán,

Tzintzuntzan and its barrios—especially Ihuatzio and Pátzcuaro—were important settlements located around what is now called Lake Pátzcuaro. Archaeological and ethnohistorical research suggests that Tzintzuntzan had a population of 25,000–35,000, while the surrounding Pátzcuaro Basin might have had as many as 200,000 inhabitants, and the area controlled by the Tarascans in Michoacán, Jalisco, and Guanajuato might have reached 1.5 million (van Young 2000:141).

The indigenous populations of the west-central region were numerous and diverse, although we know very little about their demographic characteristics. For example, only five fragments have survived of a regional survey made in 1523–1524 by Antonio de Caravajal, sent by Hernán Cortés to the Tarascan region in order to determine how the regional settlements might be divided into future *encomiendas*. A recent analysis of the Caravajal documents suggests that population density was low outside of the main settlements. It appears that the settlement pattern was dispersed, rather than nucleated, and that many of the smaller places located near their *cabeceras* disappeared during the early colonial period in the process of bringing people to live in *congregaciones*, whereas towns located at a greater distance from their cabeceras have continued to exist to the present day (Espejel Carbajal 2011).

Outside of the large central region dominated by the Tarascans, ethnolinguistic groups included Guachichil, Guamare, and Zacateco speakers to the east and north of the Río Grande de Santiago. To the west of the Tarascan Empire lived large groups of Caxcanes, Cocas, Coras, Huicholes, Tecuexes, Tepecanos, and Tepehuanes, as well as smaller groups, including the Nahuatl and Otomí. To the east of the Tarascan-dominated zone and serving as a buffer between the Tarascans and the Aztecs lived Matlatzincan, Mazahuan, and Otomí populations.

The early years after the arrival of the Spaniards were especially difficult for the indigenous populations of the west-central region. After suffering the depredations of troops led by Nuño de Guzmán, they witnessed the more benign, but equally transformative, efforts of the Franciscans and other representatives of the Catholic Church and the colonial government. For instance, Bishop Vasco de Quiroga arrived in Tzintzuntzan in 1539 but the next year moved his headquarters from there to the barrio of Pátzcuaro, located on the southern end of the lake that now bears its name. From there he and his fellow Franciscans carried out programs (such as the hospitals at Santa Fe de la Laguna on the northern shore of Lake Pátzcuaro) that were meant to improve and sustain the lives of the natives. Unfortunately, their efforts could not overcome the impact of European diseases that eventually reduced greatly the native populations. Some ethnohistorians estimate that the region's population fell by 90 percent from its preconquest levels, a drop similar to what took place in the central highlands of the Aztec Empire.

The Colonial Period

Figure 2.1 (based on Beals 1932) shows the geographical distribution of the major language groups in west-central Mexico for the period before 1750.

During the colonial period, many of the indigenous populations in west-central Mexico slowly began to recover their earlier numbers. In addition, the "empty" spaces in the region (especially the coastal areas) attracted immigrants from elsewhere in Mexico. Spanish sources suggest that by the early 1800s the populations in the west-central region had reached 30–40 percent of their pre-contact levels. Of these slowly rising numbers, 40–60 percent were considered as natives rather than as mestizos (van Young 2000:146).

Even Tzintzuntzan, once the capital of a powerful empire, had fallen on hard days. For 1639, the population was reported as some 200 *vecinos* (heads of families), indicating that the town had fallen to about 1,000 inhabitants (Rea 1882:80), and the process of mestization was already apparent. By 1748, the community was said to have 45 families of Spaniards, 52 of mestizos and mulattoes, and 150 of Indians. In sum, Tzintzuntzan had some 407 *gente de razón* (Europeans, literally "people of reason") and 496 *indios* (Foster 1948:20–21).

By the middle of the eighteenth century, the rest of the Lake Pátzcuaro region included communities, all with churches and clergy: Ichupio (60 families, apparently all Indian); Cucuchucho (18 Indian families); Cucupao (modern Quiroga, 30 Spanish, 60 mulatto and mestizo, and 60 Indian families); Santa Fe (120 Indian families); and San Jerónimo Purenchéchuaro (35 Indian families). In addition, communities in the highlands to the west and in the adjacent valley known as La Cañada had only Indian populations, with rare mention of a few Spaniards.

During the colonial period, many indigenous communities were subjected to the challenges imposed by the institution known as the *hacienda*. The economic power of the haciendas, which were able to take over the best lands in the region, meant that many communities in the areas where haciendas were located were subjugated and became dependencies in what was an extension of the feudal system of serfdom imported from Spain to the New World. Although some communities were able to maintain their status as indigenous towns (*pueblos*), this usually required years of struggles in the Spanish legal system. Tzintzuntzan was not the only community that spent many years before achieving success in regaining its status as a *ciudad* within the colonial hierarchy of localities, a title that it maintains today, despite having a local population below 4,000.

By the end of the colonial era, populations were rising throughout Mexico, and considerable demographic pressures were being felt in indigenous communities. As production increasingly was exported to urban areas and even abroad, local economies suffered. Villages were more subject to external economic and political forces, and their distinctive indigenous characteristics were

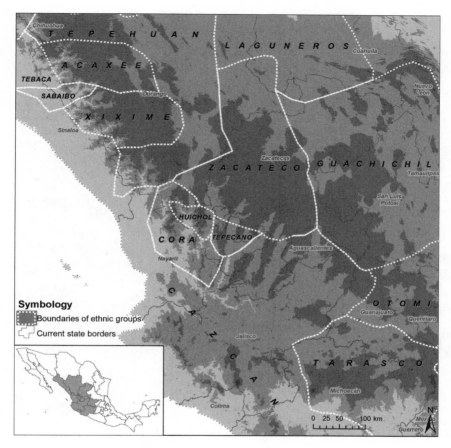

Figure 2.1. This map shows the geographical distribution of the major languages in west-central Mexico for the period before 1750 (GIS map, based on the map entitled "Ethic Groups of Northern Mexico" in Beals 1932).

submerged into a generalized "Indian" peasantry vis-à-vis the dominant mestizo population.

The Nineteenth Century

The nineteenth century became a century of "survival" for the indigenous peoples in west-central Mexico. During the century from the independence movement to the revolution, the little that we know of these peoples comes from visitors' accounts and the occasional governmental effort to enumerate their communities. Unfortunately, little reliable demographic data on the indigenous groups can be found in these sources. For example, based on a visit to the

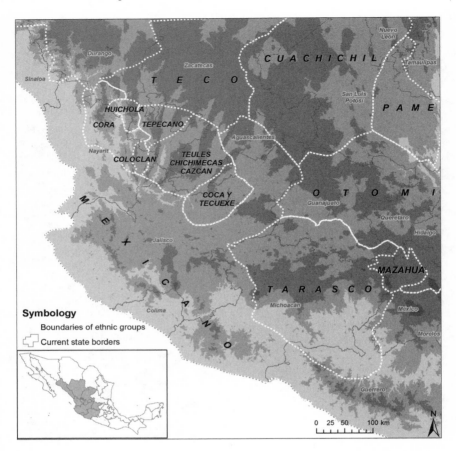

Figure 2.2. This map shows the geographical zones from east to west for Mazahua; Otomí; Tarasco; Coca and Tecuexe; Teules, Chichimecas, and Caxcan; Tepecano; Coloclan; Cora; Huichola; Teco; and Mexicano (along the entire coastline from Guerrero to Sinaloa) (GIS map based on Orozco y Berra 1864).

region, Alexander von Humboldt described Tzintzuntzan as "only a poor Indian village, though it still preserves the pompous title of *ciudad*" (1811:208). A bit later, Tzintzuntzan is described as "a miserable pueblo of Indians" (Martínez de Lejarza 1824:165–166). By contrast, Carl Lumholtz (1902:2:451) passed through the area in 1896 and called Tzintzuntzan mestizo rather than Indian in composition.

One of the few significant publications of the century focused on the geographical distribution of indigenous languages in Mexico. The author, Manuel Orozco y Berra (1864), provided a useful map, from which we have extracted the west-central portion. Figure 2.2 shows the geographical zones from east to west for Mazahua; Otomí; Tarasco; Coca and Tecuexe; Teules, Chichimecas, and Caxcan; Tepecano; Coloclan; Cora; Huichola; Teco; and Mexicano (along the entire coastline from Guerrero to Sinaloa).

The Early Twentieth Century

The situation in the early part of the twentieth century was one of great turmoil for west-central Mexico, with the expansion of the *ejido* programs in the 1930s following the Cristero Rebellion in the 1920s, which came in the wake of the Mexican Revolution of the 1910s. Understandably, the census data for that period are not considered to be very reliable; moreover, the census did not address directly the question of speakers of indigenous languages at the municipal level but only at the state level. Thus, it is not possible to make detailed regional comparisons as we can for the period from 1940 onward.

The Period from 1940 to 2000

During the twentieth century, the population of Mexico expanded greatly both in numbers and in its geographical distribution. These tendencies placed considerable pressure on the areas where indigenous populations had been living on the margins of "modern" society during the colonial and national periods. As Mexico became more urban, industrial, and market oriented, the traditional ways of life of indigenous communities were threatened. One result was an initial decline in their populations, especially as a result of immigration to the booming cities during the period after the 1940s and to the United States, where indigenous men and women worked alongside mestizos, and all were considered to be "Mexicans" rather than distinguished by ethnic or linguistic groupings.

In the region of west-central Mexico, these tendencies are visible from the data available in past decennial national censuses of population and housing. Tables 2.1, 2.2, and 2.3 show what happened to the indigenous language–speaking population in the region from near the end of the global economic depression and the beginning of the *bracero* labor treaty (1942) with the United States at the start of World War II, to the oil boom of the 1970s, to the NAFTA treaty with Canada and the United States (1994) and beyond.

In each of these three censuses, Michoacán had by far the most speakers of indigenous languages. The number of speakers has increased throughout the region, especially since 1970. The distribution of speakers within the region has changed considerably as indigenous men, women, and children have joined millions of other Mexicans in emigrating from rural areas to urban places. These data also suggest that the Mexican government recently has done a much better job of carrying out the decennial census in marginal rural zones than it did in 1940 and even in 1970. Certainly, the numbers reflect the changing

Table 2.1. Distribution of Speakers of Indigenous Languages for West-Central Mexico: 1940 (Sorted by Number of Indigenous Language Speakers per State).

State	Population 5+ years old	Population 5+ years old speaking an indigenous language	Percent of population 5+ years old speaking an indigenous language
Michoacán	1,007,826	62,181	6.17
Sinaloa	418,177	9,327	2.23
Guanajuato	895,727	6,539	0.73
Nayarit	186,251	5,504	2.96
Durango	408,541	1,823	0.45
Jalisco	1,222,439	1,517	0.12
Aguascalientes	140,646	33	0.02
Zacatecas	479,673	32	0.01
Colima	68,290	20	0.03
Total	4,827,570	86,976	1.80

Table 2.2. Distribution of Speakers of Indigenous Languages for West-Central Mexico: 1970 (Sorted by Number of Indigenous Language Speakers per State).

State	Population 5+ years old	Population 5+ years old speaking an indigenous language	Percent of population 5+ years old speaking an indigenous language
Michoacán	1,923,182	62,851	3.27
Sinaloa	1,025,956	11,979	1.17
Nayarit	450,015	9,476	2.11
Jalisco	2,725,357	5,559	0.20
Durango	770,043	4,848	0.63
Guanajuato	1,868,238	2,272	0.12
Zacatecas	770,079	1,000	0.13
Colima	200,016	406	0.20
Aguascalientes	278,196	283	0.10
Total	10,011,082	98,674	0.99

Table 2.3. Distribution of Speakers of Indigenous Languages for West-Central Mexico: 2000 (Sorted by Number of Indigenous Language Speakers per State).

State	Population 5+ years old	Population 5+ years old speaking an indigenous language	Percent of population 5+ years old speaking an indigenous language
Michoacán	3,423,064	121,849	3.56
Sinaloa	2,241,298	49,744	2.22
Jalisco	5,541,530	39,259	0.71
Nayarit	762,894	36,749	4.82
Durango	1,264,011	24,931	1.97
Guanajuato	4,049,950	10,689	0.26
Colima	457,777	2,932	0.64
Zacatecas	1,188,634	1,837	0.15
Aguascalientes	821,404	1,244	0.15
Total	19,750,562	289,234	1.46

circumstances of transportation infrastructure into (and out of) challenging natural environments. In addition, the recent rise in ethnic and cultural consciousness among ethnic populations in Mexico has contributed to a greater sense of pride in having an indigenous heritage and the ability to speak an indigenous language.

Figures 2.3, 2.4, and 2.5 show the distribution of *municipios* (roughly equivalent in political terms to a county in a state in the United States) with speakers of indigenous languages for west-central Mexico. The presence of major "core" areas (central, continuously occupied parts of an indigenous territory) is apparent in all three censuses for 1940, 1970, and 2000.

Among the hundreds of municipios of the west-central region, only a relatively small number contain a significant proportion of speakers of indigenous languages. Tables 2.4, 2.5, and 2.6 show that the zones of high linguistic concentration have gone through significant changes since 1940.

Looking at the changes from 1940 to 2000, the most remarkable is the resurgence and expansion of the populations of the Huichol and Cora populations at the intersection of the states of Nayarit, Durango, and Jalisco. In 1940 only two municipios—Nayar in Nayarit and Mezquital in Durango—had more than 15 percent of their populations over five years old as speakers

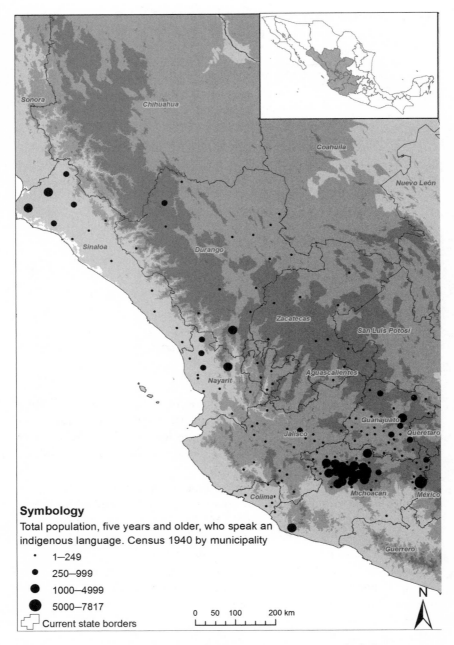

Symbology

Total population, five years and older, who speak an indigenous language. Census 1940 by municipality

- ·   1—249
- ●   250—999
- ●   1000—4999
- ●   5000—7817
- ⬚   Current state borders

0   50   100   200 km

N

Figure 2.3. This figure indicates the distribution of municipios in which there were reported speakers of indigenous languages (age five years and older) for the 1940 census. Actual numbers of speakers are represented by the size of the dot marking the location. See accompanying text and tables for discussion of changes over time.

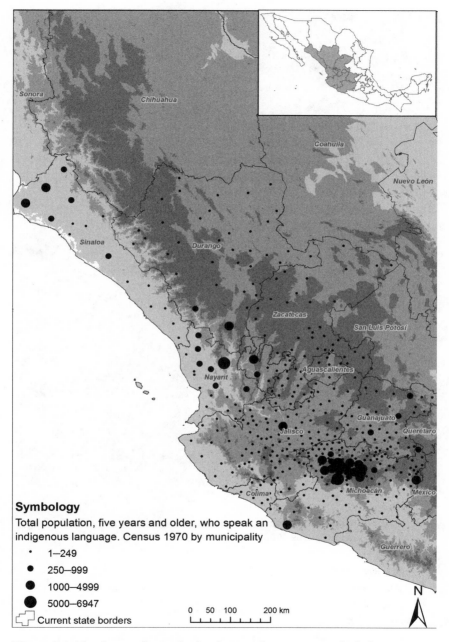

Figure 2.4. This figure indicates the distribution of municipios in which there were reported speakers of indigenous languages (age five years and older) for the 1970 census. Actual numbers of speakers are represented by the size of the dot marking the location. See accompanying text and tables for discussion of changes over time.

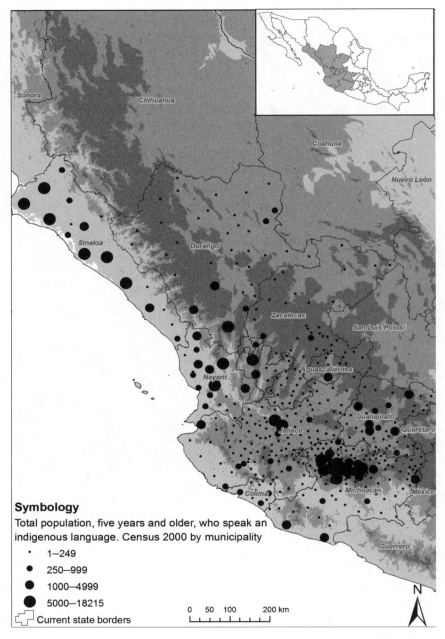

Figure 2.5. This figure indicates the distribution of municipios in which there were reported speakers of indigenous languages (age five years and older) for the 2000 census. Actual numbers of speakers are represented by the size of the dot marking the location. See accompanying text and tables for discussion of changes over time.

Table 2.4. Distribution of Speakers of Indigenous Languages for Municipios in West-Central Mexico: 1940 (Sorted by Percentage of Indigenous Language Speakers per Municipio, with a Minimum of 15 Percent).

State	Municipio	Population 5+ years old	Population 5+ years old speaking indigenous language	Percent of population 5+ years old speaking indigenous language
Michoacán	Cherán	3,113	2,511	80.66
Michoacán	Charapan	2,402	1,748	72.77
Michoacán	Paracho	8,512	5,389	63.31
Michoacán	Chilchota	7,747	4,437	57.27
Nayarit	Nayar	6,524	3,718	56.99
Michoacán	Quiroga	7,386	4,073	55.14
Michoacán	Parangaricutiro	5,684	2,754	48.45
Michoacán	Tzintzuntzan	4,630	2,030	43.84
Michoacán	Erongarícuaro	4,499	1,946	43.25
Michoacán	Tangamandapio	6,539	2,735	41.83
Michoacán	Nahuatzen	7,125	2,852	40.03
Michoacán	Los Reyes	11,128	4,285	38.51
Michoacán	Tingambato	4,390	1,677	38.20
Michoacán	Aquila	3,318	1,050	31.65
Durango	Mezquital	4,053	1,213	29.93
Michoacán	Zitácuaro	30,451	7,817	25.67
Michoacán	Ziracuaretiro	3,622	756	20.87
Michoacán	Tangancícuaro	12,965	2,405	18.55
Michoacán	Coeneo	12,171	2,110	17.34
Michoacán	Zacapu	14,177	2,334	16.46
Sinaloa	Del Fuerte	27,540	4,487	16.29
Total		187,976	62,327	33.16

Table 2.5. Distribution of Speakers of Indigenous Languages for Municipios in West-Central Mexico: 1970 (Sorted by Percentage of Indigenous Language Speakers per Municipio, with a Minimum of 15 Percent).

State	Municipio	Population 5+ years old	Population 5+ years old speaking indigenous language	Percent of population 5+ years old speaking indigenous language
Nayarit	Nayar	9,364	6,016	64.25
Michoacán	Charapan	7,158	3,525	49.25
Michoacán	Cherán	8,427	4,134	49.06
Michoacán	Chilchota	14,571	6,947	47.68
Michoacán	Tzintzuntzan	7,513	2,637	35.10
Michoacán	Quiroga	13,480	4,611	34.21
Durango	Mezquital	8,894	2,903	32.64
Jalisco	Mezquitic	8,720	2,694	30.89
Michoacán	Paracho	15,432	4,415	28.61
Michoacán	Nahuatzen	11,168	2,781	24.90
Michoacán	Tangamandapio	11,894	2,959	24.88
Michoacán	Tingambato	5,484	906	16.52
Michoacán	Aquila	11,009	1,640	14.90
Total		133,114	46,168	34.68

of indigenous languages, totaling 7,771 speakers. By 1970 the municipio of Mezquitic (Jalisco) had joined the group, and the number of speakers reached 11,613. By 2000 the core region of Huichol and Cora speakers had expanded to include the municipios of Bolaños in Jalisco and La Yesca in Nayarit, and the total number of speakers had grown to 47,988.

In contrast to the expansion of Huichol- and Cora-speaking populations, the core region of Purépecha speakers has been reduced since 1940, at least when measured by the presence of 15 percent or more speakers in a municipio. In 1940 there were 16 such municipios, but this number declined sharply to 9 in 1970 and then recovered a bit to 11 in 2000. The total number of speakers also has gone down and then rebounded: in 1940 the 16 municipios had 44,042 speakers; in 1970 the 9 municipios had just 32,915; and in 2000 the 11 municipios had 76,898.

Table 2.6. Distribution of Speakers of Indigenous Languages for Municipios in West-Central Mexico: 2000 (Sorted by Percentage of Indigenous Language Speakers per Municipio, with a Minimum of 15 Percent).

State	Municipio	Population 5+ years old	Population 5+ years old speaking indigenous language	Percent of population 5+ years old speaking indigenous language
Nayarit	Nayar	21,948	18,215	82.99
Durango	Mezquital	22,799	16,630	72.94
Jalisco	Mezquitic	11,817	7,652	64.75
Michoacán	Chilchota	26,695	15,116	56.62
Michoacán	Charapan	9,543	5,250	55.01
Jalisco	Bolaños	4,395	2,125	48.35
Michoacán	Nahuatzen	20,247	8,590	42.43
Michoacán	Paracho	26,978	10,372	38.45
Michoacán	Tangamandapio	22,562	8,158	36.16
Michoacán	Cherán	14,161	4,969	35.09
Michoacán	Quiroga	21,073	7,130	33.83
Nayarit	La Yesca	10,986	3,366	30.64
Michoacán	Erongarícuaro	11,617	2,572	22.14
Michoacán	Coeneo	20,559	3,892	18.93
Michoacán	Los Reyes	49,900	8,914	17.86
Michoacán	Tzintzuntzan	10,845	1,935	17.84
Michoacán	Aquila	18,970	2,966	15.64
Total		325,095	127,852	39.33

The core region for Mexicano (Nahuatl) speakers in west-central Mexico has been the municipio of Aquila along the coast of Michoacán. It is the only municipio with at least 15 percent of its five-year-old and older population speaking Mexicano. In 1940 Aquila had 1,050 indigenous language speakers, representing almost 32 percent of the five-year-old and older population. By 1970 the census reported an increase to 1,640 speakers, but this represented only about 15 percent of the population. By 2000 the number of speakers had increased to 2,966 but held steady at almost 16 percent.

The Contemporary Situation

In 2010, at the time of the most recent Mexican national census, the population of the nine-state region encompassing Aguascalientes, Colima, Durango, Guanajuato, Jalisco, Michoacán, Nayarit, Sinaloa, and Zacatecas had reached 23,240,916 persons. This population was distributed among 440 municipios. In this region, only six municipios had no speakers (five years old and older) of indigenous languages. The total number of persons five years old and older who were reported in the census as speakers of an indigenous language was 318,771, equivalent to only 1.4 percent of the regional population.

As figure 2.6 shows, the contemporary distribution of the population speaking an indigenous language in this nine-state region is thinly spread among nearly all municipios, at the same time that it is concentrated in relatively few municipios.

The mean size of the population of speakers of indigenous languages is 724, but the median is just 46. The variance between the median and the mean reflects the large number of municipios with small numbers of speakers of indigenous languages. Table 2.7 shows the ranges for all 440 municipios.

Another way of looking at this distribution is to focus on the relatively few municipios with large numbers (table 2.8). Their distribution reveals two tendencies: (1) there are some core regions with high populations, and (2) a large number of indigenous speakers have migrated to urban areas, especially to the metropolitan areas of state capitals. This top half of the first quartile ranges from 25,179 down to 1,004 speakers.

These 55 municipios, representing one-eighth of all 440 municipios in the region, have more than half of the region's population, while their population of speakers of indigenous languages totals seven-eighths of all indigenous language speakers in the region. Most of the largest urban places (and their municipios) are included in table 2.8, both at the top and at the bottom.

One can also see on the list those municipios traditionally associated with core indigenous populations, especially in the mountainous regions where the states of Jalisco, Nayarit, and Durango meet; in west-central Michoacán; along the coastal area of Michoacán, Colima, and Jalisco; and in the eastern area of Michoacán abutting the states of México and Hidalgo. These core regions become more visible when the data are rearranged by percentages of speakers of indigenous languages. In fact, more than half of the indigenous language speakers in west-central Mexico are concentrated in just 19 small- to midsized municipios—ranging from Bolaños, Jalisco, with 5,910 persons of five years of age and older, to Los Reyes, Michoacán, with 55,119—located in what today are considered "marginal" zones in the region.

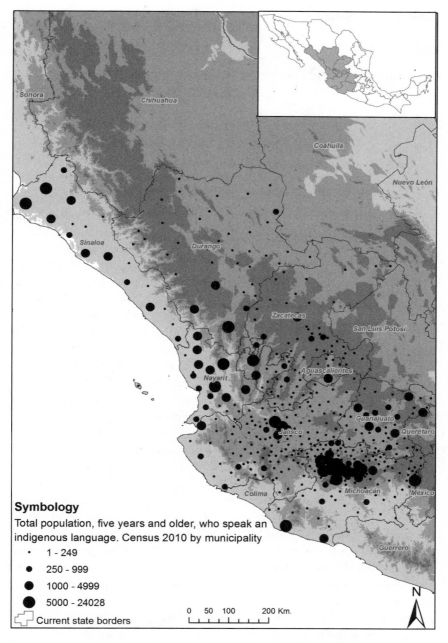

Symbology

Total population, five years and older, who speak an
indigenous language. Census 2010 by municipality

- ·   1 - 249
- ●   250 - 999
- ●   1000 - 4999
- ●   5000 - 24028

⬚ Current state borders

0   50   100   200 Km.

N

Figure 2.6. This figure indicates the distribution of municipios in which there were
reported speakers of indigenous languages (age five years and older) for the 2010
census. Actual numbers of speakers are represented by the size of the dot marking the
location. See accompanying text and tables for discussion of changes over time.

Table 2.7. Distribution of Speakers of Indigenous Languages for West-Central
Mexico: 2010.

Quartile	Municipios	Population range	Median population in quartile
1	110	189–25,179	861
2	110	46–188	96
3	110	17–45	27
4	110	0–16	8

Table 2.9 shows all municipios in which at least 15 percent of the population
(five years old and older) speaks an indigenous language. These municipios can
be further combined to reveal the existence of three distinctive language zones.
The largest zone is dominated by the Purépecha language and encompasses
the eleven highland municipios of Chilchota, Charapan, Nahuatzen, Tangamandapio, Paracho, Quiroga, Cherán, Erongarícuaro, Coeneo, Los Reyes, and
Tzintzuntzan, all located in Michoacán. In 2010 the eleven municipios had
83,709 indigenous language speakers, about a 10 percent increase during the
first decade of this century. Perhaps the most telling case is that of the municipio of Tzintzuntzan, capital of the powerful Purépecha Empire in the two centuries before the arrival of the Spaniards but reduced over the centuries into a
demographically insignificant municipio; in fact, it only became a municipio in
1930 by an executive order of Gen. Lázaro Cárdenas, then governor of the state
of Michoacán in the period before he became president of Mexico. In the 1940
census 44 percent of the municipal population was reported as being speakers
of Tarascan, whereas by 2010 the percentage had dropped to just 15 percent.
The second important zone is the home of speakers of the Huichol and
Cora languages. This mostly mountainous area, now known as the Gran Nayar,
encompasses six municipios: Nayar and La Yesca (in Nayarit), Bolaños and
Mezquitic (both in Jalisco), and Mezquital (Durango), with Huajicori (Nayarit)
having joined the group. In 2010 this area's population of indigenous language
speakers reached 69,104. Both in absolute and percentage terms, this demographic and geographical expansion of the Huichol and Cora populations in the
Gran Nayar has been remarkable and would have been impossible for scholars
and politicians in the 1930s to have imagined. Perhaps one of the greatest challenges for the populations living in the Gran Nayar is that it is divided among
three states and in each case is located at a great distance from large urban areas.
Moreover, the political representation of the Huichol and Cora speakers is diluted because they are located in municipios in three different states.

Table 2.8. Distribution of Speakers of Indigenous Languages for Municipios in West-Central Mexico: 2010 (Sorted by Number of Indigenous Language Speakers per Municipio, with a Minimum of 1,000 Speakers).

State	Municipio	Population 5+ years old	Population 5+ years old speaking an indigenous language	Percent of population 5+ years old speaking an indigenous language
Nayarit	Nayar	28,859	25,179	87.25
Durango	Mezquital	27,921	22,102	79.16
Michoacán	Chilchota	32,561	19,003	58.36
Michoacán	Uruapan	277,961	18,020	6.48
Jalisco	Zapopan	1,115,381	12,339	1.11
Jalisco	Mezquitic	15,438	11,591	75.08
Michoacán	Los Reyes	55,119	10,680	19.38
Michoacán	Paracho	31,104	9,916	31.88
Michoacán	Nahuatzen	24,093	9,850	40.88
Michoacán	Tangamandapio	24,764	8,544	34.50
Nayarit	Tepic	341,956	7,462	2.18
Michoacán	Quiroga	23,087	7,355	31.86
Michoacán	Aquila	20,610	6,940	33.67
Sinaloa	El Fuerte	88,599	5,957	6.72
Michoacán	Charapan	11,034	5,784	52.42
Jalisco	Guadalajara	1,357,921	5,471	0.40
Michoacán	Zitacuaro	138,603	5,196	3.75
Sinaloa	Ahome	378,618	5,188	1.37
Nayarit	La Yesca	11,970	4,990	41.69
Michoacán	Pátzcuaro	78,681	4,863	6.18
Michoacán	Cherán	16,086	4,310	26.79
Michoacán	Morelia	650,219	3,811	0.59
Jalisco	Bolaños	5,910	3,777	63.91
Michoacán	Coeneo	18,720	3,727	19.91
Durango	Pueblo Nuevo	42,950	3,314	7.72
Guanajuato	León	1,286,359	3,191	0.25
Jalisco	Tlaquepaque	540,360	3,175	0.59
Durango	Durango	509,077	2,801	0.55

continued

Table 2.8. Continued

State	Municipio	Population 5+ years old	Population 5+ years old speaking an indigenous language	Percent of population 5+ years old speaking an indigenous language
Michoacán	Erongarícuaro	13,139	2,750	20.93
Sinaloa	Culiacán	772,198	2,733	0.35
Nayarit	Ruiz	20,927	2,545	12.16
Jalisco	Puerto Vallarta	224,799	2,389	1.06
Guanajuato	San Luis de la Paz	102,143	2,163	2.12
Guanajuato	Tierra Blanca	16,111	2,065	12.82
Jalisco	Tlajomulco de Zúñiga	352,469	2,035	0.58
Sinaloa	Guasave	260,023	2,012	0.77
Sinaloa	Navolato	122,039	2,012	1.65
Michoacán	Tzintzuntzan	12,224	1,790	14.64
Nayarit	Rosamorada	31,036	1,767	5.69
Aguascalientes	Aguascalientes	717,057	1,752	0.24
Jalisco	Tonalá	421,256	1,719	0.41
Michoacán	Tangancícuaro	29,195	1,602	5.49
Colima	Tecoman	100,826	1,537	1.52
Sinaloa	Mazatlán	399,659	1,507	0.38
Nayarit	Huajicori	9,912	1,465	14.78
Michoacán	Lázaro Cárdenas	156,440	1,450	0.93
Nayarit	Acaponeta	33,081	1,344	4.06
Nayarit	Santa Maria del Oro	20,173	1,324	6.56
Sinaloa	Sinaloa	79,328	1,275	1.61
Guanajuato	Celaya	418,059	1,262	0.30
Michoacán	Zamora	166,229	1,211	0.73
Colima	Manzanillo	144,196	1,159	0.80
Zacatecas	Fresnillo	187,031	1,142	0.61
Guanajuato	Irapuato	474,567	1,004	0.21

Table 2.9. Distribution of Speakers of Indigenous Languages for Municipios in West-Central Mexico: 2010 (Sorted by Percentage of Indigenous Language Speakers per Municipio, with a Minimum of 15 Percent).

State	Municipio	Population 5+ years old	Population 5+ years old speaking an indigenous language	Percent of population 5+ years old speaking an indigenous language
Nayarit	Nayar	28,859	25,179	87
Durango	Mezquital	27,921	22,102	79
Jalisco	Mezquitic	15,438	11,591	75
Jalisco	Bolaños	5,910	3,777	64
Michoacán	Chilchota	32,561	19,003	58
Michoacán	Charapan	11,034	5,784	52
Nayarit	La Yesca	11,970	4,990	42
Michoacán	Nahuatzen	24,093	9,850	41
Michoacán	Tangamandapio	24,764	8,544	34
Michoacán	Aquila	20,610	6,940	34
Michoacán	Paracho	31,104	9,916	32
Michoacán	Quiroga	23,087	7,355	32
Michoacán	Cherán	16,086	4,310	27
Michoacán	Erongarícuaro	13,139	2,750	21
Michoacán	Coeneo	18,720	3,727	20
Michoacán	Los Reyes	55,119	10,680	19
Nayarit	Huajicori	9,912	1,465	15
Michoacán	Tzintzuntzan	12,224	1,790	15
Total		382,551	159,753	42

Finally, the coastal municipio of Aquila (Michoacán) has a high concentration of Mexicano (Nahuatl) speakers. The 2010 census revealed a dramatic jump in numbers of speakers to 6,940 and in percentage to 34 percent.

Summary

In sum, the population trajectory of the indigenous populations of west-central Mexico has reflected their traditional settlement patterns dating back to before the arrival of the Spaniards. The situation in the early twenty-first century also has resulted from these populations' responses to the imposition of religious, political, economic, and social institutions that largely have been inimical to the maintenance of their communities and cultures. Only recently has a resurgence of cultural and linguistic consciousness been visible in the region. Because indigenous persons now reside not only in marginal rural areas but also in major cities and in the United States, they have learned to operate more successfully in the arenas of power—though they are far from achieving their goals of adequate representation in state and national politics and economic affairs. This is especially true as indigenous communities throughout the region (and all of Mexico, for that matter) find themselves—their artistic productions, their musical performances, and their historical buildings—being converted into commodities for sale in the expanding national and international tourist marketplace. How the indigenous peoples of the west-central region cope with this situation is likely to be significant in the next round of transformations regarding their places in the Mexican cultural landscape.

Note

All data in the decennial census tables presented here were extracted and analyzed by the authors from the respective Mexican national census volumes. (These were accessed in the Benson Latin American collection at the University of Texas, Austin. During the time of our research, volumes of the census were being borrowed and scanned by Google Books, but as of the current date we have not found them anywhere online.)

II

Constructing the Historical Horizon of "Contact"

3

Territory and Resistance in West-Central Mexico, Part 1

Introduction and Archaeological Background

Phillip C. Weigand

In the northeastern corner of the Plaza de Armas of the town of Magdalena, Jalisco (the prehispanic settlement of ancient Guaxíxicar or Xochitepec), is a dignified bust of the indigenous leader Guaxicar (Coajicar). Of course, since no actual renditions of him exist, the bust is entirely imaginative. The sense of tribute and pride, though, is very real. Ignored in the official histories of Mexico taught to schoolchildren and adults alike in western Mexico (hereafter referred to as Occidente) and neglected for centuries, Guaxicar was one of the Occidente's most important historic personages. Though the cause of indigenous independence for which he and his people fought did not succeed, Guaxicar belongs in the company of the better-known (though also neglected) Caxcan leaders of the Rebelión de Nueva Galicia such as Tenamaxtli, Tenquitatl, and Xiuhtecuhtli. The solitary bust in Magdalena is Guaxicar's only formal monument. It is accompanied by a handful of other small monuments in Zacatecas and Jalisco that mark one of the most dramatic social movements that has ever taken place in the Occidente.

The Rebelión de Nueva Galicia was one of the key events that marked the Spanish conquest of the ancient Mesoamerican world and the beginning of the European colonial order. For the Occidente, it was *the* key event, for it served as the major watershed between the indigenous period (including the time of ineffectual, though disruptive, *entradas*) and the real colonial consolidation of the core areas within this vast region.

The formal histories of the Rebelión are usually written as narratives and almost exclusively from the Spanish perspective (see López-Portillo y Weber 1935, 1939; Parry 1968; Pérez Verdía 1951). In addition, they most frequently focus upon the Caxcan resistance, usually called the Mixtón War (1540–42), to the near exclusion of the rest of Nueva Galicia, at best treating the non-Caxcan elements as footnotes to the main events and at worst ignoring them altogether. Even within the Caxcan theater of the Rebelión, the major focus is always upon its final phase, the siege of the Mixtón fortress. In the Western historiographic tradition, the indigenous leaders usually are mentioned only in their role as foils for the Spaniards, the major exception being the Tenamaxtli / Bartolomé de Las Casas interview (Ruiz Medrano 1994).

While there is no doubt about the importance of the overall Caxcan theater and its final phase, the Mixtón battle, this emphasis distorts the historical character of indigenous resistance to the Spaniards in the Occidente. Indeed, there were strategic and tactical reasons to first eliminate or neutralize the Caxcanes before attempting to consolidate the rest of Nueva Galicia. Thus, the physical course of two of the three conquest efforts (those led by Spaniards Francisco Cortés de San Buenaventura (1524–31), Nuño de Guzmán (1529–34), and Antonio de Mendoza (first viceroy of New Spain, 1535–50) in the Occidente had a very explicit logic. However, these reasons have never been considered nor even fully recognized in explaining the sequence of events with the conquest of the Occidente, including, of course, the Rebelión and its suppression.

In addition, the indigenous societies of the Occidente that participated in the Rebelión are given little if any historical depth beyond their mere presence in the area upon the arrival of the Spaniards. Of course, this lack of historical depth was in the past due largely to the paucity of reliable settlement archaeological information for the area in question (see Schöndube 1980 for an example of the traditional interpretation of the Occidente's prehispanic period). Now, however, settlement (both zonal and communal hierarchies, as well as architecture) and landscape information (e.g., irrigation features, terraces, and the paleoenvironment) does exist, even though it is still highly incomplete, quite provisional in many cases, and very unevenly distributed among different zones (see Beekman 1996; Beekman and Weigand 2000; Braniff 2001; Cach 2003; Hers 1989a, 1989b; Hers et al. 1993; Jiménez Betts 1988, 1992; López and Ramos 1999; Nelson 1995, 1997, 2003; Ohnersorgen and Varian 1996; Oliveros 2004; Weigand 1982, 1985, 1993a, 1993b, 1996a, 1996b, 2004a; Weigand and Beekman 1999; Williams 1996).

Another problem exists with the use of the extant historical sources (e.g., Tello 1973) that offer comments about the origins of the Caxcan states. These sources often are deployed quite selectively in narratives concerning the Rebelión, usually resulting in a deemphasis on the protohistorical record. An interesting situation has evolved in the historiography of the Rebelión de Nueva Galicia wherein the historians examining the event do so largely in an ahistorical manner, certainly insofar as an indigenous perspective is concerned.

This chapter examines the indigenous background of the Rebelión and contextualizes that event as far as possible in archaeology and in the few non-conquest-oriented ethnohistorical texts that do exist for the area. By reinterpreting some of this latter documentary material, I hope to offer new insights about the events that became known as the Rebelión de Nueva Galicia. The purpose of this study is not to outline the actual course of the Rebelión nor to engage in another retelling of those events as viewed through the Spanish sources, except when they help us understand the particulars of indigenous actions and reactions. While these events generally are well known (see López-Portillo y Weber 1935, 1939; Muriá 1980; Parry 1968; Pérez Verdía 1951), the nature of the Rebelión is not so well understood. New studies, often based in archives (see Román Gutiérrez 1993; Ruiz Medrano 1994), continue to amplify the documentary data set in important ways. Thus, my goal here is to explain the Rebelión de Nueva Galicia from the perspective of the societies indigenous to the Occidente at the time the Europeans appeared, including a summary of how these societies had evolved over the centuries preceding the European arrival. This contextualization is badly needed because the Caxcanes, in particular, are viewed by the historiographic tradition as having appeared on the historical scene in full flower, without a history of their own. In this sense, I examine a social situation in which, in Eric Wolf's (1982) term, "the people without history" actually have a historical context.

The Rebelión that brought Tenamaxtli (the personage who came to symbolize the Caxcan resistance) and Guaxicar (the symbol of the highland Jalisco and Nayarit resistance) together represents the culmination of millennia of cultural developments and contacts between two very different ecological areas. While these two areas were geographical neighbors, they experienced radically different sociocultural and evolutionary backgrounds.

As neighboring regions, Jalisco and Nayarit had always interacted with one another in both trade and warfare. They had exchanged ideas, and they had affected each other over a long period of time. But what brought these two areas together for a brief period during the early sixteenth century was something far more fundamental: a common enemy, that is, the Europeans, their diseases, and their actions. Nonetheless, the Rebelión de Nueva Galicia, while widespread, most probably was not a coordinated event, or series of events, throughout the various theaters of the Occidente. Nor did all of the indigenous societies of the area participate at the same level; indeed, many did not take part at all.

Historiographical Considerations: The Trans-Tarascan Zone

The term "trans-Tarascan" is defined as the neighboring area of upland lake and river valleys that existed to the west and northwest of the frontiers of the Tarascan state (figure 3.1). This term should only be used for the late Postclassic period (ca. A.D. 1250–1520, the period inclusive of the first rumblings of the Tarascan state to its culmination), though the area itself had a regional character long before the Postclassic period. During the late Postclassic, this area was caught between the expansive societies of the Tarascans to the south and southeast and various of the Caxcan states (especially those of Teul, Juchipila, and Nochistlán) to the north and northeast. From this situation emerged a series of small states that were to form the core of the western theater of the Rebelión de

Approximate territorial limites

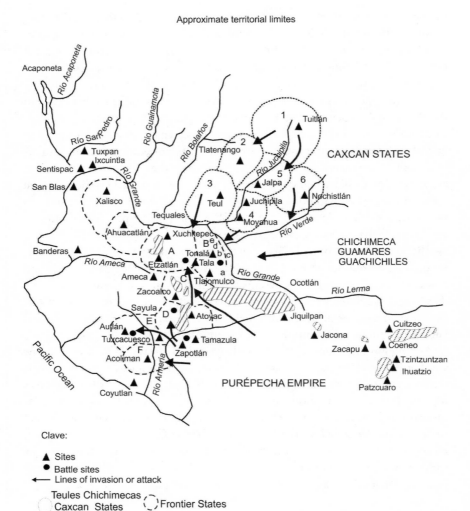

Clave:

▲ Sites
● Battle sites
← Lines of invasion or attack

Teules Chichimecas
Caxcan States
Frontier States

1. Tutitlán	A Etzatlán	Tonala's Fortifications
2. Tlatenanco	B Tonalá	a Las Paredes
3. Teul	C Zacoalco	b Coyula
4. Juchipila	D Sayula	c Atenco
5. Jalpa	E Autlán	d Huentitan
6. Nochistlán	F Acolimán	e Mesa Colorad

Figure 3.1. The trans-Tarascan "double frontier" on the eve of the Spanish conquest.

Nueva Galicia. All of the Spanish leaders involved in the attempts at conquest of this region (Cortés de San Buenaventura, Guzmán, and Mendoza) appreciated its richness and potential for the colonial order (Aiton 1927; Guzmán and Cortés 1937; Marín Tamayo 1992).

This zone comprises the fertile upland lake and river valleys of central, west-central, and southern Jalisco; from Zapotlán el Grande and Sayula in the south, to Tonalá in the east, and to Etzatlán and Ahuacatlán in the west. The canyon of the Río Grande de Santiago forms the approximate northern boundary of the trans-Tarascan zone. Most of these valleys have extremely rich soils composed of varying combinations of highly organic lake sediments and volcanic ash. The area is very well watered, depending upon a summer monsoon for the majority of its precipitation and frequent winter rainstorms for the rest. These latter rains are now few and far between, as they were originally generated as part of a microclimate dependent on a vast pine-oak forest cover. This forest cover has almost completely disappeared, altering in turn the composition of bottomland soils due to erosion and causing desertification, reflected in far higher temperatures. There were few periods of frost in the valleys, and, with irrigation, agriculture was possible throughout the year in many areas. Thus, the strategic resource profile was superior in every category, and large prehispanic populations were noted at the time of European contact by almost every observer (see summaries in Cook and Borah 1971–1979; Sauer 1948).

In addition, the rare resource profile was superior. The area abounds in minerals and other commodities deemed useful by prehispanic peoples everywhere within Mesoamerica: many varieties of obsidian, quartz crystals, malachite, azurite, copper, silver, gold, opals, tropical feathers, shell, and salt (Weigand 1993a; Weigand and García de Weigand 1994, 1996). Only jade and chemical turquoise were not naturally found within this large region, yet trade for these two minerals began as early as the Formative period (Harbottle and Weigand 1992; Ramos and López 1996; Weigand and Harbottle 1992).

Traditionally, the social aspects of the late Postclassic cultures of the trans-Tarascan zone have been discussed solely from the perspectives of the European source materials compiled during the conquest and the early colonial period. While these sources are obviously and incontestably invaluable, they are used without any contextualization in the archaeological record. Nor are they considered from the perspective of the sociodemographic changes evident, at least by inference, for the immediate preconquest period, after the first effects of the European presence had already been felt (these changes were recorded in some of those same documents).

There are major weaknesses for the historiographical tradition of this region. The primary documentary sources of the early Spanish period are not extremely detailed. Unfortunately, there is no preserved equivalent of the 1541 *Relación de Michoacán* (RM 2000) for the trans-Tarascan zone. Even the *Relaciones geográficas* of 1579–1585 (Acuña 1988) are either extremely brief or, in most cases, missing altogether for the zone. The extant documents, including chronicles of the various conquests (Aiton 1927; Guzmán and Cortés 1937; Pérez Bustamante 1928), do not deal with many of the questions that we now consider to be anthropologically important and pertinent. The documents offer very little on such matters as settlement patterns (zonal or community), irrigation works, economic structure including trade and exchange, almost all themes of social organization, and religious matters, except in the most superficial sense. Furthermore, as mentioned, the archaeological information discussed for the zone usually has been restricted to fine arts such as ceramics and figurines (see Bell 1971). Indeed, until recently, no further systematic archaeological information existed.

In addition, there are major questions regarding the character and veracity of the ethnohistorical and archival data sets that have not been posed systematically. Aside from some disagreements among different sources, even on the major points such as population estimates, there is excellent reason to believe that the conquest period documents are not dealing with a pristine state of affairs in their reportage on the native societies of the trans-Tarascan zone or, for that matter, other regions of western Mesoamerica, if by "pristine" we mean a situation unaffected by any type of European contact whatsoever.

But perhaps more significant, the temporal lapse between the first arrival of Europeans in Veracruz and their appearance in the Occidente, though not prolonged, afforded enough time for the initiation of considerable sociological and demographic changes. Without the concept of an "epidemiological front" (Crosby 1977), the Spaniards were not capable of systematically evaluating the types of changes under way in the Occidente that either preceded or accompanied their first explorations. In the eleven-year period between 1519 and Guzmán's expedition in the Occidente, which resulted in the most comprehensive series of early documents for the area (Guzmán and Cortés 1937), there elapsed sufficient time for the disruption of the elaborate exchange routes of the Mesoamerican trade structure in which the trans-Tarascan zone was fully embedded.

The products from this zone that circulated within the trade structure were cacao, feathers, salt, copper, gold, silver, malachite, azurite, chrysocolla, tin, shell, cotton, hematite, cinnabar, pyrite, lead, specular iron, opal, quartz, chalcedony, chert, obsidian, and rhyolite (Weigand 1993a). Except for the *tierra caliente* area (the hotlands of Michoacán between the Transvolcanic Axis and the coastal mountain range at the Pacific coast) controlled by the Tarascans (Pollard 1987; Warren 1968), this zone, along with Nayarit, produced more metal than any other area in ancient Mesoamerica. Dorothy Hosler's (1994) study shows the diversity of this technology. She maintains that this technology reached the Occidente from South America, but this argument, while no doubt true, needs two qualifiers: (1) the Occidente was probably already predisposed to accept this infusion of ideas in technology and artifact forms from the south, as it seems likely that some experimentation with the appropriate ores and metals was already under way; and (2) there was a long tradition of malachite and azurite mining within the Occidente and adjacent areas, such as the Chalchihuites area of Zacatecas, that began long before the introductions occurred (Weigand 1982, 1993a). Origins of metallurgy aside, as they do not affect the argument, copper and tin artifacts (along with objects of gold [Kelley 1985], silver, and specular iron) were without doubt an important part of the Occidente's material contribution within some sectors of the Mesoamerican trade structure.

In addition, the most valuable products of much of the northwestern sectors of ancient Mesoamerica, including the southwestern United States, passed through the trans-Tarascan zone en route to consumers elsewhere. Turquoise, in particular, should be mentioned to illustrate this point, as it became the gemstone par excellence, surpassing jade in the symbol structure of Mesoamerica (Harbottle and Weigand 1992; Weigand and Harbottle 1992). However, all these trade networks, which were in operation in 1519, were either no longer functioning or seriously impaired by 1530. The collapse of the Mesoamerican trade structure in that interim had profound sociopolitical implications for the Occidente. Similar trade structure collapses elsewhere among nonindustrial civilizations, while at first affecting the elites, have always had profound social and economic implications (Abu-Lughod 1989; Braudel 1984).

During the same period, epidemics of European origin began to have a severe impact on the Occidente's populations. Undoubtedly, epidemic diseases preceded the arrival of the Spaniards at varying times in different areas within the trans-Tarascan zone. The "virgin soil" epidemics (Crosby 1977; McNeill 1976) reinforced the disintegrative factors of the trade structure's ongoing collapse. Their effect on the Tarascans is recorded in some detail, as the diseases arrived prior to the first Spanish expeditions, thereby conclusively sapping the Tarascans' resolve to resist the Spaniards (RM 2000; Warren 1977; see also Cook and Borah 1971–1979). By 1527, the eve of Guzmán's expedition to the Occidente, the epidemics were becoming generalized throughout the Tarascan population. By 1530, epidemics were appearing throughout the trans-Tarascan zone, occurring as far away as the Río Acaponeta valley in Nayarit (Guzmán 1960; Guzmán's documents in Marín Tamayo 1992; Tello 1973).

In the Tarascan area, it was the nobility, merchants, and military who were first affected by the diseases. This pattern is common in the first appearance of a virgin soil pandemic. Hypothetically, this same pattern would have prevailed in the trans-Tarascan zone. The nobility, merchants, and military are the first to be exposed due to their key interregional contact positions. From them the spread of diseases would proceed into their respective local populations. Generally, in complex societies, serious disorganizational effects result when the elites are so impacted, to the point of political disruptions and collapses over broad areas. For the Occidente, the epidemiological front preceded the actual appearance of the first Europeans. This disease front, plus the ongoing and accelerating breakdown of the trade structure, demonstrates that the Spaniards could not possibly have reported upon a pristine situation.

Aside from the aforementioned societal disarrangements, another problem that affects our ability to understand the historiography of the trans-Tarascan zone is the rivalry, hostility, and outright hatred between two of the most important conquering groups involved in the primary military expeditions and the first territorial redistributions throughout the region. The factions led by Cortés and Guzmán were never really reconcilable (Guzmán and Cortés 1937; see Brand 1971 and Marín Tamayo 1992 for summaries). As the winner of that contest, the Cortés faction had the opportunity to present itself to posterity in a more favorable light. The result is that Guzmán's accounts are often questioned as unreliable, except where their information supports the observations of the Cortés faction. For example, the Cortés and Guzmán sources disagree about the demographic configuration of many areas within the trans-Tarascan zone and about the level of violence that was present in the area after Cortés's incursion. Guzmán presented the case for higher population estimates and a fair amount of disruptive violence and disorganization in the trans-Tarascan area in the wake of Cortés's supposed conquest. These contentions were criticized on the basis that Guzmán wanted to increase his importance as a conqueror in the eyes of the Hapsburg king.

A historiographical tradition has evolved that demonizes Guzmán and demeans the contributions of those like Tello (1968), who took his documentation seriously (see also Brand 1971). Certainly, Guzmán's conquest was unnecessarily brutal. In addition, it seems that some of Guzmán's allies—Tarascans and Tlaxcaltecas alike—often were out of control, operating with some independence from his command. This situation was not unique to Guzmán; after the Rebelión had been suppressed, Mendoza dismissed a large number of his allies in the Occidente, introducing a great measure of chaos into an already heavily impacted area (Aiton 1927; Pérez Bustamante 1928). Despite Guzmán's brutal actions in the Occidente, other criteria must be considered when evaluating his firsthand observations.

Thus, an understanding of the trans-Tarascan zone for the contact period suffers from a selective use of the documentary record. This selectivity by historians and anthropologists is made even more problematic because the available primary sources are so scant and so scattered. Donald Brand's summary has had an extremely strong influence on the characterization of the area. Most researchers, though, have forgotten his explicit qualifiers: "Although many of the 'facts' of such material are highly debatable, this brief article can only be summary and dogmatic. Of the utmost importance are the evaluation and critical selection of the written sources that are available. No use is made of archaeological data" (Brand 1971:633). As will be discussed in more detail below, his comments concerning Tello seem especially overdrawn and weak. Just as important, as already mentioned, there now exists a data set generated by archaeologists that should be used in coordination with the primary documentary records, especially since a sixteenth-century social and political conflict colored their trustworthiness and since the earliest sources are not reporting a pristine indigenous situation.

Ethnohistorical sources (aside from the Guzmán vs. Cortés dispute) reflect another controversy in the historiography of the trans-Tarascan zone, a controversy that appears to be represented in two schools of thought. Since these schools have no formal appellations, we will coin names for the purpose of discussion: Maximalist and Minimalist.

The Maximalist school is said, with good reason, to be the creation of wishful thinking, infused with strong elements of regional pride and romantic inclinations. Its adherents posit the existence of a large political and cultural entity for the trans-Tarascan zone, called Chimalhuacán, which existed in the area when the Spaniards first arrived (see López-Portillo y Weber 1935; Pérez Verdía 1951). According to most of these accounts, Chimalhuacán was a great confederation comprised of four large semiautonomous units. Xalisco, Acolimán, Aztatlán, and Tonallán are the most frequently identified. Within each of these great subunits were the smaller *provincias* so named by the Spaniards.

A variety of criteria are used in support of the existence of Chimalhuacán, though the documentary evidence for this confederation is extremely slight if not nonexistent. In the primary documentation (i.e., Cortés, Guzmán, or Mendoza) and the seventeenth-century summaries thereof (Tello), the term "Chimalhuacán" simply does not appear. However, given what we have said above about the "virgin soil" epidemiological front, plus the evidence for archaeological complexity and specialization during the late Postclassic (see below), confederations of some sort within the trans-Tarascan zone should remain within the realm of the possible. It is just that they are not mentioned in the earliest documents, and thus the specifics of Chimalhuacán (such as the internal organization into four zones, as an example) are entirely unsupported. Therefore, Chimalhuacán (as posited in the historical literature) is an artifact of the historians themselves rather than an artifact of the archaeological and historical record.

The attraction of the Chimalhuacán confederacy is that it lends an attractive prehispanic dimension to the concept of "Gran Jalisco." Central Mexico has the Aztec Empire, even Texcoco and the Toltecas; Yucatán has the Maya; Oaxaca has the Zapoteca and Mixteca kingdoms; Michoacán has the Tarascan Empire . . . What might Jalisco have had in a similar vein? Chimalhuacán offered that ancient dimension and its corollary: a stronger and more dignified sense of regional pride, which helped stress the natural and cultural differences between Nueva Galicia / Intendencia de Guadalajara / Jalisco and the rest of Mexico, especially central Mexico.

However, dismissing Chimalhuacán entirely may not do justice to the more abstract concept of interregional alliances or states. Indeed, there is strong archaeological evidence for far-ranging cultural, perhaps political, provinces in the zone under discussion for various time periods, including the Classic period's Teuchitlán Tradition (Weigand 1993b, 2004a). These latter occurrences, though, are based on the hard evidence of archaeological field data rather than romantic reconstructions entirely independent of any real data set.

The Minimalist school represents the opposite extreme in its characterization of the prehispanic societies of the non-Tarascan Occidente. Formed in part as a natural and well-intentioned reaction to the Maximalist theories, the Minimalist school postulates a fragmented cultural and political landscape for the archaeological cultures of the highland lake and river valley zone of Jalisco for all time periods (see Brand 1971; Díaz 1987; Schöndube 1980). According to this interpretation, the region was characterized by fairly small valleys surrounded by great mountain chains and transected by deep canyons. Within each valley were fairly self-contained cultures and societies with relatively low organizational and demographic levels. Intergroup contacts were largely based in trade and incessant warfare. This position usually needs to take a critical view of the Guzmán/Tello accounts.

The environmental descriptions implicit in this view of the Occidente, which stress fragmentation into small, isolated valleys surrounded by canyons and mountains, are simply wrong. Vast, high-quality, well-watered, flat agricultural areas, with easy access between them, exist from the coastal plains of much of Nayarit, the Valle de Las Banderas of Jalisco, and most all of Colima, to the aforementioned highland lake valleys of west-central, central, and southern Jalisco. To emphasize the canyons and mountains, excluding these areas from consideration, cannot be considered a legitimate ecological description of the Occidente.

When archaeological data are used in the Minimalist argument, they are almost exclusively ceramics and figurine styles. The great variability of these styles, apparent from most of the time periods, is used to buttress this interpretation. Isabel Kelly's (1948) and Pedro Armillas's (1948a) very preliminary documentations of "ceramic provinces" for the Occidente were the initial inspirations for this interpretation. To define the fragmented social landscape through time, beginning millennia ago, the correlation of the "ceramic provinces" and cultures was posited, forgetting or ignoring the fact that archaeological cultural systems cannot be defined in that way. Certainly, Kelly never intended her suggested provinces to be interpreted in this fashion, as she viewed her suggestions only as the first step in an ongoing documentation of the Occidente's prehispanic past. Armillas insisted that his ideas about ceramic provinces were simply heuristic devices to be employed in the ongoing anthropological investigation of this area's archaeological cultures (personal communication). But the ceramic provinces became fossilized, and, once turned into cultures, they could be related to the small-scale societies that some of the Spanish accounts defined. A tight and very logical argument was woven to suggest that the Occidente always had been characterized by fragmentation and low levels of sociocultural development.

Both of the aforementioned schools operate with complete independence from settlement pattern and landscape studies. The Minimalist school, while much closer to a literalist reading of some of the early sources, also appears to have a firm set of idées fixes concerning the nature and history of society in the western sectors of ancient Mesoamerica. These preconceptions include the belief that high culture and civilization in western Mesoamerica were late and, at least in large part, derivative from central Mexico, though the Occidente made a stimulating and original contribution to the final product. The sweep of Puebla-Mixteca influences into the Occidente, which indeed occurred, often has been mentioned in this context. The corollaries to this belief are that there was neither monumental architecture nor social complexity in the Occidente until the Postclassic period, and even then, except for the Tarascan zone, both were still at fairly low levels. This interpretation of the evolutionary character of prehispanic society in the trans-Tarascan zone is termed the "simplicity complex" elsewhere (Weigand 1985, 1993b).

Octavio Paz (1970, 1972) criticized a school of thought that he called the *punta de vista nahua*. His analysis, rich in metaphor, discussed a *pirámide de poder* in which the entire course of ancient Mesoamerican civilization is interpreted as slowly, but inevitably, focusing on the Central Valley of Mexico. The contemporary centralist presuppositions in this argument are clear, and, indeed, this position represents a current political philosophy. It has little to do with the reality of ancient Mesoamerica. In many respects, the Minimalist interpretation embodies centralism. The careful and thoughtful work by Schöndube, with its focus on regional origins for the early societies of the Occidente, while within the Minimalist school, is an exception to this last statement. However, both the Minimalist and Maximalist schools are equally remote from a processual and anthropological perspective concerning the archaeological data set.

The Archaeological and Demographic Setting: The Trans-Tarascan Zone

As systematic and large-scale landscape-oriented surveys were started in the western lake valley zone of Jalisco, it became evident that the Minimalist view was fundamentally flawed. The area around the Volcán de Tequila, which in time became the northern core of the trans-Tarascan zone, was the nucleus for a remarkable cultural development—called the Teuchitlán Tradition—during the late Formative and Classic periods. While this early cultural system is still poorly understood, a number of recent studies have explored many aspects of its character in some detail. It certainly was the Occidente's first experiment in a highly complex sociocultural system(s).

It is the architecture of the Teuchitlán Tradition that so clearly sets it off from the rest of Formative and Classic period Mesoamerica. Based on the theme of concentric circles, the buildings are very symmetrical and highly proportional. The late circles, such as the Guachimontón precinct near Teuchitlán (figure 3.2), are monumental and complex. They most frequently have attached or adjacent ball-courts, which also are monumental, and elite residential or administrative compounds. The greatest circle at the Guachimontón precinct is over 125 m in diameter and 400 m in circumference. This precinct has a total of ten circles and two ball-courts. A program of excavation and restoration has been carried out at this complex (Weigand 2004a).

The Classic period architecture is clearly formal in design and morphology (Weigand 1996a). There are hundreds of these circular precincts in the immediate area, so this architecture marks, beyond reasonable doubt, the limits of a well-defined core of complex sociocultural development. This development far outstripped the level of architectural and settlement complexity for most of the rest of the Occidente during the Classic period. The differential sociocultural evolution obtained within this core became characterized by a "key economic area" (Chi 1936), defined as a zone wherein the landscape is modified to maximize agrarian output, often to support a concentrated population, and marked by monumental building activities (Weigand 2004a).

The monumental buildings and substantial habitation zones have been explored by extensive surface surveys, accompanied by systematic excavations at five precincts: Guachimontones and Huitzilapa (López and Ramos 1999; Ramos and López 1996), Llano Grande and Navajas, and Bugambilias. The Teuchitlán Tradition, while beginning around 1000–800 B.C., reached its apogee between 350 B.C. and A.D. 450–500, though the extant ^{14}C dates mark only the period 350 B.C.–A.D. 150.

The largest of the habitation zones may have had some urban characteristics (figure 3.3). It covered ca. 24,000 ha of ceremonial precincts, ball-courts, elite residential areas, obsidian workshops, habitations for the nonelite, terraced in-fields, and *chinampas* (floating gardens used in Mesoamerican horticultural systems). The population of this habitation zone may have reached 25,000 by ca. A.D. 150. While it does not have anywhere near the population density seen at Teotihuacan, for example, it is the greatest such demographic concentration yet reported in the Occidente for the late Formative and early Classic periods.

The neighboring valleys outside the Volcán de Tequila core did not have the same level of architectural development nor the concentration of religious and administrative buildings and habitations, although circular structures are found as far away as the Comala area in Colima, at twenty-two localities in

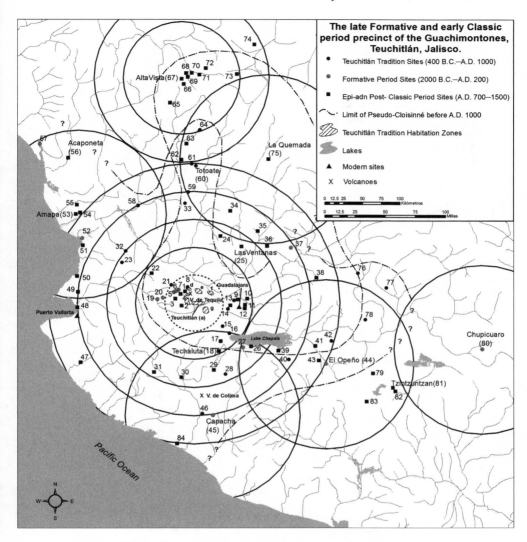

Figure 3.2. The late Formative and early Classic period precinct of the Guachimontones, Teuchitlán, Jalisco.

Guanajuato (Cárdenas 1999), the Bolaños valley of Jalisco (Cabrero García 1989, 1991; Weigand 1985), the Chapala basin, and various areas in Nayarit. It appears as if the core was surrounded by a neighboring hinterland, in some cases much less developed, that probably functioned as resource procurement and communications outposts to other, well-developed Mesoamerican socio-cultural systems. Undoubtedly there was no single polity that extended over the vast region marked by this distinctive circular architecture. Much more likely is

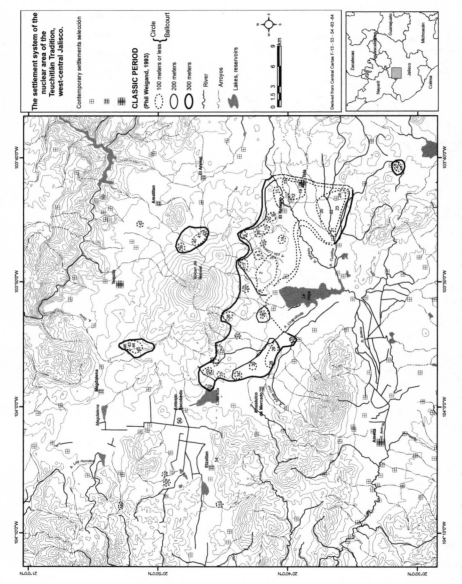

Figure 3.3. The settlement system of the nuclear area of the Teuchitlán Tradition, west-central Jalisco.

a type of organization called a "segmentary state," in which "the spheres of ritual suzerainty and political sovereignty do not coincide. The former extends widely toward a flexible, changing periphery. The latter is confined to the central, core domain" (Southall 1988:52).

For reasons still poorly understood, the Teuchitlán Tradition entered into a period of decline, probably starting around A.D. 400, to a complete demise ca. A.D. 500. This is the initiation of an epoch of dramatic changes throughout the Mesoamerican ecumene. While these observations help us understand the civilization-wide context for the Teuchitlán Tradition's disappearance, they do not explain what actually and specifically transpired in the Occidente.

The reorganization was so thorough in this area as to strongly suggest the arrival of outsiders. The appearance of the open and semiclosed U-shaped ceremonial buildings, sunken rectangular or square patios, and great rectangular platforms suggest the Bajío, the Lerma valley in general, and the Chapala basin as the points of origin for at least some of the changes. These structures occur at Santa Crúz de Bárcenas (Ahualulco), Ixtpete (Guadalajara), Higueras (Tala), and Ocomo (Oconahua) within the area that used to be the core of the Teuchitlán Tradition, as well as at quite a number of other sites in the Occidente at approximately the same time.

Specific conditions favoring change may be related to the development and spread of metallurgy in the Occidente at a slightly later date. The Teuchitlán Tradition, with apparent success, had engaged in regional and extraregional trade for a very long period prior to the epi-Classic period. The mainstays for this trade probably included blue-green gemstones, quartz crystals, high-quality obsidian artifacts, shell artifacts, possibly pseudo-cloisonné ceramics, and probably perishable commodities such as cotton textiles and feather work. Metallurgy, with the evident direct corollary of new mining sites and distribution networks, may have allowed competitors to open new opportunities in this area's sector of the Mesoamerican trade structure. In addition, this new wealth may have helped attract outsiders. The social forms represented by the circular buildings and ball-courts may have become quite cumbersome and thus may no longer have had the flexibility to respond to the quickly changing economic and political situations, especially if these changes were accompanied by migrations.

The sudden appearance of "corral"-type architecture during the epi-Classic strongly suggests cultural affinities farther north (see Deltour-Levie 1993). In addition to the northern "corral"-type architecture, the linguistic data set also points to the north. The distribution and dialectation of the western Uto-Aztecan languages indicate a fairly long presence in the Occidente (Valiñas 1993), perhaps even beginning prior to the period under consideration here. Without a doubt, the "Tepiman corridor" indicates the overall spread of these languages, including those represented in the Occidente (Kroeber 1934; Miller 1983; Sauer 1934). The spread of the Uto-Aztecan languages into the

Occidente apparently came along two routes: the intermountain valleys of the Sierra Madre Occidental, and the Pacific coastal plain and adjoining piedmont. It is in this latter area, especially in the south, that dialectation appears to have been more developed. Unfortunately, the Uto-Aztecan languages of the trans-Tarascan zone are so poorly known that their classification is tenuous at best. Tecuexe, Coca, Totorame, Huichollan (Huichol and Cora), and Tecual appear to be the major groupings within or near the trans-Tarascan area. In the composite, they all appear to belong to the coastal/piedmont group and to be very distinct (as well as distant) from Caxcan and the Uto-Aztecan languages of central Mexico. Since these languages appear to be closely related, I have termed the grouping "Totorame."

Does the collapse of the Teuchitlán Tradition mark the arrival of Tecuexe/Coca into the trans-Tarascan zone (see Baus de Czitróm 1982, 1985)? Does the collapse of the Chalchihuites mining complex in Zacatecas (see below) mark the beginning of the Caxcan push to the south, hence displacing the Tecuexe from areas they inhabited in the north? As mentioned, Totorame without doubt was somehow involved in the demise of the Teuchitlán system, but how remains an open question. If Totorame was involved during the period of transition, then what were the languages spoken during the period of Teuchitlán's ascendancy? It seems evident that these Classic period societies were already multiethnic. Were they also multilingual, perhaps including the earliest dialects of southern Uto-Aztecan? Is there a link between the circular architecture of the Teuchitlán Tradition and the *yácata* (the Purépecha term for "pyramid") structures of the later Tarascans? It so, could that link be used to suggest that Purépecha may have been spoken in this area (Manrique 1994)?

The end of the Teuchitlán Tradition was revolutionary. Everything, from architecture to culinary ceramics, changed during a relatively brief period of time. While there were most certainly continuities from the Classic into the Postclassic period, we are dealing with changes of epochal proportions. The differences between this phase of dramatic and thoroughgoing changes and those occasioned by the arrival of the Europeans some 600 years later are many. The major difference is the lack of a virgin soil pandemic associated with the collapse of the Teuchitlán Tradition. Therefore, the opportunity existed for a major demographic continuity between the epochs. But the social and cultural impacts of the changes were extreme and profound.

The epi-Classic and Postclassic social systems that replaced the former tradition were the direct forerunners of the societies that the Spaniards encountered in the sixteenth century. They appear to have been more compact societies, though this statement should not be taken to imply that they were necessarily simple or small scale. They had been in place, in constantly changing configurations, for about eight or nine centuries when the Occidente's second major sociocultural revolution, the arrival of the Europeans and their diseases, took place.

This time period can be divided roughly into two segments, the first of which appears to be the more complex in architecture and settlement structure. The last phase, before the arrival of the Europeans, was special: the trans-Tarascan zone had become a contested zone, having a double frontier of successful and expansionary states in the north and northeast (the Caxcanes) and a predatory, territorially based empire in the south and southeast (the Tarascans).

The Epi-Classic and Early Postclassic Periods

The epi-Classic and early Postclassic periods show remarkable diversity within their repertoire of architectural forms. For example, open and semiclosed U-shaped structures have been located at Santa Crúz de Bárcenas (also known as Tabacál, figure 3.4), El Grillo, Tepehuaje, Portezuleo, and Ocomo (figure 3.5), as well as at a number of other localities.

Distinctive sunken patios are found at such sites as Techaluta (figure 3.6), Navajas, and Tepehuaje (figure 3.7). The great flat-topped rectangular or square Ixtépete-style platforms form another component in the epi-Classic and early

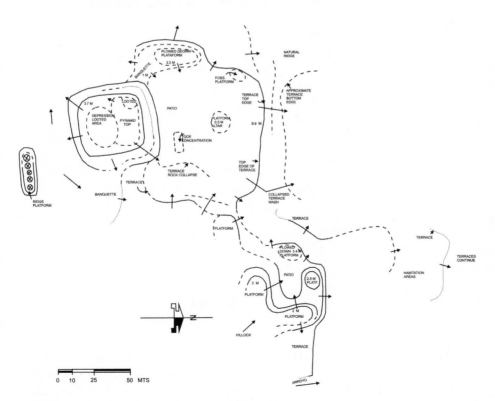

Figure 3.4. The Tabacal precinct, near Ahualulco, Jalisco.

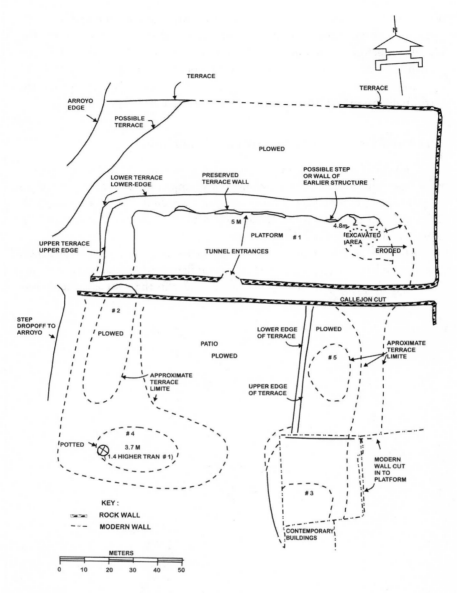

Figure 3.5. The Palacio de Ocomo, Oconahua, Jalisco.

Postclassic architectural repertoire. The structure at Ixtépete itself is best known, but others exist at Coyula, Las Paredes, Huaxtia, and Higuerita, plus a number of other sites in the Chapala and lower Lerma valleys, such as Yurécuaro (figure 3.8).

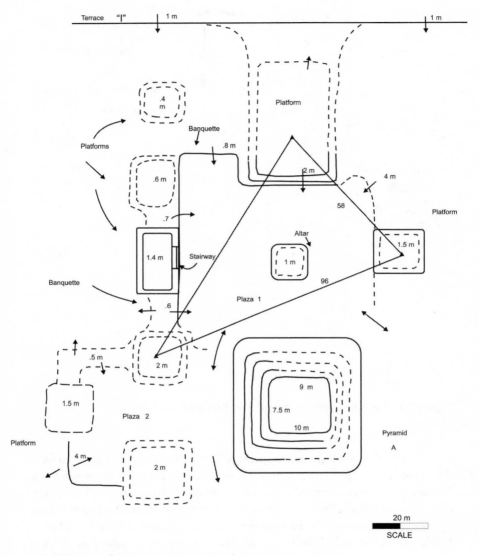

N

Terrace "I"

Platforms

Platform

Banquette

Platforms

Banquette

Stairway

Altar

Plaza 1

Plaza 2

Platform

Pyramid A

SCALE
20 m

Figure 3.6. The Playa de Techaluta "A" precinct, Techaluta, Jalisco.

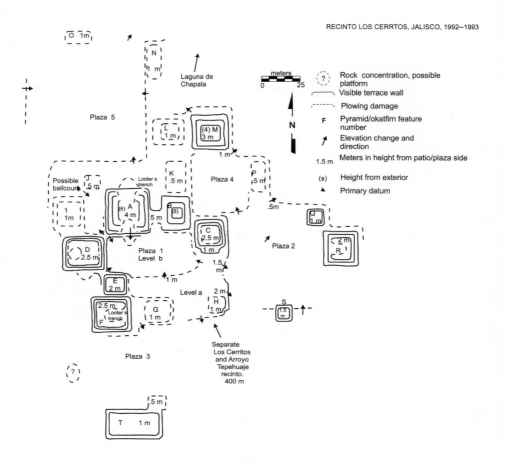

Figure 3.7. The major complex at Tepehuaje, Chapala basin, Jalisco.

The "corral" type of structure appears to be involved with the transition from the Classic to the epi-Classic period. These structures are not monumental, nor do they seem to be ceremonial or administrative. They resemble habitations more than anything else. Their inspiration is northern, from the intermontane canyons and mountains of the southern sector of the Sierra Madre Occidental. While the sites of the Volcán de Tequila area seem in part specialized in obsidian procurement, it appears that the sites of the Atoyac basin are fully specialized in salt working. These salt workings are especially noteworthy in the Cerros Colorados area and the Playa de Carmelita zone, though they occur in a number of other zones as well. Aside from the relatively rich agricultural land of the upper playa and piedmont (areas that were sometimes terraced), salt production may help explain the architectural elaboration in this valley.

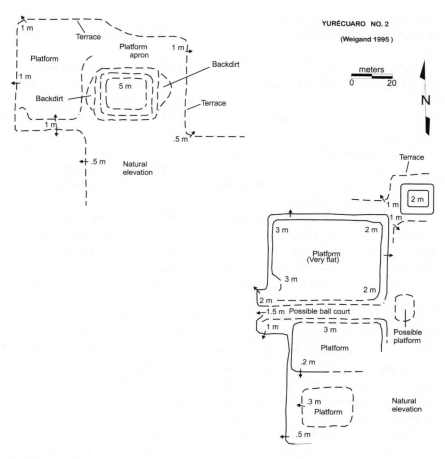

Figure 3.8. The Yurécuaro #2 precinct, near Yurécuaro, Michoacán.

This period, while poorly defined and poorly understood, was a time of re-markable change and reorganization. The societies that developed during these phases were heavily influenced from the outside, especially the Bajío and the middle/lower Lerma valley. The open and semiclosed U-shaped buildings, the sunken patios, and the great Ixtépete-style platforms are especially prominent from that perspective. Influences have been postulated from even farther afield within the realm of fine arts; noteworthy are the Puebla-Mixteca polychrome and plumbate ceramics and the molded Mazapan figurines. Problems with these postulations abound, however. For example, the Mazapan figurines were clearly made in the Occidente, where they are found in the hundreds, along with molds for their manufacture. The Puebla-Mixteca horizon has chronologi-cal difficulties, too. As originally postulated, the Puebla-Mixteca complex was responsible for the Aztatlán horizon in the Occidente, thus bringing civilization to that area from its central Mexican heartland. This postulation is simply no longer feasible.

Moreover, this area was innovative in its own right. Jade and turquoise were traded from afar and illustrate that the Occidente was actively participating in exchange throughout the Mesoamerican trade structure. These gemstones, along with obsidian, were worked into a remarkable series of artifacts. Regional polychrome ceramics, metallurgy, and the construction of large and important settlement systems all mark the dynamic character of these phases in the area. Mining, especially for obsidian, was very well developed. The large mining complex at La Joya, Municipio de Magdalena, which has hundreds of mines or quarries, was expanded during this time period.

Not enough landscape and settlement-oriented surveys have been accomplished to comment reliably on demographic density or social complexity except in a fairly impressionistic fashion. Small zones, however, have been fairly thoroughly surveyed. The results suggest a decrease in large-area integration after the Teuchitlán Tradition's demise, though not necessarily accompanied by an overall population collapse. Rather, there is good evidence to suggest that populations were rearranged. Valleys that had been heavily populated during the Formative period and relatively depopulated during Teuchitlán's apogee became heavily populated once more. Apparently, no site or settlement system ever again concentrated as many people as in the Teuchitlán region during the late Formative and early Classic periods. Once the influences of Teuchitlán were gone, the neighboring valleys experimented and built anew. Intervalley traditions, marked in architecture and, to a lesser degree, in ceramics, developed.

Since only a few of these sites survived into the period of Tarascan ascendancy and expansion to the west and northwest, accompanied by the initial Caxcan expansion into the south and southwest, the dislocations that the initial military and political stirrings of those polities caused throughout the broader area, including the Chapala basin, might in part be responsible for their abandonment and/or decline. However, this observation cannot be generalized to include all the early Postclassic sites and site systems throughout the Occidente.

The initial period of Tarascan military and political activity must have been preceded by something else. There are firm indications that this was the case within the Caxcan region. The changes around A.D. 1200–1300 that set the stage for Tarascan and Caxcan expansion might have included still further demographic dislocations over a broad zone, resulting in new or quite modified sociocultural configurations.

The prior period of sociocultural change during the epi-Classic period appears to have been more dramatic, but this interlude of transformation is no better understood. With the alteration and/or collapse of the early Postclassic sites, settlement systems, and their cultures, the sociocultural dispositions encountered by the Spaniards came into being.

The Chalchihuites Tradition and Caxcan Origins

The Caxcanes have been treated in the history of Nueva España and Nueva Galicia as the principal and most dramatic actors of the Rebelión de Nueva Galicia and in its last phase, the Mixtón War. Indeed, often the Rebelión and the war are confused or, more frequently, telescoped into one event focused upon the Caxcanes. In the normative historical accounts, such as those by Pérez Verdía (1951) and Parry (1968), the Caxcanes have been given little or no historical depth beyond their adversarial role in the actual war.

Actually, Caxcan polities evolved within a long developmental sequence of regional cultures that participated in a common tradition (called the Chalchihuites Tradition by archaeologists). This tradition probably began ca. 1,300 years before the Spaniards arrived in the area. The themes of Chichimeca warfare, mining, and long-distance commerce predate the colonial world by approximately that same length of time.

The Mixtón War, as an integral component of the Rebelión de Nueva Galicia, was a wider and deeper historical movement than most historians have recognized. The Rebelión de Nueva Galicia permanently affected the sociopolitical character of Nueva Galicia itself, being in effect but the first stage of the subsequent 180-year war against incorporation into the Spanish colonial system.

The collapse of complex culture in this zone, apparently during the ninth or tenth century A.D., may have set into motion the demographic and sociocultural dislocations from which the Caxcanes ultimately emerged. Major ecological adaptive themes were related to the cultural variability evident in the vast area from Durango to northern Jalisco and southern Zacatecas between A.D. 200 and 1500. Here we shall focus on a social system operating within and across these differing regions, each with its own resources and potentialities and each, of course, with its own cultural and subcultural expressions.

Traditions are multicultural through time and over space. They involve the landscape (the largest "artifact" that humans can produce), the settlement pattern (both zonal and community), architecture, agricultural and hydraulic features, and rare resource procurement patterns. Other artifact sets, such as ceramics and lithics, are crucial, but only so long as they are fully contextualized.

The cultural variation within a tradition is often related to regional specialization, social hierarchies, and ethnic variability within societies. Viewing cultures as tightly integrated, localized systems (however variable in content), operating largely at the material level, is more profitable than stretching the concept to explain social organization within a region. Following this reasoning, it is the mining and ceremonial complex of the Chalchihuites area that constitutes the Chalchihuites "culture" ca. A.D. 200–900.

In the Occidente, the integrating societal theme was the dedication of many of the local sociocultural resources to the extraction and procurement of selected minerals in the service of the Mesoamerican trade structure. Socially, the Chalchihuites mining complex seems to have been among the strategically placed "outposts in the surrounding periphery" (Algaze 1993:310). The massive output of these mines could not have been consumed locally. Therefore, the Chalchihuites culture must have been integrated into a far larger social system. According to Algaze's comparative analysis for early civilizations throughout the world, these outposts are common occurrences in the early life histories of ancient civilizations, reflecting their ability both to project their cultural power and to serve their expansive economies.

The mines themselves were complex. The longest tunnel/chamber mines explored to date were well over 1 km in underground length. There were approximately 800 mines in the area, though, of course, not all were monumental. The wealth acquired from these mines allowed the development of rich, though small-scale, ceremonial and administrative architectural complexes in an area not endowed with good agricultural resources.

The Chalchihuites culture probably had no more than 8,000–12,000 people at any one time during the period of its apogee during the Alta Vista and Vesuvio phases (ca. A.D. 400–800/900). The Chalchihuites culture can be characterized by its ability to (1) extensively mine and exchange the products of that mining, as well as to attract or procure exotic minerals from other areas; (2) build elaborate, if small-scale, specialized buildings; and (3) sponsor innovative ceremonialism, which included skull racks, human sacrifice, cannibalism, and Tezcatlipoca symbolism.

With reference to the first point, the people of the Chalchihuites culture were engaged in exploratory and possibly expeditionary mining and trade for chemical turquoise in places as far away as north-central and southwestern New Mexico, the Concepción del Oro area, and several other places not yet identified but probably in the Mulatos (Zacatecas) and Salinas (San Luis Potosí) areas. In effect, the Chalchihuites culture was a very well organized and innovative participant in a far larger social system. The high degree of specialization in mining and mineral trade was its hallmark.

In the Chalchihuites area, the first systematic evidence for the Tezcatlipoca ceremonial complex appeared during the Alta Vista and Vesuvio phases. The god Tezcatlipoca and the accompanying symbol set apparently formed one of the major sociocultural innovations along this sector of the northern Mesoamerican frontier. The spectacular pseudocloisonné vessels, showing multiple representations of this god, are accompanied by trophy skulls and complex ceremonies involving human sacrifice, including skull racks and cannibalism.

By ca. A.D. 800–900, at the end of the Alta Vista and Vesuvio phases, the Chalchihuites culture had begun a rapid decline back to the small village level of organization (known to archaeologists as the Retoño and Calichal phases) similar to that from which it had developed 400 or 500 years before during the Canutillo phase. By ca. A.D. 900–1000, the area had apparently declined even further, and it was abandoned by most of its inhabitants. Certainly, the elaborate elements of the ceremonial and mining system were gone. The area had become much more like a Loma–San Gabriel "culture." In sum, the collapse of the Chalchihuites culture should be viewed as a decline into a less organized mode within the same tradition.

The settlement pattern in the Chalchihuites area suggests a complex set of multicultural themes for the polity. Accompanying the peak period of mining and ceremonialism (A.D. 400–800/900), there was a significant Loma–San Gabriel presence within the core of the culture. Hence, the Chalchihuites culture, as a regional social system, may have been multiethnic.

When the area's mining and long-distance trade/exchange economy collapsed, it was the "civilized" members of the system who left. While never numerous, they had been innovative and very well organized. Their exit from the area, even if spaced over a century, would have had an impact throughout the entire region. The collapse of the Chalchihuites culture set into motion the southern movement of elements of the groups later to be called Caxcanes and the southeastern movement of elements of the groups that may even have been related to the Tolteca-Chichimeca. The rise and fall of such a complex culture had a very wide influence over the evolution of many sociocultural developments within the zone, including the south. As a multiethnic, multicultural, and composite social system, the Chalchihuites culture is the best candidate for being a major historical element (both culturally and physically) for the groups later called the Caxcanes.

The Caxcanes and the Malpaso Area

Recent fieldwork has offered a new view of the Citadel of La Quemada in the region's culture history, demonstrating an earlier developmental sequence than previously had been postulated. The new, earlier dates have good architectural associations and place the initial construction phases of the Citadel around A.D. 500–600. During the epi-Classic period (ca. A.D. 700–900), dramatic sociocultural changes took place in the Teuchitlán region. During this period the magnificent stairways and fortifications were probably finished. Many of the great rooms, courts, and ball-courts plus the Hall of Columns were begun or finished within these two centuries, if not before.

The 200+ km network of roads around the valley floor was probably in place during the epi-Classic. In all, a vast amount of construction was initiated within approximately the same time frame that the Chalchihuites mining and trading complex flourished and as it began to decline. While the Citadel at La Quemada and Alta Vista are roughly contemporary, the sequence at Alta Vista suggests a slightly earlier apogee.

The Armillas expedition to La Quemada during the 1960s recovered many carbon samples. Some of these were from the *cuartel* (barracks) area of the Citadel. Many of these dates are fairly late, clustering within the period of A.D. 900–1100. Beyond any reasonable doubt, there are firm dates for an early Postclassic occupation on the Citadel that most likely was not as intense as the earlier phases. Indeed, the Malpaso valley was never abandoned, as the historical evidence for a late Postclassic/contact period occupation is unequivocal. The Chiriños expedition of 1530 represented the first Spanish foray into the valley, and they found it well populated.

A parallel for La Quemada's rather confusing construction history exists at the Peñol de Juchipila. This fortified site was largely constructed before the Caxcan period, yet no one doubts its historical function as the palace of the Caxcan leader Xiuhtecutli.

By ca. A.D. 800–900 La Quemada was one of the greatest fortifications of the Mesoamerica architectural experience (see Armillas 1948b, 1951, 1964, 1969). Volumetrically, the revetments, terraces, and walls (i.e., the fortifications themselves) represent the greatest investment in labor to be documented from the Citadel. All other construction activity, while also impressive in volume and design detail, pales in comparison. The fortifications were probably the last of the massive construction projects to be completed. At certain places on the Citadel, they are clearly superimposed on, even obstructing, earlier structures. They may have been finished just as or slightly before the Chalchihuites zone was abandoned by most of its miners and civilized occupants.

La Quemada certainly represented the apex of a large and complex settlement hierarchy. While no population estimates for the Malpaso valley have been offered for its apogee period, it undoubtedly was considerably larger than that for the Chalchihuites region. The extensive road system within the valley must have played an important role in social control and for provisioning the Citadel. The map by Carl de Berghes (1989 [1855]) of the roads shows the central focus that the Citadel played in the valley system. It is one of the greatest road systems yet documented for Mesoamerica.

Aside from many basic similarities in architectural design (court/platform complexes, small pyramids, the Hall of Columns) and in ceramics, there are major thematic differences between the Malpaso and Chalchihuites zones:

1. There was no major mining complex within or near the Malpaso valley that compares even slightly with the massive mining operation in the Chalchihuites zone. There were, though, tin crystal mines beneath the Citadel. These mines may be the "caves" that early sources mentioned beneath the Citadel.

2. While there does not appear to have been a monumental road system in the Chalchihuites zone, a highly formal "procession" way passed in front of Alta Vista to connect that center with a platform site that overlooked the nearest mining complex (Kelley 1993). The road system in the Malpaso valley was one of the most highly developed in Mesoamerica.

3. No site in the Chalchihuites zone was as fortified as La Quemada, although minor fortifications were built at a number of sites such as El Chapín, Gualterio, Pedrogoso, and the Cerro de Moctezuma in the Chalchihuites area. The first three had no ceremonial or major residential elements within the fortified perimeter; the last is predominantly a ceremonial and elite residential site located on a highly defensible hill (Kelley 1971). All these fortified or semifortified sites overlooked mining areas.

4. The major settlement within the Chalchihuites zone was Alta Vista (Kelley 1971, 1993). Undefended by major fortifying features, it was located on an open and level pasture, while the major settlement of the Malpaso zone (La Quemada) was highly fortified, located upon a massive rock, high above the valley floor.

5. The architectural techniques used at Alta Vista were more varied than appears to have been the case for La Quemada.

6. The Malpaso zone participated within the elegant, negative polychrome ware sphere of exchange. This sphere was oriented strongly toward the south and southeast and included the Juchipila valley and sections of the Altos de Jalisco. The core for the development of these wares may have been the middle Lerma area.

7. La Quemada had a strong association with formal ball-court ceremonialism, which, while present in the Chalchihuites area, was not as well developed architecturally.

These differences had social importance, giving Malpaso participation within the Chalchihuites Tradition a different structural form and focus. If the Chalchihuites culture can be characterized as a mining system, then perhaps La Quemada can be characterized as a military one. Both, of course, had strong agricultural bases and very well developed trade/exchange relationships with their neighbors and more distant societies. But their thematic social differences are pronounced. In each of these zones, specialization was evident in ways that either precluded or excluded similar developments in the other. If they were contemporaneous, as recent ^{14}C dates suggest, then their participation in the events and the economic structure of the frontier must have been differentiated and specialized within a common regional system. However, society along the northern periphery of Mesoamerican civilization appears to have changed with the collapse of the Chalchihuites zone. The other components within this system, such as the Malpaso valley and its great Citadel at La Quemada, were not unaffected. When the Chalchihuites culture declined, the rest of the northern sector of the Chalchihuites Tradition was not far behind. The Chalchihuites Tradition settlements in various areas of Durango (especially the Guadiana zone) increased in importance. As ongoing work (Hers 1989a) at Hervideros shows, a continuing synthesis of Loma–San Gabriel and Chalchihuites cultural elements already was firmly under way. La Quemada may have lasted a few centuries longer, perhaps at a lesser level of importance. However, its southern neighbors continued to flourish and grew in prominence. With the demise of the northern sectors of the Chalchihuites Tradition, it appears that a series of interrelated dislocations to the south and southeast were under way.

4

Territory and Resistance in West-Central Mexico, Part 2

The Rebelión de Nueva Galicia and Its Late Postclassic Prelude

Phillip C. Weigand

A major problem exists for archaeological survey and exploration concerning late Postclassic sites: many of the most important ones are still occupied, as there are strong continuities of settlement between the late Postclassic, colonial, and contemporary periods. Only a very few major contact period sites are uninhabited today, though many smaller ones fall into this category. This has made demographic, social, and economic interpretations for the late Postclassic period difficult, at best.

To mitigate these difficulties, archaeologists have spent years examining present-day trenches and pits that were dug for sewer, water, and telephone lines within settlements such as Etzatlán, hence gaining insights into the earlier levels of these settlements. Most Postclassic settlements covered by contemporary habitations were much more dispersed than are the modern settlements. Therefore, scholars have been able systematically to examine their margins, where specific buildings and/or complexes have been preserved.

Augmenting the written record and field surveys are two remarkable sixteenth-century maps. The *Pintura del Nuevo Reino de Galicia* (also called the *Mapa de Compostela*) (Acuña 1988:facing 150) was compiled sometime during the 1540s. The map by the Flemish cartographer Abraham Ortelius, *Hispaniae Novae Sivae Magnae Recens et Vera Descriptio*, was published in 1579. These two maps are among the finest documents we have for identifying towns, toponyms, and settlement patterns for the trans-Tarascan area and the Caxcan zone. A later colonial reproduction of both maps by Willem Janszoon Blaeu, in 1638, illustrates these place names and settlement patterns "Nova Hispania et Nova Galicia" (figures 4.1 and 4.2).

René Acuña, in his brief analysis of the *Pintura del Nuevo Reino de Galicia*, postulates that the map must be dated after 1546. He bases his assessment on several points, some of which may be erroneous. Due to the mention of the "minas ricas de los Zacatecas," he believes the *Pintura* must follow the founding of the city of Zacatecas. His second reason concerns the complex depiction of

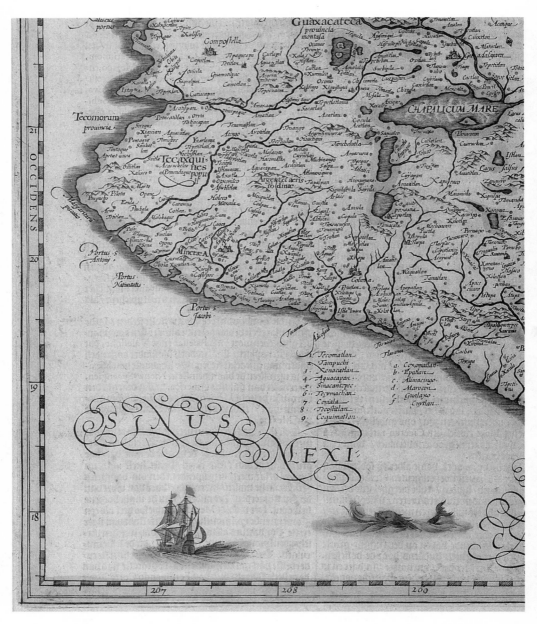

Figure 4.1. A fragment of "Nova Hispania et Nova Galicia" by Willem Janszoon Blaeu corresponding to the region depicted in *The Pintura del Nuevo Reino de Galicia*.

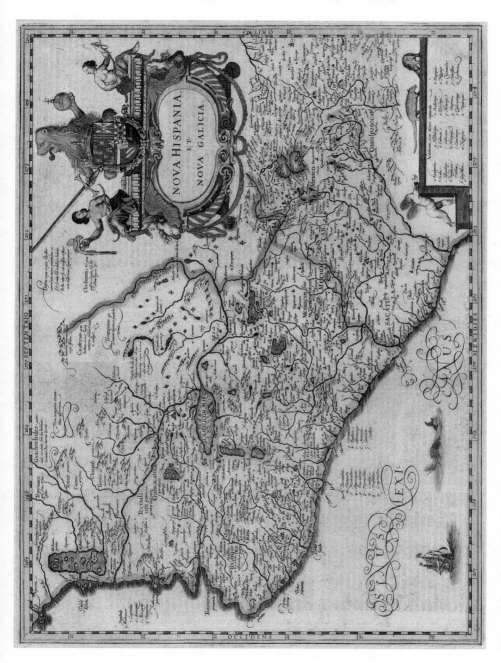

Figure 4.2. A later colonial reproduction by Willem Janszoon Blaeu of the 1579 Ortelius map, *Hispaniae Novae Sivae Magnae Recens et Vera Descriptio.*

Guadalajara's architecture and the likelihood that the city was already in its final location. The former reason is by far the least compelling. The Zacatecas area is shown still with indigenous architecture and *flecheros*, whereas everywhere else on the *Pintura* the Spanish presence is unequivocally marked by European-style buildings, without the company of bow-and-arrow-bearing warriors. "Los Zacatecas" is a clear reference to the ethnic group of that name and not the Spanish settlement, which is not portrayed on the *Pintura*. For this area, the term *minas* often means "outcrops" and not necessarily actual formal mines (see del Hoyo 1978; Topete del Valle 1978). However, since this area had had indigenous mines beginning in the Classic period a thousand years before the Spaniards arrived on the scene (Weigand 1993a), which indicates that the Indians were skilled in working with minerals, dating the *Pintura* on this point is not convincing. In addition, since both the Caxcan and Tequal areas are portrayed in active warfare, the Rebelión de Nueva Galicia might not have been fully resolved when this map was drawn.

Guadalajara's location on the *Pintura* is certainly in the Atemajac valley, but the drawing is not exact enough to ascertain the exact site. It could just as easily be at Tonal (and hence a reference to 1533) as at Atemajac (and, therefore, 1542). Both Tonal and Atemajac (as Amaxac) appear on the *Pintura* well outside the quadrangle enclosing Guadalajara. However, given the elaborateness of Guadalajara's architectural depiction, it seems very probable that the site is meant to be the 1542 location.

In all likelihood, the *Pintura* telescopes various time periods, thus illustrating a historical dynamic of about ten years in the format of a single depiction from the final perspective of the early 1540s. In this sense, it is not a true cartographic-style map but rather a mixture of elements, including formal motifs commonly seen in *lienzos* (painted cloths), codices, and maps. I suggest that its drafting date is no earlier than 1542 but certainly pre-1546.

Another of the sixteenth century's finest examples of cartography for Mesoamerica is the Ortelius map (see Boehm de Lameiras 1995). The copy I examined was taken from a photograph of a 1579 original, thus avoiding some of the pitfalls in using later Dutch copies and redrafts. Ortelius's map was compiled from many reports of differing quality and descriptive content.

Since it was never ground-checked by Ortelius or his associates, and since few other maps existed for cross-checking, the map has numerous errors and mislocations. Given the many differences in spellings and locations of settlements and rivers, it is unlikely that Ortelius was able to consult a copy of the *Pintura* when he compiled the section of the overall map that deals with the Occidente. Ortelius's geography of the trans-Tarascan area is confused, to say the least, especially the Teuchitlán-Tala basin. The Etzatlán basin is more accurately portrayed, though here too errors arose—for example, the Bolaños-Chapalagana-Guaynamota drainages were completely confused.

A comparison of the two maps gives the general impression that the *Pintura*, while a more elementary example of cartography, is the more accurate of the two in terms of the realistic spacing of the settlements, the locations of rivers, and, in some cases, the presence of religious architecture. The Ortelius map, in contrast, certainly has more toponyms. In addition, it is an example of true cartography, without the motifs so prominently featured on the *Pintura*.

Using both maps as survey guides, I have attempted to locate all the places on them in order to evaluate their late Postclassic character. In the survey process, I found hundreds of late sites that did not appear on either map. Some of these "missing" sites played major roles in the events of the late Postclassic and the Rebelión de Nueva Galicia, especially Xochitepec (Magdalena). Some sites, such as Tala, appear to have been destroyed by Tarascan raids in the period immediately before the Spanish conquest. Nuño de Guzmán described Tala as "large ruins of collapsed structures that, so it seemed, had been large towns worthy of admiration" (my translation of Tello 1968:120).

In the area that formed the core of the indigenous leader Guaxicar's polity, I have studied three other major sites: Atitlán, Etzatlán, and Xochitepec (or Guaxíxicar). Atitlán, an island site in the now drained Laguna de Magdalena, located near San Juanito, had a large obsidian workshop and obviously specialized in that activity. It was a tributary to Etzatlán in the period just before the Spaniards arrived. Etzatlán appears to have been the major site in this area during the late Postclassic period. The toponym appears as Yzatlán on the *Pintura* and Ortelius maps and also as Itzatlán (Hernán Cortés in Tello 1968:55), plus a number of other variations. While this settlement was some distance from the active military frontier facing the Tarascans, it is mentioned as being directly involved in the warfare against them (Guzmán and Cortés 1937), thus playing a critical role in the political order of the entire zone. It is to Etzatlán that Francisco Cortés de San Buenaventura came after his mixed successes along the Pacific coast. Apparently, he was aware of Etzatlan's existence even before leaving Colima and probably viewed Etzatlán as the key center in this sector of the highland lake districts of Jalisco. Its wealth in strategic and rare resources, coupled with a large population, made Etzatlán an important center and a crucial point of control for the entire region. Tello (1968) suggests that Etzatlán had a population of 18,000 inhabitants, though this estimate must be calculated from a series of figures that he offers in several areas of his text. Most historians and archaeologists have assumed that this figure refers to the population of the entire polity and not just to the center itself. In light of our studies of present-day utility trenches in Etzatlán and throughout the Etzatlán-Magdalena valley, we must reconsider Tello's estimates. Within the valley there is unmistakable evidence for a highly specialized settlement hierarchy consisting of at least four tiers. Aside from the largest sites such as Etzatlán, which had palaces and pyramids, there were smaller administrative centers—such as Oconahua/Ocomo (see below) and Atitlán (with its highly specialized obsidian workshop)—with palaces and ceremonial elements, villages with or without small ceremonial features, farmsteads, fortifications, mining camps with or without ceremonial features, canoe ports, and isolated shrines.

Modern Etzatlán, with around 12,000 inhabitants and covering ca. 350 ha, is surrounded by the late Postclassic ruin. This ruin covers 600+ ha, though it is spatially discontinuous and can be described as a center of *barrios* (neighborhoods). A literalist reading of the Spanish sources for this settlement's demographic profile thus might count only the main barrios clustered around the major ceremonial area.

Clearly, the first Spaniards in the area regarded Etzatlán as a special place. While Cortés encountered no resistance when he entered the center, this lack of resistance reflected disorganization from the ongoing and cumulative effects of epidemics and/or the collapse of the regional trade structure. We know that the Tarascans, too, did not seriously resist the Spaniards (Beltrán 1994; Warren 1977). The Tarascans, who had proven capable of holding at bay the Mexica at every turn (Beltrán 1994; Hernández Rivero 1994), were so impressed with the Spanish destruction of Tenochtitlán and so demoralized by the impact of disease on their nobility that they offered no resistance. These important psychological factors might have been at play in the Etzatlán case, as well as more broadly throughout the trans-Tarascan zone.

Etzatlán's early centrality in the Spanish regional system probably reflected its prehispanic status. The monumental fortified convent—started and finished in the early to mid-1530s—was the greatest structure of its kind between Compostela and Guadalajara (González Romero et al. 2000). On the *Pintura*, the convent is shown as the most prominent building in that area. The convent became the center of religious affairs for much of the area bounded by Compostela, Guadalajara, Zacoalco, and Ahuacatlán. Apparently, this convent was built atop a ceremonial pyramid. Opposite it, an open *capilla* ("chapel," the only one in the Occidente) was built over a smaller pyramid, thus completing the hispanization of the ancient center.

In its role as a center of wealth and prominence, Etzatlán (1) was forced to support two groups of mutually hostile Spaniards, one of which (led by Guzmán) had a poorly disciplined Tlaxcaltecan and Tarascan army of possibly 20,000 soldiers under its command; (2) undertook, albeit unwillingly, the aforementioned monumental building project for several years; (3) sustained its existence and provisioned the Europeans despite at least two population flights, which, along with diseases, reduced its demographic profile considerably; (4) provided space for another major army after the collapse of the Rebelión de Nueva Galicia; and (5) remained viable after the first drafts for labor in the local and Zacatecas silver mines began. Etzatlán was obviously placed under too much strain to prosper given these conditions, but these events reflected its resources, demography, and organization during the early contact period.

Xochitepec (modern-day Magdalena) was the center from which Guaxicar ruled his realm. The settlement is not mentioned in the Guzmán and Cortés (1937) account. Both maps show a region, though, with clear indications that the zone was not pacified when the drawings were made. The Ortelius map calls the area "Guaxacate cus provincia montasa." The *Pintura* calls the general area by two names, "Guaxíxicar de gue[r]a" and "Guaxacatlán de guer[r]a," the latter located in the west, south of the Tequales, and shown in flames. The Ortelius map shows the "Tecoalium provincia, gentes indomitas" to the west and Guaxacatlán (with a church) across the Río Santiago to the north. Just north of Guaxacatlán, in the mountains, is a notation concerning cannibals ("Antropophagi hic sunt"). Despite the disagreements between the two maps, the major point is that the general area was not yet firmly within the colonial order. This may explain why *Pintura* shows the route of the *camino real* between Compostela and Guadalajara as considerably to the south of the Xochitepec area.

Most of the site of Xochitepec is covered by the eastern suburbs of modern Magdalena and its garbage dump. What little is left has been heavily damaged by plowing and looting. When Antonio de Mendoza's group entered Xochitepec after defeating the Caxcanes in 1542, the settlement still had more than 3,000 inhabitants (Tello 1968:328). These were the remnants left behind after the effects of the Rebelión, the diseases, and Guaxicar's retreat from the area into the mountains and canyons beyond. Since Guaxicar took with him his still undefeated army, the settlement must initially have been considerably larger. Indeed, a larger figure (4,000) is given by Tello (1968:128) when discussing Oñate's visit with Guaxicar, but this figure still represented a 25 percent decline in population over ten years.

Mendoza's party received the surrender of the town (but not Guaxicar) at Hyguera, which was located upon the shores of the Laguna de Magdalena, one league west of Xochitepec. The site of Hyguera is probably within contemporary Magdalena at the site of the town's well, where a massive grove of eponymous hyguera trees still grows. Xochitepec was located between Hyguera and Tequila, which is shown on both maps. On the *Pintura*, a third zone—labeled "Tecoles de guerra"—of nearby warfare is shown across the Río Santiago from Tequila. Thus, the Xochitepec zone was surrounded on three sides by areas still engaged in warfare. The names Tecol(es) and Tequil(a), along with Tecoal(ium), Tequal(es), and Qual(es), are all close cognates, probably indicating a common ethnicity and/or language for the central Río Santiago canyon and at least some of southern and central Nayarita.

At Xochitepec, the only structures still visible and relatively undamaged appear to be residential or, possibly, small-scale administrative compounds. The best-preserved, largest compounds are composed of platforms around very small, interior patios. These patios are probably sunken. They measure ca. 60 by 50 m. The only possible ceremonial and/or administrative compound is represented by two small pyramids that are located on a north-south axis, are connected by a common banquette, and face a semienclosed patio. This structure is over 100 m long and about 80 m wide. This structure had adobe bricks in the profile exposed by a looter's trench. Most platform fill, however, is mixed rock and prepared earth. There is evidence to suggest that some of the larger platforms had veneer finishing.

The Caxcan Southern Expansion

The expansion of the Caxcanes into the river valleys to the south of the Tlaltenango, Juchipila, and Verde drainages had an important corollary; that is, it was achieved at the expense of the remaining elites in the northern settlement system, especially in the Malpaso zone. Although the Malpaso valley was never abandoned, the collapse at Tuitlán meant that the Malpaso valley became a periphery to a newer core of sociopolitical activity farther south. It was demoted from its core status but not relegated to a place outside the Caxcan world or the Chalchihuites Tradition.

The invasion of the southern river valleys may have placed too much of a strain on the Malpaso region for it to have continued to support a great center such as Tuitlán. Since the southern expansion of the Caxcan elite appears to have started in the early thirteenth century, Tuitlán must have been abandoned shortly after that period.

Even if the decline of Tuitlán was gradual, the repercussions must have been felt over a wide area. It is tempting to see this collapse and the accompanying dislocations as having been intimately related to the last of the major migrations of Chichimeca into central Mexico and the Cuenca de México, including groups later called the Culhua Mexica and Azteca.

The linguistic evidence, summarized by Leopoldo Valiñas (1993), supports the early colonial contention that the languages of the Caxcanes and those from central Mexico were sufficiently similar to have been mutually intelligible. This linguistic similarity argues strongly for a short period of linguistic separation between the Caxcanes in the Occidente and the Nahuatl speakers of central Mexico. Some point within the late Postclassic certainly would have been appropriate for this separation, since a longer period would have considerably lessened the possibility for mutual intelligibility that so impressed colonial observers.

The southern river valleys already had considerable developmental histories of their own, including large populations, long before the Caxcan expansion took place. The first cycle of conquest or territorial warfare targeting the southern valleys occurred while Tuitlán was still occupied. The successes were celebrated with a sacrifice of 200 children (large collections of disarticulated and/or burned human bone occur at the Citadel [Peter Jiménez Betts, personal communication]). One result of the first invasion discussed in the accounts is that Tuitlán sent a governor of its choice to Teul. Apparently, as a part of this same campaign or very shortly afterward, Juchipila and Tlaltenango were conquered. This campaign produced refugees who relocated in the *barranca*, or arroyo, of the Río Grande de Santiago in the San Cristobal zone. The probable date given for this campaign is 290 years before the Spaniards arrived, or the early thirteenth century (Tello 1968:27). Juchipila at this time apparently recognized the authority of the temple at Teul, though this too may have had pre-Caxcan roots. As an alternative, Juchipila's recognition of the religious power of Teul may be a reference to the physical shift in power that was under way: the growth of Teul as the major Caxcan center and the concomitant collapse of Tuitlán. It is certain that Teul held this central position when the Spaniards arrived in the Caxcan zone. While Teul's authority was not political in the sense of a united polity but rather moral/religious, it nonetheless carried the obligation for tribute from the other Caxcan polities.

Another, later conquest was initiated toward the Río Verde valley. The target was Teocaltiche, a center of warlike Tecuexes who had allied themselves with their neighbors, the Zacatecas and Guachichiles, to resist the invasion. The Caxcanes prevailed and went on to Nochistlán. This event is also given a date: 260 years before the Spaniards arrived, or the middle of the thirteenth century (Tello 1968:29). Just after that date, apparently, the major Caxcan centers that the Spaniards encountered were in place (in the sense of the presence of these possible new conquest dynasties). The dates may be real or imagined, but without archaeological confirmation they are all we have at present. They may include ceremonial considerations; for example, 260 years is exactly five Mesoamerican centuries. Therefore, an exact placement in the Christian calendar is not possible, and these dates should be used only as referents for a general time frame.

By the time the Spaniards arrived, Teul had become the main ceremonial center for the entire Caxcan region, or Caxcana. The elaborate temple and fortification complex at Teul probably had pre-Caxcan roots in the same fashion as the buildings of the Peñol de Juchipila. The roots of the Teul complex probably belong to the Classic period, as my examination of surface finds of ceramics and architectural profiles of the many looters' pits strongly suggests.

The Caxcanes, in another section of Tello's narrative, were simply called the "naciones de Teutl" and "las Provincias del Teul" (1968:318, 205–206; see also Marín Tamayo 1992). It is important to note that "naciones" and "provincias" are plural in all these references. The Spaniards recognized a confederacy of some sort among these highly active and warlike neighbors. This loose polity was based upon mutual but hierarchically structured religious obligations and on kinship ties among the Caxcan leaders. These ties give the area a feeling of much more cohesion, and they support the proposition that the initial conquering force was constituted from a closely knit group. Ritual obligations and kin ties were obviously used to mitigate some of the political and territorial ambitions and conflicts that were endemic in the region. This confederacy is reminiscent of the internal relationships within the Triple Alliance during the first stages of the growth of Culhua Mexica power. In this sense, Teul perhaps can be regarded as the heir to the Caxcan political system first set into motion at Tuitlán and possibly even slightly earlier in the Chalchihuites region.

Despite their confederation under at least the minimal or nominal religious tutelage of Teul and their kinship ties among the regional elite, Caxcan polities were frequently at war with one another. For example, the *Relación del Pueblo de Teucaltiche* (Acuña 1988:305–306) describes warfare by the Caxcan leadership against other Caxcan polities (Xuchipila, Xalpa), groups in the barranca of the Río Grande de Santiago, nearby areas within the Altos of Jalisco (Yahualica), the "indios chichimecas de guerra" (Acuña 1988:305), and others of their immediate neighbors. While the other *Relaciones* are far less explicit, it seems certain that warfare among the Caxcanes, despite their religious confederacy, was chronic and that warfare against their non-Caxcan neighbors, including the Chichimeca, was incessant.

I offered a reconstruction of the possible political and territorial order of much of the Occidente just prior to the conquest in chapter 3 (and see figure 3.1). It is obvious that Caxcan expansion toward the south was still under way until interrupted by the Spaniards' arrival in the early sixteenth century. Up until that date, Caxcan expansion had always been accompanied by colonization, though in most cases the actual colonists may have been only an elite. This deliberateness may help explain the relatively slow Caxcan spread into the Occidente, as compared to the much quicker movements of other Tolteca-Chichimeca or the Azteca into the southeast. Most but certainly not all Caxcan expansion and colonization had occurred in areas that were already closely related in cultural terms, such as into the southern river valleys of Zacatecas, where much of the region was composed of cultural groups already within the Chalchihuites Tradition. The Caxcanes were able to expand beyond the limits of those groups ethnically related to them.

Though the barranca of the Río Grande de Santiago may have offered a partial barrier against Caxcan expansion, the real barrier was the existence of fairly well organized political entities in the trans-Tarascan area (Weigand 1993a, 1993b). These states, no matter how fragmented by the general disturbances inherent in their "double frontier" situation, were not and had never been participants in the Chalchihuites Tradition except as partners in trade and exchange. Their own roots were considerably different and more complex. Thus, during their expansion into this area the Caxcanes might have encountered more sociocultural resistance than they had experienced elsewhere. Caxcan raids and warfare were carried into the barranca zone and beyond, directly threatening Tonalá, Xuchitepec, and even Etzatlán. In effect, between the southern Caxcanes and the trans-Tarascan polities the barranca region was a fluid boundary, a sociomilitary frontier of considerable importance and significant antiquity.

The Caxcanes must have been aware of the Tarascan Empire (and vice versa), whose frontier was located in another contested region between the Río Verde and Río Lerma. Within this region, though, was located the Peñol de Coyna (also Cuina), a polity that the Spaniards felt was a crucial site for the control of the lower Lerma valley (cf. Tello 1968:100–104). Coyna had a population of 8,000 at the time of the Guzmán invasion, and they were enemies of the Tarascans (Tello 1968:103). Of course, this animosity does not mean that they were necessarily allies of the Caxcanes. The Tarascan military presence, based from Jacona (for the lower Lerma, Chapala, and Tonalá frontier) and Tamazula (for the Acolimán, Sayula, and Tala frontier), had been felt throughout the trans-Tarascan region for at least sixty years prior to the arrival of the Spaniards. Some of the targets of conquest or raiding were shared between the Tarascans and the southern Caxcan polities of Nochistlán, Juchipila, and Teul. Given the military capacities of the Caxcanes and the Tarascans, a large-scale conflict between them for greater control of the trans-Tarascan zone certainly loomed as a serious possibility until brought to an abrupt end by the Spaniards.

The Tarascans' Frontiers to the North and Northwest

In the trans-Tarascan zone, the first documented cycle of conquest from the east preceded the arrival of the Europeans by more than a half-century. These first attempts at conquest came from the Michoacán lake zones, which, after the collapse of the Teuchitán Tradition, emerged as the dominant civilization in the Occidente. It is informative to examine the Tarascan strategies and goals in this region before turning to the later Spanish invasion and the indigenous response known as the Rebelión de Nueva Galicia.

The Purépecha polity had well-attested difficulties in its conquest attempts, or military raids, among its western and northwestern neighbors (Beltrán 1994; Bravo Ugarte 1962; Gorenstein and Pollard 1983; León 1904; Pollard 1987, 1993; Ponce 1968; RM 2000; Stanislawski 1947; Tello 1968). Acolimán, a territorial kingdom centered in the modern state of Colima, was apparently conquered by the Tarascans at least once and possibly twice, yet it later managed to regain its independence and, in the process, extend its own territory and influence. The Tarascans never did conquer their other western neighbors, such as Autlán, despite a number of raids. In addition, their northwestern neighbors remained unconquerable, though apparently not for lack of trying. There were at least three possible campaigns toward the northwest. Documentary evidence for these campaigns varies greatly in quality, and every account has its difficulties. One of the best is embedded in the Guzmán chronicle concerning the visitation to Tala. In this account, the Tarascans had not been the first to destroy ancient Tala, but their destructive raid was so thorough that the site remained uninhabited even after sixty years of inactivity.

Concomitant with the Tarascan military campaigning, there appear to have been some political realignments in the trans-Tarascan zone. To face the common enemy, interregional alliances (e.g., Sayula-Acolimán and Etzatlán-Tala) may have come into being. This side effect of Tarascan campaigning in the area could hardly have been a desired result from their perspective. Such alliances would have placed a series of reorganized states of proven military capacity directly upon the northwestern frontier of the Tarascan Empire. The net result may have been to produce greater political consolidation in areas that otherwise would have been more fragmented. Although details are imprecise about when and where battles took place, the destruction of Tala seems to have occurred around A.D. 1470. The other campaigns probably took place around this same time and afterward. Tarascan military targets, aside from Tala, apparently included the Sayula-Atoyác basin, the northern shore of the Laguna de Chapala, and the upper Santiago valley via such places as Ocotlán, Tonalá, Coyna, and Tlajomulco.

Given the inability of the Purépecha to effect conquests in this zone, it appears that whatever they accomplished was Pyrrhic at best. Of course, it may be that the goal of Tarascan military activity was disruption and booty rather than complete conquest. Since commerce in ceramics (Noyola 1994), turquoise (Weigand 1992), probably metals (Pollard 1987), and possibly salt (Liot 2000) existed across the trans-Tarascan / Tarascan frontier zone, too much military activity might have been counterproductive. As Pollard (1987, 1994) has pointed out, Tarascan expansion outside of the Pátzcuaro-Jacona corelands had an undeniable logic that involved control over rare resource areas, especially those that had metals.

A relatively nearby hinterland of mineral-rich provinces was conquered fairly early in the history of Tarascan expansion: Churumuco, Sanchiqueo, Jicalán, and Inguarán for their copper deposits; Pungarabato for tin; Zinapecuaro for obsidian; Ixtlán for salt (which was paid to Jacona); and, farther away and apparently somewhat later, Tamazula for silver. With firm control established over these nearby silver-, tin-, copper-, salt-, and obsidian-mining areas, the Tarascans could consider the expansion of their rare resource procurement system or, at least, a system of raiding that would allow improved access to those resources.

There are three categories of economic targets—rare resources, routes of access, and strategic resources—that might have interested the Purépecha in the trans-Tarascan region. These targets were distributed in two quite different ecological zones, which, to some extent, were concomitant with the types of resources involved: the coastal (and largely tropical) ecotones and the highland lake/river basins.

Rare Resources

The trans-Tarascan zone was abundantly endowed with mineral, crystal, and organic materials of proven value within the regional exchange systems and the larger Mesoamerican trade structure. A number of high-quality obsidian deposits show signs of significant exploitation (e.g., La Joya). The silver deposits in the Sierra de Ameca were mined in the prehispanic period and those in the Bolaños canyon possibly as well. Copper deposits were widely distributed, with those from the Sierra de Ameca showing signs of ancient exploitation, as did those from the Bolaños canyon and the Sayula valley. Blue-green gemstones were found in all of these copper- and silver-mining areas, but the mines in the Sierra de Ameca seem to have been particularly well developed. Placer gold was available in the river valleys, especially those of the coastal piedmont zone, in both Colima and Nayarit. Opal deposits show some indication of ancient exploitation in the Magdalena and Hostotipaquillo zones. Salt deposits were exploited widely, with the best highland source in the Atoyác-Sayula valley and the best coastal sources in Colima and Nayarit. Tropical birds and their feathers were widely distributed in Colima, Jalisco, and Nayarit. Cacao came mostly from that same coastal area. Shells, especially from Nayarit and Colima, were valuable. All of these items had high value for the Tarascans and could have provided motives for their expansion efforts.

Routes of Access

Some rare resources such as turquoise were not available as deposits in or near the trans-Tarascan zone but had to be transported across the region for trade and exchange elsewhere in Mesoamerica. Given the high value of turquoise in Mesoamerica (Harbottle and Weigand 1992; Weigand and Harbottle 1992), the Tarascans may have sought to control or influence a larger section of the actual route. On the other hand, the only routes that the Purépecha seemed concerned with were those into the nearby rare resource areas of the trans-Tarascan region.

Strategic Resources

If the Tarascans wished to control natural resources at a distance from their homeland, some efforts in colonization or garrisoning would have been required. They were capable of this, as their successful efforts in the Tamazula and *tierra caliente* zones appear to show. However, this would have placed a heavy administrative strain on a state that had already expanded well beyond its immediate hinterland. Colonization, or any other type of direct control over trans-Tarascan strategic resources, seems to be the least probable of the three economic motives for expansion.

Thus, the best explanation for Tarascan expansion seems to involve the desire to improve access to selected rare resources, most probably salt, metals, obsidian, and tropical products such as cacao, shell, and feathers. Military activity, then, could be seen as an incentive to collaborate in trade on more favorable terms rather than as a lever to gain direct control. Given the sociomilitary organization of the Purépecha state, had they wished to conquer nearby neighbors in the trans-Tarascan region, this most likely could have been accomplished. But in the early sixteenth century, this does not seem to have been their primary focus.

Perspectives on the Rebelión de Nueva Galicia

The intent here is not to review details of the actual conquest of the trans-Tarascan or Caxcan region. Instead, my comments will be limited to the early Spanish strategic considerations for control over both zones and the reactions of the indigenous societies of the two areas in question (Aiton 1927; Marín Tamayo 1992; Guzmán and Cortés 1937; Tello 1968; Weigand 1993a, 1993b).

While the Cortés de San Buenaventura tour of selected sections of the trans-Tarascan region was only minimally an effort at systematic military conquest, it seems to have done more to disrupt the area than to reorganize it—a fact that Guzmán emphasized during the legal contest that followed his efforts at conquest in the Occidente. Cortés's direct military efforts were relatively mild when compared to the storm that followed with Guzmán and Mendoza.

It was Guzmán who devised a strategy for the conquest of the Occidente, though it is uncertain how much of this strategy was planned and how much resulted from chance, especially since its initial application failed in the face of the Rebelión de Nueva Galicia. Mendoza (Aiton 1927), following the same strategy, was more successful in dealing with the Rebelión; perhaps he should be regarded as the real conqueror of the Occidente.

While both Cortés and Guzmán targeted the northern trans-Tarascan zone for major military campaigns, they entered the area from different directions. Although both routes made sense in terms of Mesoamerican cultural systems of trade and exchange, only Guzmán's offered the Spaniards the opportunity for gaining lasting control over the trans-Tarascan zone.

While both Cortés and Guzmán realized that a firm base in the Tarascan zone was required for successes farther west or northwest, only Guzmán grasped that a Tarascan base would be insufficient. For Guzmán, the ideal base already existed. When he left the Tarascan capital at Tzintzuntzan, his first attempt to penetrate the Occidente was to secure a direct route across the Lerma into the

Tonalá region via the strategic site of Coyna, using the northern shore of the Laguna de Chapala as his southern flank. This maneuver was successful, but he soon realized that the Caxcan presence on his northern flank would leave exposed any adventure into the rich valleys of the trans-Tarascan region, which eventually would form the heartlands of the colonial system in the Occidente. Guzmán sent an expedition into the Caxcan region at the same time that he continued the western penetration deeper into the trans-Tarascan zone (Tello 1968:120). While this expedition ultimately failed to achieve its goal of military neutralization of the Caxcan polities, it was the correct military strategy for the conquest of the entire region. He must have realized that portions of the trans-Tarascan zone were in fact part of a military frontier, half of which was still completely active and uncontrolled.

This first application of Guzmán's strategy for control over the Occidente was destined to fail because he did not invest enough effort to bring it to fruition. The Guzmán party burned the pan-Caxcan center at Teul in 1530 or shortly thereafter, though he had found this center and many others in the area empty of most of their populations. Apparently, Guzmán correctly perceived that a destructive blow at this symbol of Caxcan unity would have a great psychological impact on the native peoples. His military thrust into the Caxcana was based on recognition that, after the Tarascans, the Caxcanes represented the best-organized and most militarized threat in the Occidente. Only after they were neutralized would a move into the fertile trans-Tarascan zone make sense. With the raid into the Caxcana and the destruction of Teul, Guzmán thought that he had neutralized both sides of the trans-Tarascan double military frontier.

Guzmán attempted to establish firm Spanish control over three settlements in order to build a chain of influence throughout the area: Nochistlán (a prominent Caxcan settlement and the first site of Guadalajara, meant in part to control the entire Caxcan region), Etzatlán (to control the northern trans-Tarascan region), and Compostela (to control the westernmost highlands and access to the Pacific coast). Effective control over these three strategic places and their surrounding regions would insure long-term control over the entire zone.

Guzmán's system failed, however, because of three factors: (1) infighting among the Spaniards involved with the initial *entradas* into the Occidente destroyed the prospects for a unified command over the entire zone, especially since it was the middle link in the chain (Etzatlán) that remained outside Guzmán's effective control; (2) the Caxcanes rebelled and expelled the Spaniards from Nochistlán early in the 1530s, thus entirely eliminating that control point; and (3) the northward departure of the large armed Spanish contingent under Francisco Vázques de Coronado for Quivira/Cíbola in 1540 emptied the area of many of its potential fighting forces and resources.

Despite construction of the monumental convent at Etzatlán, begun in 1534 (González Romero et al. 2000), this region was in rebellion and beyond effective Spanish control by 1538. Thus, just as the Rebelión de Nueva Galicia was achieving its full momentum, two of Guzmán's three strategic bases lost their effectiveness. Apparently, Guaxicar (of Xochitepec) neutralized the overall Etzatlán area just as Tenamaxtli (of Nochistlán) and Xiuhtecutli (of Juchipila) had already neutralized Spanish control within most of the Caxcana (Ruiz Medrano 1994).

However, the Spaniards had had two major successes among the Caxcanes. First, they managed to neutralize Teul prior to the outbreak of the Mixtón War. In addition to the Spaniards' success at Teul, Miguel de Ybarra, the Spanish *encomendero* of Nochistlán, had managed to have Xiuhtecutli assassinated, probably in 1541. Xiuhtecutli had been the highly effective leader of Juchipila, with apparent renown throughout the Caxcana. These were important accomplishments because they required the Caxcanes to establish a new center and rallying point in order to organize a concerted effort against the Spaniards and also to reconfigure their leadership. Since Caxcan leadership was closely interrelated through kinship ties, this part of the restructuring probably followed an established pattern.

Choosing a new site to mirror the theme of Caxcan unity probably posed a greater challenge. Given the ongoing religious revitalization among the Caxcanes (Ruiz Medrano 1994) in the face of the growing Spanish presence, accompanied by ongoing epidemics and general sociocultural disintegration, this overall reorganization was not too difficult to accomplish.

The site known as Peñol de Mixtón was chosen for the last crucial battles through which the Spaniards were attempting to crush the Caxcan wing of the Rebelión. Where was this site? The Cerro del Indio and the Cerro de Santa Cruz seem to be the most likely candidates. Both are in the immediate area of Juchipila, as a number of documents mention. Prehispanic Juchipila was located at the Peñol de Juchipila (Cerro de Las Ventanas), so this description, plus the mention of the Peñol de Mixtón as being opposite Apotzol, also corresponds. The Peñol de Juchipila is described as extending far into the valley. Neither the Peñol de Juchipila nor the Peñol de Mixtón has an architectural complex; thus, the site for the battles was chosen for its military potential rather than as a place with a ceremonial and/or administrative heritage.

In addition, the Peñol de Mixtón was located in a central place as far as the Caxcan resistance was concerned. Nochistlán was too close to the Spaniards, though a very spirited defense of the Peñol de Mixtón occurred when Mendoza first entered into the Caxcana. The Peñol de Mixtón is located in the geographical heart of the Caxcana and nearer to the remaining active allies and antagonists—Tlaltenango, Jalpa, Juchipila, and their many tributaries—in the war against the Spaniards.

The first battle near Mixtón—in 1541, prior to Mendoza's arrival in the Occidente—was a conclusive Caxcan victory. The battle appears to have been fought on the valley floor near the Peñol de Mixtón rather than on the surrounding slopes and peaks. This victory, however, undoubtedly added luster to the general choice of the site as the focal point for the second battle, over which Mendoza presided. Once the defenders had been almost starved out, the actual attack took place. The Caxcan forces were defeated conclusively at Mixtón. While large numbers were killed, were captured, committed suicide, or were dispersed, the Caxcanes were not completely eliminated from the scene. The victory was firm enough, however, for Mendoza to control all the major centers of Caxcan population and to continue his efforts to suppress the rest of the Rebelión.

Mendoza thus continued Guzmán's strategy: only after controlling the Caxcana (which Guzmán had failed to accomplish) did Mendoza invade the extremely fertile trans-Tarascan region. By 1542 he had ousted Guaxicar from Xochitepec and eliminated the last vestige of resistance at Ahuacatlán. Guaxicar, however, had not sensed defeat and had his forces still intact. Just as Tenamaxtli and his retinue had escaped Spanish recapture after Mixtón to relocate among the Nayaritas, Guaxicar and his army did the same.

The Roots of the Rebelión

The vast field of violence sown by Guzmán created the conditions for the beginning of the Rebelión. Up to this point, the conquest of the Occidente had been relatively peaceful, probably due to the psychological disarray over the epidemic diseases, the collapse of Tzintzuntzan and Tenochtitlán, and the ebb of trade. Xalisco revolted in 1530 and Ahuacatlán in 1532. The Caxcanes successfully expelled the Spaniards from Nochistlán during the same time period. Thus, the Rebelión de Nueva Galicia included both the trans-Tarascan and Caxcan regions. The movement against the Spaniards gained momentum due to the illegal or quasi-legal actions of the Spaniards themselves. Aside from the ongoing dislocations of native cultures and social organization, the immediate causes for the Rebelión were related to the economic transformations of the landscape and to illegal slave raids.

Economic Transformations

After conquest, much of the Occidente was subdivided into *encomiendas*, many of which abused their limited privileges. The introduction of a new elite into an area undergoing the initial stages of demographic collapse put a great strain on the existing social order. Both Cortés and Guzmán placed tribute loads on selected native polities, although Guzmán's demands were especially heavy. While many of the new obligations were paid in foodstuffs and direct labor, some tribute was paid in precious materials such as metals, thus intensifying extractive activities for these commodities. Mining by the Spaniards was at first based at localities shown to them by the native peoples. The *Pintura* shows that, as early as ca. 1540, the Spaniards recognized four major zones with mines or mining potential. Two of them (Tepeque and Zacatecas) were in the Caxcana or Nayarita zone; the other two (in the Sierra de Ameca south of Etzatlán and at Guachinango) were in the trans-Tarascan zone. As the invaders gained familiarity with the region's geology, they began their own operations using labor drafts. The introduction of cattle into the area also brought changes to the landscape, often degrading indigenous field systems.

Illegal Slaving

Soon after the conquest, illegal slave raids began to be conducted in the trans-Tarascan region. For example, a major slave raid during 1535 ravaged the zone from Tequila to Ahuacatlán, including the Xochitepec area of the Etzatlán basin. It may have been this raid that set this zone into open revolt. Incidents of rebellion became more frequent, and by 1538 the entire zone in which the raid had occurred had fallen out of Spanish control. Shortly thereafter, the Rebelión had become widespread throughout the trans-Tarascan region.

Revitalization and the Native Response

An intense social corollary of the confrontation of the indigenous peoples with the Spaniards was a wave of religious revitalization in the Occidente. This movement quickly gained strength throughout the entire Caxcan and trans-Tarascan zones. The flavor of the religious sentiments among the Caxcanes and peoples of the trans-Tarascan region closely parallels that in other parts of the Spanish colonial realm.

This revitalization movement provided a sense of unity to the Rebelión that otherwise would have been difficult to achieve, especially given the hostilities between the trans-Tarascan and Caxcan states prior to the arrival of the Europeans and the differences in cultural traditions between the two zones. Participants in the Rebelión came to share a ceremonial ideology that offered a well-grounded rationale for joint military action against the Spaniards. Among the key targets were the Spanish religious personnel, the most famous being Fray Antonio de Cuellar and Fray Juan Calero. Both had been based in the fortress-convent in Etzatlán, and both were killed within the general area during 1541 in separate incidents.

By this date, almost the entire zone—from Guaynamota in the west to Juchipila in the north and Purificación in the south—was in revolt. Guaxicar became the maximum leader, or *cacique*, for the zone between Xocotlán, Hostotipaquillo, and Guaxacatlán, thus dominating a highly important and central sector of the western theater of the Rebelión. In 1541 Oñate recognized that the Rebelión was so widespread that it would take a grand strategy to suppress it. His highest priority was reinforcements to replace the forces lost by Manuel de Ybarra's defeat near Juchipila and by the departure of Coronado's expedition. With Mendoza's arrival from Mexico City to deal with the Rebelión, the balance of power shifted between Nueva Galicia and Nueva España. Mendoza recognized that the Caxcan area was the most highly organized and dangerous sector of the Rebelión. His troop strength was impressive, with estimates ranging from 20,000 to 50,000 indigenous auxiliaries. Whatever the numbers may have been, there had not been battles like these since the siege and capture of Tenochtitlán twenty years earlier.

Mendoza's line of march was marked by two serious battles before he reached the Peñol de Mixtón (Aiton 1927; Tello 1968). Both Coyna and Nochistlán offered determined resistance. At Mixtón, the final act of the Caxcan phase of the Rebelión was played out. On December 16, 1541, formal resistance at the Peñol de Mixtón ended, with most of the Caxcan forces dispersing and thereby escaping. Among them was Tenamaxtli, who had escaped from the Spaniards after the collapse of Nochistlán. A great number of Caxcan defenders appeared to have taken refuge within the Nayarita, a zone roughly defined as the area wherein the Tepecano, Huichol, Tequal, and Cora survived and developed during the colonial period. Rather than pursuing those fleeing natives, Mendoza chose to destroy the Caxcan centers, then allocated or reallocated encomiendas, and finally dispersed much of the Caxcan population, either through slavery or resettlement, to other areas within Nueva Galicia and in the north.

While the defeat and loss of the Peñol de Mixtón spelled the effective end of the Rebelión in the Caxcan theater, the trans-Tarascan region and the Nayarita zone remained as obstacles to Spanish dominion in the Occidente. After leaving the Caxcana devastated, Mendoza shifted his campaign to the trans-Tarascan region.

After crossing the barranca of the Río Santiago, Mendoza's party regained the highlands near Tequila. They went directly to the town of the leader Guaxicar, where the Spaniards received the surrender of the area at Hyguera, though Guaxicar and his army eluded capture. The Spanish force briefly laid siege to Ahuacatlán, and this battle constitutes the last major engagement of the western theater of the Rebelión. Only the Nayarita theater remained.

In Etzatlán, two native leaders—don Fernando and don Diego—surrendered during the final phase of the Rebelión. Cortés had assigned Etzatlán as an encomienda to Juan de Escareño, who subsequently was discharged from his holding for absenteeism around 1535. After this, Etzatlán was reorganized as a *corregimiento* (a country subdivision for administrative purposes). The center was reorganized again in 1540 as an *alcaldía-mayor* (a later *organización* of the corregimiento) (Gerhard 1972).

In 1542 the last of the indigenous auxiliaries of Mendoza's army were released in and around Etzatlán, probably still numbering well above 10,000. They were simply set loose on the countryside without any provision for their orderly return to Michoacán or central Mexico. This plague of poorly disciplined ex-soldiers—combined with the accelerating pandemic(s), starvation, and slaughter resulting from the Rebelión, slave taking, and plundering—marked the definitive sociocultural collapse of native polities in this sector of the Occidente.

The Guerra de los Nayaritas

The Rebelión de Nueva Galicia did not end when the Spaniards officially concluded it in 1542. The indigenous societies remaining in the Nayarita region of the Occidente were not officially in rebellion but had not been conquered. The presence of two of the most powerful leaders of the Rebelión de Nueva Galicia among the Nayaritas, along with unknown numbers of their retainers and elements of their armies, must have had a major impact in the region.

While Tenamaxtli eventually returned to the Spanish world and was extensively interviewed by Bartolomé de Las Casas, thus preserving his unique indigenous account of Caxcan life and the events of the Mixtón War, Guaxicar apparently remained at large. In addition, it is uncertain how many of Tenamaxtli's retinue stayed behind in the Nayarita zone after he returned or, for that matter, how many Caxcanes took refuge among them. When the Caxcanes of Tuitlán first invaded and captured Teul, Tlaltenango, and Juchipila, possibly during the course of the early thirteenth century, those events had provoked a flight of refugees into the Nayarita zone.

In other words, Tenamaxtli and his retinue were following a recognized route into a traditional region of refuge. Guaxicar's association with the Nayarita hinterlands, in terms of proximity and tradition, was just as intimate, especially with the area called Tequal and/or Xurute. Within the Nayarita zone, many toponyms reflect his presence, influence, and/or heritage. If, indeed, both Guaxicar and Tenamaxtli were in residence among the Nayaritas in 1542, the Rebelión could not be considered at an end. Having such a large entourage of highly experienced soldiers and leaders among them offered a promising start for the Nayaritas who were opposed to being incorporated into the colonial order.

The impact of the long-term war against the Nayaritas was considerable. Continuous raiding from the Nayarita mountains seriously affected the stability of Nueva Galicia's economy, especially with the incessant cattle rustling and capturing of colonists. Such raiding demonstrated the political and religious weakness of the colonial order in the zones neighboring the Nayaritas, thus serving as an example for the marginally conquered peoples to the north and often inspiring them to similar rebellious acts. The Nayarita zone served as a refuge region for runaway slaves, renegades wanted by the authorities, and other general misfits, revolutionaries, and refugees. The constant attention required to contain the raiding was costly in military, evangelistic, and economic resources. The presence of the Nayarita enclave within the empire gave the Occidente a frontier character long after other such enclaves had been eliminated everywhere else.

The Nayaritas were never politically unified, except perhaps toward the very end of the Guerra de los Nayaritas in the late seventeenth and early eighteenth centuries. The political fragmentation within this zone was probably far greater than in any other region that the Spaniards had encountered in the Occidente. The extremely rugged terrain no doubt facilitated this fragmentation, but it also meant that the Nayaritas were able to withstand, with relatively small forces, numerous Spanish attempts at penetration.

In sum, the Guerra de los Nayaritas represented a continuity of the Rebelión de Nueva Galicia. The interchange of personnel, closeness in sociocultural traditions, shared languages and dialects, and long mutual history meant that the two events are best understood as parts of a continuing process of resistance against the Spanish invaders. The Nayaritas understood the value of active resistance, and, in this sense, their role in the events of the Rebelión was critical. While the first phase of the Rebelión de Nueva Galicia only lasted a decade, the Guerra de los Nayaritas endured for generations, until it was brought to an end—after 180 years of resistance—when the Spaniards finally were able to sack and burn the Nayaritas' stronghold at Tonati in 1722.

Acknowledgments

I appreciate very much the comments and suggestions made by Elizabeth Mozzillo, Andrew Roth, Brigette Boehm, and Francisco Román Gutiérrez. I owe a special debt of gratitude to Ethelia Ruiz Medrano, who has shared several of her unpublished manuscripts and archival sources, as well as her invaluable commentary. Errors, of course, are mine.

5

The Prehispanic Heritage of the Tarascans (Purépecha)

Helen Perlstein Pollard

In 1522 the Tarascan king ruled over a domain of more than 75,000 km² in the west-central highlands of Mexico, including the modern state of Michoacán. The Tarascan Empire was at that time the second largest in Mesoamerica and was ethnically dominated by a population the Spaniards called Tarascos, who spoke a language known as Tarasco or Purépecha. The modern Purépecha of central and northern Michoacán are the descendants of those people. But while the empire only emerged in the two centuries before the Europeans' arrival, Purépecha culture can be identified at least two millennia earlier. This deep cultural tradition, and the massive transformations it underwent with the emergence of a centralized state and an expansionist empire, has confronted the colonial and postcolonial worlds during the last five hundred years. In this chapter I argue that a significant part of the Purépecha response can be understood only through the long lens of history.

Tarascan Prehistory

The past two decades have seen the establishment of major archaeology programs in Michoacán, resulting in the first chronometrically dated and stratigraphically defined sequences of occupation from several of the lake basins of central and northern Michoacán, regional surveys in these same lake basins, and targeted surveys for salvage projects in other parts of the state. With regard to ethnohistorical research, scholars have transcribed and analyzed sixteenth- and seventeenth-century documents in Spanish and Purépecha and have published new editions of the *Relación de Michoacán* (RM 2000), the primary extant document describing the Tarascan Empire in the early sixteenth century. These new sources of archaeological and ethnohistorical data make it possible to test models of long-term sociopolitical change, stability, and ethnogenesis.

Recent salvage survey and excavation projects (Esparza López 1999; Novella et al. 2002; Pulido Méndez 2003; Silverstein 2000, 2001) in the Balsas and Tepalcatepec River Basins, in the Balsas tributaries north to Uruapan, in the southeast-central Balsas, and along the coast of Michoacán have confirmed that ethnic Purépecha populations were limited to central and northern Michoacán until the expansion of the Tarascan Empire (Pollard 1994). Based on their reading of sixteenth-century documents, Woodrow Borah and Sherbourne Cook (1960, 1963) estimated the population of the Tarascan Empire at 1.3 million; more recently, Ulises Beltrán (1994:119–120) estimated the 1524 population at 750,000 divided into three regions: about half in the Bajío, about one-third in the Sierra, and one-sixth in the Lowlands, always emphasizing the high concentration of population in central and northern Michoacán.

While little systematic research has taken place in the Meseta Tarasca of western Michoacán, all of the zones of highest population density at contact—including the Zacapu, Pátzcuaro, and Cuitzeo Basins—have been the focus of major archaeological projects. Regional archaeological surveys (Arnauld and Faugère-Kalfon 1998; Fisher et al. 2003; Healan 1997; Michelet 1995; Migeon 1998; Pollard 2000, 2008; Valdez and Liot 1994) in the Zacapu, Pátzcuaro, Cuitzeo, and Sayula Basins suggest that population density reached its highest level under the empire. Tribute records indicate that the Cuitzeo Basin was densely populated. Indeed, the largest concentration of tributaries recorded in the empire was located in north-central Michoacán from the Zacapu Basin east to the Cuitzeo Basin (Beltrán 1982). Moreover, the data also suggest that the largest and most populous settlements, whether ceremonial centers or cities, also date to the period of the empire during what is known to archaeologists as the late Postclassic (Pollard 2003a).

Purépecha Cultural Tradition, State Emergence, and Colonial Transformation in the Lake Pátzcuaro Basin

Containing the imperial capital at Tzintzuntzan and major state religious complexes at Pátzcuaro and Ihuatzio, the Pátzcuaro Basin was the geopolitical core of the empire during the late Postclassic. Estimates of demographic and settlement trends within the Purépecha heartland of the Tarascan core are based on regional archaeological surveys in the Zacapu and Pátzcuaro Basins and through documents pertaining to the Pátzcuaro Basin, especially the capital, Tzintzuntzan. Taken together, the archaeological, ethnohistorical, and historical evidence confirms the presence of a distinguishable Purépecha cultural tradition in the Pátzcuaro Basin by the late Preclassic period and the emergence of a politically centralized and socially stratified state in the same basin during the middle Postclassic period. Moreover, as the political and economic core of the Prehispanic state, the Pátzcuaro Basin was the earliest region affected by the new colonial order. Indeed, by 1524 Cortés had already taken Tzintzuntzan and its dependencies as his personal *encomienda*.

In 1990 a pilot project of excavations at the site of Urichu, located in the southwestern portion of the Pátzcuaro Basin, was designed to test a model of the emergence of the empire based on the ethnohistory of the unification of the

Table 5.1. Central Michoacán: Phases.

Period	Local phases
Late Postclassic	Tariacuri (A.D. 1350–1525)
Middle Postclassic	Late Urichu (A.D. 1000\1100–1350)
Early Postclassic	Early Urichu (A.D. 900–1000\1100)
Epiclassic	Lupe–La Joya (A.D. 600\700–900)
Middle Classic	Jarácuaro (A.D. 550–600\700)
Early Classic	Loma Alta 3 (A.D. 350–550)
Late\Terminal Preclassic	Loma Alta 1 and 2 (150 B.C.–A.D. 350)
Middle Preclassic	Chupícuaro (≥500–150 B.C.)

state recounted in the *Relación de Michoacán* (2000). In 1995–1996 the area of study was extended to include the two adjacent contemporary centers of Xaracuaro and Pareo. The goal of the project was to determine the demographic, economic, and political resources available to the local elites during the period of political and economic transformation associated with the emergence of the state. In the summer of 2001, the final phase of the study was expanded to the site of Erongarícuaro, where survey and excavation of elite centers in the southwestern part of the basin were conducted.

As a result of these studies, it is possible to define six occupation phases that extend from the late Preclassic to the late Postclassic (100 B.C.–A.D. 1525). Four of the six phases are defined stratigraphically from the excavations at Urichu and with chronologies based on fifteen radiocarbon dates from Urichu. The fifth phase is defined by the distinctive polychrome ceramics at several study sites and dated by associations outside of the basin. The excavations at Erongarícuaro added two additional radiocarbon dates and documented a sixth phase (Table 5.1).

Development of Purépecha Culture

Based on maize pollen from sediment cores dating to 1500 B.C., the Pátzcuaro Basin probably was first inhabited by sedentary or semisedentary agriculturalists during the early to middle Preclassic period. Settlements were focused on lake-related activities. Unfortunately, due to deforestation, terrace abandonment, and large-animal grazing since contact, the more recent prehistoric sites are now buried under up to 4 m of eroded soil. As a result, additional evidence of such early occupations will probably be revealed only as a side effect of modern construction activity around the lake. Evidence from the Bajío and Cuitzeo Basin and the following period suggests that it is likely that these populations were culturally part of the Chupícuaro tradition (Darras 2006; Darras and Faugère 2005; Darras et al. 1999; Porter Weaver 1969).

Loma Alta and Jarácuaro Phases

On the basis of research in the southwestern Pátzcuaro Basin, it is possible to document Loma Alta phase settlements at Jarácuaro, Urichu, and Erongarícuaro (Pollard 2000, 2005b, 2008). There is evidence of a Loma Alta occupation in Tzintzuntzan based on sherds of the Agropecuaria and Tres Palos types incorporated in late Postclassic deposits (Carot 2001:71). Of the deposits with radiocarbon dates, Loma Alta 2 settlement is documented at Erongarícuaro and in irrigation canals found in the deposits between Charahuén and Nocutzepo (Fisher et al. 1999). The analysis of stable isotopes (of carbon and nitrogen) in three human bone samples from Loma Alta 2 burials at Erongarícuaro indicates that diets were based on maize and are similar to those of individuals from the later phases in the Pátzcuaro Basin (Laura Cahue, personal communication 2002). Loma Alta 3 settlement is documented at Urichu, at Erongarícuaro, in the lacustrine zone of Xaracuaro, and in repeated use of the irrigation canal documented between Charahuén and Nocutzepo.

Within the borders of the Purépecha cultural tradition, two extensive zones of obsidian were located, one in the Zinapécuaro-Ucareo zone in northeastern Michoacán and the other in the Zináparo zone in north-central Michoacán. Both were used by prehispanic populations from the Preclassic to colonial periods (Darras 1998, 1999; Healan 1997), and both sites are represented among artifacts analyzed from the Loma Alta phase at Erongarícuaro (Pollard 2005b). So far, Erongarícuaro is the only site of the Loma Alta phase with evidence of architectural remains and a size of over 20 ha. Additional excavation will make it possible to distinguish whether the settlement was a village or town with a ritual center.

Thus, we can document lacustrine and nonlacustrine settlements, canal irrigation, and intensified agricultural production. During the centuries between 100 B.C. and A.D. 600, the level of the lake fluctuated between approximately 2,033 and 2,035 m above sea level (Fisher et al. 2003). The evidence of the density and size of settlements in the southwestern area of the basin suggests a population for the entire basin of only 5,000–8,000 people (Pollard 2000). The absence of rounded and notched ceramic disks (associated with fishing) in the deposits at Erongarícuaro and its distance from the lake suggest that communities were already economically distinct, with some focused on a lacustrine adaptation (Phillips 2002; Pollard 2000). Long-distance exchange is documented in obsidian tools from northeastern Michoacán (Ucareo) and central Mexico (Pachuca) and in Thin-Orange pottery from central Mexico.

The eponymous type-site for the Loma Alta phase, located in the lacustrine zone of the Zacapu Basin northwest of Pátzcuaro, was excavated in 1983 by the Zacapu Project under the direction of Dominique Michelet, CEMCA (Arnauld et al. 1993; Michelet et al. 1989). Excavations were carried out during the 1980s and again in the mid-1990s by Patricia Carot, CEMCA (Carot 2001; Carot and Fauvet-Berthelot 1996; Carot et al. 1998; Carot and Ponce López 1997; Pereira 1996). Based on the first excavations, it was believed that the site was a mortuary settlement on a hill in the marshes used from 100 B.C. until A.D. 550. Two long trenches were excavated to reveal the existence of an architectural complex that included a sunken plaza with a central altar, walls of worked stone, and stairways (Carot et al. 1998). The architectural complex is similar to that found in the salvage excavations at Santa María (in the suburbs of Morelia, Michoacán) and many others known from the Lerma River Basin in Guanajuato (Fernández–V. Medina 2004; Filini 2004; Manzanilla López 1988; Pereira et al. 2007).

Other similarities between the Erongarícuaro site and the type-site at Loma Alta include the *bajareque* (wattle-and-daub) fragments, the type of construction of the worked-stone walls, and the range and type of artifacts found, including the associated figurines. Not yet confirmed at Erongarícuaro is the degree of links to the Teotihuacán culture of central Mexico found at Loma Alta in the form of Thin-Orange ceramics (only one sherd chemically confirmed at Erongarícuaro) and of cloisonné, although the presence of relatively high frequencies of Pachuca obsidian is evidence of long-distance trade with central Mexico.

The recent documentation of the Loma Alta phase in many parts of central and northern Michoacán has provided clear evidence of a period of transition between the earlier Chupícuaro society of the late Preclassic and the later societies of the Classic and Postclassic from which the Tarascan state emerged and Purépecha culture developed. Loma Alta has been found in the Pátzcuaro Basin, the Zacapu Basin (the Lomas, El Palacio, and Las Milpillas sites), and Morelia (Santa María) and at several sites in the Cuitzeo Basin (Queréndaro, Zinapécuaro) (Carot 2001), and it is closely related to the Mixtlán phase of the Bajío. At the type-site in the Zacapu Basin, the appearance of sunken plaza / platform architecture in the Loma Alta 2b phase (A.D. 250–350) is associated with construction materials of basalt and clay brought from almost 10 km away and a new burial tradition in which richness of interment is directly related to proximity to platform centrality (Pereira 1996). These burial deposits are currently the best evidence for the timing of the emergence of social ranking among the populations of central Michoacán. In all cases they document the existence of small-scale, socially ranked agrarian societies. Only expanded excavation at these sites will enable us to determine the characteristics of households and of the political economies that dominated the region.

Lupe—Early Urichu Phases

During the Epiclassic Lupe phase, at least seven settlements occupied the south-western portion of the Pátzcuaro Basin; four were lacustrine, and three were at some distance from the lake, including villages at Urichu and Erongarícuaro (Pollard 2000). Based on size and artifact density, I estimate the population to have been between 600 and 1,000 for the survey area and 6,000 and 7,000 for the basin (see table 5.2).

Lake levels continued to fluctuate during this phase but were never very low. A deeply buried irrigation canal associated with maize phytoliths attests to the use of wetland agriculture. Sherds and basalt artifacts associated with the irrigation canal are the only evidence of a Lupe Phase occupation near Charahuén and indicate that Epiclassic sites are underrepresented due to colonial era and more recent soil erosion.

In the adjacent Zacapu Basin, archaeological surveys have located ten or eleven sites with plazas and ball-courts dated to the late Lupe phase (Michelet 1992). The number of settlements increased during the Lupe phase, especially toward the Lerma River, in light of a major expansion of obsidian mining at the Zináparo complex (Darras 1999). Thus, the impact of changes in central Mexico can be seen in the Purépecha political economies.

Excavations at the sites of Urichu and Erongarícuaro reveal the presence of local elites during the Classic and Epiclassic periods (Pollard 1995; Pollard et al. 2001). In addition to the material remains from the Pátzcuaro Basin, there is evidence of Classic and Epiclassic period elite at Loma Santa María (Manzanilla López 1988), Tingambato (Lagunas Rodríguez 1987; Piña Chan and Oí 1982), Guadalupe in the Zacapu Basin (Arnauld et al. 1993; Michelet 1992; Michelet et al. 1989; Pereira 1999), and Tres Cerritos in the Lake Cuitzeo Basin (Macías Goytia 1989; Macías Goytia and Vackimes Serret 1988). While there are no published chronometric dates from Tingambato or Tres Cerritos, we can nonetheless use available data to place the evidence from the Pátzcuaro Basin within a regional context.

In the period from A.D. 500 to 700, elites resided in centers throughout central Michoacán. Their broadly shared heritage from the Chupícuaro and Loma Alta societies is reflected in the ceramic tradition and in many aspects of mortuary behavior, including, for example, the dominance of primary extended burials and the association of shell beads with the burials of children and, occasionally, adult females (Porter Weaver 1969). By the late Classic period the elite were buried in group tombs that were similar to each other in their methods of construction and their uses over multiple generations (Pollard and Cahue 1999). At all sites, only some families have formal tombs. They were buried with precious goods imported from other regions of Mesoamerica. Such grave goods, along with cranial deformation and dental mutilation, distinguished

Table 5.2. Late Postclassic Pátzcuaro Basin (Tariacuri Phase): Central Places.

	Size	Population	Administration	Ritual	Market	Craft production	Elite residence
Tzintzuntzan	901 ha[a]	30,000	Imperial and basin capital (1 and 2)	State	Regional	Basic, ritual, and elite	Royal dynasty\upper and lower nobility
Ihuatzio	125 ha[b]	4,000	(Treasury)	State		Ritual and elite	Upper and lower nobility
Pátzcuaro	100 ha[b]	<4,000	(Treasury)	State		?	Lower nobility
Erongarícuaro	228 ha	7,500[c]	Rank 3 center	Local (?)		Basic, ritual, and elite	Upper and lower nobility
Urichu	90 ha	4,000	Rank 4 center	Local		Basic, possibly elite	Lower nobility

[a]GIS mapping by C. Stawski has a new estimate for the capital, replacing the earlier figure of 674.
[b]Estimated.
[c]Caravajal's list of 1524 indicates a similar population to Urichu (Warren 1985), but others do not (see text).

elite families from the rest of the population. Local elite status was partially derived from their participation in the macroregional exchange system by which such goods were obtained. Many of the goods are Toltec in design (flutes, censers, projectile points), and the burials of these elites, including children, not only reveal their role as intermediaries with distant powers but also self-define the males as warriors, with projectile points, atlatls, maces, and the costumes of warriors (Pereira 1999).

Despite their common cultural tradition, the elites varied in the size and architectural complexity of the centers they controlled and the degree of internal social ranking. There is variation observed in the size of tombs, characteristics of individuals buried, and number of grave goods per person. Urichu appears to have had primarily males buried in the single excavated tomb, but females, children, and infants were buried under floors and within *laja* "boxes" (small stone cists). Unlike the Guadalupe tombs from the Zacapu Basin only 20 km away, which included no polychrome vessels, most vessels from Urichu had both polychrome and resist (negative) decoration (Pollard and Cahue 1999).

From A.D. 700 to 900 the burial tradition continued at Urichu, presumably representing direct descendants of the earlier elite. However, the number of grave goods per individual rose dramatically. Indeed, the sex of the individual with the greatest number of associated goods in the tomb is currently undetermined, but he or she is buried with projectile points and whole prismatic blades, items that in the late Postclassic were associated with males and with the hunter-warrior deity Curicaueri (Pollard 1993:137, 179). At Urichu the capacity of local elites to obtain and bury foreign trade goods seems to have increased, as did their ability to use local producers of polychrome and resist ceramics.

During the early Urichu phase (A.D. 900–1100) in the southwestern portion of the Pátzcuaro Basin, the number of sites increased, and the number of hectares occupied almost doubled. The lake level began to drop during this phase, and lacustrine settlements moved to the new lake margins, as revealed by new settlements below 2,031 m above sea level. By the end of this phase at least one settlement was at 2,028 m above sea level (based on my personal observation in May 2004), probably indicating the lowest lake levels in the last two millennia. Soil erosion was low to moderate around these newer settlements (Fisher et al. 2003). There is evidence of continued canal irrigation near Charahuén, deeply buried under colonial era eroded soil. Within the survey zone, ten sites were located, including the first small settlements on islands and in marsh zones that later were underwater, and the first evidence of settlement in the southwestern upland zone near modern Ajuno. A new area at Urichu was occupied with terraces, mounds, and retaining walls similar to those recorded from the Zacapu Basin. Using site size and artifact density, I estimate the population to have been 1,000–2,000 for the survey area and about 12,000 for the basin (see table 5.2).

Because this phase has not been isolated in other archaeological projects, except near the obsidian source of Ucareo (Healan 1997), making comparisons is difficult. However, at Urichu and the other early Postclassic settlements in the Pátzcuaro Basin, gray-black obsidian was still primarily from the Zináparo complex, while the Ucareo obsidian continued to flow eastward, probably through networks dominated by merchants from the Toltec state (Mastache et al. 2002). Ceramic production and distribution remained highly localized (Pollard et al. 2001).

This phase marked the last use of the tomb in area 5 at Urichu and the end of multiple-use tombs in Michoacán. The last three burials in the tomb at Urichu are the richest, with objects imported from central Mexico, some of which may be ritual paraphernalia from Tula or in Toltec style (flutes, a censer). This suggests that markers of status remained similar during the period.

Late Urichu Phase

This phase includes the two centuries during which the Tarascan state formed and to which the legendary accounts of state emergence and ethnic affiliation pertain. Archaeological evidence comes from excavations at Urichu and surface surveys in the southwestern portion of the Pátzcuaro Basin. There is some comparative data from the Zacapu and Cuitzeo Basins, although the phase has not been chronometrically isolated in these regions.

In the middle Postclassic period, the number of sites in the Pátzcuaro Basin increased, and the area of occupation again doubled. A large proportion of the new sites was located on recently exposed islands and on fertile lacustrine soil exposed by an episode of lake regression (Fisher et al. 2003). The lake level was at its lowest since first human occupation of the basin. Soil erosion was local and focused around newer settlements. Within the survey area, 105 collection units were located, 32 of which were hamlets and towns, with the remainder being household clusters located adjacent to the lakeshore or in marshes. Settlement expanded onto islands as the lake level dropped but also markedly expanded in upland zones and on to the *malpaís* (badlands) in defensible locations. A current survey by Christopher Fisher and myself in the southeastern portion of the basin (2009–10) is documenting major settlement expansion on the malpaís separating the Pátzcuaro and Cuitzeo Basins. Using site size and artifact density, I have estimated the population at 4,000–7,800 for the survey area, with up to 48,000 people for the basin. This represented a major population growth in both the basin and surrounding central and northern Michoacán. Nevertheless, basic resources such as obsidian, basalt, and pottery were being produced, distributed, and consumed in patterns unchanged since the Classic period.

In the last decades of this phase, the lake level rose again, reaching its contact period level of 2,041 m above sea level. This resulted in the abandonment of low-lying communities and agricultural land and the relocation of marsh production zones. Given the size of the population existing in the basin and the existence of sociopolitical elites in the larger communities, competition over expanding, diminishing, and shifting resources must have become fierce.

Moreover, environmental data suggest that similar patterns would have been occurring throughout central and northern Michoacán. In the Zacapu Basin, the Postclassic was marked by an increase from 61 sites to 96 (Arnauld and Faugère-Kalfon 1998:16) and a shift from primarily lakeshore occupation to a marked increase in the number of sites located in the badlands above Zacapu and the uplands toward the Lerma River. In the early Postclassic, the site of El Palacio was the first occupied and appears to have been the largest, at least in terms of having the most public architecture. In general, settlement appears to maximize access to agricultural land, defensive position, and continued development of the nearby obsidian mines of Zináparo. Sunken patios disappear from public architecture and are replaced by square rooms with columns and covered porticos reminiscent of La Quemada. The late Postclassic phase includes 83 sites; the drop in numbers comes from the reduction of sites immediately adjacent to the Zináparo obsidian mines. There is an increase in sites along the southern lakeshore associated with the intensification of agriculture. On the badlands the density of settlement increases to urban levels, and up to 20,000 people are estimated to have inhabited the 13 sites covering 5 km^2 (Migeon 1998). The sites themselves include multiple barrios, each with public centers dominated by *yácatas* (pyramids), with one plaza complex larger than all others. Michelet (1995) interprets this as reflecting relatively rapid movement of individual communities onto the malpaís, clustering together for defensive purposes, and shortly thereafter (A.D. 1250) each reorganizing under the control of a single authority.

Thus, the Purépecha cultural heartland came to be composed of several competing chiefly / small state societies. This was a transition period when settlements shifted and elite mortuary patterns changed. Both the archaeological and ethnohistorical records suggest that patterns of leadership and control were in flux. While the legendary histories record several episodes of migration of non-Purépecha populations into the region, so far these population movements are not visible in the archaeological record.

The Political Economy of State and Empire: The Tariacuri Phase

Tzintzuntzan was the largest of some 90+ Tarascan settlements around the Pátzcuaro Basin during the late Postclassic period. Of the basin's estimated total population of 80,000 in 1522 (Gorenstein and Pollard 1983), Tzintzuntzan had about 35,000 (Pollard 1977, 2003a). Its secondary and tertiary administrative centers, each with 5,000–15,000 people, included Erongarícuaro, Ihuatzio, Pátzcuaro, and Urichu (see Table 5.3) (Pollard 1980, 1995, 2003a).

During what archaeologists call the Tariacuri phase, low-lying sites were flooded, and settlements shifted to the new lakeshore and to areas of high agricultural fertility farther away from the lakeshore. The lake level was relatively high (more than 2,041 m above sea level), and earlier settlements were below water (O'Hara 1993). Soil erosion was minimal, even as settlements expanded to uplands due to widespread terracing and other soil management strategies (Fisher et al. 2003). The number of sites and area occupied in the southwestern survey area doubled to more than 90, including Erongarícuaro, Urichu, Pareo, the island of Xaracuaro, and densely occupied towns with public architecture at Tócuaro, Arocutín, Charahuén, Ajuno (Axuni), and many smaller villages, hamlets, and isolated homesteads (Pollard 2000). Using site size and artifact density, I estimate the population to have been 7,000–13,000 for the survey area and 80,000 for the basin, confirming previous estimates based on historical documents. A number of communities were functionally differentiated, and settlements varied considerably in their areas and populations. Tzintzuntzan was a regional primate center not only on the basis of its population size but also because of its control of the administrative, tributary, market, religious, and social hierarchies.

Table 5.3. Population of the Lake Pátzcuaro Basin.

Period	Local phase	Survey area	Basin
Early colonial 2	Valladolid (Morelia) (A.D. 1580–1650)	—	10,000
Early colonial 1	Pátzcuaro (A.D. 1540–1580)	—	20,000
Conquest	Tzintzuntzan (A.D. 1522–1540)	—	—
Late Postclassic	Tariacuri (A.D. 1350–1522)	10,000	80,000
Middle Postclassic	Late Urichu (A.D. 1100–1350)	6,000	48,000
Early Postclassic	Early Urichu (A.D. 900\1000–1100)	1,500	12,000
Epiclassic	Lupe–La Joya (A.D. 600–900\1000)	800	6,500
Classic	Loma Alta 3 / Jaracuaro (A.D. 350–600)	400–600	4,500
Early Classic	Loma Alta 2 (100 B.C.–A.D. 350)	—	—

Note: Prehispanic phases are defined by excavations at Urichu (Pollard 2000) and Erongarícuaro (Pollard 2003). Survey area population was determined by site area and ceramic artifact density using the methods developed for the Basin of Mexico (see Fisher et al. 2003). Basin estimates for the late Postclassic and early colonial periods are based on historical population figures and the archaeological surveys of Tzintzuntzan and Ihuatzio (see Gorenstein and Pollard 1983; Pollard 2003); for the earlier periods, basin estimates are extrapolated from the survey area estimates.

Figure 5.1. Sites in Guanajuato, Michoacán, Jalisco, Colima, and Nayarit.

Few areas of the Tarascan Empire have been systematically surveyed. As a result, the basin's settlement structure has been calculated by consulting documentary sources, especially early colonial maps (e.g., Gorenstein and Pollard 1983). Figures 5.1 and 5.2 illustrate the similarities and differences of the documentary and archaeological information on late Postclassic settlements. Not surprisingly, smaller and more dispersed settlements were reported more often in the archaeological surveys than in the historical documents. A similar pattern of underdocumentation of small settlements has been found in the adjacent Zacapu Basin (Migeon 1991).

The data from all surveyed regions in central and northern Michoacán suggest that population density reached its zenith during the late Postclassic period. Moreover, the largest and most populous settlements within any single

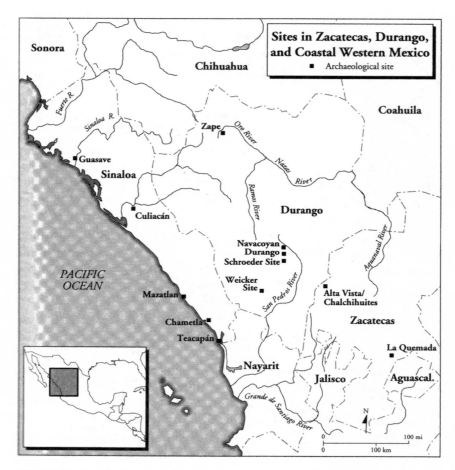

Figure 5.2. Sites in Zacatecas, Durango, and coastal western Mexico.

region, whether ceremonial centers or cities, also date to the late Postclassic. Not all of this population growth was due to macroregional population increases. There also is evidence for population movement from the Zacapu region into the Pátzcuaro Basin, as well as a north-to-south shift in population within the Zacapu region. These population movements suggest that the political and economic power of the state had a centripetal effect on settlement patterns, especially in the relocation of regional elites into the capital. The evidence from Huandacareo in the Cuitzeo Basin (Macías Goytia 1990) and Zirizicuaro, to the east of Uruapan (Pulido Méndez 2003)—both Tarascan administrative centers during the late Postclassic—suggests that the Tarascans constructed additional public spaces in those areas in order to carry out and display administrative functions, including the burial of local and imperial leaders.

Given the denser occupations, which occurred during a time of high lake levels when previously irrigable lands were flooded, new economic mechanisms were required to support local populations. By A.D. 1300, lake levels had begun to rise again, forcing lakeshore communities and fields to be abandoned (Fisher et al. 1999; Fisher et al. 2003; O'Hara 1993; O'Hara et al. 1993). By 1522 the core of the Tarascan state in the Lake Pátzcuaro Basin was not viable economically on purely local terms. It thrived only by the exchange of goods and services through local and regional markets and various state institutions (Pollard 1993). Both the type and the quantity of goods imported varied within the Pátzcuaro Basin by social class and community. While the documentary record indicates the existence of markets, the tributary relationships of many communities, and the nature of goods acquired by state long-distance merchants, detailed sourcing analyses of archaeological collections are clarifying the complex nature of the production, distribution, and consumption patterns of obsidian, pottery, shell, and metal objects (for greater detail see Pollard 2003b; Pollard et al. 2001).

Analysis of obsidian artifacts, for example, suggests that the pattern of procurement observed at Tzintzuntzan, the Tarascan capital, where more than 90 percent of the obsidian came from the Zinapécuaro-Ucareo mines, was not characteristic of the Lake Pátzcuaro Basin as a whole, even during the late Postclassic period. Ucareo obsidian, dominant at the capital, is a prominent feature at only two of the other three elite centers sampled (the ritual and elite residential zones of Erongarícuaro and Urichu). This suggests that the differential distribution of Ucareo obsidian at the capital and its significance at Urichu and Erongarícuaro, associated in all cases with prismatic blade technology, may be due less to market exchange than to direct intervention by the state. Thus, we now have evidence to suspect that the Tarascan central dynasty directly controlled either the Ucareo obsidian mines or the distribution of prismatic blades from those mines.

In all phases, small quantities of obsidian from sources outside of Michoacán have been found in Tarascan sites. All of the yellow-green obsidian was from Pachuca, primarily in the form of prismatic blades, with a dark green obsidian from Pénjamo. All, however, were from the highlands of central and western Mexico and probably were obtained through long-distance merchants. Thus, the emergence of state-sponsored, long-distance merchants may have led to a larger number of sources being represented, but the greater variety was distributed primarily in the capital.

Metal objects of gold, silver, copper, and bronze alloys were produced within the territory of the empire and used for ritual, status, and utilitarian purposes (Hosler 1994; Pollard 1993; Warren 1968). The documentary record indicates that some of the mining, smelting, and production of objects was carried out by full-time craft specialists and tenants under the direct control of the state ("Minas de cobre" [1533], in Warren 1968). The production of ingots of smelted ore took place at smelting centers in the Balsas River drainage, and some portion of the crafting of objects took place in the Tarascan capital, possibly within the king's palace (Pollard 1993). Other metals or smelted ingots were obtained through the state tribute system, particularly for gold and silver. Metal moving through the tribute system is recorded for the frontier zones of the southeast and the west, but there is no direct evidence of independent production of metal goods sold in local or regional markets. Within the Tarascan territory, metal objects are associated with ritual and elite deposits, although utilitarian objects like needles and axes are more widely distributed. Although postconquest looting of metal objects has severely limited (and biased) our samples from the core of the Tarascan Empire, sourcing evidence from metal artifacts excavated from late Postclassic sites of Atoyac (in the Sayula Basin) and Urichu (in the Pátzcuaro Basin) suggests that metal artifacts found in Michoacán were produced from ores mined in the Balsas Basin and adjacent Jalisco (Hosler and Macfarlane 1996). At both sites the metal objects were associated with elite administrators' residences, probably reflecting redistribution of state goods.

Most of the objects found both within and outside the Tarascan sphere have been dated to the late Postclassic, that is, to the period after Tarascan imperial expansion. Copper artifacts are known from early Postclassic occupations only in the Balsas (Infiernillo and La Villita) and Chapala Basins (Tizapán el Alto and Cojumatlán) (Hosler 1994; Pulido Méndez 2003), probably reflecting routes of communication of this technology from the Pacific coast. Thus, it is not possible to discuss changes in the production and distribution of metals during the Postclassic, at least based on the evidence from within Michoacán. Clearly, the Tarascan Empire emerged in a region that was already part of the western Mexican metallurgical tradition. Nevertheless, it appears that the emergence of a centralized state in the Pátzcuaro Basin and its subsequent expansion beyond the lake region were associated with a marked increase in the scale of production and, possibly, a restricting of the control over the technology, raw materials, and products to core elites, especially the royal dynasty.

The royal dynasty officially allocated all access to land, water, forests, and mineral resources (Pollard 1993). In practice, access to land was distributed within communities by traditional kin ties, and land was acquired by kings for support of state administrators (*angámecha*) and state temples. In addition, there were state copper mines, obsidian mines, forests, fisheries, and craft workshops. For the Pátzcuaro Basin, there were no obsidian or copper mines, but the documentary record is unclear about the status of fishing and forestry rights, that is, the degree to which they were seen as resources traditionally held by specific communities or resources to which communities were allowed access by the king. Sixteenth-century documents suggest the latter, but, if so, this was a change in the ideology of resource ownership that would only have emerged with the unification of the state in the middle Postclassic period.

According to the *Relación de Michoacán*, the division between nobility and commoner was virtually absolute, as lineages did not cross class boundaries, and marriages were within one's class. Among the nobility, a distinction was made among the royal dynasty, the upper nobility, and the lower nobility; commoners varied by ethnicity (although overwhelmingly Purépecha), occupation, and whether they were slaves. Within the Pátzcuaro Basin, members of the royal dynasty were located in the capital (Tzintzuntzan) and at the sacred religious center of Ihuatzio; members of the upper and lower nobility were found in 11 settlements, including Erongarícuaro, Urichu, Pareo, and Xaracuaro (Gorenstein and Pollard 1983). Archaeological surveys and excavations at Tzintzuntzan and Ihuatzio and in the southwestern portion of the basin have confirmed this pattern and defined the material correlates of elite status in residential and mortuary contexts. During the late Postclassic, elites and commoners located in secondary and tertiary centers of the basin like Urichu—a tertiary center that paid tribute to Erongarícuaro, which in turn collected tribute from some 20 settlements for forwarding to Tzintzuntzan—consumed the same goods as did the residents in the capital. The people of Urichu also shared Tarascan elite/commoner identity and participated in a single social system (Gorenstein and Pollard 1983).

The creation of the Tarascan state was accompanied by the establishment of a new ideology that made the Pátzcuaro Basin the center of cosmic power. The roots of this ideology came from the different cultural traditions that characterized Postclassic Michoacán populations. The patron gods of the now-dominant ethnic elite were elevated to celestial power, while the various regional deities and worldviews—themselves products of generations of change—were elevated, incorporated, or marginalized. The clearest evidence of this process involves the joining of the ethnic Chichimec or Uacúsecha deity Curicaueri with the ethnic "islander" or Purépecha goddess Xarátanga. In the prophetic language of a great epic, "Curicaueri will conquer this land, and you for your part will stand with one foot on the land and one on the water . . . and we shall become one people" (RM 2000:40). Their joint worship at Ihuatzio and Tzintzuntzan was a direct product of this unification, reinventing them as husband (sun) and wife (moon).

In the ritual of *Equata consquaro*, before the recounting of the official Tarascan history in Tzintzuntzan, the chief priest would turn to the east and invoke the goddess Cuerauáperi, turn to the west and invoke the goddess Xarátanga, turn to the north and invoke the solar god of Zacapu (Querenda-Angapeti), turn to the south and invoke the gods of the hot lands, and finally look up to the sky and invoke the spirit of Curicaueri, the great sun (Pollard 1993:135). This union of deities previously associated with distinct ethnic/political groups can also be seen in the ritual centers constructed in the Tarascan core. A specialized pyramid form, the yácata, consisting of a keyhole shape, was constructed at major religious centers associated with the Tarascan sun god, Curicaueri. The greatest number (five) were located in Tzintzuntzan, but at Ihuatzio there were not only three yácatas but also two rectangular pyramids associated with Xarátanga adjacent to a ball-court. According to the legendary history, the Ihuatzio pyramids were built on the orders of the goddess Xarátanga, and it was here that the gods were to be fed at midday. Stone Chacmool sculptures were placed in front of the yácatas at Tzintzuntzan and Ihuatzio, scenes of major ceremonies celebrating the state and cosmic order.

The centrality of the Pátzcuaro Basin in state rituals and the union of the two major deities, not to mention the value of metallurgy to the royal dynasty, were reflected in the location of the official state treasuries. The chests of gold (Curicaueri, the sun deity) and silver (Xarátanga, the moon deity) were located in the king's palace at Tzintzuntzan and on the islands of the lake, including Apupato, Janitzio (Xanecho), Pacandan, the Urandeni, and Utuyo (RM 2000:323–324).

Finally, the centrality of the Pátzcuaro Basin was reflected in characteristic attitudes of urban elites to the largely nonurban population. Ethnohistorical documents refer to native speech as either "lengua de Cintzuntza" (language of Tzintzuntzan) (Lagunas 1983 [1574]:146) or Purépecha (language of the people/commoners); the dominant language of the Tarascan state generally was referred to as Tarascan. While dialect divergence within Tarascan is often believed to be relatively recent, Lagunas made it clear in 1574 that he was basing his dictionary and grammar on Tarascan as spoken in the Pátzcuaro Basin. This version he viewed as the "courtly, cultured and universal language of Michoacán, to be preferred to the incongruous, barbarous and badly pronounced language that they use in some towns, inasmuch as the language of Michoacán is all one" (Lagunas 1983 [1574]:343).

Ethnicity and the State

Based upon mortuary evidence from the site of Urichu, it has been proposed that changes in the burial practices of local elites show a transformation of these elites from highly ranked local chiefs into a socially stratified elite class associated with the emergence of the Tarascan state (Pollard and Cahue 1999). Two distinctive mortuary patterns that represent the Classic-Epiclassic and late Postclassic periods are documented. These patterns vary in the age and sex composition of differing mortuary facilities, the preparation and treatment of the bodies, the mortuary facilities, the types of burial goods, and the location of the burials within settlements. This transformation involved a shift in elite identity from one primarily associated with imported finished goods from distant powerful centers and control of prestige goods networks to an identity primarily associated with locally produced, distinctively Tarascan goods and control of tributary, military, political, and ideological networks (for specific evidence, see Pollard and Cahue 1999).

For instance, late Postclassic elite identity as expressed at Urichu is specifically associated with finely decorated pottery, metal ornaments, and tools that were both locally produced and imported from other basin centers in distinctive Tarascan shapes and designs. Elite burials and ritual platform assemblages from Urichu are indistinguishable from those excavated at Tzintzuntzan and, like those at Ihuatzio, include both rectangular pyramids and a yácata (Pollard 1995)—in spite of the distinctly different ethnic identity ascribed (in the legendary history) to their elites before unification of the state. Thus, within the Tarascan core, the emergence of a new political economy was also associated with a new state religion and a new regional elite identity. Inequalities in wealth, status, and power, as revealed by the material record, were at their greatest for the prehispanic era.

For the Purépecha (commoners) of central and northern Michoacán, this new society was a major transformation on the macrolevel but also permitted continuities on the household and village scales. The social continuity represented by the long cultural tradition from the Preclassic to the Postclassic is visible in ceramic technology, ceramic designs, use of negative (resist) on polychrome pottery, types of figurines, mortuary patterns, basic technology, diet, and household organization of labor. The specific types of artifacts, such as the use of molcajetes with punctate instead of incised lines in the interior bases and the absence of mold-made figurines throughout the sequence, emphasize the degree of continuity at the level of the household, despite major changes in the political economies that took place during those 2,000 years. In addition, there is evidence of specific continuities in ideology that existed among adjacent phases. For example, the recent excavations at Chupícuaro sites reveal burials within round platforms similar to those found at the site of Loma Alta (Carot et al. 1998; Darras et al. 1999). I suggest that this continuity in the material culture and ideology was matched by a continuity in language and that Purépecha was spoken throughout these two millennia in central and northern Michoacán.

As the political and economic core of the prehispanic state, the Pátzcuaro Basin was the earliest region affected by the new colonial order. In 1524 Cortés took Tzintzuntzan and all its dependencies (i.e., the entire Pátzcuaro Basin) as his personal encomienda. Tribute was assessed at 600 cargas of maize, 45 cargas of beans, 25 cargas of chile, and 20 cargas of fish to be delivered to the mines every thirty days (Warren 1985:281). Since other regions of central Michoacán had been supporting the Tarascan nobility through the imperial tribute system, and these regions were now given as encomiendas to other Spaniards, this immediately placed the Tarascan king and the upper nobility resident in Tzintzuntzan in conflict with the new colonial power.

Despite significant changes in the power, status, and material culture of the native elite, for the Purépecha the first century of European colonization was characterized by epidemics and famines that decimated the population (see Table 5.2); the *congregaciones* of 1593–1605, which nucleated populations in settlements along the lakeshore; the loss of hereditary governing rights by native leaders in Pátzcuaro in 1595; and the emergence of large landowners descended from the native royal dynasty and upper nobility. These native landowners, sometimes related by kinship to Spaniards born in New Spain whose ancestors had married into the Tarascan royal dynasty (e.g., the heirs of Beatriz de Castilleja), invested in the new economy and formed alliances with powerful Spaniards (Kuthy 1996). As a tributary empire, the Spanish Empire was to a great extent structurally similar to the now-defeated Tarascan Empire. In this sense, the next great transformation to affect the Purépecha would not come until the eighteenth century—and in many ways it is a transformation still in progress.

III

Native Organization and Colonial State Formation

6

Visions of the Past

The Tarascan Kingdom and the Late Colonial Primordial Titles from Michoacán

Hans Roskamp

Introduction: The Genre of "Primordial Titles"

One of the most challenging categories of native history involves what are known as "primordial titles," that is, the seventeenth- and eighteenth-century documents that describe the origins of indigenous towns and their territories. Although the best-known examples have come from the central valleys of Mexico, they also have been found in western and southern parts of the region. All such documents share recognizable characteristics but at the same time show variations in form and content, even among the texts from a specific area. Generally made by local scribes or regional specialists, each title represented a distinctive composition based on similar documents from neighboring settlements, royal grants and dispositions, and, above all, oral traditions. Many titles give the impression that they were produced in the sixteenth century or even in the prehispanic period and that they received the approval of the Spanish authorities and/or indigenous kings, even though they lack official signatures or seals. Frequently their contents are not structured chronologically; that is, historical events and persons from different time periods are confused or presented as contemporaneous.

The main purpose of this indigenous genre was the protection of communal territory against invasions from neighboring settlements and agricultural enterprises. The majority of the documents were made after A.D. 1650, a period in which general population growth and the expansion of Spanish properties increased the demand for agricultural land (Gruzinski 1993:121; Lockhart 1992:411; Wood 1991:186, 1998b:201).[1] They were produced primarily for a local indigenous audience and not for external use, even though they usually ended up being invoked in court cases. Titles portrayed the increasing strength of the communities and their growing concern about invasions from outside and urged present and future generations to safeguard corporate rights and possessions (Wood 1991:177, 179, 1998a:169, 1998b:210, 220, 227; cf. Haskett 1996:101). The preservation of titles in their communities was clearly a by-product of their use in legal disputes and other procedures (Lockhart 1992:411; cf. López Caballero 2003:27). Intended to serve as timeless protective instruments, ready to be used in case the community's interests were threatened, titles had to be securely guarded in the local archives. Furthermore, their contents had to be communicated periodically to the town's inhabitants, for whom the titles became the official, unquestioned, and almost sacred foundational history of the community and its landholdings.

The primordial titles were used whenever the territorial integrity of the community was threatened by its indigenous, mestizo, or Spanish neighbors. Although the exact moments in which this occurred varied according to local or regional circumstances (especially the frequency and intensity of land problems), it is possible to identify several crucial periods. As previously noted, the documents were generally made in the late seventeenth into the eighteenth century, when the communities suffered continuing invasions of their lands. During that period many indigenous authorities responded to a governmental program that required the presentation of their documentation as well as a payment to the Spanish Crown, thus allowing them to obtain regulation and reconfirmation of their territory (the so-called *título de composición*) (Pérez Escutia 1990). Another crucial period came during the second half of the nineteenth century, when the Liberal government tried to modernize rural areas, with the result that communal holdings were converted into private properties that in many cases were sold to outsiders. A third moment in which primordial titles were presented as documentary evidence to safeguard the community's interests was the restitution of the communal lands after the Mexican Revolution, which, in many cases, generated severe conflicts that even today remain unresolved. The neoliberal agrarian reform of 1992 constitutes the latest attack on the territorial integrity of indigenous communities and once again permits the sale of their lands. These changes have not been accepted by indigenous groups, who continue in their long-term struggles to prevent the loss of their communal lands and territorial identity (Decreto de la Nación Purhépecha 1995).

Because of their claim to be official documents from the sixteenth century or even from the prehispanic period, their unusual manner of presenting information, and their inclusion of incorrect or contradictory data, many primordial titles were (and still are) rejected as forgeries by the authorities and neighboring communities (Lockhart 1992:411).[2] Others, however, have been accepted as authentic, even when their problematic character has been identified (García Castro and Arzate Becerril 2003). This production and presentation of manipulated evidence in court should not be regarded as an exclusively indigenous practice; on the contrary, it has to be placed in the broader context of the general human desire to legitimize territorial, political, and economic claims, even when this means resorting to illegitimate methods. In the eighteenth century, for example, when the Spanish city council of Guayangareo-Valladolid in Michoacán (the present-day state capital of Morelia) was involved in a conflict about its privileges and rights, a series of supposedly sixteenth- and seventeenth-century royal grants were produced that are completely contradicted by contemporary official sources (Herrejón Peredo 2000:290).

Regarding the purposes of primordial titles, James Lockhart (1992:413–414; cf. Wood 1991:178) argues that they were intended to provide an authentic internal view of local history and rights; deliberate falsification would have occurred only in situations of extreme pressure and perhaps due to the loss of local historical traditions. Serge Gruzinski suggests that what seems an obvious forgery according to the criteria of colonial law and modern historiography was perhaps a result of confusion or could even "express a different apprehension of the past, a singular grasp of the event and of history" (1993:99, 125). According to Joanne Rappaport (1990:10), the non-Western historical consciousness generally does not separate earlier events from contemporary concerns and, rather than describing what really happened, instead focuses on what should have occurred. If we accept that the titles served primarily to defend or even expand the indigenous community's interests, it is not surprising that historical information was selected, arranged, structured, or even invented to produce an effective instrument for the legitimation of territorial and other claims. The final result depended on the creative abilities of the authors, the availability of written and oral information, and the specific needs and economic capacity of the communities. Variations in these factors explain the sometimes significant differences in contents, length, presentation, and historicity among titles from neighboring settlements. For example, whereas some were limited to the use of only local skills and data, others had access to regional specialists and paid them to elaborate their titles, as in the case of the Toluca area and the northwestern part of Michoacán (Carrillo Cázares 1991; García Castro and Becerril 2003; Haskett 1996:104; Wood 1986, 1987).

Although their legal value was, and still is, questioned, primordial titles have become important sources for the study of how indigenous town governments tried to defend or even expand their interests by elaborating and presenting hybrid documents containing specific visions of a community's past as well as its supposed rights and privileges. Titles also provide evidence of how their authors perceived and constructed the corporate or communal identity (Florescano 2002:196; Lockhart 1992:416, 418; Wood 1998b). Comparison of their contents with colonial chronicles and legal documents can help to separate verifiable and accurate data on certain events from those that are imprecise, mistaken, or invented. Many titles contain information that describes past events that actually happened and correspond with what we would now call historical reality (Menegus Bornemann 1999; Wood 1998b:216). The same comparison of colonial documents can also lead to the identification of sources used by the authors of the titles, which in some cases provide our only (though indirect) access to older manuscripts now lost.

The primordial titles were new creations and reinterpretations that responded to very specific needs in the seventeenth and eighteenth centuries; nevertheless, they form part of a flexible and dynamic indigenous historical tradition that originated before the arrival of the Spaniards and was first registered in pictorial writings (Florescano 2002:221; Oudijk and Romero Frizzi 2003). In this chapter, I examine the case of Michoacán, where only a few seventeenth- and eighteenth-century primordial titles relate the foundation and identity of their towns to the official history of the prehispanic Tarascan kingdom (*irechaqua*) that was ruled by the Uacúsecha, or eagle, lineage.

The Foundational History of the Tarascan Kingdom and Its Capital, Tzintzuntzan

Between 1539 and 1541 the Franciscan Jerónimo de Alcalá wrote a chronicle about prehispanic Tarascan society based on his own observations and information provided to him by members of the ruling Uacúsecha (eagle) lineage. This valuable ethnohistorical source, known today as the *Relación de Michoacán* (RM 2000), also includes a version of the official history that the *petamuti* (high priest) presented to local and regional elites at the annual celebration known as *Equata consquaro* in Tzintzuntzan.

According to the petamuti's discourse, the founding father of the lineage was Hireti or Uacús Thicatame, who initiated the cult of the lineage's patron deity, Curicaueri, and at a distant but unspecified time established himself on a mountain near the town of Zacapu. After the next generations of the lineage dwelled in Guayameo, an omen caused the group to split up and settle in different places. Uapeani II and Pauacume II moved to the south side of Lake Pátzcuaro and established matrimonial and political relations with the people of the islands, causing great discontent among the lords of Curinguaro, who subsequently assassinated the two rulers. Tariácuri succeeded his father, Pauacume, and was said to be destined by the divine forces to subject all his enemies and other lords in the region to the realm of the Uacúsecha and Curicaueris. Together with his allies from Jarácuaro and other settlements, he initiated a major series of raids and conquests that, after his death, was continued by his son Hiquingaje as well as by his nephews Tangaxoan I and Hiripan, respectively lords of Pátzcuaro, Tzintzuntzan, and Ihuatzio. This triple alliance, founded by Tariácuri, continued these expansionist policies and installed its own obedient rulers in the recently annexed territories, replacing many of the old local elites, including their mortal enemies from Curinguaro. Although Hiripan managed to increase the power and importance of Ihuatzio, it was Pauacume's son, Tzitzispandaquare, who turned Tzintzuntzan into the sole capital of the Tarascan kingdom, a position consolidated by his successors Zuangua and Tzintzicha Tangaxoan (RM 2000).

Table 6.1. List of the Uacúsecha Rulers (According to the *Relación de Michoacán*).

Hireti Thicatame	
Sicuirancha	Son of Hireti Thicatame
Pauacume	Son of Sicuirancha
Uapeani	Son of Pauacume
Curatame	Son of Uapeani
Uapeani II and Pauacume II	Sons of Curatame
Tariácuri	Son of Pauacume
Hiquingaje	Son of Tariacuri
Tangaxoan I	Son of Aramen
Hiripan	Son of Zhétaco (son of Uapeani II)
Tzitzispandaquare	Son of Tangaxoan I
Zuangua	Son of Tzitzispandaquare
Tzintzicha Tangaxoan	Son of Zuangua
Francisco Tariacuri and Antonio Huitzimengari	Sons of Tzintzicha Tangaxoan

In this retelling of the foundational history, the high priest emphasized that the Uacúsecha king (called *irecha* or *cazonci*) was the representative on earth of Curicaueri, the god who had ordered the expansion of the Tarascan kingdom through the conquest of neighboring groups and settlements. This vision of the past explained and legitimized the existing order, urging both elites and subjects not only to remember their origins but also to obey and serve the supreme leader and the gods to whom they owed their own rights and privileges. This annual narration by the petamuti in Tzintzuntzan and its presentation by minor priests in other settlements assured that the story was known, preserved, and respected in every corner of the Tarascan kingdom.

Considering that the petamuti's discourse contained the official history of the Uacúsecha lineage, recounted the origin and expansion of the Tarascan kingdom, and described the foundation and power of its capital, Tzintzuntzan, it is not surprising that elements from such a story were used to claim and defend a privileged position in the colonial period after 1522. The last native king, Tzintzicha Tangaxoan, was named governor of the province of Michoacán, being succeeded first by his adoptive brother Pedro Cuiniharangari and later by his sons Tariácuri and Huitzimengari. Tzintzuntzan was named "city of Michoacán" and converted into the sole capital of the civil and religious authorities. However, in 1538 its status was reduced to that of being a subject town of its former barrio Pátzcuaro, which usurped all its authority and became the new governing center of the entire region. These political changes met with strong opposition (even among Spanish settlers) and were the starting point of a long struggle by the indigenous nobles to regain the recognition of Tzintzuntzan's— and therefore also their own—autonomy and supremacy.

The indigenous nobles made use of information and visions of the prehispanic past that were deeply rooted in the local oral tradition and recorded in contemporaneous documents. However, they added their pact with the Spanish authorities and the Christian god, who jointly ended the old order and started a new "enlightened" order in which the nobles also played a primary role. For example, in the so-called *Códice de Tzintzuntzan* and a related document in alphabetic writing (both probably made around 1567), the indigenous nobles stated that the last native king resided in Tzintzuntzan, where he peacefully received the conqueror Cristóbal de Olid (sent by Hernán Cortés) and friars of the Franciscan order, who founded their convent and the first church, thus starting the evangelization of the Tarascan noblemen and their subjects (Roskamp 1997). Another document, a coat of arms that combines native and European iconographical conventions, shows the Habsburg royal eagle protecting the Uacúsecha lineage and their capital, Tzintzuntzan, and guiding them on their ascending way to the only true Christian god and acceptance of the new faith. Alternatively, the coat of arms also might have expressed the position of the ruling elites as descendants and servants of the sun god, Curicaueri, and their role in expanding the power of Tzintzuntzan in his name. This heraldic document was first used in 1593, when the former capital finally managed to recover the title of *ciudad* (city) to become an independent jurisdiction again, though smaller, less powerful, and now separated from Pátzcuaro (Roskamp 2002).

A study by Felipe Castro Gutiérrez (2003) indicates that during the sixteenth to eighteenth centuries Tzintzuntzan's restored autonomy was periodically threatened by Pátzcuaro and Valladolid (Morelia), obliging the local indigenous authorities to protect their principal rights and privileges, at which they were more or less successful until the beginning of the nineteenth century. The alphabetic and pictorial manuscripts from the sixteenth century were carefully preserved in the local archives (and some periodically copied) to avoid their destruction or loss, while at the same time additional documents were also being made. When, in the second half of the eighteenth century, the Franciscan Pablo Beaumont consulted the collection, using the information in his *Crónica de Michoacán*, the coat of arms from 1593 probably had disappeared or at least been replaced by a second heraldic document that not only showed the last three prehispanic kings of Tzintzuntzan as European rulers with crowns and scepters but also stressed the role of Tzintzicha Tangaxoan in the evangelization process and the defense of the Christian faith. Apparently, the coat of arms was copied several times in order to use it as a kind of protective shield. Whereas Beaumont probably saw a now lost eighteenth-century copy, the municipal building in

Tzintzuntzan still preserves a version that was elaborated for the indigenous governor Lorenzo Rojas in 1802, indicating that the authorities must have been aware of the glorious past of their city and the need to conserve written and oral memories to assure the independence of the community in the present as well as into the future (Roskamp 1997, 2000).

The major part of the colonial documentation once found in the local archive of Tzintzuntzan has disappeared, and the population does not consider itself to be indigenous anymore. Nevertheless, many inhabitants still have at least a general notion of the remote past, which continually confronts them in the form of the prehispanic *yácatas* and the Franciscan convent, which have been the subject of archaeological and historical studies (including restoration projects) and attract a considerable number of national and foreign tourists. These factors and special circumstances, combined with information obtained through published monographs (see Castro-Leal 1986; Foster 1948; Rendón Guillén 1980, 1996), influence the perception and knowledge that individuals have of the local and regional past, which they express in oral and written form.[3]

A Different Vision of the Past: The Foundation of Xiuhquilan

The expansionist and propagandistic politics of the prehispanic Uacúsecha, including the replacement of conquered elites by members of their own lineage, matrimonial alliances, and the inclusion of local gods into their own pantheon and religious ideology, were very effective. Other early colonial sources from different places in the region, including, for example, the late sixteenth-century *Relaciones geográficas*, confirm domination by this lineage and Tzintzuntzan, paying little or no attention to other traditions and visions. These did not cease to exist, however, and in at least some instances they were preserved, expressing a strong local identity and a different (re)construction of the past. For example, in 1565 the colonial lords of the old Jicalán (or Xiuhquilan) used a *lienzo* (cotton cloth), on which they painted the origin of their settlement and their ancestral rights to minerals and mines. The document describes how they were created by the gods in a precious bowl of greenstone and started their long journey in search of the promised land, guided by their patron deity, Tezcatlipoca. Departing from the east coast of Mexico, they moved in a westerly direction and passed Mexico-Tenochtitlan on their way to Michoacán, where they founded Xiuhquilan and began to exploit the mineral resources in the region long before they became voluntary tributaries of the Tarascan kingdom. This is a story also shared, albeit with some variations, by the inhabitants of Tetlama. Whereas the Uacúsecha made clear that they considered themselves to be warriors and hunters (*chichimeca*) who spoke the Tarascan or Purépecha language, the Xiuhquilteca and Tetlamantlaca identified themselves as artisans and sedentary people (*nonoalca* and *tolteca*) who communicated in Náhuatl. Xiuhquilan and Tetlama used these descriptions of the past as evidence in late sixteenth-century conflicts with Tarascan communities, emphasizing that they were the first to settle in the region. However, they clearly recognized the expansion and supremacy of the Uacúsecha in the late Postclassic era and also at the beginning of the colonial period (Roskamp 1998:81–195, 2001).

The lienzo disappeared before 1638–1639 and, until the third quarter of the nineteenth century, remained in the neighboring community of Jucutacato. It was recovered there by Luisa Magaña, member of a cacique family from Jicalán who, around the year 1876, gave it as payment to her physician, Pablo García Abarca. Magaña may have used the lienzo as a title during the privatization and redistribution of communal lands authorized by the government of Michoacán on August 17, 1872 (Archive of the Registro Agrario Nacional [RAN], file San Francisco Jicalán—Municipio de Uruapan, box 1, folder Deslindes Comunales, fols. 18–19; Roskamp 1998:83–87). This would indicate that the Magaña family, at least, maintained some general idea about the existence, the contents, and the importance of the lienzo, especially regarding the antiquity and the territorial identity of the town. The ethnic and cultural distinctiveness of its original founders, as expressed in the pictorial document, was probably of lesser concern or perhaps even completely forgotten. There are strong indications that by the beginning of the seventeenth century, Tarascans not only resided in but also occupied major political positions in Jicalán, probably contributing to the rapid loss of the Náhuatl language and also to gradual changes in the community's self-perception (Roskamp 1998:168).

In 1882, years after the division of the community's territory, the lienzo was transferred to the collection of the Mexican Society for Geography and Statistics (SMGE) in Mexico City, where it is still kept today. The people of Jicalán seem to have lost track of the document and perhaps even of its contents and apparently were not able to use it as evidence in the postrevolutionary struggle for the restitution of all their original communal lands, initiated in 1927 (reinitiated in 1954) and finally granted by the Mexican president on November 12, 1980 (RAN, file San Francisco Jicalán—Municipio de Uruapan, box 1, folder Derechos agrarios, trabajo de depuración censal realizada por Ma. De Jesús Rodríguez, fol. 16). Only in recent years have a few residents started to rediscover it in the form of several published studies that will undoubtedly leave their traces in some local versions of the town's history and identity.[4] At present, the village is no longer considered indigenous; however, a small group of inhabitants still holds the rights to the communal territory and tries to defend its rights to the *rancho* of Jicalán el Viejo, the prehispanic and early colonial settlement of Jicalán also mentioned in the sixteenth-century lienzo. Although the lienzo does contain the oldest reference to possession of these specific lands, it is not likely that it will be presented as an argument in favor of Jicalán's claims. The authorities now have and use the presidential resolution from 1980, which includes a detailed written description and a map of the territorial boundaries (including the rancho of Jicalán el Viejo).

Primordial Titles and the Tarascan Foundations in Michoacán

The link between the local past and the ruling Uacúsecha lineage was remembered not only in the aforementioned sources from Tzintzuntzan and in sixteenth-century documents from subject towns but also in several late colonial primordial titles from other communities that once formed part of the Tarascan kingdom. Although they frequently contradict parts of the petamuti's discourse, on other occasions they show interesting similarities, as may be seen in the following selection of manuscripts from different regions in Michoacán.

An interesting document (in alphabetic writing) from the former island of Jarácuaro, in Lake Pátzcuaro, describes how eight Uacúsecha kings arrived in the north. Only two of them, Hareme (Harame) and Tsintsichan (Tzintzicha), also appear in the official genealogy of the Uacúsecha (see the *Relación de Michoacán*). After settling on a mountain in the vicinity of Zacapu they traveled southward to Jarácuaro, where the king, Tsipetaqua, built his palace and marked all the lands that belonged to the community, thus becoming its first ruler. Quitsique, probably his eldest son, expanded their dominions and took possession of nearby Uricho. His grandchild Sinderindi later settled in the same territory. This document was supposedly made in 1596 and signed by several people who appear to be local authorities and members of the council of elders (León 1904:410). Despite the many differences, the place of origin (a mountain near Zacapu) and the migration route of the ruling lineage clearly resemble the petamuti's story.

A second and more extensive title (also in alphabetic writing) from Jarácuaro includes a similar vision of the origin and migration of the Uacúsecha but attributes a major role to King Ziuangua, who reached the place after a migration that took him to Valladolid (present-day Morelia), Capula, Cútzaro, Tzintzuntzan, and the isle of Janitzio. Upon his arrival in Jarácuaro he stuck three arrows into three stakes that he had previously set on fire, thus founding and taking possession of the settlement. At the same time he also constructed a well and used additional arrows to mark the territorial borders. According to the document, his sons were called Tzintzicha, Tzitzispandaquare, and Tariácuri. All appear in the official genealogy of the Uacúsecha, although they were not contemporaneous rulers, and none was a direct descendant of any of the others. After a violent conflict with the neighbors from Pareo about the use of natural resources, Tzintzicha departed for neighboring Tócuaro, where he took possession of the land.[5] Afterward he told Tarimpoecha, an old lord of Curínguaro, to destroy the settlement of Pátzcuaro, an order that was carried out with the help of several allies. Through the victory Tzintzicha obtained the status of supreme ruler of the entire region. In this same period he and the other lords were notified about the imminent arrival of the Spanish conquerors and their leader, "the marquis" (Hernán Cortés). They all gathered in Tzintzuntzan in 1519 and decided to prepare ambushes to surprise and kill the invaders. However, the plan was not carried out, and instead the Europeans received a peaceful welcome (García Alcaraz 1970).

In addition to the migration and additional activities of the Uacúsecha lords in the region, there are other themes in this primordial title that remind us of the petamuti's discourse. A first example is the long-term conflict between the Uacúsecha from Pátzcuaro and their principal enemies from Jarácuaro and Curinguaro, who, according to the *Relación de Michoacán,* eventually succumbed to their adversaries. A related theme is the later liquidation of Pátzcuaro's rulers by their relatives from Ihuatzio during the period in which the two settlements and Tzintzuntzan formed a triple alliance. In the primordial title the two separate episodes addressed by the petamuti might have been merged into a single event, constituting a new vision of the past in which Jarácuaro obtained a victory over Pátzcuaro. It is also possible that this late colonial town document refers to events not mentioned in the official Uacúsecha history but perhaps registered in other documents and oral narratives. A third theme is the initial resistance to and later acceptance of the Spanish conquerors, also mentioned in the last part of the *Relación de Michoacán* and the *Códice de Tzintzuntzan* (Roskamp 1997). A last example is the use of arrows by prehispanic rulers to take possession of the land and to mark its boundaries and water wells, a theme that also appears in the primordial titles from Tócuaro, Nahuatzen, and Carapan (among others). The text and several illustrations of the *Relación de Michoacán* clearly indicate that bows and arrows were considered to be divine instruments that emphasized the identity of the Uacúsecha as experienced hunters and warriors (chichimecas). The arrow, in particular, constitutes a symbol of the power and force of the ruling lineage, comparable to the scepter carried by European kings.

The second primordial title from Jarácuaro, which does not include the date of its supposed manufacture, was copied in 1825, at which time a brief text was added that contains instructions about how it had to be preserved. Whenever the sands of time were about to cause its destruction, it had to be duplicated and adapted so that it could be understood by future generations, who were urged not to lose either the original manuscript or the copies. Every year, on the feast day of the patron, Saint Peter, the document had to be read in public and in the presence of the *viejos,* old male members of the community who generally formed a council and were considered to be local authorities. Afterward it had to be guarded safely again, only to be taken out and presented to the supreme government in case the territorial integrity of the community was threatened.

At present the documentation still forms part of the local archive of Jarácuaro (García Alcaraz 1970).

An example of an undated seventeenth- or eighteenth-century pictorial title from the Sierra Tarasca is the Lienzo de Nahuatzen, which provides a description of the prehispanic foundation of this town on the slopes of the mountain of San Marcos, as well as its later relocation in the valley at the time of the Spanish conquest (Roskamp 2004). The origin of Nahuatzen is attributed mainly to Huitzimengari and his father, the last Uacúsecha king, Tzintzicha Tangaxoan, in this title erroneously presented as contemporaneous rulers. They were assisted by local warriors and nobles from neighboring Sevina and Cheran, such as Quanibi, Vanotsi, Quahrame, Canari, and especially Cuincacahtsi, who, according to the document, was present during the majority of the ceremonies in which different parts of the lands of Nahuatzen were taken into possession. The descendants of the original founders are don Antonio and his wife, Magdalena, who became the first Christian rulers of the town and allies of the Spanish king, being succeeded by don Pedro and his spouse, Lucia.

Another primordial title from Nahuatzen (alphabetic writing), probably from the early twentieth century, tells a different story and only focuses on the second settlement, founded in the valley (Acosta 1998). It explains how in 1525 Nana Guari-Huapa, the daughter of the moon, settled in a place called El Tzirimu to sell food and beverages to travelers, establishing friendship with neighbors from Cheran and Sevina who eventually sold her two pieces of land located exactly on the dividing line between the two towns. In 1534 she decided to leave and donated her property to the inhabitants of Xharacatan, a move that caused heavy opposition from Cheran and Sevina, forcing the new owners to present the problem to the Uacúsecha king, Tzintzicha (Tangaxoan), at the capital in Tzintzuntzan. The king finally gave them their official titles and sent a group of priests and warriors to the Sierra in order to take possession of the lands and found the new community of Yahuatzen, a name that later became Nahuatzen.

In both primordial titles from Nahuatzen, the final foundation of the community and the marking of its landholdings are attributed to the kings from Tzintzuntzan, although the importance of the neighbors from Cheran and Sevina is also emphasized. According to the pictorial document, the latter were actively participating in the events as allies of the ruling lineage. The alphabetic document mentions their initial donation of the lands to Nana Guari-Huapa, although it stresses their later opposition to the foundation of Nahuatzen by the Uacúsecha king, Tzintzicha. The relation between the Sierra and the ruling elites from the Lake Pátzcuaro region can also be found in the petamuti's discourse. When King Tariácuri was being persecuted by his enemies from Curinguaro, his nephews Hiripan and Tangaxoan fled to the Sierra villages of Pichataro, Sevina, and Cheran. Pichataro, along with nearby Comachuen, later offered military aid to Tariácuri when he had regained his strength and continued the expansion of his kingdom. Afterward, his nephews and son conquered several settlements in the Zacapu region and also subdued Cheran and Sevina (Espejel Carbajal 2000:307–308).

The lienzo disappeared from Nahuatzen shortly before 1886, when Abraham Molina, the representative of the local landowners, sent it to the prefect in Uruapan, who forwarded it to Morelia, where it ended up in the local museum. Probably after 1892 but before the turn of the century, it was stolen from the collection and sold in Mexico City, where some years later (but before 1930) it reappeared in the National Museum of Anthropology and History (Roskamp 1998:66–70). Comparison of the two titles shows no evidence that the older pictorial document was used to produce the more recent alphabetic manuscript, perhaps reflecting the lienzo's lack of availability during a considerable period between 1892 and 1930. Even after it reappeared in the Mexican capital, the information probably did not reach the Sierra community. Therefore, it was the alphabetic title kept in the archive of Nahuatzen that was copied in 1934 by Leopoldo Molina, who at that time was the president of the local administrative committee. This copy was handed over to the agrarian authorities when they asked for the presentation of official titles to initiate the process of restitution and donation of land to the community.

The most extensive and detailed set of primordial titles from Michoacán belongs to Carapan, a town in the Cañada de los Once Pueblos. As in the previous cases, the documental corpus (one document in alphabetic and four in pictorial writing) explains how the Uacúsecha kings conquered the entire region and founded Carapan and also marked its boundaries and its springs. After the arrival of the Spaniards, Carapan's rights were supposedly reconfirmed by the colonial descendants of the Uacúsecha and the Spanish royal couple. Although the chronological order differs from the one registered in the *Relación de Michoacán*, the majority of the prehispanic rulers are mentioned, adding Carapu (from whom the name Carapan was derived) as a member of the Uacúsecha. The final foundation of the village was accomplished by Sirundame (a soldier of the king, Zuangua), who gathered people from the Sierra towns of Sevina, Aranza, and Piritan and guided them to the area where he officially took possession of the lands and springs in the name of his ruler, Zuangua, father of Tzintzicha Tangaxoan (Roskamp 1998:199–282, 2003). Such participation by warriors from the Sierra in the military campaigns that the Uacúsecha undertook in the region is also explicitly mentioned in the Lienzo de Nahuatzen, one of the titles from Jarácuaro, and the petamuti's discourse registered in the *Relación de Michoacán*.

The primordial titles from Carapan were made at the end of the seventeenth and the beginning of the eighteenth century, when the community wanted to separate itself from the jurisdiction of Chilchota and also had land conflicts with the neighboring town of Ichan. The documentation disappeared at the end of the nineteenth century, although the community managed to preserve a copy of one of the pictorial documents (Lienzo de Carapan II) and a copy of a map from 1894. The latter was produced by an engineer named Percy and seems to indicate the same boundaries marked in the colonial documentation. Although we do not know whether the residents of Carapan used these documents when they asked the agrarian authorities for the restitution of their communal lands in 1918, they did refer to them in 1957 when they had a land conflict with the neighboring town of Tacuro. On this occasion they also mentioned the existence of the original lienzo (II) in the Michoacán Museum in Morelia, as well as another copy that hung on a wall in the nearby Hotel Virrey de Mendoza (RAN, file San Juan Carapan, boxes 75 and 76). Although the Carapan authorities recognized the importance of the lienzo, they had only a very general understanding of its contents and no knowledge about the other titles that once had been kept in the community.

When I conducted my analysis of primordial titles of Carapan, including their location in public and private collections, as well as publication of the original documentation, I not only provided photographic copies to the town but also worked with several local authorities to identify toponyms and to reconstruct the original territory claimed in the titles. Although the rediscovery and study of the primordial titles has certainly not been of interest to all community members, don Vidal Alejo has embraced them as the only true local history and clear proof that Carapan was always the most important and extensive settlement in the Cañada de los Once Pueblos. Alejo, my main collaborator during my fieldwork in the region, is an important local political leader who also participated as a treasurer in the municipal government of Chilchota. Having read my published research and added his own (re)interpretations of the original documentation, he continually tries to explain the contents and importance of the documents to other community residents (including the current authorities and the council of elders), hoping that they will come to appreciate the story of their community's origin. At the same time, he considers these documents to be valuable historical arguments that strengthen Carapan's most recent claims for autonomy and the creation of an indigenous municipality separate from Chilchota.

Continuity and Change in Indigenous Visions of the Remote Past

Several seventeenth- and eighteenth-century primordial titles from Michoacán mention the prehispanic Uacúsecha and relate them to the founding of specific communities and the marking of their territorial boundaries. Whereas some documents include accurate and extensive references that coincide with elements from the official history of the lineage (recorded in the petamuti's discourse), others include information that is less certain. The occasional discrepancies between these documents and the primordial titles are related to several issues: the knowledge and selection of information by the authors, their writing and painting skills, their level of access to older documentation and oral tradition, the quantity and quality of available data, the exact purpose of the document, and the financial capacities of the community, especially when outside specialists were hired.

It is difficult to reconstruct how individual primordial titles were created. However, in the case of the documents from Carapan we have convincing evidence that the authors were specialized regional writers who used several older manuscripts from the ancient capital of Tzintzuntzan. They had direct access to the coat of arms that had been given to Tzintzuntzan in 1593 and made a general reinterpretation of its contents, due to their understanding only part of its original meaning. Other documents that they consulted must have contained fairly precise genealogical data on the Uacúsecha lineage—including, for example, the names of Tzintzicha Tangaxoan's wives, who are not mentioned in any other available source. Furthermore, the titles mention efforts (also recorded in the *Relación de Michoacán*) by a cacique called Timas to get rid of the last king, Tzintzicha Tangaxoan, at the time of the conquest.

The use of trained and paid specialists who were able to consult the archives in Tzintzuntzan explains the richness of the documental corpus from Carapan. Titles from other villages in the region were less extensive, less impressive, less detailed, and probably also less expensive, though not necessarily less effective. The known documents from the Lake Pátzcuaro region, relatively close to Tzintzuntzan, contain more references to the prehispanic period and to the Uacúsecha than do examples from other parts of the former Tarascan kingdom, the only exception being the titles from Carapan. This suggests that the historical tradition of the former ruling lineage was better preserved in the center of Michoacán than in the surrounding areas. This could be explained by the Uacúsecha's greater control, including their propagandistic and legitimizing historical vision, in the core of the Tarascan kingdom than in the periphery. Towns in central Michoacán, such as Jarácuaro, were the first to establish relationships with the Uacúsecha and even played an important and active role in the expansion of the lineage's dominions.

The colonial indigenous towns did not appeal to only one version of the prehispanic past; rather, they frequently used different versions—sometimes compatible, sometimes contradictory. To protect their landholdings and other corporate interests, they followed different strategies, which varied according to the community, region, and historical context. Although the primordial titles from Carapan formed a coherent corpus and were all preserved in the local archives, some documents came to be considered more important than others. The oldest lienzo, for example, was reinterpreted in another document copied in the nineteenth century. Information about the boundaries was extracted to form a modern map (Roskamp 1998:199–282). In the case of Jarácuaro, the short document was replaced by a different document, more extensive but apparently its contemporary, probably based on the primordial title from the neighboring community of Tócuaro but adding references to the conflict that Jarácuaros and Curínguaros had with the Uacúsecha. Nahuatzen lost its seventeenth- or eighteenth-century pictorial document and eventually, at the beginning of the twentieth century, had to produce a new one, this time in alphabetic writing. Although both manuscripts seem to agree that the town was founded by the Uacúsecha, the details of the two stories are otherwise completely different.

A significant number of the primordial titles urge future generations of community members to preserve and maintain the historical documents in good condition (and, if necessary, to make copies) in order to protect the community against any threat and assure its continuing existence in time and space. The transmission and understanding of their contents were crucial and were probably assured by periodic public readings or even enactments during important festivities such as, in the case of Jarácuaro, the day of the patron saint. Just as the petamuti's discourse had served to protect the status quo before the arrival of the Spaniards, the ritualized consultation of colonial primordial titles in the presence of authorities and commoners reaffirmed the original bond of the community members with their ancestors, marked the town's territory, and strengthened the promise to defend its integrity.

The mere preservation of documents did not always ensure that knowledge about their contents also was preserved, as shown by the example of Comachuen in the Sierra Tarasca. Although this community still possesses a pictorial primordial title, it is in the hands of a former local official who does not recognize the present authorities and therefore refuses to give them the local historical archive. Because of this internal quarrel, the document cannot be used in their current land conflict with the neighboring town of Tingambato. Furthermore, the inhabitants do not comprehend fully the manuscript's meaning, not only because of a rupture in the periodic transmission of its message to the community members but also because of their failure to develop new local experts. Interpretative problems occur most commonly when complex pictorial documents can be read only by a specialist, especially if the titles are written in Purépecha.

The loss of the primordial titles themselves may also have severe consequences for the transmission and preservation of local history. These documents were regarded as "birth certificates" of the communities in question, sacred writings that contained and constituted the heart and identity of the settlement and its corporate group. The physical presentation of the titles and other documentation, even if their contents were preserved in the oral tradition, in colonial and modern courts (at least when related to land issues) was and remains crucial. For example, we have seen that Nahuatzen lost its colonial lienzo and several decades later was forced to create a document that served the same function in order to meet the requirements of external authorities.

The interpretation and public reading of the titles were probably tasks for local elites such as scribes, members of the council of elders, and official authorities, who represented the community and were the ones expected to use the documents as political instruments. However, the commoners must have had some understanding, even if this were sustained through an oral tradition, of the titles and their significance to the community. Even in cases in which the original document disappeared, some communities or families managed to remember its existence and general message. The sixteenth-century Lienzo de Jicalán is such a case, known as it was to the Magaña family from Jicalán and also to inhabitants from the neighboring village of Jucutacato.

An important cause of the ruptures and transformations in the transmission of the primordial titles and their contents was the physical disappearance of the documentation, which often—but not always—occurred when an external threat obliged communities to present written evidence of their claims in the courts. It was not unusual for the documents to "disappear" in the judicial process, either actually being destroyed or finding their way into private collections or public archives. In addition, problems inside communities have sometimes caused former authorities to fail to pass on historical documentation to their successors. In some cases, these authorities have even profited personally by selling the title, as in the case of a local official in Tócuaro, who sold that community's title to the National Museum of Anthropology in Mexico City in 1958.[6]

Although many Tarascan communities were founded during the prehispanic period, they all experienced major changes in the early colonial period when they were moved, regrouped, and restructured around the church and the civic-religious institution known as the *hospital*, which formed the center of their well-defined territories. In this sense, the surviving communities and their territories were more colonial than prehispanic. The most extensive and complete documents, like the titles from Carapan and Nahuatzen, deal with both the prehispanic and colonial foundations, thus presenting a relatively complete reconstruction of the past.

Primordial titles were by no means the only expressions of corporate identity and historical memory. Many settlements that emphasized their colonial foundation were aware that in primordial times their lands were inhabited by their "pagan" forefathers. Ruins of prehispanic pyramids (yácatas), for example, can be found throughout the region. On the other hand, the towns that exclusively stressed their precolumbian origin did not ignore the importance of the Spanish conquest and the imposition of the Christian faith. The data provided in the titles surely were selected in view of their final purpose: the legitimation of land claims and enhancement of political status. They were not meant to be objective and all-inclusive descriptions or reconstructions of the past. Written documentation was often produced primarily for external purposes, especially for legal and other procedures implemented by colonial and modern bureaucracies.[7]

Consider the case of Nurío Tepaqua, a town in the heart of the Sierra Tarasca. According to information provided in 1991 by don Juan Chavez, in the prehispanic period a large settlement existed on Nurío huata (Nurío Mountain). It was divided into several sections or *barrios* dedicated to and named after the principal crafts of their inhabitants: Ukata urío (ceramics), Tiamo urío (metal), Takushi urío (textiles), and Katsikua urío (sombreros or hats). These groups decided to leave the mountain in order to flee from the foreign invaders when the Spaniards were arriving in Michoacán. The people from Katsikua urío, for example, guided by their leader, Popocha, wanted to go to Lake Pátzcuaro in order to join the inhabitants of Uricho, who originally came from a former village called Iurucho (located at the foot of the mountain of Nurío). They descended and started to travel in the direction of Pomacuaran, where they stopped to spend the night, giving a signal with their trumpets. The authorities and other inhabitants from Pomacuaran and Urapicho heard the noise and came to investigate what was happening. After having been informed of Popocha's plans, they decided not to let the group move on, because the products from Nurío huata were important to the regional economy, and, furthermore, its warriors played a crucial defensive role and could protect neighboring settlements from the Spaniards. An agreement was reached, and Popocha was allowed to choose a site on the border between Pomacuaran and Urapicho to found a new settlement.

Popocha located an appropriate place with sufficient springs: Canindo, Chapakato, Zinzu, Tahpitiru, Huanzindicuaro, Nuricho, and Inchandicurini. His agreement with Urapicho and Pomacuaran included a promise that the new settlement and land of Nurío could never be taken away. In return, its inhabitants agreed to participate in the organization and performance of the annual religious festivals (predominantly of the patron saints) celebrated in the two original communities, a tradition that lasted until the beginning of the twentieth century. When the Spaniards finally arrived in the region, the people of Nurío were converted to Christianity, and their settlement received the name of Santiago Nurío Tepakua. The last word means "bigger part," used to indicate that the majority of the inhabitants of Nurío were now baptized and had abandoned their old religion.

When the Spaniards ascended the mountain of Nurío, they found the old settlement and noticed that it was still inhabited by a small population. They destroyed the pyramids and used the material to build two chapels, one in a section of town that came to be called San Simón Nurío Caracua (the last word means "high") and another in Santo Tomás. The people who belonged to the latter refused to accept the new religion and decided to depart, first hiding their water well (Ocumscataru, "where they covered the water") and also burying the major bell of their chapel (which sometimes is still heard by present-day inhabitants of Nurío). They left in the direction of the Cañada de los Once Pueblos, where they finally established themselves in the fertile land near the Río Duero, calling their new town Santo Tomás. At that time, the only other settlements in the region were Chilchota, Huancito, and Carapan. The people from San Simon Nurío Caracua also opposed the Christian faith, but, due to pressure from the Spaniards and from the town of Nurío Tepakua, they decided to leave the mountain. However, they refused to establish themselves in Nurío Tepakua, which had, without any opposition, collaborated with the conquerors and their priests. Instead they asked Pomacuaran to give them their own piece of land, a petition that was denied and in the end obliged them to join Nurío Tepakua.

Additional information from other sources confirms the basic elements of this version of Nurío's foundation. A preliminary survey of the archaeological zone located on Nurío huata indicates that the ruins of two buildings probably pertained to sixteenth-century Catholic chapels, not only proving the probable division of the settlement into at least two barrios but also suggesting that evangelization began while people still were on the mountain. Furthermore, interviews with inhabitants of Santo Thomas yielded a similar version of the origin of this Cañada town—that it was founded by a group that formerly lived on the mountain of Nurío. Colonial documents mention the existence in the sixteenth century of the two separate settlements that were called Nurío and indicate that at the beginning of the seventeenth century San Simon was joined into Santiago Nurío Tepacua or into San Miguel Pomocuaran (Archivo General de Notarias del Estado de Michoacán, Morelia, ramo Títulos de tierras y aguas, tomo 1, legajo 9, fols. 416–430).

It is possible that the foregoing narrative about the foundation of Nurío was originally the subject of an even older but now lost primordial title. At least during the past century and a half, the story seems to have been passed on in oral form and has probably undergone several adaptations, depending not only on the selection and skills of the narrators and their listeners but also on the precise context in which the story was told. When I heard don Juan Chavez's version in 1991, he was actively involved in peace negotiations between Nurío and the neighboring communities of San Felipe de los Herreros, Pomacuaran, Urapicho, and especially Cocucho. These negotiations were concerned with settling a severe conflict about territorial boundaries that can be traced back to the seventeenth century. Furthermore, Chavez is a regional leader who always has been active in movements for indigenous autonomy, respect for indigenous culture and language, and improvement of living standards. At the same time, he is unusually familiar with colonial sources, especially the *Relación de Michoacán*, of which he has a copy. Thus, his activities and knowledge probably influenced and shaped his detailed and balanced transmission of the founding history of

Nurío that had been told to him by his father, grandfather, and other family members.

Conclusion

As the case of the Tarascan region of Michoacán demonstrates, primordial titles, other colonial documents, and oral traditions are valuable sources for the study of how origins and corporate identity have been produced by representatives of certain prehistoric and historic communities and have been retold by subsequent generations of narrators. Although such traditions are not in themselves objective reconstructions of the past, they generally do include information that corresponds to historical reality and therefore should not be dismissed as being fakes, inventions, or fantasy. The strength and survival of historical themes and conventions through time varies according to the community, the family, and even the individual. In this sense, indigenous historical traditions and collective memories in places like Michoacán need to be understood as dynamic, complex, and related versions of the past that continue to be transmitted in written and oral form with inevitable transformations, ruptures, and even (re)inventions. They still provide communities and individuals with effective instruments with which to defend their rights and privileges against outside threats. Like the prehispanic petamuti's discourse, the primordial titles constitute sacred histories that need to be understood as a complex combination of logical construct, cosmological representation, religious and political symbolism, and historical fact.

Notes

1. Margarita Menegus Bornemann (1999:141–142, 153–154) suggests not only that the production of titles had already started at the end of the sixteenth and beginning of the seventeenth century but also that they were a direct response to the *congregación* of the dispersed indigenous population in villages and the subsequent distribution of their unoccupied land to Spanish colonists.

2. Although in most cases the rejected documents were probably given back to the communities, Stephanie Wood (1987:480; 1998a:170; 1998b:227) has encountered cases in which they were confiscated or even destroyed.

3. In his reflections on the construction of a Purépecha identity, historian Naoki Yasumura (2003) mentions the hybrid nature of the historical visions of some people from Tzintzuntzan who identify themselves with the glorious prehispanic past yet do not consider themselves in any way related to the present-day indigenous groups and culture; they even discriminate against them.

4. The same story applies to the town of Jucutacato, where the lienzo remained for more than 200 years. At the time it was taken away by Magaña, it was known as the *sábana* and was used as a precious mortuary garment in the local church to cover a huge crucifix during the 40-day Lenten period before Holy Friday. Even today its important

religious function, along with its "theft" by a neighbor from Jicalán, are remembered by some families. A painted artistic interpretation of the document by José Luis Soto, mixed with elements from Tarascan iconography and cosmology, hangs on a wall in the Municipal Office (Roskamp 1998:84–85).

5. This part of the story can also be found in the primordial title of Tócuaro (León 1904:405–406).

6. Annotations that accompany the original titles of Tócuaro in the Codices Collection, National Library of Anthropology and History, Mexico City. In an exceptional and early case (1805) from the Zacapu region, an indigenous pictorial document from an unidentified community passed into the hands of a priest, Juan José Pastor Morales, who might have used it as a title to his Hacienda of Bellas Fuentes (Moxó 1968).

7. Yasumura (2003:669) divides the historical narratives in two main categories: (1) the ones that center on the community and contain its collective memory; and (2) personal memories whose main subject is the individual.

7

Identity and Ethnicity in Colonial Michoacán

Corporatism, Social Contract, and Individualism among the Tarascans

Felipe Castro Gutiérrez

In the Beginning Was the Name

Dealing with the history of an indigenous people leads us into certain conceptual problems that cannot be ignored. Every time we speak of "the Tarascans" or "the Caxcans," we risk creating an abstract entity out of a group that had no other existence apart from that of being a demographic aggregate. It tends to be taken for granted that the speakers of a certain language comprise a homogeneous group simply because the sources lead us to think this and because it makes for a convenient narrative resource.

The real problem, however, is that these linguistic conglomerates did not always share common ideas, attitudes, or behaviors. Hence we must ask: To what degree can we really speak of an indigenous linguistic group as a homogeneous community and not just as a series of populations that, incidentally, shared a common language? For instance, the Nahua peoples (who were distributed all the way from Veracruz to the coast of Michoacán) had little or no sense of collective identity. A more delimited argument could be based on the existence of linguistic groups with shared histories and traditions. The identity of a certain group is not simply a reflection of its past or of its "objective" cultural conditions. Rather, it corresponds to a selection (or adjudication) of features that may be real but may also be mythical (Vázquez León 1992; Yasumura 2003).

For centuries, the minority indigenous languages of Mesoamerica have undergone a gradual process of absorption and even extinction. The great contemporary linguistic diversity of Mexico (with over 50 native languages) is a pale reflection of earlier times. In the prehispanic era, speakers of distinct languages were often intermixed and formed part of the same polity. Among the Tarascans, for example, there were nobles with family names that suggest Nahua origins, such as the Acatli and the Coneti.

The ever-present risk consists in creating an ethnic group that did not exist centuries ago. The growing ethnic consciousness (which includes defining themselves as a "nation") that the Tarascans currently demonstrate does not mean that this has always been the case. Rather, a group's identity may be geographical, political, historical, racial, or religious. On the other hand, a collective identity forms part of a set of reciprocal images that not only distinguish among cultural groups but also constitute one aspect of their strategies of domination, adaptation, and resistance.

One of the most surprising elements of the prehispanic history of the "Tarascans" of Michoacán is that we do not know what they used to call themselves. Though the origin of the term "Tarasco" (commonly used to refer to this group in modern Western languages) remains dubious, it is quite clear that it was a Spanish creation that was not used by the speakers themselves. The word "Michoacán" itself comes from Nahuatl ("the place of the people who have fish") and probably originated among the region's ancient, pre-Tarascan settlers. This does not mean that it could not have been adopted by the Tarascans themselves, but there are no references that might lead us to think that they referred to themselves as *michoaque* or "Michoacanos."

The *Relación de Michoacán* (2000), our main source for this period, mentions the *enéani* (etymology unknown), the *çacapuhireti* ("inhabitants of Zacapu, the stone") and the *uanácaze* ("those who pass by") as the primary lineages that unified the kingdom, although the same can be said of the *uacúsecha*, who are mentioned only incidentally in this source (Márquez 2000). The *Relación de Michoacán* also speaks repeatedly of the Chichimecas, a name applied to certain warrior groups who arrived belatedly on the central Mesoamerican scene.

The contemporary indigenous inhabitants of the central highlands of the state of Michoacán prefer to be called Purépecha (or variants such as Phurhépecha and P'urhépecha), a circumstance that has led current scholars to adopt this term in keeping with prevailing principles of "political correctness" applied in other contexts (such as those of the Tarahumaras/Raramuris or the Pápagos/O'odham). Based on the method of associating related roots and suffixes, Francisco Miranda has suggested that the term "Purépecha" could be interpreted (rather magnificently) to mean "people from other places whose vocation is war, which has allowed them to acquire their own place in which they move freely" (1988:29–30). However, in the first dictionaries compiled by early missionaries, this word is associated with "villein" or the "common people" and linked to a verb like *purepechaenstani*, which means "to become cowed or intimidated" (Gilberti 1987 [1558]). It seems, then, that the word "Purépecha" referred to the common folk and was thus inappropriate to denote the governing elite. When the elite sector later disappeared and the remnant population consisted mainly of "Purépechas," this term came to be applied to the entire society deep into the past (see Martínez Baracs 2003).

This situation is unusual because an essential part of ethnogenesis—the creation of a sense of group identity—involves the determination of the group's name (the "ethnonym") both within the population and vis-à-vis others outside of the group. This raises an important question: Could it be that the prehispanic polity of Michoacán had a nucleus of identity that was not, properly speaking, "ethnic"?

Lineages and Collective Identity

The *Relación de Michoacán* describes a political system in which lords were elected from among the members of "royal" lineages, though their legitimacy did not rest upon purely dynastic principles or the idea of a "chosen people." On the contrary, it was strongly linked to religion: the *cazonci*, or king, was a man who occupied "god's place" on the earth (RM 2000:558). Those who aspired to this position had to accumulate merit by keeping the fires of the temples stoked with wood, doing penance, and sacrificing captives to feed the deities. Deeds such as these allowed a man to accumulate divine favor, which was then made manifest through hallucinatory dreams in which the gods promised dominion over the earth (RM 2000:494–499). It was, as Jean Marie Le Clézio (1985) has said so well, a sacred conquest.

Authority was always associated with the physical possession of the god Curicaueri, represented concretely by a blade of obsidian. The *Relación* tells us that "in their time this people said that those who were to be lords were to have [the god] Corícagueri with them, and if they did not, they could not become lords. And therefore the lords guarded [the god] with great care, and after them their sons" (Castro's translation, RM 2000:460, see also 481, 484). It was Curicaueri who decreed the dominion of the Uacúsechas over all other lords and who in some cases showed "liberality" by pardoning their lives and returning their lands.

The reconstruction of the political system of Michoacán, as developed by various authors, indicates a situation in which ethnic groups were arranged in a social hierarchy. The source of this interpretation is the *Relación* itself, because, as Helen Perlstein Pollard (2003b:57–59) has pointed out, it describes three levels of integration within the polity. At the top were the Chichimeca conquerors. They were followed by associated lords who, once conquered, were obligated to supply firewood to the temples and warriors for battle, in addition to cultivating the cazonci's fields. There also were groups of vassals (such as the Otomi) who were deployed along the frontiers for military service but who kept their own rulers. The Tarascan kingdom's policy of assimilation, based on a differentiated restriction of access to the power and prestige that accrued to subordinated local elites, was distinctive among Mesoamerican polities. The success of this policy might explain the remarkable internal solidity of the kingdom of Michoacán, which contrasted so starkly with the Mexicas' constant wars of reconquest and the almost immediate defection of their vassals upon the arrival of the Spaniards.

The different groups found within the kingdom of Michoacán were also linked by kinship ties that integrated the dominant lineages, the local lords, and even the peasants into a vast network of relations of subordination and reciprocity. This element was certainly present in many other large Mesoamerican polities, but in Michoacán it took on a particularly elaborate form.[1]

The importance of kinship among the Michoacanos is clearly visible, even from ancient times, when the Uacúsechas were a recently arrived group in the lake area pursued by more powerful groups. The account of the formation of this particular polity abounds with lords who considered themselves brothers, fathers-in-law, brothers-in-law, and uncles. For example, the important lord of Xarácuaro called his counterpart in Tariarán "brother"; while the lord of Syrauéni referred to Tariácuri, the cazonci of the Chichimeca Uacusechas, as "son." This latter personage, in turn, was a son-in-law of the lord of Cuirínguaro. Some of these appellations seem to have been simple forms of courtesy (not so different from those used by European nobles, who often referred to each other as "cousin"), while other terms indicate actual familial relationships.

In the Michoacán polity, relations of subordination were established when the lord of a dominant group gave a daughter or sister as wife to the lord of a subordinate group (RM 2000:570, 609). Inheritance was determined through the female line, so this was an indirect way of appropriating polities and their subordinated deities. The history of the agitated conjugal life of Tariácuri is revealing. His wife was a daughter of Chansori, the powerful lord of Cuirínguaro, who justified the union by saying to her, "It will please the gods for you to bear a child by him, and thus we shall take away Curicaueri, who is a very great god" (RM 2000:402, 404). Tariácuri's wife was the cause of continual interference by his father-in-law and brothers-in-law into their domestic affairs. When he finally repudiated her and went to visit Zurumban, the lord of Tariarán, in search of an alliance, the latter sent several young women to his chamber during the night, hoping that he would sleep with them; but Tariácuri, in order to avoid falling into a perilous relationship, spent the entire night staying awake talking with his councilors (RM 2000:418, 419). The Tarascan lords literally lived under threat from their own sexuality. It is likely that the endogamy the Spaniards observed among the indigenous nobility resulted from the need for descendants without the dangerous political repercussions of exogamous alliances.

Although information in this respect is fragmentary, it may be that this "family" organization not only embraced the nobility but extended outward to include the common people. The *Diccionario grande de la lengua de Michoacán* (Warren 1991), compiled by an unknown missionary in the sixteenth century, gives the following meanings for the word "Purépecha": "vassal," "plebeians," "villein," and, more precisely, "villein of lineage." The only explanation for this last shade of meaning is that the clergyman detected a difference between "villein" and one who, despite his inferior condition, placed himself in a network of kinship relations.

Another intriguing detail is that the verb "to possess the land" (*minguareni*) also meant "to become related by marriage" (Velásquez Gallardo 1952 [1539]). Therefore, having possession of land implied contracting kinship. Similarly, a second term that indicated possession of land (as in the phrase "Hi hapinga yni tareta," which means "I possess this field") (Gilberti 1987:160 [1558]), contains the root *hapi*, which was used to indicate a subordinate relationship. Thus, "servant" was also expressed as *hapingata* ("one who is possessed") (Gilberti 1987:80 [1558]).

All of these elements suggest a sociopolitical organization based on an interwoven hierarchy of noble lineages that established their dominion over people who were considered kin but who lived in different towns or neighborhoods (see Beltrán 1994:100–107). Ethnicity does not seem to have played a particularly significant role in this social organization. Actually, this system presents suggestive similarities with a model of social organization described many years ago by Paul Kirchhoff (1955) and applied to societies in which legitimacy, authority, and access to resources are derived not from social classes but from descending circles of hierarchical kinship (see Monzón 1996).

In his study of Tepeaca, Hildeberto Martínez proposed that when ancient indigenous documents use the word *barrio* (neighborhood), we should understand this to mean "localized tributary sub-units governed by local heads (*mandones*) and belonging to different lords" (1984:105–107). This interpretation may well be applicable to the case of Michoacán. It is revealing that the word for "neighborhood" in Purépecha (*yrenariquareponi*) means "living with one another in the place of origin," which indicates that human settlements existed as a function of personal and kinship relations.

If this is true, then we will have found an explanation for the absence in Tarascan of terms equivalent to *calpulli*, which was so characteristic of Nahua society. The calpulli was a subordinate peasant organization that occupied lands in its own right and had a certain capacity to govern its domestic affairs. Nothing similar seems to have existed in Michoacán, where the political organization was apparently more similar to that of the *teccalli*, or "noble houses," of certain Nahua groups, though with the peculiarity that, in the case of Michoacán, it included both the lands and the peasants who lived in different towns.

It was in these lineages in Michoacán that the Spanish conquerors found the necessary and indispensable intermediaries who allowed them to govern a very large population and extensive territory with which they were poorly acquainted. The descendants of those who were called "natural lords" were recognized as chieftains (*caciques*) and *principales* (the Indian equivalent of an *hidalgo*, or lesser nobility). They were exempt from paying tribute and performing personal services and had the right to bear arms, to ride on horseback, to participate in local government, to conserve the lands of their ancient patrimony, and to obtain pensions and other lucrative concessions (López Sarrelangue 1963:111, 112). Among their own kind, they were always called with the honorific title *acha*, which is equivalent to the term "don" among Spaniards.

The most distinguished of these cacique families were the Huitziméngari, descendants of the cazonci. The direct male descendants of this lineage were recognized during the sixteenth century as the caciques and virtual hereditary rulers of Pátzcuaro. Bishops and friars sought their support, the conquerors procured marriage alliances with their female heirs, and the viceroys turned to them for matters of great import, such as gathering contingents of indigenous warriors to defend the frontier against the Chichimecas (Gerhard 1992:330, 334, 343). By the same token, their rights over a vast expanse of land were recognized, allowing them to cultivate fields, pasture their cattle, and operate grain mills and sugar refineries. In this way, these Indian noblemen enjoyed the obedience of numerous indigenous tenant farmers (*terrazgueros*), who paid rent and provided them with gifts of bread, flowers, and fruits as signs of allegiance (Archivo Histórico Municipal de Pátzcuaro [AHMP] 1625, 25 fols.). In the mid-sixteenth century—though the practice was prohibited, at least in theory—these caciques continued to receive tribute directly from the Indians (Archivo Histórico del INAH [AHINAHN] 1597, 171).

Of course, the caciques of Pátzcuaro were no longer imbued with sacred legitimacy. They could neither remove local town governors from their posts nor lead armies in forays to achieve new conquests and thus extend their domains. Nonetheless, even though they had ceased to be the main authority figures in Michoacán, they continued to play a dominant role in indigenous society.

In official documents, the Huitziméngari were often referred to as the "caciques of Michoacán," a designation that implicitly established a distinction between them and other caciques and governors who had jurisdiction only over their subject towns and neighborhoods. In the surviving Tarascan texts, the authorities of each town were referred to by the Spanish title of *gobernador* (governor), while the Huitziméngari continued to be called *irecha*, or "lord" (Archivo General de la Nación, Mexico City [AGN] 1635, 213–214). Some towns, such as Jicalán and Urecho, disputed dominion over certain properties, basing their positions on authorizations supposedly granted in the mid-sixteenth century by don Pablo and don Antonio Huitziméngari (Roskamp 2001).

As late as 1579, the *corregidor* of Sirándaro affirmed that the Indians, "during the era of their gentility, came and went from Mechoacán loaded with goods from this lowland, and their lords had them as slaves; so, even today, their descendants still respect the sons of the nobles of Mechoacán, saying that their fathers were their slaves and captives, and for this reason, they love them and hold them in reverence, paying them no other tribute" (Acuña 1987:265–266, my translation).[2] This reference to "slaves" cannot be interpreted literally according to the Western understanding of the concept. Those men were *teruparaquaebaecha* and *acípecha*, which mean "those who worked the patrimonial lands of the nobles." In referring to these men, the *Relación de Michoacán* says, "They are their relatives, slaves from the wars whom their ancestors had taken or that they had saved from starvation, who were loaned corn, or men who were caught stealing in their fields, or slaves purchased from merchants" (RM 2000:571, 572). Once again, social relationships were expressed in kinship terms: the "slaves" were "relatives" of the nobles, which should be interpreted as meaning that they belonged to the same "house" or lineage.

Similar situations occurred in Uruapan, where several successive caciques of the Coneti family occupied the governorship without interruption (AHMP 1596, 147); and in Charo, Capula, and Ucareo, where sons succeeded their fathers in the post of governor (Martínez Baracs 1998:75; Paredes Martínez 1994:60, 120). The Coneti were probably of Nahua origin, if their family name is any indication, as it is a Hispanicized form of *conetl*, which means "child" in that language. The last of the cacique-governors of Pátzcuaro, don Constantino Huitziméngari, was probably also considered Nahua because his mother was of that origin, and descendancy among Tarascans was adjudicated following the maternal lineage. He was accused of illegally favoring his relatives, the Jiménez Acatli (or "Cane"), who, judging by their surname, must also have belonged to the so-called Nauatlatos or Nahuales (Paredes Martínez 1994:327–328).

Other features of the indigenous political organization also indicate the survival of prehispanic elements. The councilmen (*regidores*) and local judges (*alcaldes*) of the city council (*ayuntamiento*) of Pátzcuaro at that time belonged, almost invariably, to important noble families such as the Cuara, Tsitsiqui, Cuiris, Ramírez, Tzurequi, Chocho, and Pehmu. Those men were proud to have been "domestics" (part of the "family" in the wide sense, not menial workers) or stewards (*mayordomos*) of the Huitziméngari (López Sarrelangue 1963:247–257). In fact, the verb "to govern," *urengarihpeni*, also meant "to have servants."

Prior to the arrival of the Spaniards, there had been deputies (*diputados*) or "head stewards" (*mayordomos mayores*) responsible for gathering tribute and directing the guild corporations. As late as the mid-sixteenth century in Pátzcuaro, there were still stewards of the quarry workers, mat makers, fishermen, tanners who were in charge of sandal production, feather workers, carpenters, and boatmen. Others were in charge of collecting tribute or overseeing public works (RM 2000:559–563). This evidence suggests that the caciques still maintained a certain degree of control over all of these economic activities (López Sarrelangue 1963:285).

The vigor and importance of the lineage-based organization of indigenous society allowed the caciques to preserve a large share of their influence and authority during the early colonial period. Despite the enormous changes and violent ruptures brought about by the conquest, the ancient order survived, at least to a degree, behind the new hierarchies and institutions. This was more evident in the administrative centers of greater importance because in the secondary towns, where only a lower rank of nobility had existed, Hispanicization took place more quickly and completely.

Toward the end of the sixteenth century, however, various processes converged to dissolve the survivals of the old social and political order. Obviously, the Crown was hostile to the hereditary privileges that it had had to combat in Spain. For this reason, and from very early times, the viceroys had proceeded to establish *repúblicas*, that is, a territorial jurisdiction administered by *cabildos* and presided over by governors who were elected annually (Paredes 2003). The few exceptions of permanent, hereditary governing rights, such as Pátzcuaro and Uruapan, ceased to be so in the last decade of the sixteenth century. From that time on, the position of governor circulated among a few families of principales, that is, those descended from, or said to be descended from, the "noble" families, including secondary lineages and persons who had ascended by serving or assisting the Spanish clergy. Without doubt, family prestige and influence continued to be important factors in the appointment of mayors, councilmen, and governors, but families no longer occupied such positions through hereditary ascription.

The continuities in the social system had indirect consequences for the transition from extended to nuclear families. In prehispanic Michoacán, both of these forms of family organization seem to have existed.[3] However, since medieval times the Catholic Church had struggled in Europe against the strength of lineages because they fragmented the solidarity of the Christian community. For this reason, the church sought to impose the model of the nuclear family, in which authority resided in the father. The Crown also preferred this form of family organization, because homes were thought of as the basic fiscal unit. Although the success of this innovation was unequal and incomplete, it no doubt contributed to weakening the authority of patriarchs. A recurring theme in cases of family violence from Michoacán saw husbands attacking their fathers-in-law due to their repeated attempts to intervene in domestic disputes involving their married daughters (Castro Gutiérrez 1998). Clearly, patriarchal authority was being called into question.

The serious epidemics of the late sixteenth century also contributed to the decline of the noble families. On the one hand, the old, complex kinship relations had been battered and fragmented by the deaths of innumerable people. On the other, the indigenous nobles saw their authority seriously diminished. It just was not the same being the indispensable intermediary between the government and large populations of thousands of inhabitants as being the head of a town with only a few dozen tributaries.

After the conquest, indigenous nobles tended to sell their lands quickly, usually to Spanish settlers. There may well have been an underlying reason for this apparently irrational conduct: after all, the fields would have been of little use if their owners had no workers to labor on them or tenant farmers to pay them rent. The nobles might have argued that their ancient patrimonial lands had been transformed into Spanish-style private property, but most indigenous people continued to identify the possession of land with governing hereditary rights. Once these rights had disappeared, the common people no longer saw any reason to continue paying a rent that they associated with the tribute they owed to the governor. This situation occurred among the Indians of San Pedro Charantxen, who long had paid rent for their lands to the caciques don Pablo and don Antonio Huitziméngari. Many years later, when one heir of the Huitziméngaris, don Juan Puruata, sued them for lack of payment, the surprised farmers replied that they had continued to pay rent to the governor of Pátzcuaro, don Constantino Huitziméngari, because "they understood that payment was due to the government of the city" (Archivo Parroquial de Pátzcuaro [APP] 1621–1622, fol. 41r).

The religious program of *congregaciones* was the final blow to the influence of the nobles. Shortly after the conquest, the clergy proceeded to unite dispersed settlements into larger towns that would be simpler to administer. Between 1593 and 1605, the viceroys did the same, though more systematically, by making use of their coercive powers. These so-called congregaciones, together with the founding of new towns, had the indirect consequence of providing access to communal lands to recently congregated tenant farmers, who were thus freed from the dependence, respect, and labor they had traditionally owed to their former lords. The nobles no longer granted land concessions in the towns, nor did they derive any benefit from belonging to a lineage.

The Emergence of a Communitarian Identity

The gradual dissolution of the ancient organization of lineages, however, did not bring with it a collective ethnic identity. Rather, this emerged, at least in part, from another deliberate colonial policy. In the northern reaches of the viceroyalty, the Spaniards had found only scattered indigenous settlements that lacked any tradition of centralized political control. This led the Spaniards to create ethnic groups as a means of control. Thus, they established towns and named as the communal authorities indigenous persons to whom they granted a certain amount of authority in matters such as public order, tribute, and religion. Moreover, general captains (*capitanes generales*) were set up to preside over a series of towns in which the same language was spoken (Mirafuentes Galván 1992). In the center of the viceroyalty, in contrast (as Gibson [1981:35–37, 168–170] pointed out long ago), the Spanish opted to break up the large polities and to organize each town of a certain hierarchy as a *república*, each of which had a municipal organization consisting of councilmen and local judges, presided over by a governor, who answered directly to the state and the church. In reality, the orders and judicial decisions involving conquered peoples rarely mention any ethnic affiliation, referring to them invariably as either *naturales* or "Indians" (this latter, a judicial category) and as residents of a certain town.

In the case of Michoacán, changes went far beyond the simple emergence of new institutions. Towns there had existed as sets of families that obtained access to land as a result of being subjects of certain noble lineages. Now, however, they were granted a juridical status and could elect their authorities, make decisions concerning common property, and present petitions directly to the viceroy. This political reform had enormous repercussions: paradoxical as it may seem, the imposition of Spanish domination led to the decentralization of authority in indigenous society.

Local nobles, who earlier had played only a minor role, came to exercise great influence in decision making and in everyday affairs. It is hardly surprising that they found the new colonial order quite to their liking. This organization soon took root and was so vigorous that its basic features endured until the nineteenth century. Such was its success that this communitarian organization came to be considered "distinctive" and "typical" of Indian culture, and people forgot that it was, in its origins, a novelty that had a precise historical origin linked closely to the particular administrative, fiscal, and religious necessities of the Spanish Empire.

From that time on, people's fundamental identity centered on their town of residence. Despite its undeniable importance, the family no longer constituted the nucleus of communitarian identity, nor was it the determining factor in acquiring or possessing land. Gradually, it was replaced by a new associational and contractual concept: an indigenous man (and his family) belonged to a town because he paid tribute, provided personal services, and participated in the tasks and affairs of a particular república. This situation is reflected quite clearly in the arguments presented in certain judicial procedures. For example, in 1781 Pedro Martín, a principal from Atécuaro, stated that he had held all council offices, from the lowest to the highest, and that it was a "legal disposition and an inviolable and immemorial custom that any individual who served in this manner would receive common lands to seed and pastures" (Archivo de Notarías de Morelia [ANM] 1781, 520–604). A similar argument was presented by Juan Thomas, an Indian from Tarejero living in Atécuaro, when he stated during a dispute over lands in 1768 that when he came to live in that town the "elders and mayors" had given him a place to live and work, with the obligation to participate in the municipal posts (*cargos*) and to pay communal fees and royal tributes (ANM 1768, 452–497). Similarly, as land in certain towns became scarce over time, young people began to complain that they could not obtain plots for themselves, although they were *pensioneros* who paid contributions, helped to provide for the priest, and held posts in the república (ANM 1778, 467–495).

This deep-rooted residential identity linked every town to the state and the church but did not foster solidarity or intercommunity mobilizations. The election of officials of the república, the fiestas, the veneration of patron saints, and the confraternities and hospitals all reflected and reinforced this localized worldview. For the Indians, their universe was their town, the space where they found sustenance, security, and protection. Beyond its boundaries, there were only entities that were best kept at arm's length, regardless of whether they were indigenous or Spanish.

This isolation of communities emerged clearly in cases of serious conflicts. In other areas of the viceroyalty, large-scale rebellions occurred in which several towns united to challenge the colonial order, for example, in Tehuantepec in 1660 and later in the Maya area and along the northern frontier (Katz 1990). But this was not the case in Michoacán. There, the space that the indigenous people identified as their own was clearly marked and restricted to their towns. The residents of each space defended their own resources and what residents called "rights and privileges," neither seeking nor obtaining the support of their neighbors. Though towns did come to have common adversaries (especially those located on the edges of haciendas), rarely did they show any form of solidarity (Castro Gutiérrez 1998:5–21).

In fact, these indigenous towns were fully capable of fighting each other with the same rancor with which they confronted the Spanish landowners. In the late seventeenth century, Santa Fe and Cocupao began a series of quarrels over boundaries that continues today. The people of Nurío fought a pitched battle with the residents of San Felipe de los Herreros in a dispute over land. Hundreds of cudgel- and axe-wielding men from the two towns participated, several men were seriously injured, and one man was killed. Another collective melee took place when groups from Quinceo challenged the people of Capacuaro. In another case, the Indians of Pungarabato expelled the people of Huetamo "with great temerity and violence," attacking them with knives and other weapons and even burning their houses. People from Nahuatzen once invaded the lands of Tarejero, threatened passersby, and wounded or cut off the ears of their neighbors' cattle. Jucutacato did not hesitate to turn to an influential Spanish lawyer to intimidate the governor of Uruapan into signing an agreement through which residents actually ceded much of their lands. Even close relationships based on collaboration and companionship could come to a bad end: Guayameo and Sirándaro, towns that at one time had considered themselves co-owners, had a falling out when the latter sued the former and obtained as patrimony some lands it had previously rented there, leaving its neighbor with its commons severely reduced. The worst example of depredation was provided by the Indians of Purungueo, who invaded the lands of Tiquicheo so completely that one tenant farmer led his cattle right into the cemetery to pasture. There, according to the local Indian judge, the cows "proceeded to eat the houses."

In sum, what we find in Michoacán from the early years of the seventeenth century is a series of peasant corporations that shared a common past and the same language but demonstrated no mutual support nor any idea of a shared destiny. With respect to that historical period we can only use the term "the Tarascans" to refer to a kind of literary convention that describes a set of towns in which the same language was spoken. Of course, the people there were aware that they shared a common past, but they do not seem to have deduced from that any kind of consequent interest or importance for their private interests. Over time, of course, collective movements did emerge from those towns, as did a vigorous consciousness of historical identity, which is more vibrant in the twenty-first century than it has been in centuries past.

Notes

1. The lords who were subject to the Mexicas had to give the daughters or sisters of local nobles to the *tlatoani* of Tenochtitlan as concubines; their sons, educated in the metropolis, gradually modified the composition and loyalties of the conquered nobility. The most noteworthy case is that of Cuitláhuac, lord of Iztapalapa, who was the next-to-last tlatoani Mexica.

2. The people of Siríndaro were *apanecas* but also "captives" from other provinces such as Zacatula and Colima. The cazonci had brought them back to settle—and sustain with tribute—a large garrison at Cutzamala to protect the kingdom from the Mexicas (Acuña 1987:265–266).

3. Data on this topic are very scarce and can be derived from the first population count carried out in 1523–24 by the *visitador* Antonio de Caravajal (cited in Warren 1977:387–408). In this count, many cases show a notorious difference between the "families" reported by the indigenous authorities (*mandones*) and those registered by the Spanish magistrate. Though this has been attributed to an effort to conceal tributaries, another plausible explanation is that the units of counting were distinct: while the Indians counted by "houses" cohabited by distinct generations, the Spanish took into account all married men.

8

Indigenous Space and Frontier in Sixteenth-Century Nueva Galicia

José Francisco Román Gutiérrez

Spanish Settlement on an Indigenous Frontier

Eighteen years separated Nuño de Guzmán's arrival in Nueva Galicia in 1530 and the establishment in 1548 of the *audiencia* and chancellery as the regional representative of Spanish royal authority. During that interregnum colonial administration was in the hands of three governors (Nuño de Guzmán, Diego Pérez de la Torre, and Francisco Vázquez de Coronado), various lieutenant-governors (Cristóbal de Oñate on three occasions), and two *alcaldes mayores*. It was not until 1548 that the first of the four magistrates (*oidores*) named to the audiencia and chancellery of Nueva Galicia took up his position at the city of Compostela, eventually moving to Guadalajara in 1560.

The colonial government authorities held a royal mandate to assure the preservation and well-being of the Indians and their conversion to Christianity and civilization as exemplified by Spanish culture. In reality, the conquest, the economic interests of different Spanish groups, and the specific development of events made such principles impractical; indeed, violations of those "rules" was the norm from the beginning. At the outset of the conquest of Nueva Galicia under Guzmán, the capture and trade of Indian slaves was one of Guzmán's (and his lieutenants') most lucrative activities. When his government came to an end in 1536, Guzmán was accused by the resident judge of having enslaved thousands of Indians without just cause (Archivo General de Indias, Seville [AGI], Guadalajara 5, traslado de los cargos hechos a Nuño de Guzmán durante el juicio de residencia, Compostela, a 5 de mayo de 1537).

During that initial stage in the conquest of Nueva Galicia, the exploitation of conquered Indian villages' labor and other resources was also under Guzmán's authority. With complete disregard for the norms established by the Spanish army in relation to the distribution of plunder obtained through conquest, he personally controlled several of the largest and most important settlements and assigned other villages to his most loyal followers (AGI, Guadalajara 5).

With the change of governor (first Pérez de la Torre, then Vázquez Coronado), the exercise of such broad powers was reduced, as was the practice of benefiting the members of one's closest friends. The promulgation of the New

Laws in 1542–1543 in no way protected Indian towns from being placed into the *encomienda* and *corregimiento* systems, which were, in effect, disguised forms of slavery, especially with the consolidation of the mining towns of Guachinango and Zacatecas. Despite its softened tone, the official description of the magistrate Hernán Martínez de la Marcha's *visita* to Nueva Galicia in 1549–1550 revealed that Indian labor in the mines was controlled by strong pressures emanating from the economic interests of the Spanish miners (AGI, Justicia 306, 1557, 1560–1561, "Residencia de los licenciados Hernando Martínez de la Marcha, Lorenzo Lebrón de Quiñones, Miguel de Contreras y Guevara y Alonso Oseguera, oidores, alcaldes mayores de la Audiencia de Guadalajara. Por Pedro Morones, oidor, alcalde mayor de dicha Audiencia," fol. 343v).

Because of its size, the territory of Nueva Galicia presented enormous challenges to the colonial order, which was just beginning to take shape. Descriptions by travelers and residents and the reports of the mandatory visitas by colonial, ecclesiastical, and religious officials never failed to mention the complex geography and topography of the area, its extreme climatic conditions, and its biological diversity—all of which combined to make it very difficult for new groups (Spanish or Indian) to settle in northern New Spain. The administrative regions and institutions in sixteenth-century Nueva Galicia were divided into three domains: first, the areas where sedentary Indian villages were more numerous; next, the most lucrative areas for economic development; and third, the outposts created for defensive purposes and as links along the roadways.

The seat of the civil government for all of Nueva Galicia was established in Compostela by Nuño de Guzmán, and that city also was chosen by the Spanish Crown as the seat of a bishopric. While those decisions seemed right in light of Guzmán's design to expand the jurisdiction farther north, the drastic decline of the Indian population and the disappointing results of the expeditions that went beyond San Miguel Culiacán soon exposed Compostela's limitations as a seat of government. However, the seat was not moved to the city of Guadalajara until the decade of 1560, when the civil officials there (governors, alcaldes mayores, and magistrates) finally implemented the provisions of the Council of the Indies.

In contrast, the first bishop of Nueva Galicia, Pedro Gómez de Maraver, having arrived in Compostela in December 1546, remained for less than a month before deciding to move to Guadalajara. He argued that too few Spaniards resided in Compostela and that the great distance to the main indigenous villages made bringing the Indians into the church extremely difficult, beyond the evangelizing efforts of the Franciscans and the few missionaries who were there at that time. Moreover, in the aftermath of the Mixtón War, the region of Compostela was surrounded by rebel Indian groups protected by the mountainous terrain of the Sierra Madre Occidental. Upon the discovery of the Zacatecas mines in 1546 and the economic boom that followed, interest in the region turned toward sites that were more strategically located in terms of controlling

Indian villages, that offered better living conditions for Spaniards, and that would facilitate exploiting the Zacatecas silver mines, which for sheer volume were the most productive in all of New Spain in the 1550s.

In other words, once the true value of the mines had been demonstrated, it became more important to consolidate the area around the silver deposits in northern Nueva Galicia and, by the same token, to exploit the more numerous conquered sedentary Indian villages there, where some degree of acculturation had been achieved through fifteen years of Spanish dominion. It is no accident that a 1550 painting of Nueva Galicia done in conjunction with the visita by the magistrate Hernán Martínez de la Marcha—the only one of four commissioned paintings subsequently sent to the emperor, Charles V—shows a marked contrast between Compostela and Guadalajara. The first is shown as an isolated city in the sierra with warlike Indians all around it; the second is set in the midst of valleys and towns already incorporated into the encomienda and corregimiento systems (see Borah 1994:9). The portrait of the original seat of the audiencia (Compostela) also shows the long journey to the mines in both Zacatecas and Mexico City and the absence of access routes to the territories in the northwest. The location of the bustling city of Guadalajara, on the other hand, was shown to be precisely situated between the Guachinango and Zacatecas mines, while the painting also highlighted the city's several entrance and departure points to and from the kingdom of Nueva Galicia. Finally, of course, Guadalajara was also much closer to the capital of the Viceroyalty of New Spain.

The Crown not only confirmed the change of the episcopal seat from Compostela to Guadalajara but also ordered the transfer of the audiencia because of the benefits this would bring to the Royal Treasury as a consequence of the discovery and exploitation of the mines in Zacatecas and, later, in San Martín, Sombrerete, Fresnillo, Chalchihuites, Nieves, and Mazapil, almost all of which were founded between 1546 and 1567. What continued to worry the colonial administration most, however, was the hostility of the Chichimec Indians, especially those of the Zacateca and Guachichil nations, whose ancestral territories had been invaded. After twenty years of armed conflict with the Spaniards, these Indians had learned to adapt their battle strategies.

The dimensions, biological diversity, contrasting environments, and coexistence of nomadic and sedentary Indians in that territory, which aspired to become a kingdom within the viceroyalty, were just some of the difficulties that the Spanish administration encountered, and it did so with varying degrees of success. The dispersed nature of the settlements and a less than homogeneous control over the area revealed regions with unstable population bases, especially in the mining zones. By 1575 the authorities of Nueva Galicia still had not managed to establish more than sixty-one clearly identifiable settlements subject to their jurisdiction through the system of corregimientos and *alcaldías mayores*. By that time, the audiencia had been moved from Compostela to Guadalajara, most of the encomiendas had been transformed into corregimientos, attacks by the Chichimecs were a constant along the roads and in the more isolated settlements, and tensions were running high between the magistrates in Guadalajara and the viceroy and audiencia of Mexico over the control of the northern reaches of Nueva Vizcaya. Alcaldías mayores were established in those places where the indigenous population was still fairly dense and in the mining settlements as a means of assuring the Crown's income from silver extraction. This distribution, as well as the spatial reorientation that resulted from the discovery and exploitation of the silver deposits, is shown in table 8.1.

Certain enclave areas in Nueva Galicia—such as the provinces of Colima and the frontiers with Michoacán and Nueva Vizcaya—were subject to the jurisdiction of New Spain and thus were placed beyond the administrative control of the audiencia of Guadalajara. As a result, even more pressure was exerted on Indian villages located there, and villagers could be carried away as tribute to work in the mines (see Contreras de Guevara 1569, cited in Fernández Sotelo 1994). The distance from those areas to Mexico City was daunting for any Indian or Spaniard who may have wished to challenge the imparting of justice, and it was a journey fraught with danger in both directions (Calvo 1997:21–25, 83–84). This was a constant source of demands by Indians and Spanish visitors during diverse historical moments in Nueva Galicia until at least 1570 (Orozco y Jiménez 1922:52–54; AGI, Justicia 305, fols. 155r–158v, mandamientos del 15 de abril de 1555, dictados por el oidor Lorenzo Lebrón de Quiñones).

There was a clear asymmetry between Indian settlements and Spanish towns in the four regions—Culiacán, Purificación, Compostela, and Guadalajara—described in the information that the audiencia of Nueva Galicia sent to the Crown in 1575. What stands out in the first area is the dramatic demographic decline in the early postconquest years, the gravity of which was reported in the several visitas undertaken in the mid-1600s by officials from Nueva Galicia and New Spain. Together with the difficult working conditions, slavery, and wars, the plagues and epidemics brought from the Old World ravaged the Indian population. In 1575–1576 one of the most calamitous epidemics of the century broke out in New Spain and Nueva Galicia, causing high mortality among the Indians. In a narrative written years later, this episode was associated with an astronomical event and thus acquired the character of an omen: "In the year 1576 a great pestilence and mortality among the *naturales* fell upon these lands that lasted for more than one year [and] ruined and destroyed most of New Spain, which was left with almost no Indians. A month before the mortality began a great sign was seen in the sky, [as] three rings were visible around the sun that seemed like three bloody suns or suns inflamed with fire because of the color. The three rings were like a rainbow [and] lasted from eight until almost one, after midday" (Real Academia de Historia [RAH], Colección Juan Bautista Muñoz, Libro de antigüedades que tenía Diego Panes, fol. 172r).

Given the terrible effects of this epidemic on Nueva Galicia, Juan Bautista de Orozco (the president of the audiencia of Guadalajara) declared:

God has been served through our sins since the plague has taken away a large number of the natives. Since it has not ended, I cannot cite the number of those affected. May our Lord God solve this problem as required and may He be pleased with my desire to see the Indians settled where I have mentioned rather than being buried there. If this plague were to please God, rather than having taken the friendly Indians, He would have taken the Chichimecs and eliminated them as He is doing with the others. Thus our plans would not be necessary since He who is the true planner does what is most needed. (AGI, México 69, carta de Juan Bautista de Orozco, a Felipe II, fechada el 25 de noviembre de 1575, in Naylor and Polzer 1986:52)

The gravity of this situation was such that it became necessary to implement urgent measures that included using resources from the Royal Treasury without previous authorization from the Consejo de Indias or the Crown. On the orders of the audiencia, royal officials in Nueva Galicia used 2,363 pesos in common gold to buy medicines and food, because the absence of those goods was exacerbating mortality among the Indians (AGI, Guadalajara 31, carta de los oficiales reales, fechada en Guadalajara el 3 de octubre de 1577, informando a Felipe II sobre el cocoliztli que afectó a los indios de Nueva Galicia; AGI, Guadalajara 230 Z 1, fol. 319r, real cédula de Felipe II, a los oficiales reales de Nueva Galicia, fechada en El Pardo a 28 de abril de 1578). The Crown urged the magistrates and members of the Royal Treasury to combat the epidemic, but even as late as 1577–1578 its ravages were still being felt in many areas of Nueva Galicia. According to audiencia reports, the authorities even enlisted the *encomenderos* to confront the problem by giving food to the sick Indians under their charge (AGI, Guadalajara 6, carta de la Audiencia de Nueva Galicia, a Felipe II, firmada por Santiago de Vera, Orozco y del Riego, fechada en Guadalajara el 2 de octubre de 1577). Among the bad news sent to the Crown was a report about a drastic decline in royal income and the threat of even greater losses in 1578 due to the enormous reduction of the Indian population. To cite one representative example, miners who before the outbreak of the epidemic had been operating five mills were able to operate only one or, at best, two because of the dearth of laborers (AGI, Guadalajara 230 Z 2, fols. 45v–46r, carta de Felipe II a Gerónimo de Orozco, presidente de la Audiencia de Guadalajara, fechada en San Lorenzo de El Escorial el 5 de junio de 1578; AGI, Guadalajara 6, carta de la Audiencia de Nueva Galicia, a Felipe II, firmada por Orozco, Alarcón y Del Riego, fechada en Guadalajara, 7 de marzo de 1577).

One important source for assessing the demographic decline of the Indian population is the "Relaciones geográficas" ordered by King Philip II in the decade of 1570. The section on Ameca mentions only 193 tributaries and a total

Table 8.1. Administrative Regions of Nueva Galicia, 1575.

Culiacan Province	La Purificación Province	Compostela Province	Guadalajara Province
1. Culiacán (*pueblo de indios*)	1. Piloto y Malato	1. Compostela and mines of Espíritu Santo, and *corregimiento* of the town of Tepic	1. Cuyutlán and Calatitlán
2. Baila	2. Pampuchin and Zapotlán	2. San Juan Iztapa	2. Tonalá
3. Tacolimbo	3. La Villa de la Purificación	3. Aguacatlán	3. Tlaxomulco
4. Guana and Xifo		4. Acalo and San Esteban	4. Mezquiticacán
5. Achiotla		5. Mascota	5. Nochistlanejo
6. Town of Vizcaíno		6. San Miguel and surrounding settlements	6. Atemajac
7. Tecuberito and Los Pescadores		7. Santiago Temichoque	7. San Pedro Tlacpal (Tlaquepaque)
8. Ayone		8. Santiago Iztapa	8. Analco and Tetlán
9. Cocala and Los Guamúchiles		9. Acatispa and Pontoque	9. Poncitlán
10. El Ostral, Cuatometo, and Nabolato		10. Suchipil	10. Mexcala
11. Ilarito		11. Jalisco	11. Matlatlán
12. Tecurimeto		12. Xala	12. Cuiseo
13. Cogota		13. Acaponeta, Quibito, and Totorame	13. Tequila
14. Yegualito and El Pescadero		14. Centicpac and surrounding settlements	14. Quilitlán and Copala

15. Chilobito

16. Navito and Ayabuto

17. Town of Culiacán

15. Villa of Jerez and Valley of Tlaltenango

16. Las Salinas Viejas

17. Mochiltitic

18. Villa of Santa María de los Lagos and corregimiento of Teocaltiche

19. Mines of Acuitlapilco and Chimaltitlán and *corregidor* in the towns of Atepusguacán and Zacatlán and surrounding settlements

20. Mines of Fresnillo and San Demetrio

21. Mines of Guachinango and corregidor of Atengoychan

22. Mines of the Zacatecas

23. Mines of Xocotlán and corregimiento of the towns of Guaxacatlán, Cacalote, and Mezquitique and surrounding settlements

24. Mines of Tepeque and *corregimiento* of Juchipila and Nochistlán

25. Mines of Las Charcas

26. Mines and villa of San Martín and villa of Llerena

27. Mines of Mazapil

Source: AGI, Guadalajara 6, "Memoria de todos los cargos de alcaldías mayores y corregimientos que se proveen en todo el Nuevo Reino de Galicia y qué tanto tiene cada uno de salario y en qué personas están proveídos, y de qué tiempo a esta parte como Vuestra Majestad lo manda . . . proveyóse a diez y siete mes de febrero" de 1575.

population of 300 in 1579, compared to a population of over 2,000 Indian warriors (i.e., men in their prime) at the moment of the Spaniards' arrival in that province, a figure that extrapolates to a population above 6,000.

Large numbers of Indians had been brought down from the hills and re-settled in humid areas, an action that later facilitated the outbreak and propagation of epidemics. It was reported that they "died while coming and going with the loads of gear [*jarcías*] that they carried to the Port of Navidad [for shipment] to China" and while traveling to other places as bearers (Acuña 1988:30–31). A similar situation occurred in the towns of Zapotitlán, Tuscacuesco, Cusalapa, Compostela, Tlaltenango, Purificación, Nochistlán (only 252 tribute payers left from a total of over 4,000), Tenamaztlán (860 tribute payers and a remnant population of 2,500; the original population had been double that figure), Teocaltiche (200 Indian warriors in 1585, compared to over 1,000 before), and Xocotlán.

According to the "Relaciones geográficas," the population of those sedentary Indian towns was decimated by plagues, forced resettlement, forced labor, and abandonment in search of sites far removed from Spanish control and war. Despite the imprecise figures available, the differences are enormous: in Nochistlán, for example, the 1576–1577 epidemic caused the death of "two-thirds" (Acuña 1988:167). Similarly, mining towns that had had no sedentary Indian population before the arrival of the Spaniards either ceased to grow or had to be abandoned because of attacks by the Chichimecs. The case of the mines at Charcas in the modern state of San Luis Potosí is illustrative: around 1577 it was forced to relocate twice because of raids by the Guachichiles (AGI, Indiferente General 1090, ramo 11, no. 297, relación de Martín Despés, clérigo presbítero del obispado de Guadalajara, sin fecha, documento elaborado entre 1576 y 1577).

Near the end of the sixteenth century, tenuous lines of communication were extended from Nueva Galicia toward the north and northeast, which, together with the creation of the kingdom of Nueva Vizcaya and the opening of the mines at Santa Bárbara in 1598, resulted in the founding of the kingdom of New Mexico in light of Juan de Oñate's expedition. In the same period, the establishment of Mazapil (1567), Saltillo (1577), and Monterrey (1596) in the northeast opened a route toward the province of Texas (Alessio Robles 1978; John 1996; Rodríguez-Sala et al. 1995).

Evangelization and Indigenous Society

The second important initiative implemented by the Crown to assert its royal dominion was its evangelization project, which from its formative stage in 1531 until the mid-1570s was administered almost exclusively by Franciscans and the secular clergy. The gradual increase in the number of Franciscans in

Nueva Galicia, especially in the 1530s, proved insufficient to carry out an evangelization capable of bringing stability to the emerging society there. Convents like the ones in Etzatlán and Juchipila were key points for bringing Indians into closer contact with the new religious and social orders, but the small number of friars, the mental shock that the Indians had suffered while witnessing the destruction of their world, their subjection to encomiendas and excessive forced labor, plus the enslavement of thousands of their brethren had all combined to impede their acceptance of the "goodness" predicated by those lesser friars. Two of those Franciscans—Antonio de Cuéllar, the *guardián* at Etzatlán, and Juan de la Esperanza—paid a particularly heavy price for their evangelizing efforts, as they lost their lives in the Mixtón War (AGI, Justicia 262, pieza 2, Auto de inicio para los descargos del Virrey Mendoza en las ciudades de Guadalajara y Compostela, fol. 122r, declaración de Alonso Álvarez, 1546). Years later, the Franciscans recognized that the mistreatment, enslavement, and death of so many Indians were fundamental causes of the rebellion of 1540–1541 (Ávila Márquez 2006). Near the end of that decade, after almost fifteen years of labor among the Indians, there were only twelve friars and three convents in Nueva Galicia, a number clearly insufficient to fulfill the aims of evangelization.

By 1554 the Franciscans had developed their plan for the evangelization and social organization of the Indians and proposed founding several towns with farming families brought from Spain as a means of consolidating the territory and setting an example for the Indians. The friars felt this approach might work, since colonizing initiatives centered on the mines and mining had not produced the permanent settling of any social group (RAH, Colección Juan Bautista Muñoz A/114, carta de fray Juan de Armellones, al rey, fechada en Guadalajara el 20 de septiembre de 1554). In fact, the Franciscans repeated this proposal to the king and the Consejo de Indias several times during the sixteenth century as a peaceful means of settling the indigenous population (Al respecto, otra propuesta de la orden franciscana introdujo un matiz para consolidar a la población en campamentos mineros, AGI, Guadalajara 65, relación de fray Diego Rengel, escrita en el convento de San Francisco de Tepeyacac el 25 de diciembre de 1578; Sarabia Viejo 1978:263–265).

Indian Wars in Nueva Galicia

The Mixtón War, also known as the general rebellion of Nueva Galicia, occurred between 1540 and 1542 and would be the last war in which the Indians fought using their precontact weapons and strategies. The Mixtón uprising forced the Spaniards to mount an enormous war effort using primarily Indians from the Valley of Mexico plus a large contingent of Spanish soldiers, almost all of whom had had extensive experience in conquest situations in different areas of Mesoamerica. Moreover, it was the only armed conflict led personally by the viceroy, who was forced to leave his seat in the city, an event that would never again occur in the following 270 years of colonial rule. More than a religious war against Christianity and its symbols and rituals, the Mixtón War was a movement that sought to revitalize the threatened Indian identity. The starting point (as all contemporary sources agree) was a message (*tlatol*) sent by nomadic Indians (Chichimecs of the Zacateca nation) to the Caxcans, sedentary Indians living in Juchipila.

Any evaluation of that message must take into account its capacity to call both nomadic and sedentary Indians to collective armed action, given that these two groups have traditionally been considered as separate and, often, in permanent opposition due to conflicts over boundaries and means of subsistence. Images in documents of the period show contrasting customs, lifeways, and social structures that seem to suggest irreconcilable differences between nomadic and sedentary groups. However, the existence of the tlatol and its dissemination by the Zacateca Indians to every indigenous town in Nueva Galicia suggests that they must have shared certain religious beliefs and deities.

The testimony of the military leader and political administrator Cristóbal de Oñate in 1547 regarding "el habla del diablo" (the speech of the devil) is relevant, as it was given just a few years after the end of the Mixtón War. When the general rebellion broke out in Nueva Galicia, Oñate was the person most familiar with the region, its features, the Indian groups who lived there, and their lifeways. In his statement, Oñate expressed the meaning of the tlatol for those groups: "And be it known also that at the time of the rebellion there were some towns that informed [this] witness and his superiors that they protect the cattle and haciendas that they had in their towns and that they provide Spaniards who were there to resist the other rebellious Indians who carried the devil's message, *because if the devil's message ever entered those towns, they would have no choice but to rise up*" (AGI, Justicia 262, pieza 2, Auto de inicio para los descargos, fol. 172v, declaración de Cristóbal de Oñate, 1547).

Those who lived through the rebellion in Nueva Galicia and later testified in judicial acts, both Indians and Spaniards, all agreed that the starting point of the war was the tlatol from the Zacateca Indians, which was carried to the Caxcans in Juchipila and from there was propagated by those groups to every corner of Nueva Galicia. The uprising spread over the entire territory, including areas where the Spaniards had not yet penetrated. In effect, the peoples who received the tlatol "could not but rebel." The Indians who participated in the message from the "great devil" renounced Christian beliefs and returned to their ancient gods and rites, while those who remained neutral because they did not receive the tlatol or because they rejected it were often attacked by the rebels. Oñate stated that "the rebel Indians marauded over the lands of those who were in peace and as they refused to rise up with them captured as many as they could" (AGI, Justicia 262, pieza 2, Auto de inicio para los descargos, fols. 174v–175r, declaración de Cristóbal de Oñate).

How could this message from the nomadic Zacateca Indians have had such an impact on sedentary groups living so far from their habitual roaming areas and even among the nomadic groups that inhabited the mountainous western sierra? This can only be explained through ancestral cultural connections, symbolic exchanges, and shared gods and rites, the strength of which were unquestioned by the peoples who received the message. Though living under Spanish dominion and the evangelizing pressures of the Franciscans, the Indians closed ranks and united in a widespread uprising because of the religious force of the tlatol, the threat of attacks against those who did not accept it, and the real possibility of that threat being carried out.

Testimonies by Indian witnesses provide clues that reveal that the "great devil" who produced the tlatol was Tezcatlipoca, the "Lord of the Smoky Mirror," one of the most complex and enigmatic gods of the precontact world (Olivier Durand 1997). In 1547 the indigenous governor of Juchipila, the Caxcan town from which the message of the uprising was spread by Zacateca messengers, spoke of the conditions in which the rebellion in Nueva Galicia began:

> Some eight years ago, while this witness was in Juchipila, the usual [leader] of the town was Juyteque. One night this witness saw that certain Zacateca Indian messengers arrived, met with Cuish, and went with him to Juyteque and told him to join them, that they brought as their [leader] the word and deed of Tezcatepocal the devil, to say that all the land should come together and that the fathers and grandfathers and ancestors would resuscitate and join with them and that they should kill all the Christians in this province of México and rise up and take the land; and from that moment they would not have to work, as the corn and other seeds would grow in just one day, and to tell them that all those who did not wish to believe the word of their devil would die with the Christians. That speech was kept secret by Juyteque for some days until he and his people joined the uprising with the other insurrectionists and rebels, and from that moment this witness saw that Juyteque was in rebellion and would not obey the clergy or Hernán Flores, his master, and in this way they led them to understand many such frivolities and trickeries, that were later revealed as lies and deception, all of which this witness knew that the messengers had said and spread to many towns. (AGI, Justicia 262, pieza 2, Auto de inicio para los descargos, fols. 439v–440r, declaración de Juan Juchipila, and fol. 444r, declaración de Martín, 1547)

Though from another region and historical period, the tradition of Indian rebellions among the Chichimecs was reinforced by another "call to arms" from Tezcatlipoca, issued during the earlier era in which the Toltecs were dominated by the Olmecs and Xicallancas and, exhausted by mistreatment, were lamenting their fate. At that moment, Tezcatlipoca appeared before them to ease their dejection and raise their spirits to fight their oppressors, promising that they would become the lords of those towns. The indigenous record of that deity's words is most illuminating:

> Do not be desperate, as we are in our land. It is my concern. After all, am I not two, am I not three? We shall destroy the Olmecs, the Xicallancas. *And this is how we shall begin the war to destroy them: we shall compose a song, dance [and] intone the* pancuicatl *[song]. Then Tezcatlipoca sang. . . . And when he had sung he told them: "Listen well, as this shall be your song.* Pay heed. Do not faint! Do not go to the Olmecs and Xicallancas to take their properties, but rather the insignias they use, the club [*macana*] and shield. Go to them, make them receive the song, your enemies will dance with it, the tlatoque of the Olmecs and the Xicallancas. Hey! Pay heed!" (Kirchhoff et al. 1976:152–153, my translation, emphasis added)

After receiving the tlatol from Tezcatlipoca, the two Toltec lords undertook the journey to Chicomoztoc to call to arms the seven Chichimec tribes that were "asleep" there and to make them allies in their war against the Olmecs and Xicallancas. In several codices, Tezcatlipoca was identified with war, with discord among people, and with the ability to seduce and direct human action (Olivier Durand 1997:43 ff.).

Tezcatlipoca was a god of northern origin in whom both nomadic and sedentary Indians shared a belief. He survived the destruction of the ancient indigenous cultures in the north and west and played a major role in the rebellion in Nueva Galicia in 1540 (Olivier Durand and Román Gutiérrez 2008; Román Gutiérrez 1988). From an archaeological perspective, Phil Weigand has argued that this deity also was present in the Chalchihuite culture, where "the first systematic evidence of this god's ceremonial complex appears" (see chapter 3 in this volume).

Thus, there were deeply shared religious and cultural roots among nomadic and sedentary Indian groups in the territory of Nueva Galicia that, despite the conquest and a decade of evangelizing, retained sufficient strength to convince the Indians to mount the largest rebellion in the colonial history of New Spain (Ruiz Medrano 1994). Though it ended in defeat for the indigenous peoples, the Mixtón War exercised an enormous influence on Indian religiosity in the sixteenth century, as shown in the ongoing Chichimec uprisings that later spread into northern Nueva Vizcaya.

Black Ash Dye

Through the Mixtón War the Indians sought to recover their ancient traditions and to distance themselves from all signs of foreign-imposed Christian identity. On the other side, the colonial authorities—in this case, Viceroy Mendoza—went to extraordinary lengths to justify a war that, according to some contemporary commentators, would cause severe problems in the Viceroyalty of New Spain (Ruiz Medrano 1994:365 ff.). By collecting testimonies about the war, the administration wished to legitimize its actions and demonstrate the grave peril that the rebellion in Nueva Galicia represented for the entire colonial system. A particular effort was made to expose the anti-Christian nature of the rebellion. Testimonies were collected that, because they reflected the interests of the viceroy, allow us to gain a better understanding of the rebellion and the beliefs and gods on which it was based. To give one example: upon receiving the tlatol of war and various ritual and material insignia from the Zacateca messengers, the Indians who chose to participate painted their hair and faces with black ash dye (*tile*), an act that the Spaniards interpreted as a mockery of the sacrament of baptism.

Witnesses to the uprising affirmed that they had seen the rebel Indians repudiate baptism, the sacrament that made them Christians. Many rebels had been involved in the evangelizing process in Nueva Galicia either under the Franciscans or through their encomenderos. Although these acts of repudiation were visible, the Indians' thought processes and commitment to erasing all signs of Christian baptism were not. A judicial process began in January 1547, six years after the defeat of the Indians at Mixtón Hill. In several cities and villages of Nueva Galicia, a total of 37 Spaniards and 31 Indian participants were called by prosecutors who had been sent by Viceroy Mendoza to collect "favorable" testimonies. With regard to the act (of imposing the black ash dye) that the Spaniards interpreted as an expression of the Indians' intent to wipe away Christian baptism, the only Spaniard who testified was Oñate. Though he admitted that he had never witnessed such acts directly, he stated: "Later [I heard] those pardoned here say they had rejected the faith and washed their heads to wipe away the baptism they had received, and that they were repentant of the time they were Christians" (AGI, Justicia 262, pieza 2, Auto de inicio para los descargos, fol. 175r, declaración de Cristóbal de Oñate, 1547). No other Spanish witness from Nueva Galicia gave an account of this practice.

In contrast, 10 Indian testimonies provided a more complete description of this ceremony. Washing the head and face with black dye, as the governor of Iztlán was said to have done with other town principales and lords, was evidence of a rejection of Christian baptism and of the faith that had been transmitted to the new believers (AGI, Justicia 262, pieza 2, Auto de inicio para los descargos, fol. 139r, declaración de Juan, 1547).

The association of the color black with Tezcatlipoca is well known, but the Zacateca Indians to whom the Spaniards attributed the outbreak of the rebellion in 1540 (and identified as the spell-casting carriers of the tlatol) also were noted for their use of that color. In ceremonies associated with Tezcatlipoca, the "Lord of the Smoky Mirror" (a black obsidian mirror described in several codices and chronicles), priests painted their faces and bodies black with soot from candles or torches. Also associated with this deity was the use of ground charcoal and ash for the same purpose. Friar Diego Durán, who wrote about indigenous gods and rites, left a graphic description of Tezcatlipoca's food, the composition of which resulted in a black color, similar to the dye with which his priests painted themselves. The use of black after the conquest to evoke darkness and suggest the invisibility of the gods may have meant, as Guilhem Olivier Durand (1997:211–212) has suggested, a return to the ancient religion. On the use of black, there is a salient reference from the Yanhuitlán Codex: "I ordered the fathers to go to the hills and make charcoal and bring it, grind it and make a dye, and don Francisco [removed his clothes], painted himself with soot, and said: 'Now I am no longer a Christian but as I used to be,' then he perforated his ears and perfumed himself with copal" (Olivier Durand 1997:215–216, my translation; see also Durán 1971:47, 119).

In the *relación* from the village of Jerez, written in 1584, we find another reference to the identification of the Zacateca Indians with black: "The nation of Indians of this region that has been depopulated were of the Zacateca nation, which in their language means 'black head'" (Acuña 1988:138). Those Indians called on the lords and *principales* of the Caxcan villages to carry the *tlatol* to all the Indians in Nueva Galicia. In reference to them, Diego Vázquez Alonso, a principal of Apozol, declared that "*as they were credible persons* [people] came from many areas of Caxcan and Tonalá to hear them and join them." Similarly, the governor of Apozol described the Zacateca Indians as having the ability to invoke the sacred (AGI, Justicia 262, pieza 2, Auto de inicio para los descargos, fols. 187v, 448v, 452r, 1547, emphasis added).

But what was it that made them "credible persons" in the eyes of other sedentary Indians? The following hypothesis is plausible: the Zacateca messengers were recognized as priests and spokespersons of Tezcatlipoca and, as such, had the power to convene and meet with the Indian lords of the Caxcan towns, several of whom washed their faces and then painted them with the black dye to transform themselves into messengers who would carry the *tlatol* to other Indian towns. According to judicial statements from 1547 (AGI, Justicia 262, pieza 2, Auto de inicio para los descargos, fols. 129v, 139r, 141v, 143r, 144v, 446v, 1547), this happened with the lords of Tetitlán, Iztlán, Mezpan, Aguacatlán, Suchipil, and Juchipila, and with some Indians (e.g., Pedro Quéchul from Tetitlán) who were not of the nobility or local elite.

This ritual, always performed at Indian altars in the hills in front of images of the "demon," were accompanied with perfume, probably incense (León-Portilla 1992:49), human sacrifice, and offerings of hearts. It seems to have been invested with an unquestioned solemnity, even though it took place in the midst of a war against the Spaniards. A second hypothesis holds that rebellion and resistance to the Spaniards demanded—it could hardly be otherwise—performing rigorous rituals presided over by Tezcatlipoca himself as a means of fulfilling the auguries and actions that would bring the defeat of the Christians of Nueva Galicia and New Spain (see Olivier Durand 1997:43–46).

Coloring one's head and face with black dye can be interpreted as an act of incarnating the deity, or at least some of his attributes, before spreading the tlatol. In his chronicles, Friar Durán referred to processes of incarnating ancient gods in the early period of Spanish dominion through certain ritual functions, mentioning specifically the case of Tezcatlipoca (1971:71–72).

The supposed rejection of Christian baptism went hand in hand with the symbolic act of washing the head "and applying black dye to the face, as it was understood that the devil would be very angry if they did not do so, thus they did it and made sacrifices" (AGI, Justicia 262, pieza 2, Auto de inicio para los descargos, fols. 137v–138r, declaración de Pedro Quéchul, and fols. 138v–139r, declaración de don Juan, 1547; see also Durán 1971:37, 47). But let us look at other elements of that ritual process. The *alguacil* of Cuzpaltlan stated that the tlatol messengers also carried flint blades and other objects (AGI, Justicia 262, pieza 2, Auto de inicio para los descargos, fol. 457r, declaración de Juan, 1547). Another Indian witness from Cuzpaltlan stated that, in addition to flint blades, they also bore feathers, all wrapped in deerskin (AGI, Justicia 262, pieza 2, Auto de inicio para los descargos, fol. 460r, declaración de Martín, 1547; see also Durán 1971:99). Upon receiving the tlatol from the carriers, one of the two governors of Tetitlán gave them bells to offer to the "devil" (AGI, Justicia 262, pieza 2, Auto de inicio para los descargos, fol. 140v, declaración de Pedro, 1547; see also Durán 1971:99). On the topic of the squash that also accompanied the message, five Spanish and two Indian witnesses mentioned that it was part of the "call to war" (AGI, Justicia 262, pieza 2, Auto de inicio para los descargos, fol. 400r, declaración de Hernando, 1547). Another source speaks of arrows carried by the tlatol messengers, with "beads, *nóminas*, and colored threads." In sixteenth-century Castilian, nóminas were small bags or bundles (AGI, Justicia 262, pieza 2, Auto de inicio para los descargos, fol. 400r, declaración de Tomás Gil, 1547; Covarrubias Orozco 1984:830) in which Indians kept sacred objects to protect them from evil. According to Friar Bernardino de Sahagún's informants, all of these objects, reported fragmentarily by different witnesses, reflect characteristics of the god Tezcatlipoca: "On his head there was a *flint headdress, he had stripes at the level of his eyes*, his earrings were of gold twisted into spirals. He bears a *pot made of quetzal feathers*, his bracelets were of *flint. His legs are striped with black lines*, and on his legs he has rattles, *bells, round bells*, [and] obsidian-colored sandals. On his arm he has a shield trimmed with feathers and a banner made of paper, the perforated mirror in one hand, with which he looks at the people" (León-Portilla 1992:117, emphasis added). Arrows wrapped in deerskin were another material vehicle that gave substance to the tlatol. In addition to confirming the genuineness of the message transmitted by the carriers, the arrows were a clear call to begin the war: "[The] arrows were sent from one town to another to attract them to the devil's tlatol" (AGI, Justicia 262, pieza 2, Auto de inicio para los descargos, fol. 191v, declaración de Diego Vázquez, and fol. 210v, declaración de Juan de Ojeda, 1547; see also Durán 1971:99). The Indian towns that had refused to join the rebellion were later brought into the war when they received the message accompanied by a threat: if they did not participate in the fight against the Spaniards, they would be destroyed.

Revitalization

In the general scheme of the Indian rebellion, expelling the Spaniards was considered not only an act that would manifest the power of the ancient gods but one that would bring the recovery of the world that had been lost to the conquest. That return was not to be a simple "going back" but a new creation in every sense of the word. The "ancestors and grandfathers shall come back to life" and bring an abundance of food to the rebels, no matter where they were, in no more than five days (AGI, Justicia 262, pieza 2, Auto de inicio para los descargos, fol. 137v, declaración de Pedro Quéchul, 1547).

The uprising in Nueva Galicia began on the eve of St. John's Day, June 23, 1540, a significant date for two reasons: first, its proximity to the summer solstice, an astronomical and calendrical event of great ritual importance recognized by all prehispanic groups in Mesoamerica and among the groups of hunter-gatherers known as Chichimecs (Aveni 1994); second, the coincidence of planting time with the arrival of the summer solstice. Under such circumstances, mobilizing for war would have prevented the sedentary Indians from carrying out the agricultural activities that provided their sustenance. This explains the importance of the promise that the ancestors would bring food upon the Indians' return.

On this point, a declaration by one of the principales from the town of Suchipil (or Suchipila) in the Aguacatlán valley is particularly important. He affirmed that "the Indians of this province made very few plantings" in anticipation of the return of the ancestors and the death of the Christians (AGI, Justicia 262, pieza 2, Auto de inicio para los descargos, fol. 144v, declaración de Alonso, 1547), a statement that seems to relate the return of the "natural" abundance that existed in preconquest times (i.e., sources of sustenance that would magically provide abundance upon the return of the ancestors and the death of the Christians) to the impossibility of planting at the onset of the agricultural cycle because the Indians would be busy fulfilling the prophecies disseminated by the Zacatecan and Caxcan messengers.

The return to the "old times" augured by the resuscitation of the ancestors held out another promise, one related to the destruction of the living conditions imposed by the conquest. The brutal enslavement begun by Nuño de Guzmán and extended by the encomiendas and corregimientos, together with the public labors that the Indians were forced to perform, had ruptured all the work processes of the indigenous societies. Thus, the return to the old order was also the promise of a respite from the hardships the Indians had suffered under the thumb of their Spanish conquerors.

The dispute between Spaniards and Indians was not limited to a conflict of religions, differentiated labor systems, and opposing cultural forms. It also included confrontations over effective territorial occupation, another facet of the conflict expressed in the promise that the Indians would recover the full territorial dominion they had enjoyed before it was destroyed by the Spanish occupation. One declaration that indicates this was made by a man from Etzatlán who expressed in his testimony ideas of the return of deceased relatives, an abundance of food, a return to the peace that the conquerors had taken from them, the absence of plantings at the outset of the rebellion, and the recovery of power by the Indians. (AGI, Justicia 262, pieza 2, Auto de inicio para los descargos, fol. 151r, declaración de Francisco, 1547)

In addition to "washing" and painting their hair and faces black as a way of recovering the signs of their ancient gods, the rebel Indians set out to destroy Christian images, crosses, temples, and convents in an attempt to eradicate all traces and visible signs of the conquerors' religion. Those actions culminated with the already mentioned deaths of two Franciscans, who were shot with arrows and beaten with clubs. (AGI, Justicia 262, pieza 2, Auto de inicio para los descargos, fol. 156v, declaración de Antonio, and fol. 222v, declaración de Diego Hurtado, 1547)

The death of the two friars was acutely important in the context of the war and the area of Nueva Galicia: they were the first Franciscans to suffer martyrdom in the entire Viceroyalty of New Spain; in fact, they were the first martyrs among all the orders active there (see Zurita 1999:672–680). The Indians' desecration of Christian images, blasphemies, and destruction of crosses and churches completed the profile of a war in which both sides advanced the symbols and agents of their respective religious beliefs in a nonnegotiable confrontation over the dominion and status of the sacred. Perhaps as a response to the destruction of the Indian altars and images that Guzmán had ordered in 1530, the villages called to war by the tlatol in 1540 battled against what they believed to be one of the sources of Spanish power. To demonstrate the weakness of the new gods, "in some of their altars the Indians had an image of Our Lady . . . sewn on a seat where to mock her rebel Indians in the province of Aguacatlán would sit." A Spanish soldier also reported seeing images of the Virgin and other saints sewn in similar fashion (AGI, Justicia 262, pieza 2, Auto de inicio para los descargos, fol. 103v, declaración de Juan Pascual, and declaración de Jerónimo Pérez de Arciniega, 1547). Another Spaniard wrote that the Indians who took refuge in the mountains spoke with "belligerent and ugly words that cause great shame to Christians because they defame and disdain the Lord our God and his sacred Catholic faith," thus belittling a principle that the conquerors held in highest esteem: respect for and submission to Christianity by those who had been indoctrinated and incorporated into the church (AGI, Justicia 262, pieza 2, Auto de inicio para los descargos, fol. 121r, declaración de Alonso Álvarez, 1547).

In several geographical areas of Nueva Galicia, Indians also held up tortillas to simulate the consecration of the Communion wafers (*hostias*), an act that the Spanish may have interpreted as another attack on Christianity by the rebels. Indeed, in one of the Indian temples or altars on the Mixtón Hill, one perhaps installed there during the rebellion itself, an observer saw "one of the rebel Indians, who had been a Christian and lived among Christians . . . raise a corn tortilla like a communion wafer to mock the sacred sacrament" along with other ceremonies, including the scattering of perfumes (AGI, Justicia 262, pieza 2, Auto de inicio para los descargos, fol. 233r, declaración de Francisco Cornejo, 1547).

The case of using corn tortillas as Communion wafers suggests two possible interpretations: because corn was the staple grain of Mesoamerican cultures, tortillas stood out in many ancient rites, as the "Historia Tolteca-Chichimeca" shows, but this does not preclude their blasphemous use as a weapon against the Spaniards. Whatever the case, all of the witnesses' statements on raising tortillas suggest that this act was indeed carried out in the context of indigenous rituals (AGI, Justicia 262, pieza 2, declaraciones de Pedro, señor de Tetitlán; Juan, gobernador de Iztlán; Pedro, señor de otra parte de Tetitlán; Diego, señor de Mespan; Pedro, principal de Aguacatlán; fray Pedro de la Concepción, guardián del convento de Etzatlán; Cristóbal de Oñate, minero de Zacatecas; Francisco Cornejo, vecino de Guadalajara; Francisco, indio de Tequila; Juan, señor y gobernador de Juchipila; Martín, señor y gobernador de Apozol; and Martín, principal y naguatlato de Juchipila, fol. 446v, 1547).

The "Historia Tolteca-Chichimeca" contains another very suggestive element: the day on which the Toltecas Icxicouatl and Quetzalteueyac arrived at Colhuacatepec (Crooked Hill), site of the mythical cave of Chicomoztoc, which housed the eight Chichimec tribes (Quauhtinchantlaca, Moquiuixca, Totomiuaque, Acolchichimeca, Tzauhcteca, Zacateca, Texcalteca, and Malpantlaca), to call them to the fight as allies against the Olmecs and Xicallancas, "they sat there and performed their rites to invoke their creator and inventor." The next day, Icxicouatl said to Quetzalteueyac: "Make it thin" (*tlacanaua* in Náhuatl), and so he did. This expression was used to refer to the gods having extended and thinned the land during the act of creation. According to contemporary studies in the Huasteca, the word *tlacanaua* literally means "to make tortillas"; therefore, the act of "thinning" may be understood as symbolizing the creation of the world, with the tortilla representing the world created by the gods in a mythology in which one of the Chichimec tribes—the Zacatecas—participated (Kirchhoff et al. 1976:162–163). There are still more references to the use of tortillas in ritual: during the Izcalli fiesta, offerings given consist of tortillas prepared in front of an image of the god of fire, Xiuhtechutli; also, young people made small tortillas in their homes to offer to the gods at dawn (Sahagún 1959–1981:161, 194; see also León-Portilla 1992:47). Finally, Durán tells us that tortillas were offered to the god Tezcatlipoca (1984:53).

The Great Devil

In another ritual feature of the rebellion, the Zacateca and Caxcan Indians spread messages of the destruction that the ancient gods would bring down upon the native peoples if they remained in the Christian religion and did not rise up against the Spaniards. The order to destroy all Spaniards was delivered with greater emphasis still, as they were identified as Christians, the invaders of their lands, and the agents of the extirpation of their religious beliefs. The Indian god—called the "great devil" by the judicial authorities—would help them win the rebellion against the Christians, the Spaniards, and other Indians and "would create a great opening in the earth into which all Christians would be sucked, and then a great flame of fire would come sent by the devil and the Christians and all Indians who did not wish to take up arms and rebel would be swept up and burned and, that done, they would go on to Mexico [City], subdue it and do the same" (AGI, Justicia 262, pieza 2, Auto de inicio para los descargos, fols. 134r–134v, declaración de don Cristóbal, 1547).

Perhaps the presaging of the destruction of the Christians was part of the Indians' war strategies. They spoke of a generalized destruction that would "cleanse" Nueva Galicia and New Spain of all types of Christians, be they Spaniards or Indians. Indeed, in some towns the tlatol announced that the Christians in Mexico City had already been destroyed and that the rebellion was now aimed at exterminating those of Nueva Galicia (AGI, Justicia 262, pieza 2, Auto de inicio para los descargos, fols. 137r–137v, declaración de Pedro Quéchul, 1547). Alonso López, the encomendero of Iztlán, found out from one of the principales of that town and from an interpreter (*nahuatlato*) that the rebels "were going to kill all Christians" (AGI, Justicia 262, pieza 2, Auto de inicio para los descargos, fol. 107r, 1547). The indigenous lord of Tetitlán admitted that he had joined the uprising because the Indians of Iztlán and the Caxcans had told him that they were to kill all the Christians in the land (AGI, Justicia 262, pieza 2, Auto de inicio para los descargos, fol. 129v, 1547). Juan Fernández de Hijar, a Spanish captain who was active in the war, pointed out that the rebel Indians boasted that "they would kill all the Christians in New Spain with three arrows, as well as those who come by sea and from Castile" (AGI, Justicia 262, pieza 2, Auto de inicio para los descargos, fol. 243v, 1547). A principal from Juchipila stated that the aim of the rebel Indians was to take back their lands, in the material and symbolic senses of dominion and power, adding that in order to do so they intended to "kill all the Christians [on the land]," as announced in the tlatol (AGI, Justicia 262, pieza 2, Auto de inicio para los descargos, fol. 445r, 1547). Another principal, this one from the town of Contla and also an active agent in the Mixtón rebellion, stated that the Indians intended to "kill all the Christians and to be free on the land with their artfulness and sorcery of old" (AGI, Justicia 262, pieza 2, Auto de inicio para los descargos, fol. 463r, 1547).

Resistance after the Mixtón War

One of the immediate consequences of the Mixtón War and the Indian defeat was the demise of the lords and elders of the Caxcan towns. The lord of Juchipila—Xiuhtecutli, or Juytecle—was one of the first to die at the hands of Spanish justice. With him, 10 other lords suffered the same fate after they were found guilty of rebellion (AGI, Justicia 262, pieza 2, Auto de inicio para los descargos, fol. 445v, declaración de Martín, 1547; Román Gutiérrez 1996:29).

Some other towns were only superficially aware of the rebellion, as in the case of the Indians of Tepique (Tepic), whose lord stated that he had learned of events through comments by a variety of Indians but had never acted directly on either side, Indian or Spanish. The salient point is that processes of communication continued to exist among villages despite the conflagrations and the magnitude of the conflict (AGI, Justicia 262, pieza 2, Auto de inicio para los descargos, fols. 136r–136v, declaración de don Francisco, 1547).

Other groups maintained an active resistance even after the defeat at Mixtón. Some Caxcans who had been displaced from their hometowns and others who lived in areas that the Spanish found hard to reach (e.g., the Sierra Madre Occidental) were still repelling Spanish attempts to impose control at the end of the decade of 1540, while others who earlier had been settled in that area continued to wage religious warfare against the Spaniards, despite the defeat of the main rebel forces a few years earlier.

Let us look briefly at some illustrative cases documented by the magistrate Martínez de la Marcha during his visita to Nueva Galicia in 1549. At the Tepeque mines, a mining district later known as Bolaños, Indians from the town of Pochotitlán declared that they had been threatened by a cacique named Chapuli and a large group of warring Indians from Nochistlán (the village of the leader Tenamastle), who had entered their town, burned down the church, killed several Indians, and carried away four young women. Certain Indians who managed to speak to the invaders asked them what the motive of the attack was; the response was that Chapuli had ordered them "to kill and destroy all of them, and after that the Christians" (AGI, Guadalajara 46, no. 33, translated from information provided by Toribio de Bolaños, 1549).

Several participants in the Mixtón War made statements on the similarity of the protests with which the war had begun and the actions occurring seven years after its conclusion (AGI, Guadalajara 46, no. 34, "probanza de lo de Coringa," realizada por el oidor Hernán Martínez de la Marcha en la ciudad de Compostela el 6 de noviembre de 1549, fols. 1r–1v, declaración de Juan Pascual, 1549). It turns out that, from their refuge in the mountains of the Sierra Madre Occidental in northern Nueva Galicia, the rebels continued to attack Indian towns like Tequila and Colotlán and the Tepeque mines, all of which were at peace under the Spanish encomienda system:

> Now what that Indian Coringa began to do, in the same way as before, as this witness is from that area and has been where said Indian Coringa is and lives, [he] saw Indian cantors leave the church and go to the sierra where the tlatol of the uprising is [found] and [saw] that all the Indians that are at peace and in Christian doctrine were adopting bad ways, doing the dances of old, and not planting or attending what they had planted, but letting the weeds grow up in their corn and cotton fields because of their [belief] in the past uprising, and they say they must not stop dancing until their mothers and fathers resuscitate, and that with dancing and singing they shall come, secretly, so the Christians do not hear of the uprising in the land, and [they will] kill all the Christians as they did the other time they rebelled. (AGI, Guadalajara 46, no. 34, "probanza de lo de Coringa," realizada por el oidor Hernán Martínez de la Marcha en la ciudad de Compostela el 6 de noviembre de 1549, declaración de Juan Pascual, fols. 1v–2r)

Indian resistance thus continued in hard-to-reach areas under various guises and with the ritual and religious character that had motivated the Mixtón War, as evidenced well by a Spaniard who participated in the events of 1540–1542 and those of the subsequent years in the territory of Nueva Galicia:

> At that time said Coringa sent Indians who were at peace a squash with three arrows inside and told them it was a sign of war against the Christians, that they must dance and not obey the Spanish Christians in any way because while dancing they would secretly take up arms against the Christians without being perceived; then that same Coringa sent another messenger to tell the Indians who were at peace that the devil Tayán was coming burdened with the dead, that in three years he would not reach the place where they were and that they should hurry to dance, and after this he sent another [to say] that if they wanted to see their fathers and mothers resuscitated they should hurry to dance and that the women were to dance naked in the flesh, as thus the devil had ordered, and that if one were to die that said death was to be reported to the Chichimec fools, so it was ordered by Tayán, and the Christians were to be [tied to] stones so that while

they slept a wind would come and hurl them into the salty sea from whence they came from Spain. (AGI, Guadalajara 46, no. 34, "probanza de lo de Coringa," fols. 2v–3r, 1549)

A final reference to this period mentions attacks by Tezol Indians from the town of Talistacan on the Indians of Tequila, the former led by their cacique and principal, Elote. An Indian woman who witnessed those events and whose spouse was imprisoned and accused of carrying out attacks, sacrificing Indians in ritual acts, and returning to prehispanic forms of religiosity left the following description: "This witness . . . saw Elote the cacique and other prisoners and many other *macehuales* from his town enter one end of the town of Tequila on the Río Yztaque and take five Christian Indian men and women and sacrifice them at the altar as I have said and eat them in the same manner" (AGI, Guadalajara 46, no. 37, Sancho de Bullón, declaración de la indígena de nombre Amoche, fols. 1v–2r, 1549).

What stands out in the statement by the main Indian leader accused of these attacks—the cacique Elote—is that he and his men were also motivated by the devil Tlacateculote, a name that referred to one of the manifestations of Tezcatlipoca as a wizard. In 1541 those Indians had raided the town of Tequila, killing three Indians and carrying away fifteen others to be offered as sacrifices on their altar. Around the year 1544 they went to the town of Téul, where they killed many people and captured several Indians, whom they took to Talistacan to be sacrificed in their temple. By 1546 the Franciscans had arrived in that town to convert them to Christianity, but the Indians rejected them and even spoke of killing them (AGI, Guadalajara 46, no. 37, declaración de Elote, fols. 3v–4r, 1549).

For some ten years after the defeat of the Indians of Nueva Galicia in the battle of Mixtón, Indian leaders such as Tenamastle, Chapuli, Coringa, Elote, and Zomón kept the resistance alive. In late 1550 and early 1551, the cacique Chapuli died and was replaced by Itopote Ilinza, who immediately called for a new uprising and attacked some of the Indian followers of Tenamastle, who, perhaps weary of persecutions and dissension among the indigenous lords, had decided to turn himself in to Pedro Gómez de Maraver, the bishop of Guadalajara, thus beginning a journey that would take him all the way to Valladolid, Spain. Meanwhile, Coringa and his troops were threatening to attack the province of Centiquipaque. Martínez de la Marcha told the king: "I have been told and heard [that] the tlatol and sound of those Indians of the sierra have done, still do, and are expected to do evil" (AGI, Guadalajara 51, carta de Hernán Martínez de la Marcha, al rey, Compostela, a 18 de febrero de 1551, fols. 7r–7v). Despite the discovery of the Zacatecas mines in 1546 and the rapid population shift toward those deposits, it was not until the early 1550s that a route was forged into the territories of northern Nueva Galicia. This had the double effect of extending the frontier and opening a new war front. The Chichimec nations never again confronted the Spaniards in such numbers or in places where their warriors could be contained and besieged (as happened in the mesas and mountains). Rather, they carried out furtive attacks on small groups, assaulted travelers, and raided the least protected villages using the element of surprise against Spanish soldiers (Sarabia Viejo and Román Gutiérrez 1992:614–620).

The Franciscans never forgot the strategic role of towns like Téul and Juchipila in the Mixtón rebellion, especially because of their religious and ethnic importance. Of all the convents founded in the territory of Nueva Galicia, only those established in Téul and Juchipila continued to operate until the late sixteenth century. In 1586 the Franciscans in Guadalajara dissuaded Friar Alonso Ponce from making a visita to those convents because "it was a very dangerous road [where] his life was at risk," so instead he sent "an old and very honorable friar." In the sierra around Téul there were Indian groups that had not been converted and continued to put up resistance to the Spanish colonizing projects (Ciudad Real 1993:98).

Cycles of Warfare

The Mixtón War, which lasted from 1540 to 1542, was followed by an uninterrupted period of Indian attacks (Carrillo Cázares 2000; Powell 1977, 1980) that continued to manifest ritual elements, as in the case of the indigenous caudillos from the Tepeque region. Another widespread rebellion occurred between 1560 and 1561, just a few years after the founding of several key mining settlements in New Spain and Nueva Galicia. Raids by the Zacatecans and Guachichiles targeted primarily the mining areas, their supply zones, and local roads.

Pedro de Ahumada Sámano (a miner, soldier, and commercial representative of the second marquis del Valle, Martín Cortés, in the mining zones of northern New Spain) was commissioned by Viceroy Luis de Velasco and the audiencia of Nueva Galicia to organize the war effort and prevent the loss of settlements where silver-mining operations were under way. When drafting his relación, Ahumada wrote that the losses caused by Chichimec raids surpassed one million gold pesos. The intensity of those attacks increased in the late 1550s, with concerted action of Zacateca and Guachichil Indians along an axis from the town of San Miguel, in the modern state of Guanajuato, to the mines at Avino, Durango.

In his relación, Ahumada described the onset of the attacks and the confederation of Indians in terms similar to those used by participants in the Mixtón War twenty years before. Once again there were Zacateca and Guachichil Indians, but they were trying to convince the Caxcan nation, which was then at peace, to join their uprising (AGI, Patronato Real 182, ramo 5, 1562, "Relación de Pedro de Ahumada," fols. 1r–1v). The Zacateca nation was described as a large bloc whose presence in the region varied from *rancherías* around San Miguel to the mines at Zacatecas, Sain, Chalchihuites, San Martín, Avino, Poana, and Peñol Blanco. In contrast, the Guachichiles were divided into three large groups. The concerted action of these two nations kept the Spanish troops commanded by Pedro de Ahumada in constant movement until an uneasy peace was achieved in late 1561 (Sarabia Viejo 1978:457–459; see also Powell 1977).

After that period, Indian attacks continued to flare up in Nueva Galicia, but not as part of a general plan of rebellion. In the late 1570s, the Zacatecans and Guachichiles stepped up their belligerence against the Spanish and their settlements, spurred to action by the enslavement of noncombatant Indian women and children, who, upon their capture, were treated as part of the soldiers' pay. Assaults on traders on the roads and in the mining towns at times forced the temporary or even permanent abandonment of certain localities (Román Gutiérrez 2005).

In 1580–1581 news came of an uprising in which Indians from different regions had allied to fight the Spanish. On this occasion, transit from the cities of Mexico, Puebla, Guadalajara, and Valladolid (today Morelia) to the Zacatecan mines and other extraction areas in the north was a perilous adventure in which those who dared to attempt the journey put their lives at risk. In early 1580, the situation in Nueva Galicia was worrisome for Spanish residents and the authorities. Though officials at the Royal Treasury had provided the funds needed to maintain a garrison, the 36 soldiers deployed there proved to be woefully inadequate in the face of a resistance movement that, instead of focusing on one place, launched attacks on different stretches of the roads and in Indian towns and villages (AGI, Guadalajara 33, carta de los oficiales reales de Zacatecas Alonso de Caballero, Francisco López de Ibarra y Juan de Llanos, al rey, a 8 de marzo de 1580, Zacatecas). The president of the audiencia of Guadalajara, Jerónimo de Orozco, took personal command of the soldiers and set out to fight the Chichimecs. In one of his reports, he described the process that led to the rebellion:

> With things as they were in this kingdom, I received news by letter from Friar Francisco Gil of the Franciscan Order, resident in the convent of the province of Acaponeta, and from other persons that the Indians of certain towns in that province that had been in peace for many years and who were and are Christians and had always been under the administration of the clergy of that Order had risen up and rebelled against Your Royal Service and that together and at the point of war had gone to other Christian Indian towns and killed many, burned towns and churches, and robbed and taken ornaments, bells, and the belongings of the Indians. And that they had joined and confederated with the Chichimec Indians of the sierra of that region, and altogether perhaps three or four thousand decided to ravage and destroy the entire province and neighboring towns.

(AGI, Guadalajara 6, carta del doctor Jerónimo de Orozco, al rey, fechada el 28 de septiembre de 1580 en las minas de Zacatecas).

Once again, the Zacateca and Guachichil Indians were participants in the uprising. Among other measures, the audiencia of Guadalajara approved sending parties of soldiers to the mining towns of Mazapil and Sombrerete to contain the attacks, while the construction of presidios at strategic points on the roads was accelerated. Once the area had been partially pacified, the Franciscans petitioned for the division of the provinces of Michoacán and Jalisco and the union of the latter with the *custodia* of Zacatecas. In addition, they proposed that violent tactics be abandoned and that attempts be made to attract the Indians through peaceful means. Since the Mixtón War, violence and confrontation had only succeeded in intensifying conflicts between Chichimecs and Spanish. The Franciscans also pointed out that the Chichimecs would receive them in their towns as long as they were not accompanied by soldiers.

The Third Mexican Provincial Council, held in 1585, condemned the "war of fire and blood" that had been carried out up to that point and recommended the use of peaceful measures by colonial authorities and the continuation of the Franciscans' evangelizing efforts. In the decade of 1590, the first systematic steps were taken to build peace: the authorities attempted to change the material basis of Chichimec subsistence by giving them food, clothes, and tools, financed by the Crown, and congregating them in towns. There, living with other Indian groups like the Tlaxcaltecans, sedentarization was achieved on the basis of family links and farming (AGI, México 22, no. 11, carta del virrey Velasco, al rey, del 2 de marzo de 1590, en México, fols. 5r–5v, 1590; AGI, México 22, no. 37, carta del virrey Luis de Velasco, al rey, en México, a 4 de marzo de 1591, fol. 4v).

No new uprisings broke out until 1601, when the extension of the frontier of colonial control into the northern reaches of Nueva Galicia and southeastern Nueva Vizcaya led to conflict. In the province of Topia, the Acaxee and Sobaibo Indians called on other nations to join their rebellion. Though it seems that the former soon returned to the fragile peace in which they had lived, the Sobaibos opted to continue fighting. Declarations rendered by some rebel Indian prisoners revealed that "they fought both because the devil spoke with them the night before and told them to await the Spanish and to be of good morale, as he would help them. They all confessed to eating human flesh, and many idols, churches, and crosses were found burned" (AGI, Guadalajara 28, gobernador de Nueva Vizcaya, Rodrigo de Vivero, envió al virrey de la Nueva España, Conde Monterrey, fechada el 9 de abril de 1602).

This new outbreak included many of the elements that had been present in the Mixtón War sixty years earlier. At some point between September 1601 and March 1602, the Acaxees suffered a terrible defeat and opted to make peace, but the Sobaibos did not. In that year, while Bishop Alonso de la Mota y Escobar was making his visita to the diocese in the region of the uprising, an Indian from the town of Chacala, Sinaloa, called Perico (who had been a priest and was a noted authority on ancient rites) proclaimed himself "bishop" of the Indians, perhaps emulating Mota y Escobar, because he strove to obtain the Christian symbols that gave the Spaniards their strength. He also "rebaptized the Christians through different ceremonies and unmarried those couples that had been wed according to the rite of the church. He was to be called God the Father or the Great Father" (Alegre 1956:113–114, my translation), and he proclaimed himself God of the Holy Spirit, "giving the others to understand that he came from the sky to teach a new doctrine for their salvation, [and] taught them ill-sounding prayers to persuade a great number of people of the Sobaibo nation of his doctrine" (AGI, Guadalajara 49, expediente no. 8, fol. 326r, información de méritos y servicios de Miguel Sánchez, a 7 de abril de 1604).

According to the testimonies of the Spanish authorities, the goal of those rebels was to liberate their nations' lands and ravage Nueva Galicia, where some Indian towns had joined the conspiracy. The Indian bishop Perico named two Indians as his aides, baptizing them as Santiago and San Pedro. Later, perhaps because of the complexity of his goals or to complete the set of religious elements he needed to oppose the Christians, he designated twelve Indians as assistants, a move that clearly paralleled the number of apostles (Román Gutiérrez 1993:410–411). But the Spanish authorities soon trapped the bishop and his "apostles": Perico was drawn and quartered, and his lieutenants were hanged, thus bringing the conflict to an abrupt end (AGI, Guadalajara 49, expediente 7, información de méritos y servicios de Bartolomé de Mesa, fechada el 31 de marzo de 1604, en Guadalajara, fols. 2v–3v). A comprehensive description of the uprising and its manifestations was left by a soldier who witnessed the military actions:

> Eating meat from the bodies [of those] they killed, blocking and controlling the royal roads, [they] threatened to ravage and burn the mines at Topia and the villages of Culiacán and Sinaloa and to kill their inhabitants, and having carried out said damages, they convened and called the Indians of the ravine and sierra in Topia to join the uprising. . . . This was the most widespread of the uprisings seen among the Indians as the tlatoles spread through the sierra to the Indians at Chiametla, Acaponeta, Guadiana, Sinaloa, and Culiacán, and all were about to rise up with them. (AGI, Guadalajara 49, expediente no. 8, fol. 326r, información de méritos y servicios de Miguel Sánchez, a 7 de abril de 1604)

Among the material causes of this rebellion were the mistreatment of Indians at the mines (e.g., those who worked in Topia) and the smallpox and measles epidemics that had decimated the Tepehuan nation. In an effort to eradicate those diseases, "the shamans organized traditional dances [*mitotes*]" (Genotte

2006:140–141). It is probable that this ferment of nonconformity spread to the Acaxee and Sobaibo nations (AGI, Guadalajara 6, carta de los oidores Vera, Pareja y Palma de Mesa, de la Audiencia de Guadalajara, al rey, informando sobre la rebelión de los indios de las minas de San Andrés, fechada el 20 de abril de 1602; AGI, Guadalajara 230 Z 2, real cédula de Felipe III al presidente y oidores de la Audiencia de Guadalajara, fechada en Aranjuez el 29 de abril de 1603, fol. 90v).

But there was still one more resistance movement to come in this cycle of warfare: the Tepehuan uprising of 1616, a broad rebellion that sought to expel the Spaniards from the northern lands. On this occasion the immediate targets were the Jesuit and Franciscan missionaries who administered the missions where the Indians had been congregated. Once again, the backdrop included a "general confederation of the Indians of this kingdom." Friar Juan Gómez of the Franciscan Order wrote to Phillip III that,

> "having received news of the uprising of the Tepehuan Indians and other nations of this government," he knew that "it was carried out by a mestizo named Mateo Canelas, son of a Tepehuan Indian woman and a Portuguese man, who today captains it and accompanies them [and] was the first mover and instrument of this war, treason, and uprising." [A]s a result of the damages caused—in addition to the destruction of many temples, towns, and convents, the deaths of over one hundred Spaniards, children and adults, including Jesuits, Dominicans, and Franciscans—he petitioned the king "to order with severe sanctions that no one of that nation [Portugal] be allowed on the land, as on many occasions Your Highness has so ordered." (AGI, Guadalajara 67, expediente no. 20, carta de fray Juan Gómez, a Felipe III, fechada en Durango el 20 de mayo de 1617, fol. 1r)

The Tepehuan rebellions of 1616 and 1619 continued the cycle of approximately 20 years between uprisings. Most contemporary testimonies, and most scholars who have studied these Indian movements, define them as "millenarian uprising[s] based on a new anti-Christian religion that pulled many neighboring nations of the Tepehuanes into the struggle against the Spanish, beyond the frontiers of their territory such that it came to include almost the entire province of Nueva Vizcaya" (Giudicelli 2006:163). Among the nations that rebelled with the Tepehuanes were the Tarahumaras, Conchos, Lobosos, Salineros, Cahuametos, Acaxees, Xiximes, Humes, Humases, Hinas, Coras, Nayaritas, and other peoples who, like the Zacatecans, had been displaced from their lands and moved into the Tepehuan area (Giudicelli 2006:166–167).

One witness reported that "the tlatol that has been spread [says] this and is known to all those of the nation" (AGI, Guadalajara 8, ramo 11, no. 47, fols. 40r–41v, n.d.). Any Indian who did not obey the orders of that god faced the punishment of being devoured by the land. Finally, a small stone sculpture representing a deity was carried to each town as a call to war against the Spanish

(Giudicelli 2006:169). This rebellion ended with the defeat and punishment of the Tepehuanes and many of their allies. At the same time, the authorities strengthened their defenses in the area by building more presidios and deploying more Spanish soldiers with Indian auxiliaries.

A Century of Confederation and War

After 1540–1541, the tlatol of war reappeared in 1560–1561, 1580–1581, 1601–1602, and 1616–1619, showing a regularity that went hand in hand with violent rejections of the practices of the colonizers who had reduced and enslaved thousands of Indians and almost completely destroyed the Indians' world. As late as the year 1600, however, several Indian nations in Nueva Galicia and Nueva Vizcaya were still practicing their ancient rituals and venerating their gods, despite their contacts with the evangelization process in New Spain. For example, early in the seventeenth century a Spanish captain named Jerónimo Pérez de Arciniega found ritual paraphernalia in towns in the sierra and other isolated sites that included idols, arrows, clothing, and quantities of offerings used in Indian rites, all of which he burned "to make the Indians understand that his intention in taking them from the sierra was not to exploit [their possessions] but to show them that the gods they adored were false, because a man like him was able to burn them together with their offerings" (AGI, Guadalajara 36, expediente 10, información de méritos de Jerónimo Pérez de Arciniega, fechada en Guadalajara, a 10 de julio de 1600, fol. 9r).

Throughout the sixteenth century, many Indians of Nueva Galicia and Nueva Vizcaya continued forms of religiosity that predated Christianization. Their commitment to these religious practices was so powerful that it could unite groups in general rebellions against the Spaniards across that vast territory. Attacks on travelers, mining settlements, villages of congregated Indians, and Spanish towns and villages occurred practically nonstop from 1531 to the early seventeenth century. The Indians maintained confederations (as the Spanish called them) characterized by common ritual elements and recognized the tlatol from a god or gods (that emphasized the figure of Tezcatlipoca) in confrontations that sought to eradicate the Spanish presence. The dissemination of the tlatol was always initiated by nomadic Indians as a means of calling their sedentary neighbors to war, as if they possessed a tradition strong enough to incite their neighbors to rebel. The prehispanic world of western and northwestern Mexico had lived with a permanent structure of warfare for hundreds of years, and this had left its mark on the region (Hers 2006:282–283). The possibility that such a structure might have survived into the sixteenth century is related to the religiosity of that indigenous world and opens a new direction for understanding the life of the Chichimecs of that region and their relations with sedentary Indian nations.

IV

The Past in the Present

9

The *Historia* of Islands

New Huichol Territorial Claims to Ancestral Places

Paul Liffman

In this chapter I examine how, in the wake of the Mexican constitutional changes of the 1990s, a set of indigenous discourses about territoriality was expanding at the same time that the sacred sites to which those discourses applied were being reduced in both number and size. The discourses dealt with *kiekari,* a Huichol (Wixarika; plural = Wixaritari) term often translated into Spanish as *territorialidad* (territoriality) or *cultura* (culture), and the shrinking set of sacred sites known as Tatei Xapawiyemeta (Our Mother Fig Tree Rain Place). In tracing this discursive history of sacred territory, I compare the meanings attributed to kiekari in the political process of making land claims with those produced as part of Huichol practices across a stage measuring at least 90,000 km^2 of western Mexico since the Postclassic period. The current actors on this stage include Huichol subsistence agriculturalists, intellectuals and ceremonial experts, members of an NGO, an emergent indigenous organization, and regional universities, among others.

It has become increasingly important to understand how people use their religious practices as a basis for making territorial claims in national and international arenas. The 1990s were a period of major structural change and political ferment in Mexico, and Huichols found novel ways to represent to non-Indian publics the territoriality that their people have sustained for generations through traditional subsistence and ceremonial practices.

Following the Salinas de Gortari government's recognition of indigenous peoples (by adopting Convention 169 of the International Labor Organization [ILO] and amending Article 4 of the Mexican Constitution in 1992) and concomitant with the growth of numerous autonomous indigenous movements (including the Ejército Zapatista de Liberación Nacional [EZLN] rebellion of 1994), the mid-1990s saw an upsurge in ethnically based claims by indigenous peoples in Mexico and throughout Latin America who had adopted similar strategies or were inspired by them (de la Peña 1999). The other major neoliberal change to the Mexican Constitution—the amendment of Article 27—essentially ended the revolutionary legacy of agrarian reform. Aware of this paradox, Huichol leaders framed some of their agrarian demands in terms of Article 4 even as the demise of Article 27 signaled that market forces could now ignore indigenous land tenure to an extent unequaled since the Liberal development-oriented regime of the late nineteenth century. The historical question is: To what extent can post-*indigenista*, multicultural inclusiveness win the formal recognition of territorial structures amid the neoliberal commodification of land?

Huichol claims about their territories included both the performance of ceremonies and oral/written arguments offered in regional, multiethnic contexts. Behind these claims lay the Huichols' historically and culturally profound premises about how canonical places are replicated hierarchically and why they expect reciprocity from the state in return for sacrifices and shamanistic services. Such premises are expressed in a genre of origin narrative they call *historia* in Spanish. Historia, then, expresses a sense of territoriality in which places are reproduced throughout the vast geographical area encompassing economic and ceremonial exchanges across time. Through their historical sacred narratives about these exchanges, Huichols have constructed a virtual sociocultural order that they call kiekari. While this virtual order may lack the groundedness of the dramatic sacrifices and ceremonial exchanges upon which it is predicated, it still reflects their fundamental logic.

As such, the Huichol case reminds us of Marshall Sahlins's model (1981, 1985, 2000) of how indigenous cultural categories can shape neocolonial political and economic circumstances. In this case, increasingly assertive Mexican indigenous peoples are struggling to make claims within mestizo-controlled state institutions, thereby recasting the terms of political negotiation and the nature of their own cultures. The Huichols have narrowed the structural reach of their sense of territoriality into a few canonical exemplars. This narrowing has occurred because Huichol territory has been whittled away and so restricted in terms of access that it has been rendered noncontiguous. It has also occurred because of a neoliberal historical turn that explicitly empowered indigenous status even as it continued to limit the economic possibilities of rural people such as the Huichols. In particular, government cultural heritage regulations restrict official recognition of sacred sites to single exemplars rather than the broad sets of places that Huichols have tended to group under a single toponym. This externally induced foreclosing of the rural world challenges indigenous claims toward their historical lands.

We can identify three general types of land claims:

1. standard agrarian claims such as the *"restitución y titulación de bienes comunales"* (restitution and titling of communal resources) that are made in the *tribunales agrarios* (agrarian courts) and based on the *Código agrario* (Agrarian code);

2. expanded claims that are pressed in the courts but based on emergent legal categories rooted in recent constitutional reforms and international treaties that recognize "traditional" cultural practices and social relations; and

3. broader territorial and cultural claims in the public sphere that are based on a combination of these emergent legal categories and universal claims to historical rights for indigenous peoples.[1]

These claims are also based on a widely shared sense of Indians' cultural significance to the Mexican nation as a whole and on their increasingly explicit representations of a land-based ethnic identity. In this chapter I examine episodes of the third type during the mid-1990s that were produced by Huichol Indians from three *comunidades indígenas*—San Andrés Cohamiata (Tateikie), Santa Catarina Cuexcomatitlán (Tuapurie), and San Sebastián Teponahuaxtlán (Wautïa)—which straddle the contested borders of the states of Jalisco, Nayarit, Zacatecas, and Durango in the formidable Sierra Madre Occidental.

While claims for exclusive communal property rights (the first category of claims described above) may include both ceremonial and agricultural-residential dimensions, claims regarding places elsewhere in the kiekari (in its extended sense of ancient, shared, multiethnic, and seminomadic trading, hunting, and gathering territory) are based primarily on ceremonial usage. Under these claims, Huichols seek rights for hunting deer, gathering peyote, selling their art, and conducting their ceremonies, including protection for votive objects left in such places, but they do not demand residential or agricultural rights. At the same time, non-Huichols dispute the ceremonial nature of such uses and customs on the grounds that these practices impinge upon current animal populations, property rights, or other national norms; that is, the greater good of the nation trumps the lesser good of the Huichols.

Despite differences between these different claims, they have been linked by the use of kiekari as an encompassing category in the context of the new legal dimension opened by Mexico's adherence to ILO Convention 169 and by a modified definition of the juridical status of Indian peoples in Article 4 of the national Constitution. This is a unified indigenous political strategy based on a convergence among local, national, and international agencies.

My objective, then, was to understand the Huichols' regional political discourse by looking at how they are elaborating a key cultural category—kiekari—that not only encompasses the people's struggle to reclaim their heritage but also, in its broader sense, has become virtually synonymous with Edward Burnett Tylor's notion of "culture." The various meanings different kinds of Huichol people give to the category "kiekari" point to the complexity and potential contradictions entailed in the notion of "territorialization" as practices that link power and space (Vandergeest and Peluso 1995:388–389), regardless of whether the actors are agents of the state or, as in this case, are subordinated people and their intermediaries (de la Peña 2001). These claims on territory refer to traditional subsistence activities, social organization, and ceremonial practice (known as *yeiyari*) as the main forms of territorialization. In short, for the Huichols, yeiyari subsumes kiekari.

Kiekari and the Sacrificial Logic of Land Claims

By 1995 Huichol ceremonial rights had been acknowledged in a sweeping (though weak) federal resolution on Wirikuta, the highly contested peyote country that constitutes the eastern terminus of the kiekari in San Luis Potosí and, as this book goes to press, prized real estate for transnational mining corporations (San Luis Potosí 1994). These rights had heretofore been focused on tiny fenced-in lots enclosing the most obvious central features of some key ancestral places like Tatei Matinieri (the springs at the gateway to Wirikuta) and Haramaratsie (a cave opposite a sea pillar at the Pacific shore at the western terminus of the kiekari, also coveted by large-scale hotel developers). In contrast, the northern and southern places of Hauxa Manaka and Xapawiyemeta remained virtually without meaningful recognition or protection, but as we shall see, they are the focus of comparable territorial disputes.

Insisting on more than the general recognition of indigenous customs mentioned in Article 4, Huichols say that they are entitled to land rights as *payment* for shamanistic services because, through sacrifice, they maintain reciprocal relations with divine ancestors who, in turn, maintain the health of the whole region's ecosystem. Instead of deeming themselves to be clients of the state, the Huichols argue in effect that the state is *their* client and that their ritual acts of sacrifice are a mode of production that both undergirds and dwarfs capitalism in importance. Thus, kiekari takes on a political-economic role in Huichol imaginings of territoriality.

Contrary to Benedict Anderson's (1991) vision of "fraternity" as a reliable hallmark of Latin American nationalism, Claudio Lomnitz (2001:337) points out that hierarchies, dependencies, and asymmetries (whether familial or community based) are fundamental characteristics of such nationalism. Indeed, in and through their ceremonial practices, Huichols strive for balance between their sense of hierarchy and "fraternity." On the one hand, the Huichols' patriarchal model of hierarchy concentrates access to the largesse of the ancestor-divinities who control the landscape and the elements in the hands of a small ceremonial elite; on the other, the collateral kin term *'iwama* (brothers) is a generalized cultural category for ethnic identity among all Huichols.

The Huichols' state-like "imaginings of a people tied to a territory" (Lomnitz 2001:352) rely principally on religious practice, land, and blood as markers of identity. This is a more ancient form of inventing community than the language-based collective with which Anderson identified eighteenth- and nineteenth-century England and Holland. The case of the Huichols raises the question of how different these "representations" can be and yet still be considered part of a national discourse. That is, while new legal measures instituted by the neoliberal regimes of the 1990s were intended to provide indigenous peoples with the right to represent their cultures *to* the state, their representation *of* the state has remained consistent with a Huichol worldview that keeps the state in the background.

Thus, Huichols do not so much posit a democratic, modern social order based on "fraternity" as they emphasize an organic, caste-like, regional division of labor. Their shamans provide the fundamental ecological conditions for the survival of all; therefore, the dominant political order in turn is expected to reciprocate by providing appropriate and necessary material benefits to the Huichols (Zingg 1938; see also Dumont 1980). This reciprocal logic is reminiscent of the Spanish colonial administrative model, which itself was based on a broader European feudal concept of social harmony within a hierarchy defined in religious terms.

The Huichols' sense of their place in the regional system also reflects their historical role as traders in ceremonial goods (turquoise, peyote, feathers) and as ceremonial specialists serving other societies throughout the Gran Nayar region of western Mexico since preconquest times.[2] These terms of exchange between Huichols and regional clients are coterminous with the general form of reciprocity within Huichol society: as sacrificial mediators with ancestors, *mara'akate* (shamans) are entitled to the lion's share of the sacrifice. They deem this to be fair because they expend their tremendous strength divining in consecutive all-night chants or curing rituals and complying with the attendant prohibitions. In effect, shamans sacrifice themselves by undertaking ventures into the harrowing nocturnal underworld, just as Huichol *hikuritamete* (peyote people) walked forty days in the desert to hunt and return with the deer-heart plant. To phrase it in spatial terms, in return for articulating their national and cosmological territory, they feel justified in claiming a measure of its resources, just as governments do.

The conflicting interests of the diverse actors on the regional and national stages point to the need to refine our conception of intermediation and verticality in relations between indigenous peoples and the state. Our models must take into account the internal contradictions and the limits to their ability to embody the discourses they share, reshape, and appropriate anew from both local and global sources (de la Peña 1986; Wolf 1956, 1957). As Huichol cultural imaginings embedded in the concept of kiekari confront national political realities, the impact on local structures of meaning becomes more central. Therefore, before saying more about contemporary sacred place claims, it is important to sketch the history of the word *kiekari* itself.

Kiekari: The Etymology of a Discourse

Although the historical usage of a term may be far from its current definition, the rapid transformation of kiekari into a politicized category on the regional level and the continued currency of its morphological components as everyday elements in Huichol speech demonstrate the daily struggle over the meaning of this word (Voloshinov 1986 [1930]). Even though its meanings have been reshaped and expanded, kiekari has mundane roots. It derives from the morpheme *ki*: in the beginning was the "house"—the dwelling. It is as if the Greek word *oikos* (which also means "house" and is at the root of "ecology" and "economy") were still current in modern English. So, for Huichols, the notion of the domestic unit as a prototype of the political and cosmological order is very close to the semantic surface of the words used to describe various levels of natural and cultural production and reproduction. A compound form of *ki* is *kie* (in Spanish, equivalent to *ranchería*, or extended family house cluster, the basic unit of Huichol society). By adding *kari* (a nominalizing suffix that implies abstraction or generalization), *kie* becomes *kiekari*; thus, a more literal, etymologically appropriate translation than "territoriality" would be "domain" (or even the funky neologism "rancherity"). In short, this term is a powerful resource for constructing new social and political identities.[3]

The most encompassing concept of kiekari that I encountered on the ground was the processual model of hierarchical exchange that emerges from sacrifice. This model is based on the image of a network of paths, or, in Huichol terms, *nanari* (roots), that connect kiete (rancherías) to structurally homologous *tukite* (temples) and finally to the primordial creation places known as *kakaiyarita* (ancestral places). In the political context described in this chapter, however, kiekari is represented more in terms of specific, permanent ancestral *places* than in terms of the sacrificial *relationships* that create a fluid, multitiered hierarchy linking rancherías, temple districts, and the place of a sacrifice.

Just as ancient ancestors are considered to be more divine and more inclusive of all Huichols, the process of claiming ancestral places beyond the zone of contemporary Huichol habitation depends on having representatives of the largest possible number of temple districts trekking there to perform the sacrificial acts that reaffirm these long-standing relationships with the ancestors. Huichol claims to such extended spaces and places run afoul of government programs for *patrimonio cultural* (cultural heritage) that mandate precise, bounded definitions of singular *lugares sagrados* (sacred places), despite the range of social relations and economic activities extending beyond them.[4] This official definition of territoriality also ignores the indigenous cultural logic that asserts kinship between a potentially expandable set of synonymous, iconically linked places predicated on ancient ancestors' movement between them. Instead, government policies place a premium on demonstrating the "traditional" legitimacy of the actors who can connect a place to the greatest number of *tukipa* (temple compounds) within recognized Huichol lands.

An Island of Historia: Xapawiyemeta

I now present a general sketch of the negotiations to guarantee Huichol pilgrims access and other rights to Tatei Xapawiyemeta (Our Mother Fig Tree Rain Place). This family of structurally similar places is characterized by being an island or outcropping with a cave or other passage to the underworld, with a *chalate* (giant fig tree) on top. As such, Xapawiyemeta is one of the five cardinal Huichol kakaïyarita that demarcate the kiekari as the primordial exchange sphere. Historically, Huichols depended on the entire area for hunting, gathering, and the long-distance exchange of precious goods such as turquoise, feathers, peyote, and salt (Durin 2003a, 2003b; Weigand 1985).

Much of the region is now regaining economic importance as more Huichol vendors of ethnic art and migrant farmworkers go from visiting it seasonally to inhabiting it permanently. The Nayarit coast has always been economically essential to the survival of the sierra cultures, whereas the eastern reaches where Wirikuta lies are now primarily of ceremonial importance (though they too were formerly sources of trade goods). It is not clear that economic activity in a capitalist wage labor context will remain associated with ceremonial activity for most people, but *cargo* holders continue to combine commercial and religious goals on journeys to ancestral places. In any case, Huichols have always treated the whole 90,000 km^2 kiekari as a living archive of primordial divine ancestral action, that is, as a fundamentally ceremonial space. It is a territory defined by places and by the paths that connect those places where parties of pilgrims pass, leave offerings, and collect essential substances for reproducing *'iyari* (life force).[5]

To gain a more complete understanding of Huichol territorial logic for Xapawiyemeta, we need to appreciate the term's multisited qualities, that is, how identically named places replicate each other synecdochically in much the same way as ranchería shrines and regional temples do. The case of the "main" Xapawiyeme place is especially telling. To make this point, I examine details of the August 1995 meetings held under the auspices of the Universidad de Guadalajara on the sacred island in Lake Chapala and in its eponymous lakeside town. This ethnography of place making and narrative of performance will clarify the confluence of economic, ethnic, and cultural factors operating in the struggle over Huichol territoriality and the challenge it presents to state power.

Sacred Multisitedness

The multiple, hierarchical, historically contingent replication of extended family rancherías and ceremonial centers also characterizes a more expansive territorial process (Liffman 2000, 2002). Here, people assign sacred toponyms and sacrificial relationships to multiple places and thereby create the possibility of making different kinds of claims on them. In contrast, the 1930s anthropologist Robert Zingg upheld the cartographic convention that a toponym should apply to one, and only one, place within a bounded set of sites; he considered that parallel toponyms must be "mistaken." In point of fact, Huichols reproduce toponyms with particular mythological references to accommodate the vision that a place generates for people who visit it. That is, a place-name may fit a number of sites that fulfill a general set of topographic and narrative criteria that conform to a geographically based storyline. This mythological basis for toponymy becomes concrete when people perform sacrificial practices there, thereby claiming it as a kakaɨyarita. This may reflect a very old Mesoamerican geopolitical logic of territorial expansion, even a kind of "Huichol manifest destiny."

In my experience, no toponym is applied to more places than Tatei Xapawiyemeta (Our Mother Fig Tree Rain Place). In the abstract, decontextualized, cosmological formulas most often produced by and for the anthropological literature, this rain mother is associated with "The South," but this is not entirely correct. It is true that Tatei Xapawiyeme is represented as a blue serpent or an 'imukwi lizard who appears in lagoons and brings rain from the south and consequently is identified with maize (Lumholtz 1900:13–14). However, her association with *xapa* (*chalate*, giant fig trees) may be the most potent symbolic referent: the xapa is the Huichol banyan tree in terms of both its visual impact and its mythological role.[6] Its massive trunk spreads downward and outward into thick roots visible as they enter the earth, and a huge spreading canopy thrusts out overhead.

Xapa has an association with the birth of culture itself: Watakame and the little black dog-woman who gave rise to the Huichol people are said to have survived the primordial flood in a dugout fig tree canoe, and their primordial voyage included Xapawiyemeta. The appearance of a xapa atop a rocky, obsidian-rich island with a cave inside constitutes a quintessential emergence point for the neighboring Náyeri (Cora) people as well (Coyle 2001). Or as one of Zingg's Huichol informants put it, Tatei Xapawiyeme "chose a great rock, since she was very 'delicate' [sacred]," and Ur-mother Takutsi Nakawe brought her water, so Xapawiyeme became a spring (1938:346). Given these generously broad topographical characteristics, it should come as no surprise that there are several major Xapawiyeme places in the southern and eastern quadrants of Huichol territory.

To put the places in (a somewhat Huichol) narrative order: We first encounter Tatei Xapawiyeme, a water-related deity born in Haramara, the sea that surrounds the world. As we move inland from the Pacific, the westernmost Xapawiyeme place identified by the explorer-collector Carl Lumholtz (1900:14) was at the Laguna de Laja near Mascota, above Puerto Vallarta and the Bahía de Banderas. This bay was the center of a major prehispanic coastal polity that Postclassic period Huichols may well have visited on hunting, trading, or tribute-paying trips down the Ameca River valley from the Magdalena area. Not far upstream from the Laguna de Laja is another Tatei Xapawiyeme lagoon near Talpa, Jalisco.

These places were scarcely being visited by the Huichols when Lumholtz conducted his expedition for the American Museum of Natural History in the 1890s, but if they represent a deep Mesoamerican trade and sacrifice network, he caught the last fleeting shadows of a 1,500-year-old regional system. Both Lumholtz (1900) and Phil C. Weigand (personal communication 1992) identified another quintessential Xapawiyeme on an island known as Las Cuevas in Lake Magdalena, the highest in the chain of broad, shallow lakes that stair-step southeastward down to Chapala and constitute the cradle of Classic period West Mexican civilization, most notably the urban complex around Lake Teuchitlán (Townsend 1998).

Unfortunately for Huichol ceremonial territoriality, Lake Magdalena was drained in the 1950s to expand the local *ejido's* arable land. Nevertheless, the island with its caves is still there and continues to be visited occasionally by Huichols from Wautia (San Sebastián Teponahuaxtlán), as it had been by many indigenous groups for both religious and mining purposes for the preceding two or three thousand years (Weigand, personal communication 1992; Weigand 1993a).[7] Like Lumholtz's Talpa and Mascota Xapawiyemetas of the 1890s, this ceremonial center was also on the edge of oblivion in the 1990s but is now the focus of a revival under the auspices of a local nongovernmental organization.

Figure 9.1. Xapawiyemeta, the former island of Las Cuevas in the now-desiccated Lake Magdalena. Courtesy Patronato de La Cueva of San Juanito de Escobedo, Jalisco.

Figure 9.2. Cave at the base of the Las Cuevas Xapawiyemeta site, Lake Magdalena. Courtesy of Patronato de La Cueva of San Juanito de Escobedo, Jalisco.

Figure 9.3. Archaeologist-ethnohistorian Phil C. Weigand and an unidentified associate surveying altar niches carved into the cave at the base of the Las Cuevas Xapawiyemeta site. Courtesy of Patronato de La Cueva of San Juanito de Escobedo, Jalisco.

Moving east across the trans-Tarascan lake zone, we find that contemporary *kawiterutsixi* (ceremonial elders) of Tutsipa (Tuxpan de Bolaños) in the community of San Sebastián still take offerings to Villa Corona in the *municipio* of Tuxcueca, Jalisco, although the precise location of Tatei Xapawiyeme's emergence there was not clear to the delegation of elders who surveyed the area in 1995. Other nearby Xapawiyeme places are said to be at the Chimulco hot springs (now a major tourist site) and at Valencia. In response to the government's call for demarcation, the Tutsipa kawiterutsixi and shamans were said to be *heinitsika*, "dreaming" or divining the places' locations. In this sense, trekking to places is interwoven with dreaming them—a process similar to that used for selecting new communal authorities on the feast of San Francisco (October 4) each year and announcing the results on the feast of the Virgin of Guadalupe (December 12).

By far the most commonly visited Xapawiyeme place is on the Isla de los Alacranes, a small wooded volcanic outcropping that rises perhaps 15 m out of Lake Chapala. One Huichol consultant, Werika (b. 1962), told me that his maternal grandfather (b. ca. 1915) had told him that *his* "uncle" used to go to this place on Lake Chapala. Werika reports that his ancestors would sit up all night chanting at the edge of the water with their candles lit and their ritual implements at hand until the next day, when a passing canoe might take them to the island. It is surprising, therefore, that Lumholtz and later Zingg fail to mention this site.

Now Chapala has become a concentrated symbol for Xapawiyeme in an era when Huichols no longer intimately traverse the landscape of western and central Mexico on foot as they once did. Much the same can be said of the other cardinal sacred places, Wirikuta, Haramaratsie, and Hauxa Manaka. Increasing rural insecurity and fencing, on the one hand, and wage labor time commitments and motorized transportation, on the other, are transforming Huichol territoriality. These new commodified patterns of organizing time and space are making kiekari noncontiguous and mediated by greater dependency on state or market subsidies for its continued viability.[8]

The Isla is a few kilometers south of the bustling tourist and resort town of Chapala, located on the lake's north shore 50 km south of downtown Guadalajara, Mexico's second city. Commercial launches regularly ply the waters separating the small lakeside town of Chapala from the island, charging each of the roughly twenty passengers several dollars for the leisurely half-hour cruise to spend an hour or two on what may appear to the tourists to be no more than a pleasant, shaded island. Tourists stroll on part of the tiny island's narrow, developed perimeter, where they can purchase knick-knacks identical to those sold back on the Chapala shore, lunch on the polluted lake's little white fish, and wash them down with a cold beer or *refresco*. Afterward, if so inclined, they can take in the blue panorama of Mexico's largest lake if they are among the few tourists willing to stroll up the sloping 50 m path to the volcanic outcropping at the island's center. Once there, the tourists may notice niches littered with curious homemade bundles of painted cane arrowshafts, tiny gourd bowls, 5 cm embroidered squares of white muslin cloth, and hand-formed 10 cm beeswax candles. This is the context for the meetings at which representatives of lakeside municipalities and the three Huichol communities expressed their conflicting claims regarding the Isla de los Alacranes.

Moving onward from the lake region to the sierra, we encounter a mountain-top on the eastern side of the Sierra Huichol that Zingg called the one and only Xapawiyeme place: "This Huichol told me that Rapauwíeme [*sic*] is a goddess who lives on the top of a hill three days away from Tuxpan, toward the East. All Huichols carry votive arrows and bowls, and other objects, and my informant said he had done this many times" (1938:346). In terms of the region's cultural geography and Huichols' Olympian endurance as trekkers, Zingg's vague "three days east" of Tutsipa could be as much as 120 km in the general direction of the former Tepecano and Caxcan areas, that is, somewhere between Juchipila or Nochistlán and La Quemada. In effect, Zingg seems to be referring to the Juchipila River valley, known for its numerous Mesoamerican conquest era for-tified mountaintop sites (*peñoles*).

Finally, according to a Tuxpan man whom I met at Teekata, where he and the San Andrés people I was accompanying were fulfilling their ceremonial ob-ligations, Xapawiyeme also has a *brazo* (arm) in the heart of the sierra.[9] His metonymic expression suggests the same kind of connectedness among places that Werika does: hierarchical ranking as much as horizontal connections along a path. This notion of hierarchical extension finds its ultimate embodiment in the *xukurite* (gourd bowls) kept in the tukite, which also are manifested in ritual offices and in ritual narrative as microcosmic representations of the entire kiekari (Kindl 2000).[10]

Clearly, a bundle of topographical features connected to other similar places by a geographical narrative combine to define a place's "Xapawiyeme" status. Indeed, more recently Huichols have claimed a Xapawiyeme place near Man-zanillo, Colima, (Rosa Rojas, personal communication 1997). Located 200 km down the coast from the Bahía de Banderas, this is the rain mother's southern-most and most coastal place to date.

I have already suggested that one form of such connectedness among the var-ious places was the eastward journey taken by Xapawiyeme after her emergence from the sea: a sinoidal succession of equivalent units. As my friend Werika put it, there is a root (*nana*) connecting these dispersed Xapawiyeme places. What appears to be novel about this sense of rootedness is that when people are talk-ing about where they live, they rank analogous places in an ascending hierarchy from *xiriki* (ranchería shrine) to *tuki* (regional temple) to increasingly distant primordial ancestral places (kakaɨyarita) like Teekata (the sacred place in the center of Huichol territory) and Xapawiyemeta. However, within the family of narratively connected Xapawiyeme kakaɨyarita, no such hierarchy is evident.

The recent governmental mandate to identify a paramount place, or primus inter pares, in order to focus limited cultural heritage funding on the most sig-nificant sites not only has had the effect of restricting the breadth of indigenous territorial claims but also has skewed Huichol sacred places into a new kind of hierarchy. Werika considers that the nana root of Xapawiyeme extends from the place on the Isla de los Alacranes toward more out-of-the-way sites like Villa Corona and beyond. In effect, the cosmologically important ceremonial places are shifting as political and economic forces reshape Huichol territoriality. For instance, among the various Haramaratsie places along the Pacific coast to the west, the one at the port of San Blas, Nayarit, is paramount, surely due to its importance as a trade and tribute center since the eighteenth century. And while there are various sites that embody aspects of Wirikuta along the path to the easternmost place on the San Luis Potosí steppe, Wirikuta itself unquestionably remains paramount. This is because of its abundance of a crucial ceremonial good (peyote), the number of related places at hand, and the cultural equation between geographical distance, historical depth, and religious importance that has been applied to it.

How can we account ethnographically for the sheer proliferation of identically named places? Is "Xapawiyemeta" a fuzzy set of places defined by a bundle of topographic and geographic features that can be ranked according to the speech events in which they are indexed? To summarize this logic as concisely as possible: at particular moments each community (or tuki group or even individual ceremonial elder) seems to have a different interpretation of where exactly Xapawiyeme's place is located. Part of this ambiguity can be resolved by considering that the term *Xapawiyemeta* can refer not only to specific places but also to the general ancient *region* of Xapawiyeme, or the trans-Tarascan exchange sphere ultimately traceable to the center point at Teekata. This region may be identified even more extensively as the trans-Tarascan lake region extending east from Magdalena to Chapala along the south side of the Río Grande de Santiago, the westernmost arm of the central Mexican plateau,[11] and from Chapala northeast to the Tepecano region between the Ríos Bolaños and Juchipila. In terms of the Huichol narrative that orders this landscape, it would be appropriate to understand the succession of Tatei Xapawiyemetas *processually* as this divine ancestor's migration paths that uncoil in a sine wave eastward from her emergence place(s) in the Pacific Ocean through one lake after another and eventually northward toward the Huichol heartland. Moreover, this model could have been significant in terms of Mesoamerican geopolitics: the general association between ceremonial treks and commercial exchange in the premodern world (see Polanyi 1968) makes the search for connections between ancestral places and prehispanic centers of resources and political legitimacy a potentially useful direction for future archaeological and ethnohistorical research.

From Multiple Meanings to Patronage

Who, then, are the principal actors, and what are the interests at stake in claims to a major ancestral place such as Xapawiyemeta? What do Huichols demand of regional governmental authorities who control access to ancestral places? How do Huichols represent their expansive territorial logic to nonindigenous audiences? Specifically, how do Huichol cultural brokers convince their counterparts in the state that indigenous cultural practices deserve territorial respect and material support?

Some of the answers emerged during a trip to the Isla de los Alacranes in Lake Chapala prior and an encounter between Huichol activists and elders and regional government authorities. A Huichol delegation sent to survey an area of the ancestral island that they wish to protect had hired two launches and made the twenty-minute ride out from the town of Chapala. Shortly after arriving, and in the spirit of the ancient practice of performing interethnic shamanistic services, a Huichol shaman prepared to perform a cure on a non-Huichol administrator of the Universidad de Guadalajara's Centro Universitario de Apoyo a las Comunidades Indígenas (Center in Support of Indigenous Communities). Meanwhile, a mestizo tourist, his wife, and their daughter observed and videotaped—whether for their own consumption or for distribution through the Internet to the world at large—the spectacle of the Huichol delegation surveying the area of the ancestral island that the Huichols wish to fence off from public access. At the same time and in front of these nonparticipant observers, a Huichol community leader, shaman, and schoolteacher prepared to leave an offering for consumption by the ancestors (*kakaiyarixi*) in a cleft in the rock outcropping at the highest point on the island, the symbolic epicenter of the whole struggle. At the same time, a young Huichol activist and schoolteacher also videotaped the proceedings, perhaps to raise the political consciousness of his students and other community members. Above the whole group an ancient chalate fig tree graced the rocky crest of the island with its shade and strong, elegant form.

Diverse actors are involved in Huichol access claims on the island. These include (1) the fishermen's and boatmen's unions, which effectively restrict Huichol access to the island; (2) the authorities of the busy tourist town of Chapala, who seek to turn Huichol ritual into a spectacle for the benefit of many, but not the Huichols; (3) the numerous U.S. and Canadian tourists and expatriates, who constitute a sympathetic audience for indigenous custom; (4) the University Center, which works on development and land claims initiatives with indigenous communities in Jalisco; (5) the nongovernmental organization known as AJAGI, or Asociación Jalisciense de Apoyo a los Grupos Indígenas (Jalisco Association in Support of Indigenous Groups), which has worked in grassroots sustainable development and on behalf of Huichol territorial claims; (6) "postmestizo" representatives of a group identified with La Nueva Mexicanidad, a range of indigenous-style cultural movements primarily composed of urban mestizos who identify themselves as "mixed-blood Indians" and in this case as communal authorities of nearby small towns (see Friedlander 1975; Rostas 1995); (7) the new Huichol leadership, of less mixed blood but composed of professionals and technicians with broad experience if not bicultural identities, who nominally lead the land claim effort; (8) various *kawiterutsixi* (community elders and counselors), who have been invited to serve as consultants because of their exact knowledge of ancestral practices and places; and (9) the anthropologist, who was brought along primarily to serve as an authenticating witness for the event on the island.

The expansiveness of Huichol cultural territoriality is constrained by Mexican legal, political, and economic realities. Most of the actors at the event on the island wished to reduce the vast quadrant of the prehispanic exchange sphere encompassed by the indigenous term *Xapawiyemeta* to a solitary "sacred place." From the nonindigenous perspective, the Huichols' claim had to be narrowed dramatically, because the multiplicity of sites identified with a particular category makes no sense within the Mexican legal system. Even the single claim to one Xapawiyemeta raised acute economic and political issues: the place has great economic importance to many people in the region and especially to the small city of which it has become such a significant part.

Despite the complexity of the cast and the underlying expansiveness of the Huichols' claims, their requests were quite humble. They requested chain-link fencing material to erect around the rocky outcropping at the center of the island and sought permission to build a small *xiriki* (a 2 or 3 m^2 roofed shrine structure). They also asked for help to ameliorate the cost of transportation in commercial motor launches to the Isla de los Alacranes and to end the endemic theft of ritual offerings from the place. Beyond these issues, the Huichols adamantly contested the Chapala authorities' efforts to transform Huichol ceremonial practices into tourist-oriented spectacles.

Their demand that the authorities respect the Huichols' human rights seemed to infringe on local cultural sensibilities as well as political and economic interests, especially when one Huichol leader announced, "These sites are our churches; respect them." The Huichols also made a far more radical and ancient claim upon the governmental representatives when one shaman proclaimed that the very survival of the planet depends on Huichol sacrificial activities: "The rain which benefits everyone comes because the shamans make it come." At this point, the Huichols were insisting on their entitlement to material assistance from the state, based on a premise that the political leaders of the state could not easily accept. From the Huichols' perspective that their ceremonial practices at their sacred sites are essential to the world, their requests for a fence and a shrine seemed hardly too much to ask.

In meetings held with a variety of regional representatives, the political authorities were polite but unhelpful. They did not acknowledge the sanctity of Xapawiyemeta nor its provenance in a religious tradition established in the area for at least twice as long as their own. They failed to publicly recognize the damage done by oblivious tourists whose eyes and cameras carried away images of the place and whose hands stole sacred offerings that would be transformed into curios to decorate their houses. Perversely, the authorities' main basis for supporting Huichol ritual activities at all was precisely that Indian ceremonialism might attract more tourists to the region or provide an interesting educational field trip experience for local schoolchildren.

Like the tourist-hungry government officials, Huichols also depend on the market for "magical ethnic art." In addition, Huichols are valued by local mestizos who perceive that indigenous ritual activity authenticates the practices of nonindigenous New Age groups.

Although absent from these meetings, another potentially important group is the sizable North American expatriate and tourist community, which numbers more than 5,000 members during the pleasant winter dry season. The largest of three U.S. community organizations in the region was the Lake Chapala Society, with 1,600 members, many of them retirees enjoying the enhanced purchasing power of their U.S. Social Security checks in Mexico. Many "old gringos" have expressed interest in indigenous themes, which are reported on with some regularity by the area's English-language newspaper, the *Guadalajara Reporter* (Sean Godfrey, personal communication 1995). In fact, the editors and I arranged for the Xapawiyemeta claim to receive coverage in that publication (see September 15, 1995), and up to a point Huichol strategists have considered crafting their statements to reach this group of resident readers.

In addition to the government, other social sectors militating against a positive reception of Huichol claims on the Isla de los Alacranes have considerable importance in the region's general economic and political circumstances. For example, the union of fishermen who use the island and the tour operators who run motor launches to and from it do not find it in their immediate interest to subsidize Huichol pilgrims. Likewise, the merchants who enjoy federal permits to operate food stalls and small restaurants along the edges of the shady island are not disposed to cede access rights to any part of it. Neither are local vendors of mass-produced artisanal products, who fear competition from Huichol pilgrims whose handmade beaded bowls and jewelry have an aura of indigenous authenticity.

Federal officials are ill disposed to upset the status quo by granting "special" concessions to indigenous people just passing through on their way to the lake from the mountainous northern reaches of the state of Jalisco, much less Durango or Nayarit. Finally, this controversy reflects the deep-seated racism in the region toward those referred to with the patronizing diminutive "Huicholitos." Because the authorities see Indian virtues as being limited to the preconquest past, they do not consider contemporary "Huicholitos" worthy of being modern partners in sharing territory and tourist revenues.

Near the end of the proceedings, a partially bilingual Huichol speaker declared that, despite all the talk, it is still difficult to assure access to the ancestral places in Chapala and in San Luis Potosí. He explained the logic of such territorially extensive ceremonial practices: "It pains the heart if a family member, livestock, or the cornfield dies. There in the home community are all kinds of problems. The temple officials are the legitimate representatives who should confront all this."

Here we see a close identification of traditional authority—in this case, the temple ceremonial officials—with the reproduction of territoriality: as a result of their sacrificial practices, "cuando se moja es para todos" (when it [the earth] gets wet, it is for everyone). Once, in a ceremony in Tateikie (San Andrés Cohamiata), a ritual authority asserted this meteorological ethnocentrism to me even more bluntly: "Huichols make the weather." This is a classic Huichol claim: their ceremonial activity benefits everyone in the region. Now, before a multiethnic audience, they claim that their importance extends to the whole planet.

Huichol brokers invoke a general model of regional reciprocity and equality to justify their access to ancestral places and to demand more of the state resources on which they now depend. They gesture toward Zapatista discourses calling for indigenous autonomy and haughtily insist on maintaining the ancient system of ranked ethnic difference and sacrificial territorialization. At the same time, the authorities seek to restrict Huichol territoriality, transform Huichol cultural performances into tourist spectacles, and invert identity politics so that some nonindigenous persons may claim "indigenous" authenticity. In sum, the Huichol situation and the ongoing debates about their ceremonial practices illustrate the challenges faced by native peoples throughout the world. They seek strategies for their cultural survival in a context that undercuts the possibilities for economic and political autonomy at the same time that the authorities offer new declarations of indigenous cultural rights.

Notes

This chapter is based on dissertation research supported by fellowships from the Department of Education Fulbright-Hayes program, the Wenner-Gren Anthropological Foundation, and the Secretaría de Relaciones Exteriores of Mexico. That research also benefited immensely from the institutional and collegial support of the Centro de Investigaciones y Estudios Superiores en Antropología Social, the Asociación Jalisciense de Apoyo a los Grupos Indígenas, and the Anthropology Department at the University of Chicago. I also wish to thank Andrew Roth of the Colegio de Michoacán for inviting me to participate in this forum. A condensed version appears in my book *Huichol Territory and the Mexican Nation* (University of Arizona Press, 2011).

1. However, these claims would not fully coincide with the Zapatista definition of territorial autonomy; we are dealing here with five Mexican states containing major national population centers. The demands are for free movement, site protection, and access to renewable plant and animal resources.

2. In traditional rural areas, belief in the efficacy of Huichol shamanism is still widespread. I was struck by the moral authority of the old *curandera* and *mara'akame* doña Andrea Ríos, eldest daughter of don José Matsïwa Ríos, who was Peter Furst's and Barbara Myerhoff's famed anthropological informant, as she performed a classical (and very expensive) sucking cure on a poor mestizo worker in Atonalisco, Nayarit (see Furst 1972; Myerhoff 1974).

3. In its historical usage, kiekari refers not only to the ranchería but also to other levels of social organization both within and beyond the *comunidad*: "village" and "city" (McIntosh and Grimes 1954:24). In its most encompassing sense, it means "the cosmos" (Neurath 2002) or, by adding a localizing suffix to form *kiekaritsie*, it is "the world"; or, by instead adding quantifiers, one can say *kiekari naititama* (all the inhabited places). In the same way, *kiekame* (*kie* + *kame*, a personalizing suffix) is an "inhabitant" (whether human or not) of any environment but more properly the synecdochical "elder of the *kie*" or, in a more general sense, a "citizen" of Mexico (Grimes 1981:89). The extended form, *kiekarikame* (pl. *kiekaritari*), also denotes "inhabitant" but not "ranchería elder." In short, this lexical set is a powerful resource for constructing new social and political identities. Without neglecting its more common uses, Neurath focuses on *kiekari* principally as the cosmological space demarcated by the five cardinal points—in which the central point is an *axis mundi* connecting diurnal zenith and nocturnal, subterranean nadir—and represented iconically in the architectonics of the *tukipa* (temple compound). On the other hand, *kwiepa* denotes "lands" (*kwie* = land + *pa* = place), which applies more to the idea of rural property.

4. In the early 1990s this program included ritual displays by ceremonial elders when government recognition of key ancestral places and zones included permission to construct shrines at Haramaratsie (San Blas, Nayarit) and Tatei Matinieri (Yoliatl, San Luis Potosí). *Kawiterutsixi* were invited to bear community seals, the communal *gobernador's* staff of authority, deer rifles, and a huge votive candle, to be anointed in sacrificial animal blood before state authorities. In turn, these officials would provide seals (i.e., permission for ritual deer hunting and peyote gathering) plus funds for these ceremonial activities both at home and on the road, as well as for registering ancestral places with the Instituto Nacional Indigenista. This territorial recognition, however, remained of very limited scope.

5. The other main meaning of *'iyari* is "heart," which, in the Huichols' sacrificial economy, is clearly a central value linking ceremony to production.

6. The word *xapa* formerly may have referred to more species of fig tree than *chalate* since it also denotes "paper," and *amate* (fig tree bark) was the source for the paper used in prehispanic codices. It is again used in contemporary indigenous painting, especially in Guerrero.

7. Mineral knowledge seems to persist among Huichols: a young agrarian activist who was part of the *kawiteru* delegation identifying Xapawiyemeta places in the region in April 1995 gave me one of three little chunks of unworked high-grade obsidian that he had picked up at the Xapawiyeme place near Villa Corona, Jalisco. Since at that point he was being reintroduced to his culture after a twenty-year lapse (and not given to amateur geology), he must have been taught the significance of obsidian by the *kawiterutsixi*, despite the fact that it no longer has economic uses and only rarely appears to be

employed ceremonially as a votive offering (Weigand 1970). The very process of making the survey of sacred places in the region was part of teaching territorial principles to the younger activists, just as participating in ceremonies is the main way to gain ritual knowledge and construct Huichol identity in general. (This intrinsic efficacy of practice—particularly trekking to ancestral places—to impart potent knowledge explains the reticence to let outsiders join in rituals.) I did not see any obsidian on the Isla de los Alacranes Xapawiyemeta, but we could postulate obsidian as one of a few signal qualities of Xapawiyeme-ness.

8. In terms of these places' official recognition, Haramaratsie has received some protection and transportation subsidies, with at least a brick *xiriki* (which can serve as a small shelter) inside a tiny fenced area. Hauxa Manaka has only received a gubernatorial decree specifying a tiny place amid clearcutting operations in the Tepehuan indigenous comunidad of San Bernalillo, Durango. In Wirikuta the protected places are noncontiguous, and there has periodically been talk of building a new San Luis Potosí–Saltillo superhighway through there, despite the generally worded state decree respecting Huichol cultural practices throughout some 75,000 ha of mestizo-controlled, largely ejidal lands.

9. *Brazo* could also refer to "hand," given the single term *mama* for both body parts in Huichol—in either case glossed as an "extension" considering the implicit subordination of the hand and arm to the torso. The *kawiteru* Pedro de Haro (personal communication 1993) employed a more political metaphor, reminiscent of those I have cited elsewhere (2000) for Wirikuta: "juzgado de primera instancia" (district court).

10. As Kindl shows, the bowl's round shape is iconic with the world, and its function as a cup for liquids also evokes the water sources that so many ancestral places contain.

11. In fact, the westernmost Xapawiyemeta places at Talpa and Mascota described by Lumholtz occupy the very last edge of this mesa at around 1,200 m elevation.

10

The Defense of Territory in the Costa-Sierra Nahua of Michoacán

John Gledhill

$\mathbf{A}$s James Lockhart (1992, 1999) has pointed out, there was a fundamental difference between the indigenous concepts of territoriality embedded in the Nahua *altépetl* and the notions that guided the interventions of the Spanish colonial regime and the Mexican postrevolutionary state in indigenous affairs. For the Nahuas of central Mexico, the altépetl linked people to place and implied sovereignty. Although the roots of the word—*atl* (the water[s]) and *tepetl* (the mountain[s])—literally referred to territory, Lockhart argues that its principal meaning was an organization of persons exercising dominion over a given place, a meaning that allowed the Nahuas to apply it to any sovereign or potentially sovereign entity, whatever its scale. As a sociopolitical conceptualization projected onto space, the altépetl was not understood in indigenous terms as an urbanized center dominating a hinterland. In the course of the year, each of the four, six, or eight *calpolli* (great houses) constituting the altépetl, each of which was a microcosm of the whole in itself, would deliver its labor and products for the maintenance of the rulers (*tlatoani*), temples, and public works in a strict and invariant order of rotation that was expressive of precedence and hierarchy. There was no "center" above and beyond the units that constituted the altépetl, to one of which the ruler himself, as an incarnation of the whole, inevitably belonged (Lockhart 1999).

For the colonial authorities, in contrast, the self-governing "indigenous communities" created after the reversion of private *encomiendas* to Crown control were defined precisely in terms of the spatial and political hierarchical relationship between a central town (*pueblo cabecera*) and subject communities (*pueblos sujetos*). The colonial regime was interested principally in the role of the former as a tribute collection point and as a center from which political and religious administration could be effected in an orderly manner.

In contrast to the colonial regime, the postrevolutionary state insisted on redefining the proper relationship between territory and persons at the level of the "agrarian community." State authorities adopted a modernist vision in which the quantity of land legally possessed by the community had to be precisely measured and demarcated rather than indicated only by vague references to often transitory features of the natural landscape, as was frequently the case in colonial land titles. Moreover, the state insisted on knowing the number of individuals who possessed officially recognized rights to the use and management of agrarian community resources. The postrevolutionary state also prescribed the formal procedures under which land was to be administered by assemblies of beneficiaries. The work of these local-level organs of agrarian governance was to be directed by officials whose powers and responsibilities were specified by federal law and whose elections would be conducted at regular intervals in accord with officially specified norms.

Indigenous communities with communal landholdings were allowed to reemerge alongside the Cárdenas-era *ejidos* as a result of successive modifications to the agrarian laws after 1940 (Sandoval et al. 1999). The Mexican state generally left the details of internal management of resources to the communities themselves. Furthermore, in some indigenous regions, such as the Cañadas de Ocosingo and Tojolabal zones of southern Chiapas (Leyva Solano and Ascencio Franco 1996; van der Haar 2004), the state exercised remarkably little influence in practice over how local people adapted state-mandated institutional forms to their own purposes, just as they had done with many of the secular and religious institutions originally imposed on them by the Spaniards.

The relative tolerance of state agents and institutions toward heterodox arrangements at the local level was not sufficient to prevent conflict under certain conditions. In the case discussed here—the Nahua indigenous community of Ostula, located in the coastal sierras of the state of Michoacán—conflict was heightened because the community had never lost de facto control over its communal territory since the colonial period. Although the people of Ostula accepted, up to a point, the state's model of how agrarian communities should be organized, the Ostula community rejected (and continues to reject) the official definition of its agrarian boundaries—and has done so in a militant manner. Ostula originally sought restoration of state guarantees for possession of its territory, *not* a redefinition of its rights, even when the law declared the community nonexistent as a legal entity.

The case of Ostula, seen in the light of Lockhart's understanding of the altépetl, shows the importance of the link between dominion over space and a unique organized social group bearing its own identity and traditions via a notion of sovereignty. Regardless of how "Ostula" is defined externally and in juridical terms, this "indigenous community" defines itself through the intimate practices of living, dying, working, worshiping, marrying, and maintaining other relations of sociality within the space that it perceives as its sovereign territory. In this perception, the social-cultural unit and the spatial unit are indivisibly articulated, so that any subtraction from the size or integrity of the land threatens the people.

Divergent Local Histories

Until the late nineteenth century, there were seven distinct *pueblos de indios* in the coastal region. Of these, only three—Pómaro, Coire, and Ostula—still existed by the start of the Mexican Revolution. The others suffered total dispossession as a result of the implementation of nineteenth-century Liberal legislation to privatize corporate landholdings attached to the indigenous communities previously recognized by the Spanish Crown (Gledhill 2004; Sánchez Díaz 1988).[1] Even after progress toward completing the Liberal land reform was halted by the outbreak of revolutionary violence, the three surviving populations were officially defined as "ex-communities" until modifications to the Agrarian Code after 1940 reopened the possibility for indigenous communities based on communal landowning to receive official recognition.[2]

The nineteenth- and early twentieth-century land reforms in this region of Michoacán had initially been promoted by the criollo elite of the district capital, Coalcomán, located in the high sierra. They were determined to impose modernization through large-scale capitalist enterprise, including foreign investment.[3] The indigenous communities represented a significant barrier to such initiatives, since their territories not only contained valuable forests and pastureland but also blocked Coalcomán's access to the sea.[4] Not surprisingly, the regional elites of the late nineteenth century enthusiastically embraced European biological models of race, arguing that colonists from Europe should replace an indigenous population characterized by congenital "unproductiveness," "indolence," and stubborn resistance to "enlightenment." Although the 1910 Revolution halted further arguments on that front, immigration of non-indigenous ranchers continued into zones occupied by indigenous communities in Coalcomán district.

Coalcomán had long been attracting mestizo immigrants from the ranching and muleteering communities on the other side of the Michoacán *tierra caliente* depression. This influx accelerated at the end of the nineteenth century with the construction of railways and the decline of the mule trade.[5] As concentration of control over property increased, newcomers were obliged to make a livelihood as sharecroppers (Cochet 1991). Many began to think that moving into the indigenous territories would present a better option. Although the class structure of Coalcomán promoted an accelerating "march to the sea" after the revolution, rancheros of relatively modest means had already intermarried extensively with the women of the soon-to-be-extinguished indigenous community of Maquilí before its lands were privatized in 1906 (Archivo del Poder Ejecutivo del Estado de Michoacán, Morelia [APEM], *Hijuelas del reparto de bienes comunales, Distrito de Coalcomán*, libro I, foja 85, 1905).

The fighting prowess of these ranchero immigrants made Coalcomán the most important center in western Michoacán for the *cristero* rebellion against the postrevolutionary state in the period 1926 to 1929. During that period Gregorio Guillén, Coalcomán's leading cristero general, established his base inside the territory of the Pómaro indigenous community. Given the strength of the local cristero movement, Lázaro Cárdenas—state governor from 1928 to 1932 and president of the republic from 1934 to 1940—adopted a politics of compromise that left the region outside the control of national government and immune to reformist policies until the end of the 1950s, thus allowing Guillén to maintain control over the indigenous community of Pómaro as his personal fiefdom until he was assassinated in 1959 by his nonindigenous enemies.

For coastal Nahua communities subjected to the political dominion of mestizo municipal *cabeceras* run by ranchero "political chiefs," the threats to their way of life during the Porfiriato were little changed by the revolution. For example, mestizo interlopers who had settled on communal lands embargoed in 1914 by the state treasury for nonpayment of taxes took over the civil governmental posts in Coire in the 1930s (Cochet 1991). When a majority of the members of the indigenous community voted to expel them in 1936, these mestizo officials reacted by killing fifteen people before President Cárdenas dispatched troops to protect the community from further attacks. In 1928 another "political chief" based in Aquila had sponsored an armed invasion of the communal lands of Ostula (Registro Agrario Nacional [Archivo General Agrario], Mexico City [RAN], Santa María Ostula, *Bienes comunales*, exp. 1523-b, foja 91). These threats produced what at first sight seems a purely defensive reaction. When in 1948 the French historian François Chevalier visited Ostula, it had become an archetypical "closed corporate community" (Foster 1967; Wolf 1957). Women who married mestizos were expected to leave, and an old colonial law had been revived that forbade nonindigenous outsiders to stay within its borders for more than two days. Chevalier also recorded that a luckless mestizo lighthouse keeper, whose presence could not be avoided without offending higher authorities, was subject to constant surveillance by the Ostulans. He had to be provisioned by sea, since he was not even allowed to cultivate a little garden "on the grounds that the bees would need the whole communal forest" (Chevalier 1995, my translation). Chevalier concluded that this resistance would prove to be a futile effort to stem the inexorable tide of mestizo hegemony.

Chevalier's pessimistic assessment was to prove incorrect, however. The mestizo advance was halted at the borders of the communal territory of Ostula, which continues to jealously defend those borders against the *ejidatarios* and ranchers of the coastal mestizo settlement of La Placita and the inland settlements of Maquilí and Aquila. Chevalier (1995) believed that he was witnessing a vanishing world of "villages of Indians [dressed] in white, silent or speaking Náhuatl, on foot or with their donkeys," about to be engulfed by the world of horse-riding, lasso-wielding rancheros with their broad-brimmed sombreros, singing loudly after work. Instead, the people of Ostula proved capable of renewing their long-standing struggle to force the state to recognize their communal territorial rights.

In the community of Ostula, these rights have always been regarded as the power to decide, within a community assembly, on the disposition of all resources within community borders, even the mineral resources that the state, capitalist corporations, and promoters of "economic modernization" deem to be of "national interest." Not long after Chevalier's visit, an event occurred that suggested that the Ostulans were doing something more than simply keeping their heads down in the face of external threats.

In 1950 don Esteban Santos, with three other family heads, moved from Ostula down to the coast, where they established the settlement of La Ticla. Don Esteban organized this expedition, inviting the other families to join him, after reports had been given to the communal assembly that a federal deputy was trying to organize the occupation of this area by a group of commercial farmers from Manzanillo, Colima, and that these would-be "squatters" (as the Ostulans put it) had petitioned for irrigation works to be constructed there.

Although the communal authorities had not instructed these pioneers to immigrate toward the coast, the assembly strongly supported their initiative. Mindful of the continuing threat of invasions and the problems posed by lack of official recognition of the community's territorial rights, within a few years the assembly voted to elect representatives to negotiate the reconfirmation and titling of its communal lands. Furthermore, a pattern of strategic movement toward community frontiers had already been established in earlier conflicts with invading ranchers, as well as in colonial-era boundary disputes between Ostula and its neighbor Coire. Ostula had also faced a similar challenge earlier in the postrevolutionary period, when a smaller group of rancheros had settled in the community and secured control of the official civil government of the community as a *tenencia* of Aquila municipality. But these interlopers were expelled peacefully after a very short period of tolerance.

If we consider the historical fates of the different Náhuatl-speaking indigenous communities originally living in the area during the colonial period, we observe a continuum of outcomes. Very limited mestizo penetration took place in Ostula; an externally brokered compromise finally led to the grudging reincorporation (as "second-class citizens") of mestizo invaders into the indigenous community of Coire in 1963; and, in the extreme case of Pómaro, a considerable proportion of communal territory passed into the control of mestizo immigrants.

Until 1964 the community of Pómaro accepted some mestizo families as commoners with the same rights as its members of indigenous ancestry on the grounds that these mestizos had supported them in their fights against other mestizos who planned to drive all the indigenous people from the land (Ramírez García 1982). Despite the community's decision to decree that "it is strictly

prohibited to accept in any settlement [*ranchería*] any additional person coming from outside since not a meter more will be given to such persons" (Cochet
1991:204), the mestizo infiltration of Pómaro territory continued unchecked.
By the 1990s, members of the indigenous community (including those who
were incorporated mestizos and their descendants) controlled less than half of
the 75,000 ha of communal land officially in their possession under the state's
certification and titling program (Cochet 1991).

Language, Culture, and Community Organization

When the North American geographer Donald Brand visited Ostula a few years
after Chevalier, he remarked that "the government of the anachronistic *comunidades de indígenas*" continued alongside the form of government mandated for
the tenencias of municipios, with the officials serving in the latter roles being
"for public consumption" and not the "real government" (Brand 1960:118).
Although he was right on that score, like Chevalier he was wrong in assuming
that what he saw was simply an anachronism inherited from a colonial past.

Ostula's resilience was a reflection of particular institutions. All the Nahua
communities of this region were postcolonial creations. During a catastrophic
first century of colonization, the lives of the aboriginal inhabitants were completely transformed by forced and spontaneous resettlement, which threw together groups that had spoken different languages and installed radically new
forms of community political and religious organization. At the start of the seventeenth century, Náhuatl was in general use as a lingua franca, but the really
significant changes occurred from the middle of the century onward, when the
profitability of the production of cacao and cash crops introduced by the Spaniards collapsed, leading to a general withdrawal of the remaining nonindigenous
residents from the area. The now Náhuatl-speaking communities reoriented
themselves toward a larger network of economic and cultural relations with
other Nahua groups that stretched from Jalisco and Colima down to Guerrero,
enjoying a high measure of autonomy not simply in their economic and religious
life but even, by the late eighteenth century, in regional self-defense, which the
Spanish Crown was obliged to entrust to militias made up of indigenous archers.

This history makes continuity from the preconquest period extremely unlikely, even if new practices that were equally "indigenous" entered the region
from other centers of postcolonial Nahua culture. What might have survived, or
perhaps been revived, was a very un-European way of exploiting the resources
of an ecologically diversified local territory through a "broad-spectrum" strategy
that combined agriculture and animal husbandry with the "harvesting" of forest and maritime resources (Gledhill 2004). Although they were self-sufficient,
communities such as Ostula traded salt and wax candles in commercial quantities with the nonindigenous world beyond their borders. Indigenous families

from the area also migrated to rent abandoned hacienda lands to the south in the eighteenth century with a view to commercial production of cotton, also grown for domestic use in the home communities. Although a good deal of the interregional trade of the communities was handled by muleteers, even in the period when those communities became most "closed" to outsiders, their (male and female) members still carried local products to markets in Colima and sometimes drove their own cattle to market. More important, however, was the way this relative openness in economic relations was accompanied by responsiveness to changes in the larger world beyond community boundaries.

In the insurgency that initiated the struggle for independence from Spain, the archer coast guards from Ostula and Maquilí fought alongside mestizos from the nonindigenous *congregación* of Cohuayana, the emerging commercial hub of the region in the late colonial period (Brand 1960). Such alliances with mestizos represented links to particular figures in the mestizo world not associated with perceived threats to indigenous interests. These links also demonstrated a desire to be included in the new nation on "new terms" under which indigenous people would cease to be a subordinate, tribute-paying caste. It seems unlikely that Ostulan community leaders saw these "new terms" as a way for their community members to have the status of individual "free and equal citizens." On the contrary, they would have seen the weakening of Spanish colonial power as an opportunity to consolidate their possession of the territories that defined their historical identity and traditions. In effect, the insurgency provided a "victory" regarding its territorial claims that Ostula had been vigorously pursuing in the colonial courts.

While the traditional economic system of the Ostulans made the integrity of an ecologically diverse territory a priority, their indigenous perceptions of territory were tied to a holistic understanding of what it meant to be Ostulan. What made such perceptions so important in the case of Ostula was the way in which control over territory articulated with other peculiarities of the community's postcolonial culture.

Even in the seventeenth century, Ostula was emerging as a religious center within its region, and the following centuries saw a progressive elaboration of its systems of saint cults, associations, fiestas, and religious cargo systems. During the late nineteenth century, the Virgin of Guadalupe was adopted as the community patron, a further indication of the Ostulans' efforts to "belong" to the wider national society. The Ostulan ritual process as a whole is characterized by a consistent symbolic parodying of the claims to secular and religious authority of non-Indians. In this way, community members assert their moral standing as "true Christians" capable of managing their own affairs.

In the past, religious organization in Ostula was rigidly hierarchical and strongly patriarchal. The civil-religious *cabildo* survived as the basic structure of community governance until the end of the 1930s. Within that structure, power was concentrated in the hands of eight *cabecillas*, or "advisors," to elected community officials. This form of authority continued to operate even after the separation of civil and religious authorities. In 1960 the community rose up against the abuses of authority perpetrated by a group headed by the agrarian representative after he tried to create a political boss system (*cacicazgo*). When the community assembly rejected the arbitrary rule being imposed by the self-declared political boss, he reacted by conspiring with the civil authorities to bring in a local detachment of federal troops, which arrested and tortured dissident members of the community. Thanks to the intervention of the procurator of indigenous affairs (based in Uruapan), the community assembly in Ostula engineered a settlement in which the boss resigned and the victims were compensated. Unfortunately, the boss's faction continued to contest power for the next twenty years, provoking further internal conflicts.

These conflicts repeatedly blocked the consolidation of power by political bosses and reinforced the sovereignty of the community assembly. They also reflected the tensions provoked by socioeconomic differentiation within the community and between those settling on the coast and those who remained around the main settlement of Santa María Ostula. Most striking about Ostula's recent political history is not the factionalism and conflict but the resilience of community institutions in the face of continuing crises.

Although the backstage rule of the cabecillas ended in ignominy, it had served the community well in earlier crises. The cabecillas were men of high social prestige but not necessarily great wealth who had mastered the arts of rhetorical Náhuatl and were considered persons capable of good judgment and "deliberation." Their reputations were constantly tested in communal assemblies, and their abilities were linked to the community's religious culture. The continuing integration of the civil and religious orders ensured that an ethos of "service" was manifested by those who participated in public life. At least some of the figures who acted as cabecillas traveled outside Ostula, sometimes as far as the city of Colima, where strong official discrimination against indigenous people made it essential to speak Spanish and abandon the traditional white *manta* for a pair of trousers.

Strong internal organization and engagement with the external world were the keys to Ostula's ability to adapt to a changing world while maintaining a rigorous defense of its territorial integrity and religiously encoded "culture of resistance." The way religious and secular community service combined in Ostula helps make the robustness of its communal institutions more intelligible. Ostula also differed from its neighbors Coire and Pómaro on the issue of language competence. Increasingly, effective management of bureaucratic relations required competence in Spanish.

At the beginning of the twenty-first century, nearly all Ostula leaders were monolingual Spanish speakers. Only a few elderly men remained fluent in the indigenous language, and even these spoke Spanish perfectly as their first language. For many anthropologists, abandonment of an indigenous language signals a willingness to abandon indigenous "culture" and "identity," but this is clearly not the case in Ostula. On the contrary, the language shift was occurring when the community was taking more determined steps to shut out mestizos and to defend its territory and cultural practices.

This "outward orientation" by the "real rulers" of Ostula through the nineteenth and twentieth centuries reveals much about its peculiar kind of hybrid political culture. On October 15 of each year, Ostula ends its celebrations of the fiesta of Santa Teresa with a ceremony to mark the handing over of the now annually rotated office of the parish church's *fiscal* (and his group of helpers), as well as the cargos for the Virgins of the Nativity and the Sorrows. The choirmaster who presides over the ceremony summons the agrarian, civil, and religious authorities of the modern pueblo to reconstitute the extinct cabildo, thereby briefly restoring the unity of civil and religious power. The public summoned to witness the events in the church atrium are told that the "ancestors" designed this ceremony to incarnate the "usos y costumbres" of the community, to give an account of the essence of its traditions and Catholic culture "in case important personages from Mexico City might come as researchers to investigate its indigenous culture."

The event was established long before the shift in the 1980s of state policy from assimilationism to a more multicultural posture. Although federal schoolteachers arrived in the 1920s, the resistance of Coalcomán's ex-cristero political bosses delayed imposition of the culture of the postrevolutionary state through education until the 1960s, when representatives of the Instituto Nacional Indigenista came to town. The Santa Teresa ceremony already existed as a local effort to seek the state's support in holding back the tide of mestizo advance during Ostula's campaign for official rerecognition of the community's lands. The actions associated with the Santa Teresa fiesta illustrate how the people of Ostula have become conscious of the distinctive features of their own cultural order and have objectified them as a distinct "tradition" (see Comaroff and Comaroff 1992).

Such objectification appeared frequently in the petitions and complaints directed by community leaders toward state and federal governments during the 1960s and 1970s. A striking example is a letter sent in 1967 by the Comisariados de Bienes Comunales (Commissary of the Community Commons) of Coire, Ostula, and Pómaro to President Gustavo Díaz Ordaz protesting a scheme to redistribute communal lands to the heads of landless households without regard to their ethnic identities or the existence of legally recognized indigenous communities. In its protest, the letter draws a sharp distinction between "Mexicans" and indigenous people, explicitly challenging the regional criollo-mestizo stereotypes that painted the Nahuas as lacking the capabilities required to create a "modern" economy. The communities' rights to preserve exclusive control over their communal lands were defended in terms of the antiquity of their colonial "primordial titles."[6] Testimony from the middle of the nineteenth century suggests that during earlier epochs the sharpest divisions were among the indigenous communities themselves, as reflected in strict observation of norms of community endogamy (Romero López 1993 [1864]). The developments of the late nineteenth and early twentieth centuries changed the situation radically, as the indigenous versus mestizo distinction became the focus of indigenous concerns about the growing aggression of mestizo colonists.

The conjunction of land reform schemes and accelerating mestizo colonization produced fundamental changes in interethnic relations and in indigenous struggles to retain "autonomy" in this region. The defense of territory and "autonomy" in the management of community affairs involved an *active* engagement with change in the external world and the acceptance of changes that seemed beneficial and compatible with indigenous goals. Ostulans did not dream of a lost preconquest past but saw themselves as members of a postcolonial society in which they could claim a more dignified place. Yet their situation inevitably drew them into new kinds of engagements due to the pressures created by the growth of the local mestizo population.

Once the leaders of Ostula embarked on the official process for regaining legal tenure of their communal lands, they were obliged to accept the new forms of organization imposed by the nation-state, in particular with regard to agrarian matters. New authority structures were created, and communal assemblies that dealt with agrarian matters were now subject to rules regarding quorums. Conflicts arose repeatedly over who had a right to participate in such assemblies, since the state only recognized the voting rights of those adult males who were named officially as beneficiaries under the new legal procedures. When factional conflicts erupted over the management of the new official agrarian community, the intervention of state bureaucrats became unavoidable, even though community members generally found backstage ways of resolving conflicts about how community affairs should be managed.

Although a significant degree of control over internal affairs has been maintained by the assembly as a sovereign body, the gains from the new relationship with the state have been limited. The presidential resolution on Ostula's territorial claims has never been fully executed, since it has proven impossible for the parties to reach agreement on the question of the community's land boundaries.

Battles over Territory in the Twentieth Century

Ostula's representatives delivered their petition for confirmation and titling of their communal lands to the Departamento Agrario in January 1952, though its publication in the *Diario Oficial* was delayed until March 1954 (RAN, Santa María Ostula, *Bienes comunales*, exp. 1523-b, foja 39, 1954). The petitioners presented titles, which were declared valid, dating from 1802 and 1803, the epoch of the territorial conflicts with Coire. In July 1959 the government sent an engineer to Ostula to carry out the technical-informational work necessary to proceed with the formal titling process.

The engineer's report, submitted in October, revealed problems with the already executed presidential resolution on Coire. The disputes among Ostula, Coire, and Pómaro continued after 1959 because the engineer's work in Ostula was subsequently deemed defective by another official sent to the region in 1966. According to this second official, the 1959 map of the western boundary of the Pómaro community had been drafted without conducting a proper survey on the ground. As a result, the center of the Pómaro community had been mislocated and had left Ostula in possession of a strip of territory that had been previously adjudicated to Coire. Although these anomalies generated demands for a resurvey of boundaries and the re-placing of boundary markers, from this period onward the principal conflicts were not among the indigenous communities themselves but between Ostula and its neighboring nonindigenous landholders of Aquila and Maquilí and between Coire and the mestizo population enclave on its northern borders.

Ostula also had a problem with a small group of mestizo families that had invaded its territory under the auspices of Aquila's political chief in 1928. The Ostula assembly denied the mestizos any voice or vote in community affairs, instead treating them as renters (*arrendatarios*). This "zero tolerance" posture rendered impossible the compromises eventually reached in Coire.[7] The irony of the situation of the handful of "enclaved" mestizos within Ostula's territory is that several outsiders had married indigenous women despite the community's general insistence that women should leave in such circumstances, and these men genuinely wished to be allowed to participate in the collective social and religious life of the community.

Ostula was already involved in its boundary disputes with the mestizo *pequeños propietarios* (small landholders) of Aquila when the engineer arrived in 1959, and since the mestizos' representatives did not present themselves when he was producing his (erroneous) plan of Ostula's territory, he relied on the information supplied by Ostula community members. He reported that no serious boundary disputes existed on the borders between the community and Aquila and Maquilí and proclaimed that he had brokered a boundary agreement between the community and the ejido of Coahuayutla (RAN, Santa María Ostula, *Bienes comunales*, exp. 1523, foja 23, 1959). Everything seemed set for a swift move to a presidential resolution recognizing the 19,032 ha of communal property free of disputes that the engineer had identified as the territory of Ostula. Yet, within the year, a community revolt against the conduct of the recently elected community representative for indigenous landholdings made further delays inevitable. New agrarian authorities were elected with an overwhelming majority of votes in the assembly. Two years later, a project plan was approved (RAN, Santa María Ostula, *Bienes comunales*, exp. 1523-b, foja 15, 1961), but it took a further three years for the presidential resolution to be signed. In October 1964 newly elected agrarian authorities of Ostula certified that the community's territory had been properly surveyed and was duly demarcated with boundary markers. It rapidly became apparent that the signatures had been obtained under pressure and reflected the lack of experience of the new authorities. In June 1966 yet another request was sent to the government to request that technical personnel be sent again to carry out the work of marking the community's boundaries (RAN, Santa María Ostula, *Bienes comunales*, exp. 1523-b, foja 98, 1966). This request arrived with another document sent by the municipal president of Aquila, requesting that troops be deployed to provide the "necessary guarantees" for the work to be carried out (RAN, Santa María Ostula, *Bienes comunales*, exp. 1523-b, fojas 96–97, 1966).

The requested official arrived in Ostula in September 1966. He reported that he could not conduct his work because the people of Ostula refused to accept the boundaries defined by the *plan proyecto* and presidential resolution (RAN, Santa María Ostula, *Bienes comunales*, exp. 1523-b, foja 97, 1966). The Ostulan position was stated in a letter sent to President Díaz Ordaz by the incoming agrarian authorities via the municipal committee of the PRI two months later (RAN, Santa María Ostula, *Bienes comunales*, exp. 1523-b, fojas 133–134, 1966). In their letter, the Ostulans accused government officials of having received bribes from the mestizo small landholders to allow communal territory to be invaded. The letter further claimed that government officials had refused to reconnoiter the community's boundaries and had failed to locate the points marked on the plan and trace the necessary lines to close the perimeter. The Ostulans argued that these deficiencies in the official mapping process were deliberately designed to permit invasions. The letter ends by requesting that "a way be found to give recognition to the primordial boundaries of the property title that protect our interests."

The following year, the government conducted a general study of boundary problems in the region and concluded that the problems lay in "differences of criteria" between the indigenous community members and their mestizo neighbors, who consistently thwarted efforts to make agreements stick (RAN, Santa María Ostula, *Bienes comunales*, exp. 1523-b, foja 102, 1967). From the government's perspective, the only way forward was to insist that the communities accept the officially approved maps. Bureaucrats argued that brigades of engineers should be dispatched yet again and that the communities should be persuaded to sign permanent and binding agreements. This stance ignored the reality on the ground. Ostula had suffered invasions of a frequently violent kind, and the mestizo authorities from Aquila were calling for a new *reparto* of communal lands that would include landless mestizos.

The agrarian bureaucracy was even less inclined to think through the deeper implications of "differences of criteria" that included repeated references to "primordial" rights and titles rooted in an early colonial past. The available documents demonstrate that the relations between these places were known through ancient boundary markers and the kinds of straight lines that peasants draw when they survey the landscape with their eyes. From the indigenous perspective, the landscape was not just a collection of "geographical" features but a collage of places saturated with historical meanings known through local oral historical traditions. The indigenous peasants "knew" their territory in an intimate kind of way. This intimate knowledge was not only "practical" and economic, acquired by traveling within the landscape and learning by experience and instruction how to make use of its varied resources, but also social. Places were invested with meanings related to the histories of families that had opened up the land for cultivation and to incidents that evoked the history of social relations between families and between the human and supernatural worlds.

Social relationships are always embedded in the ways in which human populations interact with their environment. In the Ostula case, attachment to the physical landscape within which people "dwell" reflects the historical uniqueness of the social group, so that a "place-people" has emerged with a distinctive "culture" and "traditions." In contrast, bureaucrats impose geographical maps onto social space without being sensitive to the ethnic interaction and agrarian conflict taking place on the ground. In their preferences for demarcating spaces in terms of straight lines between known points, the engineers (and the bureaucrats to whom they report) are working with a cosmology that both idealizes and diminishes the social, economic, and political "reality" in which territory has meaning for community members.

The consequences of this disjuncture between bureaucratic and indigenous perspectives rapidly became apparent. In 1971 a further effort was made to resolve Ostula's boundary disputes with Aquila (where an attempt was under way to reconstruct its own lost indigenous community), as well as with the small landholders of Maquilí and La Placita. All the interested parties were called to a meeting in Ostula to present the documents that supported their property claims. Nevertheless, the work was again suspended due to irreconcilable differences between all parties, including the community members of Aquila (RAN, Santa María Ostula, *Bienes comunales*, exp. 1523-b, fojas 164–164, 1971).

As a result of this stalemate, the situation passed into the hands of the Comisión Agraria Mixta in Morelia. A meeting was called that was attended by representatives from Maquilí, Aquila, Coire, and Ostula. Lengthy and contentious discussion focused on the problems caused by the fact that the first engineer's survey had not been conducted properly, thus causing errors affecting several communities. The principal result of the meeting was that another engineer was ordered in March 1972 to return to Ostula to complete the work abandoned in the previous year.

Despite interventions by various other governmental agencies, including the National Indigenous Institute, a new survey team was not dispatched to Ostula. As a result, disputes continued to break out between Ostula and the mestizo ranchers from a nearby municipio who drove their cattle into communal territory for grazing. In 1978, after yet another set of new community authorities had requested the governor's intervention in the drawn-out land conflict, the regional delegate of the Secretaria de la Reforma Agraria responded to state authorities by noting that his organization was overworked and that it was futile to repeat the effort to rectify the situation in Ostula so long as the community refused to accept the approved plan (RAN, Santa María Ostula, *Bienes comunales*, exp. 1523, fojas 60–61, 1978).

Although a new survey team did eventually make an appearance, its members did not carry out any survey work but restricted themselves to organizing meetings designed to deal with the conflicts between Maquilí's small landholders and the people of Ostula. Any possibilities of further effective resolution of the Maquili-Ostula conflict were laid aside with the outbreak of the most serious round of factional conflict in Ostula's history. The conflict escalated and endured because it reflected an increasing polarization of the community around questions of illegal logging, abuse of authority, and social inequality. By the end of the 1980s, it also reflected the emergence of political alternatives beyond the long-ruling Partido de la Revolución Institucional, as well as the emergence of radical indigenous political groups. Ultimately, the Nahua communities of Ostula and the region were incorporated into wider indigenous movements.

Even when factional conflict within the community was most intense, contending parties would come together in matters that related to the defense of territory. This was true not only during the 1980s but also during 2001–2003, when the community's ability to act was seriously prejudiced by conflicts between authorities aligned with the Partido de la Revolución Democrática and their opponents aligned with the PRI. In the end, the undermining of the authority of the PRD faction actually led, after new authorities were elected, to an armed occupation of disputed terrain by a large number of Ostulans in June 2003. This development may also have been encouraged by the "demonstration effect" of recent examples of successful direct action by indigenous groups against ejidatarios in other states, although the potential crisis was defused by the intervention of figures from the PRD-controlled state government.

Most striking about the long debates in community assemblies that preceded this escalation of conflict was the constant reiteration of the theme that it was essential that younger people be taken around the community perimeter to learn the precise boundaries of their community. Even in the midst of factional conflict, the contending parties suspended hostilities to make possible these tours of the perimeter. The internal conflicts that broke out after 1978 effectively ended efforts to force the agrarian bureaucracy to complete the work of boundary demarcation and to define accurately the community's territory. The "differences of criteria" that always have driven the issue of boundary conflicts and land-use policies remain as contested as ever.

Toward an Uncertain Future?

Differences between the Mexican state and Ostula's indigenous people reflect a genuine "clash of cultures." The chief benefit of relations between the Ostula region and the state, especially in recent years, was the influx of social development aid and improvements to infrastructure. Unfortunately, even these investments were not sufficient to transform the "marginalized" socioeconomic status of the region's Nahua indigenous communities. Furthermore, even these limited gains had problematic consequences, especially a culture of patron-client relations between individual community members and the municipal authorities. Even when mestizo mayors were replaced by indigenous officials after 1998, these new leaders continued to reproduce the same patterns of political clientelism that had always been the order of the day in Ostula and its region.

The period after the land settlement of 1964 also produced a degree of assimilation of ranchero cultural styles by the indigenous population. Yet emphasis on the distinctiveness of regional indigenous cultural traditions has been promoted by state government policies encouraging cultural and ecotourism in the area, as well as by social development and antipoverty programs that preferentially target indigenous groups.

The Nahuas of the Michoacán coast were relatively late entrants to the new wave of indigenous mobilization triggered by the 1994 revolt of the Zapatista Army of National Liberation (EZLN, Ejercio Zapatista de la Liberación Nacional) in Chiapas. Initially, participation in the wider state and national indigenous movement was restricted to a few local political leaders linked into wider networks created by the Catholic Church and the PRD. The state movement itself is dominated by Purépecha professionals based in the central highlands of Michoacán whose political activism long predates the EZLN rebellion. The Purépechas represent the majority of an indigenous population that remains a very small minority (3.5 percent) of the total state population. Still weakly articulated to external centers of political power, the coastal Nahuas faced some tricky choices in their cultural politics. On the one hand, they needed to assert their distinctiveness to gain spaces within new structures of indigenous political representation; on the other, they needed to move toward more inclusive definitions of who is "indigenous" to strengthen the movement's overall political influence.

At the community level, bilingual teachers born and raised in the area's villages are at the forefront of this latest round of mobilization. Given their professional self-interest in the rescue of indigenous culture and language, there have sometimes been tensions between the teachers and the agrarian and civil authorities, who are more closely articulated to the everyday problems of both peasant families and the increasing number of community members involved in migration to the United States. The potential contradictions of a politics of indigenous identity and recognition divorced from socioeconomic questions are readily apparent. Some teachers' pursuit of wider ambitions through the political party system also became a further source of factional conflict within their communities.

Yet factionalism and internal community conflicts in Ostula also demonstrated the resilience of systems of community governance based on the sovereignty of communal assemblies. Ostula's retention of a rich religious life based on the principle of community service played an important role in restraining tendencies toward caciquismo in the past. Although the growing numbers of young people leaving for the United States and staying there posed some threat to the survival of established cultural patterns, including the system of community cargos, the latter underpinned a capacity for democratic management of community affairs that continued to manifest itself in the embrace of new models of indigenous autonomy and self-determination. In 2006 new leadership in Ostula aligned the community with the EZLN's Other Campaign and the Sixth Lacandón Declaration. Subcomandante Marcos paid a personal visit to Ostula, now declared a "community in resistance" to the government's Program for the Certification of Communal Rights (PROCECOM). The defense of the community's boundaries against rancher encroachments had come to be seen as crucial to defeating new plans to allow private-sector interests to expropriate the community's beaches and mineral resources, plans now seen as enjoying the support of all mainstream political forces in the state, including, up to the state elections of 2011 and national elections of 2012, both a PRD-controlled state government and PAN-controlled federal government. Ostula's Commission for the Defense of Communal Property thus took an increasingly aggressive attitude toward 700 ha of land that the community claimed had been usurped by ranchers from La Placita. This led in July 2008 to the killing of the commission's president, primary school teacher Diego Ramírez Domínguez, whose naked and battered body was dumped in the disputed terrain. Less than a year later, following a confrontation in which heavily armed men fired upon men, women, and children from Ostula, the community turned its communal police into a self-defense force (capturing three of the alleged perpetrators, later handed over to the public prosecutor) and took control of the disputed territory, initiating the construction of a new settlement within it and announcing that its name would be changed from La Canahuancera to the Náhuatl name Xayacallan.

After the seizure of the disputed terrain, the *perredista*, or PRD, state government undertook to negotiate a solution based on indemnification of the ranchers for the value of the land involved and to recognize Ostula's police as a legitimate self-defense force, but no concrete steps were taken to regularize the situation legally, opening the way to continuing violence: two more Ostulans serving as town councilors in Aquila were kidnapped and "disappeared," and by 2010 the community had finally attracted the attention of human rights NGOs as it denounced intensifying attacks from "paramilitary" forces. The suggestion was that the ranchers had sought help from the cartels. Having become independent of the Gulf cartel, the Zetas were now fighting a war of "narco-messages" and severed heads with a newer crime organization whose members they originally trained, La Familia Michoacana. La Familia, whose leaders made regular public declarations and adopted the model of a religious cult, claimed to be engaged in a moralizing project that opposed the local consumption of drugs and offered the population the protection that it did not receive from the Mexican state. It achieved a deep infiltration of local government and police forces, a reflection not only of its economic power in a situation of economic stagnation, made worse by the impact of the crisis in the United States on immigration, but also of widespread popular resentment about the way that the government of President Felipe Calderón used federal security forces and the military in the state. Although the La Familia cartel began to unravel following the death of its principal leader, nicknamed "the craziest one," in a federal security operation at the end of 2010 and the subsequent arrest of others, two of the original founders who remained at large formed a rival organization with a similar orientation, the Knights Templar (Los Caballeros Templarios), and the conflict with the Zetas continued on its sanguinary course. In Ostula the killing of community leaders intensified, including those who had played the leading roles in the retaking of the disputed land. The absence of any significant action to halt this extermination on the part of either federal or state security forces prompted many *comuneros* to suspect that yet more powerful economic interests were at work. The twenty-first century is thus repeating the history of the late nineteenth and early twentieth centuries. Entangled in the violence of actors who do not belong to their local social world yet have the capacity to reach inside its borders, Ostulans once again feel that they are fighting for survival.

Thus, the question for the future is not whether the surviving coastal Nahuas in Michoacán have the will to defend themselves against their immediate neighbors and threats to their control of territory. The question is whether they can survive the violence that such resistance provokes given the levels of impunity that all levels of government seem willing to grant the immediate perpetrators of that violence and the interests behind them. Also at issue is whether the Nahua can build a unity movement among different indigenous communities in the coastal region and use this newfound unity to negotiate a stronger position within the larger indigenous movement. Given that Coire and Pómaro actively supported Ostula in the 2009 confrontation with La Placita, that the community became firmly integrated into the National Indigenous Congress, and that Ostula has continued to receive strong support from Cherán, engaged in its own autonomy movement on the basis of local self-defense (see chapter 11, this volume), this does seem possible. Recent developments have also weakened the grip of political parties over indigenous political life. Yet whatever the future may be for new styles of politics within indigenous communities, the case of Ostula and its neighbors in the southwestern coastal region of Michoacán shows that territorial control is integral to indigenous conceptions of identity in a way that motivates passionate action.

Notes

1. The indigenous community of Coalcomán was the first to suffer dispossession. The criollo elite that established itself in this old colonial administrative center used a combination of fraud and violence to steal the lands of the indigenous population, whose communal lands were converted into individual parcels under Liberal land reform laws implemented in 1871. Indigenous protests continued until 1892, when the Coalcomán elite massacred the remaining opposition (Sánchez Díaz 1988). The community of Maquilí rapidly lost its indigenous population after its communal lands were divided in 1906. In its case, the principal beneficiaries of the dispossession were invading mestizo ranchers. In the case of Maquilí, as in those of the neighboring communities of Aquila and Huizontla, the instrument of dispossession was the authorities' fiscal revaluation of the community's forest lands, which subsequently became a major commercial prize for regional and foreign logging interests (Gledhill 2004).

2. The provision for "restitution" of communal lands adopted by the postrevolutionary state only applied to land that had been lost as a result of illegal usurpation under the terms of the federal disentailment law of 1856 (the Ley Lerdo). Furthermore, the state preferred to make land grants (*dotaciones*) to establish the new type of agrarian communities (ejidos) that it sponsored as a means of turning the peasantry into "modern citizens" and political clients. The state was operating within the framework of a cultural policy in which assimilation—the "Mexicanizing the Indian" cultural version of nineteenth-century ideologies of "whitening as progress"—was seen as a necessary step forward for communities that had stubbornly retained their "indigenous" identities. In contrast to historic communal holdings, the land granted to communities as ejidos remained state property to which the beneficiaries merely enjoyed inheritable use rights rather than collective ownership.

3. In 1805 an iron and steel works opened in the relatively remote settlement of Coalcomán to take advantage of its iron ore deposits (Brand 1960). Although the Revolution of 1810 disrupted the town's development, the revival of mining in the 1820s and the growth of cattle-ranching encouraged further nonindigenous immigration. Although military operations disrupted life in the region from 1834 onward, followed by the Liberal-Conservative wars and guerrilla actions against the French, after 1867

conditions became more stable. This made it possible to make a dramatic leap into capitalist industry, agriculture, commercial logging, and cattle raising.

4. A port at Maruata Bay, in the indigenous territory of Pómaro, did finally secure official recognition in 1875. It played an important role in the export of timber by North American companies until the revolution. Ten years earlier, Maruata had already been inhabited by some three hundred residents, at least some of whom were attracted by pearl fishing and contraband trading (Romero López 1993 [1864]; Sánchez Díaz 1988), but it ceased to operate as a general export outlet for coastal products before the close of the nineteenth century (Sánchez Díaz 1988).

5. The ranchers had originated in the highlands of Jalisco, crossing the plains between Chapala and Zamora to establish themselves in the towns of Cotija and Peribán, respectively a major center of muleteering and a center for interregional trade in cattle and oxen. The sparsely populated sierra of Coalcomán became their next zone of colonization. As the building of railroads reduced the opportunities available to Cotija muleteers, they focused on the more isolated parts of their original routes from the tierra caliente down to the coast and into Colima. This spearheaded at the turn of the twentieth century a second wave of migration, which had an increasing impact on coastal indigenous communities. As a result, Coalcomán was one of the few towns in Michoacán to gain population throughout the decade of revolutionary war (Cochet 1991).

6. *Títulos primordiales* are indigenous documents (usually written in Náhuatl) that, although often failing to meet official legal criteria, provide accounts of the foundation of a community, construction of churches, and other important events, thus codifying a community's own historical memory and thereby grounding its claims to its territory (Gruzinski 1991; see chapter 6 in this volume). Claims in this region were frequently based on mythologized foundation charters in which Hernán Cortés personally guaranteed a community peaceful possession of its lands in perpetuity. Ostula and Coire did, however, possess legally recognized titles in the late colonial period, and all the communities were able to produce documentation deemed satisfactory as a basis for the titling and confirmation of communal land in the second half of the twentieth century.

7. These families were finally accepted as members of the newly reconstituted indigenous community of Aquila in 1987. In 1971, in the context of another campaign to produce a definitive resolution of boundary problems with Aquila, the assembly had determined that the families in the ranchos of Troncón de Aguacate y La Laguna, neighboring La Mina, should be allowed to remain in the community's territory on condition that they accepted their status as arrendatarios and would never again seek recognition as members of the community. See RAN, Santa María Ostula, *Bienes comunales*, exp. 1523-b, foja 183, 1971.

11

Ritual and Public Spheres in an Ethnic Celebration of Communal Sovereignty

The Purépecha Transition

Andrew Roth-Seneff

A Highway in the Highlands

In 1988, two weeks after the creation of the Democratic Revolution Party (Partido de la Revolución Democrática, PRD), several busloads of townspeople from the Purépecha Highlands in the state of Michoacán arrived at Los Pinos, the president's residential complex, for a meeting described as a forum for "collaboration and dialogue." The event was organized by the Federation of Purépecha Professionals as part of the Program for Collaboration and Development in the Purépecha Highlands, which operated within a larger public works project called the Michoacán Plan. At the meeting, President Carlos Salinas de Gortari addressed his "Purépecha compatriots" and promised that within the year the federal government would begin to pave the second most important roadway in the highlands. He also invited those present to return to their towns and villages and encourage their communities to participate in this major development project (Méndez Alfaro 1989).

Before the meeting at Los Pinos, the only paved road in the highlands connected the Guadalajara–Morelia highway to Uruapan, the second largest city in the state and the gateway to the rich agricultural hotlands and Michoacán's Pacific coast. That road had been paved four decades earlier in a massively funded federal development project headed by former president Lázaro Cárdenas (Calderón 1999; Castile 1972; Nelson 2000). That a second major roadway would be upgraded and paved was exciting news not only because of the commercial possibilities it offered for greater participation in agroindustrial activities in the well-watered regions surrounding the highlands but also because the roadwork itself, as well as the extraction of volcanic gravel from the surrounding extinct volcanoes (to be used in rebuilding the roadbed), promised immediate economic relief to many Purépecha communities (Roth-Seneff et al. 2004).

At the same time, however, the project was controversial. The election of Carlos Salinas in July 1988 and the beginning of his presidency in December 1988 had deeply divided Michoacán. This state is home to the Cárdenas family,

whose patriarch, Lázaro Cárdenas (1895–1970), was the architect of postrevolutionary land reform in Mexico, and of the Institutional Revolutionary Party
(Partido Revolucionario Institucional, PRI), which held power from the 1930s
until 2000. By 2002 this family had produced four state governors, and Cuauhtémoc, Lázaro's only son and the PRI governor of Michoacán from 1980 to
1986, had precipitated a major rupture in the PRI.

One faction of that party, referred to as the "technocrats" or "neoliberal re-
formers," which had been in power since 1982, successfully blocked Cuauhtémoc Cárdenas's efforts to be selected as the PRI presidential candidate in 1987.
In response, Cárdenas first formed an opposition movement within the party,
called the Revolutionary Democratic Movement. But when he was passed over
once again as a precandidate for the PRI presidential nomination, he left the
party to build an opposition movement, the Democratic Current (Corriente
Democrática), which formed a multiparty coalition. This coalition created the
National Democratic Front for the 1987 presidential election and ultimately
became the aforementioned PRD.

Cuauhtémoc Cárdenas ran against Salinas in 1988 in a highly controversial election; many voters questioned the results and the legitimacy of Salinas's
victory. This was especially the case in the Purépecha Highlands, where the
Cárdenas legacy is profoundly influential. There was, in fact, a generational split
between those Cardenista supporters of Lázaro Cárdenas still affiliated with the
PRI and the so-called *neo-cardenista* supporters of his son, Cuauhtémoc, in the
PRD. This split surfaced, for example, in professional Purépecha organizations
associated with the highland town of Zacán.

By 1991 Zacán had produced three federal congressmen, two in the PRI
and one in the political movement that was evolving into the PRD. The con-
gressman involved in the opposition movement had very famously broken with
decades of political protocol during Salinas's first State of the Union address
by interrupting the speech with shouts of "Michoacán! You must speak about
that!" after Salinas, in his address, stated that "submitting to the popular will;
recognizing triumphs, genuinely obtained, is an expression of the society's political maturity" (Beltrán del Río 1993:112, my translation). These Purépecha
political leaders, along with many of the hundreds of highly educated Purépecha professionals with links to Zacán, got their start with the support of a professional organization created in the late 1960s and early 1970s.

This civil organization was founded to promote the material and cultural
"progress" of the highlands and, especially, of Zacán. The group began formally
in 1971 as the Association of Zacán Professionals. Informally, regular social
meetings had begun years earlier at the home of one of the founders in Uruapan. By 1971 the group had a charter, an elected directorship, and a formal
mandate: "To contribute to the general betterment of the people [*pueblo*] in
moral, material, and cultural aspects . . ., goals gradually achieved thanks to

the state government and, above all, the determined support of the Universidad Michoacana de San Nicolás de Hidalgo" ("Documento de la Asociación de Profesionista de Zacán," in Martínez Buenabad 2000, my translation).

This association began with a slogan, "For the progress of our people," and a membership of 84 professionals. The rector of the Universidad Michoacana at the time, Dr. Melchor Díaz Rubio, was named lifetime president, and Cuauhtémoc Cárdenas was a frequently invited guest at the association's meetings. Within four years' time, a factional fight emerged over the degree to which the group had been compromised through its strong ties to the state government and the university's bureaucracy. The result was the creation of a second association, one that operated largely from Mexico City under the name Ambakentsani ("to become transparent" in Purépecha).

By 1986 this second association would be transformed again, ironically, into a group that provided key logistical support to the PRI in the highlands (Beltrán del Río 1993). The original Zacán association founded in Uruapan, in contrast, was divided between supporters of the PRD and the PRI. In spite of these divisions, the leaders of both associations pragmatically participated in organizing the Federation of Purépecha Professionals and utilized this federation both to organize the meeting in Los Pinos with Salinas and, afterward, to control the direction of the roadwork program. In November 1989, Salinas arrived by helicopter to a much-publicized meeting in Zacán for the formal inauguration of an almost completed two-lane paved highway.

Ritualized Spheres of Exchange and the Public Sphere

The organization of public works in the Purépecha Highlands in the context of a major postelectoral conflict and, in particular, the mobilization of Purépecha communities in an act favorable to the PRI presidency after a very controversial vote raises a complex issue. What was the nature of the political mobilization involved? Was it ethnic and, therefore, a powerful identification that cut across political and class affiliations and allowed the Purépecha (peasants and professionals, *priistas* and *perredistas*) to come together and thereby benefit from a major public works project? Or, rather, was such a strategic mobilization and spectacle in support of the legitimacy of the controversial Salinas administration based on a complex system of clientelism in which the Purépecha leadership, already well established in the state's bureaucracy, could demonstrate power to their political bosses by mobilizing the "masses" in the towns, villages, and ranches of the highlands not through ethnic identification but within a system of patronage that could then be resignified in terms of ethnicity in speeches ("my fellow Purépecha compatriots") and in the press?

Another, more general way of posing this problem for Mexico and much of postcolonial Latin America and its cultural histories concerns both the relation with and the difference between ritualized spheres of exchange and a modern national public sphere. The Purépecha have a long history of participation in ritualized spheres of exchange that reaches beyond their contact with the Spanish. For example, one of the key institutions of the Purépecha towns and villages created in the sixteenth century is known in Purépecha as the *yurhíxu*. This term refers to a Marian institution of social assistance, a hospital, established by the Franciscan order under Bishop Vasco de Quiroga, who arrived in the Tarascan region in 1533.[1] As the Tarascan population was "congregated" into towns and villages, a church dedicated to a patron saint and a hospital dedicated to the Virgin of the Immaculate Conception would be erected in each central plaza. Indeed, one township, Santa Fe de la Laguna, was a hospital-town; that is, the entire town encompassed the institution of the hospital and a Marian cult of social assistance. These indigenous congregations in towns controlling smaller nearby hamlets were called Indian republics and were protected by both imperial law and the church from their non-Indian Spanish or mixed counterparts within the empire.

The root of the word for hospital in Purépecha, *yurhíxu*, is probably *yurhi*, which means "blood." The word *yurhixe* appears in a sixteenth-century Tarascan dictionary as "virgin" (Lagunas 1983 [1574]). Also, the Purépecha expression *yurhits queri* means "girl, maiden of age" (Warren 1991), which in etymological terms would be understood as "she who has started bleeding," while *yurixu* literally translated would be the "home of the bleeding." Hence *yurhíxu* is the "home of the virgin or virgins" and could refer to a prehispanic institution (a house for maidens) in which, upon reaching the age of menstruation, the daughters of the nobility were prepared for marriage alliances. To name the colonial institution *yurhixu* suggests that the formation of the colonial state and the key institutions of its Indian republics formed a hybrid and often contradictory process that combined institutionalized practices of both Tarascan and Spanish origin (Monzón and Roth Seneff 1999).

These institutions—church, hospital, communal treasury—were organized around ritualized spheres of exchange that defined the Indian republics. The church and hospital had (and continue to have) an annual calendar of religious celebrations honoring Jesus, Mary, and the saints. During the colonial period the calendar was administered by brotherhoods (*cofradías*) with "officers" in hierarchical positions of service (e.g., *prioste*, *mayordomo*, *fiscal mayor*, and *Kengue*, among others) in the religious system and positions (*cargos*) such as governor and secretary in the civil system of each Indian republic. Both religious and civil institutions had their properties managed by the brotherhoods and officials (called *cargueros*). It was common to keep a written record of the holdings of the holy images that resided in and gave meaning to institutions such as the hospital or the church. Each such record is called a *pindecuario* in Purépecha. Though they originated in the sixteenth century, several of these documents terminated abruptly in 1767 after a series of uprisings in the Tarascan area against the Spanish Empire's Bourbon reforms initiated an extended, complex, and changing campaign against the corporate properties of the Indian republics (Castro Gutiérrez 2004).

What I have called ritualized spheres of exchange organized around the religious and civil institutions of the Indian republics—that is, Indian towns organized corporately on a base of a commons (commonly held land and natural resources)—had a central core of exchange that involved not only the *barrios* (roughly, neighborhoods) of each town or village but also a much wider exchange circuit with surrounding towns and villages. For instance, Holy Week and the celebration of Corpus Christi traditionally bring together several related villages and towns in a complex coordination and rotation of collective celebrations: (1) in the Zacapu Valley, Tiríndaro, Naranja, Tarejero, Azajo, and Comanja (Friedrich 1977); (2) in the southwestern area of Lake Pátzcuaro, Erongarícuaro, Urichu, and Xarácuaro, plus several ranches (Castilleja 2007); and (3) on the southwestern rim of the Purépecha Highlands: San Juan Parangaricutiro, Santiago Angáhuan, San Salvador Kumbatizio, San Pedro Zacán, Santa Ana Zirosto, and San Francisco Corupo.

In order to understand the transformations of this civil-religious system during almost two and a half centuries (1780–2012), it is useful to distinguish among a civil system, a religious system, and family-based fiesta sponsorship (Chance 1992; Chance and Taylor 1985). The liberal reforms of the nineteenth century were aimed at transforming the ritualized spheres of communal exchange into a modern national public sphere. But, as Eric Wolf has noted (1986), the dismantling of the corporate structure of the Indian republics with their ritualized spheres of exchange led to new local and regional forms of participation in several projects of state reform, namely, nineteenth-century liberal reform, mid-twentieth-century corporate postrevolutionary reform, and the current neoliberal reform of the late twentieth and early twenty-first centuries.

The historical transformations of the civil-religious system of the Indian republics were complex and varied. Wolf (1986) also observes that attempts to typify these general processes are problematic. For instance, in Zacán in 1791, the local priest used the hospital as his residence, which suggests that at least one of the principal communal institutions was no longer in operation (Castro Gutiérrez 2004). On the other hand, this same hospital was part of a major ecclesiastic and artistic revival in the Purépecha Highlands at the time of the mid-nineteenth-century Liberal reforms (Sigaut 2008). Meanwhile, in communities like Santa Fe and Puácuaro in the Lake Pátzcuaro area, a village elite emerged through control over the local religious fiesta cycle, often with support from powerful neighboring landholders (Hernández 2004; Zárate 2001).

On the basis of major reviews of historical and ethnographic case studies (Chance 1992; Chance and Taylor 1985), the few generalizations that can be made about transformations in these ritualized spheres of exchange involve the separation of the civil and religious spheres and the loss of corporate holdings for fiesta sponsorship. Throughout the Liberal reforms of the nineteenth century, but especially in the last two decades of Porfirio Díaz's dictatorial presidency (1890–1910), the institutions of the former Indian republics became differentiated into a civil system based on a municipal hierarchy of elected administrators and a religious system that maintained the traditional offices with their duties of service to the church, the hospital, and, especially, religious images. These images, traditionally housed both in the hospital's chapel and in the sanctuary building, were increasingly distributed to private homes and neighborhood chapels, as family-based fiesta sponsorship came to replace the earlier corporate sponsorship exercised by the religious brotherhoods. In short, the municipal offices of president, *regidor*, and *jefe de tenencia*, among others, replaced the offices of the republics (governor, *alcalde*, secretary), while at the same time the civil-religious *cabildo* (institutionalized leadership) of the Indian republics became an exclusively local religious authority. In addition, advancement through the religious hierarchy and eventual membership in the cabildo as an elder, or *principal* (*tarhepeti* in Purépecha), was achieved through family fiesta sponsorship organized around the residential pattern of the town or village barrios, often grouped together into half-sections or moieties (e.g., "the barrios above the central plaza" and "those below").

The postrevolutionary land reforms introduced important changes into the civil hierarchy by creating an elected hierarchy for the control of the commons (*ejido*) resources—basically land, forests, and water—and, most important, by establishing a general assembly as the supreme sphere of authority for the community. In many Purépecha towns, the figure of the cabildo was largely replaced by a general assembly often controlled by "elected" agrarian officials. In the context of these changes, the hierarchy of religious offices associated with fiesta sponsorship was greatly reduced or simplified. Nevertheless, in the last two decades (1990–2010), state reforms have removed government support and protection for this local indigenous management of the commons, and the authority of the cabildo has increased notably in many places. Currently, the *tarhipiticha* (cabildo members) in many Purépecha communities have a powerful voice in meetings of the general assembly and are often asked by the elected agrarian and municipal authorities to ratify, assess, or bless community decisions. As we will see, it is also the case that many younger Purépecha professionals have chosen to advance through the hierarchy of religious offices and fiesta sponsorship, thereby gaining cabildo authority while also holding civil (political or agrarian) elected positions.

It is clear that the nineteenth-century Liberal reforms were aimed at creating a modern national public sphere and explicitly dismantling the corporate institutions of a supposedly "ancient regime." Equally clear is the subsequent process of postrevolutionary state formation, which involved a project that sought to reorganize rural Mexico into middle- to large-scale corporate production units oriented toward national and international markets. Tied to this project was a major effort to "acculturate" and "integrate" rural Mexico, especially the indigenous population, into a national culture predefined as Spanish speaking and composed of individual citizens with rights and obligations. There is less clarity concerning the recent series of constitutional reforms that have obliged rural Mexico to participate in the global economy and have provoked debate and dialogue concerning the definition and preservation of Mexican national culture.

These very different periods of state reforms, each involving the intense participation of the Purépecha population, are all part of a continuing and contentious confrontation between, on the one hand, the historically rooted but constantly transforming ritualized forms of exchange among the Purépecha and, on the other, an increasingly simultaneous (thanks to evolving telecommunications and intelligent technology) modern public sphere. At the turn of the twentieth century, the mobilizations of Purépecha villagers, townspeople, and ranchers during the postelectoral struggles of 1988–1989, the efforts at cultural revitalization and ethnic mobilization, and the demands for local political autonomy based on custom are but several chapters of this ongoing drama of contentious confrontation, a process inseparable from the emerging roles of Purépecha women and community cabildos in local politics.

Gender and Cabildo Politics

One of the towns that most strongly opposed Salinas's election and supported Cárdenas and the PRD was Cherán, a municipal seat located in the center of the Purépecha Highlands. After the presidential elections in July 1988, Cárdenas's supporters in Cherán participated in acts of protest and civil disobedience, closing down the highlands' main highway and commandeering buses to travel to Morelia to participate in massive protests in the central plaza of the state capital. In December 1988, a plebiscite was held in Cherán through which a "popular" municipal president was put in office and the "elected" PRI leader was removed. The central plaza and municipal offices were taken over, and "popular" government was initiated in January 1989.

The women of the town participated actively in the presidential elections, the postelectoral protest, and the support of the "popular" government and played a key role in protecting the central plaza and the opposition government. Using their gender as a weapon against the machismo of the federal and state police, they aggressively confronted policemen, even scalding several with boiling water or hot coffee. Through their efforts, Cherán maintained its autonomy from the PRI administration, and for the next twelve years the PRD would control this municipal seat.

Lise Nelson (2000) has described how this political participation impacted the women of Cherán, leading to the creation of new social networks built not out of kinship or ritualized forms of patronage but rather through political participation in both organized protests and party and barrio meetings. She notes that there was a marked difference between women over 50 (many of them widows) who participated actively in local politics and younger women who enjoyed noticeably less freedom of movement outside the home. Nevertheless, in 1998 a female schoolteacher from Cherán was elected to an assembly post (*regidora*) in the municipal government, the first woman ever elected to office there.

The social drama of the takeover of the town hall and the plaza in Cherán and its defense against what were perceived as corrupt local "elected" politicians supported by the Salinas administration led, first, to an enthusiastic period of participation in a popular government in which women were treated as active and equal members and as heroic defenders of the town. This collectively charismatic period was not, however, long-lived. The PRD soon established itself as a male-dominated authoritarian presence, while municipal politics again became a personalized sphere of favors and patronage. Nevertheless, Nelson (2008) has documented the change in political discourse in Cherán, especially among women, a discourse that became openly concerned with the issues of citizenship and equality and, more particularly, with an equitable distribution of municipal resources. Prior to the 1988 struggle, politics in Cherán were under the control of a local *cacique*, or strongman, who was openly opposed only by a small faction equally interested in taking power (Calderón 2004). After the successful struggle for local control, new political attitudes and demands developed, and women began to speak out critically about male-dominated crony politics.

Cherán's women had a similar central role in April 2011 during a major collective communal response to a criminal network illegally trafficking in Cherán's forests. In the early hours of April 15, members of a barrio in Cherán blocked trucks loaded with timber leaving the city. Faced with threats of reprisal, the community organized to control all access to the city. In every barrio, neighbors gathered around bonfires and took turns patrolling their areas. A communal solidarity emerged as Cherán organized around barrio committees and a general consensus arose over the role of party politics in opening the city to the dangers of organized crime. As the self-imposed siege continued, community members voted to end party politics in Cherán and thus not participate in the state elections for municipal leaders or governor. Instead, they petitioned to establish a local government based on custom. In September 2011 the High Court of the Electoral Tribune of Federal Judicial Power (Sala Superior del Tribunal Electoral del Poder Judicial de la Federación) recognized Cherán's right to form a local custom-based government. In January 2012 Cherán became the first Purépecha city with a local government composed of three representatives from each of the city's four barrios. These twelve men and women are called *k'eri janhaskaticha* (senior mentors) and compose a governing council.

Another example of the struggle for political change and greater local autonomy occurred in Tarecuato, a Purépecha town on the central western edge of the highlands. There, the neo-cardenista rupture in the PRI and the electoral and postelectoral conflict of 1988–1989 were assimilated and accommodated into a preexisting communal division between, on the one hand, a charismatic Catholic movement instigated in 1982 by the (then) new parish priest and, on the other, the communal organization of collective service (*faena, cargueros*) and religious celebrations, coordinated by the cabildo. The parish priest had introduced a new program of collective organization in which the town's five barrios were renamed and organized around "little communities" of worship. The communities in each barrio initiated a series of conflicts with the residents of the other barrios over the control of their respective chapels and the saintly images associated with them. The members of this charismatic Catholic movement were dedicated to organizing and promoting a direct and inspired reading of the scriptures. In addition, they stressed the importance of their daily and rapturous involvement with the Holy Ghost, above and beyond any form of devotion to saintly images. Nonetheless, they were also clearly organized to take control of each barrio's traditional religious spaces, as well as those chapel images that were generally kept in the houses of the family elected each year by the cabildo to lead the associated celebrations.

Conflicts between the two groups were constant and over the years evolved into a clear split between the cabildo and the local priest, each of whom enjoyed the support of an important number of followers. In addition, several young professionals in Tarecuato were involved in a new ethnic organization, the Independent Purépecha Front, which in 1994 became the Purépecha Nation. These young professionals had strong ties to the PRD, which by 1994 had elected a party member as municipal president (mayor) in Tangamandapio, the municipal seat, and taken control of the local government in Tarecuato. In addition, they actively sought and, through kinship links, established a working relationship with the cabildo (Rivera Farfán 1998).

Tarecuato, hence, was divided: on one side, the cabildo, the institution that organized the traditional religious cycle of celebrations and represented the town's communal barrio organization, and on the other, an active and growing charismatic Catholic movement that sought to resignify and reorganize the communal barrio structure into "sectors" and "little communities." The priest who introduced and led the charismatic movement had strong ties to the PRI that allowed him access to important government support for several communal projects. In contrast, the cabildo, through its support from the young professionals of the Purépecha Nation, had the support of the PRD and local government (Rivera Farfán 1998).

This division was clearly apparent in 1995, when Tarecuato was host to the celebration of the Purhépecheri Jimanhi Wéxurhini (Purépecha New Year's Celebration). A year earlier, in 1994, just two months after the takeover of San Cristobal de las Casas by the Zapatista National Liberation Army, the Purépecha New Year was programmed to be celebrated in a rather isolated ranch called Ucasanastacua on the shore of Lake Pátzcuaro, between the towns of Ihuatzio and Tzintzuntzan. However, the scheduled event had a change of venue. Instead of an isolated ranch favorable to a largely Purépecha turnout and to political speeches in Purépecha (which, indeed, had occurred the year before at the Cocucho celebration [Roth-Seneff 1993]), the event was moved to the grand plaza in Pátzcuaro. An additional change at the beginning of the celebration was the announcement that it would honor Purépecha women; hence, only women would coordinate the activities and would control all public speaking. It is noteworthy that this change was made in January, right after the PRI government's head of the National Commission for the Integral Development and Social Justice for Indigenous Peoples, Beatriz Paredes, had held a national meeting with indigenous leaders, where the Purépecha were represented by founders of the Purépecha New Year's Celebration (Roth-Seneff 2010).

At the Pátzcuaro celebration, a delegation of women from the charismatic movement in Tarecuato formally asked to be the 1995 hosts of the event, and their request was approved. These women were the closest collaborators with Tarecuato's charismatic priest. One in particular was placed in charge of requesting the celebration and then hosting it. Through her involvement in the charismatic movement, this young woman had traveled nationally and internationally to speak at indigenous leadership events and had become an extremely articulate and forceful public speaker.

The celebration in Tarecuato only further exacerbated the divisions in the town. In 1992, when the tenth anniversary of the Purépecha New Year's Celebration was held in the town of Ichupio, the then Independent Purépecha Front openly questioned the organization of the event and the degree to which it represented the Purépecha nation as a whole (Zárate 1994). By 1995 this organization had become the Purépecha Nation, and its members in Tarecuato were supported by the cabildo and PRD town government against the priest with his links to the PRI (Rivera Farfán 1998). They openly questioned the political presence of the PRI state government in the organization of the event and decided to boycott the celebration. As a result, the charismatic Catholic movement was left completely in charge, resulting in a far more openly religious and political spectacle than on any previous occasion: the poster celebrating the event listed the PRI state government in order to recognize its financial support in the creation and presentation of the event, which was inaugurated by a formal Mass, followed by a parade of Tarecuato women all in traditional dress, and all the members of the charismatic movement, who collectively greeted the small delegation of PRI elected officials and candidates attending as distinguished guests. At the close of the event, one of the founders of the Purépecha New Year's Celebration from the highland town of Cheranástico made a speech in Purépecha in which he spoke of the division in Tarecuato and stressed that the celebration was one of unity and "juchari uinapikua" (our strength). He announced that henceforth requests to host the event could only be made with the town's authorities present and openly in support. In Tarecuato, just after the event, the cabildo and town officials announced they would host the IVth Annual Congress of the Purépecha Nation in three months' time—proof of Tarecuato's support for indigenous autonomy from government intervention (Rivera Farfán 1998).

The conflict at the Purépecha New Year's Celebration in 1995 and the creation of a local government in Cherán based on custom in 2012 are clear indications of a continuing and contentious transformation of local forms of control organized around ritualized spheres of exchange. This transformation involved (and involves) changes in both the politics of gender and a newly recognized political role for cabildos in local politics. But most important, these changes appear to emerge through a process of objectification in which the practices of local ritualized spheres of exchange inform strategies for organizing practice at the extralocal level (Dietz 1999; Roth-Seneff 1993, 2010; Zárate 1994). The emerging organization of the Purépecha New Year's Celebration is an excellent example.

The Purépecha New Year's Celebration

The annual cultural celebration of Purépecha revitalization, symbolized by the lighting of a new fire, began in 1983, when Purépecha leaders (teachers, professors, medical doctors, engineers, etc.) and promoters of Purépecha culture (priests, anthropologists, teachers, professors, regionally recognized artists, etc.) met at the ruins of a prehispanic site in the town of Ihuatzio in order to march to the *yácatas* (pyramids) above Tzintzuntzan, the ancient center of the Tarascan Empire (Roth-Seneff 2010). Over the years, the preparation and organization of the Purépecha New Year's Celebration has evolved around the spheres of ritual exchange associated with the organization and preparation for town celebrations honoring patron saints. The New Year's Celebration also adds elements from Purépecha cosmology and Mesoamerican practices, as well as from the traditions and customs of the towns in the core area inhabited by Purépecha speakers.

The most striking elements in the composition of the celebration are (1) the selective tradition, which established the eve of February 2 as the start of each Purépecha New Year; (2) the symbols of Purépecha ethnicity; (3) the celebration's protocol; and (4) the civil-religious system, which organizes the celebration and through which, I will argue, a modern Purépecha public sphere is beginning to come into existence.

The selective tradition was created from a complex series of significant associations among cosmologies, custom, the Mesoamerican calendar, and the constellation Orion (*hararu jóskua* in Purépecha), and that tradition lies behind the determination of the date of the Purépecha New Year. The most complex of these associations is between the Nahuatl or Aztec term *tonalpohualli*, its Purépecha counterpart, *huriyatamiyucua*, and Curicuaueri, the Purépecha sun god. The Mesoamerican calendar is literally a "sun count" (*tonal*, "sun"; *pouhualli*, "count" in Nahuatl; also *huiryata*, "suns," and *miyucua*, "count" in Purépecha), an obvious reference not only to the solar cycle but also to the sun as an object of veneration. Curicaueri or Curicuaueri (he who emerges making fire [*curica* or *curicua*, from *curicani*, "to make fire," and *ueri*, "he who emerges"]) is the principal god of the Purépecha group called Uacusecha (the eagle clan) and the god of war associated with the sun. The Uacusecha established the Tarascan state, with its capital at Tzintzuntzan, under the leadership of the representative of Curicaueri on Earth, the Caltzontzin.

The huriyatamiyacua, or Purépecha sun count, is a variant of the Mesoamerican calendar composed of eighteen months, each with twenty days, and five days left over annually (18 × 20 = 360 + 5 = 365). Each month was named after its ritual feast day. Of the fifteen known names of prehispanic Tarascan ritual feasts, thirteen are mentioned in a text compiled in Tzintzuntzan between 1539 and 1541 (Warren 2000) that records the Uacusecha version of Tarascan history up to the Spanish conquest. Four of the ritual feast days mentioned in the text appear in association with a corresponding date on the Julian calendar, and two more ritual feast days are mentioned in a Jesuit history published around the turn of the seventeenth century. One of these dates corresponds to the last month of the Aztec calendar with its ritual feast, called Izcalli. This is February 2, and Izcalli corresponds in meaning to the Purépecha ritual feast Tzintaquarénsquaro. Both refer to resurrection. Both could also reflect the process of incorporating Christian Catholic celebrations into the Mesoamerican calendar.[2] Hence, numerous associations can be made between the Mesoamerican calendar and sun worship, as well as between Christian celebrations and the annual solar cycle: for instance, the winter equinox approximates the celebration of the Nativity, while February 2 marks two Mesoamerican months, or 40 days (the Judeo-Christian traditional "quarantine" period after childbirth, followed by a purification rite for mother and child). In Mexico, February 2 is the celebration of Our Lady of the Candles (Candlemas Virgin), when candlelight and fire are associated with purity.

At Candlemas, in all Purépecha towns, that year's candles for the lighting of home altars are blessed in the church, and in some towns (e.g., Capacuaro and Tacuro [Valente Soto, cited in Roth-Seneff 1993]), it is customary to light fires outside the home on the eve of Candlemas, a practice similar to the traditional fires lit to celebrate the Christian New Year's Eve in the region. Also, children engage in the same New Year's custom of burning a type of herb, *tobardillo* (*Calliandra californica*), in the fires (Jerónimo Mateo 1998). Hence, there exists an association between the new fire and the celebration of rebirth and resurrection that culminates on February 2.

The association of Candlemas Eve and Orion is more complex. Among the Purépecha, the constellation Orion is most commonly known as hararu jóskua (*jóskua*, "star," and *hararu*, a borrowing from the Spanish *arado*, "plow"). Orion has no seasonal zenith or nadir but is the most visible constellation during winter in the northern hemisphere. The founders of the Purépecha New Year's Celebration argue that Orion's greatest visibility or "zenith" is reached on the eve of February 2.

Clearly, the new fire is the central symbol of the Purépecha New Year's Celebration. The fire dominates along with a calendar stone and the Purépecha flag, though several other iconic symbols or images have been incorporated into the celebration over the past almost–thirty years: a stone fish, a white obsidian arrowhead, a stone dog or perhaps coyote, and a framed photograph of the late Father Agustín García Alcaraz, an anthropologist and priest who was a founder of the New Year's Celebration. As with the new fire, several Purépecha symbols represent the relationship between fire, sun, and the god Curicaueri, a relationship that is represented in the central part of the Purépecha flag.

This flag was created during an armed struggle in which the Purépecha community of Santa Fe de la Laguna retook lands occupied by ranchers from the neighboring town of Quiroga. At the flag's center, a large fire surrounds a white arrowhead and a clenched fist. This center is framed like a coat of arms, with four arrows that point cardinally to the four sides of the flag. Again, fire and a white arrowhead represent the war god, Curicaueri (he who emerges making fire), the hand clenched in a fist is an expression of the slogan "juchari uinapikua" (our strength), and the four colors of the four sections of the flag represent the four subregions of the Purépecha homeland: blue for the Pátzcuaro Basin; green for the Purépecha Highlands; yellow for the narrow Duero River Valley, called the Canyon of the Eleven Towns (La Cañada de los Once Pueblos, or Eráxami in Purépecha); and red (or purple) for the Zacapu Basin. The dominant solar symbolism is also present in the white obsidian arrowhead (*ts'inapu urápiti*), another reference to the sun god, Curicaueri.

The calendar stone is a lapidary register of the ritual sphere of exchange that sustains and organizes the celebration. It has a 10 cm^2 base and a 5 cm^2 top with four vertical faces on which the symbols emblematic of each host town are inscribed, along with the year when the celebration was held in Mesoamerican numeration. Two faces of the stone are filled with the names of ten host towns each, and a third now has nine hosts registered, taking the event to 2012. Thus, from below to above and moving clockwise, the calendar stone will eventually register 40 years of celebrations and ritualized reciprocity among host towns, and if the bottom and top faces of the stone are utilized, the count could reach the 52-year cycle in which the ritual day cycle and the sun cycle in the Mesoamerican calendar coincide. The stone fish, a gift from the town of San Andres Tsiróndiro when the New Year was celebrated there in 1986, is often placed on top of the calendar stone, thereby creating a toponymic reference to Michoacán (from *michi*, "fish," and *-can*, a locative in Nahuatl: "land or place of the fish") and to the indigenous homeland represented by the Purépecha towns inscribed on the stone and recently captured in a newly coined word in Purépecha, Purhéecherio, which refers to this homeland. Another symbol, the stone dog or coyote, was introduced in 1994, when the celebration began in the ranch of Ucasanastacua only to be moved to the central plaza of Pátzcuaro at the house of the descendants of the last Caltzoni or vicar of Curicaueri, the Huitziméngari.[3]

Although each celebration of the Purépecha New Year reflects the ideas and creativity of the host town, a protocol has evolved over the years and become formalized by the "principals" or "elders," the founders and former hosts of the event. This protocol revolves around the insertion of these new symbols of Purépecha ethnicity into the traditional ceremonial context of patron saint celebrations. At the same time, it reflects a certain tension between, on the one hand, the cultural celebration of Purépecha dance, dress, food, song, music, and games and, on the other, a solemn ceremony of ritual respect for an ethnicity tied to Curicaueri and the annual ritual of lighting a new fire.

This ritual of respect revolves around the dominant symbols of the new fire, the Purépecha flag, and the calendar stone and the secondary symbols with their more local references to specific Purépecha communities or prominent personalities. Similar to the images kept in the homes of persons who have taken charge of a particular year's cycle of celebrations for a specific saint or manifestation of the Virgin associated with the church or hospital, the dominant symbols are kept during the year prior to the annual celebration in the homes and the church of the host town's authorities. On the day of the celebration— February 1—they are placed on an altar decorated and filled with offerings of bread in the form of animals and fruit and a local sugarcane alcohol called *charanda*. Since the celebration of the Purépecha New Year in the town of Tarecuato in 1995, it has also become common to hold a midday Mass with the symbols present. Afterward, the symbols are paraded through the town on the same route used for religious images during patron saint processions. Along the route, they are accompanied by *wanachecha* (young maidens who decorate and care for the symbols just as they do for patron saints and Virgins), as well as by the authorities responsible for the event. Everyone is dressed in the traditional style of their respective towns: men in embroidered white cotton trousers, shirt, and red sash, carrying a poncho and wearing a sombrero; women in embroidered blouses and long dresses, the colors of which identify their town of origin, covered by aprons and with rebozos that may also identify a town or subregion. Everyone is adorned with ribbons whose colors represent the subregions of *p'urhéecherio*, or the Purépecha homeland, as mentioned previously. It is common for the procession of the symbols to end with a solemn act honoring the Purépecha flag, in which a salute is given with the left arm raised, hand clenched into a fist, to symbolize "juchari uinapikua" (our strength).[4]

The protocol of the event also involves petitions from the authorities of towns aspiring to host the celebration the following year. These authorities must make a formal request at the beginning of the assembly of all the former hosts. It is also appreciated if a town's representatives offer a public greeting to the town hosting the event. These representatives must demonstrate that they have the support of the local elected officials, and it is also considered correct for a town to request hosting the celebration at least twice before being granted the honor. In addition, the town must have a history of participation in past celebrations, which involves preparing and bringing traditional dance groups or musicians, a team to compete in the traditional Purépecha game of *wárhukua*, or individual players for a traditional game of chance called *kuiliche*.[5]

Both current and former hosts of the celebration are associated with the prehispanic Tarascan figure of the *petamuti*. According to the sixteenth-century description of the Tarascan state prior to the Spanish conquest, the petamuti were the authorities responsible for preserving Tarascan heritage and genealogical memory, as well as for controlling public discourse. By organizing and carrying out the celebration in their respective towns, the hosts of the Purépecha New Year's Celebration are entitled to participate in the assembly held during each celebration and to receive petitions from towns that aspire to host the celebration. Their deliberations over the next host generally last two to three hours and are carried out during the evening and night when different Purépecha towns, villages, hamlets, and urban barrios perform traditional dances, music, songs, oratory, and, on some occasions, short theater pieces. This cultural festival is also the space for discourses on cultural revitalization and Purépecha collective rights, but, most centrally, it constitutes a cultural exchange between the host village and all Purépecha settlements that formally share their music, poetry, song, dance, drama, and opinions.

The celebration culminates with the lighting of a new fire. As the new fire begins to blaze, the hosts for the following year are publicly announced, and the Purépecha symbols are formally exchanged along with gifts of bread, fruit, and sometimes small pieces of pottery tied to ribbons and hung around the necks of the new hosts, who must then dance with the symbols accompanied by all the former hosts. Also, a series of speeches is made: public expressions of gratitude by the new hosts for the recognition received; pledges of support for the upcoming celebration by the petamuti, or former hosts; and recognition of the support and help received during the current celebration.

Conclusion

More than two decades ago, the Mexican anthropologist Guillermo de la Peña suggested that we reflect on "the capacity of indigenous institutions to transform themselves into vehicles for the unalienated, democratic revindication of ethnic identity" (1987:294, my translation). The problem posed by de la Peña is compelling and ethnographic. Indeed, this chapter is an effort to present a contemporary case of an emerging "unalienated, democratic revindication of ethnic identity" among the Purépecha of central western Mexico in the state of Michoacán. However, as another Mexican-raised anthropologist, Claudio Lomnitz (2001), has argued more recently, the problem is particularly complex for Indo-Mexican society because it demands an examination of the relations between popular ritual and state ritual, especially as to how and when they may serve to promote or prevent the development of modern public spheres.

As Lomnitz has noted, there is an inverse relationship between the social weight of political ritual and the development of what Habermas describes as "a sphere which mediates between society and state, in which the public organizes itself as the bearer of public opinion" (Eley 1994:298; citing Habermas 1974:49). The weight of political ritual in the Purépecha Highlands is well exemplified by the 1988–2012 period. The use of the Federation of Purépecha Professionals to orchestrate "ethnic" participation in a major public works project at the controversial and contentious beginning of the Salinas administration is one example. Likewise, patriarchal and clientelist politics reemerged in the municipal seat of Cherán after a collectively charismatic period of popular government, a change during which Purépecha women began to participate actively in local politics. More recently and with strong support from the women of Cherán, a unified, autonomously organized defense against both organized crime and its possible association with local party politics has evolved into the first Purépecha local government based on custom.

The political rituals of the Mexican state have clearly undermined the construction of a modern public sphere characterized by increasing political participation and the growing appropriation of ideals of citizenship, leading to new conditions for voluntary associations and identification (Eley 1994). However, the political struggles of the last three decades have led to some notable changes. While the political actions of the Federation of Purépecha Professionals were clearly orchestrated to ritually legitimize the controversial Salinas administration, new Purépecha organizations were emerging at the same time. In Tarecuato, the organization called the Purépecha Nation managed an alliance with the town's cabildo, and its members successfully sought local political office, which allowed both strategic political gains in their municipality and a successful opposition to a Catholic religious movement allied with the dominant political party, the PRI (Rivera Farfán 1998). Also, in Cherán, in the context of reemerging factional political domination, local opposition continued and continues. An early result was the election of a female candidate to a midlevel municipal office (Nelson 2000) and, more recently, the first legally recognized act of local autonomy by a Purépecha municipality.

The evolution of the Purépecha New Year's Celebration, which is based on popular ritual forms that revolve around the ever-emerging and transforming communal celebration of patron saints and Virgins, is an important background to the changes of the last three decades. These communal celebrations have considerable historical depth and are based on local and regional ritualized spheres of exchange. As the celebration of the Purépecha New Year's Celebration has evolved over three decades, the pattern of a ritualized sphere of exchange operating at the village, town, or regional level has come to objectify the *p'urhéecherio*, or four subregions of the Purépecha homeland, an objectification based on ritualized exchanges among the towns, villages, hamlets, and urban barrios during the hosting and celebration of each New Year.

After thirty years, this celebration has become a central process in an emerging extralocal ethnic sphere of exchange based on voluntary association and identification. The representations and relations that emerge from the Purépecha New Year's Celebration, the nascent Purépecha organizations, and the last three decades of local political struggles appear to indicate a movement toward an "unalienated, democratic revindication of ethnic identity."

Notes

1. Here, I follow Felipe Castro Gutiérrez (chapter 7, this volume) in the use of Tarascan to refer to the indigenous population in colonial times and Purépecha as the contemporarily accepted term.

2. Alfonso Caso cites, *apud* León, a text by Ramírez from 1600 on how the Purépecha population "began to celebrate in their manner many fiestas that are celebrated in our mother the Church, such as the one called Peuánscuaro, or Nativity, and the one called Tzintaquarénsquaro, or Resurrection" (1944:11–36, my translation). Caso also shows (through a continuous sequence of Purépecha 20-day months constructed from the four months named in the sixteenth-century text, the *Relación de Michoacán*, and accompanied by their Christian calendar date) that the month that ends the Tarascan year with its five remaining extra days would have to be February 23 or May 18.

3. The Huitziméngari house was occupied by Purépecha organizations in 1992 and proclaimed Purépecha patrimony. The house originally belonged to Antonio de Huitziméngari, a son of the *caltzontzin*, Tzintzicha Tangaxoan, who was killed by the Spaniards during the conquest and was a godson of the first viceroy of New Spain, Antonio de Mendoza.

4. In Mexico, the national flag is saluted with the right hand, palm down, crossing the chest.

5. *Wárhukua* has similarities with hockey. It is played with carved sticks and a ball made from natural rubber. At the New Year's Celebration it is common to set the ball on fire. *Kuiliche* involves moving pieces over 52 spaces based on the throwing of slotted sticks that determine the number of movements according to the vigesimal system based on 20 and units of 5, which is what gives the game its name in Purépecha; kuiliche refers to a configuration of 5. Given its numerical references to the Mesoamerican calendar and cosmology (every 52 years the 260-day Mesoamerican ritual calendar of 20 cycles of 13 named days coincides with the solar calendar of 18 months of 20 days plus 5 additional days) and the discovery of the pattern of the game inscribed on stones in archaeological sites in the Purépecha region, it is likely that kuiliche was derived from prehispanic divinatory practices, as Hans Roskamp has noted (personal communication 2003).

References Cited

Abu-Lughod, Janet. 1989. *Before European Hegemony: The World System A.D. 1250–1350.* Oxford University Press, Oxford.

Acosta, Gabriela. 1998. Desde "tiempo inmemorial": Los origenes de Nahuatzen, Michoacán. *Boletín del Archivo General Agrario* 2:49–56.

Acuña, Rene (editor). 1987. *Relaciones geográficas del siglo XVI: Michoacán.* Universidad Nacional Autónoma de México, Mexico City.

———— (editor). 1988. *Relaciones geográficas del siglo XVI: Nuevo Galicia.* Universidad Nacional Autónoma de México, Mexico City.

Aiton, Arthur Scott. 1927. *Antonio de Mendoza, First Viceroy of New Spain.* Duke University Press, Durham, North Carolina.

Alegre, Francisco Javier. 1956. *Historia de la provincia de la Compañía de Jesús de Nueva España*, Vol. 9. Edited by Ernest J. Burrus and Félix Zubillaga. Institutum Historicum S.J., Rome.

Alessio Robles, Vito. 1978. *Coahuila y Texas en la época colonial.* Biblioteca Porrúa 70. Editorial Porrúa, Mexico City.

Algaze, Guillermo. 1993. Expanding Dynamics of Some Early Pristine States. *American Anthropologist* 95(2):304–333.

Anderson, Benedict. 1991. *Imagined Communities: Reflections on the Origin and Spread of Nationalism.* Verso, London.

Ansolabehere, Karina. 2006 ms. Diversidad retórica: Suprema Corte de Justicia y diversidad cultural. V Congreso de la Red Latinoamericana de Antropología Jurídica, September.

Armillas, Pedro. 1948a. Fortalezas mexicanas. *Cuadernos Americanos* 5:143–163.

————. 1948b. Provincias arqueológicas, cronología y problemas del occidente de México. In *El occidente de México*, pp. 211–216. Sociedad Mexicana de Antropología, Mexico City.

————. 1951. Mesoamerican Fortifications. *Antiquity* 25:77–86.

————. 1964. Condiciones ambientes y movimientos de pueblos en la frontera septentrional de Mesoamérica. In *Homenaje a Fernando Márquez-Miranda*, Publicaciones del Seminario de Estudios Americanistas y Seminario de Antropología Americana, pp. 62–82. Universidades de Madrid y Sevilla, Madrid.

————. 1969. The Arid Frontier of Mexican Civilization. *Transactions of the New York Academy of Sciences*, Series 2, Vol. 31:697–704.

Arnauld, Charlotte, and Brigitte Faugère-Kalfon. 1998. Evolución de la ocupación humana en el Centro-Norte de Michoacán (Proyecto Michoacán, CEMCA) y la emergencia del Estado Tarasco. In *Génesis, culturas y espacios en Michoacán*, edited by Véronique Darras, pp. 13–34. CEMCA, Mexico City.

Arnauld, Marie Charlotte, Patricia Carot, and Marie-France Fauvet-Berthelot. 1993. *Arqueología de las Lomas en la cuenca lacustre de Zacapu, Michoacán, México.* Cuadernos de Estudios Michoacanos 5. Centre d'Études Mexicaines et Centraméricaines, Mexico City.

Aveni, Anthony F. 1993. Observadores del Cielo en el México Antiguo, traduction by Jorge Ferreiro. Fondo de Cultura Económico, Mexico.

Ávila Márquez, Humberto. 2006. *Tenamaztle: Defensor pionero de los derechos humanos.* Gobierno del Estado de Zacatecas, Instituto Zacatecano Cultural, Zacatecas.

Batres, Leopoldo. 1903. *Visita a los monumentos arqueológicos de "La Quemada," Zacatecas.* Imprenta de la Vda. de Francisco Díaz de León, Mexico City.

Baus de Czitróm, Carolyn. 1982. *Tecuexes y Cocas: Dos grupos de la región Jalisco en el siglo XVI.* Colección Científica, Serie Etnohistoria No. 12. Instituto Nacional de Antropología e Historia, Mexico City.

———. 1985. The Tecuexes: Ethnohistory and Archaeology. In *The Archaeology of West and Northwest Mesoamerica,* edited by Michael S. Foster and Phil C. Weigand, pp. 93–115. Praeger, Westview, Connecticut.

Beals, Ralph L. 1932. *The Comparative Ethnology of Northern Mexico before 1750.* Ibero-Americana 2. University of California Press, Berkeley.

Beekman, Christopher. 1996. Political Boundaries and Political Structure: The Limits of the Teuchitlán Tradition. *Ancient Mesoamerica* 7(11):135–147.

Beekman, Christopher, and Phil C. Weigand. 2000. *La cerámica arqueológica de la tradición de Teuchitlán, Jalisco.* El Colegio de Michoacán and La Secretaría de Cultura del Estado de Jalisco, Zamora, Michoacán.

Bell, Betty. 1971. Archaeology of Nayarit, Jalisco, and Colima. In *Archeology of Northern Mesoamerica,* edited by G. Ekholm and I. Bernal, pp. 694–753. Handbook of Middle American Indians, Vol. 11, R. Wauchope, general editor. University of Texas Press, Austin.

Beltrán, Ulises. 1982. Tarascan State and Society in Prehispanic Times: An Ethnohistorical Inquiry. Unpublished Ph.D. dissertation, University of Chicago.

———. 1994. Estado y sociedad tarascos en la época prehispánica. In *El Michoacán antiguo: Estado y sociedad en la época prehispánica,* edited by Brigitte Boehm de Lameiras, pp. 31–163. El Colegio de Michoacán, Zamora.

Beltrán del Río, Pascal. 1993. *Michoacán, ni un paso atrás.* Libros de Proceso, Mexico City.

Berghes, Carl de. 1989 [1885]. *Beschreibung der überreste Aztekischer Niederlassungen auf ihrer Wanderung nach der Thale von Mexico durch den gegenwärtigen Freistaat von Zacatecas.* Dietrich Reimer, Berlin.

Boehm de Lameiras, Brigitte. 1995. Poblamiento en el occidente de México en el Mapa de Ortelius. Paper presented at the Simposio sobre Arqueología y Etnohistoria de las Cuencas del Occidente de México, Colegio de Michoacán, Zamora.

Bonfil Batalla, Guillermo. 1996. *México profundo.* University of Texas Press, Austin.

Borah, Woodrow. 1954. Race and Class in Mexico. *Pacific Historical Review* 23(4):331–342.

———. 1994. *Tendencias de precios de bienes de tributo real en la Nueva Galicia, 1557–1598.* El Colegio de Jalisco and El Colegio de Michoacán, Mexico City.

Borah, Woodrow, and Sherbourne F. Cook. 1960. The Population of Central Mexico in 1548. *Ibero-Americana* 43:75–103.

———. 1963. The Aboriginal Population of Central Mexico on the Eve of the Spanish Conquest. *Ibero-Americana* 45.

Brand, Donald D. 1960. *Coalcomán and Motines de Oro: An ex-distrito of Michoacán, México.* Martinus Nijhoff for the Institute of Latin American Studies, The Hague; and University of Texas Press, Austin.

———. 1971. Ethnohistorical Synthesis of Western Mexico. In *Archeology of Northern Mesoamerica,* edited by G. Ekholm and I. Bernal, pp. 632–656. Handbook of Middle American Indians, Vol. 11, R. Wauchope, general editor. University of Texas Press, Austin.

Braniff, Beatríz (editor). 2001. *La Gran Chichimeca: El lugar de las rocas secas.* Jaca Books / CONACULTA, Mexico City.

Braudel, Fernand. 1984. *Wheels of Commerce: Civilization and Capitalism,* Vol. 2. Harper and Row, New York.

Bravo Ugarte, Jose. 1962. *Historia sucinta de Michoacán: El estado tarasco.* Editorial Jus, Mexico City.

Cabrero García, Ma. Teresa. 1989. *Civilización en el norte de México: Arqueología de la Cañada del Río Bolaños (Zacatecas y Jalisco)*. Universidad Nacional Autónoma de México, Mexico City.

————. 1991. Cultura arqueológica de Bolaños (Zacatecas y Jalisco): Una frontera cultural. *Ancient Mesoamerica* 2(2):193–203.

Cach, Eric (editor). 2003. Arqueología del centro de Jalisco. Special issue of *Seminario de historia mexicana* 4(1). Universidad de Guadalajara, Guadalajara.

Calderón, Marco. 1999. *Violencia política y elecciones municipales*. El Colegio de Michoacán, Zamora.

————. 2004. *Historias, procesos políticos y cardenismo: Cherán y la Sierra Purhépecha*. El Colegio de Michoacán, Zamora.

Calvo, Thomas. 1997. *Por los caminos de Nueva Galicia: Transportes y transportistas en el siglo XVII*. Universidad de Guadalajara / CEMCA, Guadalajara.

Cárdenas, Efraín. 1999. *El Bajío en el Clásico: Análisis regional y organización política*. El Colegio de Michoacán, Zamora.

Carot, Patricia. 2001. *Le site de Loma Alta, Lac de Zacapu, Michoacán, Mexique*. Paris Monographs in American Archaeology 9, BAR International Series 920. Archaeopress, Oxford.

Carot, Patricia, and Marie-France Fauvet-Berthelot. 1996. La monumentalidad del sitio de Loma Alta, Michoacán, revelada por métodos de prospección geofísica. In *Las cuencas del occidente de México: Época prehispánica*, edited by Eduardo Williams and Phil C. Weigand, pp. 83–103. Colegio de Michoacán / ORSTOM / CEMCA, Zamora.

Carot, Patricia, Marie-France Fauvet-Berthelot, Luis Barba, Karl Link, Agustín Ortiz, and Albert Hesse. 1998. La arquitectura de Loma Alta, Zacapu, Michoacán. In *El occidente de México: Arqueología, historia y medio ambiente*, Perspectivas regionales, Actas del IV Coloquio de Occidentalistas, edited by R. Avila, J. Emphoux, L. Gastélum, S. Ramírez, O. Schöndube, and F. Valdez, pp. 345–361. Universidad de Guadalajara, Guadalajara.

Carot, Patricia, and Rocío Ponce López. 1997. Á propos de la découverte d'un lot de sculptures sur le site de Loma Alta, Zacapu, Michoacán. *Trace* 31:64–69.

Carrillo Cázares, Alberto. 1991. Chiquisnaquis un indio escribano, artífice de títulos primordiales (La Piedad siglo XVIII). *Relaciones* 48:187–210.

————. 2000. *El debate sobre la guerra chichimeca, 1531–1585: Derecho y política en la Nueva España*. El Colegio de Michoacán, Zamora.

Caso, Alfonso. 1944. El calendario de los tarascos. *Anales del Museo Michoacano* 3:11–36.

Castile, George. 1972. *Cherán: The Adaptation of an Autonomous Community in Michoacán, Mexico*. University of Arizona Press, Tucson.

Castilleja González, Áida. 2007. Construcción social y cultural de categorías referidas a espacio: Un estudio en Pueblos Purépecha. Unpublished Ph.D. dissertation, Escuela Nacional de Antropología e Historia.

Castro Gutiérrez, Felipe. 1998. Condición femenina y violencia conyugal entre los purépechas durante la época colonial. *Mexican Studies* 14(1):5–21.

————. 2003. Tzintzuntzan: La autonomía indígena y el orden político en Nueva España. In *Autoridad y gobierno indígena en Michoacán*, edited by Carlos Paredes Martínez and Martha Terán, pp. 285–303. El Colegio de Michoacán, CIESAS, INAH, and Universidad Michoacana de San Nicolás de Hidalgo, Zamora.

————. 2004. *Los tarascos y el imperio español, 1600–1740*. Universidad Nacional Autónoma de México and Universidad Michoacana de San Nicolás de Hidalgo, Mexico City.

Castro-Leal, Marcia. 1986. *Tzintzuntzan, capital de los tarascos*. Gobierno del Estado de Michoacán, Morelia.

Chance, John K. 1992. Changes in Twentieth-Century Mesoamerican Cargo Systems. In *Class, Politics, and Popular Religion in Mexico and Central America*, edited by Lynn Stephens and James Dow, pp. 27–42. American Anthropological Association, Washington, D.C.

Chance, John K., and William Taylor. 1985. Cofradías and Cargos: An Historical Perspective on the Mesoamerican Civil-Religious Hierarchy. *American Ethnologist* 12(1):1–26.

Chevalier, François. 1995. Avant-propos. *Histoire et Société de l'Amérique Latine* 3. Available online at http://www.sigu7.jussieu.fr/hsal/hsa195/fc95.html.

Chi, Ch'ao-ting. 1936. *Key Economic Areas in Chinese History, as Revealed in the Development of Public Works for Water Control*. G. Allen & Unwin, London.

Ciudad Real, Antonio. 1993. *Tratado curioso y docto de las grandezas de la Nueva España: Relación breve y verdadera de algunas cosas de las muchas que sucedieron al padre fray Alonso Ponce en las provincias de la Nueva España siendo comisario en aquellas general de aquellas partes*. Edited by Josefina García Quintana and Victor M. Castillo Farreras. Universidad Nacional Autónoma de México, Mexico City.

Cochet, Hubert. 1991. *Alambradas en la sierra: Un sistema agrario en México; La sierra de Coalcomán*. CEMCA, El Colegio de Michoacán, and ORSTOM, Mexico City.

Comaroff, John, and Jean Comaroff. 1992. *Ethnography and the Historical Imagination*. Westview Press, Boulder, Colorado.

Constitución Política de los Estados Unidos Mexicanos. http://inf04.juridicas.unam.mx /ijure/fed/9/1.htm?s=.

Cook, Sherbourne F., and Woodrow Borah. 1971–1979. *Essays in Population History: Mexico and the Caribbean*. Vol. 1, 1971; vol. 2, 1974; vol. 3, 1979. University of California Press, Berkeley.

Covarrubias Orozco, Sebastián de. 1984. *Tesoros de la lengua castellana o española*. Ediciones Turner, Mexico City.

Coyle, Philip E. 2001. *Flowers and Ash: Náyari History, Politics and Violence*. University of Arizona Press, Tucson.

Crosby, Alfred. 1977. *The Columbian Exchange: Biological and Cultural Consequences of 1492*. Greenwood Press, Westport, Connecticut.

Darras, Véronique. 1998. La obsidiana en la *Relación de Michoacán* y en la realidad arqueológica: Del símbolo al uso o del uso de un símbolo. In *Génesis, culturas y espacios en Michoacán*, edited by Véronique Darras, pp. 61–88. CEMCA, Mexico City.

———. 1999. *Tecnologías prehispánicas de la obsidiana: Los centros de producción de la región de Zináparo-Prieto, Michoacán*. Cuadernos de Estudios Michoacanos 9. CEMCA, Mexico City.

———. 2006. Las relaciones entre Chupícuaro y el centro de México durante el preclásico reciente: Una crítica de las interpretaciones arqueológicas. *Journal de la Société des Américanistes* 92:69–110.

Darras, Véronique, and Brigitte Faugère. 2005. Cronología de la cultura Chupícuaro: Estudio del sitio La Tronera, Puruagüita, Guanajuato. In *El antiguo occidente de México: Nuevas perspectivas sobre el pasado prehispánico*, edited by Eduardo Williams, Phil C. Weigand, Lorenza López Mestas, and David Grove, pp. 255–281. El Colegio de Michoacán and Instituto Nacional de Antropología e Historia, Guadalajara.

Darras, Véronique, Brigitte Faugère-Kalfon, Christophe Durlet, Catherine Liot, Javier Reveles, Rosalba Bérumen, Omar Cervantes, and Cybèle David. 1999. Nouvelles recherches sur la culture Chupícuaro (Guanajuato, Mexique). *Journal de la Société des Américanistes* 85:343–351.

Decreto de la Nación Purhépecha. 1995. *Relaciones* 61/62:163–167.

de la Peña, Guillermo. 1986. Poder local, poder regional: Perspectivas socioantropológicas. In *Poder local, poder regional*, edited by Jorge Padua and Alain Vanneph, pp. 27–56. El Colegio de México, Centro de Estudios Sociológicos / CEMCA, Mexico City.

———. 1987. La institución municipal contra las instituciones indígenas: Comentario. In *El municipio en México*, edited by Brigitte Boehm de Lameiras, pp. 293–295. El Colegio de Michoacán, Zamora.

———. 1999. Territorio y ciudadanía étnica en la Nación Globalizada. *Desacatos: Revista de antropología social* 1:13–27.

———. 2001. Apuntes sobre los indigenismos en Jalisco. *Estudios del hombre* 13–14:95–118.

del Hoyo, Eugenio. 1978. Juannes de Tolosa, "descubridor de minas." *Anuario de historia* 1:187–195. Universidad Autónoma de Zacatecas.

Deltour-Levie, Claudine (editor). 1993. *L'architecture des villages préhispaniques dans la Sierra de Nayar: Prospections de la mission archéologique belge au Mexique, Projet Sierra del Nayar.* Université Catholique de Louvain, Louvain-la-Neuve.

Díaz, Clara Luz. 1987. *El Occidente de México.* GV Editores, Mexico City.

Diccionario grande de la lengua de Michoacán. 1991. Book 2, Vol. *Tarasco-Español.* Edited by J. Benedict Warren. Fimax Publicistas, Morelia.

Dietz, Gunther. 1999. *La comunidad purhépecha es nuestra fuerza: Etnicidad, cultura y región en un movimiento indígena en México.* Abya-Yala Press, Quito.

Dumont, Louis. 1980. Homo hierarchicus: *The Caste System and Its Implications.* Translated by Mark Sainsbury, Louis Dumont, and Basia Gulati. University of Chicago Press, Chicago.

Durán, (Fray) Diego. 1971. *Book of the Gods and Rites and the Ancient Calendar.* Translated and edited by Fernando Horcasitas and Doris Heyden. University of Oklahoma Press, Norman.

———. 1984. *Historia de las indias de Nueva España e islas de la tierra firme*, Vol. 1. Edited by Ángel María Garibay K. Editorial Porrúa, Mexico City.

Durin, Séverine. 2003a. Antiguas rutas de comercio a larga distancia y destinos actuales de los peregrinos wixaritari (Huicholes). Paper presented at the Primer Coloquio Internacional del Noreste, Saltillo, Coahuila, October 6–7.

———. 2003b. Sur les routes de la fortune: Commerce à longue distance, endettement et solidarité chez les Wixaritari (Huichol), Mexique. Unpublished Ph.D. dissertation, Institut des Hautes Études de l'Amérique Latine, Université de Paris.

Durkheim, Emil. 1997 [1893]. *The Division of Labor in Society.* Free Press, Simon & Schuster, New York.

Eley, Geoff. 1994. Nations, Publics, and Political Cultures: Placing Habermas in the Nineteenth Century. In *Culture, Power, History*, edited by Nicholas B. Dirks, Geoff Eley, and Sherry B. Ortner, pp. 297–334. Princeton University Press, Princeton, New Jersey.

Embriz Osorio, A., and Laura Ruíz Mondragón. 2003. Los indicadores socioeconómicos de los pueblos indígenas y la planeación de la política social en México. In *Las dinámicas de la población indígena: Cuestiones y debates actuales en México*, edited by François Lartigue and André Quesnel, pp. 85–114. CIESAS–IRD–Miguel Ángel Porrúa, Mexico City.

Esparza López, Juan Rodrigo. 1999. Aplicación de las técnicas nucleares PIXE y NAA para el estudio de las redes de comercio de la obsidiana en Tierra Caliente, Michoacán. Licenciatura thesis, Escuela Nacional de Antropología e Historia.

Espejel Carbajal, Claudia. 2000. Guía arqueológica y geográfica para la Relación de Michoacán. In *Relación de las ceremonias y rictos y población y gobernación de los indios de la provincia de Mechuacán* [Jerónimo de Alcalá], edited by Moisés Franco Mendoza, pp. 301–312. El Colegio de Michoacán and Gobierno del Estado de Michoacán, Zamora.

————. 2011. Distribución de la población en el centro de Michoacán a la llegada de los españoles: Análisis de la visita de Antion de Caravajal (1523–1524). In *Patrones de asentamiento y actividades de subsistencia en el occidente de México: Reconocimiento a la doctora Helen P. Pollard*, edited by Eduardo Williams and Phil C. Weigand, pp. 73–100. El Colegio de Michoacán, Zamora.

Fernández Sotelo, Rafael Diego. 1994. *La primigenia audiencia de la Nueva Galicia, 1548–1572: Respuesta al cuestionario de Juan de Ovando por el oidor Miguel Contreras y Guevara.* Instituto Cultural Ignacio Dávila Garibi, Cámara Nacional de Comercio de Guadalajara, and El Colegio de Michoacán, Mexico City.

Fernández–V. Medina, Eugenia. 2004. Evidencias de una tradición mesoamericana en Zaragoza. In *Las tradiciones arqueológicas del Occidente de México*, edited by Efraín Cárdenas García, pp. 291–305. El Colegio de Michoacán, Zamora.

Filini, Agapi. 2004. *The Presence of Teotihuacan in the Cuitzeo Basin, Michoacán, Mexico.* BAR International Series 1279. Archaeopress, Oxford.

Fisher, Christopher, Helen P. Pollard, and Charles Frederick. 1999. Intensive Agriculture and Socio-political Development in the Lake Pátzcuaro Basin, Michoacán, Mexico. *Antiquity* 73(281):642–649.

Fisher, Christopher T., Helen P. Pollard, Isabel Israde, Victor Hugo Garduno, and Subir K. Banerjee. 2003. A Reexamination of Human Induced Environmental Change within the Lake Pátzcuaro Basin, Michoacán, Mexico. *Proceedings of the National Academy of Sciences* 100(8):4957–4962.

Florescano, Enrique. 2002. El canon memorioso forjado por los *Títulos primordiales. Colonial Latin American Review* 11(2):183–230.

Foster, George M. 1948. *Empire's Children: The People of Tzintzuntzan.* Institute of Social Anthropology, Publication No. 6, Smithsonian Institution, Washington, D.C.; Imprenta Nuevo Mundo, Mexico City.

————. 1967. *Mexican Peasants in a Changing World.* Little, Brown, Boston.

Franco Mendoza, Moisés (editor). 2000. *Relación de las ceremonias y rictos y población y gobernación de los indios de la provincia de Mechuacán.* [Jerónimo de Alcalá, 1541]. El Colegio de Michoacán and Gobierno del Estado de Michoacán, Zamora. [Cited in text as RM for *Relación de Michoacán.*]

Friedlander, Judith. 1975. *Being Indian in Hueyapan: A Study of Forced Identity in Contemporary Mexico.* St. Martin's Press, New York.

Friedrich, Paul. 1977. *Agrarian Revolt in a Mexican Village.* University of Chicago Press, Chicago.

Furst, Peter T. 1972. *Flesh of the Gods: The Ritual Use of Hallucinogens.* Praeger, New York.

García Alcaraz, Agustín. 1970. Un códice tarasco inédito. *Montaña* (January–February):27–33.

García Castro, René, and Jesús Arzate Becerril. 2003. Ilustración, justicia y títulos de tierras: El caso del pueblo de La Asunción Malacatepec en el siglo XVIII. *Relaciones* 95:49–92.

Genotte, Jean-François. 2006. La evangelización de los tepehuanes de los valles orientales de Durango (1596–1604): Las primeras misones jesuitas. In *La Sierra Tepehuana: Asentamientos y movimientos de población*, edited by Chantal Cramaussel and Sara Ortelli, pp. 129–146. El Colegio de Michoacán, Zamora.

Gerhard, Peter. 1972. Colonial New Spain, 1519–1786: Historical Notes on the Evolution of Minor Political Jurisdictions. In *Guide to Ethnohistorical Sources*, edited by Howard F. Cline and John B. Glass, pp. 63–137. Handbook of Middle American Indians, Vol. 13, Part 2, R. Wauchope, general editor. University of Texas Press, Austin.

————. 1992. *Síntesis e índice de los mandamientos virreinales: 1548–1553.* Instituto de Investigaciones Históricas, Universidad Nacional Autónoma de México, Mexico City.

Gibson, Charles. 1981. *Los aztecos baja el dominio español, 1519–1810.* Siglo Ventiuno, Mexico City.

Gilberti, Maturino. 1987 [1558]. *Arte de la lengua de Michuacán.* Edited by J. Benedict Warren. Fimax, Morelia.

Giudicelli, Christophe. 2006. Alianzas y asentamientos de guerra durante la guerra de los tepehuanes de 1616–1619. In *La Sierra Tepehuana: Asentamientos y movimientos de población*, edited by Chantal Cramaussel and Sara Ortelli, pp. 163–179. El Colegio de Michoacán, Zamora.

Gledhill, John. 2004. *Cultura y desafía en Ostula: Cuatro siglos de autonomía indígena en la costa-sierra nahua de Michoacán.* El Colegio de Michoacán and El Gobierno del Estado de Michoacán, Zamora.

———. 2012. Violence and Reconstitution in Mexican Indigenous Communities. In *Violence, Coercion, and State-Making in Twentieth-Century Mexico: The Other Half of the Centaur*, edited by Will G. Pansters, pp. 233–251. Stanford University Press, Stanford, California.

Gluckman, Max. 1960. Rituals of Rebellion in South-East Africa. In *Order and Rebellion in Tribal Africa*, pp. 110–136. Glencoe, London.

Godoy Rangel, Leonel. 2010. "Iniciativa de Decreto" para la reforma del Constitución del Estado Libre y Soberano Michoacán de Ocampo, February 10, 2010. http://transparencia .congresomich.gob.mx/media/documentos/trabajo_legislativo/dictamen_82_24-10-12 .pdf.

González Romero, Roberto, Phil C. Weigand, and Acelia García. 2000. *El Templo/Convento de la Concepción de Etzatlán, Jalisco, y su contexto prehispánico.* Secretaría de Cultura del Estado de Jalisco, Guadalajara.

Gorenstein, Shirley S. 2000. Western and Northwestern Mexico. In *Mesoamerica*, edited by Frank Salomon and Stuart B. Schwartz, pp. 318–357. Cambridge History of the Native Peoples of the Americas, Vol. 1, Parts 1–2, Richard E. W. Adams and Murdo J. Macleod, general editors. Cambridge University Press, Cambridge.

Gorenstein, Shirley, and Helen Perlstein Pollard. 1983. *The Tarascan Civilization: A Late Prehispanic Cultural System.* Vanderbilt University Publications in Anthropology 28. Vanderbilt University, Nashville, Tennessee.

Grimes, Joseph E., et al. 1981. Huichol: Apuntes sobre el léxico. Technical Reports to the National Science Foundation, Department of Modern Languages and Linguistics, Cornell University, Ithaca, New York.

Gruzinski, Serge. 1991. *La colonización de lo imaginario: Sociedades indígenas y occidentalización en el México español.* Fondo de la Cultura Económica, Mexico City.

———. 1993. *The Conquest of Mexico: The Incorporation of Indian Societies into the Western World, 16th–18th Centuries.* Polity Press, Cambridge.

Guzmán, Nuño Beltrán de. 1960. *Crónicas de la conquista de Nueva Galicia y memoria de Guzmán.* Instituto Jalicense de Antropología e Historia, Guadalajara.

Guzmán, Nuño Beltrán de, and Hernán Cortés. 1937. *Nuño de Guzmán contra Hernán Cortés, sobre los descubrimientos y conquistas en Jalisco y Tepic.* Boletín General de la Nación, Vol. 7, Nos. 3–4.

Habermas, Jürgen. 1974. The Public Sphere. *New German Critique* 3:49–55.

Harbottle, Garman, and Phil C. Weigand. 1992. Turquoise in Pre-Columbian America. *Scientific American* 266(2):78–85.

Haskett, Robert. 1996. Paper Shields: The Ideology of Coats of Arms in Colonial Mexican Primordial Titles. *Ethnohistory* 43(1):99–126.

Healan, Dan M. 1997. Pre-Hispanic Quarrying in the Ucareo-Zinapecuaro Obsidian Source Area. *Ancient Mesoamerica* 8:77–100.

Hernández, Claudia Tomic. 2004. Estado, campo social y construcciones de comunidad: El caso de Puácuaro, Michoacán, 1916–1936. In *Recursos contenciosos: Ruralidad y reformas liberales en México*, edited by Andrew Roth-Seneff, pp. 129–160. El Colegio de Michoacán, Zamora.

Hernández Rivero, José. 1994. La arqueología de la frontera tarasco-mexíca: Arquitectura bélica. In *Contribuciones a la arqueología y etnohistoria del occidente del México*, edited by Eduardo Williams, pp. 115–155. El Colegio de Michoacán, Zamora.

Herrejón Peredo, Carlos. 2000. *Los orígenes de Morelia: Guayangareo-Valladolid*. Frente de Afirmación Hispanista, El Colegio de Michoacán, Mexico City.

Hers, Marie-Areti. 1989a. Existió la cultura Loma San Gabriel? El caso de Hervideros, Durango. *Anales del Instituto de Investigaciones Estéticas* 60:33–57.

———. 1989b. *Toltecas en Tierras Chichimecas*. Instituto de Investigaciones Estéticas, México, Universidad Nacional Autónoma de México.

———. 2006. La cultura chalchihuiteña: Un antiguo camino de Tierro Adentro. In *Rutas de la Nueva España*, edited by Chantal Cramaussel, pp. 277–197. El Colegio de Michoacán, Zamora.

Hers, Marie-Areti, et al. 1993. *L'architecture des villages prehispaniques dans la Sierra del Nayar*. Edited by Claudine Deimar-Levie. Universite Catholique de Louvain, Louvain-la-Neuve.

Hindley, Jane. 1996. Towards a Pluricultural Nation: The Limits of Indigenismo and Article 4. In *Dismantling the Mexican State?*, edited by Rob Aitken, Nikki Craske, Gareth A. Jones, and David E. Stansfield, pp. 225–243. St. Martin's Press, New York.

Hosler, Dorothy. 1994. *The Sounds and Colors of Power: The Sacred Metallurgical Technology of Ancient West Mexico*. MIT Press, Cambridge, Massachusetts.

Hosler, Dorothy, and A. Macfarlane. 1996. Copper Sources, Metal Production, and Metals Trade in Late Postclassic Mesoamerica. *Science* 273:1819–1824.

Humboldt, Alexander von. 1811. *Political Essay of the Kingdom of New Spain*. 2 vols. London.

Jerónimo Mateo, Gilberto. 1998. P'urhépecha Jimbani Uéxurhini. In *Vocabulario práctico bilingüe P'urhécha*, edited by Juan Velázquez Pahuamba, Gilberto Jerónimo Mateo, Edelmira Estrada Basilio, and Raúl Máximo Cortés, p. 128. 2nd ed. Conaculta, INEA, Morelia, Michoacán.

Jiménez Betts, Peter. 1988. Ciertas inferencias de la arqueología del sur de Zacatecas. In *Primera Reunión Sobre las Sociedades Prehispánicas en el Centro-Occidente de México, Memoria*, pp. 39–50. Centro Regional de Queretaro / INAH.

———. 1992. Una red de interacción del noroeste de Mesoamerica: Una interpretación. In *Origen y desarrollo de la civilización en el occidente de México*, edited by B. Boehm and P. C. Weigand, pp. 177–204. El Colegio de Michoacán, Zamora.

John, Elizabeth A. H. 1996. *Storms Brewed in Other Men's Worlds: The Confrontation of Indians, Spanish, and French in the Southwest, 1540–1795*. University of Oklahoma Press, Norman.

Katz, Friedrich (editor). 1990. *Revuelta, rebelión y revolución: La lucha rural en México del siglo XVI al siglo XX*. Ediciones Era, Mexico City.

Kelley, J. Charles. 1971. Archaeology of the Northern Frontier: Zacatecas and Durango. In *Archeology of Northern Mesoamerica*, edited by G. Ekholm and I. Bernal, pp. 768–801. Handbook of Middle American Indians, Vol. 11, R. Wauchope, general editor. University of Texas Press, Austin.

———. 1985. The Chronology of the Chalchihuites Culture. In *The Archaeology of West and Northwest Mesoamerica*, edited by Michael S. Foster and Phil C. Weigand, pp. 269–287. Westview Press, Boulder, Colorado.

———. 1993. Archaeological Excavations at Alta Vista, Chalchihuites: Seasons of 1991–1993. Paper presented at the Seminario de Arqueología: Perspectivas sobre la Arqueología de la Periferia Septentrional de Mesoamerica, Zacatecas, Mexico.

Kelly, Isabel. 1948. Ceramic Provinces of Northwest Mexico. In *El occidente de México: Memorias de la 4a mesa redonda de la Sociedad Mexicana de Antropología*. Sociedad Mexicana de Antropología, Mexico City.

Kemper, Robert V., and Julie Adkins. 2004. De la "moderna área Tarasca" a la "tierra natal P'urhépecha": Conceptos cambiantes de identidad étnica y regional. *Relaciones* 25(100):227–278.

Kindl, Olivia. 2000. The Huichol Gourd Bowl as a Microcosm. *Journal of the Southwest* 42(1):37–60.

Kirchhoff, Paul. 1955. The Principles of Clanship in Human Society. *Davidson Journal of Anthropology* 1(1):1–11.

Kirchhoff, Paul, Lina Idena Güemes, and Luis Reyes García. 1976. *Historia Tolteca Chichimeca*, vol. 2. CISINAH, INAH, SEP, Mexico City.

Kroeber, A. L. 1934. *Uto-Aztecan Languages of Mexico*. University of California Press, Berkeley.

Kuthy, Lourdes. 1996. Strategies of Survival, Accommodation and Innovation: The Tarascan Indigenous Elite in Sixteenth Century Michoacan. Unpublished Ph.D. dissertation, Michigan State University.

Lagunas, Juan Baptista de. 1983 [1574]. *Arte y diccionario: Con otras obras en lengua michuacana*. Casa Pedro Balli, Mexico City.

Lagunas, (Fray) Juan Baptista de. 1983 [1574]. *Arte y diccionario con otras obras en lengua michuacana*. Facsimile edition, edited by J. Benedict Warren. Morelia: FIMAX Publicistas.

Lagunas Rodríguez, Z. 1987. Análisis de los restos óseos humanos procedentes de la tumba núm. 1 de Tinganio, Tingambato, Michoacán. *Avances en antropología física*, vol. 3. Cuaderno de trabajo 4:7–72. Instituto Nacional de Antropología e Historia, Mexico City.

Le Clézio, Jean Marie. 1985. *La conquista divina de Michoacán*. Fondo de Cultura Económica, Mexico City.

León, Nicolás. 1904. *Los tarascos: Notas históricas étnicas y antropológicas*. . . . Museo Nacional, Mexico City.

León-Portilla, Miguel (editor). 1992. *Ritas, sacerdotes y atavíos de los dioses* [Bernardino de Sahagún]. Universidad Nacional Autónoma de México, Mexico City.

Lévi-Strauss, Claude. 1966. *The Savage Mind*. University of Chicago Press, Chicago.

Leyva Solano, Xochitl, and Gabriel Ascencio Franco. 1996. *Lacandonia al filo del agua*. Fondo de la Cultura Económica, Mexico City.

Liffman, Paul. 2000. Gourdvines, Fires, and Wixárika Territoriality. *Journal of the Southwest* 42(1):129–166.

———. 2002. Huichol Territoriality: Land Conflict and Cultural Representation in Western Mexico. Unpublished Ph.D. dissertation, University of Chicago.

———. 2010. *Huichol Territory and the Mexican Nation: Indigenous Ritual, Land Conflict, and Sovereignty Claims*. University of Arizona Press, Tucson.

Liot, Catherine. 2000. *Les salines prehispaniques du bassin de Sayula (Occident de Mexique): Milieu et techniques*. Archaeopress, Oxford.

Lockhart, James. 1992. *The Nahuas after the Conquest: A Social and Cultural History of the Indians of Central Mexico, Sixteenth through Eighteenth Centuries*. Stanford University Press, Stanford, California.

———. 1999. *Los nahuas después de la conquista: Historia social y cultural de la población indígena del México central, siglos XVI–XVIII*. Fondo de la Cultura Económica, Mexico City.

Lomnitz, Claudio. 2001. *Deep Mexico, Silent Mexico: An Anthropology of Nationalism*. University of Minnesota Press, Minneapolis.

López, Lorenza, and Jorge Ramos. 1999. Excavating the Tomb at Huitzilapa. In *Ancient West Mexico: Art and Archaeology of the Unknown Past*, edited by Richard Townsend, pp. 53–70. Art Institute of Chicago, Chicago.

López Caballero, Paula. 2003. *Los títulos primordiales del centro de México*. Consejo Nacional para la Cultura y las Artes, Mexico City.

López-Portillo y Weber, José. 1935. *La conquista de la Nueva Galicia*. Instituto Jalicense de Antropología e Historia, Guadalajara.

———. 1939. *La Rebelión de Nueva Galicia*. Instituto Panamericano de Geografía e Historia, Mexico City.

López Sarrelangue, Delfina. 1963. *La nobleza indígena de Pátzcuaro en la época virreinal*. Universidad Nacional Autónoma de México, Mexico City.

Lumholtz, Carl. 1900. Symbolism of the Huichol Indians. *American Museum of Natural History, Memoirs in Anthropology* 3(1):1–228.

———. 1902. *Unknown Mexico*. 2 vols. Charles Scribner's Sons, New York.

Macías Goytia, Angelina. 1989. Los entierros de un centro ceremonial tarasco. *Estudios de Antropología Biológica*, Serie Antropológica 100, 531–559. Universidad Nacional Autónoma de México, Mexico City.

———. 1990. *Huacandareo: Lugar de juicios, tribunal*. Colleción Científica No. 222. Instituto Nacional de Antropología e Historia, Mexico City.

Macías Goytia, Angelina, and Katina Vackimes Serret. 1988. Tres Cerritos, Cuitzeo, Michoacán. In *Primera reunión sobre las sociedades prehispánicas en el centro-occidente de México*. Cuaderno de trabajo 1:161–164. Centro Regional de Querétaro, Instituto Nacional de Antropología e Historia, Mexico City.

Maine, Henry Sumner. 1986 [1861]. *Ancient Law: Its Connection with the Early History of Society and Its Relation to Modern Ideas*. University of Arizona Press, Tucson.

Manrique, Leonardo. 1994. Las lenguas prehispánicas en el México actual. *Arqueología Mexicana* 1(5):6–13.

Manzanilla López, Rubén. 1988. Salvamento arqueológico en Loma Santa María, Michoacán. In *Primera reunión sobre las sociedades prehispánicas en el centro-occidente de México*. Cuaderno de trabajo 1:151–160. Centro Regional de Querétaro, Instituto Nacional de Antropología e Historia, Mexico City.

Marín Tamayo, Fausto. 1992. *Nuño de Guzmán*. Siglo Veintiuno Editores, Mexico City.

Márquez, Pedro. 2000. El significado de las palabras p'urhepecha en la *Relación de Michoacán*. In *Relación de las ceremonias y rictos y población y gobernación de los indios de la provincia de Mechuacán* [Jerónimo de Alcalá], edited by Moisés Franco Mendoza, pp. 695–726. El Colegio de Michoacán and Gobierno del Estado de Michoacán, Zamora.

Martínez, Hildeberto. 1984. *Tepeaca en el siglo XVI: Tenencia de la tierra y organización de un señorio*. CIESAS, Mexico City.

Martínez Baracs, Rodrigo. 1998. *Michoacán en el último libro de gobierno novohispano de don Antonio de Mendoza, 1550*. Yehuetlatolli A.C., Mexico City.

———. 2003. Etimologías políticas michoacanos. In *Autoridad y gobierno indígena en Michoacán: Ensayos a través de su historia*, edited by Carlos Paredes Martínez and Marta Terán, pp. 61–91. El Colegio de Michoacán / CIESAS / INAH / UMSNH, Zamora.

Martínez Buenabad, Elizabeth. 2000. Agentes de la modernidad: Profesionalización y la representación de identidad étnica y comunal en San Pedro Zacán, Michoacán. Unpublished M.A. thesis, Colegio de Michoacán.

Martínez de Lejarza, Juan José. 1824. *Análisis estadístico de la provincial de Michuacán en 1822*. Mexico City.

Mastache, Alba Guadalupe, Robert H. Cobean, and Dan M. Healan. 2002. *Ancient Tollan, Tula and the Toltec Heartland*. University of Colorado Press, Boulder.

McIntosh, Juan B., and José Grimes. 1954. Niuqui iquisicayari: Vocabulario Huichol-Castellano—Castellano-Huichol. Instituto Lingüístico de Verano, Mexico City.

McNeill, William. 1976. *Plagues and Peoples*. Anchor Press, Garden City, New York.

Méndez Alfaro, Medardo (editor). 1989. *Revista Michoacán* 1(5).

Menegus Bornemann, Margarita. 1999. Los títulos primordiales de los pueblos de indios. In *Dos décadas de investigación en historia económica comparada en América Latina: Homenaje a Carlos Sempat Azzadourian*, edited by Margarita Menegus Bornemann, pp. 137–161. El Colegio de México, CIESAS, Instituto Mora, and UNAM, Mexico City.

Michelet, Dominique (editor). 1992. *El proyecto Michoacán, 1983–1987: Medio ambiente e introducción a los trabajos arqueológicos*. Collection Études Mésoaméricains II-12, Cuadernos de estudios michoacanos 4. Centre Français d'Études Mexicaines et Centraméricaines, Mexico City.

———. 1995. La zona occidental en el Posclásico. In *Historia antigua de México*, vol. 3, edited by L. Manzanilla and L. López Luján, pp. 153–188. Grupo Editorial Miguel Angel Porrúa / INAH / UNAM, Mexico City.

Michelet, Dominique, M. C. Arnauld, and Marie-France Fauvet-Berthelot. 1989. El proyecto del CEMCA en Michoacán. Etapa I: Un balance. *Trace* 16:70–87.

Migeon, Gerald. 1991. Les sites Tarasques de la région de Zacapu: Confrontation des données archéologiques et ethnohistoriques. In *Vingt études sur le Mexique et le Guatemala réunies à la memoire de Nicole Percheron*, edited by A. Breton, J.-P. Berthe, and S. Lecoin, pp. 95–115. Presses Universitaires du Mirail, Université de Toulouse–Le Mirail.

———. 1998. El poblamiento del malpaís de Zacapu y de sus alrededores, del Clásico al Posclásico. In *Génesis, culturas y espacios en Michoacán*, edited by Veronique Darras, pp. 35–45. CEMCA, Mexico City.

Miller, Wick. 1983. Uto-Aztecan Languages. In *Southwest*, edited by Alfonso Ortíz, pp. 113–124. Handbook of North American Indians, Vol. 10, William C. Sturtevant, general editor. Smithsonian Institution, Washington, D.C.

Mirafuentes Galván, José Luis. 1992. El "enemigo de las casas de adobe": Luis del Sáric y la rebelión de los pimas altos en 1751. In *Organización y liderazgo en los movimientos populares novohispanos*, edited by Felipe Castro Gutiérrez, Virginia Guedea, and José Luis Mirafuentes Galván, pp. 147–176. Universidad Nacional Autónoma de México, Mexico City.

Miranda, Francisco. 1988. Prólogo. In *La relación de Michoacán*, edited by Francisco Miranda, pp. 29–30. Secretaría de Educación Pública, Mexico City.

Monzón, Cristina. 1996. Términos de parentesco p'urhépecha en tres documents del siglo XVI: Resultados iniciales. *Amerindia* 21:101–110.

Monzón, Cristina, and Andrew Roth-Seneff. 1999. Referentes religiosos en el siglo XVI: Acuñaciones y expresiones en lengua tarasca. In *The Language of Christianisation in Latin America: Catechisation and Instruction in Amerindian Languages*, edited by Sabine Dedenbach-Salazar Sáenz and Lindsey Crickmay, pp. 169–181. Verlag Antón Sauerwein, Bonn.

Moxó, D. Benito María de. 1968. Disertación sobre una antigua pintura de los indios tarascos. *Anales del Museo Michoacano*, facsimile of the original, 1888–1891, Biblioteca de facsimiles mexicanos 1:96–105. Guadalajara.

Muriá, José María. 1980. *Historia de Jalisco*. Gobierno de Jalisco, Secretaría General, Guadalajara.

Myerhoff, Barbara G. 1974. *Peyote Hunt: The Sacred Journey of the Huichol Indians*. Cornell University Press, Ithaca, New York.

Naylor, Thomas H., and Charles W. Polzer, S.J. 1986. *The Presidio and Militia on the Northern Frontier of New Spain: A Documentary History. Volume One: 1570–1700.* University of Arizona Press, Tucson.

Nelson, Ben A. 1995. Complexity, Hierarchy, and Scale: A Controlled Comparison between Chaco Canyon, New Mexico, and La Quemada, Zacatecas. *American Antiquity* 60(4):597–618.

————. 1997. Chronology and Stratigraphy at La Quemada, Zacatecas, Mexico. *Journal of Field Archaeology* 24(1):85–109.

————. 2003. A Place of Continued Importance: The Abandonment of Epiclassic La Quemada. In *The Archaeology of Settlement Abandonment in Middle America*, edited by T. Inomata and R. W. Webb, pp. 77–89. University of Utah Press, Salt Lake City.

Nelson, Lise Kirsten. 2000. Remaking Gender and Citizenship in a Mexican Indigenous Community. Unpublished Ph.D. dissertation, University of Washington.

————. 2008. Espacio y etnografía en un contexto globalizado. In *Sendas en la globalización: Comprensiones etnográficas sobre poderes y desigualdades*, edited by Francisco Gómez Carpinteiro, pp. 205–225. Benemérita Universidad Autónoma de Puebla, Consejo Nacional de Ciencia y Tecnología, and Casa Juan Pablos, Mexico City.

Neurath, Johannes. 2002. *Las fiestas de la casa grande: Procesos rituales, cosmovisión y estructura social en una comunidad huichola.* INAH, Mexico City; and Universidad de Guadalajara, Guadalajara.

Novella, Roberto, Javier Martínez González, and Antonieta Mogul Cos. 2002. *La costa norte de Michoacán en la época prehispánica.* BAR International Series 1071. Archaeopress, Oxford.

Noyola, Andrés. 1994. Análisis preliminar de la cerámica del fraccionamiento, San Juan, Atoyac, Jalisco. In *Contribuciones a la arqueología y etnohistoria del occidente de México*, edited by Eduardo Williams, pp. 55–91. El Colegio de Michoacán, Zamora.

O'Hara, Sarah. 1993. Historical Evidence of Fluctuations in the Level of Lake Pátzcuaro, Michoacán, México over the Last 600 Years. *Geographical Journal* 159(1):51–62.

O'Hara, Sarah, F. Alayne Street-Perrott, and Timothy P. Burt. 1993. Accelerated Soil Erosion around a Mexican Highland Lake Caused by Prehispanic Agriculture. *Nature* 362:48–51.

Ohnersorgen, M. A., and M. D. Varian. 1996. Formal Architecture and Settlement Organization in Ancient West Mexico. *Ancient Mesoamerica* 7:103–120.

Olivier Durand, Guilhem. 1997. *Moqueries et métamorphoses d'un dieu aztèque: Tezcatlipoca, le "Seigneur au miroir fumant."* Institute d'Ethnologie, Musée de l'Homme, Paris.

Olivier Durand, Guilhem, and José Francisco Román Gutiérrez. 2008. *Tezcatlipoca y la guerra del Miztón.* In *Las vías del noroeste II. Propuesta para una perspectiva sistémica e interdisciplinaria*, edited by Carlo Bonfiglioli, Arturo Guitiérrez, Marie-Areti Hers, and Maria Eugenia Olavarría, pp. 131–147. Universidad Nacional Autónoma de México, Mexico City.

Oliveros, Arturo. 2004. *Hacedores de Tumbas en El Opeño, Jacona, Michoacán.* El Colegio de Michoacán and the Ayuntamiento de Jacona, Zamora.

Orosco y Jiménez, Francisco. 1922. *Colección de documentos históricos inéditos o muy raros: Referentes al Arzobispado de Guadalajara.* Tip. Y Lit. Sucursales de Loreto y Ancira, Guadalajara.

Orozco y Berra, Manuel. 1864. *Geografía de las lenguas y carta etnográfica de México: Precedidas de un ensayo de clasificación de las mismas lenguas y de apuntes para las inmigraciones de las tribus.* Imprenta de J. M. Andrade y F. Escanate, Mexico City.

Oudijk, Michel R., and María de los Ángeles Romero Frizzi. 2003. Los títulos primordiales: Un género de tradición mesoamericana, del mundo prehispánico al siglo XXI. *Relaciones* 95:17–48.

Paredes, Carlos. 2003. Instituciones coloniales en poblaciones tarascas. In *Autoridad y gobierno indígena en Michoacán: Ensayos a través de su historia*, edited by Carlos Paredes Martínez and Marta Terán, pp. 131–152. El Colegio de Michoacán / CIESAS / INAH / UMSNH, Zamora.

Paredes Martínez, Carlos (editor). 1994. "Yo por mi visto . . .": Mandamientos, ordenanzas, licencias y otras disposiciones virreinales del siglo XVI. Casa Chata Editiones, CIESAS, Michoacán University, Michoacán.

Parry, J. H. 1968. *The Spanish Seaborne Empire*. Penguin Books, London.

Paz, Octavio. 1970. *Postdata*. Siglo XXI, Mexico City.

———. 1972. *Puertas al campo*. Siglo XXI, Mexico City.

Pereira, Gregory. 1996. Nuevos hallazgos funerarios en Loma Alta, Zacapu, Michoacán. In *Las cuencas del occidente del México: Época prehispánica*, edited by Eduardo Williams and Phil C. Weigand, pp. 105–129. Colegio de Michoacán / CEMCA, Zamora.

———. 1999. *Potrero de Guadalupe: Anthropologie funéraire d'une communauté pré-tarasque du nord du Michoacán, Mexique*. BAR International Series 816. Archaeopress, Oxford.

Pereira, Gregory, Dominique Michelet, and Gerald Migeon. 2007. Cerro Barajas, Guanajuato. *Arqueología mexicana* 15(87):77–82.

Pérez Bustamante, Ciriaco. 1928. Los orígenes del gobierno virreinal en las Indias Españolas, Don Antonio de Mendoza, primer virrey de la Nueva España (1535–1550). Anales de la Universidad de Santiago. Vol. 3. Santiago de Compostela, Spain.

Pérez Escutia, Ramón. 1990. Composiciones de tierras en la provincia de Michoacán en los siglos XVII y XVIII. *Tzintzun* 12:5–22

Pérez Verdía, Luis. 1951. *Historia particular del estado de Jalisco*. 3 vols. 2nd ed. Gráfica, Guadalajara.

Periódico Oficial del Estado Libre y Soberano de San Luis Potosí. April 3, 2010.

Phillips, Catherine Anderson. 2002. Neglected Artifacts: A Study of Re-worked Ceramic Sherds from the Lake Pátzcuaro Basin, Mexico. Unpublished M.A. thesis, Michigan State University.

Piña Chan, Román, and Kuniaki Oí. 1982. *Exploraciones arqueológicas en Tingambato, Michoacán*. Instituto Nacional de Antropología e Historia, Mexico City.

Polanyi, Karl. 1968. *Primitive, Archaic, and Modern Economies: Essays of Karl Polanyi*. Edited by George Dalton. Anchor Books, Garden City, New York.

Pollard, Helen Perlstein. 1977. An Analysis of Urban Zoning and Planning in Prehispanic Tzintzuntzan. *Proceedings of the American Philosophical Society* 121(1):46–69.

———. 1980. Central Places and Cities: A Consideration of the Protohistoric Tarascan State. *American Antiquity* 45(4):677–696.

———. 1987. The Political Economy of Prehispanic Tarascan Metallurgy. *American Antiquity* 52(4):741–752.

———. 1993. *Tariacuri's Legacy: The Prehispanic Tarascan State*. University of Oklahoma Press, Norman.

———. 1994. Factores de desarrollo en la formación del Estado Tarasco. . . . In *El Michoacán antiguo*, edited by Brigitte Boehm de Lameiras, pp. 187–250. El Colegio de Michoacán y El Gobierno del Estado de Michoacán, Zamora.

———. 1995. Estudio del surgimiento del Estado Tarasco: Investigaciones recientes. In *Arqueología del occidente y norte de México*, edited by Eduardo Williams and Phil C. Weigand, pp. 29–63. El Colegio de Michoacán, Zamora.

———. 2000. Informe final al Consejo de Arqueología, INAH. Proyecto desarrollo del Estado Tarasco: Los Señoríos Urichu, Xaracuaro, y Pareo (1990–1998).

————. 2003a. Central Places and Cities in the Core of the Tarascan State. In *Urbanization in Mesoamerica*, edited by William T. Sanders and Alba Guadalupe Mastache, pp. 345–390. University of Pennsylvania Press, Philadelphia.

————. 2003b. El gobierno del estado tarasco prehispánico. In *Autoridad y gobierno indígena en Michoacán: Ensayos a través de su historia*, edited by Carlos Paredes Martínez and Marta Terán, pp. 49–60. El Colegio de Michoacán / CIESAS / INAH / UMSNH, Zamora.

————. 2005a. From Imperial Core to Colonial Periphery: The Lake Pátzcuaro Basin 1400–1800. In *The Late Postclassic to Spanish Era Transition in Mesoamerica*, edited by Rani Alexander and Susan Kepecs, pp. 65–76. University of New Mexico Press, Albuquerque.

————. 2005b. Michoacán en el mundo mesoamericano prehispánico: Erongarícuaro, Michoacán y los estados teotihuacano y tarasco. In *El antiguo occidente de Mexico: Nuevas perspectivas sobre el pasado prehispánico*, edited by Eduardo Williams, Phil C. Weigand, Lorenza López Mestas, and David C. Grove, pp. 283–303. El Colegio de Michoacán–INAH, Guadalajara.

————. 2008. A Model of the Emergence of the Tarascan State. *Ancient Mesoamerica* 19(2):217–230.

Pollard, Helen P., and Laura Cahue. 1999. Mortuary Patterns of Regional Elites in the Lake Patzcuaro Basin of Western Mexico. *Latin American Antiquity* 10(3):259–280.

Pollard, Helen P., Amy Hirshman, Hector Neff, and Michael Glascock. 2001. Las elites, el intercambio de bienes y el surgimiento del área nuclear tarasca: Análisis de la cerámica de la cuenca de Pátzcuaro. In *Estudios cerámicos en el occidente y norte de México*, edited by Eduardo Williams and Phil C. Weigand, pp. 289–309. El Colegio de Michoacán, Zamora.

Ponce, Alonso. 1968. *Relación breve y verdadera de algunas cosas de las muchas que sucedieron al padre fray Alonso Ponce en las provincias de la Nueva España. . . .* Guadalajara: Seminario de Cultura Mexicana.

Porter Weaver, Muriel Noe. 1969. A Reappraisal of Chupícuaro. In *The Natalie Wood Collection of Pre-Columbian Ceramics from Chupícuaro, Guanajuato, Mexico*, edited by Jay R. Frierman, pp. 81–92. University of California Press, Berkeley.

Powell, Phillip W. 1977. *La guerra chichimeca*. Fondo de Cultura Económica, Sección de Obras de Historia, Mexico City.

————. 1980. *Capitán Mestizo: Miguel Caldera y la frontera norteña; la pacificación de los chichimecas (1548–1597)*. Fondo de Cultura Económica, Sección de Obras de Historia, Mexico City.

Pulido Méndez, Salvador. 2003. Salvamento arqueológico en dos carreteras de Michoacán: Resultados de las investigaciones. *Arqueología* 29:45–62.

Ramírez García, Higinio. 1982. *La agricultura moderna y tradicional en la costa nahua de Michoacán*. Unidad Regional Pátzcuaro, Dirección General de Culturas Populares, Secretaría de Educación Pública, Uruapan.

Ramos, Jorge, and Lorenza López. 1996. Datos preliminares sobre el descubrimiento de una tumba de tiro en el sitio de Huitzilapa, Jalisco. Special section on western Mesoamerica, *Ancient Mesoamerica* 7(1):121–134.

Rappaport, Joanne. 1990. *The Politics of Memory: Native Historical Interpretation in the Colombian Andes*. Cambridge University Press, Cambridge.

Rea, Alonso de la. 1882. *Crónica de la Orden de N. Seráfico P. S. Francisco, Provincia de San Pedro y San Pablo de Mechoacán en la Nueva España*. Second Edition. Mexico: Imprenta de J. R. Barbedillo.

Redfield, Robert. 1953. *The Primitive World and Its Transformations*. Cornell University Press, Ithaca, New York.

Rendón Guillén, Alberto. 1980. *Tzintzuntzan: Breve reseña histórica y turística.* Fonapas, Mexico City.

———. 1996. *Tzintzuntzan: Monografía municipal.* Gobierno del Estado de Michoacán, H. Ayuntamiento de Tzintzuntzan, Morelia.

Rivera Farfán, Carolina. 1998. *Vida nueva para Tarecuato: Cabildo y parroquia ante la nueva evangelización.* El Colegio de Michoacán, Zamora.

Rodríguez-Sala, María Luisa, Ignacio Gómezgil R. S., and María Eugenia Cué. 1995. *Exploradores en el septentrión novohispano.* Miguel Angel Porrúa Grupo Editorial, Mexico City.

Román Gutiérrez, José Francisco. 1988. Chalchihuites, el nacimiento de un dios. Unpublished M.A. thesis, Unidad Académica de Ciencias Sociales, Universidad Autónoma de Zacatecas.

———. 1993. *Sociedad y evangelización en Nueva Galicia durante el siglo XVI.* El Colegio de Jalisco, Zapopan; INAH, Mexico City; and Universidad Autónoma de Zacatecas, Zacatecas.

———. 1996. Los indígenas de Juchipila alrededor de 1540–1547. *Estudios Jaliscienses* 23:21–29.

———. 2005. Comerciantes y minería en Nueva Galicia durante de siglo XVI. In *La tierra nómada: Seminario permanente de estudios de la Gran Chichimeca,* edited by Andrés Fábregas Puig, pp. 229–256. Universidad de Guadalajara, Guadalajara.

Romero López, José Guadalupe. 1993 [1864]. *Noticias estadísticas del partido de Coalcomán en 1863.* Universidad de San Nicolás de Hidalgo, Instituto de Investigaciones Históricas, Morevallado Editores, Morelia.

Roskamp, Hans. 1997. Pablo Beaumont and the Codex of Tzintzuntzan: A Pictorial Document from Michoacan, West Mexico. In *Cuadernos de Historia Latino-Americana,* No. 5, edited by Maarten Jansen, Luis Reyes, and Raymond Buve, pp. 193–245. Asociación de Historiadores Latinoamericanistas Europeos (AHILA), Ridderkerk, The Netherlands.

———. 1998. *La historiografía indígena de Michoacán: El lienzo de Jucutácato y los títulos de Carapan.* Research School CNWS, Leiden University, Leiden.

———. 2000. El carari indígena y la heráldica novohispana: Los escudos de armas de Tzintzuntzan, Michoacán. Paper presented at the international colloquium on emblematics "Esplendor y ocaso de la cultura simbólica." Zamora.

———. 2001. Historia, mito y legitimación: El lienzo de Jicalan. In *La tierra caliente de Michoacán,* edited by Eduardo Zárate Hernández, pp. 119–151. El Colegio de Michoacán and Gobierno del Estado de Michoacán, Zamora.

———. 2002. La heráldica novohispana del siglo XVI: Un escudo de armas de Tzintzuntzan, Michoacán. In *Esplendor y ocaso de la cultura simbólica,* edited by Herón Pérez Martínez and Barbara Skinfill Nogal, pp. 227–268. El Colegio de Michoacán and CONACYT, Zamora.

———. 2003. Los "Títulos Primordiales" de Carapan, Michoacán: Legitimación e historiografía en una comunidad indigena. In *Autoridad y gobierno indígena en Michoacán,* edited by Carlos Paredes and Marta Terán, pp. 305–360. El Colegio de Michoacán, Centro de Investigaciones y Estudios Superiores en Antropología Social, Instituto Nacional de Antropología e Historia, Universidad Michoacana de San Nicolás de Hidalgo, Zamora.

———. 2004. El lienzo de Nahuatzen: Origen y territorio de una comunidad de la Sierra Tarasca. Unpublished manuscript.

———. 2010. Memoria, identidad y legitimación en los "Titulos Primordiales" de la región tarasca. In *Caras y máscaras del México étnico: La participación indígena en las formaciones del Estado mexicano,* vol. 1, *Dominio y libertad en la historia indígena de México,* edited by Andrew Roth-Seneff, pp. 39–53. El Colegio de Michoacán, Zamora.

246   *References Cited*

Rostas, Susanna. 1995. Los Concheros, la Mexica y mexicanidad: Una nueva identidad et-
nopolítica y religiosa. Paper presented at the XVII Congreso de Historia de las Religiones,
Mexico City, August.
Roth-Seneff, Andrew. 1993. Región nacional y la construcción de un medio cultural. El Año
Nuevo P'urhépecha. *Relaciones: Estudios de historia y sociedad* 14(53):241–272.
———. 2010. Forjando el debate nacional y el *p'urhepecheri jimpanhi wéxurhini*. In *Reformas
del estado en América Latina: Movimientos sociales y mundo rural en el siglo XX en América
Latina*, edited by Antonio Escobar Ohmstede, Fernando I. Salmerón Castro, Laura R.
Valladares de la Cruz, and Ma. Guadalupe Escamilla Hurtado, pp. 555–589. UNAM,
Mexico City.
———. In press. P'urhepechari Jimpanhi Wéxurhini—Año Nuevo Purépecha. In *Los pueblos indígenas de Michoacán: Atlas etnográfico*, edited by Aída Castilleja González. Colección Etnografía de los Pueblos Indígenas de México, Serie Divulgación. Instituto Nacional de Antropología e Historia, Mexico City.
Roth-Seneff, Andrew, Elizabeth Martínez Buenabad, and Manuel Sosa. 2004. "A nombre de
la comunidad": Política étnica y reforma neoliberal en la Meseta P'urhépecha. In *Recursos
contenciosos: Ruralidad y reformas liberales en México*, edited by Andrew Roth-Seneff, pp.
181–208. El Colegio de Michoacán, Zamora.
Roth-Seneff, Andrew, and Hans Roskamp. 2004. El paisaje prehispánico y la tradición oral
en la Meseta P'urhépecha. In *Tradiciones arqueológicas*, edited by Efraín Cárdenas García,
pp. 35–53. El Colegio de Michoacán, Gobierno del Estado de Michoacán, Zamora.
Roth-Seneff, Andrew, and Manuel Sosa. 2003. Tradiciones del estado, usos y costumbres y
desarrollo communal: El caso del astillador de Angahuan, Michoacán. In *Estudios Michoacanos X*, edited by Oscar González, pp. 117–139. El Colegio de Michoacán, Gobierno
del Estado de Michoacán, Zamora.
Ruiz Medrano, Ethelia. 1994. Versiones sobre un fenómeno rebelde: La guerra del Mixtón
en Nueva Galicia. In *Contribuciones a la arqueología y etnohistoria del occidente de México*,
edited by Eduardo Williams, pp. 355–378. El Colegio de Michoacán, Zamora.
———. 2010. *Mexico's Indigenous Communities: Their Lands and Histories, 1500–2010*. University Press of Colorado, Boulder.
Sahagún, (Fray) Bernardino de. 1959–1981. *Florentine Codex: History of the Things of New
Spain*. Translated and edited by Charles E. Dibble and Arthur J. O. Anderson. School of
American Research, Santa Fe, New Mexico.
Sahlins, Marshall D. 1981. *Historical Metaphors and Mythical Realities: Structure in the Early
History of the Sandwich Islands Kingdom*. University of Michigan Press, Ann Arbor.
———. 1985. *Islands of History*. University of Chicago Press, Chicago.
———. 2000. *Culture in Practice: Selected Essays*. Zone Books, New York.
Sánchez Díaz, Gerardo. 1988. *El suroeste de Michoacán: Economía y sociedad, 1852–1910*.
Universidad de San Nicolás de Hidalgo, Instituto de Investigaciones Históricas, Morelia.
Sandoval, Zazil, René Esparza, Teresa Rojas Rabiela, and Regina Olmedo. 1999. *Guía de
restitución y dotación de tierras y de reconocimiento, confirmación y titulación de bienes comunales*. Registro Archivo General Agrario and CIESAS, Mexico City.
San Luis Potosí. 1994. Decreto que declara sitio de patrimonio histórico, cultural y Zona
sujeta a Conservación Ecológica del grupo étnico "Wirrarika" a los lugares sagrados y a la
ruta histórico cultural ubicada en los municipios de Villa de Ramos, Charcas y Catorce
del Estado de San Luis Potosí. Periódico Oficial no. 57, special issue, 22 September.
www2.ine.gob.mx/publicaciones/libros/360/slp.html (accessed 21 November 2014).
Sarabia Viejo, María Justina. 1978. *Don Luis de Velasco, virrey de Nueva España, 1550–1564*.
Escuela de Estudios Hispano-Americanos, Seville.

Sarabia Viejo, María Justina, and José Francisco Román Gutiérrez. 1992. Nueva España a mediados del siglo XVI: Colonización y expansión. In *Congreso de Historia del Descubrimiento, Actas*, Vol. 2, pp. 614–620. Real Academia de Historia, Confederación Española de Cajas de Ahorros, Madrid.

Sauer, Carl. 1934. *The Distribution of Aboriginal Tribes and Languages in Northwest Mexico.* Ibero-Americana 5. University of California Press, Berkeley.

———. 1948. *Colima of New Spain in the Sixteenth Century.* Ibero-Americana 29. University of California Press, Berkeley.

Schöndube, Otto. 1980. Las exploraciones arqueológicas en el área tarasca. In *La cultura purhé, fuentes e historia*, edited by Francisco Miranda. El Colegio de Michoacán, Fonapas Michoacán, Zamora, Michoacán.

Sigaut, Nelly. 2008. El cielo de colores. In *Del territorio a la arquitectura en el obispado de Michoacán*, edited by Carlos Salvador Paredes Martínez et al., pp. 269–304. Universidad Michoacana de San Nicolás de Hidalgo and CONACYT, Morelia.

Silverstein, Jay E. 2000. A Study of the Late Postclassic Aztec-Tarascan Frontier in Northern Guerrero, Mexico: The Oztuma-Cutzamala Project. Unpublished Ph.D. dissertation, Pennsylvania State University.

———. 2001. Aztec Imperialism at Oztuma, Guerrero: Aztec-Chontal Relations during the Late Postclassic and Early Colonial Periods. *Ancient Mesoamerica* 12:1–30.

Southall, A. W. 1988. The Segmentary State in Africa and Asia. *Comparative Studies in Society and History* 30(1): 52–82.

Stanislawski, Dan. 1947. Tarascan Political Geography. *American Anthropologist* 49(1):46–55.

Tönnies, Ferdinand. 1957 [1887]. *Gemeinschaft und Gesellschaft (Community and Society).* Michigan State University Press, East Lansing.

Tello, Antonio. 1968. *Crónica miscelánea de la Sta. Provincia de Xalisco.* Vol. 1, book 2. UAH / U de G / Gobierno del Estado de Jalisco, Guadalajara, Jalisco.

———. 1973. *Crónica miscelánea de la Sta. Provincia de Xalisco.* Vol. 2, book 2. UAH / U de G / Gobierno del Estado de Jalisco, Guadalajara, Jalisco.

Topete del Valle, Alejandro. 1978. Información de méritos y servicios de Juan de Tolosa. *Anuario de Historia* 1:181–185. Universidad Autónoma de Zacatecas.

Tortolero, Alejandro. 2008. *Notarios y agricultores: Crecimiento y atraso en el campo mexicano, 1780–1920.* Siglo XXI, UAM-I, Mexico City.

Townsend, Richard F. (editor). 1998. *Ancient West Mexico: Art and Archaeology of the Unknown Past.* Thames and Hudson, New York.

Valdez, Francisco, and Catherine Liot. 1994. La cuenca de Sayula: Yacimientos de sal en la frontera oeste del estado tarasco. In *El Michoacán antiguo*, edited by Brigitte Boehm de Lameiras, pp. 285–305. El Colegio de Michoacán and El Gobierno del Estado de Michoacán, Zamora.

Valiñas, Leopoldo. 1993. Las lenguas indígenas mexicanas: Entre la comunidad y la nación. Paper presented at the Coloquio de Occidentalistas, Universidad de Guadalajara.

van der Haar, Gemma. 2004. *Land Reform and the Constitution of Community in the Tojolabal Highlands of Chiapas, Mexico.* Rozenberg Publishers, Amsterdam.

van Young, Eric. 2000. The Indigenous Peoples of Western Mexico from the Spanish Invasion to the Present. In *Mesoamerica*, edited by Richard E. W. Adams and Murdo J. Macleod, pp. 136–186. Cambridge History of the Native Peoples of the Americas, Vol. 2. Cambridge University Press, Cambridge.

Vandergeest, Peter, and Nancy Lee Peluso. 1995. Territorialization and State Power in Thailand. *Theory and Society* 24(3):385–426.

Vásquez León, Luis. 1992. *Ser indio otra vez: La purepechización de los tarascos serranos.* CNCA, Mexico City.

Velásquez Gallardo, Pablo. 1952 [1539]. Título de tierras de Cherán Hatzincurin. *Tlalocan* 3(3):238–245.

Voloshinov, V. N. 1986 [1930]. *Marxism and the Philosophy of Language.* Translated by Ladislav Matejka and I. R. Titunik. Harvard University Press, Cambridge.

Warren, J. Benedict. 1968. Minas de cobre de Michoacan, 1533. *Anales del Museo Michoacano* 6:35–52.

————. 1977. *La conquista de Michoacán, 1521–1530.* Fimax, Morelia.

————. 1985. *The Conquest of Michoacan.* University of Oklahoma Press, Norman.

———— (editor). 1991. *Diccionario grande de la lengua de Michoacán.* Vol. 2, *Tarasco–Español.* Fimax Publicistas, Morelia.

————. 2000. Fray Jerónimo de Alcalá, autor de la *Relación de Michoacán.* In *Estudios introductorios a la Relación de Michoacán,* edited by Moisés Franco Mendoza, pp. 37–56. El Colegio de Michoacán and Gobierno del Estado de Michoacán, Zamora.

Weigand, Phil C. 1970. Ceremonial Re-use of a Fluted Point by the Huichol Indians. *American Antiquity* 35(3):365–367.

————. 1982. Mining and Mineral Trade in Prehispanic Zacatecas. In *Mining and Mining Techniques in Ancient Mesoamerica,* edited by P. C. Weigand and G. Gywnne. *Anthropology* 6:87–134.

————. 1985. Considerations on the Archaeology and Ethnohistory of the Mexicaneros, Tequales, Coras, Huicholes, and Caxcanes of Nayarit, Jalisco, and Zacatecas. In *Contributions to the Archaeology and Ethnohistory of Greater Mesoamerica: Essays in Honor of Carroll L. Riley,* edited by William J. Folan, Jr., pp. 126–187. Southern Illinois University Press, Carbondale.

————. 1992. *Ensayos sobre el Gran Nayar: Entre Coras, Huicholes, y Tepehuanes.* CEMCA/ Intituto Nacional Indigenista/El Colegio de Michoacán, Mexico City.

————. 1993a. *Evolución de una civilización prehispánica: Arqueología de Jalisco, Nayarit y Zacatecas.* Colegio de Michoacán, Zamora.

————. 1993b. The Political Organization of the Trans-Tarascan Zone of Western Mesoamerica on the Eve of Spanish Conquest. In *Culture and Contact: Charles C. Di Peso's Gran Chichimeca,* edited by Anne I. Woosley and John C. Ravesloot, pp. 91–217. University of New Mexico Press, Albuquerque.

————. 1996a. The Architecture of the Teuchitlán Tradition of the Occidente of Mesoamerica. Recent Research in the Lake Basins of Highland Jalisco. *Ancient Mesoamerica* 7(1):91–101.

————. 1996b. La evolución y ocaso de un núcleo de civilización: La Tradición Teuchitlán y la arqueología de Jalisco. In *Las Cuencas del Occidente de México: Epoca prehispánica,* edited by E. Williams and P. C. Weigand, pp. 185–245. El Colegio de Michoacán, ORSTOM, and CEMCA, Zamora.

————. 2004a. La tradición Teuchitlán del Occidente de México. In *Tradiciones Arqueológicas,* edited by Efrain Cárdenas, pp. 217–241. El Colegio de Michoacán and El Gobierno de Michoacán, Zamora.

————. 2004b. Los antecedentes mesoamericanos de los murales kiva de los Hopi de Awatovi, norte de Arizona: Análisis y escenario. *Relaciones* 25(100):313–340. El Colegio de Michoacán, Zamora.

Weigand, Phil C., and Christopher Beekman. 1999. The Teuchitlan Tradition: Rise of a State-like Society. In *Ancient West Mexico: Art and Archaeology of the Unknown Past,* edited by Richard Townsend. Art Institute of Chicago, Chicago.

Weigand, Phil C., and Acelia García de Weigand. 1994. Minería Prehispánica en Jalisco. *Estudios jaliscienses* 17:5–21. Colegio de Jalisco, Zapopan, Jalisco.

————. 1996. Salinas y salineras: Manufacturas prehispánicas de sal en el Occidente de México. In *Antropología en Jalisco: Una visión actual.* Vol. 9, pp. 5–23. La Secretaría de Cultura del Estado de Jalisco, Guadalajara.

Weigand, Phil C., and Garman Harbottle. 1992. The Function of Turquoise in the Ancient Mesoamerican Trade Structure. In *The American Southwest and Mesoamerica: Systems of Prehistoric Exchange,* edited by J. E. Ericson and T. G. Baugh, pp. 159–177. Plenum Press, New York.

Williams, Eduardo. 1996. Desarrollo cultural en las cuencas del Occidente de México: 1500 aC–1521 dC. In *Las Cuencas del Occidente de México: Epoca prehispánica,* edited by E. Williams and P. C. Weigand, pp. 15–59. El Colegio de Michoacán, ORSTOM, and CEMCA, Zamora.

Williams, Raymond. 1977. *Marxism and Literature.* Oxford University Press, Oxford.

Wolf, Eric R. 1955. Types of Latin American Peasantry: A Preliminary Discussion. *American Anthropologist* 57(3, pt. 1):452–471.

————. 1956. Aspects of Group Relations in a Complex Society: Mexico. *American Anthropologist* 58:1065–1078.

————. 1957. Closed Corporate Peasant Communities in Mesoamerica and Central Java. *Southwestern Journal of Anthropology* 13(1):1–18.

————. 1982. *Europe and the People without History.* University of California Press, Berkeley.

————. 1986. The Vicissitudes of the Closed Corporate Peasant Community. *American Ethnologist* 13(2):325–329.

Wood, Stephanie. 1986. Don Diego García de Mendoza Moctezuma: A Techialoyan Mastermind? *Estudios de Cultura Náhuatl* 19:245–268.

————. 1987. Pedro Villafranca y Juana Gertrudis Navarrete: Falsificador de títulos y su viuda (Nueva España, siglo XVIII). In *Lucha por la supervivencia en la América colonial,* edited by David G. Sweet and Gary B. Nash, pp. 472–485. Fondo de Cultura Económica, Mexico City.

————. 1991. The Cosmic Conquest: Late-Colonial Views of the Sword and Cross in Central Mexican Títulos. *Ethnohistory* 38(2):176–195.

————. 1998a. El problema de la historicidad de los *títulos* y los códices *Techialoyan.* In *De tlacuilos y escribanos,* edited by Xavier Noguez and Stephanie Wood, pp. 167–207. El Colegio de Michoacán, El Colegio Mexiquense, Zamora.

————. 1998b. The Social and Legal Context of Náhuatl *Títulos.* In *Native Traditions in the Postconquest World,* edited by Elizabeth Hill Boone and Tom Cummins, pp. 201–231. Dumbarton Oaks, Washington, DC.

Yasumura, Naoki. 2003. Polifonía en la construcción de lo purépecha. In *Autoridad y gobierno indígena en Michoacán: Ensayos a través de su historia,* edited by Carlos Paredes Martínez and Marta Terán, pp. 643–673. El Colegio de Michoacán / CIESAS / INAH / UMSNH, Zamora.

Zárate, Eduardo. 1994. La fiesta del Año Nuevo Purhépecha como ritual político: Notas en torno al discurso de los profesionales indígenas purhépechas. In *El verbo oficial: Política moderna en dos campos periféricos del estado mexicano,* edited by Andrew Roth-Seneff and José Lameiras, pp. 99–124. El Colegio de Michoacán, ITESO, Zamora.

————. 2001. *Los señores de utopia. Etnicidad política en una comunidad p'urhépecha: Santa Fe de la Laguna-Ueamuo.* 2nd ed. El Colegio de Michoacán / CIESAS, Zamora.

Zingg, Robert M. 1938. *The Huichols: Primitive Artists.* G. E. Stechert, New York.

Zurita, Alonso de. 1999. *Relación de la Nueva España: Relación de algunas de las muchas cosas notables que hay en la Nueva España y de su conquista y pacificación y de la conversión de los naturales de ella,* edited by Ethelia Ruiz Medrano, Wiebke Ahrndt, and José Mariano Leyva. CONACULTA, Mexico City.

Editors and Contributors

Editors

Andrew Roth-Seneff is a professor of anthropology at the Colegio de Michoacán and a member of the Mexican National System of Researchers. His research is focused on Purépecha popular culture and its ethnographic and historical referents. His articles and essays have been published in numerous journals in Mexico, Puerto Rico, the United States, and the United Kingdom, and he has edited five books concerned with analyzing and interpreting the relation between the organization of regional culture and historical changes in discourse frames, most recently, *Caras y máscaras del México étnico*, vol. 1 (2010) and vol. 2 (2011). He currently serves as provost of the Colegio de Michoacán.

Robert V. Kemper (1945–2013) was a professor of anthropology at Southern Methodist University. His regional interests included Mexico and the United States, and his research and teaching ranged from urban anthropology (especially migration) to bilingual education to tourism. For over forty years he carried out long-term research among the people of Tzintzuntzan, Michoacán, Mexico, where he worked on topics of migration and community transformation since 1969. He authored and edited several books on these topics, as well as numerous articles and book chapters.

Julie Adkins is an instructor in anthropology at the University of Texas, Arlington. Her regional interests are the United States, Mexico, and Central America, and her research interests are urban poverty and homelessness, development and NGOs, and volunteer tourism. Combining these interests, she has recently published (with Tara Hefferan and Laurie Occhipinti) two edited volumes: *Bridging the Gaps: Faith-Based Organizations, Neoliberalism, and Development in Latin America and the Caribbean* (2009) and *Not by Faith Alone: Social Services, Social Justice, and Faith-Based Organizations in the United States* (2010).

Contributors

Phillip C. Weigand (1934–2011) was a distinguished scholar in the archaeology, ethnohistory, and ethnography of western and northwestern Mesoamerica. In over 27 books and monographs and 130 articles and chapters, as well as the development of a major archaeological site (Teuchtitlan in Jalisco, Mexico), Weigand made seminal contributions to the archaeology and ethnohistory of central western Mexico.

Helen Perlstein Pollard is a professor of anthropology at Michigan State University. Her research has been focused on Tarascan archaeology and ethnohistory, emphasizing urbanization and the formation of the Tarascan state. In addition to over 40 chapters and articles on the Tarascans in the Postclassic Mesoamerican world, she is the author of *Tariacuri's Legacy: The Prehispanic Tarascan State* (1993) and (with Shirley Gorenstein) *The Tarascan Civilization: A Late Prehispanic Cultural System* (1983).

Hans Roskamp is a professor of ethnohistory at the Colegio de Michoacán and a member of the Mexican National System of Researchers. His research has focused on the analysis of sixteenth- through eighteenth-century pictorial and alphabetical documents that the indigenous nobles and commoners used to legitimize their claims to certain rights and privileges. He has published numerous articles and chapters on these topics in Mexico, the United States, and Europe, as well as the monograph *Los códices de Cutzio y Huetamo: Encomienda y tributo en la tierra caliente de Michoacán, siglo XVI* (2003).

Felipe Castro Gutiérrez is a titular research professor at the Instituto de Investigaciones Históricas at the Universidad Nacional Autónoma de México and a member of Academia Mexicana de Ciencias and the Mexican National System of Researchers. He has published extensively on the colonial history of the Purhépecha Indians of Michoacán, including the monographs *Los Tarascos y el Imperio Español, 1600–1740* (2004) and *Nueva ley y nuevo rey: Reformas borbónicas y rebelión popular en Nueva España* (1996).

José Francisco Román Gutiérrez is a professor of history at the Autonomous University of Zacatecas and a member of the Mexican National System of Researchers. His research is focused on the early colonial period in northern and western Mexico and on the cultural patrimony of the Spanish Empire in these regions. His most recent publications are *Los sabores de la tierra: Raíces y tradiciones de la comida zacatecana* (2009), winner of the Gourmand World Cookbook Award (2010), and in collaboration, *Los recetarios de Majoma: La cocina de una hacienda del semidesierto zacatecano* (2012) and *¡Puro bola y mirasol! Andanzas del chile en Zacatecas* (2012).

Paul Liffman is a professor of anthropology at the Colegio de Michoacán and a member of the Mexican National System of Researchers. He has done extensive fieldwork in the Gran Nayar region of western Mexico, with a focus on territoriality in the Huichol community of San Andrés Cohamiata, and has recently published *Huichol Territory and the Mexican Nation: Indigenous Ritual, Land Conflict, and Sovereignty Claims* (2010).

John Gledhill is Max Gluckman Professor of Social Anthropology at the University of Manchester, an academician of the UK Academy of Learned Societies in the Social Sciences, and a fellow of the British Academy. His research has focused on the ethnography and history of rural society, politics, and social movements in Latin America, alongside broader comparative analyses of the social and political implications of globalization. Among his numerous books and articles are his monographs *Casi Nada: Agrarian Reform in the Homeland of Cardenismo* (1992), *Power and Its Disguises: Anthropological Perspectives on Politics* (2nd ed., 2000), both of which have also been published in Spanish, and *Neoliberalism, Transnationalization and Rural Poverty: A Case Study of Michoacán, Mexico* (1995) and *Cultura y desafío en Ostula: Practicando la autonomía indígena en la costa-sierra Nahua de Michoacán* (2004).

Index

Page numbers in *italics* represent illustrations.

PRINCIPLES OF
FARM MACHINERY
Third Edition

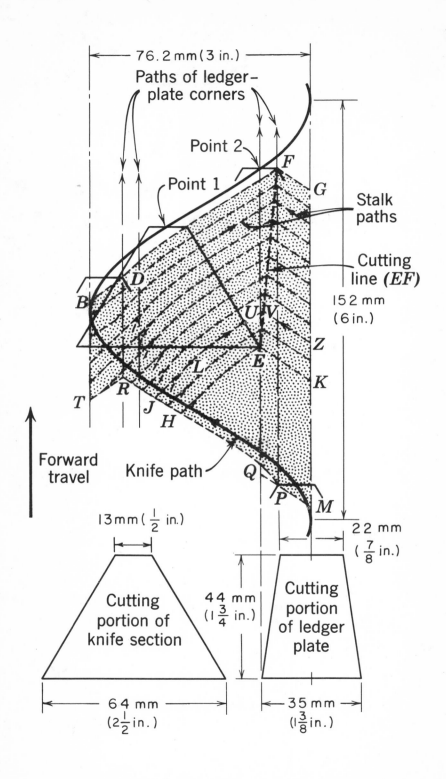

76.2 mm (3 in.)
Paths of ledger-plate corners
Point 2
Point 1
F
G
Stalk paths
Cutting line *(EF)*
152 mm (6 in.)
D
B
U V
E
Z
K
T
R
J
H
L
Forward travel
Knife path
Q
P
M
13 mm ($\frac{1}{2}$ in.)
22 mm ($\frac{7}{8}$ in.)
Cutting portion of knife section
44 mm ($1\frac{3}{4}$ in.)
Cutting portion of ledger plate
64 mm ($2\frac{1}{2}$ in.)
35 mm ($1\frac{3}{8}$ in.)

PRINCIPLES OF FARM MACHINERY

Third Edition

R. A. Kepner

Professor of Agricultural Engineering,
University of California,
Davis, California

Roy Bainer

Emeritus Dean of the College of Engineering,
and Emeritus Professor of Agricultural Engineering,
University of California,
Davis, California

and

E. L. Barger

Former Director of Product Planning,
Massey-Ferguson, Ltd.

AVI PUBLISHING COMPANY, INC.
Westport, Connecticut

Library of Congress Cataloging in Publication Data

Kepner, Robert Allen, 1915-
    Principles of farm machinery.

    Includes index.
    1. Agricultural machinery. I. Bainer, Roy,
1902- joint author. II. Barger, Edgar Lee,
joint author. III. Title
S675.K43 1978   631.3   78-16078
ISBN 0-87055-252-X

Printed in the United States of America

Preface To The Third Edition

The primary objective in preparing a new edition of *Principles of Farm Machinery* at this time was to incorporate SI (metric) units of measure. Engineering colleges and schools in many universities are moving rapidly toward the use of the SI system in teaching engineering courses. In this Third Edition, U.S. customary units are also shown in most places because responses to a questionnaire sent to all agricultural engineering departments in the United States and Canada were overwhelmingly in favor of the dual-unit presentation. Customary units have been omitted in some places where the significance of the numbers is in their *relative* values rather than their absolute magnitudes or where including dual units would unduly complicate the presentation of a graph. Problems have only SI units.

The portion of Chapter 2 dealing with costs has been updated and rewritten. New material has been added pertaining to large-hay-bale systems, axial-flow threshing cylinders and rotary separation in grain combines, and handling and storing seed cotton. Minor updating has been done where appropriate throughout the remainder of the book. We did not make an exhaustive search of all pertinent literature published since the Second Edition was prepared in 1971, but papers appearing in the Transactions of the ASAE during this period were reviewed and appropriate ones are cited.

Principles of Farm Machinery emphasizes functional requirements, principles, and performance evaluation of field machines, but also includes some design-related material. It is intended primarily as a textbook for an upper-division engineering course in field machinery. Prerequisites should include a course in static mechanics. Knowledge pertaining to strength of materials and dynamics would be helpful but is not essential.

Reference lists at the ends of the chapters indicate the source of much of the technical material in the book and provide a handy guide for more detailed study of a particular subject. Such information should be helpful to the practicing agricultural engineer as well as to others in the farm machinery industry.

In 1975, agricultural engineering students at the University of Missouri-Columbia, under the direction of Professor C.E. Goering, developed a page-by-page SI conversion supplement for the Second Edition. Having their results available as a means of checking our conversions for the Third Edition was most helpful. Massey-Ferguson, Inc., Des Moines, Iowa, provided funds for typing, drafting, and other incidental expenses. Special appreciation is expressed to Karin Clawson for typing the revised portions of the manuscript, to James Bumgarner for preparing the line drawings, to

Dennie Kepner (wife of the senior author) for assistance in proofreading, and to electronics engineers for developing pocket computers such as the HP-55.

R. A. KEPNER
ROY BAINER
E. L. BARGER

April, 1978

Preface To The Second Edition

There has been a tremendous amount of research and development in the area of farm machinery since the First Edition was published 17 years ago. Several thousand technical reports have been published during this period. Reviewing a substantial portion of these and deciding what information should be included in the Second Edition has been a formidable task.

To provide space for new information without greatly increasing the length and cost of the book, four chapters and most of the appendix material included in the First Edition have been deleted. No ASAE standards or recommendations are included in their entirety because these are now readily available and kept up-to-date in the Agricultural Engineers Yearbook. The chapter on construction materials was deleted because of the considerable amount of space that would be required to cover this subject adequately.

Several new chapters or major portions of chapters have been added. Although much of the basic information from the First Edition has been retained, the entire book has been rewritten and up-dated. Substantial changes have been made in the organization and sequence of presentation in some subject areas. Half of the line drawings and 60% of the halftones are new in the Second Edition.

As in the First Edition, some problems are included at the ends of most chapters. Instructors are urged to develop additional problems appropriate to their specific teaching objectives.

Responses to a questionnaire sent to all agricultural engineering departments in the United States and Canada in 1970 provided valuable guidance regarding the general subjects to be included and the manner of presentation. Some instructors would prefer that the book be design-oriented, but the predominant use appears to be in more general farm machinery courses. Accordingly, the Second Edition continues to emphasize functional requirements, principles, and performance evaluation, but with some design-related material included. Ideally, there should be two textbooks, one on principles and one on design.

We wish to acknowledge the assistance of the following persons, each of whom reviewed preliminary drafts of one or more chapters: N.B. Akesson, K.K. Barnes, G.P. Barrington, A.M. Best and members of his engineering staff, D.C. Bichel, H.D. Bruhn, B.J. Butler, D.M. Byg, W.J. Chancellor, G.F. Cooper, T.E. Corley, J.B. Dobie, K.J. Fornstrom, R.B. Fridley, W.R. Gill, J.R. Goss, R.C. Hansen, E.D. Hudspeth, Jr., D.R. Hunt, W.H. Johnson, J.J. Mehlschau, M. O'Brien, J.G. Porterfield, C.B. Richey, C.E. Schertz, W.L. Sims, B.A. Stout, H.E. Studer, G.R. Tupper, P.K. Turnquist,

J.C. Vance, and W.E. Yates. Comments and suggestions from these experts were extremely helpful and represent significant contributions to the final product.

Massey-Ferguson, Ltd., Toronto, Canada, provided funds for typing, drafting, and other incidental expenses. Without this support, the revision probably would not have been undertaken. We are grateful to the University of California for providing facilities and especially to the Department of Agricultural Engineering for permitting part of the writing to be done on University time. Special appreciation is expressed to Karin Clawson and Joanne Weigt, who typed the manuscript, and to James Bumgarner who prepared the line drawings.

R. A. KEPNER
ROY BAINER
E. L. BARGER

December, 1971

Preface To The First Edition

In preparing this textbook, the authors have attempted to present the subject of farm machinery from the engineering viewpoint, emphasizing functional requirements and principles of operation for the basic types of field machines. Where feasible, machines for a particular cultural practice (such as planting) have been treated on the basis of the unit operations performed by the functional elements of the machine. Methods for testing or evaluating the performance of certain types of field machinery are included in the appropriate chapters.

Principles of Farm Machinery is designed primarily as a textbook for an upper-division course in farm machinery that might be required of all professional agricultural engineering students, regardless of their expected field of specialization. Prerequisites should include a course in static mechanics. Knowledge pertaining to strength of materials and to dynamics would be helpful but is not essential.

In discussing the various machines, only a minimum amount of descriptive material has been included. We have assumed that the reader will be generally familiar with the common types of farm machinery, either from actual experience or from other course work. A student without this background should, from time to time, consult references of a more descriptive nature (trade literature, non-technical textbooks, etc.). The laboratory provides additional opportunity for the student to become familiar with the details of specific machines.

This book represents a summarization and integration of a vast amount of engineering information not heretofore available in one volume. Reference lists at the ends of the chapters indicate the sources for much of the material and provide a handy guide for more detailed study of any particular subject. Such information should be helpful to the practicing agricultural engineer as well as to others in the farm machinery industry.

The subject matter deals primarily with the more common types of field machines but also includes general discussions of materials, power transmission, economics, and hydraulic controls, as applied to farm machinery. The chapter on seed cleaning is included only because of its relation to the separating and cleaning functions in seed-harvesting equipment. There are many examples of specialty equipment and localized special problems that require engineering attention and offer a real challenge to the farm machinery development engineer, but space does not permit their consideration in this book.

It is recognized that there is considerable variation in the type of approach and technical level of treatment for the various subjects presented. Unfortunately, this inconsistency is an indication of the present status of farm machinery. For some types of equipment, considerable engineering information and analytical material are available in the literature, but for other types there is little or nothing other than descriptive material. This situation, however, is changing rapidly and will continue to improve in the future.

Lack of standardization of nomenclature is one of the difficulties confronting a person who writes about farm machinery. The authors have given considerable thought to this problem in an attempt to select the most descriptive and logical terms and perhaps contribute in some degree to future standardization of nomenclature. For example, what we describe as a vertical-disk plow is known in the industry by any one of half a dozen names, including the one we selected.

In a group of closely related books such as The Ferguson Foundation Agricultural Engineering Series, some overlapping of subject matter is unavoidable and perhaps even desirable. For example, the subject of hydraulic controls is discussed in our book as well as in the tractor book of this series. This duplication is felt by the authors to be justified because of the increasing importance of the subject and because of the direct relation of hydraulic controls to farm machinery and its design.

The authors wish to express their appreciation to the many individuals and organizations whose material we have freely used in preparing this manuscript. Farm machinery manufacturers and others have been most cooperative in supplying illustrative material. We are particularly indebted to the Ferguson Foundation, Detroit, Michigan, for sponsoring this work, and to Mr. Harold Pinches of the Foundation for his encouragement and assistance. Credit is given to the University of California for providing the services and facilities so necessary in such an undertaking.

The preliminary, offset-printed edition was reviewed by many of the leading agricultural engineers, both in industry and in state colleges and universities. Specific suggestions received from approximately fifty of these reviewers, over half of whom were men in industry, represent an important contribution to the accuracy and completeness of the book. We are sincerely grateful for the help received from these men. Our special thanks go to Messrs. N.B. Akesson, A.W. Clyde, and F.W. Duffee for assistance with the subject matter in their respective fields of specialization. Appreciation is expressed to Mrs. Hazel Porter for her cooperation and patience in typing the manuscript, to Messrs. Maurice Johnson and Gerald Lambert who prepared most of the line drawings for illustrations, and to all others who assisted in any way.

ROY BAINER
R. A. KEPNER
E. L. BARGER

October, 1955

Contents

Research and Development
In Farm Machinery

1.1. Introduction. The application of machines to agricultural production has been one of the outstanding developments in American agriculture during the past century. The results are to be seen in many aspects of American life. The burden and drudgery of farm work has been reduced and the output per worker has been greatly increased. Farm mechanization has released millions of agricultural workers to other industries, thus contributing to America's remarkable industrial expansion and to the high standard of living that now prevails in this country.

Our constantly expanding population has required and will continue to demand an ever-increasing agricultural production of foods and fibers. Some of the increased production that has been realized during the past century must be credited to advances in nonengineering phases of agricultural technology such as better crop varieties, the more effective use of fertilizers and pesticides, and improved cultural practices. A major factor, however, has been the increased utilization of nonhuman energy and of more effective machines and implements.

Mechanization has been aided by, and in some cases made feasible only because of, the contributions of plant scientists and others in the biological sciences. Plant breeders have produced varieties better suited to mechanical harvesting. Examples are dwarf varieties of grain sorghum having uniform growth, stormproof cotton, hybrid corn varieties with less tendency to lodge, and tomatoes that all ripen over a short period of time and can withstand the rough treatment from a mechanical harvester. Cultural practices for some crops have been changed to modify growth habits and obtain plants better suited to mechanical harvesting.

1.2. Reasons for Mechanization. Reduction of labor requirements has been the principal motivating force in agricultural mechanization. Whereas in 1870 over half of the entire labor force in the United States was still on farms,[7] only one U.S. laborer out of 12 in 1960 and one out of 26 in 1976 was engaged in agriculture.[22] Mechanization is particularly advantageous when it can minimize a high peak labor demand that occurs over a relatively short period of time each year, as in harvesting certain fruits and vegetables.

Historically, advances in farm mechanization have been made where a strong demand for labor in other industries has withdrawn workers from the

1

land and forced wage rates up. Severe labor shortages and high wage rates during World War I and World War II, together with the simultaneous demands for increased agricultural production, have had a marked influence on the mechanization of certain operations in the United States. Before World War II, for example, the mechanization of sugar beet harvesting was held back by the reluctance of processors to accept the product obtained with mechanical harvesters. But the labor shortage resulting from the war forced the industry to modify its standards, improve processing equipment, and accept mechanically harvested beets in order to prevent a drastic reduction in crop area. Current labor problems are forcing mechanization of fruit and vegetable harvesting at an abnormally fast rate.

Mechanization encourages better management of farm enterprises and makes it possible by providing more free time for planning and study. The average size of farms in the United States doubled between 1945 and 1969, while the total crop area remained approximately the same.[22] The increased size and the higher level of mechanization, with resulting large capital investments, require increased emphasis on management.

Mechanization contributes to timeliness which, in turn, often increases profits. Many field operations must be performed within rather short periods of time if optimum results or maximum returns are to be obtained. With high-capacity mechanized units, operated 24 h per day if necessary during these critical periods, such operations can be completed in a minimum of time. Other contributions or objectives of farm mechanization are the improvement of working conditions and the performance of jobs that would otherwise be difficult or impossible by hand methods.

Overall cost reduction as a result of mechanization is highly desirable but not always imperative. In some situations farmers may prefer to mechanize, even though their net profits may be slightly reduced, to avoid problems inherent in procuring and managing large labor forces.

1.3. Mechanization in the Future. History indicates that the process of mechanization is dynamic, with no ultimate goal in sight. Under our system of competitive free enterprise, each manufacturer must continually improve his products and develop new ones in order to maintain a profitable position and grow or survive. Safety, comfort, and convenience for the operator will continue to receive a great deal of attention. As operators are isolated more and more from the functional portions of a machine, monitoring systems and automatic controls for complex machines become increasingly important. Automation of certain field operations, including automatic guidance systems, is already beyond the dream stage.

As larger and larger tractors are introduced, tillage tools must be designed for higher speeds or to efficiently utilize other than drawbar power so that traction is not a limiting factor. There is a great deal of room for developing more efficient tillage tools that will require less energy per hectare to produce the desired effect on the soil.

Although considerable progress has been made in mechanizing the harvest of fruits and vegetables, much remains to be done in this area. Mechanical harvesting of these crops is difficult because of the varied characteristics of the different plants and because most fruits and vegetables are delicate and perishable. Pruning of trees and vines in the conventional manner is difficult to mechanize because of the human judgment required in this operation. Changes in cultural practices to permit hedge-row pruning will facilitate mechanization. Tobacco, one of the ten most valuable crops in the United States, still requires a tremendous amount of hand labor.

The economic adaptation of certain types of machines to small farms is a problem that needs more attention before our agriculture can become completely mechanized. On many farms the area planted to a particular crop is too small to justify the ownership of expensive equipment such as hay balers, hay cubers, cotton pickers, tomato harvesters, and the like. Joint ownership and contract or custom operations are alternatives to individual farmer ownership, but they have their limitations and disadvantges from the farmer's standpoint.

Simplification of the more complex machines, which is in direct contrast to present development trends, is needed and is a real challenge to agricultural engineers.

1.4. Characteristics of Farm Machinery Engineering. Agricultural engineering is the application of engineering knowledge and techniques to agriculture. The successful agricultural engineer must recognize that there are basic differences between agriculture and other industries.

The biological factor is an important consideration in engineering applications because soils and plant materials usually are involved. The farm machinery engineer needs to be familiar with the basic principles and practices in agriculture. Cultural practices may need to be changed, or new crop varieties developed, to make mechanization of a particular operation feasible or to increase the effectiveness of a machine. Processing equipment and standards may need to be revised to accommodate mechanically harvested crops. The quality or yield of a crop is sometimes reduced by the use of a machine, the resulting monetary losses being chargeable against the machine.

The agricultural industry is basically decentralized or dispersed, with nearly 3 million operating units in the United States (2.8 million farms in 1976[22]), and is greatly affected by climatic conditions. Power must be taken to the work, rather than bringing work to a centralized power plant. Most field operations are seasonal in nature, often with only a short period of time available in which to perform the task. Consequently, field machinery in many cases has a low annual use (i.e., very few hours of operation per year).

It has been said that the field of farm machinery design presents a greater

challenge to an engineer's ability than any other field of engineering endeavor. Farm machines must perform satisfactorily over wide ranges in a
considerable number of variables. They may be operated where the temperature is well above 40°C or where it is below freezing, and are subjected
to rain, snow, and sleet. Instead of resting on a solid factory floor or moving
over a smooth road, they must operate over uneven terrain through dust,
sand, mud, and stones. They must be designed to handle wide variations in
crop and soil conditions. Operators often are relatively unskilled, partly
because of the limited usage of the machines.

In addition to the difficult environmental conditions, farm machines are
subjected to rather stringent economic limitations. Manufacturing costs
must be kept to an absolute minimum so that the limited amount of operation will not put the cost per hour into a prohibitive range. Therefore, farm
machinery designs must be as simple as possible, must utilize the lowest-cost
materials that are available and satisfactory for the job, and must permit the
widest manufacturing tolerances that are consistent with good performance.

1.5. Types of Problems Encountered. The student approaching the subject
of farm machinery engineering might well consider the types of problems
most frequently encountered in this field, together with the general methods
ordinarily employed in pursuing these problems. Although the variety of
problems that might be encountered is wide, most of them can be grouped
into the following general classification.

1. Development of a new type of machine.
2. Improvement of a machine, development of a new model similar to
   existing machines, or design changes to reduce the manufacturing cost
   of a machine.
3. Comparative testing of several machines or evaluation of the performance of a particular machine.
4. Investigation of the effects of a machine or a mechanized system upon
   crop production and/or economics.
5. Studies relating to the more efficient utilization of existing machines or
   their adaptability to special situations.
6. Research studies of fundamental problems not specifically related to a
   particular machine, such as the study of soil dynamics in relation to
   tillage and traction.

Commercial manufacturing organizations are, of course, concerned
primarily with the development and improvement of farm machinery, the ultimate goal being to obtain a product that is useful and acceptable to the
farmer and that can be manufactured and sold at a profit. To this end, the
farm machinery industry is doing an increasing amount of research, the
results of which can be applied to some particular class or group of
machines.

Public-service agencies such as state agricultural experiment stations and the United States Department of Agriculture (USDA) may undertake any of the types of problems listed above, but their major emphasis and responsibilities are in research activities (items 3-6). Research problems related to mechanization often require the cooperation of several branches of science and hence can be investigated most effectively by state or federal experiment stations. Cooperative research between public agencies and the farm equipment industry is common, often being partially supported by a manufacturer through grants, fellowships, or equipment loans.

The development or improvement of a machine, when undertaken by a public-service agency, often involves either a special problem of a localized nature (geographically) or one that is likely to require a great deal of development work and close coordination with research workers in other agricultural fields (such as plant breeders, botanists, entomologists, etc.). Emphasis in such a program is generally placed upon determining functional requirements, testing basic principles, and developing functional elements, with the final design of a production model being left to the manufacturer.

Whether the engineer is conducting research, developing a machine, or dealing with any of the other types of problems that may be encountered, he should adopt a positive approach and have faith and determination that the problem will be solved. The need for clear thinking and keen observation throughout the job cannot be overemphasized. Open-mindedness and tolerance are also important.

RESEARCH

Ellison[8] has defined research as "study that is planned to gain basic information not available in the form (in which) it is desired." Research results are fundamental and are comparable with results secured by the same methods at other times. Development work, testing, surveys, investigations, and experimentation may all be parts of a research program but do not in themselves constitute a complete research cycle.

1.6. Research Procedure. A research procedure is primarily an orderly process for analyzing, planning, and conducting an inquiry.[8] The first and probably the most important single consideration is the recognition of and selection of a problem needing solution. Otherwise the research may be meaningless. The second step is the accumulation of existing information related to the problem, together with a careful and objective analysis of these data and of the factors (variable or constant) involved in the problem. The variables must then be associated in such a way as to establish their functional interdependence. A good basic analysis should uncover every fundamental fact and relationship without prejudice or favor.

The formation of a hypothesis and the organization of experiments based upon this hypothesis is next in order. Often a considerable amount of time must be spent on experimental methods and instrumentation before a direct attack can be made on the main objective. If the preceding steps have been performed carefully and objectively, the execution of the selected procedure and subsequent analysis of the results should lead to the ultimate research objectives.

Adequate records (both written and photographic) of experimental conditions and results are important. The findings should be compared with and checked against those of similar research performed by other agencies, and the data should be analyzed and interpreted so as to give the maximum amount of useful information, particularly in regard to general principles. Prompt and effective publishing of the results constitutes an important part of the research procedure.

1.7. Designing an Experiment. When a research problem involves the soil or biological materials, there are always unknown or partially known, uncontrolled variables that may affect the results. This is also true to a lesser extent with manufactured materials or products. In such cases, experimental statistics should be employed in designing the experiment and in analyzing the results. The engineer should either enlist the aid of a statistician or refer to appropriate publications on experiment design and statistical analysis.[5] Proper statistical design will ensure maximum usefulness and reliability of the results, assuming the tests are conducted carefully and measurements made accurately.

Two essential characteristics of a good experiment design are the inclusion of several replications of each treatment or each material and randomization of the treatments. The number of replications needed depends upon the anticipated magnitude of the uncontrolled variations. At least 2 replications are necessary to be able to estimate the variability or experimental error, but at least 4 should be used in most cases. Increasing the number of replications decreases the experimental error associated with the observed difference between two treatments, thus reducing the amount of difference required for statistical significance.

Randomization is the process of determining in a purely random manner which plots or experimental units are to receive a given treatment. Randomization must be entirely objective, as by drawing numbered slips of paper representing the different treatments or by using tables of random numbers published in statistical references.[5] Randomization is necessary to minimize bias from uncontrolled variables so that one treatment is no more likely than another to be favored in any replicate, thus ensuring that the statistical estimate of error is valid.

Experiment designs based on statistics have been developed for the simultaneous study of 2 or more factors or variables, each at 2 or more levels, in one experiment. This design, known as a factorial experiment, gives the effects of each variable and also any interactions between variables.[13] An interaction may be defined as the failure of one variable to react the same throughout regions or levels of another variable. The number of plots required per replication is the product of the numbers of levels for all the variables.

DEVELOPMENT PROCEDURES

The word "development" implies the gradual advancement of a plan toward a specific goal and describes the overall process by which most farm machines evolve. Hard work, objective thinking and planning, and numerous disappointments are characteristic of a typical machinery development program.

Early farm machinery developments were often crude and haphazard, with the cut-and-try system predominating. Present-day farm machinery design, however, is rapidly becoming more scientific, with the development of a machine being based increasingly upon fundamental principles and information obtained by research methods.

Present-day development programs, whether in industry or in public-service agencies, tend to follow to a considerable extent the research pattern described in Section 1.6. Functional and physical tests of components and machines, both in the laboratory and in the field, are an indispensable part of any development program.

Throughout the history of agricultural mechanization, the farmer has played an important role in the development of equipment to meet his needs. The ideas for many of our present-day farm machines originated on the farm, and in many cases the first models were built by farmers or under their supervision. During early field tests of a new commercial model, the assistance and cooperation of farmers and operators are invaluable assets to the manufacturer, sometimes spelling the difference between success and failure for the machine.

1.8. Improvement of Existing Machines. Most machinery projects of manufacturers are evolutionary developments involving improvements of existing machines or new designs similar to existing machines. Some projects originate because of economic considerations, even though the existing device is entirely satisfactory from both the functional and mechanical standpoints. Problems involving the reduction of costs or the substitution of more readily available materials are examples.

A new design to replace an older model usually is put into production only if the manufacturer thinks it offers more value to the farmer in relation to its manufacturing cost and will maintain or increase sales. Greater value to the farmer might be evidenced in improved quality of work, more efficient use of power or human labor, greater durability, easier servicing and maintenance, etc. Specifications for new designs are based on features of successful competitive machines, surveys of customer satisfaction, service experience with existing machines, market analysis, projected trends in yields and cultural practices, and recent technological developments.[19]

In a typical situation, the sales, service, and product engineering groups develop and agree upon the specifications for the new design, including allowable cost and estimated sales. The product engineering group then designs and develops a new model that meets the specifications and incorporates other improvements. If the new design represents a major departure from existing models, the development procedure may be similar to that described below for a new type of machine.

1.9. Development of a New Type of Machine. Some new machines are revolutionary or unconventional developments that provide new and better methods of doing a job. One example is the small combine, which was introduced in the 1930s and quickly replaced the grain binder and stationary thresher.[19] More recent examples are the hay cuber, which provides an improved method of handling hay, and the tomato harvester, which drastically reduces labor requirements.

The first step in developing a new type of machine is recognition and evaluation of the problem. In public-service agencies, farm machinery development projects (as well as other types of problems) are frequently initiated at the request of some influential outside group or organization whose members will be directly benefited by the results, or at the suggestion of personnel within the research agency who recognize the importance of the problem. Cooperative projects between agricultural engineers and various agricultural science groups are common in experiment-station work. In any case, a proposed project should first be studied and evaluated in regard to the potential application of the results and its value to the farmer in terms of labor saving, increased crop returns, improved quality, increased income, etc.

Projects in commercial organizations to develop new types of machines may originate as a result of favorable market research or because the judgment of experienced engineers or top-level administrators indicates their desirability. Market research in itself may be misleading because it is difficult to get a reliable reaction from farmers as to the probable acceptability or potential applicaton of a proposed new type of machine with which they have had no experience. Hence, a considerable amount of experience and judgment is needed to arrive at an estimate for the sales potential. Other factors, such as the engineering and economic feasibility of the proposed machine, are also considered in evaluating the project and deciding whether to undertake it.

1.10. Determination of Functional Requirements and Fundamental Relations. In either industry or a public research agency, the next step in the development of a new machine is to establish a set of functional requirements or specifications. In other words, what must the machine do? Under what conditions is it expected to operate satisfactorily? The answer to the first question includes consideration of such factors as the optimum distribution and placing of seeds by a planter, the desired effect of a tillage implement upon the soil, or the required action and permissible tolerances of a harvesting machine in regard to recovery and quality of product. General experience or field investigations and surveys may be involved in answering the second question.

The assistance and recommendations of other technical groups (such as plant scientists, soil scientists, entomologists, and crop processors) are frequently needed in establishing the functional requirements. Oftentimes a compromise must be made between conflicting requirements or between ideal requirements and those attainable with a practical machine.

Closely following this second step, and often directly associated with it, is a critical review and evaluation of existing information (or machines) and past experiences related to the problem. Fundamental relationships that might be of value in solving the problem should be determined, either by field investigations or by laboratory research. What characteristics of the plant, for example, can be utilized to advantage in accomplishing the desired end result? What limitations are imposed by plant or soil characteristics?

1.11. Design and Development of Experimental Machine. At this point the engineer should accumulate ideas for several alternative solutions to the problem, using both imagination and logic and including ideas suggested by other people. All possibilities should be evaluated objectively and the most promising ones selected for further consideration.

The first experimental designs are primarily functional and generally deal with machine elements rather than a complete machine, the chief objective being to test and develop (or discard) certain ideas or principles of operation. Although durability and the refinement of mechanical details are not important in these early models, except to the extent necessary to permit adequate functional testing, the mechanical and economic practicability of the ideas should be given increasing consideration as the development progresses. The ultimate objective is, of course, to be able to perform the specified functions satisfactorily with as simple and efficient a unit as possible. Several complete experimental units may need to be built and tested before a satisfactory design is evolved.

The development program up to this point might be conducted by either a public-service agency or a manufacturing organization, but any further design and testing would always be done by a manufacturer.

1.12. Design of Production Prototype Model. If the results from the development of the experimental unit are favorable and indicate that the machine has economic possibilities, a mechanically sound unit, suitable for commercial production, is designed. Consideration is given to factors such as forces involved, power requirements, inertia of moving parts, mass, balance, durability, ease of servicing and adjusting, safety, comfort, compliance with industry standards, and costs. Close coordination is maintained between representatives of the engineering, production, and sales departments regarding materials, fabrication procedures, and other factors contributing to the most economical manufacture of a machine that will perform properly and give the required life with a minimum of repairs.

Analytical design procedures are being employed to an increasing extent, although many noncritical structural members are designed by proportion or by comparison with other similar applications, because of the saving of time and the difficulty in predicting the extreme loads likely to be encountered.

A good design from the sales standpoint takes into consideration customer appeal and anticipated consumer prejudices. Simplicity, ease of operation, comfort and safety for the operator, attractive styling, and a general appearance that suggests capacity and ruggedness are factors that contribute to customer and operator appeal.

1.13. Construction and Testing of Prototype Machines. If the machine represents a new development, it is customary to build a limited number of production prototype or pilot units. They may undergo tests and modifications for several years before the design is placed in production. The prototype machines are generally built by experimental-shop methods but follow the proposed production design rather closely. These machines are operated by farmers in various geographical areas, preferably under a wide range of conditions, and their performance is checked periodically by field engineers and design engineers. Laboratory tests are also conducted to determine points of excessive stress and any other indications of possible durability shortcomings. Accelerated fatigue tests may be needed for certain critical parts.

1.14. Manufacture of Production Model. The proposed production design is modified as required, based on the results of the field and laboratory tests of the prototype units and on suggestions of cost estimators, quality control people, manufacturing representatives, and others who have carefully reviewed the design. The final design is then released for production.

Depending upon the nature and extent of the design changes made in this step, the complexity and type of machine, and the expected degree of variability in operating conditions, the manufacturer may decide to make a limited preproduction run of perhaps 25 to 50 machines the first year. Then, if serious mechanical or functional problems develop, there are comparatively few machines to take back or rebuild. If the preproduction machines are a success, the design goes into full production the following year.

Although this might be considered as the final step in the evolution of a machine, engineering problems still continue to manifest themselves in such forms as desirable improvements, obtaining satisfactory life, the use of new and improved materials and fabrication methods to reduce costs, and expanded applications of the machine.

1.15. Use of Electronic Computers. Both analog and digital computers are being used increasingly in farm machinery design, research, and teaching. The use of computers to solve complex design problems gives the engineer more time for creative thinking and productive engineering. The high speed of computer operation makes it possible to obtain answers for a greater number of design variations than would be feasible with manual calculations, and to select the optimum combination of parameters. New, streamlined techniques of design and production may become feasible.[25] Theoretical analyses involving complex equations virtually unsolvable by manual means can be made with the aid of computers.

An analog computer deals in quantities representing the magnitude of the problem variables. It is particularly well-suited to problems involving the solution of differential equations. Programming involves setting up mathematical equations that describe the physical system to be simulated. The output is usually a graphic display showing the relation of two variables. Accuracy is comparable with that from a slide rule. The operator can observe the results as they are computed and can, if desirable, immediately make another run after adjusting some parameter.

Examples of farm machinery problems solved with an analog computer are (a) determination of trajectories of broadcast fertilizer particles, (b) kinematic and dynamic studies of a universal joint in the classroom,[27] and (c) analyzing and correcting a problem of instability under certain conditions with an existing tractor and semimounted plow.[27] The analog is an excellent classroom teaching tool, partly because the methods used to set up, program, and obtain a solution to the problem relate to both the mathematical description and the physical behavior of the system.[27]

A digital computer deals with pure numbers and simple arithmetic and has storage and logic capabilities. It can solve many types of engineering problems in a short time with great precision. Highly complex problems are better suited to the digital computer than to the analog, particularly if they are repetitive. Programming differential equations is more involved for a digital computer than for an analog computer because any nonarithmetical problem must be transformed, through numerical analysis methods, into simple arithmetic steps before it can be programmed for a digital computer. However, many digital computer systems have available subprograms to perform integration, thus relieving the user of the task of writing his own integration program.

Digital computers have gained more rapid acceptance than analog computers in the farm equipment industry, perhaps partly because of the use of digital computers in payroll preparation and inventory accounting as well as in engineering. Examples of problems on which digital computers have been used are (a) to establish empirical equations for soil-particle paths across existing plow moldboards and determine acceleration rates along the paths, as a basis for theoretical analysis and comparing plow-bottom performances,[4] (b) as an aid in designing suspension systems and frame structures for large field machines,[21] (c) to compute dimensions for various profiles of cams on a cotton-picker drum, so that a considerable number of profiles could be tested and compared,[3] (d) in designing gears, and (e) to perform tedious calculations involved in statistical analysis of test data.[3]

1.16. Standardization. Many ASAE standards, recommendations, and data documents, covering all fields of agricultural engineering, have been developed. Up-to-date versions of all these are included in each issue of Agricultural Engineers Yearbook, which is published annually by the American Society of Agricultural Engineers (ASAE) and automatically distributed to all members. As the need arises, existing documents are revised or new ones developed. The 1977 Yearbook includes 44 standards, 16 recommendations, and one data (Agricultural Machinery Management Data) that pertain to both implements and tractors or to implements alone.

Certain types of ASAE standards and recommendations are developed jointly with the Society of Automotive Engineers or the Farm and Industrial Equipment Institute. ASAE standards and recommendations are all of the "consensus" type and their use is entirely voluntary. However, the degree of conformance among U.S. farm equipment manufacturers is high. Some of the objectives and advantages of standardization relating to farm tractors and implements are:

1. To promote interchangeability between implements and tractors of different makes and models.
2. To promote safer operation of implements and tractors.
3. To reduce the variety of components required to service the industry.
4. To promote uniformity in the methods of specifying equipment capacities, sizes and ratings.

Standards related to farm equipment have been developed by organizations in many other countries. Some of these are quite similar to standards in the United States, but others impose considerably different requirements in various countries. These differences cause problems for U.S. manufacturers who sell equipment in foreign countries. Attention is being given to international standardization through the International Standards Organizaton (ISO),[24] although progress is slow. ISO is a nongovernment organization with consultative status to the United Nations. Membership is held by national standardization bodies of the member countries (American National Standards Institute, for the United States.)

The farm machinery designer needs to be familiar with any ASAE or foreign standards or recommendations pertinent to the project on which he is working. He should also be familiar with other applicable standards, such as those pertaining to materials or component parts.

TESTING FARM MACHINERY

1.17. Types and Planning of Tests. Farm machinery testing may involve determination of (a) functional performance characteristics, (b) power requirements for a machine or components, (c) stresses from static or dynamic loading, (d) durability, (e) wear rates, and (f) external forces acting upon a machine (such as soil forces on a tillage implement). Manufacturing organizations are concerned with all of these types. Tests conducted by public-service agencies such as state and federal experiment stations usually involve functional performance, power measurements, or determining the external forces acting on an implement.

The nature of functional tests varies widely, depending upon the type of machine or implement under consideration and upon the test objectives. Functional requirements and some of the test methods are discussed in subsequent chapters that deal with specific types of machines.

As with research, proper planning and careful execution of tests are of extreme importance. Whenever feasible, tests should be designed to permit statistical analysis of the results, as discussed in Section 1.7. This is important for accelerated durability tests in the laboratory as well as for functional field tests.

1.18. Use of Strain Gages and Brittle Lacquers. Electrical-resistance strain gages, used with appropriate electronic instruments, have many applications in farm machinery testing. The principal advantages are their small size (lengths as short as 3 mm), their direct attachment to the surface of the element being tested, and the ability to be used for dynamic strain measurements as well as for static measurements. High-frequency fluctuations in loads or stresses, such as cyclic torque variations in a rotary-power drive line, can be measured with appropriate, fast-responding instruments.

An important use of strain gages is for determining stresses in structural members. To ensure that maximum stresses are evaluated, proper location and orientation of the gages on the test member are important. A brittle, strain-sensitive lacquer can be applied to the part in the preliminary step to study stress patterns and determine the proper locations for strain gages. The brittle lacquer coating, when strained beyond a predetermined value, cracks at right angles to the direction of the principal tensile strain. Lacquers are available with various strain ratings. Since these lacquers are quite sensitive to humidity, they are best used in a controlled-atmosphere room.

After the locations and directions of the highest stresses have been established with the brittle lacquer, strain gages are applied and measurements made under load. If the yield point of the material in the test member has not been exceeded, the stress at the strain-gage location is determined by multiplying the measured strain by the modulus of elasticity of the material.

Strain gages are also employed as the sensing units in transducers such as torque meters for measuring rotary power, drawbar dynamometers, and pressure indicators. The principle of load determination with strain gages is to introduce the load into some member whose resulting deformation can be measured with one or more strain gages. Except for the simplest arrangements, calibration of a load-measuring device is usually required.

Strain gages are sometimes applied directly to a machine member to measure the total load on the member, as on the plunger pitman of a hay baler. Dynamic torque can readily be measured by applying strain gages directly to a section of shaft or tubing on the machine, provided the torsional stiffness is not too great and the collector that connects the rotating strain-gage circuit to the stationary instrument circuit is of a type that has stable contact resistance.

1.19. High-Speed Photography. High-speed motion-picture photography is a valuable aid in both farm machinery research and product development. The two principal types of applications are in studying the mechanical behavior of rapidly moving parts and in studying the behavior of crop materials passing through a machine at high speed. When film that has been exposed at 5000 frames per second is viewed at a normal projection speed of 16 frames per second, the resulting time magnification is about 300 to 1. Slower exposure speeds can be used if less time magnification is needed.

Because of the extremely short exposure times obtained in high-speed photography, special lamps must be used to obtain the extremely high level of illumination that is required. Timing may also be a problem. At a speed of 5000 frames per second, a full 30-m roll of film will pass through the camera in 1 to 1½ s and will be up to normal operating speed only during perhaps the last half of this period. If the event to be filmed occurs for only a short time (say ⅓ s) the operation of the camera must be accurately synchronized with the event.

1.20. Public Testing Agencies.[12] Public testing of farm machinery and/or tractors is being done by at least 25 agencies in more than 20 countries. The British National Institute of Agricultural Engineering (NIAE) has operated as a public farm machinery testing agency for many years. The oldest such agency in the world is the Agricultural Machinery Testing Institute at Uppsala, Sweden. These are probably the two best known farm machinery test agencies. Tests are voluntary in both countries — that is, there is no requirement for tests before equipment can be sold.

The NIAE tests are primarily functional, including power measurements. A fee is charged for all tests, and reports are published only at the option of the manufacturer. The manufacturer cannot advertise or otherwise indicate that the NIAE recommends or endorses any machine tested. The Swedish Institute carries out extensive field trials for both functional and durability evaluation. No fee is charged for testing production models, but a report is automatically published as soon as a machine is placed on the open market. For a fee, the Swedish Institute will undertake the confidential evaluation of a machine during its development stage, publishing the report only if the manufacturer so desires.

The evaluation technique used by most public testing agencies makes use of a standard or baseline reference machine selected on the basis of its popularity. Each machine tested is compared with the standard machine by conducting concurrent tests under identical conditions. Some agencies, however, make comparative evaluations by concurrently testing a group of machines of the same class. This procedure permits valid comparisons only within the group.

Tests by public agencies provide reliable data obtained on a controlled basis by impartial observers. This information is useful to both the consumer and the design engineer.

1.21. Test Programs in Industry. In any test program of a farm machinery manufacturer, the ultimate objectives are to provide information needed for design and to prove completed designs or discover weaknesses so they can be corrected. Although the final proof of a design must come from field tests and field experience, laboratory tests are assuming an increasingly important role in farm machinery development programs. When a laboratory test for either a complete machine or a component can be designed to essentially duplicate field loading and pertinent environmental conditions, a great deal of time can be saved and development costs are reduced.

Laboratory tests are conducted under controlled conditions that permit repetition of tests with reasonably good reproducibility of results. Laboratory tests provide quick comparisons between different designs, and the results are immediately available to all concerned persons. Accelerated durability tests can be conducted 24 h per day if necessary, and testing is not limited to certain seasons of the year as is the case with most field tests.

Field testing involves functional and physical testing of complete machines under varying and essentially uncontrolled conditions of crop, soil, weather, and terrain, but with the machines doing the work they were intended to do. In the early stages of development, tests of an experimental machine may be confined to a limited number of field conditions in order to reduce the number of variables. But as the development progresses, the scope of the tests is expanded to include a wide range of expected operating conditions. The main purposes of field testing by a manufacturing organization are:

1. To check the functional design of a machine or machine elements.
2. To establish normal and peak power requirements.

3. To obtain information on durability of the complete machine and machine elements.
4. To provide stress and load data for the various machine elements as a basis for future rational design and as a guide for accelerated laboratory tests.

Experimental stress analysis in the laboratory is a powerful tool that is being used increasingly in farm machinery design. In many cases, structural members are statically indeterminate or the loads are not known, so reliable calculation of stresses is impractical or impossible. By simulating maximum or exaggerated field loads and employing strain gages and brittle lacquers as discussed in Section 1.18, maximum stresses and locations of stress concentrations can be determined. Design modifications, if necessary, can then be made immediately without waiting for time-consuming and costly field experience to expose the problems. Overdesigned parts are also revealed, thus permitting a more economical design in some cases. Stress values determined under normal loading can be used to predict fatigue life by referring to the S-N fatigue curves* for the particular material involved.

The laboratory lends itself particularly well to comparative functional testing of machine components such as the threshing cylinder or the cleaning shoe on a combine or the cutterhead on a field chopper. High-speed photography is often employed in tests of this nature. Although the results may not be comparable with those from field tests, they can indicate trends and thus be of great value in developing components. By storing crop materials needed for a particular type of test, the test period can be extended beyond the field season.

Determination of the uniformity of seed distribution from a planter is an example of a functional test that can be performed more reliably in the laboratory than in the field. With some types of complete machines, preliminary functional tests in the laboratory prior to the field-testing season can save time in the development program.

1.22. Accelerated Durability Tests. One of the major objectives in laboratory testing by farm machinery manufacturers is to obtain information on durability of machines or components in as short a time as possible. To do this it is necessary to develop laboratory equipment and test procedures that will essentially duplicate field operating conditions in regard to the magnitude and distribution of loads and stresses and in some cases the frequency of stress peaks, and in regard to pertinent environmental conditions such as dust, water, etc.

One of the problems in laboratory durability testing is correlating the laboratory results with field experience. To be valid, laboratory tests must always be based on actual field conditions, as determined by field measure-

---

*An S-N curve for a material shows fatigue life, in number of stress cycles, as a function of the average stress.

ments. However, because of the extremely variable conditions encountered in many field operations, it is sometimes difficult to accurately establish representative load conditions. It is also almost impossible to duplicate all pertinent field conditions in the laboratory. The usual method of establishing a correlation is to compare laboratory results and field experience with an existing production model that is similar to the new model and has been in the field for several years.

Many farm machinery manufacturers have rigid-surfaced test tracks, usually of concrete, with built-in bumps having various shapes and spacings. These tracks are used in accelerated structural durability tests of complete machines. Different sections of a track may have bumps all the way across, bumps staggered for the right-hand and left-hand wheels of the machine being tested, or bumps only along one side of the track.

A test track provides a means of duplicating stresses produced in a machine as a result of its movement over the ground in normal field work. To establish the stresses to be developed in the track test, it is necessary to determine the normal and peak stresses developed in critical members during actual field operation, usually with strain gages. The only variables in track testing are the choice of existing bump pattern to use (if more than one pattern is available) and the forward speed. The speed is adjusted to produce a strain pattern that is essentially the same as that produced in field operation.

Accelerated results are obtained by using a higher frequency of loading than in field operation (more bumps per minute) and by continuous operation. Durability is established in terms of the total number of stress cycles. With a properly designed and properly used test track, it is possible to obtain dependable results in one month that would require 2 or 3 years of field testing[15] and might represent 8 to 10 years of normal field operation.

Many ingenious devices have been developed by test engineers for accelerated laboratory testing of the power-transmission systems on complete machines and of machine elements. In testing rotary-power drive components, stress peak magnitudes and frequencies are important and must be simulated in the test setup. Bearings, chains, and other drive components that operate in the open may need to be tested in a dust box, water bath, or other adverse environment. In many cases the only reduction in overall test time, as compared with field tests, comes from continuous operation. For wear, however, test acceleration factors up to 2 (i.e., 1 h of laboratory time = 2 h of field time) have been found satisfactory.[15]

HUMAN FACTORS IN DESIGN

1.23. Factors Involved in Man-Machine Relationships. Technological advances have greatly reduced man's physical burdens through the use of machines, but man's mental work has been increased. The person who operates modern farm equipment must make many decisions and perform many functions to use the machines properly. The demand for more decisions may result in mistakes that lead to serious accidents.

Research has shown that several environmental variables and machine characteristics can materially affect a person's performance when operating a machine. Among these are air temperature and humidity, air purity (freedom from dust and other pollutants), noise level, vibration, seat design, arrangement of work space, placement of controls and instruments, the shape and coding of controls, the amount of physical effort required for controls, and overall visibility of the machine components and functions that need to be watched. Some of these are discussed, in relation to tractor design, in the textbook, *Tractors and Their Power Units*.[1]

In addition to the above factors, there are other man-machine relationships that do not necessarily affect the operator's comfort or efficiency but are directly associated with safety. Some of these are discussed in Section 1.24.

Although human factors are of greatest concern in tractors and self-propelled implements, the farm machinery designer should consider man-machine relationships for every machine or implement with which he is involved. Design engineers need not necessarily become human factors experts, but they must be aware of human factors concepts to avoid creating hidden sources of man-machine conflicts. Some farm equipment manufacturers include a human factors engineer or a safety engineer on the development team for a machine and some others have separate groups.

Equipment designed with the proper application of human factors principles can result in increased efficiency and productivity, decreased operator effort, increased reliability, improved safety, improved flexibility, increased comfort, and better operator and consumer acceptance.[2]

Basically, the factors that are likely to affect the operator's efficiency and productivity are related to comfort, convenience, and visibility. The increasing use of enclosed cabs on grain combines and some other self-propelled machines, as well as on tractors, is one way of improving comfort. These cabs provide partial isolation from noise, have comfortable seats designed to reduce the effects of vibration and bumps, and are equipped with blowers that pressurize the cabs with filtered air. Heaters and/or air conditioners are usually available. Although cabs improve man-machine relations in regard to comfort, they introduce a new problem, particularly in grain combines, by isolating the operator from sensory indications of trouble.

In the usual farm situation, an operator is likely to use a number of different kinds and makes of tractors and self-propelled machines, often interchangeably. Both convenience and safety are improved if the motions, general locations, and identifications of operator controls are standardized.

Progress has been made toward this end by the adoption of ASAE standards that provide guidelines for the location and direction of motion of operator controls on tractors and self-propelled machines and establish a recommended system of universal symbols for identifying operator controls on agricultural and industrial equipment.

Power steering on self-propelled machines and powered controls for machine adjustments minimize the physical effort needed to operate a machine and thus reduce operator fatigue.

Visibility is an important consideration in designing a self-propelled machine such as a grain combine. The designer should determine what parts of the machine and surroundings the operator needs to see and the frequency and degree of visibility required in each situation. He should then design and locate the operator's station to best meet these needs, considering operator convenience and man's visual limitations. Instruments should be located so that those most frequently observed require the least amount of transfer of vision from the normal line of sight.

1.24. Product Safety. The development of increasingly complex machines and an increasing social awareness of accident prevention has made product safety a dominant consideration in the design of farm tractors and implements. Product safety represents a great challenge for farm equipment manufacturers. No other industry produces equipment to be used under conditions more difficult to control.[11] The farmer-operator is a free agent. He operates his equipment under a wide variety of conditions, where, when, and how he chooses. He may or may not use safeguards provided by industry, as he sees fit.

The designer is faced with the task of optimizing design and operator instructions to achieve the greatest possible assurance that the operator will voluntarily respond to the opportunities for safe practice. Safety warning signs are considered an integral part of the design and should highlight, mark, or otherwise identify all hazardous locations. The designer must avoid covering a machine so thoroughly with protective shields that accessibility for servicing and adjusting is sacrificed. Otherwise, the shielding is likely to be removed and not replaced.

Product safety is closely related to man-machine relationships and to man's physical, physiological, and psychological limitations. The more efficient and trouble-free a machine can be made, the safer it will be. The fewer times an operator has to leave his seat to correct some functional or mechanical problem, the less chance there is of injury.

Some of the most common safety problems with which farm machinery designers need to be concerned are:

1. Protection from moving parts, particularly power-transmission components.

2. Unshielded functional components. Some components, such as a mower sickle or the snapping rolls on a corn picker, are incompatible with shielding.
3. Protection against falls from elevated areas (provide rails).
4. Proper design of ladders and steps.
5. Minimizing exposure of the operator to agricultural chemicals while filling or using application equipment.
6. The relation of human reaction time to the design and effectiveness of emergency safety controls.
7. Warning systems for use when moving an implement on public roads. An ASAE standard for safety lighting has been adopted. An emblem to identify slow-moving vehicles has been developed and standardized, and is a legal requirement in many states.

With product design and testing as its base, product safety also involves accident analysis, alertness to the need for specific changes, development of industry standards, dealer and customer education, research, and field modifications when needed. Each manufacturer should continually strive for the highest possible degree of machinery safety consistent with the requirements of acceptable machine functions and increased cost. The engineer should keep abreast of new technological developments used in other industries and should apply them when appropriate.

Federal legislation on occupational safety and health, enacted in December, 1970, will have a continuing significant impact on product safety. Agricultural equipment manufacturers, as well as others, are expected to comply with Federally enforced standards and regulations promulgated under the legislation. Practical and economically sound safety standards can best be developed by the farm equipment industry in cooperation with the appropriate Federal agency. Agricultural engineers have made considerable progress in developing safety standards, with 11 ASAE standards and 2 ASAE recommendations pertaining to safety for farm implements and/or tractors included in the 1977 Agricultural Engineers Yearbook.

Even without legislative regulations, safety standards are an important part of an industry-wide product safety program. However, the engineer should recognize that standards are generally a compromise covering a broad range of variables and tending to oversimplify the problems. The designer should not forget the mission objectives in safety, and should regard standards as minimal requirements.

Product liability is a growing force in promoting product safety in all consumer industries. Lawyers and judges, through court decisions, are continually establishing the law regarding product liability. Court decisions have established that there is manufacturer's liability for negligent design or defective products that cause injury. A defective product is one that is not reasonably safe for the reasonably foreseeable uses.[17]

Some of the kinds of negligence that may result in a defective product and manufacturer's liability for personal injury are[17] (a) true drawing-board design errors, (b) failure to install adequate safety devices, (c) employment of safety devices that fail in use, (d) construction from unsafe or unsuitable materials, (e) failure to plan for unintended but reasonably foreseeable use or misuse, (f) failure to foresee improper maintenance, and (g) negligent failure to warn customers of hazards.

REFERENCES

1. BARGER, E. L., J. B. LILJEDAHL, W. M. CARLETON, and E. G. McKIBBEN. Tractors and Their Power Units, 2nd Edition, Chap. 12. John Wiley & Sons, New York, 1963.
2. BELLINGER, P. L. Man-machine compatability. Agr. Eng., 50:17-19, 21, Jan., 1969.
3. CADE, W. M. The new look in today's farm machinery test lab. Western Farm Equipment, 58(10):25-27, Oct., 1961.
4. CARLSON, E. C. Plows and computers. Agr. Eng., 42:292-295, 307, June, 1961.
5. COCHRAN, W. G., and G. M. COX. Experimental Designs, 2nd Edition. John Wiley & Sons, New York, 1957.
6. COOMBS, G. B. E. Experimental stress analysis as a tool in industry. Farm Mach. Design Eng., 4:20-21, 24-25, July, 1970.
7. COOPER, M. R., G. T. BARTON, and A. P. BRODELL. Progress of farm mechanization. USDA Misc. Publ. 630, 1947.
8. ELLISON, W. D. Research procedures. Agr. Eng., 22:249-252, July, 1941.
9. GOERING, C. E., L. N. SHUKLA, and B. D. WEATHERS. Is the analog computer obsolete? Agr. Eng., 50:142-143, Mar., 1969.
10. HEITSHU, D. C. Place of research in farm machinery design. Agr. Eng., 31:501-502, Oct., 1950.
11. JOHNSON, W. Product safety and the agricultural engineer. Agr. Eng., 48:553, 598-599, Oct., 1967.
12. KYLE, J. T. Farm machinery testing by public agencies. Agr. Eng., 44:432-433, 437, Aug., 1963.
13. LeCLERG, E. L. Statistics in agricultural engineering research. Agr. Eng., 39:88-91, Feb., 1958.
14. McKIBBEN, E. G. The evolution of farm implements and machines. Agr. Eng., 34:91-93, Feb., 1953.
15. MILLER, W. G. Correlation of design and testing. Agr. Eng., 36:23-25, Jan., 1955.
16. PFUNDSTEIN, K. L. Corporate product safety for farm and industrial equipment. Agr. Eng.,52:309-311, June, 1971.
17. PHILO, H. M. Legal liability of the agricultural engineer. Agr. Eng., 49:517-520, Sept., 1968.
18. PYLE, H. Setting ASAE goals for agricultural safety. Agr. Eng., 52:15-16, Jan., 1971.
19. RICHEY, C. B. A machine is produced. USDA Yearbook of Agriculture, 1960, pp. 51-60.
20. SILVER, E. A. How research and development aid machinery design. Agr. Eng., 36:806-807, 812, Dec., 1955.
21. SMITH, R. E. How computers cut design time. Agr. Eng., 47:648-651, Dec., 1966.
22. Statistical Abstract of the United States, 1977. U.S. Bur. Census, 1977.
23. TANQUARY, E. W. Standardization of farm equipment. Agr. Eng., 38:606-609, Aug., 1957.
24. TANQUARY, E. W. Standardization: world-wide. Agr. Eng., 44:486-487, 496, Sept., 1963.

25. VAN GERPEN, H. W. Using digital computers in farm equipment design. Agr. Eng., *49*:394-395, July, 1968.
26. WALKER, H. B. Balancing agricultural engineering research. Agr. Eng., *35*:479-481, 485, July, 1954.
27. YOERGER, R. R., and R. E. REINTS, Jr. Bridging the gap with a general-purpose analog. Trans. ASAE, *10*(6):808-812, 1967.
28. ZINK, C. L. Safety in farm equipment: the manufacturer's concern. Agr. Eng., *49*:74-75, Feb., 1968.

2

Implement Types,
Field Capacities, and Costs

2.1. Introduction. Although the first requirement of a machine is that it be able to perform its intended function satisfactorily, the management and economic aspects of the machine application are also of great importance. In fact, the engineer soon finds that his approach to a farm machinery design problem is largely controlled by economic considerations. To work most effectively, he should have a thorough understanding of the factors affecting field capacities and of the economic principles governing the costs of owning and operating field machines.

2.2. Types of Implements. In this chapter and throughout the entire text, reference is made to four general types of field implements, based upon their relation to the power unit. These are defined and discussed in the following paragraphs.

A *Pull-type* or trailed implement is one that is pulled and guided from a single hitch point and is never completely supported by the tractor.

A *mounted* implement is one that is attached to the tractor through a hitch linkage in such a manner that it is completely supported by the tractor when in the raised position. The linkage usually provides rotational stability about the longitudinal axis and it permits depth or height control by vertical support from the tractor, if desired, while the tool is in the operating position.

A *semimounted* implement is attached to the tractor through a horizontal or nearly horizontal hinge axis and is partially supported by the tractor, at least during transport, but is never completely supported by the tractor. In the usual situation the hinge axis is transverse at the rear of the tractor and the hitch provides rotational stability about the longitudinal axis. The implement may respond directly to tractor steering, but if a vertical hinge axis is superimposed on the horizontal axis (as on large, semimounted plows), the rear of the implement is guided by its own wheel or wheels.

A *self-propelled* machine is one in which the propelling power unit is an integral part of the implement.

2.3. Mounted and Semimounted Implements. Mounted or semimounted equipment is basically less expensive than equivalent pull-type equipment. The support wheels and accompanying frame structure required on pull-type implements are eliminated, and a single depth or height control system, which is part of the tractor, serves for all or most of the mounted and semimounted implements used with any one tractor. Maneuverability, visibility, ease of transport, and the advantages gained by draft sensing and vertical-load transfer through the control system make mounted implements popular. Standardization of the three-point hitch and quick-attaching couplers, to permit interchangeable use of different makes of equipment, has made attaching and detaching of mounted and semimounted implements a simple and easy operation.

The physical size and mass of equipment that can be mounted on the rear of a tractor and fully supported by it are limited by the carrying capacity of the tractor chassis and by transport stability limitations of the combination. Semimounting, in which the tractor carries only part of the mass, overcomes these limitations and still retains the advantages of maneuverability, lower investment cost, and the ability to utilize the tractor's draft-sensing system. Semimounting, in preference to full mounting, is particularly appropriate for moldboard plows having more than 4 or 5 bottoms, because their mass and great length would produce an excessive moment on the tractor, thus causing instability during transport.

2.4. Self-propelled Machines. Over 95% of the grain combines sold in 1969 and over 90% of all windrowers for either hay or grain were self-propelled units. Most cotton pickers are self-propelled and increasing percentages of several other types of harvesting equipment are self-propelled.

In comparison with pull-type units, self-propelled machines tend to provide more flexibility and better maneuverability, better visibility and control by the operator, and improved mobility. With field harvesting equipment, field opening losses are minimized because the cutting or gathering unit is across the front of the machine rather than projecting to one side. The principal disadvantage is the greater initial investment, which means that a self-propelled machine must have a relatively large annual use to be economically comparable with a pull-type machine.

One approach to the problem of reducing per-hectare costs of self-propelled machines for small areas and increasing their versatility is to provide a self-propelled carrier consisting of a skeleton frame or chassis equipped with a power unit and controls, upon which various types of harvesting units or other equipment can be mounted. The interchangeable machine bodies might include a combine, corn picker, field chopper, hay baler, cotton picker, and perhaps others. Considerable engineering ingenuity is required to provide a carrier that will accommodate such a variety of machines and properly satisfy their basic requirements. There has been some interest in this type of machine since the late 1940s, and at least one self-propelled carrier with several interchangeable machine bodies is commercially available.[19]

FACTORS AFFECTING FIELD CAPACITY

2.5. Terms Related to Field Performance of Machines. The rate at which a machine can cover a field while performing its intended function is one of the considerations in determining the cost per unit area for the operation.

The *theoretical field capacity* of an implement is the rate of field coverage that would be obtained if the machine were performing its function 100% of the time at the rated forward speed and always covered 100% of its rated width.

The *theoretical time per hectare* is the time that would be required at the theoretical field capacity.

Effective operating time is the time during which the machine is actually performing its intended function. The effective operating time per hectare is greater than the theoretical time per hectare if less than the full rated width is utilized.

The *effective field capacity* is the actual average rate of coverage by the machine, based upon the total field time as defined in Section 2.6. Effective field capacity is usually expressed as hectares per hour [acres per hour].

Field efficiency is the ratio of effective field capacity to theoretical field capacity, expressed as percent. It includes the effects of time lost in the field and of failure to utilize the full width of the machine.

Performance efficiency is a measure of the functional effectiveness of a machine, as for example, the percent recovery of usable product by a harvesting machine.

2.6. Effective Field Capacity. The effective field capacity of a machine is a function of the rated width of the machine, the percentage of rated width actually utilized, the speed of travel, and the amount of field time lost during the operation. With implements such as harrows, field cultivators, mowers, and combines, it would be practically impossible to utilize the full width of the machine without occasional skips. The required amount of overlap is largely a function of speed, ground condition, and the skill of the operator. In some cases the yield of a crop may be so great that a harvesting machine cannot handle the full width of cut, even at the minimum forward speed obtainable.

The rated width of implements with spaced functional units, such as row-crop planters or cultivators, grain drills, and field cultivators, is the product of the number of units (rows, grain-drill furrow openers, or cultivator standards, for example) times the spacing of the units. In other words, the rated width is assumed to include one-half space beyond each outside unit. Row-crop machines utilize 100% of their rated width, whereas open-field implements with spaced functional units are subject to losses from overlapping.

The maximum permissible forward speed is related to such factors as the nature of the operation, the condition of the field, and the amount of power available. With harvesting equipment, the limiting factor may be the maximum rate at which the machine can effectively handle the crop. Typical operating speeds are included in Appendix B.

Lost time is the most difficult variable to evaluate in relation to field capacity. Field time may be lost as a result of adjusting or lubricating the machine, breakdowns, clogging, turning at the ends, adding seed or fertilizer, unloading harvested products, waiting for crop transport equipment, etc. In relation to effective field capacity and field efficiency, as defined and discussed in this chapter, lost time does not include time for setting up or daily servicing of the equipment or time lost due to major breakdowns. It does include time for minor repairs in the field and for any lubrication required in addition to the daily servicing, as well as the other items mentioned above. The total field time is considered to be the sum of the effective operating time plus the lost time.

Time spent in traveling to and from the field is usually included in figuring the overall cost of an operation, but is not considered in determining effective field capacity or field efficiency because the machine should not be penalized for the geographical location of the enterprise.

The effective field capacity of a machine may be expressed as follows:

$$C = \frac{SW}{10} \times \frac{E_f}{100} \qquad (2.1)$$

$$[\, C = \frac{5280\ S \times W}{43,560} \times \frac{E_f}{100} = \frac{SW}{8.25} \times \frac{E_f}{100} \,]$$

where C = effective field capacity, in hectares per hour [acres per hour]
$\quad\ \ S$ = speed of travel, in kilometres per hour [miles per hour]
$\quad\ W$ = rated width of implement, in metres [feet]
$\quad\ E_f$ = field efficiency, in percent

Renoll[18] suggests predicting effective field capacities on the basis of total minutes per hectare, which is the sum of the theoretical time per hectare plus the time per hectare required for turns plus the time per hectare required for "support functions." He classifies all items of lost time other than turning as support functions; these are evaluated or estimated individually and then totaled.

2.7. Time Losses in Turning. Turns at the ends or corners of a field represent a loss of time that is often of considerable importance, especially for short fields. Regardless of whether a field is worked back and forth, laid out in lands, or worked by traveling around the perimeter, the total number of turns per unit of area with a given width of implement is inversely proportional to the length of the field. For a given rectangular field, worked either in the long direction or around the field, the required total number of round trips (exclusive of opening or finishing lands as in plowing) would be the same for any of the three methods. Working back and forth requires two 180° turns per round, whereas either of the other methods involves four 90° turns per round trip.

The time required for turns in back-and-forth operations, as in row crops, is also influenced by irregular field shapes, the amount of turning space in the headlands, the roughness of the turning area, and the implement width. Renoll,[16] in an 8-year study with 1-row, 2-row, and 4-row equipment (102-cm [40-in.] row spacing), found that turning times were typically 12 to 18 s per turn when the turning areas were smooth, but were 10 to 30% greater when the areas were rough. The time per turn was increased as much as 50% if the turning areas were so narrow that the tractor had to be backed during each turn.

The time per turn on smooth headlands averaged about 5% greater with a 4-row planter or cultivator than with a 2-row unit.[16] The difference was 20 to 25% on rough headlands. In tests involving wider implements, Barnes and his associates[3] found that times per turn averaged 40 to 50% greater for 6-row cultivators and planters than for 4-row units.

Renoll[15,17] suggests employing a factor that he terms "field machine index" to indicate how well a particular field is adapted to row-crop operations. He defines this index as the percentage ratio of (effective operating time) ÷ (effective operating time + turning time). Comparative index values for different fields are determined by actual time studies with the same machine. His tests indicate that the field machine index for a particular field tends to be about constant for various row-crop operations.

Idle travel across the ends of a field represents another loss that is often unavoidable and is particularly important where wide lands are laid out in short fields. If w is the total width of each land (i.e, width of each area worked out as a unit), the average theoretical distance across each end is ½ w. Then, if the length of the field is L, the average total travel per round is $2L + w$ and the percentage of idle travel distance is

$$I = \frac{w}{2L + w} \times 100$$

Dividing numerator and denominator by w gives

$$I = \frac{100}{(2L/w) + 1} \tag{2.2}$$

In actual practice the maximum travel across the end of a land would be a little greater than w, and the minimum travel as the land is narrowed down would be limited by the turning radius of the machine or tractor. Thus, in computing I, a value of w somewhat greater than the width of the land should be assumed.

2.8. Time Losses That Are Proportional to Area. Some time losses, such as those from rest stops and adjusting or checking the equipment, usually tend to be proportional to the effective operating time (or to total field time) as the operating speed or implement width is increased. Idle travel across the ends tends to be proportional to effective operating time if the normal operating speed is maintained across the ends.

Other time losses, such as those caused by field obstructions, clogging, adding fertilizer or seed, and filling spray tanks, often tend to be more nearly proportional to area than to operating time. The time per hectare for back-and-forth turns in row-crop operations tends to remain about constant (or decrease only slightly) as the operating speed is increased, because the speed is usually reduced for turning unless normal operating speeds are low. Time losses due to the unloading of harvested crops tend to be proportional to the yield as well as the area.

Time losses that tend to be proportional to area become increasingly important as the width or speed of an implement is increased, because they then account for a greater percentage of the decreased total time per hectare. Thus, changing from a 4-row planter to a 6-row planter at the same forward speed may increase the output by only 30% instead of 50%.

The relative importance of interruptions proportional to area may be determined from the following equation, which is based on the definition of field efficiency.

$$E_f = 100 \; \frac{T_o}{T_e + T_h + T_a} \qquad (2.3)$$

where T_o = theoretical time per hectare [per acre]
$\quad T_e$ = effective operating time = $T_o \times 100/K$
$\quad K$ = percentage of implement width actually utilized
$\quad T_h$ = time lost per hectare [per acre] due to interruptions that are not proportional to area. At least part of T_h usually tends to be proportional to T_e.
$\quad T_a$ = time lost per hectare [per acre] due to interruptions that tend to be proportional to area

In actual practice, the relations between many types of time losses and effective operating time or area fall somewhere in between the extremes represented by T_h and T_a. As indicated in Section 2.7, the time per turn for row-crop planting or cultivating increases somewhat as the implement width is increased, so that turning time for the wider unit is a higher percentage of the total time but usually a smaller amount per hectare. Filling seed hoppers, when only a small amount of seed per hectare is needed, may require less time per hectare for a wide planter than for a narrower one because the time required to dismount from the tractor, walk to the hoppers, and return would be about the same for both sizes and would be a significant percentage of the total time lost in adding seed.

2.9. Time Losses Related to Machine Reliability. The probability of equipment breakdowns, with resultant loss of field time, is inversely related to machine reliability. Success reliability may be defined as the statistical probability that a device will function satisfactorily under specified conditions during a given period of time. For example, if a device has a 1000-h success reliability of 90%, an average of 10% of the devices will fail within 1000 h and 90% will have a life exceeding 1000 h. Another way to express success reliability is as the mean time interval between failures.

The reliability of a combination of components or machines is the product of the individual reliability factors. The expected percent reliability for a combination of n items is

$$y = 100 \frac{(x_1)(x_2)(x_3)....(x_n)}{100^n} \tag{2.4}$$

where x_1, x_2, x_3, ... x_n, are the expected reliabilities of the individual devices, in percent. It should be noted that reliabilities indicated by equation 2.4 are only the statistically expected values. The reliabilities of individual units of any specific type vary widely from the expected values. The expected reliability and the variability factor may be determined statistically from observations of a group of individual units.[14]

A complex machine such as a combine has a far greater chance of failure than a simple machine, even though the success reliability of all its individual components may be high. For example, a machine with only 10 parts, each having a success reliability of 97% for a given time period, would have an overall reliability of only 74%. Although design is the main factor in success reliability, manufacturing procedures and the manner in which the equipment is maintained and used are also important.[11] Optimum design is a compromise that balances the cost of obtaining high reliability against the benefits of minimizing the failure frequency.

A survey of over 1500 farmers in Indiana and Illinois[11] indicated that success reliability was not greatly influenced by age of either complex or simple machines. In this survey, reliability was based upon random, unpredictable breakdowns and did not include the effects of normal wear. On the average, there was a 60 to 80% probability of having one or more breakdowns per year, starting with the first year of a machine's life. For those machines having breakdowns, the average loss of field time per year usually was more than 8 h for combines, 3 to 6 h for corn pickers, 1 to 4 h for plows, and less than 2 h for row-crop cultivators and planters. The major time losses typical of breakdowns with complex harvesting equipment may represent serious economic losses because of timeliness.

The time-use reliability of individual machines becomes increasingly important when several machines or machine units are used in combination. For an individual implement, a 5 or 10% time loss from breakdowns, adjustments, clogging, or other stops related to the machine is generally not considered serious. But if 4 such units, each with a time-use reliability of 90%, are used in series, the expected overall time-use reliability of the combination is reduced to 66%. Time-use reliability, as discussed in this section, is based on the effective operating time and the time lost from stops required for the individual machines in the combination. Time losses due to turning, rest stops, filling seed or fertilizer hoppers, and the like would be about the same regardless of the number of machines, but must be included in determining the field efficiency of the combination.

Because of the reduced reliability with a combination of machines, preventive maintenance becomes relatively more important than when only a single machine is used. All machines in a combination should be able to operate the same length of time between servicings, and the capacities of various units should be reasonably well matched.

2.10. Determining Time Losses and Field Efficiencies. Times studies have been made by a number of investigators to determine field efficiencies and provide information for operations analysis. Detailed time studies involve continuous observation and timing of each activity involved in the field operation, for one or more full-day periods. If $K = 100\%$, the field efficiency is the percentage of the total field time during which the machine was actually performing its function, and may be determined directly from the time data.

An example of a detailed time study for a one-row cotton picker[17] is presented below. The observed times have been reduced to a per-hectare basis.

Activity	Minutes per hectare
Turn at row ends	6.4
Dump basket	11.4
Clean machine	5.7
Idle travel	2.7
Travel to and from wagon	8.9
Pack basket	5.2
Other down time	1.7
Actual picking	89.0
Total time per hectare	131.0

From these results, the field efficiency is

$$E_f = 100 \times 89.0 / 131.0 = 68\%$$

If only the field efficiency is desired from a field study, this can be obtained by observing the total field time for one or more days, the average speed while the implement is actually performing its function, the total area covered, and the rated width of the machine. The actual average rate of coverage can then be related to the theoretical field capacity to determine the field efficiency (equation 2.1).

The results of field studies by various investigators have been analyzed and summarized,[8] yielding typical field-efficiency values, as follows:

Most tillage operations (plowing, disking, cultivating, etc.)	75-90%
Drilling or fertilizing row crops or grain	60-80%
Drilling *and* fertilizing row crops or grain*	45-65%
Combine harvesting	65-80%
Picking corn	55-70%
Picking cotton (spindle-type picker)	60-75%
Mowing hay	75-85%
Raking hay	75-90%
Windrowing hay or grain with self-propelled windrower in field with irrigation levees	65-80%
Windrowing hay or grain with self-propelled windrower in field with no levees	75-85%
Baling hay (bales discharged onto ground)	65-80%
Baling hay (with bale wagon trailed behind)	55-70%
Field chopping	50-75%
Spraying*	55-65%

2.11. Improving Field Efficiencies. As field machines become more complex and expensive, it is increasingly important to obtain maximum output from them. Minimizing lost time in the field is one way to improve the field capacity. Engineers can contribute to high field efficiencies by designing machines that have maximum reliability and minimum service requirements.

Time studies often indicate potential areas of improvement in machinery management. An excessive amount of turning time may suggest the need for improving the condition or width of the headlands or changing the turning pattern. Excessive down time may mean that a better system of preventive maintenance is needed.

The development of more efficient equipment and systems for handling materials in the field offers considerable potential for increasing field efficiencies.[2,17] Seed, fertilizer, herbicides, insecticides, and other materials must be transported to the field and loaded onto field machines. Harvested

---

*Based on reference 5 and other sources.

products must be discharged and hauled to storage areas. In planting-fertilizing operations, handling bagged materials in the field can easily occupy 25% of the total field time. Bulk handling of dry fertilizers, or the use of liquid fertilizers and transfer pumps, could substantially reduce the materials handling time and thus increase the field efficiency.[2] Renoll[18] found that changing the method of handling water for the pre-emergence chemical in a particular planting operation increased the planter capacity from 1.4 ha/h to 1.6 ha/h.

COST OF USE

2.12. Cost Factors. The total cost of performing a field operation includes charges for the implement, the tractor power utilized, and labor. Implement and tractor costs are divided into two categories — fixed costs and variable or operating costs. Fixed costs are related to machine ownership and occur regardless of whether or not the machine is used. Fixed costs *per hour* are inversely proportional to the amount of annual use. Operating costs are directly related to the amount of use and include repairs and maintenance, fuel and lubricants, and servicing. Depreciation is a fixed cost if the machine life is determined by obsolescence or if the machine is arbitrarily fully depreciated before it wears out (as for tax purposes). But, if based on the operating time required for the machine to wear out, depreciation becomes a variable cost.

As mentioned in Chapter 1, farm machinery is characterized by low annual use. Surveys have indicated that, considering the United States as a whole, the average annual use of most field machines (excluding tractors, trucks, and wagons) seldom exceeds 15 full days. Machines such as combines, balers and other hay harvesting equipment, and perhaps corn pickers, may be used as much as 20 to 40 days per year. Because of the limited annual use, fixed costs often represent a large part of the total machine costs, particularly for the more expensive types of equipment.

2.13. Depreciation. Depreciation is the reduction in value of a machine with the passage of time. In the usual situation, with field machines being operated only a few days per year, obsolescence is the most important factor affecting depreciation. A machine may become obsolete because of the development of improved models, changes in farm practices, etc. Where a machine has a relatively high annual use, as on many of the larger farms in the western states and with custom operations, wear becomes the predominant factor in determining the useful life.

Among the various systems employed in calculating depreciation are the straight-line, declining-balance, estimated-value, and sum-of-the-years-digits methods. These are described and compared in references 5 and 12.

If the average cost of machine use during the machine's entire useful life is desired, the straight-line method is the most practical and the most common. It is the simplest method and gives a constant annual charge for depreciation throughout the life of the machine. In the straight-line method, the amount of annual depreciation is equal to the new cost minus the trade-in or salvage value at the end of the assumed life, divided by the estimated life in years. It is common practice to assume a trade-in or salvage value equal to 10% of the new cost, although some investigators assume zero salvage value.

The declining-balance, estimated-value, and sum-of-the-years-digits methods give rapid depreciation during the early years and slower depreciation as the machine becomes older. These methods are more suitable than the straight-line method for determining the market value of a partially depreciated machine and for tax valuation. For income tax purposes, depreciation is often based on a much shorter life than would be justified on the basis of obsolescence or wear.

With the declining-balance method, the depreciation for any year is a constant percentage of the remaining value at the beginning of the year. The estimated-value method is based on determinations of actual market values for machines of different ages, established through farm sales and auctions and by farm equipment dealers and published as recognized "guides" and "blue books."

Data from these price handbooks can be analyzed to determine the relation between age and remaining farm value expressed as a percentage of the new list price. This has been done in references 1 and 5, combining all tractors into one group and all types of implements into 1 or 3 groups.

Estimated-value relations developed in this manner give realistic depreciation values for *average* machines under the conditions represented by the analysis. They do not cover situations where high annual use results in faster-than-average depreciation. In the absence of more specific information, they should be used when year-by-year machine costs are desired as a basis for deciding when to replace a machine.

2.14. Machine Life. A value for the useful life of a machine is needed to estimate depreciation by any method except the one based on estimated market values. Estimates of either obsolescence life or wear-out life are rather arbitrary. Usually there is no definite time at which a machine suddenly becomes unrepairable. Rather, there is a gradual increase in repair costs until eventually it becomes uneconomical to continue making repairs. Likewise, obsolescence is usually a relative matter based on comparison of features of a new model with those of an existing, old machine.

Suggested values for obsolescence life and wear-out life for various types of implements are included in Table 2.1. If the annual use exceeds the value given in the third column, the machine is likely to wear out (from an economic standpoint) before it becomes obsolete. In calculating depreciation, use either the obsolescence life or the wear-out life, whichever is the smaller. For example, a combine used 250 h per year would wear out in 8 years, but if used only 150 h per year it would become obsolete (in 10 years) before it wore out.

Note that for most implements the hours per year for wear-out life to equal obsolescence life represents more than 15 normal days of use. This

Table 2.1. LIFE AND REPAIR COSTS OF MACHINES

Machine	Years Until Obsolete	Wear-out Life, Hours	Hours per Year for Wear-out Life to Equal Obsolescence Life*	Repair Costs, Percent of New Cost	
				Average per Hour	Total During Wear-out Life
Tractors					
Wheel-type	10	10 000	1 000	0.010	100
Track-type	15	15 000	1 000	0.007	105
Tillage implements					
Cultivator	12	2 500	208	0.048	120
Disk harrow	15	2 500	167	0.048	120
Disk plow	15	2 500	167	0.048	120
Moldboard plow	15	2 500	167	0.080	200
Spike-tooth harrow	15	2 500	167	0.040	100
Spring-tooth harrow	15	2 000	133	0.060	120
Seeders					
Grain drill	15	1 200	80	0.075	90
Row-crop planter	15	1 200	80	0.075	90
Harvesting equipment					
Bale wagon, automatic	10	2 000	200	0.040	80
Combine, self-propelled	10	2 000	200	0.025	50
Corn picker	10	2 000	200	0.038†	75
Cotton picker	10	2 000	200	0.035†	70
Cotton stripper	10	2 000	200	0.030†	60
Field chopper, pull-type	10	2 000	200	0.040	80
Hay baler, aux. eng.	10	2 000	200	0.030	60
Hay baler, PTO	10	2 000	200	0.040	80
Mower	10	2 000	200	0.150	300
Rake, side delivery	10	2 500	250	0.060	150
Sugar beet harvester	10	2 500	250	0.030	75
Windrower, self-propelled	10	2 500	250	0.040	100
Miscellaneous					
Fertilizer equipment	8	1 200	150	0.100	120
Forage blower	12	2 000	167	0.030	60
Wagon (rubber tired)	15	5 000	333	0.018	90

*When average annual use exceeds this number of hours, machine will wear out before it becomes obsolete.

†If machine is mounted type, add total of 1% of new cost for each time machine is mounted *and* dismounted (normally once a year).

means that the *average* farm machine in the United States probably is discarded before it is worn out. However, many machines with low annual use remain in service for a longer period than indicated by the obsolescence-life values.

2.15. Interest on Investment. Interest on the investment in a farm machine is a legitimate cost, since money spent in buying a machine cannot be used for other productive enterprises. The rate of interest should reflect prevailing rates.

Strictly speaking, the annual charge for interest should decrease over the life of the implement as the value decreases. If a variable depreciation rate is used, the interest charge for each year should be based on the remaining value of the implement at the beginning of the year. If straight-line depreciation is assumed, then a constant annual interest charge is desired so the total fixed costs each year will be the same. In this case, the interest charge is based on the average investment during the life of the machine. With straight-line depreciation, the average investment is equal to one-half the sum of the new cost and the trade-in or salvage value.

2.16. Taxes, Insurance, and Shelter. These are minor items in the total fixed costs, but should be included. Property taxes are assessed on the remaining (depreciated) value of farm machinery at the same rate as on other farm property. There are wide variations among states in regard to property taxes. Many states have sales taxes. Although the sales tax is all paid at the time of purchase, the charge for it may be distributed over the life of the machine.[9,12]

Farm machinery is sometimes insured against loss, although the owner frequently elects to carry the risk himself. In either case, a charge against the implement is justified. Insurance costs are based on the remaining value of the equipment.

Although it is difficult to demonstrate conclusively that protection from the weather results in monetary savings, shelter is considered desirable for many types of farm machinery. The charge for housing is related to the physical size of the machine and usually ranges from 0.5 to 1% of the new cost of the machine. This charge should remain constant over the life of the machine.

Note that some of these minor items are related to the remaining value of the machine each year, whereas others are based on the new cost. To simplify their inclusion, a total annual charge equal to 2% of the new cost is suggested if straight-line depreciation is assumed, and 4% of the remaining value at the beginning of each year if a variable-depreciation system is used.

2.17. Repairs and Maintenance. Repair costs are difficult to estimate because of wide variations resulting from differences in operating conditions, management, maintenance programs, local costs, etc. Repair-cost records of individual farmers vary in their accuracy, form, and completeness. Cost surveys must include a large number of farms in order to provide reasonably reliable average values. These average results are not directly applicable to any specific situation, but do provide a basis for general cost estimating.

Repair costs include maintenance (adjusting for wear, daily service and lubrication, etc.) as well as the cost of all parts and the labor to install the parts. Repair costs per hour of use increase with age but tend to level off as a machine becomes older.[11] The amount of change in repair rate (cost per hour) with age is influenced by the type of machine. Tillage implements and other machines that require frequent sharpening or replacing of cutting elements have relatively high initial repair rates and relatively small increases in repair rates as they become older.

Data obtained in a 1966 survey of over 1500 farmers in Indiana and Illinois[6] provided information on repair costs versus age for tractors and 10 kinds of implements. By assuming a definite useful life for each kind of machine, it was possible to establish approximate mathematical relations between total accumulated repair costs and percent of assumed life.[6] Similar relations, but with somewhat different constants, are included in reference 1. These equations indicate a more rapid increase in repair rate during the early years than during later years. If the Indiana-Illinois data are plotted as repair rate versus age in years, the repair rate eventually becomes about constant.[11] Relations that reflect the increase of repair rate with age should be utilized when estimates of year-by-year machine costs are needed.

When *average* costs during the useful machine life are acceptable, it is simpler to apply a uniform annual charge for repairs. This is done in conjunction with straight-line depreciation. Table 2.1 includes average repair costs per hour during the indicated wear-out lives, as well as the total life repair costs. The cost of daily servicing is included. These values are based on references 1, 4, 5, 7, and 8. For some machines there was considerable variation among the references in regard to suggested repair-cost factors.

2.18. Fuel, Lubricants, and Miscellaneous Supplies. With tractors and other powered equipment, the cost of fuel and lubricants (including engine oil and filters) must be included in the total machine charge. Power requirements can be estimated by referring to the table of draft and power requirements in Appendix A. For a given draft D, in kilonewtons [pounds force], and a given speed S, in kilometres per hour [miles per hour], the required drawbar power for mounted, semimounted, or pull-type implements, in kilowatts [horsepower], is

$$\text{dbp} = \frac{DS}{3.6} \tag{2.5}$$

$$[\ \text{dbp} = \frac{D \times 5280\ S}{60 \times 33{,}000} = \frac{DS}{375}\ ]$$

The draft for most pull-type, nontillage implements is in the form of rol. ing resistance. The pull required to overcome rolling resistance is determined by multiplying each wheel's load normal to the soil surface (in force units) by the appropriate coefficient of rolling resistance obtained from Appendix C, and adding the resistances for all wheels.

Table 2.2. TRACTOR FUEL CONVERSION[12]

Loading, Percent of Maximum PTO Power	PTO Kilowatt-hours per Litre			PTO Horsepower-hours per Gallon		
	Diesel	Gasoline	LP Gas	Diesel	Gasoline	LP Gas
100	2.60	1.92	1.59	13.2	9.7	8.1
80	2.53	1.78	1.52	12.9	9.0	7.7
60	2.36	1.57	1.40	12.0	8.0	7.1
40	2.02	1.23	1.16	10.3	6.3	5.9
20	1.37	0.79	0.75	7.0	4.0	3.8

Averages from 103 Nebraska Tractor Tests after 1965, with fuel consumptions increased by 15% to represent typical fuel usage for tractors on farms. Values apply specifically to operation at full governed speed, but probably are reasonably accurate for part-throttle settings.

Fuel requirements for tractors can be estimated from Table 2.2, provided the maximum PTO (power take-off) power rating of the tractor and the actual PTO power requirement are known. The drawbar power output is always less than the PTO output because of drive-wheel slippage, tractor rolling resistance, and friction losses in the drive train between the engine and the wheels. The sum of these losses may be represented by a tractive-and-transmission (T & T) coefficient, which is defined as the ratio of drawbar power to PTO power. References 1 and 12 include a nomograph from which drawbar power and percent wheel slip can be determined for two-wheel-drive tractors in relation to PTO or axle power,* static force on drive wheels, travel speed, soil condition, and implement type (mounted, semimounted or pull-type). Table 2.3 shows typical values of T & T coefficients determined from the nomograph for a semimounted implement.

Coefficients for four-wheel-drive tractors would be somewhat higher than those for two-wheel-drive tractors. Track-type tractors seldom have more than 5% slip, even on soft soils. Tractive-and-transmission coefficients for them probably would be at least 0.8 to 0.85 on firm soil and 0.7 to 0.75 on soft soils.

---

*Axle power is considered to be approximately 96% of PTO power.

Table 2.3. TRACTIVE-AND-TRANSMISSION COEFFICIENTS
FOR TWO-WHEEL-DRIVE TRACTORS

Loading, Percent of Max. Avail. PTO Power	Tractive-and-Transmission Coefficient*					
	Firm Soil		Tilled Soil		Soft or Sandy Soil	
	6.5 km/h [4 mph]	8 km/h [5 mph]	6.5 km/h [4 mph]	8 km/h [5 mph]	6.5 km/h [4 mph]	8 km/h [5 mph]
80	0.73	0.75	0.60*	0.61	**	**
70	0.75	0.75	0.61	0.61	**	**
60	0.75	0.74	0.61	0.59	**	0.51
50	0.74	0.72	0.60	0.56	0.51†	0.50
40	0.72	0.68	0.55	0.49	0.50	0.45

*Determined from Fig. 1 in reference 1, for a semimounted implement and a rear-axle static force of 0.625 kN per PTO kilowatt [105 lbf/hp]. Average values from Nebraska Tractor Tests in 1973-1976 (with ballast and operator) were 0.66 kN per PTO kW for all tractors with maximum PTO outputs between 37 and 86 kW [50 and 115 hp] and 0.59 kN per PTO kW for all tractors with maximum PTO outputs betwen 86 and 136 kW [115 and 182 hp].

**Excessive wheel slip (over 18%).

†Wheel slip = 16 to 18%. Values for other conditions in the table were from 4% to 15%.

The PTO power corresponding to the required drawbar power is determined by applying the appropriate T & T coefficient. If part or all of the power to the implement is supplied directly through the PTO, this is added to the PTO power needed for the drawbar pull. In determining the size rating (maximum PTO power) needed for a particular job, or the maximum size or speed of an implement for a given tractor, the normal loading should not exceed 80% of the maximum available power.

As an example, assume a disk harrow with a draft of 18 N [4050 lbf] is to be pulled at 6.5 km/h [4 mph] in a firm, untilled field, by a diesel tractor having a maximum PTO power rating of 60 kW [80.5 hp]. The problem is to determine the average fuel consumption rate. From equation 2.5, the required drawbar power is

$$dbp = \frac{18 \times 6.5}{3.6} = 32.5 \text{ kW } [43.6 \text{ hp}]$$

Referring to the second column in Table 2.3, the T & T coefficient on a firm soil ranges from 0.73 to 0.75 for 80% to 40% loading. Use a value of 0.74 for this problem. Then the PTO power needed to develop 32.5 kW at the drawbar is 32.5/0.74 = 43.9 kW [58.9 hp]. Since the maximum available PTO power is given as 60 kW, the actual load is 100 × 43.9/60 = 73% of the maximum power. Interpolation between 60% and 80% in the diesel column in

Table 2.2 gives a fuel conversion factor of 2.47 kW·h/L. Fuel consumption, then, is 43.9/2.47 = 17.8 L/h [4.70 gal/h].

Table 2.2 can also be employed in estimating fuel requirements for self-propelled machines or for engines on pull-type implements if the power requirements are known or can be estimated. For tractors and for implements having engines, the total cost of lubricants (including engine oil and filters) can be taken as 15% of the cost of the fuel used.[5,8]

Twine or wire for hay balers is an example of miscellaneous supplies that should be included in cost calculations. Average requirements per megagram [per ton] are given in Section 15.7.

2.19. Total Cost of Performing a Field Operation. The total cost is generally desired on either a per-unit-area or production-unit basis. Determination of the total cost per unit of work involves the following factors.

1. Annual use of implement, in hours or hectares.
2. Effective field capacity of implement, in hectares per hour.
3. Total annual fixed costs for implement.
4. Total operating costs per hour (repairs, fuel and lubricants) for implement.
5. Cost per hour or per hectare for tractor power required by implements that are not self-propelled.
6. Labor cost per hour.

In some harvesting operations, field losses and/or quality reduction resulting from the use of a machine must also be considered, since the grower's potential income is thereby reduced. This charge against the operation is particularly important when comparing two or more harvesting methods.

For quick reference, total annual fixed costs are indicated in the table below for six straight-line depreciation rates. The interest rate is taken as 9% of the average investment and the total for taxes, insurance, and shelter is 2% of the new cost.

Assumed life, years	Assumed salvage value, percent of new cost	Total annual fixed costs, percent of new cost
10	0	16.5
12	0	14.8
15	0	13.2
10	10	16.0
12	10	14.5
15	10	13.0

Determination of tractor power costs involves the same factors that have been discussed for implements. The hourly cost is based on the total annual operating time for the tractor rather than the annual use with the particular implement involved. In the absence of specific data for the tractor, a fair approximation, based on 1976 costs, is to assume 12¢/h per maximum available PTO kilowatt* [9¢/h per PTO hp] for 2-wheel-drive diesel tractors.

Labor charges should be based upon prevailing wage rates. The labor cost per hectare is inversely proportional to the field capacity of the machine. The use of a larger implement for a given total area per year decreases the labor cost per hectare but increases the implement fixed costs per hectare.

2.20. Examples of Cost Determination. For the first example, consider a 4.9-m [16-ft] self-propelled combine with a 70-kW [94-hp] diesel engine, operating at 5 km/h [3.1 mph] and used to harvest 200 ha [494 acres] of grain per year. Assume the average required engine power is 60% of the maximum available. Other pertinent factors are: New cost = $29 000, interest rate = 9%, diesel fuel cost = 10.5¢/L [40¢/gal], operator's wage = $3.50/h. Determine the total harvesting cost per hectare [per acre].

Section 2.10 indicates field efficiencies from 65 to 80% for combines. Assume a value of 70%. Then, from equation 2.1, the effective field capacity is

$$C = \frac{5 \times 4.9}{10} \times \frac{70}{100} = 1.72 \text{ ha/h } [4.25 \text{ acres/h}]$$

The total operating time per year, then, is 200/1.72 = 116 h. Reference to the third column in Table 2.1 indicates that for 116 h of annual use, depreciation should be based on the obsolescence life, which is shown as 10 years. Assume a 10% trade-in value. Table 2.1 indicates that average repair costs per hour = 0.025% of the new cost.

From Table 2.2, the diesel-fuel conversion factor at 60% loading is 2.36 kW·h/L. The actual average power requirement is 70 × 0.60 = 42 kW [56.3 hp]. Therefore, fuel consumption is 42/2.36 = 17.8L/h [4.70 gal/h].

Calculations for the various charges and the total cost per hectare [per acre] are as follows:

Annual Fixed Charges

Depreciation	$\dfrac{29\,000 - 2900}{10} =$	$2610.00
Interest	$0.09\left(\dfrac{29\,000 + 2900}{2}\right) =$	1435.50

---

*Advertised tractor ratings usually are maximum PTO power unless stated otherwise.

Taxes, insurance, shelter (Section 2.16)	$0.02 \times 29\ 000$ =		580.00
Total fixed costs per year			$4625.50

Cost per Hour

Fixed costs	$\dfrac{4625.50}{116}$ =		$ 39.88
Repairs	$\dfrac{0.025}{100} \times 29\ 000$ =		7.25
Fuel @ 10.5¢/L	0.105×17.8 =		1.87
Lubricants (15% of fuel cost)	0.15×1.87 =		0.28
Labor	=		3.50
Total cost per hour			$ 52.78

Total Cost per Unit Area

Per hectare	$52.78/1.72$ =		$ 30.69
Per acre	$52.78/4.25$ =		$ 12.42

In this example, total fixed costs could have been calculated by applying the factor shown in Section 2.19 for a 10-year life with 10% trade-in value.

As a second example, consider a 5-bottom 46-cm [18-in.] semimounted moldboard plow, pulled at 6.5 km/h [4 mph] with a wheel tractor loaded to 75% of its maximum available power. The average draft of the plow is 25 kN [5600 lbf]. The new cost is $4400 and the annual use is 125 h. Assume 10% salvage value. As in the first example, the interest rate is 9% and the operator's wage is $3.50/h. Again, the total cost per hectare [per acre] is desired.

Table 2.1 indicates that depreciation for the plow should be based on the obsolescence life, which is 15 years. From Section 2.19, the total annual fixed costs are 13.0% of the new cost. Table 2.1 indicates an average hourly repair cost of 0.08% of the new cost.

The width of cut is $5 \times 46/100 = 2.30$ m. Assume a field efficiency of 85% (Section 2.10). Then, from equation 2.1, the effective field capacity is

$$C = \frac{6.5 \times 2.30}{3.6} \times \frac{85}{100} = 1.27 \text{ ha/h [3.14 acres/h]}$$

The actual drawbar power requirement for 25 kN draft at 6.5 km/h is

$$\text{dbp} = \frac{25 \times 6.5}{3.6} = 45.1 \text{ kW [60.5 hp]}$$

Since plowing usually would be done in a firm field, a T & T coefficient of 0.74 for 75% loading is appropriate (Table 2.3). Since the tractor is to be loaded to 75% of its maximum power, the size required for an actual drawbar power of 45.1 kW would be

$$\frac{45.1}{0.74 \times 0.75} = 81.2 \text{ maximum available PTO kW [109 hp]}$$

Assume a power cost of 12¢/h per available PTO kilowatt, as suggested in Section 2.19.

The details of the various charges are as follows:

Annual Fixed Costs for Plow

Total (13.0% of new cost)	0.13×4400	= $572.00

Cost per Hour

Fixed costs for plow	$\dfrac{572.00}{125}$	= $ 4.58
Repair costs for plow	$\dfrac{0.08}{100} \times 4400 =$	3.52
Tractor power	$0.12 \times 81.2 =$	9.74
Labor	$\doteq$	3.50
Total cost per hour		$ 21.34

Total Cost per Unit Area

Per hectare	$21.34/1.27$	= $ 16.80
Per acre	$21.34/3.14$	= $ 6.80

2.21. Effect of Annual Use Upon Costs. Figure 2.1 shows the relation of total cost per hectare to the total hours of annual use for the machines and conditions of the two preceding examples. For the self-propelled combine, the initial investment is high and fixed costs represent a large part of the total cost, even for an annual use of 150 h. The total cost per hectare becomes prohibitive as the annual use is reduced to 50 h (which represents 86 ha per year in this case).

The moldboard plow is an example of an implement for which power and labor costs are relatively high in relation to fixed costs. But even so, the total cost per hectare increases considerably as the annual use is reduced below about 100 h.

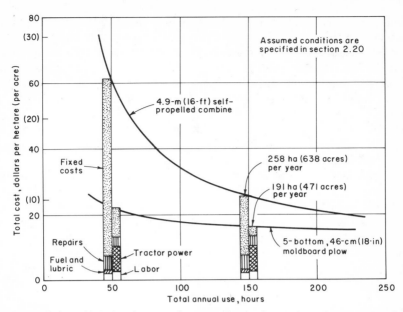

Fig. 2.1. Relation of calculated cost per hectare to hours of annual use, for two types of field machines.

2.22. Determining the Optimum Size of an Implement. Selecting the optimum width or size of an implement for a particular enterprise minimizes the total cost per hectare for performing the operation. For a given area to be covered with a specific type of implement, the use of a unit that is too small will result in high costs per hectare, primarily because of the excessive amount of labor required. If the implement is too large, total costs per hectare will be high because of the greater fixed costs.

By making a series of cost calculations for various implement widths, a least-cost width between these two extremes can be determined. Hunt[12,13] developed an equation that expresses the total annual cost for the implement, power, and labor in terms of all the contributing factors, including total area and implement width. He assumed that total area, field efficiency, implement fixed-cost percentage per year, and the tractor fixed-cost amount per hour all remain constant, independent of the implement width, and that the implement new cost and implement and tractor operating costs per hour are directly proportional to the width. By differentiation he obtained a second equation from which the magnitude of the least-cost width can be calculated for any given area.

An example of the application of Hunt's equations is shown by the lower curve in Fig. 2.2. The rapid increase in cost as the width is decreased below the least-cost value is due primarily to the increased amount of labor required per hectare because of the lower field capacity. The increase in costs to the right of the least-cost width occurs primarily because implement fixed costs increase more rapidly than the sum of labor costs and tractor fixed costs per hectare decreases. Note that there is less economic penalty from choosing an implement that is too large than from choosing one that is too small. The right-hand portion of the curve would be even flatter for tillage tools.

Expensive machines have a more sharply defined least-cost width than shown in Fig. 2.2 for grain drills, and the cost increases much more rapidly as the width is increased beyond the least-cost value. Thus, choosing the correct size is more important for high-cost machines than for low-cost ones.

Timeliness in performing a field operation has an economic value if crop yield and/or quality are reduced because of the length of time required to perform the operation. With many crops there is a gradual reduction in yield or quality as planting or harvesting is delayed beyond the optimum calendar time or period. In other cases there is the probability of adverse weather causing the complete loss of the unharvested portion of a crop.

Hunt[12,13] and Bowers[5] have established timeliness factors for several operations and crops for which applicable results of agronomic field experiments are available. These timeliness factors indicate the rates at which potential crop values decrease with time of performing certain operations. There are some differences between the values recommended by these two men, perhaps reflecting differences in environmental and growth conditions.

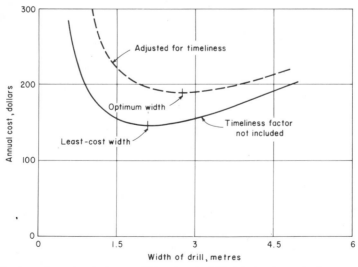

Fig. 2.2. Annual cost in relation to widths of grain drills for planting 32 ha/year. (D. Hunt.[12])

By adding a timeliness term to his least-cost-width equation, Hunt arrived at an optimum-width equation that charges timeliness losses against the implement. When timeliness is a factor, the effect is to increase the optimum implement width as indicated by the upper curve in Fig. 2.2.

2.23. Justification for Machine Ownership. It is evident from Fig. 2.1 that expensive machines such as a self-propelled combine are not economically practical for individual ownership on small farms. As pointed out in Chapter 1, this is one of the serious problems of mechanization. Custom operations and joint ownership by several farmers are two methods of increasing the annual use and thus reducing unit costs. But with either arrangement the individual farmer sacrifices timeliness and independence in scheduling his operations.

In some cases, particularly on small farms, the choice may lie between hand labor and a more expensive mechanical method. If the cost difference is not too great, the machine operation may be preferred because of the elimination of problems associated with obtaining and managing hand laborers. Convenience, mobility, and other similar factors are difficult to evaluate but have a definite bearing on economic considerations.

2.24. Managing Farm Machinery. As the size of farms continues to grow and machinery investments increase, efficient management of machines becomes more and more important to the success of an enterprise. Management includes determining the costs for performing a particular operation, selecting the best size and type of equipment for each application, matching machinery components in a complete system, establishing an effective maintenance program, determining the optimum age for replacing a particular machine, scheduling farm operations for the best use of the machine, and consideration of other factors.

Computer analysis is becoming increasingly important in making certain types of machinery-management decisions and is employed in some large farming enterprises. An ASAE conference devoted entirely to "Computers and Farm Machinery Management" was held in December, 1968.[7]

Detailed coverage of all aspects of farm machinery management is beyond the scope of this text. The reader who is interested in pursuing this subject further should consult books by Bowers[5] and Hunt[12] and other appropriate references listed at the end of this chapter.

REFERENCES

1. Agricultural machinery management data. Agricultural Engineers Yearbook, 1976, pp. 322-329. ASAE, St. Joseph, Mich.
2. BARNES, K. K. Materials handling in the field. Implement & Tractor, *74*(21):50, 73, Oct. 17, 1959.
3. BARNES, K. K., T. W. CASSELMAN, and D. A. LINK. Field efficiencies of 4-row and 6-row equipment. Agr. Eng., *40*:148-150, Mar., 1959.

4. BARNES, K. K., and P. E. STRICKLER. Management of machines. USDA Yearbook of Agriculture, 1960, pp. 346-354.

5. BOWERS, W. Fundamentals of Machine Operation — Machinery Management. Deere & Company, Moline, Ill., 1975.

6. BOWERS, W., and D. R. HUNT. Application of mathematical formulas to repair cost data. Trans. ASAE, *13*(6):806-809, 1970.

7. Computers and Farm Machinery Management, Conf. Proc., 1968. ASAE, St. Joseph, Mich.

8. Costs and use, farm machinery. Agricultural Engineers Yearbook, 1963, pp. 227-233. ASAE, St. Joseph, Mich.

9. FAIRBANKS, G. E., G. H. LARSON, and D. S. CHUNG. Cost of using farm machinery. Trans. ASAE, *14*(1):98-101, 1971.

10. HUNT, D. A FORTRAN program for selecting farm equipment. Agr. Eng., *48*:332-335, June, 1967.

11. HUNT, D. Equipment reliability: Indiana and Illinois data. Trans. ASAE, *14*(4):742-746, 1971. (See also Implement & Tractor, Apr. 7, 14, May 7, 1971.)

12. HUNT, D. Farm Power and Machinery Management, 6th Edition. The Iowa State College Press, Ames, Iowa, 1973.

13. HUNT, D. R. Efficient machinery selection. Agr. Eng., *44*:78-79, 88, Feb., 1963.

14. McKIBBEN, E. G., and P. L. DRESSEL. Over-all performance of series combinations of machines as affected by the reliability of individual units. Agr. Eng., *24*:121-122, Apr., 1943.

15. RENOLL, E. Field machine index use and application. Trans. ASAE, *18*(3):493-496, 1975.

16. RENOLL, E. S. Row-crop machinery capacity as influenced by field conditions. Auburn Univ. Agr. Expt. Sta. Bull. 395, Auburn, Ala., 1969.

17. RENOLL, E. S. Some effects of management on capacity and efficiency of farm machines. Auburn Univ. Agr. Expt. Sta. Circ. 177, Auburn, Ala., 1970.

18. RENOLL, E. S. A concept for predicting capacity of row-crop machines. Trans. ASAE, *15*(6):1028-1030, 1972.

19. Uni-System, the New Idea. Farm Machine Des. Eng., *1*:25-27, Dec., 1967.

PROBLEMS

2.1. A farmer using a 4-bottom 41-cm moldboard plow at 6.5 km/h covers 8 hectares in 9.5 h. The draft is 15 kN. Calculate:

(a) Field efficiency.

(b) Drawbar power.

2.2. In harvesting grain with a 5-m combine, the time required for emptying the grain tank averaged 8.5 min/ha. Turning, adjusting, and other miscellaneous interruptions amounted to 12% of the effective operating time. The average width of cut was 0.3 m less than the rated width and the forward speed was 4 km/h.

(a) Calculate the field efficiency.

(b) Calculate the effective field capacity.

(c) What would the field efficiency be if the grain tank were unloaded on-the-go, with no time lost during unloading?

2.3. Plot curves of field efficiency versus row length, for lengths from 0.2 to 1.5 km, when planting corn with a 4-row planter at 5 km/h or 8 km/h. Row spacing = 100 cm and the average turning time at each end is 15 s for either down-the-row speed (assuming the operator throttles down from 8 km/h to turn). The time required for filling seed hoppers and other miscellaneous interruptions is 5.4 min/ha plus 7% of the effective operating time.

2.4. A field chopper discharging into a trailed wagon averages 27 Mg/h at a field efficiency of 65% when there is no waiting for wagons. The average load per wagon is 4.5 Mg and it takes 1.5 min to change wagons. If the operator must occasionally wait for an empty wagon and the delay averages 1.8 min per load, by how much is his average output (megagrams per hour) reduced? What is the field efficiency?

2.5. A 4-m grain drill is pulled at 7 km/h with a wheel-type tractor having 35 PTO kW. The new cost of the drill is $3000 and the labor cost is $3.50/h. Calculate the following, indicating the basis or reference for any assumptions made.

(a) The total cost per hectare for drilling 40 ha/year.

(b) The cost per hectare if the annual use is 100 ha.

(c) The number of hours required to plant 100 ha.

2.6. A farmer has a choice of buying a 4-bottom 41-cm moldboard plow for $3000 or a 5-bottom 45-cm plow for $4200. Assume that the cost per hectare for tractor energy would be the same in either case. With either plow, operating speed = 6.5 km/h and field efficiency = 82%.

(a) If the labor cost is $3.50/h, what is the minimum number of hectares plowed per year that would justify the purchase of the larger plow (i.e., the break-even point)?

(b) How many hours per year would each plow be used at the break-even area?

(c) How would increased labor costs affect the size of the break-even area?

2.7. A PTO-driven, twine-tying baler is pulled with a tractor having a maximum PTO rating of 35 kW. The average baling rate (including lost time) is 6.5 Mg/h. New costs are $4500 for the baler and $9500 for the tractor. Assume a 10% trade-in value for each machine and an interest rate of 9%. Annual use for the tractor is 800 h. Fuel consumption (gasoline) is 10.5 L/h, fuel cost = 12¢/L, baler twine cost = 85¢/kg, and the operator's wage = $3.50/h. Calculate the total baling cost per megagram for

(a) 500 Mg/year.

(b) 1800 Mg/year.

2.8. A gasoline tractor with a maximum PTO rating of 35 kW is pulling a PTO-driven baler at 7 km/h in a reasonably smooth alfalfa field. The PTO power requirement for the baler is 12 kW. The baler mass is 2.1 Mg and the average OD of the tires is 0.75 m. Estimate the rate of fuel consumption.

3

Mechanical Power Transmission and Power-Take-Off Drives

3.1. Introduction. This chapter is intended to acquaint the student with some of the characteristics of the mechanical rotary power transmission elements most common on agricultural machines. Emphasis is placed upon the differences between agricultural applications and industrial drive systems, with only a minimum of space devoted to subjects that are adequately treated in machine design textbooks, engineering handbooks, or other similar references. As the student studies various types of machines during the course, he should observe and evaluate specific applications of the various drive systems and their components.

BEARINGS AND SEALS

3.2. Applications. Bearings and seals are needed on axles of ground-driven rotating components as well as in power-transmission systems. Both types of applications are included in the following discussion. Bearings on agricultural implements are often required to operate under extremely dusty or dirty conditions. Development of suitable bearings, seals, and lubricants for these conditions has been a real challenge, but great progress has been made in recent years.

Sealed, factory-lubricated ball bearings are now employed extensively on most types of harvesting equipment and in many other applications, the added initial cost being justified by reduced repair costs and less daily servicing time. Although the trend is to install these bearings with no provision for relubrication, some do have fittings to permit occasional replenishment of the lubricant. Regreasing at intervals of several years is said to have some merit in maximum-service applications where excessive heat tends to break down the grease.[11] But there are also likely to be problems from such things as the use of an incorrect type of grease, contamination of the grease from dirt on the fitting or in the gun, and collection of dust and dirt around the seal lips because of excess grease purging through the seals.[9]

Self-alignment of bearings on open shafts is an important feature in many agricultural applications, to compensate for manufacturing tolerances and variable deflection of supporting members. Self-aligning mountings may range from a plain cast-iron sleeve body fitted loosely in a hole in a plate to a

48

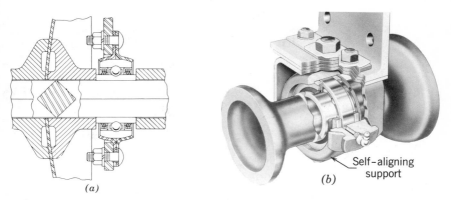

(a)   *(b)* Self-aligning support

Fig. 3.1. Specially designed disk-harrow bearings with triple-lip seals, in self-aligning mountings. (*a*) Spherical OD on outer race, with flange mounting; seals integral with bearing. (Courtesy of New Departure Div., General Motors Corp.) (*b*) Trunnion mounting for self-alignment; seals separate from bearing but with lips riding on bearing inner ring. (Courtesy of Deere & Co.)

spherical-OD ball bearing held in stamped flanges as shown in Fig. 3.1*a*. Another method of providing self-alignment for axle bearings is by means of a trunnion support for the bearing housing, as shown in Fig. 3.1*b*.

   3.3. Plain Bearings. Proper design calls for adequate contact area, dirt exclusion, and effective lubrication. Plain bearings can take thrust loads only if they are made with circumferential ribs or end flanges. Plain bearings on open shafts are usually unsealed. Lubrication by grease gun serves to flush out dirt and maintain a grease seal at the bearing ends, as well as to lubricate. Plain bearings with little reservoir space may require lubrication daily or even twice a day to prevent excessive friction and wear. Such bearings are, for the most part, being eliminated from new designs. In some cases, centralized lubricating systems are installed. These have tubes leading to the individual bearings from a hand pump on a grease reservoir.

   Common bearing materials are bronze, oil-impregnated sintered metal, oil-soaked wood (usually maple), hardened steel, white cast iron, and plastics. Wood is no longer used extensively, but one application for which it is well-suited is on combine straw-walker cranks, where split bearings are needed for practical assembly. Hardened steel bearings and hardened steel shafts are used to some extent on heay-duty tillage implements.[11] Plastic bearings have good corrosion resistance and may not need lubrication, but they require fairly large molding tolerances and are subject to cold flow under heavy loads.[11]

   White iron bearings are relatively inexpensive and are still used to some extent on the smaller tandem disk harrows and in certain other low-speed applications, in preference to antifriction bearings. Chilled or white cast iron is made by rapid cooling after pouring special, low-silicon cast irons. The resulting material is very hard and brittle and has excellent resistance to abrasive wear such as that caused by dirt getting into bearings.

3.4. Antifriction (Rolling-Contact) Bearings. Antifriction bearings are available for almost any type of application. Ball bearings may be fitted into machined housings or they may be installed as self-aligning pillow-block or flange-mounted units. Idler sprockets and sheaves with integral, sealed ball bearings are employed extensively on farm machines. Although most ball bearings are designed primarily for radial loading, they can take a moderate amount of thrust. Some ball bearings are designed specifically for thrust loads or combination loads.

In some cases, special bearing designs have been developed specifically for farm machinery applications. Two notable examples are disk-harrow bearings (Fig. 3.1) and tine-bar bearings for hay rakes (Fig. 3.2). Disk bearings are subjected to fairly heavy radial and thrust loads at low speeds and operate in contact with dirt most of the time. Self-aligning mountings and effective seals are imperative. Disk bearings are available with either square or round holes. (Some disk gang bolts are square.)

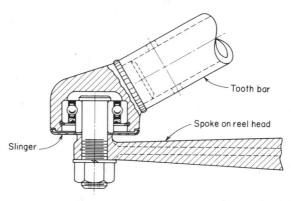

Fig. 3.2. Specially designed tine-bar bearing on the reel of a side-delivery hay rake. (Courtesy of New Departure Div., General Motors Corp.)

Plain roller bearings have a high radial load capacity but no end-thrust capacity. They are most suitable for low-speed applications such as on the axle of a grain drill. They are more sensitive than ball bearings in regard to misalignment, dirt, and grit. A needle bearing is a form of roller bearing employing a maximum number of small-diameter rollers without a cage or spacers. Because of their comparatively small radial dimensions and their exceptionally high load capacity, particularly at low peripheral speeds, needle bearings are well-suited to applications involving oscillating motion. They may be installed without a race, with only an outer race, or with both

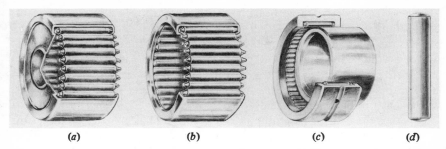

Fig. 3.3. Common types of needle bearings. (a) and (b) Bearings with outer races only, (c) bearing with inner and outer races, (d) spherical-end roller used in transmissions, etc. (Courtesy of The Torrington Co.)

inner and outer races (Fig. 3.3). When the shaft (or the housing) is to serve as a race, it should be hardened and precision-ground to close tolerances. As with other types of straight roller bearings, needle bearings are very sensitive to dirt and misalignment.

Tapered roller bearings are designed to take both radial and thrust loads, the relative capacities depending upon the amount of taper. These bearings are used in pairs, in housings that maintain accurate alignment, as illustrated in Fig. 7.3. Axial adjustment is usually provided for the inner race. In addition to being adjustable, tapered roller bearings are more tolerant of dirt than are other types of antifriction bearings. They have many applications in farm machinery design.

3.5. Load Capacities of Antifriction Bearings. Manufacturers publish tables that give the load ratings for different bearings at various speeds, based upon a specified average life. These data can be adjusted to give ratings for other life expectancies by means of factors included in the catalogs. In general, the life of an antifriction bearing, in terms of stress cycles, appears to vary about as the inverse cube of the load. Since these bearings fail primarily because of fatigue, the life in hours is inversely proportional to the rotational speed. In many slow-speed and heavy-duty farm-machinery applications, the size of the bearing is determined by the size of shaft needed to carry the load rather than by capacity limitations of the bearing.

3.6. Seals. Antifriction bearings require effective seals, but the close fits and absence of wear result in a greater potential for good seal performance than with plain bearings. Sealing is usually effected by a sharp-cornered lip held against the rotating shaft or a rotating surface on the bearing by its own elasticity or by spring pressure (garter spring). Synthetic rubber compounds and leather are the most common seal materials. Compatibility of seal compounds and lubricants is an important consideration.[16] Some lubricant formulations may cause premature failure of synthetic rubber seals.

Sealed, factory-lubricated bearings have the seals as an integral part of the bearing assembly, as in Fig. 3.1*a* and 3.2. The arrangement shown in Fig. 3.1*b* has the seals as separate units but the lips run on the smooth, concentric surface on the bearing inner ring. The seals shown in Fig. 3.1 are triple-lip, developed for the extremely severe dirt conditions encountered in disk-harrow applications. Sealed bearings designed for less severe applications usually have only single-lip seals.

Note that the bearing assembly shown in Fig. 3.2 has an external flange or slinger that rotates with the hub and protects the lip of the seal from hay that might wrap around the hub or tine bar.

V-BELT DRIVES

3.7. Applications. V-belts are employed extensively in agricultural machinery applications in which it is not necessary to maintain exact speed ratios. V-belts tend to cushion shock loads, do not require lubrication, and are less critical to misalignment than are other types of drives. They can be operated at speeds as high as 33 m/s [6500 ft/min], although speeds in agricultural machinery applications seldom exceed 15 m/s [3000 ft/min]. V-belts are not suitable for heavy loads at low speeds.

V-belts may be used singly or in matched sets, although single belts are the most common on agricultural machines. Banded, multiple V-belts are sometimes employed on drives having high power requirements, pulsating loads, and inherent instability problems. A banded belt consists of a matched set of two or more conventional V-belts with a thin tie band connecting their tops. Tying the strands together minimizes lateral belt whip and improves the load distribution among the belts.

Because a V-belt wedges into the sheave grooves, it can transmit a given amount of power with less overall shaft pull than a flat-belt drive. V-belts can be operated with relatively small arcs of contact, as in close-center shaft arrangements with large shaft-speed ratios. A single belt on an implement often drives several components in an arrangement known as a serpentine drive. V-belts permit considerable latitude in possible orientation and arrangement of the shafts involved in a drive.

V-belts are adaptable to clutching arrangements. A close-fitting guard may be needed to maintain proper belt orientation and move the belt away from the driver when the tension is released. Under certain conditions it is convenient or economically desirable to drive a relatively large flat pulley with V-belts from a smaller, grooved sheave.* This is known as a V-flat drive.

---

*In this chapter, "pulley" means a wheel that has an essentially flat face, and a sheave is a grooved wheel for V-belts.

Table 3.1. AGRICULTURAL V-BELT CROSS-SECTIONAL DIMENSIONS,
SHEAVE GROOVE ANGLES, AND DIFFERENCES BETWEEN SHEAVE
EFFECTIVE OUTSIDE DIAMETERS AND PITCH DIAMETERS.*

Type	Belt Cross Section	Nominal Belt Width		Nominal Belt Depth		Sheave Groove Angle,	Effective OD Minus PD for Std.-Groove Sheave	
		mm	in.	mm	in.	deg.†	mm	in.
Conventional V-belts								
	HA	12.7	0.50	7.9	0.31	30 - 38	6.35	0.250
	HB	16.7	0.66	10.3	0.41	30 - 38	8.89	0.350
	HC	22.2	0.88	13.5	0.53	30 - 38	10.16	0.400
	HD	31.8	1.25	19.0	0.75	30 - 38	15.24	0.600
	HE	38.1	1.50	23.0	0.91	32 - 38	20.32	0.800
Double V-belts								
	HAA	12.7	0.50	10.3	0.41	30 - 38	6.35	0.250
	HBB	16.7	0.66	13.5	0.53	30 - 38	8.89	0.350
	HCC	22.2	0.88	17.5	0.69	30 - 38	10.16	0.400
	HDD	31.8	1.25	25.4	1.00	30 - 38	15.24	0.600
Adjustable-speed V-belts								
	HI	25.4	1.00	12.7	0.50	26	7.6	0.30
	HJ	31.8	1.25	15.0	0.59	26	9.4	0.37
	HK	38.1	1.50	17.5	0.69	26	11.4	0.45
	HL	44.4	1.75	19.8	0.78	26	13.2	0.52
	HM	50.8	2.00	22.2	0.88	26	15.2	0.60

*ASAE Standard S211.3.[2]
†For V-belts and double V-belts, sheave groove angle increases as diameter is increased.

3.8. V-Belt Types and Standardization. Three types of V-belts specially designed for agricultural machines are known as agricultural V-belts, agricultural double V-belts, and adjustable-speed belts. These are illustrated in Table 3.1. Banded belts made from agricultural V-belts are also available. Agricultural V-belts and double V-belts are distinguished from the corresponding cross-sectional sizes of industrial V-belts by the prefix, H.

The cross-sectional dimensions of agricultural V-belts are identical with those of industrial belts but the construction is different because of the different type of use. Agricultural V-belts are more likely to be subjected to excessive shock loads, heavy pulsating loads, and other adverse conditions. Whereas V-belts in an industrial drive are expected to last for several years of continuous operation, a life expectancy of 1000 to 2000 h is adequate for most farm machinery applications. Hence, agricultural V-belt loadings can be higher than in industrial applications.

Double V-belts are employed in serpentine drives where the direction of rotation of one or more shafts is reversed, thus requiring that power be transmitted to grooved sheaves from both the inside and outside of the belt. Adjustable-speed belts are discussed in Section 3.12.

The ASAE has established a standard for agricultural V-belts.[2] This standard covers cross-sectional dimensions (Table 3.1), belt lengths generally available, groove specifications, minimum diameters for idlers, procedures and examples for calculating required belt lengths, installation and take-up allowances, twisted-belt drives, and belt-measuring specifications.

The ASAE standard is similar in many respects to the standard established by the Rubber Manufacturers Association (RMA) for industrial V-belts. There are minor differences in groove dimensions and in available belt lengths. The RMA standard specifies pitch lengths for belts, whereas the ASAE standard specifies *effective outside* lengths. The RMA standard is intended primarily for two-sheave drives and includes formulas and charts for power ratings. The ASAE standard covers a broad range of drive configurations and does not include power ratings. In designing an agricultural drive, the allowable load is related to the expected number of hours of actual operation for a specific drive.

3.9. Mechanics of V-Belt Drives. A V-belt transmits power by virtue of a difference in belt tension between the point at which it enters a sheave and the point at which it leaves. This difference in tension is developed through friction between the belt sidewalls and the sides of the sheave groove. The wedging effect as the belt is pulled into the groove because of belt tension greatly increases the potential driving force.

As a belt bends to conform to the sheave curvature, the outer section stretches and the inner section is compressed. The location of the neutral axis, which establishes the pitch diameter of the sheave, is determined by the position of the load-carrying cords within the belt cross section. Differences between sheave effective outside diameters and pitch diameters are included in Table 3.1. Pitch diameters, rather than outside diameters, should always be used in calculating speed ratios and belt speeds.

The tension difference, or effective pull, that is required to transmit the load at each driven sheave can be obtained from the following equation.

$$T_t - T_s = 1000 \ \frac{kW}{V} \tag{3.1}$$

$$[\ T_t - T_s = \frac{33,000 \times hp}{V} \ ]$$

where T_t = tight-side tension, in newtons [pounds force]
T_s = slack-side tension, in newtons [pounds force]
kW = power transmitted, in kilowatts [hp = horsepower]
V = belt speed, in metres per second [feet per minute]
$T_t - T_s$ = effective pull, in newtons [pounds force]

It is customary to calculate tensions on the basis of a design power load that is somewhat greater than the average load to be transmitted, thus allowing for the effects of overloads or fluctuating loads. The design power for each driven wheel in a drive system is determined by multiplying the actual power by an appropriate service factor. Recommended values for service factors in agricultural machinery applications are included in reference 6 and range mostly from 1.2 to 1.5.

3.10. Tension Ratio. If the ratio between the tight-side and slack-side tensions is too great, belt slippage will be excessive. Slippage in a properly designed drive should not exceed 1 to 2%. If the ratio is smaller than it needs to be, unnecessarily high tensions will be needed for a given effective pull, thereby reducing belt life. The maximum allowable tension ratio is[10]

$$R_a = \frac{T_t}{T_s} = e^{k\theta} \tag{3.2}$$

where e = base of natural logarithms = 2.7183
θ = arc of contact, in radians, = deg $\times$ $\pi/180$
k = a coefficient that reflects the friction and wedging effect between the belt and the sheave or pulley

In designing a drive with a V-belt in a V-sheave, a tension ratio of $R_{a\pi} = 5$ (allowable tension ratio for 180° arc of contact) is commonly assumed.[6] This gives a value of $k = 0.512$. A somewhat higher tension ratio is permissible if automatic tensioning is provided. For a V-belt running on a flat pulley, a value of $R_{a\pi} = 2.5$ is satisfactory ($k = 0.292$).

When the arc of contact is less than 180°, the allowable tension ratio is less, as indicated by equation 3.2, thus requiring higher values of T_t and T_s for a given effective pull and power. For example, if an effective pull of 360 N is required for the design power, values of T_t and T_s would be 450 N and 90 N if the arc of contact on a grooved sheave is 180° ($R_{a\pi} = 5$). But if the arc of contact is only 120°, the maximum allowable tension ratio is 2.9, requiring tensions of 549 and 189 N. Flat, backside idlers are often employed to effect tensioning and, at the same time, increase the arcs of contact on the loaded sheaves.

In a two-sheave drive without an idler, the smaller sheave is the critical one in regard to tension ratio (slippage) because it has the smaller arc of contact. In a V-flat, two-wheel drive without an idler, the sheave and the flat pulley have equal maximum allowable tension ratios when the arc of contact is about 130° on the sheave and 230° on the flat pulley. When a drive has more than one driven sheave or pulley, tensions must be determined in a cumulative manner. All tensions in the system must be adjusted so that no wheel has a tension ratio greater than its allowable value. In a multiwheel drive, the driver is usually the one most likely to slip.

3.11. Stresses and Service Life. Stresses in a V-belt drive arise from the effective pull needed for the power load, slack-side tension needed to prevent slippage, bending around each wheel, and centrifugal forces acting on the belt. The bending tension T_b in the outer fibers of a belt with a given cross section is inversely proportional to the wheel diameter. The tension due to centrifugal force may be expressed as[10]

$$T_c = w V^2 \qquad\qquad (3.3)$$

$$[\, T_c = 8.63 \times 10^{-6} w V^2 \,]$$

where T_c = centrifugal tension, in newtons [pounds force]
  w = belt mass, in kilograms per metre of length [pounds per foot of length]

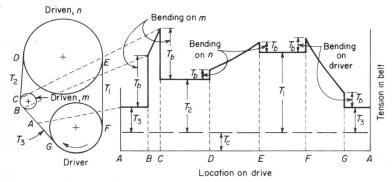

Fig. 3.4. Belt tensions in relation to position on a three-sheave drive. (Gates Rubber Co.[6])

The tensions in a three-sheave drive are illustrated in Fig. 3.4. T_3 is the slack-side tension and the differences, $T_2 - T_3$, $T_1 - T_2$, and $T_1 - T_3$, represent the effective pulls needed to transmit the power. Note that there is one peak tension at each wheel. It has been determined experimentally that a V-belt usually fails from fatigue caused by repetition of peak tensions and that the average fatigue life of a belt is predictable if loads are accurately known or can be estimated.[1,6]

The Gates Rubber Company has developed a design method for predicting the service life of a V-belt that includes the effects of the following factors.

1. The number of wheels on the drive.
2. The design power for each wheel (including an appropriate service factor for each driven wheel).
3. Belt speed.
4. The arc of contact for each wheel.

5. The sequence of loaded wheels and idlers on the drive.
6. The pitch diameter of each wheel.
7. The stress-fatigue characteristics and cross-sectional dimensions of the particular type and cross section of belt being considered.
8. Belt length.

This method is described in detail in reference 6, which includes details of all other steps involved in designing an agricultural V-belt drive.* The Gates manual also includes a table of recommended acceptable design service lives for belts on various farm implements or components. Adams[1] describes a design method that is similar to the Gates method.

The Gates system is based on the determination (from an empirical equation or nomographs[6]) of a "fatigue rate" corresponding to the peak tension for each wheel at a given belt speed. The units of the fatigue rate are millimetres [inches] of belt length per 100 h of life. The fatigue rates for the individual wheels are added together to obtain the total fatigue rate for the particular size and type of belt being considered for the drive. The calculated average service life of the belt at a given speed is

$$\text{Life, in hours} = \frac{(\text{Belt length, in millimetres [inches]}) \times 100}{\text{Total fatigue rate}} \quad (3.4)$$

For a given tight-side tension and wheel pitch diameter, increasing the belt speed increases the fatigue rate, primarily because of the greater frequency of stress cycles but also because of increased centrifugal tension at high speeds. (The transmitted power would be increased also.)

The relation of fatigue rate to tension and speed for each type or quality of belt and each cross section is determined experimentally by means of durability tests in the laboratory, from which constants in a generalized equation are evaluated. A typical curve for one speed is shown in Fig. 3.5. Essentially, a tension-fatigue-rate curve is the inverse of the usual S-N curve (fatigue cycles versus stress).

In designing a drive, the sequence of the driven sheaves or pulleys affects the magnitudes of the peak tensions and hence the service life. If a multiple-sheave drive can be arranged so the belt leaving the driver comes to the driven sheaves in order of increasing power requirements, the magnitudes of tension peaks for the low-power sheaves will be minimized. Exceptionally small-diameter sheaves should be in belt spans of lesser tension to avoid the combination of a high tight-side tension and a high bending tension. An idler, if used, should be in the span with the least tension.

Increasing the sheave diameters on a particular drive, if feasible, reduces both the bending stresses and the required effective pull and may even permit

---

*In 1977, copies of this design manual[6] were available from the Gates Rubber Company, free of charge, to instructors and students.

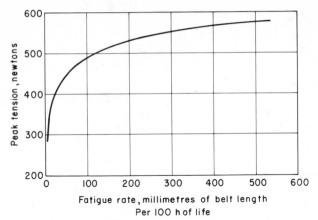

Fig. 3.5. Typical relation between tension and fatigue rate for one V-belt cross section and quality and one speed. (Gates Rubber Co.[6])

the use of a smaller belt cross secton. Centrifugal tension is seldom a limiting factor at speeds encountered in agricultural machinery drives.

3.12. Variable-Speed V-Belt Drives. An adjustable-pitch V-belt sheave has provision for moving one face axially with respect to the other, thus changing the radius at which the belt operates. Some adjustable-pitch sheaves can be changed only when stopped, but others can be changed while in motion (Fig. 3.6). In this textbook, the term "variable-speed drive" implies the ability to change the speed ratio over the entire range of control while the drive is in operation and under load.

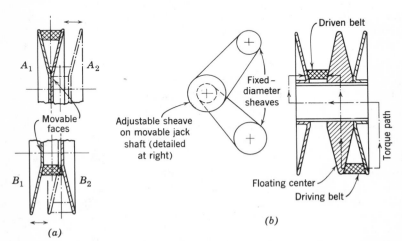

Fig. 3.6. (a) Arrangement with two adjustable-pitch sheaves on fixed centers. (b) Double adjustable-pitch sheave with floating center. (E.G. Kimmich and W.Q. Roesler.[10])

Variable-speed V-belt drives have been employed extensively in the propulsion drives of self-propelled combines and to a lesser extent on other self-propelled machines, although hydrostatic drives are becoming increasingly popular for this type of application. Combine threshing cylinders and header reels sometimes have variable-speed V-belt drives. Cylinder drives represent rather severe conditions because of the high average power requirements at relatively low belt speeds and momentary extreme overloads from "slugging."

Belts designed specifically for variable-speed drives are wider than conventional V-belts in relation to their thickness. The extra width is necessary to obtain reasonable ranges of speed ratio as well as increased load capacities. Relatively thin belts are needed because minimum operating diameters are necessarily small in this type of drive. Also, the thickness subtracts from the total in-and-out movement of the belt for a given depth of sheave face.

With adjustable-speed sheaves and V-belts* that conform to the ASAE standard (Tables 3.1 and 3.2), maximum speed-range ratios ranging from 1.75 for HI belts to 1.9 for HM belts are obtainable when one adjustable-pitch sheave of the minimum allowable diameter is used in conjunction with a fixed-diameter sheave.† The range for a given belt size varies inversely with the sheave diameter, since the maximum change in pitch diameter is fixed by the 26° groove angle and the belt top width (Fig. 3.6a).

Table 3.2. DIAMETERS OF ASAE STANDARD
ADJUSTABLE-SPEED SHEAVES‡

Belt Cross Section	Recommended Minimum OD		Maximum PD with Min. OD		Maximum Belt Diam. Change	
	mm	in.	mm	in.	mm	in.
HI	177.8	7.00	170.2	6.70	72.1	2.84
HJ	222.2	8.75	212.8	8.38	94.7	3.73
HK	266.7	10.50	255.3	10.05	117.3	4.62
HL	311.2	12.25	298.0	11.73	140.2	5.52
HM	355.6	14.00	340.4	13.40	162.8	6.41

‡ ASAE Standard S211.3.[2]

Because the belt moves axially as its radial position on the nonadjustable face of the sheave is changed, the belt will be in alignment for only one speed ratio when an adjustable-pitch sheave is used in combination with a fixed-

*"Adjustable-speed" is used herein to describe the sheaves and belts for a variable-speed drive, to conform to ASAE Standard S211.3. Although S211.3 also refers to "adjustable-speed drives," use of the term "variable-speed drive" in relation to agricultural machinery is common practice.

†Maximum speed ratios were 1.99 to 2.06 prior to the 1968 revision of the ASAE standard.

diameter sheave. The position of proper alignment should be at the midpoint of the adjustment range. In this type of arrangement, speed adjustment may be accomplished by (a) providing an axial thrust spring on the adjustable-pitch sheave and moving an idler, (b) having a spring-loaded idler and moving the adjustable sheave face by means of a mechanical linkage, or (c) providing a thrust spring and varying the shaft center distance.

The speed range for a combination of 2 adjustable-pitch sheaves is the product of the 2 individual ranges. When both sheaves have the minimum recommended diameter, the maximum speed ratio varies from 3.0 for HI belts to 3.7 for HM belts. The most common arrangement is with the two sheaves on fixed centers, as shown in Fig. 3.6a. If the faces A_1 and B_2 are fixed axially while A_2 and B_1 are moved simultaneously, proper belt alignment is maintained at all speed ratios because the entire belt moves axially.

For equal axial movements of the two adjustable faces, the required belt length will be greater for each extreme of adjustment than for the adjustment that makes the two legs of the belt parallel. Hence, if A_2 and B_1 are moved by an interconnecting mechanical linkage, a spring should be provided in the linkage between the two sheaves to compensate for the changes in required belt length and maintain the proper belt tension.

A simpler arrangement with two sheaves on fixed centers is to provide an axial thrust spring on one sheave and mechanically move the adjustable face of the other sheave. The design procedure for such a thrust spring is included in reference 6. This system provides automatic belt tensioning.

A third arrangement has two adjustable-speed belts in tandem and a double adjustable-pitch sheave with floating center section, as shown in Fig. 3.6b. The speed ratio is changed by moving the adjustable-pitch sheave along a path that keeps the sum of the required belt lengths constant as the floating center changes its lateral position. This system is subject to belt misalignment as discussed above for arrangements employing a single adjustable-pitch sheave.

GEARS AND CHAIN DRIVES

Both of these types of drive give constant speed ratios, gears being adapted to close-center, intersecting, or crossing shafts, and chain drives being used for parallel shafts with moderate center distances. Gears are usually enclosed so they can be protected and properly lubricated, whereas chain drives on agricultural machinery frequently operate in the open with periodic oiling, or sometimes with no lubrication at all on slow-speed chains in a dusty or dirty environment. Since gear applications on farm machinery are in general very similar to industrial applications, and since detailed design and selection information is available from many standard sources, no further discussion on this subject will be included here.

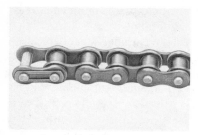

Standard-pitch roller chain

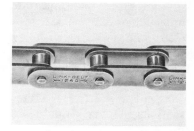

Double-pitch roller chain

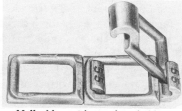

Malleable-cast-iron, detachable-
link chain

Pressed-steel, detachable-link chain

Fig. 3.7. Four types of drive chain common on farm machines. (Courtesy of Link-Belt Co.)

3.13. General Considerations for Chain Drives. The pitch of a chain is the effective length of one link. Standard-pitch roller chain, double-pitch roller chain, and detachable-link chain (Fig. 3.7) are all common on agricultural machines. Standardized dimensions for each of these types have been adopted by the American Standards Association (ASA).

In general, the load capacity of a chain is based upon the rate of wear rather than the ultimate strength. Because wear is mainly due to the hinge action as the chain engages or leaves a sprocket, the rate of wear is greater with small sprockets than with large ones. The rate of wear is also directly related to chain speed and inversely related to chain length. As a chain wears, the pitch length increases and the chain rides farther out on the sprocket teeth. The more teeth a sprocket has, the sooner the chain will ride out too far and have to be replaced. For this reason, speed ratios should not exceed 10 to 1 for standard-pitch roller chain or 6 to 1 for other chains.[14]

Power ratings published in chain catalogs are for the relatively long life expected in industrial applications. As in designing V-belt drives, actual power requirements are multiplied by appropriate service factors to obtain design power. Because of the shorter life requirements on agricultural machines in comparison with industrial applications, somewhat greater loadings are often acceptable. However, unfavorable environmental conditions may tend to shorten the life.

Chain selection for extremely slow drives is sometimes based on ultimate strength rather than wear rate. With roller chains, the recommended maximum ratios of working load to ultimate strength range from 0.2 at 0.13 m/s [25 ft/min] to 0.1 at 1.3 m/s [250 ft/min].[12] Conventional, steel detachable chain has inherent stress concentration points that promote early fatigue failures if the chain is loaded to more than 10% of its ultimate strength. The pull required for a given power and speed can be determined from equation 3.1. T_s is assumed to be zero, since a chain should run with essentially no slack-side tension. Chain speed in m/s = (chain pitch, mm/1000) × (number of teeth on sprocket) × (sprocket r/min ÷ 60).

Since a sprocket is essentially a polygon with as many sides as there are teeth or pitches, either the chain speed or the angular velocity of the sprocket must vary as the chain engages or leaves the sprocket. The fewer teeth there are on the sprocket, the greater is the speed variation. Theoretically, a 10-tooth sprocket would give a variation of about 5%. Practically, however, small speed variations as well as sudden load shocks tend to be absorbed or cushioned by the natural elasticity of the chain and the catenary effect of the driving side. Although sprockets with as few as 6 teeth are available, sizes with less than 17 or 18 teeth are not recommended for high-speed drives.

3.14. Detachable-Link Chain. Steel detachable-link chains are used extensively on agricultural implements, both for transmitting power and in conveyors and elevators. This is the least expensive type of chain and it is well-suited for moderate loads at speeds not exceeding 2 to 2.5 m/s [400 to 500 ft/min]. Under dirty conditions, detachable chains are subject to greater wear than roller chains because of the loose-fitting, open hooks. Detachable chains usually are not lubricated, because the lubricant would tend to retain grit particles in the joint.

An improved type of steel detachable-link chain, developed in the early 1950s, is said to have one-third more tensile strength than conventional steel detachable chain, and more than twice the fatigue strength.[17] The hook is rolled up from material in front of the link rather than from the material punched out from the center. This "high-fatigue" steel detachable chain is more expensive than the conventional type.

3.15. Standard-Pitch Roller Chain. Drives of this type are satisfactory at linear speeds from less than 0.5 m/s [100 ft/min] up to 20 m/s [4000 ft/min] and are well-suited for heavy loads requiring a compact drive. The maximum permissible speed decreases as the pitch is increased. Multiple-width chains of short pitch can be used for extremely compact drives at high speeds. Roller chains are precision-built and under favorable conditions may have efficiencies as high as 98 to 99%.[12]

Sprockets may be driven from either the inside or the outside of a roller chain. Although oil-bath lubrication is recommended for high-speed drives, this system often is not practical on agricultural machines. Standard-pitch roller chain is several times as expensive as steel detachable chain.

3.16. Double-Pitch Roller Chain. This type of chain employs the same pins, bushings, and rollers as standard-pitch roller chain, but the side plates have twice the pitch. Thus, double-pitch chains have the same strength and precision as corresponding standard-pitch chains but less mass. They are less expensive than standard-pitch roller chains, but considerably more expensive than steel detachable chain. Double-pitch chains are suitable for slow and moderate-speed drives. Because the roller diameter is only $\frac{5}{16}$ of the pitch, there is ample space for sprocket teeth, and precision, cast-tooth sprockets are satisfactory (more economical than machine-cut teeth).

To further reduce the cost of this type of chain, an *agricultural* double-pitch chain has been developed that is dimensionally the same as the regular double-pitch chain but has a lower cost because of different materials and because the joints have more clearance, thus permitting greater manufacturing tolerances. Performance is said to be somewhat inferior to that of regular double-pitch chain.[17]

3.17. Self-Lubricating Chain. During the 1950s several companies developed chains that are physically interchangeable with standard-pitch and double-pitch roller chains but which are self-lubricating.[5] This type of chain has oil-impregnated, sintered-steel bushings at the joints, replacing the bushings and rollers of conventional roller chain. It was designed for applications where external lubrication is impossible or impractical. Many farm machinery applications fall into this category. Because this chain does not have rollers, it is not recommended for high speeds or extremely heavy loads.

The cost of standard-pitch or double-pitch self-lubricating chain is the same as that of the corresponding size of conventional roller chain. Ultimate strengths are perhaps 5 to 20% lower. Laboratory tests and field experience have indicated that, for a given load and a given allowable percentage elongation due to wear, the service life of a self-lubricating chain is several times as great as that of *nonlubricated* conventional roller chain. But, where a conventional chain can be adequately lubricated, it will out-perform the self-lubricating chain.

OVERLOAD SAFETY DEVICES

In many types of farm machinery, a single power source drives various components that have widely differing power requirements and are subject to varying degrees of possible overload. In such a system some overload protection is almost mandatory, especially for the lower-powered components. Three general types of safety devices commonly used in rotary drives are: (a) those that depend upon shearing of a replaceable connecting member in the drive, (b) units in which spring force holds two corrugated members together, utilizing the principle of the inclined plane, and (c) devices depending entirely upon friction.

3.18. Shear Devices. This type of device is simple and relatively inexpensive, but the sheared element must be replaced after each overload. Thus, it is most suitable where overloads are rather infrequent. Shear devices can be designed for almost any desired load rating, although pin or key sizes become rather small for low torque ratings unless a material with low shear strength is selected. Typical arrangements for shear devices are:

1. Shear key between shaft and hub (usually brass key, with tapered shaft and bore).
2. Diametral shear pin through hub and shaft (gives double shear).
3. Flange-mounted shear pin parallel to shaft, as illustrated in Fig. 3.8.

Regardless of the arrangement, the driving and driven members must rotate freely with respect to each other after the shear element has failed. With either of the first two types, the shaft or bore is likely to be scored by the sheared element. Removal of the hub from the shaft may be necessary in the first type to replace a sheared key.

The flange-mounted shear pin is the most easily replaced, but the unit is more costly than a diametral pin and not as well-adapted to low torques because of the greater radius to the shear section. For experimental testing, interchangeable pins necked down to different diameters can be used to vary the load at which failure occurs. In production units, a full-sized pin of an ordinary material (such as hot-rolled steel) is desirable for convenience of replacement by the operator.

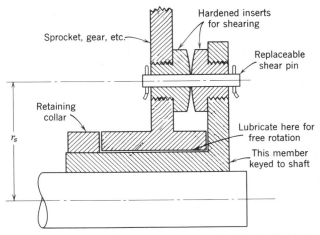

Fig. 3.8. An arrangement with a flange-mounted shear pin. The hardened shearing inserts could be omitted, particularly if overloads are expected only infrequently or if necked-down shear pins are used.

The torque at which a flange-mounted shear pin will fail is

$$T = r_s(\frac{\pi}{4} d_1^2 S_s) \times 10^{-3} \qquad (3.5)$$

$$[\, T = r_s\, (\frac{\pi}{4} d_1^2\, S_s)\,]$$

and the power is

$$kW = \frac{2\,\pi\,NT}{60 \times 1000} = 8.225\, N\, r_s\, d_1^2\, S_s \times 10^{-8} \qquad (3.6)$$

$$[\, hp = 1.246\, N\, r_s\ d_1^2\, S_s\ \times 10^{-5}\,]$$

where T = torque, in newton-metres [pound-force-inches]
N = shaft speed, in revolutions per minute
r_s = distance between shaft center and shear-pin center (Fig. 3.8), in millimetres [inches]
d_1 = diameter of shear pin at shear section, in millimetres [inches]
S_s = ultimate shear strength of shear pin, in megaspascals [pounds force per square inch]

Similarly, a diametral shear pin (double shear) will fail when

$$kW = 8.225\, N\, D\, d_1^2\, S_s \times 10^{-8} \qquad (3.7)$$
$$[\, hp = 1.246\, N\, D\, d_1^2\, S_s \times 10^{-5}\,]$$

where D = shaft diameter (diameter at which shear occurs), in millimetres [inches]

3.19. Jump Clutch. A jump clutch has rounded, mating jaws or corrugations that are held together by an adjustable spring. In Fig. 3.9, part A is

Fig. 3.9. Typical arrangement of a jump clutch. (Courtesy of International Harvester Co.)

keyed to the shaft and part B, the driving member, is free to rotate on the shaft when an overload occurs. The overload torque required to rotate B with respect to A and cause jumping is a function of the slope of the inclined corrugation faces, the coefficient of friction between the faces, the effective radius from the shaft centerline to the contact area, and the force required to compress the spring and permit axial movement of B with respect to A.

The spring must have sufficient deflection available so it is not compressed solid before the relative displacement of the two corrugated faces is sufficient to permit jumping. Although friction between the corrugated faces influences the magnitude of the torque required for jumping, the unit would function (at a lower torque) even if the coefficient of friction were zero.

Because of its automatic resetting feature, the jump clutch is more suitable than shear devices where overloads may occur rather frequently. There is no slippage until the load exceeds the setting of the unit, and then the operator is warned audibly that an overload has occurred. Jump clutches are more expensive than shear devices and are not well-suited to large loads because of the excessive physical size required. When they are jumping, they impose high shock loads upon the drive system.

The magnitude and variability of the friction force required to slide the movable member axially can have an important effect upon the torque required to cause jumping. To minimize the axial friction force, the torque should be transmitted to or from the movable member at a relatively large radius, as with a sprocket or sheave, rather than through splines or a key in the shaft.

3.20. Friction Devices. A properly designed belt drive can serve as a friction safety device, although its performance is affected by variations in belt tension and by the increase in coefficient of friction as the percentage of belt slip increases. The performance is more consistent with a spring-loaded idler than with a fixed adjustment.

Single-plate clutches with two friction surfaces, similar to tractor or automotive clutches, are often used for overload protection. The spring pressure is adjusted to drive normal loads but slip under abnormal loads.[8] In comparison with jump clutches, friction safety clutches have the advantages of more consistent breakaway torque and no damaging peaks during slippage. However, tests have shown that the momentary dynamic torque capacity under sudden load application may be 2 to 3 times the static value.[8]

Friction clutches are very effective in protecting a drive from high-frequency peak torques, as discussed in Section 3.29. But under some conditions it is possible to have a friction clutch slipping sufficiently to become overheated without the operator being aware of the overload.

UNIVERSAL JOINTS

3.21. Single Joints. The type of universal joint generally used on farm machinery is known as the Cardan or Hooke joint (Fig. 3.10). A single joint operating at an angle does not deliver uniform angular output velocity. Figure 3.11 shows the lead or lag of the driven shaft for one-half revolution, with the universal operating at various joint angles α. The cycle repeats itself for each 180° of rotation. The rotational fluctuation is small when the joint

Fig. 3.10. A Cardan or Hooke universal joint. Roller bearings are commonly used in power-transmission joints. The ends of the trunnions of the center cross and the bottoms of the bearing caps are precision ground, thereby forming thrust bearings. (F.M. Potgieter. Agr. Eng., Jan., 1952.)

angle is 10°, but when the angle is 40° the total fluctuation for a single joint is 15°.

The curves in Fig. 3.11 are based on the well-known equation[18]

$$\frac{\tan \phi_2}{\tan \phi_1} = \cos \alpha \qquad (3.8)$$

where ϕ_1 = angle of rotation of the driving shaft from the initial position shown at the upper left in Fig. 3.11

ϕ_2 = corresponding angle of rotation of the driven shaft

α = joint angle (Fig. 3.11)

The lead or lag of the driven shaft is $\phi_2 - \phi_1$, a negative sign indicating lag. The peak lag and peak lead occur when the average angle of rotation of the 2 shafts is 45° or 135°, respectively, from the indicated reference position in Fig. 3.11. Thus the peak lag occurs when the driving shaft is past 45° by an amount equal to half the peak lag, as indicated by the broken line in the lower half of Fig. 3.11.

The relation between the angular velocities of the output and input shafts is[18]

$$\omega_2 = \omega_1 \frac{\cos \alpha}{1 - \sin^2 \alpha \sin^2 \phi_1} \qquad (3.9)$$

where ω_1 = angular velocity of the input (driving) shaft

ω_2 = angular velocity of the output (driven) shaft

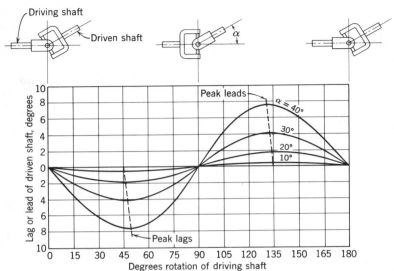

Fig. 3.11. Lead or lag of shaft driven by a cardan-type universal joint, in relation to rotational position of the driving shaft.

The velocity ratio, ω_2/ω_1, is maximum when $\phi_1 = 90°$ and minimum when $\phi_1 = 0°$ or $180°$. From equation 3.9, the maximum ratio is $1/\cos \alpha$ and the minimum ratio is $\cos \alpha$. With uniform input velocity, the angular-velocity fluctuations of the output shaft are about $\pm 15\%$ when the joint angle is $30°$ and $\pm 6\%$ for a joint angle of $20°$.

3.22. Multijoint Combinations. When two universal joints are connected in series, the angular displacement and velocity fluctuations will cancel if (a) the joint angles are equal, and (b) the joints are 90° out of phase. The output shaft will then have a uniform angular velocity (assuming uniform input velocity), but the intermediate shaft must still be accelerated and decelerated twice during each revolution.

If the 3 shafts connected to the 2 joints all lie in the same plane, the proper phase relation is obtained by having the yokes on the intermediate shaft in line. The output and input shafts may be parallel or the joint angles may be additive. If the shafts connected to one of a pair of joints are in a different plane than the shafts connected to the other, the proper phase relation is obtained by having the yokes on the intermediate shaft out of line by an amount equal to the angle between the 2 planes, so these 2 yokes will lie in the 2 planes simultaneously.

When three or more universal joints are used in series, the problem of orienting the shafts and joints to produce uniform angular velocity (or minimize fluctuations) in the final driven shaft is rather complex. If the joint angles are known or assumed, the best phase relations can be determined by vector analysis. Reference 18, which is an excellent treatise on all phases of universal-joint relations and applications, includes a description of the vector-analysis method and of another system called "90° system phasing" that is sometimes applicable. The theory behind the vector method is discussed in reference 3.

If the best combination of phase relations for a particular combination of joint angles is not acceptable, one or more of the joint angles must be changed and the analysis repeated. Another approach is to study different combinations with a model setup having degree indicators at each joint.

3.23. Joint-Angle Limitations. The maximum permissible angle between shafts depends upon the type of drive, the torsional flexibility of the shafts, the inertia of the rotating parts, the speed, and the desired life. Figure 3.12 illustrates the effect of joint angle upon the magnitude of cyclic peak torques for a specific drive situation. In these tests a 22.4 kW electric dynamometer was driven at 560 r/min by a tractor, through a typical power-take-off arrangement. With a single joint, peak torque values increased rapidly with joint angle and the increase was substantial even at only 8 to 10° joint angles.

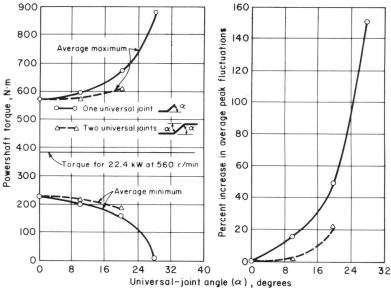

Fig. 3.12. Effect of universal-joint angularity on maximum and minimum instantaneous peak torque values when transmitting 22.4 kW. (M. Hansen.[7])

Even when 2 joints were properly phased and operated at equal angles, peak torques were increased 20% when the joint angles were changed from zero to 20°. The velocity fluctuations in the intermediate shaft were at least partly responsible for the increase in peak torques. Although angles considerably greater than 20° in 2-joint systems may sometimes be acceptable — continuously under some conditions and intermittently under others — maintaining minimum joint angles during normal operation is important.

Torque fluctuations can be reduced by introducing torsional elasticity into the drive. V-belts also help absorb the angular fluctuations. Constant-velocity universal joints have been developed primarily for vehicle front-wheel drives, but these are too expensive for farm machinery applications.

3.24. Universal-Joint Shafts. Provision for axial movement of the shafts in a drive containing universal joints is important. This is usually provided by telescoping shafts and tubes or by splined connections. If the sliding connection is between two joints, the telescoping part should be keyed in some manner to ensure assembly with the correct orientation of yokes.

A universal joint operating at an angle and transmitting torque tends to try to eliminate its angle and bring the two shafts in line, thus setting up bending moments in the shafts. These secondary couples are cyclic, with 2 stress reversals and 2 peaks occuring in each revolution. The shaft connecting two universal joints needs to be stiff enough to prevent whip but should have a low polar moment of inertia to minimize torque variations due to its velocity fluctuations. It is particularly important that the operating speed be below the critical speed* of the shaft. For these reasons, non-telescoping connecting shafts are usually tubular members.

POWER-TAKE-OFF DRIVES

3.25. Applications. Mechanical power-take-off (PTO) drives on tractors have been available for many years, and their use has steadily increased. Remote hydraulic motors, powered from the tractor hydraulic system, are a relatively recent development. This type of drive is discussed in Chapter 4.

The introduction of the independently controlled PTO in the 1940s greatly increased the versatility of power-take-off drives in comparison with the transmission-driven PTO. An independent power-take-off is connected directly to the engine through its own clutch, thus permitting forward travel to be stopped without interrupting the operation of the implement.

Power-take-off drives are used on many types of trailed or mounted harvesting equipment, on many sprayers, and on rotary or vibratory tillage implements. Pull-type field forage choppers, corn pickers, and stalk cutters and shredders employ PTO drives almost exclusively. The larger pull-type combines, although relatively few in number, all have PTO drives. The availability of large tractors with 1000-rpm PTO outlets capable of transmitting the full tractor power output have made this type of drive feasible for these larger machines.

*The critical speed of an assembly is the speed at (or above) which excessive vibration sets in.

3.26. Standardization of Power-Take-Off Drives. The development and adoption of an ASAE standard that now specifies two PTO speeds has provided a basis for easy attachment and interchangeable use of PTO-driven implements with various makes and models of tractors.[2] Prior to 1958, the only standard speed was 536 r/min. But with the advent of larger tractors, this speed was too low to transmit the available power without excessive torque. Consequently, a second standard speed, 1000 r/min, was adopted in 1958. The other standard speed was changed to 540 r/min at the same time. Two shaft sizes are specified for the 1000-r/min speed and one for 540 r/min.

The standard includes dimensional specifications for the PTO shafts on the tractor and the relative locations of the shafts and the drawbar hitch point. The splines for the two speeds are different to prevent accidentally connecting an implement to the wrong speed. Some of the pertinent specifications are shown in the following table, in which the dimensions A, B, C, and D refer to Fig. 3.13. All dimensions are in millimetres [inches].

	540 r/min	1000 r/min	1000 r/min
Shaft diameter	35 [1⅜]	35 [1⅜]	45 [1¾]
Dimension A	356 [14.0]	406 [16.0]	508 [20.0]
Dimension C	330 to 432	330 to 432	432 to 533
	[15 ± 2]	[15 ± 2]	[19 ± 2]
Dimension D	152 to 305	152 to 305	203 to 254
	(203 preferred)	(203 preferred)	(229 preferred)
	[6.0 to 12.0]	[6.0 to 12.0]	[8.0 to 10.0]
	[8.0 preferred]	[8.0 preferred]	[9.0 preferred]
Dimension B	-25 to + 127	-25 to + 127	-25 to + 127
	[-1.0 to + 5.0]	[-1.0 to + 5.0]	[-1.0 to + 5.0]

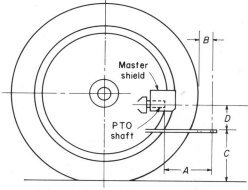

Fig. 3.13. Standardized locations for the PTO shaft and drawbar hitch point on agricultural tractors. The hitch point is to be directly beneath the extended center line of the PTO shaft.
(ASAE Standard S203.8.)

The standards also contain specifications regarding safety shields. Considerable attention has been given to this matter because PTO drives have been a substantial contributor to injuries and fatal accidents caused by farm machines. Early safety shields consisted of a telescoping sheet-metal cover tunnel that was pivotally attached to the implement and could easily be attached to the master shield on the tractor. Tunnel shields are effective when in place, but frequently they are removed and not replaced.

A more foolproof arrangement is an integral, smooth tube that surrounds the shaft and has a bell housing to partially cover each universal joint (Fig. 3.14). The tube is journaled on the PTO shaft and normally rotates with it,

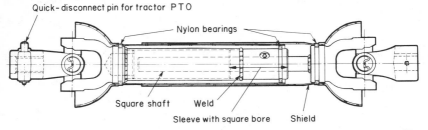

Fig 3.14. A telescoping PTO shaft with integral safety shield. (Courtesy of Neapco Products, Inc.)

but can stop if contact is made with a person or any foreign object. the PTO standards specify this type of shield. *Full* integral shielding goes one step further by providing complete coverage of each joint with interlocking bell housings. A standard has been developed for this type of shielding.[2]

3.27. Power-Take-Off Drives with Two Universal Joints. Figure 3.15 shows a typical two-joint PTO drive for a pull-type implement. Ideally, the

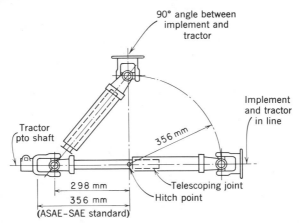

Fig. 3.15. Plan view of a PTO drive with two universal joints, for a pull-type implement.

hitch point should be midway between the two joints so the joint angles would be equal for any turning position of the implement with respect to the tractor. In practice, however, it has been found that if the ASAE standard dimension of 356 mm [14 in.] from the hitch point to the end of the PTO shaft (540 r/min) is used, it is necessary to have the rear universal a little farther from the hitch point to obtain sufficient telescoping action for sharp turns.

With this arrangement, the two joint angles are not equal when the implement is on a turn (Table 3.3) and there will be an increasingly serious fluctuation of angular velocity as the implement is turned more sharply. The standard distances from the PTO shaft to the hitch point are greater for the two 1000-r/min systems (Section 3.26), so the problem of unequal angles is minimized or eliminated for the higher PTO speed.

Table 3.3. COMPARISON OF UNIVERSAL-JOINT
ANGLES FOR POWER TAKE-OFF DRIVES
ILLUSTRATED IN FIG. 3.15 and 3.16

Angle Between Implement and Tractor, Degrees	Angles in Universal Joints, Degrees			
	Two-Joint Drive		Three-Joint Drive	
	Front Joint	Second Joint	Front Joint	Second, Joint
0	0	0	0	0
30	16	14	12	18
50	27	23	21	29
70	38	32	33	37
90	50	40	51	39

Some pull-type implements with 2-joint drives have the rear joint considerably farther behind the hitch point than shown in Fig. 3.15, usually because it is more convenient and economical to mount the rear joint on the shaft of a gear box whose position is fixed by other considerations than to install a 3-joint system. Such an arrangement causes large velocity fluctuations on sharp turns and, hence, should be employed only when relatively light loads are involved.

3.28. Three-Joint Power-Take-Off Drive. Figure 3.16 shows the plan view of a three-joint PTO drive having the implement shaft normally in line with the tractor PTO shaft. Note that the telescoping action is between the 2 rear joints, with a fixed-length shaft between the 2 front joints. This type of drive requires more longitudinal space than the two-joint arrangement, but a longer telescoping distance can be provided. It is well-suited for corn

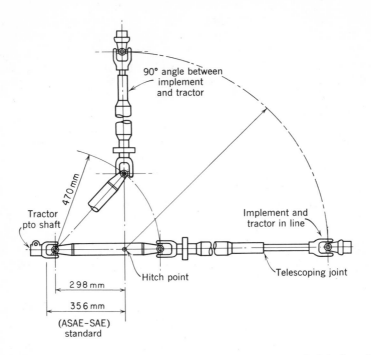

Fig. 3.16. Plan view of a typical three-joint drive having the implement shaft in line with the tractor PTO shaft. (F.M. Potgieter. Agr. Eng., Jan., 1952.)

pickers, field choppers, pull-type combines, and other implements with long tongues. It is not suitable for hay balers having short tongues.

With a fixed distance between the two front joints, it is geometrically impossible to have these joints equidistant from the hitch point for all turning angles of the implement. Thus a compromise is made, with the second joint being closer to the hitch point when the implement is not turning and farther than the front joint when the implement is turned 90° from the tractor.

With the arrangement shown in Fig. 3.16, the rear joint operates practically straight at all times and hence creates only minor velocity fluctuations. The joint angles for the two front joints are indicated in Table 3.3 for various implement turning angles. Note that the second joint has the greater angle for a 70° implement turn but a smaller angle than the front joint for a 90° turn. The drive will be quite rough for an implement turn of 90°.

If the driven shaft of the implement is offset from the centerline of the tractor PTO shaft so that the normal operating angle of one or both of the intermediate shafts is greater than about 15 to 20° from the line of the PTO shaft, serious velocity fluctuations may occur on sharp turns in the field.

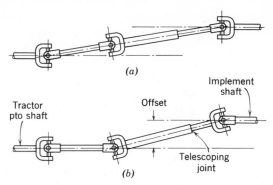

Fig. 3.17. Plan views of two arrangements for a three-joint, offset PTO drive. Note the difference in phasing of the right-hand joint in the two arrangements.

Figure 3.17 shows two possible arrangements for obtaining the offset. With the joints phased as indicated, either system theoretically provides uniform velocity of the driven shaft when the implement and tractor are in line. On sharp turns the lower arrangement is considerably better than the upper one, having smaller maximum joint angles and much less fluctuation in angular velocity. For a given amount of offset, it has the disadvantage of requiring greater joint angularities in the normal operating position.

Application of the vector-analysis method mentioned in Section 3.22 might yield a better combination of joint angles and phase relations for the offset-shaft situation. Any combination that looked promising would need to be checked for various implement turn angles.

3.29. Loads Imposed on Power-Take-Off Shafts. Extensive tests with fast-responding hydraulic and electronic torque meters have indicated that *average* power or torque requirements have little value as a basis for designing PTO drive parts.[7] Maximum instantaneous (high-frequency) peak torques are of far more importance because of the resulting fatigue stresses. These peak loads vary tremendously and are influenced by the following factors (in addition to joint angles as discussed in Section 3.23).

1. The amount of kinetic energy stored in the rotating parts of the tractor.
2. The moment of inertia of the implement's rotating parts.
3. The amount of resilience in the drive between the heavy rotating parts of the tractor and the rotating parts of the driven implement.
4. The PTO power available from the tractor.
5. The average power required to operate the implement.
6. The type of load (peak torque requirements of the implement).

The first three of the above items have a great deal more influence on the magnitude of peak torques than do the last three.[7] This is particularly true when PTO drives are used on implements such as balers, hammer mills, field choppers, and combines, which have variable loads capable of causing very rapid changes in PTO rotating speeds. Hansen[7] measured maximum and average torque values with these implements operating under various conditions that might be encountered in regular service. His results show that, even under normal operating conditions, peak torques for the baler were 4 to 6 times as great as the average values. With a field chopper and a combine, peak torques under normal conditions usually were about twice as great as the average values.

Peak torques can be limited to any desired value by the use of a friction slip clutch in the PTO drive, as indicated by the two lower curves in Fig. 3.18. However, many implements that are subject to occasional plugging or infrequent overloads now take advantage of the fact that PTO drives can absorb occasional peak loads about twice as great as the maximum allowable values for infinite fatigue life. A protective device cannot be expected to limit loads to values within the infinite-fatigue-life specifications and yet permit occasional torsional loads of twice that magnitude. In these cases it is particularly important that the normal high-frequency torsional peaks of the implement be within the infinite-fatigue-life limit of the drive so the protective device can be adjusted to allow the occasional higher loads.

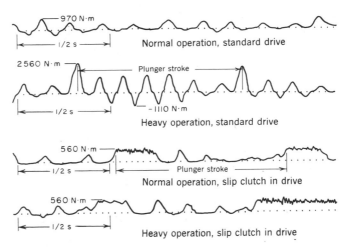

Fig. 3.18. Torque-meter charts for a PTO-driven baler with and without a friction slip clutch. (M. Hansen.[7])

3.30. Recommended PTO Load Limits. Excessive PTO loads from an implement can cause premature failure in either the tractor components or the implement drive system. The implement designer has the responsibility for investigating the PTO load characteristics of his implements and making any practical corrections that will reduce excessive peak torques. Designing for minimum joint angles during normal operation (implement not turning) is important. Overload safety devices should be provided when needed.

To assist tractor manufacturers and implement manufacturers in providing suitable PTO drive systems, the ASAE has adopted an official recommendation entitled, "Operating Requirements for Power-Take-Off Drives" This recommendation[2] discusses the importance of proper hitching, adequate telescoping action of the power shaft, and provision to prevent locking of universal joints when the implement is on a sharp turn. It specifies the maximum bending load to be imposed upon the tractor PTO shaft and recommends torque-limit settings for power-line protective devices under various types of loading.

Tests have indicated that when a conventional, square telescoping shaft is transmitting large amounts of torque, the axial force required for telescoping action can be as high as 65 to 90 kN [1500 to 2000 lbf], even when greased.[15] A dry shaft may require 90 kN when transmitting only 15 kW [20 hp].

To protect against damage due to excessive telescoping force, the ASAE recommendation specifies that an implement which is capable of being loaded with a continuous PTO torque in excess of 340 N·m [3000 lbf-in.] (which represents 35 kW [47 hp] at 1000 r/min and 19 kW [26 hp] at 540 r/min) is to be equipped with a low-friction telescoping shaft incapable of transmitting an axial thrust of over 6.67 kN [1500 lbf]. Driveline shafts with either recirculating-ball or nonrecirculating-ball telescoping sections are available to meet this need.

REFERENCES

1. ADAMS, J., Jr. V-belt design for farm machinery. Agr. Eng., 42:348-349, 353, July, 1961.
2. Agricultural Engineers Yearbook, 1976. ASAE St. Joseph, Mich.
3. BERRY, J. H., and C. L. CALLUM. Speed fluctuation in multijoint power lines. Agr. Eng., 34:308-311, May, 1953.
4. CURTIS, G. W. Tapered roller bearing practice in current farm machinery applications. Agr. Eng., 30:285-293, June, 1949.
5. EDGERTON, W. R. Self-lubricating chain drives in farm machinery design. ASAE Paper 64-610, Dec., 1964.
6. Gates Agricultural V-belt Drive Design Manual. The Gates Rubber Co., Denver, Colo., 1976.
7. HANSEN, M. Loads imposed on power-take-off shafts by farm implements. Agr. Eng., 33:67-70, Feb., 1952.
8. HETH, S. C. Development of safety clutch for tractor PTO drives. SAE Preprint 589, 1955.
9. HOWE, R. S., Jr. and G. H. RALEY. Trends in ball bearing design for farm machinery. Agr. Eng., 39:152-155, 171-172, Mar., 1958.
10. KIMMICH, E. G., and W. Q. ROESLER. Variable-speed V-belt drives for farm machines. Discussion by L. J. Confer and W. S. Worley. Agr. Eng., 31:334-340, July, 1950.

11. KUETHER, D. O. Farm equipment bearing developments. Implement & Tractor, *80*(22):20-22, 53, Oct. 21, 1965.
12. Marks' Standard Handbook for Mechanical Engineers, 7th Edition, Section 8, p. 88. T. Baumeister, Editor-in-Chief. McGraw-Hill Book Co., New York, 1967.
13. MOOERS, N. F., and R. J. MATT. Evaluating an agricultural ball-bearing seal. Agr. Eng., *50*:582-585, Oct., 1969.
14. PEARCE, B. L. Chains. Mechanical Drives Reference Issue, Chapter 1. Machine Design, *39*(22):4-7, Sept. 21, 1967.
15. SAIBERLICH, E. W. Why telescoping PTO's don't telescope — easily. SAE J., *68*(1):49-50, Jan., 1960.
16. STEPHENS, C. A. Oil seals and lubricants. Agr. Eng., *46*:264-267, 275, May, 1965.
17. THUERMAN, J. H., and E. A. PAUL. Recent agricultural chain developments. Agr. Eng., *37*:613-617, Sept., 1956.
18. Universal Joint Layout and Selection Data Book. Rockwell-Standard Corp., 1964 (now North American Rockwell Corp., Detroit, Mich.).

PROBLEMS

3.1. An HB-section V-belt is to transmit 5 kW at a belt speed of 17 m/s. The included angle between the sides of the belt cross section is 38° and the belt density is 1.25 gm/cm^3. The arc of contact on the smaller sheave is 150°. Tensioning is accomplished by changing the position of an adjustable idler (not automatic).

(a) Calculate T_t and T_s.

(b) Calculate the centrifugal tension, T_c.

3.2. A V-belt drive has 2 sheaves with effective outside diameters of 125 mm and 348 mm. One shaft is to be movable for take-up and the desired center distance is about 460 mm.

(a) Using ASAE Standard S211 and the examples therein, select the best normally available *effective* belt length for an HA belt and determine the maximum and minimum center distances needed for installation and take-up.

(b) Calculate the r/min of the larger sheave if the smaller sheave turns at 1250 r/min.

3.3. Lay out to scale a variable-speed drive of the type shown in Fig. 3.6*b*. Assume that at one extreme of the speed range (shown in Fig. 3.6*b*), sheave pitch diameters, from top to bottom, are 152, 254, 137, and 229 mm; center distance from top sheave to adjustable-speed sheave = 460 mm; center distance from adjustable-speed sheave to lower sheave = 430 mm; and the angle between the 2 lines joining the 3 centers is 100°. Determine the path of movement of the adjustable-sheave shaft center that will keep the sum of the required belt lengths constant. Refer to ASAE Standard S211 for the method of determining the relation between belt length and center distance, or use graphical methods with a large scale. Plot at least four points along the path. State basic assumptions and indicate the procedure used.

3.4. A 330-mm-OD adjustable-pitch sheave, operating at a constant r/min, drives a 305-mm-OD adjustable-pitch sheave through an HK-section V-belt. The center distance between the shafts is fixed, as in Fig. 3.6*a*. Using dimensions given in Table 3.1, calculate the ratio of maximum r/min to minimum r/min for the driven sheave.

3.5. (a) Compute the theoretical percentage variation in speed of a chain as it leaves an 8-tooth sprocket rotating at a uniform speed.

(b) Repeat for an 18-tooth sprocket (which is about the minimum size normally recommended for high speeds).

3.6. A 9-tooth sprocket operating at 200 r/min drives a 23-tooth sprocket through No. 45 steel detachable-link chain. The pitch of this chain is 41.4 mm and the ultimate strength is 9.34 kN. Calculate:

(a) Average linear speed of chain, in metres per second.

(b) Recommended maximum power, in kilowatts.

(c) Average torque applied to the driven shaft when the recommended maximum power is being transmitted.

3.7. (a) Specify the location of a 2.38-mm flange-mounted steel shear pin $(S_s = 310$ MPa) which will fail at 4.5 kW when the speed is 650 r/min.

(b) What size diametral shear pin would be required if the shaft diameter is 25 mm?

3.8. The 2 universal joints of a pair are operating at joint angles of 30° and 22°, respectively. The input shaft, intermediate shaft, and output shaft are all in the same plane, and the yokes on the two ends of the intermediate shaft are in line.

(a) Calculate the lead or lag in each joint for each 15° increment of rotation of the *input* shaft, from 0 to 90°.

(b) Plot lead or lag versus degrees rotation of the input shaft, showing a curve for each joint and one for the system. On each joint curve, indicate where the peak occurs.

(c) What change might be made in this drive system to provide uniform rotation of the output shaft?

3.9. Let ω_1, ω_2, and ω_3 be the instantaneous angular velocities of the input, intermediate, and output shafts of a two-joint drive system.

(a) Assuming the 2 joints are 90° out of phase and have joint angles of α_1 and α_2, derive an expression for the maximum value of the velocity ratio ω_3/ω_1 during each cycle. At what value of ϕ_1 does the maximum ratio occur? (Note: will depend upon whether α_2 is larger or smaller than α_1.)

(b) Compare maximum velocity ratios at 30°, 50°, and 70° implement turn angles for the 2 systems represented in Table 3.3. In each case give the value of ϕ_1 at which the maximum ratio occurs.

3.10. (a) For each of the PTO drive arrangements shown in Fig. 3.15 and 3.16, calculate the amount of telescoping action required in turning the implement through a 90° angle.

(b) For each arrangement, determine the additional amount of telescoping required if the inside rear wheel of the tractor drops into a 300-mm ditch while the implement is turned at 90°. The tractor PTO shaft centerline is 200 mm above the level of the drawbar hitch point and the tractor rear wheel tread is 1.52 m. Assume all shafts remain horizontal.

4

Hydraulic Power Transmission and Implement Controls

4.1. Introduction. Hydraulic controls and actuators for adjusting the depth or position of implements and functional components have been used extensively for many years. Tractor hydraulic control systems are utilized for mounted or pull-type equipment, with remote cylinders for pull-type implements considered to be part of the tractor systems. Most types of self-propelled machines also have hydraulic control systems.

The implement designer needs to be familiar with the various types of hydraulic systems on tractors in order to utilize them to the best advantage. He should work with the tractor engineer to ensure maximum compatibility between the implement requirements and the tractor system. The implement designer has the full responsibility for any hydraulic systems employed on self-propelled machines.

Hydraulic control systems, in addition to providing conveniently located and easily operated control levers, are extremely flexible in regard to application possibilities. Hydraulic actuators (cylinders, motors, etc.) may be mounted in any desired location on the tractor or the implement, with oil being transmitted to and from them through flexible hoses. Depth or position can be changed easily and safely while the machine is moving, and the speed of changing is adjustable or controllable. With appropriate sensing devices, cylinders can be made to respond automatically to changes in some parameter, as in automatic control of implement draft or automatic control of the header height on a combine.

An electric remote-control system to replace certain hand functions on pull-type implements became commercially available in 1970.[15] This system is designed for low-force functions only, and is intended to supplement hydraulic controls. One application is on field choppers, where electric-motor-driven units can be utilized to rotate the delivery spout, change the spout deflector angle, and control the feed-roll drive. Performing operations of this type by hand from the tractor operator's station, through ropes, levers, or cranks, is awkward and hazardous at best and becomes difficult or impractical when the tractor is equipped with a cab. For low-force applications, electric actuators are said to be simpler, more compact, and less expensive than hydraulic controls and actuators.[15]

A major development in agricultural equipment during the 1960s was the application of hydrostatic propulsion drives to self-propelled machines and tractors and the increasing use of hydrostatic drives (hydraulic motors) for certain types of functional components on self-propelled harvesting equipment and on some pull-type implements.

Hydrostatic rotary drives provide stepless change of output speed under load, easy reversal of rotation, automatic overload protection with a simple pressure relief valve, and no damage from stalling the hydraulic motor. Hydraulic drives simplify the transmission of power to locations remote from the power source and are especially advantageous on machines with complex drive requirements. They are better than mechanical systems if the power-requiring unit must be movable through a wide range of positions with respect to the power source.

Hydraulic power transmission systems are more expensive than mechanical systems. Hence, they are used primarily in situations where some of the characteristics mentioned in the preceding paragraph are important enough to warrant the extra expense or where the annual use is relatively high. Hydraulic pumps and motors usually have efficiencies of 75 to 90%, but multiple-function *systems* can be extremely inefficient if the components are not properly balanced in regard to pressure and flow requirements. Low efficiencies are not serious for intermittent operation but they are of concern for continuous operation because of heat-dissipation requirements and the waste of engine power.

4.2. Basic Components of a Hydraulic System. In a *hydrostatic* power transmission system, energy is transmitted between the pump and one or more actuators in a closed path, usually at relatively high fluid pressures and relatively low velocities. Power inputs and outputs at a given flow rate are reflected as changes in fluid static pressure. By contrast, a *hydrodynamic* drive such as a torque converter involves high fluid velocities, and the energy transfer to the output unit comes mainly from changes in kinetic energy of the fluid. All hydraulic systems discussed in this chapter operate on the hydrostatic principle.

The basic elements of a hydraulic system include a reservoir, a pump, one or more actuators, control valves, and associated plumbing. With a fixed-displacement pump or a closed-loop system, one or more pressure relief valves are needed to protect system components. Relief valves are desirable for added protection when a pressure-compensated, variable-displacement pump is employed. Adequate filtration and the use of fluids having proper characteristics for hydraulic systems are important. When substantial amounts of power are to be transmitted continuously, heat exchangers are usually provided to cool the oil.

4.3. Types of Systems. The hydraulic systems employed on agricultural machines may be classified as

1. Constant-flow, variable-pressure systems.
2. Constant-pressure systems.
3. Variable-flow, variable-pressure systems.

In a constant-flow system, a fixed-displacement pump operates continuously, the output being bypassed back to the reservoir at low pressure when not needed for any function. The two usual bypass methods are through open-center valves and through pilot-operated bypass valves. When all the open-center valves in a circuit are in the neutral position, an open bypass from the pump back to the reservoir is provided through the valves. In the pilot-operated bypass arrangement, all control valves are of the closed-center type. When all valves are in the neutral position, the bypass valve opens to permit pump flow to the reservoir at a low pressure. This system is described in more detail in Section 4.14.

Most implements with hydraulic systems (other than hydrostatic propulsion drives) and most medium- and small-size tractors have constant-flow systems. This arrangement is simple and is well-adapted to systems involving intermittent performance of a limited number of control functions. The operating pressure is only as great as needed for a particular function at a particular time, and the pump operates at low load when not needed. However, when pump capacities are greater than 38 to 57 L/min [10 to 15 gpm], the pressure loss through the open-center valve or bypass valve may be sufficient to cause oil-heating problems. Most medium- and small-size tractors with constant-flow systems have pump capacities of 19 to 38 L/min [5 to 10 gpm]. Complications are introduced if two or more functions must be performed concurrently.

Constant-pressure systems are not common on implements, but are being used increasingly on the larger tractors. One method of maintaining an essentially constant system pressure is by means of a variable-displacement, pressure-compensated pump, usually of the radial-piston type (Section 4.4). The pump displacement (and hence its flow) changes in response to system pressure to meet the flow demands of the system while maintaining the predetermined system pressure. Another method involves a combination of an accumulator tank with compressed gas in the upper portion, a fixed-displacement pump, and an unloading-type bypass valve for the pump. With an accumulator system, the pressure varies between predetermined maximum and minimum pressures that may differ by 10 to 15%. The change in gas volume as oil is withdrawn or pumped in provides a finite storage capacity between the cut-in and cut-out pressures.

A constant-pressure system provides much greater flexibility than a constant-flow system, with simpler valving and circuits for multiple functions. The full pressure is available for any number of functions in parallel at any time, and one function does not affect the others. Response is fast, since pressure is always available. But whenever the pump is needed it must operate against the full system pressure even though the demand may be for only a low pressure. The throttling required to reduce the pressure to that needed by the actuator produces heat which must be dissipated and represents wasted energy.

Rated pressures for constant-flow, variable-pressure systems on tractors are mostly 8 to 14 MPa [1200 to 2000 psi]. Constant-pressure systems usually have rated pressures of 12 to 18 MPa [1800 to 2600 psi]. System relief valves are normally set about 25% higher than the rated pressure.

Variable-flow, variable-pressure systems are basically closed-loop arrangements, with oil recirculating between the pump and a motor. The flow is usually varied by changing the pump displacement but could be varied by changing the pump speed. The pressure adjusts itself to accommodate the motor load at any particular flow rate. The hydrostatic propulsion drive, which is discussed in Section 4.25, is an example of a closed-loop system.

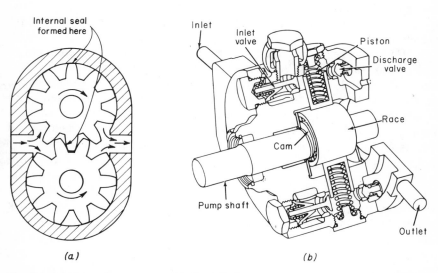

(a)   (b)

Fig. 4.1. (a) External-gear pump. (b) Fixed-displacement radial-piston pump with rotating cam. (b, courtesy of Deere & Co.)

4.4. Hydraulic Pumps. External-gear pumps (Fig. 4.1a) are widely used for rated system pressures up to about 14 MPa [2000 psi]. They are simple, compact, and much less expensive than piston pumps. The volumetric efficiency can be as high as 90% but may be substantially lower due to internal

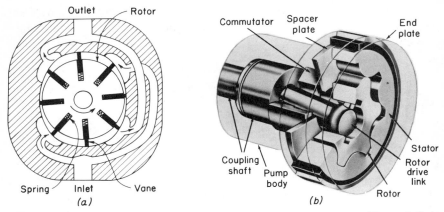

Fig. 4.2. *(a)* Balanced vane motor. *(b)* Internal-rotor gear motor. *(b*, courtesy of Deere & Co.)

leakage past the gears. Two other types of gear pumps have a gear within a gear (internal-gear type) or an internal gear-rotor similar to Fig. 4.2*b*. Vane pumps are sometimes used on agricultural equipment. They are similar to the vane motor shown in Fig. 4.2, except that vane springs are not needed.

Multiple-cylinder piston pumps are the usual choice when rated pressures are above 14 MPa [2000 psi]. They are seldom used at pressures below 10 MPa [1500 psi] because of their greater cost and complexity in comparison with gear or vane pumps. Piston pumps have high volumetric and overall efficiencies. Radial-piston pumps of the type shown in Fig. 4.1*b*, usually with 8 or 9 cylinders, are used in tractors having constant-pressure systems. An arrangement (not shown) that puts pressurized oil in the crankcase controls the piston stroke by holding the pistons away from the cam when less oil flow is needed, thus providing the variable-displacement feature.[9]

Axial-piston pumps may have the pistons parallel with the driving member (in-line type), or the housing and parallel cylinders may be angled from the driving member (bent-axis type). With the in-line type (Fig. 4.10), relative rotary motion between the tilted swashplate and the cylinder block causes the pistons to move in and out. The magnitude of the piston stroke depends upon the tilt of the swashplate. In a variable-displacement pump, the cylinder block rotates and the swashplate tilt is adjustable to permit changing the oil flow rate and direction of flow. A fixed-displacement pump has the swashplate at a fixed angle, similar to the motor shown in the right-hand portion of Fig. 4.10. Either the swashplate or the cylinder block may rotate. The principal application of axial-piston pumps on farm machines is in hydrostatic propulsion drives (Section 4.25).

4.5. Hydraulic Motors. Hydraulic motors convert fluid power to a rotary, mechanical output. Hydraulic motors are similar in design to hydraulic pumps and the same general types are available. Some units can be used interchangeably as motors or pumps. External-gear motors (similar to Fig. 4.1a), internal gear-rotor motors (Fig. 4.2b), and balanced vane motors (Fig. 4.2a) are common on implements utilizing hydraulic power to drive functional components.

Axial-piston motors are used in hydrostatic propulsion drives for self-propelled machines (Fig. 4.10). Like axial-piston pumps, they may have either fixed displacement or variable displacement. However, a variable-displacement motor is not reversible under load because the speed ratio would become infinite as the motor displacement approached zero. The minimum displacement is usually limited, by mechanical stops, to about half the maximum displacement.

The motor shown in Fig. 4.2b is a popular version of the internal-gear or rotor type that has high torque outputs and is suitable for operation at speeds as low as 10 r/min. The rotor has one tooth less than the stator and the profiles are such that each rotor tooth is always in contact with the stator, thus forming a continuous seal. As the rotor rolls around the inner periphery of the stator, "orbiting" around the shaft center, each tooth engagement and withdrawal results in a piston-like action. A commutator valve plate, rotating with the shaft, ports oil into and out of each space between stator teeth in phase with the withdrawal and engagement actions. Incoming oil under pressure forces the tooth withdrawal, thus causing rotation of the rotor and shaft.

Vane motors are usually of the balanced type as shown in Fig. 4.2a. An unbalanced motor has a circular rotor within an eccentric, circular housing and has only one inlet and one outlet. The difference between the inlet and outlet pressures causes an unbalanced force situation that puts heavy loads on the shaft bearings. The balanced version has 2 inlets 180° apart and 2 outlets. With either type, sliding vanes in the slotted rotor are held out against the housing by springs and centrifugal force. The springs are needed in a motor (but not in a pump) to provide sealing while the unit is getting up to speed. Incoming oil under pressure pushes against the vanes to cause rotation.

Selection of a motor type for a particular application involves consideration of factors such as the cost per kilowatt, pressure range, operating speed range, starting-torque characteristics, volumetric efficiency, overall efficiency, the need for reversibility, mass, and physical size. These and other factors are compared broadly in references 6, 7, and 9. In general, piston motors are the most efficient (85 to 95% overall), the most versatile, and the most costly type. Overall efficiencies are usually 60 to 90% for gear motors and 75 to 90% for vane motors.[9]

4.6. Directional Control Valves. Directional control valves start, stop, and direct fluid flow to cylinders, motors, and other actuators. Spool-type valves are widely used, primarily because of the great variety of valving arrange-

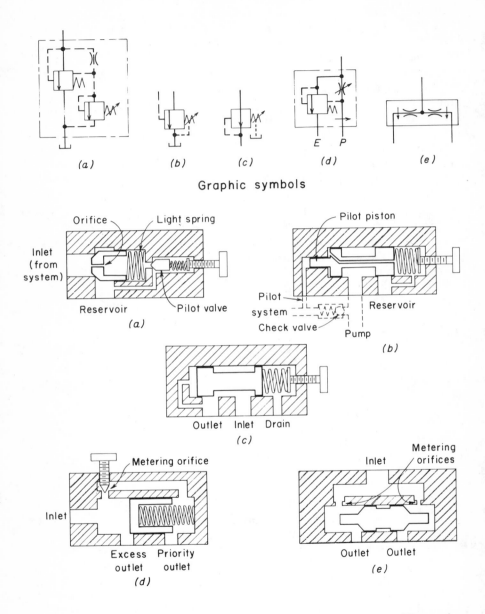

Graphic symbols

Fig. 4.3. *(a)* Pilot-operated relief valve. *(b)* Direct-acting unloading valve. *(c)* Direct-acting pressure-reducing valve. *(d)* Adjustable, pressure-compensated bypass or priority flow divider valve. *(e)* Pressure-compensated proportional flow divider valve. Any of these can be either adjustable or nonadjustable. Graphic symbols, shown at top, are discussed in Section 4.11.

ments which they offer and because they can be hydraulically balanced. Fluid flow between annular ports is controlled by lands on a sliding spool that cover and uncover the ports (Fig. 4.5 and 4.6). The land edges can be notched, tapered, or chamfered to permit feathered control at partial flow rates.

Spool valves must be accurately machined and fitted to minimize leakage past the spool. In multifunction systems, several valves may be stacked in a compact control package, as in Fig. 4.6. Valves may be actuated manually, mechanically, hydraulically, electrically, or pneumatically.

Check valves pass flow freely in one direction but do not permit flow in the opposite direction. Spring-loaded ball-type or poppet-type check valves are used extensively in hydraulic systems. A direct-acting ball-type check valve is shown in Fig. 4.3b. The spring is light so the opening pressure is not over 35 to 70 kPa [5 to 10 psi]. Pilot-operated check valves (Fig. 4.5) prevent reverse flow until the ball or poppet is unseated by pilot pressure from another part of the circuit, acting through a piston and push rod.

4.7. Pressure Control Valves. Relief valves limit the maximum pressure that can be developed in a hydraulic circuit. Direct-acting relief valves, such as the one shown in Fig. 4.5, are satisfactory for relatively low flow rates and infrequent operation. But with high flow rates the full-flow pressure is considerably higher than the "cracking pressure" because of the increased spring force as the valve opens wider.[9] This difference is known as pressure override and reduces the allowable system operating pressure for a given full-flow relief pressure.

A pilot-operated relief valve, such as the one shown in Fig. 4.3a, relieves over a wide flow range with very little pressure override, although the response is slower than with a direct-acting valve. The pilot section is a small, spring-loaded relief valve that controls the main valve. When the pilot valve is closed, the main valve is held closed by the light spring and by system pressure acting on the larger piston area at the spring end. When the system pressure rises enough to overcome the force of the pilot-valve spring and open the pilot valve, flow through the orifice creates a pressure drop across the piston. This pressure differential opens the main valve and holds it open until the system pressure drops and allows the pilot valve to close.

Figure 4.3b shows an unloading valve that is used to direct pump output back to the reservoir at low pressure when the system pressure is satisfied. The valve opens when the system pressure, transmitted to the pilot piston through the pilot port, is sufficient to overcome the force of the adjusting spring. A check valve, installed as shown by the broken-line portion of the drawing, holds the system pressure while the pump is bypassing. Accumulator systems employ a variation of this type of valve,[7] designed to provide the differential between cut-out and cut-in pressures that is needed for accumulator reserve capacity.

A pilot-operated unloading or bypass valve designed to respond to low pilot pressures is shown in Fig. 4.5. This type of arrangement is suitable for constant-volume systems, whereas unloading valves of the type described in the preceding paragraph are for constant-pressure applications.

When one part of a circuit is to be maintained at a constant pressure that is below the operating pressure in the main circuit, a direct-acting or pilot-operated pressure reducing valve usually is used. A direct-acting, adjustable valve that maintains constant reduced pressure is shown in Fig. 4.3c. This is a normally open valve. As the outlet pressure increases and approaches the preset control value, the spool moves against the spring force to restrict the outlet as required to maintain a constant outlet pressure.

A pressure sequence valve allows flow to a second cylinder or other limited-motion function only after the first one has been fully satisfied. The valve is placed in the supply line to the second function and is set to open at a pressure somewhat above that needed for the first function. Thus it directs flow to the second function only when the pressure rises after the first function has been completed. The most common application on agricultural equipment is in delayed-lift arrangements for front-mounted and rear-mounted cultivator tool bars on tractors. The simplest type is like an in-line check valve with a heavy spring. A reverse-free-flow check valve is needed in parallel with the sequence valve to permit flow in the opposite direction.

4.8. Flow Control Valves and Flow Divider Valves. Flow control devices are used to control actuator speeds by either restricting the flow or diverting the excess flow. Either method causes a pressure drop that is converted into heat and represents wasted energy. Manual valves and orifices are non-pressure-compensated restrictive devices, since the flow rate is related to the pressure drop. Nevertheless, needle valves and orifices are useful in many hydraulic-circuit situations. For example, a needle valve is used to control the lowering rate of mounted implements supported through a single-acting cylinder on the tractor rockshaft.

Figure 4.3d shows a pressure-compensated priority flow divider valve. It maintains a constant flow rate from the priority outlet, bypassing the excess to other functions in the system or to the reservoir. Pressure compensation is achieved by automatic operation of the balanced spool to maintain a constant pressure drop across the metering orifice. The pressure drop across the orifice is determined by the spool cross-sectional area and the spring force, and is relatively small. The regulated flow rate then depends upon the area of the metering orifice, which is adjustable in the example shown. Nonadjustable valves usually have the metering orifice through the spool. A pressure relief valve is often built into a priority valve to protect the priority circuit.

A common application for a priority valve is for the power-steering function in a multifunction hydraulic system. At low engine speeds most or all of the pump output may be needed for power steering. As the engine speed is increased, the power-steering flow remains constant (usually at some value between 8 and 11 L/min [2 and 3 gpm]) and the excess flow becomes available for other functions. In some systems, a valve of this type is employed to bypass excess flow back to the reservoir.

A restrictor-type, pressure-compensated flow control valve is similar to the valve shown in Fig. 4.3d except that there is no excess or bypass outlet (or this outlet is merely plugged). The inlet flow is controlled by throttling the outlet (the "priority" outlet, in Fig. 4.3d). If a restrictor valve is used in an open-center (constant-flow) system, any excess flow must be discharged through the relief valve, which means the pump must operate against relief pressure.

A pressure-compensated proportional flow divider takes a single flow and divides it between 2 outlets or functions in proportion to the areas of the 2 inlet metering orifices (Fig. 4.3e). The spool is in balance only when the pressure-drops through the two metering orifices are equal. The flow divider shown would direct about 75% of the flow to the right-hand outlet. With appropriate orifice sizes, the ratio could be anything from 50-50 to perhaps 90-10.[9]

4.9. Hydraulic Cylinders. Hydraulic cylinders may be either double-acting or single-acting. A double-acting cylinder (Fig. 4.5 and 4.7) is powered in both directions. Pressure oil enters at the blind end to extend it and at the rod end to retract it. Oil from the opposite end is returned to the reservoir or directed to some other series function. An effective seal around the piston rod must be provided at the rod end of the cylinder. For a given oil pressure, a greater force is exerted on the extending stroke than on the retracting stroke because the rod cross-sectional area subtracts from the effective piston area for the retracting stroke.

A single-acting cylinder can exert thrust only in the extending direction. For the retracting stroke, the control valve is opened to permit oil flow back to the reservoir and an external force such as the force of gravity on an implement, or some type of spring loading, causes the retracting movement. The rod end of the cylinder is vented to the atmosphere through a porous breather or filter that keeps out dirt and dust. A double-acting cylinder can be used as a single-acting cylinder by properly venting the rod-end port.

In some single-acting cylinders there is no piston on the end of the piston rod. Instead, the rod is only slightly smaller than the cylinder bore and the end of the rod serves as the piston. There is no piston seal, as is required with a piston-type cylinder. The only seal is at the rod end of the cylinder. No air vent is needed. This type of device is known as a *ram-type* cylinder.

4.10. Power, Work, and Speed Relations. At this point it may be helpful to review certain definitions and basic relations. Hydraulic power is the rate of fluid energy output from a pump or input to a motor. It may be determined from

$$\text{ph} = 0.01667 \, Q \, \Delta P \tag{4.1}$$

$$[\, \text{ph} = \frac{Q \, \Delta P}{1714} \,]$$

where ph = hydraulic power, in kilowatts [horsepower]
    Q = fluid flow rate, in litres per minute [gallons per minute]
    ΔP = pressure change, in megapascals [pounds force per square inch]

Shaft power (sp) is the mechanical input to a pump or output from a motor. The *overall* efficiency for a motor is 100 × sp/ph and for a pump is 100 × ph/sp. The *volumetric* efficiency of a motor is 100 × (theoretical flow rate, based on displacement and speed) ÷ (actual flow rate). The volumetric efficiency of a pump is 100 × (actual flow rate) ÷ (theoretical flow rate). *Mechanical* efficiency reflects losses due to internal friction, bearing friction, etc. Mechanical efficiency is equal to overall efficiency divided by volumetric efficiency.

The hydraulic power input to a motor, based on the difference between the motor inlet and outlet pressures, must be multiplied by the overall efficiency to obtain the useful power output (shaft power). The torque output is proportional to the motor displacement and mechanical efficiency and to the pressure drop across the motor. The speed is inversely proportional to the displacement per revolution and directly proportional to the motor's volumetric efficiency and to the oil flow rate.

The total work capacity of a cylinder, in kilojoules [foot-pounds-force], is

$$W = \Delta P \, ALE \tag{4.2}$$

$$[\, W = \Delta P \times A \times \frac{L}{12} \times \frac{E}{100} \,]$$

where A = effective piston area, in square centimetres [square inches] (cylinder cross-sectional area for extending stroke; cylinder area less rod area for retracting stroke)
    L = length of piston stroke, in millimetres [inches]
    E = cylinder efficiency, in percent (100 × ratio of mechanical-energy output to fluid-energy input)

The total time for extending or retracting a cylinder, in seconds, is

$$t = 0.0060 \frac{AL}{Q} \tag{4.3}$$

$$[\, t = \frac{60 \, AL}{231 \, Q} = 0.260 \frac{AL}{Q} \,]$$

Any pressure losses in the system that are not caused by a motor or other actuator represent power losses that are converted to heat and reduce the efficiency of the system. The pump efficiency must also be included in determining system efficiency.

4.11. Graphic Symbols. Graphic symbols for fluid-power diagrams have been standardized by the American National Standards Institute (ANSI)* and are used extensively for circuit representation. A partial listing of these (adopted in 1966) is included in Appendix D. These symbols are easy to draw and they emphasize the functions and methods of operation of components, rather than construction.

Symbols for five types of valves are shown in Fig. 4.3, supplementing those included in Appendix D. The symbols for valves *a, d* and *e* in Fig 4.3 are composites developed from basic symbols and rules in the ANSI standard. Pilot-operated valves such as *a* are often represented by the simpler symbols for direct-acting valves (shown in Appendix D). Simplified symbols of various types are also commonly employed for valve *d*.

Graphical representation may be combined with a cutaway or pictorial diagram if one wishes to emphasize the internal arrangement or functioning of particular components. Figure 4.5 shows a comparison between a schematic cutaway drawing and a graphical diagram.

HYDRAULIC CONTROL SYSTEMS

4.12. Single-Acting and Double-Acting Cylinders. Both single-acting and double-acting cylinders are used on tractors to control mounted implements. Most built-in lift systems have single-acting cylinders. With single-acting cylinders, the rate of downward movement of the implement is a function of the implement mass and inertia, the magnitude of vertical components of soil forces, and the resistance to flow of the oil being expelled from the cylinder. Lowering time is more consistent with a double-acting cylinder because of its positive action in either direction.

With a single-acting cylinder, an implement may be allowed to "float" (ie., seek its own depth or position) by merely locking the control valve in the lowering (open) position. A control valve for double-acting cylinders can be designed with a float position in which both cylinder ports are connected to the reservoir port. The lift linkage can be designed to provide a floating effect with either type of cylinder without requiring the piston to float.

Some pull-type implements, such as disk harrows, grain drills, land levelers, and others, require that the controlling device be able to exert force in either direction. Consequently, most cylinders intended for in-

---

*ANSI is the internationally recognized standardization organization for the United States.

terchangeable use on pull-type implements are of the double-acting type. Provision is often made to mount the same cylinder on pull-type implements and on the tractor for the control of mounted implements.

Single-acting cylinders are adequate for applications on self-propelled machines that involve lifting components such as headers and the picking units on various types of harvesters. There are also numerous situations where double-acting cylinders are required. Cylinders utilized on self-propelled machines have a considerable range of diameters and lengths to match the widely differing thrust and stroke needs.

4.13. Single-Cylinder Systems. Two basic single-cylinder systems are shown by graphic-symbol diagrams in Fig. 4.4. One is for a single-acting cylinder. Both are constant-flow systems with open-center valves — the most common arrangement for single-cylinder systems.

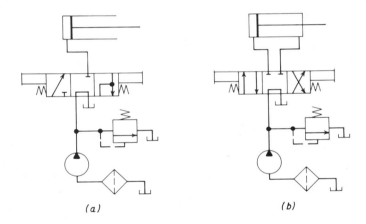

(a)   (b)

Fig. 4.4. Basic, single-cylinder, open-center hydraulic control systems, shown with manual control and spring-return to center position. *(a)* Single-acting cylinder and 3-way (3-port) control valve. *(b)* Double-acting cylinder and four-way control valve.

4.14. Parallel Cylinders in a Constant-Flow System. Most present-day tractors and most self-propelled machines that have hydraulic control systems have two or more individually controlled cylinders operated from the same pump. It is desirable and sometimes necessary to be able to operate two cylinders concurrently. If these cylinders were controlled by two parallel-connected, open-center valves like the ones in Fig. 4.4, it would be impossible to operate one cylinder alone because the pump output would all bypass through the other open-center valve.

One solution to this problem is to install a flow divider between the pump and the two parallel control valves. Then only a portion of the pump output would be bypassed through the inactive control valve and the remainder would go to the activated cylinder. Furthermore, if both cylinders were operated simultaneously, each would get only its proportion of the total flow, so both would move simultaneously and independently. But neither cylinder can ever receive more than its predetermined proportion of the pump output, and the pump must always bypass against the flow-divider

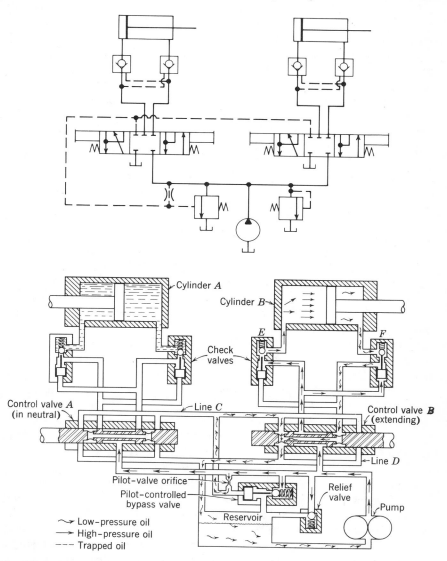

Fig. 4.5. Parallel-cylinder system with parallel control valves, a pilot-operated bypass valve, double-acting cylinders, and pilot-operated cylinder check valves.

pressure drop.

Another solution in a constant-flow system is to use parallel, closed-center valves with a pilot-operated bypass valve to permit the pump to operate at low pressure when all control valves are in neutral. Such a system is shown in Fig. 4.5. This same system works for more than two cylinders or for only one cylinder. The graphic-symbol diagram shows both valves in the "hold" or neutral position. In the schematic cutaway drawing, control valve *A* is shown in the neutral position and valve *B* is in the "extend" position.

As long as one or more of the control valves in such a system is held in an operating position (as shown for valve *B*), there is a direct passage from pilot line *C* to return line *D* and back to the reservoir. Because the small-diameter pilot-valve orifice greatly restricts the flow to line *C*, the pressure on the bypass-valve piston is low and the spring holds the bypass valve closed.

When all control valves are returned to neutral, there is no longer any passage from line *C* to line *D*. Then, since there is no flow through the pilot-valve orifice, the pressure on the bypass-valve piston becomes equal to that in the pump discharge line. Since the piston area is several times that of the ball seat, the valve opens and remains open under low pressure until one or more of the control valves is moved from neutral and again opens line *C* to line *D*.

Cylinders in parallel can also be controlled independently by a stacked, series-parallel arrangement of open-center valves. Such an arrangement, with two identical valve units clamped together between header plates, is illustrated in Fig. 4.6. One valve may be removed or more may be added. Valve *A* is shown in the neutral position, whereas valve *B* has been moved to the right to operate cylinder *B*. When all valves are in neutral, the pump output flows through the open-center passages in series and thence back to the reservoir. When any valve is moved from neutral, the bypass path is closed (as shown for valve *B*) and oil under pressure becomes available to this cylinder and to cylinders connected to any other valves that might be operated simultaneously. Thus, while the valves are in series when bypassing the oil from the pump to the reservoir (i.e., all valves in neutral), the simultaneous operation of two or more cylinders is in parallel.

The series-parallel arrangement with stacked valves is quite common on farm equipment. The parallel valves shown separately in Fig. 4.5 can also be stacked, but this arrangement is found mostly on tractors.

If only one control valve of a parallel-cylinder system without flow dividers is operated at any particular time, the behavior is identical with that of a single-cylinder system. The full pump output is available to the cylinder. If two or more control valves are operated at the same time, with unrestricted flow to all cylinders, the one with the lowest pressure requirement will be moved first. The other cylinder or cylinders cannot operate until the system pressure rises after the first cylinder reaches the end of its stroke. In actual

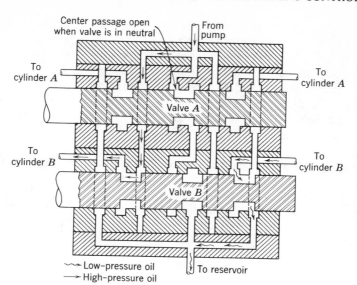

Fig. 4.6. Stacked, series arrangement of open-center valves for operating cylinders in parallel.

practice, an expert operator can obtain simultaneous motion of two cylinders by feathering (throttling) one or both control valves to restrict the flows.

Headers on combines and self-propelled windrowers usually have two parallel cylinders controlled by the same valve. In this type of application, torsional rigidity of the unit being lifted, or an interconnecting torsional member, ensures simultaneous, equal movements of the two cylinders.

In parallel-cylinder operation, the total oil displacement or overall piston travel time is equal to the sum of the values for the individual cylinders, regardless of whether or not the pistons move simultaneously. But the full rated system pressure is available for each cylinder if needed.

4.15. Cylinders in Series. Selective control of individual, double-acting cylinders in a multicylinder system can also be obtained by a series arrangement of open-center control valves, in which the pump is connected to the input side of only the first valve. The return line from each valve is connected to the input side of the next valve in the series, this being the only interconnection between valves. The return line from the last valve goes to the reservoir. A stacked arrangement of valves can be used, or the valves may be physically separated.

With this arrangement, the pump output will be bypassed through all valves in series as long as they are all in the neutral position. If any one valve is moved from neutral to extend or retract its cylinder, the system behaves like a single-cylinder system. If two or more control valves are operated at the same time, a series arrangement of the cylinders is obtained, with positive simultaneous movement of the pistons. The oil from the low-pressure side of one cylinder is forced through the control valve into the high-pressure side of the next cylinder being operated. The oil from the low-pressure side of the last cylinder in the series is returned to the reservoir.

When two or more cylinders operate in series, the rate of movement of the first piston is the same as it would be for a comparable single-cylinder system and the relative movements of any two successive cylinders are inversely proportional to the effective cross-sectional areas of the interconnected sides. If two equal-diameter cylinders have the rod end of one connected to the blind end of the next one while being extended, the latter will move more slowly because the effective cross-sectional area is greater.

The total pressure required for a series system is the sum of the pressure differentials required by the individual cylinders, plus line friction losses. The pressure differential required for any one cylinder, neglecting cylinder friction losses, may be determined from the relation,

$$P_i A_i = P_o A_o + 10\,T \qquad (4.4)$$

$$[\,P_i A_i = P_o A_o + T\,]$$

where P_i = cylinder inlet pressure, megapascals [pounds force per square inch]

P_o = cylinder outlet pressure, megapascals [pounds force per square inch]

A_i = effective piston area at inlet end, square centimetres [square inches]

A_o = effective piston area at outlet end, square centimetres [square inches]

T = cylinder thrust force, kilonewtons [pounds force]

To determine the required system pressure, one must start with the downstream cylinder, assuming P_o for that cylinder is zero (or some value that represents friction loss in the return line to the reservoir). The calculated P_i for the last cylinder then becomes P_o for the next cylinder upstream if friction loss in the connecting lines is neglected.

4.16. Series Cylinders with a Single Control Valve. Matched, series cylinders provide an excellent means for controlling the depth of wide, multi-section, pull-type implements.[11] The sections are hinged together and the depth of each section is controlled by a separate cylinder acting against the support wheels for the center section or against outrigger gage wheels for the additional sections. The cylinders are connected in series, with the rod end of each double-acting cylinder passing oil to the blind end of the next cylinder on the lifting stroke, thus producing positive, simultaneous movement of all cylinders. The inlet to the first cylinder and the outlet from the last one are connected to the tractor hydraulic remote control outlets.

Bore sizes are progressively smaller so the rod-end effective piston area of each cylinder matches the blind-end piston area of the next cylinder. Thus the rates of extending or retracting are the same for all cylinders. The full stroke lengths are equal also. A bypass orifice from each cylinder's bore into its rod-end port is located so the piston seal passes and uncovers it just before the piston reaches the end of the extending stroke. This arrangement permits a small amount of oil to bypass from one cylinder to the next when the cylinders are fully extended and the control valve is still in the "lift" position, thus initially purging any air and subsequently resynchronizing the cylinders each time the implement is fully raised. A limit stop on the largest cylinder will control the depth at all cylinders.

A similar arrangement has been applied for depth control or automatic draft control of wide, single-section mounted implements.[12] Matched, series cylinders on two outrigger wheels are connected in series with the tractor's built-in rockshaft cylinder and operate in a manner similar to that described above. Hydraulic lifts for combine header reels employ two matched, series cylinders to obtain equal height adjustments for both ends.

4.17. Multiple Cylinders in a Constant-Pressure System. With a constant-pressure hydraulic system, any number of cylinders or other functions can be operated concurrently, in parallel. Each will be independent of the others as long as the system's flow capacity is not exceeded. The full system pressure is available for each cylinder, and the flow rate is limited by fixed restrictions, flow control valves, or throttling with the main control valve. The energy represented by the difference between the system pressure and the required cylinder pressure is converted to heat and wasted. The principal application of constant-pressure systems has been on tractors.

4.18. Cylinder Check Valves. A system with pilot-operated check valves in the oil lines between the main control valve and the power cylinder is illustrated in Fig. 4.5. While cylinder B is extending, check valve E operates in the normal manner, but check valve F must be held open by pilot pressure from the high-presure end of the cylinder to permit oil to leave the low-pressure end.

Check valves of this type prevent cylinder creep due to leakage past the valve spools and they protect against the load dropping because of pressure loss if a second, parallel cylinder is actuated while the first one is still actuated. They also provide a safety feature for operators and other persons because it is impossible to lower an implement or component by merely moving the control lever when the oil pump in a constant-flow, variable-pressure system is not operating.

A pilot-operated check valve is adaptable to a single-acting cylinder if a four-way control valve is used so it can apply pressure to the check-valve piston when the control lever is moved to the "retract" position.

4.19. Nudging-Type Hydraulic Controls. In a limit-control or nudging system, a cylinder is activated to raise or lower an implement or perform some other function by moving the control lever to either side of its neutral position. The piston in the cylinder continues to move until the lever is returned to neutral or until the travel is limited by a stop or by the piston reaching the end of its full stroke. The control arrangements shown in Fig. 4.4 are for nudging systems. Note that the control-valve spools are spring-centered.

Implement depth or component position is controlled by quickly returning the lever to neutral when visual observation indicates that the desired depth or position has been reached. Incremental changes are made by momentarily "nudging" the lever from its neutral position. Most cylinder controls on self-propelled implements are of the nudging type.

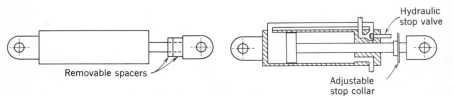

Fig. 4.7. Two arrangements for limiting the retracting stroke of hydraulic cylinders in nudging-type control systems.

Tractor remote cylinders for use on either pull-type or mounted implements may have stops of various types to limit the piston travel on the retracting stroke and thus predetermine a working depth for the implement. The common arrangements include (a) mechanical stop on the cylinder (Fig. 4.7 *left*), (b) hydraulic shut-off actuated by piston movement (Fig. 4.7 *right*), and (c) electric remote control of solenoid-operated hydraulic valves, with adjustable, electrical limit switches on the cylinder or linkage. All of these systems are adjustable but a change of stop setting usually involves halting the implement and raising it slightly to free the stop.

Nudging-type systems on tractors frequently have a detent arrangement to hold the control valve in either of its extreme positions while the implement is being raised or lowered, thus freeing the operator's hand for other purposes. When the piston reaches the limit of its travel, the detent is released automatically by hydraulic or mechanical means, and spring action returns the control valve to neutral. It can also be returned to neutral at any time by hand. Control levers sometimes have an intermediate, indexed position between neutral and each extreme, which provides slow-speed movement of the piston for making small changes in depth adjustment.

4.20. Automatic Position Control Systems on Tractors. Virtually all tractors with hitches for mounted implements have built-in lift systems with automatic position control. In this type of control system, any given position of the control lever in its quadrant represents a specific position or depth of the implement. Thus the operator can preselect and identify an implement position by the location of the hand lever, and the cylinder will automatically move the implement to the corresponding position or depth.

The basic linkage for an automatic position system is indicated in Fig. 4.8a. The solid outlines represent a stabilized condition, the control valve being in neutral. If the control lever is then moved from *A* to *A'*, joint *C* is moved to the left while joint *E* momentarily remains in the same position, thus moving *D* and the control-valve spool to the left. This actuates the power cylinder, which raises the implement until *D* is returned to the neutral position.

With the control valve again in neutral, the new position of the lift arms and connecting linkage is as shown by the broken-line outlines. Similarly, moving the control lever in the opposite direction results in lowering of the implement. In effect, *D* acts as a pivot point in determining the relative equilibrium positions of the control lever and the implement.

Theoretically, automatic position control can be applied to any type of cylinder and control-valve arrangement. But since a mechanical interconnection between the control lever and the piston or implement linkage is required, automatic position control is most readily adapted to mounted implements.

4.21. Automatic Draft Control. With automatic draft control, the position of the hand lever represents a given implement draft rather than a par-

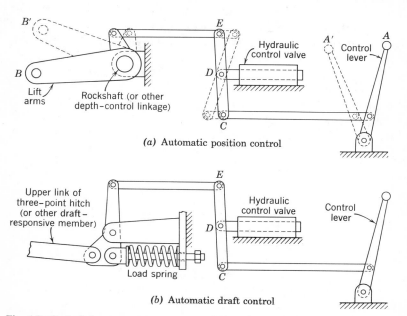

(a) Automatic position control

(b) Automatic draft control

Fig. 4.8. Basic linkage arrangements for automatic position control and automatic draft control.

ticular depth. Variations in draft cause the implement to be raised or lowered automatically as required to restore the draft to the preselected value.

As indicated in Fig. 4.8b, the linkage for automatic draft control is similar to that for automatic position control except that the top end of equalizer link CE is moved in response to deflection of the load spring rather than by movement of the implement lift linkage. With the control lever in a given position, any change in draft changes the amount of deflection of the load spring, thus moving the control valve from its neutral position, D. The hydraulic system then acts to change the implement depth as required to restore the draft and load-spring deflection to the preselected values and thus return the control valve to neutral.

In the arrangement illustrated, the draft-sensing member is always in compression. It is evident that, for any given position of the control lever, there is only one compressed length of the load spring that will bring the control valve to neutral. But if the control lever is moved to the left in Fig. 4.8b, less compression of the load spring, and hence less draft, is required for equilibrium.

With the larger sizes of tractors, mounted equipment may extend quite a distance to the rear and the upper link of a three-point hitch is likely to be in tension part of the time. Lower-link sensing is generally employed in such cases, although systems on some tractors can respond to either tension or compression in the upper link. Sensing torque in the tractor-wheel driveline is a recent development for automatically controlling the draft of mounted, semimounted, or pull-type implements.[19]

Most tractors with automatic position control also have automatic draft control. In some cases, the operator selects one or the other by merely moving an auxiliary lever. Other tractors have a combination of draft control and position control in which the load-spring linkage and lift linkage are interconnected by an equalizer link so they both affect the control valve. The result is a compromise between a constant implement depth and constant draft. The relative degree of control from these two parameters may or may not be adjustable.

4.22. Automatic Controls on Implements. Hydraulic control systems provide an excellent base for automatic control of certain parameters on implements. In general, these include attitude or slope (self-leveling combines), height, lateral position (automatic guidance), and performance (combine loading). The sensing device is on the implement. The tractor's hydraulic system may provide the control power for pull-type or mounted implements, or a separate system may be provided on the implement. Self-propelled machines, of course, have their own hydraulic systems.

The signal from the sensing device is transmitted to a hydraulic control valve, usually either through direct mechanical connection or electrically to a solenoid-operated control valve. The control valve then actuates a cylinder to move the machine component in the proper direction to reduce or eliminate the error signal. Minimum time lapse between the change in the control-parameter value and sensing of the change is desirable. This involves locating the sensor close to the point where the changes occur.

Two-point controllers (sensing devices) continually call for either a positive or a negative correction. Three-point controllers have a neutral or dead zone between the two correction zones. In either type, the response rate may be constant or it may be related to the magnitude of the error signal. A solenoid-operated control valve usually provides a constant response rate, whereas direct mechanical actuation of a control valve can give proportional response. Dynamic response characteristics must be considered in relation to response rates. Damping may be needed to minimize cycling.

One of the first commercial applications of automatic controls on implements was in self-leveling hillside combines, during the early 1950s. In this type of application, sensitivity, speed of response, stability, and adequate safety devices for protection in malfunction situations are all extremely important considerations. Specially designed four-way control valves had to be developed and manufactured to extremely close tolerances for a model that has a damped pendulum as the sensing device and provides both lateral and fore-and-aft leveling.

Considerable attention is being given to the automatic control of feed rates into combines to minimize seed losses due to overloading.[5,8] Automatic height control is being applied to combine headers,[3] cotton pickers and strippers,[17] and other harvesting equipment. In some European countries, height sensors have been applied to mounted plows to control depth.[2] When the field surface is uneven, these give more uniform depth than the tractor's automatic position control system because the sensor can be placed close to the plow bottoms. Automatic guidance systems for pull-type sugar beet harvesters have been developed to keep the root-lifting wheels or blades centered on the row and thus reduce losses.[2,13]

Most automatic controls on implements are for open-center hydraulic systems. However, control valves suitable for height sensing with the constant-pressure hydraulic systems common on the larger tractors have been developed.[17]

4.23. Standardization of Tractor Remote Cylinders for Pull-Type Implements. Remote cylinders used for the control of pull-type implements are considered to be part of the tractor hydraulic system. To permit interchangeable use on various makes of pull-type implements, an ASAE-SAE standard was developed. This standard[1] specifies cylinder mounting and operating dimensions, maximum cylinder outline dimensions, clearance allowances required on implements, and hose-length requirements.

Cylinders with a 203-mm [8-in.] stroke are specified for tractors having up to 60 maximum drawbar kilowatts [80 hp]. Cylinders for tractors with over 60 kW may have either a 203-mm or 406-mm [8-in. or 16-in.] stroke. Full-stroke operating times at maximum full-load engine speed are to be 1½ to 2 s for 203-mm-stroke cylinders and 3 to 4 s for 406-mm-stroke cylinders. The thrust capacity with either size cylinder is to be at least 500 N per maximum drawbar kilowatt [150 lbf/hp]. At the specified full-stroke operating times, this thrust represents 9 to 12% of the maximum drawbar power.

Implements are to be raised, or disk harrows deangled, on the extending stroke. Stops needed for variable-stroke control are to be incorporated in the cylinder or hydraulic system, rather than being part of the implement, and are to be applied to the retracting stroke.

4.24. Designing Lift Linkages for Pull-Type Implements. The tractor engineer has the responsibility for providing a hydraulic control system that will develop the minimum cylinder thrusts specified in the ASAE-SAE standard. The implement designer should be concerned with minimizing peak lifting loads, keeping these loads within the available capacity of the power lift, and generally making the most effective use of the control system.

In designing a lift linkage, the engineer should remember that the total *work* capacity of a hydraulic cylinder is primarily a function of the effective piston area, the available system pressure, the length of stroke, and friction losses in the hydraulic system and cylinder. The lifting time, on the other hand, is related to the piston displacement and the pump capacity at the required lifting pressure. The operating times specified in the ASAE-SAE standard represent a compromise between high power requirements of rapid lifting and greater travel distances for slower lifting.

The total work (or the average force for a cylinder with a given stroke) required to lift an implement is influenced by the lifted mass of the implement, the soil reaction, friction in the linkage, inertia forces and surges, and the height of lift. The ideal linkage, from the standpoint of the hydraulic system, would be such as to require a constant cylinder thrust throughout the stroke, at least under extreme load conditions. This would give maximum work output with minimum pressures. Frequently, however, the initial design of a linkage results in high peak forces during some portion of the cycle, as illustrated by the work diagram shown in Fig. 4.9.

Assuming it is desired to take corrective measures to obtain a more uniform thrust requirement throughout the stroke, the first steps are to determine, either graphically or experimentally, the relation of implement lift to piston travel and to plot the results. Then divide the piston travel into equal increments on the graph and measure the area under the cylinder thrust curve (i.e., the work) for each increment and for the full piston travel.

The average height of the work curve (total area divided by total piston stroke) represents the desired uniform thrust. Dividing each increment of work area by this average thrust gives the theoretical portion of the piston

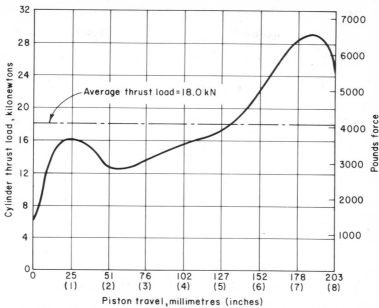

Fig. 4.9. Work diagram for lifting a 3-bottom 41-cm moldboard plow stalled in hard ground. The first peak is attributed to the load required to break ground, and the high peak near the end is due to increased lifting rates as slack in the rear furrow-wheel linkage is taken up. (R.D. Barrett. Agr. Eng., Oct., 1949.)

stroke that should be used for the amount of implement lift represented by the original increment of piston travel.

As an example, take 25-mm increments of piston travel for the work diagram in Fig. 4.9. Assume that with the existing linkage the curve of implement lift versus piston travel indicates that the implement is lifted 23 mm during the first 25 mm of piston travel and an additional 31 mm during the next 25-mm increment. Dividing the measured work areas for these first 2 increments by the average thrust (18.0 kN) indicates that only 18 mm of piston travel should be used in lifting the implement through this first step of 23 mm, and 21 mm of piston travel for the second lift step of 31 mm.

Thus a piston travel of 18 mm for a lift of 23 mm represents one point on the ideal lift curve, and a total piston travel of 39 mm for a total lift of 54 mm represents the next point. Similar treatment of successive increments will yield a complete ideal curve, against which the results of proposed modifications in the linkage can be compared.

If the uniform thrust obtained by redesigning the linkage still exceeds the available capacity, additional corrective measures that may be taken include (a) reduction of total friction in the linkage, (b) reduction of total lift height, (c) reduction of implement mass, (d) elimination of unnecessary horizontal movement of the implement in the soil, resulting from the lifting action, and (e) use of auxiliary springs.

Most tillage implements require more thrust to lift them when stopped than when traveling, the increase being as much as 50 to 100% for some implements.[20] It is generally assumed that the *rated* pressure of the hydraulic system should not be exceeded while lifting a traveling implement, but that the full relief pressure can be considered as available for the occasional instances when a stalled implement must be raised.[20] This gives an additional available thrust of perhaps 25% for such emergencies.

Where power-control loads are light so that uniformity of thrust is not important, it is possible to incorporate other desirable features into the system. For example, greater fineness of control for a tillage implement can be obtained by arranging the linkage to give a low lift rate in the range of usual working depths. If, on the other hand, a quick lift is desired, as for a mower cutterbar, the design can be such as to utilize only a portion of the piston stroke for the full lift.

HYDRAULIC POWER TRANSMISSION

4.25. Hydrostatic Propulsion Drives. The most common type of hydrostatic propulsion drive found on agricultural equipment consists of a variable-displacement axial-piston pump driving a fixed-displacement or variable-displacement axial-piston motor in a closed-loop circuit. Axial-piston pumps permit simple, positive control of the variable displacement. Axial-piston motors provide good reversibility and, if desired, may have variable-displacement control. Piston-type pumps and motors have higher volumetric and overall efficiencies than other types.

The closed-loop feature means that the oil is recirculated between the pump and motor in a closed path without passing through the reservoir. Low-side pressure is maintained at 1.0 to 1.4 MPa [150 to 200 psi] by a charging pump that also bypasses a small percentage of the main oil flow through a cooler and a supply reservoir.

Figure 4.10 shows a hydrostatic drive system having a fixed-displacement motor. The charge-pump output enters the closed loop at whichever port of the variable-displacement pump is the inlet (depending on the direction of motor rotation) and the excess leaves the loop at the motor through the charge-pressure control valve. The shuttle valve automatically connects the low-pressure side of the loop (which may be either leg) to the charge-pressure control valve. Free-flow oil from the charge-pressure control valve circulates through the motor and pump housings to cool them, then through a heat exchanger to cool the oil, and finally into the reservoir.

Two servo cylinders change the swashplate angle to increase or decrease the pump displacement or reverse the flow, in response to changes in the

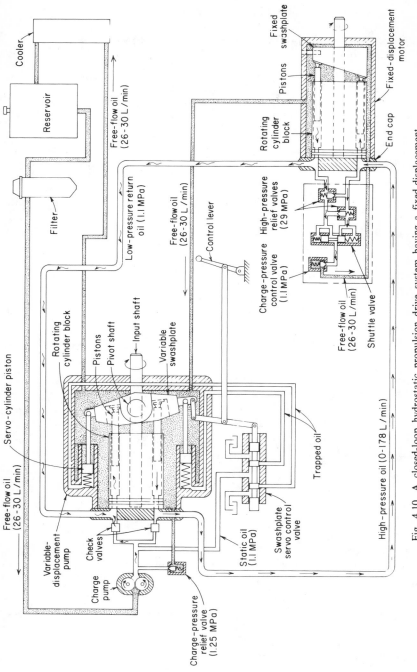

Fig. 4.10. A closed-loop hydrostatic propulsion drive system having a fixed-displacement motor. (**B.F.** Vogelaar.[18])

control-lever position. The servo control has a built-in centering device for the neutral position with some degree of free movement to eliminate the need for precise positioning of the control lever for zero speed. Oil supplying the energy for the servo control comes from the charge pump through a four-way control valve. The control action is similar to that in automatic position control systems on tractors, as described in Section 4.20.

Hydrostatic propulsion drives first became commercially available on self-propelled combines in 1965.[14,18] Within less than 5 years nearly all combine manufacturers in the United States had hydrostatic drives available on one or more models and hydrostatic drives were common on self-propelled windrowers. Some advantages of hydrostatic propulsion drives in comparison with other types of drives are

1. They provide infinitely variable speed control from full reverse to full forward, under load, with a single control lever. No separate clutch is needed.
2. The closed-loop feature provides positive speed control under all conditions. The ground speed at any control-lever setting is essentially constant, regardless of positive or negative propulsion power requirements.
3. They provide dynamic braking when moving and static braking in neutral.
4. The control is position-responsive (i.e., speed is related to lever position).

Hydrostatic drives are less efficient than full mechanical power transmission systems, especially under reduced loading.[18] This characteristic, however, is not of great consequence in combines because usually the major portion of the engine output is required to drive functional components. Most other self-propelled machines have relatively low propulsion power requirements in comparison with tractors providing drawbar power. Hydrostatic drives are more expensive than other types, but costs are being reduced by improved technology and by increased production as their use expands.

Whereas the torque available from a variable-speed mechanical drive increases as the output speed is reduced, the maximum torque from a hydraulic motor is limited by the relief pressure and remains essentially constant as the speed is reduced. For this reason, a multispeed, gear-type transmission is usually used in conjunction with the hydraulic motor on combine drives. Although the full speed range down to zero can be obtained in the highest transmission gear, the use of a lower gear for low forward speeds increases the available torque. For a given low-speed maximum torque requirement, the use of a multispeed mechanical transmission permits the use of a smaller pump and a smaller motor.[18]

Self-propelled windrowers need to be able to reverse one drive wheel while the other one is still moving forward, in order to make square turns. This is accomplished by having two hydrostatic drive systems, one for each wheel.[4] Controls for the two variable-displacement pumps are interconnected to permit changing both speeds either equally or differentially. The motors also have variable displacement, with the minimum displacement (about half of the maximum) being employed to obtain road speeds.

When a hydrostatic drive has a variable-displacement motor, it is desirable to have the controls arranged so the motor displacement cannot be reduced until the pump displacement is at its maximum adjustment. A hydrostatic drive can have 2 parallel-connected motors at the 2 drive wheels, driven from a single pump. This arrangement eliminates the differential gears and drive axles. Hydraulic motorized wheels, with radial-piston or rotor-type motors built into the hubs and having bolt circles to take standard vehicle disk wheels, are commercially available.

In common usage, the term "hydrostatic propulsion drive" refers to the type of drive described in the preceding paragraphs. Another type of propulsion drive that is much less expensive has a fixed-displacement pump driving a fixed-displacement motor in an open-loop circuit. Speed is controlled by means of an adjustable bypass flow divider or with an adjustable flow regulator valve in parallel with the motor as in Fig. 4.11. Speed control is not as smooth or as positive as with a closed-loop system. The motor can overrun the pump (i.e., no braking action) unless a suitable restriction or pressure control is provided between the motor outlet and the reservoir.

4.26. Hydraulic Power Transmission in Multifunction Systems. If a hydraulic system includes both motors and cylinders but requires only intermittent operation of the motors and only one function at any one time, a simple, open-center circuit with series-parallel valves is satisfactory. But if one or more motors are to be operated continuously, or if two or more functions must be operated simultaneously, flow dividers or flow regulators are needed. If no more than 2 or 3 functions are involved, these might be operated in series, provided their flow requirements were the same and the sum of their pressure requirements did not exceed the rated pressure for the system.

The pump for a system having several functions in parallel must have enough capacity to meet the total needs for all components that might be operated at any one time. The components should be selected such that their required operating pressures match as closely as possible, because the pump must always deliver its full flow capacity against the highest pressure required by any function that is being operated. Excess pressure not needed for other functions operated at the same time must be absorbed by throttling.

When a system includes continuously operating motors, it is often advantageous to divide it into two or more independent circuits with a separate

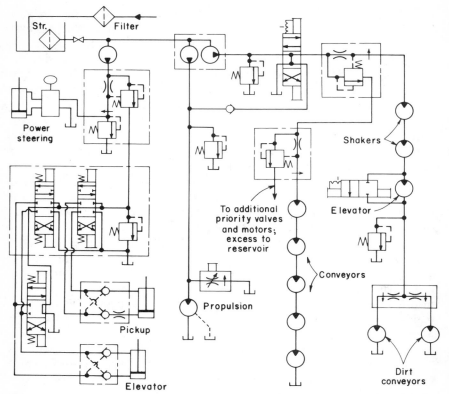

Fig. 4.11. Multifunction hydraulic system for a self-propelled tomato harvester. (Courtesy of FMC Corp.)

pump for each (but usually with a common reservoir). Tandem gear or vane pumps, with two or more pumping units in the same housing and on the same shaft, are available for this purpose. Single pumps may also be used. Each motor is connected to a separate pump which automatically adjusts its discharge pressure to the motor needs (up to the relief pressure). Motor speed can be controlled by a bypass flow divider without affecting any other components of the system.

Two or more motors loaded in proportion to their ratings might be operated in parallel from the same pump, provided the loads maintain a reasonably constant relationship and moderate speed variations can be tolerated. In most cases all cylinders in a system would be served by one pump.

Hydraulic motors are sometimes connected in series for driving conveyors that operate in sequence. This arrangement ensures approximate synchronization of speeds even though the loads vary. If one motor stalls because of an overload or stops for any other reason, all conveyors in the system are automatically stopped. To produce a given torque at a given speed, 2 series-connected motors would need to be twice as large as 2 parallel motors because of the smaller pressure differential across each motor.

Figure 4.11 shows the circuit diagram for a multifunction system having three pumps. One pump is for power steering and the lift cylinders, one is for the propulsion drive, and the third supplies all other motors. The output from the third pump can be directed to the propulsion motor for increased road-travel speeds. Note the groups of series motors supplied through priority flow dividers, the parallel dirt-conveyor motors supplied through a proportional flow divider, and the series-priority arrangement of the three directional control valves for the lift cylinders.

4.27. Tractor Hydraulic Remote Motors. For many years the principal function of hydraulic systems on agricultural tractors was to provide energy for tractor control functions and implement controls. But as hydraulic control functions have expanded and system capacities increased, tractor hydraulic systems have become more important as a significant potential means of utilizing engine power. Since most tractors have outlets for connecting remote cylinders, it is only logical that consideration be given to providing remote motors that can be connected to these same outlets.

As a first step, an ASAE standard for remote hydraulic motors[1] was adopted in 1968. The motor is considered to be part of the tractor. Hose lengths are to permit mounting the motor anywhere within a specified spherical radius from the tractor drawbar hitch point. Mounting dimensions and shaft sizes are specified. The rated operating speed is 1000 r/min, corresponding to the higher standard speed for mechanical power-take-off drives. Motors are to be reversible and have variable speed control. Minimum motor outputs are to be 3.7, 7.5, and 11.2 kW [5, 10, and 15 hp] for 3 tractor size ranges, at 80% of minimum relief pressure. These minimum capacities represent 10 to 25% of the maximum drawbar power.

For certain implement applications that are within the limited power capabilities of tractor hydraulic remote motors, this type of drive offers significant advantages over mechanical PTO drives or small engines in regard to versatility, compactness, and ease of variable speed control. More heat-dissipation capability is needed for continuous motor operation than for intermittent operation of cylinders and other tractor control functions. Although many tractor hydraulic systems are now designed to permit remote motor operation, others do not have adequate oil-cooling capacity for continuous operation of motors.

REFERENCES

1. Agricultural Engineers Yearbook, 1976, pp. 224-228. ASAE, St. Joseph, Mich.

2. BATEL, W., and R. THIEL. Automatic control of agricultural machines. Grundl. Landtech., Heft *14*:5-13, 1962. NIAE transl. 206.
3. BREDFELT, R. T. Automatic header height control for self-propelled combines. Agr. Eng., *49*:666-667, Nov., 1968.
4. CASE, C. Development of a hydrostatic driven windrower. ASAE Paper 67-676, Dec., 1967.
5. EIMER, M. Progress report on automatic controls in combine-harvesters. Grundl. Landtech., *16*:41-50, 1966. NIAE transl. 207.
6. Farm Equipment Hydraulics. Reprint of seven articles published from Jan. 7, 1966 through Apr. 7, 1966. Implement & Tractor.
7. Fluid Power Handbook and Directory. Industrial Publishing Co., Cleveland, Ohio, 1969.
8. FRIESEN, O. H., G. C. ZOERB, and F. W. BIGSBY. For combines: controlling feed rates automatically. Agr. Eng., *47*:434-435, Aug., 1966.
9. Fundamentals of Service — Hydraulics. Deere & Co., Moline, Ill., 1967.
10. HERSHMAN, G. L. Tractor hydraulics — good field, no hit. SAE Trans., *66*:612-619, 1958.
11. HOOK, R. W. Hydraulic depth control of multi-section machinery. Agr. Eng., *49*:732-733, Dec., 1968.
12. HOOK, R. W., and K. E. MURPHY. Providing depth control for integral flexible implements. Agr. Eng., *51*:560-561, 563, Oct., 1970.
13. KRAVCHENKO, A. S. Automatic guidance of beet harvesters along the rows. Trakt. Selkhozmash., *33*(10):34-35, 1963. NIAE transl. 187.
14. KRUKOW, E. J. Harvesting grain hydraulically. Agr. Eng., *47*:424-427, Aug., 1966.
15. MYERS, G., and D. SCHWIEGER. John Deere forage harvester electrical remote control system. ASAE Paper 70-680, Dec., 1970.
16. POOL, S. D. Controls for full-leveling hillside combine. Agr. Eng., *37*:245-248, Apr., 1956.
17. SANDERSON, L. F. Height sensing with a closed-center hydraulic system. Agr. Eng., *52*:18-19, Jan., 1971.
18. VOGELAAR, B. F. Developing a hydrostatic drive for self-propelled combines. Agr. Eng., *47*:70-72, Feb., 1966.
19. WILSON, R. W. Implement control by tractor driveline torque sensing. ASAE Paper 71-A609-NP, Dec., 1971.
20. WORTHINGTON, W. H., and J. W. SIEPLE. Hydraulic capacity requirements for control of farm implements. Agr. Eng., *33*:273-276, 278, May, 1952.

PROBLEMS

4.1. The hydraulic control valves of a multicylinder system are manipulated to connect two cylinders in series as indicated in the accompanying diagram. Each cylinder has a bore of 76

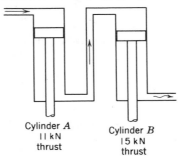

Cylinder *A*
11 kN
thrust

Cylinder *B*
15 kN
thrust

mm and a piston-rod diameter of 25.4 mm. The thrust loads are indicated on the diagram. The pump output is 32 L/min. Calculate:

(a) Required pump pressure, neglecting line losses.

(b) Rate of piston movement for each cylinder, in millimetres per second.

(c) Power input to the pump, assuming an overall system efficiency of 60%.

4.2. Develop a graphic-symbol diagram for three series-parallel stacked valves similar in function to those shown in Fig. 4.6.

4.3. It is desired to control the front gangs and the rear gang of a mounted row-crop cultivator with a single control lever and to have automatic delayed lifting and automatic delayed lowering of the rear gang. Using graphic symbols, show an arrangement that will delay motion of the rear cylinder until the front cylinder reaches the end of its stroke (in either direction). Show only the portion of the circuit downstream from the directional control valve. Indicate an appropriate opening pressure for each pressure sequence valve if the system rated pressure is 8 MPa and the maximum lifting pressure required for each cylinder is 2 MPa. (The symbol for a pressure sequence valve is the same as for a pressure relief valve except that the outlet line goes to the next function instead of to the reservoir.)

(a) For a system in which both cylinders are double-acting.

(b) For a system in which the rear cylinder is single-acting (the usual situation for a three-point hitch). The system relief valve should not be required to operate while either piston is moving.

4.4. Assume that, for the conditions represented in Fig. 4.9, the actual increments of plow lift for successive 25.4-mm increments of piston travel were 23, 31, 36, 41, 48, 69, 91, and 99 mm (438 mm total lift). Plot this assumed curve of plow lift versus piston travel (cumulative values). Then, using the curve in Fig. 4.9, determine the ideal lift curve for constant thrust requirement. Plot this ideal curve on the same graph with the assumed actual lift curve. Tabulate your data and results.

4.5. The output torque from a gear-rotor motor is 82 N·m at 275 r/min. The required flow rate is 34 L/min, the motor displacement is 105 cm^3 per revolution, and the motor overall efficiency is 72%. The total pressure loss in lines, valves, and fittings is 0.41 MPa. The pump overall efficiency is 75%. Calculate:

(a) Power output from the motor.

(b) Required pressure drop across the motor.

(c) Volumetric efficiency of the motor.

(d) Overall system efficiency, assuming all of the pump output passes through the motor.

4.6. The speed of the motor in Problem 4.5 is reduced 25% by bypassing part of the pump output. The torque requirement is unchanged. Assume the pump and motor efficiencies and the total pressure loss in the lines to and from the motor remain the same as in Problem 4.5. Calculate:

(a) Pressure drop across the motor.

(b) Flow rate through motor.

(c) Overall system efficiency.

Soil Tillage and Dynamics

5.1. Introduction. This chapter considers some of the general aspects of tillage and tillage methods, including a brief coverage of some of the principles of soil dynamics as applied to tillage. In general, no attempt has been made to describe soil failure patterns or the mechanisms of soil failure.

Although soil-dynamics research was conducted as early as 1920, there has been a marked upsurge in this area of research since about 1950, from which has come a tremendous number of scientific papers. Gill and Vanden Berg have analyzed, summarized, and coordinated soil-dynamics research results reported through 1964, relating these results to basic principles and concepts. Their efforts resulted in a 500-page reference book[10] that represents a major contribution in the field of soil dynamics.

In spite of the rapid advances made in recent years, tillage is still far from being an exact science. Although one of the major objectives of tillage is to provide optimum environmental conditions for plant growth, we cannot quantitatively specify or identify the desired soil conditions. Forces applied to a tillage tool to produce a given effect upon the soil can be accurately measured but we cannot reliably predict the effects of changes in tool design. Consequently, it is not surprising that the design of tillage equipment is still largely an art rather than a science.

The importance of optimizing tillage operations and improving tillage tool design becomes apparent when one considers that just in the United States more than 225×10^9 Mg [250 billion tons] of soil are estimated to be stirred or turned each year. To plow this soil once requires 2×10^9 litres [500 million gallons] of gasoline or diesel fuel.[10]

Throughout this chapter, reference is made to tillage tools and tillage implements. A tillage tool is defined as an individual soil-working element, such as a plow bottom, a disk blade, or a cultivator shovel. A tillage implement consists of a single tool or a group of tools, together with the associated frame, wheels, control and protection devices, and any other structural and power transmission components.

5.2. Tillage Objectives. Tillage may be defined as the mechanical manipulation of soil for any purpose. In agriculture, some of the objectives of tillage are:

1. To develop a desirable soil structure for a seedbed or a rootbed. A granular structure is desirable to allow rapid infiltration and good

retention of rainfall, to provide adequate air capacity and exchange within the soil, and to minimize resistance to root penetration. A good seedbed, on the other hand, is generally considered to imply finer particles and greater firmness in the vicinity of the seeds.

2. To control weeds or to remove unwanted crop plants (thinning).

3. To manage plant residues. Thorough mixing of trash is desirable from the tilth and decomposition standpoints, whereas retention of trash in the top layers reduces erosion. On the other hand, complete coverage is sometimes necessary to control over-wintering insects or to prevent interference with precision operations such as planting and cultivating certain crops.

4. To minimize soil erosion by following such practices as contour tillage, listing, and proper placement of trash.

5. To establish specific surface configurations for planting, irrigating, drainage, harvesting operations, etc.

6. To incorporate and mix fertilizers, pesticides, or soil amendments into the soil.

7. To accomplish segregation. This may involve moving soil from one layer to another, removal of rocks and other foreign objects, or root harvesting.

5.3. Tillage Methods. Tillage operations for seedbed preparation are often classified as primary or secondary, although the distinction is not always clear-cut. A primary tillage operation constitutes the initial, major soil-working operation; it is normally designed to reduce soil strength, cover plant materials, and rearrange aggregates. Secondary tillage operations are intended to create refined soil conditions following primary tillage. The moldboard plow is most commonly used for primary tillage, but disk plows, heavy-duty disk harrows, chisel-type tools, blade-type subsurface tillers, and rotary tillers are also employed. Plows and disk-type implements cut, shatter and at least partially invert the soil. Chisel-type tools and subsurface blade tillers break up the soil without inverting it. A wide variety of implements, including some of those mentioned above, is used for secondary tillage and for cultivation when planting.

Considerable attention in recent years has been directed toward the potentialities of multipowered tillage tools, i.e., tools which obtain their energy in more than one manner. Rotary tillers, oscillating tillage tools, and powered spading machines are examples. These tools obtain part of their energy from a rotary source, usually the tractor PTO. Reduced draft requirements and greater versatility in manipulating the soil to obtain a desired result are two reasons for considering these more complex types of equipment. If draft requirements can be reduced by utilizing at least part of a tractor's output through nontractive means, the tractor can be made with less mass, which will reduce its cost and reduce soil compaction.

Rotary tillers have low or negative draft requirements, but total power requirements are high and pulverization may be excessive. Forced vibration or oscillation of a tillage tool may substantially reduce draft requirements, but the total power input is usually not decreased and may be increased. Spading machines, developed in Europe, have articulated spades or diggers that lift and invert the soil. Although energy requirements are reasonable, current models are mechanically complex and lack durability.[23]

5.4. Minimum-Tillage Systems. Engineers and crop and soil scientists are generally agreed that more tillage is being done than is necessary to assure maximum net income from crop production. In some cases, soil compaction from the tractor and implements in a sequence of secondary tillage operations may virtually eliminate the effects of primary tillage operations. Continuous-width tillage operations are usually designed to produce a good seedbed, even though the degree of soil pulverization and the firmness may be excessive for optimum root growth.

In recent years there has been increasing interest in minimum-tillage systems as a means of reducing row-crop production costs and improving soil conditions. Minimum tillage is a broad principle that can be applied in many ways. The major objectives are

1. To reduce mechanical-energy and labor requirements.
2. To conserve moisture and reduce soil erosion.
3. To perform only the operations necessary to optimize the soil conditions for each type of area within a field (e.g., row area versus inter-row area).
4. To minimize the number of trips over the field.

In some minimum-tillage systems, till-and-plant combination units follow plowing, chiseling, or other primary tillage, with narrow strips receiving shallow secondary tillage just ahead of the planter. Other types of combination units perform zone or strip tillage just ahead of the planters in untilled soil or in soil that was plowed during the previous fall. Several arrangements of combination units that will perform minimum-tillage and planting operations are commercially available.

The principal application of minimum-tillage systems has been in corn, although zone tillage has been used successfully in cotton[2] and a number of other row crops. Minimum-tillage corn is often planted through sod or small-grain residue. In the so-called "no-tillage" system, a fluted coulter or other appropriate tool cuts and tills a strip 5 to 8 cm [2 to 3 in.] wide through the stubble or mulch and the planter follows immediately behind. Among the early approaches to minimum tillage in corn were (a) combining the plowing and planting operations, and (b) planting in wheel tracks immediately after plowing. For various reasons, neither of these methods has received much acceptance.

Lister-planting in untilled fields is a form of minimum tillage that is practiced with corn and other row crops in some areas. Each row is planted in the bottom of a lister furrow or on a raised plateau strip in the furrow, in a combined operation. In the coastal plains of the Carolinas and Georgia, for example, various kinds of annual row crops are planted in small-grain residue without previous tillage.[12]

Experience has indicated that minimum tillage, under suitable conditions and with some row crops, is a practical way to conserve resources and reduce production costs, usually without reducing yields.[25] Minimum-tillage systems may introduce new management problems, particularly when surface plant residues are involved. Insect problems may be increased and effective chemical weed control is essential.

5.5. Stubble-Mulch Tillage. The chief objectives of stubble-mulch tillage are to reduce wind and water erosion and to conserve water by reducing runoff. This practice is widely accepted in the Great Plains and other arid or semiarid regions. Stubble-mulch tillage involves cutting the roots of weeds and other plants and leaving the crop residue on the surface or mixed into the top few centimetres of soil. The proper disposition of the residue depends upon the amount present and the subsequent operations involved. The large amounts of residue at or near the surface protect the soil but introduce problems in planting (since the planter must penetrate the mulch) and in cultivation if row crops are included in the crop rotation.

Special, blade-type subsurface tillers have been developed to perform either the initial or subsequent tillage operations without stirring or turning the tilled layer. V-shaped sweeps designed for this purpose may have cutting widths ranging from 0.6 to 2.4 m [2 to 8 ft]. Straight blades operated at right angles to the direction of travel are sometimes used for the initial tillage operation. Rod weeders are also employed. In extremely heavy mulches where some of the residue must be mixed into the top few centimetres of soil, vertical-disk plows and disk harrows may be used. Field cultivators, chisel plows, rotary hoes, and skew or mulch treaders are also employed in some situations.[24] In tilling summer-fallow wheat stubble, 4 tillage operations at about 1-month intervals may be required to control weeds.[24]

5.6. Definitions of Force, Energy, and Power Terms. In considering tillage force and energy relations it is important that the student be thoroughly familiar with the fundamental definitions and relations of mechanics. Pertinent terms, along with additional concepts used specifically in connection with farm machinery, are defined in this section.

Force is any action that changes or tends to change the state of rest or motion of a body. A force is completely specified by its magnitude and direction and the position of its line of action. Common units are the newton in the SI system and the pound in the customary system.

Pull on an implement is the total force exerted upon the implement by a power unit. With tillage implements it is generally at some angle above the horizontal, and it may or may not be in a vertical plane parallel to the line of motion.

Draft is the horizontal component of pull, parallel to the line of motion.

Side draft is the horizontal component of pull, perpendicular to the line of motion.

Specific draft is the draft per unit area of tilled cross section, usually expressed as newtons per square centimetre [pounds force per square inch.]

Torque is the moment of a force tending to produce rotation about a point. It is the product of the force times its radius of rotation and is commonly expressed as newton-metres [pound-force-inches]. A *couple* consists of two equal and opposite forces that are parallel but not concurrent. The magnitude or moment of a couple is equal to the product of one of the forces times the perpendicular distance between the two forces. A couple may tend to produce rotation about any point in the plane of the two forces. Thus, torque is a special case of a couple with the center of rotation on the line of one of the forces.

Work is the product of force (in the direction of motion) times the distance through which the force acts. Common units are the joule in the SI system and the foot-pound-force in the customary system.

Power is the rate of doing work. Common units are the kilowatt in the SI system and the horsepower in the customary system. One *kilowatt* is one kilojoule of work per second. One *horsepower* is 550 ft-lbf of work per second.

Drawbar power (dbp), in relation to either a pull-type or a mounted implement, is the power actually required to pull or move the implement at a uniform speed.

Kilowatt-hour [horsepower-hour] is the quantity of work performed when one kilowatt [one horsepower] is used for one hour.

5.7. Forces Acting upon a Tillage Tool or Implement. The engineer is concerned with the forces acting upon a tillage implement from the standpoints of total power requirements, proper hitching or application of the pulling force, designing for adequate strength and rigidity, and determination of the best shapes and adjustments of tools. A tillage implement (or tool) moving at a constant velocity is subjected to three main forces or force systems, which must be in equilibrium. These are

1. Force of gravity acting upon the implement.
2. The soil forces acting upon the implement.
3. The forces acting between the implement and the prime mover. If torque from rotary power transmission is not involved, the resultant of these forces is the pull of the power unit upon the implement.

Clyde[4] subdivides the total soil reaction into *useful* and *parasitic* forces. He defines useful soil forces as those which the tool must overcome in

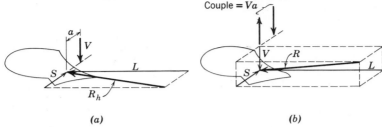

Fig. 5.1. Two ways of expressing the total soil reaction on a tillage tool when a rotational effect exists. (a) Two nonintersecting forces, R_h and V. (b) One force R, plus a couple Va in a plane perpendicular to the line of motion. (A. W. Clyde.[5])

cutting, breaking, and moving the soil. Parasitic forces are those (including friction or rolling resistance) that act upon stabilizing surfaces such as the landside and sole of a plow or upon supporting runners or wheels. Under a given set of operating conditions with a specific implement, the operator has little control over the useful soil-resistance forces. However, both the designer and the operator have some control over parasitic forces.

When a tool is not symmetrical about the vertical, longitudinal plane through its centerline, the useful soil forces usually introduce a rotational effect. Two ways of expressing the total soil reaction on a tillage tool for the general case in which a rotational effect exists are shown in Fig. 5.1. Other methods that have been used by different investigators include

1. A wrench, i.e., one force plus a couple in the plane perpendicular to the force.
2. Three forces on mutually perpendicular axes and three couples in the planes of intersection of the axes.
3. Three forces in three major planes.

Results of force measurements may be accurately represented by any of these five methods, and results expressed in one form can be transposed to another form by methods of statics. One method may be more desirable than the others in a particular situation, depending upon the intended use of the data. Vanden Berg[21] points out that the unique line of action of a single resultant force can be shown only by the wrench method because this system represents the minimum couple.

5.8. Symbols Used in Tillage Force Analysis. The most common symbols occurring in the several chapters dealing with tillage implements are identified in the following list. Others are identified as they appear in the various sections.

R = resultant of all useful soil forces acting upon the tool or implement (Fig. 5.1b). Where useful and parasitic forces cannot be determined separately, R includes both.

L = longitudinal or directional component of R (Fig. 5.1)

S = lateral component of R (Fig. 5.1)
V = vertical component of R (Fig. 5.1)
R_h = resultant of L and S (Fig. 5.1a)
R_v = resultant of L and V (i.e., component of R in a vertical, longitudinal plane)
a = lateral distance between V and R_h, for tools having a rotational effect (Fig. 5.1a)
Va = couple tending to rotate the tool about the longitudinal axis (Fig. 5.1b)
Q = resultant of all parasitic forces acting upon the implement
Q_h = component of Q in a horizontal plane. It includes stabilizing side forces and the accompanying longitudinal friction forces.
Q_v = component of Q in a vertical, longitudinal plane. It includes vertical support forces and the accompanying longitudinal friction forces or rolling resistance.
P = resultant pull exerted on the implement by the power unit
P_h = component of P in a horizontal plane
P_v = component of P in a vertical, longitudinal plane.
W = force of gravity acting on the implement, through the center of gravity
H = horizontal center of resistance of the implement, which is the point of concurrence of R_h and Q_h, or of two R_h components as in a disk harrow
G = point of concurrence of Q_v and the resultant of W and R_v. It might be called the vertical center of resistance.

The subscripts x, y, and z, as applied to P and Q, refer to force components in the longitudinal, lateral, and vertical directions, respectively.

5.9. Mechanics of Tillage. The reactions of soils to forces applied by tillage tools are affected by the resistance of the soil to compression, the resistance to shear, adhesion (attractive forces between the soil and some other material), and frictional resistance.[15] These are all dynamic properties in that they are made manifest only through movement of the soil.[10] Acceleration forces are not a soil property but are also present. Nichols[15] has shown that reactive forces of all classes of soils are dominated by the film moisture on the colloidal particles,* and are thus directly related to the soil moisture and colloidal content.

Soils may be classed as plastic and nonplastic, the term plastic implying that the soil is moldable within a certain range of moisture contents and that it will retain its molded shape after drying. Sands or other soils containing less than 15 to 20% colloids or clay are generally considered to be nonplastic.

---

*Colloidal particles are disk- or plate-shaped particles that characterize clay soils. Pure sand has zero colloidal content.

If a plastic soil is saturated with water and then allowed to dry, it passes through the following stages, in order: sticky, plastic, friable (crumbly), and hard (cemented). The friable stage represents optimum conditions for tillage. Soil compaction by tillage implements and power units, which is a serious problem in some areas, is promoted by working the soil when too wet.

Practically all tillage tools consist of devices for applying pressure to the soil, often by means of inclined planes or wedges. As the tool advances, the soil in its path is subjected to compressive stresses which, in a friable (un-cemented) soil, result in a shearing action. The shearing of soils is con-siderably different from the shearing of most solids, in that the reaction may extend for a considerable distance on either side of the shear plane because of internal friction and the cohesive action of moisture films.

Cohesion may be defined as the force that holds two particles of the same kind together. Internal friction results from interlocking of particles within the soil mass. Cohesion and internal friction are sometimes referred to as real physical properties of the soil. In reality they are only parameters of shear, as indicated in the following equation.[10]

$$\theta = \frac{\pi}{4} + \frac{\phi}{2}$$

$$\tau = C + \sigma \tan \phi \qquad \sigma = \frac{\sigma_1 + \sigma_3}{2} + \frac{\sigma_1 - \sigma_3}{2} \cos 2\theta \qquad (5.1)$$

where τ = shearing stress at soil failure
  C = cohesion
  σ = stress normal to plane of shear failure
  ϕ = angle of internal friction

$$\tau = \frac{\sigma_1 + \sigma_3}{2} \sin 2\theta$$

Based on equation 5.1, cohesion might be rationalized as the shear stress with zero normal load. Values for C and ϕ may be determined by measuring the shear stress for several values of normal stress σ. Shear strength has an important influence on the draft of a tillage tool.

Failure of a soil by compression is generally associated with a reduction in volume. Failure by shear and failure by compression are not independent phenomena, but occur as some combined action.[10] Failure or yielding of a soil can also be evidenced as plastic flow without the usual shattering and developing of shear failure surfaces. An example is the "flowing" of a wet clay soil around a subsoiler shank as the tool moves through the soil.[10]

Soil cutting may be defined as a slicing action that does not result in any other major failure such as shear. Conditions under which pure cutting can occur are determined by the soil characteristics and moisture content and, to some extent, by the degree of confinement.[10] In many tillage operations, cutting is not a clearly defined, independent action.

5.10. Friction and Adhesion. All tillage operations involve a sliding action of soil over some surface of the tool. Friction of soil against a tool having large contact areas represents a significant component of the draft require-ment. Friction is also involved when two rigid bodies of soil move with respect to each other. This phenomenon is distinctly different from the internal friction included in equation 5.1.[10] Unless large normal loads or speeds are involved, rigid-body soil-on-soil friction is usually assumed to follow the law for simple friction,[10] in which

$$\mu = \frac{F}{N} = \tan \psi \tag{5.2}$$

where μ = coefficient of friction (soil on soil)
F = frictional force tangent to the surface
N = normal force (perpendicular to the surface)
ψ = friction angle

In this idealized relation, μ is independent of the normal load, the contact area, and the speed of slipping.

Friction of soil on a tillage tool is usually soil-on-steel, but is sometimes soil-on-plastic (e.g., on plow bottoms covered with plastic). When soil slides on metal, adhesive forces between the soil and the metal have a marked influence on the friction force. The adhesive forces are primarily due to the moisture films, and their magnitude varies with the moisture content. The adhesive force has the effect of increasing the normal (perpendicular) load on the surface, thus increasing the tangential friction force. Since it is impractical to separate the effects of these two components, the usual practice in laboratory testing is to represent their combined effect by an "apparent coefficient of friction" which is identified as μ' (to distinguish it from μ in equation 5.2).

The general relation between soil-metal friction and soil moisture content, as described by Nichols,[16] is shown in Fig. 5.2. In the friction phase, adhesive forces are small and the coefficient of friction is essentially independent of

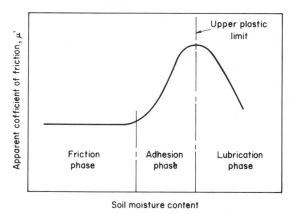

Fig. 5.2. Characteristic curve showing the effect of moisture content upon the apparent coefficient of friction between soils and steel.

moisture content. Soils in a friable condition usually have moisture contents in this range. In the adhesion phase, moisture films develop between the soil particles and the metal, thus creating adhesive forces that cause the apparent coefficient of friction to increase rapidly with moisture content. When the soil has enough moisture to act as a lubricant, the apparent coefficient of friction decreases as more water is added.

The transition moisture contents between phases increase with clay content, being higher for clay soils than for sandy soils. Apparent coefficients of friction are higher for clays than for sandy soils. Typical ranges for soil on smooth steel having an ordinary polish, as reported by various investigators, are 0.2 to 0.5 for sand, 0.3 to 0.65 for loams, and 0.35 to 0.8 for clay soils. The lower portion of each range represents values in the friction phase.

The type and smoothness of the material on which the soil slides affects the apparent coefficient of friction. Materials such as Teflon, which resist wetting, do not develop large adhesive forces with the soil and therefore have substantially lower apparent coefficients of friction (Fig. 5.3).

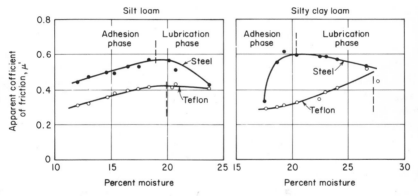

Fig. 5.3. Comparison of apparent coefficients of friction for steel and Teflon, in relation to moisture content. (W. R. Fox and C. W. Bockhop.[6])

Several investigators have found that soil-metal apparent coefficients of friction decrease as normal loads become large, particularly in moist clays and clay loams.[10,17]

5.11. Soil Strength Characterization by Penetration Resistance. Soil strength is the ability or capacity of a soil in a particular condition to resist or endure an applied force.[10] Penetration resistance is a composite parameter that involves several independent properties of a soil but is generally considered to reflect the strength of the soil. To measure penetration resistance, a simple, instrumented probe known as a penetrometer is pushed into the soil and the force is observed in relation to penetration depth. Penetrometer force readings per unit of base cross-sectional area provide indications of relative strengths of different soils and of uniformity versus depth in a particular soil condition.

ASAE Recommendation R313, adopted in 1968, specifies dimensions for two proposed standard sizes of cone penetrometers and also includes a procedural method for obtaining readings. The adoption and general acceptance of this recommendation has greatly enhanced the usefulness of penetrometer data.

5.12. Abrasion by Soils. Abrasiveness is a dynamic property of soils that has a cumulative effect rather than an immediate effect. When a large amount of soil slides over the surface of a tillage tool, abrasive wear may change the size, shape, or roughness of the tool enough to make it ineffective, especially if soil pressures against the tool are high. Soil characteristics or conditions that affect abrasiveness include the hardness, shape, and size of the soil particles, the firmness with which the particles are held in the soil mass, and the soil moisture content. The abrasive resistance of metals is influenced mainly by the composition of the material and by its hardness, strength, and toughness. The effects of some of these factors are discussed in Section 7.9 in relation to disk-blade wear and durability.

A layer or coating of a special, abrasion-resistant alloy is often applied along the cutting edges of tillage tools to reduce wear rates, especially for operation in sandy or sandy loam soils. This process is known as hard facing or hard surfacing. Hard-facing materials of different compositions are available for specific combinations of abrasion and impact conditions. These materials, sold under various trade names, are extremely hard and some are quite brittle. They are generally nonferrous, chromium-cobalt-tungsten alloys, or high-carbon iron-base alloys containing such elements as chromium, tungsten, manganese, silicon, and molybdenum. They are applied to plowshares, subsoiler points, chisel cultivators, and other tillage tools by means of the electric arc or an acetylene torch.

5.13. Tillage-Tool Design Factors.* The purpose of a tillage tool is to manipulate (change, move, or form) a soil as required to achieve a desired soil condition. Three abstract design factors — initial soil condition, tool shape, and manner of tool movement — control or define the soil manipulation. The results of these three independent input factors are evidenced by two output factors, namely, the final soil condition and the forces required to manipulate the soil. All five factors are of direct concern to a tillage implement designer.

Of the three input factors, the designer has complete control only of the tool shape. The user may vary the depth or speed of operation and may use

---

*This section is based primarily on material from reference 10, but reference 20 contains an excellent discussion of design considerations for various basic operations that may be performed by tillage implements.

the tool through a wide range of initial soil conditions. However, tool shape cannot be considered independently of manner of movement or initial soil condition. The orientation of a tool shape with respect to the direction of travel must be defined. Different initial soil conditions sometimes require different shapes. For example, many different shapes of moldboard plows have been developed for different soil types and conditions.

The shape that is of concern in design is the surface over which soil moves as a tillage tool is operated. Gill and Vanden Berg[10] classify three shape characteristics as macroshape, edgeshape, and microshape. The term macroshape designates the shape of the gross surface, whereas edgeshape refers to the peripheral and cross-sectional shapes of the boundaries of the soil-working surface. Notched and smooth disk blades have different edgeshapes but the macroshapes may be the same. Microshape refers to surface roughness.

Most tillage-tool shapes have been developed by cut-and-try methods or on the basis of qualitative analysis. The manipulation-shape relation has received greatest emphasis in the development of moldboard plow bottoms, whereas force-shape relations have been of concern in subsoilers and chisel-type tools. Mathematical descriptions of shapes are the most versatile means of representation, but tools such as moldboard plows have complex shapes that cannot easily be represented in mathematical form. Graphic representation is often employed for plow bottoms, although mathematical analyses have been attempted and computer analysis of plow-bottom shapes is increasing.

The shape of the cutting edge can materially affect draft as well as vertical and lateral components of soil forces. For example, disk blades sharpened from the concave side penetrate more readily than blades sharpened from the convex side. Worn plowshares reduce the vertical downward force V, tend to cause soil compaction, and sometimes substantially increase draft.

The roughness of a surface over which soil slides (microshape) influences friction forces. Surface roughness is related to the initial polish and the effect of abrasive wear, and may result locally from rust, scratches, or small depressions. Frictional resistance can account for as much as 30% of the total draft of a moldboard plow.[23] Microshape can also have an important effect on other aspects of soil movement, such as scouring. Factors affecting scouring are discussed in Chapter 6 because this performance characteristic is of major concern with moldboard plows.

Manner of movement involves orientation of the tool, its path through the soil, and its speed along the path. For tools that travel in a straight line (i.e., not rotary or oscillating tools), the path is usually identified by merely specifying the depth and width of cut. Orientation of a tool having a particular shape may significantly influence both the soil manipulaton and the forces. Often the linkage system used to position a tool affects both depth and orientation. When sufficient power is available, speed is the easiest design factor to vary. Increasing the speed generally increases draft but also affects soil movement and breakup.

5.14. Measuring and Evaluating Performance. As indicated in the preceding section, tool forces and change in soil condition are the two basic aspects of tillage-tool performance. The tool should accomplish the necessary soil manipulation with a minimum of energy input, and the final soil condition must be acceptable when compared with the desired conditions. The force systems acting on tillage tools can be represented mathematically and the forces can be measured. But quantitative assessment of performance is difficult because no method has been developed for adequately describing soil conditions or for specifying the conditions needed for the intended use.

Three aspects of final soil condition that may be of interest, depending upon the function or purpose of a specific tillage operation, are (a) the degree of soil breakup, (b) segregation of clod sizes in relation to depth, and (c) uniformity of mixing throughout the tilled depth. Soil breakup may be measured by sieving a soil sample that represents the entire tilled depth. Gill and Vanden Berg[10] describe a rotary sieve designed for this purpose. The results may be expressed in terms of the actual size distribution of the clods, a mean-mass diameter,* or a pulverization modulus.

Segregation of clod sizes, perhaps with the larger clods on or near the surface, is sometimes desired but in other situations may be undesirable. Many types of tillage tools tend to have this effect, in varying degrees. Sieving distinct layers of the soil profile provides a means for measuring the segregating performance of tillage tools.

Often an objective of tillage is to mix the soil to obtain uniform distribution of clods or moisture. In other instances, applied materials such as pesticides or fertilizers need to be uniformly mixed with the soil. Uniformity of mixing can be evaluated by applying tracer materials to the soil surface and determining their distribution after tillage. Easily identifiable granules or pellets, radioactive materials, fluorescent materials, dyes whose concentrations in soil samples can be determined by spectrophotometry, and sodium or potassium chlorides have been employed.

Evaluation of performance involves comparing the actual final soil condition with the desired condition. The desired condition is determined entirely by the intended use of the tilled soil. The acceptable level of functional performance, assuming it is below the desired level, may be tempered by economic considerations and other factors. Performance also includes field capacity and energy utilization efficiency, which must be considered when

---

*Mean-mass diameter is the 50% value from a curve of cumulative mass percentage versus clod diameter.

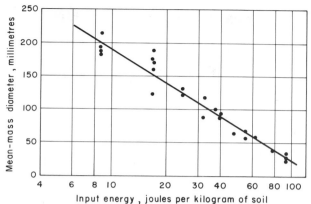

Fig. 5.4. Relation between energy input and the resultant clod size from a drop-shatter test with a silty clay loam at 12 to 16% moisture. (W. R. Gill and W. F. McCreery.[9])

comparing two or more implements. Placement and degree of size reduction of plant residues are other factors that sometimes must be included.

To determine the energy utilization efficiency of a tillage implement when the primary objective is soil breakup, the equivalent energy represented by a reduction in clod size must be determined experimentally. This has been done by applying energy to the soil in a controlled manner and measuring the effect in terms of clod size. Gill and McCreery[9] developed a drop-shatter method in which soil samples are dropped from a known height onto a rigid surface and the kinetic energy expended in falling is related to the resulting mean-mass diameter. Successive dropping of remaining large clods yields a relationship between mean-mass diameter and total kinetic energy input (Fig. 5.4).

In other methods of determining the equivalent energy input, forces to shatter the soil have been applied by slow compression,[3] by striking the soil with a pendulum device,[3] or by a rotating blade similar to that of a rotary tiller. None of the methods measures the absolute energy required for pulverization, since failure mechanisms may differ from those in an actual tillage system. The results from different methods do not necessarily give the same answers.[3] A new test must be conducted for each new soil condition. Nevertheless, these methods do provide a useful means for comparing the results of different tillage operations.

To evaluate a tillage operation in terms of energy utilization, the actual tillage energy input per unit volume is calculated from the measured draft, width of cut, and depth of cut. The equivalent energy input determined by one of the methods described above is divided by the actual tillage energy input to obtain a dimensionless ratio that might be called the energy utilization factor. This factor does not represent tillage efficiency in the strict sense because the reference equivalent energy input is not an absolute minimum.

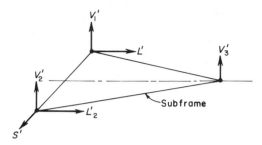

Fig. 5.5. An arrangement for completely restraining a tool subframe through six force transducers. The "prime" superscripts are used to indicate forces exerted on the subframe by the main carrier, as distinguished from L, S, and V components of R (Section 5.8).

5.15. Measuring Soil Forces on Tillage Tools. If a tool is attached to a subframe that is entirely supported from a carrier frame through six appropriately oriented force transducers (Fig. 5.5), the resultant soil reaction can be determined completely. The carrier, usually pulled by a separate power unit, moves the tool through the soil at controlled speeds, depths, and lateral orientations while resulting forces are measured. For accurate results a track or guidance system for the carrier is needed to maintain constant width and depth of cut in the test zone.

With such an arrangement, tools having any combination of translational and rotational soil reactions can be tested. Parasitic forces may be included in the measured soil reaction, or they can be eliminated or minimized by adjustment of the tool or by removing any stabilizing or supporting surfaces. The effect of gravity on the tool is eliminated from the force considerations by taking initial load readings with the tool suspended and then dealing only with load changes caused by the soil reaction. The results or outputs from the 6 force transducers can be combined into any of the 5 forms indicated in Section 5.7.

Force measurements on full-size tools may be made with mobile field test units or by means of laboratory facilities having soils in large bins. Soil-bin systems permit conducting tests under carefully controlled and uniform soil and operating conditions. This arrangement is particularly suitable for basic research and for repetitive tests involving the comparison of different designs or tool adjustments under various soil conditions. Quantitatively, the results do not necessarily represent field conditions. Field test units yield results that are more typical of actual operating conditions but are influenced by the inherent variability of soil conditions, even within one field. Field results provide a better basis for structural design than do soil-bin results.

Clyde did much of the pioneering work in tillage force analysis and measurement at Pennsylvania State University. He developed a mobile field test unit in about 1935 and used this for many years.[4] Lateral control of this unit, which he called the tillage meter, was obtained by metal wheels running in movable steel-channel guides. Depth was controlled by two rubber-tired wheels running on undisturbed ground. Emphasis was placed on determining soil resistances under actual field conditions with easily tilled, typical, and rather difficult soils, to give a range of conditions as a basis for design and operation.

Gill and Vanden Berg[10] describe two mobile field dynamometer units being used by research agencies in Europe. Neither of these employ guide rails. The NIAE unit is tractor-mounted and has small outrigger tracks to control depth. The other unit, in Germany, is on a three-wheel, pull-type carrier. Where width of cut must be controlled, as with plows or disk tools, two similar tools are mounted on the carrier in the same relation they would have on a complete implement, and the rear tool is instrumented. Several implement manufacturers and other organizations in the United States also have mobile test units.

The USDA's National Tillage Machinery Laboratory at Auburn, Alabama, is a well-known soil dynamics research center that has soil bins and has been in operation since about 1936. This laboratory has 9 outdoor and 2 indoor soil bins in which full-size wheels, tracks, vehicles, and tillage tools may be operated.[10] Each bin is 6.1 m [20 ft] wide, 0.6 m or 1.5 m [2 ft or 5 ft] deep, and 58 m or 76 m [190 ft or 250 ft] long. The soils vary in mechanical composition from sand to predominantly clay. They were selected to provide a wide range of soil characteristics. Rails on the walls between bins support the wheels of all soil-fitting and test units. Equipment is available for packing, pulverizing, stirring, leveling, or sprinkling the soil and for protecting it from the weather. A power car pulls the tool carrier and can be operated at speeds from 0.3 to 16 km/h [0.2 to 10 mph].

Several agricultural equipment manufacturers, several state agricultural experiment stations, and the National Tillage Machinery Laboratory have small indoor soil bins intended primarily for research with scale models or simple tillage tool shapes. The number of these facilities is continually increasing. In some cases the tool moves along a stationary bin that may be 6.1 to 18.3 m [20 to 60 ft] long. In other arrangements the soil is moved past the stationary tool in a rotating annular-ring trough, in a linearly moving short bin, or on a belt.

Most, if not all, present-day test units employ strain-gage force transducers. Forward speed is usually measured with a tachometer generator which gives an electric signal that can be put onto one channel of the same instrument used for the force transducers. Eight-channel recording oscillographs, eight-channel magnetic tape recorders, and X-Y recorders are commonly employed. In at least one case, all transducer output signals are fed directly into an analog computer where all required processing is performed during the test.[22]

When one particular component or portion of a tool is being studied, it is often desirable to isolate the component and measure only the forces acting upon it. For example, the share of a moldboard plow can be supported from behind by two cantilever beams that structurally isolate it from the rest of the plow bottom but still hold it in its correct functional position. Strain gages can be applied to the support beams to measure one or more force components or for measuring the complete force system on the share. Determining the complete system requires 6 force measurements — in this example, axial force and bending in 2 transverse directions for each beam. Sometimes force transducers can be incorporated directly into the structural members that normally support the tool or component.

When determining forces by means of bending-moment measurements, bending moments need to be measured at two sections of the beam in order to determine the applied normal force accurately.[13] The two sections should be as far apart as possible (for maximum response) and the cross sections must be identical. The bridge circuit is connected so the difference between the two moments is measured. Any moments resulting from eccentric force components parallel to the beam axis then cancel in the transducer readings, since such a moment would have a uniform magnitude over the full length of the beam. Axial forces produce no response, since they affect all the strain gages equally.

5.16. Measuring Draft of Pull-Type Implements. As defined in Section 5.6, draft is the component of pull in the direction of travel. The simplest device for measuring pull is a spring-type dynamometer (essentially a heavy spring scale) that is connected between the tractor drawbar and the implement hitch and is read directly. Because of rapid fluctuations in load, such a dynamometer is suitable only for rough measurements. A hydraulic type, transmitting pressure to a Bourdon gage calibrated in force units, is easier to read than the spring type because force fluctuations can be damped considerably by using a viscous fluid or having a restriction in the line to the gage. Some hydraulic dynamometers record the pull on a strip chart driven by a ground wheel.

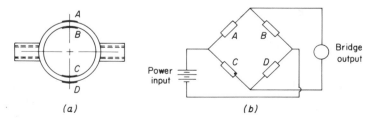

Fig. 5.6. *(a)* Ring-type force transducer for measuring axial forces, showing the strain-gage arrangement; *(b)* bridge circuit for the strain gages. (A. L. Neuhoff.[14])

Strain-gage dynamometers are often used for measuring drawbar pull. Various configurations are employed, but usually the strain is measured in a member subjected to bending. Having opposing gages in tension and compression provides maximum response and simplifies temperature compensation. A ring-type force transducer with strain gages arranged as shown in Fig. 5.6 has good sensitivity to axial tension or compression forces and the response is not affected by overall bending loads.

To provide a complete picture of implement draft and power requirements, it is necessary to measure speed and the width and depth of cut in addition to determining the draft. Because of wide fluctuations in soil conditions and draft, even within a short run, it is desirable to record at least the pull in relation to travel distance. Integration of the area under the curve then gives the total work and average pull. Speed may be determined by timing a measured or automatically recorded travel distance or with a tachometer generator driven from a ground wheel.

If a conventional dynamometer is connected directly in the line of pull of the implement, the measured force represents the total pull rather than the draft component. Then the inclination of the line of pull from the horizontal, and the horizontal angle from the direction of travel, must be measured so the draft can be calculated from the pull. Zoerb[26] describes a direct-connected strain-gage dynamometer that has the strain gages on a vertical shaft supported by two ball bearings (acting as a simple beam) in such a way that the gages sense only the draft component of the pull. By exciting the strain-gage bridge circuit with the voltage output from a tachometer generator, he was able to obtain direct readings of power.

The draft of plows is commonly expressed as newtons per square centimetre of furrow slice [pounds force per square inch of furrow slice]. This is defined in Section 5.6 as *specific draft*. For some implements, such as planters, kilonewtons [pounds force] per row may be specified. For most other tillage implements, draft is usually given in kilonewtons per metre of width [pounds force per foot of width], sometimes also indicating the depth. Typical ranges for implement draft are included in Appendix A.

5.17. Measuring Hitch Forces on Mounted and Semimounted Implements. Draft can be measured by installing strain gages on the front and rear sides of lateral, cantilevered pins that support the front ends of the links on a three-point hitch. A simple beam, rather than a cantilever beam, can be used for the upper-link attachment point. Four gages on each support are accurately positioned so that they respond only to bending moments in a horizontal plane. A single reading for draft can be obtained by connecting the outputs from the three bridge circuits (one per support) in parallel or connecting all the gages into one bridge circuit. Measuring the difference between bending moments at two sections for each support beam, as described in Section 5.15, eliminates the effects of moments caused by friction in the

Fig. 5.7. Three-directional, subtractive double-bending-moment force transducers incorporated into the lower links of a three-point hitch (upper link not used in this instance because
the implement was a semimounted plow). The "rod" in the left foreground is one of two sliding
potentiometers that sense the location of the links. (R. W. Morling.[13])

link ball joints.[13] Scholtz[19] minimized the effects of ball-joint friction by
making the lower-link cantilever beams 165 mm [6½ in.] long (to ball center). He measured the bending moment only at one section of each beam.

The hitch-pin system for measuring draft is suitable only when the implement receives no support through the hitch lift links or if the lift-link forces
and angles are measured. Because the lift links are not vertical (Fig. 5.7),
any force in them would have a longitudinal component that would affect the
response from the lower-link transducer beams. The forces in the lift links
could be measured with ring-type transducers (Fig. 5.6) and combined into a
single reading. The lift-link angles in a vertical, longitudinal plane must also
be known to determine the correction for the draft readings.

If longitudinal, vertical, and lateral force components acting upon the implement are all to be determined, simultaneous measurements must be made
of (a) axial forces and bending moments in 2 directions in the 2 lower links
(measured behind the lift links), (b) axial force in the upper link, and (c) the
directions of all 3 links. Strain gages can be installed directly on the lower
links or on modified straight links, provided adequate response in all three
directions is obtainable. A more sensitive arrangement consists of special
links that transmit axial forces and bending moments through a cantilever
beam perpendicular to the link axis, employing the subtractive double-

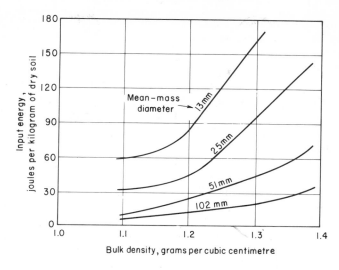

Fig. 5.8. Influence of bulk density and desired clod size on the energy input from a pendulum for a silty clay loam at 28% moisture. (H. P. Bateman, M. P. Naik, and R. R. Yoerger.[3])

bending-moment principle (Section 5.15) for each of the three directional force components.[13] An arrangement of this type is shown in Fig. 5.7. A ring-type force transducer would be used in the upper link.

5.18. Energy Requirements for Soil Breakup. As indicated in Fig. 5.4, the energy required for soil breakup is related to the desired degree of pulverization. The amount of energy required to produce a given degree of pulverization depends primarily upon the soil strength and the energy utilization efficiency of the implement. Soil strength is related to the nature of the soil and to its physical condition. Clay soils have higher breakup-energy requirements than sandy soils or loams. Climate, cropping practices, cultural practices, and other factors influence the physical condition. For a given soil, energy requirements increase with bulk density, as illustrated in Fig. 5.8.

The strength of an initially moist soil increases considerably as the soil dries out, particularly with clays and clay loams, thereby increasing the pulverization energy requirements.[8] When tools have large soil-engaging surfaces, increased friction in the adhesion stage increases energy requirements if the soil is too wet. Thus, scheduling tillage operations so they will be performed at optimum moisture contents can be important in relation to minimizing energy requirements. In arid regions, irrigation prior to tillage may reduce power requirements and/or increase the degree of pulverization. Secondary tillage operations should be performed before the clods have time to dry out.

Depth of cut, width of cut, tool shape (including cutting edges), tool arrangement, and travel speed are factors that may affect draft and the energy utilization efficiency for a specific soil condition. The effects of these parameters vary with different types of implements and with different soil conditions. In assessing the effects upon draft, any accompanying effects upon the degree of soil pulverization must also be considered. In some cases the increased soil breakup may be sufficient to prevent appreciable reduction of the energy utilization efficiency. The question must then be asked whether the increased pulverization is advantageous in a particular situation.

With chisel-type implements, average specific draft in a primary tillage operation generally shows a slight or moderate increase with depth, particularly in the heavier soils. Field tests sometimes show a large increase at depths below the normal tillage depth because of variations in soil conditions (e.g., compacted layers). The effect of depth upon the specific draft of moldboard plows is influenced by shape and size, as discussed in Chapter 6. Improper location of wheels, runners, or adjacent tools so they interfere with the normal soil failure pattern can increase draft.[20] Shape and orientation of tools are significant factors in regard to draft. These are discussed in the chapters dealing with specific types of implements.

Gill and McCreery[9] conducted tests with sections of moldboard plow bottoms having widths of 51, 102, 152, and 203 mm [2, 4, 6, and 8 in.] and taking cuts 25 to 203 mm [1 to 8 in.] wide in a silty clay loam soil at the National Tillage Machinery Laboratory. The specific drafts for the 51-mm and 25-mm cuts were 40% and 140%, respectively, greater than the average for the 102-mm, 152-mm, and 203-mm cuts. But the clod mean-mass diameter decreased from 218 mm to 38 mm [8.6 to 1.5 in.] as the width of cut was reduced. Energy utilization factors, based on the drop-shatter method (Section 5.14) increased from 0.14 with a 203-mm cut to 0.65 with the 51-mm cut and 0.79 with the 25-mm cut. Tests with a 66-cm [26-in.] disk blade taking 25-mm to 203-mm cuts resulted in higher specific drafts at the 25-mm and 51-mm cuts, but not much change in the energy utilization factor over the entire range of widths.

These tests demonstrate the principle of using small cuts in a consolidated soil to obtain maximum fragmentation, and suggest that the most efficient method of producing a given clod mean-mass diameter is to apply the forces in such a manner that the soil breakup all occurs in one step.[9] This is the opposite approach from present practice, which is to break a mass of soil down into smaller sizes by a series of tillage operations. Implements operating in a loose soil often tend to merely rearrange the clods without much additional breakup.

The effects of plowing followed by 4 combinations of secondary tillage operations were observed in field tests conducted under 7 combinations of soil and previous cropping conditions.[11] In 4 fields, in which all tillage operations for a particular field were performed within a 3-h period, clod mean-mass diameters after plowing ranged from 33 mm to 61 mm [1.3 to 2.4 in.].

The first disking after plowing reduced the clod size by 20 to 35% but additional diskings, or harrowing after disking, usually had no great effect on average clod size. Plowing reduced the bulk density by about 25% and all secondary tillage operations increased it.

5.19. Effect of Speed Upon Draft. Increased forward speed increases the draft with most tillage implements, mainly because of the more rapid acceleration of any soil that is moved appreciably. Soil acceleration increases draft for at least two reasons — first, because acceleration forces increase the normal loads on soil-engaging surfaces, thereby increasing the frictional resistance, and second, because of the kinetic energy imparted to the soil. Since acceleraton forces vary as the square of the speed and since draft also includes components that are essentially independent of speed, it seems logical to represent the relation between speed and draft by an equation of the form

$$D_s = D_o + KS^2 \qquad (5.3)$$

where D_s = draft at speed S
D_o = static component of draft, independent of speed
S = forward speed
K = a constant whose value is related to implement type and design and to soil conditions

The magnitude of the effect of speed upon draft depends on the relative magnitude of the components that are independent of speed and the components that increase with speed, as influenced by implement type and design and by soil type and condition. For example, test results presented in later chapters indicate that increasing the forward speed from 4.8 km/h to 9.6 km/h [3 mph to 6 mph] increased the draft by 90% and 40% for a disk plow in 2 different soil types, by an average of 50% for conventional-shaped moldboard plows in a variety of soils, and by 15% for a subsoiler.

5.20. Scale-Model Studies. Field testing of tillage tools is complicated by the natural variability of soil conditions. The use of large soil bins for testing full-size tools requires an expensive installation of highly specialized equipment. Another approach, offering economy, convenience, and good control of conditions, is the application of similitude principles in scale-model laboratory testing of tillage tools. Scale models are employed in many different areas of engineering, but it is only since about 1960 that there has been much interest in model studies with tillage tools.

The usual objectives of scale-model testing are (a) to be able to predict prototype (full-size) system performance from values measured on a small and relatively inexpensive system, or (b) to gain understanding of the nature, magnitude, and effect of the physical parameters of the system. Scale-model studies are based on the concept of similarity between the prototype system and the model, with the same physical laws governing both systems.

Two systems will exhibit similar behavior if geometric, kinematic, and dynamic similarities are achieved.[7] Obtaining geometric similarity is a relatively simple matter. For dynamic similarity, the ratios of all forces affecting the system must be the same in the model as in the prototype. The problem is to identify and determine all such forces. Kinematic similarity usually follows if geometric and dynamic similarities are present.[7]

The first and most important step in planning a model study is the identification of all measurable physical variables which, when properly combined, will completely describe the physical phenomena under study.[1] Then the principles of dimensional analysis are applied to group these variables into a series of independent, dimensionless terms that are used as the basis for the design of the model.

If true scaling of all the relevant factors is achieved, a good prediction of the performance of the prototype system can be obtained by merely multiplying the model performance by an appropriate scale factor. Usually, however, there are elements that cannot be scaled. These result in significant nonsimilarities or distortions. Scaling soil properties is one of the major problems.

An alternative to attempting to define and measure all soil properties so they could be scaled is to use the same soil for both the prototype and the model. The resulting distortion is then accounted for empirically by observing the trend of results obtained with models of several sizes (having different scale factors) and developing a prediction factor to compensate for the distortion.[18]

5.21. Research with Simple Tillage Tools. In recent years considerable research effort has been devoted to testing simple-shaped tillage tools as a means of studying the fundamental principles of soil reactions to applied forces. These tools are usually flat plates that are moved through the soil either in a vertical position (90° lift angle) or inclined with the bottom edge forward (acute lift angles). Plates having widths of 25 to 100 mm [1 to 4 in.] are usually operated as tines, with the full-width portion extending above the ground surface. Wide plates (some up to 76 cm [30 in.]) are more likely to be submerged and operated at lift angles less than 45°, to study the action of a soil being lifted. Tests with simple tools are conducted in the field, in outdoor soil bins, and in indoor bins of various sizes.

REFERENCES

1. BARNES, K. K., C. W. BOCKHOP, and H. E. McLEOD. Similitude in studies of tillage implement forces. Agr. Eng., 41:32-37, 42, Jan., 1960.
2. BATCHELDER, D. G., and J. G. PORTERFIELD. Zone tillage machines and methods for cotton. Trans. ASAE, 9(1):98-99, 1966.
3. BATEMAN, H. P., M. P. NAIK, and R. R. YOERGER. Energy required to pulverize soil at different degrees of compaction. J. Agr. Eng. Res., 10:132-141, 1965.

4. CLYDE, A. W. Measurement of forces on soil tillage tools. Agr. Eng., *17*:5-9, Jan., 1936.
5. CLYDE, A. W. Technical features of tillage tools. Pennsylvania Agr. Expt. Sta. Bull. 465 (Part 2), 1944.
6. FOX, W. R., and C. W. BOCKHOP. Characteristics of a Teflon-covered simple tillage tool. Trans. ASAE, *8*(2):227-229, 1965.
7. FREITAG, D. R., R. L. SCHAFER, and R. D. WISMER. Similitude studies of soil machine systems. Trans. ASAE, *13*(2):201-213, 1970.
8. GILL, W. R. Soil-implement relations. Conf. Proc.: Tillage for Greater Crop Production, 1967, pp. 32-36, 43. ASAE St. Joseph, Mich.
9. GILL, W. R., and W. F. McCREERY. Relation of size of cut to tillage tool efficiency. Agr. Eng., *41*:372-374, 381, June, 1960.
10. GILL, W. R., and G. E. VANDEN BERG. Soil Dynamics in Tillage and Traction. USDA Agr. Handbook No. 316, 1967.
11. LUTTRELL, D. H., C. W. BOCKHOP, and W. G. LOVELY. The effect of tillage operations on soil physical conditions. ASAE Paper 64-103, June, 1964.
12. McALISTER, J. T. Mulch tillage with lister-planters. Trans. ASAE, *9*(2):153-154, 1966.
13. MORLING, R. W. Soil force analysis as applied to tillage equipment. ASAE Paper 63-149, June, 1963.
14. NEUHOFF, A. L. Measuring force in two or more members with one instrument. Agr. Eng., *40*:456-457, Aug., 1959.
15. NICHOLS, M. L. The dynamic properties of soil: I. An explanation of the dynamic properties of soils by means of colloidal films. Agr. Eng., *12*:259-264, July, 1931.
16. NICHOLS, M. L. The dynamic properties of soil: II. Soil and metal friction. Agr. Eng., *12*:321-324, Aug., 1931.
17. O'CALLAGHAN, J. R., and P. J. McCULLEN. Cleavage of soil by inclined and wedge-shaped tines. J. Agr. Eng. Res., *10*:248-254, 1965.
18. SCHAFER, R. L., C. W. BOCKHOP, and W. G. LOVELY. Prototype studies of tillage implements. Trans. ASAE, *11*(5):661-664, 1968.
19. SCHOLTZ, D. C. A three-point linkage dynamometer for mounted implements. J. Agr. Eng. Res., *9*:252-258, 1964.
20. SPOOR, G. Design of soil engaging implements (in two parts). Farm Machine Des. Eng., *3*:22-25, 28, Sept., 1969; *3*:14-19, Dec., 1969.
21. VANDEN BERG, G. E. Analysis of forces on tillage tools. J. Agr. Eng. Res., *11*:201-205, 1966.
22. WEGSCHEID, E. L., and H. A. MYERS. Soil bin instrumentation. Agr. Eng., *48*:442-445, 463, Aug., 1967.
23. WISMER, R. D., E. L. WEGSCHEID, H. J. LUTH, and B. E. ROMIG. Energy application in tillage and earthmoving. SAE Trans., *77*:2486-2494, 1968.
24. WOODRUF, N. P., and W. S. CHEPIL. Influence of one-way disk and subsurface-sweep tillage on factors affecting wind erosion. Trans. ASAE, *1*:81-85, 1958.
25. ZIMMERMAN, M. Which way will tillage go? Implement & Tractor, *83*(26):28-30, Dec. 21, 1968.
26. ZOERB, G. C. A strain gage dynamometer for direct horsepower indication. Agr. Eng., *44*:434-435, 437, Aug., 1963.

PROBLEMS

5.1. The line of pull on an implement is 15° above the horizontal and is in a vertical plane which is at an angle of 10° with the direction of travel.

(a) Calculate the draft and side-draft forces for a pull of 11 kN.

(b) What drawbar power would be required at 5.5 km/h?

6

Moldboard Plows

6.1. Introduction. The moldboard plow is one of the oldest of all agricultural implements and is generally considered to be the most important tillage implement. Plowing accounts for more traction energy than any other field operation. Although yield studies have indicated that under certain conditions with some crops there is no apparent advantage in plowing, the moldboard plow is still by far the most-used implement for primary tillage in seedbed preparation.

Through the years there has been a vast amount of development and research work pertaining to moldboard plows. Yet plow-bottom design (as with other tillage tools) is still largely dependent upon cut-and-try methods. Many excellent plow bottoms have been developed, but there are still important soil types and conditions for which present equipment is not suited, such as the heavy, waxy soils found in parts of Texas, Alabama, and Mississippi and sticky, "push-type" soils in Hawaii.

6.2. Types of Moldboard Plows. Mounted plows for small and medium-size tractors have been popular ever since the advent of hydraulically controlled integral hitches. As tractor sizes were increased, sizes of mounted plows increased to some extent, but their size is limited because the rearward overhang of large plows causes tractor instability in the transport position. Semimounted large plows were developed to overcome the instability problem while retaining most of the advantages of mounted implements. This type of plow has become very popular since its introduction in the United States in about 1960. The value of semimounted one-way moldboard plows manufactured in the United States in 1966 was more than twice the combined value of mounted plus pull-type one-way plows.[21]

Mounted plows usually have two to five 30-cm, 36-cm, or 41-cm [12-in, 14-in, or 16-in.] bottoms. Semimounted and pull-type plows usually have four to eight 36-cm, 41-cm, or 46-cm [18-in.] bottoms. Semimounted plows are more compact and more maneuverable than pull-type plows, are less expensive, and put more vertical load on the tractor rear wheels (thereby improving tractive ability).

In the usual arrangement, a semimounted plow is supported at the front by the tractor, through a horizontal hinge axis on the hitch linkage that prevents rotation of the plow about its longitudinal axis (Fig. 6.1). When the tractor has lower-link draft sensing (Section 8.14), the horizontal hinge axis is merely a cross member between the two lower links.

136

Fig. 6.1. A semimounted moldboard plow with automatic-steered rear furrow wheel. *A* — three-point hitch frame, *B* — horizontal hinge axis, *C* — vertical hinge axis for plow frame, *D* — steering arm that remains parallel with hitch crossbar, *E* — steering rod for rear wheel, *F* — selective lift cylinder for rear end of plow. (Courtesy of Massey-Ferguson, Inc.)

The rear wheel of a semimounted plow is automatically steered, being linked to a stationary arm on the hitch assembly in such a way that the rear of the plow follows around the tractor tracks on a turn. This arrangement provides good maneuverability and good trailing around curves in contour plowing. A remote cylinder for the rear-wheel lift, plus the integral lift system for the tractor hitch, provides selective raising or lowering of the front and rear ends of the plow when lowering it into the ground or lifting it out.

Semimounted plows often have rubber-tired gage wheels that run on the unplowed ground near the rear of the plow. Some also have a castered front gage wheel that runs in the previous furrow. Mounted plows usually have steel rear furrow wheels to absorb some of the side thrust from the bottoms. Gage wheels are sometimes used, especially for the larger mounted plows.

6.3. Two-Way Plows. Most moldboard plows are designed to turn the furrow slices only to the right. Two-way plows, however, have two sets of opposed bottoms that can be used selectively. With this arrangement, all the furrows can be turned toward the same side of the field by using the right-hand bottoms for one direction of travel and the left-hand bottoms on the return trip. The 2 sets of bottoms are mounted on a common frame that is rotated 180° about a longitudinal axis to change from one set to the other. In most cases, rotation is accomplished with a hydraulic cylinder that is part of the plow. The plow bottoms are rotated up 90° on the retracting stroke, pass over-center due to their inertia, and are let down on the other side on the extending stroke. Gage wheels and rear furrow wheels are automatically repositioned as the plow-bottom frame rolls over, unless each set of bottoms has its own wheel (which is usually the case with mounted plows).

Mounted 2-way plows usually have two to four 36-cm or 41-cm [14-in. or 16-in.] bottoms per set. Semimounted or pull-type units seldom have more than 5 bottoms, but they are usually 41-cm or 46-cm [16 in. or 18-in.]. Because 2 sets of bottoms are needed, 2-way plows are more expensive than comparable one-way plows and are, of course, much heavier.

One-way plows require laying out a field in lands, starting with back furrows (two furrow slices thrown back-to-back) and ending with dead furrows (two open furrows together). A two-way plow eliminates the back furows and dead furrows, leaving the field more nearly level for irrigation or drainage. Two-way plows are also advantageous for terraced fields or contour plowing and for small fields of irregular shape.

6.4. The Plow Bottom. Essentially, a moldboard plow bottom is a three-sided wedge with the landside and the horizontal plane of the share's cutting edge acting as flat sides and the top of the share and the moldboard together acting as a curved side. The primary functions of the plow bottom are to cut the furrow slice, shatter the soil, and the invert the furrow slice to cover trash. The size of a moldboard plow bottom is the width of furrow it is designed to cut.

For many years, most plows had shares of the type shown in Fig. 6.2a. This type of share has a vertical portion, known as the gunnel, that acts as a forward extension of the landside. Gunnel-type shares are removed and shar-

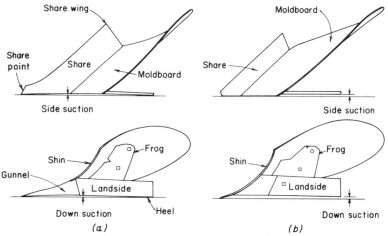

Fig. 6.2. Typical moldboard plow bottoms. *(a)* With gunnel-type share, showing method of measuring suction when no rear furrow wheel or depth-control devices are used. *(b)* With throw-away share, indicating clearances when a rear furrow wheel is used.

pened by forging when they become worn or dull. Practically all plows now manufactured have throw-away shares of the general type shown in Fig. 6.2b. These shares are available with various point shapes. The most common shape of throw-away share is made by merely shearing specially rolled strip stock to the proper length and shape and pressing attachment bolts into countersunk holes. Narrow-cut shares cover somewhat less than the full width of the furrow slice. Over-cut shares extend 2 to 5 cm into the previous furrow to prevent tough roots from sliding around the end.

Because the new cost of throw-away shares is perhaps one-third that of gunnel-type shares, they can economically be replaced when dull or worn, rather than being resharpened. Moldboard shins are also replaceable on many plows, since this is another cutting edge and is subject to considerable wear.

As with any cutting tool, the moldboard plow bottom requires clearance behind the cutting edges. The vertical clearance is known as down suction and the lateral clearance as side suction (Fig. 6.2). When there is insufficient suction, it is difficult to maintain the desired depth or width of cut. Clearance values may range from 5 mm to 13 mm [$^3/_{16}$ to ½ in.], depending on the design of the plow bottom and whether or not a rear furrow wheel or a gage wheel is employed.

6.5. Materials for Moldboards and Shares. Wear resistance in abrasive soils and scouring in sticky soils such as clays and clay loams are two important problems that influence the choice of materials for plow bottoms. Moldboards are usually made from soft-center steel. This is a 3-ply steel, the outer layers being high-carbon steel (usually C-1095, which has 0.90 to 1.05% carbon) and the center layer being low-carbon steel (such as C-1010, which has 0.08 to 0.13% carbon). After heat treatment, the outer layers are somewhat brittle but extremely hard, giving a smooth surface that wears well and scours well in most soils. The center layer, because of its low carbon content, does not respond to the heat treatment. It remains soft and tough, thus providing shock resistance. Similar characteristics can be obtained by carburizing a low-carbon steel on both sides.

Shares are generally made from C-1095 solid steel and hardened by heat treating to provide wear resistance. For extremely abrasive conditions, as in sandy soils, shares and replaceable shins are sometimes made from chilled cast iron (described in Section 3.3). These provide greater wear resistance than steel, but are brittle and therefore subject to breakage if obstructions are encountered.

6.6. Attachments for Moldboard Plows. Rolling coulters are employed to help cut the furrow slice and to cut through trash that might otherwise collect on the shin or beam and cause clogging. Four types of coulters are illustrated in Fig. 6.3. Plain coulters are used in sod or relatively clean fields.

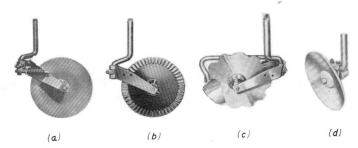

(a)   (b)   (c)   (d)

Fig. 6.3. *(a)* Plain coulter with spring-cushion mounting to permit coulter to ride over obstructions; *(b)* ripple-edge coulter; *(c)* notched coulter with jointer attachment; *(d)* front view of concave coulter or disk jointer. (Courtesy of J. I. Case Co.)

Notched coulters and ripple-edge coulters work well in heavy trash. A coulter is usually mounted with its axis directly above or a little ahead of the share point and with the disk blade in a plane 13 to 19 mm [½ to ¾ in.] to the left of the shin (with a right-hand bottom). A large-diameter coulter goes through heavy trash better than a smaller one but does not penetrate hard ground as readily.

A stationary jointer is a miniature plow bottom that is usually used in conjunction with a rolling coulter (Fig. 6.3c) and cuts a narrow, shallow furrow ahead of the shin. Its function is to move the trash and roots from this strip toward the main furrow in such a manner as to ensure complete coverage by the plow bottom. Disk jointers, which are concave disks set at an angle to the direction of travel (Fig. 6.3d) are sometimes used in place of the coulter-stationary-jointer combination. Moldboard extensions, weed hooks to fold tall plant growth over just in front of the plow bottom, and various other devices are sometimes employed to improve trash coverage.

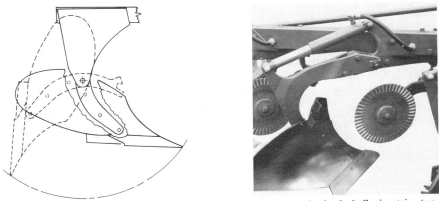

Fig. 6.4. Two types of overload protection for plow-bottom standards. *Left:* Spring-trip standard. *Right:* Hydraulic, automatic reset standard. *(Right,* Courtesy of Deere & Co.)

6.7. Beam Overload Protection. The wide acceptance of mounted and semimounted plows brought about the need for individual overload protection devices for plow standards (beams). The trend toward increased forward speeds further accentuates this need. Figure 6.4 shows two general types of devices that have been developed to provide protection in fields where obstructions are likely to be encountered.

When the load against the share exceeds the preset value of a spring-trip device, the trip releases and permits the plow bottom to swing rearward about a horizontal, transverse axis. In most spring-trip arrangements the pivot point is well behind the share point (Fig. 6.4 *left*), causing the point to move downward in relation to the pivot point. Unless the obstruction will permit the share point to actually move downward, the entire implement is raised by the tripped bottom, which results in considerable extra force on the plow point and the frame, especially at high speeds.

Because of eccentric loads imposed upon the hinge and beam when an obstruction is encountered, careful design is necessary to ensure that friction will not represent a large portion of the release resistance. Some spring-trip units are designed to provide a cushioning effect before the trip releases, so that not all overloads will cause tripping. Whenever a spring trip releases, the operator must stop and either back up or raise the plow out of the ground so the plow bottom will return to its normal position.

Hydraulic-reset overload devices (Fig. 6.4 *right*) provide cushioning and automatic resetting by means of hydraulic cylinders connected to a constant-pressure source. If the tractor has a constant-pressure hydraulic system, the overload cylinders can be connected to this source through a pressure reducing valve. Otherwise, an accumulator partially filled with an inert gas is provided on the plow and is charged up to the pressure needed for the desired maximum overload condition. Hydraulic reset systems have the standards pivoted directly above the share point so the point does not go deeper or raise the rest of the plow when an overload occurs.

6.8. Types of Moldboards. Because soil types and plowing conditions vary widely, many different shapes of moldboards have been developed. Some moldboards are essentially cylindrical sections, some tend toward a spiral or helical shape, and others are modifications of these geometric shapes. From the functional standpoint, common types include general-purpose bottoms, stubble bottoms, deep-tillage bottoms, sod bottoms, blackland bottoms, and slat moldboards.

A sod bottom has a long, low moldboard with a gradual twist (spiral) that completely inverts the furrow slice with a minimum of breakup, thus covering vegetative matter thoroughly. A stubble bottom has a relatively short and broad moldboard that is curved rather abruptly near the top, resulting in a greater degree of pulverization than with other types. The general-purpose bottom lies in between these two extremes and is suitable for a wide range of conditions. Special shapes of general-purpose bottoms have been developed for plowing efficiently at relatively high speeds. The blackland bottom has a relatively small moldboard area, and its shape tends to promote scouring in soils such as the heavy blacklands of Texas. A less common type is the slat moldboard, which has portions of the moldboard cut out and is sometimes used in extremely sticky soils.

6.9. Expressing Moldboard Shapes. Some means of identifying a moldboard shape is needed in comparing and analyzing the performance of different plow bottoms and for manufacturing purposes. Several methods of expressing the shape mathematically or identifying it by empirical methods have been devised.[9] White[29] reported in 1918 that many plow bottoms had surfaces that could be fitted by equations representing hyperbolic paraboloids. Although he was unable to quantitatively relate these equations to either the forces or the resultant soil condition, he did demonstrate that existing plow-bottom shapes can be represented mathematically.

Nichols and Kummer,[14] in a study involving 22 typical plows of various shapes, found that the entire surfaces of all plows studied could be covered by arcs of circles moved along and rotated about the line of travel of the share wing tip or about a line directly above the wing tip. They describe a method of reducing their measurements to a mathematical equation that would express the entire surface of a particular plow but concluded that the complexity of such a relation would make it of little value.

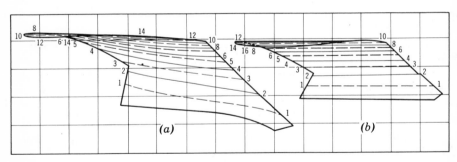

Fig. 6.5. Plan views of two 36-cm [14-in.] general-purpose plow bottoms, showing contours for 25.4-mm [1-in.] vertical intervals. (a) Conventional moldboard with warped surface. (b) Moldboard with cylindrical surface and share. (I.F. Reed.[20])

Reed[20] identified plow-bottom shapes by measuring coordinates for horizontal contours at 25.4-mm [1-in.] vertical intervals and plotting the results on a plan view of the bottom as illustrated in Fig. 6.5. Soehne[23] employed a light-interception method to obtain horizontal contours and also contour lines in vertical planes parallel to the landside. He projected a narrow strip of light onto the white-painted plow surface and recorded the reflected light trace by means of a camera located on a line at right angles to the plane of the light beam. The plow bottom was moved to obtain a family of horizontal contour lines and a family of vertical contours, as illustrated in Fig. 6.12. Representation of plow-bottom shapes by contour lines is a common practice.

Ashby,[1] in 1931, proposed a set of nine standard measurements or parameters of plow-bottom shape. Soehne,[23] in 1959, defined a number of shape parameters that he considered important. Both investigators attempted to relate their parameters to performance. Neither system provides a complete description of the surface shape. Soehne's shape parameters are discussed in Section 6.24.

6.10. Reactions of Soils to Moldboards. The wide range of soil conditions encountered in tillage materially affects the reactions of the soil on moldboard surfaces. Nichols and Reed[15] classify the various soil conditions and describe the reactions as follows:

1. Hard cemented soils. These soils break into large irregular blocks ahead of the plow, with no definite pattern to the soil reactions.
2. Heavy sod. Because of the surface reinforcement from the mass of roots, normal shear planes are not generally observed. However, normal soil reactions occur below the sod.
3. Packed or cemented surface. This is a rather unusual situation, with relatively loose soil immediately beneath the packed surface. Blocks of the surface layer are broken loose irregularly and lifted like boards.
4. Freshly plowed soil. In this condition, the soil has insufficient rigidity and resistance to compression for the plow to function properly.
5. Push soils. These soils, when settled, act somewhat like freshly plowed soil. Adhesion of the soil to the moldboard builds up a pressure ahead of the plow bottom, which, because of insufficient rigidity in the furrow slice, causes the soil to be pushed to one side rather than being elevated and turned.
6. Normal soil condition. The soil has settled and reached a firm condition, primarily as a result of natural agencies, and is within its proper moisture range for good plowing.

Under normal soil conditions the movement of soil on the moldboard is due to the resistance of the soil ahead of the plow, and the average speed of movement of the soil across the moldboard would be expected to approximate that of the plow. Except for an increase in volume as a result of pulverization, there is no evidence of any appreciable dimensional change of the furrow slice in passing over a properly functioning plow.[7] There are, of course, changes in direction which result in substantial acceleration forces.

6.11. Pulverizing Action. As a plow moves forward, its double wedging action exerts pressure both upward and toward the open furrow. Nichols and

Reed[15] found that the stresses set up by this action cause blocks of soil to be sheared loose at regular intervals on parallel, inclined shear planes. These primary shear planes extend forward from the plow point at an angle of about 45° in both the horizontal and vertical planes, retaining their relative positions as they move across the moldboard surface (Fig. 6.6). The soil

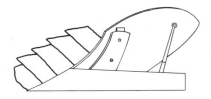

Fig. 6.6. Diagram indicating the development of primary shear planes, as observed in the plane of the landside and shin through a glass surface. (M. L. Nichols and I. F. Reed.[15])

blocks formed by the primary shearing action break down as they move up the moldboard, forming secondary shear planes at right angles to the primary shear planes. Further pulverization is caused by the sliding of these soil blocks over each other.

Nichols and Kummer[14] show that pulverization is promoted if the moldboard curvature is such as to produce simultaneous movement on all primary shear planes (Fig. 6.6) as the plow moves forward. They demonstrate that theoretically this involves uniformly accelerated motion of the soil in the direction of the shear planes and is accomplished by a surface whose vertical profiles in planes parallel to the landside have the mathematical form

$$z = ae^{bx} \tag{6.1}$$

where z and x are the vertical and longitudinal coordinates, a and b are constants, and e is the base of natural logarithms.

Equation 6.1 indicates an increasing rate of curvature from front to rear of the moldboard. Measurements on a number of typical, successful plows showed that vertical profiles in the central or pulverization areas of all moldboards studied could actually be fitted by equations of this type.[14] The lower, or front, portion was steeper than indicated by the equation, in order to obtain strength and suction. Because of inversion requirements, the upper portion was also steeper than the equation would indicate.

6.12. Turning and Inversion. Since the cutting edge of the share is normally at an angle of about 40 to 45° from the direction of travel, elevation of the shin side of the furrow slice begins before elevation of the wing side. Thus, turning and inversion start immediately. Most of the turning, however, is accomplished by the upper part of the moldboard.[14] The final action is to push or throw the soil from the upper moldboard into the preceding furrow, the amount of throw depending largely upon the forward speed and the direction of release of the soil. The inversion of the soil and the accom-

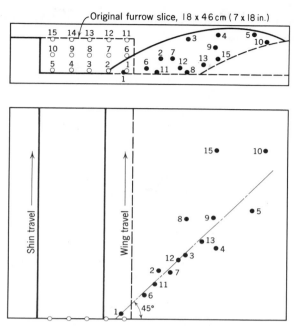

Fig. 6.7. Movement of soil during plowing, as determined by placing small blocks in the unplowed furrow slice and noting their final positions in the turned soil. (M. L. Nichols and I. F. Reed.[15])

panying forward movement during plowing are indicated in Fig. 6.7 for typical conditions, as determined by Ashby and reported by Nichols and Reed.[15]

Nichols and Kummer[14] found that in a group of typical plows the turning and inversion of the furrow slice on the upper portion of the moldboard was accomplished by uniform-pressure curves similar in principle to the spiral easement or transition curves employed in highway and railroad engineering. The shape is such that soil moving around the curvature has a constant rate of acceleration due to turning.

6.13. Scouring. One of the most important aspects of the sliding action of soil is scouring of a tool. Scouring means the movement of soil across a tool surface without sticking, and fast enough to avoid soil buildups. Payne and Fountaine[18] studied the mechanics of scouring along simple surfaces and concluded that the ability to scour is affected by the coefficient of soil-metal friction, the coefficient of soil-soil friction, the angle of approach of the tool, soil cohesion, and soil adhesion.

Scouring will occur as long as the frictional resistance at the soil-tool interface is less than the resistance at a parallel soil-soil interface. When scouring is adequate, soil flows over the tool along a path that is determined by the shape of the tool. In nonscouring situations, soil flows over a layer of soil attached to the tool surface, usually resulting in increased draft and poor performance.

In practice, the soil-metal friction angle is usually less than the angle of soil shearing resistance. Therefore, an increase in pressure against the moldboard will increase soil shearing resistance more than the soil-metal frictional resistance and so will improve scouring.[26] Nonscouring is likely to occur at low spots or other surface irregularities, in areas of abrupt change in surface direction, and in other low-pressure areas. An increasing rate of curvature from front to rear along the soil path tends to equalize soil-metal contact forces and thus improve scouring by avoiding low-pressure areas.[7]

As explained in Section 5.7, adhesive forces due to moisture films have a marked influence on friction. Adhesion may be reduced by employing a material that resists wetting. Bacon[3] reported in 1918 that moldboards coated with plaster of Paris or covered with hoghides scoured better in sticky Texas soils than did steel, iron, glass, brass, or aluminum. He also cites instances in which heat apparently improved scouring by reducing adhesion. Kummer[11] found that wood slats impregnated with paraffin or linseed oil scoured better than steel slats on a slat moldboard in clay soils, presumably because of less adhesion. A slat moldboard scours better than a solid moldboard because the smaller contact area results in reduced adhesive forces and increased soil pressure.

Teflon (polytetrafluoroethylene) is a nonwetting plastic that is being used in Hawaii to make moldboard plows scour in push-type nonabrasive soils. Sheets of the material are merely bolted onto the moldboard and are replaced when worn out.[28] In USDA tests at the National Tillage Machinery Laboratory,[6] a Teflon-covered plow bottom scoured well in a heavy, push-type clay soil where a steel plow would not scour, and the draft at 5.6 km/h [3½ mph] was 23% less with the Teflon-covered bottom. A layer of this soil would stick to the steel surface, causing soil to move over soil and resulting in poor inversion. Both bottoms scoured satisfactorily in a clay soil that had high adhesion but good cohesive strength. The draft at 5.6 km/h in this soil was 12% less with the Teflon-covered plow bottom than with the steel plow.

Excessive wear has been the principal factor restricting the use of low-friction plastic coverings on tillage tools. The life of the Teflon coverings in the nonabrasive Hawaii soils apparently is acceptable, but the USDA tests[6] indicated a life of only 20 ha [50 acres] per 36-cm [14-in.] bottom for 5-mm-thick [0.2-in.-thick] Teflon sheets in a fairly abrasive clay soil. High-density polyethylene had a much higher wear rate than Teflon but is considerably less expensive.

Another approach to reducing soil-metal friction and improving scouring is by applying air to the soil-engaging surface to provide an air cushion or boundary layer which separates the two surfaces that are moving relative to each other.[9,30] Air from a compressor driven by the tractor is delivered to a plenum chamber on the back side of the moldboard and passes through a network of small holes to the front of the moldboard. The effectiveness of this scheme is influenced by the permeability of the soil to airflow, since flow resistance is required to build up air pressure between the soil and the moldboard. Laboratory tests have indicated that use of the air-lubrication principle can substantially reduce the draft of tillage tools in some soils and does improve scouring, but that as much as five air kilowatts may be required to save one draft kilowatt.[30]

Employing a moving surface to transport the soil is another means of reducing friction. Kummer's studies[11] included tests in which the solid moldboard was replaced by endless belts and by a series of wooden rollers. In 1950, Skromme[22] reported the development of a belt-type moldboard to obtain scouring in the push-type soils in Hawaii. This plow would cut a furrow 81 cm [32 in.] wide and 33 cm [13 in.] deep and was operated at 4 km/h [2½ mph]. Plows with rollers or belts replacing most of the moldboard have also been developed in Europe. The moving parts in arrangements such as these are costly and introduce problems in design and maintenance.

6.14. Forces Acting Upon a Plow Bottom. The useful soil forces acting upon a moldboard plow bottom are those resulting from the operations of cutting, pulverizing, lifting, and inverting the furrow slice. These soil forces practically always introduce a rotational effect on the plow bottom. Parasitic forces include those that act upon the side and bottom of the landside (including friction), as well as the rolling resistance of support wheels.

In the following discussion, the force R and its components L, S, V, R_h, and R_v refer to the resultant of all useful soil forces. The term Q indicates a parasitic force, whereas P, P_v, P_h, and P_x (draft) include the effects of both useful and parasitic forces and the force of gravity on the implement. These terms are defined in more detail in Sections 5.7 and 5.8.

In discussing force relations for an unsymmetrical tillage tool such as a plow, it is convenient to give separate consideration to horizontal components and to the components in a vertical plane or planes parallel to the direction of travel, referring to these as horizontal force relations and vertical force relations. In each case the force components are all projected into one plane. Couples are treated separately.

6.15. Horizontal Force Relations. Figure 6.8a shows a typical location of R_h for general-purpose plows with shares in good condition, based on many field tests conducted by Clyde over a wide range of soil conditions.[5] S is shown as 24% of L in this situation. S/L ratios from results reported by other researchers (landside removed, coulter forces not included, coulter usually on) were mostly as follows: sand,[19] 0.35 to 0.45; sandy loams,[8,16,19] 0.25 to 0.40; clay loams,[6,13] 0.20 to 0.30.

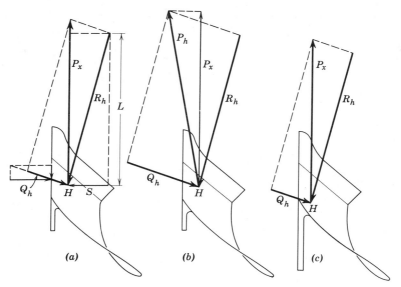

Fig. 6.8. Typical location of R_h and its relation to the landside force and the pull. *(a)* Straight pull, *(b)* angled pull, *(c)* long landside. (A. W. Clyde.[5])

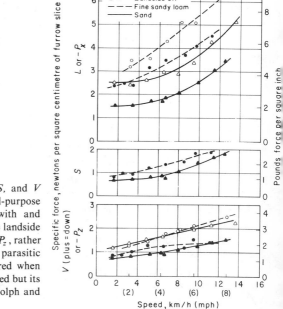

Fig. 6.9. Effect of speed upon *L*, *S*, and *V* forces for a 36-cm [14-in.] general-purpose plow bottom tested in soil bins with and without the landside. Forces with the landside on should be identified as $-P_x$ and $-P_z$, rather than *L* and *V*, since they include parasitic forces. Side forces were not measured when the landside was on. A coulter was used but its forces are not included. (J.W. Randolph and I.F. Reed.[19])

Soil-bin tests conducted at the National Tillage Machinery Laboratory[19] indicated that all three of the soil-force components increase with speed (Fig. 6.9). Field tests in a silty clay and a silty clay loam at speeds from 3.2 to 11 km/h [2 to 7 mph] (without landsides)[13] showed rates of increase similar to those for the fine sandy loam in Fig. 6.9 (but with considerably higher specific drafts because the soils were heavier). In both groups of tests, S/L ratios for a particular bottom changed very little with speed.

Referring again to Fig. 6.8, if the horizontal component of pull were equal and opposite to R_h, there would be no side force on the landside and the draft force would be equal to $-L$. When the horizontal pulling force is in the direction of travel (P_x in Fig. 6.8a), a parasitic side force is automatically introduced on the landside to counteract S. Q_h is the resultant of this side force and the accompanying friction force on the landside. Assuming a value of 0.3 for the coefficient of friction in the friction phase, the draft P_x is, in this example, greater than L by $0.3S$. A pull angled to the left, as in Fig. 6.8b, increases the landside force and would increase P_x still more. Observed increases in P_x due to the addition of a landside are indicated by differences between curves in the upper graph of Fig. 6.9. The differences shown for the sand seem excessive in relation to the magnitude of the side forces.

Point H, the intersection of R_h and Q_h in Fig. 6.8, represents the horizontal location of the center of resistance of the plow bottom. Increasing the landside length (Fig. 6.8c) moves Q_h to the rear, thus relocating H farther back. H is also closer to the landside because the line of R_h does not change. Taking most of the side force on a rear furrow wheel has a similar effect. Soil conditions and other factors also cause R_h (and H) to vary somewhat from the position shown.[5]

6.16. Vertical Force Relations. A moldboard plow bottom by itself generally has a downward-acting vertical component of the useful soil force (suction). The magnitude of V in relation to L varies widely, being influenced by soil type, soil condition, depth of cut, share edgeshape and sharpness, and other factors. The tests mentioned in the second paragraph of Section 6.15 indicated that V increases with speed (Fig. 6.9), but with a tendency in some soils for a slight reduction of V/L ratios as speed is increased. V/L ratios from the soil-bin tests represented by Fig. 6.9 ranged from 0.5 to 0.6 for the sand and from 0.35 to 0.45 for the fine sandy loam. Results reported for field tests in various soil types and conditions, presumably with shares in reasonably good condition,[5, 8, 13, 27] give V/L ratios ranging from 0.1 to 0.3.

Penetrating ability, as reflected by the magnitude of the downward V, is an important characteristic of a tillage tool. With mounted or semimounted implements, V contributes directly to the vertical load on the tractor rear wheels and also increases the load transfer from the front wheels to the rear wheels, thereby providing additional tractive ability. (See Section 8.16.)

Shares with downward-pitched points extending forward beyond the line

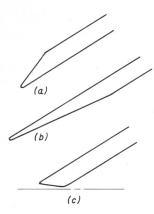

Fig. 6.10. New and worn share edgeshapes. (a) New, top-beveled; (b) new, bottom-beveled; (c) worn share.

of the share edge have greater suction (downward V) than straight shares, particularly at shallow or moderate depths, because the point is wedging farther ahead into undisturbed soil.[13] Tests have shown that throw-away shares beveled on top (Fig. 6.10a) have substantially less downward V than shares beveled on the bottom.[13,16]

The cutting edges of plow shares and most other tillage tools wear to a profile like that shown in Fig. 6.10c, with the leading portion of the bottom slightly higher than the rear portion. This sled-runner effect reduces V for the plow bottom and also increases soil compaction by pushing down on the furrow bottom. Share wear can reduce V for the plow bottom to zero and even make it act upward. Differences of 440 to 890 N [100 to 200 lbf] between worn and new shares on 36-cm [14-in.] bottoms have been observed.[5,13,16] Lack of penetrating ability often determines when shares must be discarded.

Rolling coulters must always be forced into the ground, which means that their V is always upward (Fig. 6.11a). The V component for the plow-coulter combination may be either up or down, as indicated in Fig. 6.11b, depending primarily upon the resistance of the soil to coulter penetration. When plowing with 28-cm [11-in.] bottoms in a 3-year-old pasture on moist sandy loam soil, Tanner and Dean[27] found that the upward V on the coulter was about twice as great as the downward V on the plow bottom, resulting in net upward forces of 220 to 440 N [50 to 100 lbf].

Sod requires more coulter penetrating force than does bare soil. A large-diameter coulter requires more force to penetrate to a given depth than does a smaller coulter. As a soil becomes drier, the upward force on the coulter usually increases and the downward V for the plow bottom alone would be expected to decrease. Coulters are sometimes removed to improve penetration under difficult conditions, and are not always used even under good conditions.

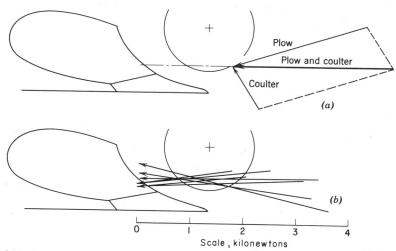

Fig. 6.11. (a) Typical division of R_v (resultant of L and V) between plow bottom and coulter in spring plowing of moist sod (moderately hard ground). (b) Typical values and locations of R_v from tests over a wide range of soil conditions, with a 36-cm [14-in.] plow cutting 18 cm [7 in.] deep at about 4.8 km/h [3mph]. (A.W. Clyde.[5])

6.17. Couples. A right-hand plow bottom by itself is generally subjected to a counterclockwise couple as viewed from the rear. The highest value reported by Clyde[5] is about 225 N·m [2000 lbf-in.]. A rolling coulter decreases this couple, and in hard ground changes it to clockwise (up to 125 N·m [1100 lbf-in.] has been observed). In a complete plow this rotational effect is counteracted primarily by parasitic support forces on the wheels of the plow or tractor or on the bottom surfaces of the plow.

6.18 Draft of Plows. The specific draft of plows varies widely under different conditions, being affected by such factors as the soil type and condition, plowing speed, plow-bottom shape, friction characteristics of the soil-engaging surfaces, share sharpness and shape, depth of plowing, width of furrow slice, type of attachments, and adjustment of the plow and attachments. A great deal of work has been done in evaluating the various factors and investigating possible means for reducing draft. O'Callaghan and McCoy[17] have developed a mathematical method for predicting draft, based on experimentally determined equations for soil flow paths. Their method is described briefly in Section 6.23.

Soil type and condition are by far the most important factors contributing to variations in specific draft. Values of specific draft range from 1.4 to 2 N/cm² [2 to 3 lbf/in.²] for sandy soils, up to 10 to 14 N/cm² [15 to 20 lbf/in.²] for heavy gumbo soils. Sandy or silt loams may have specific drafts from 2 to 5 N/cm² [3 to 7 lbf/in.²], whereas 4 to 8 N/cm² [6 to 12 lbf/in.²] would be typical for clay loams and heavy clay soils.

Soil moisture content is an important factor in regard to both draft and quality of work. A dry soil requires excessive power and also accelerates wear of the cutting edges. In USDA soil bin tests, an increase of moisture content from 9.1 to 11.7% reduced the specific draft in a fine sandy loam by 15 to 35%.[19]

Other pertinent soil factors include the degree of compaction, the previous tillage treatment, and the type or absence of cover crop. For example, the USDA tests[19] showed a 15 to 35% increase in draft when the apparent specific gravity of a fine sandy loam was changed from 1.68 to 1.83.

6.19. Effect of Depth and Width of Cut. Most available evidence indicates that the specific draft of a plow generally decreases as the depth is increased to some optimum depth/width ratio and then increases as the depth is increased further. The initial decrease of specific draft with increased depth is logical because the total force for cutting the bottom of the furrow slice should be independent of depth. The increase in specific draft beyond the optimum depth is probably due in part to choking of the thick furrow slice in the curvature of the moldboard.[19] Deep-tillage plow bottoms have higher moldboards than standard bottoms. Randolph and Reed observed that the minimum specific draft for a number of 36-cm [14-in.] bottoms was at depths of 13 to 18 cm [5 to 7 in.].[19]

Results from a limited number of soil-bin tests in a sand indicate that, for this one soil condition, varying the width of cut with a 30-cm [12-in.] bottom and a 41-cm [16-in.] bottom (landsides removed) had little effect on the specific draft for the bottom alone.[14] But landside friction, draft due to a coulter, and rolling resistance of the plow wheels, which were not included, would change very little and hence would cause the implement specific draft to increase as the width of cut is reduced. Getzlaff,[8] in field tests with 26-cm plows, found that the specific draft increased as the width of cut was reduced below 26 cm.

6.20. Effect of Plow-Bottom Shape and Design. The shape of the moldboard has a definite influence on draft, although the relative effects are influenced by soil type and conditions, speed, and perhaps other factors. Soehne[24] conducted a detailed study of the effects of shape, speed, and soil type on draft and performance. His results show that the order of ranking within a group of plow bottoms, in terms of specific draft, may be quite different at two different speeds or in different soils. Reed[20] also found distinct differences in specific draft for different types of plow bottoms and even among various bottoms within the general-purpose classification. In general, shapes that give the best trash coverage or the greatest degree of pulverization tend to have the highest drafts, although the converse is not necessarily true.

Share edgeshape can significantly affect draft. Three different shapes tested on a 36-cm [14-in.] plow bottom in a clay soil at the National Tillage

Machinery Laboratory had drafts of 1.18, 1.29, and 1.41 kN [266, 290, and 317 lbf] when new.[16] Morling[13] compared 6 types of commercially available throw-away shares, using a 36-cm [14-in.] plow bottom in 3 soil types. Deep-suck shares (having points extended forward somewhat similar to the shape of a gunnel-type share), shares with the points upset to make them thicker, and shares with top bevel (Fig. 6.11a) had 10 to 20% more draft than the reference, modified-curve share. Flat shares had 3 to 10% more draft than the modified-curve share. Some of the shares with higher draft have offsetting, desirable characteristics such as good penetration or good durability in rocky soils.

Worn shares may have substantially greater draft than new shares[9,16] but sometimes have about the same or slightly less draft.[13,16] Share wear occurs rapidly in many types of soil, particularly when the moisture content is low. Draft increases of 15% or more after only a few hours of field operation have been reported.[9]

Changes in design or materials to reduce soil-metal friction offer considerable potential for reducing draft. According to Wismer and his associates,[30] friction on moldboard-plow surfaces may represent as much as 30% of the total draft. Several ideas for reducing friction are discussed in Section 6.13, in relation to scouring. These include covering the soil-engaging surfaces with Teflon, providing an air film between the soil and the metal for air lubrication, and employing moving surfaces to transport the soil. As indicated in Section 6.13, covering a plow bottom with Teflon reduced the draft by 23% in a soil where steel would not scour and by 12% in a soil where both scoured.

6.21. Effects of Attachments and Rear Furrow Wheel. Results from several sources,[5,17,27] indicate that the draft of a rolling coulter may be 10 to 17% of the total for the plow-coulter combination. There is little or no information available to show the relative draft of a plow-coulter combination as compared with a plow without a coulter. It is likely that any difference would be rather small under usual conditions.

A 43-cm [17-in.] disk jointer with the face set at an angle of 10 to 12° from the direction of travel was compared with a coulter-stationary-jointer combination on the same plow, in 3 soil types at the National Tillage Machinery Laboratory.[9] At 4.8 km/h [3 mph] the total draft of the plow plus the disk jointer was about 10% less than the draft with the coulter-jointer combination on the plow. The difference was about 15% at 7.2 km/h [4.5 mph]. Other tests with 41-cm and 46-cm [16-in. and 18-in.] bottoms in sandy loam and clay loam have shown that removing the stationary jointer from the coulter-jointer combination reduced the plow draft by about 7%.[2]

Comparative tests in loam soils[2,5] indicate perhaps 5 to 7% reduction in draft by taking most of the side thrust on the rear furrow wheel rather than all on the landside. The soil-bin results shown in Fig. 6.9 indicate a draft reduction of 30 to 40% in a sand and about 20% in a fine sandy loam when the landside was removed and all the side force was absorbed by the test car. The percentage reductions would be less if the draft of a coulter were included.

6.22. Effect of Speed Upon Draft and Performance. McKibben and Reed[12] consolidated the many speed-versus-draft test results reported between 1919 and 1949. They plotted the percent increase in draft as a function of speed, taking the draft at 4.83 km/h [3 mph] as 100% in each case. These data include several hundred runs with moldboard plows, mostly at speeds from 1.6 to 13 km/h [1 to 8 mph]. A few runs are shown for disk plows and a few for a subsoiler. The data for moldboard plows can be represented reasonably well by the relation

$$D_s/D_r = 0.83 + 0.00730\,S^2 \qquad (6.2)$$

$$[D_s/D_r = 0.83 + 0.0189\,S^2]$$

where D_r = draft at reference speed, 4.83 km/h [3 mph]
D_s = draft at speed S, in same units as D_r
S = speed, in kilometres per hour [miles per hour]

The form of equation 6.2 differs slightly from the form of equation 5.3 (Section 5.19), in that K from equation 5.3 becomes a function of D_r (or a function of D_o in equation 5.3, since $D_o = 0.83\,D_r$ in this case).

Equation 6.2 represents average conditions for average moldboard shapes commonly used prior to 1949. It cannot be applied to any specific situation, but is of general interest. It indicates that the average increase in draft between 3.2 and 6.4 km/h [2 and 4 mph] was only 25%, whereas the increase between 4.8 and 9.6 km/h [3 and 6 mph] was 50%. Different moldboard shapes and different soil conditions have different rates of draft increase with speed, and hence different constants in equation 6.2 or equation 5.3. Soehne's results[24] with a large number of commercially available plow bottoms included some that could be fitted quite closely by equation 6.2 and other shapes that had substantially less increase of specific draft with speed.

Although soil breakup may increase as speed is increased, this is not necessarily the case. Soehne compared 4 general types of plow bottoms in 2 soils at 4.35 km/h and 12.2 km/h [2.7 mph and 7.6 mph]. In one soil there was very little difference in clod size distribution from the two speeds, and in the other soil the differences were not of any great consequence. Different designs are needed for high speeds to produce the desired performance without excessive draft.

6.23. Graphical Analysis in Plow-Bottom Design. Since procedures have not been developed for designing moldboard shapes by means of theoretical analysis and mathematical relations, new plow-bottom designs usually are based on modifications or deviations from existing bottoms that are known to perform satisfactorily. Graphical analysis of soil flow paths across a moldboard is a useful tool for comparing existing and proposed bottoms and predicting some of the effects of shape changes. Flow paths may be determined from scratch marks made when the plow bottom is moved through the soil for a relatively short distance at a constant speed after spraying the surface with a suitable lacquer.[23] Flow paths are not necessarily the same for different forward speeds.

Three-dimensional coordinates of points along each of several flow paths are measured and an empirical equation developed for each flow path. Velocities and accelerations are then determined from the first and second derivatives of these equations. Digital computers have been employed to fit polynomial curves to the measured coordinates and to compute velocities and accelerations along the flow paths.[4,17] Computers provide more accurate fits than manual calculations and permit investigating a much greater number of possible designs.

Although the quantitative significance of such mathematical relations has not been established, comparisons of results for existing plow bottoms permit qualitative evaluations. For example, Carlson[4] compared two bottoms whose performance characteristics had been established through years of field experience. Acceleration rates for the one considered to be the better performer were much more uniform than those of the other bottom and were considerably lower than for the other bottom on the rear portions of the moldboard. Actually, this comparison tends to substantiate the findings of earlier investigators that uniform soil acceleration along the flow paths is desirable for good performance.

O'Callaghan and McCoy developed a method for predicting the draft of a plow bottom, based on experimentally determined equations for soil flow paths.[17] They considered the forces on a 25-mm by 25-mm soil prism extending the full depth of the soil layer on the moldboard. They derived equations to show separately the components of work done in overcoming friction, gravity, acceleration, and adhesion as this prism is moved from any one position to another position along a soil flow path. From these relations they could determine the total work done on an elementary prism in moving along a particular flow path from the front of the bottom to the discharge point. Their equations also permitted determination of V and S, from which parasitic drag forces on the landside and plow bottom could be calculated. Total draft forces predicted by this method checked reasonably well with experimental results obtained in a sandy loam soil.

6.24. Plow-Bottom Shapes for High Speeds. As a first step in investigating plow-bottom shapes for high speeds, Soehne[23] determined graphical representations for the shapes of about 25 existing plow bottoms, using the light-interception method described in Section 6.9. He also observed their performances in the field and measured draft and lateral throw as a function of speed.[24] He utilized equation 5.3 (Section 5.19) to analyze the effect of speed upon draft, calling K the coefficient of dynamic plowing resistance. He concluded from his tests that the most important factor affecting the values of K for different plow bottoms was the lateral directional angle of the rear of the moldboard. He also defined certain other shape parameters and attempted to relate them to performance, particularly in regard to high-speed plowing (8 to 11 km/h [5 to 7 mph]). Several high-speed bottoms were designed and tested, each design starting from a proven bottom for normal speeds.[25]

In general, Soehne's studies indicate that a high-speed plow bottom must be relatively flat, elongated, and pointed so that vertical and lateral soil velocity components will not be much greater than for conventional bottoms at lower speeds. In order to achieve satisfactory inversion, the moldboard must be relatively strongly twisted. Uniform twisting from the landside to the moldboard end provides satisfactory performance for a greater range of reduced speeds than with a moldboard having most of the twist near the end. The moldboard edge needs to be higher towards the furrow side than with a conventional bottom so soil is not sprayed over it at high speeds.

Figure 6.12 compares the shapes of 2 similar plow bottoms designed for speeds of 5.3 km/h and 8 km/h [3.3 mph and 5 mph]. Values for the shape

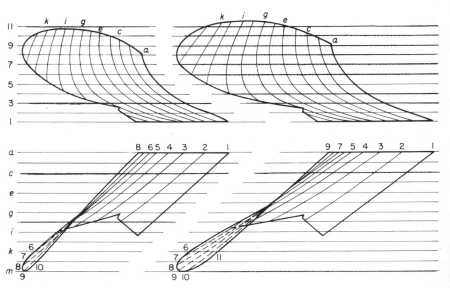

Fig. 6.12. Contour representation of conventional plow bottom that worked well at 5.3 km/h [3.3 mph] (left), and shape developed from it for 8 km/h [5 mph] (right). Each contour line is projected from the plane identified by the same number or letter in the opposite view. (W. Soehne and R. Moller.[25])

parameters that Soehne considered most important are indicated in the following table.[25]

	Conventional bottom		High-speed bottom	
Speed, km/h [mph]	5.3	[3.3]	8.0	[5.0]
Working width, cm [in.]	30	[12]	30	[12]
Working depth, cm [in.]	22	[8.7]	22	[8.7]
Maximum moldboard height, cm [in.]	35	[13.8]	40	[15.8]
Share point angle (between share edge and line of travel), deg.	43		37	
Share lift angle at share point, deg.	22		17	
Share lift angle at share rear end, deg.	18		13	
Lateral direction angle on horizontal contour No. 6				
At front of moldboard, deg.	43		37	
At rear of moldboard, deg.	40		26	

In comparison with conventional plow bottoms operating at 4.8 to 5.6 km/h [3 to 3½ mph], high-speed bottoms operating at their normal speeds should be designed to produce about the same amount of inversion and soil breakup with little difference in the furrow shape or the draft. To ensure adequate soil breakup, the share point angle, share lift angles, and lateral direction angle at the front of the moldboard should be reduced only by relatively small amounts.[25]

REFERENCES

1. ASHBY, W. A method of comparing plow bottom shapes. Agr. Eng., *12*:411-412, Nov., 1931.
2. ASHBY, W., I. F. REED, and A. H. GLAVES. Progress report on draft of plows used for corn borer control (mimeographed). USDA Bur. Agr. Eng., 1932.
3. BACON, C. A. Plow bottom design. ASAE Trans., *12*:26-42, 1918.
4. CARLSON, E. C. Plows and computers. Agr. Eng., *42*:292-295, 307, June, 1961.
5. CLYDE, A. W. Technical features of tillage tools. Pennsylvania Agr. Expt. Sta. Bull. 465 (Part 2), 1944.
6. COOPER, A. W., and W. F. McCREERY. Plastic surfaces for tillage tools. ASAE Paper 61-649, Dec., 1961.
7. DONER, R. D., and M. L. NICHOLS. The dynamic properties of soil: V. Dynamics of soil on plow moldboard surfaces related to scouring. Agr. Eng., *15*:9-13, Jan., 1934.
8. GETZLAFF, G. E. Comparative studies on the forces acting on standard plow bodies. Grundl. Landtech., Heft *5*:16-35, 1953. NIAE transl. 6.
9. GILL, W. R., and G. E. VANDEN BERG. Soil Dynamics in Tillage and Traction, pp. 171-181, 221-238, 246-248, 316-318. USDA Agr. Handbook No. 316, 1967.

10. JOHNSON, O. E. Design factors in a spring-trip beam assembly for moldboard plows. Discussions by W. H. Silver and R. W. Wilson. Trans. ASAE, 3(2):61-65, 1960.
11. KUMMER, F. A. The dynamic properties of soil: VIII. The effect of certain experimental plow shapes and materials on scouring in heavy clay soils. Agr. Eng., 20:111-114, Mar., 1939.
12. McKIBBEN, E. G., and I. F. REED. The influence of speed on the performance characteristics of implements. Paper presented at SAE National Tractor Meeting, Sept., 1952.
13. MORLING, R. W. Soil force analysis as applied to tillage equipment. ASAE Paper 63-149, June, 1963.
14. NICHOLS, M. L., and T. H. KUMMER. The dynamic properties of soils: IV. A method of analysis of plow moldboard design based upon dynamic properties of soil. Agr. Eng., 13:279-285, Nov., 1932.
15. NICHOLS, M. L., and I. F. REED. Soil dynamics: VI. Physical reactions of soils to moldboard surfaces. Agr. Eng., 15:187-190, June, 1934.
16. NICHOLS, M. L., I. F. REED, and C. A. REAVES. Soil reaction: to plow share design. Agr. Eng., 39:336-339, June, 1958.
17. O'CALLAGHAN, J. R., and J. G. McCOY. The handling of soil by mouldboard ploughs. J. Agr. Eng. Res., 10:23-25, 1965.
18. PAYNE, P. C. J., and E. R. FOUNTAINE. The mechanism of scouring for cultivation implements. NIAE Tech. Memo. 116, 1954.
19. RANDOLPH, J. W., and I. F. REED. Tests of tillage tools: II. Effects of several factors on the reactions of fourteen-inch moldboard plows. Agr. Eng., 19:29-33, Jan., 1938.
20. REED, I. F. Tests of tillage tools: III. Effect of shape on the draft of 14-inch moldboard plow bottoms. Agr. Eng., 22:101-104, Mar., 1941.
21. RICHEY, C. B. Design and development of a semimounted reversible plow. Trans. ASAE, 12(4):519-521, 1969.
22. SKROMME, A. B. A belt moldboard plow. Agr. Eng., 31:387-390, Aug., 1950.
23. SOEHNE, W. Investigations on the shape of plough bodies for high speeds. Grundl. Landtech., Heft 11:22-39, 1959. NIAE transl. 87.
24. SOEHNE, W. Suiting the plough body shape to higher speeds. Grundl. Landtech., Heft 12:51-62, 1960. NIAE transl. 101.
25. SOEHNE, W., and R. MOLLER. The design of mouldboards with particular reference to high-speed ploughing. Grundl. Landtech., Heft 15:15-27, 1962. NIAE transl. 146.
26. SPOOR, G. Design of soil engaging implements. Farm Machine Des. Eng., 3:22-25, 28, Sept., 1969.
27. TANNER, D. W., and J. R. DEAN. The soil forces acting on the body and on the disc coulter of a plough. J. Agr. Eng. Res., 8:194-201, 1963.
28. TRIBBLE, R. T. The "Teflon"-covered moldboard plow. ASAE Paper 58-615, Dec., 1958.
29. WHITE, E. A. A study of the plow bottom and its action upon the furrow slice. ASAE Trans., 12:42-50, 1918.
30. WISMER, R. D., E. L. WEGSCHEID, H. J. LUTH, and B. E. ROMIG. Energy application in tillage and earthmoving. SAE Trans., 77:2486-2494, 1968.

PROBLEMS

6.1. (a) By what percentage is the draft (P_x) of a plow bottom increased if the horizontal component of pull is at an angle of 10° from the direction of travel rather than being straight ahead (Fig. 6.8, b versus a)? Assume R_h is at an angle of 12° from the direction of travel and the coefficient of friction on the landside is 0.33.

(b) By what percentage is the perpendicular force on the landside increased? Graphical solution is suggested, with the scale at least four times that of Fig. 6.8.

6.2. The total draft of a 4-bottom 41-cm moldboard plow when plowing 18 cm deep at 6 km/h was 15 kN.

(a) Calculate the specific draft in newtons per square centimetre.

(b) What is the actual power requirement?

(c) If the field efficiency is 75%, what is the rate of work in hectares per hour?

6.3. A 4-bottom 36-cm moldboard plow is to be operated at a depth of 18 cm in a soil that has a specific draft of 5 N/cm² at 4.83 km/h. Field efficiency is 80% and 125 ha/year are to be plowed. Assume that the average relation between draft and speed indicated by equation 6.2 applies in this situation, that total plow costs (fixed costs plus share replacement and other repairs) are $5.00/ha and are independent of speed, and that the energy cost is 16¢ per actual drawbar kilowatt-hour. The operator's wage is $3.50/h.

(a) Express the effective field capacity (ha/h) as a function of speed (km/h)

(b) Determine the most economical speed (minimum cost per hectare) for plowing under the above conditions. Suggested procedure: set up an algebraic relation between speed and cost per hectare, and then differentiate to obtain minimum cost.

(c) How would this speed be changed by increased labor costs? By increased energy costs? By decreased hectares per year?

7

Disk Implements

7.1. Introduction. The disk harrow ranks close to the moldboard plow in importance as a tillage implement in the United States. Heavy-duty disk harrows are used for primary tillage, for controlling weeds, and for cutting up and mixing stubble or cover crops with the soil. Lighter units are often used in seedbed preparation subsequent to plowing.

The popularity of disk plows has decreased drastically since the early 1950s. United States domestic shipments averaged over 30 000 standard disk plows and 13 000 vertical-disk plows per year from 1950 through 1954,[11] but annual shipments from 1971 through 1975 averaged only about 1000 standard disk plows and 1500 vertical-disk plows.[1] By comparison, shipments of disk harrows during the 1971-1975 period averaged about 100 000 units per year and moldboard-plow shipments averaged about 50 000 per year.[1]

Blades on disk harrows and disk plows are concave, usually representing sections of hollow spheres. The action of a concave disk blade is somewhat similar to the action of a moldboard plow bottom in that the soil is lifted, pulverized, partially inverted, and displaced to one side. Disk plows move all the soil toward the same side, whereas disk harrows have opposing gangs that move the soil in opposite directions.

Multiple-disk implements leave a scalloped furrow-bottom profile. The theoretical height of the untilled apexes above the lowest points in the furrow bottoms is directly related to disk spacing and inversely related to disk diameter and the angle between the disk face and the direction of travel.[5,13] In actual practice, the upper portions of the scallops may be broken out as adjacent soil is moved.

Disk implements can cut through crop residues, will roll over roots and other obstructions, and can be operated in nonscouring soils by using scrapers. They do not provide complete coverage of trash, which may be either an advantage or a disadvantage, depending upon the tillage objectives.

7.2. Force Representation for a Disk Blade. The net effect of all soil forces acting on a disk blade as a result of the operations of cutting, pulverizing, elevating, and inverting the furrow slice, plus any parasitic forces acting on the disk, can be expressed in any one of several ways. In Fig. 7.1a, the resultant effect is expressed by two nonintersecting forces, one being a thrust force T, parallel to the disk axis, and the other being a radial force U. This method is particularly advantageous in calculating loads on disk support

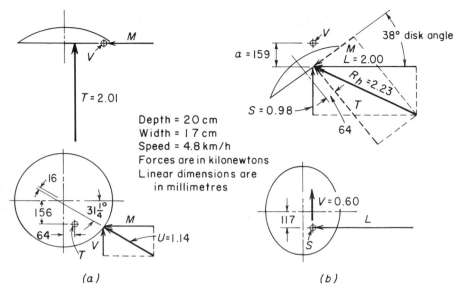

Depth = 20 cm
Width = 17 cm
Speed = 4.8 km/h
Forces are in kilonewtons
Linear dimensions are
in millimetres

(a)   (b)

Fig. 7.1. Example of resultant soil forces acting upon a 61-cm [24-in.] vertical disk blade under field conditions in a silt loam soil, the total effect being represented by two nonintersecting forces: (a) a thrust force T, plus a radial force U, and (b) a horizontal force R_h , plus a vertical force V. (A.W. Clyde.[3])

bearings. (See reference 2 for a description of the procedure.) The thrust force is always well below the disk centerline because the soil acts against the lower part of the disk face. The radial force, which includes the vertical support force on the disk blade, must pass slightly to the rear of the disk centerline to provide the torque necessary to overcome bearing friction and cause rotation of the disk.

The resultant effect can also be expressed by either of the methods illustrated in Fig. 5.1, which are based on the longitudinal, lateral, and vertical components, L, S, and V and resultants of these forces. This type of force representation, illustrated in Fig. 7.1b, is more useful than the other when considering the effects of soil forces upon an implement as a complete unit. In Fig. 7.1b, the L and S components are combined into the horizontal resultant R_h so that the entire effect is represented by the two nonintersecting forces V and R_h (as in Fig. 5.1a). Because these two forces do not intersect, they introduce a couple Va that tends to rotate the implement about the axis of forward travel (the distance a is identified in Fig. 7.1b). This couple is always clockwise for a right-hand disk plow as viewed from the rear, which is opposite to the effect on a moldboard plow without a coulter.

The forces indicated in Fig. 7.1a can be obtained directly from those in Fig. 7.1b (or vice versa) by proper application of the methods of statics.

Although the numerical values in Fig. 7.1 are for a disk on a vertical-disk plow, the same two methods of representation can be applied to a tilted disk, as on a standard disk plow, or to disks on a disk harrow.

DISK PLOWS

7.3. Standard Disk Plows. A standard disk plow consists of a series of individually mounted, inclined disk blades on a frame supported by wheels. A tractor-mounted disk plow has only a rear furrow wheel. Disk plows are most suitable for conditions under which moldboard plows do not work satisfactorily, such as in hard, dry soils, in sticky soils where a moldboard plow will not scour, and in loose, push-type soils such as peat lands. A moldboard plow, in soils and moisture conditions where it works properly, does a better job than a disk plow and has a lower specific draft.

Standard disk plows usually have from 3 to 6 disk blades, spaced to cut 18 to 30 cm [7 to 12 in.] per disk. The disks are tilted backward at an angle of 15 to 25° from the vertical (tilt angle in Fig. 7.2), and are usually operated with the horizontal diameter of the disk face at an angle of 42 to 45° from the direction of travel (disk angle, Fig. 7.2). Disk diameters are commonly 61 to 71 cm [24 to 28 in.]. Scrapers are furnished as regular equipment on most standard disk plows. These assist in covering trash and prevent soil buildup on the disks in sticky soils.

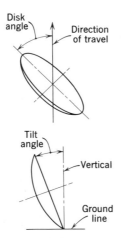

Fig. 7.2. Identification of disk angle and tilt angle for a plow disk.

Reversible disk plows (usually mounted or semimounted) have an arrangement whereby the disk angle can be reversed at each end of the field to permit one-way plowing.

Under most conditions, and particularly in hard, dry soils, any disk tool must be forced into the ground by the effect of gravity upon its mass, rather

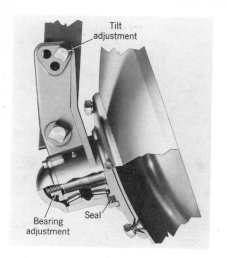

Fig. 7.3. Tapered roller bearings used to support the disks on a standard disk plow. (Courtesy of International Harvester Co.)

than depending upon suction as does a moldboard plow. Consequently, standard disk plows are built with heavy frames and wheels (total masses of 180 to 540 kg [400 to 1200 lb] per disk blade), and even then, additional mass must sometimes be added. Whereas the moldboard plow absorbs side forces mainly through the landside, a disk plow must depend upon its wheels for this purpose. Because of the large, off-center thrust forces encountered, the disks are supported through antifriction bearings, usually tapered roller bearings (Fig. 7.3).

7.4. Vertical-Disk Plows. The vertical-disk plow is also known by various other names such as one-way disk, disk tiller, harrow plow, and wheatland plow. It is similar to a pull-type, standard disk plow in regard to the frame, wheels, and depth control, but the disks are uniformly spaced along a common axle or gang bolt and clamped together through spacer spools so the entire gang rotates as a unit (as in a disk harrow). This implement is used in the Great Plains area and in other grain-growing regions for shallow plowing (often only 8 to 10 cm [3 to 4 in.]) and mixing the stubble with the soil.

The disks of a vertical-disk plow are somewhat smaller than those of a standard plow, the most common diameters being between 51 and 61 cm [20 and 24 in.]. They are generally spaced 20 to 25 cm [8 to 10 in.] apart along the gang bolt. The width of cut per disk depends upon the spacing and upon the angle (adjustable) between the gang axis and the direction of travel. Disk angles range from 35 to 55°, with 40 to 45° being most common.

Widths of cut obtainable with various sizes of vertical-disk plows range from about 2 to 6 m [6 to 20 ft]. Some of the larger sizes have several gangs of disks in line, joined by flexible couplings. Since vertical-disk plows are primarily for relatively shallow plowing, they are built much lighter than standard disk plows (usually 45 to 90 kg [100 to 200 lb] per disk).

7.5. Soil Reactions on Plow Disks. The influence of different variables upon soil reactions has been investigated in a series of tests made under carefully controlled soil conditions at the USDA's National Tillage Machinery Laboratory.[6] Two soils were used, one a fairly heavy clay loam at moisture contents of 14.9 to 17.6% and the other a fine sandy loam at 8.5 to 10.7% moisture. Most of the tests were with a 66-cm [26-in.] plow disk having a 56.9-cm [22.4-in.] radius of curvature. The results reported for these tests include values of L, S, V, and the calculated thrust T, but do not indicate the values of a or the magnitudes of the couples involved. Clyde reports that in field tests with the Pennsylvania State University tillage meter, the magnitude of the Va couple for a plow disk has usually ranged from 125 to 215 N·m [1100 to 1900 lbf-in.] (always clockwise for a right-hand disk).[3]

The effects of speed were determined for a disk angle of 45°, a tilt angle of 18 to 20°, a depth of 15 cm [6 in.], and widths of cut of 18 cm and 23 cm [7 in. and 9 in.].[6] When the speed was increased from 4.8 km/h to 9.6 km/h [3 mph to 6 mph], the draft L increased 40% in the clay loam and 90% in the fine sandy loam. The rate of increase in the clay loam was slightly less than the average rate for moldboard plows indicated in Section 6.22. The side force S also increased with speed because the soil is thrown farther to the side.

The vertical upward force V decreased as the speed was increased. Thus, with the blade tilted, increasing the speed would improve soil penetration under these soil conditions. Tests by other investigators indicate that if the blade is vertical the effect is reversed and penetration is decreased at higher speeds.

The effect of disk angle is indicated for 2 soils and 2 tilt angles in graphs (a) and (b) of Fig. 7.4. Note that in these tests the draft was a minimum in each case at about a 45° disk angle. The increased draft at greater angles is probably due in part to greater throw of the soil. At smaller disk angles the draft tends to increase because of greater contact area between the furrow wall and the convex (rear) side of the disk. This increasing contact is also indicated by the reduction in measured side force at smaller angles, particularly in the fine sandy loam. Penetration is improved by increasing the disk angle, since the upward V decreased considerably.

Increasing the tilt angle, within the 15 to 25° range normally encountered in disk plows, increases the draft and the vertical upward force but decreases the measured side force (Fig. 7.4c). Thus, penetration is better at the smaller tilt angles.

It was also found in the USDA tests that increasing the disk concavity (i.e., smaller radius of curvature) increased the vertical upward force somewhat, especially in the heavier soils, and tended to increase the draft. Comparative tests with 51-cm and 66-cm [20-in. and 26-in.] disks at a 45°

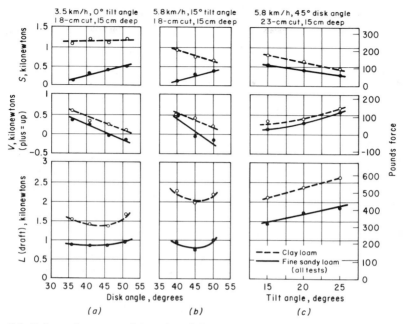

Fig. 7.4. Soil reactions versus disk angle and tilt angle for a 66-cm [26-in.] disk having a 56.9-cm [22.4-in.] spherical radius of curvature. (E.D. Gordon.[6])

disk angle slightly favored the larger disk in regard to draft and penetration when the disks were vertical but favored the smaller disk at a tilt of 19°.

The USDA tests indicated that soil type and soil condition have the most pronounced effect on soil reactions, as evidenced by the comparative results for the two soils in Fig. 7.4. It should be kept in mind that these results were obtained in carefully prepared soils that had not been subjected to the effects of plant growth and other field environment conditions.

Field tests with a 61-cm [24-in.] plow disk in 2 soil types in Australia[12] yielded relationships for V and S versus disk angle and for S versus tilt angle that were similar to those shown in Fig. 7.4. When operating at a 9-cm [3½-in.] depth in a sandy clay loam, L increased about linearly between disk angles of 32½° and 55°. In tests at a depth of 13 cm [5 in.] in a gray silty clay, L increased with disk angle when the width of cut was 20 cm [8 in.], decreased with a 10-cm [4-in.] cut, and remained constant when the cut was 15 cm [6 in.].

7.6. Adjustments for Disk Plows. With some disk plows, the width of cut per disk blade can be changed by rotating the entire frame in a horizontal plane and adjusting the wheels to compensate for the changed frame angle. Reducing the width of cut by this method reduces the total draft. Penetration in hard ground is improved because the total gravitational force acting upon the implement is distributed over a narrower cutting width and because the accompanying increase in disk angle reduces the upward V as indicated in Fig. 7.4.

Penetration of a standard disk plow is also improved by decreasing the tilt angle. If penetration is not difficult, the use of a larger tilt angle will result in better inversion of the furrow slice. A large tilt angle is best for sticky soils.

DISK HARROWS

7.7. Types and Characteristics. The three general types of disk harrows are illustrated in Fig. 7.5. A *single-acting* disk harrow has two opposed gangs of disk blades, both throwing soil outward from the center of the tilled strip. This type is seldom used except when ridges or raised beds are to be split out. A *tandem* disk harrow has two additional gangs that throw the soil back toward the center as a second operation, thus tilling the soil twice and leaving the field more nearly level, but with unfilled furrows along both sides of each pass.

An *offset* disk harrow has one right-hand gang (i.e., a gang that moves the soil to the right) and one left-hand gang, operating in tandem. As will be explained in a later section, the forces acting upon an offset disk harrow are such that, when it is operating with no side draft, the center of the tilled strip is considerably to one side of the line of pull. This feature makes the offset disk harrow especially well-suited for working under low-hanging branches in an orchard. This type of disk harrow is usually designed for normal right-hand offset, as illustrated in Fig. 7.5.

When the front gangs of a tandem disk harrow (or the two gangs of a single-acting disk harrow) are arranged as shown in Fig. 7.5, a narrow strip of untilled soil is left between the center blades. This problem can be overcome by having a staggered arrangement of the two front gangs with the inner blade of one front gang operating directly behind the inner blade of the other front gang.

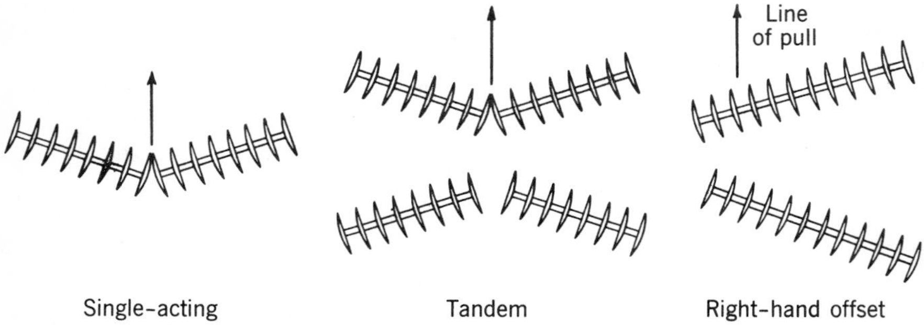

Single–acting   Tandem   Right–hand offset

Fig. 7.5. Gang arrangements for the three general types of disk harrows.

Traditionally, tandem disk harrows have been built lighter than offset disk harrows and have been used extensively for secondary tillage operations. The main use for offset disk harrows has been (and still is) for primary tillage. In recent years, however, models of tandem disk harrows with blade sizes, blade spacings, and masses per unit width that are comparable with those of offset disk harrows have become available. These heavy-duty tandem models (Table 7.1) have about the same primary-tillage capabilities as offset disk harrows.

Some small, light-duty disk harrows (Table 7.1) are tractor-mounted. Most (if not all) current models of pull-type tandem disk harrows have wheels between the front and rear gangs that are used for leveling and depth control, to raise the implement for turning, and for transport. The wider units have hinged outer sections that provide flexibility for uneven fields and can be folded upward hydraulically to reduce the width for transport. Although some current models of offset disk harrows do not have wheels, the trend in recent years has been toward models with wheels. Offset models more than about 6 m [20 ft] wide usually have hinged joints between the ends of gang sections.

Table 7.1. TYPICAL SIZES AND MASSES OF DISK HARROWS

Type	Blade Diam., cm [in.]	Blade Spacing, cm [in.]	Available Widths, m [ft]	Mass per Unit of Width, kg/m [lb/ft]
Tandem, mounted	41,46,51,56 [16,18,20,22]	18-23 [7-9]	1.5-4.0 [5-13]	150-270 [100-180]
Tandem, wheel-type				
Light-duty	46,51,56 [18,20,22]	18-24 [7¼-9¼]	2.4-6.4 [8-21]	270-370 [180-250]
Medium-duty	46,51,56 [18,20,22]	19-24 [7½-9¼]	3.4-9.5 [11-31]	370-480 [250-320]
Heavy-duty*	56,61,66 [22,24,26]	23-28 [9-11]	3.4-13.7 [11-45]	480-700 [320-470]
Offset, pull-type				
With wheels†	56,61,66,71 [22,24,26,28]	23-28 [9-11]	2.1-7.3 [7-24]	400-750 [270-500]
No wheels†	61,66,71 [24,26,28]	23-28 [9-11]	2.7-9.1 [9-30]	390-650 [260-440]

Data based on analysis of manufacturers' information available in February, 1977. Ranges cover most, but not all disk harrows of any particular classification.

*At least one model has 61 or 66 cm [24 or 26 in.] blades and masses of 720 to 900 kg per metre of width [480 to 600 lb per foot of width].

†A few models have 71 to 81 cm [28 to 32 in.] blades spaced 28 to 34 cm [11 to 13½ in.] apart and masses of 750 to 1100 kg per metre of width [500 to 740 lb per foot of width].

Pull-type offset disk harrows without wheels have powered, adjustable angling for depth control, turning, and transport. Angling devices are usually operated with a remote hydraulic cylinder. Gang angles can be adjusted manually on most mounted and wheel-type disk harrows while they are raised, sometimes by merely removing a pin but more often by loosening clamps or removing bolts. Depth control on wheel-type units is usually obtained by raising or lowering the implement through its wheels.

When a disk harrow has wheels, the pull member or hitch between the frame and the tractor drawbar must be rigid or semirigid in the vertical direction to provide uniform depth control for front and rear gangs. The pull member is usually hinged to the frame and has an adjustable control arm linked to the lift mechanism on the cylinder or axle to give a generally parallel lifting action. Sometimes a spring is incorporated in this linkage to provide some flexibility for irregular ground surfaces.

7.8. Bearings. Bearings on disk-harrow gangs are subjected to both radial and thrust loads of considerable magnitude and operate in contact with dirt most of the time. Some mounted tandem disk harrows are available with white cast iron bearings, but most disk-harrow gangs have sealed ball bearings. Tapered roller bearings are usually employed in the wheels. Bearings are discussed in Sections 3.3 and 3.4.

7.9. Disk-Harrow Blades. Although most disk-harrow blades are sections of hollow spheres, blades having a truncated-cone shape are also used. Typical blade diameters and spacings are indicated in Table 7.1. The larger sizes and wider spacings are preferable for cutting up heavy cover crops and for other primary tillage, and they permit greater operating depths than do smaller blades. The maximum operating depth for a disk harrow is usually about one-fourth of the disk diameter.

Small-diameter disks penetrate more readily than do large disks, i.e., they require less vertical force to hold them to a given depth. Reducing the concavity (larger radius of curvature) and sharpening disks from the concave side rather than the convex side also improve penetration (less vertical force required, or greater depth for a given vertical force). These effects are related to the size of the bearing area in contact with the soil on the convex side of the disk.[8]

Some disk harrows are equipped with cut-out or notched blades, usually with one cut-out for approximately each 2.5 cm [1 in.] of radius. Cut-out blades penetrate a little better than plain blades because of the reduced peripheral contact area. They cut heavy trash more readily because they tend to pull it under instead of pushing it ahead. They are also more expensive and wear more rapidly.

Blade wear rates and resistance to impact shocks and fatigue are of concern to users and to manufacturers. In laboratory and field tests with disk-harrow blades made from SAE 1080 steel and heat treated to various hardnesses,[10] the lowest wear rate was obtained when the hardness was in the range from 44 to 48 on the Rockwell C scale (Rc). Wear rates were greater when steel of the same composition was either harder or softer. When steels having carbon contents from 0.45 to 0.95% were tested, the wear rate for any particular hardness decreased as the carbon content was increased. The wear rate with SAE 6160* steel was a little greater than for SAE 1080 steel at any given hardness.

Results from additional laboratory tests[10] indicated that both impact and fatigue resistance for disk blades made from SAE 1080 steel decreased rapidly as the hardness was increased from Rc36 to Rc52. Disks made from cross-rolled steel were definitely superior to disks from straight-rolled steel. In general, field experience has indicated that alloy steels (such as SAE 6160) have better impact resistance than carbon steel and will stand up better in large disks subjected to extreme impact loads under severe operating conditions.[10]

7.10. Soil Reactions on Disk-Harrow Blades. Tests were conducted with single 51-cm [20-in.] disk-harrow disks at the National Tillage Machinery Laboratory to determine the effects of adjustments and design parameters upon the soil reactions.[7] The tests were conducted at 4 km/h [2.5 mph] in a sandy soil having 8.4% moisture, with the disk faces vertical (zero tilt angle). The effect of disk angle on L, S and V forces is shown in Fig. 7.6 for a constant depth and constant width of cut. All forces decreased as the disk angle was increased to 25°, primarily because the bearing area on the convex (back) side of the disk decreased. At angles greater than 25 to 30° the backside bearing area presumably was small.

Increasing the radius of curvature from 47.8 cm to 66 cm [18.8 in. to 26 in.] (less concavity) decreased L, S, and upward V moderately when the disk angle was 12° and slightly when the angle was 23°, but had little effect at 35°. When the width of cut was increased from 5 cm to 15 cm [2 in. to 6 in.] at a disk angle of 23° and a depth of 10 cm [4 in.], the specific draft (L per unit area) decreased slightly, and the upward V per unit of furrow cross-sectional area decreased.

Clyde conducted a series of field tests in a silt loam soil to determine soil reactions on groups of four or five 46-cm and 56-cm [18-in. and 22-in.] disk-harrow blades, using the Pennsylvania State University tillage meter.[3,4] In these tests the value of V was varied by applying different masses to the disk assemblies and then allowing the disks to seek their own depth during the run. The results for the 56-cm [22-in.] disks are shown in Fig. 7.7. Average values of a are indicated, from which the magnitude of the soil couple Va about the axis of forward motion can be determined.

---

*SAE 1080 is a carbon steel with 0.80% carbon. SAE 6160 is an alloy steel containing 0.60% carbon, 0.70 to 0.90% manganese, and 0.80 to 1.10% chromium.

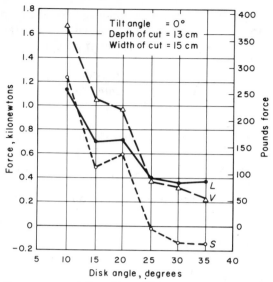

Fig. 7.6. Soil reactions versus angle for a 51-cm [20-in.] disk with a 53.8-cm [21.2-in.] spherical radius of curvature, operated at 4 km/h [2.5 mph] in Lakeland sand having a moisture content of 8.4%. (W.F. McCreery.[7])

The 0.45 to 0.55 kN [100 to 120 lbf] upper limit of V per disk in Fig. 7.7 represents a mass of about 445 kg per metre of width [300 lb per foot of width] for a tandem or offset disk harrow.* This upper limit is somewhat less than the average mass of present-day offset or heavy-duty tandem disk harrows (Table 7.1). The total V for a pull-type disk harrow without wheels is approximately equal to the gravitational force on the implement and any added mass. If a disk harrow has wheels (or is tractor-mounted), the mass of the implement merely establishes the maximum V for the condition when the wheels or tractor are carrying no vertical load from the implement. The magnitude of V when the wheels are being used for depth control depends mainly upon the soil condition, depth of penetration, and disk angle.

The tests with 46-cm [18-in.] blades having a concavity of 44 mm [1¾ in.] and a spacing of 17 cm [6⅝ in.] were at values of V from 90 to 310 N [20 to 70 lbf] per disk. These force values represent 110 to 375 kg of mass per metre of width [75 to 250 lb per foot of width] and cover the usual mass range for light-duty tandem disk harrows (Table 7.1). Ratios of L/V and S/V for both sizes of disks are summarized in the following table.

---

*Calculations based on ASAE Standard S290, "Determining the cutting width and the designated weight of disk harrows", indicate 8.50 blades per metre of width for a 6-m tandem disk harrow and 9.02 blades per metre for a 6-m offset disk harrow.

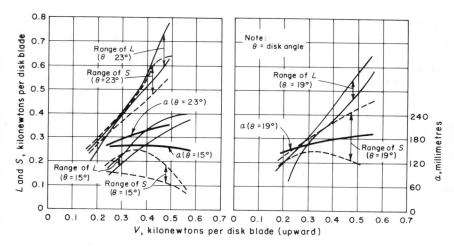

Fig. 7.7. Soil reactions on 56-cm [22-in.] disk blades with 63-mm [2½-in.] concavity and 23-cm [9-in.] spacing, in a fairly compact silt loam with a moisture content of 19 to 24% at a speed of 4.8 km/h [3 mph]. The product of $V \times a$ gives the rotational moment about the x axis. R_h usually met the plane of the disk face near the vertical centerline and R_v met it 13 to 20 cm [5 to 8 in.] above the bottom. (A.W. Clyde.[3])

Disk angle	46-cm [18-in.] blades		56-cm [22-in.] blades	
	L/V ratio	S/V ratio	L/V ratio	S/V ratio
15°	0.5-0.75	0.6-0.9	0.7-0.85	0.15-0.8
19°	0.7-1.0	1.0-1.3	0.95-1.1	0.4-1.1
23°	0.9-1.2	1.25-1.55	1.3-1.5	1.2-1.4

These ratios are for previously untilled soil. Ratios at a given angle may be somewhat different for the rear gangs of a tandem or offset disk harrow because they operate in soil that has been loosened by the front gangs.

Note in Fig. 7.7 that at disk angles of 19° and 15° the observed values of S varied widely for a given V. When the disk angle was 15°, S decreased as the depth increased. These effects probably were due to varying amounts of side support resulting from contact between the back side of the disk blades and the furrow walls. The 23° disk angle apparently was large enough to provide clearance behind the cutting edge at all depths. The wide spread of S was not evident in the tests with 46-cm [18-in.] blades, perhaps because they had less concavity than the 56-cm [22-in.] blades.

7.11. Forces Acting Upon a Disk Harrow. McKibben is credited with making the first complete force analysis on a disk harrow. His studies,[9] which included qualitative field observations, were initiated soon after the commercial appearance of the offset disk harrow, primarily to determine the factors responsible for its ability to operate in an offset position with no side draft.

Soil reactions on an individual blade have already been discussed and are illustrated diagrammatically in Fig. 7.1. The combined soil reactions for a group or gang of disks can be considered as acting upon a single disk blade in the average position of all blades (i.e., at the center of the gang). The forces acting upon a complete disk harrow are then (a) the resultant soil reaction on each gang, (b) the force of gravity acting upon the implement and any extra mass added, (c) any supporting soil forces provided by wheels or as a result of being mounted on a tractor, (d) the pull of the power source. For uniform motion these forces must be in equilibrium. If there is to be no side draft, the sum of the side components of all soil reactions must equal zero.

Vertical force relations for a complete disk harrow are discussed under hitching of pull-type implements in Chapter 8.

7.12. Horizontal Forces. Figure 7.8b shows the horizontal forces acting upon an offset disk harrow without wheels (or with wheels carrying no load) when it is operating with no side draft. The location of the horizontal center of resistance H is determined by the intersection of R_{hf} and R_{hr}. For the condition of no side draft, the hitch linkage of the disk harrow must be adjusted so the hitch point F_0 is directly in front of H.

If the hitch linkage is changed to move the implement either to the right or to the left from the no-side-draft position, side draft is introduced and the operating conditions of the harrow are changed. If, for example, the hitch point in Fig. 7.8b is moved from F_0 to F_2, the force equilibrium is momentarily destroyed and the side component of the new pull, acting at point H, rotates the implement counter-clockwise about F_2.

Rotation continues until the disk angles of the two gangs have readjusted themselves (the front increasing and the rear decreasing, since the total included angle remains constant) so that the difference between their lateral force components S_f and S_r becomes equal to the side draft P_y (as in Fig. 7.8a). Note that the magnitudes of L_f and L_r and the position of H also change during this readjustment. The change in disk angles shown between positions *(b)* and *(c)* seems small, but Clyde[4] states that these results were consistent with those from other tests with this implement.

In changing from condition *(b)* to condition *(a)*, the amount of soil moved by the rear gang is decreased. Conversely, in the extreme right-offset position (Fig. 7.8c), the rear gang is doing most of the work. Even with no side draft (Fig. 7.8b), the rear gang operates at a greater angle and moves more soil than the front gang, because it is in softer soil. In orchards this condition results in a gradual movement of soil away from the trees.

The force relations for a tandem disk harrow are symmetrical about the implement centerline because both front gangs are operating under the same

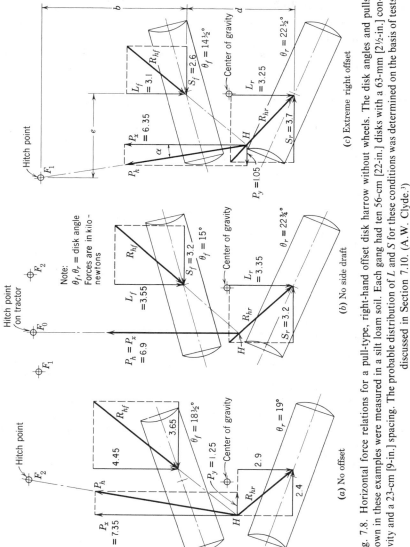

Fig. 7.8. Horizontal force relations for a pull-type, right-hand offset disk harrow without wheels. The disk angles and pulls shown in these examples were measured in a silt loam soil. Each gang had ten 56-cm [22-in.] disks with a 63-mm [2½-in.] concavity and a 23-cm [9-in.] spacing. The probable distribution of L and S for these conditions was determined on the basis of tests discussed in Section 7.10. (A.W. Clyde.[3])

(a) No offset

(b) No side draft

(c) Extreme right offset

Note:
θ_f, θ_r = disk angle
Forces are in kilo-newtons

Hitch point on tractor

Hitch point

Hitch point

Center of gravity

F_2
F_0
F_1

$P_h = P_x$
$= 6.9$

R_{hf}
L_f
$=3.55$
$S_f = 3.2$
$\theta_f = 15°$

R_{hr}
H
L_r
$= 3.35$
$S_r = 3.2$
$\theta_r = 22¾°$

F_2
P_h
P_x
$= 7.35$

R_{hf}
4.45
3.65
$\theta_f = 18½°$

$P_y = 1.25$
Center of gravity

R_{hr}
H
2.9
2.4
$\theta_r = 19°$

b
d

Hitch point
F_1

e

P_x
$= 6.35$
α
P_h

$L_f = 3.1$
R_{hf}
$S_f = 2.6$
$\theta_f = 14½°$

Center of gravity

L_r
3.25
R_{hr}
H
$P_y = 1.05$
$S_r = 3.7$
$\theta_r = 22½°$

soil conditions (untilled), with the side components equal and opposite to each other, and both rear gangs are in tilled soil. Thus H for the 2 front gangs and H for the 2 rear gangs are both on the centerline and the implement operates with no side draft and no offset.

7.13. Amount of Offset Obtainable. Let e be the amount of offset from the hitch point to the center of cut, α = the horizontal angle of pull, d = the longitudinal distance between the centers of the two gangs, and b = the longitudinal distance from the center of the front gang to the hitch point (Fig. 7.8c.) Taking moments about F_1 yields the following relation, assuming that R_{hf} and R_{hr} pass through the centers of the gangs.

$$eL_f + eL_r + bS_f - (b + d)S_r = 0$$

from which

$$e = \frac{b(S_r - S_f) + dS_r}{L_f + L_r} = b \tan \alpha + \frac{dS_r}{L_f + L_r} \qquad (7.1)$$

For the condition of no side draft, $S_f = S_r = S$ and $\alpha = 0$. Then, from equation 7.1, the offset with no side draft is

$$e_o = \frac{dS}{L_f + L_r} \qquad (7.2)$$

Equation 7.2 states that the amount of offset obtainable without side draft is a function only of the distance between gangs and of the relative magnitudes of the lateral and longitudinal soil reactions. The soil-force relations, however, are affected by soil condition, disk angles, disk-blade size and concavity, and other factors. S/L increases as the disk angle is increased and, according to Clyde,[4] is greater in firm soils than in soft soils.

7.14. Couples Acting on Disk-Harrow Gangs. It is a well-known fact that the concave end of a disk-harrow gang tends to penetrate more deeply than the convex end. This condition exists because the soil-force component T, perpendicular to the disk blades, is applied well below the axle (Fig. 7.9) while the balancing force T' is applied at axle height (through the bearings), thus forming a couple Tf.

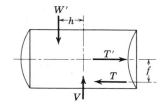

Fig. 7.9. Vertical and thrust forces acting upon a disk-harrow gang.

With uniform penetration, V will act approximately at the center of the gang. To obtain uniform penetration with a single gang, the resultant downward force W' (force of gravity on the gang and any extra mass added, minus any upward component of pull) must act at a distance h from the center of the gang (toward the convex end) such that

$$W'h = fT \qquad (7.3)$$

It is a relatively simple matter with single-acting and tandem disk harrows to obtain uniform penetration by having the couples of the laterally opposed gangs counteract each other through the frame. The design problem is more complex in the case of an offset disk harrow because the opposing couples subject the frame between the gangs to torsion. Adequate torsional stiffness and appropriate adjustments for lateral leveling of one gang with respect to the other are important.

Another complicating factor in an offset disk harrow is that the couple of the front gang is usually considerably larger than that of the rear gang because the rear gang is operating in looser soil. For example, in the tests represented by Fig. 7.8b, the front couple was 723 N·m [6400 lbf-in.] whereas the rear couple was only 462 N·m [4090 lbf-in.]. The larger front couple results in a tendency for the right side of the entire harrow, and particularly the right end of the front gang, to run deeper than the rest of the harrow (considering a right-hand offset disk harrow). Transport wheels, if used for depth control, tend to minimize the problems of uneven penetration.

REFERENCES

1. Annual statistics issue. Implement & Tractor, 91(22):16-70, Nov. 7, 1976.
2. CLYDE, A. W. Load studies on tillage tools. Agr. Eng., 18:117-121, Mar., 1937.
3. CLYDE, A.W. Improvement of disk tools. Agr. Eng., 20:215-221, June, 1939.
4. CLYDE, A.W. Technical features of tillage tools. Pennsylvania Agr. Expt. Sta. Bull. 465 (Part 2), 1944.
5. GILL, W.R., and J.G. HENDRICK. The irregularity of soil disturbance depth by circular and rotating tillage tools. Trans. ASAE, 19(2):230-233, 1976.
6. GORDON, E.D. Physical reactions of soil on plow disks. Agr. Eng., 22:205-208, June, 1941.
7. McCREERY, W.F. Effect of design factors of disks on soil reactions. ASAE Paper 59-622, Dec., 1959.
8. McCREERY, W.F., and M.L. NICHOLS. The geometry of disks and soil relationships. Agr. Eng., 37:808-812, 820, Dec., 1956.
9. McKIBBEN, E.G. A study of the dynamics of the disk harrow. Agr. Eng., 7:92-96, Mar., 1926.
10. REED, I.F., and W.F. McCREERY. Effects of methods of manufacture and steel specifications on the service of disks. Agr. Eng., 35:91-94, 97, Feb., 1954.
11. STRICKLER, P.E., and H.V. SMITH. Farm Machinery and Equipment. Number and value of shipments for domestic use, 1935-39 to 1966. USDA Econ. Res. Serv. Statistical Bull. 419, 1968.

176   PRINCIPLES OF FARM MACHINERY

12. TAYLOR, P.A. Field measurements of forces and moments on wheatland plow disks. Trans. ASAE, *10*(6):762-768, 770, 1967.
13. THOMPSON, J.L., and J.G. KEMP. Analyzing disk cuts graphically. Agr. Eng., *39*:285-287, May, 1958.

PROBLEMS

7.1. Each gang of an offset disk harrow without wheels has 13 61-cm blades spaced 24 cm apart. The total mass is 1400 kg. In operation, V_f = 8.7 kN and V_r = 5.3 kN. The disk angles are 16° for the front gang and 22° for the rear gang. Based on information presented in Section 7.10 and Figs. 7.8 and 8.2, the estimated L/V is 0.9 for the front gang and 1.2 for the rear gang, and the estimated S/V is 0.7 for the front gang and 1.1 for the rear gang. Calculate
 (a) Draft
 (b) Side draft.
 (c) Kilonewtons of draft per kilogram of mass.
7.2. The resultant effect of all soil reactions upon each 56-cm blade of a 7-blade disk-harrow gang is represented by the values indicated for the radial force U and the axial thrust force T in the accompanying diagram.[3,4] U actually passes slightly to the rear of the disk center to provide

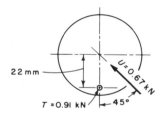

torque for rotating the gang but is shown through the center to simplify the problem. The gang is supported by two combination radial-thrust bearings 1.15 m apart and equidistant from the plane of the resultant radial force for the gang. The total mass of the rotating assembly (disks, spools, gang bolt, etc.) is 115 kg and the center of gravity is midway between the bearings.
 (a) Determine the radial force on each bearing. Use graphical methods where feasible. Suggestion: see reference 2.
 (b) Determine the total thrust force. Discuss its probable distribution between the two bearings, and factors that might affect the distribution.
 (c) What is the magnitude of the couple that must be resisted by the frame (and counteracted by an opposing gang) to provide uniform penetration depth if no extra mass is added?
7.3. A disk-harrow gang with 56-cm blades is operating at a disk angle of 19°, with a V of 0.35 kN per disk.
 (a) Taking the average values indicated in Fig. 7.7, construct a force diagram similar to Fig. 7.1*b*
 (b) By application of static mechanics, determine the location and magnitude of the corresponding radial and thrust forces as in Fig. 7.1*a*.
7.4. A right-hand offset disk harrow is operating with disk angles of 15° and 21°, respectively, for the front and rear gangs. The centers of the two gangs are 2.45 m and 4.25 m behind a transverse line through the hitch point on the tractor drawbar. The horizontal soil-force components are: L_f = 3.1 kN, S_f = 2.65 kN, L_r = 3.35 kN, S_r = 3.8 kN. Calculate:
 (a) The horizontal angle of pull (from the line of travel)
 (b) The horizontal pull, P_h
 (c) The amount of offset of the center of cut with respect to the hitch point.
7.5. Draw carefully a diagram to show the horizontal force relations for a tandem disk harrow (similar to Fig. 7.8). Assume that for each gang the disk angle is 19° and L/S = 1.2.

8

Hitch Systems and
Hitching Tillage Implements

8.1. Introduction. This chapter considers force relations involved in hitching pull-type implements, as well as force relations, design parameters, and performance characteristics of hitch systems for mounted and semimounted implements. Symbols and terminology employed in the force analyses are defined in Sections 5.7 and 5.8. Factors affecting useful soil forces, methods of measuring these forces, and some information regarding their magnitudes and directions have been discussed in Chapters 5, 6, and 7.

The useful soil force components L, S, and V (or resultants R_h and R_v) and the implement gravitational force W are the independent force variables involved in analyzing either a simple drawbar hitch arrangement or integral hitch systems. The parasitic soil forces Q and the pull P are dependent variables that may be influenced by the hitch arrangement. The analysis procedures in this chapter assume that W and the components of the useful soil force are known or can be estimated. Another approach for determining the force relations between the implement and the tractor is to actually measure the magnitude and direction of the pull (or its components) by some method such as those described in Sections 5.16 and 5.17.

It is common practice in analyzing force relations for hitching tillage implements to give separate consideration to horizontal components of R, Q, and P, and to W and the components of these forces in a vertical plane (or planes) parallel to the line of motion. These considerations are referred to as horizontal hitching and vertical hitching.

The primary objective of proper hitching for pull-type implements having adjustable pull members is to establish the locations and/or magnitudes of the resultant parasitic support force $(Q_h$ or $Q_v)$ and the pull $(P_h$ or $P_v)$ that are the most desirable from the standpoints of the effects of the pulling force upon the tractor and the magnitude and distribution of parasitic forces acting upon the implement. Force relations for mounted or semimounted implements in a given soil condition are determined primarily by the design of the hitch linkage and implement and by the method of controlling implement depth, rather than by hitch adjustments.

177

VERTICAL HITCHING OF PULL-TYPE IMPLEMENTS

8.2. Types of Vertical-Hitching Situations. Pull-type tillage implements generally fall into one of the following three categories in regard to vertical-hitching arrangements and the effects of hitching upon the force system.

(a) Implements with hinged pull members that have support wheels or support runners to gage the depth. The pull member acts as a free link in the vertical plane. Examples are moldboard plows, disk plows, and drag-type spring-tooth harrows.

(b) Implements with hinged pull members that do not have gage wheels or runners. The only support is through the soil-working units, and parasitic forces cannot be separated from the useful soil forces. Examples are disk harrows without wheels, spike-tooth harrows, and tandem-gang rotary hoes.

(c) Single-axle implements with rigid pull members. Examples are field cultivators and chisels, subsoilers, and disk harrows that have wheels for transport and depth gaging.

Force relations are shown in the following sections for one example of each type, and hitch adjustment recommendations are included for some other types. One must remember that in all the force analyses, the direction and magnitude of R_v may vary widely from those shown, even within one field.

8.3. Implements Having Hinged Pull Members and Support Wheels or Runners. Figure 8.1 shows the vertical force relations for a pull-type moldboard plow. For uniform motion, W, R_v, P_v, and Q_v must be in equilibrium. Knowing the magnitudes and locations of the implement gravitational force W and the useful soil force R_v under the particular operating conditions involved, the first step in analyzing the hitch is to combine these forces graphically into the resultant AB (Fig. 8.1).

The line of pull is established next. It must pass through the hitch point F on the tractor and the hitch hinge axis selected at E, since the pull member acts as a free link in the vertical plane. The line of pull and the resultant AB intersect at G. The line of action of the support force Q_v is now drawn through G, although its magnitude is not yet known. In Fig. 8.1, Q_v is shown with some backward slant to include the rolling resistance of the wheels furnishing the vertical support. If the support were mostly on sliding surfaces, more slant would be needed to include the friction force.

Since P_v must be in equilibrium with AB and Q_v, the magnitudes of Q_v and P_v can be determined by moving AB along its line of action to DG and then completing the force parallelogram as indicated.

The top example in Fig. 8.1 represents a desirable hitch adjustment for a moldboard plow, with Q_v located well behind the front wheels so there is

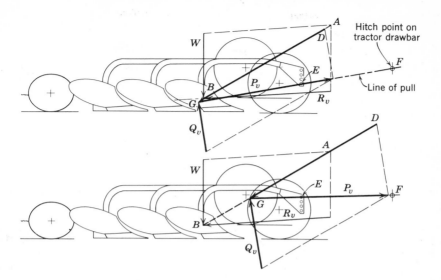

Fig. 8.1. Vertical force relations for a pull-type implement having support wheels and a hinged pull member.

enough load on the rear wheel for stable operation. The lower example illustrates an extreme condition in which the hitch point E is so high on the plow that Q_v is about under the front wheels, with practically no load being carried on the rear wheel. The rear of the plow will be very unstable, particularly when momentary variations in the direction and magnitude of R_v are considered.

Hitching at too low a point on the implement has the opposite effect. The resultant support force Q_v is moved toward the rear, thus reducing the load on the front wheels. Increasing or decreasing the slope of P_v without changing the location of G decreases or increases Q_v but does not change its location. Having too great a slope for P_v can cause difficulty in maintaining the desired depth, particularly with a relatively light implement that has little or no suction, such as a spring-tooth harrow.

Clyde[5] recommends that for moldboard plows the preliminary adjustment of the hitch height on the plow frame be such that P_v passes through a point slightly below the ground surface and directly above the average location of all share points. For disk plows the suggested trial point for establishing the line of pull is at the ground surface midway between the centers of the front and rear disks.[5] If the rear furrow wheel of a disk plow has the proper amount of lead toward the plowed ground and still tends to climb out of the furrow, the hitch point on the plow frame should be lowered, thus putting more of Q_v on the rear wheel.

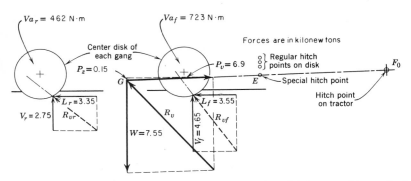

Fig. 8.2. Vertical force relations for a pull-type offset or tandem disk harrow without wheels and with no hinge axis between the front and rear gangs. Numerical values are for the conditions indicated in Fig. 7.8b (A. W. Clyde.[5])

8.4. Implements with Hinged Pull Members but Without Gage Wheels or Runners. Vertical force relations for an offset or tandem disk harrow without wheels are shown in Fig. 8.2. The only support from the soil is through the disk blades. The position of point G is established by the intersection of W and the line of pull P_v. The soil forces R_{vf} and R_{vr} automatically adjust themselves, by means of depth changes, so their resultant R_v passes through point G and is in equilibrium with W and P_v.

Raising the hitch on the implement frame raises G and moves R_v closer to the front gang, thus increasing R_{vf} and decreasing R_{vr}. The result would be increased depth of penetration for the front gang and decreased depth for the rear gang. In the example shown, R_{vf} is greater than R_{vr} because the front gang is operating in firm soil and the rear gang is in loosened soil.

8.5. Single-Axle Implements with Rigid Pull Members. When a single-axle implement receives vertical support only through its wheels, the location of Q_v is fixed. The line of Q_v must pass slightly behind the axle centerline (Fig. 8.3) in order to supply torque to overcome wheel-bearing friction and cause rotation of the wheels. Point G is fixed by the intersection of AB and Q_v, and the line of pull is through G and the vertical hitch point F at the tractor drawbar. The only possible hitch adjustment is changing the height of the drawbar at F, which would change the slope of P_v. In the example shown, with R_v having a downward slope, moving the wheels rearward with respect to the soil-engaging tools would increase the slope of P_v and reduce the magnitude of Q_v.

The force relations for a disk harrow having wheels to gage the depth would be basically the same as the relations shown in Fig. 8.3, but R_v would have a steep upward slope as shown in Fig. 8.2. The fore-and-aft location of R_v would be determined by the relative depths and soil resistances of the front and rear gangs. The relative depths would be related to the attitude of the frame, as established by the vertical adjustment of the rigid pull member.

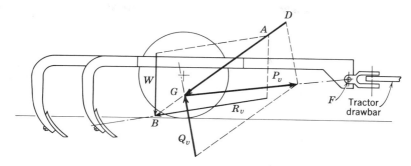

Fig. 8.3. Vertical force relations for a single-axle, pull-type implement receiving vertical support only through its wheels.

HORIZONTAL HITCHING OF PULL-TYPE IMPLEMENTS

8.6. Types of Horizontal Hitching Situations. Most tillage implements, with the exception of moldboard plows, disk plows, and offset disk harrows, are symmetrical about their longitudinal centerlines. The side components of the soil forces are balanced, the horizontal center of resistance is at the center of the tilled width, and the horizontal line of pull is in the direction of travel.

Plows and offset disk harrows can withstand substantial amounts of side draft (lateral component of pull), and proper hitching is necessary to minimize adverse effects on the tractor and the implement. Moldboard plows absorb side forces through the landsides, disk plows through the furrow wheels, and offset disk harrows by automatically changing the disk angles to create a difference between the soil-force side components for the front and rear gangs. Pull-type disk plows have essentially free-link pull members, whereas moldboard plows and disk harrows have laterally rigid pull members. Horizontal hitching for moldboard plows and disk plows is discussed in the two following sections. Horizontal force relations for an offset disk harrow were covered in Section 7.12.

It is not always possible to have the horizontal center of resistance of an implement directly behind the center of pull of the tractor, particularly for narrow implements and wide-tread tractors. If the implement can withstand side forces, the alternatives are a central angled pull passing through the center of pull of the tractor, an offset straight pull, or an offset angled pull. If the implement cannot withstand side draft, the only alternative is an offset straight pull. The center of pull of the tractor is generally considered to be midway between the rear wheels and slightly ahead of the axle, since the differential divides the torque to the wheels about equally.

A central angled pull does not affect tractor steering, whereas the offset pulls do. An angled pull (either central or offset) introduces a side force on the tractor rear wheels which is sometimes of sufficient magnitude to be objectionable. An angled pull is undesirable with some implements, even though the implement can resist the side forces. Usually, some compromise in hitching is best, with part of the adverse effect being absorbed by the tractor and part by the implement. For implements such as the moldboard plow and the offset disk harrow, the lateral location of the center of resistance can be controlled somewhat by design relations (Sections 6.15 and 7.12).

8.7. Horizontal Hitching of Pull-Type Moldboard Plows. As indicated in Section 6.15, the location of the horizontal center of resistance H for a moldboard plow bottom is determined by the point of intersection of the parasitic force Q_h, acting upon the landside, and R_h. The lateral location of H varies somewhat, depending upon soil conditions, length of landside, amount of side force taken by the rear furrow wheel, etc. For hitching purposes the location is often assumed to be about one-fourth of the width of cut over from the landside and a little behind the rear edge of the share. The line of pull is determined by the location of H and the location of the drawbar hitch point F (Fig. 8.4), since the pull member is laterally rigid.

The ideal hitch is obtained when the tractor tread can be adjusted so the center of pull is directly ahead of the horizontal center of resistance. In some cases, however, a sufficiently narrow wheel tread cannot be obtained or is not practical, even with one rear wheel in the furrow. With large plows, the tractor is sometimes operated with both wheels on unplowed ground, primarily to reduce soil compaction from the wheel in the furrow. When a central, straight pull cannot be obtained, it is common practice to divide the effects of the offset, as indicated in Fig. 8.4, so that the line of pull passes a little to the right of the center of pull but not enough to cause steering troubles. Fortunately, a moldboard plow will operate satisfactorily even when the line of pull is at a considerable angle from the line of travel.

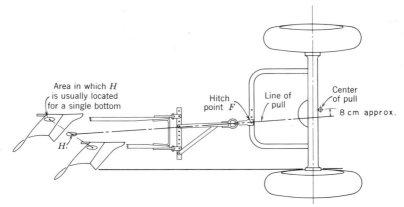

Fig. 8.4. Recommended horizontal hitching for a moldboard plow pulled by a wide tractor. (R. J. McCall and A. W. Clyde. Pennsylvania Agr. Ext. Circ. 259.)

8.8. Horizontal Hitching of Pull-Type Disk Plows. The horizontal force relations (Fig. 8.5) are somewhat different for a disk plow than for a moldboard plow, because all the side thrust must be taken through the wheels and because the pull member on a disk plow (DF in Fig. 8.5) is essentially a free link in regard to horizontal forces. Whereas the horizontal line of pull on a moldboard plow must pass through the hitch point on the tractor and through a center of resistance established primarily by the plow and soil characteristics, the horizontal line of pull for a disk plow is determined by the location of hitch points D and F. The position of the horizontal center of resistance H and the location of the resultant side force Q_h are then established by the point of intersection of P_h and R_h.

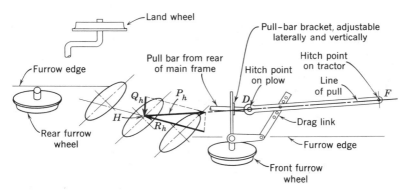

Fig. 8.5. Horizontal force relations and hitching for a pull-type disk plow. Although a standard disk plow is shown, the relations are basically the same for a vertical-disk plow.

For the side force to be divided equally between the front and rear furrow wheels, the line of Q_h must pass midway between them. With most pull-type disk plows this condition will be approximated if the hitch is adjusted so the line of pull passes through a point slightly to the left of the average position of all disk centers (thus establishing H in the desired location).[5] If hitch point D in Fig. 8.5 is moved to the left on the plow frame, H and Q_h will be moved toward the rear of the plow, and the rear furrow wheel will carry a greater proportion of the side thrust. Moving D to the right (or F to the left) puts more of the side thrust on the front wheel.

HITCHES FOR MOUNTED IMPLEMENTS

8.9. Design Considerations and Types of Linkages. Two types of hitch linkages are common on present-day tractors. Practically all rear-mounted hitches are of the three-point, converging-link type, and parallel-link hitches are employed extensively for front-mounted cultivators. Single-axis hitches have been superseded by three-point hitches in new designs. Any of these three types can be operated with the hitch members acting as free links in vertical planes or with the implement supported through the lift mechanism of the tractor (restrained links).

Some of the factors that should be considered in designing or evaluating a system for mounting tillage implements on the rear of a tractor are:

1. Ease of attachment and adjustment; versatility; and safety.
2. Standardization to permit interchangeability.
3. Uniformity of tillage depth as the tractor passes over ground-surface irregularities.
4. Ability to obtain penetration of the implement under adverse conditions, particularly with implements such as disk harrows and disk plows.
5. Rapidity with which tools such as plows and listers enter the ground.
6. Trailing characteristics of the implement around contours and on side hills.
7. Effect of the implement upon the tractive ability of the tractor (vertical load transfer from front wheels to rear wheels).
8. Effect of the raised implement upon the transport stability of the tractor.

8.10. Three-Point Hitches. Following the introduction of hydraulic control systems on tractors in the late 1930s, quite a number of different hitch arrangements for rear-mounted implements were developed. From these evolved the present-day, standardized three-point hitch systems (Fig. 8.6) that are used worldwide by tractor manufacturers. The two lower links converge toward the front and are free to swing laterally within limits. They may also be locked so they are laterally rigid, which is desirable in some nontillage applications. The upper link and the lower links converge vertically toward the front.

The ASAE-SAE standards for 3-point hitches[1] specify all dimensions related to the 3 connecting points between the implement and the tractor, as well as minimum limits for lift height, lateral leveling adjustments, and side sway, and the minimum lift force to be available at the hitch pins. Link lengths and the amounts of horizontal and vertical convergence are not specified. Dimensions are included for 4 hitch categories for different ranges of maximum drawbar power, as follows: category I — 15 to 35 kW [20 to 45 hp], category II — 30 to 75 kW [40 to 100 hp], category III — 60 to 168 kW [80 to 225 hp], and category IV — 135 to 300 kW [180 to 400 hp].

Quick-attaching couplers for three-point hitches have been developed to facilitate the attachment of implements that are too heavy to be nudged into position by one man. These have been standardized to fit onto the standard three-point linkage systems. An example is shown in Fig. 8.6. The hitch links can be connected directly to the implement if the coupler is not used. Quick-

Fig. 8.6. Three-point hitch with quick-attaching coupler. (Courtesy of Deere & Co.)

attaching couplers allow the operator to couple or uncouple an implement without leaving the tractor seat, thus contributing to both convenience and safety.

8.11. Free-Link Operation of Three-Point Hitches. With free-link operation, depth is controlled by gage wheels or other supporting surfaces on the implement. Although depth control form mounted moldboard plows can be obtained through vertical support from the rear furrow wheel and the heel of the rear landside, gage wheels running on the unplowed ground are more common when free-link operation is desired.

The vertical force relations for free-link operation with a moldboard plow having a gage wheel are shown in Fig. 8.7. In free-link operation, the convergence of the links in a vertical plane provides a vertical hitch point or instantaneous center of rotation as shown at F_v. The location of F_v can readily be changed by modifying the arrangement of the links and it shifts automatically as the implement is raised or lowered. The broken-line position of the links in Fig. 8.7 illustrates how F'_v is lower than F_v and farther to the rear when the tool is entering the ground. This shift promotes more rapid

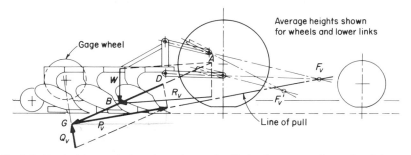

Fig. 8.7. Vertical force relations for a three-point hitch when operated as a free-link system.

entry of tools that have appreciable bottom support surfaces (such as a moldboard plow).

The force analysis is basically the same as for a single-axle, pull-type implement (Section 8.5) except that the line of pull P_v must pass through the virtual hitch point F_v rather than through a real hitch point. All the vertical support in this example is assumed to be on the gage wheel, thus establishing the line of action of Q_v. The slope represents the coefficient of rolling resistance. W and R_v are first combined into the resultant AB, and the location of G is established by the intersection of AB and Q_v. P_v then passes through G and F_v.

Raising F_v, by modifying the linkage, would reduce Q_v and increase the load on the tractor rear wheels, as will be explained in Section 8.16. However, Q_v must not be reduced to the point where the implement becomes unstable due to momentary variations in R_v. Increasing the plow length by adding more bottoms would move W, R_v, Q_v, and G farther to the rear. P_v would then have less slope but would be higher above the ground at the tractor wheels.

Gaged, free-link operation gives more uniform depth than either automatic position control or automatic draft control when the field surface is irregular and the soil resistance varies substantially, particularly with the larger sizes of mounted moldboard plows. Gage wheels are sometimes used in preference to the other systems in light soils where the draft is relatively low. Wide field cultivators and chisels often have gage wheels to minimize depth variations across the width of the implement.

8.12. Restrained-Link Operation of Three-Point Hitches. In restrained-link operation, the implement gets all or most of its vertical support from the tractor, the hitch links being free only when the tool is entering the ground. As soon as a moldboard plow, for example, reaches its working depth, it is held by the hydraulic system. Its landside and rear furrow wheel must have clearance above the furrow bottom so the plow can go deeper when the controls call for greater depth.

Since the implement obtains no support from the soil, P_v is merely the equilibrant of W and R_v as indicated in Fig. 8.8. The lift links are in tension and the implement exerts downward bending moments on the portions of the lower links behind the lift links. Reference 2 describes a method for graphic determination of the forces acting upon the hitch links when P_v is known.

With restrained-link operation, the effect of the implement upon the tractor when the implement is at its operating depth is independent of the hitch linkage arrangement. The only significance of the virtual center of rotation F_v is that, with single-acting lift mechanisms (the usual arrangement for integral systems), the line of pull cannot pass below this point. However, when the tool is entering the ground, the location of the virtual center of rotation affects the pitch of the tool, just as it does with full free-link operation.

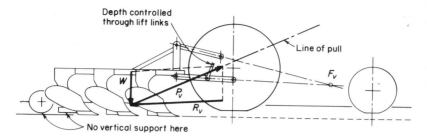

Fig. 8.8. Vertical force relations for a mounted implement when supported by restrained links. W and R_v are the same as in Fig. 8.7.

Operating with restrained links rather than free links increases the vertical load on the tractor rear wheels and thereby provides greater tractive ability. This is because the support forces that would act upon the gaging units in a free-link system are transferred to the tractor rear wheels when the links are restrained and because the higher location of P_v at the rear wheels increases the load transfer from the front wheels to the rear wheels.

But when the implement is suspended at a fixed height with respect to the tractor, as with automatic position control (Section 4.20), depth fluctuations caused by ground-surface irregularities are greater than with a gaged, free-link system. The magnitude of this problem increases in direct proportion to the amount of overhang of the implement behind the tractor rear axle.

In some European countries, height sensors that actuate the hydraulic lift system are attached to the frames of mounted plows in the vicinity of the plow bottoms.[3] This arrangement gives good depth control, even in undulating fields, while retaining the advantage of extra rear-wheel loading obtained with restrained-link operation.

8.13. Automatic Draft Control. This is a type of restrained-link system in which the depth of the implement is automatically adjusted to maintain a preselected, constant draft, as explained in Section 4.21. If the soil resistance is uniform, depth fluctuations caused by irregular ground surfaces are less with automatic draft control than with automatic position control, but may still be appreciable.[7] In a field with nonuniform soil conditions, depth will vary as a result of the variations in soil resistance, regardless of whether the field is smooth or undulating. Dwyer[9] has made a theoretical analysis of the operation of automatic draft control systems over undulating surfaces, in which he considered the effects of all forces acting upon the plow and of the response sensitivity. He checked his analysis with the results of field tests.

In smooth fields, automatic draft control maintains the average draft within the available power or tractive ability of the tractor. It also acts to dynamically increase vertical-load transfer to the drive wheels when high draft requirements of short duration are encountered. When an overload occurs, the automatic draft control system attempts to lift the implement against gravity and its inertia and against any downward soil force components. This lifting action behind the tractor results in a counterbalancing lifting action on the front wheels, thus momentarily transferring vertical load to the drive wheels from both the implement and the front wheels and minimizing wheel slippage until the draft overload has been reduced. If the excessive soil resistance persists over any appreciable distance, the implement depth is reduced proportionately.

Wilson[14] reports the results of field tests with a 5-bottom mounted plow in which 36 draft corrections per minute were observed in loam and 12 per minute in a sandy soil. The average duration of the draft corrections was 0.2 s. During the corrections an average of 1.8 kN [400 lbf] above the normal was transferred from the plow and 1.3 kN [300 lbf] from the front wheels, thus momentarily adding 3.1 kN [700 lbf] of vertical load to the tractor rear wheels.

8.14. Draft Sensing. *Upper-link* draft sensing was employed on all early automatic draft control systems and is still used extensively on small and medium-size tractors. With mounted implements of appropriate sizes for these tractors, the upper link is almost always in compression when the tools are in the ground.

However, the long overhang of plows for large tractors causes the line of pull to pass above the lower-link hitch points in many cases, thus putting the upper link in tension. In the normal operating range, the upper link may be subject to either tension or compression. It can provide no signal if the line of pull passes directly through the lower-link hitch points. Consequently, most of the larger tractors have lower-link sensing or tractor driveline torque sensing (Section 4.21).

8.15. Vertical Hitching Relations for a Semimounted Plow. A semimounted plow is usually attached only to the two lower links, as shown in Fig. 8.9. If the tractor has upper-link sensing, automatic draft control can be obtained only by using an A-frame as shown in Fig. 6.1, in which the horizontal hinge axis is slightly below the lower-link hitch pins so the upper link is subjected to compression. The line of pull passes through the horizontal hinge axis in either case.

In this example, as in Fig. 8.7, all the vertical support force from the soil is assumed to act upon the rear furrow wheel. Actually, the plow bottoms probably provide some support, which would put Q_v somewhat forward from the rear wheel. W is shown larger in proportion to R_v than in Fig. 8.7 and 8.8 because semimounted plows are about 50% heavier per bottom than are mounted plows.

Since P_v must pass through the horizontal hinge axis provided at the three-point hitch, locating the hinge axis higher on the frame would raise P_v and thereby increase the vertical-load transfer to the tractor rear wheels.

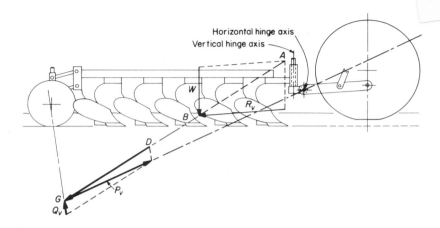

Fig. 8.9. Vertical force relations for a semimounted plow. All the vertical support from the soil is assumed to be at the rear furrow wheel.

Wilson[14] found that the momentary dynamic load-transfer increases due to automatic draft corrections in two soil types were less than half as great as for a comparable mounted plow, probably because of the shorter moment arms involved in lifting the semimounted plow.

Field observations with a five-bottom, semimounted plow indicated very little difference between automatic position control and automatic draft control in regard to uniformity of depth in undulating ground conditions.[14]

8.16. Vertical Effects upon the Tractor. When the magnitude and line of action of P_v are known, the effect of the implement upon the drive-wheel loading of the tractor can readily be determined. The force relations in a vertical plane are shown in Fig. 8.10. R_r and R_f are the vertical supporting soil reactions upon the wheels, and R_t is the tractive effort. R_r is slightly in front of the rear axle (perhaps 25 to 50 mm [1 to 2 in.]) because of the rolling resistance of the tractor. P_v' is the pull of the implement upon the tractor. It is equal and opposite to P_v' and may be from a pull-type, mounted, or semimounted implement. P_z' and P_x' are the vertical and horizontal components of P_v'. The distance y is the height above the ground at which P_v' intersects the vertical line of action of R_r. W_t is the force of gravity on the tractor, acting through the center of gravity.

Taking moments about C_2 yields the following relation.

$$R_r x_1 - W_t x_2 - P_z' x_1 - P_x' y = 0$$

from which

$$R_r = W_t \left(\frac{x_2}{x_1}\right) + P_z' + P_x' \left(\frac{y}{x_1}\right) \tag{8.1}$$

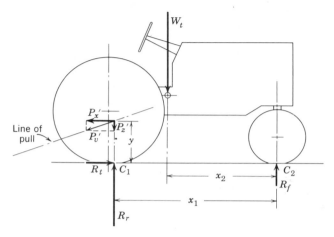

Fig. 8.10. Vertical force relations for a tractor when pulling an implement at a uniform velocity on level ground.

Taking moments about C_1 gives

$$W_t (x_1 - x_2) - P'_x y - R_f x_1 = 0$$

from which

$$R_f = W_t \left(\frac{x_1 - x_2}{x_1} \right) - P'_x \left(\frac{y}{x_1} \right) \qquad (8.2)$$

These equations indicate that the effect of the implement pull is to add the vertical force P'_z to the rear wheels and to transfer from the front wheels to the rear wheels a vertical force equal to $P'_x y/x_1$, thus increasing the tractive ability.

Instability of the tractor when the implement is in the raised or transport position is sometimes a limiting factor for rear-mounted equipment. Front-end masses may be needed to counterbalance heavy implements having long overhangs. Borchelt and Smith[4] suggest that implements should be designed to produce moderately high lines of pull to provide maximum load transfer for good tractive performance, but not high enough to cause front-end instability.

8.17. Horizontal Effects of Hitching. The trailing characteristics of a mounted tillage implement should be such that a reasonably uniform width of cut is maintained when operating around a curve (such as on a contour) without adversely affecting the tractor steering. If a rear-mounted implement is not permitted any lateral movement with respect to the tractor, the implement will cut to the outside when operating on a curve and steering response may be poor because of the side forces introduced by the implement. These effects are particularly objectionable with an implement such as a plow. A laterally swinging hitch gives easier steering, but the implement ordinarily cuts to the inside on a corner as explained in the following paragraphs.

Figure 8.11 shows the plan view of a mounted implement on a three-point hitch. The lower links converge toward the front and are free to swing laterally. With the tractor operating on a slight curve as indicated, M is the instantaneous center of rotation of the two lower links but is not a virtual hitch point. Because the line of action of the force in the top link does not pass through M, the sum of the forces in the three links lies along some line BH which passes between M and the tractor centerline. H is the horizontal center of the resistance of the implement and BH is the line of pull. P_h' is the pull of the implement upon the tractor and is in equilibrium with F_{1h}, F_{2h}, and F_{3h}. The direction of P_h' can be determined from the linkage geometry in the vertical and horizontal planes.

A nondirectional implement (i.e., one that has little or no resistance to side forces) tends to move along the line of pull when the tractor is on a curve, the linkage adjusting itself so that BH is perpendicular to a radius drawn through H and the turning center for the tractor. The effect is the same as that of a trailed implement pulled from a point within the small area A_1 on the tractor centerline. The implement cuts the corner more than it would if M were the virtual hitch point. The total amount of corner cutting is the distance from H to arc CD, as indicated in Fig. 8.11.

Some implements, such as a moldboard plow or a cultivator equipped with a guiding coulter or fin, are directional. Within reasonable limits they tend to go in the direction in which they are pointed, rather than in the direction of pull. In this case the implement is pulled toward the virtual hitch zone A_2, representing the intersection of the implement centerline and the tractor

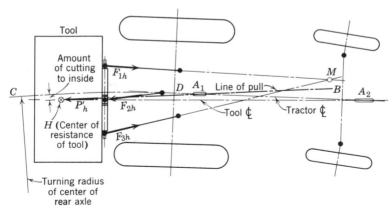

Fig. 8.11. Trailing characteristics with horizontally converging pivotal links (three-point hitch) when operating around a curve.

centerline (Fig. 8.11), and the implement adjusts itself so A_2H is perpendicular to the radius line through H. Since A_2 is farther forward than A_1, a directional implement cuts the corner even more than an implement that is free to move in the direction of pull.

For ideal trailing of any implement around a curve (no corner cutting), the horizontal hitch point (real or virtual) should be on the tractor centerline, equidistant from the center of resistance of the implement (H) and the center of pull of the tractor (D). On a side hill, however, where the rear of the tractor tends to slide downhill, the lateral position of the implement will be affected least when the hitch point is well forward on the tractor. A hitch point somewhat forward of the rear axle is also best in regard to ease of steering. Thus a compromise must be made to determine the best overall location for the horizontal hitch point for mounted implements.

As indicated in Section 6.2, a semimounted moldboard plow has a rear wheel that is automatically steered in such a way that the rear of the plow follows around the tractor tracks on a turn. This arrangement provides good trailing around moderate curves in contour plowing, with less corner cutting than would be experienced with a comparable mounted plow. The directional characteristics resulting from landside pressures limit the sharpness of curves on which the rear wheel can be effective when the curve is concave toward the plowed ground.

8.18. Parallel-Link Hitches. Hitches with parallel links are used on most mounted row-crop cultivators because raising or lowering the gang or tool bar changes the depths of all shovels by the same amount and does not change the pitch of the shovels. Lateral rigidity of the hitch is important to permit cultivating close to plants.

Depth of cultivation is sometimes controlled through the lifting mechanism (restrained-link operation) but free-link operation with gage

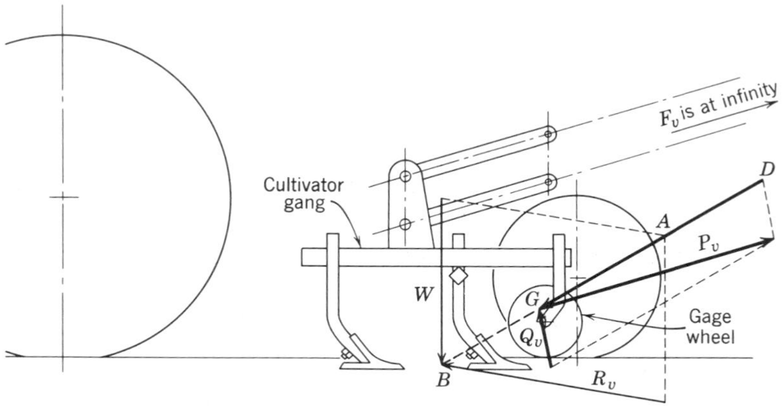

Fig. 8.12. Vertical force relations for a parallel-link hitch operated as a free-link system.

wheels is common on wide tool bars and on multiple-gang cultivators. The virtual hitch point for free-link operation (Fig. 8.12) is at the intersection of the parallel links or, in other words, at infinity. Thus P_v with such a system must be parallel with the links, and the magnitude of Q_v for given operating conditions can be changed by changing the slope of the links. Moving the gage wheel forward or backward has no effect on the magnitude of Q_v.

8.19. Load-Transfer Systems for Pull-Type Implements. The vertical-load transfer effects of rear-mounted implements have been mentioned in preceding sections. Load transfer with pull-type implements as a means of increasing the tractive ability of the larger tractors is equally important. Most major manufacturers now have such systems available.

Basically, a load transfer system for pull-type implements has some sort of arrangement for applying a moment to the implement pull member which tends to lift the rear end of the pull member and the front of the implement. The pull member must be strong enough to withstand these forces. The effect upon the tractor is similar to that with mounted implements, in that vertical load from the implement and from the tractor front wheels is transferred to the tractor drive wheels. This transfer tends to reduce the depth of some types of implements. The maximum acceptable amount of implement vertical-load reduction is influenced by soil conditions, implement mass, implement type, and method of controlling or gaging depth. Tractor front-end stability and steering response may also be limiting factors.

Load-transfer systems currently available usually require some modification or additions to the implement pull member, plus mounting special devices on the tractor, usually on the three-point hitch. Some arrangements pull the implement from the lower links and utilize the lower-link draft sensor to vary the lifting force on the implement as the draft changes. The maximum amount of load transfer is determined by the setting of the automatic draft control lever. Other systems pull from the regular tractor drawbar and exert a constant lifting force by means of an adjustable, constant hydraulic pressure applied to the rockshaft lift cylinder.

Both types of hydraulic control systems provide flexibility for operation over uneven ground without any great change in the amount of load transfer. The automatic draft control adds vertical load to the drive wheels only as it is needed. The constant-pressure system provides load transfer for increased braking ability when pulling wagons or trailers.

REFERENCES

1. Agricultural Engineers Yearbook, 1976, pp. 282–289. ASAE, St. Joseph, Mich.
2. BARGER, E. L., J. B. LILJEDAHL, W. M. CARLETON, and E. G. McKIBBEN, Tractors and Their Power Units, 2nd Edition, Chap. 15. John Wiley & Sons, New York, 1963.

3. BATEL, W., and R. THIEL. Automatic control of agricultural machines. Grundl. Landtech., Heft *14*:5-13, 1962. NIAE transl. 206.
4. BORCHELT, M. C., and O. A. SMITH. Lower link sensing in implement hitches. Agr. Eng., *43*:450-453, 468, Aug., 1962.
5. CLYDE, A. W. Technical features of tillage tools. Pennsylvania Agr. Expt. Sta. Bull. 465 (Part 2), 1944.
6. CLYDE, A. W. Pitfalls in applying the science of mechanics to tractors and implements. Agr. Eng., *35*:79-83, Feb., 1954.
7. COWELL, P. A., and S. C. LEN. Field performance of tractor draught control systems. J. Agr. Eng. Res., *12*:205-221, 1967.
8. DAVIS, W. M. Implement requirements in relation to tractor design. Agr. Eng., *42*:478-483, Sept., 1961.
9. DWYER, M. J. The effect of draught control response on the performance of agricultural tractors. J. Agr. Eng. Res., *14*:295-312, 1969.
10. JOHANNSEN, B. B. Tractor hitches and hydraulic systems. Agr. Eng., *35*:789-793, 800, Nov., 1954.
11. LONG, M. E. Weight transfer with trailing implements. Implement & Tractor, *82*(23):22-25, Nov. 7, 1967.
12. MURPHY, K. E., M. C. BORCHELT, and M. P. GASSMAN. Power weight transfer for towed implements. Agr. Eng., *51*:28-30, Jan., 1970.
13. PERRSON, S. P. E., and S. JOHANNSON. A weight-transfer hitch for pull-type implements. Trans. ASAE, *10*(6):847-849, 1967.
14. WILSON, R. W. Mounted vs. semi-mounted plows for large tractors. ASAE Paper 61-648, Dec., 1961.

PROBLEMS

8.1. If the wheels in Fig. 8.3 are mounted on plain, grease-packed bearings with 63-mm-diameter bearing surfaces and the coefficient of friction of the bearings is 0.15, what must be the distance from the wheel centerline to the line of Q_v to cause rotation of the wheel? Draw a free-body diagram of the wheel. Neglect the force of gravity on the wheel, but indicate all other forces and the point of contact between the axle and the hub.

8.2. Determine the proper wheel tread for a tractor to pull a 4-bottom 36-cm moldboard plow without side draft. Assume rear tire width = 330 mm and clearance between the tire and the furrow wall = 25 mm. Show pertinent dimensions on a diagram.

8.3. Take accurate measurements on a tractor having a moldboard plow attached through a three-point, converging-link hitch.

(a) By graphical methods, determine the location of the virtual hitch point when the plow is operating at a depth of 15 cm, with a free-link system.

(b) Locate the virtual hitch point when the front plow point is just touching the surface of the ground (as the plow starts to enter the ground).

8.4. Assume that P_v = 9.9 kN in Fig. 8.7. Determine the force in the top link and the total force in the two bottom links, indicating whether tension or compression. Scale the dimensions and angles from the text and solve by graphical methods. Also determine the draft.

8.5. Compare free-link operation with restrained-link operation, in regard to the effects on front and rear wheel loading of a tractor, for the conditions represented by Figs. 8.7 and 8.8. W and R_v for the implement are the same in both cases. For free-link operation, P_v = 9.9 kN at a slope of 11° and y (Fig. 8.10) is 150 mm. For restrained-link operation, P_v = 10.15 kN at 25° and y = 71 cm. The effective wheelbase of the tractor (x_1 in Fig. 8.10) is 2.03 m.

When operated 36 cm [14 in.] deep in a highly compacted clay soil, the straight-standard tool had a draft of 12.4 kN [2790 lbf]. The moderately curved subsoiler had 16% less draft than the straight tool but only 1% more than the tool with the most curve. In another comparison, tilting the straight standard backward 15° from vertical reduced the draft 12% and using a curved standard reduced it 28%.

Fig. 9.2. Three shapes of subsoilers compared in draft tests. (M. L. Nichols and C. A. Reaves.[22])

9.4. Effect of Depth and Speed upon Draft of Chisel-Type Implements. Results obtained by various investigators are not consistent in regard to the effect of depth upon specific draft. It is likely that the effect of depth is influenced by the tool shape and orientation, soil type, and soil condition. The results indicate a general tendency for a moderate increase in specific draft as depth is increased in firm soils.

Most of the available data on the effects of speed is for flat-plate tines at low speeds and is not very meaningful in relation to field operation. Payne,[25] however, conducted tests up to 9.6 km/h [6 mph] with vertical, flat-plate tines. In 3 soil types the draft increase between 4.8 and 9.6 km/h [3 and 6 mph] was 11 to 16%. Reed[27] conducted tests with 2 field cultivators (probably having sweep-type shovels) in 2 loam soils and found an increase of 4 to 13% between 4.8 and 9.6 km/h [3 and 6 mph]. McKibben and Reed[21] reported results for a subsoiler at speeds from 4 to 14.5 km/h [2½ to 9 mph] that can be fitted with an equation of the same form as equation 6.2 (Section 6.22) but with constants of 0.944 and 0.0024 [0.944 and 0.0062]. The draft increase between 4.8 and 9.6 km/h was 16%.

Tool surface area, lift angle, depth, and soil condition undoubtedly influence the magnitude of the speed effect for chisel-type implements. In some cases a linear relation between draft and speed can be assumed over a limited range of speeds.

9.5. Vibratory or Oscillatory Tillage*. There has been a considerable

---

*The terms vibratory (or vibrating) and oscillatory (or oscillating) are used interchangeably in research reports and in this text.

amount of research on vibratory tillage, the primary incentives being the potentialities of this system for reducing draft, improving the overall energy utilization efficiency in soil breakup, and providing some control over the degree of pulverization. Draft reduction is especially desirable with high-draft implements such as subsoilers. Gunn and Tramontini[11] did some of the pioneering work with oscillating tillage tools in the early 1950s, but most of the research in this area has been reported since 1957. Reference 32 presents a comprehensive review of published research results pertaining to vibratory tillage. Less extensive summaries are included in references 10 and 19.

Much of the research has been with simple, plane-surface tools, usually in laboratory soil bins. However, field tests have been conducted with full-size tillage tools such as subsoilers and moldboard plows. Oscillating subsoilers have been manufactured and sold in the United States.

Operating parameters for a vibratory tillage system include travel speed, oscillation frequency, amplitude, direction and pattern of oscillating motion, tool shape, tool lift angle, and soil physical characteristics. Several investigators have reported good correlation between draft reduction and parameters of various forms that reflect the ratio of travel speed to oscillating velocity. Another parameter that has been employed is cycles per unit of travel distance, which includes the effects of travel speed and frequency but not amplitude.

9.6. Effects of Oscillating Tillage Tools. Research results indicate that, with appropriate combinations of values for the above parameters, draft requirements can be reduced by as much as 50 to 75% in comparison with non-oscillated tools. Soil breakup is also improved by tool oscillation.[32] The effects reported for various parameters vary widely, but in general it has been found that draft reduction is increased by increasing the vibration velocity and is decreased by increasing travel velocity.

The effects of frequency and amplitude tend to diminish rapidly as their values are increased beyond optimum values. Several investigators found that the effects of vibration were most pronounced at frequencies that resulted in a forward travel per cycle which was about equal to, or slightly less than, the spacing of natural shear planes caused by a nonoscillating tool.[32] This relation would make the optimum frequency a function of soil physical characteristics. Frequencies in most tests have been from 10 to 50 Hz (cycles per second). Zero-to-peak amplitudes from 2.5 to 13 mm [0.1 to 0.5 in.] were common.

Although oscillation of tillage tools has reduced draft, there has usually been very little reduction in total energy requirements, and sometimes a substantial increase. Oscillation conditions that cause large reductions in draft are usually not the best in regard to total energy requirements. For example, tests with hoe-type simple tools in a soil bin[32] indicated a total energy increase of 150 to 200% when the tools were oscillated in such a manner as to reduce the draft by 80% in comparison with no oscillation. But with a combination of frequency and amplitude that reduced the draft only 40 to 50%, the total energy was about equal to that for the nonoscillating condition.

Total-energy comparisons reported by various investigators are contradictory in many cases. Gunn and Tramontini[11] conducted field tests with a simple, inclined blade like a subsoiler, operating 19 cm [7½ in.] deep, and found a slight reduction in total energy when the tool was oscillated horizontally. Verma[32] cites one report on a subsoiler test in which vibration reduced the total energy requirements by 35% and another subsoiler study in which the draft was reduced by 20 to 40% but with no reduction in total energy. Wismer and his associates[34] report subsoiler tests in which vertical oscillation usually increased the total energy requirements.

Eggenmuller[7] oscillated the share and the entire moldboard of a plow bottom in opposition to each other. He tried only one combination of oscillating directions, which he selected on the basis of previous experience with simple tools. With an amplitude of 9 mm [0.35 in.] and a frequency of 20 Hz, the draft was 50 to 60% less than with no oscillation, but the total energy requirement was 30 to 40% greater. Other investigators[14] vibrated the share and lower portion of the moldboard "in the direction of the resulting soil reaction," using an electromagnetic vibrator. At 4.8 km/h [3 mph] and 50 Hz, the draft was reduced 28% and the total energy was reduced 20%. At 6.4 km/h [4 mph], vibration caused no decrease in draft and increased the total energy. Eggenmuller probably wasted most of the energy used to vibrate the upper portion of the moldboard, and he may not have had the optimum direction of oscillation.

9.7. Principles of Vibratory Tillage. Research efforts reported prior to 1970 have not provided a complete understanding of the principles involved in vibratory tillage and the reasons for observed draft reductions. There is evidence indicating that vibration causes physical changes to take place in the soil that tend to reduce the shear strength.[32] As indicated in Section 9.6, the natural period of soil shearing by a nonoscillating tool seems to have an important effect.

Boyd and Nalezny[3] developed a mathematical model for a horizontally vibrating blade in which a spring represented the elasticity of the soil and blade. Velocity and dynamic effects were neglected. Soil-bin test results in a silty sand at a speed of 0.18 km/h [0.11 mph] checked well with calculated results.

Eggenmuller[6] concluded from an analysis and laboratory tests that for maximum draft reduction a tillage tool should be oscillated in such a manner that there is a definite separation of the cutting and soil-lifting operations to minimize soil-metal friction, as illustrated in Fig. 9.3. In this example, the tool is pivoted at a point above and somewhat ahead of the cutting edge so that on its forward stroke the cutting edge moves downward along path AB. If the forward motion of the implement frame during one cycle is slightly less than the oscillation amplitude, the cutting edge on its return stroke will

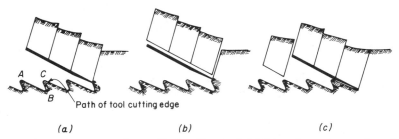

Fig. 9.3. Idealized operation of an oscillating tillage tool. (*a*) Separation and upward acceleration of the soil; (*b*) soil lifted from tool by inertia, at the beginning of the cutting stroke; (*c*) end
of cutting stroke. (A. Eggenmuller.[6])

move slightly rearward with respect to the earth, along *BC*.

The shearing action takes place on the return stroke (Fig. 9.3*a*). Since
there is little or no forward motion of the tool during this operation, the
energy for shearing, lifting, and accelerating the soil upward does not contribute to the draft. The upward motion of the soil, plus the fact that the soil
is loose, minimizes the friction against the upper surface of the tool during
its forward stroke (between Fig. 9.3*b* and 9.3*c*). The tool makes the new cut
at a flat angle with very little lifting of the block being cut. If the relation
between the oscillation angle, the tool lift angle, and the forward travel per
cycle is correct, there will be adequate clearance beneath the tool body. In
this idealized situation, the principal draft requirements are to overcome
cutting resistance and the minimal frictional forces of the newly cut soil
sliding on the upper surface of the tool.

The wide variation in experimental results regarding the effect of oscillation upon total energy requirements suggests that much more research and
analysis is needed to determine the most efficient manner of applying energy
to the soil through the vibratory mode. The fact that appreciable reductions
in total energy have been obtained under certain conditions should provide
incentive for further work.

Velocity-displacement relations heretofore have been basically sinusoidal.
Other patterns might be more effective. Perhaps the return motion should be
different from the forward motion. The application of energy through sonic
waves is said to have intriguing possibilities in the construction industry for
cutting through rocks and hard earth.[32] The use of sonic waves may be
worthy of investigation in relation to soil tillage.

9.8. Multipowered Rotating Tillage Tools. Many different configurations
and arrangements, including vertical-axis units, longitudinal-axis units, and
transverse-axis units, have been used for multipowered rotating tools. The
most common type consists of blades attached to flanges along a horizontal
shaft that is perpendicular to the direction of motion. This arrangement is
identified herein as a conventional rotary tiller.

Vertical-axis powered rotary tillage machines, developed in Europe, were

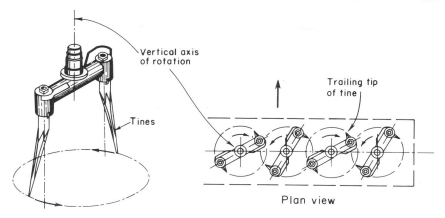

Fig. 9.4. Basic arrangement for a vertical-axis rotary tiller. Gears on the upper ends of the rotor shafts transmit power from one rotor to the next and provide counter rotation of adjacent rotors.

introduced into the United States in about 1970. These machines have a series of two-tine vertical rotors across the width of the machine. The tine paths of adjacent rotors overlap, as indicated in Fig. 9.4. Vertical-axis machines are comparable with horizontal-axis rotary tillers in regard to soil pulverization and power requirements, but do not work well in loose surface trash.[5,24] They are intended mainly for secondary tillage, as in final seedbed preparation.

Rotary spading machines have been employed in Europe for a number of years. A spading machine has a transverse, powered rotor with spades attached to arms mounted on it. The spades dig in from the front, cut soil sections loose, and lift them at the rear. In one type of spading machine, each blade tilts when the soil section has been partially lifted, causing the lump of soil to fall off. In another type the spades are on fixed arms and the soil is pushed off of them by stationary retainers at the rear. Spading machines are comparable to moldboard plows in regard to soil pulverization and energy requirements.[5] Like rotary tillers, they obtain most or all of their energy from the tractor PTO. Mechanical complexity and lack of durability are problems. Trash coverage is poor. Forward speeds are limited to about 2 km/h [1¼ mph].[24] They are said to work best in heavy soils.

Moldboard plows, on which the rear portions of the moldboards are replaced with powered rotors, have been produced commercially in the United States and in Europe.[2] The rotors usually have teeth to assist in soil pulverization. Draft is less than for a conventional moldboard plow,[23] but total power requirements are greater.[2] Soil pulverization under some conditions can be adequate for a final seedbed but is unsatisfactory in dry, compact soils. Trash coverage is poor, and the driven rotors make this implement more complex and expensive than conventional plows. Plows on which most or all of the moldboard is replaced with belts or rollers have also been developed, a primary objective usually being to improve scouring (Section 6.13).

9.9. Conventional Rotary Tillers. Swiss-made rotary tillers were introduced into the United States in about 1930, and soon afterwards several American manufacturers started making this type of equipment.[17] Early models were primarily small, garden-type units. Currently, a number of manufacturers have heavy-duty tractor-mounted or pull-type units for open-field work with widths ranging up to 4 m [13 ft] or more. Tractors for these units, when used for primary tillage, should have about 0.3 maximum available PTO kilowatts per centimetre of tilling width [one horsepower per inch of width].

The use of rotary tillers for primary tillage in open-field work is still rather limited in the United States, principally because of the high power requirements and excessive soil pulverization. The high degree of pulverization, although not desirable for root beds, does make either conventional or vertical-axis rotary tillers good for seedbed strip tilling and for preparing precision-shaped, raised beds for planting. Conventional rotary tillers are good for cutting up vegetative matter and mixing it throughout the tilled layer, but coverage is not as complete as with a moldboard plow. They are also effective for mixing chemicals into the soil and for cultivation in certain row crops. Rotary tillers are widely used for rice in Japan[16] and other Asiatic countries. Rice paddies in these countries are often "puddled" by means of underwater rotary tillage.

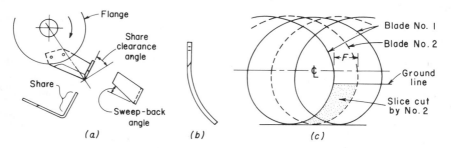

Fig. 9.5. *(a)* Three views of an L-shaped blade for a conventional rotary tiller; *(b)* curved blade; *(c)* paths of cutting edges or tips for 2 blades 180° apart, in relation to forward travel.

Many types and shapes of blades have been developed, but hoe-type blades such as the one shown in Fig. 9.5*a* appear to be superior to other types in most respects and are widely used. L-shaped blades are better than hook-shaped or pick-type (pointed) blades in trashy conditions, they are more effective in killing weeds, and they do not pulverize the soil as much.[1] Variations of the hoe type have gradual curves (Fig. 9.5*b*) or larger-radius bends for special situations such as operating on the sides of plant beds. Straight, nearly-radial blades with the narrow edges of thin rectangular cross sections facing the direction of motion are sometimes employed on mulchers designed primarily for secondary tillage.

The rotor usually rotates in the same direction as the tractor wheels, although reverse rotation has been investigated by various workers. Each blade cuts a segment of soil (Fig. 9.5c) as it moves downward and toward the rear. Most rotary tillers make either 2 or 3 cuts per revolution (along any one longitudinal line). The bite length F is defined as the amount of forward travel per cut. The slice thickness varies during the cut, and the cutting force also varies. Vinogradov and Leont´ev[33] have analyzed the forces acting upon a blade and have measured force in relation to time during a single cut. They also observed the cutting action with high-speed motion pictures.

Because of the high peak torques developed during each cut, it is important to stagger the blades in the different courses, with equal angular displacements between them, so no two blades strike the soil at the same time.[10] The stagger pattern should be approximately symmetrical about the longitudinal centerline.

The useful soil force on a forward-rotating rotary tiller has an upward component V and a forward-acting component L. The relative magnitudes of these components are influenced by many factors, including depth, rotor diameter, bite length, soil type and condition, type of blade, and share clearance angle (Fig. 9.5a). The upward component reduces the amount of implement gravitational force that must be supported by gage wheels or the tractor; under some conditions it causes the rotor to "walk out" of the ground. Furlong,[9] in tests with several shapes of hoe-type blades on a rotor having a width of 0.61 m [24 in.] and a diameter of 46 cm [18 in.], found that upward forces varied widely, increased rapidly with depth, and averaged over 4.4 kN [1000 lbf] for a 15-cm [6-in.] depth in a silt loam.

The forward component results in a negative draft and negative specific energy requirement for traction, both increasing in magnitude with increased bite length (Fig. 9.7b). The forward thrust from the negative draft can be troublesome in regard to tractor stability and design.[34] In Furlong's tests with various blades, the negative power requirement represented by the forward thrust was usually less than 7% of the rotor power when the bite length was 5 cm [2 in.] but amounted to 20% of the rotor power when the bite length was 15 cm [6 in.].

9.10. Pulverization Effects and Energy Requirements of Conventional Rotary Tillers. Bite length, depth of cut, rotor speed, blade shape, soil type, and soil condition are important parameters that can affect the degree of pulverization and the specific-energy requirements. As previously mentioned, excessive pulverization under some conditions, and high power requirements, are major problems that have limited the application of rotary tillers for overall primary tillage operations.

Frevert[8] found a considerable increase in clod size between bite lengths of 4.0 and 8.1 cm [1.6 and 3.2 in.], but no appreciable increase at greater bite

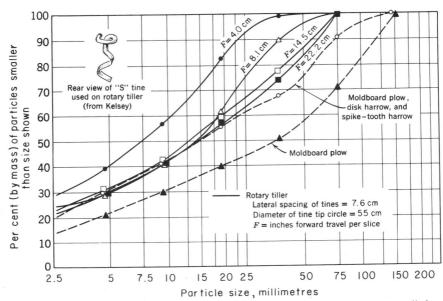

Fig. 9.6. Soil particle-size distribution resulting from various tillage treatments applied to clover stubble on a silt loam soil having a moisture content of 28%. (R. K. Frevert.[8])

lengths (Fig. 9.6). His results indicated that even with a bite length of 15 to 23 cm [6 to 9 in.] the degree of pulverization was as great as obtained by the successive use of a moldboard plow, a disk harrow (twice over), and a spike-tooth harrow. It should be noted that his blade shape differed somewhat from the L shape currently prevalent. Furlong[9] found an increase in clod size between 5-cm and 15-cm [2-in. and 6-in.] bite lengths when the depth was 5 cm or 10 cm [2 in. or 4 in.] but no change when the depth was 15 cm [6 in.]. Other investigators have found little effect of bite length upon clod size, or a moderate increase. Thus, although it is generally recognized that increasing the bite length tends to reduce pulverization, the effects in a specific situation seem to be influenced by other factors.

Hendrick and Gill[12] have analyzed and summarized the results of various research studies involving conventional rotary tillers. They concluded that there is no consistent relation between depth of cut and the degree of pulverization, but suggest that hood and shield shape can have significant effects on the soil breakup. Results included in their report show that clod size may be reduced somewhat by increasing the rotor speed and forward speed proportionately (constant bite length).

Bite length is one of the important factors affecting power requirements. Increasing the bite length by either increasing the forward speed or decreasing the rotor speed reduces the specific-energy requirements as illustrated in Fig. 9.7, until the bite length becomes so great that there is insufficient

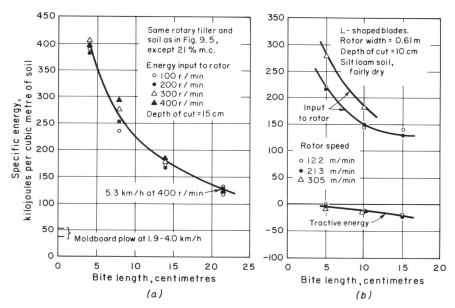

Fig. 9.7. Effect of bite length upon specific-energy requirements for a conventional rotary tiller. The indicated units of specific energy correspond numerically to 10 times the specific draft of plows expressed in newtons per square centimetre. *(a)* — (R.K. Frevert.[8]), *(b)* — (data from D.B. Furlong.[9])

clearance on the back side of the blade. PTO-driven rotary tillers usually have rotor speed-change arrangements to permit some choice of bite length for a particular situation.

If the rotor speed and forward speed are increased proportionately, the specific-energy requirement usually increases. This effect is shown by the spread of points for a 7.6-cm [3-in.] bite length in Fig. 9.7*a* and by the differences between the two curves in Fig. 9.7*b*. Richardson[28] found a substantial effect of speed in 1955 field tests but only a small effect in 1956 tests in the same field.

Energy requirements are influenced by the ratio of the depth to the rotor diameter. Increasing the diameter for a given depth of cut makes the slices thinner, which should tend to reduce the energy requirements, but also makes the cutting paths longer (more friction energy). The combined effect of these factors is to cause a reduction of specific energy to a minimum value as the depth is increased to about 70 to 75% of the diameter.[12]

Note that even the lowest rotor specific-energy requirement shown in Fig. 9.7*a* was about three times as great as for a moldboard plow in the same soil. However, the additional energy and cost for disking and harrowing after plowing must be included to give a fair comparison, and the rotary tiller should be credited with the increase in fuel efficiency obtained when a tractor transmits power through the PTO rather than through the wheels. Also, the power represented by the forward thrust of the tiller must be subtracted from the rotor power to obtain the net input. Although the negative specific energy from thrust can be substantial for long bite lengths (lower curve in Fig. 9.7b), many investigators do not even measure thrust.

Some attention has been given to combination implements in which chisels or other fixed (passive) tools are attached to the rear of a conventional rotary tiller and operate directly beneath the rotor. The rotor pulverizes the upper portion of the tilled layer and the fixed tools loosen the lower portion, leaving it in a less pulverized condition than the upper layers. The chisels help cancel the rotor's negative draft and its upward V. The average specific-energy requirement for the entire tilled depth is considerably less than for rotary tillage to the full depth.[2]

9.11. Mixing Chemicals into the Soil. In some cases fertilizers, pesticides, or other chemicals are broadcasted onto a field and then mixed in by means of one or more tillage operations. Another common practice is incorporating pesticides in narrow bands prior to planting row crops. Uniform distribution in the proper depth zone is particularly desirable when incorporating herbicides, in order to obtain good weed control without applying excessive amounts of expensive materials and without producing concentrations that might later injure crop plants.

Several investigators have compared the mixing characteristics of different kinds of tillage implements.[13,26] Hulburt and Menzel[13] found that in either a well-pulverized soil or a previously untilled field, twice over with a conventional rotary tiller gave excellent uniformity throughout the 15-cm [6-in.] depth. After only one pass, however, there was considerably more of the added material in the top 5 cm than in the next 5 cm, and only a small amount below 10 cm. Rotary tilling gave better results than disking 2 or 3 times, spring-tooth harrowing, plowing, or combinations of these operations.

Matthews[20] tested 7 commercially available devices designed to incorporate chemicals in bands 18 to 36 cm [7 to 14 in.] wide. Descriptions are not given but it is probable that most or all of these were ground-driven, rotating devices. In most cases, at least 75% of the material was in the top one-third of the 7.6-cm [3-in.] tillage depth and lateral uniformity was poor.

The effects of various parameters upon the performance of conventional rotary tillers for band incorporation have been studied. L-shaped blades gave better lateral and vertical distribution than slightly curved knife-type blades.[29] Bite lengths of 2.5 to 5 cm [1 to 2 in.] were better than longer bites.[15,29] With simulated L-shaped blades 38 mm [1½ in.] wide, increasing the share clearance angle (Fig. 9.5a) from 15° to 60° improved vertical distribution when the tilling depth was 13 cm [5 in.].[15]

Carter and Miller[4] found that with L-shaped blades operating 5 cm [2 in.]

deep the best mixing was obtained when the blade peripheral velocity was 3 to 6 times the forward velocity, regardless of rotor diameter. Changing relative velocities (peripheral minus forward) between 120 and 240 m/min [400 and 800 ft/min] had little effect upon uniformity, but results were poorer with relative velocities either lower or higher than this range. L-shaped blades placed 40% of the material below a 3-cm [1.2-in.] depth in this velocity range, whereas rotors with 25-mm [1-in.] angle irons parallel to the axis put 60% deeper than 3 cm.

REFERENCES

1. ADAMS, W. J., Jr., and D. B. FURLONG. Rotary tiller in soil preparation. Agr. Eng., 40:600-603, 607, Oct., 1959.
2. BERNACKI, H. Rotary tillage combined with passive tools. ASAE Paper 70-637, Dec., 1970.
3. BOYD, R. J., and C. L. NALEZNY. Simple model simulates soil cutting of vibrating plow. SAE J., 76:79-82, Apr., 1968.
4. CARTER, L. M., and J. H. MILLER. Characteristics of powered rotary cultivators for application of herbicides. Trans. ASAE, 12(3): 305-309, 1969.
5. COOPER, A. W., W. R. GILL, G. E. VANDEN BERG, and C. A. REAVES. Plow, soil type define soil breakup energy needs. SAE J., 7(9):88-90, Sept., 1963.
6. EGGENMULLER, A. Oscillating tools for soil cultivation. Kinematics and testing of single tools. Grundl. Landtech., Heft 10:55-70, 1958. NIAE transl. 228.
7. EGGENMULLER, A. Field experiments with an oscillating plow body. Grundl. Landtech., Heft 10:89-95, 1958. NIAE transl. 151.
8. FREVERT, R. K. Mechanics of tillage. Unpublished thesis. Iowa State Univ., 1940.
9. FURLONG, D. B. Rotary tiller performance tests on existing tines. Tech. Rept. 1049, Central Eng. Dept., FMC Corp., San Jose, Calif., 1956.
10. GILL, W. R., and G. E. VANDEN BERG. Soil Dynamics in Tillage and Traction, pp. 265-288. USDA Agr. Handbook 316, 1967.
11. GUNN, J. T., and V. N. TRAMONTINI. Oscillation of tillage implements. Agr. Eng., 36:725-729, Nov., 1955.
12. HENDRICK, J. G., and W. R. GILL. Rotary tillage design parameters. Part I — Direction of rotation; Part II — Depth of tillage; Part III — Ratio of peripheral and forward velocities. Trans. ASAE, 14(4):669-683, 1971.
13. HULBURT, W. C., and R. G. MENZEL. Soil mixing characteristics of tillage tools. Agr. Eng., 34:702-704, 706, 708, Oct., 1953.
14. KALHUZHNIE, G. D., and M. M. GORKHAM. Investigation of an oscillating plow bottom. Mekh. Elektrif. Sel. Khoz., 22(6):45-46, 1964. National Tillage Machinery Laboratory translation.
15. KAUFMAN, L. C., and B. J. BUTLER. Increment of cut-and-rake angle interaction during granular incorporation by rotary tillage. Trans. ASAE, 10(6):718-722, 1967.
16. KAWAMURA, N. Progress of rotary tillage in Japan. ASAE Paper 70-639, Dec., 1970.
17. KELSEY, C. W. Rotary soil tillage. Agr. Eng., 27:171-174, Apr., 1946.
18. KOEFED, S. S. Kinematics and power requirement of oscillating tillage tools. J. Agr. Eng. Res., 14:54-73, 1969.
19. LARSON, L. W. The future of vibratory tillage tools. Trans. ASAE, 10(1):78-79, 83, 1967.
20. MATTHEWS, E. J. Chloride tracer evaluation of herbicide incorporation tools. Trans. ASAE, 13(1):64-66, 1970.

21. McKIBBEN, E. G., and I. F. REED. The influence of speed on the performance characteristics of implements. Paper presented at SAE National Tractor Meeting, Sept., 1952.
22. NICHOLS, M. L., and C. A. REAVES. Soil reaction: to subsoiling equipment. Agr. Eng., 39:340-343, June, 1958.
23. PANOV, I. M., and V. A. SHMONIN. Test of trailed five bottom plow with rotating moldboards. Traktory Sel. Khoz., 6:21-23, 1967. Nat. Tech. Info. Service transl. PB-177009T.
24. PASCAL, J. A. Rotary soil working machines. Farm Mechaniz., 19(211):24-26, 29, Mar., 1967.
25. PAYNE, P. C. J. The relationship between the mechanical properties of soil and the performance of simple cultivation implements. J. Agr. Eng. Res., 1:23-50, 1956.
26. READ, K., M. R. GEBHARDT, and C. L. DAY. Distribution of Trifluralin in the soil when mixed with disk harrow and power rotary cultivator. Trans. ASAE, 11(2):155-158, 1968.
27. REED, W. B. Techniques for determining an equation for the draft of cultivators using several independent variables. ASAE Paper 66-123, June, 1966.
28. RICHARDSON, R. D. Some torque requirements taken on a rotary cultivator. J. Agr. Eng. Res., 3:66-68, 1958.
29. SCHMID, D. R. Granular incorporation with rotary tillage. ASAE Paper 66-116, June, 1966.
30. SPOOR, G. Design of soil engaging implements — practice. Farm Machine Des. Eng., 3:14-19, Dec., 1969.
31. TANNER, D. W. Further work on the relationship between rake angle and the performance of simple cultivation tools. J. Agr. Eng. Res., 5:307-315, 1960.
32. VERMA, B. P. Oscillating soil tools — a review. Trans. ASAE, 14(6):1107-1115, 1121, 1971.
33. VINOGRADOV, V. I., and Y. S. LEONT'EV. The interaction of rotary working tools with soil. Traktory Sel. Khoz., 9:29-31, 1968. Nat. Tech. Info. Service transl. PB-183829T.
34. WISMER, R. D., E. L. WEGSCHEID, H. J. LUTH, and B. E. ROMIG. Energy application in tillage and earthmoving. SAE Trans., 77:2486-2494, 1968.

PROBLEMS

9.1. Compare the energy requirements for rotary tilling to a depth of 15 cm and the total energy required for preparing a seedbed by plowing to the same depth with a moldboard plow, disking twice with a light-duty tandem disk harrow, and then finishing with a spike-tooth harrow. For the rotary tiller take F = 22 cm with an energy requirement of 124 kJ/m^3 of tilled soil (from Fig. 9.7a). The specific draft of the moldboard plow in the same soil was about 4.8 N/cm^2 at 4 to 5 km/h. Assume the draft per metre of width is 2.2 kN for the disk harrow and 0.6 kN for the spike-tooth harrow.

9.2. A 2.5-m rotary tiller is mounted on a tractor having a maximum PTO rating of 78 kW. The tillage depth is to be 15 cm and the tractor is to be loaded to 75% of its maximum rating. If the energy requirements are represented by the lower curve in Fig. 9.7b, what would be the forward speed under the following conditions?

(a) Bite length = 15 cm (rotor specific energy = 131 kJ/m^3 and tractive energy = −21 kJ/m^3).

(b) Bite length = 7.5 cm (rotor specific energy = 180 kJ/m^3 and tractive energy = −7 kJ/m^3).

10

Crop Planting

10.1. Introduction. Crop planting operations may involve placing seeds or tubers (such as potatoes) in the soil at a predetermined depth, random scattering or dropping of seeds on the field surface (broadcasting), or setting plants in the soil. Machines that place the seed in the soil and cover it in the same operation create definite rows. If the rows or planting beds are far enough apart to permit operating machinery between them for intertilling or other cultural operations, the result is known as a row-crop planting; otherwise, it is considered to be a solid planting. Thus, grain drilled in rows 15 to 36 cm [6 to 14 in.] apart is a solid planting, whereas sugar beets, with rows commonly 51 cm [20 in.] apart, are grown as a row crop.

With appropriate planting equipment, seeds may be distributed according to any of the following methods or patterns.

1. Broadcasting (random scattering of seeds over the surface of the field).
2. Drill seeding (random dropping and covering of seeds in furrows to give definite rows).
3. Precision planting (accurate placing of single seeds at about equal intervals in rows).
4. Hill dropping (placing groups of seeds at about equal intervals in rows).

Solid planting is generally done by one of the first two methods, whereas row-crop planting may involve any of the methods except broadcasting.

10.2. Row-Crop Planting Systems. Planting may be done on the flat surface of a field, in furrows, or on beds, as illustrated in Fig. 10.1. Furrow planting (or lister planting) is widely practiced under semiarid conditions for row crops such as corn, cotton, and grain sorghum because this system places the seed down into moist soil and protects the young plants from wind and blowing soil. Bed planting is often practiced in high-rainfall areas to improve surface drainage. Flat planting generally predominates where natural moisture conditions are favorable.

A variation of furrow planting provides a flat plateau perhaps 7.5 cm [3 in.] high and 25 cm [10 in.] wide in the bottom of the furrow.[21] The advantages mentioned above for furrow planting are retained and, in addition, the small furrows beside the plateau keep water from standing on the row or washing soil onto the row if a heavy rain occurs.

Minimum-tillage planting systems are discussed in Section 5.4. These include strip tillage, the "no-tillage" system which is actually narrow-strip

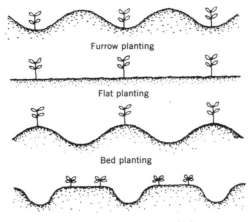

Fig. 10.1. Various types of surface profiles for row-crop planting.

tillage), lister planting, till-and-plant combinations following plowing or other primary tillage, and planting in wheel tracks immediately after plowing. These systems are sometimes employed with crops such as corn, soybeans, and sorghum.

Bed planting is common for certain types of row crops in irrigated areas. With close-spaced row crops such as sugar beets, lettuce, and certain other vegetable crops, two or more rows are sometimes planted close together on a single bed (Fig. 10.1), thereby leaving more width in the spaces between beds for the operation of equipment. For example, beds might be on 102 or 107-cm [40 or 42-in.] centers, with 2 rows 30 to 40 cm [12 to 16 in.] apart on each bed.

Combination bed-shaping and planting units are sometimes used for vegetables, sugar beets, and other similar crops in irrigated areas. A unit of this type might simultaneously pulverize the seedbed strip with a rotary tiller, incorporate pesticides, form the bed to a firm, flat-top shape, apply fertilizers, and plant the seed. Sled runners between the beds guide and support the implement while it is in operation, thus minimizing height variations. The result is an overall precision operation in which the seeds and chemicals are accurately placed at specific locations with respect to each other and with respect to the top and sides of each bed. If the relationships have been properly selected, results should be better and more uniform than from separate operations.

Tests in Texas with cotton have shown that precision shaping of flat-top beds, followed by planting at a uniform depth after the beds have been settled by spring rains, resulted in a substantial improvement in yield uniformity and increased total yields.[28] Cone-shaped guide wheels running against the sides of the beds (Fig. 11.8) provided accurate centering of the planting units. Subsequent use of these guide wheels on a cultivator permitted close cultivation at relatively high forward speeds.

10.3. Plant Population and Spacing Requirements. The primary objective of any planting operation is to establish an optimum plant population and plant spacing, the ultimate goal being to obtain the maximum net return per hectare. Population and spacing requirements are influenced by such factors as the kind of crop, the type of soil, the fertility level of the soil, the amount of moisture available, and the effect of plant and row spacing upon the cost and convenience of operations such as thinning, weed control, cultivation, and harvesting.

With many crops, such as corn, there is a fairly narrow range of plant populations that will give maximum yields under a particular combination of soil and fertility conditions, the optimum number of plants per hectare increasing as the productivity of the soil is increased. For other crops, such as cotton and the small grains, there appears to be a rather wide range of plant populations over which yields do not vary appreciably, the principal requirement from the yield standpoint being to keep the number of plants per hectare above some minimum value.

Most crops can tolerate moderate variations in uniformity of plant spacing in the row without seriously affecting yields, provided the average population density (or land area per plant) is within the optimum range. Uniform spacing is important with certain crops, however. Uniform spacing of corn plants along the row becomes increasingly desirable as yields are increased. For a given plant population per hectare, reducing the row spacing and having plants farther apart in the row has increased yields in comparison with the conventional 102-cm [40-in.] row spacing.[19] Uniform spacing of single plants is needed for crops such as lettuce, sugar beets, onions, and carrots, because of the space needed for development of the usable portion of the plant.

Factors other than yield are sometimes of considerable importance in establishing the best population or spacing for a particular crop and set of conditions. In upright crops, increased populations may increase the tendency for stalks to lodge or break, which is undesirable from the harvesting standpoint. On the other hand, increasing the plant population for cotton usually tends to raise the height of the lowest fruiting nodes, which is an aid to mechanical harvesting. Narrow row spacings in corn or cotton may increase yields but they also increase the costs of planting and cultivating and require changes in the design of harvesting equipment.

Cotton and corn are sometimes planted in hills, especially under conditions where surface crusting is likely to be a problem. The mutual reinforcement from a compact group of seedlings increases the crust-penetrating ability.

10.4. Functions of a Seed Planter. With the exception of broadcasters, a seed planter is required to perform all of the following mechanical functions.

1. Open the seed furrow to the proper depth.
2. Meter the seed.
3. Deposit the seed in the furrow in an acceptable pattern.
4. Cover the seed and compact the soil around the seed to the proper degree for the type of crop involved.

The planter should not damage the seed enough to appreciably affect germination. The seed should be placed in the soil in such a manner that all the factors affecting germination and emergence will be as favorable as possible. Since timeliness is of extreme importance in the majority of planting operations, it is desirable that a planter be able to perform these functions accurately at fairly high rates of speed.

The primary function of a broadcaster is to meter the seed and distribute it with reasonable uniformity over a given width of land. Covering is a separate operation or is omitted entirely under some conditions.

10.5. Factors Affecting Germination and Emergence. Important factors that affect germination and emergence include the viability of the seed (percent germination under controlled laboratory conditions), soil temperature, availability of soil moisture to the seeds, soil aeration, and mechanical impedance to seedling emergence (i.e., the resistance of the soil to penetration by the seedling). These are influenced by the soil type, the physical condition of the soil, the depth of planting, the intimacy of contact between the seeds and the soil, the degree of compacting of the soil above the seeds, and formation of surface crusts after planting. Final field stand is also influenced by post-emergence losses due to diseases, insects, and adverse environmental conditions.

Field emergence rates of 80 to 90% are typical for corn and other crops that tolerate a fairly wide range of planting conditions. In such cases, planting the proper amount of seed to obtain the desired final stand is not a serious problem. With sugar beets and many of the smaller-seed vegetable crops, however, field emergence is so low and unpredictable (often only 35 to 50%) that it is customary to plant a considerable excess of seed and then thin as required to obtain the desired stand.

10.6. Effects of Planter or Planting System upon Emergence Factors. It should be apparent that planter performance cannot control all the factors involved in emergence. But the planter can have an important influence on many of these factors, and good planter performance is essential for obtaining an adequate stand with crops whose emergence is critical. Precise depth control, placement of seeds into moist soil, and noncrusting conditions above the seeds are important for small-seed vegetables and some other crops.

Packing of the soil by the planter can affect the availability of moisture, the availability of oxygen, and mechanical impedance. Laboratory tests in Michigan with beans, corn, and sugar beets in sandy clay loam indicated that pressures of 34 or 69 kPa [5 or 10 psi] applied to the soil surface after planting usually suppressed emergence, whereas 3.4 kPa [½ psi] did not.[24] Pressures of 34 and 69 kPa applied at seed level, however, improved emergence when adequate moisture was available immediately below the seeds. These results indicate that planters should be designed to pack the soil below the seed level, press the seeds into the compacted soil, and cover the seeds with loose soil.

Seedling thrust forces during emergence and factors affecting thrust requirements (impedance) are of interest in analyzing planter performance and developing new designs. Drew and his associates[10] measured thrust forces actually developed by corn and cotton seedlings during emergence in sandy loam. Values were usually 2.2 to 2.7 N [0.5 to 0.6 lbf]. Morton and Buchele[20] pushed probes representing seedlings upward through a layer of soil to determine the effects of various factors upon emergence energy requirements. Buchele and Sheikh[8] developed a mathematical relation for the maximum required seedling thrust in terms of soil cohesion, internal friction, soil-to-seedling friction coefficient, seedling diameter, and soil depth. In one experimental check, the measured force for an artificial seedling with a cone-shaped tip was 3.1 N [0.70 lbf] and the calculated force was 3.6 N [0.81 lbf].

Mechanical impedance can be reduced and percent emergence increased by covering the seeds with an anticrusting amendment such as vermiculite and applying a stabilizing binder. This has been done experimentally in the field with lettuce seed[9,12,14] and in the laboratory with various kinds of seeds. Although excellent results have been obtained, the added operations and the amounts of vermiculite and binder required make the planting system somewhat expensive and quite bulky.

Another approach for improving emergence is encasing single seeds in capsules or tablets of vermiculite or other similar material. In tests with lettuce, Harriott[14] obtained best results with cylinders (tablets) 19 mm [¾ in.] in diameter and 6 mm [¼ in.] thick, formed by axial compression and planted on edge with the top flush with the soil surface. Natural cleavage planes tended to be perpendicular to the direction of original compression. The tablets were made from vermiculite with polyvinyl acetate and water as a binder. Johnson and his associates[17] obtained similar results with tomatoes and cucumbers, using 19-mm-diameter [¾-in.-diameter] tablets 6 mm or 13 mm [¼ in. or ½ in.] thick.

Pesticides, as well as starter nutrients, can be included in the tablets. Although the tablets would be rather expensive (Harriott estimated $62/ha [$25/acre] for lettuce in 1970), an appropriate planting unit could merely press the tablets into the soil, thus providing precision spacing of single seeds and accurate depth control. The same size tablet could be used for various seed sizes.

10.7. Devices for Metering Single Seeds. Devices for metering single seeds usually have cells on a moving member or an arrangement to pick up single seeds and lift them out of a seed mass. The horizontal-plate planter is the most common example of the cell type. Two types of hopper bottoms are shown in Fig. 10.2. Edge-cell, edge-drop plates are well-suited for planting relatively large, flat seeds like corn. The stationary ring surrounding the plate should fit well for best performance, because it forms one side of the cells. Plates with round or oval holes instead of edge cells are used interchangeably for drilling or hill dropping seeds of various row crops. A large selection of plates is necessary to meet the requirements for the many types and sizes of seeds and spacings.

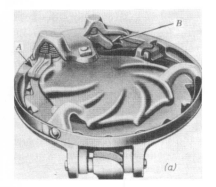 

Fig. 10.2. Hopper bottoms for horizontal-plate planters. *(a)* With edge-drop plate for corn. Note the spring-loaded cutoff *A* and the spring-loaded knockout pawl *B*. *(b)* Hopper bottom suitable for precision drilling of sugar beets or coated seeds. Note the round-hole plate and the positive-acting, toothed knockout wheel *A*.

A horizontal-plate planter has a spring-loaded cutoff device (Fig. 10.2) that rides on top of the plate and "wipes" off excess seeds as the cells move beneath it. A spring-loaded knockout device pushes the seeds from the cells when they are over the seed tube. The unit shown in Fig. 10.2*b* is a precision-planting arrangement, having small-diameter, accurately sized cells and a positive knock-out device that extends nearly through the cells.

Inclined-plate metering devices (Fig. 10.3 and 10.4) have cups or cells around the periphery that pass through a seed reservoir fed under a baffle from the hopper, lift the seeds to the top of the plate travel, and drop them into the delivery tube. A stationary brush is usually employed for more positive unloading. Seeds are handled more gently than with horizontal-plate units because there is no cutoff device. The metering unit in Fig. 10.4 has an edge-cell plate with sizes available to fit various kinds of small

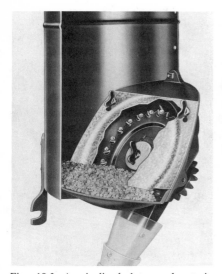

Fig. 10.3. An inclined-plate seed-metering device.

Fig. 10.4. An inclined-plate seed-metering device designed for precision planting of small vegetable seeds. (Courtesy of Deere & Co.)

vegetable seeds. The plates and the surrounding ring are accurately machined to provide uniform cell sizes for precision metering.

Vertical-rotor metering devices of the type shown in Fig. 10.5 are often used for precision planting of vegetables and sugar beets. Some units omit the seed tube, placing the rotor as low as possible and discharging directly

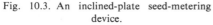

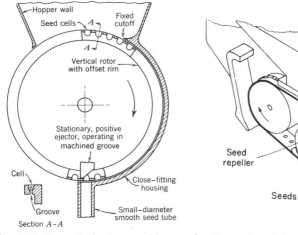

Fig. 10.5. A vertical-rotor precision seed-metering device.

Fig. 10.6. A belt-type precision seed-metering device. (After Stanhay, Ltd.)

into the furrow. Vertical-rotor units are also available that have seed cups which move up through a shallow seed reservoir, pick up single seeds, carry them over the top of the circle, and discharge them during the downward travel.

Another type of precision metering device has cells in a belt, sized to fit the seeds (Fig. 10.6). Seed from the hopper enters the chamber above the belt through opening A and is maintained at a controlled level. As the belt moves clockwise, the counter-rotating seed repeller pushes back excess seeds so there is only one in each cell. Seeds in the cells are conveyed over the base and discharged from the belt beneath the seed repeller wheel. Lack of a positive unloading device causes some variability in seed spacing.

Two types of single-seed metering devices that do not have cells are shown in Fig. 10.7, 10.8, and 10.9. Either type can accommodate normal variations in seed size and shape encountered with a particular kind of seed. The unit shown in Fig. 10.7 is designed for all types of corn. Twelve spring-loaded, cam-operated fingers on radial arms rotate, gripping one or more seeds as they pass through the seed reservoir. All but one seed is released as each finger passes over two small indents near the top of the stationary disk. As the finger continues to rotate, it passes over an opening in the disk and kicks the remaining kernel into one of 12 cells in the adjacent, rotating seed wheel. The seed wheel discharges the individual kernels into the furrow.

The pneumatic (air-pressure) metering system shown in Fig. 10.8 has a centralized hopper and metering unit that serves 4, 6, or 8 rows. The ground-driven seed drum has one circumferential row of perforated seed pockets for each planter row. A shallow reservoir of seed is automatically maintained in the drum by gravity flow from the hopper. A PTO-driven fan supplies air to the drum, maintaining a pressure of about 4 kPa [0.6 psi] in the drum and in the hopper. Air escapes through the holes in the seed pockets until a seed enters the pocket. Then differential pressure holds each seed as the revolving drum carries it up past a stationary brush near the top that knocks off any excess seeds. Air-cutoff wheels on top of the drum momentarily block the holes, causing the seeds to drop into the seed-tube manifold. Air flow through the tubes carries the seeds to the planting units and deposits them in the furrows. This system is designed for crops such as corn, beans, and grain sorghum, a different drum being employed for each kind of seed.

The pneumatic principle is also utilized in single-row metering devices for unit planters. Small blowers driven by electric motors connected to the tractor's electrical system provide air pressure in the metering chamber (Fig. 10.9). Seeds held against the holes in the rotor seed pockets are carried upward and around in a counterclockwise direction in the unit shown in Fig. 10.9. The seeds are released into the seed tube when the pockets pass a baffle that cuts off the inner air pressure to the front (left-hand) portion of the rotor. Different disk rotors are used for different kinds of seeds.

Fig. 10.7. Exploded cutaway view of finger-pickup type of seed-metering device for corn. The rotating seed wheel and the stationary disk behind the fingers are close together in actual operation. (Courtesy of Deere & Co.)

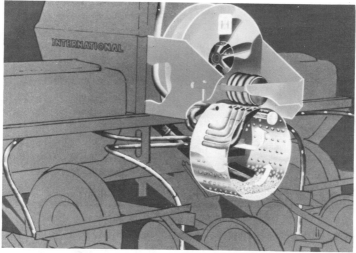

Fig. 10.8. Pneumatic seed-metering and distribution system designed for crops such as corn, beans, and grain sorghum. (Courtesy of International Harvester Co.)

Fig. 10.9. Single-row pneumatic seed-metering device on a unit planter. (Courtesy of White Farm Equipment Co.)

A number of seed-metering devices employing the vacuum-pickup principle have been developed experimentally[12,13,27] and at least one manufacturer had a planter with a vacuum pickup device commercially available in 1977. Most of these have had a central vacuum pump with valving to each pickup orifice and a seal between the stationary piping and the rotating pickup assembly. One metering unit, however, had a self-contained vacuum-and-pressure pump cylinder for each pickup orifice.[12] A stationary cam extended the piston to produce pressure for unloading the seeds and a spring retracted it to develop the vacuum for seed pickup. Vacuum-pickup devices can perform effectively, even with small, irregular-shaped seeds like lettuce,[12] but they are sensitive to dust and dirt.

With any of the metering devices described above, the average spacing of seeds or hills is determined by the ratio of the linear or peripheral speed of the seed pickup units (cells, fingers, etc.) to the forward speed of the planter and by the distance between the seed pickup units on the metering unit. Plates, belts, or rotors with different numbers of cells are available for some types of metering units, but changing the speed ratio is the most common method of changing seed spacing.

10.8. Seed-Tape Planting Systems. In this type of precision planting system, seeds are deposited either singly or in groups (hills) on a water-soluble tape in a laboratory or production facility under controlled conditions. Equipment is available for singling and spacing small, irregular-shaped seeds on tape with a high degree of accuracy. In one seed-tape system that has been used commercially, the seeds are placed on the tape at the desired field spacing and a continuous strip of tape is unreeled and placed beneath the soil by a simple planting unit.[11,18] The tape is a polyethylene oxide that is stable under normal atmosphere conditions but dissolves in 1 or 2 min when placed in moist soil.

The continuous-tape system has been used for commercial plantings of lettuce, tomatoes, cucumbers, and some other vegetable crops. The tape is expensive and good soil preparation is imperative.[18] A large amount of tape per hectare is needed, especially for close-spaced rows (e.g., 20 km/ha for 51-cm row spacing). Precise depth control is difficult to maintain but planting can be done at relatively high forward speeds. Seed spacing in the row is predetermined when the seed tape is made and is precise in the field. Increased yields, in comparison with planting bare seeds, have been reported for lettuce and cucumbers.[11]

Chancellor[9] developed a system in which single seeds were spaced 10 mm [0.4 in.] apart on soluble paper tape. He developed a planter that would cut the tape into single-seed sections and deposit these sections in cone-shaped pockets pressed into the soil. He included an arrangement to meter a charge of noncrusting soil amendment (vermiculite) into each pocket to cover the tape. Perforations along one side of the tape synchronized the depositing of seeds on the tape and the cutting of tape into sections by the planter. With this system, seed spacing is adjustable.

10.9. Bulk-Flow Seed Metering Devices. Three common types of metering devices that deliver a more-or-less continuous flow of seeds are illustrated in Fig. 10.10, 10.11, and 10.12. Fluted-wheel and internal double-run force-feed metering devices are used to a limited extent on row-crop planters but their main application is on grain and grass drills. The fluted-wheel feed is generally favored over the double run where only relatively small seeds are to be handled. The double-run feed is suitable for large seeds as well as for the small grains. Only one side is used at any one time, the side selected depending upon the seed size.

The rate of seeding with the fluted wheel is controlled by moving the wheel axially to change the length of flutes exposed to the seed in the feed cup. The primary method of controlling the seeding rate with the double-run feed is by changing the speed ratio between the ground wheels and the feed shaft.

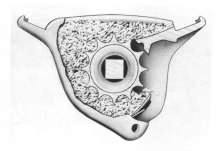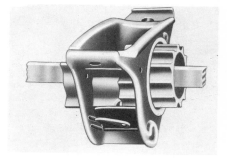

Fig. 10.10. Fluted-wheel seed-metering device. (Courtesy of Deere & Co.)

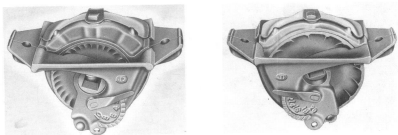

Fig. 10.11. Internal double-run seed-metering device, showing large and small sides of the wheel, for large and small seeds. (Courtesy of Deere & Co.)

Broadcast seeders usually have stationary-opening metering devices. The seeding rate is controlled by adjusting the size of opening. Agitators are provided above the openings to prevent bridging and to reduce the effect of seed head on the flow rate. The stationary-opening principle is applied in a little different manner on the unit illustrated in Fig. 10.12, which is used extensively for planting vegetables and to some extent for other row crops. The agitator merely moves the seed back and forth across the selected metering hole. Several interchangeable plates with different hole-size ranges are available.

10.10. Furrow Openers. Examples of both rotating and fixed types of furrow openers are shown in Fig. 10.13. The choice among these types or others similar to them is influenced by a number of factors. The optimum

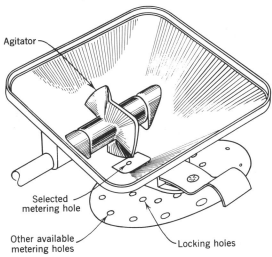

Fig. 10.12. Stationary-opening seed-metering device with agitator, as employed on some vegetable seeders (hopper not shown).

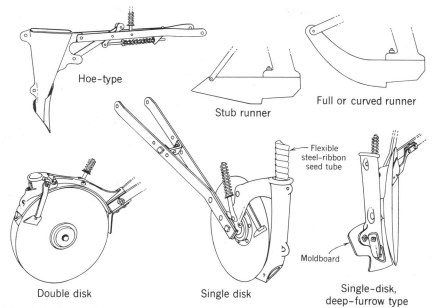

Fig. 10.13. Some of the common types of furrow openers. The single-disk openers are slightly concave; the double disks are flat and contact each other at the lower front.

depth of planting varies widely with different crops and is influenced by soil moisture conditions, soil temperature, time of year, etc. Some seeds are rather sensitive to environmental conditions and require careful control of the planting depth, whereas others can tolerate a considerable range of conditions.

The full runner is a simple device that works well at medium depths in mellow soil free of trash and weeds. It is suitable for the average conditions encountered by corn and cotton planters. Horizontal plate-type depth gages may be attached to the runner for soft soils. The stub runner is sometimes used on corn planters in rough or trashy ground.

Hoe-type openers, when equipped with spring trips as shown in Fig. 10.13, are suitable for stony or root-infested soils. They, or similar shovel-type openers, may also be used for deep placement of seeds if the soil is relatively free of trash. Some vegetable planters have shoes or runners considerably smaller than those shown (Fig. 10.4).

Disk-type openers are suitable for trashy or relatively hard ground. In wet, sticky soils they are more satisfactory than fixed openers because they can be kept reasonably clean with scrapers. The single-disk opener, used on some grain drills, is more effective than the double disk in regard to penetration and cutting of trash. Single-disk openers with moldboard attachments, as shown at the lower right in Fig. 10.13, are used for furrow planting of grain, the drilled surface being left as a series of furrows and ridges. Double-disk openers are particularly well-adapted to medium or shallow seeding of row crops that are critical in regard to planting depth, because the depth can be controlled rather accurately with removable depth bands (Fig. 10.15).

Another type of furrow opener developed for planting sugar beets has a narrow flange, perhaps 32 mm [1¼ in.] high, centered on the flat rim of a wheel. The wheel *presses* a V-shaped groove in the soil, thus providing firmer soil in the seed zone than is obtained with a disk or runner. Planting depth is determined by the height of the flange. Field tests with sugar beets have shown considerably higher emergence than with double-disk openers.[5]

10.11. Covering Devices. Among the many types of covering devices employed on seeders are drag chains, drag bars, scraper blades (Fig. 10.4), steel presswheels, rubber-covered or zero-pressure pneumatic presswheels, disk hillers, and various combinations of these units. As indicated in Section 10.6, a covering device should place moist soil in contact with the seeds, press the soil firmly around the seeds, cover them to the proper depth, and yet leave the soil directly above the row loose enough to minimize crusting and promote easy emergence.

Some kinds of seed are more critical than others in regard to these factors. Thus simple drag chains, which merely cover the seeds with loose soil, are satisfactory for grain drills under most conditions where there is ample moisture. In loose, sandy soils or for furrow drilling of grain in heavy residue, narrow presswheels with steel or rubber rims may be used behind the openers; they tend to give increased stands and yields in areas where moisture is a limiting factor.

Figure 10.14 shows some of the types of presswheels employed on row-crop planters. Open-center, concave, steel presswheels are common for corn and other large-seed crops. Zero-pressure pneumatic presswheels are used extensively for vegetables and some other crops. Their continual flexing tends to make them self-cleaning. Tires with narrow center ribs (Fig. 10.14) press soil down firmly around the seeds and have given good results in sugar

Fig. 10.14. Various types of presswheels used on row-crop planters. (Courtesy of Allis-Chalmers.)

beets. A drag chain behind the flanged presswheel fills the remaining groove with loose soil. Narrow rubber-tired seed packer wheels (25 mm [1 in.] wide and 200 to 250 mm [8 to 10 in.] in diameter), running directly behind the opener to press the seed into the bottom of the furrow before the seed is covered, sometimes improve emergence, especially with cotton.

10.12. Row-Crop Planter Arrangements. Most row-crop planters are adaptable to a variety of crops by merely changing seed plates, hopper bottoms, or some other element of the metering device. Tool-bar-mounted unit planters (Fig. 10.15) are popular because of their great versatility in regard to row spacings and types of seed that they can plant. These are mounted on a tractor tool bar, a pull-type tool carrier, or a combination bed-shaping and planting unit of the type described in Section 10.2. Many different combinations of furrow openers, metering units, and covering devices are employed. The seed-metering device on a unit planter is usually driven from the presswheel but in some cases is driven by a gage wheel or by double-disk openers.

Mounted or pull-type planters can plant 2, 4, 6, 8, or 12 rows, covering widths as great as 9 m [30 ft]. Two pull-type planters can be connected side-by-side for even greater widths. Tractor-mounted planters more than about 6 m [20 ft] wide usually have fold-up outer sections to reduce the width for transport.

Fig. 10.15. A tool-bar-mounted unit planter with double-disk opener and depth bands. Note the parallel-link attachment. The presswheel drives the metering unit through interchangeable sprockets. (Courtesy of Deere & Co.)

With either unit planters or pull-type planters having independently mounted row units, the depth of each unit is controlled by its presswheel, a gage wheel, shoes on runner openers, or depth bands on double-disk openers (Fig. 10.15). Seed hoppers are mounted on the individual row units, directly above the furrow openers, and should be as low as feasible.

Fertilizer attachments, with which bands of chemical fertilizers can be placed in the soil at prescribed locations with respect to the seed, are available for most row-crop planters and are widely used for certain crops. Attachments for applying pesticides are also common. Centralized fertilzer hoppers, each serving several rows, can be used on pull-type planters, thus minimizing filling time.

10.13. Grading and Processing Seed. One of the requirements for accurate seeding of row crops with cell-type metering devices is that the seeds or seed-containing units be of uniform size and shape. For best results this involves accurate grading of the seed within acceptable size limits, as well as selection of the proper seed plate. Seeds that are too large for a given size of cell will remain in the hopper or will protrude from the cell and be damaged as the plate passes the cutoff. Small seeds will either give multiples in the cells or the top seed will protrude and may be damaged by the cutoff. Smooth seeds approaching a spherical shape are best adapted to precision planting.

The introduction of hybrid corn varieties has resulted in wide variations in seed size and shape. This poses a difficult grading problem, particularly since each of the three major dimensions must be considered. Accurate classification requires a large number of grades, and planter seed plates are needed to fit each grade. Improved planter performance, however, usually justifies the added expense of better graded seed. The metering devices illustrated in Fig. 10.7 and 10.8 can handle all sizes and shapes of corn kernels, but no published information is available to indicate metering efficiency.

In some cases the individual seed units are actually modified as to size, shape, or surface condition to make them more suitable for precision planting. One of the earliest examples of seed processing on a commercial basis was the modification of sugar beet seed balls to produce smaller seed units that were roughly spherical in shape and had only one seedling-producing germ per unit instead of one to five germs as natural seed balls had at that time.[3] The resulting high percentage of single plants greatly reduced hand-thinning costs and made mechanical thinning feasible.

Monogerm sugar beet seed was developed by plant breeders in 1948 and has now virtually replaced processed multigerm seed. Monogerm seed must also be processed to be suitable for precision planting because in its natural state it is somewhat pancake-shaped and has a rough, corky outer periphery (Fig. 10.16a). Processing is usually done with a seed decorticator (developed originally for multigerm seed[3]) or a rice polisher. Either process removes

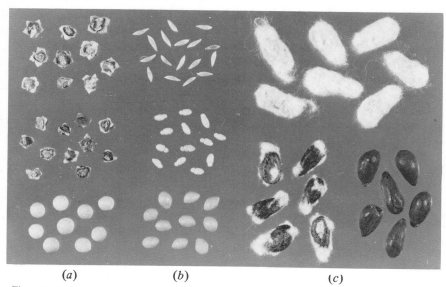

(a)   *(b)*   *(c)*

Fig. 10.16. Examples of seed processing. *(a)* Sugar beet seed—natural ungraded (top), processed, and coated. *(b)* Lettuce seed—bare seed (top), minimum-coated, and full-coated. *(c)* Gin-run fuzzy cotton seed (top), mechanically delinted seed (lower left), and acid delinted seed (lower right). All seeds are shown at approximately their actual sizes.

much of the corky material and tends to smooth up the periphery but still leaves the seeds discus-shaped. Accurate screening to close size tolerances and a careful fit of cell sizes are necessary for good metering results.

Small, irregular-shaped seeds are sometimes coated with an inert material to make the seed units larger and more nearly spherical so they can more readily be singled by metering devices.[25] The pellets are screened to a uniform size. The coating material must be durable enough to withstand handling and shipping and porous enough to permit respiration of the enclosed seed. It should soften rapidly when in contact with moist soil and permit adequate moisture transfer to the seed to promote germination and emergence. Each pellet should contain only one seed, and the seed must not be damaged.

Monogerm sugar beet seed is sometimes coated to improve its metering characteristics and thereby reduce the percentage of doubles. Coating has also been tried on various types of vegetables, with varying degrees of success and acceptance. Coated seeds germinate more slowly than bare seeds and are more critical in regard to soil preparation, planting depth, and moisture conditions. A recent development for lettuce that tends to reduce the magnitude of these problems is a minimum-coating process in which the mass ratio of coating material to seed is about 10 to one instead of 50 to one as in full coating. Full-coated, minimum-coated, and bare lettuce seeds are shown in Fig. 10.16b. The minimum coated seed can be metered satisfactorily by cell-type precision metering devices and germinates faster than full-coated seed.[16] Minimum coating is an established practice with lettuce[22] and is also used on some other vegetable crops such as tomatoes and carrots.

Cotton is another type of seed that is much easier to plant uniformly after it has been processed. Because gin-run cotton seed is covered with fuzzy lint (Fig. 10.16c), the seeds stick together in a fluffy mass and will not flow freely. Special planting units are required, and accurate seed distribution is difficult if not impossible to attain. Seed that has had the lint removed by either mechanical or chemical means can readily be handled by the same types of planting units employed for other row crops, and more uniform planting rates can be obtained than with fuzzy seed. Delinted seed is now used for most cotton planting.

10.14. Precision Planting. Precision planting implies accurate spacing of single seeds in the row, precise control of planting depth, especially for shallow planting of vegetable crops, and creating a uniform germination environment for each seed. The principal problem in developing plate-type precision planters for corn has been to obtain accurate metering and uniform seed dropping at high forward speeds. Corn planters are available that will do an acceptable job at speeds of 8 to 11 km/h [5 to 7 mph].

The primary objective in precision planting of sugar beets, vegetables, and other crops that require thinning because emergence rates are low and unpredictable is to obtain single plants spaced far enough apart so that thinning can be done mechanically or with a minimum of hand labor. In addition to reducing thinning costs, precision planting makes the timing of the thinning operation less critical, reduces competition between adjacent plants before thinning, and reduces the shock to the remaining plants during thinning. The more uniform maturing that can result from precision planting increases the feasibility of nonselective harvesting of crops such as lettuce. Metering devices of the types shown in Fig. 10.2b, 10.4, 10.5, and 10.6 are commonly used for sugar beets and small-seed vegetables. Maximum forward speeds are considerably lower than for corn.

The principal requirements for precision planting with a cell-type metering device are:

1. The seeds must be uniform in size and shape, preferably about spherical.
2. The planter cells must be of the proper size for the seeds. Plates and other critical parts of the metering device must be accurately made.
3. The seeds must have adequate opportunity to enter the cells. Plate speed and exposure distance of the cells in the hopper are the basic parameters, with low speed being more effective than long exposure distances.
4. A good cutoff device is needed to prevent multiple cell fill without causing excessive seed breakage.

5. Unloading of the seeds from the cells must be positive.
6. The seeds must not be damaged enough to appreciably affect germination.
7. The seeds must be conveyed from the metering unit to the bottom of the furrow in such a manner that the spacing pattern produced by the metering device is maintained (discussed in Section 10.16).
8. The seeds should be placed at the proper depth in a narrow furrow with a minimum of bouncing or rolling in the furrow.

As with any planting operation, the seeds should be uniformly covered and the soil compacted around them to the proper degree.

10.15. Factors Affecting Cell Fill and Seed Damage. The percent cell fill for a given planter is influenced by such factors as the maximum seed size in relation to cell size, the range of seed sizes, the shape of the seeds, the shape of the cells, the exposure time of a cell to seed in the hopper, and the linear speed of the cell. Percent cell fill is defined as the total number of seeds discharged divided by the total number of cells passing the discharge point. According to this definition, 100% cell fill does not necessarily mean that every cell contains a single seed but merely implies that any empty cells are offset by extra seeds in multiple fills. The most uniform seed distribution is usually obtained with combinations of seed size, cell size, and cell speed that give about 100% average cell fill.

Figure 10.17 shows the relation of cell fill to speed when metering corn with edge-drop, horizontal-plate planters. The broken-line curve shows very

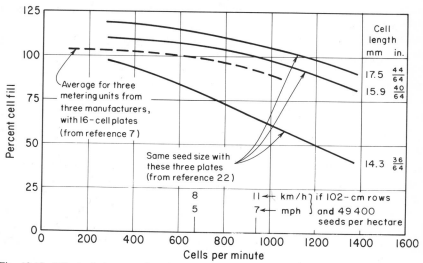

Fig. 10.17. Effect of plate speed and cell size upon percent cell fill for corn with edge-drop, horizontal plates. (Row spacing of 102 cm [40 in.] assumed for data from reference 23, which was reported as travel speed for 49 400 seeds per hectare [20,000 seeds per acre].)

little increase in cell fill (i.e., very few doubles) as the speed was reduced below the point of 100% fill, indicating that perhaps the seed was more uniform and the cell size better matched to the seed than for any of the other 3 curves. In tests with processed sugar beet seed in 2 horizontal-plate, precision planters (similar to Fig. 10.2b), Barmington[4] found a linear decrease in cell fill from 122% at a cell speed of 3 m/min [10 ft/min] to 27% at 55 m/min [180 ft/min], with 100% fill at about 15 m/min [50 ft/min]. Similar results were obtained with vertical-rotor planters.

The effect of cell speed appears to be much greater for rough-surfaced seeds than for large, smooth seeds like corn. Doubles are more likely to occur at low speeds with small seeds than with large seeds. When planting seeds such as sugar beets, the best performance of a cell-type metering unit can be obtained only within a relatively narrow range of cell speeds. With large seeds such as corn, cell fill is not greatly affected by speeds below that which produces 100% fill, and the main consideration is to keep plate speeds relatively low. For a given spacing in the row and a given forward speed, increasing the number of cells in the plate reduces the linear cell speed.

Comparison of the solid curves in Fig. 10.17 shows the effect of cell size upon percent cell fill. Although the 14.3-mm [36/64-in.] plate had been recommended by the seed producer for this particular lot of seed,[23] it obviously was too small. The largest cells (top curve) had an excessive percentage of doubles at low speeds and damaged the seed excessively at high speeds.[23] The effect of the relation between seed size and cell size was also shown by tests with processed sugar beet seed in a horizontal-plate planter having 4.37-mm [11/64-in.] diameter cells, in which seed closely graded to size limits of 2.78 to 3.18 mm [7 to 8/64 in.], 3.18 to 3.57 mm [8 to 9/64 in.], and 3.57 to 3.97 mm [9 to 10/64 in.] gave cell fills of about 140, 100, and 90%, respectively.[4]

In general, experience has indicated that the cell diameter or length should be about 10% greater than the maximum seed dimension and the cell depth should be about equal to the average seed diameter or thickness. Performance is improved by grading the seed within close size tolerances. Cell size is less critical with pneumatic (air-pressure) metering devices and is not a factor with vacuum pickup devices.

Most seed damage in horizontal-plate or vertical-rotor metering units is caused by the cutoff device. The percentage of damaged seeds increases as the cell speed is increased. Damage is also greater if the cells are too large. Damage can be minimized by making the cutoff device flexible and gentle or by employing designs in which individual seeds are lifted out of the seed mass so that no cutoff is needed, as with inclined-plate, pneumatic, and vacuum-type metering units.

10.16. Controlling Seed Between Metering Device and Furrow. Precise metering is of little value unless the seeds are controlled so that each requires the same time from the meter to the furrow and unless bouncing and rolling in the furrow are minimized. These factors are especially critical for close spacings in the row and/or for high forward speeds. When drilling at 4.8 km/h [3 mph] with seeds spaced 50 mm [2 in.] apart in the row, a seed that is delayed $1/25$ s will be overtaken by the next seed.

Variations in drop time can be minimized by one of the following:

1. Having a short, smooth, small-diameter drop tube with the discharge end close to the bottom of the furrow.
2. Discharging the seed directly from the metering device within a few centimetres of the furrow bottom.
3. Mechanically transferring the seed from the metering unit to the furrow as is done with transfer wheels on some hill-drop planters (Fig. 10.18).

Slow cell speeds, or trajectory-shaped seed tubes for high plate speeds, minimize bouncing within the seed passage.[2]

Seed movement in the furrow can be minimized by having a narrow furrow and by imparting a rearward velocity component to the discharged seed to at least partially offset the forward velocity of the planter. Improved uniformity has been obtained in tests with plate-type corn and cotton planters by angling the seed tube rearward 15 to 30° from the vertical.[7,26] High downward velocities (as from long drop distances) tend to increase seed bouncing and displacement in the furrow.

10.17. Hill Dropping. Seed plates with cells large enough to hold a full hill of seeds can be used for hill dropping, but there is likely to be considerable scattering of the seeds, particularly at high forward speeds. Seed dispersion may result from time delays as the seeds leave the plate cells, time delays as they fall through the seed tube, or scattering when they strike the furrow.[2]

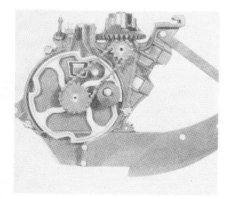

Fig. 10.18. Rotary valve for hill dropping. (Courtesy of White Farm Equipment Co.)

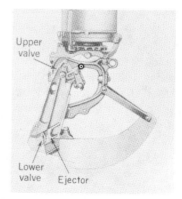

Fig. 10.19. Reciprocating valves for hill dropping, shown in closed positions.

More accurate hill spacing and closer grouping of seeds within a hill can be obtained with a rotary valve or transfer wheel of the type shown in Fig. 10.18 than with hill-drop plates. This wheel accumulates the desired number of seeds for a hill as they are discharged from the metering plate and discharges them close to the furrow bottom at a low velocity relative to the ground.

Valve mechanisms of the type shown in Fig. 10.19 were originally developed for checkrow corn planting but can also be used for random hill dropping. Rotary valves, however, are more suitable for high-speed operation. In a reciprocating-valve arrangement, a cam on the feed shaft opens the two valves simultaneously for each hill. Seeds that had been momentarily resting on the lower valve are ejected down and rearward a relatively short distance into the furrow, while seeds accumulated on the upper valve are released to fall down onto the lower valve. Spring action closes both valves.

10.18. Planter Testing. Although the ultimate criterion for evaluating a complete planting operation is the stand obtained in the field, these results are influenced by seed viability and environmental factors beyond the control of the planting machine. The effects of different types of furrow openers or presswheels can only be determined by field emergence trials, but the performance of a seed-metering device can be checked more readily and more reliably in the laboratory than in the field.

The regularity of seed spacing can be observed rather simply by mounting the hopper and metering device on a suitable stand and passing a grease-coated board beneath the seed tube at a rate representing the ground speed of the planter. The resulting seed pattern is representative of the performance of the metering device with its seed tube but does not show the effect of bouncing in the furrow. Photosensitive devices and electronic units have also been used to record the paths or frequencies of falling seeds.

The performance of a metering device alone is often expressed as the percentages of skips, singles, and doubles (or multiples). Various methods have been employed to evaluate or compare seed distribution patterns. Some investigators have assumed an acceptable range or tolerance for the seed spacing and then determined the percentages of spaces within this range. Sometimes the unacceptable spaces are segregated into those that are too short and those that are too long. Another method involves measuring each space and then calculating the standard deviation and the coefficient of variability.

The most common method of determining cell fill is to weigh the seed collected while a certain number of cells pass the discharge point, count the number of seeds in a known mass, and then calculate the total number of seeds collected. Damage is determined on a mass basis by screening out the broken particles of seed. Another method is to count the number of seeds collected or recorded by one of the arrangements for determining regularity of spacing. The counting method gives a direct indication of the number of seeds discharged by each individual cell and the probability of a cell's selecting zero, one, two, or any other number of seeds, whereas the weighing method merely indicates the overall average.

10.19. Broadcast Seeding. Seeds may be broadcasted with centrifugal-type spreaders, with drop-type broadcasters that have spaced openings along the full length of a hopper (similar to a grain drill without furrow openers), or by distribution from helicopters or fixed-wing aircraft. If broadcasted seed is to be covered, this is done as a separate operation, usually with a spike-tooth harrow.

The centrifugal-type broadcaster, also known as an endgate seeder, provides a rapid and inexpensive method of seeding crops such as the small grains and some grasses. It is particularly useful for fields that are small, wet, irregularly shaped, or have surface or subsurface obstructions. Seed is metered from the hopper through an adjustable opening with an agitator above it, or sometimes with a fluted wheel. The metered seed is dropped onto one or 2 horizontal, ribbed disks (spinners) that rotate at 500 to 1000 r/min (sometimes faster) and spread the seed as a result of the centrifugal discharge force. The width of strip covered generally ranges from 6 to 15 m [20 to 50 ft], being influenced by the physical characteristics of the seed (size, shape, density, etc.), the speed and height of the spinners, and the configuration of the spinners. Distribution is not as uniform as with a grain drill and is affected by wind. Centrifugal broadcasting is discussed in more detail in Section 12.10.

10.20. Airplane Seeding. The first reported use of an airplane for seeding rice was in 1929, when it became necessary to replant some California fields that had already been flooded.[6] At the present time most of the rice planted in California, as well as considerable areas in other states, is presoaked and broadcasted onto either flooded or dry fields by airplane. Other crops such as wheat, barley, and pasture grasses have been seeded by airplane to a limited extent. Aircraft are particularly valuable for reseeding hilly rangelands or burned-over areas. Pellets containing groups of seeds are often used for range reseeding. The equipment for aircraft seeding is the same as that used for aircraft broadcasting of granular fertilizers, which is discussed in Section 12.11.

10.21. Grain Drills. In comparison with broadcast seeders, grain drills tend to give higher yields because of the greater uniformity of seed distribution and the more uniform seeding depth. The maximum depth of the furrow openers is controlled in gangs, usually through suitable adjustments in the lift arrangement. Each opener, however, is held down by spring pressure and can raise independently to pass over irregularities.

A fertilizer-grain drill has a divided hopper, the front section being for seed and the rear section for fertilizer (Fig. 10.20). The fertilizer may be

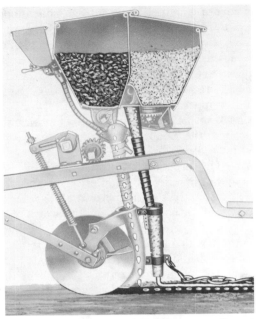

Fig. 10.20. Phantom view of fertilizer-grain drill with grass-seeding attachment on front.

deposited through the same tubes with the seed or through separate passages behind the seed tubes. Fertilizing units are also available as removable attachments for plain grain drills. Fertilizing equipment is discussed in more detail in Chapter 12. Attachments for drilling small grass seeds are available for either plain or fertilizer drills. An auxiliary hopper equipped with small-diameter fluted wheels is provided (Fig. 10.20), the grass seed either being deposited through the grain seed tubes or allowed to fall onto the soil behind the furrow openers. The operations of drilling grain, distributing fertilizer, or seeding grasses can be performed independently or in any desired combination.

Most grain drills have double-disk or single-disk furrow openers, but some have hoe-type openers for deep planting. Spacings generally range from 15 to 36 cm [6 to 14 in.], with 15.2, 17.8, and 20.3 cm [6, 7, and 8 in.] being common for standard drills. The wider spacings are primarily for furrow drilling (as with the single-disk, deep-furrow opener in Fig. 10.13).

10.22. Potato Planting. Potatoes are generally grown from seed pieces cut from the whole tubers, although small potatoes are sometimes planted without cutting. Since planting rates are in the order of 900 to 1700 kg/ha [800 to 1500 lb/acre], large seed hoppers are necessary and potato planters are usually pull-type implements (1-, 2-, or 4-row). Fertilizing units with hoppers holding several hundred kilograms per row are available for most potato planters and are integral units on some of them. The fertilizer is deposited in bands on either or both sides of the row by means of disk openers. The seed furrows are generally made with runner or shoe-type openers. Concave covering disks bury the seed pieces to a depth of perhaps 10 cm [4 in.] and leave a ridge over each row.

Automatic potato planters have vertical, rotating picker wheels with devices to either pierce or grip individual seed pieces and then drop them into the furrow. The picker-pin type, shown in Fig. 10.21, is the most common.

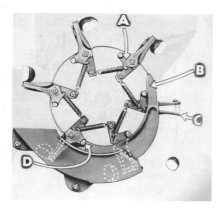

Fig. 10.21. A picker-pin feed mechanism for an automatic potato planter. In the left-hand view, the cam *B* causes the picker head to release the seed piece at *C*. The cam drop-off at *D* allows the spring-loaded arm to snap shut and pierce a new seed piece. The right-hand view shows how the seed is fed from the hopper into the picking chamber to maintain a uniform level.

Each arm or head of the picker wheel has two sharp picking pins that pierce a seed piece in the picking chamber (at point *D*) carry it over to the front, and then release it above the furrow (at point *C*). To avoid excessive picker-head speeds in high-speed planting (e.g., 8 km/h [5 mph]), 2 wheels per row, each with 6 to 8 picker heads, are mounted side by side with the arms staggered. The position of the picker pins on each head is adjustable to accommodate various sizes of seed pieces. The spacing of seed pieces in the row is controlled by the speed ratio between the ground wheels and the picker wheels.

10.23. Transplanting. Some kinds of crops, including tobacco, cabbage, sweet potatoes, and tomatoes, may be propagated in special beds and then transplanted in the field. If any appreciable area is involved, mechanical aids are usually employed. Mechanical plant setters are also suitable for planting small trees in reforestation work and for other kinds of nursery stock.

The essential components of the simpler transplanting machines are a furrow opener, provision for carrying a supply of plants, low seats for operators who place plants directly in the furrow, and presswheels or press plates to cover the roots and firm the soil around them. A water supply tank is usually provided, with appropriate valving for either intermittent application of water around each plant or continuous application along the row. Plants are spaced in response to a mechanical clicking device or other appropriate signal.

Machines designed for setting plants in prepared seedbeds are generally equipped with runner-type furrow openers. The principal requirements are that the furrow be of uniform depth and that it be wide enough to accommodate the plant roots without crowding. Presswheels are used in pairs, tilted outward at the top and sometimes with the fronts angled slightly away from the row.

Some transplanting machines have mechanical transfer devices that are hand-fed but which automatically place the plants in the furrow. This arrangement allows the operators to work in more comfortable positions and tends to give more uniform placement in the furrow. The transfer device must be carefully designed to ensure that the plants will not be damaged and to preclude any possibility of injury to the operator. Proper timing of the release is required so that the plants will remain upright as the roots are covered.

Huang and Splinter[15] developed a fully automatic transplanter for plants in small pots. The pots were of a conventional type that is sometimes used for hand transplanting and disintegrates rapidly when placed in the soil. Grid frames containing the potted plants were carried on the transplanter and automatically shifted to place the pots, one at a time, over an opening above a drop tube that guided the pots into the furrow.

REFERENCES

1. ABERNATHY, G. H., and J. G. PORTERFIELD. Effect of planter opener shape on furrow characteristics. Trans. ASAE, 12(1):16-19, 1969.
2. AUTRY, J. W., and E. W. SCHROEDER. Design factors for hill-drop planters. Agr. Eng., 34:525-527, 531, Aug., 1953.
3. BAINER, R. The processing of sugar beet seed. Agr. Eng., 29:477-479, Nov., 1948.
4. BARMINGTON, R. D. The relation of seed, cell size, and speed to beet planter performance. Agr. Eng., 29:530-533, Dec., 1948.
5. BARMINGTON, R. D. Trends in sugar beet planter design in Colorado. J. Am. Soc. Sugar Beet Technologists, 12(2):141-147, 1962.
6. BATES, E. N. California rice land seeded by airplane. Agr. Eng., 11:69-70, Feb., 1930.
7. BRANDT, R. G., and Z. FABIAN. Developing a high-speed precision planter. Agr. Eng., 45:254-255, May, 1964.
8. BUCHELE, W. F., and S. G. SHEIKH. Application of soil mechanics to plant emergence. ASAE Paper 67-655, Dec., 1967.

9. CHANCELLOR, W. J. Seed tape system for precision selection and planting of small vegetable seeds. Trans. ASAE, *12*(6):876-879, 1969.
10. DREW, L. O., T. H. GARNER, and D. G. DICKSON. Seedling thrust vs. soil strength. Trans. ASAE, *14*(2):315-318, 1971.
11. From Union Carbide: Evenseed planting. Agr. Eng., *52*:187, Apr., 1971.
12. GIANNINI, G. R., W. J. CHANCELLOR, and R. E. GARRETT. Precision planter using vacuum for seed pickup. Trans. ASAE, *10*(5):607-610, 614, 1967.
13. HARMOND, J.E. Precision vacuum-type planter head. USDA ARS 42-115, 1965.
14. HARRIOTT, B. L. A packaged environment system for precision planting. Trans. ASAE, *13*(5):550-553, 1970.
15. HUANG, B. K., and W. E. SPLINTER. Development of an automatic transplanter. Trans. ASAE, *11*(2):191-194, 197, 1968.
16. INMAN, J. W. Precision planting — a reality for vegetables. Agr. Eng., *49*:344-345, June, 1968.
17. JOHNSON, P. E., C. G. HAUGH, G. F. WARREN, G. E. WILCOX, and B. A. KRATKY. To plant vegetables with seed wafers. Agr. Eng., *51*:566, Oct., 1970.
18. KNOOP, J. G. Seeds on a spindle. The Farm Quarterly, *23*(5):64-68, 110-111, Fall, 1968.
19. MEDERSKI, H. J., D. M. VanDOREN, and D. J. HOFF. Narrow-row corn: yield potential and current developments. Trans. ASAE, *8*(3):322-323, 1965.
20. MORTON, C. T., and W. F. BUCHELE. Emergence energy of plant seedlings. Agr. Eng., *41*:428-431, 453-455, July, 1960.
21. PORTERFIELD, J. G., E. W. SCHROEDER, and D. G. BATCHELDER. Plateau profile planter. ASAE Paper 59-105, June, 1959.
22. ROBINSON, F. E., K. S. MAYBERRY, and H. JOHNSON, Jr. Emergence and yield of lettuce from coated seed. Trans. ASAE, *18*(4):650-653, 1975.
23. RYDER, G. J. High planting speed cuts corn yields. Plant Food Review, *4*(4):12-16, Winter, 1958.
24. STOUT, B. A., W. F. BUCHELE, and F. W. SNYDER. Effect of soil compaction on seedling emergence under simulated field conditions. Agr. Eng., *42*:68-71, Feb., 1961.
25. TAYLOR, D. Growers find coated seed aids in precision planting. California Farmer, *220*(8):19-20, Oct. 19, 1963.
26. WANJURA, D. F., and E. B. HUDSPETH, Jr. Metering and seed-pattern characteristics of a horizontal edge-drop plate planter. Trans. ASAE, *11*(4):468-469, 473, 1968.
27. WANJURA, D. F., and E. B. HUDSPETH, Jr. Performance of vacuum wheels metering individual cotton seed. Trans. ASAE, *12*(6):775-777, 1969.
28. WILKES, L. H., and P. HOBGOOD. A new approach to field crop production. Trans. ASAE, *12*(4):529-532, 1969.

PROBLEMS

10.1. (a) What seed spacing is required when planting corn in rows 102 cm apart if the desired plant population is 6000 plants per hectare and an average emergence of 85% is expected?

(b) If the edge-drop seed plate has 16 cells and a diameter of 200 mm, what is the linear cell speed in metres per minute when planting at 8 km/h?

10.2. A horizontal-plate planter has plates with 72 cells on a 165-mm-diameter circle. The effective radius of the drive wheel (presswheel) is 195 mm. A 16-tooth sprocket on the presswheel drives an 18-tooth sprocket on the feed shaft. A 12-tooth bevel gear on the feed shaft drives a 27-tooth gear on the plate shaft.

(a) Calculate the seed spacing in the row for 100% cell fill.

(b) If a plate speed of 15 m/min gives 100% cell fill, what forward speed (kilometres per hour) is required for 100% fill?

10.3. A planter has a vertical-rotor metering device similar to the one in Fig. 10.5, but with no seed ejector. The unit is operated without a seed tube, the seeds being released at the lowest point of travel and falling freely by gravity to the furrow bottom 90 mm below. The peripheral speed of the rotor is 21 m/min and the ground speed is 5 km/h. How far does a seed move horizontally (indicate whether forward or backward) between the point of discharge and the point of impact in the furrow,

(a) if the rotor turns in the same direction as the ground wheels?

(b) If the rotation is opposite?

(c) At what angle from the vertical does the seed strike the bottom of the furrow in each case? Neglect air resistance.

10.4. During a cell-fill test with sugar beet seed in a horizontal-plate planter having a plate with 72 cells on a 167-mm-diameter circle, 28.75 g of undamaged seed and 0.95 g of damaged (screened) seed were collected during 50 revolutions of the ground wheel in 68 s. A 6.40-g sample contained 556 seeds. The seed plate makes 0.76 revolutions for each revolution of the ground wheel. Calculate:

(a) Average percent cell fill (including damaged seed).

(b) Linear speed of cells, in metres per minute.

(c) Percent seed damage.

10.5. The seed tube on a plate-type corn planter is angled 20° rearward from the vertical and the seed plate is 560 mm above the furrow bottom.

(a) What is the horizontal rearward component of the seed velocity with respect to the planter when the seed reaches the furrow? Neglect the effects of friction and seed bouncing in the tube.

(b) What would be the horizontal velocity of the seed with respect to the ground, in kilometres per hour, if the planter speed is 7.25 km/h?

11

Row-Crop Cultivation, Flaming, And Thinning

11.1. Methods of Controlling Weeds. Since a large part of this chapter is devoted to equipment and practices whose primary function is to control weeds, a brief discussion of the general problem and the methods of combating weeds seems appropriate. The control of weeds and grasses has always been one of the greatest time- and labor-consuming operations in the production of crops.

In addition to requiring extensive control measures, weeds rob crop plants of nutrients and water, often serve as hosts to insects and other pests that prey on crop plants, and create equipment problems, especially in harvesting and processing of certain crops.

Mechanical cultivation or tillage is still the most important method for controlling weeds and is generally the most economical method where it can be used. The weeds may be uprooted, covered, or cut off. The principal problem in the tillage method is killing weeds and grasses in the crop row.

In the early stages of growth for some crops, implements such as the rotary hoe and the spring-tine or pencil-point weeder can be operated directly over the rows to uproot small weed seedlings from among established crop plants. The action of these tools depends upon differential resistance between the weeds and the crop plants, and there is generally some crop mortality. Indiscriminate or "overall" coverage of both the middles and the rows with implements of this type is fast and economical, and power requirements are low. Individual-row, rotary-hoe attachments are often mounted between the sweeps or shovels of a row cultivator for early cultivations.

Selective burning or flaming is an effective means of controlling in-the-row weeds in certain crops, such as cotton, corn, grain sorghum, and soybeans, whose stems are not injured by a short exposure to an intense heat. This method, however, cannot be applied during the early stages of crop growth.

Chemical herbicides are widely used for weed control at various stages of crop planting and growth. A number of types of selective chemicals are available that, if applied to the soil at the correct rates, will kill certain kinds of weeds or grasses and not be injurious to a particular type of crop plant. The margin of safety between adequate weed control and crop injury is small with some herbicides and some crops. Selective systemic herbicides, such as

2,4-D, are available that will kill broadleaf plants and not injure grasses when sprayed on the foliage. Others, such as dalapon, will kill grasses without injuring certain types of broadleaf plants.

Pre-plant or pre-emergence application of granular or liquid herbicides to the soil in a band perhaps 18 to 25 cm [7 to 10 in.] wide, centered on the row, is a common practice and can provide effective weed control in the early stages of crop growth. Pre-plant applications are usually incorporated into the soil. Pre-emergence treatments are usually applied to the soil surface in conjunction with the planting operation (behind the presswheel). If needed, post-emergence treatments may be applied to the soil surface adjacent to the row, either when the plants are young or at later stages of crop growth. Adequate moisture is required for activating most soil-applied herbicides and to sprout the weeds.

Directed post-emergence spraying with general-contact weed killers (which kill most kinds of vegetation) is practical with row crops that are resistant to injury from such sprays applied at the plant base. The nozzles must be carefully placed and directed so the spray does not strike the foliage or tender portions of the stalks.

Sometimes the crop itself is effective in combating weeds by shading them, but other methods of control are required until shade takes over. Hand hoeing and finger weeding are effective weed-control methods, but these are time-consuming, tedious, and costly operations. If other methods are not fully effective and weeds in the row get out of control, hand hoeing is about the only method that can be used.

The selection of a method or methods for controlling weeds is influenced by the type and age of crop, the type and size of the weeds or grasses, timeliness, the equipment available, and other factors. Good weed control usually involves a combination of the available methods plus timeliness and good farming. Weeds in the middles are usually controlled by cultivation, whereas weeds in the crop row may be controlled by any one or more of the methods described above. Weeds and grasses in the row are most effectively controlled when not more than 25 to 50 mm [1 to 2 in.] tall.

ROW-CROP CULTIVATORS

In general, the most important reason for row-crop cultivation is to promote plant growth by eradicating weeds. Additional functions in irrigated areas are to prepare the land for the application of irrigation water and to improve water penetration. In certain crops, preparation of the field for harvesting operations is an important consideration in the final cultivations. Incorporation of chemical fertilizers or pesticides into the soil is another function of cultivation.

As tractor sizes have increased, row-crop cultivator widths have also become greater. Because power requirements per metre of width are relatively low, the maximum width of row-crop cultivators is limited primarily by factors such as maneuverability, the effects of unbalanced draft variations from tools offset a great distance from the tractor centerline (i.e., steering stability of the tractor-cultivator combination), implement mass, and structural considerations. Rear-mounted or front-mounted cultivators are available that will cover widths as great as 9 m [30 ft]. The maximum number of rows ranges from eight 102-cm [40-in.] rows to sixteen 51-cm [20-in.] rows. Some cultivators are designed to cover only two 102-cm rows, but most cultivators now being manufactured cover at least 4 rows.

11.2. Tractors for Mounted Row-Crop Cultivators. The tricycle-type, all-purpose tractor with adjustable wheel tread was developed primarily for mounted cultivators and other row-crop equipment. Four-wheel tractors with both front-wheel and rear-wheel treads adjustable are widely used, especially for the larger cultivators. A 3-wheel tractor can turn sharper than a 4-wheel tractor but is less stable on turns or side hills and cannot straddle a single row or bed. High-clearance row-crop tractors, having minimum vertical clearances of more than 760 mm [30 in.] beneath the axles, are available for straddling tall crops.

11.3. Types of Mounted Cultivators. The most common type, which might be described as a separated-gang cultivator, has either one or two independent gangs per row that drop down between the rows as shown in Fig. 11.1

Fig. 11.1. A rear-mounted, separated-gang cultivator. Note the attachment points for the three-point hitch, the spring-loaded guide coulter at the left (there is also one at the other end), the parallel-link gang supports, and the gage wheels on individual gangs. (Courtesy of International Harvester Co.)

Fig. 11.2. A front-mounted, separated-gang cultivator with gage wheels on individual gangs. (Courtesy of Deere & Co.)

and 11.2. This arrangement provides maximum vertical clearance for the plants. The size of a separated-gang cultivator is designated as the number of rows covered, which is determined by the number of gangs provided. The gang spacing is adjustable for different row spacings.

Cultivators designed specifically for sugar beets and vegetables with close row spacings have continuous tool bars that extend across the tops of the plants as shown in Fig. 11.3. A separated-gang cultivator can be converted to a continuous-tool-bar unit by merely clamping tool bars across the separate gangs. A continuous-tool-bar arrangement is adaptable to a wide range of row spacings, the maximum number of rows depending upon the length of the tool bars and the row spacing. Good lateral stability between tools is characteristic of this type of cultivator and is an essential requirement for cultivating extremely close to plants. Vertical clearance is limited by the maximum practical length of the tool standards.

11.4. Gang Attachment Linkages and Depth Control. Separated gangs and front-mounted, continuous-tool-bar arrangements are attached to the cultivator frame through parallel links. Then raising or lowering a gang does not affect the tool pitch, and the depths of all tools change by the same amount. Good fits and wide contact areas at the link pivot points are needed to minimize lateral movement, especially with separated gangs.

Rear-mounted, continuous-tool-bar cultivators are attached directly to the three-point hitch. If the vertical distance between the upper and lower hitch points (mast height) is normal, vertical convergence of the links causes tool pitch and the relative depths of fore-and-aft spaced tools to change as the cultivator is raised or lowered. Reducing the mast height to make the upper and lower links parallel when in the operating position would minimize these effects.

Fig. 11.3. A rear-mounted, continuous-tool-bar cultivator with 2 gage wheels and 2 rigid guiding coulters. (Courtesy of Deere & Co.)

Satisfactory depth control can sometimes be obtained with narrow cultivators in smooth fields by adjusting the tool bar or gang heights in relation to the tractor. But for wide units, gage wheels on individually floating gangs are highly desirable and widely used (Fig. 11.1, 11.2, and 11.3). Gage wheels allow each gang to follow ground-surface irregularities or to compensate for lateral tilting of the tractor and/or cultivator frame with a minimum of depth variation.

Gang attachment linkages or lift linkages sometimes have springs that exert a downward force on the gang to aid in obtaining penetration. Otherwise, the only downward forces are the force of gravity on the gang and any downward component of soil forces (suction) on the tools.

As discussed in Section 8.18, the maximum depth obtainable with a parallel-link hitch when a gage wheel is used (free-link operation) or when the gang is suspended from the tractor is that which causes the resultant of R_v and W to become parallel with the hitch links. The support force Q_v on the gage wheels, or the restraining force in the lift links, would then be zero. If hold-down springs are employed, their effect should be combined with the gravity force. Penetration with a parallel-link system can be improved by raising the rear ends of the links with respect to the gang or lowering the front ends, thereby reducing the upward component of pull on the gang.

11.5. Characteristics of Rear-Mounted and Front-Mounted Cultivators. A rear-mounted cultivator that is laterally rigid is not satisfactory for cultivating close to plants because the initial response to a steering correction is in the opposite direction from that of the front wheels. The general adoption of the three-point hitch has eliminated this problem because the horizontal convergence of the lower links provides a virtual hitch point which, for a directional implement, is usually in the vicinity of the front axle (Section 8.17). One or two guide coulters (Fig. 11.1 and 11.3) provide lateral stability for the cultivator and make it directional. A visual steering guide is attached to the front axle of the tractor, directly over a row. Because the virtual hitch point is well forward, the implement tends to average out short-time variations in steering.

Front-mounted cultivators are laterally rigid with respect to the tractor and respond directly to steering. More continuously precise steering control is required for close cultivation than with rear-mounted units on a three-point hitch, but the operator has good visibility of the work. When a front-mounted cultivator is used, a rear gang is also needed if the soil is to be loosened behind the tractor rear wheels. When separated gangs are employed on a front-mounted cultivator, special extensions are needed to reach under the tractor body.

Front-mounted cultivators are somewhat more difficult to attach or remove than are rear-mounted units because parts of one or more gangs are directly behind the front wheels. To facilitate mounting or dismounting, the frames are usually hinged (Fig. 11.2) so they can be swung out and forward (i.e., rotated 90°) for removal, after detaching the inner ends from the sides of the tractor frame. The tractor can then be backed out without interference from the gangs. Several bolts must be loosened or removed but only a minimum amount of manual manipulation or lifting is needed to attach or detach most present-day front-mounted cultivators.

If the frame of either a rear-mounted or a front-mounted cultivator is relatively wide, small amounts of tractor tilting can cause enough vertical motion at the outer extremities of the frame to be objectionable, even with independently gaged gangs. To overcome this problem, rear-mounted cultivators more than about 6 m [20 ft] wide often have a gage wheel near each end of the main cross beam or frame, in addition to the individual-gang gage wheels. Front-mounted cultivators over 6 m wide usually have each half semimounted, with a longitudinal hinge axis at the tractor frame and a caster wheel at the outer end.

Carrier wheels and a hitch member to permit endways transport are available for most rear-mounted cultivators over 6 m wide. The wide, semimounted front cultivators have provision for swinging the two halves forward so they are together in front of the tractor for transport. The caster wheels still support the outer (front) ends of the frames.

11.6. Lift Arrangements. Each half of a front-mounted cultivator has a rockshaft above the main cross beam with a lift arm and lift link for each separated gang (two for a continuous-tool-bar gang). One remote (external) hydraulic cylinder may lift both halves, or two cylinders may be employed to permit selective lifting of one half before the other (sometimes desirable in odd-shaped fields). When a rear-mounted cultivator is lifted through the three-point hitch, the main cross beam first lifts alone and then it picks up each gang as the gang linkage reaches the lower limit of its travel with respect to the main cross beam.

When both front and rear gangs are employed, some method of delaying the raising or lowering of the rear gang is desirable so all operations can be started and stopped at about the same position with respect to the ends of the rows. Two hydraulic cylinders operated from a single control valve can be arranged to provide an automatic delay for the rear gang by means of two hydraulic pressure sequence valves, one for lifting and one for lowering (Section 4.7). Another common arrangement has independent controls for the front and rear cylinders, thus providing selective lifting or lowering with the timing determined by the operator.

11.7. Cultivating Tools and Attachments. Many types and combinations of cultivating tools are used in row crops, the selection being influenced by such factors as type and size of crop plants, soil type and field condition, and the purposes for which cultivation is being performed. A few of the common types of shovels and sweeps are illustrated in Fig. 11.4. Various sizes and

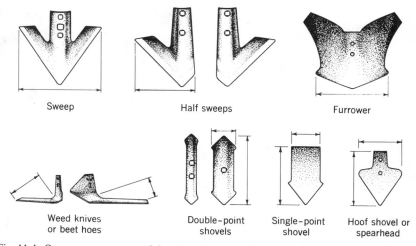

Fig. 11.4. Some common types of shovels and sweeps. The dimension lines indicate the manner of specifying the size of each tool.

shapes of these tools are available. Among the many other types of equipment are tools such as disk weeders and disk hillers for moving dirt to or from the row (Fig. 11.3), rotary hoe units, and special rotary cultivating equipment for row crops.

Row shields are often needed in close cultivation of small plants to prevent covering of the plants with dirt or clods. Stationary row shields are illustrated in Fig. 11.1 and rotary shields in Fig. 11.8. Special fenders or shields are sometimes needed to prevent large plants from being damaged by the tractor wheels or the cultivator frame.

Sweeps are used extensively for weed control, since shallow cultivation is generally desired. Special sweeps have been developed that can be operated at high speeds (often 8 km/h [5 mph] or more in crops such as corn and cotton) without throwing excessive amounts of dirt. When subsurface or mulch tillage is practiced, the crop residue tends to clog sweeps and prevent penetration. Disk hillers have given good results in these areas.

Fig. 11.5. Rotary-hoe attachment for a row-crop cultivator. (Courtesy of Deere & Co.)

Rotary-hoe attachments for row-crop cultivators (Fig. 11.5) are very effective at 8 to 10 km/h [5 to 6 mph] for early post-emergence cultivation of corn, cotton, and other crops. They are run directly over the rows while the crop plants are small but after they have well-established root systems. The hoe wheels uproot small, tender weeds and break any crust that might be present, without serious injury to the crop plants. They also serve as excellent rotary shields for the sweeps or other shovels in the middles. They allow sweeps to work at high speeds without covering, even when the plants are small. Continuous-width rotary hoes with staggered-wheel, tandem gangs are used in some flat-planted crops, covering the middles as well as the crop rows.

Rolling cultivators of the type shown in Fig. 11.6 are quite versatile tools for shallow cultivation and work well at high forward speeds. The twisted blades have a slicing action that moves soil laterally as well as uprooting small weeds and mulching the soil. The gangs can be adjusted to move soil either toward or away from the row and can be oriented to till a flat surface or the sloping side of a bed.

Fig. 11.6. Rolling-cultivator units with twisted blades that provide a slicing action and can move soil laterally as well as mulching. Right-hand and left-hand units are usually used in pairs. (Courtesy of Lilliston Corp.)

11.8. Cultivator Adjustments. The three basic adjustments for cultivator tools are the relative horizontal positions (lateral and fore-and-aft), the depth, and the pitch. Some tools, such as disk hillers and other tools for moving dirt to or from the row, also require a directional adjustment. This adjustment may be obtained by using standards whose upper portions have a circular cross section so they can be rotated in the clamps. Vertical adjustment of the standards in the clamps is provided so the relative depths of tools on a gang can be adjusted. Clamps should be easy to remove or shift.

Standards for separated-gang cultivators ordinarily have an adjustable joint for changing the pitch of individual tools, whereas continuous-tool-bar cultivators generally have one-piece standards and provision for rotating the entire tool bar or gang to adjust the pitch. Some tools, such as weed knives (Fig. 11.4), have slotted holes for pitch adjustment at the point of attachment to the standards.

In general, a cultivator is set up for the same number of rows that were planted at one time, since the guess rows (row spaces between adjacent planter trips) will always have some variation in width. For close cultivation it is important that the tool spacings correspond accurately with the spacing of the planter units. The tools that are to be operated closest to the row are usually placed in the most forward positions on a gang.

11.9. Protective Devices for Cultivator Standards. Continuous-tool-bar cultivators for beets and vegetables seldom have any protection for individual tools or standards, but spring-trip standards are common on separated-gang cultivators. Their purpose is to provide overload protection in case the tool encounters a stone, root, or other solid object. Friction-release standards are less expensive than spring-trip standards but also less reliable.

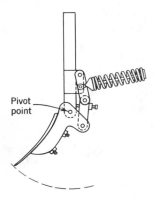

Pivot point

Fig. 11.7. Spring trip on a cultivator standard.

A typical arrangement for a spring trip is shown in Fig. 11.7. Ideally, the force on the shovel required to operate the spring trip should be large enough at the start of tripping to hold the shovel rigid until an obstruction is encountered and should then decrease as the shovel moves rearward. An inherent defect in most spring trips is that the pivot point is located behind the point of the tool, which causes the shovel to try to go deeper when the device trips (Fig. 11.7) and thus introduces high stresses in the standard.

11.10. Rotary Cultivation. Powered rotary cultivators are used for weed control and shallow mulching in certain crops, particularly those with close-spaced rows such as sugar beets and various vegetable crops. The upper view in Fig. 11.8 shows a rotary cultivator in operation in a bed planting and also shows cone-shaped guide wheels that run against the sides of the beds and keep the cultivator centered on the beds. A second pair of cones might be used on the front of the cultivator for more positive control.

The lower views in Fig. 11.8 show two types of rotary cultivating units. L-shaped blades (left) are the most common and are the type on the machine pictured above. Curved blades would be used if the sides of the bed were being tilled. In the example shown, ground-driven disks, free-wheeling on the rotor shaft, act as plant shields (lower left). Stationary, sliding shields are employed on some models. With either type of rotor, the widths of individual units or overall widths of pairs can be changed to accommodate various row spacings. The vertical crop clearance is limited by the radius of the tillage units.

Rotary cultivators are very effective weeders and mulchers. When equipped with suitable shields, the rotors can be operated extremely close to young plants having small root systems. It is not uncommon to leave an un-

Fig. 11.8. *Top:* A rotary cultivator with L-shaped blades. Cone-shaped guide wheels keep unit centered on the beds. *Lower left:* Diagram showing the operation of the L-shaped blades and the ground-driven disk shields. (Courtesy of International Harvester Co.). *Lower right:* Cylindrical type of rotor with blades parallel to the axis. (Courtesy of Cultro, Inc.)

tilled strip only 6 to 8 cm [2½ to 3 in.] wide in young sugar beets and vegetable crops. Such close cultivation, with either rotary cultivators or other cultivating tools, must be done at low forward speeds to permit accurate steering and reduce operator fatigue.

FLAME WEEDING

11.11. General Applications of Flaming. Control of unwanted vegetation by flaming has been practiced for many years in such places as railroad right-of-ways and drainage ditches. The practical application of *selective* flaming to control weeds and grasses within a specific row crop dates back to the early 1940s, when research demonstrated its feasibility in cotton. Since then, flame weeding has been tried in many different row crops with varying degrees of success and economic feasibility.[2]

Since about 1960, a considerable amount of research effort has been devoted to other applications for flaming. Thermal defoliation of cotton has been accomplished effectively (Section 19.14) with no adverse effects upon yields.[13] Flaming is sometimes employed to control weeds around the trees in orchards. Flaming alfalfa during the latter part of the dormant period has given effective, economical control of the alfalfa weevil.[14] Flame drying of standing grain sorghum to permit earlier harvesting has been tried.[2] These are just a few examples of agricultural applications of flaming that have been or are being investigated.[14]

11.12. Principles of Selective Flame Weeding. The differentiation in burning depends upon the weeds being small and tender and upon the crop plants having stems that are resistant to the intense heat and being tall enough so that flame directed at the ground in the row will not strike the leaves or other tender parts. Since large clods or ridges of soil are likely to deflect the flame up into the row, it is essential that the tops of the plant beds be as flat and smooth as possible. Accurate control of the flame path with respect to the ground surface in the row is important.

To be most effective, flame weeding must be done when the weeds and grasses are not over 25 to 50 mm [1 to 2 in.] tall. The theory of selective flaming is that the heat intensity (fuel rate) and the exposure time are adjusted so that enough heat is applied to the weeds and grasses to cause expansion of the liquid in the plant cells and consequent rupture of the cell walls but not enough heat to cause actual combustion. Thus, the effect of flaming may not become fully apparent until several hours after the operation has been performed.

Tests in cotton have indicated that the length of exposure time, as determined by the forward speed, has more effect upon crop damage (and weed control) than does fuel rate.[3,15] Forward speeds are usually 4.8 to 6.4 km/h [3 to 4 mph].[11]

11.13. Row-Crop Applications. By far the greatest amount of research and the most extensive applications of selective flaming have been in cotton. Control of weeds and grasses in the row is a serious problem in some areas, particularly in relation to the effects on mechanical harvesting. Cotton is well-suited to flame weeding, although it is likely to be damaged if flamed with conventional equipment before the plants reach a height of 180 to 200 mm [7 to 8 in.].[3,11]

Interest in flame weeding of cotton (and other crops) increased during the 1950s but declined in most areas during the mid and late 1960s as the use and effectiveness of pre-emergence and post-emergence herbicides increased. The principal area employing flaming in cotton to any appreciable extent in the early 1970s was the mid-south states, where certain kinds of broadleaf weeds and vines in the row cannot be controlled satisfactorily with chemicals.[11]

The most effective utilization of flaming is as one component of an overall weed-control system. Until the crop plants become large enough to withstand the flame, weeds and grasses in the row must be controlled by other means such as pre-emergence and post-emergence herbicide applications.

Flaming and shallow cultivation of cotton are usually carried on as a combined operation during midseason. Sweeps are used to clear the middles of weeds and the flames are directed to destroy the small weeds and grass in the rows. The operation is repeated at frequent intervals, since flaming is most effective when the weeds are small. Periods of extended rainfall may result in weed infestations becoming so thick and vigorous that flame weeders will not be effective in cleaning the rows. Flaming alone is used if weed control is necessary during the latter part of the season after the cotton has been "laid by" (i.e., cultivation discontinued) and until the first bolls open.

Flame weeding usually has no significant effect on cotton yields.[3,15] Fuel requirements are 35 to 55 L/ha [4 to 6 gal/acre] per flaming. Three to five flamings may be needed in addition to the early herbicide applications. Equipment for flame weeding is more expensive than equipment for chemical weed control, but there is no problem of toxic residues and a broader range of weeds can be controlled. Flaming requires more trips through the field than does chemical control and the procedure is less well-defined. Whereas mechanical cultivation tends to stir up a new set of weed seeds each time, neither flaming nor chemical control methods do this.

Crops such as corn, soybeans, and grain sorghum can also be flamed without adverse effects. Research has indicated that flaming corn in the Midwest, if properly done in conjunction with other weed-control methods, does not reduce yields.[10] Flaming usually should not begin until the corn is at least 250 mm [10 in.] tall. However, if a severe weed infestation exists when the corn is not over 50 mm [2 in.] tall, all the vegetation in the row can be flamed off and the corn will recover with no measurable effect on yield.[10] Soybeans should not be flamed until they are at least 250 mm [10 in.] tall nor while they are blooming or setting pods.

11.14. Components of a Flame Weeder. Present-day burners operate on LP (liquified petroleum) gas, which is usually propane or a mixture of butane and propane. These fuels exist in the gaseous state at ordinary atmospheric pressure and temperatures but liquefy when subjected to moderate pressures. Thus LP gas is stored and handled in pressurized tanks as a liquid, and at normal temperatures the tank supplies the pressure needed by the burners. Absolute vapor pressures of butane and propane, respectively, are 152 and 634 kPa at 10°C [22 and 92 psi at 50°F], 262 and 986 kPa at 26.7°C [38 and 143 psi at 80°F], and 421 and 1462 kPa at 43.3°C [61 and 212 psi at 110°F].

Two general types of burners are employed. One type, known as a liquid burner or self-vaporizing type, has a vaporizing tube on top of the burner housing. The other type employs a separate vaporizer connected to the tractor engine cooling system. The basic components of a system having vapor burners are shown in Fig. 11.9. Fuel rates of 7.5 to 15 L/h [2 to 4 gal/h] per burner are typical. One configuration of a vapor burner is shown in Fig.

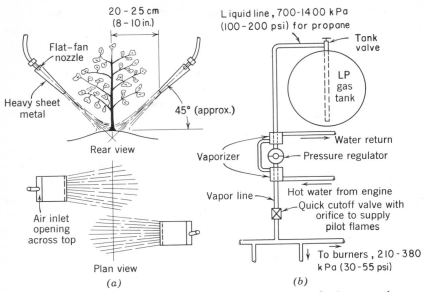

Fig. 11.9. (a) Essential features and approximate proportions for a flat burner, and recommended placement of burners with respect to a row of cotton. (b) Basic components of a typical LP-gas fuel system employing vapor burners.

11.9a. A properly designed burner should produce a broad, thin flame that is steady and well-controlled.[3]

Although mechanical cultivation is generally employed to control weeds in the middles, devices are available for flaming the middles between flat-planted rows. These usually consist of two standard burners with the flame directed downward and rearward under a low metal hood that covers the width to be flamed.[12]

A flame weeder developed at the Iowa Agricultural Experiment Station in 1966 flames both the rows and the middles in flat-planted crops and protects the crop plants by means of an air-curtain heat barrier.[7,8] This design is intended to be less sensitive to ground-surface irregularities than conventional cross flaming and to permit flaming when the crop plants are smaller.

Burners for flame weeding are usually supported on skids hinged to a rear-mounted tool bar (usually one skid per middle) or on parallel-link arrangements having gage wheels. In a combined flaming and cultivating operation, burners are attached to the independently gaged cultivator gangs. Accurate control of the burner height with respect to the ground surface in the crop row is essential for best results, especially when the plants are small. Guide coulters are needed for lateral stability, as on rear-mounted cultivators.

11.15. Burner Placement and Flaming Practices. The usual arrangement of burners is with two staggered burners directed across each row from opposite sides (cross flaming). The optimum burner placement is influenced to some extent by the type and size of crop and the type of burner. Recommendations of different manufacturers may vary somewhat. Typical recommendations for flat burners in cotton[12] are indicated in Fig. 11.9a. The burners may be set at 45° or as flat as 30°.[3] Under normal conditions the flame should strike the ground about 50 mm [2 in.] from the row center, on the near side. The burners are staggered along the row to prevent any flame interference that might cause deflection upward into the foliage of the crop plants.

Parallel flaming may be employed for small plants and crops with low resistance to flaming.[2,12] The burners are placed almost parallel to the row on each side, 75 to 125 mm [3 to 5 in.] from the row center. The burner outlets are 100 to 150 mm [4 to 6 in.] above the ground surface and are directed downward at about 45° toward the rear. Only the cooler edges of the flame contact the crop plants. Pre-emergence (and sometimes post-emergence) chemical herbicide band treatments are needed to control early weeds in the row. As the crop plants develop more flame resistance, the burners may be directed more toward the row or cross flaming is employed. The Iowa air-curtain flame weeder mentioned in the preceding section is essentially a parallel flamer.

11.16. Water-Spray Shields for Flaming. Water-spray shielding for the crop plants was developed at the Arkansas Agricultural Experiment Station and first field tested in 1968.[11] Shielding is accomplished by mounting a conventional fan-type spray nozzle about 50 mm [2 in.] above the burner mouth and directing it so the spray discharge is parallel with the flame. The spray crosses the row about 40 mm [1½ in.] above ground level. The recommended nozzle sizes have discharge rates of 0.5 to 0.7 L/min [⅛ to ³⁄₁₆ gpm] of water at the recommended pressures of 410 to 480 kPa [60 to 70 psi]. The smaller size applies 84 to 94 L/ha [9 to 10 gal/acre] at a speed of 6.4 km/h [4 mph] with a row spacing of 102 cm [40 in.] and half this amount per hectare at 12.8 km/h.

Water-spray shielding causes a drastic reduction in air temperatures above the spray (i.e., above 40 to 50 mm [1½ to 2 in.] height in the row), thereby greatly increasing the versatility of flaming. Smaller plants can be cross flamed safely. Cotton plants only 100 to 125 mm [4 to 5 in.] tall are not damaged if the beds are smooth and uniform and the burners precisely guided.[11] Larger plants can be flamed at high speeds with large-flame burners. Water-shielded burners have given effective weed control in cotton at a speed of 13 km/h [8 mph], with no damage to cotton leaves higher than 100 mm [4 in.] above ground level.[11] Standard-size burners with water shielding can be operated at slower-than-normal speeds (e.g., 3.2 km/h [2 mph]) where weed infestations are heavy. The development of water shielding has caused renewed interest in flame weeding of cotton.

PLANT THINNING

11.17 Reasons for Thinning. With some row crops, such as sugar beets, many vegetables, and cotton, emergence rates are generally low and rather unpredictable because of the inability to control all the pertinent factors. It is common practice with these crops to plant a considerable excess of seed and then to thin the plants to the desired stand after emergence. Ideally, it would be desirable to eliminate the thinning operation by planting to the desired final stand. Evidence indicates that, with cotton, it is possible in many cases to do this without affecting yields adversely.

11.18. Methods of Thinning Plants. Blocking or thinning of row crops may be accomplished by hand methods, with mechanical devices, with flame, or with chemicals. Hand thinning is basically a selective operation but is tedious work, is costly, and involves high peak labor requirements. Mechanical or chemical thinning devices may be either random or selective.

Prior to about 1965, all commercially available thinners were random stand reducers. Selective mechanical and chemical thinners were introduced in the 1960s and, although much more expensive, are rapidly replacing random thinners in crops such as sugar beets.

Random blockers or thinners alternately remove all plants for a specific distance along the row and then skip a specific length of block. They take out weak or strong plants indiscriminately and may leave multiple plants or no plants at all in the block skipped. They do, however, give a reasonably consistent and predictable average reduction in stand. Uniformity of distribution of plants along the row is important. Selective thinners leave the first plant encountered beyond a predetermined minimum distance from the preceding retained plant. Becker[1] has developed a method for predicting the probable distribution of plant spacings before thinning and after either random or selective thinning, in terms of percent emergence.

11.19. Random Blockers and Thinners. Random mechanical thinning is generally done with down-the-row thinners but may be done by cross blocking with machines that operate across the rows. Cross blocking is accomplished by cross cultivation with sweeps, knives, or other cutting tools of the proper width mounted on a cultivator tool bar so as to give the desired widths of cuts and skips. Cross blocking is suitable only for flat-planted fields. Depth control is not as good as with down-the-row thinners.

Down-the-row random mechanical thinners may be of the power-driven rotary type (driven from the tractor PTO or from a ground wheel on the thinner), power-driven oscillating type, or direct ground-driven type. The axis of rotation of a power-driven cutting head often is parallel to the direction of travel. Various arrangements of blades are employed. Blades may be adjustable or removable, or interchangeable cutting heads are provided, to obtain the desired lengths and spacings of skipped blocks. Power-driven rotary units usually have individual depth-gage wheels.

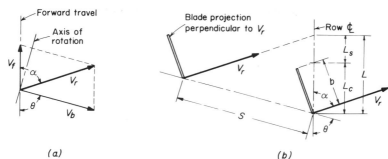

(a)   *(b)*

Fig. 11.10. *(a)* Velocity relations for a down-the-row rotary thinner at lowest point of blade travel. *(b)* Paths of successive blades with respect to the row. (Peripheral relations "unwrapped" onto a horizontal plane.)

A direct ground-driven thinner rotates because of contact with the ground and must be operated with its axis at some acute angle from the direction of travel, as shown in Fig. 11.11. Adjustable or interchangeable blades may be mounted on the ends of spokes or merely project radially outward from a circular mounting plate, or a disk may have cut-outs between peripheral sections that act as blades.[9]

A large-diameter rotary thinner gives less variation in depth of cut across a specified band width than does a smaller wheel, thus permitting a little more variation in steering accuracy.

Chemical or flame random thinners have metal boxes or hoods at regular intervals on a wheel or conveyor. These cover the blocks or spaces to be skipped while the flame or chemical spray is applied continuously along the row. These types of thinners have been employed only to a very limited extent.

11.20. Action of Rotary, Down-the-Row, Random Thinners. The vector diagram in Fig. 11.10*a* indicates the general velocity relations for a rotary thinner and Fig. 11.10*b* shows the paths of successive blades with respect to the row. The various symbols are defined as follows:

V_f = forward velocity of machine
V_b = peripheral velocity of blade with respect to the machine
V_r = resultant velocity of blade with respect to the row, at bottom of blade travel
θ = angle between plane of rotation and direction of forward travel
α = angle between V_r and direction of forward travel
D = diameter of cutting head
N = number of blades on cutting head
S = blade spacing around periphery = $\pi D/N$
b = effective blade length (projection perpendicular to V_r)
L = center distance between blocks in the row
L_c = length of row cut out
L_s = length of row skipped (length of block)

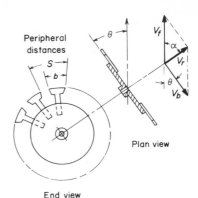

Plan view

Fig. 11.11. Schematic representation of a direct ground-driven thinner, showing velocity relations at lowest point of blade travel.

End view

Since a blade rotates through the peripheral distance S in the same time that the machine moves forward a distance L, it follows that

$$L = S \frac{V_f}{V_b} = \frac{\pi D V_f}{N V_b} \tag{11.1}$$

From the geometry of Fig. 11.10b it can be shown that

$$\frac{L_c}{L} = \frac{b}{S \sin (\theta + \alpha)} \tag{11.2}$$

and

$$\frac{L_s}{L} = 1 - \frac{L_c}{L} \tag{11.3}$$

Angle α can be determined graphically, as indicated in Fig. 11.10a.

If the axis of rotation is parallel to the line of travel, θ is 90° and equation 11.2 becomes $L_c/L = b/S \cos \alpha$.

When a rotary thinner is driven by direct contact with the ground, the direction of skidding (along V_r) must be approximately along the axis of rotation as shown in Fig. 11.11, assuming there is no appreciable rotational resistance in the bearing and axle assembly. The sum of $\theta + \alpha$ is then 90°, which makes $L_c/L = b/S$ (from equation 11.2). Also, it may be seen from Fig. 11.11 that $V_b/V_f = \cos \theta$, so that equation 11.1 becomes $L = S/\cos \theta$.

11.21. Determination of Required Setup for a Random Thinning Operation. Adjustment of a random thinner depends upon the desired plant spacing and desired percent stand reduction. The spacing is determined by the number of blades and the ratio between the rotor speed and the forward speed (equation 11.1). When a down-the-row random thinner is run over the field once, the theoretical average percentage of plants left, in terms of the stand just before the operation, is $100 \times L_s/L$. Factors affecting L_s/L are indicated in equations 11.3 and 11.2.

The ratio of the desired final number of plants per unit of area or row length to field counts of the average existing stand indicates the percentage of plants to be retained. If more than half of the plants are to be removed, a twice-over sequence is sometimes used for sugar beets. The second operation is done with narrower knives than used for the first time over and with more cuts per metre (usually twice as many). The percentage ratio of the final stand to the initial stand is then

$$R = 100 \, (L_{s1}/L_1)(L_{s2}/L_2) \qquad (11.4)$$

11.22. Selective Mechanical or Chemical Thinning.[5] Between 1966 and 1969, four different models of electronic, selective thinners (sometimes known as synchronous thinners) became commercially available in the United States. Three were newly developed and one had been available previously in Germany. Each of these has a sensor that detects the first plant occurring beyond the pre-selected minimum distance from the preceding plant that was retained. The sensor controls knives or a chemical spray in such a manner that intervening plants are killed and each selected plant is saved.

Two basic types of sensing devices have been employed. In one type, the selected plant completes an electric circuit to ground when an electrically charged probe contacts it, thus activating a circuit controlling the device which eliminates the unwanted plants. Measurements on several kinds of crop plants indicated that plant resistances are in the order of 2 to 10 megohms.[6] The other type of system employs a phototransistor (electric eye) and light source, aimed across the row just above the soil surface, to detect the plant to be saved.

The four models have distinctly different methods of eliminating the unwanted plants. One of the machines employing a probe sensor has a hydraulically powered knife that is hinged along an axis directly above the row and swings across the row once at a high rate of speed, in front of the probe, each time it is activated. The recommended cutting depth is about 6 mm [¼ in.]. The length of the knife determines the minimum plant spacing. As the machine moves down the row, the probe senses the first plant encountered beyond the cut-out section and again activates the knife. No memory device or timing device is needed.

The German unit has a rapidly rotating hoe wheel with eight L-shaped knives and with its axis directly above the row (Fig. 11.12). The knives are tangentially hinged to the hub and are held in the working position by latches that restrain spring-loaded plungers. The row is hoed continuously except when a plant is to be saved. Immediately ahead of the rotor is a sensing probe (visible below the hub in Fig. 11.12). A ground-driven timing wheel drives a disk in the electrical control box that deactivates the probe after each cycle and reactivates it when the predetermined minimum plant spacing has been traversed.

Fig. 11.12. Hoeing head of a German-made selective thinner. (H. Fiola.[5])

Fig. 11.13. Under-cutting knives and electric-eye sensor on a selective thinner. One of two canted leaf-lifter wheels is shown at right. (Courtesy of Eversman Mfg. Co.)

When the probe contacts the next plant encountered after being reactivated, the signal causes a solenoid at the rotor to unlatch the knives. The spring action then swings the knives rearward and inward so they pass above the plant to be saved. When the desired length has been skipped, the solenoid is de-energized and cam action returns the knives to their normal, latched positions.

The third design (Fig. 11.13) has two narrow knives that swing in from either side of the row, move along in momentarily stationary positions with respect to the frame, and undercut the plants to be removed. Plant selection is accomplished with an electric eye, and spacing is determined with a time-delay switch. Prior to the selection of a plant, the rear knife is in the row. When the system is activated by the signal from the electric eye, the rear knife withdraws from the row and the front knife simultaneously enters it, the spacing between the knives establishing the block to be skipped. After the rear knife is past the block, it re-enters the row and the first knife withdraws.

The fourth thinner also employs an electric eye to sense the plant to be saved, but it kills the unwanted plants by spraying a chemical on them. The spray is shut off while the nozzle is passing over the selected plant. None of the soil in the row is disturbed. Precise and positive shutoff of the spray, with no drift, is necessary to prevent damaging the saved plants. Another selective, chemical thinner, employing a probe sensor, has been developed and tested experimentally in England.[4] Sugar beet yields were comparable with those from hand thinning.

The greatest initial use and development of selective thinners has been in sugar beets, presumably because this is the largest-area crop that requires thinning. Other crops that have been selectively thinned include cabbage, broccoli, cauliflower, lettuce, and cotton.[5]

A complete thinner includes 4 to 8 or more individually gaged row units clamped onto a tool bar or a bed sled. An accurate guidance system is imperative, especially for the thinners having mechanical cutters. Recommended operating speeds range from 2.4 to 4 km/h [1½ to 2½ mph] for the thinners with mechanical cutters and up to 6.4 km/h [4 mph] for the electro-chemical thinner.

For accurate gaging and consistent results, the soil in the row in a band at least 20 cm [8 in.] wide must be firm and smooth and have a consistent profile shape. In some cases it is necessary to roll the beds a few days before thinning in order to attain a smooth, clod-free surface. Minimum plant spacing should be at least 50 to 65 mm [2 to 2½ in.]. Otherwise, there may be doubles in some of the skipped blocks. The rows should be essentially weed-free at the time of thinning, or the weeds must be small in relation to the crop plants. The optimum plant height for thinning varies somewhat with different machines and different conditions, but is usually between 40 and 100 mm [1½ and 4 in.] for sugar beets.

REFERENCES

1. BECKER, C. F. Influence of planting rate and thinning method on sugar beet stand. Trans. ASAE, *12*(2):274-276, 1969.
2. BUCKINGHAM, F. Flame cultivation. Implement & Tractor, *78*(5):30-33, 96-98, Feb. 21, 1963.
3. CARTER, L. M., R. F. COLWICK, and J. R. TAVERNETTI. Evaluating flame-burner design for weed control in cotton. Discussion by J. L. Smilie and C. H. Thomas. Trans. ASAE, *3*(2):125-128, 1960.
4. COX, S. W. R., and K. A. McLEAN. Electro-chemical thinning of sugar beet. J. Agr. Eng. Res., *14*:332-343, 1969.
5. FIOLA, H. Electronic thinning: a special report. Western Farm Equipment, *66*(8):6-13, Aug., 1969.
6. GARRETT, R. E. Device designed for synchronous thinning of plants. Agr. Eng., *47*:652-653, Dec., 1966.
7. LALOR, W. F., and W. F. BUCHELE. Progress in the development of a selective flame weeder. Proc. Fourth Annual Symposium on Thermal Agriculture (1967), pp. 45-51.
8. LALOR, W. F., and W. F. BUCHELE. Field experiments with an air-curtain flame weeder. Agr. Eng., *50*:358-359, 362, June, 1969.
9. LeBARON, F. Mechanization in thinning. Amer. Veg. Grower, *14*(2):16-17, Feb., 1966.
10. LIEN, R. M., J. B. LILJEDAHL, and P. R. ROBBINS. Five year's research in flame weeding. Proc. Fourth Annual Symposium on Thermal Agriculture (1967), pp. 6-20.
11. MATTHEWS, E. J., and H. SMITH, Jr. Water shielded high speed flame weeding of cotton. ASAE Paper SWR 71-102, presented at ASAE Southwest Region Annual Meeting, Apr., 1971. (See also Arkansas Farm Res. *18*(6):3, 1969.)
12. PARKER, R. E., J. T. HOLSTUN, and F. E. FULGHAM. Flame cultivation equipment and techniques. USDA ARS, Prod. Res. Rept. 86, 1965.

13. PORTERFIELD, J. G., D. G. BATCHELDER, W. E. TAYLOR, and G. McLAUGHLIN. 1969 thermal defoliation of cotton. Proc. Seventh Annual Symposium on Thermal Agriculture (1970), pp. 3-5.
14. Proc., Symposium on Thermal Agriculture. Annually, beginning in 1964. Natural Gas Processors Ass'n. and National LP-Gas Ass'n.
15. TAVERNETTI, J. R., and H. F. MILLER, Jr. Mechanized cotton growing. California Agr., 7(5):3-4, May, 1953.

PROBLEMS

11.1. The front gangs and the rear gang of a row-crop cultivator are 3.7 m apart and are lifted by 2 cylinders connected in parallel to a single control valve. Pressure sequence valves (Section 4.7) in the line to the rear cylinder provide automatic delayed lifting and lowering of the rear gang. The total lifting time of the front gangs at rated engine speed is 1¾ s.

(a) At what forward speed (with rated engine speed) would the resulting delay be the proper amount?

(b) If the amount of delay is correct at rated engine speed, how would the delay distance be affected if the engine is throttled to two-thirds speed when approaching the end of the rows?

11.2. (a) Calculate the fuel cost per hectare for cross flaming cotton at 6.5 km/h. Each burner uses 11 L/h of fuel costing 11¢/L. Row spacing is 102 cm. Assume that the field efficiency is 80% and that the burners are off for 10% of the total field time.

(b) How many hectares per hour can be covered with a four-row machine?

11.3. Design the disk blade for a disk-type down-the-row thinner that is driven directly by contact with the ground and which will leave 75-mm blocks on 250-mm centers. Select a disk with a diameter that is a multiple of 50 mm (300, 350, 400, etc.). To permit easy passage of clods and trash and give good clearance for the crop plants, the cut-out notches should be at least 50 mm wide (measured circumferentially) and at least 75 mm deep (radially). The depth of cut at either edge of a 100-mm-wide band down the row should be within 13 mm of the depth at the center of the band. Calculate this difference for your design. The angle between the face of the disk and the line of forward travel should not exceed 40°. Specify the value of this angle used in your design. Draw a face view of the disk, to scale, showing all pertinent dimensions.

11.4. The average initial-stand count in a field of sugar beets is 28 hills per 2.5 m of row. The desired average final stand is 10 hills per 2.5 m. The following cutting units are available for a power-driven, down-the-row, random thinner: 10-knife head with L_c = 50 mm, 10-knife head with L_c = 38 mm, 20-knife head with L_c = 25 mm, and 20-knife head with L_c = 13 mm. The cutting head makes one revolution per metre of forward travel. Recommend the head to be used in each operation of a twice-over sequence, and calculate the probable average final stand for this combination.

12

Applying Fertilizers and Granular Pesticides

12.1. Introduction. Fertilizers are applied to the soil to increase the available supply of plant nutrients (principally nitrogen, phosphorous, and potassium) and thus promote greater yields or better crop quality. The use of commercial fertilizers has increased steadily during recent years, with nearly 34 Tg [38 million tons] being applied to United States crops in 1969.[11] Uniform distribution and proper placement in the soil have become increasingly important as factors in producing maximum crop response at minimum cost.

This chapter considers methods and equipment for applying commercial (chemical) fertilizers and granular pesticides. Application rates for granular pesticides are low in comparison with fertilizing rates, and distribution requirements are different, but the general problems and basic principles of the equipment are similar.

12.2. Types of Commercial Fertilizers and Application Methods. Dry fertilizers are applied in connection with practically every kind of field operation performed in the production of crops. Some of the application methods for dry fertilizers are as follows:

1. Broadcasted before plowing, or placed at the plowing depth by a distributor on the plow that drops fertilizer in each furrow.
2. Deep placement with chisel-type cultivators.
3. Broadcasted and mixed into the soil (or drilled into the soil) after plowing and before planting.
4. Applied during the planting operation.
5. Side-dressing applications on growing row crops (generally during a cultivating operation) or broadcasted top dressings on solid-planted crops.
6. Drilled into established pastures and other sods with special equipment.

Application rates of 225 to 560 kg/ha [200 to 500 lb/acre] per treatment are common, but rates may be as high as 1100 kg/ha [1000 lb/acre]. Where large amounts of fertilizer per hectare are needed for row crops, a portion of the total amount is often broadcasted and plowed under or worked into the soil prior to planting.

259

Anhydrous ammonia (NH_3) contains 82% nitrogen, is the least expensive source of nitrogen, and is widely used. It is a water-soluble gas at normal temperatures and atmospheric pressure but must be stored and handled as a liquid under pressure, in special cylinders or tanks similar to the LP-gas tanks required for flame weeding. The gage vapor pressure of liquified ammonia is approximately 860 kPa at 24°C and 1720 kPa at 46°C [125 psi at 75°F and 250 psi at 115°F].

Anhydrous ammonia is classified as a *high-pressure* liquid fertilizer. Plant nutrients can also be applied as *low-pressure* liquids or *nonpressure* liquids, the principal forms being aqua ammonia, solutions containing other nitrogen compounds in combination with ammonia, aqueous solutions of solid nitrogen compounds or other nutrients, and liquid mixed fertilizers. Aqua ammonia is a solution of ammonia in water. The fertilizer grade usually contains 1 part ammonia to 3 parts water, which gives 20.5% nitrogen. A saturated solution (NH_4OH) would contain 40% nitrogen.

Aqua ammonia and other aqueous solutions containing ammonia are *low-pressure* liquids. They must be kept in pressurized containers, but pressures seldom exceed 170 kPa [25 psi]. The gage vapor pressure of aqua ammonia having 20.5% nitrogen is only 14 kPa at 40°C [2 psi at 104°F] and is −21 kPa at 32°C [−3 psi at 90°F]. Mixed fertilizers and solutions not containing ammonia are *nonpressure* liquids.

To prevent losses from vaporization of ammonia, it is essential that anhydrous ammonia or low-pressure liquids be injected into the soil in deep furrows and quickly covered. Nonpressure liquids do not lose nutrients by evaporation and may be applied by any of the methods employed with dry fertilizers.

Liquid fertilizers and dry fertilizers are sometimes applied through irrigation water. Anhydrous ammonia can be introduced into an open irrigation supply stream directly from the pressure storage tank, through a metering orifice and a hose. Special injection systems have been developed for metering and introducing low-pressure or nonpressure liquids and dry materials into irrigation streams or pipelines.

Fertilizers dissolved in water may be applied directly to plants as a foliar spray, and at least part of the material will be absorbed. The main purpose of such an application is to quickly overcome some particular mineral deficiency that otherwise would seriously impair the growth or yield of the plant. Excessive concentrations of some chemicals will injure the leaves or fruit, and spray applications need to be repeated at frequent intervals.

12.3. Soil Amendments. Materials such as lime and gypsum are not fertilizers but are used to improve the chemical or physical condition of a soil. Lime is useful for correcting soil acidity and is the most common commercial soil amendment. It is usually applied before planting and then worked

into the soil but it can be applied to a crop at any stage without injury.[17]
Either centrifugal broadcasters or drop-type broadcasters are employed.
Application rates are much higher than for commercial fertilizers, ranging
from 1.1 Mg/ha [1000 lb/acre] up to several times this amount.

12.4. Placement of Commercial Fertilizers. Because movement of most
fertilizers in the soil is very limited, proper placement in relation to the seeds
or plant roots is important for maximum response and the most efficient
utilization of the nutrients.

Localized placement of fertilizer bands near the seeds at the time of
planting (rather than uniform distribution over the entire area) favors early
stimulation of the seedlings and results in more effective utilization of the
plant nutrients. However, excessive concentrations of soluble nutrients in
contact with the seeds or small roots may seriously injure the initial roots or
even impair germination. Best results with most row crops have been obtained when the bands were 25 to 75 mm [1 to 3 in.] below the level of the
seed and spaced 40 to 100 mm [1½ to 4 in.] laterally from the row on one or
both sides.[17]

Band placement during row-crop planting is accomplished with applicators that are independent from the seed furrow opener and are adjustable both vertically and laterally. Double-disk, single-disk, and runner-
type openers, similar to seed furrow openers, are commonly used. The fertilizer opener usually precedes the seed furrow opener but may be immediately behind it. Limiting the application to a single band per row simplifies
the implement and causes less disturbance of the seedbed.

Fertilizer-grain drills often deliver the fertilizer through the seed tube,
placing it in direct contact with the seeds in the furrow. Tests have indicated,
however, that when high-analysis fertilizers are applied at relatively high
rates, germination and yields may be adversely affected if the fertilizer is in
contact with the seed.[13,20] Separate disk openers are sometimes provided
behind the seed openers to permit placing the fertilizer to one side of the seed
row and below it. Some drills deliver the fertilizer through separate tubes
and deposit it behind the seeds in the same furrow after some soil has fallen
in on top of the seeds. This arrangement does not always provide good
separation, and having the fertilizer above the seed level tends to reduce its
effectiveness.[13]

Fertilizers applied as row-crop side dressings are of most immediate
benefit when placed in moist soil within the root zone, but excessive
mechanical destruction of the root system must be avoided. Side dressings
are usually applied in conjunction with a cultivating operation. The fertilizer
is generally dropped in furrows opened by regular cultivator shovels but it
can be placed at other locations or depths with separate, narrow-shovel
openers or chisels.

APPLICATION OF DRY COMMERCIAL FERTILIZERS

12.5. Types of Equipment. In general, the various distributors for dry fertilizer may be classified as those that broadcast the material onto the surface of the ground and those designed for placing the fertilizer in rows or bands beneath the surface. Equipment for row or band placement includes (a) attachments for row-crop planters or cultivators, (b) special open-field fertilizer drills, and (c) combination units such as the fertilizer-grain drill.

Drop-type or full-width-feed broadcasters have metering devices spaced at regular intervals (usually about 150 mm [6 in.]) along the full length of a hopper. Implements of this type are suitable for spreading either fertilizer or lime. Some have furrow openers available for band placement below the soil surface and can be used for side-dressing row crops by plugging part of the outlets. Drop-type broadcasters are usually pull-type implements 2.4 to 3.7 m [8 to 12 ft] wide, but are also available as mounted units and as attachments for various types of open-field tillage implements.

Centrifugal fertilizer broadcasters are similar to centrifugal seeders in that the material is metered from a hopper and distributed laterally by one or two horizontally rotating, ribbed disks. Some mounted centrifugal broadcasters can be used for either seeding or fertilizing. The use of bulk trucks and pull-type bulk handling equipment for broadcasting fertilizers and lime is a common practice. Most of these units employ centrifugal spreaders, primarily because of the compactness and simplicity in comparison with trough-type distributors. Non-uniform lateral distribution is a problem, but the availability of fertilizer formulations with large granules and reasonably close size tolerances has increased the potential for obtaining acceptable distribution patterns.

Fertilizers are broadcasted by aircraft in certain areas, particularly on rice and the small grains and on hilly pasture lands. Approximately 1.6 Mha [4 million acres] were fertilized by aircraft in the United States in 1962, the majority of this being rice fields in Texas, Arkansas, Louisiana, and California.[28] In 1967, over 3.4 Mha [8½ million acres] in New Zealand, mostly hilly pasture, were fertilized by aircraft at an average rate of about 280 kg/ha [250 lb/acre].[28] Aircraft fertilization is most likely to be employed where large areas are involved and/or where it is impractical to do the job with ground equipment (as on flooded rice fields or rough terrain). The same equipment is used for fertilizing and for seeding. Equipment and operating procedures are discussed in Section 12.11.

12.6. Design Parameters. The basic performance parameter for a fertilizer distributor is uniformity of distribution over a wide range of conditions. For drop-type units or band placement, uniformity is determined primarily by the performance of the metering devices. With centrifugal broadcasters or airplane broadcasters, lateral spreading must also be considered.

The metering device should have a positive dispensing action with fertilizers covering a range of drillabilities. (Drillability has been defined as the ease with which a fertilizer flows.[18]) It is desirable that the discharge rate be proportional to the forward speed of the implement so the application rate per hectare will be independent of speed.

The discharge rate should be independent of the depth of fertilizer in the hopper and of reasonable inclinations of the distributor. The design should be such that there are no appreciable cyclic variations in discharge rate. The rate should be adjustable in small increments and should have a definite relation to a suitable reference scale provided on the unit. Parts should be accurately made so multiple units will have equal delivery rates.

The metering device should be easy to empty and to disassemble for thorough cleaning. Many fertilizers are corrosive and will tend to "freeze" rotating parts if even small amounts are left in the distributor and become moist or wet. To facilitate emptying, hoppers should be mounted so they can be easily tipped or completely removed, or they should have hinged or removable bottoms.

Corrosion-resistant materials should be used where feasible, and particularly for the working parts. Fiberglass is being employed increasingly for hoppers. Stainless steel, particularly types 302 and 304, provides excellent corrosion resistance,[25] but is expensive. It is sometimes used for the metering components. When metal coatings (galvanizing, terne plate, etc.) are used, the effect of abrasion, followed by corrosive action after the coating has worn away, is a problem. In laboratory tests,[25] galvanized coatings had corrosion rates greater than those of bare carbon steels in some fertilizers. Cast iron is no better than carbon steel in regard to corrosion resistance,[25] but a cast part can tolerate more corrosion than a thin steel part before becoming functionally unsatisfactory.

12.7. Metering Devices. Many different types of metering devices for dry fertilizers have been developed through the years in attempting to obtain a consistent and uniform metering action under the wide variety of conditions encountered in distributing commercial fertilizers. Some of the principles employed in present-day distributors are described in the following paragraphs. The rotating members of these metering devices are generally driven from a ground wheel. Row or band placement units are automatically disengaged or engaged when the planter or cultivator is raised or lowered, either by having the ground-drive wheel (such as a planter press wheel) raised and lowered with the implement or by means of an automatic feed clutch.

The star-wheel feed (Fig. 12.1) was developed many years ago and is used on some grain drills and a few row-crop side-dressing attachments. Each wheel carries fertilizer through a gate opening into the delivery compartment. Fertilizer carried between the teeth of the feed wheel falls into the

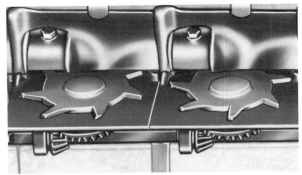

Fig. 12.1. Star-wheel feed on a grain drill. Note the adjustable-height gate above each wheel.

delivery tube by gravity, while material carried on top of the wheel is scraped off into the delivery opening. The discharge rate is controlled by raising or lowering a gate above the wheel. Two or more speed ratios are often provided. Each wheel is driven through a set of bevel gears, from a feed shaft beneath the hopper, and has a shear pin to give protection if the wheel becomes blocked with caked fertilizer or other solid objects.

Metering devices for some row-crop attachments have horizontal, rotating bottom plates that fit up against the stationary bottom ring of the hopper base (Fig. 12.2). The discharge rate is controlled by an adjustable gate over a side outlet. Note that the unit shown in Fig. 12.2 has 2 outlets, thus permitting application of 2 bands from one hopper.

Auger-type metering devices are illustrated in Fig. 12.3 and 12.4. The type shown in Fig. 12.3 has a close-fitting auger tube and the auger has a relatively large displacement per revolution. The loose-fitting or floating-auger

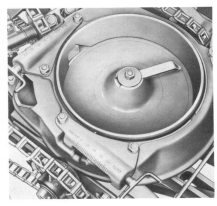

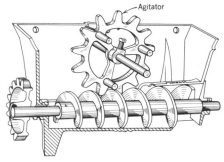

Fig. 12.2. A rotating-bottom metering device. (Courtesy of International Harvester Co.)

Fig. 12.3. A metering device with close-fitting auger. (Courtesy of John Blue Co.)

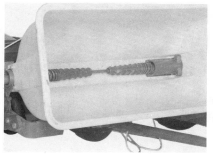
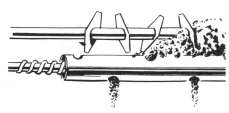

Fig. 12.4. Two arrangements of metering devices with loose-fitting augers. *Left:* For row-crop attachments. Hopper shown tipped forward for emptying. (Courtesy of White Farm Equipment Co.) *Right:* For row-crop attachments or drop-type broadcasters. (Courtesy of Barber Engineering.)

arrangement shown in Fig. 12.4 *left* is a relatively recent development that is widely used on row-crop attachments. The inside diameter of the tube is perhaps 13 mm [½ in.] greater than the auger diameter. Each of the two auger sections moves the material toward one end of the hopper, where it is discharged from the end of the tube or drops through an outlet opening. One hopper serves two rows. Augers are easily removable for cleaning.

Figure 12.4 *right* shows a variation of the loose-fitting-auger principle in which the material enters the auger tube from the top instead of from the end, is transported a short distance through the tube, and is then discharged from a bottom outlet. The tube assembly forms the bottom of the hopper and is removable. A series of openings along the tube provides multiple outlets for row-crop use or for drop-type broadcasters. With any of the auger-type distributors, the discharge rate is adjusted by changing the speed ratio between the auger and the ground wheel.

An edge-cell, positive-feed type is shown in Fig. 12.5. Metering-wheel assemblies are spaced as required along the hopper and are driven by a common shaft. Rotor widths ranging from 6 mm to 32 mm [¼ in. to 1¼ in.] are employed for different rate ranges. The discharge rate for a given rotor is controlled by changing the rotor speed.

Belt-type metering devices are sometimes employed where relatively high discharge rates are required, as on potato planters and centrifugal broadcasters with large hoppers. Some units have a flat wire belt (usually stainless steel) that drags the material along the hopper bottom (Fig. 12.6) and others employ rubberized-fabric belts. The discharge rate is controlled by an adjustable gate above the belt. The discharge can be split into two or more streams if desired.

Stationary-opening metering devices are common on drop-type broadcasters (Fig. 12.7). The rate is controlled by adjusting the size of the openings. A rotating agitator breaks up lumps and moves the material across the

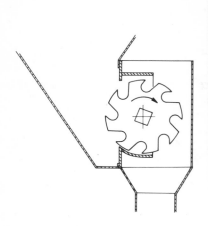

Fig. 12.5. An edge-cell, vertical-rotor
metering device.

Fig. 12.6. A wire-belt metering device on a
centrifugal broadcaster. (Courtesy of Deere &
Co.)

openings to assist in feeding and to minimize the effects of fertilizer head
changes as the hopper empties. Centrifugal broadcasters having hoppers of a
size that can be tapered down to a small bottom area usually employ
stationary-opening metering devices.

Some grain drills and drop-type broadcasters have arrangements in which
impeller wheels or fluted rolls on a feed shaft in the hopper, partially covered
by a baffle plate, convey the material to the discharge openings in a more
positive manner than the action of a conventional agitator. In the impeller-
wheel arrangement, the material is moved around the bottom of the housing
periphery and discharged through adjustable openings located behind the
impellers and somewhat above the lowest point of the housing. When fluted
rolls are employed, they drag the material across bottom openings, the discharge rate being adjusted by changing the speed ratio between the feed shaft
and the ground wheels. With either of these two arrangements, the flow
stops automatically when the rotor stops.

12.8. Factors Affecting Discharge Rates. Some present-day metering
devices have a positive action in dispensing part of the flow but also depend
partly upon gravity. A star-wheel feed, for example, has a positive action on
the material carried between the fingers but depends partly on gravity for the
flow through the gate opening above the top of the wheel. Stationary-
opening arrangements (Fig. 12.7) depend largely upon gravity. Auger feeds,
belt feeds, and cell-type units are essentially positive-displacement devices.

Discharge rates from metering devices that are not positive-acting are
materially affected by the type and condition of the fertilizer and by

Fig. 12.7. Stationary-opening metering devices on a drop-type broadcaster. (Courtesy of Avco New Idea Div., Avco Corp.)

operating conditions, the extent of the effects being related to the degree of dependence upon gravity flow. Mass rates of all types of distributors are affected by the apparent specific gravity of the material.

One of the important factors affecting discharge rates is the drillability of the fertilizer. The drillability or ease of flowing is affected by such factors as the hygroscopicity of the fertilizer, the relative humidity at which it is stored, the size and shape of particles, presence of lumps, the bulk density, and the compaction characteristics of the material.[18] Great strides have been made by fertilizer manufacturers in recent years in providing uniformly sized granular or prilled* formulations that flow readily and resist bridging and caking. Some materials, however, still have relatively poor drillability under normal conditions and others are adversely affected by storage and moisture.

In a large number of tests with a star-wheel feed unit from a grain drill, all made with the control gate raised about one-third way, Mehring and Cumings[18] found a definite relation between the kinetic angle of repose of the fertilizer and the discharge rate, as indicated in Fig. 12.8. They concluded that the drillability of a fertilizer is inversely proportional to the angle of repose and that fertilizers with angles of repose greater than about 55° cannot be metered satisfactorily with most types of equipment.

The discharge rate for a metering unit with positive volumetric displacement would not be affected appreciably by the angle of repose, provided the material flows freely enough to fully load and unload the displacement member. Closing the gate of the star-wheel feed would tend to reduce the slope of the curve in Fig. 12.8 because the positive-acting portion would become relatively more important.

---

*In the prilling process (used primarily for urea), spherical pellets are formed by dropping molten material from a tower. The pellets are screened and those not within the desired size range are recycled.

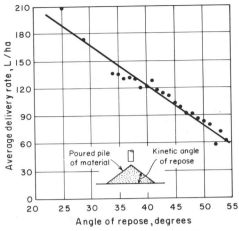

Fig. 12.8. Relation of delivery rate to angle of repose of the fertilizer, for a star-wheel feed with the gate opening at about one-third of the maximum. (A. L. Mehring and G. A. Cumings.[18])

Mehring and Cumings also found that with a free-flowing material (35° angle of repose), depth in the hopper had little effect on the discharge rate of belt-type and auger distributors. With the star-wheel and rotating-bottom types, there was little variation at depths greater than 75 to 100 mm [3 to 4 in]. Tilting the star-wheel or rotating-bottom hoppers 10° toward the discharge opening increased the discharge rate by 11 to 21% because of the increased effect of gravity. A 10° tilt in the opposite direction decreased the rate by 11 to 15% as compared with the level rate.

Lee and Karkanis[15] determined the effect of rotor speed upon discharge rate for drop-type broadcasters with 3 types of metering devices, using 2 kinds of fertilizer. One fertilizer, identified as 10-10-10,* had angular particles with 50% retained on a No. 14 Tyler sieve, a bulk density of 1040 kg/m³ [65 lb/ft³], and a 37° angle of repose. The other fertilizer, which was urea, had spherical particles (prilled) with 60 to 80% retained on a No. 14 sieve, a bulk density of 740 kg/m³ [46 lb/ft³], and a 33° angle of repose. Tests were conducted at rotor speeds representing forward speeds of 4.0, 7.2, and 10.5 km/h [2.5, 4.5, and 6.5 mph].

With stationary-opening metering units, the discharge rate at each of 3 settings increased only about 25% when the speed was increased 80% (from 4.0 to 7.2 km/h) and 15 to 30% when the speed was increased an additional 45% (from 7.2 to 10.5 km/h). Thus, increasing the speed reduced the application rate per hectare. The *volumetric* rate was about 90% greater with the urea than with the 10-10-10, presumably because of a difference in flow

*In this designation, the three numbers represent percentages by mass of nitrogen, phosphoric acid (P₂0₅), and potash (K₂0), respectively.

characteristics and the effects of gravity. With a star-wheel feed, the volumetric discharge rate at each of three settings increased in direct proportion to the speed (giving a constant rate per hectare) and was the same for both fertilizers.

The third distributor had a series of right-hand-wound and left-hand-wound wire coils on a horizontal shaft that moved the fertilizer to nonadjustable openings in the hopper bottom. The action probably was similar to that of an auger like the one shown in Fig. 12.4 *right*. The rate with each fertilizer increased in direct proportion to the speed, but the volumetric rates with the 10-10-10 fertilizer were about 15% greater than with the urea.

The discharge rates from metering devices such as belts and cell-type units, which have essentially positive displacement, would be expected to be about proportional to speed.

12.9. Factors Affecting Uniformity of Distribution. Cyclic variations due to the design of the metering device are the principal cause of irregular distribution of free-flowing fertilizers. The fingers of a star-wheel feed give definite impulses of delivery, as indicated in Fig. 12.9. Likewise, the auger feed tested by Mehring and Cumings[18] (probably similar to Fig. 12.3.) had a rather pronounced cycle corresponding to one revolution of the auger. When either of these devices metered fertilizer that had a 48° angle of repose, some 305-mm [1-ft] increments received about 4 times as much fertilizer as did other increments.

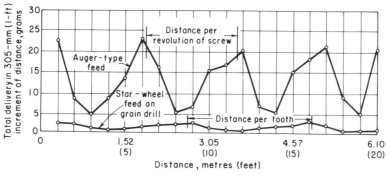

Fig. 12.9. Uniformity of distribution in relation to distance traveled, for 2 types of distributors, when metering a fertilizer that had a 48° angle of repose. Each point represents the total delivery in a 305-mm [1-ft] increment of travel. (A. L. Mehring and G. A. Cumings.[18])

Southwell and Samuel[26] tested star-wheel feeds on a drop-type broadcaster with fertilizers having 33° and 37° angles of respose and found maximum rate variations from the mean of only 5 to 14%. However, the outputs from individual wheels were collected in pairs so the variations would tend to cancel or be reduced if the wheels happened not to be in phase.

Cyclic variations with augers of the type shown in Fig. 12.4 probably would be relatively small because of the small displacement per revolution. Tests by Southwell and Samuel with a spiral-coil distributor and the 2 fertilizers described in the preceding section showed an average rate variation of 8% from the mean. The cell-type device shown in Fig. 12.5 would tend to produce cyclic variations, especially at low rotational speeds. Belt-type units and rotating-bottom units have no inherent cycling characteristics. Stationary-opening arrangements can have some cyclic tendencies due to the action of the agitator.

Fertilizers with a large angle of repose are delivered unevenly regardless of the type of metering device, because the material does not flow freely. Mehring and Cumings[18] found that all distributors they tested had wide variations in flow rates with a fertilizer having a 54° angle of repose. Devices with no inherent cyclic characteristics had relatively small variations with a fertilizer having a 48° angle of repose.

Machine vibrations, jolts, and inadequate slope of delivery tubes are factors that can produce variations in uniformity of distribution in the field. These all tend to become more serious as the angle of repose of the material is increased.

With a drop-type broadcaster, differences between average outputs from individual outlets affect transverse uniformity. Southwell and Samuel found variations between units that amounted to 20 to 31% from the mean for the stationary-opening distributor, 8 to 27% with the star-wheel feed, and 6 to 17% with the spiral-coil distributor.

12.10. Centrifugal Broadcasters. A broadcaster with a single spinner is shown in Fig. 12.6. Two counter-rotating spinners are often employed, the rotation being such that the adjacent sides move rearward. When a dual-spinner machine has a belt-type metering device, the stream is usually split with an inverted, V-shaped divider. When stationary-opening metering devices are employed, separate openings are provided for the two spinners and the lower part of the hopper has an internal, V-shaped divider. Spinner blades may be radial, forward-pitched with respect to the radius, or rearward-pitched, and may be either straight or curved. Forward-pitched blades give greater carrying distances for free-flowing materials and rearward-pitched blades unload sticky material (e.g., moist lime) more readily.

Cunningham[6] has developed rather complex equations of motion for a particle moving outward along a blade, for three basic spinner configurations. The discharge velocity and the angular displacement of the spinner between the time of particle delivery to the spinner and particle discharge from the spinner can be predicted from these equations. His equations indicate that the discharge velocity and the angular displacement are a function of spinner outside radius, the angle of the blade with respect to the radius (blade pitch), the radial distance at which the particle is delivered to the spinner, the spinner rotational speed, and the coefficient of fertilizer-to-blade friction. Particles deposited on the spinner at different locations theoretically will leave the spinner at different angular locations and with different velocities, thus providing lateral distribution. Alternate blades on a spinner may have different pitch angles or different shapes to improve distribution.[7]

Cunningham assumed a particle would immediately be accelerated to the angular velocity of the spinner and would then slide outward along the blade. Inns and Reece,[14] in analyzing the motion of a particle, assumed the particle would bounce at the initial impact with the blade but would be essentially sliding after the third impact.

Particle trajectory equations which include air-resistance effects complement the theoretical spinner equations and provide a rational method for calculating the distribution pattern width.[6] Several investigators have developed trajectory equations.[6,19,24] Reints and Yoerger[24] developed a general set of equations and used an analog computer solution to obtain trajectory curves and drag-coefficient curves for several sizes of plastic spheres, seeds, and granular fertilizers. Experimental verification checked the predicted horizontal distances within 10% in most cases. The horizontal distance is influenced by the particle size, density, and shape. Larger particles of a given density carry farther than smaller particles. The components of a dry blend may have different distribution patterns if the particles have different physical characteristics, thus causing separation of the materials. Wind also affects the carrying distance and, hence, the distribution pattern.

Uniformity of application is influenced by the shape of the pattern from the spreader and by the amount of overlap. Most patterns from centrifugal spreaders can be approximated by one of the shapes shown in Fig. 12.10.[9]

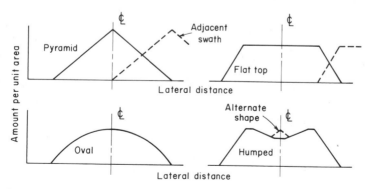

Fig. 12.10. Typical, generalized, lateral distribution patterns for centrifugal spreaders.

Pyramid and flat-top patterns give uniform distribution if they are symmetrical, straight-sided, and overlapped as shown. The pyramid pattern allows more leeway for driving error. Humped and oval patterns are undesirable from the standpoint of uniformity, but patterns of the shapes shown would give reasonably uniform distribution if the swath width were not over 40% of the overall pattern width.[9] Reed and Wacker[23] developed a laboratory setup for measuring patterns with trays 305 mm [1 ft] wide pulled past a stationary spreader and developed a computer program to determine the coefficient of variation as a function of the amount of overlap. They could then determine the optimum overlap for any pattern and the consequences if the amount of overlap varies from the optimum.

To obtain an acceptable pattern, spreaders should be adjustable to compensate for different materials and large changes in the flow rate.[9] Patterns tend to be less uniform at high rates than at low rates.[9,23] Operating parameters that may be adjustable are the location at which the material is delivered onto the spinner, rotational speed, and the pitch of the blades. Perimeter driving around the field helps compensate for an unsymmetrical pattern, whereas back-and-forth driving amplifies the effect.[23]

12.11. Aircraft Broadcasting. For many years, Stearman-type biplanes (used by the U.S. Army and Navy as trainers during World War II) were the predominant type of fixed-wing aircraft employed for applying agricultural chemicals and seeds. Since the 1950s they have gradually been replaced by new models designed or adapted for agricultural use. Current models are mostly low-wing monoplanes, although some are biplanes. Engine sizes of 170 to 450 kW [230 to 600 hp], maximum pay loads of 500 to 1100 kg [1100 to 2400 lb], and working speeds of 130 to 190 km/h [80 to 120 mph] are typical.

Fertilizers are usually applied from heights of 9 to 15 m [30 to 50 ft], the lower heights being preferable under windy conditions. Large granule sizes minimize pattern distortions due to cross winds. Swath widths depend upon the release height, the distribution pattern, and the required amount of overlap. Flagmen stationed at each end of the field guide the pilot on each pass. Bulk handling and mechanical loading devices make it possible to fill the hoppers on an airplane within a minute or less. Since the cost of applying the material is related to the mass rate per hectare, the use of high-analysis fertilizers is desirable to keep the total cost per hectare at a minimum.

Ram-air spreaders, located in the propeller blast beneath the fuselage, have been employed for many years. A spreader of this type consists of an air scoop, a venturi or restricted-throat section where the material is introduced, and a diverging section with dividers to give the proper lateral velocity components to the material being carried by the air streams. Many different designs of ram-air distributors have been developed. Most of those for spreading fertilizers or seeds are 910 to 1140 mm [36 to 45 in.] long, have a throat 610 to 760 mm [24 to 30 in.] wide and 150 to 200 mm [6 to 8 in.] high, and have a discharge area at least twice the throat area.[3] The discharge angle for the outer sections is usually at least 45° from the line of travel.

Many of the ram-air spreaders give a trapezoidal pattern with a fairly flat top so that reasonably uniform distribution can be obtained with proper overlap at swath widths of 12 to 14 m [40 to 45 ft].[3,21] However, as the material flow rate increases, the air velocity through the spreader is decreased and there is less energy available to accelerate the particles. Consequently, distribution patterns are poor for application rates greater than about 280 kg/ha [250 lb/acre].[28] This application rate represents a discharge rate of about 900 kg/min [2000 lb/min]. Another limitation of ram-air distributors is the high aerodynamic drag or power requirement, which can amount to 48 kW at 145 km/h [65 hp at 90 mph] and may cause problems in mountainous terrain.[28]

The use of centrifugal spreaders with either one or two vertical-axis spinners has increased since the early 1960s. These are commonly driven with hydraulic motors, although wind-driven models have been made. The principles are the same as for ground-rig units except that considerably higher rotational speeds are needed to obtain adequate lateral velocity and broad patterns. In tests with 457-mm-diameter [18-in.-diameter] single spinners at 1700 r/min and 11 to 14 m [35 to 45 ft] height, pyramidal patterns about 37 m [120 ft] wide were obtained with fertilizers and several kinds of grain seed.[4] This pattern would give reasonably uniform distribution with an effective swath width of 18 m [60 ft]. A spreader with two 380-mm [15-in.] spinners also gave fairly good results at 1400 to 1800 r/min. Smaller-diameter spinners produced sharp-peaked, narrow patterns, which are less desirable than wider patterns.

Power requirements for centrifugal spinners are much less than for ram-air distributors but may be as much as 15 kW [20 hp] for high flow rates.[28] Lower rotational speeds would require less power but would give narrower swath widths. When used for seeding the possibility of seeds being damaged by impacts from the high speeds must be considered. The design of the system that feeds material onto the spinner is important in relation to the pattern produced.

With a centrifugal spreader, energy utilized in imparting fore-and-aft velocity components to the material is wasted. An experimental spreader constructed in New Zealand in 1968 imparts only lateral velocities and requires only about 7.5 kW [10 hp].[28] This device consisted of two horizontal-axis paddle rotors that ejected the material in both lateral outward directions and a gate that provided free-falling material to cover the central portion of the swath. Preliminary tests at 160 km/h [100 mph] and a height of 18 m [60 ft], applying a granulated superphosphate at a rate of 335 kg/ha [300 lb/acre], produced a pattern about 24 m [80 ft] wide and indicated that good uniformity could be obtained with an effective swath width of 17.7 m [58 ft].[28]

Helicopters are used to a limited extent for fertilizing and seeding in areas not well-adapted to fixed-wing aircraft operations, such as rugged, hilly regions remote from suitable landing strips. Hourly operating costs are 2 to 3 times as great as for fixed-wing aircraft, but the productivity is also greater because of shorter ferry distances, less turning time, and less loading time.[27] Centrifugal spreaders have given good results on helicopters.[3,4]

Some helicopters have 2 side-mounted hoppers, each holding 135 to 225 kg [300 to 500 lb] of fertilizer. An alternative that is gaining in popularity is a self-contained hopper and distributor powered by its own remotely controlled small engine or by a hydraulic motor driven through quick-disconnect hoses from the helicopter hydraulic system.[4] The unit is suspended from a hook on a sling beneath the helicopter. If two self-contained units are used, the empty one can quickly be exchanged for a full one each time.

APPLICATION OF LIQUID FERTILIZERS TO THE SOIL

12.12. Nonpressure Liquids. Nonpressure liquids (defined in Section 12.2) can be applied directly to the soil surface, as on pastures and other solid-planted crops. Broadcast applications may be made with spray equipment similar to that employed for pesticides. Tank materials include mild steel, stainless steel, aluminum, and fiberglass, the choice being influenced by the kinds of fertilizer to be handled. Band applications of nonpressure liquids are sometimes made during a row-crop planting operation or as later side dressings, instead of using dry fertilizers. Nonpressure liquid fertilizer attachments are available for many planters, usually with one fiberglass tank provided for each two rows. Furrow openers and band locations are the same as for dry fertilizers except that the openers have small tubes which discharge the liquid close to the furrow bottom.

The simplest metering arrangement for nonpressure liquids is gravity flow through fixed orifices. Row-crop attachments employing this system have metering units that contain a sediment bowl, a filter, one or two orifice disks with a range of orifice sizes, and a quick-shutoff valve. Unless the tank elevation is large in relation to its depth, or bottom venting is employed, head changes will cause appreciable variations in flow rate. Bottom venting (inverted syphon) is obtained by having the tank sealed so air can enter only through an open tube that runs from the top of the tank to a point inside the tank near the bottom. The height of the bottom end in relation to the orifice then establishes the liquid head. This tube may be attached to a sealing-type filler cap. With a given orifice size and head, the application rate per hectare is inversely proportional to the forward speed.

A simple type of metering pump developed at the Tennessee Agricultural Experiment Station in the 1940s, commonly known as the squeeze pump, is used on many nonpressure liquid applicators. The basic arrangement is shown in Fig. 12.11. Units are available with as many as 20 tubes, each serving one applicator outlet. At low pressures (i.e., gravity head to the pump), this type of unit tends to give positive displacement. Since it is ground-driven, the volume from each tube is proportional to the forward travel. The application rate is adjusted by changing the speed ratio between the reel and the ground wheel.

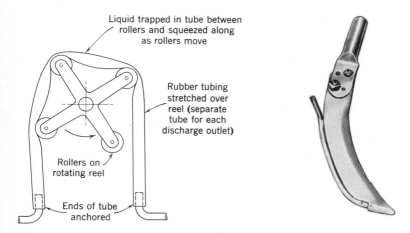

Fig. 12.11. A simple metering pump for non-pressure liquids.

Fig. 12.12. An applicator blade for anhydrous ammonia.

12.13. Anhydrous Ammonia and Low-Pressure Liquids. With anhydrous ammonia, aqua ammonia, and other low-pressure liquids, it is essential that the material be released in narrow furrows at a depth of at least 10 to 15 cm [4 to 6 in.] and covered immediately to prevent escape of ammonia. A typical, narrow applicator blade is shown in Fig. 12.12. The liquid is discharged from holes in the sides of the delivery tube near the lower end. A loose, friable soil with adequate moisture is important for good sealing and for adsorption of ammonia on the soil particles. Under some conditions, presswheels, covering shoes, scrapers, or other covering devices should follow immediately behind the applicators.

Since the release and subsequent vaporization of anhydrous ammonia is actually a refrigeration process, the applicators must be designed so the furrow opener and standard will not be chilled sufficiently to cause a buildup of ice and soil on them. To promote sealing of the furrows, the applicator blades should shed trash freely and the soil should flow smoothly around them. Spring-trip or coil-spring standards are often employed where there is danger of encountering obstructions in the soil.

Both mounted and pull-type implements are available for applying pressure liquids. Tank sizes range from 0.23 to 0.38 m³ [60 to 100 gal] on the smaller mounted units to 3.8 m³ [1000 gal] or more on some 4-wheel nurse trailers pulled behind ammonia applicators. With anhydrous ammonia, the vapor pressure in the tank can be used to discharge the liquid through a pressure-regulating valve and fixed orifices. This is the simplest and most common metering arrangement, but a constant forward speed must be maintained.

Ground-driven, variable-stroke piston pumps are also employed for metering anhydrous ammonia. The discharge rate is controlled by changing the stroke and is proportional to the forward speed. Anhydrous ammonia flows from the tank through a small heat exchanger in which it is cooled to condense any gas bubbles, through the pump where it is further cooled by the partial vaporization accompanying a reduction in pressure, back through the heat exchanger to cool incoming liquid, into a dividing manifold, and finally into the various delivery tubes. Metering pumps of this type give excellent performance but are expensive.

Low-pressure solutions are usually metered by being forced through restrictions in a distribution manifold. The application rate is controlled primarily by the pressure and the forward speed. A wide variety of pumps is employed, including centrifugal, gear, roller, piston, and others. Air compressors are sometimes employed to pressurize the tank through a pressure regulator. Variable-stroke piston pumps designed for anhydrous ammonia are also suitable for low-pressure solutions.

APPLICATION OF GRANULAR PESTICIDES

12.14. Soil-Application Methods for Pesticides. Pre-plant or pre-emergence soil applications of herbicides in bands 18 to 36 cm [7 to 14 in.] wide are used extensively for many row crops. Pre-plant herbicides may be applied as a separate operation or immediately ahead of the planting units in a combined treatment-planting operation. Pre-emergence herbicide applications (after planting but before emergence) are usually made in conjunction with the planting operation, after the seeds have been covered. Insecticides are often applied during the planting operation, the material being deposited in the furrow with the seeds. Fungicides are sometimes placed in the seed furrow.

Pesticides may be applied to the soil either as liquids or impregnated on granular carriers. One common granular carrier is processed from the mineral, attapulgite, which is a chemically inert, naturally absorbent, crystalline clay. Common size ranges are from 16/30 mesh to 30/60 mesh

(U.S. standard sieves).* Other types of carriers include palygorskite, expanded mica, bentonite, perolite, and tobacco.[8] Liquids are applied with conventional spray equipment (Chapter 13). Granular materials are applied with specially developed metering devices and spreaders which are discussed in the following sections.

Granular formulations eliminate the need for hauling water and for the mixing required with spray applications, and drift is not a problem. The application equipment is less expensive and more trouble-free, but granular materials are more expensive than liquids. Granular applications of pesticides tend to have greater persistence or longevity than liquids. Poor metering uniformity along the row and poor lateral distribution of herbicides are the principal problems with granular applications. Also, metering devices must be calibrated for each different material and for different operating conditions, whereas spraying rates can be determined from nozzle ratings and pressures.

With some herbicides and under some soil conditions, mixing the material uniformly into the top few centimetres of soil improves the reliability and consistency of the results. Theoretically, soil incorporation can be done either before or after planting. Seed placement depth is the limiting factor for incorporating behind the planter, because the mixing must not disturb the seed. Pre-plant incorporation is usually done to a depth a little greater than the planting depth, often in a combined operation. If either the depth or the band width is greater than needed, the concentration of herbicide in the soil is reduced. If the mixing is too shallow, weeds may germinate below the treated layer and survive.

Uniform mixing of the chemical within the desired incorporation zone is important for the most effective results. Ground-driven attachments such as tined rotors, paddle wheels, open-mesh wheels, rotary-hoe units, and reels are sometimes employed and are reasonably satisfactory in well-prepared, light soils. Powered rotary tillers, however, do a more uniform mixing job, especially in the heavier soils. Most ground-driven devices incorporate only to about half the stirring depth, often leaving most of the chemical in the top 25 mm [top inch]. Mixing characteristics of tillage implements are discussed in more detail in Section 9.11.

12.15. Granular-Pesticide Metering Devices. Application rates for granular pesticides are relatively low, usually ranging from 3 to 55 kg/ha [3 to 50 lb/acre]. The metering devices on most granular-pesticide applicators consist of a ground-driven vaned or fluted rotor above an adjustable discharge opening (Fig. 12.13). Hoppers for row crops sometimes have 2 or 4

---

*Sieve opening sizes are 1.19, 0.595, and 0.250 mm [0.0469, 0.0234, and 0.0098 in.] for 16-, 30-, and 60-mesh U.S. standard sieves, respectively. A 16/30 size range means the material will pass through a 16-mesh sieve but not through a 30-mesh sieve.

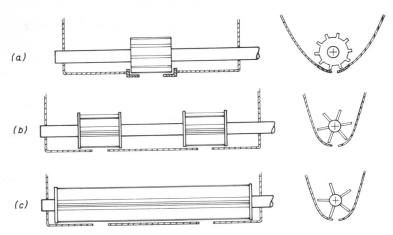

Fig. 12.13. Three types of metering devices for granular pesticides. *(a)* Neoprene fluted roll; *(b)* vane-type short rotor over each opening; *(c)* full-length vane-type rotor. Adjustable covers or slides for discharge openings not shown.

openings whose outputs can be used separately or combined. Rotors fit closely in the hopper bottoms, thus providing positive shutoff when the rotor is not turning. This sealing action apparently isolates the discharge opening from hopper head effects during operation. Several investigators[5,16] have found that depth of material in the hopper has little effect upon the discharge rate as long as the rotor is covered.

Ideally, the discharge rate should be proportional to the rotor speed so the application rate per hectare will not be affected by forward speed. Tests have shown, however, that the effect of speed upon discharge rate is variable, depending upon the type of rotor, the size of granules, and other factors. Centrifugal force may be a factor both in opposing the filling of the spaces between vanes or flutes and in assisting the unloading. The radial depth of the pockets influences the time required for unloading, since gravity is a major factor. The flow is erratic if the rotor speed is too low. If the speed is too high, there may be excessive grinding of the granules. Recommended speed ranges for vane-type rotors are usually in the order of 7 to 20 r/min. Fluted rotors are sometimes operated a little faster than 20 r/min.

Some tests with vane-type rotors have shown decreases in discharge rate as the rotor speed is increased.[5,8] Other tests with the same types of rotors have shown a moderate increase (but never proportional to speed).[2,16] In tests with different granule sizes, the rate tended to increase with speed for large granules and to decrease with increased speed when the granules were small.[8] When a rubber, fluted roll similar to the one shown in Fig. 12.13*a* was tested,[2] the discharge rate was found to be nearly proportional to the speed between 5 and 15 r/min but there was no change between 25 and 50 r/min.

Results have been reported for one commercially available unit, built in England, in which the discharge rate was very nearly proportional to the rotor speed throughout the operating range.[16] This was a force-feed device with a fluted roll, similar to fluted-wheel seed meters (Fig. 10.10) except that the discharge rate was controlled primarily by changing the speed ratio between the rotor and the ground wheels. Three interchangeable rolls, with lengths of 13, 19, and 25 mm [½, ¾, and 1 in.] were available. Holzhei and Gunkel[12] developed an experimental spiral-grooved-disk metering device that produced discharge rates proportional to speed.

Tests with vane-type rotors have shown cyclic rate variations corresponding to the frequency of the vanes passing the discharge opening. With a 6-vane rotor turning at 12.5 r/min and a forward speed of 4.83 km/h [3 mph], the length of a cycle would be 1.07 m [42 in.] along the row. Various investigators [10,12,16,22] have reported ratios between maximum and minimum cyclic rates for 76-mm to 127-mm [3-in. to 5-in.] increments along the row that ranged from 2:1 to 5:1. Cyclic variations were increased by impacts simulating field operation[10] and became more severe as the discharge opening was increased.[12] A rotor of the type shown in Fig. 12.13a, with a small displacement per flute, should have smaller cyclic variations than the vane-type units.

12.16. Lateral Distribution of Granular Herbicides. Conventional applicators obtain lateral distribution across the herbicide treatment band (usually 18 to 36 cm [7 to 14 in.] wide) by means of fan-shaped spreaders or diffusers. Dispersion is obtained with perforated dividers or screens, baffle plates, splash pins or spools, or other devices within the fan. Some applicators employ 2 fans, fed from separate hopper discharge openings, to cover a 30 to 36 cm [12 to 14 in.] width. Others have a single fan. Lateral distribution is poor with any of the currently available devices. Laboratory tests[16,22] have indicated irregular distribution patterns, with ratios between maximum and minimum discharge rates for 25-mm [1-in.] increments of width ranging from 2:1 to 5:1. The experimental spiral-disk metering device mentioned in the preceding section had an air-plenum distributor that produced a relatively uniform lateral distribution.[12]

When lateral variations of currently available applicators are superimposed upon down-the-row variations, the overall variations can become quite large. Although uniform application is considered highly desirable, allowable tolerances and the effects of variations have not been established. There is little doubt, however, that application rates could be reduced, thereby reducing costs and residue problems, if uniform distribution could be achieved.

REFERENCES

1. ADAMS, J. R., and M. S. ANDERSON. Liquid nitrogen fertilizers for direct application, USDA Agriculture Handbook, 198, 1961.
2. BECKER, C. F., and G. L. COSTEL. Metering and distributing granular carriers for pesticides. ASAE Paper 62-609, Dec., 1962.
3. BRAZELTON, R. W., N. B. AKESSON, and W. E. YATES. Dry materials distribution by aircraft. Trans. ASAE, *11*(5):635-641, 1968.
4. BRAZELTON, R. W., K. C. LEE, S. ROY, and N. B. AKESSON. New concepts in aircraft granular application. ASAE Paper 70-657, Dec., 1970.
5. CORLEY, T. E. Performance of granular herbicide applicators for weed control in cotton. Trans. ASAE, *7*(4):391-395, 1964.
6. CUNNINGHAM, F. M. Performance characteristics of bulk spreaders for granular fertilizers. Trans. ASAE, *6*(2):108-114, 1963.
7. CUNNINGHAM, F. M., and E. Y. S. CHAO. Design relationships for centrifugal fertilizer distributors. Trans. ASAE, *10*(1):91-95, 1967.
8. GEBHARDT, M. R., C. L. DAY, and K. H. READ. Metering characteristics of granular herbicides. Trans. ASAE, *12*(2):187-189, 194, 1969.
9. GLOVER, J. W., and J. V. BAIRD. The performance of spinner type fertilizer spreaders. Trans. ASAE, *16*(1):48-51, 1973.
10. GUNKEL, W. W., and A. HOSOKAWA. Laboratory device for measuring performance of granular pesticide applicators. Trans. ASAE, *7*(1):1-5, 1964.
11. HARGETT, N. L. Fertilizer summary data—1970. National Fertilizer Development Center, Tennessee Valley Authority, Muscle Shoals, Ala.
12. HOLZHEI, D. E., and W. W. GUNKEL. Design and development of new granular applicators. Trans. ASAE, *10*(2):182-184, 187, 1967.
13. HULBURT, W. C., H. J. RETZER, C. M. HANSEN, and L. S. ROBERTSON. Performance tests of commercial seed-fertilizer openers for drills and development of a new side placement opener. Proc. 38th Annual Meeting of the Council on Fertilizer Application, pp. 97-103, 1962.
14. INNS, F. M., and A. R. REECE. The theory of the centrifugal distributor. II: Motion on the disc, off-centre feed, J. Agr. Eng. Res., *7*:345-353, 1962.
15. LEE, J. H. A., and E. A. KARKANIS. Effect of ground speed and type of fertilizer on metering accuracy. Trans. ASAE, *8*(4):491-492, 496, 1965.
16. LINDSAY, R. T., and O. D. HALE. Applicators for granular insecticide and herbicide carrier materials. J. Agr. Eng. Res., *8*:231-236, 1963.
17. MARTIN, J. H., and W. H. LEONARD. Principles of Field Crop Production, 2nd Edition, Chap. 6. The Macmillan Co., New York, 1967.
18. MEHRING, A. L., and G. A. CUMINGS. Factors affecting the mechanical application of fertilizers to the soil. USDA Tech. Bull. 182, 1930.
19. MENNEL, R. M., and A. R. REECE. The theory of the centrifugal distributor. III: Particle trajectories. J. Agr. Eng. Res., *8*:78-84, 1963.
20. Methods of applying fertilizer. Recommendations of the National Joint Committee on Fertilizer Application. National Plant Food Institute, Washington, D.C., 1958.
21. NELSON, G. S. Aerial application of granular fertilizer and rice and lespedeza seed. Arkansas Agr. Expt. Sta. Bull. 671, 1963.
22. PRICE, D. R., and W. W. GUNKEL. Measuring distribution patterns of granular applicators. Trans. ASAE, *8*(3):423-425, 1965.
23. REED, W. B., and E. WACKER. Determining distribution pattern of dry-fertilizer applicators. Trans. ASAE, *13*(1):85-89, 1970.
24. REINTS, R. E., Jr., and R. R. YOERGER. Trajectories of seeds and granular fertilizers. Trans. ASAE, *10*(2):213-216, 1967.

25. SHAFFER, T. F., Jr. The use of corrosion-resistant steels for agricultural chemicals. Trans. ASAE, 7(4):439-443, 447, 1964.
26. SOUTHWELL, P. H., and J. SAMUEL. Accuracy of fertilizer metering by full-width machines. Trans. ASAE, 10(1):62-65, 1967.
27. STANGEL, P. J. Aerial fertilization in the Appalachian region. Proc. 40th Annual Meeting of the Council on Fertilizer Application, pp. 20-35, 1964.
28. YATES, W. E., J. STEPHENSON, K. LEE, and N. B. AKESSON. Dispersal of granular materials in the wake of agricultural aircraft. Trans. ASAE, 16(4):609-614, 1973.

PROBLEMS

12.1. A side-dressing fertilizer unit is to place 2 bands per row on a crop with a 1-m row spacing. It is desired to apply a fertilizer having an apparent specific gravity of 0.85 at a rate of 560 kg/ha. If the distributor is calibrated by driving the machine forward a distance of 30 m, what mass of material should be collected from each delivery tube when the distributor is properly adjusted?

12.2. A distributor for liquid fertilizer has gravity feed through fixed orifices. The tank is 460 mm deep and is top-vented. The bottom of the tank is 610 mm above the ground and the ends of the delivery tubes are 75 mm below ground level. The metering heads (including orifices) are just below the tank, but the delivery tubes are small enough so each one remains full of liquid between the orifice and the outlet end (thereby producing a negative head on the orifice).

(a) Calculate the ratio between flow rates with the tank full and with a depth of only 25 mm remaining in the tank.

(b) List three possible changes in the system that would reduce the variation in rates.

13

Spraying and Dusting

13.1. Introduction. Chemical pesticides have played and will continue to play a major role in the rapid advancement of agricultural production. Crop quality and yields have been improved and the use of chemical herbicides has greatly reduced labor requirements for weed control. But the widespread use of pesticides has resulted in some serious environmental and health problems. These problems are of direct concern to both the user and the equipment designer.

Drift (aerial transport) from the treated area may result in poisonous or toxic chemicals being deposited on adjacent crops intended for either human or animal consumption. Some insecticide chemicals, when eaten by dairy cows, tend to concentrate in the fats and milk, thereby creating a hazard in human consumption of these products.[28] Drift of potent herbicides such as 2,4-D may cause injury to adjacent, susceptible crops. The drift problem is most acute for aircraft applications but is also evident when dusting or spraying with ground rigs.

Pesticide residues can also enter the general environment by transport out of the treated field on harvested crops, in ground water or surface runoff water, and by wind picking up deposited materials. Some pesticides have low rates of degradation under natural conditions. Accumulations of chemicals, particularly the chlorinated hydrocarbons such as DDT, have been injurious to certain wildlife and fish species. Insecticides have in some cases created ecological unbalances, destroying predators, parasites, and crop pollinators, and generating resistant strains of the insects for which control is needed.[28]

Although these problems have existed to some extent for many years, there has been a great increase in public awareness and concern about them since the early 1960s. Federal and state agencies have adopted tolerance specifications indicating the maximum amounts of many specific pesticide chemicals permissible on certain crops at the time the crops are offered for sale. The use of some chemicals having a low rate of natural degradation has been greatly restricted.

Improvement of application equipment and techniques to permit the effective use of smaller dosages of chemicals and to reduce drift and harmful residues has become increasingly important as one means of minimizing the problems associated with the use of chemical pesticides.

13.2. Types of Equipment and Applications. Present-day agricultural pest control equipment includes (a) boom-type field sprayers, (b) high-pressure orchard and general-purpose sprayers (2.75 to 5.5 MPa [400 to 800 psi]), (c) airblast sprayers, which utilize an air stream as a carrier for sprays, (d) aircraft sprayers, (e) granular applicators, (f) ground-rig dusters, and (g) aircraft dusters. Aerosol generators, which atomize liquids by thermal or mechanical means, are widely used for the control of mosquitoes and other disease-transmitting vectors, but have only limited application for agricultural pest control.

Among the many uses for the various types of pesticide application equipment are the following:

1. Application of insecticides to control insects on plants.
2. Application of fungicides to control plant diseases.
3. Application of herbicides to kill weeds, either indiscriminately or selectively (Section 11.1).
4. Application of preharvest sprays to defoliate or condition crops for mechanical harvesting (Chapters 17 and 19).
5. Application of hormone (growth-regulating) sprays to increase fruit set or prevent early dropping of the fruit.
6. Application of sprays to thin fruit blossoms.
7. Application of plant nutrients (sprays) directly to the plant foliage (Section 12.2).
8. Application of biological materials such as viruses and bacteria, in sprays, to control insect pests.

Because dusts have a much greater drift hazard and lower deposition efficiency than sprays, most pesticide applications other than granular soil treatments are now in the form of sprays, usually water emulsions, solutions, or suspensions of wettable powders. Consequently, most of the material in this chapter pertains to spraying. The application of granular pesticides to the soil is discussed in Sections 12.14, 12.15, and 12.16.

In recent years there has been a trend toward reduced liquid application rates per hectare, using higher concentrations of the active ingredient, primarily to reduce the amount of water that must be hauled and handled. There has also been some interest in so-called ultra-low-volume (ULV) spraying, which is defined as the application of undiluted, technical-grade, liquid pesticides (i.e., no water added). Application rates may range from 9 L/ha [1 gal/acre] to only a few hundred mL/ha.[15,30] Grasshoppers and cereal leaf beetles have been controlled with ULV aircraft applications of Malathion at rates as low as 0.59 L/ha [0.063 gal/acre].[28] ULV applications of several pesticides with a modified airblast sprayer gave excellent control of insects and mites in an apple orchard.[15] Drift is a serious problem because of the fine atomization required for adequate coverage, limiting ULV applications to relatively non-toxic materials or to large areas where drift is not a hazard.

13.3. Specifying Particle Sizes and Size Distributions. Most types of atomizing devices produce a wide band or spectrum of droplet sizes under any given set of conditions. The range and distribution of droplet sizes, as well as some measure of the average size, are important in pesticide applications. Graphical representation of droplet size distribution provides a convenient means of comparing different atomizing devices and different conditions. The data are usually plotted on probability paper. The ordinate is some function of droplet diameter (usually the logarithm or the square root) and the abscissa is the cumulative percentage of number of droplets, droplet diameter, droplet surface area, or droplet volume. The choice of abscissa depends upon what dimension is most important in a particular application. Cumulative volume percentage is commonly employed for agricultural sprays (Fig. 13.1). Various types of distribution functions have been introduced to mathematically identify droplet size distributions.[28] The relation between the 15%-volume diameter and the 85%-volume diameter is sometimes used.

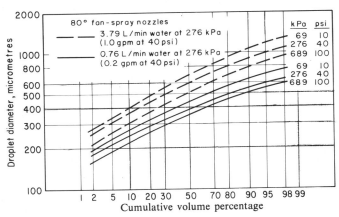

Fig. 13.1 Droplet size distributions, based on cumulative volume, for two sizes of fan-spray nozzles. (Spraying Systems Co.[23])

Average droplet size is expressed by one (or more) of several forms of median or mean diameters. A median diameter divides the spray into two equal portions on the basis of number, cumulative length (diameter), surface area, or volume. The volume median diameter (VMD), for example, divides the droplet spectrum into two portions such that the total volume of all droplets smaller than the VMD is equal to the total volume of all droplets larger than the VMD. The mass median diameter (MMD), which is sometimes used in place of the VMD, is numerically equal to the VMD. The volume or mass median diameter and the number median diameter (NMD) are the most commonly used parameters for agricultural sprays. The volume median diameter for a given sample is larger than the number median diameter because it places relatively more emphasis on the larger droplets.

The various kinds of *mean* diameters are based on arithmetic averages of diameters, surface areas, or volumes of individual droplets or upon ratios of the totals of any 2 of these 3 measures (such as volume/surface, which is the Sauter mean).

Dusters have no direct influence on particle size, except as they affect agglomeration of particles during application, but the average size and range of sizes can be controlled to some extent by the processor. Size distribution is determined by sieving and the average is often expressed as a number median diameter.

13.4. Particle Size in Relation to Effectiveness and Drift. The size of particles is a significant parameter in relation to the penetration and carrying ability of hydraulic sprayers, the efficiency of "catch" of sprays or dusts by plant surfaces, uniformity and completeness of coverage on plant surfaces, the effectiveness of individual particles after deposition, and drift of materials out of the treated area.

Coarse atomization is good for drift control, but more complete coverage of the plant surfaces with smaller droplets may give more effective control with fungicides, insecticides, and many herbicides. Large droplets, however, give satisfactory results with sprays of the translocation type, such as 2,4-D. For a given application rate the number of droplets is inversely proportional to the cube of the diameter. Thus an application of 10 L of liquid per hectare [1.07 gal/acre] would give only 190 droplets per square centimetre of land area if they were all 100 μm in diameter but would give 1520 50-μm droplets or 23 800 20-μm droplets.

Particle size is also important in relation to the ability of the particles to impinge upon plant surfaces, especially when carried by an air stream. As an

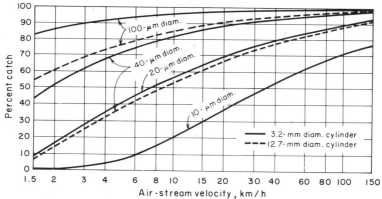

Fig. 13.2. Effect of droplet size and velocity of approach upon the dynamic catch of two sizes of cylinders. (F.A. Brooks.[6])

air stream approaches an obstruction, all particles of a particular size will be removed from a central portion of the approaching stream but all particles of the same size that are outside of this central width will be carried around the obstruction. The efficiency of dynamic catch is defined as the percentage of the total frontage of approaching air stream (having the same cross-sectional area as the obstruction) that is cleaned of droplets of a particular size.[6] A catch efficiency of 100% for particles of a particular size means that air sweeping through the foliage would be stripped of all particles of that size only in a cross-sectional area equal to that presented by the foliage. Increasing the size of the particles or the velocity of approach increases the percentage of catch because of the greater momentum of the particles (Fig. 13.2). The catch also varies inversely with the size of the obstruction (broken-line curves in Fig. 13.2).

13.5. Factors Affecting Drift. Drift is of particular concern when deposits of toxic or harmful materials must be avoided or minimized in some or all fields near the treated area. The basic parameters affecting drift and deposits from drift are the rate of fall of particles, the initial height and other effects of the application equipment, wind velocity and direction, atmospheric stability, and other meteorological factors. The meteorological relations that affect aerial transport of sprays or dusts, and deposits from drift, are complex and are beyond the scope of this chapter. However, reference 28 contains a comprehensive discussion of the various factors affecting drift, including analytical considerations and experimental results.

Size is by far the most important particle property affecting the rate of fall and associated drift distances.[28] Small particles settle more slowly than large particles because the aerodynamic drag forces are greater in relation to particle mass. For example, the theoretical distances that water droplets would be carried while falling 3 m [10 ft] in straight air flow having a uniform horizontal velocity of 4.8 km/h [3 mph] would be only 15 m [50 ft] for 100-μm droplets but about 1.6 km [1 mile] for 10-μm droplets.[6] In actual practice, atmospheric turbulence would cause small particles, such as the 10-μm size, to be carried much farther than indicated by the theoretical, nonturbulent relation. Figure 13.3 shows the relation between the volume median diameter of deposits and the drift distance for an actual test with a fixed-wing aircraft.

Evaporation of water or other volatile materials from droplets while in flight reduces the droplet size and thus adversely affects both deposition efficiency and drift. The water phase in oil-water mixtures sprayed from aircraft usually evaporates in about the first hundred metres of drift.[29] Small droplets evaporate more rapidly than large droplets. At 30% relative humidity and 25.6° C [78° F], the theoretical time for a water droplet to be reduced to 10% of its initial volume is 0.8 s for a 40-μm droplet and 4.2 s for a 100-μm droplet.[28]

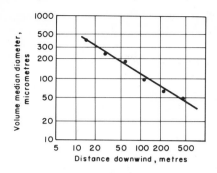

Fig. 13.3. Relation between downwind drift deposits and volume median diameter from spraying at a 1.5-m [5-ft] application height with a fixed-wing aircraft. The wind velocity at a height of 2.44 m [8 ft] was 7.25 km/h [4.5 mph] and the temperature inversion between heights of 2.45 m and 9.75 m [8 ft and 32 ft] was 2.1°C [3.7°F]. (H.H. Coutts and W.E. Yates,[10] and personal communication.)

Drift is minimized by employing atomizing devices that produce sprays having large volume median diameters. For example, in aircraft tests, total drift deposits 305 m [1000 ft] downwind were doubled when the VMD produced by the nozzles was decreased from 420 μm to 290 μm.[29] With the usual types of atomizing devices, increasing the VMD increases the sizes throughout the distribution spectrum, thus reducing the number of small droplets. However, the increased size of the largest droplets reduces the efficiency in regard to uniform coverage. Since small droplets are usually preferable from the standpoint of coverage and effectiveness, whereas large droplets are best in regard to drift, the ideal situation would be to produce a spray having uniform-sized droplets or a narrow size spectrum.

Drift is also influenced by the discharge height and direction and by equipment-induced air turbulence and air currents. Aircraft and airblast sprayers create considerable air movement. Hydraulic ground-rig sprayers have the potential for minimum discharge heights and minimum air turbulence, both of which favor minimum drift.[12]

Drift and inefficient deposition are far more serious with dusts than with sprays because of the smaller particle sizes. Most commercial dusts have number median diameters of 1 to 10 μm.[28] Theoretically, a 10-μm dust particle with a specific gravity of 2.5 would require over 100 s to settle 0.9 m [3 ft] and a 1-μm particle would require over 3 h.[28] Tests have indicated that over 70% of the dust applied by airplane may drift away from the treated area.[6]

13.6. Electrostatic Charging of Dusts and Sprays. Extensive research has been conducted over a period of many years on the development and evaluation of equipment for electrostatic precipitation of pesticidal dusts. At least two commercial electrostatic dusters have been made available in the United States, and there is some use of electrostatic dusters in Europe.[21] Techniques for charging fine sprays from hollow-cone and pneumatic-atomizing nozzles were developed in the 1960s.[22]

The primary objective of charging spray or dust particles is to increase the percentage deposition on plant surfaces. The electrostatic force generally has no great effect on the large particles and it does not affect the basic trajectory from the application equipment to the target.[28] But if a charged particle reaches the plant or target area and has insufficient inertia to cause impingement, the charge increases the probability of deposition. Charging dusts has improved the control of insects and diseases on a number of different crops.[9] Charging dusts or sprays has increased deposits on cotton plants by ratios of 2 or 3 to one.[4,22] The increased deposition efficiency, particularly for small particles, would reduce the amounts of drift.

Electrostatic dusters and sprayers are more complicated and more expensive than conventional equipment. A number of practical problems regarding their design and their effectiveness over a wide range of atmospheric conditions have not been completely solved.

ATOMIZING DEVICES

13.7. Types of Atomizing Devices. In general, devices for atomizing liquids utilize one or more of the following principles.

1. Pressure or hydraulic atomization, which depends upon liquid pressure to supply the atomizing energy. The liquid stream from an orifice or a nozzle is broken up by its inherent instability and its impact upon the atmosphere or by impact upon a plate or another jet.
2. Gas atomization, in which the liquid is broken up by a high-velocity gas stream. The breakup may occur either entirely outside of the nozzle or within a chamber ahead of the exit orifice.
3. Centrifugal atomization, in which the liquid is fed under low pressure to the center of a high-speed rotating device, such as a disk, cup, cylindrical screen or cage, or brush, and is broken up by centrifugal force as it leaves the periphery.
4. Low-velocity jet breakup, in which a nonviscous, low-velocity stream, after emerging from a small orifice or tube, breaks up into a system of droplets as a result of external and/or internal disturbances and the effect of surface tension (sometimes referred to as the Rayleigh-type breakup).

Hydraulic nozzles and low-velocity jet breakup are discussed in Sections 13.8 and 13.10. Pneumatic-atomizing (two-fluid) nozzles, in which compressed air is employed for atomization, have been used on some special, low-volume sprayers because fine atomization can be obtained at low liquid pressures. The drift hazard from the extremely fine particles limits the use of this type of equipment to applications of relatively nontoxic materials. Some European airblast sprayers introduce the liquid into the air stream at a very low pressure and rely entirely on air shear to obtain atomization.[8]

High-speed rotating cages covered with fine-mesh screen gauze (40- to 80-

mesh) have been employed to a limited extent on aircraft, and at least one manufacturer has produced airblast sprayers having rotary-screen atomizers. Rotary atomizers operating in still air at relatively low liquid flow rates can be employed to produce uniform droplets of controlled sizes for laboratory studies. But when they are employed on aircraft or on airblast sprayers, the rapidly moving air stream affects the atomization process and produces droplets having a considerable range of sizes (Fig. 13.5). Volume median diameters obtained in aircraft tests of rotary atomizers (50 to 135 μm)[14,32] are relatively small compared with those from the types and sizes of hydraulic nozzles commonly used in agricultural spraying.

13.8. Hydraulic Nozzles. Five types of hydraulic nozzles found on agricultural sprayers are illustrated in Fig. 13.4. A sixth type, disk-type hollow-cone nozzles, is the same as Fig. 13.4b except that the axial opening in the whirl plate is omitted. Removing the whirl plate from Fig. 13.4b produces a seventh type, namely, a jet or solid-stream nozzle, which is often employed on aircraft sprayers.

In a hollow-cone nozzle, the liquid is fed into a whirl chamber through a tangential side-entry passage or through spiral passages in a whirl plate or core insert to give it a rotary velocity component. The orifice is located on the axis of the whirl chamber and the liquid emerges in the form of a hollow conical sheet which then breaks up into droplets.[19] With any of the three arrangements shown in Fig. 13.4a, b, and c, various size combinations of whirl devices and orifices are generally available. The core-insert type is

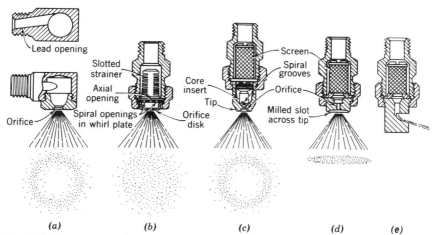

Fig. 13.4. Five types of nozzles found on agricultural sprayers. (a) Side-entry hollow-cone, (b) disk-type solid-cone, (c) core-insert hollow-cone, (d) fan-spray, and (e) flooding. Omission of the axial opening in the whirl plate of (b) would result in a disk-type hollow-cone nozzle (which is more common than the solid-cone type). Screens are seldom used in the larger sizes of flooding nozzles.

found mainly in small-size nozzles. It is used only to a limited extent in agricultural spraying.

The construction of a solid-cone nozzle is the same as that of a hollow-cone nozzle except for the addition of an internal axial orifice (Fig. 13.4b). The axial stream is atomized and fills in the central section of the hollow-cone pattern.

A fan-spray nozzle of the type shown in Fig. 13.4d has a narrow, elliptical orifice formed by the intersection of a slot milled across the face and a hemispherical surface cut out from the inside. The liquid emerges as a flat, fan-shaped sheet which is then broken up into droplets.[19] In a flooding nozzle (Fig. 13.4e), liquid emerging through a circular orifice impinges upon a curved deflector which produces a fan-shaped sheet having a relatively wide spray angle at pressures as low as 70 kPa [10 psi]. Flooding nozzles are often operated with the axis vertical, as shown, but may be operated with the axis horizontal (spray aimed downward).

13.9. Hydraulic Nozzle Flow Rates and Spray Angles. Fan-spray nozzles and core-insert hollow-cone nozzles are available with water flow rates as low as 80 mL/min at 275 kPa [0.02 gpm at 40 psi], but clogging is a problem with nozzles this small. Minimum sizes for disk-type hollow-cone nozzles and flooding nozzles are about 0.4 L/min at 275 kPa [0.1 gpm at 40 psi]. Maximum sizes range from 9.5 to 11 L/min at 275 kPa [2.5 to 3 gpm at 40 psi] for disk-type hollow-cone nozzles, up to 115 L/min [30 gpm] for fan-spray nozzles, and even higher for flooding nozzles.

In general, the flow rate for a particular nozzle is about proportional to the square root of the pressure. For nozzles with geometrically similar passages, the discharge rate is about proportional to the orifice area. Because core-type hollow-cone nozzles and the smaller sizes of disk-type hollow-cone nozzles have an appreciable pressure drop in the whirl devices, the flow rate increases more slowly than the orifice area if the whirl openings are not enlarged proportionately. With some nozzles the pressure drop through the whirl device is low enough that it does not have any great effect on the flow rate.

Fan-spray and hollow-cone nozzles employed on boom-type field sprayers generally have spray angles of 60 to 95° (included angle of cone or fan). Flooding nozzles of the sizes common in agricultural spraying have spray angles of 100 to 150°. Spray angles of most types of hydraulic nozzles decrease considerably as the pressure is reduced in the range below 345 to 520 kPa [50 to 75 psi]. With a given whirl device in a hollow-cone nozzle, increasing the orifice size increases the spray angle because of the greater whirl velocity.

Operating pressures below about 140 kPa [20 psi] are undesirable for hydraulic nozzles other than the flooding type because of the small spray angles and poor atomization.

13.10. Low-Velocity Jet Breakup. This system is of considerable interest because of the possibility of obtaining rather uniform, predictable droplet sizes, thereby reducing drift. Pressure low enough to produce essentially nonturbulent flow (preferably 7 to 35 kPa [1 to 5 psi]) causes liquid to emerge from a circular orifice or capillary tube as a cylindrical column or filament. At some distance from the orifice, natural or induced disturbances and surface-tension forces cause the filament to break up into rather uniform large droplets interspersed with occasional satellite droplets that are much smaller. The diameter of the main droplets is roughly twice the orifice diameter when the breakup is controlled by the natural wave length of the liquid column (rather than by externally induced disturbances).[20,28] Minimum droplet size is limited by the difficulty of precisely forming and maintaining small orifice holes or capillary tubes. For example, 127-μm [0.005-in.] diameter openings would produce droplets having a nominal diameter of about 250 μm. A large number of openings is required, and dispersion from each stream is poor.

A multi-capillary-jet unit for use on helicopters was introduced in the late 1960s.[28] This unit has 3120 capillary tubes on a 7.9-m [26-ft] boom. At least 2 sizes of openings, with diameters of 0.33 and 0.71 mm [0.013 and 0.028 in.], have been employed. Operating pressures are less than 14 kPa [2 psi]. The boom is mounted well forward and the outlets are aligned 180° from the direction of flight to prevent secondary breakup from air shear or turbulence. The primary droplet size with the 0.33-mm diameter tubes is 800 to 1000 μm.[25] The number of satellite droplets at speeds of 48 to 80 km/h [30 to 50 mph] seems to be less than with low-speed or stationary operation. Low-velocity jets, spaced 64 mm [2½ in.] apart, have also been used on boom-type field sprayers, employing lateral vibration of the boom or rotary oscillation of groups of jets to obtain lateral distribution between the jets.[28]

It has been demonstrated in the laboratory that extremely uniform, controllable droplet sizes can be obtained from a low-velocity jet if a high-frequency pulsation is applied to the liquid just before it enters the orifice or as it leaves the orifice.[3,20,28] Three ways in which this has been done are by vibrating the orifice disk,[28] by employing a magnetostrictive* device to induce vibration in the liquid just before it enters an orifice in a rigid plate,[20] and by inducing cyclic pressure pulsations in a small liquid chamber just ahead of the orifice.[3,25] With any of these systems the rate of droplet formation is controlled by the excitation frequency, the rate of flow through the orifice, and the physical properties of the liquid.[3] Multiple-opening orifice

---

*Magnetostriction is the cyclic, dimensional change in a nickel rod caused by magnetization from an alternating current passed through a coil surrounding a portion of the rod.

plates can be used to obtain reasonable flow rates from a nozzle.[3,25] Adequate filtering for the extremely small orifices, and the requirement that the spray solution be filterable, are practical limitations in regard to field use of such a system.

13.11. Factors Affecting Droplet Size.* The degree of atomization depends upon the characteristics and operating conditions of the atomizing device and upon the characteristics of the liquid being atomized. The principal fluid properties affecting droplet size in agricultural spraying are surface tension and viscosity. Density has little effect within the range normally encountered.[28] Increased surface tension increases the size of droplets produced by a given nozzle.

Increased viscosity increases droplet sizes by physically damping natural wave formations and thus delaying disintegration.[28] Most spray solutions have relatively low viscosities, ranging from 1.0 mPa·s [1.0 centipoise] for water to 10 mPa·s [10 centipoises] for some weed oils.[28] Within this range, viscosity differences have no great effect upon the degree of atomization.[19] During the 1960s, however, several thickening agents were introduced that greatly increase the viscosities of water-base sprays. Emulsifiers are also available which can be used to produce viscous, water-in-oil emulsions (known as invert emulsions) with up to 85% water. The objective in using these additives is to increase droplet size and thereby reduce drift.

Invert emulsions and thickened sprays behave as non-Newtonian fluids in that the apparent viscosity decreases rapidly as the shear rate is increased.[28] Thus, the mixtures are quite thick in the tank (low shear rate) but nozzles producing high shear rates reduce the effectiveness of the additives in regard to increasing droplet sizes. Tests have shown that, although the additives increased the volume median diameter, they still produced a broad spectrum of droplet sizes. VMD values with a hollow-cone nozzle in a 160-km/h [100-mph] air stream were 1250 to 2600 μm with 3 different additives, versus 500 μm with no additive.[7] When a jet (solid-stream) nozzle was tested, the values were 2500 to 7500 μm versus 1300 μm.[7] Although the larger droplets from thickened sprays do significantly reduce drift, increased application rates per hectare are required to obtain uniformity of coverage comparable with that from normal-viscosity sprays.

With any type of hydraulic nozzle, reducing the pressure increases droplet sizes (Fig. 13.1). The relationship varies with the type of nozzle, and data from various sources are not consistent. In general, reducing the pressure on a hollow-cone or fan-spray nozzle by 50%, in the range from 170 to 690 kPa [25 to 100 psi], seems to increase the volume median diameter by about 10 to 30%.[16,23,24,28] There is some evidence indicating that, with disk-type hollow-cone nozzles at pressures above 690 kPa [100 psi], the volume me-

---

*See reference 28 for a more detailed discussion of atomization principles.

dian diameter varies about as the inverse square root of the pressure.[11,23]
Increasing the orifice size of a hydraulic nozzle increases the volume median diameter. Doubling the area may increase the VMD by 10 to 30%.
[16,23,24] Increasing the spray angle of a fan-spray nozzle, while maintaining
the same flow rate at a given pressure, usually decreases the VMD. But with
a disk-type hollow-cone nozzle there is no definite relationship between
spray angle and the VMD.[23] Using a larger orifice and a smaller whirl device
to maintain a given flow rate increases the spray angle but has no consistent
effect on the VMD because the increased whirl velocity provides greater
atomization, thus tending to counteract the effect of the larger orifice.

As mentioned in Section 13.7, air shear is the primary atomizing force in
some airblast sprayers and contributes to breakup by rotary atomizers on
airblast sprayers and aircraft. Air velocity and direction also influence the
degree of atomization from hydraulic nozzles. Isler and Carlton[16] tested
several types and sizes of nozzles on a fixed-wing airplane, using No. 2 fuel
oil at 172 kPa [25 psi]. Changing the angle between the nozzle direction and
the line of flight from 180° (rearward) to 45° (down and forward)
reduced the volume median diameter by 45 to 50% with fan-spray nozzles
and by 35% with disk-type hollow-cone nozzles. With any nozzle position
within this range, increasing the forward speed from 130 to 275 km/h [80 to
170 mph] reduced the VMD for fan-spray nozzles by 45 to 55%. Changing
the nozzle angle from 180° to 90° (down) reduced the VMD by about 35%
with the fan-spray nozzles in these tests[16] and with disk-type hollow-cone
nozzles spraying a 2.8% oil-water emulsion in other tests (Fig. 13.5).

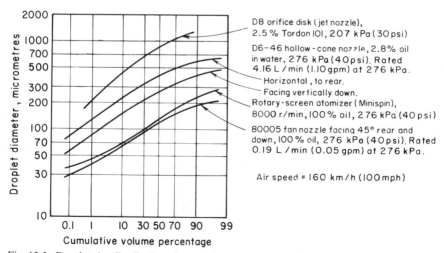

Fig. 13.5. Droplet size distributions from various types of atomizing devices on fixed-wing aircraft. (W.E. Yates and N.B. Akesson.[28])

13.12. Droplet Sizes and Size Distributions. Typical droplet size spectrums for fan-spray nozzles in still air are shown in Fig. 13.1. For a given pressure, flow rate, and spray angle, hollow-cone nozzles usually have somewhat lower droplet spectrums (smaller droplet sizes) than fan-spray nozzles.[23] Flooding-type nozzles, however, produce coarser sprays than fan-spray nozzles at pressures below about 275 kPa [40 psi].[23]

Droplet size distributions for various types of atomizing devices on fixed-wing aircraft are compared in Fig. 13.5. Note that all the curves have similar slopes and that the jet nozzle produced the largest droplet sizes. The No. 80005 nozzles and the rotary atomizers would be employed for low-volume applications because fine atomization is needed to obtain acceptable coverage.

13.13. Determining Droplet Size Distribution and Uniformity of Deposition. Droplet sizes and numbers can be determined by collecting samples of the spray (containing a dye) on glass slides coated with silicone, magnesium oxide, or other similar material or on a glossy-surfaced printing paper such as Kromekote or Lustercote.[10,14] Correction factors must be applied to determine the original sphere diameters from the observed sizes of stains or impressions. Correction factors vary with droplet size and with the physical characteristics of the spray mixture.

Droplet sizes can be measured directly if the immersion method is employed. The spray droplets are caught in a shallow dish containing a liquid or matrix that permits the droplets to sink at least partially, where they remain nearly spherical. A hydrocarbon solvent works well for water droplets.[24] A cellulose-thickened water solution containing detergent or soap can be used for oil droplets. The immersion method is primarily a laboratory technique.

Sizing and counting the collected droplets or the stains can be done directly with a microscope, or the samples or photographs of the samples can be scanned automatically with an electronic analyzer. The analyzer scans, counts, and records the number of droplets in successive size ranges selected by the operator. Equipment is available for direct automatic scanning of droplets while in flight, in laboratory testing. A stroboscopic light intermittently illuminates the area of spray being analyzed and a scan is made during each illuminated period.

Field measurements of uniformity of distribution are usually made by collecting sprayed material on distributed mylar sheets or metal plates.[2,10] A known concentration of tracer material is added to the spray mixture. The material from each collection plate is washed into a specified volume of water and the concentration of tracer is measured. Water-soluble fluorescent dyes, ordinary dyes, or metallic-salt tracers are employed, the concentrations being measured with fluorometers, colorimeters, or atomic absorption spectrophotometers, respectively. Fluorescent tracers are better than ordinary dyes for low spray-application rates. Metallic tracers are more stable in sunlight than are either fluorescent tracers or ordinary dyes.

Nozzle distribution patterns can be determined in the laboratory by spraying onto a surface that consists of a series of adjacent, sloping V troughs and measuring the liquid collected from each trough.

Uniformity of coverage on plant surfaces can be checked by adding fluorescent dyes or insoluble fluorescent materials to the spray and then viewing the surfaces with a fluorescent light (ultraviolet, with filter) after dark. A permanent record can be obtained by means of ultraviolet photography.

PUMPS FOR SPRAYERS

13.14. Piston or Plunger Pumps. Positive-displacement pumps found on sprayers include piston or plunger, rotary, and diaphragm types. These types are self-priming, and they all require automatic (spring-loaded) bypass valves to control the pressure and to protect the equipment against mechanical damage if the flow is shut off. Piston or plunger pumps are well-suited for high-pressure applications such as high-pressure orchard sprayers and multi-purpose sprayers that are designed for both high- and low-pressure spraying. They are more expensive than other types, occupy more space, and are heavy, but they are durable and can be constructed so they will handle abrasive materials without excessive wear.

The volumetric efficiency of a plunger pump in good condition is generally high (90% or more), and the discharge rate is essentially a direct function of crank speed and volumetric displacement. Crank speeds on the smaller sprayer pumps (38 L/min [10 gpm] and less) are mostly 400 to 600 r/min. High-pressure sprayer pumps (4.1 to 5.5 MPa [600 to 800 psi]) are usually operated at 125 to 300 r/min and have capacities of 75 to 225 L/min [20 to 60 gpm]. Mechanical efficiencies may range from 50 to 90%, depending on the size and condition of the pump.

13.15. Rotary Pumps. Rotary pumps are popular for low-pressure sprayers, the most common types being gear pumps (internal or external) and roller pumps (Fig. 13.6). Nylon is a common material for the rollers in roller pumps, although rubber, steel, and carbon are also used. In operation, the rollers are held against the case by centrifugal force. Rotary pumps of these types are compact and relatively inexpensive, and can be operated at speeds suitable for direct connection to the tractor PTO. Their pumping action depends upon maintaining close clearances between the housing and the gears or impellers. Although they are classed as positive-displacement pumps, leakage past the rotor causes a moderate decrease in flow as the pressure is increased.

Pressures above 690 kPa [100 psi] are not generally recommended for rotary pumps when pumping nonlubricating liquids. Gear pumps are not

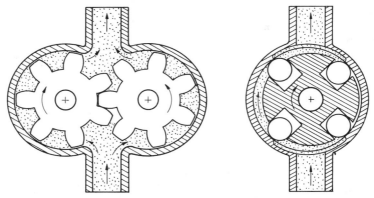

Fig. 13.6. *Left:* External-gear pump. *Right:* Roller-type rotary pump. Reversing the rotation of either type interchanges the inlet and the outlet.

satisfactory for pumping suspensions of wettable powders or any other abrasive materials, because of rapid wear and short life. Roller pumps also wear rather rapidly under abrasive conditions, but they are better than gear pumps in this respect and the rollers can be replaced economically.

13.16. Centrifugal Pumps. Because pumps of this type depend upon centrifugal force for their pumping action, they are essentially high-speed, high-volume devices (especially if high pressures are needed) and do not have positive displacement. The pressure or head developed by a given centrifugal pump at a particular speed is a function of the discharge rate, as indicated by the typical performance curves in Fig. 13.7. Note that the peak efficiency, which occurs at a relatively high flow rate, is well above 70% for this particular unit, whereas efficiencies at small flows are low.

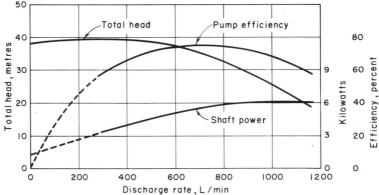

Fig. 13.7. Typical performance curves for a centrifugal pump at a constant r/min. This pump is of a size suitable for an airblast sprayer.

For a given pump and a given point on the efficiency curve, the discharge rate varies directly with the speed, the head varies as the square of the speed, and the power varies as the cube of the speed. If two or more stages are connected in series, the head and power at a given discharge rate are increased in proportion to the number of stages. Thus, multistaging provides increased pressures without increasing the capacity range.

Centrifugal pumps are popular for certain types and sizes of sprayers because of their simplicity and their ability to handle abrasive materials satisfactorily. They are well-suited to equipment such as airblast sprayers and aircraft sprayers, for which high flow rates are needed and the required pressures are relatively low, and are used on many low-pressure field sprayers. The high capacities are advantageous for hydraulic agitation and for tank-filling arrangements. Speeds in these applications are generally in the range between 1000 and 4000 r/min, depending upon the pressure required and the diameter of the impeller.

Since centrifugal pumps do not have positive displacement, they are not self-priming and do not require pressure relief valves for mechanical protection. Priming is usually accomplished by mounting the pump below the minimum liquid level of the tank or providing a built-in reservoir on the pump that always retains enough liquid for automatic priming.

13.17. Miscellaneous Pumping Systems. Diaphragm pumps are used to a limited extent for flow rates up to 19 to 23 L/min [5 to 6 gpm] where required pressures do not exceed about 550 kPa [80 psi]. Since the valves and the diaphragm are the only moving parts in contact with the spray material, these pumps can readily handle abrasive materials.

Small field sprayers have been built with an air compressor to pressurize the tank. The spray material then does not pass through the pump, but agitation of the material in the tank presents mechanical problems. The practical size of this type of system is limited by the requirement that the tank be pressure-tight and able to withstand operating pressures up to 690 kPa [100 psi] and by the cost of the larger compressors.

AGITATION OF SPRAY MATERIALS

Many spray materials are suspensions of insoluble powders or are emulsions. Consequently, most sprayers are equipped with agitating systems. Both mechanical and hydraulic systems are used. Either type, if properly designed, will provide satisfactory mixing.

13.18. Mechanical Agitation. Mechanical agitation is commonly obtained by means of either flat blades or propellers on a shaft running lengthwise in the tank near the bottom and rotating at a speed of 100 to 200 r/min. The following relations apply to round-bottom tanks with flat, I-shaped paddles sweeping close to the bottom of the tank. They are based on results originally reported by French.[11]

$$S_m = 5.39 \frac{A^{0.422}}{R^{0.531}} F_e^{0.293} \qquad (13.1)$$

$$\left[S_m = 69.2 \frac{A^{0.422}}{R^{0.531}} F_e^{0.293} \right]$$

$$sp = 3.26 \times 10^{-11} R^{0.582} S^{3.41} L \qquad (13.2)$$

$$\left[sp = 1.93 \times 10^{-11} R^{0.582} S^{3.41} L \right]$$

where S_m = minimum peripheral speed of paddles, in metres per minute [feet per minute]

A = depth of liquid above agitator shaft centerline, in millimetres [inches]

R = total combined width of all paddles, divided by tank length

L = length of tank, in millimetres [inches]

sp = shaft input kilowatts [horsepower] at any peripheral speed S

F_e = factor indicating relative difficulty of agitating a given oil-water emulsion (hydraulically or mechanically)

Values of F_e for various oil-in-water emulsions are shown in Table 13.1. These were established during tests with hydraulic agitation but are assumed

Table 13.1. VALUES OF AGITATION FACTOR F_e FOR OIL-IN-WATER EMULSIONS

Percent Oil	Percent Water	Percent Emulsifier	Jet Position (Fig. 13.8)	F_e
60	40	0	Emulsion	0.83
50	50	0	,,	1.00
40	60	0	,,	1.00
10	90	0	,,	0.89
1-2	99-98	0	,,	0.50*
40	59.9	0.1	,,	0.50
40	59.9	0.1	W.P.	0.68

*Unpublished data from Yates. Other values are from reference 27.

to apply reasonably well for mechanical agitation. French's tests were actually conducted with an emulsion containing 1 to 2% oil. No data are available to indicate mechanical agitation requirements for suspensions of wettable powders.

Paddle tip speeds in excess of about 150 m/min [500 ft/min] may cause serious foaming of some mixtures. For mechanical agitation of emulsions in flat-bottom tanks with rounded corners, the minimum tip speed from equation 13.1 must be multiplied by the factor, 1.22.[11] This increase in minimum speed causes the minimum power requirement to be approximately doubled (equation 13.2).

13.19. Hydraulic Agitation. To obtain agitation hydraulically, a portion of the pump output is discharged into the spray tank through a series of jet nozzles or orifices located in a pipe along the bottom of the tank. The energy and turbulence from the jets provide the mixing action. In tests with various sizes of cylindrical tanks, Yates and Akesson[27] found that best results were obtained when the jet nozzles were mounted as shown in Fig. 13.8. The location shown for wettable powders was satisfactory for an emulsion containing 40% oil and 60% water only when a suitable emulsifier was included in the formulation. Nozzle spacings from 75 to 710 mm [3 to 28 in.] were satisfactory for oil-water emulsions but should not exceed 305 mm [12 in.] for wettable powders.[27]

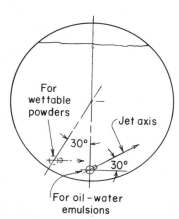

Fig. 13.8. Jet locations for optimum hydraulic agitation. (W. E. Yates and N. B. Akesson.[27])

The minimum total recirculation rates for hydraulic agitation in a cylindrical or round-bottom tank, based on complete mixing of a full tank of material in 60 s, were found to be as follows:[27]

For oil-water emulsions,

$$Q_m = 3830 \frac{V F_e}{P^{0.56}} \tag{13.3}$$

$$[\, Q_m = 1.30 \frac{V F_e}{P^{0.56}} \,]$$

For wettable powders,

$$Q_m = 1380 \frac{V F_e}{P^{0.35}} \tag{13.4}$$

$$[Q_m = 0.704 \frac{V F_e}{P^{0.35}}]$$

where Q_m = minimum total recirculation rate, in litres per minute [gallons per minute]

V = tank volume, in cubic metres [gallons]

F_p = factor indicating relative difficulty of agitating a given wettable-powder mixture

P = pressure at the agitation jet nozzles, in kilopascals [pounds force per square inch]. Ordinarily, this will be essentially the same as the spray-nozzle pressure.

The value of F_p was arbitrarily taken as 1.00 for a mixture of 120 g of wettable sulfur per litre of water [1 lb/gal], since this is a difficult material to keep in suspension.[27] Values of F_p for concentrations of 60, 12 and 6 g/L [0.5, 0.1, and 0.05 lb/gal] were found to be 0.87, 0.43, and 0.27, respectively.[27] Table 13.1 indicates that adding an emulsifier to an oil-water mixture reduces the agitation requirements and also shows that F_e is greater when the jets are in the wettable-powder optimum position (Fig. 13.8) instead of the emulsion position.

From basic hydraulic relations, the hydraulic useful power output required for any recirculation rate and pressure is

$$ph = 1.667 \times 10^{-5} Q P \tag{13.5}$$

$$[ph = \frac{Q P}{1714}]$$

where ph = hydraulic power, in kilowatts [horsepower]

Q = total recirculation rate (not necessarily the minimum required for agitation), in litres per minute [gallons per minute]

It can be shown from equations 13.3, 13.4, and 13.5 that increasing the nozzle pressure decreases the minimum flow rate required for agitation, but increases the corresponding power requirement in proportion to $P^{0.44}$ for oil-water emulsions and $P^{0.65}$ for wettable powders.

The principal advantage of the hydraulic system is its simplicity as compared with the mechanism and drive required for mechanical agitation. With hydraulic agitation, however, the spray pump must have additional capacity and the power requirements will be considerably greater than for mechanical agitation, especially at high pressures. For high-pressure sprayers, mechanical agitation is definitely the more economical system.

HYDRAULIC SPRAYERS

13.20. Types and Applications. Most hydraulic, ground-rig sprayers may be broadly classified as (a) boom-type field sprayers with maximum operating pressures of 275 to 690 kPa [40 to 100 psi], or (b) high-pressure, general-purpose or orchard sprayers with maximum operating pressures ranging from 1.7 to 5.5 MPa [250 to 800 psi] but mostly 2.75 to 5.5 MPa [400 to 800 psi]. Some high-pressure sprayers are designed primarily for orchard spraying, but most of them have booms for field spraying available as standard equipment or as an option. Hand guns can be used with high-pressure sprayers for specialty jobs such as livestock spraying, individual tree spraying, fire control, and machinery cleaning.

A sprayer must be able to handle many types of materials, including solutions of chemicals in water or oil, suspensions of insoluble materials (wettable powders), various oils, and oil-water emulsions. Many of the materials are corrosive. Others are abrasive and result in rapid wear of pumps and nozzles. Normal application rates for field spraying are usually 90 to 375 L/ha [10 to 40 gal/acre] but may range from less than 45 to over 900 L/ha [5 to 100 gal/acre].

Tractor mounting is popular for sprayers having small tanks, whereas larger units are of the two-wheel, trailed type. Sprayers are often mounted on skids so they can be placed on trailers or trucks when they are to be operated. High-clearance, self-propelled units are available for tall row crops.

13.21. Basic Components of a Hydraulic Sprayer. Figure 13.9 shows a typical schematic arrangement for a hydraulic sprayer. Mechanical agitation is usually employed for pressures above 2.1 MPa [300 psi] and hydraulic agitation for lower pressures. Tank sizes are usually between 0.2 and 1.9 m³ [50 and 500 gal]. Most tanks are now lined with, or made of, noncorrosive materials such as plastics, epoxies, fiberglass, or stainless steel.

Sprayers with maximum operating pressures of 275 to 690 kPa [40 to 100 psi] are usually equipped with centrifugal, roller, or gear pumps. Capacities

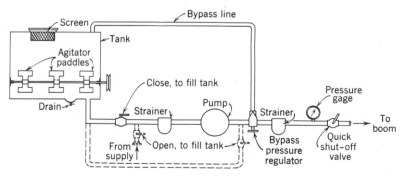

Fig. 13.9. Diagram showing the basic components of a hydraulic sprayer having mechanical agitation.

of roller or gear pumps are usually 19 to 95 L/min [5 to 25 gpm], whereas centrifugal pumps may deliver 190 to 285 L/min [50 to 75 gpm] at about 275 kPa [40 psi]. Piston pumps are employed almost exclusively for pressures above 1.7 MPa [250 psi]. Capacities of 19 to 45 L/min [5 to 12 gpm] are common for general-purpose sprayers, but piston pumps on high-pressure orchard sprayers may have capacities as high as 225 L/min [60 gpm]. On any sprayer, the pump capacity should be at least 10 to 15% greater than the maximum expected spraying requirements. The piping may be arranged to permit filling the tank with the spray pump, as indicated by the broken-line portion of Fig. 13.9.

With a positive-displacement pump (piston, roller, gear, etc.) an automatic relief valve or a bypass pressure regulator is essential for protection of the equipment. When a high-pressure sprayer is designed for intermittent use, as with a hand gun, an unloading-type bypass regulator may be employed. Because of the relatively flat head-flow characteristic of a centrifugal pump (Fig. 13.7), an automatic bypass regulator generally does not give good control over a range of pressures. The pressure from a centrifugal pump can be controlled reasonably well by changing the speed or by manual throttling. More precise control can be obtained with a diaphragm-type pressure-reducing valve in the line to the boom or nozzles.

Brass is the most common material for nozzles, but tungsten carbide or hardened stainless-steel orifice disks or tips are often employed when spraying abrasive materials such as suspensions of wettable powders. Nozzles of the sizes employed on ground rigs have built-in screens to prevent or minimize plugging. These are in addition to the screens shown in Fig. 13.9. To prevent screening out the wettable powders and to lessen the frequency of cleaning, nozzle screen openings should be only a little smaller than the orifice opening.

13.22. Booms and Nozzles on a Field Sprayer. Hydraulic field sprayers have horizontal booms with nozzles attached directly to the boom or to the lower ends of vertical drop pipes extending downward from the boom. The drop pipes are for between-the-row spraying of tall row crops. To obtain more accurate control of nozzle height, nozzles may be connected to the boom through drop hoses and mounted on individual skids that move along the ground between the rows.

Booms are mostly 6 to 15 m [20 to 50 ft] long. They are usually sectionalized and hinged to permit reducing the overall width for transport. The longer booms require fore-and-aft support as well as vertical support. Outrigger wheels are sometimes employed on long booms to maintain more uniform nozzle heights. Nozzle spacings are usually 38 to 51 cm [15 to 20 in.]. The 51-cm spacing is the most common because it provides 2 nozzles per row for 102-cm [40-in.] row spacings, which is convenient for drop pipes. However, the trend to narrower row spacings in some crops makes flexibility in nozzle spacing increasingly desirable.

Fan-spray nozzles are widely used for field sprayers because the shape of their spray distribution pattern makes uniformity of coverage less sensitive to boom height than with hollow-cone nozzles. This relation is discussed in the following section. Hollow-cone nozzles may be preferred for fungicides because of the greater degree of atomization. Flooding nozzles on drop pipes, mounted with their axes vertical as in Fig. 13.4e, are well-suited for spraying beneath row-crop foliage.

13.23. Uniformity of Spray Distribution. For open-field work (i.e., continuous coverage) the proper height of the boom above the deposition surface is a function of (a) the nozzle spacing on the boom, (b) the nozzle spray angle, and (c) the amount of overlap required for uniform coverage, as determined by the nozzle spray pattern. Fan-spray nozzles tend to have distribution profiles with gradually sloping sides as shown in Fig. 13.10a. Hollow-cone nozzle patterns tend to be similar to Fig. 13.10d but may be humped near the outer edges of the flat top.[18] In actual practice there is considerable variation in patterns from individual nozzles of a particular type and size.

Figure 13.10 shows the amount of overlap required for uniform coverage with the two types of idealized nozzle distribution patterns and the effect of variations of boom height upon the uniformity. Note that the steep-sided profiles in *(d)*, which are typical of hollow-cone nozzles, are far more sensitive to boom height variations than are the narrow-topped and gradually sloping profiles of *(a)*, which are typical of fan-spray nozzles and solid-cone

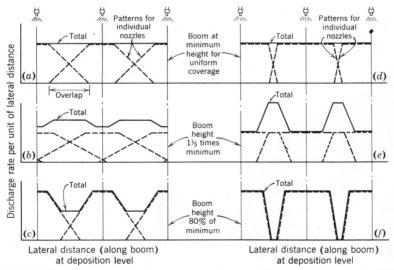

Fig. 13.10. Effect of nozzle distribution pattern and boom height upon uniformity of coverage. The broken-line curves indicate distribution patterns (at the deposition level) for individual nozzles. The solid curve in each case shows the combined discharge pattern for all nozzles (i.e., the sum of the broken-line curves.)

nozzles.[18] With either pattern the uniformity of distribution is affected less by having the boom too high (excessive overlap) than by having it too low. With nozzles having profiles of the type shown in Fig. 13.10a, the height of the boom should be such that the overall width of each nozzle spray pattern at the deposition level is about 50% greater than the nozzle spacing. More overlap is required for profiles having narrower tops, and less for steep-sided profiles.

13.24. Control of Application Rate. The amount of spray liquid applied per hectare by a field sprayer is a function of (a) the spacing of nozzles on the boom, (b) the nozzle rating or orifice size, (c) the nozzle pressure, and (d) the rate of forward travel. The relation between these variables is expressed by the following equation, in which the combined effects of nozzle size and pressure are represented by the nozzle discharge rate.

$$\text{(L/h per nozzle)} = 0.00100 \text{ (L/ha) (km/h) (nozzle spacing, cm)}$$
$$(13.6)$$
$$[\text{(gph per nozzle)} = 0.0101 \text{ (gal/acre) (mph) (nozzle spacing, in.)}]$$

The concentration of active ingredient may also be changed, which affects the required litres per hectare. Since all these factors are equally important, they must all be controlled carefully in order to obtain the desired application rate. Nozzles must have uniform flow rates and patterns; the pressure gage must be accurate, with proper allowance being made for any significant pressure losses in the lines; and the forward speed must be checked accurately by timing or with a low-range speedometer mounted on the tractor or sprayer.

13.25. High-Pressure Orchard Spraying. For many years, high-pressure sprayers were the principal means of applying liquid pesticides to orchards, using either hand guns or various types of booms or masts for automatic spraying. Airblast sprayers, however, have largely replaced high-pressure sprayers in orchards, except for some use of vertical booms or masts.

A high-pressure orchard sprayer depends upon liquid pressure to atomize the liquid and furnish the energy to carry the spray to and into the trees. Conditions that favor long carrying distances and good foliage penetration are (a) high discharge velocity from the nozzle, (b) high volume rate of discharge, (c) large droplets, and (d) small spray angle. Increasing the pressure on a given nozzle increases the carrying distance up to the point where the adverse effect of reduced droplet size offsets the benefits of higher discharge velocity and greater volume.

Sprayers having pumps with adequate capacity (at least 150 to 190 L/min [40 to 50 gpm]) may have spaced individual nozzles or groups of nozzles mounted on masts or vertical booms to cover one side of the trees as the sprayer moves along the row. Groups of nozzles provide mutual reinforcement to increase the carrying distance. Some booms consist of groups of nozzles oscillated mechanically to sweep the trees as the sprayer passes them. Application rates of 5600 to 7500 L/ha [600 to 800 gal/acre] are common for many types of mature trees.

AIRBLAST SPRAYERS

13.26. Types and Applications. Airblast sprayers (also known as air-carrier sprayers) were developed in the 1940s for applying sprays to trees. Although models designed for row-crop spraying are available and orchard models are sometimes used for row crops, the principal application of airblast sprayers is in orchards. As the name implies, airblast sprayers utilize an air stream to carry the droplets, rather than depending upon energy from hydraulic pressure. Consequently, they can utilize smaller droplet sizes than high-pressure orchard sprayers and can obtain adequate coverage with less material per hectare. The effectiveness of an airblast sprayer depends upon its ability to displace the air in all parts of the tree with spray-laden air from the machine.

In row-crop or open-field applications, the air streams from the blower or blowers distribute the spray laterally over the swath width, depositing some by impingement and some by settling after the air velocity has subsided. Fine atomization is desirable to increase the carrying distance. The larger droplets are deposited closest to the blower. Wilson[26] tested an airblast sprayer that delivered 12.3 m³/s at 145 km/h [26,000 cfm at 90 mph] and found that air velocities at distances of 1.8, 5.5, 9.1, 12.8, and 16.5 m [6, 18, 30, 42, and 54 ft] were 34, 27, 23, 9.5 and 8 km/h [21, 17, 14, 6, and 5 mph], respectively. Deposits on leaf surfaces decreased about in proportion to the air velocities. Drift problems with airblast sprayers are comparable with those from aircraft spraying.[12]

Orchard application rates with airblast sprayers may be as high as 3700 to 4700 L/ha [400 to 500 gal/acre] or as little as 45 to 90 L/ha [5 to 10 gal/acre]. With the higher rates, often referred to as dilute applications, there is usually some run-off of spray from the foliage. Rates in the order of 45 to 235 L/ha [5 to 25 gal/acre] are known as concentrate or low-volume sprays. Smaller droplets are needed for uniform coverage.

With some types of trees, concentrate applications give about as good results as dilute applications.[17,31] But in trees with dense foliage, such as citrus and olives, complete coverage is difficult to obtain even with high application rates. The principal advantage of low-volume application is the reduced amount of water that must be supplied and the resultant saving in filling and hauling times. Some dilute-application machines are also used for concentrate spraying (by changing spray nozzles), whereas other machines are designed specifically for low-volume applications.

13.27. Blowers and Outlets. Most of the large orchard-type airblast sprayers have axial-flow fans with guide vanes to direct the air radially outward through a partial, circumferential slot. Some have two opposed axial-flow fans blowing toward each other from either side of the slot. Centrifugal blowers with "fishtail" outlets or other forms of slots are also employed. Capacities are mostly 14 to 33 m³/s [30,000 to 70,000 cfm] at discharge velocities of 110 to 200 km/h [70 to 125 mph]. Some units with lower capacities have velocities above 240 km/h [150 mph]. Engine power ratings are generally over 75 kW [100 hp] for machines with 28 m³/s [60,000 cfm] capacity or more.

The discharge arrangement is such that one side of one row, or the adjacent sides of two rows, can be covered as the machine is driven along between the rows. The included angle of delivery (in a vertical plane) on each side should be adjustable to accommodate different sizes of trees. Since power requirements are high, especially for the larger units, careful design of the air system and selection of the fan or blower best suited to the operating conditions are important.

13.28. Pumps and Atomizing Devices. The most common method of introducing the spray into the air stream is through hydraulic nozzles, usually hollow-cone. The degree of atomization is primarily a function of the liquid pressure and the nozzle characteristics, although the air velocity also influences the breakup. The maximum number of outlets provided for nozzles in the air stream is usually between 10 and 40. Nozzle sizes, numbers, and distribution may be changed for different spraying conditions. To obtain uniform coverage it is generally necessary to install more or larger nozzles in the portion of the air stream which is directed to the tree tops.

Two-stage centrifugal pumps, developing about 1.4 MPa [200 psi] and delivering about 380 L/min [100 gpm], are common. These pumps can be used for rapid filling of the tank. Part of their output is often recirculated for hydraulic agitation. Some sprayers have single-stage pumps developing 520 to 1030 kPa [75 to 150 psi]. Sprayers with medium- or low-volume blowers sometimes have piston pumps with capacities of 19 to 95 L/min [5 to 25 gpm]. The high pressures obtainable with piston pumps (2.75 to 3.45 MPa [400 to 500 psi]) are advantageous in concentrate spraying because of the resulting finer atomization from hydraulic nozzles.

Air atomization is sometimes employed on airblast sprayers designed especially for concentrate applications. A number of European machines introduce the liquid at a very low pressure into high-velocity air nozzles or air streams, relying entirely on air shear to provide the breakup.[8] Compressed-air atomization is employed in at least one machine manufactured in the United States. Air atomization is capable of providing quite small droplet sizes, especially when compressed air is employed.

Small rotary-screen atomizers have been tried experimentally on a conventional airblast sprayer modified for ultra-low-volume spraying of undiluted pesticides.[15] Rotary atomizers have also been employed, by at least one manufacturer, on airblast sprayers that had several independent atomizer-propeller units driven by hydraulic motors and mounted on a boom or mast.

AIRCRAFT SPRAYING

13.29. Applications. The greatest use of aircraft in agriculture is for applying pesticide sprays. Types and characteristics of fixed-wing agricultural aircraft are summarized in Section 12.11. Only a relatively small percentage of aircraft spraying (perhaps 10% in 1970) is done with helicopters, but the percentage has increased in recent years.

The principal advantages of aircraft over ground equipment are in the speed of coverage and the resultant improvement in timeliness, and in the ability to apply the materials at times when ground equipment could not get onto the field. Coverage is not as good with aircraft spraying as with ground-rig spraying, especially in crops more than 0.9 to 1.5 m [3 to 5 ft] tall.[17] But aircraft spraying does give adequate (economic) control for many types of applications at a cost per hectare comparable with ground-rig applications. Drift of hazardous materials is one of the most serious problems in aircraft applications. Aircraft operations are hazardous, are more dependent on optimum weather conditions than are ground operations, and are less efficient and more costly on small areas.

In comparison with fixed-wing aircraft, helicopters are safer and have greater maneuverability in closely bounded or irregular-shaped fields. Because of the rotor downwash, helicopters also seem to give better penetration of sprays or dust in dense foliage on tall crops or in orchards when flown at low forward speeds (24 to 40 km/h [15 to 25 mph]).[17,31] The new cost of helicopters is about twice that of comparable fixed-wing aircraft. Ferrying time is usually much less because a helicopter can land close to the field being treated. Turning time is also less. Helicopter payloads are generally about half as great as for fixed-wing aircraft (270 to 540 kg versus 450 to 1130 kg [600 to 1200 lb versus 1000 to 2500 lb]). Because of less nonproductive time, helicopter coverage, in hectares per hour, is about the same as for fixed-wing aircraft.

Aircraft sprays are always applied in concentrate form, usually at rates of 9 to 95 L/ha [1 to 10 gal/acre]. Where terrain permits, agricultural sprays are normally applied from a height of not over 1.5 to 3 m [5 to 10 ft] above the tops of the plants. Fixed-wing aircraft are generally flown at 130 to 190 km/h [80 to 120 mph]. Helicopter speeds may be as low as 24 km/h [15 mph] over tall crops but more often are between 65 and 95 km/h [40 to 60 mph].

13.30. Pumps and Atomizing Devices. Centrifugal pumps are the most common type, primarily because of their high capacity and ability to handle abrasive materials. They may be driven by an auxiliary propeller (on fixed-wing aircraft only), from a power take off, or by an electric or hydraulic motor. Hydraulic agitation is generally employed, the entire pump output being directed back into the tank while not spraying but with no agitation during the short intervals of actual spraying.

Continuous booms with close-spaced, hydraulic nozzles (often about 30 cm [1 ft] apart) are the most common arrangement. Most booms on fixed-wing aircraft are slightly shorter than the wing length. The boom length on helicopters is sometimes as much as 3 to 4.5 m [10 to 15 ft] longer than the rotor diameter. Disk-type hollow-cone nozzles are popular, but side-entry hollow-cone, jet, and sometimes fan-spray nozzles are also employed. Boom pressures are usually between 140 and 410 kPa [20 and 60 psi]. To minimize drift, aircraft sprays applied at rates of 45 to 95 L/ha [5 to 10 gal/acre] are usually coarser than ground-rig sprays. However, lateral distribution tends to vary more with coarse sprays (as from jet nozzles) than with finer sprays.

Each nozzle on the boom is equipped with a diaphragm check valve that closes at about 35 kPa [5 psi] when the boom flow is cut off and the boom pressure released, thus preventing dribbling. The valve that diverts the pump flow from the boom back to the tank usually has a venturi suck-back arrangement (Fig. 13.11). When the pump flow is diverted into the tank (as shown), the venturi effect creates a slight suction on the boom, thereby quickly reducing the boom pressure and closing the check valves. The negative pressure also prevents leakage from faulty check valves.

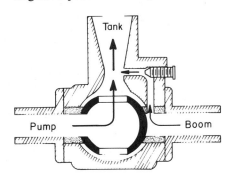

Fig. 13.11. A three-way boom shutoff valve with suck-back feature.

Rotary-screen atomizers are sometimes employed on aircraft, usually four units per airplane. The atomizers may be driven by adjustable-pitch or non-adjustable propellers or by electric motors. As indicated in Section 13.7 and Fig. 13.5, droplet sizes are relatively small, thus intensifying the drift problem but improving uniformity and completeness of coverage with extremely low application rates. These devices, rotating at speeds of 4000 to 8000 r/min and sometimes higher, require considerable maintenance and are subject to breakdowns, whereas hydraulic nozzles are not. But because they have larger metering openings than hydraulic nozzles on a boom, they are less subject to clogging at low application rates.

Low-velocity, jet-breakup systems are used on some helicopters. As indicated in Section 13.10, the capillary jets produce rather uniform, large droplets when the boom is mounted forward of the rotor and the discharge direction is carefully adjusted to be in line with the relative air flow resulting from the forward motion. Results have been less satisfactory with fixed-wing aircraft because the air turbulence causes secondary breakup and produces a broad spectrum of droplet sizes with substantial numbers of small droplets.[28]

DUSTING

Although the use of dusters has diminished greatly in recent years, primarily because of the drift problem and low deposition efficiencies, there are still some applications and situations where dusting is preferred instead of spraying. The small particle sizes (number median diameters from 1 to 10 μm) may be advantageous where complete coverage within dense foliage is important. A duster is a simpler, less troublesome machine than a sprayer, and no water is needed, but the weather must be calm for dusting. Application rates are usually 22 to 55 kg/ha [20 to 50 lb/acre].

13.31. Ground Rig Dusters. All dusters utilize an air blast in which the dust particles are airborne. Various types of blowers are employed on ground rigs. Single outlets with one or two vertical "fishtails" attached, or with peripheral openings as on airblast sprayers, are sometimes employed for vineyard or orchard dusting. Multiple-nozzle units for field or row crops have a group of flexible hoses connected to a manifold or to peripheral outlets around the blower housing. The nozzles are spaced along a supporting boom, discharging as close to the plants as is practical.

The conventional feed system consists of an adjustable opening in the bottom of the hopper, which meters dust into the blower inlet, and one or more agitators above the discharge opening. With this arrangement the feed rate may be extremely uneven and unpredictable because of variations in head, apparent density, fluidity, and compaction of the dust. A vertical-auger feed developed by the USDA[13] eliminates or minimizes the effects of most of these variables and gives rather uniform feed rates.

Electrostatic charging of dusts has been shown to substantially increase the amounts of material deposited on plants (Section 13.6). Other methods that have been employed in attempting to reduce drift and increase deposition include (a) canvas tunnels dragged along over the plants and into which the dust is discharged, and (b) the addition of an oil or water spray at the exit of the dust nozzles.

13.32. Aircraft Dusting. Dust hoppers in fixed-wing aircraft are equipped with propeller-driven low-speed agitators and usually have some type of adjustable-opening slide-gate feed control device. The metered dust enters the throat of a ram-air venturi spreader, which may be the same unit used for distributing fertilizers (Section 12.11) or may be longer and wider if designed primarily for dusts. The characteristic wing-tip vortices draw the dust out laterally but there is a tendency toward heavy deposits in the center of the swath. To improve lateral uniformity of distribution, dusting with fixed-wing aircraft usually is done at a somewhat greater height than when spraying.

Helicopters have two dust hoppers, one on each side of the plane, with agitators that are usually driven by electric motors. The feed devices are of either the slide-gate or the fluted-roll type. The engine cooling fan provides air for venturi tubes under the two hopper discharge outlets. The dust is fed into these tubes and then discharged down and outward into the rotor downdraft.

REFERENCES

1. AMBERG, A. A., and B. J. BUTLER. High-speed photography as a tool for spray-droplet analysis. Trans. ASAE, *13*(5):541-546, 1970.
2. BODE, L. E., M. R. GEBHARDT, and C. L. DAY. Spray-deposit patterns and droplet sizes obtained from nozzles used for low-volume application. Trans. ASAE, *11*(6):754-756, 761, 1968.
3. BOUSE, L. F. Use of pulsed jets to atomize various liquids. Trans. ASAE, *18*(4): 618-622, 1975.
4. BOWEN, H. D., and W. E. SPLINTER. Field testing of improved electrostatic dusting and spraying equipment. ASAE Paper 68-150, June, 1968.
5. BRANN, J. L., Jr. Factors affecting use of airblast sprayers. Trans. ASAE, *7*(2):200-203, 1964.
6. BROOKS, F. A. The drifting of poisonous dusts applied by airplanes and land rigs. Agr. Eng., *28*:233-239, 244, June, 1947.
7. BUTLER, B. J., N. B. AKESSON, and W. E. YATES. Use of spray adjuvants to reduce drift. Trans. ASAE, *12*(2):182-186, 1969.
8. BYASS, J. B., G. S. WEAVING, and G. K. CHARLTON. A low-pressure airblast nozzle and its application to fruit spraying. I. Development of equipment. J. Agr. Eng. Res., *5*:94-108, 1960.
9. CASSELMAN, T. W., C. WEHLBURG, W. G. GENUNG, and P. L. THAYER. Evaluation of electrostatic charging of chemical dusts. Trans. ASAE, *9*(6):803-804, 808, 1966.
10. COUTTS, H. H., and W. E. YATES. Analysis of spray droplet distributions from agricultural aircraft. Trans. ASAE, *11*(1):25-27, 1968.
11. FRENCH, O. C. Spraying equipment for pest control. California Agr. Expt. Sta. Bull. 666, 1942.
12. FROST, K. R., and G. W. WARE. Pesticide drift from aerial and ground applications. Agr. Eng., *51*:460-464, Aug., 1970.
13. GLAVES, A. H. A new dust feed mechanism for crop dusters. Agr. Eng., *28*:551-552, 555, Dec., 1947.
14. HILL, R. F., and R. T. JARMAN. The performance of some rotary sprayers. J. Agr. Eng. Res., *3*:205-213, 1958.
15. HOWITT, A. J., and A. PSHEA. The development and use of ultra low volume ground sprayers for pests attacking fruit. Michigan Agr. Expt. Sta. Quarterly Bull., *48*:144-160, Nov., 1965.

16. ISLER, D. A., and J. B. CARLTON. Effect of mechanical factors on atomization of oil-base aerial sprays. Trans. ASAE, 8(4):590-591, 593, 1965.
17. KILGORE, W. W., W. E. YATES, and J. M. OGAWA. Evaluation of concentrate and dilute ground air-carrier and aircraft spray coverage. Hilgardia, 35:527-536, Oct., 1964. California Agr. Expt. Sta.
18. NORDBY, A., and J. HAMAN. The effect of the liquid cone form on spray distribution of hollow cone nozzles. J. Agr. Eng. Res., 10:322-327, 1965.
19. PERRY, R. H., C. H. CHILTON, and S. D. KIRKPATRICK, Editors. Chemical Engineers' Handbook, 4th Edition, pp. 18-63 to 18-68. McGraw-Hill Book Co., New York, 1963.
20. ROTH, L. O., and J. G. PORTERFIELD. Spray drop size control. Trans. ASAE, 13(6):779-781, 784, 1970.
21. SPLINTER, W. E. Air-curtain nozzle developed for electrostatically charging dusts. Trans. ASAE, 11(4):487-490, 495, 1968.
22. SPLINTER, W. E. Electrostatic charging of agricultural sprays. Trans. ASAE, 11(4):491-495, 1968.
23. Spraying Systems Co. Curves of particle size versus pressure and accumulated volume percentages, 1966-1969.
24. TATE, R. W., and L. F. JANSSEN. Droplet size data for agricultural spray nozzles. Trans. ASAE, 9(3):303-305, 308, 1966.
25. WILCE, S. E., et. al. Drop size control and aircraft spraying equipment. Agr. Aviation, 16(1):7-13, 16, Jan., 1974.
26. WILSON, J. D. Facts you should know about air-blast spraying. Amer. Veg. Grower, 4(5):9, 32-33, May, 1956.
27. YATES, W. E., and N. B. AKESSON. Hydraulic agitation requirements for pesticide materials. Trans. ASAE, 6(3):202-205, 208, 1963.
28. YATES, W. E., and N. B. AKESSON. Reducing pesticide chemical drift. Pesticide Formulations: Physical Chemical Principles, Chap. 8. W. Van Valkenburg, Editor. Marcel Dekker, New York, 1973.
29. YATES, W. E., N. B. AKESSON, and H. H. COUTTS. Evaluation of drift residues from aerial applications. Trans. ASAE, 9(3):389-393, 397, 1966.
30. YATES, W. E., N. B. AKESSON, and H. H. COUTTS. Drift hazards related to ultra-low-volume and diluted sprays applied by agricultural aircraft. Trans. ASAE, 10(5):628-632, 638, 1967.
31. YATES, W. E., J. M. OGAWA, and N. B. AKESSON. Spray distributions in peach orchards from helicopter and ground applications. ASAE Paper 68-617, Dec., 1968.
32. YEO, D. Assessment of rotary atomizers fitted to a Cessna aircraft. Agr. Aviation, 3(4):131-135, 1961.

PROBLEMS

13.1. A 0.95-m³ round-bottom sprayer tank is 1.5 m long and has a depth of 0.9 m. Mechanical agitation is to be provided with four paddles 280 mm long (tip diameter) and 200 mm wide mounted on a shaft 150 mm above the bottom of the tank.

(a) Calculate the minimum r/min for agitating a mixture of 10% oil and 90% water.

(b) If the mechanical efficiency of the power transmission system is 90%, what input power would be needed for agitation?

13.2. (a) Under the conditions of Problem 13.1, what recirculation rates would be required for hydraulic agitation at 400 kPa and 2.75 MPa?

(b) If the pump efficiency is 50%, what pump input power would be needed for hydraulic agitation at each pressure?

(c) Prepare a table to summarize and compare the results of Problems 13.1 and 13.2. Note the decreased recirculation rate and increased power requirement when the hydraulic-agitation pressure is increased.

13.3. A field sprayer having a horizontal boom with 20 nozzles spaced 46 cm apart is to be designed for a maximum application rate of 750 L/ha at 520 kPa and 6.5 km/h.

(a) Determine the required pump capacity in litres per minute, assuming 10% of the flow is bypassed under the above maximum conditions.

(b) If mechanical agitation requires 375 input watts and the pump efficiency is 50%, what should be the engine rating if the engine is to be loaded to not more than 80% of its rated power?

(c) What discharge rate per nozzle (L/min) is required under the above conditions?

(d) If the nozzles have 70° spray angles and the pattern is such that 50% overlap is needed for uniform coverage (i.e., spray pattern 50% wider than nozzle spacing), at what height above the tops of the plants should the boom be operated?

13.4. A field sprayer is equipped with nozzles having a rated delivery of 0.42 L/min of water at 275 kPa. The nozzle spacing on the boom is 51 cm. Each kilogram of active ingredient (2, 4-D) is mixed with 80 L of water and the desired application rate is 0.95 kg of chemical per hectare. What is the correct forward speed for a nozzle pressure of 200 kPa?

13.5. A hollow-cone spray nozzle deposits most droplets between two concentric circles. Assume the diameter of the inner circle is 70% of the diameter of the outer circle and that the distribution of droplets is uniform between the circles. Plot the theoretical distribution pattern that would be expected as the nozzle is moved forward past a transverse line. Graphical solution is acceptable.

13.6. At a deposition level 430 mm below the tip of a particular fan-spray nozzle, the discharge rate across a 20-cm width at the center of the sprayed strip is essentially constant at 15 mL/min per centimetre of lateral distance. On each side of this 20-cm center strip the discharge rate per centimetre of width decreases uniformly to zero at a lateral distance of 36 cm from the nozzle centerline.

(a) Plot the distribution curve, to scale (similar to broken-line profile in the upper left diagram of Fig. 13.10).

(b) On the same graph, draw a curve for this nozzle at a deposition level 585 mm below the nozzle tip. Show how you obtained this curve.

(c) Calculate the nozzle spray angle.

(d) If nozzles having this pattern are 50 cm apart on the boom, what tip height above the deposition level would give uniform coverage?

13.7. An airblast sprayer is to be operated at 4 km/h and the desired application rate is 19 L per tree. The tree spacing is 9 × 9 m and each nozzle delivers 4.0 L/min at the operating pressure of 415 kPa.

(a) If one-half row is sprayed from each side of the machine, how many nozzles will be needed?

(b) How many hectares can be covered with a 2-m³ tank full of spray?

14

Hay Harvesting: Cutting, Conditioning, and Windrowing

14.1. Introduction. Hay is grown on more than half of all the farms in the United States, with the area averaging about 20% of the total harvested crop land. Hay production in the United States amounts to over 90 Tg [100 million tons] annually, with alfalfa being the major crop. In addition, forage crops are harvested extensively for silage. Minor methods of using forage crops include direct feeding of freshly harvested green hay and the production of dehydrated pellets or meal.

Forage handling is complicated by the nature of the product. Hay is a crop of great bulk and mass, containing 70 to 80% water (wet basis) when first harvested. For storage it must be dried, either naturally or artificially, to a safe moisture content of about 20 to 25%. Long loose hay or extremely loose bales can tolerate slightly higher moisture contents without serious damage. The relatively low cash value per hectare for hay crops limits the economic feasibility of mechanization for small areas. In addition, hay is frequently grown on rolling land and steep slopes or under other conditions unfavorable to mechanization.

Although mechanization problems are not all solved, the decade beginning about 1955 witnessed the development and/or first general use of a considerable number of important types of hay harvesting equipment. Among these are self-propelled windrowers; combination mower-conditioners; flail mowers designed especially for hay; automatic bale pickup and stacking wagons (self-propelled and pull-type); bale accumulators and associated handling equipment; bale-thrower attachments for field balers; hay cubers and wafering machines; van-type trailers with windrow pickups and impeller-blowers for fully mechanized loading and stacking of long loose hay; and mechanical, loose-hay stack movers. Large-roll and large-rectangular-bale balers are an even more recent development.

These, plus improved models of previously existing types of equipment such as cutterbar mowers, reel-type and finger-wheel side-delivery rakes, conventional field balers, shear-bar-type field choppers, impact-type field choppers, mechanically unloading chopped-forage wagons, forage blowers, sweep rakes and stacking aids for long loose hay, and other minor haying implements, provide the farmer with a wide array of combinations for the various hay or silage harvesting methods.

313

The general methods, in terms of the final field form of the harvested product, include baling, cubing or wafering, direct-cut field chopping for green feed or grass/legume silage, field chopping for wilted grass/legume silage or low-moisture grass/legume silage, field chopping of cured or partially cured hay, and handling in the long loose form.

14.2. Quality of Product in Relation to Harvesting Methods. In general, all methods of harvesting and storing forage crops involve some loss of yield and reduction in quality. Losses of 5 to 15% of the dry matter have been found to occur from respiration and enzyme action during normal field curing.[22] When hay is handled dry, leaf shatter can result in substantial dry-matter losses. Because alfalfa leaves are higher in protein than are stems, the quality of the remaining product is reduced by the dry-matter loss. Alfalfa leaves contain about 70% of the total protein in the plant and 90% of the carotene (a source of vitamin A).[22] Prolonged exposure to sun, dew, and rain increases the loss of nutrients.

In humid climates, where adverse weather conditions are likely to prevail, any harvesting procedure that reduces the time between cutting and storing tends to minimize losses in yield and quality. Partial curing in the field, followed by artificial drying in the barn or stack with forced circulation of either heated or unheated air, is one method of reducing the time the hay is in the field.

Alfalfa losses from three harvesting methods under normal weather conditions were compared in USDA tests in Maryland.[14] Protein yield losses, in terms of the total protein yield of the standing crop just before harvest, amounted to 32% for field-cured long loose hay, 26% for barn-cured hay, and 14% for silage.

Tests were conducted in California to determine the effects of raking alfalfa hay (at 8 km/h [5 mph] with an oblique reel-head rake) or packaging it (baling or wafering) under extremely dry conditions, in comparison with performing these operations under desirable moisture conditions.[7] The "properly handled" treatment was raked at 40 to 50% moisture* when the hay was tough from dew, and was baled or wafered in the morning at 13 to 16% moisture, before the hay was dry enough to cause appreciable leaf shatter. Dry raking was done in the afternoon at 10 to 15% moisture and dry packaging was done in the afternoon at 5 to 7% moisture.

Under these extremely dry conditions, raking dry and packaging at the proper moisture content reduced the baled yield by 25% in comparison with proper handling. Raking properly and packaging dry reduced the yield only 4%. Raking dry and packaging dry reduced the yield 35%. Average crude protein contents were less than the corresponding preharvest values by the

---

*In more humid climates, raking can sometimes be done at a somewhat lower moisture content without excessive leaf shatter.

following percentage points: handled properly—1.4, raked dry—3.1, packaged dry—1.8, raked and packaged dry—4.3. The overall preharvest average was 23.6%. The greater reduction in protein content for the dry treatments indicates that the dry-matter losses were predominantly leaves. When the hay was fed to sheep, quality reductions were reflected in smaller mass gains. Conditioning reduced curing times but had little effect upon yields or quality in any of the raking and packaging treatments because no weather detrimental to quality was encountered.

CUTTING

14.3. Principles of Cutting. In order to have cutting take place, a system of forces must act upon the material in such a manner as to cause it to fail in shear. This shear failure is almost invariably accompanied by some deformation in bending and compression, which increases the amount of work required for the cutting operation. A common way of applying the cutting forces is by means of two opposed shearing elements which meet and pass each other with little or no clearance between them. Either one or both of the elements may be moving, and the motion may be linear with uniform velocity, reciprocating, or rotary.

A single cutting element, either moving or stationary with respect to the machine, is sufficient if the nature of the operation permits a fixed surface, such as the ground, to act as one of the shearing elements (as with weed knives on cultivators). If the material being cut is adequately supported and is relatively strong in bending (sugar beets, for example), the material itself may transmit the force required to oppose a single cutting element. An impact cutter has a single, high-speed cutting element and relies primarily upon the inertia of the material being cut to furnish the opposing force required for shear.

14.4. Impact-Type Cutters. The impact-cutting principle is applied in two types of implements that are commonly described as rotary cutters and flail shredders A rotary cutter has knives rotating in a horizontal plane (as on a rotary lawn mower), whereas a flail shredder has knives rotating in vertical planes parallel with the direction of travel.

These implements were first developed for cutting up stalks, small brush, cover crops, and other vegetative matter to facilitate incorporation into the soil, for cutting weeds, and for other similar jobs. In the early 1950s, stalk cutters and shredders were adapted to chopping forage crops as a low-priced alternative for conventional, shear-bar-type field choppers. More recently, special flail shredders have been developed for mowing hay.

Rotary cutters with effective widths of 1.0 to 2.1 m [3½ to 7 ft] have a single rotor, usually with 2 (but sometimes 4) knives on the ends of radial arms. Wider units have at least 2 or 3 rotors, each generally cutting a width of 0.7 to 2.1 m [28 to 84 in.]. The total cutting width may be as much as 6.1 m [20 ft]. Peripheral speeds generally range from 51 to 76 m/s [10,000 to 15,000 ft/min]. Knives or support arms can be shaped to create an updraft which raises lodged material and lifts cut material for further size reduction. Knives are usually attached to the support arms through vertical hinge axes so they can swing back if an obstruction is hit. Rotary cutters are hazardous because of the tendency to throw solid objects outward from beneath the housing in a violent manner. They also tend to leave the material windrowed.

Flail shredders have free-swinging knives or flails, 50 to 150 mm [2 to 6 in.] wide, attached to the rotor in 3 or 4 rows and staggered so the cuts overlap slightly. Some of the many shapes of knives employed are shown in Fig. 14.1. The knives are sometimes attached through a loop or a chain link,

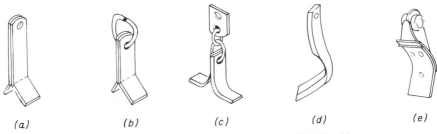

(a)   (b)   (c)   (d)   (e)

Fig. 14.1. Some types of knives employed on flail shredders.

rather than through a pivot axis, to provide greater flexibility for rocky conditions. Cutting widths of present-day units are mostly in the range from 1.2 to 6.1 m [4 to 20 ft]. Peripheral speeds are somewhat lower than for rotary cutters, usually ranging from 46 to 56 m/s [9000 to 11,000 ft/min] but sometimes being lower. Maintenance costs are higher than for rotary cutters but loose debris is less of a problem.

14.5. Flail Mowers. In the first attempts to employ flail shredders for mowing hay, excessive field loss was a major problem, primarily because of short pieces not recovered in raking or picking up from the windrow. Losses have been reduced by using lower peripheral speeds (43 m/s [8500 ft/min] or less) and by designing the shroud so it bends the plants forward for basal cutting and provides clearance above the rotor to minimize recutting (Fig. 14.2).[19] The lacerating effect and successive impacts of knives on the stems of the cut material result in a conditioning effect that increases the drying rate.

A flail mower has a full-width, adjustable gage roller located immediately behind the rotor (Fig. 14.2) to provide accurate control of cutting height and prevent scalping of high spots. Cutting widths are usually 1.8 to 3.0 m [6 to

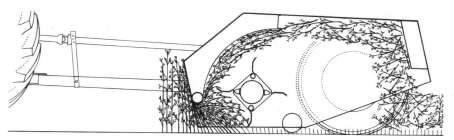

Fig. 14.2. Schematic, cross-sectional view of a flail mower. (Courtesy of Avco New Idea Div., Avco Corp.)

10 ft]. Pull-type flail mowers are generally offset so the tractor wheels run on cut hay rather than on the standing crop. Some of these units have cross-conveyor augers or movable deflector shields to permit windrowing the hay as it is cut. With mounted flail mowers, the tractor wheels knock down some of the standing crop but the flails are reasonably effective in picking it up.

Even with flail shredders specially designed for mowing hay, recovered yields for upright crops are usually at least 5 to 10% less than from conventional mowing and raking.[1,11,15,19,20] But under severely lodged conditions the flail mower may recover substantially more than a conventional mower.[15] Power requirements are considerably higher for a flail mower than for a conventional mower.

14.6. Types and Functional Parameters of a Mower Cutterbar. A mower cutterbar must be able to cut satisfactorily from 25 to 50 mm [1 to 2 in.] above ground level up to 100 mm [4 in.] or more. It must be able to cut a wide variety of crop materials, from thin-bladed grasses to thick, tough stalks, cleanly and without clogging. The cutting parts should be protected from rocks and should be capable of cutting through occasional mounds of soil without damage.

Many attempts have been made to replace the reciprocating knife with continuous-moving cutting units such as chain knives, band knives, and helical-rotor cutters, but none have reached the stage of functional and commercial feasibility. A variation of the conventional cutterbar that has received limited acceptance has two opposed, reciprocating knives and no guards. The absence of guards greatly reduces the tendency to plug in tangled, matted, or damp crops but may present problems under stony conditions. Double-knife mowers are dynamically balanced. They can be operated at higher forward speeds than conventional mowers and they produce more uniform stubble heights, but their new cost is considerably higher.

14.7. Conventional Mower Cutterbar. The construction and mounting of a typical mower cutterbar are illustrated in Fig. 14.3. Not shown are the

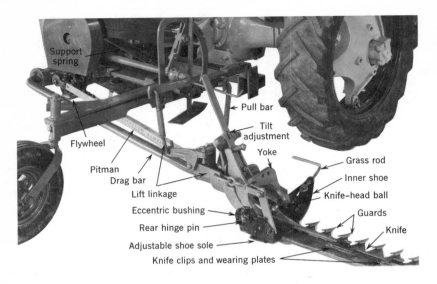

Fig. 14.3. A semimounted mower with pitman drive.

outer divider and shoe assembly and the grass board. The function of the grass board, which is attached to the rear of the outer divider, is to clear the cut material from a narrow strip next to the standing crop and thus provide a place for the inner shoe to operate on the next trip. The guard spacing is almost universally 76.2 mm [3 in.]. The knife stroke is usually 76.2 mm [3 in.], but other strokes from 63 to 95 mm [2½ to 3¾ in.] have also been employed with a 76.2-mm guard spacing.

The height of cut is gaged by adjustable shoes at the ends of the cutterbar. The adjustable support spring shown in Fig. 14.3 acts through the lift linkage to counterbalance most of the cutterbar gravitational force so that the cutterbar "floats" along the ground. The lift linkage can be adjusted to change the relative amounts of load (force) carried on the inner and outer shoes. These loads should be just enough to prevent bouncing of the cutterbar. The optimum loads are influenced by the roughness of the field and the forward speed. Typical values are 360 to 440 N [80 to 100 lbf] on the inner shoe and 90 to 130 N [20 to 30 lbf] on the outer shoe.

Figure 14.4 shows a cross-sectional view of a cutting unit. The ledger plates ordinarily are serrated on the under side and are replaced occasionally but never sharpened. The cutting edges of the knife sections may be either smooth or underserrated, both types being resharpened at frequent intervals by grinding the beveled top surfaces. Underserrated knives are good for coarse-stemmed crops because they reduce the tendency for stalks to slip forward. However, underserrated knives give trouble in grasses because the

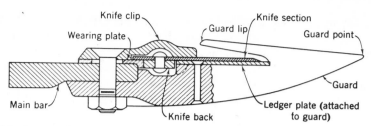

Fig. 14.4. Cross-sectional view of cutterbar, showing knife section directly over ledger plate.

fine stems tend to wedge under the blade. Knife clips and wearing plates are mounted together and are usually spaced 3 or 4 guards apart (Fig. 14.3). The wearing plates provide vertical support for the rear of the knife sections and also absorb the rearward thrust of the knife. They have a fore-and-aft adjustment but must be replaced when the top surface wears down sufficiently to tip the knife and cause an appreciable vertical clearance between the ledger plates and the points of the knife sections.

14.8. Knife Drive Systems. The knife may be driven through a long pitman attached to the knife head by means of a ball-and-socket joint, as shown in Fig. 14.3, or the transition from rotary motion to reciprocating motion is accomplished with a drive unit supported entirely on the inner shoe. One arrangement for a shoe-mounted drive unit is shown in Fig. 14.5.

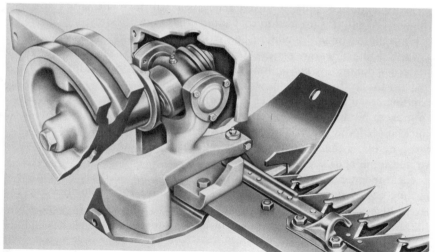

Fig. 14.5. A drive unit mounted on the inner shoe of the cutterbar, employing a wobble-joint drive to obtain knife motion and having a reciprocating counterweight. The hinge pins that support the cutterbar are placed in line with the sheave axis so that the vertical angle of the cutterbar does not affect belt tension. (Courtesy of International Harvester Co.)

This system, often called a wobble-joint drive, is simple and is sometimes employed (usually without a counterweight*) to drive sickles on other types of harvesting equipment. The axis of the main drive shaft, the yoke axis, and the vertical axis of oscillation all intersect at a common point. As the main shaft rotates, the component of motion of the angled throw in a vertical plane is absorbed by the yoke while the motion in a horizontal plane oscillates the fork about its vertical axis.

Chen[6] has developed equations of angular motion for a wobble joint (bent-shaft oscillator). It can be shown from his angular-displacement equation that the relation between linear displacement of a reciprocating member and the rotational angle of the input shaft would be sinusoidal only if the oscillating arm had a radial slider on it so the moment arm (perpendicular distance) between the reciprocating member and the center of oscillation remained constant.

Drives mounted on the inner shoe are more trouble-free than conventional pitman drives and are not affected by the vertical angle of the cutterbar, but pitman drives are less expensive. Shoe-mounted drives often include an arrangement to provide full dynamic balancing for the knife (discussed in Section 14.15). Crank speeds on most mowers are 850 to 1000 r/min for conventional pitman drives, 1000 to 1200 r/min for dynamically balanced systems, and 800 to 1150 r/min for drives mounted on the inner shoe but not having full dynamic balancing.

Most tractor mowers have a V-belt in the drive that provides overload protection and cushions high-frequency peak torques and shock loads. If there is no belt, it is important that some other type of safety device, such as a jump clutch or a slip clutch, be provided.

14.9. Knife Clearances and Cutting Velocities. Because many of the materials commonly cut with a mower are weak in bending, it is important to hold the knife sections down close to the ledger plates. This is done by bending down the knife clips (Fig. 14.4) until there is only enough clearance to prevent binding. If the clearance is allowed to increase and approach the thickness of the material being cut, deformation in bending produces a wedging effect that increases power requirements and may result in failure to cut some stalks.

Clearance tends to be less critical if the cutting unit is designed so that all cutting occurs during portions of the stroke where knife velocities are relatively high. A combination of impact and shear can then be utilized, rather than depending upon shear alone. Since the peak knife velocity with a 76.2-mm [3-in.] stroke at 1000 r/min is less than 4 m/s [800 ft/min] (as compared with 50 m/s [10,000 ft/min] for an impact cutter), there is probably very little cutting by impact of the knife sections alone.

---

*"Counterweight" is a descriptive term that refers to a counterbalancing mass.

14.10. Register and Alignment. Two adjustments that are important to proper functioning of a mower having a pitman drive are known as knife register and cutterbar alignment. A knife is in proper register when the midpoint of the stroke is centered between adjacent guards. If the stroke is the same length as the guard spacing, the knife sections are centered in the guards at each end of the stroke. Adjustment is commonly made by moving the entire cutterbar in or out with respect to the pitman crankshaft.

If a cutterbar is in proper alignment, the pitman and the knife will be in line (in plan view) when the mower is operating in the field. To allow for the rearward deflection of the outer end of the cutterbar during operation, it is customary to adjust the mower so that, when not operating, the outer end of the cutterbar has a lead of about 20 mm per metre of bar length [¼ in./ft]. Lead is measured by stretching a string parallel to the vertical plane of the pitman and determining the difference in horizontal fore-and-aft distances from the string to the knife back at the inner and outer ends. One method of adjusting lead is by rotation of an eccentric bushing on one of the hinge pins (Fig. 14.3).

Mounting the drive unit directly on the inner shoe of the cutterbar (as in Fig. 14.5 and 14.8) eliminates the problems of maintaining alignment and register.

14.11. Attachment of Mowers to Tractors. Rear-mounted mowers are compact, maneuverable, and easily mounted, and are the most popular type. Semi-mounting provides better control of cutterbar height on irregular surfaces. Two-wheel, pull-type mowers are the best type for making square corners when mowing around a field and are easiest to attach, but they are somewhat less maneuverable than mounted or semimounted units. Side mounting gives good visibility of the work and direct response to steering but is the least desirable arrangement for mowing around a field. All types are generally PTO-driven, except that hydraulic motors are sometimes employed for side-mounted mowers.

Cutterbar lengths range from 1.52 to 2.75 m [5 to 9 ft], with the 2.13-m [7-ft] size being the most common. The adverse effects of the offset drag force of the cutterbar become increasingly important as the cutterbar length is increased, especially with pull-type mowers because of their small mass.[13]

Since the inertia of all but the smallest tractors is relatively high, it is important that the cutterbar be provided with a safety break-away coupling that will allow the bar to swing back if it strikes an obstruction. This safety device becomes increasingly important for the large tractors and as forward speeds are increased.

14.12. Cutting Pattern for a Conventional Mower. Figure 14.6 shows the cutting pattern, based upon a theoretical analysis,[17] for a conventional mower when operated with a feed rate (forward travel per cut) of 76 mm [3 in.]. The shaded portion represents the land area from which stalks are cut

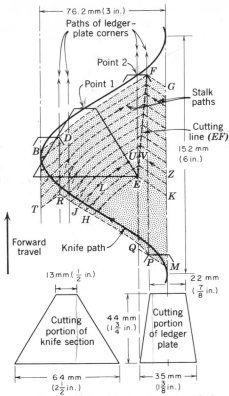

Fig. 14.6. Graph of knife displacement versus forward travel, with theoretical stalk-deflection paths superimposed, for a conventional mower when operated with a forward travel of 76 mm [3 in.] per stroke. (R. A. Kepner.[17])

during the stroke under consideration. All stalks originating in this shaded area are cut along line *EF*. As the mower moves forward and the knife section moves from left to right, cutting begins when the front center of the section is at point 1, such that the rear corners of the cutting portions of the knife and the ledger plate just come together (at *E*). Cutting finishes at *F* when the knife center is at point 2.

According to this analysis, all stalks originating along a typical path *ZV* are deflected by the guards and ledger plates to point *V* as the mower moves forward. The knife section deflects all stalks originating along *JLUV* to point *V*, where they are cut by point *U* of the knife. The slope of *ZV* is the sum of the angle of the ledger-plate edge with respect to the direction of travel and the friction angle between the stalks and the ledger plate. Similarly, the slope of *JL* represents the condition under which stalk slippage along the knife edge (toward the rear corner of the knife section) is impending or occurring. Between L and V, the slope of the path of point U on the knife is less than the slope of JL, and no slipping occurs.

The coefficients of friction assumed in Fig. 14.6 are (a) between stalks and serrated ledger plates, tan 20° = 0.364, and (b) between stalks and smooth knife edge, tan 17° = 0.306. These values are based upon friction-angle measurements originally reported by Bosoi and reproduced in reference 17. Johnston[16] observed cutting of groups of 300-mm [12-in.] flax straws in the laboratory, using high-speed motion pictures. He found that with a 76-mm [3-in.] feed rate there was little slipping of stalks along the advancing knife edge except during the first 13 mm [½ in.] of the stroke and that stalks sliding along the ledger plate were gradually bent forward due to friction.

If the included angle between the two cutting edges is too great, stalks will tend to slip forward rather than being cut. The maximum permissible angle depends upon the coefficients of friction between the stalk and the cutting edges.[17] The primary function of serrations on the cutting edges (discussed in Section 14.7) is to increase the coefficient of friction. Johnston[16] found that inertia of the stalks is also a significant factor, preventing forward slip under conditions where static tests indicated the stalk should be expelled uncut.

It will be noted in Fig. 14.6 that for a feed rate of 76 mm [3 in.] there is a sizable shaded area behind stalk paths HE and EK, from which stalks must be crowded forward in order to be cut by the rear portion of the knife. In this example, which would represent a forward speed of 9.7 km/h [6 mph] if the crank speed were 1050 r/min, the area behind HEK is equal to 25% of the total area cut per stroke. Such a condition is undesirable because of the bunching effect at the rear of the knife and the resulting large cutting force required at the start of the cutting, and because of the excessive stalk deflection involved.

14.13. Stalk Deflection. In Fig. 14.6 the theoretical maximum deflection of the rear stalks is from M (point of stalk origin) to E (point of cutting), a distance of 61 mm [2.4 in.]. The maximum deflection of side stalks is from B to F, a distance of 81 mm [3.2 in.]. Deflections for a feed rate of 38 mm [1½ in.] instead of 76 mm were found to be 20 mm [0.8 in.] from M to E and 71 mm [2.8 in.] from B to F. Thus it is seen that deflection of side stalks is rather large with the conventional cutterbar, even at low feed rates, whereas the deflection of rear stalks becomes large as the feed rate is increased.

Excessive stalk deflection, particularly when cutting close to the ground, results in stubble of uneven length. It also increases the tendency for the stalks to slip forward out of the cutting unit and thus be cut higher or missed entirely. For best performance when cutting within 50 to 75 mm [2 to 3 in.] of the ground, the maximum deflection of rear stalks (from M to E) should not exceed the amount indicated in Fig. 14.6, which represents a maximum feed rate of 76 mm [3 in.] for the conventional cutterbar.

Side deflection can be minimized by having a short stroke or by an arrangement to obtain two cuts per stroke. Thus, doubling the number of guards on a conventional mower (as is occasionally done for certain crops) reduces the side deflection. This change also increases the permissible forward speed for a given feed rate and crank speed, since the number of cuts per stroke is doubled, but the reduced width of opening between guards may cause feeding problems. If the cutterbar is equipped with 2 reciprocating knives, each having a stroke equal to half the knife-section spacing (38-mm stroke, for example), the side deflection is reduced and yet there is ample width of feed opening when the knives are at the ends of their strokes.

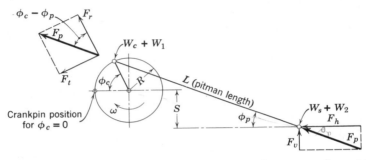

Fig. 14.7. Forces due to inertia of the reciprocating parts in a mower pitman drive.

14.14. Forces Due to Knife Inertia. Figure 14.7 shows the typical arrangement of a pitman drive and the inertia-force relations for the reciprocating knife, the pitman, and the crankpin. In analyzing the unbalanced forces, the pitman mass is assumed to be divided into compoents W_1 and W_2 concentrated at the two ends, W_1 being subjected to rotary motion and W_2 having reciprocating motion. W_s is the mass of the knife and W_c is the mass of the crankpin. Uniform angular velocity of the crank is assumed. If the ratio $R/\sqrt{L^2 - S^2}$ is less than 0.25, the inertia force of the reciprocating parts can be represented by the following approximate relation, using any consistent set of units.[25]

$$F_h = (W_s + W_2) R\omega^2 (\cos \phi_c + \frac{KS}{R} \sin \phi_c - K \cos 2\phi_c) \qquad (14.1)$$

where F_h = inertia force of the knife and the W_2 portion of the pitman mass

ω = angular velocity of the crank, in radians per second

ϕ_c = angle of crank rotation beyond reference position indicated in Fig. 14.7

L = length of pitman

R = radius of rotation of crankpin

S = height of crankshaft centerline above the plane of the pivot connection between the knife and the pitman

$$K = R/\sqrt{L^2 - S^2}$$

Note that the inertia force varies as the square of the crank speed and as the first power of the stroke. The magnitude of the peak values of F_h at the two ends of the stroke are slightly different because ϕ_p (Fig. 14.7) is different. Careful attention must be given to the algebraic signs of the trigonometric functions for values of ϕ_c or $2\phi_c$ greater than 90°.

Because of the angle between the pitman and the knife, a periodic vertical reaction F_v, alternating upward and downward, is introduced at the knife head. If the knife-head guides are loose, flexing of the knife may cause early fatigue failure of the knife back.

14.15 Counterbalancing and Vibration Control. Counterbalancing is not imperative if the mass of the machine or component supporting the cutterbar is large in comparison with the reciprocating force, as on a self-propelled windrower or a grain combine. But counterbalancing and/or vibration isolation is needed on a field mower because its frame is relatively light. Vibration sets up stresses in many parts of the mower structure, increasing maintenance requirements and the possibility of early fatigue failures.

The rotating counterweight commonly provided on the flywheel of a pitman-type drive does not give complete balancing because its centrifugal force is constant whereas the inertia force of the reciprocating parts is a function of the crank angle ϕ_c. The usual compromise is to provide sufficient mass opposite the crankpin to counterbalance $W_c + W_l$ and half of the maximum unbalance F_r (Fig. 14.7) that results from F_h. The vertical vibration component introduced by the counterweight is then about equal to the reduced maximum horizontal component of the knife plus counterweight.

One approach that has been taken to reduce vibration on pitman-type drives is to support the crankshaft in a casting that is isolated from the main frame through flexible, rubber mountings. The drag bar (coupling bar) that supports the cutterbar is attached to the crankshaft housing. The crankshaft assembly and cutterbar then reciprocate, as a unit, in the opposite direction from the knife but at an amplitude much smaller than the knife stroke because of the greater mass.

Essentially full dynamic balancing of reciprocating parts can be obtained by the addition of a second, driven reciprocating mass that moves in direct opposition to the first mass and is as closely in line with it as is feasible. Figure 14.8a shows one such arrangement. Experience has indicated that a certain degree of cutterbar vibration is desirable in some situations to help move the cut material back across the top of the bar. The drive shown in Fig. 14.5 has a reciprocating counterweight that is offset from the line of motion of the knife and thus introduces a cyclic couple on the cutterbar in the horizontal plane.

The two opposed, reciprocating knives of a double-knife mower provide essentially full dynamic balancing. If only one cut per stroke is obtained, this

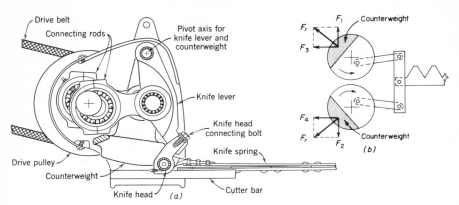

Fig. 14.8. Two methods of providing full dynamic balancing. (a) Reciprocating counterweight. (L. E. Elfes.[8]) (b) Twin flywheels with opposed counterweights.

arrangement requires only half the stroke of a comparable single-knife cutterbar, thus permitting higher crank speeds for the same peak inertia forces.

Another design employs twin, counter-rotating flywheels mounted on the inner shoe with short pitman drives to a bar across the knife head (Fig. 14.8b). For any rotational angle of the counterweighted flywheels, F_r is constant but components F_1 and F_2 cancel each other and the sum of $F_3 + F_4$ cancels the inertia force of the knife (assuming sinusoidal motion of the knife, which is not quite correct).

Full dynamic balancing minimizes vibration at a given crank speed. It also permits the use of higher crank speeds and, hence, greater forward speeds.

14.16. Cutting-Energy and Power Requirements for a Mower. With a 2.13-m [7-ft] mounted mower having a conventional type of cutterbar and a drive of the type shown in Fig. 14.8a, Elfes[8] made limited tests in moderately heavy, mixed hay and obtained the following results.

	Avg. equivalent max. knife load		Average PTO power		Average peak PTO power	
	kN	lbf	kW	hp	kW	hp
Inertia and friction load (no cutting)	1.82	410	1.27	1.70	4.61	6.18
Mowing at 7.9 km/h	2.54	570	1.90	2.55	5.22	7.00
Increase due to cutting	0.72	160	0.63	0.85	0.61	0.82

These results, obtained with a crank speed of 942 r/min and a feed rate of 68.1 mm [2.68 in.] per stroke, indicate an average PTO input of only 0.91 kW per metre of cutterbar length [0.37 hp/ft] but peak values (one peak per stroke) of about 2.4 kW/m [1 hp/ft]. At 1255 r/min the average PTO input was about 1.2 kW/m [0.5 hp/ft]. The total power requirements for the mower would include the draft due to the cutterbar drag. It is not known how well these power requirements would apply to other types of mowers or to other cutting conditions. Harbage and Morr[13] measured no-load pitman thrusts of 2.85 and 6.05 kN [640 and 1360 lbf] for a 2.13-m [7-ft] mower at crank speeds of 970 and 1360 r/min, respectively. The thrust at 1250 r/min was 4.9 kN [1100 lbf] when mowing bluegrass with a new knife. With a dull knife, the pitman thrust at 1070 r/min was 9.72 kN [2185 lbf].

Laboratory studies have been made to determine the effects of various parameters upon the energy required to cut individual stalks or groups of stalks. Chancellor[5] found that the energy required to cut groups of stalks into 13-mm [½-in.] lengths, at velocities comparable with mowing, ranged from 0.33 to 2.0 kW·h per megagram of dry matter [0.4 to 2.4 hp-h/ton]. To make one cut per stalk, as in mowing, Chancellor's maximum energy requirements represent less than 10% of the 0.63-kW increase due to cutting that Elfes obtained in his field tests. Prince and his associates[24] also found that the increase in knife force due to cutting in the field was about ten times as great as predicted on the basis of laboratory tests with single stalks. The increase in knife force may be partly attributable to increased knife friction during cutting.[24]

HAY CONDITIONING

In common usage, the term *hay conditioning* refers to any form of mechanical treatment of freshly cut hay in the field that is performed to increase the natural drying rate. The objective of conditioning is to reduce the field curing time and thus minimize the possibility of loss due to bad weather. Hay conditioning is not particularly beneficial in areas where there is little likelihood of rain during the harvest season, but can result in substantial savings in the midwestern and eastern sections of the United States, where summer rains occur frequently.

Conditioning has the greatest effect on thick-stemmed plants, such as alfalfa and sudan grass, because the stems normally dry more slowly than the leaves. Laboratory tests with various mechanical, chemical, thermal, and electrical treatments applied to alfalfa indicated that crushing the stems to increase the amount of exposed surface is one of the most effective ways to increase the drying rate.[23] Fastest drying in other laboratory tests was obtained when the stems were severely crushed or were penetrated at intervals of perhaps 5 to 10 mm [several places per inch] with a small nail, rather than being twisted, smashed at 50-mm [2-in.] intervals, or cut up into 50-mm lengths.[22] After hard crushing (more severe than would be acceptable in a field operation) the stems dried faster than the leaves.

14.17. Types of Conditioners. Flail mowers have a conditioning effect because of the lacerating, cutting, and breaking of stems by the flail knives. Separate pull-type conditioners, combination mower-conditioners, and self-propelled windrowers with conditioner attachments all employ pairs of rolls that either (a) crush the stalks continuously or intermittently or (b) bend and crack the stalks transversely at intervals of 25 to 50 mm [1 to 2 in.] with little or no crushing. These two types of conditioners are known as crushers and crimpers. A crimper has two steel, fluted rolls that are intermeshed but usually synchronized through external drive gears so the ribs do not contact each other. Springs hold one of the pair of crimper rolls against stops that limit radial overlap to perhaps 10 to 16 mm [⅜ to ⅝ in.]. The springs permit the rolls to spread if a slug of hay or some foreign object is encountered.

The rolls of a *crusher* are held together by adjustable springs. One roll is made of rubber, either laminated from rubber-and-cord disks or molded. The other roll is usually steel but sometimes rubber. To improve pickup and/or feeding, steel rolls usually have spiral or herringbone flutes formed by welding bars onto a drum, or in some cases have an open, squirrel-cage arrangement of steel bars around the periphery. Rubber rolls may or may not be fluted. One design with two rubber rolls has intermeshing, herringbone or chevron-shaped flutes that crimp the stalks in addition to crushing them.

Crimper or crusher roll diameters are usually between 125 and 250 mm [5 and 10 in.]. Peripheral speeds are mostly 7.1 to 9.1 m/s [1400 to 1800 ft/min] for crushers and 6.6 to 7.6 m/s [1300 to 1500 ft/min] for crimpers. High ratios between peripheral speed and forward speed are desirable to produce thin layers between the rolls.[3] Crimpers have a more aggressive feeding action than do crushers.

Separate conditioners usually pick up mowed hay from the swath, but windrows can be put through them. The bottom roll acts as the pickup. Mower-conditioners with not over 2.75-m [9-ft] cuts have conditioner rolls with lengths approximately equal to the width of cut, and the hay is fed directly to the rolls from the cutterbar. Self-propelled windrowers, except for a few 2.75-m models that have full-width conditioners, put the *windrow* through the conditioner. Some self-propelled windrowers feed the hay directly from the cross conveyors into the conditioner, whereas other models drop the hay onto the stubble and the conditioner then picks it up. Separate conditioners and mower-conditioners now being manufactured are predominantly crushers, but both crushers and crimpers are common on self-propelled windrowers.

14.18. Separate Conditioners. Separate conditioners came into prominence in the 1950s but production declined steadily during the 1960s.[27] Mower-conditioners have largely replaced separate conditioners. Originally, conditioning was often a separate operation, performed with a second tractor following the mower. Subsequently, mowers were made available with hitches and PTO extensions to permit pulling a conditioner behind the mower. The conditioner then picks up the swath adjacent to the one being cut. This arrangement still involves two implements and is cumbersome and inconvenient to use. Most separate conditioners have effective widths of 1.83 to 2.13 m [72 to 84 in.] and are designed to pick up the swath from a 2.13-m [7-ft] mower.

14.19. Mower-Conditioners. Although combination mower-crushers were tried experimentally in the early 1930s, the first generally acceptable commercial model did not appear until 1964.[27] Three years later, 12 manufacturers had retail sales totaling almost 12 000 units.[27] Basically, a pull-type mower-conditioner consists of a cutterbar, a reel, a pair of full-width conditioning rolls, and a deflector (Fig. 14.9). The most common cutting width

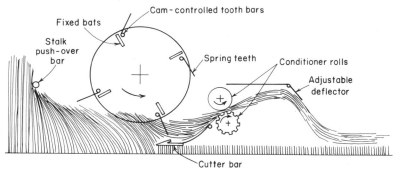

Fig. 14.9. Schematic, cross-sectional view of a mower-conditioner. Side deflectors that can be used to form a windrow are not shown.

is 2.75 m [9 ft], but widths range from 2.13 to 3.65 m [7 to 12 ft]. The 3.65-m [12-ft] models have rolls 2.13 to 2.75 m [7 to 9 ft] long with short, auger-type cross conveyors at the outer ends of the header. The conditioned hay can be left evenly spread in a swath a little narrower than the cut, or side deflectors behind the rolls can be adjusted to obtain various windrow widths and positions. Windrows cure more slowly than hay in the swath but can be straddled with the tractor and sometimes eliminate the raking operation.

The cutterbar is similar to that of a conventional mower except that the guards are more pointed and slender to improve performance in tangled or lodged crops and are made in pairs to provide greater support in mounting. Chrome-plated knife sections are sometimes employed. Because of the excellent wearing qualities of the hard plating, resharpening of these is not necessary. Chromed sections may be top-serrated (since they are not resharpened), under-serrated, or smooth. Knife speeds are usually 600 to 800 cycles per minute (somewhat slower than on mowers).

Wide runners at the ends of the header are adjustable to control the cutting height, most of the header gravitational force being carried on counterbalance springs. Each end of the header should float independently. Reels are of the pickup type and have cam-controlled tooth bars as shown in Fig. 14.10 *left*. Provision should be made for increasing the reel speed and moving the reel forward and downward when hay is lodged. In California tests with a self-propelled windrower, a reel peripheral speed twice the forward speed did a good job in badly lodged alfalfa but a ratio of 1.35 was too slow.[10]

Because of the pickup reels, both mower-conditioners and self-propelled windrowers can effectively cut lodged or leaning hay from any direction, seldom plug, and are not affected by strong winds. They can be used for hybrid grasses 1.5 to 3 m [5 to 10 ft] tall, as well as in tangled crops. In areas where conditioning is needed, mower-conditioners have greater capacity than a combination of a mower and a separate conditioner. The new cost of mower-conditioners is much lower than that of self-propelled windrowers, which makes them more suitable for small or medium areas.

14.20. Field Drying Rates and Curing Times. A great many field tests have been conducted by various state agricultural experiment stations to evaluate the effectiveness of hay conditioners and determine problems associated with their use. In general, tests in humid areas have indicated that, under reasonably good drying conditions, conditioning can reduce curing times by about one day, often permitting the hay to be baled or stored (at 20 to 25% moisture content) on the afternoon of the day following cutting.[2,4,9,21] In some cases, hay that has not over 75% initial moisture and is mowed early in the morning can be baled or stored by late afternoon of the same day.[4,9,26]

It is common practice in geographical areas where there is little likelihood of rain during the curing period to bale hay in the early morning when it is damp from night pickup of moisture, rather than in the afternoon. This procedure minimizes leaf shatter. Conditioning following conventional mowing is not generally practiced in these areas, but tests at the California Agricultural Experiment Station[18] indicated that mowed-and-conditioned hay dried to an early-morning moisture content of 20% in 3 to 5 days, whereas unconditioned hay required 2 days longer. Conditioning had little effect upon quality.

Conditioning should be done as soon as possible after mowing, to maximize the time of the accelerated drying resulting from conditioning. The effectiveness of a crusher is increased by reducing the thickness of the hay layer passing between the rolls and by increasing the roll pressure.[3,26] Excessive roll pressure, however, bruises leaves and tends to increase field losses by clipping off tips and leaf clusters. When crushing from the swath, pressures of 4.4 to 5.3 kN per metre of roll length [25 to 30 lbf/in.] have given good results.[3,26] Most comparative tests have shown crushers to be slightly more effective than crimpers when conditioning hay from the swath.[2,9,15,21,26] However, there is no evidence to establish such a relation for conditioning windrows as on a self-propelled windrower. Flail-mowed hay left in the swath will cure about as fast as crushed hay.[11,15,19] In Wisconsin tests,[1] an alfalfa-brome mixture dried at the same rate when cut with a mower-conditioner and left in the swath as when conditioned as a separate operation.

Numerous field tests have indicated that hay which is windrowed immediately after mowing and conditioning requires about the same curing time as unconditioned hay left in the swath until the moisture content is 40 to 50% or less. When harvesting an alfalfa-brome mixture, windrows made with a flail mower[1,12] or a mower-conditioner[1] dried at about the same rate as unconditioned hay. Several investigators[9,10,12,15] found that conditioned windrows made with self-propelled windrowers dried more slowly during the first day than did unconditioned hay in the swath, but had about the same moisture content by the end of the second day. In California tests,[10] conditioned windrows made with a self-propelled windrower dried to an early-morning moisture content of 20% one day sooner than mowed, unconditioned hay (5 days versus 6 days).

Conditioning is less advantageous under adverse weather conditions than in good drying weather. Conditioned hay picks up moisture more rapidly than unconditioned hay, either from rain or from normal night-time increases in relative humidity.[9,18] High soil moisture content also reduces the drying rate.

14.21. Field Losses from Conditioning. Observations of potential losses by shaking on a 51-mm-mesh [2-in.-mesh] screen, and of actual losses by picking up missed material after windrowing and baling, indicate that losses due to conditioning with a separate conditioner or with a mower-conditioner may be greater than from mowing without conditioning by 1 to 4% of the yield.[1,2,18] These losses are of little consequence in situations where conditioning appreciably reduces the probability of losses resulting from rain or other adverse conditions. As indicated in Section 14.5, losses from flail mowers may be 10% or more, especially when the aggressiveness of these machines is adjusted to give drying rates comparable with crushing.

WINDROWING

14.22. Methods of Windrowing. Most methods of harvesting hay, as well as some seed harvesting and green-crop harvesting operations, involve windrowing. As previously mentioned, hay can be windrowed in conjunction with the cutting operation by means of flail mowers, mower-conditioners, or self-propelled windrowers. Windrowing as a separate operation is usually done with side-delivery rakes. In harvesting hay by mowing and raking, the raking operation is usually done after the hay has dried to a moisture content of 50% or less. Side-delivery rakes are also employed to turn windrows, when necessary to improve drying, and for combining small windrows to permit operating balers at greater output rates.

14.23. Self-Propelled Windrowers. The first extensive use of self-propelled windrowers for harvesting hay was in about 1960. These machines are well-suited for harvesting large areas in localities where weather is not a serious hazard. Their high initial cost makes them uneconomical for small areas, particularly if mowed hay normally is not conditioned.[10] The steering system based on differential speeds of the drive wheels, with the rear wheel or wheels castered, makes self-propelled windrowers extremely maneuverable and well-suited to back-and-forth cutting in fields having irrigation levees. Models having dual hydrostatic propulsion drives (Section 4.25) are common.

Fig. 14.10. Two types of headers for self-propelled windrowers. *Left:* Auger cross conveyor and reel with cam-controlled tooth bars. (Courtesy of Sperry New Holland.) *Right:* Draper-type header with parallel-slat pickup reel. (Courtesy of Deere & Co.)

Two types of headers are shown in Fig. 14.10. The auger cross feed is the most common type on hay machines but is too aggressive for grain. The draper type is employed on windrowers intended for both grain and hay. The maximum width that should be cut with a hay windrower is limited primarily by the maximum size of windrow that will cure in an acceptable time. Windrowers with cutting widths of 3.65 and 4.25 m [12 and 14 ft] are popular in irrigated areas where hay yields per cutting are usually 2.2 to 3.4 Mg of dry matter per hectare [1 to 1½ tons per acre].[10] When high-capacity balers are employed, two windrows are raked together prior to baling. As on mower-conditioners, the cutting height is gaged by runners, and header counter-balance springs are employed.

Knife speeds are about the same as on mower-conditioners (600 to 800 cycles per minute), but strokes are often 6 to 10 mm [¼ to ⅜ in.] greater than the 76.2-mm [3-in.] guard spacing. Chrome-plated knife sections are used almost universally. Conditioning attachments are usually 0.9 to 1.4 m [3 to 4½ ft] wide, but the direct-feed, full-width-conditioner system of pull-type mower-conditioners has also been applied to some 2.75-m [9-ft] self-propelled machines.

14.24. Effects of Self-Propelled Windrowers upon Yields and Quality. Baled-hay yields from windrowing and from mowing and raking were compared for a total of 12 cuttings in California tests.[10] All of the four fields had irrigation levees. In a field with relatively high levees spaced 8.5 m [28 ft] apart, yields from the windrowed checks were 9 to 13% less than from mowed-and-raked checks. Much of the difference was due to taller stubble left by the windrower adjacent to the levee when one end of the header was on top of the levee. In fields having lower levees 11.6 or 18.3 m [38 or 60 ft] apart, the yield reduction was only 2 to 7%. The windrower yield in a badly lodged crop was 6% greater than the mowed-and-raked yield.

The California results suggest that windrowing instead of mowing should cause little difference in yields of an upright crop in a flat field with no levees. Tests have shown yields to be about the same from the two systems in New York, with more stubble loss but less leaf loss from windrowing.[15] The protein content of windrowed hay tends to be a little greater than that of mowed hay because of the taller stubble left in the field and the reduced leaf loss.[10,15]

14.25. Types of Side Delivery Rakes. Most present-day side delivery rakes are either reel-type units or finger-wheel units. Prior to 1948, all reel-type rakes were of the cylindrical-reel type. The teeth rotated in parallel positions in planes perpendicular to the reel axis, similar to the pickup reel shown in Fig. 14.10 *right*. Virtually all reel-type rakes now manufactured in the United States are of the oblique reel-head (parallel-bar) type. The reel heads are set at a horizontally acute angle from the reel axis but in parallel planes, as indicated in Fig. 14.11c.

The tooth-bar ends are shaped so the axes of the tooth-bar bearings (Fig. 3.2) are perpendicular to the planes of the reel heads. This arrangement automatically maintains the teeth in parallel positions (usually about vertical) as the reel rotates. The rotational path of any tooth is in a plane parallel to the reel-head planes. Thus the horizontal movement of the teeth with respect to the rake can be 85 to 90° (or theoretically even more) from the direction of forward motion.

Tooth pitch is changed for different hay conditions by rotating the reel frame about the reel axis. Pitching the bottom ends of the teeth forward gives a more vigorous raking action for heavy crops. Oblique reel-head rakes usually have 4 or 5 tooth bars. Raking widths range from 2.1 to 2.9 m [7 to 9½ ft], the size usually being selected to match the mowing width.

The reels of pull-type rakes are usually driven by the ground wheels, although hydraulic drives are also available. Ground drive provides the desirable feature of maintaining a constant speed ratio between reel peripheral speed and forward speed (usually between 1.35 and 1.70). The two support wheels are usually offset from each other in the fore-and-aft direction so each one can be close behind the reel for good height control. Mounted, PTO-driven rakes are lighter and less expensive than pull-type rakes, but the speed ratio is changed when the tractor is operated in different transmission gears. Pull-type rakes are more stable and have greater clearances for hay in front of the reel.

A finger-wheel rake has a series of individually floating, ground-driven wheels set at an angle to the direction of motion and overlapping each other as indicated in Fig. 14.12b. Each wheel is partially counterbalanced with a tension spring and has spring teeth around the periphery that operate in light contact with the ground. The floating feature allows the rake to adjust itself to the contour of surface irregularities such as irrigation levees or terrace channels. Wheel tooth-tip diameters are usually about 1.5 m [5 ft].

Since each wheel is set at an angle to the direction of travel, there is a velocity component perpendicular to the plane of the wheel in addition to the component causing rotation. The perpendicular component results in a dragging action of the teeth, approximately parallel to the axle. Although contact with the ground results in a clean job of raking, it tends to create a dust cloud in some fields and may cause some trash and debris to be put into the windrow. Disk shields are desirable in windy conditions to keep hay out of the spokes.

14.26. Analysis of Raking Action for Reel-Type Rakes. In analyzing and discussing both types of rakes, the following general symbols and terms will be used. Others will be identified as needed.

V_p = peripheral velocity of teeth
V_{tr} = *reel component*, which is the average horizontal component of tooth velocity with respect to the rake during the angle of rotation in which the teeth are in contact with the hay
V_f = forward velocity of rake
V_t = *resultant tooth velocity* with respect to the ground, which is the vector sum of V_f and V_{tr}
V_h = *average hay velocity* with respect to the ground as the hay is moved from the swath into the windrow along the *hay path*
V_{hr} = average hay velocity with respect to the rake as the hay is moved along the *raking front*
γ = acute angle between the raking front and the line of forward mo-

tion. With a reel-type rake, the raking front is parallel to the centerline of the reel.

θ_{tr} = *reel-component angle*, which is the angle between V_{tr} and the line of forward motion

θ_t = *resultant tooth-path angle*, which is the angle between V_t and the line of forward motion

β = angle between tooth bars on reel-type rakes

R_{pf} = ratio of tooth peripheral velocity to forward velocity = V_p/V_f

Consider the action of the teeth that rotate in plane *CD*, as indicated in Fig. 14.11. As the reel rotates, the teeth on bar *A* (Fig. 14.11b) start to rake at some angle α_1 from the centerline and continue to move the hay until the vertical clearance is sufficient to allow the teeth to pass over the roll of hay (at angle α_2 in the vertical section and line *EF* on the plan view). The total vertical clearance would then be y_2 plus the height of the teeth above the ground at their lowest point. The effective raking stroke of each tooth is $L_1 + L_2$. The forward motion of the rake during the angle $\alpha_1 + \alpha_2$ is indicated by x_1. After bar *A* drops the hay at *EF*, the reel will continue to rotate through the angle $\beta - \alpha_1 - \alpha_2$ before a tooth on bar *B* contacts the

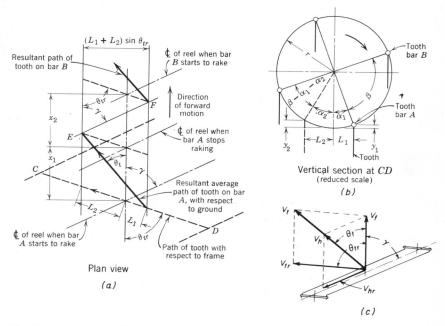

Fig. 14.11. Diagram showing the raking action, effective raking stroke $(L_1 + L_2)$, and velocity relations for reel-type rakes. Relations shown in (c) are typical, for an assumed y_2 of 76 mm [3 in.].

previously moved hay at F. The forward motion during this angle is x_2. If r is the radius of the tooth circle, then, by definition (expressing α_1, α_2, and β in degrees),

$$R_{pf} = \frac{2\pi r(\beta - \alpha_1 - \alpha_2)}{360x_2}$$

from which

$$x_2 = \frac{2\pi r(\beta - \alpha_1 - \alpha_2)}{360R_{pf}} \qquad (14.2)$$

The geometry of Fig. 14.11 indicates that

$$x_2 = L_2 \cos \theta_{tr} + \frac{(L_1 + L_2) \sin \theta_{tr}}{\tan \gamma} + L_1 \cos \theta_{tr}$$

$$= (L_1 + L_2) \left(\cos \theta_{tr} + \frac{\sin \theta_{tr}}{\tan \gamma} \right) \qquad (14.3)$$

Since $L_1 = r \sin \alpha_1$ and $L_2 = r \sin \alpha_2$, it follows that

$$x_2 = r(\sin \alpha_1 + \sin \alpha_2) \left(\cos \theta_{tr} + \frac{\sin \theta_{tr}}{\tan \gamma} \right) \qquad (14.4)$$

Combining equations 14.2 and 14.4 and solving for $\beta - \alpha_1 - \alpha_2$,

$$\frac{2\pi r(\beta - \alpha_1 - \alpha_2)}{360R_{pf}} = r(\sin \alpha_1 + \sin \alpha_2) \left(\cos \theta_{tr} + \frac{\sin \theta_{tr}}{\tan \gamma} \right)$$

$$\beta - \alpha_1 - \alpha_2 = \frac{360}{2\pi} R_{pf}(\sin \alpha_1 + \sin \alpha_2) \left(\cos \theta_{tr} + \frac{\sin \theta_{tr}}{\tan \gamma} \right) \qquad (14.5)$$

Equation 14.5 expresses the relation between rake design parameters and angular displacements α_1 and α_2. To solve this equation (assuming all rake parameters are known) it is convenient to assume a value or values for y_2 and calculate α_2 from the relation, $\cos \alpha_2 = (r - y_2)/r$, after which α_1 can be determined from equation 14.5. In practice, y_2 will vary, depending upon the position along the reel, the size of the hay crop, the stubble height, and the clearance between the reel and the ground. Reasonable values for y_2 might be 25 to 50 mm [1 to 2 in.] at the end of the reel farthest from the windrow and 150 to 200 mm [6 to 8 in.] near the windrow-end of the reel.

Velocity relations are shown in Fig. 14.11c. V_{tr} is parallel to the reel heads and V_f is in the direction of forward travel. V_{tr} will always be less than the peripheral velocity V_p. From distances in 14.11b, the relation is

$$\frac{V_{tr}}{V_p} = \frac{L_1 + L_2}{2\pi r \left(\dfrac{\alpha_1 + \alpha_2}{360} \right)} = \frac{360(\sin \alpha_1 + \sin \alpha_2)}{2\pi(\alpha_1 + \alpha_2)} \qquad (14.6)$$

Since, by definition, $V_p = V_f \times R_{pf}$, it follows that

$$\frac{V_{tr}}{V_f} = \frac{360R_{pf}(\sin \alpha_1 + \sin \alpha_2)}{2\pi(\alpha_1 + \alpha_2)} \qquad (14.7)$$

The relative magnitudes of V_{tr} and V_f (from equation 14.7) determine the resultant tooth-path angle θ_t and permit graphic evaluation of V_{tr} and V_t for a given V_f (Fig. 14.11c). In applying the above equations, care must be given to the algebraic signs of α_1, and L_1. Values of α_1, α_2, L_1, and L_2 are considered positive as shown in Fig. 14.11b. Negative values for α_1 and L_1 indicate that the start of the effective raking stroke is beyond the lowest point of tooth travel.

14.27. Analysis of Raking Action for a Finger-Wheel Rake. The action of one wheel is shown in Fig. 14.12a and velocity relations for a complete rake are shown in Fig. 14.12b. The velocity of the axle in the plane of the wheel is the component V_a of the forward velocity V_f. Since the tips of the teeth are in contact with the ground, causing the wheel to rotate, the peripheral velocity V_p is numerically equal to V_a. The wheel will act upon the hay at some average height y above the ground, with a reel (wheel) component of

$$V_{tr} = \frac{r - y}{r} V_a = V_f \frac{r - y}{r} \cos(180 - \theta_{tr}) \qquad (14.8)$$

where θ_{tr} is expressed in degrees. After assuming a value for y and calculating V_{tr}, the resultant tooth velocity V_t for a given V_f, and the angle θ_t, can be determined graphically as indicated. The direction of V_t is slightly forward of the wheel axis because it represents the path of a point on the

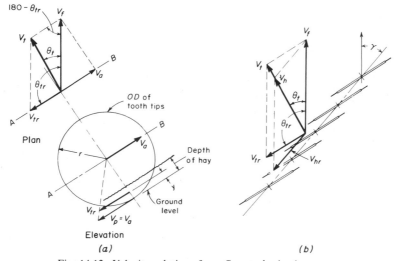

Fig. 14.12. Velocity relations for a finger-wheel rake.

tooth that is above the ground surface.

14.28. Length of Hay Path and Average Hay Velocity. After determining the resultant tooth-path angle θ_t, the theoretical average hay velocity V_h can be determined graphically in relation to the forward velocity V_f, as indicated in Fig. 14.11c and 14.12b. The assumption is made that the hay follows the resultant tooth path. This assumption neglects any effect of the stripper bars in retarding the hay movement along the raking front.

The theoretical maximum length of hay path S_h for moving hay across the full raking width W, along the resultant tooth path is

$$S_h = \frac{W}{\sin \theta_t} \tag{14.9}$$

If field observations indicate that the actual hay-path angle is not the same as θ_t, then the observed hay-path angle should be used in calculating the actual length of hay path and determining the actual average hay velocity.

14.29. Desirable Raking Characteristics. Among the factors to be considered in evaluating or comparing rake performances are the following:

1. Amount of leaf loss due to shattering.
2. Amount of hay missed.
3. Amount of trash, dirt, stones, and other debris put into the windrows.
4. Uniformity and continuity of windrow.
5. Leafy portions should be in the center of the windrow and the stems toward the outside.

Leaf loss is one of the most important considerations, particularly if the hay is a little too dry when raked. Shattering of seed crops such as beans or alfalfa would represent a similar type of loss.

14.30. Rake Design and Operating Parameters that Affect Leaf Shatter. The amount of leaf loss caused by a rake is influenced by such factors as the distance the hay is moved from the swath into the windrow, the average hay velocity, the type of hay-moving action (rolling, lifting, dragging), and any accelerating and decelerating action or periodic impacts of the rake teeth upon the hay as it is being moved. The major factor affecting the average hay velocity is forward speed. High forward speeds increase leaf shatter.

The ratio of the resultant tooth velocity V_t to the average hay velocity V_h is an index of the impacting action. This ratio should be as small as possible, the ideal limit being $V_t/V_h = 1$. It is evident from Fig. 14.11c and 14.12b that the V_t/V_h ratio is somewhat lower for the finger-wheel rake than for the reel-type rake, indicating a smoother, more gentle raking action and probably less leaf shatter.

With a reel-type rake, decreasing the peripheral speed ratio R_{pf} increases the length of hay path slightly but has the desirable effects of reducing the frequency of impacts and decreasing V_t/V_h. Increasing the number of tooth bars decreases α_1 and may slightly decrease V_t/V_h. The V_t/V_h ratio for a finger-wheel rake is minimized by having the individual wheels as nearly parallel with the raking front as is feasible (θ_{tr} nearly equal to 180 $-\gamma$). However, low ratios are less important than with a reel-type rake because of the low frequency of velocity changes. With either type of rake, increasing θ_{tr} decreases V_t/V_h and decreases the hay-path length. Increasing the raking angle γ also decreases V_t/V_h, provided the hay follows the resultant tooth path.

Although the theoretical effects of these parameters can be determined analytically, the relative importance and magnitudes of the effects of the different factors in relation to leaf loss must be determined experimentally. At the present time there is very little reliable published information on the subject.

REFERENCES

1. BARRINGTON, G. P., and H. D. BRUHN. Effect of mechanical forage harvesting devices on field-curing rates and relative harvesting losses. Trans. ASAE, *13*(6):874-878, 1970.
2. BOYD, W. M. Hay conditioning methods compared. Agr. Eng., *40*:664-667, Nov., 1959.
3. BRUHN, H. D. Status of hay crusher development. Agr. Eng., *36*:165-170, Mar., 1955.
4. CASSELMAN, T. W., and R. C. FINCHMAN. How effective are hay conditioners? Iowa Farm Science, *15*(5-6):3-6, Nov.-Dec., 1960.
5. CHANCELLOR, W. J. Energy requirements for cutting forage. Agr. Eng., *39*:633-636, Oct., 1958.
6. CHEN, P. Application of spatial mechanisms to agricultural machinery. Trans. ASAE, *16*(2):214-217, 1973.
7. DOBIE, J. B., J. R. GOSS, R. A. KEPNER, J. H. MEYER, and L. G. JONES. Effect of harvesting procedures on hay quality. Trans. ASAE, *6*(4):301-303, 1963.
8. ELFES, L. E. Design and development of a high-speed mower. Agr. Eng., *35*:147-153, Mar., 1954.
9. FAIRBANKS, G. E., and G. E. THIERSTEIN. Performance of hay-conditioning machines. Trans. ASAE, *9*(2):182-184, 1966.
10. GOSS, J. R., R. A. KEPNER, and L. G. JONES. Hay harvesting with self-propelled windrower compared with mowing and raking. Trans. ASAE, *7*(4):357-361, 1964.
11. HALL, G. E. Flail conditioning of alfalfa and its effect on field losses and drying rates. Trans. ASAE, *7*(4):435-438, 1964.
12. HALYK, R. M., and W. K. BILANSKI. Effects of machine treatments on the field drying of hay. Canadian Agr. Eng., *8*:28-30, Feb., 1966.
13. HARBAGE, R. P., and R. V. MORR. Development and design of a ten-foot mower. Agr. Eng., *43*:208-211, 219, Apr., 1962.
14. HODGSON, R. E., et al. Comparative efficiency of ensiling, barn curing, and field curing forage crops. Agr. Eng., *28*:154-156, Apr., 1947.
15. HUNDTOFT, E. B. Extension and research cooperate in evaluating forage harvesting systems. ASAE Paper 65-635, Dec., 1965.
16. JOHNSTON, R. C. R. Crop behavior during mowing. J. Agr. Eng. Res., *4*:193-203, 1959.
17. KEPNER, R. A. Analysis of the cutting action of a mower. Agr. Eng., *33*:693-697, 704, Nov., 1952.

18. KEPNER, R. A., J. R. GOSS, J. H. MEYER, and L. G. JONES. Evaluation of hay conditioning effects. Agr. Eng., 41:299-304, May, 1960.
19. KJELGAARD, W. L. Flail mower-conditioners: their place in forage harvest. Agr. Eng., 47:202, Apr., 1966.
20. KLINNER, W. E. A trial to determine the hay yields obtained by using conventional haymaking machinery and flail-type forage harvesters. J. Agr. Eng. Res., 6:315-318, 1961.
21. MILNE, C. M. Mechanical hay conditioning. Maine Agr. Expt. Sta. Bull. 590, 1960.
22. PEDERSEN, T. T., and W. F. BUCHELE. Drying rate of alfalfa hay. Agr. Eng., 41:86-89, 107-108, Feb., 1960.
23. PRIEPKE, E. H., and H. D. BRUHN. Altering physical characteristics of alfalfa to increase the drying rate. Trans. ASAE, 13(6):827-831, 1970.
24. PRINCE, R. P., W. C. WHEELER, and D. A. FISHER. Discussion on "Energy requirements for cutting forage." Agr. Eng., 39:638-639, 652, Oct., 1958.
25. RANEY, R. R. Vibration control in farm machinery. Unpublished paper. International Harvester Co., 1946.
26. ZACHARIAH, P. J., K. C. ELLIOTT, and R. A. PHILLIPS. Performance of forage crushers. West Virginia Agr. Expt. Sta. Bull. 418, 1958.
27. ZIMMERMAN, M. I & T rounds up the fast-rolling mower-conditioner market. Implement & Tractor, 83(12):30-33, May 21, 1968.

PROBLEMS

14.1. (a) How much water must be removed to obtain 1 Mg of cured hay at 20% moisture content (wet basis), starting with green hay at 75% moisture content?

(b) What percentage of this amount is removed in the swath if the hay is raked at 45% moisture content?

14.2. Consider a mower with dimensions indicated in Fig. 14.6, operating at a crank speed of 1000 r/min. Assume sinusoidal motion of the knife. Calculate:

(a) Crank angles from beginning of stroke, for start and finish of cutting.

(b) Percent of stroke during which cutting occurs.

(c) Percent of forward travel during which cutting occurs.

(d) Maximum velocity of knife, in metres per second (with respect to ledger plate).

(e) Knife velocities at start and finish of cutting.

14.3. Repeat parts (c) and (e) in Problem 14.2, assuming the same guard spacing and the same dimensions for the ledger plates and knife sections, but with a 66-mm knife stroke. Compare with results obtained in Problem 14.2 for a 76.2-mm stroke.

14.4. A mower operating at a crank speed of 1000 r/min has S = 240 mm; L = 1.06 m; R = 38 mm (see Fig. 14.7); knife mass = 4.4 kg; pitman mass = 3.4 kg, with center of gravity 0.48 m from crank end; crankpin mass = 0.35 kg. Calculate:

(a) ϕ_c and ϕ_p at each end of stroke (see Fig. 14.7 for reference position in which ϕ_c =0).

(b) Inertia force F_h at each end of stroke.

(c) Magnitude and direction of F_v at each end of stroke.

14.5. Measurements on a four-bar oblique reel-head rake gave R_{pf} = 1.48, θ_{tr} = 87°, γ = 65°, and r = 290 mm.

(a) Assuming y_2 = 150 mm, calculate α_1, α_2, and V_{tr}/V_p .

(b) Calculate V_{tr}/V_v and determine graphically the values of the resultant tooth-path angle θ_t and the velocity ratio V_t/V_h.

15

Packaging and
Handling Hay

15.1. Introduction. In general, hay is handled from the field as bales, cubes or wafers, chopped hay, or long loose hay. Baling and cubing or wafering are essentially packaging operations performed to facilitate handling, transport, and storing. Densities of baled hay generally range from 130 to 225 kg/m³ [8 to 14 lb/ft³], the higher values being for wire-tied bales. Cubes usually have a bulk density of 400 to 480 kg/m³ [25 to 30 lb/ft³]. The commonly accepted value for long loose hay (not mechanically compressed during stacking) is 65 kg/m³ [4 lb/ft³].

Field baling is a high-capacity, flexible, one-man operation with relatively low harvest losses. Over 80% of the United States hay crop has been baled each year since about 1960. Conventional field balers typically make bales having masses from 20 to 70 kg [40 to 150 lb]. Equipment is available for complete mechanical handling of conventional bales from the field into the stack or onto a commercial truck, but large annual productions are necessary for economic justification of the more sophisticated types of handling equipment. A considerable amount of hard, hand labor is still required where the production is too small to justify fully mechanized bale-handling equipment.

Field balers that can produce bales having a mass of 700 to 1400 kg [1500 to 3000 lb] are commercially available. These large bales must always be handled mechanically, but handling can be done with a relatively simple fork-lift attachment for the three-point hitch on a tractor or with a modified front-end loader.

Cubing requires a large investment in equipment and is the most expensive of all hay-handling systems, but the product flows by gravity and can be handled mechanically in bulk. Cubes are well-suited to fully mechanized, push-button storage and feeding systems, using conventional types of conveyors and elevators. Special storage facilities may be required but the volume is less than half that of baled hay. Because an extremely low moisture content (10 to 12%, or less) is necessary for cubing, this method of packaging is limited primarily to arid and semiarid areas in the western states. Cubes have given improved feeding response in comparison with baled hay, with very little waste.

Long loose hay and chopped hay are handled without packaging. Chopping, which accounts for less than 5% of the hay crop, is discussed in Chapter 16. The percentage of the hay crop handled in the long loose form decreased from about 30% in 1951 to 10% in 1961 and 7% in 1967.[10] The long loose method is employed to the greatest extent in areas where weather permits unprotected stack storage and for low-value wild hay crops. Somewhat higher storage moisture contents can be tolerated than with baled hay. Handling and storing hay in the long loose form involves the least investment in equipment. Some methods require considerable hand labor, but high-capacity equipment is available for mechanized handling on large areas. Long loose hay is usually fed locally because its low density makes transportation costly. Self-feeding from scattered small stacks is practical.

15.2. Handling Long Loose Hay. Hay is often gathered, moved short distances, and stacked with sweep rakes (also known as hay baskets or buck stackers) attached to the framework of a high-lift, front-end loader on a tractor.[14] A sweep rake has long, flexible teeth of selected wood or high-strength steel that slide under a windrow or a small stack of hay. High-lift, tractor-mounted stackers sometimes have hydraulic-powered hay push-off devices rather than requiring the teeth to be tilted downward for unloading.

Van-type stack-forming wagons (trailers) with windrow pickup devices have become increasingly popular since the late 1960s in areas where the hay is fed locally. The pickup unit impels and blows the hay into the wagon. When the wagon is full, a telescoping, rounded canopy top is forced down hydraulically to compress the load. One or more intermediate compression operations may be done at different stages of the loading operation. Unloading as a stack unit is accomplished by raising the canopy, lowering the tailgate, activating a PTO-driven chain-and-slat conveyor, and easing slowly forward as the stack is conveyed out. The sides flare out slightly from front to rear to facilitate unloading. Capacities are mostly in the range from 1.8 to 7.2 Mg [2 to 8 tons]. Densities (calculated from manufacturers' data, presumably for alfalfa) are usually 80 to 100 kg/m^3 [5 to 6 lb/ft^3].[15] The smoothly rounded top and the moderately compressed condition tend to make the stacks more weather resistant than stacks built by hand or with sweep rakes.

Special tilt-bed trucks and tractor-pulled trailers are available for moving loose-hay stacks. A PTO-driven series of parallel drag chains on longitudinal beams, or a chain-and-slat conveyor on the bed, moves the stack onto the tilted bed as the truck or trailer is backed under the stack. The speeds of the conveyor and the rearward motion of the stack mover are synchronized so that the stack is lifted without any appreciable fore-and-aft displacement. The reverse procedure is followed when unloading. Capacities range from 5 to 14 Mg [6 to 15 tons]. Long-distance hauling is not economical.[3]

CONVENTIONAL BALERS

15.3. Types and Sizes. Current models of conventional field balers are automatic-tying machines with reciprocating plungers that produce bales having rectangular cross sections. About 15% of the balers sold in 1968 and 1969 were automatic-wire-tying models and 85% were twine-tying models. Low-cost balers forming rolled, round bales wrapped with twine and weighing 23 to 32 kg [50 to 70 lb] were commercially available in the 1950s but are no longer manufactured.

Conventional balers are commonly identified as to size by the number of wires or twines placed around each bale. Most balers now have 36 × 46-cm [14 × 18-in.] or 41 × 46-cm [16 × 18-in.] bale chambers (cross-sectional dimensions) and make bales 91 to 102 cm [36 to 40 in.] long with 2 wires or 2 twines per bale. A few models, however, have 41 × 58-cm [16 × 23-in.] or 43 × 56-cm [17 × 22-in.] bale chambers and produce 3-wire (or sometimes 3-twine) bales 114 to 122 cm [45 to 48 in.] long that weigh 57 to 68 kg [125 to 150 lb]. With either 2-tie or 3-tie machines, cross tying of bales in stacking is facilitated by having the length approximately twice the width.

The principal use of three-wire balers is in the western states, in areas where a high percentage of the hay is sold and transported commercially. Smaller, 2-tie bales, weighing 23 to 36 kg [50 to 80 lb], are preferred in most other areas because they are easier to handle.

Although most field balers are pull-type machines, self-propelled models are also available. Self-propelled models provide better visibility and maneuverability but require higher annual use to justify their greater first cost. A means of varying the forward speed, independent of the baler drive speed, is desirable for flexibility in accommodating heavy and light windrows. Some self-propelled models have hydrostatic propulsion drives or two engines. Pull-type models are available with either a PTO drive or a mounted engine. The current trend is toward an increasing percentage of PTO drives because of the availability of larger tractors.

15.4. Functional Components. A plunger-type field baler includes the following functional components.

1. A unit to pick up hay from the windrow and elevate it.
2. A conveyor to move the hay to the bale-chamber entry.
3. Packers to place the hay in the chamber while the plunger is on its retracted stroke.
4. A reciprocating plunger to compress the hay and move it through the bale chamber.
5. Means for applying forces to resist the movement of hay through the bale chamber and thus control the degree of hay compression and the resultant bale density.

6. An automatic metering device for controlling bale length.
7. A means of separating consecutive bales and placing the wires or strings around each bale.
8. Automatic tying devices that operate when the bale reaches the preselected length.

15.5. Windrow Pickup, Conveying, and Feeding Devices. Most field balers employ cylinder-type pickup units with spring teeth on cam-controlled tooth bars (Fig. 15.1 and 15.2). The height is controlled either by suspension from the machine or with a gage wheel (Fig. 15.1). Counterbalance springs support most of the pickup mass. The pickup cylinder is usually driven from the engine or PTO, rather than from a ground wheel. The peripheral speed must be greater than the maximum forward speed normally encountered.

Many different arrangements are employed to move the hay from the pickup device into the bale chamber. One system has a floating cross-conveyor auger, and packer fingers timed to push hay into the chamber while the plunger is on its retracting stroke (Fig. 15.1). Other arrangements have combined cross conveyors and packers, with fingers that move back and forth across the feed table in various motion patterns, sometimes including vertical and/or rotary components. The fingers in the upper part of Fig. 15.2 are shown part way through the feed stroke. They raise up on the return stroke to clear incoming hay and then drop down as they begin to move toward the bale chamber.

Some models have fingers projecting downward from a carriage that moves back and forth across the feed table on a horizontal track. The fingers are hinged so they lift up and drag over the top of hay on the return stroke but are held approximately vertical on the feed stroke. Another system has a horizontally moving sweep fork on an arm pivoted on the baler main frame

Fig. 15.1. A field baler having a floating-auger cross conveyor. Packer fingers place the hay in the bale chamber. (Courtesy of Deere & Co.)

Fig. 15.2. Pickup unit and finger-type combined cross conveyor and packer. (Courtesy of Sperry New Holland.)

at a location forward from the bale-chamber feed opening. The fork moves the hay in a circular path from the pickup device into the bale chamber. Hinged fingers lift up and drag over the top of the incoming hay on the return stroke.

A properly functioning feed mechanism should distribute the hay charge across the bale chamber in such a manner that the resulting bale density is reasonably uniform across the bale width and height. Packer fingers may need to enter the bale chamber farther for light windrows and low baling rates than for heavy loads.

15.6. Compressing Hay and Controlling Bale Density. As the plunger moves on its compression stroke, each new hay charge is compressed until the plunger force becomes large enough to move the completed and partly formed bales along the chamber. On the return stroke of the plunger, the compressed hay is held by fixed wedges and by spring-loaded dogs that project into the bale chamber. Plunger speeds on current models are usually between 65 and 80 cycles per minute, with a trend toward higher speeds.

The density of the bales is primarily a function of the type of material, its moisture content, and the total resistance that the plunger must overcome in moving the material through the bale chamber (and up the bale chute if a trailer is used). The resistance must be adjustable to accommodate different materials and conditions. Fixed wedges may be added or removed to obtain large changes in resistance, but the principal method of controlling bale density is by squeezing together 2 sides or all 4 sides of the bale chamber at the discharge end. This convergence of the bale-chamber sides, which is adjustable, causes the hay to be compressed laterally as it moves through the chamber.

If one assumes that hay behaves as an elastic material, the portion, F_c, of the plunger force that is due to convergence of the sides may be expressed as

$$F_c = E\frac{y}{D}(2LW)\mu \qquad (15.1)$$

where E = modulus of elasticity of the hay (lateral compressive pressure divided by unit lateral deflection)

y = average lateral deflection over the length of the converging section (horizontal or vertical)

D = average depth of converging section (in the direction of deflection)

L = length of converging section

W = width of converging section (perpendicular to the direction of deflection)

μ = coefficient of friction between hay and bale-chamber sides

Ey/D is the lateral pressure on each converging side and $2LW$ is the total area of the 2 opposing, converging sides. If all 4 sides converge, as in Fig. 15.3 *left*, each pair of sides is considered independently and the two F_c values are added.

In addition to the adjustable component F_c, the total plunger force required to move the hay includes nonadjustable components due to friction on the bottom of the entire chamber resulting from the force of gravity on the hay, the effects of wedges, etc. To accommodate a wide range of conditions, the adjustable resistance should be large in comparison with the fixed resistance. Although equation 15.1 may not accurately portray the conditions in the converging section, it does give an indication of the variables involved.

One of the problems encountered in baling hay is the change of bale density as the moisture content varies from one part of the field to another, or as it changes with time. According to Raney,[21] this is because dry materials have a considerably lower modulus of elasticity and a lower coefficient of friction than do materials with a higher moisture content, and thus require more deflection of the sides to produce a given resistance force. Burrough and Graham[5] demonstrated with alfalfa that, although part of the increase in density with increased moisture content at a given adjustment is due to the additional water, the amount of dry matter per bale is also considerably greater. They also found that for a given adjustment there was an appreciable increase in density as the baling rate was increased.

When coil springs are employed as the so-called tension-control device (Fig. 15.3 *right*), the springs permit some increase in deflection if the modulus of elasticity is reduced, but the lateral force decreases, thereby reducing F_c and bale density.

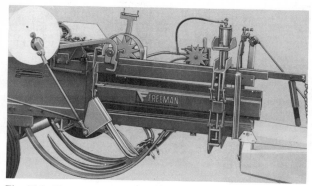

Fig. 15.3. Two types of bale tension (density) control devices. *Left:* Automatically controlled hydraulic type. (Courtesy of J. A Freeman & Son.) *Right:* Spring type. (Courtesy of International Harvester Co.)

A hydraulic tension control employs a single hydraulic cylinder to replace the two springs, as in Fig. 15.3 *left.* In most cases the hydraulic pressure is constant (but is adjustable from the operator's station) so that lateral pressure for a given adjustment is essentially uniform at all deflections. Such a system overcomes the effects of changes in the modulus of elasticity of the hay but does not compensate for any changes in the coefficient of friction. Nation[18] maintained a constant hydraulic pressure while baling a clover-ryegrass mixture at moisture contents from 15 to 49% and found that the density on a dry-matter basis remained fairly constant at about 96 kg/m³ [6 lb/ft³]. These results suggest that the coefficient of friction did not change much with this particular kind of hay.

The device shown in Fig. 15.3 *left* is designed to automatically adjust the hydraulic pressure to maintain a more uniform bale density. The cylinder pressure is controlled by a spring-loaded star wheel that runs in contact with the bale, the points penetrating to a greater or lesser depth depending upon the bale density. If the density increases, for example, the wheel is moved outward and operates a control valve to automatically reduce the oil pressure in the cylinder. Note that this model squeezes all four sides together by means of a mechanical, interconnecting linkage.

15.7. Bale Separation and Tying Systems. The plunger has a knife on the leading edge of the side toward the feeder opening (visible in Fig. 15.1 and 15.2) that acts in conjunction with a stationary ledger plate to completely separate successive hay charges by slicing. The slicing facilitates the breaking up of bales for feeding livestock and provides separation between bales in the chamber. When a bale has reached the desired length, the needles of the automatic-tying devices pass through slots in the plunger face while the plunger holds the hay in the compressed position.

The usual method of controlling bale length with an automatic baler is by means of a wheel with pointed projections around its periphery that is rotated by contact with the bale in the chamber (the left-hand star wheel in Fig. 15.3 *left*). When the material in the chamber has moved through the predetermined bale length, the metering device engages the drive clutch for the tying unit. The cycle does not begin, however, until the plunger reaches the proper position for correct timing between the needles and the plunger. At the usual plunger crank speed, the complete cycle, including needle travel, takes place in about ½ s. Uniformity of bale length is inversely related to the amount of hay compressed per plunger stroke, since each bale must contain a whole number of charges.

Wire-tied bales are tighter and more durable than bales tied with sisal twine and, for this reason, are favored where hay is sold and must be handled several times. Twine bales are looser and more tolerant of high moisture contents. Twine is not injurious to livestock and is easier to dispose of than is wire. Tests have indicated an average twine requirement of about 1.5 kg/Mg of hay [3 lb/ton].[23] Calculated wire requirements for normal sizes of 2-wire and 3-wire bales, assuming a density of 190 kg/m³ [12 lb/ft³] are about 4 kg/Mg [8 lb/ton].

Plastic (polypropylene) twine was developed in the late 1960s. Plastic twine is said to be about as strong as wire, but it is not rodent proof. It is intermediate between wire and sisal twine in cost per megagram of hay. Plastic twine does not rot but cannot be disposed of by burning. It is more uniform in diameter than is sisal twine, which is an advantage in regard to knotter performance. Plastic twine tends to be used more as an alternate for wire than as a replacement for sisal twine.

ASAE standards have been adopted for twine and for wire. These include specifications for ball or coil lengths, strengths, packaging, wire diameter, etc. Minimum tensile strengths for twine (material not specified) are 445, 667, 890, and 1112 N [100, 150, 200, and 250 lbf] for classes identified as light, medium, heavy, and extra heavy, respectively. Average strengths generally are considerably higher than these minimums. Baling wire is to have a tensile strength of 345 to 483 MPa [50,000 to 70,000 psi] and a diameter of 1.93 mm ± 0.05 mm [0.076 in. ± 0.002 in.]. These specifications represent total strengths of 1000 to 1420 N [225 to 320 lbf].

15.8. Automatic Twine-Tying Devices. The tying units on twine balers are the same in principle as those used for many years on grain binders. Figure 15.4 shows the basic components of a typical knotter. In the left-hand view, the needle has just brought the twine around the bale and placed it in the twine holder. The two outside disks of the holder now rotate through the angle between adjacent notches while the center disk remains stationary, thus pinching the twine between the spring-loaded disks and holding it as the needle withdraws. In the right-hand view, the knotter-bill assembly has

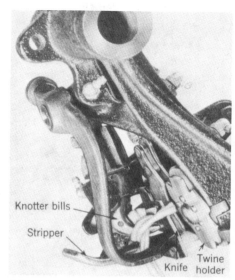

Fig. 15.4. Two views of a twine knotter head from an automatic baler. (Courtesy of International Harvester Co.)

rotated almost one turn to form a loop in the string, around the knotter bills. As the knotter-bill assembly rotates farther, the bills close over the strings held by the twine holder. Then the stripper moves forward to pull the loop off of the bills over the ends held between them, and the knife attached to the stripper arm cuts the twine.

An automatic-tying system, whether twine or wire, is a complex mechanism requiring careful adjustment and proper timing of the parts, together with adequate maintenance and replacement of worn parts.

15.9. Automatic Wire-Tying Devices. Two types of wire twisters are shown in Fig. 15.5. Each type has a clamping device that holds the end of the wire which passes from the supply coil, through the eye of the retracted needle, and around the bale being formed. When the needle has almost reached its extreme penetration position during the tying cycle, the clamping device is moved to (a) release the wire end that had been held during the bale formation, (b) shear the wire just brought in by the needle, and (c) clamp the wire from the needle, which will become the held end for the next bale. The loop-twist type has a rotating, double-disk-type holder and cutoff, visible just above the loop. The straight-twist type has an oscillating shear-and-clamp unit that alternately moves from one side to the other for successive cycles and is located behind the label, "No. 3 wire."

The twister hook of either device starts to rotate as the shearing-clamping action is taking place, and continues to turn through several revolutions af-

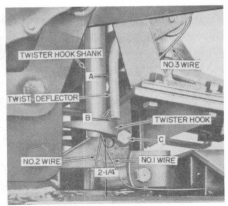

Fig. 15.5. Two types of wire twisters. *Left:* Looped twist. (Courtesy of International Harvester Co.) *Right:* Straight twist. (Courtesy of Sperry New Holland.)

ter the two ends have been released. A deflector prevents the ends from rotating with the twister hook. In the loop-twist type, the deflector causes the ends to be bent over the hook, whereas in the straight-twist type the twist deflector merely holds the ends close to the twister-hook shank. Movement of the tied bale toward the rear has just pulled the loop off of the hook in Fig. 15.5 *left*. Bale movement will pull the twisted ends of the wire down past the hook in Fig. 15.5 *right* after the twisting has been completed.

15.10. Baler Capacities. Some of the machine characteristics that affect the capacity of the baler are (a) the size of the bales, (b) the number of plunger strokes per minute, (c) capacity limitations of the pickup and feed mechanisms, (d) the amount of power available, and (e) the durability and reliability of the machine. Important operating factors include (a) size and uniformity of windrows, (b) the condition of the field surface, insofar as it limits the forward speed, (c) the condition of the hay, (d) the density of the bales, and (e) the skill of the operator.

It should be apparent from a consideration of the above items that baling capacities can vary widely. Maximum capacities claimed by manufacturers usually range from 14 to 18 Mg [15 to 20 tons] of hay per hour (sometimes higher). These capacities presumably are based on machine limitations. Often, however, overall averages are controlled by windrow size, speed limitations because of field conditions, and field efficiency (lost time). For example, if the yield were 2.8 Mg/ha [1¼ tons per acre], a windrow spacing of 8.0 m [26.4 ft] would be required to average 11 Mg/h [12 tons/h] at 6.5 km/h [4 mph] with a field efficiency of 75%.

The National Institute of Agricultural Engineering tested 7 models of 36 × 46-cm [14 × 18-in.] balers in England in 1964 and obtained maximum continuous hay outputs of 11 to 16.3 Mg/h [12 to 18 tons/h].[23] Short-time sustained rates as high as 18 to 22 Mg/h [20 to 24 tons/h] were recorded. A survey of 180 users indicated overall averages of 4.5 to 7.3 Mg/h [5 to 8 tons/h]. Von Bargen[24] reported seasonal averages of 5.1 to 7.0 Mg/h [5.6 to 7.7 tons/h] for four 41 × 46-cm [16 × 18-in.] self-propelled balers in Nebraska during 1963, 1964, and 1965 and a maximum down-the-windrow capacity of just under 14.5 Mg/h [16 tons/h].

15.11. Power Requirements. In the NIAE tests,[23] PTO power requirements for the 7 balers in hay represented energy inputs of 0.69 kW·h/Mg [0.84 hp-h/ton] for 3 balers at an average maximum feed rate* of 20.6 Mg/h [22.7 tons/h] and 0.90 kW·h/Mg [1.10 hp-h/ton] for 4 balers at an average maximum feed rate of 12.7 Mg/h [14.0 tons/h]. The type of hay and moisture content were not given. Burrough and Graham,[5] in 1953, determined power inputs to the various components of an automatic twine-tying baler over a rather wide range of conditions but with maximum feed rates of only about 5 Mg/h [5½ tons/h]. Figure 15.6 shows the relation between average plunger power requirements and feed rate for four crop conditions, as well as the total power required by all other baler components. These curves indicate that total power requirements increase less rapidly than the feed rate. For alfalfa at 23% moisture, the total energy requirements were 1.9 kW·h/Mg [2.3 hp-h/ton] at 2.3 Mg/h [2½ tons/h] and 1.2 kW·h/Mg [1.5 hp-h/ton] at 4.5 Mg/h [5 tons/h].

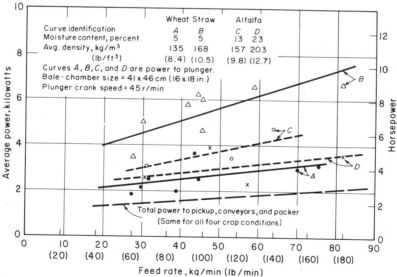

Fig. 15.6. Relation of average power requirements to baling rate. (Data from J. A. Graham. Unpublished thesis. Purdue University, 1953.)

---

*Feed rate is defined as the rate at which material enters the baler during the actual operating time (i.e., at 100% field efficiency).

Comparison of curves *A* and *B* indicates that with the rather dry wheat straw the plunger power requirements were about doubled when the bale density was increased by only 25%, from 135 to 168 kg/m³ [8.4 to 10.5 lb/ft³]. Curve *D* shows the plunger power requirements for alfalfa at 23% moisture content, which is about the upper moisture limit for safe storage of this crop. At this moisture content, the effect of bale density upon power requirements was much less than with the dry straw.

In another series of tests, using alfalfa and adjusting the density to maintain a constant amount of dry matter per bale, the plunger power requirements increased as the moisture content was reduced. The effect was most pronounced at low moisture contents, with very little change above 20 to 25% moisture.

Figure 15.7 shows the relation of plunger-face or press-plate force to plunger displacement for two feed rates, as determined by Burrough and Graham.[5] These curves are actually work diagrams for compressing the hay and moving the bales through the chamber, the area under each curve representing the total work involved. The two curves are similar except that compression starts later with the smaller hay charge and the peak force is lower. Peak forces as high as 76 kN [17,000 lbf] were encountered when baling wheat straw at 5% moisture. The small peaks in the vicinity of 300 to 400 mm displacement (Fig. 15.7) are due to shearing of the hay charge by

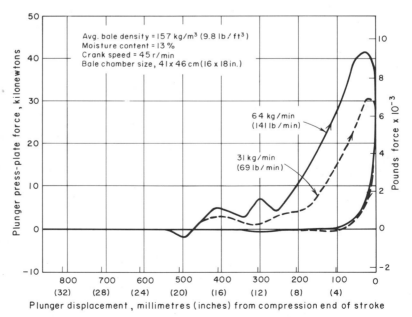

Fig. 15.7. Plunger work diagrams for two feed rates in alfalfa. Plunger friction and inertia forces are not included. (D.E. Burrough and J.A. Graham.[5])

the knife on the plunger. Their magnitude and location will vary for different baler models, usually occurring later than on the particular baler tested. Otherwise, these work diagrams can be applied to other balers by making proper allowances for bale-chamber size and crank speed.[5]

From the work diagram, plus plunger friction and inertia forces, one can determine the relation of crank torque to crank angle. Consideration of crank speed then yields plunger power as plotted in Fig. 15.6. Burrough and Graham found in their tests that the peak plunger power requirements during the compression part of the stroke were about 8 to 12 times the average plunger power when baling wheat straw at 5% moisture (curves A and B), and 7 to 9 times the average for alfalfa at 23% moisture (curve D). These peak requirements are supplied primarily from kinetic energy made available by slow-down of the baler flywheel.

The two curves in Fig. 15.7 indicate a moderate increase in peak plunger force when the feed rate was doubled. Nation[18] observed a similar effect when the feed rate was increased with a clover-ryegrass mixture.

15.12. Overload Protection. Protection is needed for the plunger and drive system because of the possibility of occasional extreme overloads from picking up foreign objects or slugs of hay, variations in hay moisture content, careless operation, or other factors. A common arrangement is a shear bolt in the drive between the flywheel and the plunger.

An automatic plunger latch is desirable to stop the plunger on its compression stroke if some malfunction has caused the needles to fail to withdraw from the chamber. The needle drive moves the spring-loaded latch into the potential latching position each time the needles enter the chamber and retracts the latch as the needles leave the chamber. The plunger stops if it strikes the latch, causing the flywheel shear bolt to fail.

A PTO-driven baler needs a friction slip clutch between the PTO shaft and the flywheel to limit the magnitude of peak torques caused by the plunger on each compression stroke (Fig. 3.18). Momentary slipping of the clutch allows the baler flywheel to slow down, thereby providing kinetic energy to meet the peak demand. An overrunning (free-wheeling) clutch is also needed in a PTO drive so the baler flywheel will not tend to propel the tractor if the engine speed is suddenly reduced without disengaging the PTO clutch.

The pickup-cylinder drive is usually protected by a slip clutch. Various types of load-limiting arrangements are employed on feed mechanisms. Additional protective devices sometimes employed include a shear pin in the drive to the tying mechanism and a device that releases if the needles strike an obstruction.

HANDLING CONVENTIONAL BALES

A wide range of equipment combinations is available for handling bales from the field into storage. Some systems offer complete mechanization with high capacities but large investments in equipment. Other systems employ relatively inexpensive equipment, making them more suitable for small areas, but require hand labor in varying amounts. The type of storage also influences the choice of system. Lack of standardization of bale sizes complicates mechanized bale handling. The most common systems are discussed in the following sections.

15.13. Bale Loaders and Bale Chutes. An early approach to the problem of reducing the hard work of handling bales by hand was the development, in the 1940s, of bale loaders for attachment to trucks or flat-rack wagons. Such a loader has its own support wheels and a gasoline engine or ground-wheel drive to operate the elevating conveyor. The loader is temporarily attached along one side of the truck or wagon through links that propel the loader and maintain its orientation with respect to the truck or wagon (a semimounted arrangement). Bales are picked up and elevated to an adjustable height as the vehicle moves along in the field. One or two men on the wagon stack the hay by hand, usually a layer at a time (increasing the delivery height as the load is built up). A similar elevator can be used for stacking at the storage site. The bale loader is relatively inexpensive, but a considerable amount of hand labor is still required.

Another system that has been used for many years involves a flat-rack wagon trailed behind the baler and a bale-chute extension so the baler can push the bales onto the wagon. As with a bale loader, the bales must be stacked on the wagon by hand and unloaded onto an elevator by hand at the storage site. Field studies have shown that trailing a wagon reduces the field efficiency of the baling operation.

15.14. Bale Throwers. Bale-throwing attachments for balers became commercially available in 1957.[25] They are fairly popular in the eastern states, especially for relatively small areas where bales are stored in the hay mow and fed on the same farm.[14]

A bale thrower tosses each bale from the baler into a trailing wagon that has high sides and sometimes has a bottom conveyor for mechanical unloading. The throwing distance is adjustable from the tractor driver's position to facilitate random filling of the wagon without hand labor. At the farmstead the bales are unloaded onto a conventional or vertical elevator and dropped into the mow in a random distribution or are hand stacked. The random stacking is adaptable to artificial drying but requires more storage volume than tight stacking. One man is needed at the wagon to position bales on the horizontal section of the elevator. Most bale throwers are designed for 36 × 46-cm [14 × 18-in.] balers. Bales are often made shorter than for conventional handling, with lengths of 61 to 81 cm [24 to 32 in.] and masses of 18 to 27 kg [40 to 60 lb].

One common type of bale thrower has 2 upward-inclined flat conveyor belts that operate continuously at maximum speeds of 10 to 13 m/s [2000 to

2500 ft/min] and contact the top and bottom surfaces of the bale being thrown. Another similar arrangement has 3 fluted rubber rolls below the bale and 3 on top of it. Power is usually obtained from the baler flywheel or some other convenient drive component. Throwing distance is controlled by a variable-speed V-belt drive. A separate engine may be employed.

Some bale throwers have intermittently operating throwing arms, pans, or toothed conveyors that are actuated when the bale contacts a trip lever. Power may be obtained from the plunger or crank on the plunger return stroke or from a rotary shaft in the baler drive system. One model[22] has a throwing pan that is automatically actuated by a hydraulic cylinder in an open-center system. The hydraulic pump is driven from the baler flywheel and the throwing distance is controllable from the tractor operator's position by adjusting the relief pressure.

Bale throwers are attached to the baler through a pivot axis so the horizontal direction can be controlled on turns. In some cases the direction is controlled automatically by connecting a guide lever to the wagon tongue. In other models the operator controls the direction from the tractor seat, either hydraulically or electrically.

15.15. Automatic Bale Wagons. Automatic bale wagons were developed in the late 1950s and are now widely used in the large hay-producing areas of the western and midwestern states. Their high first cost makes them economically impractical for small areas. Pull-type models having load capacities of 2.3 to 3.2 Mg [2½ to 3½ tons] cost only one-half to one-fourth as much as self-propelled models with capacities of 3.2 to 4.5 Mg [3½ to 5 tons]. These machines pick up individual bales in the field, automatically stack them on the wagon, and unload them mechanically, thus eliminating all hand labor. Some models can deposit the load only as a stacked unit, but others can also unload a bale at a time. Single-bale unloading is convenient for bunk feeding and for storage in a mow.

Where field conditions permit, self-propelled models can pick up bales at speeds as great as 16 to 24 km/h [10 to 15 mph], handling as much as 14 to 18 Mg [15 to 20 tons] of 3-wire bales per hour when stacking at the edge of the field.

Figure 15.8 shows three stages in the loading cycle for one type of automatic bale wagon. A pull-type model is shown, but self-propelled models of the same type are available. When the pickup deposits the second bale on the front table, a trip lever is actuated that causes the table to tip up (center view) and place the bales on the second table. Succeeding pairs push the first bales rearward on the second table. When the second table is fully loaded, it is automatically tipped up (right-hand view) to place a row of bales on the load rack. The two upright forks shown at the front of the load rack are pushed rearward as rows of bales are added. Hydraulic power on pull-type units is obtained from a pump driven by the tractor PTO.

Fig. 15.8. Three stages in the loading cycle for one type of automatic bale wagon. (Courtesy of Sperry New Holland.)

Unloading as a stack unit is accomplished by upending the loaded rack and driving forward to pull the rear forks out from under the load resting on the ground. Self-propelled units have hydraulic push-off devices to assist in withdrawing the forks without disturbing the stack. Single-bale unloading is accomplished with an arrangement that permits moving the bales forward on the load rack and discharging them, one tier at a time, onto the slightly tilted second table. The second table has a cross conveyor that removes end-to-end bales, a pair at a time. Stack retrieval is possible with some pull-type models. Independent, truck-mounted stack retrievers are available. These squeeze the bottom of the stack and have prongs that penetrate and clamp down on the top layers.

An automatic bale wagon employing a different stacking and unloading method was first used commercially in 1970. The self-propelled machine stacks the bales flat, from the bed up, a layer at a time. A stacking cage orients the bales on each layer and is lifted automatically as the layer is completed. An inclined elevator delivers bales from the pickup to the stacking cage. Any layer or layers selected by the operator can have the bales arranged in a different pattern to provide cross tying. Three-wire bales form a "package" approximately 2.4 m by 2.4 m [8 ft by 8 ft] by 7 bales high.

The completed load is moved to the rear of the stacking frame with a squeeze-type fork lift arrangement that is part of the machine. The load can be placed directly on a commercial transport truck or can be stacked on the ground, up to two loads high. Stack retrieval and truck unloading are also possible. This type of machine is more versatile than self-propelled models of the type shown in Fig. 15.8, but the new cost is substantially greater.

15.16. Automatic Bale Accumulators. A system was developed in the early 1960s that permits mechanical handling of bales in single-layer groups of eight. The basic components of this system are an automatic bale accumulator attached to the rear of the baler, a tractor-mounted grapple-fork arrangement to pick up the eight-bale groups, and a flat-bed wagon sized to accommodate the bale groups.[13]

The automatic bale accumulator is a low trailer supported by two caster wheels and attached behind the baler in a semimounted manner so it steers directly with the baler. As bales come onto the bed from the bale chute, a hydraulically powered push-over bar automatically moves pairs of end-to-end bales toward one side until eight bales are accumulated. A push-off bar on 2 conveyor chains then eases the group of bales off of the rear end of the trailer, which is perhaps 300 mm [12 in.] above the ground. The conveyor speed should be synchronized with the forward speed to keep the bale group tight. Hydraulic power for the push-over bar and the unloading conveyor is obtained from a separate pump powered by the baler or the tractor PTO.

The bale fork mounts on a general-purpose front-end tractor loader, preferably a high-lift type. To pick up a load, the frame of the bale fork is placed on top of the bales and two grapple hooks are forced into each bale hydraulically by rotating them about transverse axes just above the bales. A push plate across the rear permits initial tightening of the group by forward motion of the tractor and provides proper orientation between the bales and the fork. The bale fork may be used to load wagons, unload, stack, or remove from a stack. Bales can be stacked directly in storage structures if there is adequate maneuvering room for the tractor.

LARGE-BALE SYSTEMS

15.17. Forming and Handling Large Round Bales. Balers that make large round bales first became commercially available in 1971 and early 1972, when two manufacturers placed machines on the market.[11] By 1975, 8 manufacturers had 11 models available.[15,16] Over 40% of all balers produced in the United States during 1975 were large-round-bale machines.[1] Typical bale sizes are shown in Table 15.1.

Some roll balers form the bale by rolling up the windrow on the ground, much like rolling up a carpet. Either a chain-and-slat (raddle) conveyor with spring tines on the cross bars, or a series of side-by-side flat belts with tines attached to them, moves upward in contact with the rear of the bale being formed. Stationary, curved grid bars on the upper, forward-moving portion of the conveyor confine the bale as it approaches its maximum diameter, thereby controlling the density to some extent. When the bale reaches the desired size it is discharged by raising the rear gate (the portion of the conveyor that is behind the bale) and then driving forward.

Most roll balers lift the windrow into the machine to form the bale, rather than rolling it up on the ground. A typical arrangement is shown

Table 15.1. SOME TYPICAL SIZES AND MASSES OF LARGE ROUND BALES

Length		Max. Diameter		Max. Mass		Calc. Density	
Metres	Feet	Metres	Feet	kg	lb	kg/m³	lb/ft³
From balers that lift the windrow into the machine							
1.83	6	2.13	7	1360	3000	208	13.0
1.68	5½	1.68	5½	680	1500	184	11.5
1.52	5	1.83	6	680	1500	170	10.6
1.22	4	1.52	5	450	1000	203	12.7
1.22	4	1.52	5	385	850	173	11.3
From balers that roll up the bale on the ground							
2.13	7	1.83	6	540	1200	98	6.1
1.52	5	1.52	5	450	1000	163	8.1

Dimensions and masses are based on manufacturers' published information. Not all intermediate sizes are included in the table.

schematically in Fig. 15.9. Windrow pickup cylinders are similar to those on conventional balers, but smaller in diameter. The floor conveyor may be a series of side-by-side lugged chains, a flat belt the full width of the bale-forming chamber, or a series of closely spaced, powered transverse rollers. The bale-forming apron is either a raddle conveyor or a series of flat belts usually 100 to 150 mm [4 to 6 in.] wide with 50 to 100 mm [2 to 4 in.] spaces between them.

The idlers on the spring-loaded arm compensate for the increased length of apron required to reach around the bale as the diameter increases. Conveyor tension from the idler springs controls bale density, at least during the intermediate forming stages. The core density is low in the early stages but usually increases as the bale forming progresses. When a bale has reached the desired diameter (usually indicated by a marker on a graduated scale), the operator stops the forward motion and engages the twine-wrapping mechanism while the bale continues to rotate. The spacing of adjacent wraps

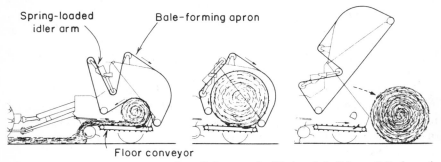

Fig. 15.9. Schematic arrangement of an off-the-ground roll baler. *Left:* Bale partially formed. *Center:* Completed bale, ready to be wrapped with twine. Note how the spring-loaded idler arm has rotated between the left and center views to provide additional length of apron to wrap around the bale. *Right:* Operator has opened the tail gate hydraulically, permitting the floor conveyor to discharge the bale. (Courtesy of Sperry New Holland.)

across the bale length (usually 150 to 200 mm [6 to 8 in.]) is controlled either manually or by a powered traversing guide. The twine ends are not tied or fastened to the bale. The wrapped bale is ejected by raising the tail gate (Fig. 15.9 *right*). Twine requirements are only one-fourth to one-half as great as for conventional bales.

The greatest use of roll balers is in areas where the hay is produced and fed on the same farm or on nearby farms. The bales are usually moved twice — first to a storage area (which may be in or at the edge of the hay field) and then to the feeding area.[3] Because the hauling distance is usually short, single-bale transport units are widely used. These may be fork-type attachments for tractor 3-point hitches, 2-wheel trailers with hydraulic lift forks, front-mounted loaders with forks or grapple hooks, or other similar arrangements.[15] Transport devices that load and haul 3 to 5 bales are also commercially available. The bales are usually stored on the ground, one layer deep, with sufficient space between bales to permit water to drain off of them. The rounded shape provides good weather resistance.

Safety in handling large round bales should be a concern of designers, local fabricators, and operators. Improper design or improper use of front-end loaders can result in serious injury or death if the elevated bale rolls down the loader booms onto the tractor and operator or if carrying the bale too high causes a tractor roll-over. Good judgement is important when ejecting bales onto a sloping field. A 700-kg bale rolling downhill has considerable destructive potential as well as being dangerous.

Long-distance hauling is expensive and generally impractical because the round bales do not stack well on trucks and maximum payloads are low. Bales 1.22 m [4 ft] long fit a highway truck better than the other sizes because they can be stacked 2 bales wide (end-to-end) within the legal width limit. Maximum densities of round bales formed by machines that lift the windrow (Table 15.1) are generally comparable with, or slightly less than, densities of conventional wire-tied bales, but the spaces between stacked round bales reduce the payload attainable within a given overall volume on a truck.

The round-bale system is fully mechanized and can be a one-man operation, but a mechanical device *must* be used any time a bale is moved. This system is economically feasible for a much lower annual production than is the use of conventional balers plus automatic bale wagons. In a 1971-73 study involving about 45 Oklahoma farms, Bowers and Rider[3] found that the round-bale system was more economical than conventional baling plus hand hauling when the annual production was greater than about 70 Mg [75 tons]. For high annual productions, however, conventional balers plus automatic bale wagons were more economical than the round-bale system. The break-even annual production was about 225 Mg [250 tons] when using a small PTO-driven automatic bale wagon.

In the Oklahoma study, seasonal average baling rates were 5.8 Mg/h [6.4 tons/h] for medium-duty conventional 2-wire balers, 7.3 Mg/h [8.0 tons/h] for heavy-duty 2-wire balers, and 6.8 Mg/h [7.5 tons/h] for roll balers. With roll balers, as much as 20 to 30% of the total down-the-windrow time per bale may be lost while stopped to wrap and eject the bale.

15.18. Large Rectangular Bales. A large-bale machine that produces bales 2.4 m [8 ft] long and having a 1.5 × 1.5-m [5 × 5-ft] square cross section was developed in England and first produced commercially in 1973. Packer fingers above a windrow pickup cylinder push the hay through a tapered feeding chute into the bale chamber. The hay is compacted by the front wall of the chamber moving about 13 mm [5 in.] into the chamber in a reciprocating motion. There is no plunger, as such, and no cutoff knife. A gate on the chamber outlet remains closed while the bale is being formed.

When the bale reaches the desired density (indicated by a gage), the operator stops the forward motion and trips the knotters. Three ties are made around the bale, using special polypropylene (plastic) twine that has a strength of 2.7 kN [600 lbf]. The rear gate opens automatically when the tying cycle is completed. The tied bale is subsequently pushed out by the next bale being formed, after which the gate closes. Maximum bale density is about 100 kg/m³ [7 lb/ft³].

A United States manufacturer developed a large rectangular baler that was first available commercially in 1978. This machine produces bales that are 2.4 m [8 ft] long and have a 1.3 × 1.2-m [4.25 × 4-ft] cross section. It has a reciprocating plunger at the inlet end of the bale chamber, similar to the arrangement in a conventional baler. The plunger operates at about 25 cycles per minute (much slower than in a conventional baler). A charge chamber is located between the windrow pickup unit and the entry to the bale chamber. When sufficient hay has accumulated in the charge chamber, a sensor automatically actuates fingers that push the hay charge up into the bale chamber while the plunger is on its retracted stroke.

Six individual wraps of plastic twine are made around each bale, in much the same manner as with conventional balers except that a double-knotter system is employed (2 balls of twine and 2 ties per wrap). Bale length is adjustable and is gaged in the same manner as on conventional balers. Density is controlled by utilizing hydraulic cylinders to squeeze together all four sides of the bale chamber at the discharge end. The cylinder pressure is controlled by a hydraulic sensor on the plunger, thereby minimizing variations in bale density.

One of the objectives in developing this unit was to be able to produce rectangular bales of a size and density suitable for commercial hauling on highway trucks. Densities up to about 240 kg/m³ [15 lb/ft³] were obtained with alfalfa during 1977 tests. This manufacturer's large-bale system includes a special machine to break up the bales for feeding, as well as other special handling equipment. A 2-wheel bale-accumulator trailer that will carry 3 bales may be pulled behind the baler, allowing the operator to drop all bales at the ends of the field.

Large rectangular bales can be handled with squeeze-type lifts mounted on tractors or special carriers, or with special attachments on front-end loaders, and they stack well.

CUBING OR WAFERING

15.19. Development. During the 1950s a great deal of interest developed in the possibility of producing small, high-density agglomerates or "packages" of hay which would retain the roughage characteristics of long hay but would have the free-flow characteristics required for bulk handling. A considerable amount of laboratory research was done by state agricultural experiment stations, and a number of manufacturers undertook development programs. Out of all this emerged 2 present-day commercial models of field cubers and 2 stationary counterparts.

Researchers and early experimental field models usually produced shapes several centimetres wide (often circular) with low length/width ratios that could be appropriately described as wafers. Current models, however, produce shapes more nearly cubical and are commonly known as cubers. The term "pellet," which was used by early researchers, is now officially described in ASAE Standard S269 as applying to an agglomeration of *ground* ingredients (individual or mixed) commonly used in animal feeds. Wafers and cubes are made from whole or chopped hay. Pellets generally have diameters not over 19 mm [¾ in.] and lengths less than 25 mm [1 in.].

The first commercial production of alfalfa cubes was in central California in 1960, with one pull-type machine producing about 900 Mg [1000 tons]. The California cube production in 1969 was 398 Gg [439,000 tons], representing 7% of the state's hay crop.[8] Lesser amounts were produced in other states, primarily Arizona, New Mexico, and Washington. The principal application of field cubing is for alfalfa hay that is sold and transported a considerable distance from the producer to the consumer.

Since 1969 there has been some interest in stationary cubing installations because of their greater versatility, better-controlled operating conditions, and higher outputs in comparison with field cubing.[8,19] Feed additives can be incorporated to produce complete rations. Artificially dried hay can be cubed in areas where natural drying is unsatisfactory. Field-chopped hay may need to be hauled from considerable distances to utilize the full capacity of a stationary cuber. The maximum haul for an economic operation is considered to be about 25 km [15 miles].

15.20. Types of Equipment. Cubes or wafers may be formed by compressing the hay in closed chambers or by extruding the hay through open-end dies. Most laboratory work has been done with closed dies, using a piston to compress a charge of hay in a cylinder. Diameters ranged from 38 to 200 mm [1½ to 8 in.]. Test results reported in 1955 to 1961[2,4,7] indicated that acceptable wafers or cubes could be formed at pressures of 24 to 34 MPa [3500 to 5000 psi].

Compression devices employed on early experimental field machines included (a) a reciprocating ram, (b) a tapered screw, (c) a roller-and-die extrusion unit, and (d) meshing rollers or gears with pockets or depressions in which wafers were formed. Type "d" operated on the closed-die principle and the other three were extrusion machines.

A more recent experimental machine[6] has a group of rubber rolls that are held together under pressure and roll the incoming hay into a tight core. The core exits from one end of the roll group and is then cut into short sections to form wafers. This is a continuous-feed process that utilizes both adhesive and cohesive binding characteristics of unchopped legumes and grasses and is said to work satisfactorily at high moisture contents (requiring subsequent artificial drying) with lower power requirements than for extrusion machines.[17]

The two models of field cubers commercially available in 1977 both utilize the roller-and-die extrusion principle. In this arrangement, a compression roller forces chopped hay through open-end dies arranged in a ring as shown in Fig. 15.10. One model employs two diametrically opposed rollers of smaller diameter than shown in Fig. 15.10. A large-diameter auger. concentric with the axis of the die ring and main shaft, feeds the material into the cubing chamber. As the main shaft turns the compression-roller support, the

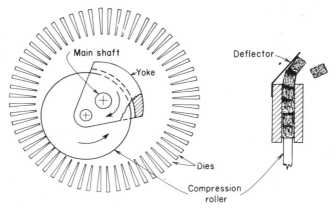

Fig. 15.10. Roller and ring-die arrangement for forming hay cubes by the extrusion process.

roller rotates because of contact with the hay and the die ring. An adjustable, cone-shaped deflector around the outer periphery of the die ring bends the extruded columns and causes them to break into pieces 25 to 100 mm [1 to 4 in.] long.

Both machines produce cubes having a 32 × 32-mm [1¼ × 1¼-in.] square cross section and bulk densities of 400 to 480 kg/m³ [25 to 30 lb/ft³]. This size is a compromise that is small enough to allow optimum feeding and have acceptable materials-handling characteristics and yet is large enough to be produced at a reasonable rate and reasonable cost. The square die shape is more practical than a round shape for a multiple-die arrangement, permitting a minimum of blocked space in the inlet face of the die assembly and being easier to machine. Dies are hardened and chrome plated to minimize wear.

The hay is chopped to improve feeding into the cubing chamber and because the cubes are more uniform than if made from long hay. One of the two commercial models picks up hay from the windrow with a small-diameter, cam-controlled pickup cylinder and subsequently chops it with a cylinder-type cutterhead set for a 35-mm [1⅜-in.] theoretical length of cut. Because the hay is quite dry when picked up, a variable-speed drive is needed on the pickup cylinder so that the speed can be adjusted for effective pickup with minimum leaf shatter. The other machine utilizes a flail-type unit to pick up the windrow and shred it.

15.21. Operating Conditions. Field cubing with current machines is confined primarily to alfalfa which, for best results, should not contain more than 10% grasses or other foreign materials.[9] Alfalfa plants have natural, soluble adhesives on the surface that are activated when the plants are moistened. The moisture content in the windrow should be not more than 10 to 12%. Water is sprayed onto the hay as it is picked up by the machine, bringing the final moisture content up to 14 to 16%.[9] For safe storage, the cubes must be dried by natural or forced ventilation (if necessary) to a moisture content of 14% or less.[9]

Good natural curing conditions are essential for cubing. The cubing operation normally begins in mid-morning and continues into the evening until increasing relative humidity causes the hay to toughen. Windrows should be wide and flat to promote uniform curing and to facilitate distribution of the water sprayed onto the hay. Self-propelled windrowers with conditioner attachments are generally employed.

Although capacities up to 5.4 Mg/h [6 tons/h] can be achieved with current field cubers, field studies have indicated that overall seasonal averages of 3.6 to 4 Mg/h [4 to 4½ tons/h] are more typical.[8,19]

15.22. Energy and Power Requirements. In laboratory tests with closed-end dies (piston and cylinder), satisfactory wafers or cubes could be formed with an energy input of 2.5 to 4 kW·h/Mg [3 to 5 hp-h/ton].[2,7] Cubing-energy requirements for a commercial machine having extrusion dies of the type shown in Fig. 15.10 were found to be about 12 kW·h/Mg [15 hp-h/ton].[12] The extrusion process has high energy requirements because it depends upon frictional resistance between the hay and the die to develop the required pressure.

Engines capable of developing at least 150 kW [200 hp] are employed on commercial cubers. Actual total power requirements for a self-propelled model were found to be about 135 kW [180 hp] at a feed rate of 7.3 Mg/h [8 tons/h] and 79 kW [106 hp] at 3.6 Mg/h [4 tons/h].[12] These inputs represent about 20 kW·h/Mg [25 hp-h/ton] as compared with 0.8 to 1.2 PTO kW·h/Mg [1 to 1.5 hp-h/ton] for conventional baling. The value for the cuber includes propulsion power, whereas the baling value does not. At 7.3 Mg/h [8 tons/h], approximately two-thirds of the total cuber power was used for the actual cubing operation.[12]

15.23. Factors Affecting Quality of Cubes or Wafers. Two important parameters of quality are durability in handling, and density of the final product. Among the factors that may affect cube or wafer quality are kind and quality of forage, moisture content, pressure, holding time under pressure, cross-sectional area of cube chamber, and die design. The ratio of die length to cross-sectional area is an important design factor for extrusion dies, and die wear also affects cube quality.

Although cubing works best with alfalfa having only small amounts of grass or weeds, other materials have been cubed by adding suitable binders. Young alfalfa can be cubed satisfactorily with less pressure than mature alfalfa.[20]

In laboratory tests with alfalfa at 12% moisture, density obtained with a piston and cylinder was found to vary linearly with the logarithm of the pressure.[7] At a given pressure, density decreased as the diameter of the compression chamber was increased from 38 mm to 86 mm [1.5 in. to 3.4 in.]. Cubes or wafers tend to expand somewhat after the pressure has been released. Laboratory tests have shown that higher pressures are required for short hold times than for longer times (e.g., ½ s versus 10 s).[20] Tests have also shown that twice as much pressure is required to produce satisfactory wafers (89 mm [3½ in.] diameter) at 20% moisture as at 10% moisture.[20]

Experience has indicated that when a cuber begins operation, capacity and cube quality improve as the dies become heated from friction of the hay being compressed. Dies should be designed with a ratio of length to cross section that will provide a die temperature of 65 to 95°C [150 to 200°F] during normal operation.

15.24. Handling Cubes. Cubes are usually collected in a special, high-dump wagon trailed behind the cuber. These wagons are dumped into a transfer truck by hydraulically lifting and rotating the large bin (3.6-Mg [4-

ton] capacity) about the upper edge of one side so that the material flows by gravity into the truck. Because the cubes are hot (50 to 60°C [120 to 140° F]) as they emerge from the dies, it is common practice to dump them from the transfer truck in shallow piles on a concrete slab for cooling and temporary storage.[9] A large-capacity power scoop is then used to transfer the cubes from the slab into a transport truck or onto a conveyor.

Commercial transport trucks are of the bottom-unloading type and meter the cubes out, by gravity, onto a conveyor at the consumer's storage facility. Various combinations of mechanical elevators and conveyors are used to fill storage structures and for subsequent mechanized feeding.

Each time there is a transfer, there is some damage to the cubes, creating some fine material. The amount of damage is related to the cube quality and the method of handling. These fines adversely affect handling and storage characteristics and can reduce feeding efficiency. Up to 10% fines, by mass, is usually acceptable.[9]

15.25. Economic Comparison with Baling. Because of the large investment represented by a field cuber and associated equipment, high annual use is imperative to make cubing economically feasible. Growers who own cubers should have enough hay area to keep the machines operating a high percentage of the available cubing time during the hay season. Custom operation is an alternative for smaller areas.

The total cost of field cubing, from the standing crop to temporary storage on the farm, was compared with the cost of harvesting baled hay with a three-wire baler and stacking it at the roadside with a self-propelled bale wagon, based on 1970 field data obtained in Central California.[19] The average cubing rate was about 3.6 Mg/h [4 tons/h]. For an annual output of 3.6 Gg [4000 tons], costs were about $4.70/Mg [$4.25/ton] more for the cubing system than for the baling system. The difference was about $5.25 [$4.75] for 2.7 Gg [3000 tons] per year. At the time of these studies, consumers were willing to pay a premium of about $5.50/Mg [$5.00/ton] for cubes in preference to bales, the difference slightly more than offsetting the additional cost of cubing.

Feeding trials and general experience with dairy cattle, beef, and sheep have shown greater feed consumption and increased production with cubes as compared with baled hay. The amount of feed wasted by the animals is also considerably less than with baled hay. These savings, plus reduced costs per megagram for commercial hauling and reduced feeding labor, have justified the price differential paid for cubes.

REFERENCES

1. Annual statistics issue. Implement & Tractor, *91*(22):16-70, Nov. 7, 1976.
2. BELLINGER, P.L., and H.F. McCOLLY. Energy requirements for forming hay pellets. Agr. Engr., *42*:244-247, 250, May, 1961.
3. BOWERS, W., and A.R. RIDER. Hay handling and harvesting. Agr. Eng., *55*(8):12-18, Aug., 1974.
4. BRUHN, H.D. Pelleting hay and grain mixtures. Agr. Eng., *36*:330-331, May, 1955.
5. BURROUGH, D.E., and J.A. GRAHAM. Power characteristics of a plunger-type forage baler. Agr. Eng., *35*:221-229, 232, Apr., 1954.
6. BUSHMEYER, R.W., D.E. KRAUSE, and C.J. RATH. Developing a roll wafering machine: a progress report. Agr. Eng., *51*:405-407, July, 1970.
7. BUTLER, B.J., and H.F. McCOLLY. Factors affecting the pelleting of hay. Agr. Eng., *40*:442-446, Aug., 1959.
8. CURLEY, R.G., J.B. DOBIE, and P.S. PARSONS. Comparison of stationary and field cubing of forage. Trans. ASAE, *16*(2):361-364, 366, 1973.
9. DOBIE, J.B., and R.G. CURLEY. Hay cube storage and feeding. California Agr. Ext. Circ. 550, 1969.
10. FERGUSON, W.L., P.E. STRICKLER, and R.C. MAX. Hay harvesting practices and labor used, 1967, 48 states. USDA Econ. Res. Serv. Statistical Bull. 460, 1971.
11. FLOYD, C.S. Making hay in the U.S.A., part 3. Looking at some recent research. Implement & Tractor, *86*(20):20-22, Sept. 21, 1971.
12. GUSTAFSON, B. W., and H. E. DE BUHR. John Deere "400" hay cuber. ASAE Paper 65-639, Dec., 1965.
13. GUSTAFSON, M.L. A new bale handling system. Agr. Eng., *44*:14-17, 32, Jan., 1963.
14. GUSTAFSON, M.L. Specialized hay handling system. ASAE Paper 64-140, June, 1964.
15. LIEN, R.M., R.G. CURLEY, and J.B. DOBIE. The big hay bale. Univ. of Calif. Div. Agr. Sciences Publ. 75-SP/3011, 1975.
16. LONG, M.E. Big baler roundup. Implement & Tractor, *90*(17):16-18, Aug. 21, 1975.
17. MOLITORISZ, J., and H.F. McCOLLY. Development and analysis of the rolling-compressing wafering process. Trans. ASAE, *12*(4):419-422, 425, 1969.
18. NATION, H.J. Further experiments to determine baler loads. J. Agr. Eng. Res., *6*:288-299, 1961.
19. PARSONS, P.S., J.B. DOBIE, and R.G. CURLEY. Alfalfa harvesting costs. California Agr. Ext. Publ. AXT-346, 1971.
20. PICKARD, G.E., W.M. ROLL, and J.H. RAMSER. Fundamentals of hay wafering. Trans. ASAE, *4*(1):65-68, 1961.
21. RANEY, R.R. The equilibrium theory of bale chamber action. Unpublished paper. International Harvester Co., 1946.
22. SOTEROPULOS, G. Development of a hydraulic bale ejector using the computer. Trans. ASAE, *16*(1):24-25, 1973.
23. Test reports for users. NIAE Rept. 445, 1965.
24. VON BARGEN, K. Man-machine performance in a baled-alfalfa-hay harvesting system. Trans. ASAE, *11*(1):57-60, 64, 1968.
25. ZIMMERMAN, M. Bale throwers. Implement & Tractor, *79*(4):30-33, May 21, 1964.

PROBLEMS

15.1. A 36 × 46-cm automatic-tying field baler averages 7.3 Mg/h at a field efficiency of 72%. The plunger makes 70 compression strokes per minute. Calculate the maximum amount of variation in bale lengths that is likely to occur. Assume a bale density of 175 kg/m^3.

15.2. A baler averages 8 Mg/h at a field efficiency of 70%. The plunger makes 75 compression strokes per minute, and the average bale mass is 30 kg. The yield is 2.8 Mg/ha.

(a) Calculate the actual number of compression strokes required per bale.

(b) Recommend the number of 2-m rake swaths that should be put into one windrow, and the corresponding forward speed required.

15.3. The average power supplied to the crank arm of a baler is 6.7 kW. During the compression portion of the stroke, the amount of energy required above the average is 4.2 kJ. This energy must be supplied by the flywheel, whose mass moment of inertia is 17.8 N·m·s^2. A 109-tooth gear on the crankshaft is driven by a 17-tooth gear on the flywheel shaft.

(a) Assuming that the crank speed is 75 r/min at the start of compression, calculate the crank r/min at the end of compression and the percentage decrease in r/min during compression.

(b) If the slow-down occurs during 55° of crank rotation, what is the average power (kilowatts) released by the flywheel during this period?

15.4. Referring to Fig. 15.7, develop a logical explanation for the following:

(a) Why the peak force is greater for 64 kg/min than for 31 kg/min.

(b) Why the high-rate peak force occurs earlier than the low-rate peak force.

15.5. A cuber of the type shown in Fig. 15.9 has 66 dies, each 32 × 32 × 150 mm.

(a) Calculate the time required for a given particle of hay to pass through the die (i.e., the cube "hold" time) when the feed rate is 5.5 Mg/h. Assume an individual-cube density of 800 kg/m^3.

(b) If the cube length averages 55 mm, how much energy per cube (in joules) is required for the actual cubing operation?

16

Forage Chopping and Handling

16.1. Introduction. With a field chopper and its complementary equipment, the hay-making or silage-making operation can be completely mechanized. The chopped material is blown directly into trailers that are towed behind the chopper or pulled beside it with a separate power source, or sometimes into trucks driven behind or beside the chopper. Chopped forage can readily be unloaded at a controlled rate by mechanical means. Elevating the chopped material into storage is generally done with an impeller-blower. Chopped forage is not free-flowing like hay cubes but is, nevertheless, readily adaptable to mechanized feeding. Equipment investment costs are high but less labor is required for the field chopping method than for baling.

Field choppers are employed in several major methods of harvesting forages, including the following:

1. Harvesting corn for silage (including delayed harvesting for low-moisture silage).
2. Direct cutting of hay for green feeding as an alternate to pasturing (or in making dehydrated alfalfa meal or pellets).
3. Direct cutting of hay for grass/legume silage (70 to 80% moisture).
4. Chopping from the windrow for wilted grass/legume silage (usually 65 to 70% moisture).
5. Chopping from the windrow for low-moisture grass/legume silage, sometimes known as haylage (40 to 60% moisture).
6. Dry chopping from the windrow for storage as hay (artificial drying needed if chopped at much above 20% moisture).

The versatility of a field chopper often permits its use for several different products, thereby increasing the annual use and decreasing the cost per megagram. The chief objective in chopping material to be stored as cured hay is to reduce the material to lengths that can be handled by an impeller-blower and moved in a pipe along with an air stream. With silage, additional important functions of chopping are to facilitate packing for exclusion of air and to make feeding easier.

The practice of making low-moisture grass/legume silage, in preference to direct-cut or wilted silage, is a recent development that is becoming increasingly popular.[12] Either wilted or low-moisture grass/legume silage involves the extra operations of mowing and windrowing (or a combined operation), but direct-cut grass/legume silage has large nutrient losses from silo seepage, may create an odor problem, and requires a preservative.[24] Low-moisture silage has low nutrient losses, and timing of the chopping operation is not critical. Less quantity of moisture must be handled than with wilted or direct-cut silage. The risk of weather damage is greater than for wilted silage but less than for field-cured hay.

Requirements for chopping and storing low-moisture grass/legume silage are more stringent than for other silages. The material must be chopped finer to obtain adequate packing. Auxiliary recutter screens have been developed for cylinder-type choppers to obtain finer and more uniform chopping. Airtight storage structures are desirable and uniform distribution is important.[24] Gum buildup in field choppers, forage blowers, and silo unloaders is a problem with low-moisture silage.[12] The amount of buildup is greater from alfalfa and other legumes than from grasses. Maximum buildup occurs with alfalfa moisture contents between 40 and 55%. There is very little buildup above 70% or below 30% moisture. A water stream is sometimes used on a forage blower while handling low-moisture silage but this solution is impractical for the chopper in the field.

16.2. Flail-Type Field Choppers.* Prior to about 1950, all field forage choppers were of the precision-cut, shear-bar type, employing either flywheel or cylinder cutterheads. Since that time, flail shredders have been adapted for field chopping. These are simpler, less expensive machines than the conventional shear-bar type, and can be used for a variety of other shredding jobs. But they are not well-suited to harvesting tall crops such as corn,[14] do not chop fine enough for good silage, and require more energy per megagram for a given average chopped length than do shear-bar choppers. They are often used for green-chopping hay that is to be fed direct, because the shredded length is not critical. They can be used to pick up previously mowed or windrowed hay but leaf losses may be large if the hay is dry.

A *direct-throw* flail chopper has a tapered discharge spout that covers the full width of cut and directs the material from the rotor into a forage wagon, utilizing kinetic energy imparted by the knives on the rotor. Cupped knives of the type shown in Fig. 14.1e are employed to provide the impelling action. Operating at high peripheral speeds (46 to 56 m/s [9000 to 11,000 ft/min]), this type of knife pumps a considerable amount of air, which contributes to high power requirements. If the knives have too much curvature they do not unload properly. Average shredded lengths may be in the order of 65 to 90 mm [2½ to 3½ in.][5,9] with some pieces over 150 mm [6 in.] long. Material this long does not pack well in silos and is difficult to remove from silos and to handle in conveyors.

Some present-day flail choppers have auxiliary, flywheel-type cut-

---

*Impact-type rotary cutters and flail shredders are also discussed in Section 14.4.

terheads, similar to those on conventional field choppers. An auger collects the material from the flail rotor and conveys it to the cutterhead located at one end of the flail rotor. The impeller-cutterhead delivers the recut material to the wagon through an adjustable spout, as on conventional field choppers. Flail knives of the type shown in Fig. 14.1d are satisfactory and pump less air than do the cupped knives employed on direct-throw machines.

The recut lengths are generally comparable with those from a conventional field chopper but tend to be less uniform because the material is not positively fed or held while being cut. The auxiliary cutterhead substantially increases the new cost. Some machines have the cross auger and an impeller-blower but no recut knives.

Power requirements are high and are influenced by the type of flail knife and other machine characteristics, the operating conditions, and the type of crop. When chopping alfalfa hay with a direct-throw flail chopper, the total energy requirement at 13.6 Mg/h [15 tons/h] was found to be 1.1 kW·h/Mg [1.3 hp-h/ton] and the average length of cut was 74.7 mm [2.94 in.].[5] With a cylinder-type cutterhead on a conventional field chopper and with an average chopped length of 57.2 mm [2.25 in.], Blevins found a total energy requirement of only 0.6 kW·h/Mg [0.7 hp-h/ton] at 13.6 Mg/h [15 tons/h].[4,5]

In other tests,[16] the PTO energy requirements for chopping a mixture of ryegrass and red clover at 13.6 Mg/h [15 tons/h] was 1.7 kW·h/Mg [2.1 hp-h/ton] for a flail chopper having S-shaped knives (Fig. 14.1d) and a flywheel-type recutter, as compared with 1.4 and 1.55 kW·h/Mg [1.7 and 1.9 hp-h/ton] for 2 direct-throw machines having cupped knives. Apparently the additional power needed for the recutter was partially offset by reduced power requirements for the different-shaped flail knives that moved less air than the cup-shaped knives. Hennen[13] reported energy requirements of 2.05 and 3.45 kW·h/Mg [2.5 and 4.2 hp-h/ton] for grass and a mixture of alfalfa and grass, respectively, with a flail chopper having a flywheel-type recutter.

SHEAR-BAR-TYPE FIELD CHOPPERS

16.3. Basic Components and General Characteristics. Shear-bar-type field choppers are available as either pull-type or self-propelled machines. Because of the general availability of large tractors, practically all pull-type models currently manufactured have PTO drives. Advertised capacities of 54 to 73 Mg/h [60 to 80 tons/h] for corn silage are common. PTO power requirements for maximum capacities of the larger choppers are over 75 kW [over 100 hp].

Self-propelled models are basically heavy-duty machines designed to withstand high annual use. Engines usually have ratings of 112 kW [150 hp] or more. A variable-speed propulsion drive is provided, either through a variable-speed V-belt drive or a hydrostatic drive.

In general, shear-bar-type field choppers include the following basic, functional components.

1. A gathering unit to cut standing plants or to pick up windrowed material.
2. A conveying and feed mechanism with spring-loaded rolls or aprons to compress and hold the material for chopping.
3. A cutterhead or chopping unit.
4. A conveying or impelling arrangement to deposit the chopped material in the transport vehicle.

16.4. Gathering Units. Field choppers have one or more of the following interchangeable gathering attachments, which makes them adaptable for a variety of jobs: (a) row-crop attachment for direct cutting of such crops as corn and sorghum for silage; (b) cutterbar unit for direct mowing and chopping of legumes and grasses for silage or direct feeding; (c) windrow pickup unit for wilted or low-moisture grass/legume silage or for cured hay. Two types of gathering attachments are shown in Fig. 16.1. Row-crop attachments are mostly for 1, 2, or 3 rows. A low set of gathering chains, not visible in the illustration, moves faster than the upper set so the stalk butts enter the feed mechanism first.

Most cutterbar attachments are similar to auger-type headers on self-propelled windrowers (Fig. 14.10 *left*). Cutting widths of 1.83 to 2.24 m [72 to 88 in.] are the most common, but a few models have widths up to 3.65 m [12 ft]. The trend toward low-moisture silage in place of direct-cut grass/legume silage has shifted emphasis away from cutterbar attachments.

Fig. 16.1. *Left:* Windrow-pickup gathering unit on a shear-bar-type field chopper. Note retracting fingers in center portion of auger. *Right:* Row-crop attachment. (Courtesy of Gehl Co.)

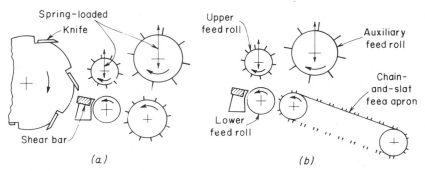

Fig. 16.2. Two common types of feed mechanisms. Top of shear bar would be horizontal for a flywheel cutterhead.

16.5. Feed Mechanisms. Two common arrangements for feed mechanisms are shown diagramatically in Fig. 16.2. A chain-and-slat apron with notched, angle-iron cross bars sometimes replaces the two upper rolls. An arrangement with three lower rolls is shown in Fig. 16.4. An auxiliary clutch or gear transmission is usually provided to permit stopping or reversing the feed mechanism from the tractor operator's seat if an overload occurs.

The functions of the upper and lower feed rolls (adjacent to the shear bar) are to compress the material to be cut, feed it positively to the cutterhead, and hold it while cutting takes place. The lower feed roll is usually smooth, whereas the upper feed roll (or apron) has transverse ribs to provide maximum holding ability. The upper and lower feed rolls should have relatively small diameters and be close to the cutting plane or arc so long pieces will not be pulled through by the knife. For the most positive feed, the peripheral speeds of all feed rolls and aprons should be the same. In determining peripheral speeds, the effective diameter of a corrugated or ribbed roller should be taken as slightly less than the outside diameter.

The upper feed rolls or apron are spring-loaded and have provision for several centimetres of vertical movement to accommodate varying amounts of material. The cross-sectional area defined by the minimum width of the feed opening at the feed rolls and the maximum operating clearance between the upper and lower feed rolls is known as the throat of the chopper. Throat area is one of the factors that may limit the capacity of a chopper, as discussed in Section 16.14.

16.6. Chopping and Impelling. Two general types of cutterheads, known as the flywheel type and cylinder type (Fig. 16.3), have been employed on conventional field choppers. With either type, the mounting or shape of the knives is such that cutting occurs progressively from one end to the other to minimize peak torque requirements. Flywheel-type cutterheads usually have

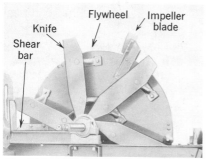 

Fig. 16.3. *Left:* A flywheel-type cutterhead. *Right:* A cylinder-type cutterhead, showing optional recutter screen. Top edge of recutter screen would normally be about level with the cylinder axis. Openings are usually in line, rather than staggered. (Courtesy of Gehl Co.)

4 or 6 knives. Most cylinder-type cutterheads have 6 knives and a diameter of 380 to 460 mm [15 to 18 in.] or 9 knives and a diameter of about 610 mm [24 in.]. With either type, some of the knives can be removed to increase the length of cut. The remaining knives must be equally spaced to maintain cutterhead balance.

A flywheel-type cutterhead has 3 or 4 impeller blades around the periphery that throw or impel the chopped material up the discharge pipe and into the wagon. Impeller-blowers are discussed in Sections 16.16 through 16.19.

Cylinder-type cutterheads either obtain a direct-throwing action from the knives in a close-fitting housing or employ a separate impeller-blower located immediately behind the cutterhead (Fig. 16.4). Direct-throw models

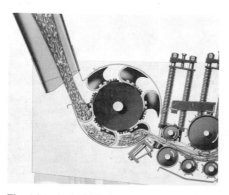 

Fig. 16.4. *Left:* Cylinder-type cutterhead with cupped knives and direct throw. (Courtesy of Allis-Chalmers.) *Right:* Auxiliary impeller-blower on a cylinder-type cutterhead. Housing swings in and is clamped to cutterhead housing during operation. (Courtesy of Hesston Corp.)

may have deeply cupped knives as in Fig. 16.4 *left*, moderately curved knives, or essentially flat knives (Fig. 16.3 *right*). Experience has indicated that direct-throw cutterheads need peripheral speeds of 28 to 30 m/s [5500 to 6000 ft/min] to satisfactorily deliver all kinds of materials to the rear of a wagon.[19] Speeds of 30 to 33 m/s [6000 to 6500 ft/min] for a PTO speed of 540 r/min are common on current models. When auxiliary impeller-blowers are employed, cylinder peripheral speeds are usually only 18 to 24 m/s [3500 to 4700 ft/min].

Flywheel-type cutterheads predominated on early models of field choppers, probably because this was the common type on stationary choppers that needed the impeller-blower capabilities for filling tall silos. Most current models of field choppers employ cylinder-type cutterheads. Because cylinder diameters are much smaller than flywheel diameters, more cuts per minute can be obtained without unnecessarily high peripheral speeds and the accompanying excessive power requirements (discussed in Section 16.13). Rigidity of the cutting components, necessary for maintaining close clearances between the knives and the shear bar, is easier to obtain than on a flywheel cutterhead. There is less damage to a cylinder-type cutterhead if a foreign object is fed into it. Built-in knife sharpeners are feasible and generally provided.

The need for extremely fine chopping of low-moisture grass/legume silage prompted the development of recutter-screen attachments for cylinder-type cutterheads (Fig. 16.3). These are sometimes used for other crops but are particularly effective for nonoriented materials such as hay or grass. Screens with square openings ranging from 13 mm to 102 mm [½ in. to 4 in.] are available. Some have elongated slots. The larger sizes are employed for low-moisture silage. A recutter screen substantially increases power requirements. An auxiliary impeller-blower, rather than direct throwing, is required on models having recutter screens available.

16.7. Chopping Lengths. The theoretical length of cut is defined as the amount of advance of the feed mechanism between the cuts of successive knives. The theoretical length is adjusted by changing the speed of the feed mechanism or the number of knives on the cutterhead. A third possible variable, the cutterhead speed, is usually not adjustable on present-day field choppers. Current production models provide adjustments to obtain minimum theoretical lengths of 3 to 6 mm [⅛ to ¼ in.]. Maximum settings range from 25 mm to 90 mm [1 in. to 3½ in.]. A 6-knife cutterhead can be operated with 2, 3, or 6 equally spaced knives. From 2 to 6 feed-mechanism speeds are provided by means of gear-shift boxes and/or sprocket changes.

The actual length of cut will approximate the theoretical length only when stalks feed in straight, as with row crops such as corn. When windrowed crops or other nonoriented materials are chopped, the actual length may average twice the theoretical setting, with some pieces being several times as long as the setting.[2,12]

A theoretical length of 6 mm [¼ in.] is generally recommended for low-moisture grass/legume silage.[12] Barrington and his associates[2] compared cutting lengths, power requirements, and densities in the silo, chopping an alfalfa-brome mixture at about 50% moisture with and without a recutter screen having 102-mm [4-in.] square openings. With a theoretical length of 6 mm [¼ in.] and no screen, approximately 12% of the mass was in pieces longer than 38 mm [1½ in.]. Adding the recutter screen reduced the long pieces to 5% of the mass. Average lengths were not determined. Recutting increased the density in the silo by 8.4%. When a 9.5-mm [⅜-in.] theoretical length plus a recutter screen was compared with a 6-mm [¼-in.] theoretical length without a screen, the silage density was increased only 3.1%.

A theoretical cut of 13 mm [½ in.] is usually considered fine enough for corn silage. Considerably longer cuts (50 to 75 mm [2 to 3 in.]) are desirable for cured hay. With any crop, chopping into lengths shorter than necessary increases the energy requirements per megagram and may reduce the capacity of the chopper.

16.8. Distribution of Power Requirements. The power required to operate a shear-bar-type field chopper is utilized in the following ways: (a) to gather, convey, and compress the material to be cut, (b) to shear the material, (c) to move the air pumped by the cutterhead and impeller-blower, (d) to accelerate the cut material to approximately the peripheral speed of the impeller, (e) to overcome losses due to friction of the cut material within the housing, and (f) to overcome mechanical losses in the machine.

Figure 16.5 shows the distribution of power as a function of feed rate, for one peripheral speed of a flywheel-type cutterhead, as obtained by Blevins[4] in tests with green alfalfa. Strain gages were installed on appropriate drive shafts to obtain power inputs to the flywheel and to the pickup and feed mechanism. Curve A, representing the power required for cutting, was obtained from tests made after removing the impeller blades and the peripheral band of the fan housing. The observed results were corrected for kinetic energy imparted by the knives and for air power as determined with no material passing through the cutterhead. The difference between curves B and A represents the calculated kinetic energy of the discharged material when operating with the fan shroud and impeller blades in place.

Curve D represents the total power input to the flywheel shaft. Curve C was obtained by measuring the air power with no material being chopped and then subtracting this amount from curve D, assuming that the air power was not affected by the feed rate. The friction power, then, is the remaining difference between curves C and B.

The difference between curves E and D represents the actual power determinations for the pickup and feed mechanism. Note that it increases more rapidly at high feed rates than at the lower rates. This power component should be relatively independent of cutterhead speed.

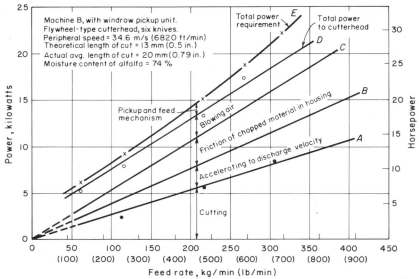

Fig. 16.5. Distribution of power in a flywheel-type field chopper at one peripheral speed of the impeller-blower and one theoretical length of cut. (F. Z. Blevins.[4])

The same power components would be involved in a direct-throw cylinder-type chopper, although the friction component and the air-blowing component probably would have different relative magnitudes.

The situation becomes more complex when a cylinder-type chopper has an auxiliary impeller-blower. The accelerating and friction components of the impeller-blower would be similar to those shown for the flywheel-type chopper. Blowing air would be a two-stage operation, part of the energy coming from the cutterhead and part from the impeller-blower. There would also be a component for acceleration of the material by the cutterhead to the cutterhead peripheral velocity, most of which might be lost in friction before the material entered the impeller-blower. A recutter screen would add still another power component, partly due to the energy required for the additional cutting and partly due to friction caused by the screen.

16.9. Air Power. According to well-established fan laws, the power required to move the air should vary about as the cube of the peripheral speed. If this power component is relatively constant regardless of the feed rate, as assumed in Fig. 16.5, the energy input to the air, *per megagram of chopped material*, varies inversely with the feed rate.

16.10. Cutting Energy. The cutting energy per megagram of material (on either dry or wet basis) varies with the moisture content, the length of cut, the condition of the cutting unit, and other factors. In 15 different groups of tests with alfalfa, Blevins[4] found that, for a given moisture content and theoretical length of cut, the cutting energy per megagram was constant, regardless of feed rate (as illustrated by curve A in Fig. 16.5). Tribelhorn and Smith,[23] when chopping 150-mm-diameter [6-in.-diameter] bundles of corn with a 508-mm-diameter [20-in.-diameter] cylinder-type cutterhead, found no change in cutting energy per megagram when the knife speed was increased from 19.4 m/s to 25.3 m/s [3820 ft/min to 4980 ft/min] and about a 10% increase between 25.3 and 29.5 m/s [4980 and 5810 ft/min.]

Richey[19] determined the cutting energy for 25-mm [1-in.] cuts by changing the theoretical length of cut from 25 or 38 mm [1.0 or 1.5 in.] to 13 mm [0.5 in.] and relating the change in total cutterhead energy requirements per megagram to the increase in number of cuts per centimetre. This procedure is based on the assumptions that (a) cutting energy per megagram is inversely proportional to the cutting length, and (b) changing the cutting length by changing the number of knives or the speed of the feed mechanism does not affect any of the energy components other than cutting. Results for alfalfa (73% moisture) with 2 flywheel-type cutterheads indicated 0.41 and 0.54 kW·h/Mg [0.50 and 0.66 hp-h/ton]* for a 13-mm [½-in.] theoretical cut. These values compare well with 0.44 kW·h/Mg [0.53 hp-h/ton] indicated by curve A in Fig. 16.5. Three comparisons with 2 cylinder cutterheads averaged 0.33 kW·h/Mg [0.40 hp-h/ton] for a 13-mm [½-in.] theoretical cut. Richey found that cutting-energy results based on differences were not consistent for cuts longer than 38 mm [1½ in.].

The right-hand graph in Fig. 16.6 shows the relation between cutting energy and cutting length for alfalfa, based on direct measurements with

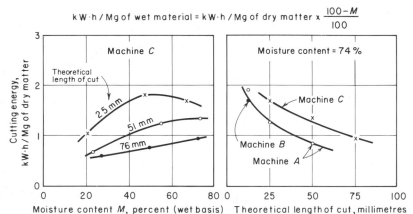

$$kW\cdot h / Mg \text{ of wet material} = kW\cdot h / Mg \text{ of dry matter} \times \frac{100 - M}{100}$$

Fig. 16.6. Effect of theoretical length of cut and of moisture content upon the cutting energy per megagram of dry matter, for alfalfa. Each plotted point represents a series of runs over a range of feed rates. Machine A had a cylinder-type cutterhead; B and C had flywheel cutterheads. (Data from F.Z. Blevins.[4])

*Unless specifically stated otherwise, feed rates and energy requirements per megagram [per ton] in this chapter are based upon the wet mass of the material as chopped.

corrections applied for kinetic energy and air power as described in Section 16.8. These results indicate that cutting energy per megagram increased less rapidly than the number of cuts per centimetre, especially for cuts longer than 25 mm [1 in.].

Hennen[13] found that reducing the theoretical cut for green corn silage from 13 mm to 6 mm [½ in. to ¼ in.] increased the total PTO energy requirement per megagram by about 35%. If the 13-mm [½-in.] cutting energy were assumed to be 35% of the total PTO energy (a reasonable assumption, based on Fig. 16.5), Hennen's cutting-energy requirements would be directly proportional to the number of cuts per centimetre.

The left-hand graph in Fig. 16.6 indicates the effect of moisture content upon the cutting energy per megagram, as measured by Blevins[4] with a flywheel-type cutterhead. In the tests with a 25-mm [1-in.] theoretical cut, and also for a 13-mm [½-in.] cut with another machine, alfalfa chopped at 45 to 50% moisture required more cutting energy per megagram of dry matter than did green alfalfa or cured alfalfa. The difference between green alfalfa and alfalfa having 45 to 50% moisture is greater on a wet-mass basis than shown for the dry-matter basis.

Liljedahl and his associates[15] employed a pendulum arrangement to provide energy for making single cuts of a mat of compressed, random-oriented alfalfa stalks 200 to 280 mm [8 to 11 in.] wide and 6 to 19 mm [¼ to ¾ in.] thick. The knife speed was 2.4 m/s [480 ft/min]. In tests with a sharp knife, they obtained a relation similar to the 25-mm curve in Fig. 16.6, with a maximum at about 40% moisture. Their energy requirements were only one-half to one-third as great as obtained by Blevins.

The laboratory tests indicated that, when cutting alfalfa at 60% moisture, a knife artificially dulled to a radius of only 0.08 mm [0.003 in.] on the cutting edge required twice as much cutting energy as did a sharp knife when the clearance between the knife and shear bar was 0.05 mm [0.002 in.] and 3 times as much when the clearance was 0.41 mm [0.016 in.]. Clearance had very little effect when the knife was sharp. It is probable that the effects of sharpness and clearance would be less at the usual cutterhead speeds of 20 to 30 m/s [4000 to 6000 ft/min] than at the speed of 2.4 m/s [480 ft/min] employed in the laboratory tests.

16.11. Friction Energy. As indicated in Fig. 16.5, a considerable amount of power may be absorbed (and wasted) by friction between the chopped material and the periphery of the housing. It can be shown analytically that the friction energy per unit of material mass, lost as a result of the effect of centrifugal force, is

$$E_f = 4.848 \times 10^{-6} \, \mu\beta V^2 \qquad (16.1)$$

$$[\, E_f = 1.522 \times 10^{-10} \, \mu\beta V^2 \,]$$

where E_f = friction energy, in kilowatt-hours per megagram of material [horsepower-hours per ton]

μ = coefficient of sliding friction between the chopped material and the housing

β = angle subtended by the average arc of housing periphery rubbed by the chopped material, in degrees

V = peripheral speed of impeller, in metres per second [feet per minute]

The angle β must represent the average arc of contact for all material passing through the unit, since all the material from a flywheel cutterhead does not strike the housing at the same place.

Note that the friction energy per megagram is independent of the feed rate but increases as the square of the peripheral speed. With large particles, such as chopped corn, there is probably very little wedging action between the impeller blades and the housing. But it is believed that with grass/legume silage the smaller particles result in considerable wedging, which increases the energy loss due to friction. Field observations of the housing becoming hot when chopping grass/legume silage provide evidence in support of this effect.[1]

Coefficients of friction for chopped materials on polished galvanized steel and stainless steel are presented for various conditions in ASAE Data D251 (Agricultural Engineers Yearbook). These data indicate average values for the coefficient of sliding friction on polished galvanized steel of 0.30 for chopped straw and 0.68 for corn or grass/legume silage at 73% moisture. Experimental determination of the friction power for 2 field choppers (as described in Section 16.8) indicated an average value of 41.8 for the product $\mu \times \beta$ in equation 16.1.[4]

16.12. Kinetic Energy. Assuming that the chopped material leaves the impeller blades or cylinder-type knives at about the peripheral speed of the impeller or cutterhead, its kinetic energy per unit mass is

$$E_{ke} = 1.389 \times 10^{-4} \ V^2 \tag{16.2}$$

$$[E_{ke} = 4.361 \times 10^{-9} \ V^2]$$

where E_{ke} = kinetic energy, in kilowatt-hours per megagram [horsepower-hours per ton]

V = peripheral speed of impeller, in metres per second [feet per minute]

Note that this component also increases as the square of the peripheral speed.

16.13. Total Energy Requirements. Figure 16.7 shows the relation of energy requirements per megagram versus impeller peripheral speed when chopping and elevating corn silage with flywheel-type stationary ensilage cutters in tests prior to 1930. In these tests Duffee[11] found that the total energy requirement at a given peripheral speed of the impeller-blower was practically the same for any actual elevating height below about 18 m [60 ft] and increased only moderately for greater heights (up to the practical height limit indicated by the broken-line curve for the particular speed). This is because the kinetic energy imparted to the material is a function of the impeller speed. Any kinetic energy not needed for elevation or for horizontal carry after discharge is wasted. Power requirements increase rapidly with speed because several of the power or energy components are proportional to the square or cube of the speed, as discussed in the preceding sections. For this reason, unnecessarily high speeds should be avoided.

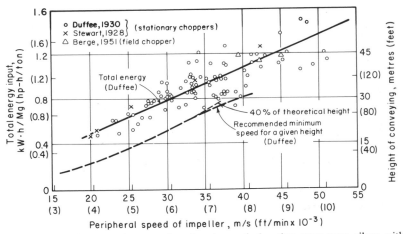

Fig. 16.7. Total energy requirements for chopping and elevating green corn silage with a theoretical cut of approximately 13 mm [½ in.] and an average feed rate of about 14.5 Mg/h [16 tons/h]. The broken-line curve indicates minimum speeds recommended by Duffee for vertical heights up to 30 m [100 ft]. (F.W. Duffee.[11])

Data from Berge[3] plotted on Fig. 16.7, and other unplotted data for lower peripheral speeds,[1] indicate that the curve in Fig. 16.7 is applicable to field choppers with flywheel cutterheads when chopping corn silage with a 13-mm [½-in.] theoretical cut. The curve should also apply reasonably well for direct-throw cylinder cutterheads, indicating a little over 0.8 kW·h/Mg [1 hp-h/ton] at 33 m/s [6500 ft/min].

Hennen[13] reports results from tests conducted by a manufacturer with several makes of field choppers and various crops during the period from

1960 to 1970. No information is given regarding the type of cutterhead, whether the chopped material was discharged by a direct-throw cylinder or by an auxiliary impeller-blower, or the magnitude of the peripheral speeds. Energy requirements at normal feed rates ranged from 1.0 to 1.5 kW·h/Mg [1.2 to 1.8 hp-h/ton] for a 13-mm [½-in.] theoretical cut with corn silage at 60 to 80% moisture and from 1.5 to 2.0 kW·h/Mg [1.8 to 2.4 hp-h/ton] for a 6-mm [¼-in.] theoretical cut with mature corn silage at 40 to 60% moisture.

Energy requirements for chopping green alfalfa (74% moisture content) with a 13-mm [½-in.] theoretical cut were obtained by Blevins[4] with 3 field choppers at peripheral speeds ranging from 20 to 46 m/s [4000 to 9000 ft/min]. His results indicate total energy requirements about 25 to 35% greater than those represented by the curve for corn silage in Fig. 16.7, which would be about 1.1 kW·h/Mg [1.3 hp-h/ton] at a typical peripheral speed of 33 m/s [6500 ft/min] for a direct-throw chopper. Richey[19] obtained comparable results with one flywheel-type chopper and one direct-throw cylinder chopper, and substantially higher energy requirements with a second flywheel-type chopper.

Hennen[13] includes results for alfalfa at 65% moisture with a 6-mm [¼-in.] theoretical cut that range from 1.55 to 2.3 kW·h/Mg [1.9 to 2.8 hp-h/ton] (peripheral speeds not stated). Some of Hennen's results probably represent choppers with auxiliary impeller-blowers.

Hennen's energy requirements for chopping low-moisture alfalfa silage at a 3-mm [⅛-in.] theoretical cut and with no recutter screen were about the same as for a 6-mm [¼-in.] theoretical cut using a recutter screen. Values ranged from about 4 kW·h/Mg [5 hp-h/ton] at 40 to 45% moisture to 2.5 kW·h/Mg [3 hp-h/ton] at 60% moisture.[13] In Wisconsin tests with a 6-mm [¼-in.] theoretical cut and an alfalfa-brome mixture at 49% moisture, adding a recutter screen with 102-mm [4-in.] square openings increased the tractor fuel consumption by 0.27 kg/Mg [0.54 lb/ton]. Assuming a fuel conversion factor of 1.65 kW·h/L (Table 2.2) and a density of 0.72 kg/L, the increase in energy requirements due to the recutter screen would be 0.62 kW·h/Mg [0.75 hp-h/ton].

Total energy requirements per ton for a forage chopper decrease somewhat as the feed rate is increased (curve E in Fig. 16.5), primarily because the power for blowing air and some minor power requirements are relatively independent of feed rate.

16.14. Capacity of Field Choppers. The capacity of a field chopper may be limited by the capacity of the feed mechanism, by the amount of power available, by the ability of the cutterhead and impeller to chop and handle the material, or by other factors.

The theoretical maximum capacity of the feed mechanism is a function of throat cross-sectional area (defined in Section 16.5), the rate of advance of material through the throat (generally considered to be the same as the linear speed of the feed mechanism), and the density of the forage as it passes between the feed rolls. The theoretical capacity T_t, in megagrams per hour [tons per hour], may be expressed by the relation

$$T_t = 6.000 \times 10^{-9} \, D \, A \, L \, N \, R \qquad (16.3)$$

$$[\, T_t = 1.736 \times 10^{-5} \, D \, A \, L \, N \, R \,]$$

where D = density of forage as it passes between the feed rolls, in kilograms per cubic metre [pounds per cubic foot]

A = throat area, in square centimetres [square inches]

L = theoretical length of cut, in millimetres [inches]

N = number of knives on cutterhead

R = speed of cutterhead, in revolutions per minute

The actual maximum working capacity of the feed mechanism will ordinarily be somewhat less than the theoretical maximum because of the difficulty in maintaining a uniform feed rate. It has been suggested that rated capacities (at 100% field efficiency) be taken as 70% of the theoretical maximum when chopping corn silage and 60% of the theoretical maximum when chopping hay.[1]

Throat widths of 430 to 585 mm [17 to 23 in.] and heights of 115 to 165 mm [4½ to 6½ in.] are typical for many current models. Throat areas range from 420 to 970 cm² [65 to 150 in.²], with 680 to 810 cm² [105 to 125 in.²] being most common. The speed of the feed mechanism is determined by the number of knives on the cutterhead, the cutterhead speed, and the desired theoretical length of cut. Reducing the feed-mechanism speed to obtain a shorter cut reduces the capacity of the feed mechanism.

The density factor is primarily a function of the type of material and its moisture content but is also influenced by the way the material enters the feed mechanism and by the pressure of the feed rolls. The effective feeding density of a given material may not be the same as the storage density and will vary somewhat for different machines. It can best be determined by actual capacity tests with the machine or machines involved. Results of research at the Wisconsin Agricultural Experiment Station over a period of many years indicate that average effective densities of 340 kg/m³ [21 lb/ft³] for green corn silage and 56 kg/m³ [3.5 lb/ft³] for hay at 26% moisture are reasonable values.[1,3]

The capacity of the feed mechanism may be the limiting factor when making short cuts in light material, such as a 6-mm [¼-in.] theoretical cut with low-moisture grass/legume silage. But when chopping corn silage with a 13-mm [½-in.] theoretical cut, the availability of power is more likely to be the controlling factor.

HANDLING CHOPPED FORAGE

Chopped forage is usually collected from the chopper in a self-unloading forage wagon pulled behind the chopper. At the storage site the wagon unloads the material at a controlled rate into a forage blower. With choppers available that can harvest more than a megagram a minute, materials handling becomes an important aspect of a field chopping system. For the most efficient operation, the size and number of wagons and the blower capacity must be closely matched to the chopper capacity. Hitching and unhitching wagons behind the chopper every 10 to 15 min can drastically reduce the field efficiency.

16.15. Forage Wagons. The typical self-unloading forage wagon has a chain-and-slat conveyor on the bed that moves the material to a conveyor located across the front of the wagon. Chain-and-slat cross conveyors are the most common type, but augers and belts are sometimes employed. A vertically stacked group of 2 or 3 toothed, rotating beaters "shaves" off the advancing load uniformly onto the cross conveyor. The cross conveyor delivers the material into the hopper of the elevator or conveyor at the storage site. When the cross conveyor is fitted with a short, inclined extension, the wagon can be used to distribute feed as the wagon is pulled along a continuous manger or bunk.

To prevent excessive losses of chopped material while loading and in transit, forage wagons are usually covered or have roof attachments available. Volumetric capacities are mostly from 8.5 to 21 m³ [300 to 750 ft³]. Many forage wagons have reversible drives on the bed conveyor to permit rear unloading of various materials such as jumbled bales from a bale thrower. Ear corn from a field picker can be collected in a forage wagon and unloaded with the cross conveyor.

The tractor PTO usually drives the conveyors and beaters. The bed-conveyor speed needs to be adjustable to control the unloading rate. Linear speeds of 0.3 to 1.5 m/min [1 to 5 ft/min] are typical. Various speed-change arrangements are used, including gear-change boxes, ratchet drives, variable V-belt drives, changing sprockets, and hydraulic motors. Gear-change boxes are the most common. A ratchet drive provides a simple means of obtaining a large speed reduction and speed adjustment, but produces intermittent motion and high peak forces. With any drive arrangement, moderate speed changes to match the unloading rate to the blower capacity may be made by changing the tractor engine speed.

A telescoping tongue is highly desirable to facilitate hitching to the rear of the chopper or to the transport vehicle. Such a device permits one man to unlatch and extend the tongue as required to make the connection, without having to accurately maneuver and position the towing machine. After hitching, the operator merely backs the machine until the tongue locks in the retracted position.

16.16. Forage Blowers. Forage blowers are popular for handling chopped material because of their simplicity, dependability, and high capacities. Basically, a forage blower consists of a feed hopper and conveyor that feeds the material into an impeller-blower similar to the units on some field choppers. Impeller-blowers depend primarily upon the throwing action of the blades rather than upon air velocity. An impeller-blower has a relatively small number of blades — usually 3 or 4 on field choppers and 6 on forage blowers. The housing is concentric, with the radial clearance between the blades and the housing periphery usually not over 3 mm [⅛ in.].

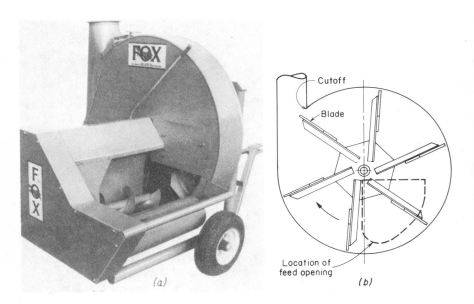

Fig. 16.8. (a) A forage blower with typical, short hopper. Most units do not have the adjustable plate to control the size of feed opening. (Courtesy of Koehring Farm Equipment.) (b) Schematic arrangement of an impeller-blower.

Short feed hoppers with auger conveyors (Fig. 16.8) are the most common arrangement on current models. This type of hopper is suitable for unloading from the front cross conveyor of a forage wagon. A blower having a 915-mm-diameter [36-in.-diameter] circular hopper and a high-speed rotary-table feed conveyor became available in 1970. Some forage blowers have tilt-up chain-and-slat conveyor tables, 2.7 to 3.7 m [9 to 12 ft] long, usually feeding into an auger hopper. The long feed tables are necessary for rear unloading from wagons without cross conveyors. Before the widespread adoption of forage wagons with cross conveyors, long feed tables feeding directly into the impeller-blower were the rule.

Forage blowers are generally designed to provide the desired peripheral speeds with the impeller-blower connected directly to the 540-r/min PTO shaft of a tractor. Some have auxiliary drives, such as sprockets and a chain from a jack shaft, for 1000-r/min PTO speeds or to permit increasing the impeller-blower speed. Impeller-blowers generally have diameters from 1190 to 1420 mm [47 to 56 in.] and peripheral speeds of 34 to 40 m/s [6700 to 7900 ft/min] at 540 r/min. Blades are usually radial or slanted backward 5 to 10°. Most discharge pipes have diameters of 229 mm [9 in.]. Rated capacities of the larger models are at least 55 to 90 Mg [60 to 100 tons] of corn silage per hour and one-third to one-half as great for dry hay.

The trend toward increased use of low-moisture grass/legume silage has influenced forage-blower design, primarily because of problems from the gummy residue. Short feed hoppers sometimes have vibrating pans or tables to improve the uniformity of flow to the auger. (These also help with other materials.) Many models have garden-hose connections to permit spraying water onto the impeller blades during operation with low-moisture silage.

16.17. Material Movement in an Impeller-Blower. When a forage particle that has entered the blower housing is contacted by an impeller blade, it is almost immediately accelerated to the angular velocity of the blade. Centrifugal force then causes the particle to move outward on the blade until it contacts the housing periphery or is discharged directly into the outlet opening. If the particle does not reach the blade tip until the blade is past the outlet cutoff point (Fig. 16.8b), the particle must make another revolution, sliding against the housing and increasing the friction losses, before it can be discharged.

As indicated in Section 16.11, friction against the housing can represent a major energy component. For the best performance of a forage blower, the feed inlet must be positioned to minimize carry-over past the feed outlet and to minimize the sliding distances around the periphery before the particles reach the outlet. Determination of the best location of the feed inlet opening with respect to the outlet is facilitated if the paths of particles on the blade are known or can be predicted.

Totten and Millier[22] present general equations for particle displacement and velocity along a blade, as derived by Kampf. These equations apply to radial or slanted flat blades and include the effect of friction between the particle and the blade. Gravitational effects are neglected and it is assumed that particle movement along the blade is not affected by air movement and that the initial acceleration to the blade velocity does not affect the particle path. Simplified equations for radial blades, assuming zero radial velocity of the particle at the initial contact and immediate acceleration to the angular velocity of the blade, are as follows:[22]

$$\frac{r}{r_o} = \frac{Ae^{B\theta} - Be^{A\theta}}{A - B} \tag{16.4}$$

$$V_r = r_o \omega \frac{e^{A\theta} - e^{B\theta}}{A - B} \tag{16.5}$$

where r_o = radius of initial contact between the particle and the blade

θ = angle of rotation of the impeller beyond the point of initial contact at r_o, in radians

r = radial distance to the particle at rotational angle θ

V_r = radial velocity of particle with respect to the blade at rotational angle θ

ω = angular velocity of impeller

e = base of natural logarithms

$A = -\mu + \sqrt{\mu^2 + 1}$

$B = -\mu - \sqrt{\mu^2 + 1}$

μ = coefficient of sliding friction between the particle and the blade

These relations are reasonably accurate for blades that are slanted small amounts from the radial position.[22] Note that the ratio r/r_o is independent of the rotational speed of the impeller and of the feed rate. The theoretical angle of rotation θ_f required for a particle to reach the housing periphery or blade tip, and the radial velocity V_{rf} when the particle reaches the blade tip, can be determined from equations 16.4 and 16.5 by letting r equal the housing radius r_f, $\theta = \theta_f$, and $V_r = V_{rf}$.

For an assumed value of $\mu = 0.7$, which is reasonable for green silage, calculated values of θ_f (converted from radians) are 102° for $r_o = 0.5r_f$, 64° for $r_o = 0.7\,r_f$, and 30° for $r_o = 0.9r_f$. Corresponding values of θ_f for $\mu = 0.3$ are 86°, 55°, and 28°.

These calculated values of θ_f indicate that, with the usual location of the feed opening on present-day forage blowers (Fig. 16.8b), there should be very little carry-over past the cutoff point with most types of chopped forage. High-speed motion pictures in a series of tests confirmed this hypothesis for green alfalfa.[22] Long-cut cured hay is more troublesome than short-cut material in regard to carry-over, sometimes hairpinning over the blade tip and creating a severe wedging condition as it is carried around the housing beyond the cutoff. Prior to the 1960s, many forage blowers had feed openings laterally centered just below the impeller axis. Carry-over was inherently more serious than with the present-day location.

If a particle is released directly into the outlet opening without striking the housing, the discharge direction in relation to the axis of the discharge pipe is determined by the direction of the resultant of V_{rf} and the tangential velocity of the blade tip and by the angle of the impeller with respect to the outlet axis when the discharge occurs. According to a relation developed by

Chancellor,[6] impact of particles discharged at an angle of 20 to 30° from the pipe axis causes a loss of 50 to 70% of the particles' kinetic energy when the coefficient of friction is 0.6.

16.18. Elevating Effect. In general, it is reasonable to assume that the chopped material leaves the impeller blades with a tangential velocity component about equal to the peripheral speed of the impeller. Theoretically, if there were no air resistance or pipe friction, material leaving the impeller blades at a vertical velocity V would be elevated to a height of $h = V^2/2g$. Actual attained heights are considerably less than the theoretical heights because of friction and aerodynamic drag and because the material must have sufficient energy at the top to carry it around the elbow and deflect it into the storage container.

Blockages will occur in the pipe if the peripheral speed for a given height is too low. Operation at speeds greater than needed for elevation results in excessive power requirements. Based on tests with stationary corn ensilage choppers having flywheel-type cutterheads, Duffee[11] recommended peripheral speeds representing a 40% elevating efficiency (i.e., actual height = 40% of theoretical height). The broken-line curve in Fig. 16.7 shows the relation between recommended speed and actual height. Field experience indicates that minimum peripheral speeds for grass/legume silage should be about 15% greater than for corn silage. When a forage blower is putting material into a barn mow, the terminal velocity from the discharge pipe or elbow must be great enough to carry the hay across to the opposite side of the mow.

Totten and Millier[22] observed flow patterns, material velocities, and air pressures at 4 levels up to 20.7 m [68 ft.] in a vertical pipe when conveying green alfalfa having a 38-mm [1½-in.] theoretical cut. They found that most of the reduction of total energy in the air-forage stream (kinetic + potential + air pressure) occurred in the lower 6.1 m [20 ft], primarily because of friction between the chopped material and the lower portion of the pipe. This observation is consistent with Chancellor's predictions of high losses from nonaxial discharge into the pipe (Section 16.17). Only 55% of the initial velocity remained at 7 m [23 ft] above the impeller axis, but 38 to 46% remained at 20.7 m [68 ft].

Chancellor and Laduke[8] analyzed the motion of a particle in a deflector elbow and concluded that, usually, more than 50% of the kinetic energy of a particle is lost in a 90° elbow. In many cases the capacity limit of a blower is determined by characteristics of the deflector elbow that contribute to plugging. They suggest several possibilities for improving the deflector design.

In general, the air velocity in the discharge pipe is lower than the velocity of the solid particles leaving the impeller blades.[20] Thus during at least the lower part of the upward motion, the air stream is absorbing energy from the solid particles. As the solid particles slow down due to the effects of gravity, friction, and aerodynamic drag, their velocity in the upper portion of the pipe may become less than the air velocity. The air will then transfer energy to the solid particles, thereby providing some pneumatic conveying effect.

Chancellor[7] derived equations for height versus time for a particle moving upward in a vertical pipe, considering separately the relations with the particle velocity greater or less than the air velocity and neglecting friction between the solid particles and the pipe. He developed a procedure for computing the effect that energy transfer between the air and the solid particles has upon the static air pressure required at the blower outlet for various airflow rates. He investigated analytically the effects of feed rate, impeller-blower speed (particle initial velocity), pipe diameter, and pipe length, for an assumed particle suspension or terminal velocity of 5.2 m/s [17 ft/s].

Chancellor concluded that under most conditions the solid material imparts energy to the air stream, thereby slowing down the solids and decreasing the static pressure required at the blower (often to a negative value). The primary function of the air stream is to reduce the effect of air resistance upon the velocity of the solid particles. His calculations show that the air velocity in the pipe has a marked influence upon the velocity of the solid particles at the top of the pipe. Partially blocking the inlet to the blower, either with material being fed in or with an adjustable gate, reduces the elevation height for a given impeller speed. Using a discharge pipe that is too large in relation to the blower size and inlet opening reduces the air velocity and adversely affects the elevating ability. A pipe that is too small increases friction losses.

16.19. Energy Requirements and Efficiencies. As a particle moves through an impeller-blower, energy is required or expended (a) because of the initial impact of the particle on the blade, (b) to accelerate the particle along the blade from the point of initial impact to the blade tip, (c) to maintain the blade's rotational velocity when the particle strikes the housing periphery, and (d) to overcome friction as the particle slides along the housing periphery.[22]

The theoretical efficiency (kinetic energy of particle leaving the blade divided by the energy input to particle) for particles that enter the blower outlet without touching the housing is 50% for radial paddles.[22] This value represents the maximum efficiency attainable with a radial-blade impeller-blower. Particles contacting the housing are subjected to additional losses from (c) and (d), above. The frictional loss due to sliding along the housing periphery is indicated by equation 16.1. Wedging of particles between the blade and the housing, especially with grasses and cured hay, can cause significant increases in friction losses. In practice, impeller-blower efficiencies, as defined above, are usually 25 to 30%.[17]

Total power requirements increase rapidly with speed because all the major power components (moving air, friction, and kinetic energy) theoretically vary as the square or the cube of the peripheral speed (discussed in Sections 16.9, 16.11, and 16.12). Deforest[10] determined power requirements in 1947 for an 8-blade impeller-blower elevating corn silage at peripheral speeds from 30 to 61 m/s [6000 to 12,000 ft/min]. Increasing the speed from 35.6 m/s to 45.7 m/s [7000 ft/min to 9000 ft/min] increased the energy requirements from 0.45 kW·h/Mg to 0.70 kW·h/Mg [0.55 to 0.85 hp-h/ton]. Smith[21] obtained energy requirements of 0.78 and 1.11 kW·h/Mg [0.95 and 1.35 hp-h/ton] at speeds of 35.6 and 43.2 m/s [7000 and 8500 ft/min], respectively, with two 4-blade (radial) impeller-blowers when elevating 24.5 Mg/h [27 tons/h] of grass/legume forage having 53% moisture.

Manufacturers' stated capacities and recommended power levels for current models yield maximum-capacity specific-energy values in the range of the values obtained by Deforest. In general, energy requirements per megagram increase as the feed rate is decreased and are greater for low-moisture grass/legume silage than for green silage.

Overall efficiencies of forage blowers are quite low compared with mechanical conveyors. For an assumed peripheral speed of 35.6 m/s [7000 ft/min], a maximum practical elevating height of 24.4 m [80 ft] for corn silage at this speed (Fig. 16.7), and an energy requirement of 0.58 kW·h/Mg [0.7 hp-h/ton], the calculated overall efficiency is 11.6%.

REFERENCES

1. BARRINGTON, G. P., O. I. BERGE, and F. W. DUFFEE. Hay harvesting machinery — forage harvester studies (mimeographed). University of Wisconsin Project 406, 1953 and 1954.
2. BARRINGTON, G. P., O. I. BERGE, and M. F. FINNER. Effect of using a recutter in a cylinder type forage harvester chopping low moisture grass silage. Trans. ASAE, 14(2):232-233, 1971.
3. BERGE, O.I. Design and performance characteristics of the flywheel-type forage-harvester cutterhead. Agr. Eng., 32:85-91, Feb., 1951.
4. BLEVINS, F. Z. Some of the component power requirements of field-type forage harvesters. Unpublished thesis. Purdue University, 1954. (See also Agr. Eng., 37:21-26, 29, Jan., 1956.)
5. BOCKHOP, C. W., and K. K. BARNES. Power distribution and requirements of a flail-type forage harvester. Agr. Eng., 36:453-457, July, 1955.
6. CHANCELLOR, W. J. Influence of particle movement on energy losses in an impeller blower. Agr. Eng., 41:92-94, Feb., 1960.
7. CHANCELLOR, W. J. Relations between air and solid particles moving upward in a vertical pipe. Agr. Eng., 41:168-171, 176, Mar., 1960.
8. CHANCELLOR, W.J., and G. E. LADUKE. Analysis of forage flow in a deflector elbow. Agr. Eng., 41:234-236, 240, Apr., 1960.
9. COWAN, A. M., K. K. BARNES, and R. S. ALLEN. Evaluation of shredded legume-grass silage. Agr. Eng., 38:588-591, 605, Aug., 1957.

10. DEFOREST, S. S. The development of a high speed drag type elevator for chopped forage. Unpublished thesis. Iowa State University, 1947.
11. DUFFEE, F. W. Ensilage cutters. CREA Handbook. Committee on the Relation of Electricity to Agriculture, Chicago, Ill., Mar. 5, 1930.
12. FINNER, M. F. Harvesting and handling low-moisture silage. Trans. ASAE, 9(3):377-378, 381, 1966.
13. HENNEN, J. J. Power requirements for forage chopping. ASAE Paper 71-145, 1971.
14. HULL, D. O., and A. M. COWAN, Jr. Development of the flail forage harvester. Iowa Agr. Ext. mimeo 850, Dec., 1956.
15. LILJEDAHL, J. B., G. L. JACKSON, R. P. DE GRAFF, and M. E. SCHROEDER. Measurement of shearing energy, Agr. Eng., 42:298-301, June, 1961.
16. PASCAL, J. A. A comparison between the performance of simple and "double-chop" flail forage harvesters. J. Agr. Eng. Res., 7:241-247, 1962.
17. PETTENGILL, D. H., and W. F. MILLIER. The effects of certain design changes on the efficiency of a forage blower. Trans. ASAE, 11(3):403-406, 408, 1968.
18. RANEY, J. P., and J. B. LILJEDAHL. Impeller blade shape affects forage blower performance. Agr. Eng., 38:722-725, Oct., 1957.
19. RICHEY, C. B. Discussion on "energy requirements for cutting forage." Agr. Eng., 39:636-637, Oct., 1958.
20. SEGLER, G. Calculation and design of cutterhead and silo blower. Agr. Eng., 32:661-663, Dec., 1951.
21. SMITH, H. K. A preliminary study of performance characteristics of four commercial forage blowers. Unpublished thesis. Purdue University, 1956.
22. TOTTEN, D. S., and W. F. MILLIER. Energy and particle path analysis: forage blower and vertical pipe. Trans. ASAE, 9(5):629-636, 640, 1966.
23. TRIBELHORN, R. E., and J. L. SMITH. Chopping energy of a forage harvester. Trans. ASAE, 18(3):423-426, 430, 1975.
24. ZIMMERMAN, M. Harvesting the hay crops — chopped materials. Implement & Tractor, 79(9):20-22, 44, Apr. 7, 1964.

PROBLEMS

16.1. The cylinder-type cutterhead on a direct-throw field chopper has 6 knives and a diameter of 460 mm. The peripheral speed is 30 m/s. The throat size is 50 × 14 cm. For a 13-mm theoretical length of cut with corn silage,

(a) Calculate the linear speed of the feed mechanism.

(b) Calculate the rated capacity in megagrams per hour, at 100% field efficiency. (Assume rated capacity = 70% of theoretical maximum.)

(c) Estimate the total power requirement at rated capacity, indicating the basis for your estimate.

16.2. Derive equation 16.1.

16.3. The total power input to the impeller-cutterhead on a PTO-driven field chopper is 22 kW and the theoretical length of cut is 13 mm. The division of power is as follows: cutting — 40%, accelerating chopped material — 20%, friction of chopped material in housing — 25%, and blowing air — 15%. If the tractor engine speed is increased 10% (thereby increasing the forward speed and the speeds of all chopper components), what would be

(a) The new total power input to the impeller-cutterhead?

(b) The new theoretical cutting length?

16.4. (a) A forage blower with a 1200-mm-diameter impeller is used to elevate corn silage to a height of 21 m. According to Duffee's recommendations, what is the minimum r/min for the blower?

(b) What are the principal effects of operating at a speed greater than necessary? What are the effects of operating at too low a speed?

16.5. Calculate the mass and volume (cubic centimetres) of corn silage carried on each impeller blade of a 6-blade forage blower operating at 540 r/min when the feed rate is 65 Mg/h. Assume a density of 320 kg/m^3.

16.6. (a) If a particle of material entering a forage blower contacts a radial blade 10° before the blade reaches its vertically downward position, at what distance from the rotor center must it contact the blade in order to be discharged directly into the outlet opening when the blade is 25° above horizontal? Assume μ = 0.7 and impeller diameter = 1270 mm.

(b) At what angle from the vertical would the particle be discharged?

17

Grain and Seed Harvesting

17.1. Introduction. Practically all grain and seed crops in the United States are now harvested with combined harvester-threshers, commonly known as combines. The greatest applications of combines are in harvesting the small grains, soybeans, and corn, but these machines are also used for a wide variety of small-area or specialty seed crops. Corn heads and the practice of harvesting corn with grain combines are discussed in Chapter 18, along with specialized corn harvesting equipment.

Direct combining, which means cutting and threshing in one operation, is the most common harvest method. Combining from the windrow involves an extra operation (windrowing) as compared with direct combining but is advantageous under certain conditions. Windrowing permits the curing of green weeds and unevenly ripened crops before threshing. The weather hazard to the standing crop is reduced because windrowing can be started several days earlier than direct combining. The principal application of windrow combining for cereal grains is in the northern section of the United States and in western Canada. Crops such as alfalfa, clovers, and flax are often harvested by the windrow-combine method.

In areas having a hot, dry climate, the system of spray curing followed by direct combining is common for small-seed legumes such as alfalfa and Ladino clover. In this method, a desiccant or a general-contact herbicide is applied to kill the top growth. The crop is then direct combined after the leaves are dry but before regrowth starts. Spray curing is most effective when the crop is uniformly mature, open, and erect. More than one spray application may be needed if the crop has a heavy, lush growth.

17.2. Development of Level-Land Combines. Although combines were common in California before the turn of the century, the large-scale adoption of these machines in the Great Plains area did not occur until the 1920s. Early combines were large, pull-type machines with headers hinged to the side of the separator body just ahead of the cylinder. Some headers were as wide as 10.7 m [35 ft]. Small, pull-type combines, mostly 1.5 to 2.1 m [5 to 7 ft] cut, became available in the mid 1930s. These were one-man machines, adaptable to the small farms in the central and eastern sections of the United States. They gained in popularity quite rapidly.

Self-propelled, front-cut combines, mostly with 3.0 to 4.3 m [10 to 14 ft] headers, came into prominence during the 1940s. Sizes have become larger in recent years, with headers up to 7.3 m [24 ft] wide available in 1977. Self-propelled combines have largely replaced pull-type machines, comprising 90 to 95% of all combines manufactured annually in the United States in 1967, 1968, and 1969.[1] Self-propelled combines have either variable-speed V-belt propulsion drives or hydrostatic drives. Infinitely variable forward-speed control is important to facilitate maintaining optimum feed rates into the combine.

Most pull-type machines currently manufactured are merely PTO-driven adaptations of self-propelled models. Header widths are usually 3.0 to 4.0 m [10 to 13 ft]. The principal interest in pull-type machines is in areas where windrow combining is common. Pull-type combines are considerably less expensive (and less maneuverable) than comparable self-propelled models.

17.3. Hillside Combines. A hillside combine has provision for keeping the body level while harvesting on slopes. Levelness is important in regard to proper functioning of the separating and cleaning units and for machine stability. The principal use of hillside combines is in the Pacific Northwest. The first hillside combines, built in about 1890,[51] were horse-drawn, ground-traction-driven machines that were leveled manually.

Automatic-leveling, self-propelled hillside combines became generally available in the early 1950s.[51] Some present-day models provide only lateral leveling, but some also have fore-and-aft leveling. Lateral leveling is accomplished by hydraulically moving one drive wheel up and the other down with respect to the body. Appropriate linkages keep all four wheels vertical. The header platform is attached to the feeder housing in such a manner as to provide a longitudinal pivot axis. A linkage between the header and the main-axle assembly automatically keeps the platform parallel with the ground beneath the drive wheels. Side leveling can compensate for maximum slopes of 30 to 45%.

Fore-and-aft leveling requires an additional mechanism to raise and lower the rear wheels with respect to the rear of the combine and a linkage connection between the rear axle and the header to keep the header height constant. Fore-and-aft leveling permits operating up or down a slope, whereas lateral leveling alone is effective only for operating approximately on the contour. Automatic four-way leveling systems for hillside green-pea combines (Fig. 21.3) have been patterned after those on grain combines.

Sensing devices are controlled by the action of gravity upon a pendulum or upon a liquid.[51] One system, for side leveling and fore-and-aft leveling, has a heavy, damped pendulum that actuates specially designed spool-type hydraulic control valves (Section 4.22). In another system, which has only side leveling,[22] a fluid reservoir exerts pressure on a diaphragm and sensitive pressure switch located at some lateral distance from the reservoir. Any side tilting of the combine body changes the pressure on the diaphragm and actuates the switch, which in turn operates solenoid valves in the hydraulic system and levels the machine. In a third type of system, the liquid is an electric conductor, such as mercury, and acts as a switch when the level in one leg of a U-tube arrangement raises or lowers.[51] Some systems have two-speed leveling, the slower speed being for small amounts of tilt.

17.4. Functional Components of a Combine. The ultimate purpose of any harvesting and threshing operation is to recover the seed, free from plant residue, with a minimum of seed loss. If the seed is intended for planting or certain other uses, minimum visible damage and internal injury are important. The four basic operations performed by a combine in recovering the seed are:

1. Cutting, or picking up from the windrow, and conveying the material to the threshing mechanism.
2. Threshing (detachment of individual seeds from the supporting parts of the plant).
3. Separating the seed and chaff from the straw.
4. Cleaning the chaff and other debris from the seed.

A general arrangement of the basic functional components of a conventional self-propelled combine is shown schematically in Fig. 17.1. Although

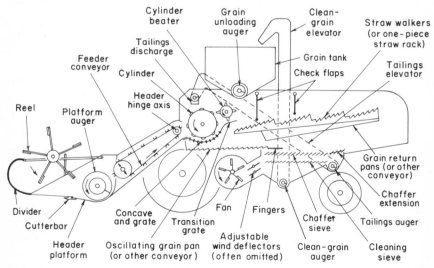

Fig. 17.1. Schematic arrangement of the basic functional components of a typical self-propelled combine.

each of the basic functions is discussed in detail in later sections, it should be helpful to the reader to first obtain an overall picture of the entire sequence of operations.

In direct combining, the reel pushes the uncut stalks against the cutterbar and then delivers the cut material onto the header platform. The header cross conveyor (usually an auger) delivers the material to the feeder conveyor, which is usually a chain-and-slat type with the lower end floating. The feeder conveyor moves the material upward to the cylinder-and-concave assembly, where it is threshed. When the concave is of the open-grate type, a high percentage of the threshed seed, as well as a considerable amount of chaff and small debris, is separated from the straw through the openings in the concave grate, falling directly onto the oscillating grain pan or some other type of conveyor (e.g., a group of parallel augers in troughs or a chain-and-slat conveyor).

The transition grate guides the material from the concave rearward to the straw carrier and provides additional separating area. The transition grate usually has either parallel fingers (rods) or a grid-type arrangement with cross bars. The cylinder beater helps strip the material from the cylinder, propels it along the transition grate, aids in further seed separation at this point, and directs the straw and unseparated seed onto the straw carrier. The straw carrier on a conventional combine may be multiple-section walkers, a one-piece oscillating rack, or a raddle conveyor preceding straw walkers.

One or two check flaps or curtains, suspended above the walkers or rack, retard the straw flow and assist in maintaining a uniform layer thickness. The front flap aids the beater in getting the material down onto the front of the walkers or rack for maximum utilization of the separation area. The flaps also prevent seeds from being thrown out the rear by the beater.

The straw walkers or straw rack agitate the material to separate out remaining seed and unthreshed heads as the straw is moved rearward to be discharged from the machine. The seed, chaff, and other small debris that fall through the openings in the walkers or rack are collected by grain return pans attached to the walker sections or by some other type of conveyor. This material is delivered to the grain pan, joining the stream of material that has passed through the openings in the concave grate.

The mixture of threshed seed, unthreshed material, chaff, and other debris is transferred from the grain pan onto the front of the oscillating chaffer sieve. As the mixture moves rearward over the chaffer sieve, an air blast directed upward through the sieve aids in separating out the free (threshed) seed and unthreshed heads and blows the light chaff out the rear of the machine. Most of the unthreshed heads ride over the chaffer sieve and drop through the larger openings of the chaffer extension into the tailings auger. Heads or pieces that pass through the chaffer sieve are delivered to the tailings auger by the cleaning sieve. The tailings are returned to the cylinder for rethreshing or sometimes, if the seed is easily damaged, to a point just behind the cylinder. Some combines have a miniature rasp-bar cylinder to rethresh the tailings, after which they are returned to the grain pan in front of the chaffer sieve.

The free seed and some debris fall through the chaffer sieve onto the cleaning sieve, which has smaller openings than the chaffer sieve. The seed passes through the cleaning sieve and is delivered to the grain tank by means of a clean-grain auger and elevator.

A somewhat different arrangement of threshing and separating units is shown in Fig. 17.2. The threshing cylinder and concave are located in the

Fig. 17.2. Cutaway view of a combine having the cylinder in the feeder housing and a raddle-type front straw separator. Note the precleaning fan just below the raddle conveyor. (Courtesy of Allis-Chalmers.)

header feeder housing and the concave is of the closed type (i.e., no openings through the concave). All the seed remains with the straw until the material is discharged above the raddle conveyor, which is the front part of the straw carrier and separator. The seed tends to fall out of the suspended straw onto the conveyor.

Figure 17.3 shows a combine in which the conventional cross-flow threshing cylinder and the straw walkers have been replaced with two independent, parallel rotors, each of which performs the threshing operation and most of the separating operation.[43] The incoming material is divided between the two rotors and fed into the threshing units by the auger sections on the front portions of the rotors. The adjacent surfaces of the rotors move downward. Each stream of material moves along the rotor in a helical path, passing first the rasp-bar threshing unit and then the separating grate beneath the rear portion of the rotor. Angled fins attached to the inside of the upper portion of the rotor housing (not shown in Fig. 17.3) cause the rotating material to move rearward. Both rotors discharge the material onto a transverse rear beater that moves the material over another separator grate and then discharges the straw from the machine. The cleaning shoe is similar to that on conventional combines. This machine first became com-

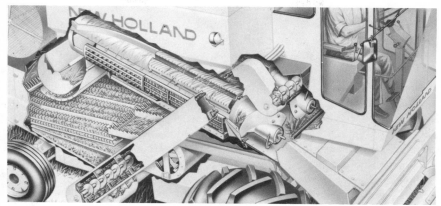

Fig. 17.3. Cutaway view of a combine having two independent, axial-flow rotors that perform the threshing and separating operations as the material moves along them in helical paths. The stream of incoming material is divided between the two rotors. (Courtesy of Sperry New Holland.)

mercially available in 1975. Single-rotor machines became available in 1977.

17.5. Definitions and Terminology. Because of some lack of consistency in terminology in published literature and general usage, it seems desirable to define certain terms that are used in this book. The terms *grain* and *seed* are used interchangeably in this chapter to represent kernels or seeds from all crops harvested with combines. Types of seed losses are identified in Section 17.6. Other pertinent definitions are as follows:*

Non-grain material includes all plant material entering the combine except the grain or seed.

Grain/non-grain ratio is the ratio of grain or seed mass to the mass of non-grain material. Unless stated otherwise (e.g., walker grain/non-grain ratio), the ratio refers to material entering the machine.

Non-grain feed rate is the rate at which non-grain material is delivered to the cylinder by the header. *Walker non-grain feed rate* and *shoe non-grain feed rate* apply to non-grain material fed onto these components.

Grain feed rate is the rate at which grain or seed is delivered to the cylinder by the header. It is the sum of the grain into the grain tank plus the losses from the rear of the machine, per unit of time.

Total feed rate is the sum of the non-grain feed rate and the grain feed rate.

---

*Terminology in this chapter generally follows the recommendations in ASAE Standard S343 (adopted in 1971) except that (a) "non-grain material" and derivatives from it are used instead of "material other than grain" and (b) "grain/non-grain ratio" is the reciprocal of the term "material-other-than-grain to grain ratio" in S343. Most literature published prior to 1971 used "grain/straw ratio."

17.6. Types and Sources of Seed Losses. Seed losses from a combine can occur in connection with any of the four basic operations listed in Section 17.4. These losses are often identified as gathering, cylinder, walker, and shoe losses. The sum of the cylinder, walker, and shoe losses is the processing loss.

Gathering losses in direct combining include heads, pods, or ears, and free seed, lost during the cutting and conveying operations. In windrow combining, total gathering losses for the harvest system include windrower losses as well as combine gathering losses in the pickup and conveying operations. Cylinder loss consists of unthreshed seed discharged from the rear of the machine, either in the straw or in the material from the cleaning shoe. Walker loss is free (threshed) seed carried over the walkers or rack (or other type of separating unit) in the straw and discharged from the machine. Shoe loss is free seed discharged over the rear of the shoe.

Cylinder, walker, and shoe losses are expressed as percentages of the grain feed rate or grain intake. Gathering loss is expressed as a percentage of the sum of the grain feed rate plus the gathering-loss rate.

Seed damage does not represent a direct loss of yield, except for seeds broken into pieces too small for recovery, but it may reduce the quality and value of the product, depending upon the intended use for the seed or grain. Thus, cracked kernels do not reduce the feeding quality of grain but are undesirable in malting barley or in rice that is to be milled. Seed damage, as it affects germination, is an important consideration when the harvested product is intended for planting. With some kinds of seed, such as lima beans, germination may be reduced by internal damage even though there is no visible evidence of damage.

17.7. Size Relations for Functional Components. The relative magnitudes of the different kinds of seed losses from a given combine depend upon the kind of crop and the harvest conditions. The engineer is faced with a compromise situation in determining the most desirable and economical combination of capacities for the different functional units in a multi-crop harvester. Header-width requirements are related to the capacities of the threshing, separating, and cleaning units, to crop yields, and to the appropriate range of forward speeds. To accommodate a range of anticipated crop conditions, various sizes of headers are available for most self-propelled models.

Size relations for 1977 models of self-propelled combines manufactured in the United States are summarized in Table 17.1 for four cylinder-width ranges. Cylinder width is a commonly used parameter of combine size. ASAE Standard S343 specifies methods for making various size measurements and for computing separating and cleaning areas.

In most combines the width of the separating and cleaning units is essentially the same as the cylinder width. Therefore, the areas given in Table 17.1

Table 17.1 SELF-PROPELLED COMBINE SIZES AND AREAS, 1977*

Cylinder Width				Header Width, Metres [Feet]		Average Area, cm² per Millimetre of Cyl. Width [in.² per Inch of Width]	
Millimetres		Inches		Avg. Min. Listed	Avg. Max. Listed		
Range	Avg.	Range	Avg.			Walkers†	Shoe Sieves
685-840	757	27-33	29.8	3.35 [11.0]	4.51 [14.8]	30.2 [119]	22.1 [87]
915-1015	983	36-40	38.7	3.87 [12.7]	6.16 [20.2]	30.5 [120]	23.6 [93]
1120-1320	1212	44-52	47.7	4.02 [13.2]	6.95 [22.8]	36.3 [143]	25.4 [100]
1395-1525	1461	55-60	57.5	3.96 [13.0]	7.32 [24.0]	34.5 [136]	25.9 [102]

*Based on data from Implement & Tractor Red Book, Jan. 31, 1977. Numbers of models listed in the four cylinder size groups, from top to bottom: 4, 9, 15, 2.
†Excluding models that have raddle-type separator preceding short straw walkers.

tend to indicate the relative lengths of the separating and cleaning units for the different size groups. The two largest groups have a little more separating and cleaning area per unit of cylinder width than do the smaller groups.

17.8. Cutting and Conveying. The cutting-and-conveying assembly, known as the header, includes the reel, the cutterbar, a platform or conveyor for receiving the cut material, and conveyors for delivering the material to the cylinder. The header is attached through a lateral hinge axis and is adjustable from the operator's station to obtain heights of cut ranging from about 5 cm up to at least 100 cm [2 to 40 in.]. The grain ordinarily is cut just low enough to recover all or nearly all of the heads. If the straw is to be saved, cutting may be at a lower height even though more material must be handled by the machine.

The cutterbar is similar in construction to that of a mower-conditioner or a self-propelled windrower but sickle speeds are lower, generally being between 400 and 550 cycles per minute. These sickle speeds are adequate for most combining but they result in considerable stalk deflection and slippage through the cutting unit when cutting an upright crop within a few centimetres of the ground at speeds above 4.8 to 6.4 km/h [3 to 4 mph]. In a crop like soybeans, the resulting stripping effect tends to increase shatter losses from the cutterbar.[30]

Fixed-bat reels (Fig. 17.1 and 17.2) have 4 to 6 wood or metal bats mounted rigidly on radial arms. Pickup reels have spring teeth attached to slats that are maintained in parallel positions by an eccentric-and-spider arrangement as the reel rotates (Fig. 14.10 *right*). Tooth pitch is adjustable by rotating the eccentric guide. Fixed-bat reels are widely used because they are simpler and less expensive than pickup reels and work well in upright crops. Pickup reels are very effective in lifting lodged (down) crops ahead of the cutterbar and also work satisfactorily in upright crops.

The position of the reel with respect to the cutterbar is adjustable both vertically and horizontally. Hydraulic height adjustment, controllable from the operator's station, is often provided. The height of a fixed-bat reel normally should be such that the top edges of the bats, at the lowest point of their travel, are a little below the lowest heads of the uncut grain. In upright grain, the reel axis is usually 150 to 300 mm [6 to 12 in.] ahead of the cutterbar.

The ratio of reel peripheral speed to forward speed (reel speed index) should be 1.25 to 1.5 under most conditions in upright crops.[20] Higher ratios may be more effective in laying the material back onto the header platform but tend to increase shatter losses. In California tests, for example, increasing the reel speed index from 1.5 to 2.8 increased barley shatter losses from 3% to 6% of the yield.[20]

When using a pickup reel in a badly lodged crop, the reel axis should be well ahead of the cutterbar (often 230 to 300 mm [9 to 12 in.]) and the teeth should clear the cutterbar by only 50 to 75 mm [2 to 3 in.]. Adjusting the slat pitch to point the teeth more rearward improves the lifting action. Low forward speeds and a lower reel speed index than for upright grain are advisable. Pickup reels are usually used in harvesting rice because this crop often lodges badly and the straw is generally wet and heavy.

The reel speed needs to be easily adjustable to accommodate different crop conditions and to compensate for different forward speeds. Variable-speed V-belt or hydraulic-motor drives, controllable from the operator's station, are often provided. Constant-ratio drives from the ground-drive system have been employed to a limited extent.

An auger cross conveyor moves the material across the header to the feeder conveyor. A retracting-finger section, which is part of the auger tube, delivers the material to the feeder conveyor. Rice combines sometimes have a short draper between the cutterbar and the auger to provide more room on the platform for handling long straw, especially when lodged. The feeder conveyor is usually a chain-and-slat unit (Fig. 17.1), but is a retracting-finger cylinder in the arrangement shown in Fig. 17.2.

17.9. Principles and Types of Threshing Mechanisms. Threshing may be accomplished by (a) impact of a fast-moving member upon the material, (b) rubbing, (c) squeezing pods, (d) a combination of two or more of these actions, or (e) some other method of applying the required forces. As an example under (e), laboratory tests have shown that wheat kernels can be removed from the heads by holding the stalks in a rotating clamp and applying centrifugal force.[29]

Many different types and configurations of threshing devices have been devised,[13] but very few have reached the stage of even limited field use. The three types generally employed in present-day combines are cross-flow rasp-bar cylinders (Fig. 17.4c), axial-flow rasp-bar cylinders (Fig. 17.3), and

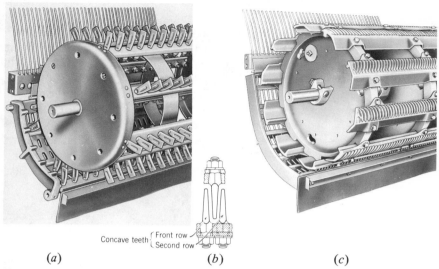

Concave teeth { Front row
              { Second row

(a)   (b)   (c)

Fig. 17.4. Two types of cylinders, showing the concave-and-grate assembly and a finger-type transition grate. *(a)* Spike-tooth cylinder. Note that the front and rear concave sections (removable) are each shown with two rows of teeth, whereas the middle section is blank (no teeth). Inset *(b)* shows the clearance relations between the teeth in the spike-tooth cylinder and those in the concave. *(c)* Cross-flow rasp-bar cylinder with open concave.

spike-tooth cylinders (Fig. 17.4a). Spike-tooth cylinders were used almost exclusively in both combines and stationary threshers prior to about 1930, but most combines now produced have rasp-bar cylinders. Spike-tooth cylinders are still used to a limited extent, principally in rice and windrowed beans.

Cross-flow rasp-bar cylinders and spike-tooth cylinders are available interchangeably on many combine models. Diameters are generally 480 to 600 mm [19 to 23.6 in.], with 559 mm [22 in.] being the most prevalent. Widths in 1977 models ranged from 685 to 1525 mm [27 to 60 in.], as indicated in Table 17.1. Spring-tooth cylinders are sometimes employed on combines intended for harvesting edible beans and on peanut combines (Chapter 20).

Most cross-flow rasp-bar cylinders have open-grate concaves with rectangular bars parallel to the cylinder axis, as shown in Fig. 17.4c. The clearance between the concave bars and the corrugated cylinder bars is adjustable. High-speed motion pictures have shown that in cereals the main threshing effect results from the impact or shattering action of the cylinder bars hitting the heads at high speeds.[2] Although rubbing undoubtedly contributes to the threshing action, the primary function of the concave appears to be holding or bringing the material into the cylinder-bar path for repeated impacts.[2]

Axial-flow (helical-flow) rasp-bar cylinders are similar to conventional cross-flow cylinders except for the number and arrangement of rasp bars on the rotor. Each of the 2 rotors shown in Fig. 17.3 has 2 pairs of rasp bars 180° apart instead of 8 to 10 uniformly spaced bars. Another arrangement, on a single-rotor machine, has three equally spaced helical rasp bars (that move the material along the rotor) and a staggered arrangement of short, axial sections between the helical bars. The cylinder diameter on the double-rotor model shown in Fig. 17.3 is 432 mm [17 in.]. Single-rotor models available in 1977 had diameters of 610 and 762 mm [24 and 30 in.].

The open-grate concaves on axial-flow cylinders are of the same general type as those used with cross-flow rasp-bar cylinders and are adjustable in a similar manner to change cylinder-concave clearances. A major functional difference is that the material passes through the threshing zone between the axial-flow cylinder and concave several times as it moves rearward in a helical path, rather than making a single pass as with a cross-flow cylinder.

The arrangement of a spike-tooth cylinder and concave is such that the cylinder teeth pass midway between staggered teeth on the concave, thus producing a combing action in addition to the high-speed impacts upon the heads. The concave assembly is adjusted laterally to give equal clearances on both sides of the cylinder teeth. The amount of radial overlap of the cylinder and concave teeth is adjustable. The lateral clearance is also changed slightly by this adjustment, since the teeth are tapered (Fig. 17.4b).

The teeth in the spike-tooth concave are mounted on perforated, removable sections, usually with two rows of teeth per section. The total number of rows of teeth needed in the concave (usually 2, 4, or 6) depends upon the crop and the threshing conditions. Perforated blank sections or grid-type grates are added to fill the concave space.

A spike-tooth cylinder has a more positive feeding action than a rasp-bar cylinder, does not plug as easily, and requires less power.[17] Rasp-bar cylinders are readily adaptable to a wide variety of crop conditions, are easy to adjust and maintain, and are relatively simple and durable. A rasp-bar cylinder with an open-grate concave has greater seed-separating capacity than a spike-tooth cylinder (discussed in Section 17.12).

On some models, the cylinder rasp bars can be replaced with rubber-faced angle-iron bars and the concave fitted with steel-jacketed rubber bars. This arrangement is sometimes called an angle-bar cylinder. Rubber-covered flat bars have also been employed on cylinders and concaves for harvesting small-seed legumes such as crimson clover, giving less damage and less un-threshed loss than conventional cylinders.[27] Rubber-covered bars wear considerably faster than steel bars.

With some podded crops, a large part of the threshing can be done with a squeezing action, a rubbing action, or a combination of the two. Rubber-covered steel rolls have been used to a limited extent for threshing beans. An experimental bean combine developed in 1937 at the California Agricultural Experiment Station[7] had a series of 3 pairs of rubber-covered rolls, operating at peripheral speeds of 1.3 to 1.5 m/s [250 to 300 ft/min], instead of a conventional cylinder. Threshing in this machine was entirely due to squeezing and rubbing of the bean pods. Satisfactory threshing of lima beans was obtained without appreciable seed damage.

A double-belt threshing unit was developed at the Oregon Agricultural Experiment Station in the late 1960s for harvesting easily damaged small-seed grasses and legumes. Two rough-surfaced belts traveling in the same direction at different speeds, with a small clearance between them, produce a rubbing and rolling action that threshes the seed. Belt backing plates are spring loaded. Laboratory tests with small quantities of soybeans have indicated that this crop also can be threshed effectively between two belts moving at different speeds, with practically no damage to the seeds.[48]

Several investigators have built and tested truncated-cone, rotary threshing units.[10,28,49] One of these[10] utilized centrifugal threshing and rubbing principles. The others depended mainly on impact and rubbing. One of the objectives in these designs has been to obtain adequate seed separation with the threshing unit so no additional separating unit (e.g., walkers) would be needed.

17.10. Performance Parameters for Threshing Cylinders. The primary performance parameters of a threshing unit are the percent of seed detached from the non-grain parts of the plant (threshing effectiveness) and the percent of seed that is damaged. Two additional parameters that are of importance because they affect the performance of the separating and cleaning units are the percent of seed separated through the concave grate (separating efficiency) and the degree of breakup of the straw. Power requirement is not a functional performance parameter but is of concern in evaluating a threshing unit. Power requirements are discussed in Section 17.29.

Most of the seed damage caused by a combine occurs in the threshing unit, primarily because of impact blows received during the threshing process. However, drag conveyors and close-fitting augers can cause damage to some types of seeds. Seed damage may be visible or it may be internal, the latter type being determinable only by germination tests or with special instruments. As explained in Section 17.6, the significance of seed damage depends upon the intended use for the seed or grain.

Maximum separation of threshed seed through the concave grate (and the transition grate) is important under the usual conditions for cereal grains in which walker losses represent an important or major portion of the total losses. Increasing the separation through the grates reduces the seed load onto the straw walkers or other type of separating unit, thereby usually reducing walker losses.[20] Reducing the grate separation efficiency from 85% to 70% would double the seed load onto the walkers. When walker losses are small, as with alfalfa and other small-seed crops under dry conditions, the amount of seed separation at the cylinder has little effect upon total losses.

Excessive straw breakup makes seed separation more difficult and causes a greater percentage of the non-grain material to go onto the shoe, either through the concave and transition grates or through the walkers. Increased amounts of non-grain material onto the shoe may appreciably increase shoe losses. Walker losses, on the other hand, would tend to be reduced because of the slight reduction in rate of non-grain material onto them.

17.11. Effects of Feeding Pattern upon Cylinder-and-Concave Performance. The orientation of the material as it enters a cross-flow cylinder has considerable effect upon cylinder-and-concave performance. Feeding butts first in laboratory tests with wheat and barley[2,15] resulted in cylinder losses at least twice as great as when fed heads first with the stalks parallel and the heads on top of the layer. The percentage of grain that failed to pass through the concave grate was also twice as high. A tangled pattern, simulating the effect of the header auger, gave about the same cylinder losses and separating efficiency as the heads-first feeding,[15,33] with somewhat more uniform feeding and lower cylinder power requirements.[15] Feeding heads first with the heads on the bottom of the layer was better than with the heads on top, but is difficult to do on a field machine.[15]

17.12. Effects of Cylinder and Concave Design Factors upon Performance. Extensive laboratory tests were conducted by the National Institute of Agricultural Engineering (NIAE) in England to determine the effects of various design parameters and operating conditions upon the performance of cross-flow rasp-bar cylinders when threshing wheat or barley at grain moisture contents ranging from 14 to 26%.[2,4,5] Cylinders were 610 mm [24 in.] wide and had diameters ranging from 381 to 686 mm [15 to 27 in.]. Concaves were of the open-grate type. Crop material was harvested with a grain binder when it reached the desired maturity and moisture content and was used within a few days. The material was fed into the cylinder by means of a 15.2-m [50-ft] variable-speed conveyor belt. Percentages of unthreshed seed, broken seed, germination, seed separation through the concave grate, and broken straw were determined.

In these tests, increasing the concave length increased the seed separation efficiency but at a diminishing rate. With wheat, for example, the first 169-mm [6.67-in.] section removed 52 to 58% of the grain and each successive 169-mm section (up to a total tested length of 678 mm [26.7 in.]) removed about 40% of the grain onto that section. Increasing the concave length increased the straw breakup and tended to increase seed damage, especially with low moisture contents and high cylinder speeds. Under easy threshing conditions there was little advantage, in regard to cylinder loss, of using concaves longer than 330 mm [13 in.]. But with more difficult conditions, increasing the length from 330 mm to 508 mm [20 in.] reduced the loss.

Operating with the concave openings omitted or covered could represent a design characteristic (as in Fig. 17.2) or it could represent a field adjustment. The effects of covering the openings in 356-mm-long [14-in.-long] concaves were determined in the NIAE tests[4] when threshing wheat at 15% and 24% moisture. Cylinder peripheral speeds ranged from 18 to 33 m/s [3500 to 6500 ft/min] and mean cylinder-concave clearances were 6 to 13 mm [¼ to ½ in.]. Seed damage was substantially greater with the openings covered than with them open, but there was no appreciable effect upon cylinder loss or straw breakup. Covering the concave openings when harvesting barley in California tests more than doubled the walker loss.[20]

Neal and Cooper[34] compared a cross-flow rasp-bar cylinder and open-grate concave with a spike-tooth cylinder and concave in regard to seed separation through the concave grate, using rice in laboratory tests. At a non-grain feed rate of 90 kg/min [200 lb/min], approximately 72% of the grain was separated by the rasp-bar concave grate but only 50% by the spike-tooth grate. A spike-tooth concave grate inherently has considerably less open area than a rasp-bar grate.

In the NIAE tests[2] there was a tendency for improved separation of wheat (but not barley) when the cylinder diameter was reduced from 533 mm to 381 mm [21 in. to 15 in.] but little effect above 533 mm. The concave length was 330 mm [13 in.]. Arnold concluded that cylinder diameter was not of major importance in regard to performance and that the diameter should be chosen to suit the desired concave length. Changing the peripheral spacing of rasp bars on the cylinder had little effect upon performance.

17.13. Effects of Operating Conditions upon Cylinder Loss and Seed Damage. Threshing effectiveness is related to (a) the peripheral speed of the cylinder, (b) the cylinder-concave clearance, (c) the number of times the material passes the concave (e.g., helical-flow cylinder), (d) the number of rows of concave teeth used with a spike-tooth cylinder, (e) the type of crop, (f) the condition of the crop in terms of moisture content, maturity, etc., and (g) the rate at which material is fed into the machine. Covering the concave openings so the heads or pods must pass over all the concave bars may be helpful for crops that are difficult to thresh. But, as indicated in the previous section, covering the concave openings sometimes increases walker losses.

Threshability varies widely with different crops and conditions. Some small-seed crops, such as the clovers, are very difficult to thresh, whereas barley and wheat are generally easy to thresh. Reducing the straw moisture content improves threshability.[2]

Cylinder speed is the most important operating parameter in regard to cylinder loss and also in regard to seed damage. Increasing the speed reduces the cylinder loss but may substantially increase damage. Susceptibility to damage varies greatly among different crops. The seeds of some dicotyledonous plants, such as beans, may be damaged excessively at peripheral speeds as low as 7.6 m/s [1500 ft/min],[6] whereas Ladino clover can withstand speeds of over 36 m/s [7000 ft/min] without appreciable damage.[11]

In general, seed damage increases as the seed moisture content is reduced.[2,6,11] Several investigators,[2,3] however, have found that germination of wheat or oats was reduced when threshed at seed moisture contents above (or below) an optimum range of about 17 to 22%. A similar relation has been observed in regard to corn kernel crackage (Section 18.10).

Figure 17.5 illustrates the effects of cylinder speed and moisture content upon cylinder loss and visible seed damage when threshing wheat in laboratory tests. Tests were conducted at 17.8, 22.9, 27.9, and 33.0 m/s [3500, 4500, 5500, and 6500 ft/min]. The "total" curves indicate that the total loss from unthreshed seed plus damaged seed would be minimized at a cylinder speed of about 23 m/s [4500 ft/min] for the low-moisture condition and 26 m/s [5100 ft/min] for the 20%-moisture condition. However, in

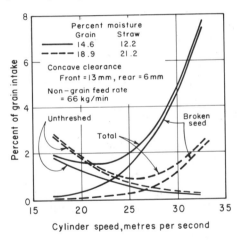

Fig. 17.5. Effect of cylinder speed upon seed damage and cylinder loss in laboratory tests with wheat, using a cross-flow rasp-bar cylinder. (Data from R.E. Arnold.[2])

determining the best cylinder speed for a field harvesting operation, the effects of cylinder speed upon walker loss and shoe loss also need to be considered. With some crops and under some conditions, high cylinder losses must be tolerated because a cylinder speed high enough to do a reasonably good threshing job will cause excessive seed damage.[11,27]

When harvesting barley in California at 7 to 9% seed moisture content,[20] visible damage amounted to 5% at 19.3 m/s [3800 ft/min], 10% at 24.4 m/s [4800 ft/min], and 15 to 20% at 29.5 m/s [5800 ft/min]. Cylinder losses were 1½ to 2% at 19.3 m/s and negligible at the higher speeds. Visible-damage percentages when harvesting barley at 12 to 15% moisture content in Minnesota[16] with a cross-flow rasp-bar cylinder and 10 to 13 mm [⅜ to ½ in.] clearance were only one-third to one-half as great at 24.4 m/s and 29.5 m/s as in the California tests with drier grain. Low visible damage and high germination are especially important for malting barley.

Reducing the cylinder-concave clearance tends to reduce cylinder losses and increase seed damage, but the effects are generally rather small in comparison with the effects of increasing cylinder speed. In laboratory tests with wheat, for example,[47] changing the clearance from 19 mm to 6 mm [¾ in. to ¼ in.] reduced the cylinder loss from 2.1% to 1.2% and increased visible damage from 5.4% to 7.8%. The Minnesota field tests[16] with barley having 12 to 15% moisture showed a moderate increase in visible damage when the clearance was reduced. Results from the California field tests[20] indicated no consistent relation between seed damage with barley at 7 to 9% moisture and clearances between 6 and 16 mm [¼ and ⅝ in.].

Arnold[2] compared front/rear clearance ratios of 3 to 1 and 1 to 1 and found very little difference in cylinder loss, visible damage, or germination of barley or wheat for any given mean clearance. Front-to-rear clearance convergence is generally desirable because the wider front opening tends to improve feeding characteristics of a cylinder.

Increasing the non-grain feed rate increases cylinder losses. Field tests have indicated that the relation is often about linear.[11,20,35,36] Increased feed rate tends to reduce seed damage, although the effect is usually small.[2,11,47] The greater density of the layer of material passing between the cylinder and the concave bars at high feed rates apparently provides more protection for the seeds, thereby reducing the probability of repeated impacts by the cylinder bars.

Field tests with barley, wheat, oats, and rye have indicated that increasing the grain/non-grain ratio usually decreases the percent cylinder loss at a given non-grain feed rate.[36]

17.14. Effects of Operating Conditions upon Straw Breakup and Seed Separation through Concave Grate. When harvesting cereal grains with combines having rasp-bar cylinders and open-grate concaves, 60 to 90% of the seed is usually separated through the concave grate.[2,20,34,41] Increasing the cylinder speed or decreasing the clearance causes more seed to be forced through the grate, as indicated in Fig. 17.6, thereby reducing the amount of seed that must be handled by the walkers. Increasing the cylinder speed makes the layer of material between the cylinder and concave less dense, and decreasing the clearance makes it thinner. Increasing the feed rate makes the layer more dense and substantially reduces the amount of seed separation (Fig. 17.6).

Arnold's laboratory tests with barley and wheat[2] confirmed the general relations shown in Fig. 17.6. He found a moderate increase of separation

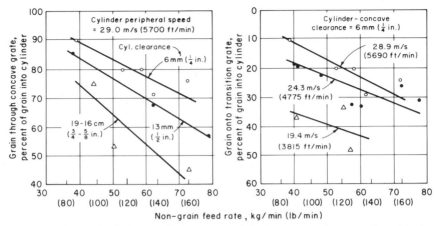

Fig. 17.6. Effects of cylinder speed, clearance, and feed rate upon the separation of barley through the concave grate of a cross-flow rasp-bar cylinder on a 3.7-m [12-ft] self-propelled combine under dry conditions. (J.R. Goss, R.A. Kepner, and L.G. Jones.[20])

percentage (63 versus 68) when the moisture content of barley was reduced from 23% to 16%, but no consistent effect of moisture content with wheat in the range from 14 to 25%. In general, his separation percentages tended to be a little higher with wheat than with barley.

Neal and Cooper[34] found in laboratory tests with rice (which generally has tough, high-moisture straw) that the percentage separation through the concave grate with a cross-flow rasp-bar cylinder was reduced from 72% to 63% when the non-grain feed rate was doubled.

Analysis of data obtained by Reed and his associates[41] in laboratory tests with wheat having a straw moisture content of 9 to 10% indicated that increasing the grain/non-grain ratio from 0.70 to 1.00 had no effect upon the separating efficiency at a given non-grain feed rate. Separation decreased from 80% at a non-grain feed rate of 90 kg/min [200 lb/min] to 70% at 180 kg/min [400 lb/min]. The cylinder width was 813 mm [32 in.]. Field tests with barley[20] also showed no effect of grain/non-grain ratio upon concave-grate separating efficiency.

The amount of straw breakup is influenced by the kind of crop and its maturity. Straw breakup increases as the material becomes drier and is increased if cylinder speed is increased. Reducing the cylinder-concave clearance generally has no great effect on straw breakup.

The percentage of non-grain material forced through the grate is increased if the cylinder speed is increased or the clearance reduced.[20] The percentage decreases slightly as the feed rate is increased.[20,41] Increasing the grain/non-grain ratio from 0.70 to 1.00 in laboratory tests with wheat[41] substantially increased the percentage of non-grain material through the concave grate at a given non-grain feed rate, reducing the walker non-grain feed rate by 7 to 9%. The increased separation probably occurred because of the higher percentage of chaffy material in the non-grain material that had the higher grain/non-grain ratio.

17.15. Summary of Effects of Certain Factors upon Cylinder Performance. Wieneke[50] developed a generalized graphical representation of the performance characteristics of a rasp-bar cylinder with open-grate concave, based upon the NIAE results cited above and upon similar research in Germany. His qualitative relations are shown in Fig. 17.7 for six of the factors discussed in the preceding sections.

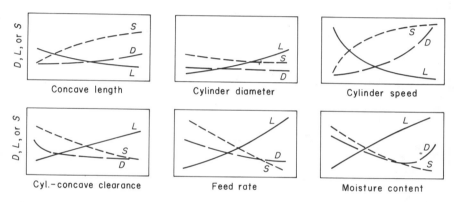

Fig. 17.7. Graphical characterization of some of the performance relations for a rasp-bar cylinder with an open-grate concave. L = cylinder loss, D = grain damage, and S = percent of grain separated through concave grate. (F. Wieneke.[50])

17.16. Cylinder Adjustment. Cylinder speed and clearance should be easy to adjust. The requirements vary with different crops and often change during the day as weather conditions change. Cylinder speed may need to be higher (or the clearance smaller) in the morning than in the late afternoon. Cylinder speeds generally are changed either by means of variable-speed V-belt drives controllable from the operator's station or by changing sprockets on a roller-chain drive.

On a few current models, clearance is adjusted by raising or lowering the cylinder. Most combines, however, have provision for moving the concave by means of a crank or a lever at the operator's station. The arrangement usually is such that both the front and rear clearances are changed simultaneously but with less change at the rear than at the front. This relation automatically provides greater clearance at the front than at the rear.

It should be evident from the preceding discussion that several important factors must be considered in selecting the best cylinder speed and, to a lesser extent, the most appropriate clearance for a particular situation.

Table 17.2 TYPICAL CYLINDER PERIPHERAL SPEEDS
AND CLEARANCES FOR VARIOUS CROPS

Crop	Peripheral Speed (Rasp-bar or Spike-tooth)		Mean Clearance for Rasp-bar Cylinder*	
	m/s	ft/min	Millimetres	Inches
Alfalfa	23-30	4500-6000†	3-10	⅛-⅜
Barley	23-28	4500-5500	6-13	¼-½
Beans, edible	8-15	1500-3000	8-19	5⁄16-¾
Beans for seed§	5- 8	1000-1500	8-19	5⁄16-¾
Clovers	25-33	5000-6500	1.5-6	1⁄16-¼
Corn, field	13-20	2500-4000	22-29	⅞-1⅛
Flax	20-30	4000-6000‡	3-13	⅛-½
Grain sorghum	20-25	4000-5000	6-13	¼-½
Oats	25-30	5000-6000	5-13	3⁄16-½
Peas	10-15	2000-3000	8-19	5⁄16-¾
Rice	23-28	4500-5500	5-10	3⁄16-⅜
Rye	25-30	5000-6000	5-13	3⁄16-½
Soybeans	15-20	3000-4000	10-19	⅜-¾
Wheat	25-30	5000-6000	5-13	3⁄16-½

*Front clearance usually should be somewhat greater than rear clearance.
†In dry climates, speeds must be kept below 25.5 m/s [5000 ft/min] to avoid excessive seed damage.[11]
§Based on data in reference 6.
‡In dry climates, some varieties require speeds of only 12.5 to 20.5 m/s [2500 to 4000 ft/min].

Typical ranges of peripheral speeds and clearances for various crops are indicated in Table 17.2. These are based upon research results and a summary of recommendations found in operator's manuals published by various manufacturers. The effect of cylinder diameter is eliminated by considering peripheral speeds rather than rotational speeds (r/min). Because of the multiple-pass feature of axial-flow cylinders, peripheral speeds can be somewhat lower and clearances a little greater than shown in Table 17.2 for cross-flow cylinders, both factors tending to reduce seed damage.[43]

17.17. Separating. As indicated in the preceding discussion, the major portion of the seed is separated from the straw at the cylinder when the combine is equipped with a rasp-bar cylinder and has an open-grate concave. Lesser amounts are separated through a spike-tooth concave grate. The first stage of separation in the arrangement shown in Fig. 17.2 is accomplished with the raddle conveyor. Concave-grate areas in 1977 models were generally 6 to 16% of the straw-walker areas.

The remaining seed and unthreshed heads or pods, as well as considerable amounts of chaff and other small debris, are usually separated by means of multiple-section straw walkers. One-piece, oscillating straw racks were often employed in the past on the smaller pull-type combines but there is little or no use of them in current models.

A walker-type separating unit has 3 to 6 side-by-side sections, each 203 to 305 mm [8 to 12 in.] wide. The sections are attached to a multiple-throw crankshaft near the front and another near the rear. The action of the straw walkers accelerates the material in a rearward and upward direction during a portion of each cycle. This action, with the aid of saw-tooth fins (Fig. 17.2) conveys the straw toward the rear of the machine as it is agitated.

Seed that passes through the openings in the straw walkers is conveyed forward and deposited on the grain pan or the front of the shoe. Some combines have trough-like bottoms attached to the individual walker sections, sloped downward toward the front, to perform the conveying operation. One-piece, oscillating grain-return pans beneath the walkers are also employed. Another arrangement has a group of parallel augers in troughs that cover the full width beneath the walkers.

Most straw walkers have crank throws* of about 102 mm [4 in.] and crank speeds of 185 to 225 r/min. One manufacturer uses a 152-mm [6-in.] throw at 157 r/min. Reference 24 states that the crank speed should be determined from the relation $r\omega^2 = 2g$, where r = crank radius, ω = crank speed, in radians per second, and g = acceleration of gravity. Under these conditions the magnitude of the centrifugal force is twice the force of gravity, which makes the net upward force at the top of the travel equal to $-g$. Speeds calculated from this relation are 188 r/min for a 102-mm [4-in.] throw and 153 r/min for a 152-mm [6-in.] throw — slightly lower than speeds indicated above as being commonly used on combines.

The possibilities of utilizing rotary separation devices instead of straw walkers have been under consideration for many years.[23,46] Combine models having 2 distinctly different types of rotary separation devices became commercially available in the mid 1970s. One of these (Fig. 17.3) has stationary grates and one or more vaned rotors that operate at rather high speeds because they are axial extensions of the rasp-bar threshing units. The crop material rubs against the separating grates as it is rotated and moved rearward. Centrifugal force causes the seeds to move outward through the straw and the grate openings. The magnitude of the centrifugal force acting upon the material is in the order of 200 times the force of gravity when the peripheral speed of the 432-mm-diameter [17-in.-diameter] rotors in Fig. 17.3 is 23 m/s [4500 ft/min] (a typical cylinder peripheral speed for cereal grains).

The other model has a rotating perforated drum into which the material is fed from a conventional rasp-bar cylinder. The drum axis is essentially horizontal, the diameter is 1.68 m [66 in.], the length is 2.74 m [9 ft], the diameter of the perforations is 13 mm [½ in.], and the rotational speed is approximately 34 r/min. A parallel auger (about 229 mm [9 in.] in diameter), located close to the inner surface of the drum near the top, strips the grain-

*Crank throw is the *diameter* of the crank circle.

straw mixture from the drum surface and, with the assistance of a blower, gradually moves the material toward the discharge end. After the stripped material has passed below the auger, centrifugal force throws most of it out against the drum again. The magnitude of the centrifugal force at the drum periphery is approximately 1.07 times the force of gravity.

The grain-and-chaff mixture that passes through the drum perforations is conveyed to the front of the machine by a group of parallel augers. There it is fed onto a conventional cleaning shoe, along with material that has been separated through the concave grate. Performance curves published by the manufacturer indicate that, at high feed rates with wheat, drum separation losses are considerably less than walker losses from a comparable-sized conventional combine.

17.18. Straw-Walker Performance. The major performance parameter of straw walkers and other separating devices is the percentage of seed and unthreshed heads or pods separated from the straw and chaff. However, the percentage of non-grain material that passes through the walkers is also of concern, since this material contributes to the shoe load. Both factors are affected by the kind and condition of the crop and by walker design. Walker losses generally account for the major portion of total losses with cereal grains[35] but may be negligible in small-seed crops such as alfalfa.[11] Non-grain feed rate and grain/non-grain ratio are the major factors affecting walker losses with a given crop.

A comprehensive series of tests was conducted at the University of Saskatchewan[40,41] to determine the effects of walker crank speed, crank throw, grain/non-grain ratio, feed rate, and other factors upon the efficiency of grain separation with straw walkers. A complete straw-walker assembly, having 4 sections 203 mm [8 in.] wide and 2.44 m [96 in.] long, was fed by a rasp-bar cylinder in the same manner as in a conventional combine. Material harvested with a grain binder was fed into the cylinder on a conveyor belt, after having been stored and conditioned to obtain the desired straw moisture content. All of the Saskatchewan tests discussed in this section were with wheat having a straw moisture content of 9 to 10%.

Tests were conducted with a 102-mm [4-in.] crank throw and a 152-mm [6-in.] crank throw, each at three different crank speeds. Walker losses at three total feed rates, scaled from graphs in reference 40, were as follows:

Total feed rate, kg/min [lb/min]	136 [300]	227 [500]	318 [700]
Percent walker loss with 102-mm [4-in.] throw			
150 r/min	2	11	34
200 r/min	1	6	18
250 r/min	2	8	17
Percent walker loss with 152-mm [6-in.] throw			
130 r/min	2	8	17
150 r/min	2	8	14
170 r/min	6	14	24

Note that lowest losses were at 200 r/min with the 102-mm throw and at 150 r/min with the 152-mm throw. These results for the two throws are not directly comparable because two different types of walkers were used. However, a series of comparative tests was conducted at total feed rates from 45 to 320 kg/min [100 to 710 lb/min], using the same walkers for both throws. Losses were about the same with the 102-mm crank throw at 200 r/min and the 152-mm crank throw at 150 r/min, but a heavier check curtain was needed with the 152-mm throw to obtain acceptable performance.

Field tests with various crops in Germany,[24] laboratory tests in Russia,[9] and general experience have also indicated that when the crank throw is 102 mm [4 in.] speeds of about 200 r/min give minimum walker losses with most seed crops. In general, excessive crank speeds may increase walker losses because the more rapid conveying reduces the time available for separation. Low speeds may hinder separation because of the thicker straw layer and may cause poor feeding.

The effects of grain/non-grain ratio were determined in the Saskatchewan studies[41] by making a series of runs at various feed rates for each of the following conditions.

1. Regular-length material (about 64 cm [25 in.]); grain/non-grain ratio into cylinder = 0.70.
2. Straw shortened to increase grain/non-grain ratio to 1.04.
3. Grain and chaff added to regular-length material to obtain grain/non-grain ratio of 0.97. (This might represent the effect of tailings recirculation.)

The walker crank throw was 102 mm [4 in.] and the crank speed was 210 r/min.

Figure 17.8 shows the effects of both grain/non-grain ratio and feed rate upon grain loss (wheat), based on the grain and non-grain feed rates onto the walkers. These graphs were obtained from analysis of data presented in reference 41. Grain/non-grain ratios onto the walkers (tabulated on the graph) were influenced by the amounts of grain and non-grain material separated through the concave grate. Note that losses increased rapidly at walker non-grain feed rates above 90 kg/min [200 lb/min].

The right-hand graph shows that the *percentage* grain loss at a given feed rate was reduced when the grain/non-grain ratio was increased by either method, but with slightly less reduction when the straw was shortened. The left-hand graph shows that adding grain to regular-length straw (thereby increasing the amount of grain onto the walkers at a given walker non-grain feed rate by about 60%) had no effect upon the *amount* of grain not separated.

The effects of grain/non-grain ratio upon the combined performance of the cylinder-and-concave assembly and the walkers in the above tests, at a

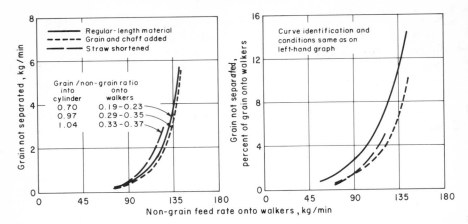

Fig. 17.8. Effect of grain/non-grain ratio and walker non-grain feed rate upon walker seed loss in laboratory tests with wheat having a straw moisture content of 9 to 10%. Walkers were fed by a rasp-bar cylinder. (Data from W.B. Reed, G.C. Zoerb, and F.W. Bigsby.[41])

non-grain feed rate of 136 kg/min [300 lb/min] into the cylinder, are indicated in the following table.

	Regular-length material	Grain and chaff added	Straw short-ened
Grain/non-grain ratio into cylinder	0.70	0.97	1.04
Walker non-grain feed rate			
kg/min	116	104	107
[lb/min]	[255]	[230]	[235]
Grain not separated by walkers			
kg/min	1.35	0.7	1.2
[lb/min]	[3.0]	[1.5]	[2.6]
Walker loss, percent of grain into cylinder	1.4	0.5	0.8

Note that increasing the amount of grain with a given non-grain feed rate into the cylinder (higher grain/non-grain ratio) reduced the kilograms per minute of grain lost over the walkers. This reduction was partly due to a greater percentage of the non-grain material passing through the concave grate.

Nyborg and his associates[36] analyzed results from numerous field tests in Saskatchewan. They found that an increase in the grain/non-grain ratio into the machine reduced walker losses (percent) at a given non-grain feed rate in all cases with wheat or rye and in most cases with barley or oats, but occasionally increased the losses with barley or oats. Walker losses in wheat, at a given non-grain feed rate, were reduced by about half in one comparison when the grain/non-grain ratio was increased from 0.84 to 1.04.[35]

Goss and his associates,[20] in harvesting dry barley, increased the grain/non-grain ratio into the machine from 1.07 to 1.70 by cutting higher. The percentage of grain separated through the concave grate remained about the same but the percentage of non-grain material carried over the walkers was reduced to the extent that the walker grain/non-grain ratio was about doubled. There was little change in walker loss (percent of grain intake) at a given non-grain feed rate into the machine, but the loss at a given walker non-grain feed rate was increased.

17.19. Effect of Walker Length upon Separation. The amount of wheat separated through each 305-mm [1-ft] increment of walker length was determined in the laboratory tests described in the preceding section.[41] The results indicated that the amount of seed not separated at any point along the walker length can be determined from the relation

$$R_L = e^{-bL} \tag{17.1}$$

where L = distance along the walkers from the effective point of delivery of material onto the walkers

R_L = decimal fraction of the seed onto the walkers that is not separated at distance L

b = constant (function of feed rate, grain/non-grain ratio, crop variety and condition, walker design, etc.)

e = base of natural logarithms

According to equation 17.1, if the walker is divided into uniform length increments the amount of seed separated in any increment is a constant percentage of the amount of seed onto that increment. The experimental results indicated that in these tests the effective delivery point onto the walkers (zero reference for L) was 150 to 230 mm [6 to 9 in.] from the front end of the walkers. If the walker loss for a given crop condition and feed rate, and the seed rate onto the walkers, are known, these values and the known effective walker length can be used to determine b for these operating conditions. The walker length required to reduce the loss to some other percentage can then be predicted from equation 17.1.

For example, assume the loss is 15% of the seed onto the walkers when L = 2.4 m (i.e., $R_{2.4} = 0.15$), and that the desired loss is 5% of the seed onto the walkers. If 70% of the grain is separated through the concave grate, these losses represent 4.5% and 1.5% of the seed into the machine. From equation 17.1, $b = -(\ln R_L)/L = -(\ln 0.15)/2.4 = 0.791$. The required length to make $R_L = 0.05$ is then

$$L = -\frac{\ln 0.05}{0.791} = 3.79 \text{ m}$$

The new length represents an increase of 58%. The increase in width re-quired to produce the same effect upon loss can be estimated by referring to the solid curve in Fig. 17.8 *right*. Indicated walker non-grain feed rates for losses of 15% and 5% are 145 and 109 kg/min [320 and 240 lb/min], respec-tively. The width would need to be increased by one-third to reduce the load per unit width by the ratio, 109/145. Thus, a 33% increase in width would have the same effect upon capacity as a 58% increase in length. Capacity can be increased more efficiently by increasing the width than by increasing the length.

17.20. The Cleaning Shoe. The functions of the cleaning shoe are to separate the threshed seed from the chaff and other plant residues that have passed through the openings in the concave grate, transition grate, and straw walkers or other separating unit; return unthreshed or partially threshed heads or pods to the cylinder; and dispose of the unwanted material.

The most common shoe arrangement has two sieves, as shown in Fig. 17.1. The chaffer (upper) sieve is usually adjustable. A common type is il-lustrated in Fig. 17.9. The pivot rods are linked together so they can all be rotated simultaneously to increase or decrease the size of the openings. Longitudinal ribs 230 to 355 mm [9 to 14 in.] apart provide intermediate support for the cross members and assist in maintaining uniformity of lateral distribution of the material on the sieve.

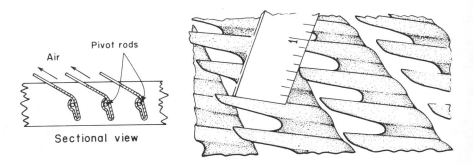

Fig. 17.9. Partial views of an adjustable-lip chaffer sieve.

The cleaning (lower) sieve separates the seed from short pieces of straw and other debris that have passed through the chaffer sieve with the seed. Cleaning sieves are usually of the adjustable-lip type, similar to the chaffer sieve shown in Fig. 17.9, but with smaller lips and openings. Round-hole sieves, however, are preferable for harvesting small-seed crops such as alfalfa, clover, and grasses, and sieves with elongated holes are occasionally used for other crops.

The chaffer sieve and shoe sieve are oscillated either together or in opposition. Opposed motions reduce the tendency for straws to stick in the chaffer openings. The sieves are held in a frame or frames supported by rocker arms oriented to give a moderate upward component on the rearward stroke. Oscillating frequencies are generally 250 to 325 cycles per minute. Areas of the chaffer sieve plus the chaffer extension on 1977 models with 2-sieve shoes averaged 11.4 to 14.7 cm^2 per millimetre of cylinder width [45 to 58 in.^{2}/in.] for the 4 size groups shown in Table 17.1. These values indicate relative increases in sieve *lengths* as the size of combines is increased. Cleaning-sieve areas averaged about 11 cm^2 per millimetre of cylinder width [43 in.^{2}/in.], with only a slight increase as cylinder width increases. As with straw walkers, increasing sieve width for the larger machines is a more effective way of obtaining greater capacity than is increasing the length.

Paddle-type centrifugal fans, with inlets at each side and extending across most or all of the shoe width, are generally employed. One or two adjustable wind deflectors are sometimes placed in the discharge duct (Fig. 17.1). Air volume is usually controlled by changing the fan speed with a variable-speed V-belt drive. Wide shoes pose a problem in obtaining uniform lateral air distribution with a two-inlet fan. For this reason, some of the larger combines are equipped with cross-flow (transverse-flow) fans. This type of fan[38] draws air in over the full width of the rotor (through an inlet parallel with the axis) and discharges it with little or no axial flow. Thus, width is not a limiting factor in regard to obtaining uniform lateral distribution. Another system for wide combines has a conventional blower at a remote location, such as alongside the separator housing. The air is ducted to the shoe, and guide vanes are used to obtain uniform distribution.

17.21. Shoe Operating Conditions. The cleaning shoe must be able to contend with a wide variety of operating conditions. The quantity and nature of the material that must be processed by the shoe is influenced by the performances of the cylinder-and-concave assembly and the straw separator, as well as by crop characteristics and condition.

The amount of non-grain material that the shoe must handle may be as little as 5 to 10% of the total intake of non-grain material under some conditions,[14,25,32] or it may be 50% or more with chaffy crops under dry conditions.[11,14,32] More than half of this material generally comes through the rasp-bar concave grate.[14] The percentage of non-grain material that goes onto the shoe generally decreases as the feed rate is increased.[14,20]

Grain/non-grain ratios for the material onto the shoe are directly related to the percentage of the non-grain material that goes onto the shoe, since the shoe handles all the grain intake except walker losses. Seed recirculated with the tailings increases the ratio. Net ratios for wheat and barley (not including recirculated tailings) may range from 10 to 15 when harvested at moisture contents of 15 to 20%, down to 2 or less for low-moisture grain.[14]

17.22. Shoe Separation Principles. Three types of separation occur in the shoe, namely, aerodynamic, mechanical (by agitation or sifting), and a combination of aerodynamic and mechanical. Aerodynamic separation depends upon the existence of a differential between the suspension velocities* of the components to be separated. Suspension velocities reported by Cooper,[14] from several sources, range from 5.1 to 9.7 m/s [1000 to 1900 ft/min] for kernels of wheat, oats, and barley, from 2.0 to 6.1 m/s [400 to 1200 ft/min] for short pieces of straw (up to 18 cm [7 in.] long), and from 1.5 to 2.5 m/s [300 to 500 ft/min] for chaff. Small seeds have lower suspension velocities than large ones.

Nearly complete aerodynamic separation for some crops can be obtained in the laboratory with vertical air streams. But the air flow through the chaffer sieve usually is at an angle less than 45° above horizontal, so only the lightest materials can be separated entirely by aerodynamic action. Particles with intermediate suspension velocities, mainly straw, may be removed by a combination of aerodynamic and mechanical actions — partly floated and partly propelled mechanically along the sieve.

Separation at low feed rates with cereal grains and large-seed crops is primarily aerodynamic, and shoe losses are usually small. As the non-grain feed rate is increased beyond a transition zone, the action becomes less aerodynamic and more mechanical, causing shoe losses to increase rapidly at high feed rates.[31]

Most combines drop the material onto the front of the chaffer sieve through and over parallel-rod fingers that tend to break up bunches. The fingers are attached to the rear of the grain pan or to the front of the shoe. A portion of the air stream is sometimes directed through the falling material. This air stream provides initial separation of much of the chaff and increases the dispersion of the material onto the sieve. These actions leave the blanket of material more open so the seeds can more readily escape downward through the material. If air is not blown through a falling stream, the velocity of the air directed to the front of the sieve should be great enough to penetrate and loosen the mat. A diminishing velocity profile from front to rear is generally desirable.

The shoe arrangement shown in Fig. 17.10 provides three drops through air streams. The triple-sieve shoe was developed primarily to cope with the heavy loads of chaff and short straw encountered in some crop conditions in the western states.[19] Field tests showed increased shoe capacity in dry barley and wheat as compared with a conventional two-sieve shoe. No differences between the two types of shoes were observed in soybeans, corn, or non-irrigated wheat because shoe loads are normally low and matting is not a problem.[19]

---

*The suspension velocity is the air velocity required to support the pieces of material against the action of gravity in a vertical air stream.

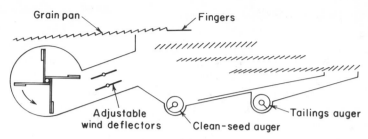

Fig. 17.10. Schematic arrangement of a three-sieve shoe with three material drops through air streams.

The combine that has the rotary-drum separator (Section 17.17) drops the grain-and-chaff mixture through an aspirator that aerodynamically removes much of the chaff before the mixture is fed onto the cleaning shoe. A blower draws air in and upward through the separation zone and then discharges the mixture of air and chaff at the rear of the machine. The air velocity is controlled by an adjustable damper.

The action of the cleaning sieve (Fig. 17.1) tends to be mechanical sifting.[14] The behavior depends upon many variables, including acceleration characteristics of the sieve motion, interactions between the sieve and the material, characteristics of the material (such as "stickiness"), and proportions of oversize and undersize constituents.[14] A thin layer aids penetration, but too high a transport velocity inhibits seed penetration because of the time factor.

17.23. Tailings. Small pieces of unthreshed heads and other material that pass through the chaffer sieve onto the cleaning sieve are discharged into the tailings auger. Ideally, unthreshed heads and pieces of heads not separated through the chaffer sieve should fall through the larger openings of the chaffer extension (Fig. 17.1). But because heads of wheat or barley have a considerably lower suspension velocity than pieces of straw and are relatively large, the shoe is not always effective in recovering them.[14]

Unthreshed heads should be the major constituent of tailings, but sometimes represent less than 10% of the total.[14,20] Free (threshed) seed often represents 50 to 90% of the total tailings.[14,20] The remainder consists of small pieces of stalk, chaff, and other plant debris. Goss and his associates[20] reported that free grain (barley) in the tailings was equivalent to 30 to 40% of the total grain intake. In other tests, with wheat and barley in California and Idaho, the tailings rate was 7% to 30% of the total net shoe input.[14]

Tailings are returned to the main cylinder or an auxiliary cylinder for reprocessing. Provision is usually made for visual inspection and sampling of the tailings from the operator's station while the combine is in operation. The quantity and composition of the tailings give some indication of the performance of the cylinder and shoe and of the possible need for adjustments or reduction of forward speed.

17.24. Shoe Performance. Shoe performance is affected by a considerable number of factors, among which are the shoe design, the type and condition of the crop, the shoe non-grain feed rate, the shoe grain/non-grain ratio, shoe adjustments, and the slope of the machine. Performance parameters are amount of seed lost, cleanliness of seed, and amount of tailings. Seeds are lost over the rear of the shoe by being blown out, bounced out, or carried out in the blanket of debris. Tailings should be kept to a minimum because the recirculated material increases the shoe load and thereby increases seed losses. Sometimes, in harvesting small-seed crops, cleanliness must be sacrificed to avoid excessive shoe losses. The trash is removed later in a recleaning operation.

Shoe losses may represent the major portion of the total loss when harvesting small-seed crops, or they may be considerably less important when harvesting cereal crops. Shoe losses increase rapidly with non-grain feed rate when the shoe is overloaded (Fig. 17.11). Uniform lateral distribution of the material delivered to the shoe from the concave grate and the straw walkers is important to avoid overloading a particular section of the shoe.

The effect of grain/non-grain ratio upon shoe loss appears to be somewhat variable, depending on the crop and its condition and perhaps to some extent on shoe adjustments. When harvesting wheat in Saskatchewan, the correlation between shoe loss and grain/non-grain ratio into the machine, at a given non-grain feed rate, was usually negative.[35,36] But analysis of data reported from laboratory tests with wheat, using a standard shoe without the cleaning sieve,[31] indicated a positive correlation at a given shoe non-grain feed rate.

When harvesting barley in California,[20] decreasing the grain/non-grain ratio by diverting the tailings or by cutting lower to increase the straw length resulted in substantial reductions in shoe losses at a given non-grain feed rate (i.e., a positive correlation). Nyborg and his associates[36] found that decreasing the grain/non-grain ratio sometimes decreased the shoe loss with barley or oats.

17.25. Effects of Shoe Adjustments and Slope. The three basic adjustments on the shoe are the size of openings in the chaffer sieve, the size of openings in the cleaning sieve (including the installation of interchangeable, fixed-hole sieves), and the volume of air from the fan. Other adjustments that may or may not be provided include the size of openings and the slope of the chaffer extension, the slopes of the chaffer and shoe sieves, and wind direction. The current trend is toward minimizing the number of possible adjustments.

If the air volume is too high, losses are increased because some seeds are lifted and blown or bounced out of the rear of the machine and the downward movement of other seeds through the blanket of material is inhibited. High air velocities also interfere with the passage of seeds through the openings in the cleaning sieve, thereby increasing the amount of free seed in the tailings.[20] The maximum amount of air that can be used is related to the minimum suspension velocity of the seeds as determined by their size, specific gravity, and aerodynamic drag characteristics.

Insufficient air results in increased amounts of trash with the clean seed and increased amounts of chaff and other plant debris in the tailings. Seed losses sometimes increase as the air velocity is reduced below an optimum range, because inadequate loosening of the mixture on the chaffer sieve causes more seed to be carried out in the blanket of material.

Goss and his associates[20] found that shoe losses with barley increased rapidly when the air volume was either too high or too low. Alfalfa losses increased only slightly as the air volume was reduced below the optimum.[11] Simpson[44] found, in laboratory tests with wheat, that shoe losses decreased as the air volume was reduced throughout the range employed in the tests, the minimum air being determined by the allowable amount of trash with the clean seed.

If the openings in the chaffer sieve or chaffer extension are too large in relation to the amount of air blast, there will be excessive amounts of chaff and other debris in the tailings. If they are too small, seeds will be carried out in the blanket of material. Increasing the opening size of an adjustable chaffer sieve has the desirable effect of increasing the slope of the air streams, thereby permitting lower total velocities for a given vertical component.

Cleaning-sieve openings that are too small cause excessive amounts of free seed in the tailings. If the openings are too large, there will be excessive amounts of trash in the clean grain.

Tilting the shoe either laterally or longitudinally generally increases shoe losses. Simpson[44] investigated the effects of fore-and-aft shoe slope because some hillside combines do not have fore-and-aft leveling. Average shoe losses in field tests with wheat were about 4% at a longitudinal slope of $+15°$ (rear end of shoe low), 1.5% at 0° slope, and 0.5% at $-15°$ slope, as long as the shoe was not overloaded. Greatly increased losses were observed in a few downhill tests where high feed rates caused the shoe to become overloaded when its discharge end was high.

17.26. Overall Combine Performance. As indicated earlier in this chapter, the relative magnitudes of the different types of seed loss vary widely among different crops and conditions. Two examples are presented in Fig. 17.11. Note that the grain/non-grain ratio was much lower in the alfalfa tests than in the barley tests. Approximately half of the total non-grain material went onto the shoe in the alfalfa tests and one-third of the total in the barley tests.

Nyborg and his associates[36] analyzed loss data collected during tests with ten different combines in wheat, barley, oats, and rye, each test series covering a range of feed rates. They found that a good fit for walker losses when a

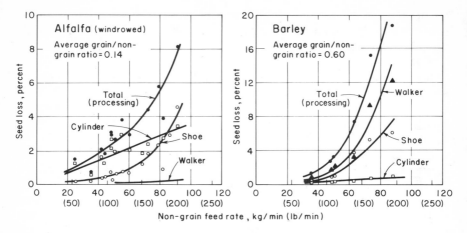

Fig. 17.11. Effect of feed rate upon seed losses for a 3.7-m [12-ft] self-propelled combine in the Sacramento Valley, California. (Data from California Agricultural Experiment Station, 1951-1955. Barley data also in reference 20.)

wide range of feed rates was included, for shoe losses when the shoe was heavily loaded, and for cylinder losses under hard-to-thresh conditions was usually provided by a mathematical model of the form

$$L = a\,(\text{NGF})^b\,(\text{G/NG})^c \qquad (17.2)$$

where L = percent loss
       NGF = non-grain feed rate
       G/NG = grain/non-grain ratio

The constants a, b, and c vary with different crop conditions, the type of loss, and different machines.

When variations in the grain/non-grain ratio were not considered, better fits usually were obtained when the independent variable was non-grain feed rate rather than total feed rate.[36] When variations in the grain/non-grain ratio were considered (as in equation 17.2), both parameters gave equally good fits.

Although the capacity of a combine may be limited by choking of one or more functional units or by the amount of power available, seed loss is usually the controlling factor. The non-grain feed rate or total feed rate corresponding to some specified percent loss (e.g., 1, 2, or 3%) is sometimes taken as an index of the capacity of a combine for a particular crop under specified conditions. ASAE Standard S343 defines combine capacity as the total feed rate at a 3% processing loss (cylinder + walker + shoe) for a stated crop, grain/non-grain ratio, grain moisture content, and non-grain-material moisture content. From the economic standpoint, the allowable loss depends upon the value of the crop in relation to harvesting costs at different loss levels.

17.27. Field Testing. For a field-performance evaluation of the functional components, simultaneous collections are made of the material discharged from the straw walkers, the material from the shoe, and the seed into the grain tank. These collections are made while the machine is traveling at a constant speed over a measured and timed distance, preferably in a uniform crop condition. The combine should be allowed to reach a stable operating condition at a constant feed rate before the collections are started. If the tailings are to be collected, they are diverted into a container for a few seconds (timed) immediately after the other collections are stopped.

Separate collections from the walkers and the shoe may be made by dragging two canvas sheets behind the machine and holding the front ends, one above and behind the other, in appropriate positions. The material collected on the top canvas consists of straw, threshed seed (walker loss), and some of the unthreshed seed (cylinder loss). The lower canvas collects the chaff and free seed from the shoe, as well as additional unthreshed seed. A number of manufacturers and other organizations have developed mechanized, semiautomatic collection devices of various degrees of sophistication.[21,35]

After weighing the collections, the material from each canvas is cleaned to recover the free seed. It is then run through a threshing cylinder or a slow-speed hammer mill to thresh out the remaining seed and is cleaned again to recover the seed that was originally unthreshed. The percentage losses at the various points are calculated on the basis of the total mass of all seed collected during the run. Manufacturers and other organizations involved in extensive field test programs generally have portable or mobile equipment for processing the samples in the field.

Gathering losses may be determined by placing a frame of known area in a number of locations at random over the field and picking up the seeds and shattered heads within the frame each time. The frame should not be placed where seed that has been lost from the rear of the machine would be included in the collection. A preharvest collection is made to determine the shatter caused by natural agencies prior to harvesting. The gathering loss is the difference between the post-harvest and preharvest determinations.

If seed damage is a problem, samples taken from the clean-grain spout are checked visually for external damage (or screened to separate broken pieces of seeds) and may also be subjected to laboratory germination tests for internal damage. Hand-threshed samples are also checked. If it is suspected that damage is occurring in parts of the machine other than the cylinder, samples should be taken from pertinent locations along the path of the seed within the machine.

Because of the influence of uncontrollable and sometimes unpredictable crop variables, runs should be replicated or preferably, a series made at varying feed rates. A control or "standard" machine should be used in all tests involving evaluations of an unknown machine or comparison of different machines.[32,35]

17.28. Laboratory Testing. Laboratory testing of functional components (cylinder, walker, shoe) has proved to be an extremely valuable tool both in development programs and in obtaining fundamental information regarding the behavior of the components. Laboratory facilities have also been developed for testing complete combines.[33]

Laboratory tests are fast and much less expensive than field testing. Conditions can be controlled more accurately, giving better reproducibility. Tests can easily be duplicated and enough runs can be made to permit statistical analysis. Components can readily be isolated for measurement, photography, and determinations of the effects of a wide range of loads and crop variables. Once the crop is stored, testing is independent of the weather and season.

The crop or crops must be properly grown, harvested, stored, and prepared for use. Some crops do not store well and, therefore, are not amenable to off-season laboratory testing. It is extremely important to feed the material into the combine or component in the same manner and condition as it would be fed during field operation, especially for the cylinder.

Laboratory functional tests cannot duplicate all aspects or the wide range of actual field conditions, but should be complementary to field testing.[33] Even though the magnitude of losses observed in laboratory tests, particularly with cleaning shoes, may be considerably less than field losses, the relative effects of design changes or adjustments should be similar.[26]

17.29. Power Requirements. Arnold and Lake[5] conducted laboratory tests with 610-mm-wide [24-in.-wide] rasp-bar cylinders to determine the effects of various factors upon cylinder power requirements. Most of the tests were with wheat having moisture contents of 12 to 15% and a grain/nongrain ratio of 0.83. They found that the power requirement decreased substantially as the cylinder diameter was increased from 305 mm to 533 mm [12 in. to 21 in.] but decreased only slightly between 533 mm and 686 mm [21 in. and 27 in.]. A closed concave required about 25% more power than an open-grate concave at cylinder speeds of 23 to 33 m/s [4500 to 6500 ft/min]. The difference was only 10% at 18 m/s [3500 ft/min]. Increasing the length of the open-grate concave from 338 mm to 508 mm [13.3 in. to 20 in.] increased the power requirement by about 10%.

At high feed rates much less power was required to thresh a thin, fast-moving input stream of material than to thresh a thick, slow-moving stream.[5] At a constant input-stream speed of 46 m/min [150 ft/min] (i.e., a typical slow stream), power increased exponentially with feed rate, with mean values of 3.0 kW [4.0 hp] at a non-grain feed rate of 45 kg/min [100 lb/min] and 7.1 kW at 68 kg/min [9.5 hp at 150 lb/min].

Power requirements tended to increase linearly with cylinder speed, the rate of increase depending upon the other operating conditions.[5] In 3 experiments, the power at 33 m/s [6500 ft/min] averaged 65% greater than the power at 18 m/s [3500 ft/min]. Cylinder-concave clearance had no great effect on power requirements with either wheat or barley. Wheat required more power than barley.

Dodds[17] conducted field tests with a 3.7-m [12-ft] self-propelled combine having interchangeable spike-tooth and rasp-bar cylinders 762 mm [30 in.] wide. Power inputs were measured to (a) the cylinder shaft, including the header drive, and (b) the main shaft, including all power input except to the propulsion drive. The combine was equipped with a straw chopper. Hollow-stem wheat, solid-stem wheat, barley, and oats were combined from the windrow. The two wheat varieties were also direct combined. Runs were made over a range of feed rates and a linear-regression equation was determined for each series of runs.

Main-shaft power requirements for a non-grain feed rate of 90 kg/min [200 lb/min], calculated from the regression equations reported for the rasp-bar cylinder, were as follows:

	Grain/non-grain ratio*	Main-shaft power, kW [hp]	
		Direct cut	Windrowed
Hollow-stem wheat	0.78	19.7 [26.4]	18.5 [24.8]
Solid-stem wheat	0.66	20.6 [27.6]	19.2 [25.8]
Barley	1.13	—	15.4 [20.7]
Oats	1.22	—	17.5 [23.4]

In all cases, main-shaft power requirements at a non-grain feed rate of 45 kg/min [100 lb/min] were 65 to 70% of the requirements at 90 kg/min [200 lb/min]. Power requirements when harvesting wheat were 75 to 85% as great with the spike-tooth cylinder as with the rasp-bar cylinder.

The NIAE[45] tested three 3.7-m [12-ft] self-propelled combines in wheat having a grain moisture content of 16 to 18% and a grain/non-grain ratio of 0.63. Total power requirements, including propulsion, were 28 to 41 kW [37 to 55 hp] at normal non-grain feed rates of 0.13 to 0.15 kg/min per millimetre of cylinder width [7 to 8.5 lb/min per inch of width]. At these feed rates, total energy requirements were 3.5 to 4.4 kW·h per megagram of non-grain material [4.2 to 5.4 hp-h per ton]. The results tabulated above for direct combining wheat in Dodd's tests, including a straw chopper but not propulsion power, indicate 3.6 to 3.8 kW·h per megagram of non-grain material [4.4 to 4.6 hp-h per ton] at a non-grain feed rate of 0.12 kg/min per millimetre of cylinder width [6.7 lb/min per inch of width].

*Personal correspondence from M.E. Dodds dated August 4, 1971.

The cylinder generally accounts for a substantial portion of the total power required by a combine.[5] Power requirements for the separating and cleaning units are small and relatively independent of feed rate.[12] Header power requirements vary with the type and field conditions of the crop, the forward speed, and the feed rate. Propulsion power requirements are influenced by the mass of the machine plus the seed in the grain tank, tire sizes, the condition of the ground surface, the slope of the ground, and forward speed. (See Section 2.19 for method of calculating rolling resistance.)

Short-time peak power requirements for the cylinder may be 2 to 3 times as great as the average requirement.[5,17] The engine needs to have considerable reserve power to be able to handle these peaks without stalling or causing undesirable speed reductions. Maximum engine power ratings on 1977 models of self-propelled combines were generally 70 to 100 W per millimetre of cylinder width [2.4 to 3.4 hp per inch of width].

17.30. Automatic Controls* and Monitoring. Automatic header-height control is desirable when it is necessary to cut close to the ground, especially when the field surface is undulating or irregular. Accurate height control is particularly important for soybeans because this crop must be cut within a few centimetres of the ground to minimize gathering losses.[30]

Automatic header-height controls have been developed as optional attachments for combines. A rotatable transverse bar, mounted directly beneath the cutterbar, has ground-contacting fingers attached to it at intervals of about 150 mm [6 in.]. The fingers rotate the bar to actuate a hydraulic control valve when height adjustment is necessary. Accuracy of control is affected by many factors, including response time and the resonance characteristics of the combine-and-header system. Rehkugler[42] has analyzed the dynamic behavior of such a system, employing analog simulation.

Attention is being given to automatic control of feed rate, by automatically changing the forward speed, as a means of avoiding overloads and maximizing harvest rates without excessive seed losses. Ideally, the feed rate should be sensed in front of the cutterbar or as early as possible in the header. The efficiency of the control system depends upon the existence of a definite and consistent relation between the sensed value and the feed rate. Some of the approaches that have been considered are:

1. Sensing torque in the cylinder drive.[18]
2. Sensing displacement of the feeder-conveyor chain caused by changes in the thickness of the layer of material.[18]
3. Sensing engine power output by measuring absolute intake manifold pressure or some other parameter.[8]

---

*See Chapter 4, and especially Section 4.22, for a discussion of hydraulic components and characteristics of automatic control systems.

4. Sensing the reaction force on the concave supports.[18]
5. Determining density of material in the feeder conveyor by means of gamma radiation.[8]

Most self-propelled combines now sold have enclosed cabs, many of them air conditioned. The resulting isolation of the operator from the sensory indications of combine performance and operational problems has created a need for a system of signal devices or monitors to provide communication from the combine to the operator.[37] Powerplant monitors (instruments and signals) have been standard equipment for many years, but the intensive application of monitors for crop-handling mechanisms and operations is a relatively new development.

The operator needs to be furnished with three types of information, as follows:[37]

1. Early-warning signals, to indicate potential problems (belt slippage, choked or overloaded functional components, overheating, low oil pressure, etc.)
2. Failure-warning signals, to indicate that some component has failed or is not functioning.
3. Process-control monitoring, such as provisions for sampling or observing tailings and clean grain, grain-loss indicators, etc.

A number of the monitoring operations on crop-handling components involve sensing shaft speeds, with the signal in the cab indicating when the speed drops below a predetermined minimum value. The manner of presenting the signals in the cab and the locations of the signal devices are important considerations in regard to their effectiveness.[37]

A grain-loss monitor was developed at the University of Saskatchewan in 1968,[39] and several commercial models have become available since then. One vibration-sensitive sounding board or tube is mounted across the full width of the combine in a position such that grain carried over the walkers in a sample portion of the straw stream will strike the sensor. A second sensor is placed in the stream of material from the cleaning shoe. In one type of monitor the impacts are converted into a voltage that is proportional to the frequency of impacts and is indicated on a meter. Another arrangement gives a digital readout of the number of impacts during a pre-selected time interval of one second or more. The seeds must be heavy enough so that the system can distinguish between seed impacts and the impacts of pieces of straw or other material. The sensors must be located where they consistently intercept a representative sample of the discharged material (difficult to do for the shoe).

17.31. Windrow Combining. Windrowing is done with a self-propelled windrower having draper-type cross conveyors (Fig. 14.10 *right*) or with pull-type windrowers. For best curing and good combine performance, the windrows should be continuous, uniform, and loose. The heads should all be laid toward the rear. The stubble in windrowed grain should be at least 15 to 20 cm [6 to 8 in.] tall to permit free air circulation beneath the windrow.

For windrow combining, the reel is removed and a windrow-pickup unit is attached to the front of the header. The pickup unit should have support runners or caster wheels operating on the ground and should be hinged to the header so it can "float" without the necessity for precise control of header height. Draper-type pickups, which have slats and spring teeth attached to inclined, flat belts, have gained wide acceptance. They handle the material more gently than cylinder-type pickups and are preferable where seed shattering is a problem. They also have less tendency to pick up stones. For best performance and minimum shattering, the peripheral speed should be 10 to 20% greater than the forward speed.

REFERENCES

1. Annual market statistics section, Implement & Tractor, 85(24):20-57, Nov. 21, 1970.
2. ARNOLD, R. E. Experiments with rasp bar threshing drums. I: Some factors affecting performance. J. Agr. Eng. Res., 9:99-131, 1964.
3. ARNOLD, R. E., F. CALDWELL, and A. C. W. DAVIES. The effect of moisture content of the grain and the drum setting of the combine-harvester on the quality of oats. J. Agr. Eng. Res., 3:336-345, 1958.
4. ARNOLD, R. E., and J. R. LAKE. Experiments with rasp bar threshing drums. II: Comparison of open and closed concaves. J. Agr. Eng. Res., 9:250-251, 1964.
5. ARNOLD, R. E., and J. R. LAKE. Experiments with rasp bar threshing drums. III: Power requirement. J. Agr. Eng. Res., 9:348-355, 1964.
6. BAINER, R., and H. A. BORTHWICK. Thresher and other mechanical injury to seed beans of the lima type. California Agr. Expt. Sta. Bull. 580, 1934.
7. BAINER, R., and J. S. WINTERS. New principle in threshing lima bean seed. Agr. Eng., 18:205-206, May, 1937.
8. BROUER, B. P., and J. R. GOSS. Some approaches to automatic feed rate control for self-propelled combine harvesters. ASAE Paper 70-632, Dec., 1970.
9. BUBLICK, S. P. Determining the main parameters of the process of crop separation. Mekh. Elektrif. Sots. Sel. Khoz., 21(2):15-17, 1963. NIAE transl. 201.
10. BUCHANAN, J. C., and W. H. JOHNSON. Functional characteristics and analysis of a centrifugal threshing and separating mechanism. Trans. ASAE, 7(4):460-463, 468, 1964.
11. BUNNELLE, P. R., L. G. JONES, and J. R. GOSS. Combine harvesting of small-seed legumes. Agr. Eng., 35:554-558, Aug., 1954.
12. BURROUGH, D. E. Power requirements of combine drives. Agr. Eng., 35:15-18, Jan., 1954.
13. CASPERS, L. Types of threshing apparatus. Grundl. Landtech., 19:9-17, 1969.
14. COOPER, G. F. Combine shaker shoe performance. ASAE Paper 66-607, Dec., 1966.
15. CSUKAS, L. Examination of the flow of crop with combine harvesters with special respect to the possible increase of performance. Jarmuvek, Mezogazdasagi Gepek, 11(3):90-97, 1964. NIAE transl. 169.
16. DeLONG, H. H., and A. J. SCHWANTES. Mechanical injury in threshing barley. Agr. Eng., 23:99-101, Mar., 1942.

17. DODDS, M. E. Power requirements of a self-propelled combine. Canadian Agr. Eng., *10*:74-76, 90, Nov., 1968.
18. EIMER, M. Progress report on automatic controls in combine-harvesters. Grundl. Landtech., *16*:41-50, 1966. NIAE transl. 207.
19. GORDON, L. L., F. D. SUMSION, and T. S. ROBINSON. Development of the MF cascade shoe. Trans. ASAE, *14*(3):448-449, 1971.
20. GOSS, J. R., R. A. KEPNER, and L. G. JONES. Performance characteristics of the grain combine in barley. Agr. Eng., *39*:697-702, 711, Nov., 1958.
21. HEBBLETHWAITE, P., and R. Q. HEPHERD. A detailed test procedure for combine-harvesters. NIAE Annual Rept., 1960-61, pp. 365-371.
22. HEITSHU, D. C. A marvel of engineering — the self-propelled hillside combine. Agr. Eng., *37*:182-183, 187, Mar., 1956.
23. HORA, O., *et al.* Means of increasing the effectiveness of combine-harvesters. Zemedelska Technika, *10*(4):151-162, 1964. NIAE transl. 196.
24. Investigations into the regulation of shaker frequency — a possibility of reducing heavy losses during harvesting. Deutsche Agrartechnik, *14*(7):293-296, 1964. NIAE transl. 199.
25. JOHNSON, W. H. Machine and method efficiency in combining wheat. Agr. Eng., *40*:16-20, 29, Jan., 1959.
26. KERBER, D. R., and J. R. LUCAS. Development of a combine cleaning system. ASAE Paper 69-622, Dec., 1969.
27. KLEIN, L. M., and J. E. HARMOND. Effect of varying cylinder speed and clearance on threshing cylinders in combining crimson clover. Trans. ASAE, *9*(4):499-500, 506, 1966.
28. LALOR, W. F., and W. F. BUCHELE. Designing and testing of a threshing cone. Trans. ASAE, *6*(2):73-76, 1963.
29. LAMP, B. J., Jr., and W. F. BUCHELE. Centrifugal threshing of small grains. Trans. ASAE, *3*(2):24-28, 1960.
30. LAMP, B. J., W. H. JOHNSON, and K. A. HARKNESS. Soybean losses — approaches to reduction. Trans. ASAE, *4*(2):203-205, 207, 1961.
31. MACAULEY, J. T., and J. H. A. LEE. Grain separation on oscillating combine sieves as affected by material entrance conditions. Trans. ASAE, *12*(5):648-651, 654, 1969.
32. MARK, A. H., K. J. M. GODLEWSKI, and J. L. COLEMAN. Evaluating combine performance: a global approach. Agr. Eng., *44*:136-137, 143, Mar., 1963.
33. NEAL, A. E., and G. F. COOPER. Performance testing of combines in the lab. Agr. Eng., *49*:397-399, July, 1968.
34. NEAL, A. E., and G. F. COOPER. Laboratory testing of rice combines. Trans. ASAE, *13*(6):824-826, 1970.
35. NYBORG, E. O. A test procedure for determining combine capacity. Canadian Agr. Eng., *6*:8-10, Jan., 1964.
36. NYBORG, E. O., H.F. McCOLLY, and R. T. HINKLE. Grain-combine loss characteristics. Trans. ASAE, *12*(6):727-732, 1969.
37. POOL, S. D., and C. RICKERD. Combine-combine operator communication. SAE Paper 680588, presented at SAE National Meeting, Sept., 1968.
38. QUICK, G. R. On the use of cross-flow fans in grain harvesting machinery. Trans. ASAE, *14*(3):411-416, 419, 1971.
39. REED, W. B., M. A. GROVUM, and A. E. KRAUSE. Combine harvester grain loss monitor. Agr. Eng., *50*:524-525, 528, Sept., 1969.
40. REED, W. B., and G. C. ZOERB. A laboratory study of straw walker efficiency. ASAE Paper 72-638, Dec., 1972.
41. REED, W. B., G. C. ZOERB, and F. W. BIGSBY. A laboratory study of grain-straw separation. Trans. ASAE, *17*(3):452-460, 1974.
42. REHKUGLER, G. E. Dynamic analysis of automatic control of combine header height. Trans. ASAE, *13*(2):225-231, 1970.

43. ROWLAND-HILL, E. W. Twin rotor combine harnesses potential of rotary threshing and separation. ASAE Paper 75-1580, Dec., 1975.
44. SIMPSON, J. B. Effect of front-rear slope on combine-shoe performance. Trans. ASAE, 9(1):1-3, 5, 1966.
45. Test for users, No. 391. NIAE, 1962.
46. Unconventional combine. Implement & Tractor, 84(23):18, Nov. 7, 1969.
47. VAS, F. M., and H. P. HARRISON. The effect of selected mechanical threshing parameters on kernel damage and threshability of wheat. Canadian Agr. Eng., 11:83-87, 91, Nov., 1969.
48. WALKER, D. S., and C. E. SCHERTZ. Soybean threshing by the relative motion of belts. ASAE Paper 70-631, Dec., 1970.
49. WESSEL, J. The threshing process within a conical rotor. Landtech. Forsch, 10(5): 122-130, 1960. NIAE trans. 100.
50. WIENEKE, F. Performance characteristics of the rasp bar thresher. Grundl. Landtech., Heft 21:33-34, 1964.
51. WITZEL, H. D., and B. F. VOGELAAR. Engineering the hillside combine. Agr. Eng., 36:523-525, 528, Aug., 1955.

PROBLEMS

17.1. The following data were obtained in a field test when harvesting barley with a 4-m self-propelled combine: length of test run = 12 m; time = 21.3 s; total material over walkers = 9.4 kg; free seed over walkers = 76 g; unthreshed seed over walkers = 60 g; total material over shoe = 4.4 kg; free seed over shoe = 289 g; unthreshed seed over shoe = 81 g; total seed collected at grain tank = 17.6 kg. The average gathering loss was 10.2 g/m². Calculate:

(a) Cylinder, walker, shoe, and total processing losses, in percent of grain feed rate.

(b) Gross seed yield, gathering loss, and processing losses, in kilograms per hectare.

(c) Gathering loss, in percent of gross yield.

(d) Walker non-grain feed rate, shoe non-grain feed rate, and total non-grain feed rate, in kilograms per minute.

(e) Percent of non-grain material retained by the walkers.

17.2. Alfalfa seed is to be harvested with a 3.7-m self-propelled combine. The yield of non-grain material is 5.6 Mg/ha, seed yield = 670 kg/ha, and field efficiency = 75%. The cost factors are: new cost of combine = $24 000; total annual fixed costs = 16% of new cost; fuel cost = $3.20/ha; cost for engine oil and lubrication = $0.30/h; operator's wage = $3.50/h; value of seed = $1.75/kg. Assume the machine is to be used for 200 h/year, the total area depending upon the speed of operation. Total processing losses (from Fig. 17.10 *left*) at non-grain feed rates of 30, 40, 50, 60, 70, 80, and 90 kg/min are 1.3, 1.9, 2.5, 3.2, 4.2, 5.5, and 7.5%, respectively.

(a) Plot a curve of total cost per hectare versus non-grain feed rate, including a charge for the value of the seed lost. From this curve, determine the most economical feed rate at which to operate.

(b) What forward speed corresponds to the most economical feed rate? What is the approximate percent seed loss at this rate?

(c) How many hectares can be harvested in the 200-h period when operating at the most economical speed?

17.3. From material presented in the text, or from other sources, develop a list of possible causes for each of the following conditions.

(a) Excessive header loss.

(b) Excessive amount of unthreshed seed.

(c) Excessive free-seed loss over straw walkers.

(d) Cracked grain.

(e) Excessive free-seed loss over rear of shoe.

(f) Excessive amount of chaff in tailings.

(g) Excessive amount of free seed in tailings.

17.4. A typical self-propelled combine with a cylinder 900 to 1000 mm wide may have a total mass of about 8.5 Mg, including grain, when the tank is full. Assume 465-660 [18.4-26] tires on the drive wheels (1.47 m OD) and 190-460 [7.50-18] tires on the steering wheels (0.86 m OD), with 77% of the load on the drive wheels. Referring to Appendix C, calculate the engine power required for propulsion with a full grain tank at 5 km/h, assuming a mechanical drive system with 10% energy loss between the engine and the wheels,

(a) On firm, level soil.

(b) On moderately firm, level soil (perhaps use coefficients of rolling resistance midway between curves for bluegrass pasture and fall rye seeding).

(c) Additional power required for going up a 5% slope.

18

Corn Picking and Shelling

18.1 Introduction. Corn is our greatest-area field crop, as well as being our most important source of feed. In recent years about 85% of the total corn plantings have been harvested for grain.[1] Although some corn is produced in every state in the United States, 80% of the total production is confined to the 12 north-central states.[1]

Interest in mechanical corn pickers developed with the adaptation of the tractor PTO to their operation during the late 1920s. However, general adoption did not take place until after World War II. The first picker-shellers appeared in the middle 1930s, but lack of suitable shelled-corn drying equipment delayed their acceptance until the 1950s.

Several attempts were made during the late 1920s and mid 1930s to adapt the grain combine for harvesting corn.[8,14,17] All the early work involved feeding the entire corn plant into the machine. The early investigators concluded that corn could be shelled and cleaned with a combine, but that the introduction of the stalks into the machine was a major problem yet to be solved. They were also concerned about lack of equipment for drying wet shelled corn.

The Illinois Agricultural Experiment Station initiated studies in 1950 to evaluate the rasp-bar cylinder as a corn husker and sheller.[9] In 1953 they developed stalk-gathering equipment for a combine.[19] The same problem experienced by the earlier investigators, that of introducing the entire plant into the combine, continued to be a major one. It was evident from these investigations, however, that the rasp-bar cylinder could shell corn satisfactorily at reasonable moisture levels.

The next step in the evolutionary process was to equip combines with corn snapping units in order to leave the stalks in the field and introduce only the ears into the machine.[8] Following the development of acceptable corn heads, the popularity of grain combines for harvesting corn increased rapidly during the 1960s. In 1970, approximately 70% of the corn produced in 5 of the principal corn-belt states was harvested by combines equipped with corn heads.[15] The number of corn heads manufactured in the United States from 1971 through 1975 was only 4% less than the total number of combines produced and was 3½ times as great as the number of corn pickers (all types).[2] Picker-sheller sales have been quite low since the early 1960s.

18.2. Types and Functional Components of Corn Harvesters. Corn harvesters may be classified as (a) snappers, (b) picker-huskers, commonly

432

known as pickers, (c) picker-shellers, and (d) grain combines equipped with corn heads. The basic components for all these types include a gathering unit to guide the stalks into the machine, snapping rolls to remove the ears from the stalks, and lugged gathering chains to assist in feeding the stalks into the rolls and moving the stalks and snapped ears rearward through the snapping zone.

A corn snapper consists of the above basic components plus an elevating conveyor to deliver the ears (mostly not husked) into a trailing wagon. The addition of a husking bed to remove the husks from the ears identifies the machine as a corn picker. A picker-sheller has a shelling unit instead of a husking unit. Sometimes these units are interchangeable. The shelled corn may be delivered to a trailing wagon or to a tank on the machine. When a grain combine is to be used for corn, a corn head is installed in place of the grain header. A corn head has the basic gathering and snapping components listed above (similar to a corn snapper) plus a conveying system to deliver the ears to the combine cylinder for shelling.

Both mounted and pull-type pickers and snappers are available. Mounted units are mostly 2-row machines, whereas 1-row, 2-row, and 3-row sizes are common with pull-type machines. Picker-shellers are usually two-row machines. Most 2-row machines have snapping-unit center distances of about 102 cm [40 in.], but narrow-row models for 76-cm [30-in.] row spacings are available. Differences of 5 to 8 cm [2 to 3 in.] between the row spacing and the snapping-unit centerline distances are tolerable in 2-row harvesters.

Corn heads for combines are mostly 2-, 3-, 4-, or 6-row units designed to handle row spacings of 92 to 102 cm [36 to 40 in.] or 71 to 81 cm [28 to 32 in.]. Five-row and 7-row heads for these row spacings, as well as 8-row heads for 51-cm or 76-cm [20-in. or 30-in.] spacings are also available. Approximately 58% of all corn heads sold in the United States in 1975 were 4-row units, 20% were 6-row units, and 9% were 2-row units.[2]

Most present-day models of corn heads have a transverse rectangular or square tubing "tool bar" (e.g., 102 × 102 mm [4 × 4 in.]) beneath the rear portion of the header. Self-contained, individual-row snapping units (including gathering chains) are clamped to the tool bar at the desired row spacing. Gear cases on the individual units are driven by a transverse hex shaft that passes through each gear case, by interconnecting stub shafts, or by some other appropriate arrangement. The two halves of each sheet-metal gathering unit and center divider usually have an adjustable amount of overlap so the row spacing on a specific corn-head assembly can be changed about 5 cm [2 in.] either way from the center position.

18.3. Gathering Units. It is a relatively simple matter for a gathering device to control stalks and feed them into the snapping units when the stalks are standing. Unfortunately, however, many stalks become lodged (leaning or broken) during the season, due to adverse weather conditions, disease, high plant populations, etc. The gathering assembly must be able to lift lodged stalks and guide them into the snapping unit with a minimum number of ears lost during the process. This requires having pickup devices close to the ground and handling the stalks gently to avoid excessive accelerations and the consequent detachment of ears.

Streamlined gatherers are shown in Fig. 18.1. The front section of each unit is hinged so the point can float along the ground surface and slide beneath lodged stalks. An adjustable support from the main section limits the lowest position of each point. For minimum loss of ears, the gathering points should be operated on the ground or as low as surface irregularities will permit. The gentleness with which lodged stalks are handled is influenced by the degree of lodging, the steepness of the top profile of the gathering points, and the forward speed.

Fig. 18.1. Front view of a four-row combine corn head, showing the streamlined gathering units. (Courtesy of Allis-Chalmers.)

The gathering units in Fig. 18.1 have a relatively low profile, which is desirable. This low profile is made possible by the use of short snapping rolls, which are characteristic of most corn heads, and because the header platform can be operated at a low height. Mounted snappers or pickers sometimes have relatively low profile angles on the gathering points, but a steeper angle is required on the flare sheets (behind the gathering points and above the snapping rolls) because of limitations imposed by the mounting of the longer snapping rolls generally employed on snappers and pickers.

Gathering chains equipped with finger links (Fig. 18.2 and 18.3) assist in moving stalks into and through the snapping zone and prevent loose ears from sliding forward to be lost. The chain speed should approximate the forward-travel speed when the stalks are upright. In lodged corn the chains

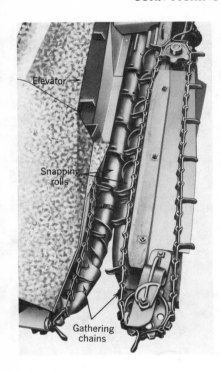

Fig. 18.2. Snapping unit having long rolls with spiral ribs and lugs. Gathering points and part of the shielding have been removed. (Courtesy of White Farm Equipment Co.)

are more effective when operated somewhat faster than ground speed. On some machines the gathering-chain speed is adjustable from the operator's platform.

18.4. Snapping Units. Two general types of snapping rolls are employed. These may be described as spiral-ribbed or spiral-lugged rolls (Fig. 18.2) and straight-fluted rolls (Fig. 18.3). Both types have tapered, spiral-ribbed points to facilitate stalk entry, and both types pull the stalks downward between the two rolls. With spiral-ribbed rolls, the ears are snapped off of the stalk when the ears contact the closely spaced rolls. Straight-fluted rolls pull the stalks down between two stripper plates (Fig. 18.3) and the ears are snapped off when they contact the plates.

Most snappers, pickers, and picker-shellers have spiral-ribbed snapping rolls. These are usually made of cast iron and have spiral ribs or lugs on their surfaces (Fig. 18.2). Their aggressiveness increases from front to rear and can be varied for different operating conditions by attaching or removing screws, bolts, or additional lugs. Roll lengths generally range from 1020 to 1270 mm [40 to 50 in.] and diameters are 75 to 100 mm [3 to 4 in.]. Peripheral speeds are usually about 180 m/min [600 ft/min].[12] The direction of wrap of the spirals is such that the ribs tend to move the stalks rearward.

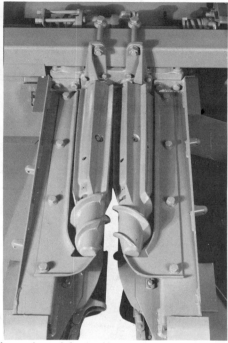

Fig. 18.3. Two views of a combine corn-head snapping unit having short, fluted snapping rolls. *Left:* Top view with shields removed, showing gathering chains and stripper plates. *Right:* Underside view showing cantilevered snapping rolls. Note the tapered, spiral-ribbed feeding points and the full-length trash knife along the outside of each roll. (Courtesy of Deere & Co.)

Because the ears are allowed to contact the spiral-ribbed snapping rolls, excessive roll shelling (butt shelling) may occur if the speed is too great or the surfaces too aggressive, especially if the corn is fairly dry.[10,12] If the surfaces are not aggressive enough, stalk slippage when the butt of the ear contacts the rolls will increase shelling because of the longer contact time. Insufficient aggressiveness under dry conditions may also result in trash accumulating on the rolls.

The clearance between the front ends of spiral-ribbed snapping rolls is adjustable and should be kept as small as possible without causing clogging and stalk breakage (6 to 13 mm [¼ to ½ in.] under normal conditions).[10] Having the rolls too far apart increases roll shelling because of stalk slippage and the tendency to pull the ears farther into the rolls. Rolls can be set closer when the stalks are damp and tough than when they are dry and brittle or are lodged. Because of the variety of crop conditions encountered, it is desirable to be able to adjust the roll clearance from the operator's station while harvesting. This feature also permits clearing clogged rolls without danger to the operator.

Straight-fluted rolls are very aggressive and tend to have a positive action in pulling the stalks through. The flutes intermesh in most designs, but one manufacturer employs rolls with sharp-edged blades that are timed so the blades bite into the stalks from both sides simultaneously. Stripper plates above the rolls (Fig. 18.3) prevent ears from contacting the rolls. Properly adjusted plates minimize the butt shelling that sometimes represents a substantial loss with spiral-ribbed rolls. Fluted rolls may be cast iron or they may be built-up units with replaceable steel flutes. Diameters are generally 90 to 125 mm [3½ to 5 in.] and roll lengths (excluding the tapered point) are mostly 400 to 600 mm [16 to 24 in.]. Peripheral speeds are considerably greater than for spiral-ribbed rolls because the shorter roll length allows less time for pulling the full stalk length down through the rolls.

Corn heads are equipped with straight-fluted rolls. Some manufacturers have developed interchangeable snapper units of this type that may also be adapted to other types of corn harvesters. Fluted rolls permit higher capacities and faster ground speeds than do spiral-ribbed rolls.[12] Fluted rolls and snapping plates remove fewer husks than spiral-ribbed rolls. This characteristic is undesirable for pickers because larger-capacity husking beds are needed, but is not a problem with combines or picker-shellers.[12]

The spacings between stripper plates and between the fluted rolls are usually, but not always, adjustable. Stripper plates should be as wide apart as possible without letting small ears pass between them. Wide spacings minimize stalk breakage and the amount of trash fed into the combine. The roll spacing is less critical than with spiral-ribbed rolls and should be adjusted to give a positive action without stalk breakage.

18.5. Trash Removal. Special trash rolls are often provided on corn pickers to remove trash and broken stalks not expelled by spiral-ribbed snapping rolls. Fluted sections may be incorporated on the upper ends of the snapping rolls (Fig. 18.4). Transverse, fluted rolls are sometimes mounted at the discharge end of a snapped-ear conveyor (Fig. 18.5). The principal function of the transverse rolls is to remove relatively long sections of stalk. Small blowers may also be used to assist in removing trash.

18.6. Husking Units. The husking unit on a picker has pairs of rolls that grasp the husks and pull them downward between the rolls. Usually, all the husks are taken at once when one is caught. Most husking beds have either 2 or 3 pairs of rolls per corn row. The rolls may be in a separate husking bed at the discharge end of a conveyor from the snapping rolls (Fig. 18.6 *left*) or they may be in line with the snapping rolls and fed by the snapping-roll conveyor (Fig. 18.6 *right*). With separate husking beds, there may be one per row or one per machine.

Husking rolls are generally 64 to 76 mm [2½ to 3 in.] in diameter and

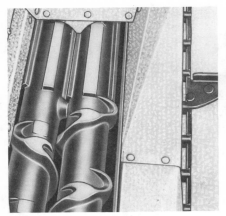 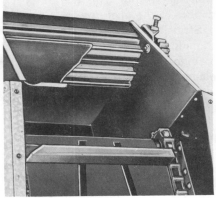

Fig. 18.4. Fluted trash rolls on the upper ends of snapping rolls. (Courtesy of Avco New Idea Div., Avco Corp.)

Fig. 18.5. Fluted-roll stalk remover at the upper end of a corn elevator. (Courtesy of White Farm Equipment Co.)

760 to 1270 mm [30 to 50 in.] long. They operate at about 500 r/min.[12] Most present-day units have cast-iron or steel rolls operating against rubber rolls (often laminated from tire-carcass stock). Various surface configurations are employed to obtain the desired aggressiveness.

Feed mechanisms, sometimes known as ear retarders (downhill) or ear forwarders (uphill), distribute the ears across the husking bed, hold them against the rolls, and move them along the rolls at a uniform rate. Devices for this purpose include rubberized paddles on transverse shafts above the rolls, rubberized finger wheels (Fig. 18.6 *left*), nylon brushes, and side-paddle chain conveyors (Fig. 18.6 *right*). Spirally grooved roll surfaces can also help advance the ears along the rolls.

A sieve arrangement of some sort is usually placed beneath the husking bed to recover shelled corn from the husks. The husk conveyor provides agitation on the sieve surface. The shelled corn falls through the sieve openings and is delivered to the wagon along with the ears. An air blast is sometimes used to assist in the separation.

The principal adjustments for a husking unit are (a) contact pressure between rolls, controlled by spring pressure, (b) aggressiveness of the rolls, as modified by adding or removing rubber buttons, pins, screws, etc., and (c) the height of the feed mechanism above the rolls. The unit should be adjusted to obtain maximum husking with minimum shelling. Excessive amounts of shelled corn in the crib may increase spoilage.[10] Husks and trash in the crib occupy storage space and reduce the natural air flow through the corn.

18.7. Shelling and Cleaning in a Grain Combine. The conventional rasp-bar cylinder in a grain combine (Fig. 17.3) is an effective device for shelling

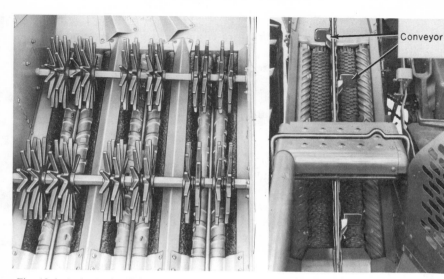

Fig. 18.6. *Left:* A 12-roll husking bed with rubber-finger presser wheels. (Courtesy of Avco New Idea Div., Avco Corp.) *Right:* A four-roll husking unit incorporated into the snapping-roll elevator. (Courtesy of Deere & Co.)

corn. The clearance between the cylinder and the concave is adjusted to about 25 to 32 mm [1 to 1¼ in.] at the front and 16 to 22 mm [⅝ to ⅞ in.] at the rear. Cylinder peripheral speeds range from 12.7 to 20.3 m/s [2500 to 4000 ft/min], often being about 15.2 m/s [3000 ft/min]. Filler plates may be attached to the cylinder between the rasp bars to prevent ears from collecting within the cylinder, but tests have indicated that the benefits (reduced shelling losses) seldom justify their use except at very low cylinder speeds.[18]

Separation of the shelled corn from the cobs, husks, and other trash is a relatively simple matter in a combine, as compared with separating small grains and other seed crops from straw and chaff. Except under extremely adverse crop or weather conditions, separating and cleaning capacity seldom is a limiting factor when harvesting corn with a combine. The chaffer and cleaning sieves are adjusted to larger openings than for the cereal grains, and a greater air blast is permissible through the cleaning shoe. Aerodynamic suspension velocities for corn kernels are considerably greater than for pieces of corn cobs and other lighter debris.[2]

18.8. Shelling and Cleaning in a Picker-Sheller. Although at least one model of picker-sheller has had a rasp-bar cylinder and concave as the shelling unit, most picker-shellers have axial-flow cage-type shellers. A cage-type sheller has a rotating cylinder with lugs, spiral flutes, or paddles around the periphery. The cylinder operates within a stationary cage that is 1020 to

1420 mm [40 to 56 in.] long and 280 to 380 mm [11 to 15 in.] in diameter. The cage periphery is made of perforated metal or parallel round bars and has openings large enough to permit easy passage of shelled kernels but not the cobs. The cylinder is operated at 700 to 800 r/min and has a peripheral speed of 6.1 to 10.2 m/s [1200 to 2000 ft/min].

Ears from the snapping units (including husks) are fed radially into an opening at one end of the cage and pass circumferentially and longitudinally along the cylinder during the shelling process.[5] Shelling is accomplished primarily by rubbing and rolling of ears and cobs against each other and against the cage (concave) and the rotating cylinder. The length of time that the ears remain in the shelling unit can be varied, by means of an adjustable cob gate at the discharge end of the cage, to accommodate different crop conditions.

The shelled corn falls through the openings in the cage and is conveyed to the tank or wagon. Light trash is removed from the shelled corn by means of an air blast or with a suction-type fan.[3] On some shelling units the material discharged from the cage passes over a cleaning shoe for final separation of shelled corn from the cobs, husks, and other trash.[5,12]

18.9. Field Losses. Machine losses with a combine or a picker-sheller include (a) gathering loss (ear loss) as the stalks enter the gathering unit, (b) snapping-roll loss (corn shelled and lost by the snapping rolls or stripper plates), (c) cylinder or sheller loss (kernels and tips not removed from the cobs), and (d) separating and cleaning losses. Snappers and pickers are subject to only the first two types of machine losses.

Preharvest losses are also important but are not related to machine performance. They consist primarily of ears that have become detached from the stalks due to natural causes. Large preharvest losses indicate a genetic weakness in some varieties and a need for further breeding work to develop plants less susceptible to lodging and with stronger bonds between the ears and the stalks.

Additional losses occur because of immaturity if the corn is harvested too early. Tests have indicated that full maturity, with maximum potential yield, may not be attained until the kernel moisture content has decreased to 26%, provided the corn reaches this moisture level before frost.[12] In cool seasons, however, frost is likely to interrupt dry-matter accumulation at higher moisture contents.[12] Harvesting with combines in the Corn Belt states often starts at a moisture content above 30%. The moisture content may be well below 20% before harvesting is completed, especially in dry climates. Drying rates generally range from 0.3 to 0.6 percentage points per day.[11,20] In a 3-year Ohio study,[7] the average moisture content during the harvest season, when harvesting with combines, was about 25%.

Shelled corn harvested at high moisture contents must be dried artificially to about 15% moisture for safe storage. Ear corn, however, can be cribbed safely without artificial drying when the kernel moisture content is about 20%.[20]

Field losses are influenced by the type of harvester, machine adjustments, forward speed, date of harvesting, moisture content, varietal differences, amount of lodging, and other factors. Results of loss studies reported by various investigators prior to 1965 are summarized and discussed in reference 12. Additional, more recent results are presented in references 7 and 21.

Preharvest ear losses and machine gathering losses increase as the season advances. The stalks become dry and brittle and tend to lodge as a result of adverse weather conditions, and the ears break off easier. High forward speeds and poor centering of the snapping unit on the row increase ear losses, especially when the stalks are lodged. Speeds of 3.2 to 4.8 km/h [2 to 3 mph] are common with combines.[7]

The increase of preharvest losses with time is illustrated by the top graph in Fig. 18.7. Preharvest losses in Iowa plot tests[21] varied considerably among 5 varieties and increased rapidly as the kernel moisture content decreased below about 25%. The 2 worst varieties had preharvest losses of over 10% of the yield at kernel moisture contents of about 20% (but only 1% loss at moisture contents of 26 to 29%, 2 or 3 weeks earlier).

Gathering losses with combines in the Iowa tests tended to follow the same pattern as preharvest losses but were only about half as great.[21] In a 3-year study of a large number of farmer-operated harvesters in Ohio, gather-

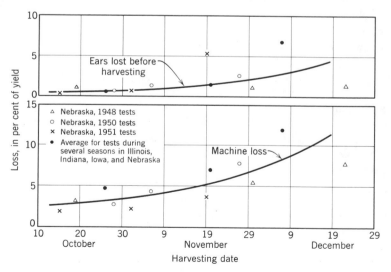

Fig. 18.7. Relation of field losses to harvest date, for corn pickers. (Data from references 4, 11, and 20.)

ing losses with combines consistently averaged twice those from conventional pickers.[7] The greater loss with combines was attributed partly to a tendency for the operators to keep the gathering points higher above the ground to minimize the possibility of feeding rocks through the cylinder. The average gathering loss for combines (reported in volume per unit area) probably represented 4 to 5% of the yield.[7]

Shelled-corn losses at the snapping rolls also increase as the kernel moisture content decreases, especially below 20%.[12,20] In general, losses with spiral-ribbed snapping rolls may be 2 to 4% at a kernel moisture content of 20%[12,13,20] and considerably greater at 15% moisture content.[12,20] Increased forward speed increases losses with spiral-ribbed snapping rolls.[12] Losses with fluted snapping rolls and properly adjusted stripper plates, as used on combine corn heads, are usually less than 1%[7,20] and are not greatly influenced by moisture content.[21]

Cylinder losses in a combine are increased if the peripheral speed is too low or the cylinder-concave clearance is too great. Cylinder losses with either a combine or a cage-type sheller seem to be related more closely to cob moisture content than to kernel moisture content, decreasing as the moisture content decreases during the harvest season.[6,18,21] Losses with the two types of shellers appear to be similar.[12] Cylinder losses for combines were usually less than 1% in studies made in Iowa[21] and Ohio[7] and often less than ½%, even at kernel moisture contents as high as 35%.

Separating and cleaning losses in a combine are generally less than ½%.[7,21] Losses may be higher, however, if the snapping unit is improperly adjusted so considerable quantities of stalk pieces and other green material are fed into the combine.[12] Separation losses with a picker-sheller are usually low when the sheller has a cleaning shoe[6] but may be high if all the separation is through the cage.[12]

All the machine losses incurred with a mechanical picker increase as the moisture content decreases during the season. The relation between harvesting date and total machine loss is illustrated in Fig. 18.7. Considering machine losses, preharvest losses, and immaturity losses, maximum harvested yields with a picker are obtained when the kernel moisture content is 30 to 35%.[12] With a picker-sheller, the decrease in cylinder loss as the season progresses shifts the zone of maximum yield recovery to a kernel moisture content of 25 to 30%.[12]

In the Ohio study of farmer-operated combines,[7] the average losses from the snapping unit, cylinder, and separating and cleaning totaled 120 kg/ha* [1.9 bu/acre] and gathering losses averaged 240 kg/ha* [3.8 bu/acre]. If one arbitrarily assumes an average yield of 5.0 to 6.0 Mg/ha* [80 to 95 bu/acre], the total average machine loss would be 6 to 7%. In the Iowa plot tests with a

*Assuming 25.4 kg [56 lb] per bushel.

combine in 5 corn varieties,[21] machine losses other than gathering losses usually totaled less than 1%. At kernel moisture contents of 25 to 20%, total machine losses (including gathering losses) were 1 to 4% and gathering losses represented 60 to 85% of the total.

18.10. Kernel Damage. Crackage is of concern because unless the fines are screened out they interfere with drying and increase the possibility of grain spoiling in storage. United States grading standards specify the maximum mass percentages passing through a 4.8-mm [12/64-in.] screen as 2% for U.S. No. 1 grade, 3% for No. 2, 4% for No. 3, etc.

Damage from a rasp-bar cylinder increases with peripheral speed, especially at speeds above 15.2 m/s [3000 ft/min].[8,18] Laboratory studies have indicated that damage is considerably less when the ears are fed into the cylinder with their axes parallel to the cylinder axis rather than longitudinally or in a random orientation.[16] Kernel moisture content has a significant effect upon damage from either a combine cylinder or a cage-type sheller. Results from various studies[7,16] indicate that crackage increases as the moisture content is changed in either direction from a minimum-crackage zone of about 20 to 22% (Fig. 18.8). A similar relation has been observed regarding the effect of moisture content upon damage to wheat or oats as determined by germination tests (Section 17.13).

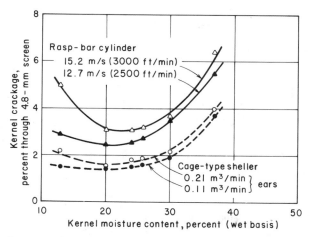

Fig. 18.8. Effect of kernel moisture content upon grain crackage from two types of shelling units, as determined with a 4.8-mm [12/64-in.] screen. (Data from D.M. Byg and G.E. Hall.[7])

Damage values based on visual inspection of kernels are several times as great as crackage percentages determined with a 4.8-mm [12/64-in.] screen. Determinations of visual damage from a cage-type sheller have not shown an increase as the moisture content was reduced below 20%.[12,18]

The crackage values in Fig. 18.8 were obtained in laboratory tests and are based on samples from all the material that passed through the shelling units.[7] Samples taken from the combine grain tank in field tests do not include kernel chips too small to be recovered by the cleaning shoe, and hence indicate lower damage percentages. In a 3-year field study of over 100 combines in Ohio, the percentage through a 4.8-mm [12/64-in.] screen ranged from 0.2 to 7.3% and averaged 1.7%.[7]

18.11. Safety in Corn-Harvester Operation. The spiral-ribbed type of snapping rolls is inherently dangerous because the rolls cannot be shielded completely. Most corn-harvester accidents are caused by the operator trying to unclog the snapping rolls while they are running and accidentally touching them with his clothing or hand. The straight-fluted type of roll is much safer than the spiral-ribbed type because the stripper plates act as shields to protect the operator. Safety is also promoted by having an arrangement to permit opening spiral-ribbed snapping rolls from the operator's station in case of clogging or imminent clogging.

REFERENCES

1. Agricultural Statistics, 1976. USDA.
2. Annual statistics issue. Implement & Tractor, *91*(22):16-70, Nov. 7, 1976.
3. BARKSTROM, R. New developments in field shelling of corn. Agr. Eng., *45*:484-485, 500, Sept., 1964.
4. BATEMAN, H. P., G. E. PICKARD, and W. BOWERS. Corn picker operation to save corn and hands. Illinois Agr. Ext. Circ. 697, 1952.
5. BELDIN, R. L., and A. B. SKROMME. Shelling attachment for mounted corn picker. Agr. Eng., *40*:87-91, Feb., 1959.
6. BURROUGH, D. E., and R. P. HARBAGE. Performance of a corn picker-sheller. Agr. Eng., *34*:21-22, Jan., 1953.
7. BYG, D. M., and G. E. HALL. Corn losses and kernel damage in field shelling of corn. Trans. ASAE, *11*(2):164-166, 1968.
8. Harvesting corn by combine. A symposium of six papers. Agr. Eng., *36*:791-800, 802, Dec., 1955.
9. HOPKINS, D. F., and G. E. PICKARD. Corn shelling with a combine cylinder. Agr. Eng., *34*:461-464, July, 1953.
10. HULL, D. O. Adjusting the corn picker. Iowa Agr. Ext. Pamphlet 161, 1950.
11. HURLBUT, L. W. How efficient is your corn harvest? Nebraska Expt. Sta. Quarterly, *1*(2):6-8, Fall, 1952.
12. JOHNSON, W. H., and B. J. LAMP. Principles, Equipment, and Systems for Corn Harvesting. Agricultural Consulting Associates, Inc., Wooster, Ohio, 1966. Available now only from Avi Publishing Co., Westport, Conn.
13. JOHNSON, W. H., B. J. LAMP, J. E. HENRY, and G. E. HALL. Corn harvesting performance at various dates. Trans. ASAE, *6*(3):268-272, 1963.
14. LOGAN, C. A. The development of a corn combine. Agr. Eng., *12*:277-278, July, 1931.
15. Machinery management. Successful Farming, *69*(8):14, June-July, 1971.
16. MAHMOUD, A. R., and W. F. BUCHELE. Corn ear orientation effects on mechanical damage and forces on concave. Trans. ASAE, *18*(3):444-447, 452, 1975.

17. McKIBBEN, E. G. Harvesting corn with a combine. Agr. Eng., *10*:231-232, July, 1929.
18 MORRISON, C. S. Attachments for combining corn. Agr. Eng., *36*:796-799, Dec., 1955.
19. PICKARD, G. E., and H. P. BATEMAN. Combining corn. Agr. Eng., *35*:500, 504, July, 1954.
20. SMITH, C. W., W. E. LYNESS, and T. A. KIESSELBACH. Factors affecting the efficiency of the mechanical corn picker. Nebraska Agr. Expt. Sta. Bull. 394, 1949.
21. WAELTI, H., W. F. BUCHELE, and M. FARRELL. Progress report on losses associated with corn harvesting in Iowa. J. Agr. Eng. Res., *14*:134-138, 1969.

19

Cotton Harvesting

19.1. Introduction. The annual production of cotton in the United States is usually 10 to 13 million bales. Over 90% of this is harvested mechanically.[5] The two types of machines used are commonly known as *pickers* and *strippers*. Mechanical pickers are selective in that the seed cotton is removed from the open bolls, whereas green, unopened bolls are left on the plant to mature for later picking. In high-yielding areas and in other areas where serious weather hazards make it important to start harvesting as early as possible, it is common practice to go over the field twice, allowing about 4 to 6 weeks between pickings. Under some conditions a second picking is not economically justifiable.

Strippers, on the other hand, are once-over machines. All bolls, whether open or closed, are removed from the plant in a single pass. Harvesting with a stripper is, therefore, usually delayed until the plants shed their leaves following the first frost. Chemical defoliants and desiccants are sometimes applied to permit earlier stripping.

Mechanical pickers are best adapted to irrigated areas and regions of high rainfall where yields are ordinarily high, the fibers are long, the bolls are of the open type, and vegetative growth is rank. Strippers have predominated in the High Plains, Rolling Plains, and Blackland areas of Texas and in Oklahoma, where the plants are small and yields are relatively low.[10] Strippers are most successful with plants having storm-resistant bolls and in areas with dry weather during the harvest season.[10] Pickers are more versatile than strippers, tolerating a wider range of plant characteristics and conditions and being affected less by grass and weeds.

The conventional row spacing for cotton has been 97 to 107 cm [38 to 42 in.]. However, considerable research relative to narrow row spacings and high plant populations has been conducted since the early 1960s.[2,13,15,17,23,25,26] There has been increasing grower interest in this system since about 1970 when continuous-width strippers suitable for narrow-row cotton became commercially available. Appreciable narrow-row plantings were made by growers in several states in 1970, and the area increased substantially in 1971 and 1972.[25,26]

Single-row, narrow spacings have been mostly 15 to 51 cm [6 to 20 in.], planted on a flat seedbed. Another common pattern has 2 rows, usually 30 to 41 cm [12 to 16 in.] apart, on beds having 102-cm [40-in.] center distances. Bed planting and the 51-cm [20-in.] single-row spacing permit cultivation for

446

weed control. Plant populations in research studies have ranged from the conventional 86 000 to 124 000 plants per hectare [35,000 to 50,000 plants per acre] to well over 494 000 plants per hectare [200,000 plants per acre].

The primary objective of narrow-row, high-population culture is to increase net profits by reducing production costs and/or increasing yields. An important means of reducing costs is by developing varieties and cultural practices that result in a short fruiting season and early maturity. Once-over harvesting then becomes feasible, fewer cultivations are required, and some late-season insecticide applications are eliminated.

Although there has been some success in meeting these objectives, results have been somewhat varied.[2,13,17,25,26] Yields may be increased 10 to 20% by narrow-row planting,[2,17,26] but under some conditions have been reduced.[25] Weed control is more difficult than in conventional row spacings. Varieties available in 1976 were not well-adapted for narrow-row plantings in some areas.

MECHANICAL PICKERS

19.2. Development. The first patent pertaining to mechanical picking of cotton was issued to Rembert and Prescott in 1850.[11] Hundreds of patents covering various types of cotton harvesting devices have since been granted. The first commercial pickers appeared in the early 1940s, but it was not until 1946 that these machines were manufactured in any appreciable volume. By 1964 there were approximately 53 000 pickers in use in the United States.[20]

19.3. Picker Arrangements and Basic Requirements. Essentially, a mechanical picker consists of the following functional units (Fig. 19.1).

1. An arrangement for guiding the cotton plants into the picking zone and providing necessary support while the seed cotton is being removed.
2. Devices to remove the cotton from the open bolls.
3. A conveying system for the picked cotton.
4. A storage basket or container in which the picked cotton can be accumulated.

Most present-day models of pickers are two-row, self-propelled machines. However, a one-row model that can be mounted on a special high-clearance tractor, interchangeably with boom-type or row-crop sprayers, was available in 1976.

A mechanical picker must be capable of gathering mature seed cotton* with a minimum of waste and without causing serious damage to the fiber, plant, or unopened bolls. To ensure the highest possible grade of ginned cotton, the harvested material should have a minimum of leaves, stems, hulls,

---

*Seed cotton consists of individual cotton seeds surrounded by lint, as produced within the "shell" (burs) of the bolls.

Fig. 19.1. Typical arrangement for a mechanical cotton picker. A model from the early 1950s is depicted, but the basic arrangement is similar on present-day pickers. (Courtesy of International Harvester Co.)

weeds, and other foreign matter entwined in the lint. How well this requirement is met depends somewhat upon how gently the plant is handled while it is passing through the machine. Streamlining of the plant passageway, the use of suitable limb lifters, and synchronization of moving picker parts with the forward travel of the machine all tend to minimize disturbance of the plant.

19.4. Spindles. The basic principle of a revolving spindle penetrating the cotton plant, winding the seed cotton from the open boll, and retreating to a doffing zone is employed by all the commercial pickers now available. The rearward movement of the spindles while in the picking zone is substantially the same as the forward movement of the machine (generally 3.2 to 5.6 km/h [2 to 3½ mph]) so that the spindles, while in the picking zone, do not move forward or backward with respect to the cotton plant. Each rotating spindle merely probes straight into the cotton plant from the side of the row, works on an open boll if it encounters one, and then withdraws straight out to the side with a minimum of disturbance and damage to the remainder of the plant. The spacing of the spindles — approximately 38 × 38 mm [1½ × 1½ in.] — is such that they can slip past unopened bolls and leave them on the plant to mature for a later picking.

Current models of mechanical pickers have either tapered spindles or small-diameter straight spindles. The spindles are carried either on bars arranged in vertical drums or on vertical slats attached to endless chain belts.

Tapered spindles, commonly employed on drum-type pickers, have 3 or 4 longitudinal rows of sharp barbs for engaging the cotton (Fig. 19.2). Their tapered shape facilitates removal of the cotton (doffing) after they leave the picking zone. Spindle speeds range from about 1850 r/min at a forward speed of 2.9 km/h [1.8 mph] to 3250 r/min at 5.0 km/h [3.1 mph].

In a series of laboratory tests,[4] speed of tapered spindles had a marked effect upon picking efficiency. For fluffy bolls, the efficiency increased from 80% at 700 r/min to 95% at 2300 r/min, remained constant from 2300 to 3900 r/min and then declined slightly at 4700 r/min. The loss at the slower speed consisted of cotton left in the burs, whereas most of the loss at higher speeds was cotton thrown by the spindles. The picking efficiency of knotty bolls that had opened before maturity (contained hard locks) increased linearly with spindle speed, from 49% at 700 r/min to 72% at 3900 r/min. These results suggest the desirability of being able to increase spindle speeds in fields of knotty cotton.

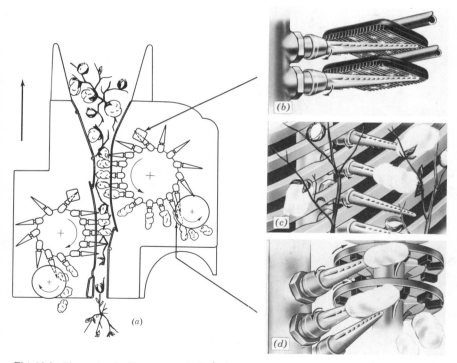

Fig. 19.2. Elements of a drum-type spindle picker. *(a)* Plan view of picking drums; *(b)* spindle-moistening pads; *(c)* spindles projecting into plant through grid section; *(d)* doffers. (Courtesy of Deere & Co.)

Horizontal spacings of 33, 40, 46, and 52 mm [1⁵⁄₁₆, 1⁹⁄₁₆, 1¹³⁄₁₆, and 2 ¹⁄₁₆ in.] were compared in these same tests, maintaining the vertical spacing at 41 mm [1⅝ in.]. The picking efficiency of fluffy cotton remained constant for the 3 smallest spacings but was significantly lower with the 52-mm spacing. With knotty cotton bolls, the efficiency decreased with each 6-mm increase in spacing.

Straight spindles are commonly employed on chain-belt pickers (Fig. 19.3). They are longer than the tapered type and are considerably smaller in diameter. They may be round or square and may have a smooth or roughened surface. In one machine the spindles are double-barbed for more aggressive action. In general, their picking ability depends primarily upon the spindles being wet when they contact the cotton. On present-day machines, spindles of this type are generally rotated at a speed of about 1250

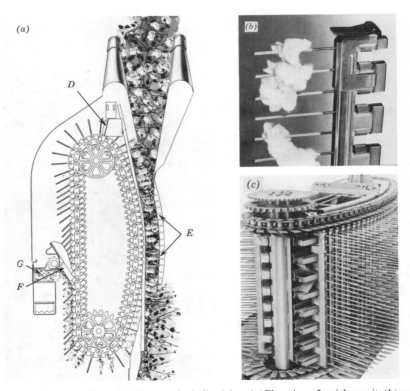

Fig. 19.3. Elements of a chain-belt type of spindle picker. *(a)* Plan view of a picker unit; *(b)* portion of a spindle slat, showing loaded spindles at left and knurled drive rollers at right; *(c)* rear view of picker unit, with some of slats removed to show the spindle drive rails; *(D)* spindle moistener; *(E)* spindles in picker zone; *(F)* spindle stripper bars; *(G)* elevator. (A prior production model, courtesy of Allis-Chalmers.)

r/min (at 4.8 km/h [3 mph]) while in the picking zone and are not driven during the remainder of the cycle.

19.5. Drum-Type Spindle Arrangements. The elements of a typical tandem-drum picker are shown in Fig. 19.2. The two drums pick from the two sides of the row in succession. A spring-loaded, adjustable pressure plate opposite each drum crowds the plants toward the spindles in the picking zone. The clearance between the pressure plate and the ends of the spindles varies from 6 to 25 mm [¼ to 1 in.], depending upon the size and density of the plants. In current high-drum machines the front drum has 15 or 16 spindle bars and the rear drum has 13 or 12 bars, with 20 spindles per bar. This gives a total of 560 spindles per row of cotton, each spindle requiring a precision-fit sleeve bearing and being driven through bevel gears by a shaft inside the spindle bar. Low-drum pickers have only 14 spindles per bar. They are suitable for low-growing or medium-height cotton.

The proper orientation of the spindle bars in relation to the row (or to the doffers) is obtained by means of a stationary cam and followers on the bars. All linear motion of the spindles while in the picking zone is at right angles to the row. The spindles enter the cotton plant through a grid section (Fig. 19.2c) which subsequently prevents the plants from being pulled into the doffing area as the loaded spindles withdraw.

In measurements made by Corley,[4] a drum-type picker moved approximately 240 mm [9.5 in.] along the row during the feed-in and return movement of the spindles. This gave a picking time of 0.20 s for a machine speed of 4.3 km/h [2.7 mph]. Four exposure times (0.16, 0.20, 0.24, and 0.28 s) compared in the laboratory showed no effect upon picking efficiencies.

19.6. Chain-Belt Spindle Arrangement. The picking process with a chain-belt unit is essentially the same as with the drum-type picker, although the chain-belt principle (Fig. 19.3) permits the spindles to remain in the picking zone for a longer time. In currently available pickers, the chain-belt units have straight spindles. The standard-height picking unit illustrated in Fig. 19.3 has 80 vertical slats, each with 16 spindles (total of 1280). High units have 22 spindles per bar. Each spindle is rotated by means of a roller in contact with a stationary drive rail (Fig. 19.3c), but only while on the picking side of the unit.

Guide strips (Fig. 19.3c, top) hold the chains in position between the main sprockets and provide the proper curvature for moving the spindles laterally into and out of the row. Each spindle slat is pivoted between the upper and lower chains. While the spindles are being rotated, the action of the drive rollers on the rails maintains the spindles in a position normal to the curvature of the drive rails. As the spindles approach the stripper (F in Fig. 19.3a), contact with a stationary restraining block or hold-back device rotates the slats to angle the spindles toward the rear and thus orient them for the stripping operation.

Machines having the chain-belt arrangement and straight spindles ordinarily pick from only one side of the row, as illustrated in Fig. 19.3. However, one manufacturer of a 2-row machine has a model on which the 2 picking units are arranged in tandem to pick a single row from both sides. This arrangement is intended for use in cotton having exceptionally high yields.

19.7. Spindle Moistening. Spindles of either type are moistened with water for two reasons: (a) as an aid to picking because cotton adheres better to a wet steel surface and (b) to keep the spindles clean. Spindles pick up a gummy substance from the plants which, if allowed to accumulate, will collect dust and trash and thus interfere with picking. The addition of a wetting agent (detergent) reduces the amount of water required for moistening and at the same time makes it more effective.

A spindle-moistening system is provided for each picking unit, water being metered in equal amounts to each level of spindles. Application is made to each spindle, just before it enters the picking zone, by means of a specially designed rubber wiping pad (Fig. 19.2b and part D in Fig. 19.3a).

19.8. Removal of Cotton from Spindles. On machines with tapered spindles, the seed cotton is removed from the spindles by means of rotating doffer plates (Fig. 19.2d). The clearance between the surface of the spindle and the rubber lugs on the doffer should be between 0.25 and 0.75 mm [0.010 and 0.030 in.]. The cotton is forced off as the doffer lug moves over the spindle surface toward the tip. With the small-diameter straight spindles, stripping is accomplished by moving the spindles axially through the spaces between closely fitted stripper shoes (F in Fig. 19.3a). Tapered spindles are rotating when doffed, whereas small-diameter, straight spindles are not.

19.9. Conveying and Carrying. A pneumatic conveying system (Fig. 19.1) is used to move the cotton from the doffing area to the storage basket on the picker. The cotton is blown through the discharge ducts against cleaning grates in the basket lid. This action removes some of the trash from the seed cotton. Machines with dual picking units have 2 separate elevating systems (2 blowers) to provide more uniform and positive conveying from each unit. Some machines use offset-fan arrangements to eliminate contact between the cotton and fan blades. Others introduce air into the conveying ducts immediately above the picker units to accomplish the same result.

Basket capacities on 2-row pickers are generally 1.2 to 1.6 Mg [2700 to 3600 lb]. Mechanical compacters are employed to achieve the higher values within this range. Baskets are emptied by hydraulically lifting and rotating them about the upper edge of one side.

MECHANICAL STRIPPERS

The cotton stripper is an outgrowth of the homemade cotton sleds that came into widespread use in the High Plains region of Texas in 1926.[19] As early as 1914, sleds equipped with a section of picket fence were employed to salvage the cotton crop in the Plains area. The practice in this region, before the stripper was introduced, was to hand-snap the cotton bolls rather than to pick the seed cotton from the burs. In 1964 there were approximately 40 000 strippers in use in the United States.[20]

Several factors have contributed to an increase in popularity of strippers in preference to pickers. They are: (1) lower first cost; (2) lower maintenance costs; (3) improved cotton varieties better adapted to stripping; (4) improved strippers employing flexible rolls, green-boll separation, and first-stage cleaning; (5) improved ginning equipment for separating trash; (6) trend toward closer row spacing; (7) good recovery of cotton in the field; and (8) higher harvesting speeds.

19.10. Principles and Development. Mechanical stripping of cotton is accomplished by forcing the plants through an area too small for the bolls to pass. The snapped bolls are collected in the machine while the plants remain in place in the row. In removing the bolls, an upward and forward force is applied to the plant. Since this force must be opposed by the root system, the plants must be firmly anchored in the row. Current models of strippers are either brush-type or finger-type units.

Brush-type strippers, used primarily on standard single-row plantings, employ a pair of rolls that are approximately 1020 mm [40 in.] long and 150 mm [6 in.] in diameter and are mounted at an angle of about 30° above horizontal (Fig. 19.4). Their surfaces are fitted with longitudinal brushes alternated with rubber flaps. The rolls are driven at about 600 r/min, with their adjacent surfaces moving upward next to the plants. Note that this is opposite to the direction of rotation of corn-snapping rolls. As the bolls are snapped off, they are moved away from the plants by the surface of the rolls and delivered onto adjacent conveyors. The flexibility of the roll surfaces permits a degree of automatic adjustment for light and heavy growth. The spacing between the rolls can be adjusted manually to meet extreme conditions.

Finger-type strippers (Fig. 19.5) were developed in the 1960s,[15,23] and have been available commercially since 1971. The fingers comb upward through the plants as the harvester moves forward. Each entire plant must pass through the narrow space between two adjacent fingers. A continuous-width finger stripper can be used for any row spacing or for random plantings. Although originally developed primarily for narrow-row cotton,[15,23] they are also used for conventional single-row spacings in low-yielding, dry-land cotton.

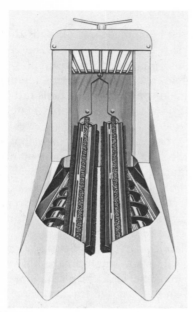

Fig. 19.4. Brush-type cotton stripper. The rolls are fitted with longitudinal brushes alternated with rubber paddles. Cotton bolls are discharged from the rolls into auger conveyors. (Courtesy of Hesston Corp.)

Fig. 19.6. Extractor unit for separating seed cotton from the burs and other foreign material. (Courtesy of Hesston Corp.)

Fig. 19.5. A continuous-width finger-type stripper. The space between fingers is about 16 mm [⅝ in.]. The reel above the rear ends of the fingers pushes detached bolls into a cross auger. A small-diameter rotating drum with longitudinal saw-tooth fins attached is located beneath the rear ends of the fingers and exerts a downward pull on the stalks.

Finger-stripper heads are simpler and less expensive than brush-type heads and require very little maintenance, but work well only under a rather limited range of conditions. They do not work satisfactorily under damp conditions, if the plants have not been well defoliated, or if the plants are large and heavily branched — conditions often encountered in irrigated narrow-row plantings.

In 1974 a conventional brush-type stripper head was modified experimentally at the California Agricultural Experiment Station to fit double rows 30 to 41 cm [12 to 16 in.] apart on beds having center distances of 97 to 102 cm [38 to 40 in.]. This stripper performed well over a wide range of plant conditions, and field losses were considerably less than with a finger stripper. But a brush-type stripper can be used only on row spacings that approximate the center-to-center distances between pairs of rolls.

Brush-type strippers for conventional single-row plantings are usually two-row units, either self-propelled or tractor-mounted. All current models of continuous-width finger-type strippers are self-propelled and have stripping heads that are 3.91 m [154 in.] wide. One model also has a 1.93-m [76-in.] head available for use in heavy-yielding cotton. Strippers of either type often have provision for separating mature cotton from the heavier, unopened green bolls with an upward-moving air stream.[14] The mature cotton is conveyed pneumatically to the storage basket on the harvester. The green bolls drop from the air stream into a container from which they are dumped onto the turnrow (headland) for possible salvage at a later date. Some strippers are also equipped with gin-type extractor units (Fig. 19.6) that remove at least a portion of the burs, sticks, and other foreign material from the seed cotton.

FACTORS AFFECTING MECHANICAL HARVESTING

19.11. Varietal Characteristics. Plant breeders in most of the cotton-producing states are continuing to develop new varieties more suitable for mechanical harvesting. Emphasis has been divided between cotton suitable for picking and cotton suitable for stripping, depending upon the area served.

Smith and Jones[19] describe the ideal variety for stripping as one producing a semidwarf plant having relatively short-fruiting, short-noded branches, storm-resistant* bolls borne singly but having fairly fluffy locks for good extracting, and a medium-size boll stem that can be pulled from the limbs with a force of 13 to 22 N [3 to 5 lbf]. Stripping a variety that produces a wide, spreading plant with numerous vegetative and fruiting branches results in low recovery of cotton and excessive field losses.

---

*"Storm resistance" in cotton (or stormproof) refers to a characteristic whereby the bolls tend to resist shattering from the burs when subjected to the action of wind and rain.

Varieties for narrow-row planting should have the general characteristics indicated above for conventional-row stripper varieties. However, because of the higher plant populations, fewer bolls per plant are needed to produce a given yield. The plants should be determinate in their growth and fruiting characteristics, with a short fruiting period and early, uniform maturity.

Tests have shown no correlation between spindle-picker performance and the size of the bolls.[4,8] Cotton bolls exhibiting too much of the storm-resistant characteristic, although well-adapted to stripping, are difficult to pick mechanically. Tests with spindle pickers in Arkansas,[22] for example, showed a picker efficiency of only 88% in a variety developed primarily for stripping, as compared with 94% in a variety more suitable for mechanical picking. Stripper efficiencies in the same varieties were 96 and 95%, respectively.

The size of the plant, the type of growth, and the nature of the boll all have more influence on the efficiency of the mechanical picker than does the yield. Where the plant characteristics are suitable, a machine will pick high-yielding cotton just as efficiently as it will low-yielding cotton.[19]

Corley[5] has pointed out that it takes approximately 100 000 cotton bolls to produce one 225-kg [500-lb] bale of lint. Since there are 4 or 5 locks in each boll, there are over 400 000 opportunities for picker losses with the harvest of each bale. Therefore, the physical characteristics of the boll influence the effectiveness of spindle pickers. In Alabama tests,[4] for example, the picker efficiency was 95% for fluffy bolls as compared with 90% for weathered bolls (subjected to 102 mm [4 in.] of rain), and 65% for knotty bolls (contained hard locks).

19.12. Plant Population and Spacing.* Plant spacing within conventional single rows seems to have no great effect on the performance of either pickers or strippers. Reasonably uniform spacing within the row is desirable for strippers because skips cause adjacent plants to grow more rank. Comparative tests at the Shafter Station (California) with spindle pickers in hill-dropped and drill-planted plots having equal plant populations (120 000 plants per hectare in 1949 tests and 88 000 in 1950 tests) showed no difference in either picker efficiency or the amount of trash collected.[21]

Other tests at the Shafter Station, in drill-planted stands ranging from 20 000 to 168 000 plants per hectare, showed very little difference in picker efficiencies for populations above 49 000 plants per hectare and only a slight decrease at the lower populations (Fig. 19.7). Picker efficiencies in Alabama irrigated-cotton tests[6] during 1960 and 1961 averaged 90.4% with 20 000 plants per hectare and increased from 93.0 to 95.1% between 49 000 and 198 000 plants per hectare. Populations from 36 000 to 141 000 plants per hectare in nonirrigated cotton had little effect on either stripper or picker efficiencies.[6]

---

*Plants per acre = 0.405 × (plants per hectare).

In actual production practice, plant populations with 102-cm [40-in.] single rows may range from 37 000 to 148 000 plants per hectare.[17] Cotton can tolerate a rather wide range of populations without greatly affecting the yields.[6,13,22]

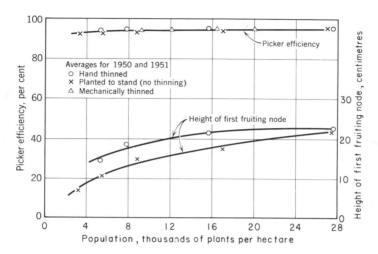

Fig. 19.7. Effect of plant population upon height of first fruiting node and upon picker efficiency. (Data from Tavernetti and Miller.[20])

Decreasing the in-row spacing (greater plant population) has the desirable effect of raising the height of the lowest fruiting branches on the plants. This relation is illustrated in Fig. 19.7. Similar results were obtained in Alabama tests[6] and in Texas.[2,13] Raising the fruiting zone makes the height adjustment for the picking or stripping unit less critical and, under adverse conditions, may improve harvester performance. The Texas results[13] showed that for a given plant spacing within the row there were no consistent differences between the average heights of the lowest fruiting branchs for single-row spacings of 13, 25, 51, 76, and 102 cm [5, 10, 20, 30, and 40 in.].

19.13. Weed Control and Cultivation Practices. Weeds and grass not only compete with the cotton plants for water and soil nutrients, but also interfere with harvesting and lower the grade of ginned cotton. Grass is extremely difficult to remove at the gin. Various combinations of late cultivation, chemical weeding, and flame weeding (Chapter 11) are employed in attempting to reduce weed populations to a minimum.

Good weed control is especially important and difficult to attain in narrow-row plantings. The development of effective pre-emergence herbicides has greatly enhanced the possibilities for effective weed control in both narrow-row and conventional plantings.

The shape of the row profiles left by the final cultivation is important in regard to mechanical harvesting. Final profiles should be uniform in height, width, and shape, should be smooth and free of clods, and should have the crest at the base of the cotton stalks.

19.14. Defoliation. When practiced in conjunction with mechanical picking or stripping, defoliation serves three valuable purposes, namely, removal of the bulk of the leaves that tend to interfere with machine harvesting, prevention of green-leaf stain on the lint, and elimination of a source of dry leaf trash that is difficult to remove at the gin. Chemical defoliation inflicts a mild injury and causes a slow drying of the leaves so that leaf abscission (detachment) can proceed in the normal manner. Chemical desiccants or a hard frost may kill the entire plant, in which case normal abscission does not occur and most leaves remain attached.

Chemical defoliants (or desiccants) are usually applied in the form of sprays, with either ground rigs or aircraft (Chapter 13). In regions where vegetative growth is extensive and defoliation is most needed, difficulty has been experienced in obtaining sufficient penetration and leaf coverage to ensure a thorough job. Two applications are sometimes made when growth is heavy.

Studies of thermal defoliation of cotton were initiated in 1962 at the Oklahoma Agricultural Experiment Station because of inconsistent results obtained with chemical defoliants.[1] A two-row field machine was developed, utilizing LP-gas burners to heat air that was mixed with the exhaust gases and recirculated through the plants in a hooded area by means of a blower. High-velocity air streams across the front and rear of the hood created air curtains or heat barriers. Results from 3 years of testing (1966 through 1968) indicated that 70% defoliation could be obtained with an exposure time of 4 to 6 s (controlled by forward speed) and corresponding air temperatures of 370 to 260°C [700 to 500°F]. Defoliation rates in excess of 90% have been achieved under some conditions. Excessive temperatures or exposure times resulted in desiccation, with the leaves dried but more of them remaining on the plants.

The cost for LP gas in these tests was about $3.70/ha, compared with $4.90 to $7.40 per hectare for the defoliation chemical, but a thermal defoliator is a fairly costly, specialized piece of equipment. Properly applied thermal treatment had no effect on cotton fiber properties.[1]

EFFECTS AND COSTS OF MECHANICAL HARVESTING

19.15 Gin Turn-Out. When seed cotton arrives at the gin it contains dirt, hulls, moisture, leaf fragments, stems, and other trash such as weeds and grass. With stripped cotton, the burs are also included. The gin must remove this foreign matter in addition to separating the lint from the cottonseed. Thus the gin plays an important role in the overall mechanization picture.

Gin turn-out (or lint turn-out) is the ratio of the mass of the recovered lint to the mass of the field-run seed cotton. For example, a gin turn-out of 36% means that approximately 635 kg [1400 lb] of seed cotton from the field are required to obtain a 225-kg [500-lb] bale of lint. The presence of excessive amounts of trash and other foreign matter reduces the gin turn-out, increases.the cost of ginning, and lowers the final grade of the lint.

Watson,[24] in 1951, reported average gin turn-outs as follows:

Hand-picked	37%
Machine-picked	36%
Machine-stripped	23%

Results reported for other areas [6,9,13,18] are in remarkably close agreement with the above figures.

Including extractors on mechanical strippers (Fig. 19.6), to give a first-stage cleaning in the field, increases the gin turn-out.

19.16. Cotton Grades. Machine-picked cotton averages lower in grade than hand-picked cotton. Although improvements in harvester operation, cultural practices, chemical defoliation, and ginning facilities have helped narrow the difference, there is still a grade reduction that may represent a loss of 5 to 10% of the crop value in comparison with hand picking.[3,18]

The principal ways in which mechanical pickers can reduce grades of lint below the grades that might be obtained by hand picking are:

1. Discoloration of lint by green leaves and by oil and grease from the machine.
2. Introduction of additional amounts of weeds, grass, and trash from the cotton plant.
3. Addition of excessive moisture (from spindle moistening) to the lint and trash, thus making trash removal at the gin more difficult and inducing graying or mildew if ginning is delayed.
4. Twisting or tangling of the lint by the spindles, thereby increasing difficulties associated with ginning.

The grade of *stripped* cotton may be reduced by the introduction of trash, because of the inherent blending of immature cotton with mature cotton, and because of weathering of the lower bolls while waiting for the upper bolls to open.[10]

19.17. Field Losses. Field losses may be in the form of cotton dropped prior to harvesting (preharvest loss), cotton left on the plants by the harvester, or cotton dropped by the harvester. Preharvest losses vary considerably among different varieties and in different areas. With conventional single-row plantings of open-boll varieties, preharvest losses are likely to be greater for stripping than for mechanical picking because stripping must be delayed longer to permit maturing of a high percentage of the bolls.[22]

Probably the greatest single factor affecting machine loss is the skill of the operator. Other factors (most of which have already been discussed) include weeds and grass in the row, varieties not well-adapted to the type of harvester used, poor row profile, uneven or insufficient headland for turning, poor defoliation, improper spindle speed in the case of pickers, climatic conditions, plant population, and the mechanical condition of the machine.

General experience with spindle pickers indicates that, with careful attention to the various production and machine-operating factors involved, machine losses will usually be 5 to 10% of the yield.[6,16,21] Under less favorable conditions, picker losses may be as great as 15 to 20%. Strippers operating in suitable varieties often have losses of only 2 to 5%.[6,15,16,19] Under comparable conditions in either open-boll or storm-resistant varieties, losses with brush-type strippers tend to be lower than picker losses.[6,22]

19.18. Costs of Mechanical Harvesting. The costs of mechanical picking are characterized by high fixed charges, because of the high new cost of the machine, and by high repair costs. Since strippers are simpler machines and have a much lower new cost than mechanical pickers, harvesting costs per hectare are considerably lower for stripping.

The amount of cotton harvested per season is an important factor in determining the harvesting cost per bale, especially for mechanical pickers. Strippers, because of their lower fixed costs, are economically feasible for smaller areas than are pickers.

When comparing pickers and strippers, charges for field losses (preharvest and machine), grade loss, and the increase in ginning costs for stripped cotton versus picked cotton must be added to the harvesting costs. When comparing two different production systems, such as narrow-row cotton versus conventional row spacings, differences in yields and in the costs of various cultural operations must also be considered.

HANDLING AND STORING SEED COTTON

In the conventional system of handling, the seed cotton is dumped from the picker or stripper basket into trailers parked on the turnrow. The filled trailers are towed to the gin and the cotton remains in them until ginned. This system creates an undesirable scheduling interdependence between the harvesting and ginning operations. Growers sometimes have to stop harvesting because all their trailers are full, waiting to be ginned. Gins may have to work short shifts or shut down temporarily because of lack of cotton if adverse weather interferes with the harvesting operation.

Storing at least a portion of the crop between harvesting and ginning alleviates both of these problems. Growers can complete their harvest at an earlier date, with less possibility of grade losses or yield reductions due to adverse weather. Gins can operate on a regularly scheduled basis and for a longer period of time, thereby reducing ginning costs per bale. Various systems of seed cotton storage were used to a limited extent by a few growers and gins in the 1960s. Following the development of new methods and new equipment in the early 1970s, there has been a dramatic increase in the amount of seed cotton stored each year. The two most common storage systems are known as ricking and moduling.

19.19. Ricking.[7] In this storage system, the cotton is dumped from the harvesters into a slip form (ricker) that is moved along the turnrow. The ricker makes continuous stacks as long as desired — usually 24 to 36 m [80 to 120 ft]. The cotton is moderately compacted, either with a mechanical device or manually, while still within the ricker. Mechanically compacted ricks are generally 2.1 to 2.3 m [7 to 7½ ft] wide and 1.5 to 1.8 m [5 to 6 ft] high. Ricks are generally covered with plastic for protection against rain and wind. The ricked cotton remains in the field until needed for ginning. It is then loaded into conventional cotton trailers, usually with a tined, scoop-type loader that can pick up as much as 680 kg [1500 lb] of seed cotton at one time.

19.20. Module System.[12] With the module system, seed cotton is dumped from the harvester baskets into a four-sided form having an openable rear door. This unit, known as a module builder, was developed by the Agricultural Engineering Department at the Texas A & M University in 1971. It has a traversing, mechanical compacter and compresses the seed cotton into high-density stacks 2.1 to 2.3 m [7 to 7½ ft] wide, 7.3 or 9.75 m [24 or 32 ft] long, and usually 1.8 to 2.1 m [6 to 7 ft] high. The width and length depend upon the dimensions of the module builder. Each module is free-standing after the module builder has been raised on its wheels and pulled forward (with rear door opened).

The modules are built on wood or metal pallets or directly on the ground. Pallet modules are hydraulically winched onto specially built tilt-bed trailers. Modules built directly on the ground can be picked up and hauled, intact, with tilt-bed module-mover trucks that have parallel roller chains running lengthwise of the bed to support and convey the module (similar to haystack movers described in Section 15.2). When loading, the forward speed of the chains relative to the truck is synchronized with the rearward speed of the truck so that the chain legs on top of the bed essentially stand still with respect to the ground as the tilted bed moves under the module. When unloading, the chains move rearward as the truck moves forward.

Modules may be hauled directly to the gin feeder station for immediate ginning or they may be stored, perferably in the gin yard, until needed by the gin. Either pallet modules or palletless modules will remain intact through several loading and unloading cycles. Modules to be stored in the field or elsewhere are covered with plastic or canvas as soon as they are completed. Modules not covered for storage are generally covered temporarily for transport.

REFERENCES

1. BATCHELDER, D.G., J.G. PORTERFIELD, W.E. TAYLOR, and G.F. MOORE. Thermal defoliator developments. Trans. ASAE, *13*(3):782-784, 1970.
2. BRASHEARS, D., I. W. KIRK, and E. B. HUDSPETH, Jr. Effects of row spacing and plant population on double-row cotton. Texas Agr. Expt. Sta. MP-872, 1968.
3. CAPSTICK, D. F., and G. R. TUPPER. Value of field and grade losses for mechanically picked cotton. Arkansas Farm Res., *12*(2):9, Mar.-Apr., 1963.
4. CORLEY, T. E. Basic factors affecting performance of mechanical cotton pickers. Trans. ASAE, *9*(3):326-332, 1966.
5. CORLEY, T. E. Correlation of mechanical harvesting with cotton plant characteristics. Trans. ASAE, *13*(6):768-773, 778, 1970.
6. CORLEY, T. E., and C. M. STOKES. Mechanical cotton harvester performance as influenced by plant spacing and varietal characteristics. Trans. ASAE, *7*(3):281-290, 1964.
7. CURLEY, R. G., et al. Seed cotton storage — an aid to both growers and ginners. California Agriculture, *27*(7):7-9, July, 1973.
8. HARRISON, G. J. Breeding and adapting cotton to mechanization. Agr. Eng., *32*:486-488, Sept., 1951.
9. HOLEKAMP, E. R., and W. I THOMAS. Picking Arizona cotton. Progressive Agriculture in Arizona, *II*(2):3, 12, July-Aug.-Sept., 1950.
10. HUDSPETH, E.B., Jr. Personal correspondence dated June 28, 1971.
11. JOHNSON, E. A. The evolution of the mechanical cotton harvester. Agr. Eng., *19*:383-388, Sept., 1938.
12. KEPNER, R. A., R. G. CURLEY, M. HOOVER, and L. K. STROMBERG. The module system for storing and handling seed cotton. California Agriculture, *28*(5):6-9, May, 1974.
13. KIRK, I. W., A. D. BRASHEARS, and E. B. HUDSPETH, Jr. Influence of row width and plant spacing on cotton production characteristics on the High Plains. Texas Agr. Expt. Sta. MP-937, 1969.
14. KIRK, I. W., and E. B. HUDSPETH, Jr. Development and testing of an improved green-boll separator for cotton-stripper harvesters. Trans. ASAE, *7*(4):414-417, 1964.
15. KIRK, I. W., E. B. HUDSPETH, Jr., and D. F. WANJURA. A broadcast and narrow-row cotton harvester. Texas Agr. Expt. Sta. PR-2311, 1964.
16. MATTHEWS, E. J., and G. R. TUPPER. Coordinated development for new cotton production systems. Trans. ASAE, *8*(4):568-571, 1965.
17. RAY, L. L., and E. B. HUDSPETH, Jr. Narrow row cotton production. Texas Agr. Expt. Sta. Current Res. Rept. 66-5, Sept., 1966.
18. SMITH, H. P. Harvesting cotton. Cotton Production, Marketing, and Utilization, Chap. 7. Edited and published by W. B. Andrews, State College, Miss., 1950.
19. SMITH, H. P., and D. L. JONES. Mechanized production of cotton in Texas. Texas Agr. Expt. Sta. Bull 704, 1948.
20. STRICKLER, P. E. Power and equipment on farms in 1964, 48 states. USDA Econ. Res. Serv. Bull 457, 1970.
21. TAVERNETTI, J. R., and H. F. MILLER, Jr. Studies on mechanization of cotton farming in California. California Agr. Expt. Sta. Bull. 747, 1954.
22. TUPPER, G. R. Stripper harvesting vs. spindle picking of open-boll and experimental stripper varieties of cotton. Trans. ASAE, *9*(1):110-113, 1966.
23. TUPPER, G. R. New concept of stripper harvesting of cotton in Arkansas. Trans. ASAE, *9*(3):306-308, 1966.
24. WATSON, L. J. The effect of mechanical harvesting on quality. Proc. Fifth Annual Cotton Mechanization Conf. (1951), pp. 25-26.

25. Western Cotton Production Conference, 1971, Proc. Includes nine papers on narrow-row cotton production.
26. Western Cotton Production Conference, 1972, Proc. Includes seven papers on narrow-row cotton production.

PROBLEMS

19.1 How many revolutions does each spindle of a cotton picker make while in the picking zone,

(a) For a drum-type arrangement in which each spindle has a rotational speed of 2700 r/min at 4.4 km/h and remains in the picking zone during 150 mm of forward travel?

(b) For a chain-belt arrangement in which each spindle has a rotational speed of 1250 r/min at 4.8 km/h and remains in the picking zone during 760 mm of forward travel?

19.2. The following data were obtained in a test of a 2-row cotton picker operating on 102-cm rows: length of test run = 20 m; time = 15.0 s; preharvest loss = 242 g of clean seed cotton; machine loss on the ground = 316 g of clean seed cotton; machine loss on the plants = 114 g of clean seed cotton; amount of material harvested = 7.4 kg; total trash in 300-g sample of harvested material = 15.7 g. Calculate:

(a) Percent trash in harvested sample.

(b) Gross yield of clean seed cotton in kilograms per hectare, including preharvest loss.

(c) Preharvest loss, in percent of gross yield.

(d) Machine performance efficiency, in percent.

(e) Harvested yield of lint, in number of 225-kg bales per hectare, assuming 35% gin turn-out.

(f) Harvest rate in hectares per hour, assuming 75% field efficiency.

20

Root Crop Harvesting

20.1. Introduction. Irish potatoes, sugar beets, and peanuts are the major root crops produced in the United States. About 600 kha [1½ million acres] of each were grown in 1975.[1] The total value of the Irish potato crop each year is about twice the value of the sugar beet crop or the peanut crop. Harvest mechanization of all three of these crops is well-advanced.

Sweet potatoes and onions are next in importance, but each represents only 2 to 3% of the total United States root-crop plantings.[1] Progress toward fully mechanized harvesting has been slower than with the three major root crops.

SUGAR BEET HARVESTING

Mechanical sugar beet harvesters were first used to an appreciable extent in 1943. Prior to the development of mechanical harvesters, sugar beets were loosened in the soil with special plows or lifter blades and then the unwanted top portions were cut off individually by hand. Virtually all the United States crop is now harvested mechanically. Reference 10 includes an excellent review of research studies and equipment development, since the early 1930s, pertaining to sugar beet harvesting.

The basic operations performed in mechanical harvesting are (a) either rotary flailing to remove top growth or cutting off the unwanted top portion of the beets at the desired height, (b) appropriate disposition of the tops to prevent interference with the other steps in the harvesting operation, (c) loosening the beets from the soil, (d) elevating the beets and separating them from clods and other foreign material, and (e) depositing the cleaned beets in a truck or trailer or in a tank on the harvester.

20.2. Topping. This operation may be performed while the beets are still in the ground (in-place topping), or it may take place in the machine after the beets have been lifted. In-place topping may be done with the harvester or as a separate operation. In the latter case, the tops are windrowed and later picked up for livestock feed. An extension may be used on the windrower to place two windrows together. In regions where the beets are processed immediately after harvesting, the vegetative top growth is usually removed with flail shredders and no further topping is done. In areas where beets are stockpiled for later processing, removal of the top portion of the beet is essential for safe storage.

464

The ideal thickness of crown to be removed in the topping operation is related to the size of the beet. Topping standards set up by the sugar beet processors for hand topping prior to the development of mechanical harvesters specified that beets up to 95 mm [3¾ in.] in diameter be topped at the lowest leaf scar and larger beets be topped 19 mm [¾ in.] above the lowest leaf scar.[15] As a basis for approaching this hand-topping standard with machine topping, Powers[15] made measurements on individual beets in fields throughout several western states.

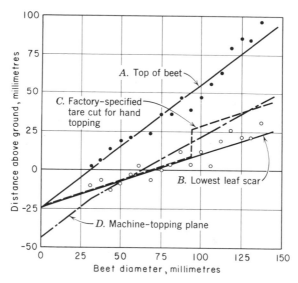

Fig. 20.1. Relation of sugar beet heights and topping planes to sugar beet diameters. (J. B. Powers.[15])

Curves *A* and *B* in Fig. 20.1 indicate the results of these measurements, showing the height of the top of the beet and the height of the lowest leaf scar in relation to the greatest diameter of the beet. Each plotted point represents the average of measurements of several hundred beets. The difference between curves *A* and *B* is the crown thickness. Curve *C* indicates the height of the topping plane above ground level if the hand-topping standards were to be met. Curve *D* represents an approximation of curve *C* that can readily be obtained with a mechanical linkage between the finder and the knife. To satisfy curves *A* and *D*, a gaging device (finder) that rides over the tops of the beets must lift the knife 0.71 cm for each centimetre the finder is raised.

A topper based on this variable-cut principle was built at the University of California,[15] and its performance approached the precision of hand topping. Some commercially available harvesters with in-place topping use the

Fig. 20.2. A three-row sugar beet topping unit employing rotating topping disks and shoe-type finders. A variable-cut linkage is used between the finders and the disks. Converging wheels lift the topped beets. Row finders for automatically centering the lifting wheels on the beet rows (not shown) are optional. (Courtesy of Deere and Co.)

variable-cut principle (Fig. 20.2). Machines that top the beets after they have been lifted (Fig. 20.4), as well as some machines with in-place topping, remove approximately the same thickness of crown from all beets, regardless of size. The thickness of crown removed can, however, be adjusted for the best average condition in a particular field.

20.3. Gaging and Cutting for In-Place Topping. Various types of finders are employed, including sliding shoes (Fig. 20.2) and power-driven wheels. Driven wheels reduce the tendency of the finder to overturn high beets in wet or loose soils.

It has been found that drawing a knife through a beet supported only below the cutting plane (as by the soil) often causes breakage of the root.[15] The break usually occurs when the knife is about two-thirds of the way through the beet and takes place along a plane sloping downward and forward from the knife at an angle of about 45°. To minimize breakage, the cutting thrust may be reduced by an opposing force applied by means of a driven finder such as a wheel. Other ways of reducing the cutting thrust are by mounting a fixed knife at an acute angle to the row or by cutting with the edge of a rotating disk. Either of these methods increases the amount of space required between beets in the row for proper topping of successive high and low beets.

20.4. Digging, Elevating, and Cleaning Beets Topped in the Ground. Beets that have been topped in place, either with the harvester or as a separate operation, are loosened from the ground and lifted onto a conveyor by means of converging wheels (Fig. 20.2). The rims of the wheels are forced

Fig. 20.3. A sugar beet cleaning bed employing rotating kicker rolls mounted on parallel shafts. The beets are propelled over the rolls and the dirt falls through the openings. (Courtesy of Oppel, Inc.)

into the ground and rotate by contact with the ground. The convergence of the lower portions of the rims, toward the rear, causes the beets (which are tapered) to be gripped and lifted. Hinged paddles rotating between the two lifter wheels at the rear (Fig. 20.3) transfer the beets onto a conveyor. Automatic row finders are available on some models. These straddle a beet row and align the lifter wheels laterally through a hydraulic control system.

A considerable amount of soil may be lifted with the beets. The main separation of soil from beets is accomplished by passing the mass over a bed of rotating, star-shaped kicker wheels (Fig. 20.3) spaced close enough together to prevent the beets from falling through. Some models provide additional cleaning by passing the beets over a bed of grab rolls (at least one of each pair having spiral ribs). Further cleaning is accomplished in rod-chain-type conveyors used to elevate the beets into trailers, trucks, or the harvester tank.

20.5. Harvesters that Lift the Beets before Topping. Machines of this type lift the untopped beets as they are plowed loose, either by gripping their top growth or by impaling the beets on a spiked wheel. With either method, the beets are lifted free of the soil and the problem of separating the roots from large clods occuring in heavy soils is eliminated. The beets are topped in the machine after being elevated.

On machines that lift the beets by their tops, a pair of inclined chains or belts, held together with spring-loaded idlers, grips the tops as a lifter blade cuts the tap roots and loosens the soil. Harvesters of this type can be used only under conditions where the tops have adequate strength to support the mass of the root. Unfortunately, in most areas of the United States the tops at harvest time cannot be depended upon to support the mass of the root. The reverse is true in the British Isles. As a result, this type of harvester is currently used in England and Ireland but not in the United States.[2] This method of lifting (with belts) has been used on other root crops, including red beets, carrots,[10] onions,[12,13] and radishes.

Fig. 20.4. *Left:* Impaling and lifting beets with a spiked-wheel sugar beet harvester. *Right:* Topping with two rotating disks. (Courtesy of Blackwelders.)

Components of a harvester that lifts the untopped beets by means of a spiked wheel are illustrated in Fig. 20.4. The spiked wheel is free-floating and is driven at a peripheral speed slightly less than the forward speed of the machine. A two-blade lifter loosens the beets as the curved spikes pierce the crowns. After the spiked wheel has elevated the beets, inclined steel stripper bars mounted between the rows of spikes (shown in Fig. 20.4 *right*) raise the beets up off of the spikes far enough to permit topping at the proper level with a pair of overlapping, rotating disks. Both the disks and the strippers are adjustable to control the thickness of top removed. After topping, a second set of strippers removes the tops completely from the spiked wheel onto a cross conveyor for windrowing. The topped beets are conveyed to a trailer or truck. This type of harvester works well in dry climates but not in areas which have substantial rainfall during the harvest season.

PEANUT HARVESTING

20.6. Harvest Methods. Current peanut-harvesting practices require a drying period between digging and picking (threshing). The basic operations involved are (a) digging, (b) shaking to remove adhering soil, (c) either wind-rowing or hand stacking, and (d) picking (removal of peanuts from the vines). Rapid progress has been made since 1950 toward complete mechanization of peanut harvesting, utilizing the windrow-combine method in preference to hand stacking and stationary threshing.

Peanuts in dry regions may be left in the windrow until they are fully cured. Combine harvesting from partially cured windrows, followed by artificial drying, is recommended as the safest practical approach in the more humid regions.[16] In a 3-year Georgia study,[18] the least hull damage was observed when combined 3 days after digging (rather than immediately or after 7 days).

20.7. Digging, Shaking, and Windrowing. In the windrow-combine method, combination machines of the type shown in Fig. 20.5 dig, shake, and windrow the peanuts. The half sweeps are operated just below the tuber zone. They should cut the tap roots without dragging the plants and should loosen the soil sufficiently to permit lifting the vines with a minimum number of pods becoming detached. The elevator-shaker should subject the plants to sufficient vibration or agitation to remove all or most of the soil without losing any nuts.

Fig. 20.5. A combination two-row peanut digger, shaker, and windrow inverter. (Courtesy of Lilliston Mfg. Co.)

Conventional digger-shakers deposit the vines in the windrows in a randomly oriented manner. Inverting-type models became available in about 1970. These have rotary devices that receive the vines from the elevator-shaker and turn them upside down before deposition, thereby leaving the nuts exposed on top of the windrows for faster drying. The model in Fig. 20.5 has an inverting device but it is not readily visible in the illustration.

Fig. 20.6. Spring-tooth cylinders and concaves in a peanut combine. (Courtesy of Lilliston Mfg. Co.)

20.8. Picking. Peanut combines have two or more spring-tooth cylinders in series that remove the nuts by a combing action (Fig. 20.6). Spring teeth project inward through slots in the concave plates to retard the passage of the vines. Cylinder speeds are low, since shelling is not desired. The separating and cleaning units are similar to those in a grain combine, but revolving stemming saws project upward through the bottom pan of the cleaning shoe to remove the stems from the peanuts.

IRISH POTATO HARVESTING

20.9. Harvest Methods and Equipment. A mechanical potato harvester (Fig. 20.7) performs the following operations, in sequence: (a) digging, (b) separation of the loose soil and small clods and stones, (c) removal of the vines and weeds, and (d) at least partial separation of the tubers from similar-sized stones and clods. From 2 to 7 hand workers may be needed on the harvester to complete the separation and to remove culls and other unwanted materials.[6] The potatoes are conveyed from the sorting belt into a bulk truck or bin. This system is known as direct mechanical harvesting.

A potato digger, used in hand harvesting, performs only the first two operations listed above. The tubers, vines, and other materials not separated

Fig. 20.7. A two-row potato harvester. (Courtesy of John Bean Div., FMC Corp.)

through the digger chain are deposited on top of the row. The potatoes are then picked up by hand and placed in containers.

Indirect mechanical harvesting involves two separate operations. The potatoes are dug and windrowed with a 2-row digger-windrower that is similar to a conventional digger but has a cross conveyor to permit placing 2 rows, or sometimes 4 or 6 rows, in a single windrow. After the potatoes have been in the windrow for 20 min to 2 or 3 h, they are picked up with a harvester of the same type used for direct harvesting but with the blade removed or modified. Separation under weedy or wet soil conditions is better than with direct harvesting, but damage may be greater. The forward speed of the indirect harvester can generally be faster than the optimum for the digger-windrower or for direct harvesting. One indirect harvester often can keep up with two digger-windrowers.

Although some potatoes are still picked up by hand in certain areas, a high percentage of the United States crop is now harvested and handled in bulk with direct-loading mechanical harvesters. Digger-windrowers and harvesters are mostly 2-row machines, but both 1-row and 2-row diggers are available. Harvesters may have either PTO drives or separate engines. Diggers and digger-windrowers generally have PTO drives.

Potatoes are easily bruised or skinned but are less susceptible when fully mature than when immature. In some areas the vines are removed with flail shredders or killed with chemicals to hasten maturity. Flailing is especially advantageous prior to hand harvesting because the whole vines interfere with picking.

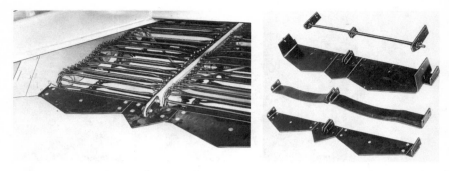

Fig. 20.8. *Left:* Blades and front of digger chains on a two-row potato harvester (or digger). *Right:* Several types of digger blades. Square rod on top unit rotates so the front moves upward, as on a rod weeder. It works well in loose, sandy soils. (Courtesy of Hesston Corp.)

20.10. Digging and Soil Separation. Various types of blades (Fig. 20.8 *right*) are employed for digging or scooping up the soil and potatoes, the choice depending upon the soil type and condition. The blade is operated just deep enough to recover all or nearly all of the tubers without cutting an excessive number. A two-row harvester operating at 3.2 km/h [2 mph] with an average blade depth of 10 cm [4 in.] lifts 7 to 9 Mg [8 to 10 tons] of soil per minute.[6]

The blade delivers the entire mass of potatoes and surrounding soil onto a rod-chain type of elevating conveyor (Fig. 20.8 *left*) that sifts out the loose, free-flowing soil, as well as small clods and stones. Two-row machines have a separate digger chain for each row. Every second or third link is usually offset upward about one link diameter from the plane of the ends. The intermediate links are either offset downward or are straight. Rod diameters of 11.1 and 12.7 mm [7/16 and 1/2 in.] and chain pitches of 39.6 to 50.8 mm [1.56 to 2.00 in.] are common. The maximum clearance between rods is limited by the minimum potato size. The longer pitches are used primarily in wet or heavy soils.[6]

Agitation is obtained by passing the digger chain over support idlers of various shapes. Changing idlers (to a different size or shape) to increase agitation improves soil separation but may increase tuber damage. Increasing the chain speed improves separation by thinning the soil layer but may increase damage.[6]

20.11. Vine Removal on Harvesters. Many harvesters discharge the material from the digger chain onto an in-line rod conveyor having a pitch large enough (100 to 125 mm [4 to 5 in.]) so the potatoes can fall through between the rods onto a cross conveyor. Stripper rolls are often placed in contact with the top of the vine conveyor, as shown at the upper right in Fig. 20.7, to assist in severing any tubers still attached to vines.

A deviner, consisting of a pair of small-diameter, counter-rotating rubber rolls (e.g., 100 to 125 mm [4 to 5 in.] diameter) is often placed at the discharge end of the cross conveyor. The rolls pull any remaining vines or weeds down between them as the potatoes and other solid objects pass over the top of the rolls.

20.12. Separating Potatoes from Stones and Clods. Separation of potatoes from similar-sized stones and clods is a major problem in some areas, such as Maine. The number of stones in the size range of potatoes may be greater than the number of potatoes.[17] To be acceptable, the separating system on a 2-row harvester must be able to operate at capacities of at least 18 Mg [20 tons] of potatoes per hour. The system should be based on a characteristic property difference that is consistent and it should not damage the potatoes.

A relatively simple and reasonably effective device that has been widely used on potato harvesters is a transversely tilted conveyor — either a solid belt or a rod-chain conveyor. This system depends upon a difference in resistance to rolling (i.e., shape). When the mixture of potatoes, stones, and clods is delivered onto the high side of the conveyor, the round potatoes roll across the belt while clods and the flatter stones remain on the high side. The adjustable divider shown in Fig. 20.7 separates the two streams. Hand sorters transfer the material that does not go into the proper channel.

Interference between objects attempting to move across the belt is a problem. A rotating brush is sometimes added to reduce the interference effect.[17] Also, there is no consistent difference in shape. Some rocks roll and some potatoes do not. The amount of tilt should be easily adjustable to obtain the maximum effectiveness under various conditions.

Devices for air separation of potatoes from stones became commercially available on harvesters in the mid 1960s and are being used increasingly in areas where stones are prevalent.[19] A blower moves air at a high velocity upward through the material carried on a rod-link conveyor chain in an enclosed area. The air stream lifts the potatoes from the input conveyor and deposits them on another conveyor. The velocity required to lift the larger potatoes is about 35 m/s [115 ft/s].[19]

The separating action is based on a combination of aerodynamic characteristics and density. Good separation from stones can be obtained by careful adjustment of the air velocity, although some flat stones may be lifted because of their relatively large frontal areas.[17] The roughness of clods, together with a lower specific gravity than for stones, causes many clods to be lifted also.[17,19] Blower power requirements are high.

A considerable amount of research has been done on other methods of separating potatoes from stones or clods. One experimental approach, based on differences in specific gravity, involved feeding the potatoes and stones over a pair of close-spaced rotating brushes that have bristles of appropriate stiffness and length.[5] The stones, being heavier than potatoes, fall through the bristles (between the brushes), while the potatoes ride over. According to Eaton and Hansen,[5] typical specific-gravity values are: potato tubers — 1.1, clods — 1.3 to 1.7, and stones — 1.5 to 2.5. Flotation in a liquid slurry is said to have given consistent separation results in England,[17] but this system is not well-suited for a field machine.

Other approaches,[17,19] have been based on infrared reflectance,[19] X-ray absorption, hardness, and electrical conductivity. Research has also been directed toward improving the effectiveness of a tilted conveyor by means such as dividing the layer of unseparated material into strips, increasing the conveyor velocity, and using rotary brushes to increase the rate of transverse movement.[17]

20.13. Minimizing Damage in Harvesting and Handling. Hansen[9] conducted a field survey involving over 30 harvesters in Colorado in 1966, 1967, and 1968. He found that in some cases as many as 25% of the potatoes were damaged severely enough to affect grade or cause storage problems.

Proper adjustment of the speed and the agitation severity of the digger chain, to maintain a protective soil blanket on the conveyor, minimizes damage in the primary conveying operation. The rods of all conveyors beyond the digger chain are covered with rubber or plastic to reduce damage. Excessive drops should be avoided. A drop of over 15 cm [6 in.] onto a hard surface may cause damage.[11] Resilience or a soft surface at impact points is helpful.

The loading conveyor on the harvester should be hinged (Fig. 20.7) so the outer end can be lowered down within 15 cm [6 in.] of the truck bottom when starting a load. The height adjustment should be watched carefully throughout the loading operation. Care must also be exercised in unloading and conveying at the storage facility.

SWEET POTATO HARVESTING

20.14. Mechanization Problems. Hand harvesting of sweet potatoes requires 150 to 185 man-h of labor per hectare [60 to 75 man-h per acre].[8] Considerable progress has been made in developing mechanical harvesters for potatoes to be processed, but problems associated with fully mechanized harvesting of fresh-market sweet potatoes have been difficult to solve.[8]

At harvest time, sweet potatoes are extremely susceptible to skinning and bruising. Damage is not of major concern for potatoes that are to be processed, because processing is usually done within 48 h after digging.[7] But damage must be minimized for fresh-market potatoes to avoid spoiling during storage. Fresh-market potatoes usually are size graded in the field (currently by hand),[3,7,8] whereas sweet potatoes harvested for processing are not field graded.

Sweet potatoes are distributed over a larger cross-sectional area in the bed than are Irish potatoes and they do not detach easily from the stems or vines.[3] The rank vine growth, covering the entire ground surface at harvest time, is difficult to handle or dispose of. In hand harvesting or semimechanized harvesting (hand sorting on a machine), the vines are commonly removed with a rotary cutter or flail shredder prior to digging.

20.15. Developments in Harvesting and Handling. Modified Irish potato harvesters are employed for sweet potatoes to be processed, but damage would be excessive for fresh-market potatoes. No size grading is done on these machines, but hand separation may be involved. The potatoes are usually handled in bulk.

Commercial machines of a semimechanized type, similar to Irish potato harvesters but designed to give gentle handling, are available for harvesting fresh-market sweet potatoes.[8] After disposing of the vines as a separate operation, the potatoes are dug and elevated to a horizontal grading conveyor from which they are removed by hand, sized visually, and carefully placed in boxes or pallet bins. A comparison between handling in bins (450-kg [1000-lb] capacity) and handling in field lug boxes (23-kg [50-lb] capacity) showed no difference in bruising or spoilage.[14] Total harvest labor requirements with either type of container were about two-thirds as great as for hand harvesting.[14]

In these comparative tests, the potatoes were placed in both types of containers by hand.[14] Possible arrangements to permit direct discharge into a bin without excessive damage include (a) a conveyor that extends down into the bin and is raised as the bin fills,[14] (b) an adjustable-height false bottom,[3] and (c) discharging into a bin partially filled with water.[3]

Experimental harvesters for fresh-market sweet potatoes have been built that pass the potatoes and vines over a horizontal section of conveyor having the cross rods far enough apart so the potatoes will drop through and, if still attached to the vines, will be suspended below the conveyor.[3,8] Detachment is accomplished by vertical shaking of the conveyor and/or by impact forces applied to the stems. Rolling coulters cut the vines at each side of the wide digger blade. Elevation and soil separation are accomplished with a rod-link chain similar to that on Irish potato diggers.

An experimental, diverging-belt size grader that handles the potatoes gently and is said to be suitable for stationary use in the field or for installation on a complete harvester has been built and tested.[7] Another experimental sizer, employing alternate elliptical and cylindrical rollers on a conveyor, was designed as one component of a proposed complete mechanical harvester.[8]

ONION HARVESTING

Onion varieties that have relatively low dry-matter content (5 to 10%) and are soft and tender (such as Sweet Spanish or Granex) are mostly hand harvested because they are easily damaged. The bulbs are undercut with a blade or with a rod-weeder type of unit (upper right in Fig. 20.8) so that the tops will cure (dry out) before the bulbs are lifted. After a curing period of a few days for fresh-market onions or at least 5 to 10 days for onions to be stored, the bulbs are lifted from the soil by hand and topped with a sharp knife. They are then placed in baskets or burlap bags and left in the field for at least 5 to 10 days for further curing before being moved to storage or to market. Hand harvesting requires about 185 man-h of stoop labor per hectare [75 man-h per acre].[12] The cost of this labor may represent 40% of the total production cost.[12]

Some varieties (such as Southport White Globe) have a higher dry-matter content and are relatively firm and resistant to mechanical damage. Mechanical harvesting and bulk handling are established practices for onions of this type.

20.16. Mechanical Harvesting. The basic functions of a mechanical harvester are undercutting the bulbs to sever the roots and loosen the bulbs, lifting, separating the bulbs from soil and trash, removing the tops, and depositing the topped bulbs in containers or bulk-handling equipment. The sequence and timing of these operations will vary somewhat, depending upon the harvesting principles employed. Bulk or bin storage with forced-air ventilation (rather than field curing) is a logical part of a mechanized harvest system.

Harvesters used for the firm varieties generally lift, top, and load all in one operation,[20] although the topped onions may be deposited in windrows and picked up later with a potato loader. Most commercially available harvesters are similar to a potato digger but include a topping unit. One type of topper has a group of side-by-side pairs of small-diameter, counter-rotating, spiral-ribbed rolls that pull the tops down between them and pinch or pull the tops off. Another similar type holds the tops between the rolls and moves the onions rearward while rotary blades cut the tops just below the rolls. A short stem is left on each bulb. With a third type, an air blast beneath the elevating conveyor blows the tops upward and they are cut off by a sickle above the conveyor. The tops must be dry for any of these types of toppers to work satisfactorily.[20] To achieve this condition, the bulbs are undercut 1 to 3 weeks before harvesting. Damage to soft varieties of onions tends to be excessive with most toppers of these types.

Lorenzen[13] developed a belt-type lifter and topper in 1949. This machine had a pair of inclined round-cross-section belts, held together by spring-loaded idlers, that gripped the tops at the same time that a blade cut off the roots. The belts then elevated the onions to the topping unit and subsequently deposited them onto another conveyor. Topping was done just above the upper portion of the pickup belts with powered overlapping disks.

LePori and Hobgood[12] also employed the belt-lift principle in a machine built in 1968. Their design included guide belts below the upper portion of the lifter belts that diverged from the lifter belts at a flatter slope. The resulting downward wedging action against the tops of the bulbs resulted in more accurate positioning for topping than in Lorenzen's harvester.

The belt-lift principle depends upon the tops being reasonably upright and strong enough to lift the bulbs from the soil. Special devices are needed to raise lodged tops (which may be 50% of the total) so the belts can grip them. Damage, even to soft onions, is minimal with this type of harvester.[12]

Another approach that has been tried experimentally for easily damaged onions is in-place topping before lifting. An in-place topper built at the Idaho Agricultural Experiment Station employed ground-driven tined wheels to lift the lodged tops so they could be removed by a rotary blade.[20] Droll and his associates[4] found that a high-speed rotary cutter was more effective than a flail topper or a sickle. They used stationary gatherers to assist in lifting lodged tops. In their tests, topping was more uniform when done before undercutting or otherwise disturbing the onions in the soil, but even then, retrimming was needed to obtain a topping job acceptable for fresh-market onions.[4]

REFERENCES

1. Agricultural Statistics, 1976. USDA.
2. ARMER, A. A. A harvester for Ireland's sugar beets. Agr. Eng., *34*:312, 314, May, 1953.
3. BURKHARDT, G. J., W. L. HARRIS, L. E. SCOTT, and E. G. McKIBBEN. Mechanical harvesting and handling of sweet potatoes. Trans. ASAE, *14*(3):516-519, 1971.
4. DROLL, R. W., R. E. ARMSTRONG, C. G. COBLE, and W. H. ALDRED. Mechanical onion top removal and related harvest practices. Trans. ASAE, *19*(6):1048-1050, 1976.
5. EATON, F. E., and R. W. HANSEN. Mechanical separation of stones from potatoes with rotary brushes. Trans. ASAE, *13*(5):591-593, 1970.
6. GLAVES, A. H., and G. W. FRENCH. Increasing potato-harvester efficiency. USDA Agriculture Handbook 171, 1959.
7. GOODMAN, H. C., and D. D. HAMANN. A machine to field size sweet potatoes. Trans. ASAE, *14*(1):3-6, 1971.
8. HAMMERLE, J. R. The design of sweet potato machinery. Trans. ASAE, *13*(3):281-285, 1970.
9. HANSEN, R. W. Injuries to potatoes during mechanical harvesting. Colorado State Univ. Expt. Sta. General Series 893, 1970.
10. HATTON, J. R., and W. A. LePORI. Saw topping unit for FMC carrot combines. ASAE Paper 71-118, June, 1971.
11. HAWKINS, J. C. The design of potato harvesters. J. Agr. Eng. Res., *2*:14-24, 1957.
12. LePORI, W., and P. HOBGOOD. Mechanical harvester for fresh-market onions. Trans. ASAE, *13*(4):517-519, 522, 1970.

13. LORENZEN, C., Jr. The development of a mechanical onion harvester. Agr. Eng., *32*:13-15, Jan., 1950.
14. O'BRIEN, M., and R. W. SCHEUERMAN. Mechanical harvesting, handling, and storing of sweet potatoes. Trans. ASAE, *12*(2):261-263, 1969.
15. POWERS, J. B. The development of a new sugar beet harvester. Agr. Eng., *29*:347-351, 354, Aug., 1948.
16. SHEPHERD, J. L. Mechanized peanut production. Georgia Agr. Expt. Sta. Mimeo. Series N.S. 163, 1963.
17. SIDES, S. E., and N. SMITH. Analysis and design of potato-stone separation mechanisms. ASAE Paper 70-683, Dec., 1970.
18. STANSELL, J. R., J. L. BUTLER, and J. L. SHEPHERD. Effect of windrow orientation and exposure times on peanut harvesting damage. Paper presented at ASAE Southeast Region Meeting, Feb., 1970.
19. STORY, A. G., and G. S. V. RAGHAVAN. Sorting potatoes from stones and soil clods by infrared reflectance. Trans. ASAE, *16*(2):304-309, 1973.
20. WILLIAMS, L. G., and D. F. FRANKLIN. Harvesting, handling, and storing Yellow Sweet Spanish onions. Idaho Agr. Expt. Sta. Bull. 526, 1971.

21

Fruit and Vegetable
Harvesting and Handling

21.1. Introduction. Many fruits and vegetables are highly perishable products that must be harvested within a very narrow time range, handled carefully, and either processed, properly stored, or consumed fresh soon after harvesting. Successful harvest mechanization requires a systems approach and involves the cooperative efforts of engineers, plant breeders, plant physiologists, biochemists, food scientists, and others. Mechanical harvesting of fruits and vegetables is truly an interdisciplinary problem.

Variety breeding, cultural practices, mechanical harvesting, materials handling, grading and sorting, and processing are all major components of a total harvest mechanization system. High-yielding, uniformly maturing varieties are highly desirable for mechanical harvesting. One way to increase potential yields for vegetables and some vine fruits is by greatly increasing the plant populations in comparison with hand-harvested crops. Increased plant populations, as well as other factors related to mechanical harvesting, often dictate major changes in planting systems, methods of controlling weeds and other pests, and other cultural practices. Old fruit trees must be reshaped and new trees properly structured for mechanical harvesting or for the most effective use of harvesting aids. Special trellises and plant training may be needed for vine and cane fruits. Effective and controllable chemical inducement of fruit abscission (i.e., separation of fruits from the stems) would be helpful for many kinds of fruit.

Mechanical harvesting can result in an extremely high rate of product output, in which case materials handling methods are of major importance. Handling must be done in a manner that minimizes damage to the product. Mechanically harvested fruits or vegetables usually contain considerable quantities of trash and cull material (immature, overripe, damaged, etc.) that must be removed, either on the harvester or as a separate operation. Processing-plant procedures and equipment usually must be changed to accommodate products that are mechanically harvested and handled.

Harvest costs for fruits and vegetables often represent 30 to 60% of the total production costs.[6] Hand harvesting usually requires large labor forces for relatively short periods of time, thereby contributing to sociological problems associated with transient or migratory workers and families. Mechanization is needed to reduce costs and to compensate for the decreasing availability of suitable labor.

479

A great deal of research has been directed toward fruit and vegetable harvesting since the early 1950s* and considerable progress has been made. Harvest mechanization has reached a high level of acceptance for a number of crops. Mechanization problems are compounded by the fact that a large number of crops with widely varying characteristics are involved. Most vegetables and many of the small fruits require individual, distinctly different types of harvesting equipment. The market potential for any one type of machine usually is small. Physical and rheological properties of each crop need to be known or determined as a basis for design.

21.2. Harvesting Methods. Although harvesting of some fruits and vegetables is fully mechanized, others must still be harvested by hand. Mechanical aids for hand harvesting have been employed to some extent but often have shown little or no advantage. Harvesting aids have generally taken the form of man positioners for tree crops, worker conveyances and supports for harvesting low-growing crops, or conveyors that receive the individual products as they are picked and carry them to a transport bin or vehicle that moves through the field at the same rate as the pickers.

In general, harvesting aids result in only moderate or small increases in productivity and they sometimes represent substantial investments. When several workers use the same equipment, the rate of output for the entire operation is usually limited by the slowest worker. Machines for individual workers may give greater average outputs but are more costly per worker than are multiman units. In developing worker conveyances for low-growing crops, it has usually been difficult to find a position that is both comfortable and efficient.

Long conveyors supported across a number of rows just above the plants have been used with reasonable success in several vegetable crops. With celery, for example, the workers cut and trim the stalks and place them on the conveyor. The stalks are conveyed to a central platform for final trimming and packing as the entire assembly moves slowly through the field.

Various methods of detachment are employed with either hand or mechanical harvesting. These generally involve cutting, pinching, pulling, bending or snapping, twisting, or some combination of these actions. Devices that comb or strip the desired product from the plants rely mainly on direct pulling, but bending may also be involved. Machines that shake the plants develop detachment forces as a result of the inertia of the portion being removed. Bending and twisting, as well as a direct pull, may be induced by the shaking. Harvesting methods which do not necessarily involve direct contact between the removal device and the fruit or stem are often referred to as mass-harvest systems.

---

*Reference 14 lists over 800 publications of fruit and vegetable harvesting and handling for 1957 through 1970, about half of which are technical or semitechnical reports. Reference 6 contains about 50 technical papers that summarize the 1968 status of fruit and vegetable harvest mechanization.

21.3. Selectivity in Mechanical Harvesting. Many fruit and vegetable crops do not mature uniformly. Several pickings are required to obtain maximum yields, selecting only the mature products each time. If such a crop is to be harvested mechanically, some characteristic that is related to maturity and identifiable by a machine must be found.

Mechanical harvesters for lettuce determine maturity by sensing head size and firmness or a combination of size and density. Selective asparagus harvesters use spear height as the basis for selecting the spears to be cut. With some fruits, including most cane berries, the force required for detachment is inversely related to maturity. Selectivity can be achieved by shaking such plants at the proper stroke and frequency. Cantaloupes also detach much more readily when ripe than when immature. Fruit size, light reflectance, and color are other characteristics than can be utilized in selective mechanical harvesting.

Selectivity in hand harvesting is often based upon visual evaluation of size, color, or shape, or an intuitive integration of these factors. With most crops it is difficult to achieve machine selectivity comparable with hand selectivity. However, machine selectivity in some crops may be superior to that from hand picking. With blackberries, for example, the machine selects mature fruit on the basis of the required detachment force, which is a better parameter of maturity than is color (the primary basis for hand selection).

The alternative to selective mechanical harvesting of crops that do not mature uniformly is nonselective harvesting (usually a once-over operation), taking mature, immature, and overripe fruit or vegetables indiscriminately. The harvest must be timed carefully to obtain the maximum yield of marketable, mature product. But even with the best timing there is usually a substantial yield reduction with nonuniform-maturing crops in comparison with selective machine harvesting or hand harvesting. The loss of potential income must be balanced against the reduced costs of one machine harvest versus selective, multiple harvests. A nonselective harvester can handle several times as much crop area as a selective harvester. High plant populations are especially desirable for nonselective harvesting of vegetables.

In general, there are relatively few crops for which selective mechanical harvesting is economically feasible. The ideal situation for mechanical harvesting is to have all or most of the crop ready to harvest at one time. Some fruits and vegetables automatically fit into this category. Plant breeders have made great strides in developing uniform-maturing varieties suitable for mechanical harvesting. They are continually working toward this goal with other fruits and vegetables that do not mature uniformly. Cultural practices, including the use of growth regulators, can also have considerable influence on uniformity of ripening.

21.4. Handling Fruits and Vegetables. Prior to the mid 1950s, most fruits and vegetables were handled in containers having filled weights of 9 to 36 kg [20 to 80 lb], which could readily be lifted and moved by hand. Because the harvest rate with a machine is high with many types of crops, small containers usually are not practical. A tomato harvester, for example, may have a short-time output of 27 Mg/h [30 tons/h], which is 454 kg/min [1000 lb/min]. Tree shaking often requires handling several hundred kilograms of fruit per minute. An efficient materials handling system is imperative in such cases in order to obtain maximum productivity.

Research and experience since the mid 1950s have demonstrated that fruits and vegetables can be handled in large containers at considerable depths with no more damage than from field boxes, and sometimes with less damage. The maximum permissible depths vary somewhat, depending upon the physical properties of the fruit, the road condition, the type of truck suspension system, and the hauling distance.[6]

As a result of research on handling characteristics, an ASAE standard has been adopted that specifies overall dimensions for 2 cross-sectional sizes of bins, 120 × 120 cm and 120 × 100 cm [47.25 × 47.25 in. and 47.25 × 39.375 in.]. Overall heights of 72 cm and 133 cm [28.35 in. and 52.36 in.] are to be available for each cross-sectional size. These heights give inside depths of about 61 cm and 122 cm [24 in. and 48 in.] for bins built onto pallets. For various reasons, bins of other sizes are sometimes used. A 120 × 120 × 72-cm pallet bin will hold about 450 kg [1000 lb] of fruit or tomatoes.

Most fruits and vegetables handle well at depths of 46 to 61 cm [18 to 24 in.].[6] Many vegetables and some of the firmer fruits can safely withstand depths up to 122 cm [48 in.] and are handled more efficiently in the deeper bins.[6] Tests have shown that in-transit accelerations of individual fruits are greater in the upper layers of the bin than in the lower layers.[30] Because of the resultant bouncing or rolling, the top layer often receives the greatest damage from hauling. The bottom fruits may be damaged by impact against the bin bottom if a protective pad is not used, or by compressive forces if the fruit is soft.

Bins or other containers should be compatible with the requirements for maintaining quality of a particular crop. Tart cherries, for example, must be cooled to 10 to 13°C [50 to 55°F] within 30 min after picking.[6] To accomplish this, the harvester deposits them in watertight bins partially filled with cool water. For some fruits and vegetables, the bins need slots or other openings in the bottom to facilitate washing, water drainage after hydrocooling, ventilation for cooling or curing, etc.

Most mechanical harvesters utilize either bins or full-load bulk handling in trailers or gondolas. The container system provides more flexibility in regard to temporary storage at the processing plant. Hand-picked, fresh-market fruits are often handled to the packing shed in bins, but care must be exercised in filling and emptying the bins to avoid bruising.

The use of bins has required the development of a variety of associated types of equipment, including special bin trailers for field use, tractor-mounted fork lifts, straddle-type carriers, sampling devices for quality determination, bin fillers, bin dumpers, etc.

Minimizing damage to easily bruised fruits and vegetables is an important consideration in designing a harvester and the associated handling equipment. Apricots or tomatoes, for example, are damaged from a single drop of more than 23 cm [9 in.] onto a firm surface or more than 41 cm [16 in.] onto other fruit.[29] Both the number and the distance of vertical drops, as at conveyor transfer points or in bin filling, must be minimized. Conveyors should be wide and operated at low speeds to handle the fruit gently. Padding should be provided on areas where impacts cannot be avoided. Some type of lowering or decelerating device to deliver the fruit into the bin just above the deposition level at a low velocity is highly desirable.[29]

21.5. Determining Economic Feasibility of Harvest Mechanization. The primary objectives of harvest mechanization are to reduce labor requirements and to increase the net income to the grower through reduced costs. Although cost reduction is not always essential, a mechanized system is not likely to be adopted if the net income would be reduced appreciably. Growers tend to use hand labor as long as it is available, adopting mechanization as a last resort.

Mechanical harvesting often causes a reduction in harvested crop value per hectare in comparison with hand harvesting, especially in nonselective harvesting of crops that do not mature uniformly or in harvesting easily damaged crops. The reduced value may be a result of reduced potential yield, actual field losses, or reduction in quality. This factor, as well as hand harvesting costs and machine harvesting costs, must be considered when making an economic comparison. The general cost relation is

$$N = H - M - LG \qquad (21.1)$$

where $N =$ increase in net income due to mechanical harvesting, in dollars per hectare

$H =$ total hand harvesting costs, in dollars per crop hectare per year

$M =$ total mechanical harvesting costs, in dollars per crop hectare per year, including machine fixed costs, machine operating costs, and labor costs

$G =$ gross income or crop value from the hand-harvested crop, in dollars per hectare

$L =$ loss factor = reduction in gross income or crop value as a result of mechanical harvesting, expressed as a decimal fraction of G

At the break-even point, defined as the condition where $N = 0$, equation 21.1 becomes

$$H - M - L_e G = 0$$

where L_e = loss factor when $N = 0$.

The break-even loss factor, then, is

$$L_e = \frac{H - M}{G} \qquad (21.2)$$

The break-even crop-value ratio R would be equal to $1 - L_e$. It is evident from equation 21.2 that the percentage loss which can be tolerated is directly related to the amount of reduction in harvest cost and inversely related to the crop value.

When a mechanical harvesting system includes handling, sorting, grading, or processing methods that differ from those used with hand harvesting, the entire system should be compared with a hand harvesting system that accomplishes the same results. Each of the factors in the above equations would then consist of totals for the system components.

In one approach for determining the economic feasibility of a proposed or existing mechanical harvesting system, machine and labor costs (M), based on known or estimated cost factors, are calculated (See Chapter 2). This may be done for the maximum crop area that one machine might be expected to handle, for a specific, assumed area within the machine's capacity, or preferably as a function of crop area. The use of two (or more) machines must be assumed for crop areas beyond the capacity of one machine. Hand harvest costs H and the hand-harvested crop value usually would be known.

After determining values for M, H, and G, the maximum allowable reduction in crop value due to mechanical harvesting (for no loss of net income) can be determined from equation 21.2. If the machine loss factor is known from tests (or a value is assumed), the effect of mechanical harvesting upon the net income can be predicted from equation 21.1.

In comparing selective and nonselective mechanical harvesting for a particular crop, it is essential to consider the effect the number of harvests has upon the loss factor. Selective mechanical harvesting of some crops reduces the loss factor L in comparison with nonselective harvesting, but in many cases the increase in M because of the greater number of harvests more than offsets any gain in harvested crop value.

In another approach, especially applicable to proposed systems,[10] the probable loss factor L and machine cost factors are assumed, based on experience with similar crops. Using these values and known values of H and G, the harvest rate required for $N = 0$ (break-even point) is calculated. An unreasonably high calculated harvest rate indicates questionable economic feasibility under the assumed conditions. Fridley and Adrian[10] have developed nomograms to facilitate this approach and have summarized pertinent background data for a number of fruits and vegetables in California.

FRUIT HARVESTING

21.6. Mechanical Tree Shakers. The basic principle involved in removing fruit (or nuts) by shaking is to accelerate each fruit so the inertia force developed ($F = ma$) will be greater than the bonding force between the fruit and the tree. Removal of walnuts and almonds with mechanical shakers became a common practice during the 1940s. The development and general application of tree shaking for mechanical harvesting of fruits has occurred since the mid 1950s.[9]

Tractor-mounted cable shakers, fixed-stroke boom shakers, and boom-type impact knockers were originally developed for nuts. Impact knockers are still used to a considerable extent on old almond trees because these trees are large and relatively rigid. An impact knocker delivers discrete axial impacts or impulses by mechanical, pneumatic, or hydraulic means, rather than having a continuous, oscillating motion. A padded head on the end of the boom is merely pushed against the limb, after which a series of several impacts is imparted to the tree. Fixed-stroke boom shakers are clamped to the limb and driven by an eccentric or crank on the tractor or other propulsion unit.

Inertia-type shakers were developed in the late 1950s and have largely replaced fixed-stroke shakers except in large nut trees. With an inertia shaker, the exciting force is derived from the acceleration of a reciprocating mass or two opposite-rotating, eccentric masses. Both arrangements shown in Fig. 21.1 provide sinusoidal force variation, or nearly so. When the rotating masses are timed as shown, the centrifugal-force components perpendicular to the boom axis cancel each other. (Force relations are shown for two side-by-side masses in Fig. 14.8b). With the slider-crank mechanism, reciprocation of the housing and drive components provides the exciting force.

An inertia shaker is attached to the supporting structure through flexible mounts or hangers, thereby isolating the vibration. Hydraulic-motor drives

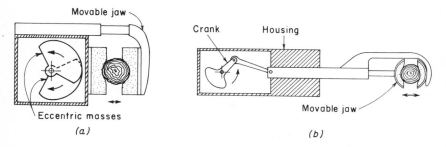

Fig. 21.1. Two common arrangements for inertia shakers. (a) Eccentric, counter-rotating masses. The two masses are generally coaxial, with one above the other, as shown. (b) Slider-crank arrangement. (R.B. Fridley and P.A. Adrian.[9])

are employed. When the exciting frequency is large in relation to the fundamental frequency of the tree component (which is the usual situation), the stroke at the clamp may be determined from the following relation.[9]

$$S = \frac{2rW}{W_s + W_t} \qquad (21.3)$$

where S =   stroke at clamp
r =   eccentricity of the unbalanced mass (crank radius in slider-crank arrangement)
W =   total unbalanced mass
W_s =   total mass of shaker, including the unbalanced mass
W_t =   effective mass of the tree component being shaken (limb or tree)

Tests have indicated that the actual stroke is influenced to some extent by the shaking frequency and by the location of the clamping point on the limb and may vary as much as ±35% from the calculated value.[9]

An inertia shaker may be attached to the trunk to shake the entire tree or to each of the primary limbs to shake only a portion of the tree at one time. The effective mass W_t generally averages 9 to 27 kg [20 to 60 lb] for limbs 5 to 15 cm [2 to 6 in.] in diameter and 360 to 450 kg [800 to 1000 lb] for trunks having diameters of 13 to 28 cm [5 to 11 in.].[9]

Trunk shakers are faster than limb shakers because attachment is easier and is needed at only one place per tree. At least 45 to 60 cm [1½ to 2 ft] of clear trunk below the lowest branches is desirable. Trunk shakers work well on reasonably rigid trees but they are not effective on willowy (limber) trees because damping, primarily from the leaves,[19] and vibration isolation caused by curved branches absorb most of the energy before it reaches the fruit. Limb shakers are more versatile than trunk shakers and are more effective where long strokes are needed, as on willowy trees such as olive and citrus.

Trunk shakers generally employ rotating masses (Fig. 21.1a). In some designs a speed differential between the two masses continually changes the direction of maximum unbalance, thereby providing successive shaking in all directions. Limb shakers usually have slider-crank mechanisms (Fig. 21.1b) because these are more compact than rotating-mass arrangements.

Typical operating frequencies are in the order of 800 to 2500 cycles per minute for trunk shakers and 400 to 1200 cycles per minute for limb shakers. Considerably higher speeds are obtainable on some models. The fundamental vibration frequencies of limbs are low in relation to shaker frequencies, generally ranging from 30 to 70 cycles per minute.[9] Strokes for deciduous fruits and nuts are often between 9.5 and 19 mm [⅜ and ¾ in.] for trunk shakers and 38 to 51 mm [1½ to 2 in.] for limb shakers.

Applying several short bursts of shaking (e.g., 5 s each) tends to provide a variable shaking frequency and creates transient conditions that contribute to the effectiveness. Removal of at least 90 to 95% of the fruit is readily accomplished with most tree fruits, including prunes, tart cherries, peaches, apricots, and apples. Others, such as olives and some citrus, are considerably more difficult to remove by shaking.

Clamps are hydraulically opened and closed. They must be properly designed and padded and properly used to avoid bark injury and the resulting chance of infection or permanent injury.[9] Padding must be flexible enough to conform to the shape of the limb or trunk but firm enough to transmit the shaking motion. Tangential loads must be minimized and radial loads distributed over enough area so the ultimate strength of the bark is not exceeded. Ideally, the shaker should be attached perpendicular to the limb or trunk. Early problems of bark damage have largely been eliminated by improved clamp designs and careful use.[9]

21.7. Shake-Catch Harvesting. Catching units used in shake-catch harvesting have low-profile collection surfaces that extend under the tree, covering all or most of the area to the outer periphery of the tree. Stationary surfaces are usually sloped toward a belt or draper-type conveyor, but some units have pans that are mechanically dumped onto the conveyor. Another arrangement, requiring a minimum of vertical clearance but more labor, has roll-out canvas sheets that are retracted toward the conveyor when loaded.

Some catching units are of the inverted-umbrella, wrap-around type, but most systems consist of a pair of catching units, one on each side of the tree. Laterally retractable sections are provided along the inner edge of one or both units to permit closure around the tree trunk. Bulk bins, into which the conveyors deliver the fruit, are carried on the catching units. When harvesting easily bruised fruits, a decelerator unit that extends down into the bin and automatically raises as the bin fills is highly desirable.

Paired catching units are often self-propelled, sometimes with front and rear steering. Good maneuverability is important because the total time per tree is only 1 to 2 min. It should be noted that front and rear steering does not necessarily improve maneuverability if the system is confusing to an operator.

Usually, two limb-type inertia shakers (one on each unit) or a trunk shaker are mounted on the catching units. Sizers are often incorporated into a conveying system to remove undersize fruit. Trash-removal facilities (such as a blower) are often included. If only a small amount of hand grading is required, this is usually done by 2 or 3 workers stationed on the catching unit.

The main collection surfaces are usually stretched fabric. A good design minimizes fruit bouncing.[11] Effective padding of all hard collection surfaces and deflector panels is necessary to avoid excessive damage to easily bruised fruits. Fruit-on-fruit impacts cause considerable damage. This type of damage can be minimized by suspending 2 to 4 layers of staggered decelerator strips above the collecting surfaces, at least over the areas where fruit is most likely to be concentrated. Neoprene tubes, 60 mm [2⅜ in.] OD and spaced on 190-mm [7½-in.] centers in each of 3 layers, have given good results with peaches.[11] Flat strips of webbing are less expensive and are used on some machines.

Pruning and shaping to obtain a suitable tree structure is important in regard to minimizing the frequency of fruits hitting branches as they fall (causing fruit damage), improving fruit removal, and facilitating movement and use of the equipment.[6,11]

Selective harvesting of a portion of the fruit from any one tree by the shake-catch method has been attempted but seldom is practical. Hence, uniform maturity is highly desirable and proper timing of the harvest is necessary to obtain the maximum yield of good, mature fruit. Selective, tree-by-tree harvesting is feasible under some conditions.[21]

21.8. Tree-Fruit Harvest Mechanization. The shake-catch method is the only mechanical harvesting system used to any extent in deciduous tree fruits. Damage to the fruit has generally limited the application of this system to fruit that is to be processed, and processing must be done within a day or so after harvesting. Even then, the damage must be relatively superficial to avoid lowering the quality of the processed fruit. High percentages of the tart cherry and prune crops are harvested mechanically, and the use of the shake-catch method for cling peaches has increased rapidly since about 1969. Variable maturity has been a deterrent to mechanical harvesting of apricots but selective, tree-by-tree harvesting could improve the situation.[6,21]

Apples are quite susceptible to bruise damage, and mechanical harvesting costs in the late 1960s were somewhat higher than for hand picking.[6] Pears are not harvested mechanically, even for processing, because the brown spots from bruises do not cook out.

Olives are difficult to harvest by shaking because the fruits are small, detachment forces are high, and the willowy branches provide excellent vibration isolation. Relatively long strokes are needed for effective fruit removal but may cause excessive limb breakage. Tests in California with specially built experimental limb-type shakers have indicated that, with properly controlled operation, 80 to 90% fruit removal is usually obtainable without excessive tree damage.[12] In general, these tests showed the desirable operating zone to be with stroke-frequency combinations ranging from 76 mm [3 in.] at 1000 cycles per minute to 38 mm [1½ in.] at 2000 cycles per minute. The resulting power requirements are several times as great as for shaking most deciduous fruits.[12]

Citrus is the major tree crop in the United States but one that has been difficult to harvest mechanically. Intensive research efforts have been directed toward mechanical harvesting since about 1960.[6] Inertia-type limb shakers, developed in Florida especially for citrus, have given satisfactory performance for citrus to be processed, removing 90% or more of the fruit.[8] Best results were obtained with relatively long strokes (203 mm [8 in.] at a maximum frequency of 270 cycles per minute).[8,26]

Another mass-harvest concept that has been investigated for citrus is the use of an oscillating air blast to shake the foliage. In one arrangement, air at 160 km/h [100 mph] is discharged from 2 side-by-side outlets 254 mm [10 in.] wide and 6.1 m [20 ft] high, directed toward one side of the tree as the machine moves down the row at about 0.4 km/h [¼ mph].[37] Mechanically moved deflectors in the outlets change the air direction at a frequency of 60 to 70 cycles per minute. This system is attractive because of its high potential capacity. Fruit-removal percentages vary widely, ranging from 60% up to 90% and above.[37] Power requirements are high and there is some leaf damage.

The development of effective abscission chemicals to reduce the force required for fruit detachment would improve the performance with either mechanical shakers or airblast shakers. Neither of these systems has been considered satisfactory for fresh-market citrus because of excessive fruit damage. The trend toward processing an increasingly high percentage of the citrus crop makes mass-removal systems more feasible than they were in the early 1960s.

Both of the above systems cause a substantial, subsequent yield reduction when used on late-crop Valencia oranges or lemons because next year's crop is already partly developed at harvest time and many of the small fruits are removed by the shaking action. Prototype systems employing limb shakers and airblast foliage shakers were operated on a limited commercial basis in Florida in 1968-69, using either catching frames or ground-pickup machines.[6] A special pickup machine for oranges was developed in Florida.[27]

21.9. Man Positioners for Harvesting Tree Fruits. Fresh-market fruits, as well as pears for either processing or fresh market, are picked by hand to minimize bruising. Man positioners are sometimes employed as harvest aids, the primary objective being to reduce the worker's nonproductive time and thereby increase his output. Single-man positioners are generally self-propelled, controlled from the picker's platform, and capable of providing three-dimensional positioning of the worker. These have not met with much success because of the high investment per worker, the need for considerable field management, and the relatively small increase in productivity (typically 20 to 25%).[6]

A system that has shown considerable promise as an interim solution to mechanization, especially in pears, requires special planting and/or training to form continuous, dense hedge rows not over 1.8 m [6 ft] thick. A multilevel picking platform moves along continually between 2 rows as workers pick the adjacent sides of the 2 rows. The fruit is placed on conveniently located conveyors that deposit it in a bin carried on the machine. The workers are stationed at different elevations, each picking from a band 0.9 to 1.2 m [3 to 4 ft] high.

One experimental model had a stair-step arrangement along one side that permitted some movement of workers to adjust for variations in fruit density.[13] This machine employed a crew of 9 to 13 workers. Tests in hedgerow-trained pears indicated that productivity per worker could be increased as much as 50 to 80% in comparison with ladder-and-bag picking and that the greatest advantage of the platform unit is realized with inexperienced workers.

Picking platforms and other types of man positioners may reduce harvesting costs, but the saving in labor is too small to be of much significance in case of a severe labor shortage.

21.10. Grape Harvesting. Mechanization of grape harvesting is complicated by wide differences in varietal characteristics, cultural methods, topography, and utilization. Costly, special trellising and retraining are needed in many cases. Research programs on mechanical harvesting were initiated at the California and Cornell (New York) Agricultural Experiment Stations in the 1950s. The first appreciable amount of harvesting with commercially available machines was in 1968, when about 30 harvesters were in use.[6] Several manufacturers had models available by 1971. Current models all employ impacts or shaking to remove clusters or individual berries by means of inertia. Most are straddle-row, self-propelled units, but pull-type straddle units are available. Some machines have vertical-stroke impacters or shakers, and others have horizontal-stroke devices.

Vertical-stroke harvesters with one impacter per row-side need special, offset trellises so the impacter can strike the bottom of the trellis wire on the upward stroke as the machine moves along the row. The vertical stroke of the impacter may be 127 mm [5 in.] or more, with frequencies of 250 to 500 cycles per minute. Vertical-stroke impacters remove some varieties, including Thompson Seedless, primarily as clusters.

Horizontal-stroke harvesters are of two distinct types. The most commonly employed principle is the use of oscillating, horizontal-stroke paddles or rods extending rearward from a vertical shaft. Shaking is accomplished by slapping the vines from the sides. A recent development (1976-1977) is the use of the continuous trunk-shaking principle. Bars or belts that move along the row on both sides of the trunks impart a lateral oscillation to the trunks. Avoiding foliage contact offers the potential of greatly reduced vine damage and defoliation, which are often problems with the rod-type shakers. With either type of harvester, overlapping, spring-loaded catch plates enter the row from each side, forming a continuous bed beneath the vines and directing the fruit onto conveyors. The plates automatically spread apart to slide around stakes, trunks, or other obstacles.

The horizontal-stroke principle was developed in New York, primarily for Concord grapes that are to be crushed. This type of harvester removes the grapes of most wine varieties as individual berries, many of the berries being broken in the process.[6] Damage is not of great concern with many grape varieties that are to be crushed, since they are collected and handled in liquid-tight bins or gondolas. Horizontal-stroke harvesters can operate in some vineyards that have simple, vertical trellises, without the necessity for special trellising or training conversions.

About 15% of California's grapes are dried for raisins, mostly on trays in the field. Raisin grapes must be handled carefully to avoid rupturing the berries. Tests have shown that if the fruiting canes of Thompson Seedless grapes (the main raisin variety) are severed at harvest time and left on the trellis wires, the leaves and fruit pedicels become dry and brittle in a few days.[35] The partially dehydrated fruit, when harvested mechanically, then detaches predominantly as single, undamaged berries.

A system for simultaneous harvesting and spreading of raisin grapes was developed at the California Agricultural Experiment Station.[35] A spreading machine towed behind the harvester or driven beside it receives the grapes in a hopper as they are harvested, unrolls paper on a prepared bed to form a continuous tray between rows, and spreads the grapes in a uniform, thin layer on the paper. After drying is complete, another machine picks up the paper and collects the raisins in bins.

21.11. Harvesting Bush and Cane Fruits. Cultivated (high-bush) blueberries, blackberries, Boysenberries, and raspberries can be harvested successfully by machines that have vibrating devices such as panels, bars, paddles, or groups of fingers. Berry harvesters have been available commercially since about 1966 and their use is increasing rapidly.[6] One type has radial, vertically vibrated fingers on free-turning vertical cylinders. Another type has 2 plywood panels that press against the canes from both sides of the row and are vibrated laterally, in unison, at about 250 cycles per minute. Others have horizontal-stroke paddles (similar to grape harvesters) or panels of fingers vibrated vertically or horizontally. Airblast cleaning devices to remove leaves and other light debris are important components.

Most varieties of blueberries and cane fruits ripen over a period of several weeks, necessitating multiple harvests at periods of 5 to 7 days. Selective mechanical harvesting is possible because mature fruits detach more easily than immature fruits. In some cases the quality is superior to that from hand picking because ease of detachment is better than color as an indicator of maturity. Multiple machine harvests tend to cause cumulative damage to canes, necessitating special pruning practices. Uniform-maturing varieties, permitting once-over harvests, would be desirable.

Problems in harvesting cane berries include excessive fruit damage and rapid post-harvest deterioration. Tests have shown that damage can be minimized by proper design of the collection, conveying, and cleaning system, and postharvest deterioration can be minimized by in-field freezing immediately after harvesting.[7] An experimental harvester for Boysenberries included facilities for freezing the berries with liquid Freon within 2 min after harvesting.[7] The berries were removed with two panels of vibrating fingers. The quality was better than from hand picking, and the 10% mass loss that occurs after hand picking was eliminated.

21.12. Strawberry Harvesting. Mechanical harvesting of strawberries presents a real challenge to both engineers and horticulturists. Strawberries are low-growing, easily bruised, and highly perishable, and require multiple harvests when picked by hand. Several agricultural experiment stations initiated harvester development programs during the 1960s, and breeding programs to develop varieties suitable for once-over harvests have been underway since 1959.[6] Although progress has been made, there was very little commercial mechanical harvesting in 1976. Excessive fruit damage and large yield reductions because of nonuniform maturity continue to be problems.

Most experimental machines have had some type of stripping or combing mechanism, often assisted by an air lift.[6] A complete harvester includes pneumatic cleaning facilities to remove leaves and trash, as well as a conveying and collection system. An experimental harvester developed at the Iowa Agricultural Experiment Station[33] had a bank of fore-and-aft-vibrating fingers that combed through the plants continually. A rearward-directed air nozzle, located at the rear of the fingers, conveyed the berries up an inclined apron to a cross conveyor and also provided pneumatic cleaning. Another experimental machine[20] employed a high-velocity air stream to lift the berries while still attached, and a stem vibrator to detach the suspended berries. Some selectivity was achieved. A machine that clips the entire plant just above the ground surface has also been tested.[5]

Machine-harvested strawberries include immature and spoiled fruit which must be removed by hand. Removal of caps (calyxes) and stems is necessary for processing. A mechanical capper developed at the Michigan Agricultural Experiment Station in the early 1970s[36] properly capped over 90% of the berries at a rate of 340 to 410 kg/h [750 to 900 lb/h] in 1974 tests. Pairs of close-spaced, counter-rotating, rubber-covered rollers on a conveyor grip the stems. The captured berries are carried up through a vertical section of the conveyor and then downward past a serrated band saw that cuts close to the rollers, removing the caps (and, with some varieties, a thin slice from each berry).

VEGETABLE HARVESTING

Mechanical harvesting and handling have been widely accepted for potatoes, green peas and lima beans, processing tomatoes, snap beans, spinach, and processing sweet corn. Considerable progress has been made in developing harvesters for many other vegetables but acceptance rates have varied considerably, depending upon the problems involved and the potential economic gain from mechanization. The status of mechanization in the mid 1970s, problems involved, and equipment are discussed for most of the important vegetable crops in the following sections. Potato harvesting and dry-onion harvesting are covered in Chapter 20.

21.13. Tomato Harvesting. Tomatoes are second only to potatoes in importance among United States vegetable crops.[6] About 85% of the crop is processed each year. More than 75% of the nation's processing tomatoes are grown in California, and practically all of these are harvested mechanically.

The first mechanical harvesting on a commercial basis was in 1961 and 1962. A cooperative research program at the California Agricultural Experiment Station, conducted during a period of over 10 years, had produced a California variety suitable for mechanical harvesting and had demonstrated the feasibility of certain principles for harvesting this variety mechanically.

The acceptance of mechanical harvesting in California was quite rapid, partly because of a severe labor shortage created by the termination, in 1964, of the Mexican-National labor-import program. Mechanization has progressed much less rapidly in other states,[6] two reasons being climatic differences and the lack of varieties suitable for mechanical harvesting.

Tomato harvesters are once-over machines that sever the plant stems, usually at or just below the ground surface (or uproot the plants), take the entire plants into the machine, and detach the fruits by shaking. Leaves, dust, and other light debris are separated from the detached fruit with blowers. On harvesters having only hand sorting, the fruits are conveyed on sorting belts past workers who remove green fruits, other culls, and any remaining clods and other debris. From 10 to 20 sorters may be needed, the number depending primarily upon the harvest rate and the maturity and condition of the fruit. Average harvest rates of 14 to 18 Mg/h [15 to 20 tons/h] are common. The sorted fruit is conveyed directly into bulk trucks or into bins on a special trailer towed beside the harvester.

Electronic color sorters for tomato harvesters became available commercially in 1975. They quickly became quite popular in spite of the high initial cost ($35 000 to 40 000 *extra*, on new harvesters, in 1976). The tomatoes and other objects are conveyed past electro-optical sensors, either single file in 8 to 12 separate channels for each of 2 assemblies, or as a continuous-width stream one layer deep. Green tomatoes, clods, and other non-red objects are ejected from the falling stream, either mechanically or with a momentary blast from an air jet. Hand sorters are still needed to remove cull red tomatoes, but only half as many sorters are needed as without electronic sorting. The advantage of electronic sorting diminishes as a field becomes more mature because there are fewer green tomatoes to remove mechanically and more culls that must be removed by hand.

Vine cutting or uprooting is generally accomplished with (a) either a V-shaped stationary knife (point leading) or two separate knives with the cutting edges at an angle of 45 to 55° from the direction of travel, (b) a sickle-bar type of cutter with stub guards, that cuts below ground, or (c) a rotating square bar that operates beneath the ground (like a rod weeder) and uproots the plants. Cutting or uprooting the plants and getting the vines onto an elevating conveyor without knocking fruit off of the plants and losing it, and without picking up excessive amounts of soil, is a problem that has not been completely solved for all conditions.

Rubber-covered, rod-link chains employed as elevating conveyors on some harvesters provide some dirt separation. Other machines have two draper-type elevating conveyors in series, with an arrangement between the conveyors that removes dirt and loose tomatoes onto special sorting belts. The good fruits are picked off of these belts and the unwanted materials are discharged onto the ground.

Some shaking units have horizontal conveying chains spaced 125 to 150 mm [5 to 6 in.] apart across the full width of the unit. Vertical fingers on the chains engage the vines. A fore-and-aft oscillating motion of the chains is superimposed on the overall net rearward motion. In one model the chains pass around a parallelogram, the top leg of which is oscillated. Another model has a unique drive arrangement that imparts a cyclic velocity reversal (160 cycles per minute) to chains having fixed sprocket-shaft locations, with the rearward (advancing) motion in each cycle being about twice as great as the forward (return) motion. A walker-type shaker has oscillating, vertical fins spaced across the separation section. The front ends of the fins have a nearly horizontal fore-and-aft motion but the rear ends have a substantial vertical component to give a more vigorous shaking action for fruits that have resisted detachment. With any of these shakers, the detached fruits fall through the openings between chains or fins onto a collecting conveyor.

Because tomatoes are quite susceptible to impact damage, the shakers and and all conveyors must be designed to minimize drop distances and impacts resulting from fruit inertia. Adequate cushioning at all critical contact points is important. In spite of great improvements since tomato harvesters first became available, excessive damage continues to be a major problem.

Fresh-market tomatoes have been harvested to a limited extent with conventional machines having special padding and other minor modifications. Some of the newer fresh-market varieties seem to be reasonably well-suited to mechanical harvesting.

21.14. Snap-Bean Harvesters. Mechanical harvesters for bush snap beans were developed commercially in the 1950s and are now widely used. Several companies in the United States and Europe have developed machines.[6] All of these employ slender steel fingers or tines that comb through the plants, removing the pods and most of the leaves and throwing them onto a belt or other conveyor. Mechanical and aerodynamic means are employed on the machine to remove most of the trash.

One type of picker has radial fingers attached to cylindrical reels and has one reel per row. Each reel axis is in a vertical plane parallel with the row. Most United States harvesters of this type are two-row models built onto modified tractors. Lifter points guide the plants into each picking unit. The reel bends the plants sharply and holds them against a sheet-metal concave backing plate, as shown in Fig. 21.2b, as the fingers comb through them. The reel and the concave are usually higher at the front end than at the rear so the tops of the plants are combed first as the machine moves along the row. Some models have a rotary brush directly above each reel to "doff" any pods or plant material remaining on the fingers.

High-speed motion pictures during laboratory tests with a commercially available machine[4] showed that when a finger acts upon the pod stem, as shown in Fig. 21.2a, the pedicel breaks due to the severe deflection and high bending stress. If the finger applies force directly to the pod, the pod is likely to break, sometimes near the stem end and sometimes remote from the end.[4] The velocity imparted to the pod usually carries it over the concave plate and throws it onto the conveyor belt, but some pods slide back down the concave and are lost. The tip speed of the fingers was about 4.6 m/s [900 ft/min] in these tests. Clearance between the concave plate and the finger tips was 16 mm [⅝ in.].

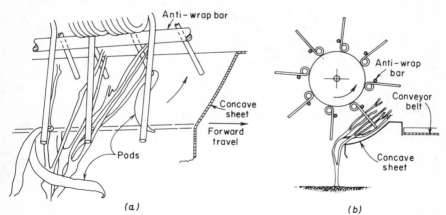

Fig. 21.2. A cylindrical-reel-type snap-bean picker. *(a)* A pod being removed by a finger contacting the pedicel. Drawing made from high-speed photograph. (B. L. Bledsoe and A. H. Morgan.[4]) *(b)* Schematic, cross-sectional arrangement of reel and concave plate.

A multirow harvester developed in England has the picking fingers attached to a chain-and-slat reel.[6] The chain and sprockets on each end form a loop about 460 mm [18 in.] high and 150 mm [6 in.] thick. The reel is 1.83 m [6 ft] long and set at a 45° horizontal angle from the line of travel, thereby giving continuous coverage across a band about 1.22 m [4 ft] wide. This arrangement is well-suited to close-spaced rows in high-population plantings. The top of the reel is tilted forward so the tops of the plants are combed first.

A multirow picker developed in the United States in the early 1970s has a header-like arrangement with the reel perpendicular to the rows. The fingers are attached to bars that are cam-controlled like on a pickup reel for a self-propelled windrower. The reel lifts the vines and strips them over a concave plate located immediately behind the lower part of the reel.

21.15. Harvesting Green Peas. Since the early 1900s, green peas have been shelled by feeding the vines into stationary machines known as pea viners.[6] Mobile green-pea combines (also used for green lima beans) were introduced in the early 1960s and have largely replaced stationary viners, primarily because of lower harvesting costs. Stationary viners are no longer being manufactured.[6] Both self-propelled and pull-type machines are available as hillside combines (Fig. 21.3). These have automatic side leveling

Fig. 21.3. Hillside green-pea combine with automatic side and fore-and-aft leveling. Note that the four main support wheels remain vertical. (Courtesy of FMC Corp.)

and fore-and-aft leveling, similar to the systems on hillside grain combines (Section 17.3). About one-third of the United States plantings are in the Pacific Northwest, much of this in hilly areas.

Green peas usually are cut and windrowed with specially designed self-propelled or tractor-mounted windrowers prior to either stationary or field shelling. Vine lifters, hinged and spring-loaded so the points can follow ground-surface irregularities, are mounted on cutterbar guards at about 305-mm [1-ft] intervals. A more recent approach has been to adapt a multirow snap-bean picking unit to the header of a self-propelled green-pea combine, thereby eliminating the windrowing operation and reducing the amount of plant material that the sheller must handle.

Shellers on green-pea combines operate on the same basic principle as used for many years in stationary viners. The vines are fed into a nearly level, slowly rotating, screen-mesh drum 1.5 to 1.7 m [5 to 5½ ft] in diameter. Inside the drum is a rapidly rotating cylinder with short lengths of paddle-type beaters mounted around the periphery. Beater overall diameters are 965 to 1090 mm [38 to 43 in.] and peripheral speeds are generally in the range from 8.6 to 12.7 m/s [1700 to 2500 ft/min]. Ribs or baffles projecting inward from the drum screen repeatedly lift the vines and pods and drop them onto the cylinder beater. The impacts from the beater paddles cause the pods to open. The peas and some small waste then fall through the openings in the drum screen onto an inclined apron or a draper conveyor.

The beater paddles are inclined at a small angle from the cylinder axis so they gradually move the vines toward the discharge end of the drum. The rate of vine movement through the drum can be controlled by changing the beater speed. Since the rate of movement is also a function of drum slope, even level-land combines often have provision for fore-and-aft leveling.

The shelled peas are cleaned pneumatically and deposited in a hopper on the machine. Pods are screened out and returned to the drum inlet.

21.16. Harvesting Sweet Corn. Mechanical harvesting of sweet corn for processing became a widespread practice during the 1950s. Conventional field-corn snappers having stripping plates above fluted stalk rolls (similar to Fig. 18.3) have been employed. The standard flutes on the stalk rolls are sometimes replaced with knives that cut part way through the ear shank to facilitate snapping. Minor modifications in the conveying system are made on some models. Two-row mounted units are the most common, one harvester replacing 10 to 15 hand pickers. A four-row, self-propelled harvester, utilizing many of the basic components of an existing design of a combine field-corn head, became available in 1970.

Since the mid 1960s there has been an increasing interest in, and acceptance of, mechanical harvesting of fresh-market sweet corn.[6] Several companies have developed pickers suitable for fresh-market corn. Field reports have indicated that these specially designed models cause little damage to the ears. Mechanical harvesters for either fresh-market or processing corn often recover substantially more corn per hectare than from hand picking because fewer ears are missed and left on the stalks. The large saving in picking labor is partly offset by increased labor required for grading and packing machine-picked fresh-market corn.

Varietal characteristics, such as variations in ear size, ease of detachment, uniformity of maturity, husk layer thickness, stalk brittleness, and ear height, have an important bearing on machine performance. Minimum husk removal, minimum damage, and uniform, short shank lengths on the harvested ears are desired for fresh-market corn.

One effective system for detaching the ears and conveying them away from the picking unit is shown in Fig. 21.4. The knives on the stalk rolls cut part way through the stalk as the stalk is pulled down. They sever or nearly sever the ear shank when an ear is encountered. The ear stop bars are narrow plates fastened to a pair of drive chains on each side of the row to form a continuous, moving "wall" on each side of the ear. The stop bars limit the downward movement of the ears before severance and then move the detached ears rearward to an elevating conveyor that deposits the ears in a hopper.

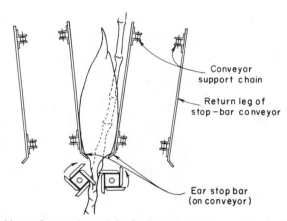

Fig. 21.4. A picking and conveying unit for fresh-market sweet corn. Spacing between stop-bar conveyors is adjustable. (Courtesy of FMC Corp.)

Parallel rolls have been employed to strip ears from stalks held between two opposed belts.[6] Another system has rubber-covered stripper bars that come downward between the stalk and the ear to produce a snapping action similar to hand picking.[6]

21.17. Harvesting Vine Crops. The first development work in mechanical harvesting of pickling cucumbers was with multiple-pick machines. Because of greatly reduced yields, cumulative damage to the vines, and other inherent problems, major emphasis since about 1965 has been on once-over harvesters.[6] Several manufacturers had once-over harvesters available commercially in 1971. These machines sever the vines just below ground level and feed the entire plants through the machine. Resilient rubber rolls pull the vines and stems through between them, pinching off the cucumbers. Damage from the harvesters has been relatively low. Considerable progress has been made in adapting cultural practices to once-over harvesting, and some progress has been made in developing more suitable varieties. In 1976, once-over harvesters were used for at least 85 to 90% of Michigan's pickling cucumbers but for only a small percentage of this crop in other states. (Michigan normally has about 20% of the 51 to 57 kha [125,000 to 140,000 acres] planted each year in the United States for processing.)

A simple and relatively inexpensive multiple-pick cucumber harvester was developed at the North Carolina Agricultural Experiment Station in the late 1960s.[22] The vines are lifted a few centimetres by small-diameter rods that pass along each side of the plant base and curve outward toward the rear. The rear portions of the rods strike the suspended fruit close to the attachment point and remove them by impact resulting from the forward motion of the harvester. Yields are greatly reduced in comparison with hand picking. Although a low-cost, selective machine of this type might be more feasible than once-over machines for small areas, this machine has had very little commercial acceptance.

Research during the 1960s has resulted in the development of experimental selective and once-over cantaloupe harvesters.[18,32] Multiple-harvest machines have not proved economical or practical because of the low production from each of the 5 to 7 harvests required. Also, special training of the vines is required. Once-over harvesting is economically impractical unless more uniform ripening can be achieved.[32] An experimental machine that picks up and loads hand-picked cantaloupes was developed in 1973.[31] The pickers place individual melons in alternate, precleaned furrows between the beds. The machine then picks them up from the furrows and deposits them in a truck. This system utilizes the worker's capability for selecting mature fruit, eliminates the onerous hand-carrying operation, retains the individual's independence regarding rate of work, and greatly increases worker productivity.

Because watermelons are large and do not mature uniformly, they do not lend themselves to mechanical harvesting. Experienced judgment is required in selecting ripe melons when picking by hand.

21.18. Lettuce Harvesting. Selective mechanical harvesters for crisphead lettuce were developed at the California and Arizona Agricultural Experiment Stations during the 1960s. Patent rights to both machines were licensed to manufacturers in the late 1960s, but commercial development was slow because of the reluctance of growers to accept selective mechanical harvesting as long as an adequate labor supply was available.[6] Experimental once-over harvesters have been developed at the Cornell Agricultural Experiment Station[34] and in Colorado.[6] Once-over harvesting is feasible in the eastern states but several selective harvests are necessary in the Southwest (where 80 to 85% of the United States crop is produced).[6]

The selector system is a major component of a selective lettuce harvester. Even if varieties and cultural practices suitable for once-over harvesting in the Southwest are developed, it is possible that selective mechanical harvesting might be more practical than sorting the entire crop as a subsequent operation to remove immature heads.[2] Both the California and the Arizona machines, as originally designed, selected mature heads mechanically on the basis of size and firmness.[6] A cutting and pickup mechanism removed the heads that had been selected. Because the sensing unit was necessarily positioned ahead of the cutting unit, a memory device capable of storing up to four signals was needed.[15]

It has been found that maturity can also be determined by using gamma or X-ray radiation through the head to sense a combination of size and density.[16,24] When the radiation across the row drops below a predetermined level, a signal is given to indicate that an acceptable head is in the beam. The radiation sensors are more complicated than the mechanical sensors but they avoid physical contact with the heads, and tests have shown them to be more accurate and more consistent than mechanical sensors.[2]

An experimental harvester that was constructed and tested in 1971 utilized the X-ray selection principle and had provision on the harvester for hand trimming and hand packing into cartons.[25] In field tests, the time required for hand trimming was the limiting factor in machine productivity. To alleviate this problem, a mechanical trimmer was developed for use on the harvester.[1] The trimmer was adjustable and did an acceptable job.

21.19. Cabbage Harvesting. Experimental, once-over cabbage harvesters were developed by several universities and small manufacturers during the 1960s, but commercial acceptance was slow.[6] About 90% of the United States crop is harvested for the fresh market, 3 to 5 selective hand cuttings generally being made.[6] Cabbage for processing is usually harvested in a once-over operation and, therefore, is more adaptable to mechanical harvesting than are most fresh-market varieties.

A successful cabbage harvester must sever the head from the stump with a clean, square cut that is close to the head, should leave the desired number of wrapper leaves (varies with the intended use), should not damage the heads appreciably, and must be able to handle a wide range of head sizes and considerable variation in alignment of plants along the row. Obtaining a satisfactory cut has been a problem. Poor alignment in the row, partly related to transplanter type and performance, tends to cause variations in orientation of heads in the harvester and thus affects cutting (when cut after lifting). Plants are likely to be spread over a band at least 20 cm [8 in.] wide.[6] Driving error increases the deviation.

Studies and field experience have indicated that the height of the cut should be gaged from a reference support surface for the head rather than from ground level. This principle was utilized in a harvester developed at the Cornell Agricultural Experiment Station which cut off the stumps after lifting the plants.[6] The heads and stumps were lifted from the soil with two powered disks that presented convex surfaces to the underside of each head in the row. The planes of the disk edges were inclined downward toward the front. The disks delivered the plants to a pair of conveyor chains that positively positioned each stump and elevated the plants to a cutoff saw. The pickup disks could satisfactorily accommodate plants located as much as 18 cm [7 in.] on either side of the pickup centerline, and a high percentage of acceptable cuts was obtained.[6]

21.20. Asparagus Harvesting. Since about 1960, many individuals and organizations have worked on the development of mechanical harvesters for green asparagus.[6] Both selective and nonselective machines became commercially available in the late 1960s. A limited amount of green asparagus for processing was harvested mechanically in 1976, mostly with nonselective machines. Large yield reductions and lack of suitable handling facilities at processing plants have inhibited the acceptance of mechanical harvesting.

A selective harvester attempts to duplicate hand harvesting, sensing and cutting spears taller than a preselected height and leaving the shorter spears for subsequent harvests. As with hand harvesting, each field must be covered daily during most of the 6 to 12 week harvest period. A nonselective harvester cuts all spears, regardless of length, at intervals of several days. With either type of harvester, cutting may be at, above, or just below ground level.

A selective harvester has a group of perhaps 8 to 12 selection channels covering a total width of 76 to 91 cm [30 to 36 in.] for each asparagus row. Each channel must have a height-sensing device, a cutting unit, and a spear-gripping or pickup unit. Wire triggers projecting from sensitive electric switches, and photo cells, have been employed as sensing devices. Knives are generally pneumatically actuated. Pairs of narrow, fingered belts grip the spears just above the sensing height and elevate them after they are cut.

Band saws and reciprocating blades have been utilized as cutting devices on nonselective harvesters. Reciprocating blades generally cut at least 2.5 cm [1 in.] above ground level, whereas band saws can cut at or slightly below ground level. The spears are elevated by a draper conveyor or with a series of rotating gripper units. A sled-type harvester developed in Michigan has a V-shaped stationary knife just ahead of an open-front bin. Sled harvesters are operated at 16 to 24 km/h [10 to 15 mph] and cut just above the ground surface. Inertia throws the spears (and some trash and clods) back into the bin.

Asparagus production per harvest is quite low compared with most crops, generally being in the order of 55 to 110 kg/ha [50 to 100 lb/acre] for daily, selective harvests. Spear tips are easily broken when the spears are turgid, as in cool weather. The maximum interval between nonselective harvests is limited by the tendency for spears to "flower" or develop open heads (which makes them culls) when they become taller than 20 to 30 cm [8 to 12 in.]. During warm weather, a height of 25 to 30 cm [10 to 12 in.] may be attained within 4 to 5 days after emergence.

Nonselective harvesters, because of the high percentage of short spears and tips cut each time, recover only about half the hand-cut yield, based on lengths acceptable for processing.[23] Selective harvesters cause substantial yield losses by cutting or damaging unselected spears[28] and because of various machine performance factors.[23] A nonselective harvester is basically simpler and more reliable than a selective harvester and can handle several times as much crop area because of higher forward speeds and the less frequent harvests. Nonselective yield losses are prohibitive in situations where spears shorter than about 15 cm [6 in.] have little value (as for fresh-market asparagus).

A cost analysis made in 1969[23] indicated that, under California conditions at that time, either system of mechanical harvesting would result in less net income per hectare than from hand harvesting. The use of greatly increased plant populations to increase the potential yield per hectare is a promising method of improving the economic feasibility.

Most mechanical harvesters deposit the spears in a bin in a jumbled manner. Present processing procedures generally require that the spears be aligned and oriented with all the heads in the same direction, which is the way hand-harvested asparagus is delivered. Automatic spear orienters have been developed, utilizing the characteristic that the center of gravity of a spear is usually closer to the butt end than to the tip.[17]

21.21 Celery Harvesting. Celery has good potential for mechanical harvesting because of the nature of its growth. Several successful harvesters have been developed on a commercial basis since the mid 1960s.[6] These grip the stalks with opposed belts and employ various kinds of knives to cut the root systems. Topping may also be done by the harvester. Bulk handling is feasible because the outer petioles, which are later removed, provide protection against damage. Mechanical stripping of the petioles is needed for a fully mechanized harvesting and handling system. The extent of mechanical harvesting was still rather limited in 1976.

21.22. Spinach Harvesting. A high percentage of the spinach crop is harvested mechanically.[6] The basic components of a harvester for spinach and other nonheading leafy vegetables are plant lifters or guides, a cutting mechanism, and an arrangement to elevate the material and deliver it into a bulk truck or trailed wagon or into crates or other small containers handled on the harvester. One type of cutting mechanism consists of a high-speed, sharpened, rotary disk for each row.

REFERENCES

1. ADRIAN, P. A., D. H. LENKER, and D. NASCIMENTO. A mechanical trimmer for crisphead lettuce — refinements, field tests, and performance. Trans. ASAE, *19*(5):835-839, 1976.
2. ADRIAN, P. A., M. ZAHARA, D. H. LENKER, W. B. GODDARD, and G. W. FRENCH. A comparative study of selectors for maturity of crisp-head lettuce. Trans. ASAE *16*(2):253-257, 1973.
3. BERLAGE, A. G., and G. E. YOST. Tree walls for the tree fruit industry. Agr. Eng., *49*:198-201, Apr., 1968.
4. BLEDSOE, B. L., and A. H. MORGAN. Pod detaching mechanisms for snap bean harvesters. Trans. ASAE, *15*(4):638-643, 1972.
5. BOOSTER, D. E. Mowing method of harvesting strawberries. Trans. ASAE, *17*(6):1053-1056, 1974.
6. CARGILL, B. F., and G. E. ROSSMILLER, Editors. Fruit and Vegetable Harvest Mechanization — Technological Implications. Rural Manpower Center Rept. 16. Michigan State Univ., East Lansing, Mich., 1969.
7. CHEN, P., and J. J. MEHLSCHAU. An over-the-row Boysenberry harvester. Trans. ASAE, *17*(2):205-208, 1974.
8. COPPOCK, G. E. Development of a limb shaker for harvesting Florida citrus. Trans. ASAE, *17*(2):262-265, 1974.
9. FRIDLEY, R. B., and P. A. ADRIAN. Mechanical harvesting equipment for deciduous tree fruits. California Agr. Expt. Sta. Bull 825, 1966.
10. FRIDLEY, R. B., and P. A. ADRIAN. Evaluating the feasibility of mechanizing crop harvest. Trans. ASAE, *11*(3):350-352, 1968.
11. FRIDLEY, R. B., P. A. ADRIAN, L. L. CLAYPOOL, A. D. RIZZI, and S. J. LEONARD. Mechanical harvesting of cling peaches. California Agr. Expt. Sta. Bull. 851, 1971.
12. FRIDLEY, R. B., H. T. HARTMAN, J. J. MEHLSCHAU, P. CHEN, and J. WHISLER. Olive harvest mechanization in California. California Agr. Expt. Sta. Bull. 855, 1971.
13. FRIDLEY, R. B., J. J. MEHLSCHAU, P. A. ADRIAN, AND J. A. BEUTEL. Multilevel platform system for harvesting hedgerow-trained trees. Trans. ASAE, *12*(6):866-869, 1969.
14. Fruit and vegetable harvesting publications — 1971 ASAE bibliography. ASAE Special Publication SP-01-71. ASAE, St. Joseph, Mich.
15. GARRETT, R. E. Control system for a selective lettuce harvester. Trans. ASAE, *10*(1):69, 73, 1967.
16. GARRETT, R. E., and W. K. TALLEY. Use of gamma ray transmission in selecting lettuce for harvest. Trans. ASAE, *13*(6):820-823, 1970.
17. GRADWOHL, D. R. Developing an orienter for mechanically harvested asparagus. Agr. Eng., *52*:312-313, June, 1971.
18. HARRIOTT, B. L., R. E. FOSTER, II, and J. H. PARK. Mechanisms, culture, and varieties for selective mechanical cantaloupe harvest. Trans. ASAE, *13*(1):48-50, 55, 1970.
19. HOAG, D. L., J. R. HUTCHINSON, and R. B. FRIDLEY. Effect of proportional, nonproportional, and nonlinear damping on dynamic response of tree limbs. Trans. ASAE, *13*(6):879-884, 1970.
20. HOLMES, R. G., and J. H. RUFF. Development of the air-suspension, stem-vibration strawberry harvester. ASAE Paper 75-1060, June, 1975.
21. HORSFIELD, B. C., R. B. FRIDLEY, and L. L. CLAYPOOL. Optimizing mechanical harvesting procedures for apricots of nonuniform maturity. Trans. ASAE, *15*(6):878-882, 1972.

22. HUMPHRIES, E. G. A second generation multiple-pick cucumber harvester. Trans. ASAE, *14*(5):886-889, 1971.
23. KEPNER, R. A. Selective versus nonselective mechanical harvesting of green asparagus. Trans. ASAE, *14*(3):405-410, 1971.
24. LENKER, D. H., and P. A. ADRIAN. Use of X-rays for selecting mature lettuce heads. Trans. ASAE, *14*(5):894-898, 1971.
25. LENKER, D. H., P. A. ADRIAN, G. W. FRENCH, and M. ZAHARA. Selective mechanical lettuce harvesting system. Trans. ASAE, *16*(5):858-861, 866, 1973.
26. LENKER, D. H., and S. L. HEDDEN. Optimum shaking action for citrus fruit harvesting. Trans. ASAE, *11*(3):347-349, 1968.
27. MARSHALL, D. E., and S. L. HEDDEN. Design and performance of an experimental citrus fruit pick-up machine. Trans. ASAE, *13*(3):406-408, 1970.
28. MEARS, D. R., J. J. MOORE, and PARASHURAM. The potential of mechanical asparagus harvesters. Trans. ASAE, *12*(6):813-815, 821, 1969.
29. O'BRIEN, M. Automatic fillers for citrus, deciduous fruit, and vegetable bins. Trans. ASAE, *12*(6):733-735, 1969.
30. O'BRIEN, M., J. P. GENTRY, and R. C. GIBSON. Vibrating characteristics of fruits as related to in-transit injury. Trans. ASAE, *8*(2):241-243, 1965.
31. O'BRIEN, M., and B. L. HARRIOTT. A melon pickup machine for reducing onerous labor. Trans. ASAE, *18*(5):803-805, 1975.
32. O'BRIEN, M., and M. ZAHARA. Mechanical harvest of melons. Trans. ASAE, *14*(5):883-885, 1971.
33. QUICK, G. R. New approach to strawberry harvesting using vibration and air. Trans. ASAE, *14*(6):1180-1183, 1971.
34. SHEPARDSON, E. S., J. G. POLLOCK, and G. E REHKUGLER. Research and development of a lettuce harvester. Trans. ASAE, *17*(2):212-216, 1974.
35. STUDER, H. E., and H. P. OLMO. The severed cane technique and its application to mechanical harvesting of raisin grapes. Trans. ASAE, *14*(1):38-43, 1971.
36. The MSU-CML strawberry capper. Agr. Eng., *56*(2):20, Feb., 1975.
37. WHITNEY, J. D., and J. M. PATTERSON. Development of a citrus removal device using oscillating forced air. Trans. ASAE, *15*(5):849-855, 860, 1972.

PROBLEMS

21.1. Consider a fruit or other object carried on a horizontal conveyor belt that has a linear velocity V and passes around a pully whose radius is R. The center of gravity of the object is at a distance d_g from the belt. Derive equations to express each of the following in terms of R, d_g, and V. Assume the object does not slip or roll on the belt, and neglect belt thickness. Specify the units for each variable.

(a) The rotational angle θ, beyond the vertical line through the pulley center, at which the object leaves the belt.

(b) The horizontal velocity component V_{hl} of the object at the time it leaves the belt.

(c) The minimum belt speed at which the object would leave the belt directly above the pulley centerline ($\theta = 0$).

21.2. (a) Using the relations developed in Problem 21.1, calculate the minimum belt speed for $\theta = 0$ when a fruit with $d_g = 28$ mm is carried on a belt that passes around a 150-mm-diameter pulley.

(b) Calculate the value of θ for a belt speed of 38 m/min.

(c) Some fruits are damaged from a free fall of over 23 cm. Calculate the impact velocity for a 23-cm fall and compare with (a).

APPENDIX

Appendix A
DRAFT, ENERGY, AND POWER REQUIREMENTS

Machine	Typical Range of Requirements	References
Tillage		
Moldboard or disk plow	2.1-4.1, 3.4-6.2, 5.5-9.7 N/cm^2	
	[3-6, 5-9, 8-14 lbf/in.^{2}] [a]	2
Lister (in firm soil)	1.8-3.6 kN per bottom	
	[400-800 lbf per bottom]	2
Vertical-disk plow (one-way disk)	2.6-5.8 kN/m [180-400 lbf/ft]	2
Disk harrow		
Single-acting	0.7-1.5 kN/m [50-100 lbf/ft]	2
Tandem (light-duty)	1.5-2.9 kN/m [100-200 lbf/ft]	2
Offset, or heavy tandem	3.6-5.8 kN/m [250-400 lbf/ft]	1, Ch. 7
Subsoiler	120-190, 190-280 N per cm depth [b]	
	[70-110, 110-160 lbf per inch depth]	2
Chisel plow or chisel-type		
field cultivator	0.23-0.69 kN/m per cm depth	
	[40-120 lbf/ft per inch depth]	3, 4
Field cultivator with sweeps,		
8 to 13 cm [3 to 5 in.] depth	1.5-4.4 kN/m [100-300 lbf/ft]	3, 4
Powered rotary tiller, conventional,		
8 to 10 cm [3 to 4 in.] bite	10-17, 17-24, 21-28 equiv. N/cm^2	
	[15-25, 25-35, 30-40 equiv. lbf/in.^{2}] [c]	2, Ch. 9
Spring-tooth harrow	1.1-2.9 kN/m [75-200 lbf/ft]	1, 2
Spike-tooth harrow	0.3-0.9 kN/m [20-60 lbf/ft]	2
Rod weeder	0.9-1.8 kN/m [60-120 lbf/ft]	2
Roller or packer	0.3-2.2 kN/m [20-150 lbf/ft]	1
Rotary hoe	0.4-1.5 kN/m [30-100 lbf/ft]	1
Row-crop cultivator		
Shallow	0.6-1.2 kN/m [40-80 lbf/ft]	2
Deep	0.11-0.23 kN/m per cm depth	
	[20-40 lbf/ft per inch depth]	2
Planting		
Row-crop planter, drilling		
seed only	0.45-0.8 kN [100-180 lbf] per row	2
Grain drill	0.4-1.5 kN/m [30-100 lbf/ft]	1
Harvesting		
Mower	1.0-2.0 PTO kW/m [0.4-0.8 hp/ft] [d]	Ch. 14
Hay baler	0.8-2.1 kW·h/Mg [1-2.5 hp-h/ton] [e]	Ch. 15
Field cuber, self-propelled	16-25 kW·h/Mg [20-30 hp-h/ton]	Ch. 15
Flail-type field chopper		
Without recutter	1.1-2.1 kW·h/Mg [1.3-2.5 hp-h/ton] [e]	2
With flywheel-type recutter	1.6-3.3 kW·h/Mg [2-4 hp-h/ton] [e]	Ch. 16
Shear-bar-type field chopper [f]		
Corn silage, 13 mm [½ in.] theor. cut.	0.7-1.6 kW·h/Mg [0.8-2 hp-h/ton] [e]	2, Ch. 16
Green grass/legume silage	0.8-2.1 kW·h/Mg [1-2.5 hp-h/ton] [e]	Ch. 16
Low-moisture grass/legume silage	1.6-4.1 kW·h/Mg [2-5 hp-h/ton] [e]	Ch. 16
Self-propelled combine in grain	3.3-4.9 kW·h/Mg [4-6 hp-h/ton]	
	of non-grain material	Ch. 17
Corn picker, 2-row	9-15 kW [12-20 hp]	1

[a] Specific drafts (force per unit of furrow cross-sectional area) for light, medium, and heavy soils, respectively.

^b Ranges are for sandy loam and medium or clay loam soils, respectively.

^c All rotary power, but expressed as equivalent specific draft. Specific energy, in kJ/m³, = 10 × specific draft, in N/cm². Ranges are for light, medium, and heavy soils. Increasing the bite length to 15 cm [6 in.] decreases energy requirements by 20 to 25% (Fig. 9.7).

^d Draft due to cutterbar drag not included.

^e Draft due to rolling resistance not included.

^f Energy requirements per unit of mass are lowest with high feed rates, low cutterhead speeds, and long cuts.

REFERENCES

1. Agricultural machinery management data. Agricultural Engineers Yearbook, 1976, pp. 322-329. ASAE, St. Joseph, Mich.
2. Costs and use, farm machinery. Agricultural Engineers Yearbook, 1963, pp. 227-233. ASAE, St. Joseph, Mich.
3. DOWDING, E., J. A. FERGUSON, and C. F. BECKER. A comparison of four summer-fallow tillage methods based on seasonal-tillage energy requirement, moisture conservation, and crop yield. ASAE Paper 66-122, June, 1966.
4. PROMERSBERGER, W. J., and G. L. PRATT. Power requirements of tillage implements. North Dakota Agr. Expt. Sta. Bull. 415, 1958.

Appendix B
TYPICAL OPERATING SPEEDS FOR IMPLEMENTS

Machine	Operating Speed km/h	mph
Tillage		
Cultivator, field	5.6-8.9	3.5-5.5
Cultivator, row-crop		
First (close) cultivation	2.4-4.8	1.5-3
Later cultivations	4.0-8.9	2.5-5.5
Disk harrow	5.6-9.7	3.5-6
Plow (moldboard or disk)	5.6-8.9	3.5-5.5
Roller (cultipacker)	4.8-9.7	3-6
Rotary hoe	8.0-18	5-11
Spike-tooth harrow	5.6-9.7	3.5-6
Spring-tooth harrow	5.6-9.7	3.5-6
Seeding		
Broadcaster	6.4-10	4-6.5
Grain drill	4.0-8.9	2.5-5.5
Row-crop planter		
Corn, cotton, soybeans	5.6-9.7	3.5-6
Most other crops, including vegetables	4.0-7.2	2.5-4.5
Harvesting		
Combine, in grain or corn	3.2-5.6	2-3.5
(Speeds may be as low as 0.8 km/h [½ mph] in some crops)		
Corn picker	3.2-6.4	2-4
Cotton picker (spindle-type)	2.4-5.6	1.5-3.5
Cotton stripper	3.2-6.4	2-4
Field chopper, shear-bar type	3.2-7.2	2-4.5
Hay baler	3.2-8.0	2-5
Mower	5.6-8.9	3.5-5.5
Mower-conditioner	5.6-8.0	3.5-5
Rake	5.6-11	3.5-7
Windrower, self-propelled	5.6-8.9	3.5-5.5
Miscellaneous		
Fertilizer spreader (broadcast)	4.8-8.0	3-5
Rotary cutter (stalk chopper)	4.8-9.7	3-6
Sprayer	4.8-8.0	3-5

REFERENCES

1. Agricultural Machinery Management Data. Agricultural Engineers Yearbook, 1976, pp. 322-329. ASAE, St. Joseph, Mich.
2. BOWERS, W. Modern Concepts of Farm Machinery Management. Stipes Publishing Co., Champaign, Ill., 1970.
3. FAIRBANKS, G. E., G. H. LARSON, and D. CHUNG. Cost of using farm machinery. Trans. ASAE, *14*(1)98-101, 1971.
4. HUNT, D. Farm Power and Machinery Management, 6th Edition. Iowa State University Press, Ames, Iowa, 1973.

Appendix C
COEFFICIENTS OF ROLLING RESISTANCE FOR PNEUMATIC TIRES

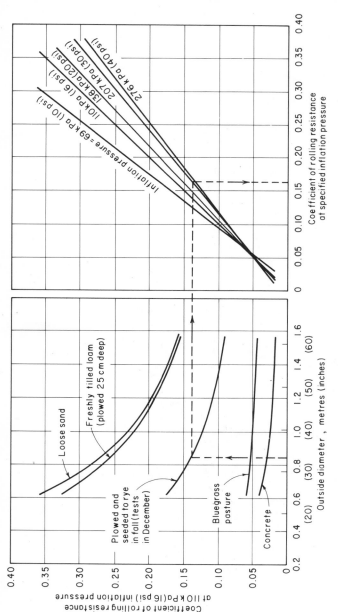

Rolling resistance, in force units = (coefficient of rolling resistance) × (vertical load on tire, in force units). (E. G. McKibben and D. O. Hull. Agr. Eng., June, 1940.)

Tire outside diameters for various size ratings may be found in ASAE Recommendation R220, in the Agricultural Engineers Yearbook. For most tires other than those classified as drive tires for tractors or self-propelled implements, the sum of the rim size plus twice the tire width (as indicated by tire size rating) is within ± 30 mm [1.2 in.] of the actual outside diameter and may be used in determining coefficients of rolling resistance from the graph.

Appendix D
GRAPHIC SYMBOLS FOR FLUID POWER DIAGRAMS
(Partial listing from American National Standard ANS Y32.10, 1966)

LINES AND LINE FUNCTIONS	
Line, working (main)	
Line, pilot (for control)	
Line, drain	
Flow direction — Hydraulic / Pneumatic	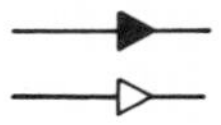
Lines crossing	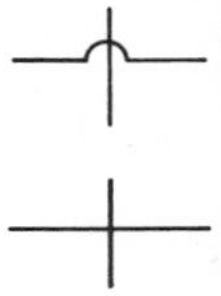
Lines joining	
Line, flexible	
Line with fixed restriction	
Station (testing, measurement, or power take-off)	
Line to reservoir* — Above fluid level / Below fluid level	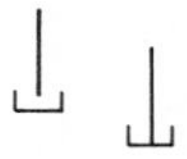
Vented manifold	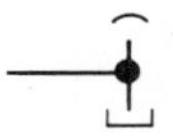
Adjustable or variable component (run arrow through symbol at approximately 45°)	
Pressure compensated units (arrow parallel to short side of symbol)	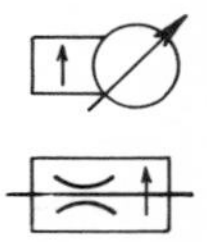
Temperature cause or effect	

PUMPS, MOTORS, AND CYLINDERS	
Pump, single, fixed-displacement	 Out / In
Pump, single, variable displacement	
Hydraulic motor, fixed displacement	 In / Out
Hydraulic motor, variable displacement	
Hydraulic motor, bidirectional	
Cylinder, single-acting	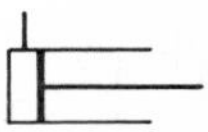
Cylinder, double-acting	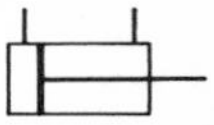

MISCELLANEOUS	
Reservoir, vented	
Accumulator, spring-loaded	
Accumulator, gas-charged	
Cooler (heat exchanger)	
Filter (strainer)	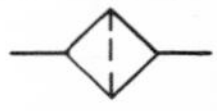
Component enclosure (may surround a group of symbols to indicate an assembly)	
Direction of shaft rotation (arrow on near side of shaft)	

*Any number of these symbols may be used in one diagram to represent the same reservoir.

510

VALVES (See also Fig. 4.3)		ACTUATORS AND CONTROLS	
Check		Spring	
On-off (manual)		Manual (general symbol; no specific type)	
Pressure relief, direct-acting (indicates infinite positioning, normally closed, for single port)		Push button	
Pressure reducing, direct-acting (indicates infinite positioning, normally open, for single port)		Push-pull lever	
Flow control, adjustable, noncompensated		Pedal or treadle	
Flow control, adjustable, pressure-compensated, with reverse bypass		Mechanical	
Two-way (two ports), two-position		Detent (vertical line indicates which detent is in use)	
Three-way (three ports), two-position		Pressure compensated	
Four-way (four ports), two-position		Solenoid, single winding	
Four-way, three-position, closed center		Reversing motor	
Four-way, three-position, two-ports open center (tandem)		Pilot pressure, remote supply	
Horizontal bars indicate valve capable of infinite positioning within limits		Pilot pressure, internal supply	
General (add divisions and internal paths)		Pilot differential	

Basic symbols may be combined in many other ways to represent different components. All symbols except accumulators, vented manifold, and lines to reservoirs may be rotated or reversed. In a circuit, each symbol should be drawn to show normal, at-rest, or neutral conditions of the component, unless multiple diagrams are included to show various phases of circuit operation.

Appendix E
SI UNITS, CUSTOMARY UNITS, AND CONVERSION FACTORS

This appendix identifies SI and U.S. customary units and symbols found in this book. It includes all of the single-unit conversion factors used in the book and most of the compound-unit conversions.

SI UNITS AND SYMBOLS

Unit Name	Symbol	Definition	Quantity
metre	m	base unit	length
kilogram	kg	base unit	mass
second	s*	base unit	time
newton	N	$kg \cdot m/s^2$	force
pascal	Pa	N/m^2	pressure
joule	J	$N \cdot m$	energy, work
watt	W	J/s	power
hectare	ha	hm^2	area (land)
litre	L	dm^3	volume (liquids)
minute	min*	60 s	time
hour	h*	60 min	time
hertz	Hz*	s^{-1}	frequency
degree	°*	$\pi/180$ radians	plane angle
degree Celsius	°C	Kelvin − 273.15	temperature

SI UNIT PREFIXES (Partial List)

Multiple	Name	Symbol	Submultiple	Name	Symbol
10^{12}	tera	T	10^{-1}	deci	d
10^9	giga	G	10^{-2}	centi	c
10^6	mega	M	10^{-3}	milli	m
10^3	kilo	k	10^{-6}	micro	μ
10^2	hecto	h			

U. S. CUSTOMARY UNITS AND SYMBOLS OR ABBREVIATIONS

Symbol or abbrev.	Unit name	Symbol or abbrev.	Unit name
bu	bushel	in.	inch
cfm	cubic foot per minute	lb	pound mass
°F	degree Fahrenheit	lbf	pound force
ft	foot	mph	mile per hour
gal	gallon	psi	pound force per square inch (pressure or stress)
gpm	gallon per minute		
hp	horsepower	r/min*	revolution per minute

CONVERSION FACTORS

Each factor is written as a number greater than one and less than 10. The number is followed by the letter E (for exponent) and a plus or minus sign with 2 digits to indicate the power of 10 by which the number must be multiplied to obtain the correct value (i.e., the number of places the decimal mark must be moved). Examples:

3.523 907 E−02 represents 0.035 239 07
3.386 389 E+03 represents 3 386.389

---

*These units and symbols are used in both the SI and the U.S. customary systems.

512

To convert from	to	multiply by
Acceleration		
free fall, standard (g)	metre per second squared (m/s²)	9.806 650 E+00
Area		
square inch (in.²)	square centimetre (cm²)	6.451 600 E+00
acre	hectare (ha)	4.046 856 E−01
acre	kilohectare (kha)	4.046 856 E−04
acre	megahectare (Mha)	4.046 856 E−07
Area/length		
square inch per inch (in.²/in.)	square centimetre per millimetre (cm²/mm)	2.540 000 E−01
Area/time		
acre per hour (acre/h)	hectare per hour (ha/h)	4.046 856 E−01
Energy or work		
foot-pound-force (ft-lbf)	joule (J)	1.355 818 E+00
foot-pound-force (ft-lbf)	kilojoule (kJ)	1.355 818 E−03
horsepower-hour (hp-h)	kilowatt-hour (kW·h)	7.456 999 E−01
Energy/mass		
horsepower-hour per ton (hp-h/ton)	kilowatt-hour per megagram (kW·h/Mg)	8.219 935 E−01
Energy/volume		
horsepower-hour per gallon (hp-h/gal)	kilowatt-hour per litre (kW·h/L)	1.969 931 E−01
Force		
pound force (lbf)	newton (N)	4.448 222 E+00
pound force (lbf)	kilonewton (kN)	4.448 222 E−03
Force/area (not pressure or stress)		
pound force per square inch (lbf/in.²)	newton per square centimetre (N/cm²)	6.894 757 E−01
Force/length		
pound force per inch (lbf/in.)	newton per centimetre (N/cm)	1.751 269 E+00
pound force per inch (lbf/in.)	kilonewton per metre (kN/m)	1.751 269 E−01
pound force per foot (lbf/ft)	kilonewton per metre (kN/m)	1.459 390 E−02
Force/mass		
pound force per pound (lbf/lb)	newton per kilogram (N/kg)	9.806 650 E+00
Force/power		
pound force per horsepower (lbf/hp)	newton per kilowatt (N/kW)	5.965 164 E+00
pound force per horsepower (lbf/hp)	kilonewton per kilowatt (kN/kW)	5.965 164 E−03
Length		
inch (in.)	millimetre (mm)	2.540 000 E+01
inch (in.)	centimetre (cm)	2.540 000 E+00
inch (in.)	metre (m)	2.540 000 E−02
foot (ft)	metre (m)	3.048 000 E−01
mile	kilometre (km)	1.609 344 E+00
Mass		
pound (lb)	gram (g)	4.535 924 E+02
pound (lb)	kilogram (kg)	4.535 924 E−01
ton	megagram (Mg)	9.071 847 E−01
ton	gigagram (Gg)	9.071 847 E−04
ton	teragram (Tg)	9.071 847 E−07
Mass/area		
pound per acre (lb/acre)	kilogram per hectare (kg/ha)	1.120 851 E+00
ton per acre (ton/acre)	megagram per hectare (Mg/ha)	2.241 702 E+00
Mass/energy (specific fuel consumption)		
pound per horsepower-hour (lb/hp-h)	kilogram per kilowatt-hour (kg/kW·h)	6.082 774 E−01

To convert from	to	multiply by
Mass/length		
pound per foot (lb/ft)	kilogram per metre (kg/m)	1.488 164 E+00
Mass/mass		
pound per ton (lb/ton)	kilogram per megagram (kg/Mg)	5.000 000 E−01
Mass/time		
pound per minute (lb/min)	kilogram per minute (kg/min)	4.535 924 E−01
ton per hour (ton/h)	megagram per hour (Mg/h)	9.071 847 E−01
Mass/volume		
pound per gallon (lb/gal)	gram per litre (g/L)	1.198 264 E+02
pound per gallon (lb/gal)	kilogram per litre (kg/L)	1.198 264 E−01
pound per cubic foot (lb/ft³)	kilogram per cubic metre (kg/m³)	1.601 846 E+01
Power		
horsepower (hp)	kilowatt (kW)	7.456 999 E−01
Power/length		
horsepower per inch (hp/in.)	kilowatt per centimetre (kW/cm)	2.935 826 E−01
horsepower per foot (hp/ft)	kilowatt per metre (kW/m)	2.446 522 E+00
Pressure or stress		
pound force per square inch (psi)	kilopascal (kPa)	6.894 757 E+00
pound force per square inch (psi)	megapascal (MPa)	6.894 757 E−03
Temperature		
degree Fahrenheit (°F)	degree Celsius (°C)	$t_C = (t_F - 32)/1.8$
Temperature difference		
degree Fahrenheit (°F)	degree Celsius (°C)	1/1.8
Torque or bending moment (including couples)		
pound-force-inch (lbf-in.)	newton-metre (N·m)	1.129 848 E−01
Velocity		
foot per minute (ft/min)	metre per second (m/s)	5.080 000 E−03
foot per minute (ft/min)	metre per minute (m/min)	3.048 000 E−01
mile per hour (mph)	kilometre per hour (km/h)	1.609 344 E+00
Viscosity		
centipoise	millipascal-second (mPa·s)	1.000 000 E+00
Volume		
gallon (gal)	litre (L)	3.785 412 E+00
gallon (gal)	cubic metre (m³)	3.785 412 E−03
Volume/area		
gallon per acre (gal/acre)	litre per hectare (L/ha)	9.353 958 E+00
Volume/time		
gallon per minute (gpm)	millilitre per minute (mL/min)	3.785 412 E+03
gallon per minute (gpm)	litre per minute (L/min)	3.785 412 E+00
gallon per hour (gal/h)	litre per hour (L/h)	3.785 412 E+00
cubic foot per minute (cfm)	cubic metre per second (m³/s)	4.719 474 E−04

REFERENCES

1. Modern metric SI measurement units and conversion. Engineering Research, International Harvester Co., Hinsdale, Ill. Revised, July, 1976.
2. Standard for metric practice. ASTM Standard E 380-76. American Society for Testing and Materials, Philadelphia, Pa. Revised, 1976.
3. Use of customary and SI (metric) units. ASAE Engineering Practice EP 285.3. Agricultural Engineers Yearbook, 1977, pp. 226-232. ASAE, St. Joseph, Mich.

Index

Adhesive forces, soil, 118, 120-121, 145-146
Agitation of spray materials, 297-300
Airblast sprayers, atomizing devices, 306-307
  blowers and outlets, 305-306
    air discharge velocities, 306
    capacities, 306
  orchard application rates, 305
    concentrate, 305
    dilute, 305
  principle, 305
  pumps, 306
  row-crop or open-field applications, 305
Aircraft, types for agricultural applications, 272, 274
  use, for fertilizing, 272-274
    for seeding, 231
    for spraying and dusting, 307, 309-310
Aircraft spraying, advantages, 307
  application rates, 307
  atomizing devices, 291, 308-309
    booms, 308
  drift, 307
    versus droplet size, 287
  droplet sizes, 287, 293
  fixed-wing aircraft, 272
  helicopters, 307-309
  operating conditions, 307
  pumps and agitation, 307-308
  venturi suck-back arrangement, 308
Alignment, in a mower, 321
Angle of repose (fertilizers), 267-270
Anhydrous ammonia, 260, 275-276
Aqua ammonia, 260, 275-276
Asparagus, harvesting mechanically, 501-502
  spear orienter, 502
Atomization, centrifugal, 288
  rotary-screen, 288-289, 306-308
  gas, 288
    in airblast sprayers, 288, 293, 306
    in aircraft spraying, 293
    with two-fluid nozzles, 288
  hydraulic, 288
  low-velocity jet breakup, 288, 291-292, 309
  specifying particle sizes and size distributions, 284-285
Atomizing devices, determining uniformity of distribution, 294-295
  droplet size determination, 294
  factors affecting droplet size, 291-293

typical droplet size distributions, 284, 293-294
Auger-type metering devices, 264-265, 269
Automatic draft control, 99-100, 186-188
  draft sensing, 100, 188, 193
  effects, 187-189
Automatic position control, 98-99, 186-187, 189
Axial-flow cylinders. *See* Threshing cylinders

Bale accumulators, for conventional balers, 356-357
  grapple forks for handling bales, 357
  for large-bale balers, 361
Bale chutes, on balers, 354
Bale density, controlling, 345-347, 360
  factors affecting, 345
  typical values, 341, 358, 360
Bale handling, conventional bales, 341, 353-357
  large rectangular bales, 360-361
  large round bales, 341, 359
Bale length, controlling, 348, 360
Bale loaders, 354
Bale sizes and masses, conventional balers, 343
  large-bale balers, 341, 358, 360
Bale throwers, on balers, 354-355
  bale sizes for, 354
Bale wagons, automatic, 355-356
Balers, conventional, 343-353
  basic components, 343
  capacities, 350-351
  compression system, 345-346
  conveying and feeding, 344-345
  overload safety devices, 353
  plunger work diagram, 352-353
  power requirements 351-352
    plunger, 351-352
  sizes, 343
  windrow pickup units, 344-345
  large-rectangular-bale, 360-361
  large-round-bale, 357-360
    applications, 359
    capacities, 360
  twine, plastic (polypropylene), 348, 360
  twine and wire, requirements, 348, 359
    standards, 348

fan-spray, 289-290, 292, 303, 308
flooding, 289-290, 294, 303
flow rates, factors affecting, 290
hollow-cone, 289-290, 293, 303, 306, 308
jet (solid-stream), 289, 292, 308
sizes available, 290
solid-cone, 289-290, 303-304
spray angles, 290
effect of pressure, 290
types (hydraulic), 289-290

Onion harvesting, 476-477
Optimum size of implement, 43-45
Oscillatory tillage. See Vibratory tillage
Overload safety devices, 63-66, 320, 353

Parasitic soil forces, 116-117
Peanut combines, 470
Peanut digging, shaking, and windrowing,
469-470
Peanut harvest methods, 468-469
Pellets, feed, 361
seed, 225-226
Penetrometers, soil, 121-122
Performance efficiency, definition, 24
Pesticides, granular, 276-279
application rates, 277
incorporation, 277
lateral distribution, 279
metering, 277-279
liquids and dusts, applying, See Sprayers
and dusters
problems in use, 282
soil-application methods, 276-277
Photography, high-speed, 14
applications, 14, 401, 495
limitations, 14
Pickup reels, 330, 332, 399-400
peripheral speeds, 330, 400
Plant emergence, factors affecting, 212-213
seed tablets to improve, 213
Plant population and spacing requirements,
211
Plant thinners, random chemical or flame, 253
random mechanical, 252-255
cross blocking, 252
determining setup, 254-255
down-the-row, 253-254
selective, 253-257
applications, 256-257
chemical, 257
mechanical, 255-256
sensors, 255

Plant thinning, methods, 252
reasons for, 252
Planter arrangements, row-crop, 223-224
Planter testing, 230-231
cell fill, 227-228, 230-231
seed regularity, 230
expressing, 230
Planters, See also Seed-metering devices
covering devices, 222-223
fertilizer attachments, 224, 232-233
furrow openers, 220-222
depth control, 221-222, 224
mechanical functions, 212
potato, 232-233
presswheels, 222
unit, row-crop, 223
Planting, precision, See Precision planting
row-crop, definition, 209
seed distribution patterns, 209
solid, definition, 209
Planting systems, row-crop, 209-210
Potato harvesting. See Irish potato harvesting;
Sweet potato harvesting
Potato planters, 232-233
Power, definition, 116
drawbar, definition, 116
hydraulic, equation, 90, 300
shaft, 90
Power and energy requirements, 506
Power-take-off drives, applications, 70
loads imposed, 75-76
recommended load limits, 76-77
shielding, 72
speeds, standard, 71
standardization, 71-72
telescoping force, axial, 77
three-joint, 73-75
two-joint, 72-73
Precision planting, cell fill, 227-228
controlling seed transfer to furrow, 228-229
definition, 209, 226
functional requirements, 226-227
objectives, 226
Presswheels for planters, 222-223
Product liability, 20-21
Product safety, 19-20
common problems, 19-20
standards, 20
Production model, 10-11
Production prototype model, 10
Public testing agencies, 14-15
Pull, center of, on tractors, 181
central angled, 181-182
definition, 115

other **AVI** books

AGRICULTURAL PROCESS ENGINEERING
  3rd Edition   *Henderson and Perry*
AN INTRODUCTION TO AGRICULTURAL ENGINEERING
  Roth, Crow and Mahoney
BASIC ENGINEERING PRINCIPLES
  Merkel
COMMERCIAL CHICKEN PRODUCTION MANUAL
  2nd Edition   *North*
DAIRY TECHNOLOGY AND ENGINEERING
  Harper and Hall
DRYING CEREAL GRAINS
  Brooker, Bakker-Arkema and Hall
ENCYCLOPEDIA OF FOOD SCIENCE
  Peterson and Johnson
ENCYCLOPEDIA OF FOOD TECHNOLOGY
  Johnson and Peterson
FOOD ENGINEERING SYSTEMS
  Vol. 1   *Farrall*
FOOD PROCESS ENGINEERING
  Heldman
FUNDAMENTALS OF FOOD ENGINEERING
  2nd Edition   *Charm*
GRAIN STORAGE — PART OF A SYSTEM
  Sinha and Muir
LABORATORY MANUAL FOR ENTOMOLOGY AND PLANT
PATHOLOGY
  Pyenson and Barké
PHYSIOENGINEERING PRINCIPLES
  Merva
PLANT PHYSIOLOGY IN RELATION TO HORTICULTURE
  American Edition   *Bleasdale*
POTATOES: PRODUCTION, STORING, PROCESSING
  2nd Edition   *Smith*
POULTRY: FEEDS AND NUTRITION
  Schaible
PRINCIPLES, EQUIPMENT AND SYSTEMS FOR CORN HAR-
VESTING
  Johnson and Lamp
PRINCIPLES OF ANIMAL ENVIRONMENT
  Textbook Edition   *Esmay*
PROCESSING AGRICULTURAL AND MUNICIPAL WASTES
  Inglett
PROCESSING EQUIPMENT FOR AGRICULTURAL
PRODUCTS
  Hall
SOILS AND OTHER GROWTH MEDIA
  American Edition   *Flegmann and George*
SOURCE BOOK FOR FOOD SCIENTISTS
  Ockerman
WHEAT: PRODUCTION AND UTILIZATION
  Inglett